W9-CZS-028

STRATEGIC MANAGEMENT

CONCEPTS AND CASES

STRATEGIC MANAGEMENT

CONCEPTS AND CASES

Eighth Edition

ARTHUR A. THOMPSON, JR.

&

A. J. STRICKLAND III

Both of The University of Alabama

IRWIN

Chicago • Bogotá • Boston • Buenos Aires • Caracas
London • Madrid • Mexico City • Sydney • Toronto

Cover illustration: *China Street Scene #2, 1923,* by Bernard von Eichman. Collection of the Oakland Museum, Gift of Louis Siegriest.

Interior illustration: Detail: *China Street Scene #2, 1923,* by Bernard von Eichman. Collection of the Oakland Museum, Gift of Louis Siegriest.

Senior sponsoring editor: *Kurt L. Strand*
Senior developmental editor: *Libby Rubenstein*
Senior marketing manager: *Kurt Messersmith*
Project editor: *Mary Conzachi*
Production manager: *Laurie Kersch*
Designer: *Heidi J. Baughman*
Interior designer: *David Lansdon*
Cover designer: *Jeanne Rivera*
Art studio: *Precision Graphics*
Art coordinator: *Mark Malloy*
Compositor: *The Clarinda Co.*
Typeface: *10/12 Times Roman*
Printer: *Von Hoffmann Press, Inc.*

Library of Congress Cataloging-in-Publication Data

Thompson, Arthur A., 1940–
     Strategic management : concepts and cases / Arthur A. Thompson,
   Jr. & A. J. Strickland III. — 8th ed.
       p.   cm.
     Includes bibliographical references and indexes.
     ISBN 0-256-14055-3   0-256-16548-3 (international student ed.)
     1. Strategic planning.   2. Strategic planning—Case studies.
   I. Strickland, A. J. (Alonzo J.)   II. Title.
   HD30.28.T53   1995
     658.4′012—dc20   94–22560

Printed in the United States of America
4 5 6 7 8 9 0 VH 1 0 9 8 7 6

To Hasseline and Kitty

PREFACE

The hallmarks of the new eighth edition package are a fresh and greatly expanded treatment of strategy implementation, an exciting and very teachable collection of 36 cases (28 of which are new or thoroughly updated), a much enhanced third edition of the companion global business simulation game, a comprehensively updated readings book with 42 new selections, and an array of pedagogically sound instructional supplements. Our objective continues to be to satisfy the market's legitimate need for a book that squarely targets what every student needs to know about crafting, implementing, and executing business strategies. Toward this end, we have enhanced and improved every piece of the teaching package—text, cases, simulation game, case analysis software, the readings book, transparencies and transparency masters, and the *Instructor's Manual*. It's our best edition ever, we think—and by a substantial margin.

WHAT'S NEW AND DIFFERENT ABOUT THE TEXT CHAPTERS

New concepts, analytical tools, and methods of managing continue to surface at rates that mandate important edition-to-edition changes in content. But whereas the topical additions and new treatments in prior editions were concentrated more heavily in the chapters relating to strategic analysis and strategy formation (because advances in the literature have for many years come faster in strategy formulation than in implementation), the most numerous changes in this edition are in the chapters pertaining to strategy implementation. In the interval since our last text revision, there have been revolutionary developments under way in the theory and practice of management. Books, journals, and the business press are full of research studies and reports about how companies are using new tools and techniques to revamp how they do business, streamline operations, restore competitiveness, and reach new heights of performance. Across the world, companies are reorganizing their work effort around teams, totally reengineering core business processes, instituting total quality management programs, competing on organizational capabilities (as much as on differentiated product attributes), and installing leaner, flatter organization structures.

But these new approaches to internal organization are more than just strategy-blind additions to the conventional wisdom about how to manage better. Each, in its own way, represents a valuable strategy-implementing tool—one whose power is magnified when seen and used as part of a larger effort to execute company strategies more competently. Incorporating these new strategy-implementing tools into the eighth edition has prompted a comprehensive overhaul of our coverage of strategy implementation and execution. We've expanded the presentation to three solid chapters, introduced a more compelling conceptual framework for thinking strategically about the tasks of implementation, and woven in all-new material on employee empowerment; team and process organization; delayering and flattening organizational structure; ways to build core competencies and hard-to-match organizational capabilities; reengineering; best practice programs; total quality management; and healthy versus unhealthy corporate cultures. The outcome is a common-sense approach to implementing and executing strategy that is in sync with recent contributions to the literature and with contemporary management practices.

In the other text chapters, you'll find new sections dealing with benchmarking techniques, value-chain analysis, competence-based competitive advantage, activity-based costing (which dovetails perfectly with value-chain concepts and strategic cost analysis), outsourcing of noncritical activities, vertical integration, and why strategy is partly planned and partly evolutionary and reactive. Once again, there's front-to-back coverage of global issues in strategic management and prominent treatment of ethical and social responsibility issues. Extensive rewriting to sharpen the presentations in every chapter has allowed us to include the new material and still cover everything in less than 320 pages—something that readers and adopters ought to welcome, given the jam-packed content of the course.

SPECIFIC CONTENT CHANGES

The overall arrangement of chapters and topical sequences in the eighth edition parallels the sequencing in the last three editions, but you'll find several noteworthy refinements in content and emphasis:

- Chapters 1 and 2 contain better explanations of how and why a company's strategy emerges from (a) the deliberate and purposeful actions of management and (b) as-needed reactions to unanticipated developments and fresh competitive pressures. We've also introduced the concept of a strategy-making pyramid to underscore that a company's strategic plan is a collection of strategies devised by different managers at different levels in the organizational hierarchy; the effect is to build a stronger case for why all managers are on a company's strategy-making, strategy-implementing team and thus need to know about and be skilled in using the concepts and tools of strategic management.

- The roles of *core competences* and organizational capabilities in creating customer value and building competitive advantage have been given added prominence in the discussions of company strengths, crafting strategy around what a company does best, and building a capable organization (Chapters 2, 4, and 9).

- The treatment of value-chain analysis has been recast and expanded, new graphics added, and emphasis placed on benchmarking costs and the performance of key value-chain activities to help determine a company's cost competitiveness and overall competitive strength (Chapter 4). There are new sections describing benchmarking techniques and activity-based costing that take value-chain analysis to a new plateau of understanding and application.

- We've built the discussion of competitive strategy around five generic approaches rather than three—overall low-cost leadership, focused low-cost, broad differentiation, focused differentiation, and being the best-cost producer—see Figure 5–1 on page 517.

- We continue to believe that global competition and global strategy issues are best dealt with by integrating the relevant discussions into each chapter rather than partitioning the treatment into a separate chapter. The globalization of each chapter, a prominent feature of the previous edition, is carried over and strengthened in this edition, and we've added more Illustration Capsules to highlight the strategies of non-U.S. companies.

- The new three-chapter module(Chapters 9–11) on strategy implementation is structured around eight tasks: (1) building an organization capable of carrying out the strategy successfully; (2) developing budgets to steer ample resources into those value-chain activities critical to strategic success; (3) establishing strategically appropriate policies and procedures; (4) instituting best practices and mechanisms for continuous improvement; (5) installing support systems that enable company personnel to carry out their strategic roles successfully day in and day out; (6) tying rewards and incentives tightly to the achievement of performance objectives and good strategy execution; (7) creating a strategy-supportive work environment and corporate culture; and (8) exerting the internal leadership needed to drive implementation forward and to keep improving strategy execution.

- The eight-task framework for understanding the managerial components of strategy implementation and execution is explained in the first section of Chapter 9. The remainder of Chapter 9 features new coverage of the management tasks of building a capable organization: creating core competences and unique organizational capabilities; developing the dominating depth in competence-related activities needed for competitive advantage; making strategy-critical value-chain activities the main building blocks in the organization structure; the pros and cons of outsourcing noncritical activities; downsizing and delayering hierarchical structures; employee empowerment; reengineering of core business processes; and the use of cross-functional and self-contained work teams. The result is a much revised treatment of organization building that ties together and makes strategic sense out of the revolutionary organizational changes sweeping through today's corporations.

- Chapter 10 surveys the role of strategy-supportive budgets, policies, reward structures, and internal support systems and explains why benchmarking of best practices, total quality management, reengineering, and continuous improvement programs are important managerial tools for enhancing strategy execution.

- Chapter 11 deals with creating a strategy-supportive corporate culture and exercising the internal leadership needed to drive implementation forward. There's all-new coverage of strong versus weak cultures, low-performance and unhealthy cultures, adaptive cultures, and the sustained leadership commitment it takes to change a company with a problem culture, plus sections on ethics management and what managers can do to improve the calibre of strategy execution.

- There are 18 new Illustration Capsules.

The use of margin notes to highlight basic concepts, major conclusions, and core truths about strategic behavior in competitive markets was well received in the previous two editions and remains a feature of this edition. Most of these notes represent an effort to distill the subject matter into a series of concise principles expressing what every student should know about strategic management. The margin notes bring the text discussion into sharper focus for readers, point them to what is important, and promote clearer strategic thinking.

Diligent attention has been paid to improving content, clarity, and style. We've taken dead aim at creating a text that is crisply written, clear and convincing, interesting to read, and comfortably mainstream, while as close to the frontiers of theory and practice as a basic textbook should be.

THE COLLECTION OF CASES

The 36 cases selected for this edition include 24 new cases, 2 carryovers from the seventh edition, 6 carryovers from the sixth edition, and 4 newly revised cases from the sixth edition (The World Automotive Industry, Toyota Motor Corp., Philip Morris, and Wal-Mart) that have been so extensively refurbished and updated as to turn them into fresh cases. We've tried to strike a good balance between currently-written cases and proven favorites. As before, the cases have been grouped into five sections. In the first section are 4 cases spotlighting the role and tasks of the manager as chief strategy-maker and chief strategy-implementer. The second section contains 14 cases that deal primarily with analyzing industry and competitive situations and the challenges of crafting business-level strategy. There are 4 cases involving strategy assessments and strategy-making in diversified companies. A 10-case grouping provides broad coverage of the managerial tasks involved in implementing strategy. The last section contains 4 cases highlighting the links between strategy, ethics, and social responsibility.

We have continued our tradition of picking cases that feature interesting products and companies and that trigger lively classroom discussions. At least 22 of the cases involve companies, products, or people that students will have heard of, know about from personal experience, or can easily identify with. Scattered throughout the lineup are 9 cases concerning international companies, globally competitive industries, and cross-cultural situations; these cases, in conjunction with the globalized content of the text chapters, give this edition a strong international flavor—in keeping with real world events and new AASCB standards. Six cases have videotape segments for use during class discussion. Then there are 3 cases involving firms listed in *The 100 Best Companies to Work for in America,* 5 cases about young start-up companies, 10 cases dealing with the strategic problems of family-owned or relatively small entrepreneurial businesses, 1 nonprofit organization case, and 16 cases involving public companies about which students can do further research in the library.

The case researchers whose work appears in this edition have done an absolutely first-rate job of preparing cases that contain valuable teaching points, that illustrate the important kinds of strategic challenges managers face, and that allow students to apply the tools of strategic analysis. We believe you will find the case collection in this edition chock full of interest, effective in the classroom, and tightly linked to the text treatments in Chapters 1–11. It's a solid, exciting, and diverse case lineup from beginning to end.

THE BUSINESS STRATEGY GAME OPTION

Version three of *The Business Strategy Game,* offered as an optional accompaniment to this eighth edition, represents a major step up in capability and performance over versions one and two. It incorporates an array of new and better features, cuts instructor processing times, and greatly reduces the potential for operator error. Our objective in preparing the new version was to make the use of a simulation as attractive and as convenient as possible. Instructor gear-up time is minimal, processing of decisions is straightforward, and the administrative requirements are modest. Version three is definitely more streamlined and user-friendly than versions one and two—thanks to some excellent feedback and suggestions from users, faster and more versatile computers, and expedited programming on our end.

The Business Strategy Game has five features that make it an uncommonly effective teaching-learning aid for strategic management courses: (1) *the product and the industry*—producing and marketing athletic footwear is a business that students can readily identify with and understand; (2) *the global industry environment*—students are provided with up-close exposure to what global competition is like and the kinds of strategic issues that managers in global industries have to address; (3) *the realistic quality of the simulation exercise*—we've designed the simulation to be as faithful as possible to real world markets, competitive conditions, and revenue-cost-profit relationships; (4) *the wide degree of strategic freedom students have in managing their companies*—we've gone to great lengths to make the game free of bias as concerns one strategy versus another; and (5) *the five-year planning and decision-making capability*—the game incorporates long-range thinking as an integral part of the exercise of running a company. These features, wrapped together as a package, provide an exciting and valuable bridge between concept and practice, the classroom and real-life management, and absorbing conventional wisdom about management and learning-by-doing.

THE VALUE A SIMULATION ADDS

Our own experiences with simulation games, along with hours of discussions with users, have convinced us that simulation games are the single best exercise available for helping students understand how the functional pieces of a business fit together and for giving students an integrated, capstone experience.

First and foremost, the exercise of running a simulated company over a number of decision periods helps develop students' business judgment. Simulation games provide a live case situation where events unfold and circumstances change as the game progresses. Their special hook is an ability to get students personally involved in the subject matter. *The Business Strategy Game* is very typical in this respect. In plotting their competitive strategies each decision period, students learn about risk-taking. They have to respond to changing market conditions, react to the moves of competitors, and choose among alternative courses of action. They get valuable practice in reading the signs of industry change, spotting market opportunities, evaluating threats to their company's competitive position, weighing the trade-offs between profits now and profits later, and assessing the long-term consequences of short-term decisions. They are called on to chart a long-term direction, set strategic and financial objectives, and try out different strategies in pursuit of competitive advantage. They become active strategic thinkers, planners, analysts, and decision-makers. And by having to live with the decisions they make, they experience what it means to be accountable for decisions and responsible for achieving satisfactory results. All this serves to drill students in responsible decision-making and improve their business acumen and managerial judgment.

Second, students learn an enormous amount from working with the numbers, exploring options, and trying to unite production, marketing, finance, and human resource decisions into a coherent strategy. They begin to see ways to apply knowledge from prior courses and figure out what really makes a business tick. The effect is to help students integrate a lot of material, look at decisions from the standpoint of the company as a whole, and see the importance of thinking strategically about a company's competitive position and future prospects. Since a simulation game is by its very nature a hands-on exercise, the lessons learned are forcefully planted in students' minds—the impact tends to be far more lasting than what is remembered from lectures. Third, students' entrepreneurial instincts blossom as they get caught up in the competitive spirit of the game. The resulting entertainment value helps maintain an unusually high level of student motivation and emotional involvement in the course throughout the term.

ABOUT THE SIMULATION

We designed *The Business Strategy Game* around athletic footwear because it is a product students can understand and because the athletic footwear market displays the characteristics of globally competitive industries in the 1990s—fast growth, worldwide use of the product, competition among companies from several continents, production in low-wage locations, and ample room for a variety of competitive approaches and business strategies. The simulation allows companies to manufacture and sell their brands in North America, Europe, and Asia, and there's the option to compete for supplying private-label sales to chain discounters. Competition is head-to head. Each team of students must match their strategic wits against the other company teams. Companies can focus their branded marketing efforts on one geographic market or two or all three, or they can deemphasize branded sales and specialize in private-label production (an attractive strategy for low-cost producers). They can establish a one-country production base or they can manufacture in all three of the geographic markets. Low-cost leadership, differentiation strategies, best-cost producer strategies, and focus strategies are all viable competitive options. Companies can position their products in the low end of the market, the high end, or stick close to the middle on price, quality, and service; they can have a wide or narrow product line, small or big dealer networks, extensive or limited advertising. Company market shares are based on how each company's competitive effort stacks up against the efforts of rivals. Demand conditions, tariffs, and wage rates vary from geographic area to geographic area. Raw materials used in footwear production are purchased in a worldwide commodity market at prices that move up or down in response to supply-demand conditions.

The company that students manage has plants to operate, a workforce to compensate, distribution expenses and inventories to control, capital expenditure decisions to make, marketing and sales campaigns to wage, sales forecasts to consider, and ups and downs in exchange rates, interest rates, and the stock market to take into account. Students must weave functional decisions in production, distribution, marketing, finance, and human resources into a cohesive action plan. They have to react to changing market and competitive conditions, move to build competitive advantage, and defend against aggressive actions of competitors. And they must endeavor to maximize shareholder wealth via increased dividend payments and stock price appreciation. Each team of students is challenged to use their entrepreneurial and strategic skills to become the next Nike or Reebok and ride the wave of growth to the top of the worldwide athletic footwear industry. The exercise is as realistic and true to actual business practice in a real-world competitive market as we could make it.

There are built-in planning and analysis features that allow students to (1) craft a five-year strategic plan, (2) gauge the long-range financial impact of current decisions, (3) do the number-crunching to make informed short-run versus long-run trade-offs, (4) assess the revenue-cost-profit consequences of alternative strategic actions, and (5) build different strategy scenarios. Calculations at the bottom of each decision screen provide instantly updated projections of sales revenues, profits, return on equity, cash flow, and other key outcomes as each decision entry is made. The sensitivity of financial and operating outcomes to different decision entries is easily observed on the screen and on detailed printouts of projections. With the speed of today's personal computers, the relevant number-crunching is done in a split second. The game is designed to lead students to decisions based on "My analysis shows . . ." and away from seat-of-the-pants approaches and the quicksand of decisions based on "I think," "It sounds good," and "Maybe it will work out."

The Business Strategy Game can be used with any IBM or compatible PC with 640K memory and it is suitable for both senior-level and MBA courses. The game is programmed to accommodate a wide variety of computer setups as concerns disk drives, monitors, and printers.

FEATURES OF THE THIRD EDITION

This much upgraded version of *The Business Strategy Game* makes things easier and better for both the players and the game administrator:

- **New Decision Variables.** Four new decision variables have been added to enhance the game's realism and provide greater strategic latitude. Each plant can now produce different quality shoes and different numbers of models, allowing both product quality and product line breadth to vary by market segment. Portions of plants can now be sold or closed. There are more options for revamping less efficient plants to make them more cost competitive. And we've changed some decision entries to give companies more flexibility in competing simultaneously in the private-label and branded segments.
- **Expanded Decision Support.** We've greatly expanded the number of on-screen calculations at the bottom of each decision entry screen, achieving a quantum improvement in player's ability to do what-iffing and immediately see the sensitivity of key outcomes without having to move to a new file and consult the projected company reports.
- **The Competitor Analysis Report.** A new set of Competitor Analysis Reports has been added that reorganizes the competitive effort information appearing in the Footwear Industry Reports into formats suitable for easy diagnosis of competitors' actions and strategies, market segment by market segment and year by year. Printouts for any year and any competitor of interest are easily obtained and easily used as a diagnostic tool.
- **Other Information Enhancements.** In addition to the Competitor Analysis Reports, we've improved the information in the Footwear Industry Report by including a whole page of cross-company comparisons of income statement and balance sheet statistics, additional plant construction data, and more infor-

mation on the private-label segment. Plus we've beefed up the Administrator's Report with more diagnostic information and cross-company comparisons.

- **A New Look.** We've given the screens a new look. The redesigned decision entry and report screens are easier to read, simpler to use, and more pleasing to the eye. There's a new menu bar that speeds access to all decision screens. It is also quicker to move from file to file.
- **The Mouse.** All programs and disks used by both players and the game administrator are now "mouse aware." The mouse may be used to make menu selections and to invoke the [Enter] and [Esc] keys when necessary.
- **Error Trapping and Entry Validation.** There's expanded error trapping capability that rejects any decision entry that falls outside the valid range or that is the wrong type (a letter versus a number).
- **Programming Refinements.** We've refined the interaction among some key variables, adjusted several algorithms, improved the methodology of calculating the strategy rating, eliminated the need for students to manually update announced changes in costs and rates (it's now done automatically on the company disk during processing), relocated the what-if entries to boxes just below the relevant decision entries, and reformatted the decision screens so that all current-year decisions can be made on 6 decision screens instead of 14. There's also a more sophisticated and user-friendly printer setup program.
- **Streamlined Processing.** Just as in the last version, we've implemented another round of streamlining in processing decisions. Instructors/game administrators have more processing flexibility and options.
- **Improved Manuals.** The *Player's Manual* has been reworked to provide better explanations of cause-effect relationships and more information on the conditions surrounding decision entries. The *Instructor's Manual* has been expanded by 20 percent to provide more details on administering a successful simulation.

At the same time, though, we've kept intact the features that users told us made them enthusiastic about the last two versions:

- There's no paperwork associated with student decisions or with returning the results. Students turn in disks with their decisions already entered. When you process the results, everything the students need is automatically written onto their company disks, and they make their own printouts. It takes only a few minutes to collect the disks and return them. A printout of the industry scoreboard and a printout of the administrator's report are automatically generated during processing.
- Decisions can be processed in 40 minutes (less than 25 minutes on a fast PC); simple procedures allow most or all of the processing to be delegated to a student assistant.
- Students will find it convenient and uncomplicated to use the PC to play *The Business Strategy Game* even if they have had no prior exposure to PCs; *no programming of any kind is involved* and full instructions are presented in the *Player's Manual* and on the screens themselves.
- A scoreboard of company performance is automatically calculated each decision period. Instructors determine the weights to be given to each of six performance measures—revenues, after-tax profits, return on stockholders' investment, stock value, bond rating, and strategy rating. Students always know

where their company stands and how well they are doing; the overall performance score can be used to grade team performance.
- An *Instructor's Manual* describes how to integrate the game into your course, provides pointers on how to administer the game, and contains step-by-step processing instructions.

THE STRAT-ANALYST SOFTWARE OPTION

We introduced this optional supplement with the fourth edition as a way of incorporating the calculating power of PCs into the case analysis part of the strategic management course. It proved both popular and effective, and we've created an updated version to accompany this edition. STRAT-ANALYST works on all IBM and 100 percent compatible personal computers with 640K memories.

The version of STRAT-ANALYST accompanying the eighth edition has three main sections. The first section contains preprogrammed, customized templates for each of 15 cases where substantial number-crunching is called for; with these templates, students can

- Obtain calculations showing financial ratios, profit margins and rates of return, common-size income statements and balance sheets, annual compound rates of change, and Altman's bankruptcy index (a method for predicting when a company may be headed into deep financial trouble).
- View charts and graphs of data in the case.
- Do what-iffing and make five-year, best-case, expected-case, and worst-case projections of financial performance.
- Get report-ready printouts of all calculations.

The number-crunching capability of STRAT-ANALYST is a big time-saver for students, and it gets them into the habit of always looking at the story the numbers tell about a company's performance and situation. Since students can do a more systematic evaluation of case data with STRAT-ANALYST than without it, instructors can insist on and expect thorough financial and operating assessments.

The second section of STRAT-ANALYST features an easy-to-use, step-by-step generic procedure for using various analytical tools and doing situation analysis. The three-part menu includes

- Industry and competitive situation analysis (keyed to Table 3–5 in the text).
- Company situation analysis (keyed to Table 4–5 in the text).
- Business portfolio analysis (keyed to Chapter 8's discussion of how to compare industry attractiveness and business strength in diversified firms).

Students can choose to use whatever situation analysis tools are appropriate and, when finished, get a neatly organized, final-copy printout of their analysis in a report format (that can then be conveniently graded by the instructor). Hints for using each situational analysis tool are provided directly on STRAT-ANALYST to guide the student in the right direction. The benefit of these three menu options is that students are prompted to consider the full array of concepts and tools and to do a systematic situation analysis rather than try to get by with spotty analysis and weakly justified opinions.

The third section of STRAT-ANALYST offers two menu selections for developing action recommendations:

1. Action recommendations pertaining to strategy formulation—development of a basic strategic direction (mission and objectives), proposing an overall business strategy, specifying functional strategies, and recommending specific action steps to develop the strategy and gain competitive advantage.
2. Action recommendations for implementing/executing the chosen strategy and correcting whatever assortment of internal administrative and operating problems may exist.

Both selections walk students step by step through areas where actions may need to be taken. A "Hints" screen appears at each step.

The whole intent of the STRAT-ANALYST software package is to give students a major assist in doing higher-caliber strategic analysis and to cut the time that it takes them to do a thorough job of case preparation. It should also build student comfort levels and skills in the use of PCs for managerial analysis purposes. The instructor profits too—from improved student performance and from increased flexibility in varying the nature of case analysis assignments.

THE READINGS BOOK OPTION

For instructors who want to incorporate samples of the strategic management literature into the course, a companion *Readings in Strategic Management* containing 48 selections is available. Forty-two of the 48 readings are new to the fifth edition. Over 80 percent have appeared since 1990. All are engaging, and all are suitable for seniors and MBA students. Most of the selections are articles reprinted from leading journals; they add in-depth treatment to important topics covered in the text and they place readers at the cutting edge of academic thinking and research on the subject. Some of the articles are drawn from practitioner sources and stress how particular tools and concepts relate directly to actual companies and managerial practices. Seven articles examine the role of the general manager and strategy; 13 articles concern strategic analysis and strategy formulation at the business unit level; 6 articles deal with strategy in diversified companies; 16 articles relate to various aspects of strategy implementation and execution; and 5 articles are about strategy and ethics management. Five articles concentrate on the international dimensions of strategic management. The readings package provides an effective, efficient vehicle for reinforcing and expanding the text-case approach.

THE INSTRUCTOR'S PACKAGE

A full complement of instructional aids is available to assist adopters in using the eighth edition successfully. The *Instructor's Manual* contains suggestions for using the text materials, various approaches to course design and course organization, a sample syllabus, alternative course outlines, a thoroughly revised and expanded set of 940 multiple-choice and essay questions, a comprehensive teaching note for each case, plus eight "classic" cases from previous editions. There is a computerized test bank for generating examinations, a set of color transparencies depicting the figures and tables in the 11 text chapters, and a package of lecture and transparency masters that thoroughly cover the text (concepts) part of the book and can be used to support the instructor's classroom presentations. To help instructors enrich and vary the pace of class discussions of cases, six videos are available. Four of these—Campus Designs, Solid Shield Americas, Mary Kay Cosmetics, and Lexmark International—can be obtained from Richard D. Irwin, Inc. The other two, Fluent Machines (A) and Food Lion, may be ordered from the producers/creators. Details are provided in the teaching notes contained in the *Instructor's Manual*.

In concert, the textbook, the three companion supplements, and the comprehensive instructor's package provide a complete, integrated lineup of teaching materials. The package offers wide latitude in course design, full access to the range of computer-assisted instructional techniques, an assortment of visual aids, and plenty of opportunity to keep student assignments varied and interesting. Our goal has been to give you everything you need to offer a course that is very much in keeping with the strategic management challenges and issues of the 1990s and that is capable of winning enthusiastic student approval.

ACKNOWLEDGMENTS

We have benefited from the help of many people during the evolution of this book. Students, adopters, and reviewers have generously supplied an untold number of insightful comments and helpful suggestions. Our intellectual debt to those academics, writers, and practicing managers who have blazed new trails in the strategy field will be obvious to any reader familiar with the literature of strategic management.

We are particularly indebted to the case researchers and to the companies whose cooperation made the cases possible. To each one goes a very special thank-you. The contribution made by timely, carefully researched cases to a substantive study of strategic management issues and practices cannot be overestimated. From a research standpoint, cases in strategic management are invaluable in exposing the generic kinds of strategic issues that companies face, in forming hypotheses about strategic behavior, and in drawing experience-based generalizations about the practice of strategic management. Pedagogically, cases about strategic management give students essential practice in diagnosing and evaluating strategic situations, in learning to use the tools and concepts of strategy analysis, in sorting through various strategic options, in crafting strategic action plans, and in figuring out successful ways to implement and execute the chosen strategy. Without a continuing stream of fresh, well-researched, and well-conceived cases, the study of strategic management would quickly lose much of its energy, focus, and excitement. There's no question that first-class case research constitutes a valuable scholarly contribution.

The following reviewers provided insightful suggestions and advice regarding ways to make the eighth edition better: James Boulgarides, California State University at Los Angeles; Betty Diener, University of Massachusetts; Daniel F. Jennings, Baylor University; David Kuhn, Florida State University; Kathryn Martell, Southern Illinois University; Wilbur Mouton, University of Toledo; and Bobby Vaught, Southeast Missouri State University.

We are also indebted to Tuck Bounds, Lee Burk, Ralph Catalanello, William Crittenden, Vince Luchsinger, Stan Mendenhall, John Moore, Will Mulvaney, Sandra Richard, Ralph Roberts, Thomas Turk, Gordon VonStroh, Fred Zimmerman, S. A. Billion, Charles Byles, Gerald L. Geisler, Rose Knotts, Joseph Rosenstein, James B. Thurman, Ivan Able, W. Harvey Hegarty, Roger Evered, Charles B. Saunders, Rhae M. Swisher, Claude I. Shell, R. Thomas Lenz, Michael C. White, Dennis Callahan, R. Duane Ireland, William E. Burr II, C. W. Millard, Richard Mann, Kurt Christensen, Neil W. Jacobs, Louis W. Fry, D. Robley Wood, George J. Gore, and William R. Soukup. These reviewers were of considerable help directing our efforts at various stages in the development of the manuscript through the first seven editions.

Naturally, as custom properly dictates, we are responsible for whatever errors of fact, deficiences in coverage or in exposition, and oversights that remain. As always we value your recommendations and thoughts about the book. Your comments regarding coverage and contents will be most welcome, as will your calling our attention to specific errors. Please write us at P.O. Box 870225, Department of Management and Marketing, The University of Alabama, Tuscaloosa, Alabama 35487-0225.

A.A.T
A.J.S.

A SPECIAL NOTE TO STUDENTS

The ground that strategic management covers is challenging, wide-ranging, and exciting. The center of attention is *the total enterprise*—the environment in which it operates, the direction management intends to head, management's strategic plan for getting the enterprise moving in this direction, and the managerial tasks of implementing and executing the chosen strategy successfully. We'll be examining the foremost issue in running a business enterprise: What must managers do, and do well, to make the company a winner rather than a loser in the game of business?

The answer that emerges again and again, and which becomes the theme of the course, is that good strategy-making and good strategy-implementing are always the most reliable signs of good management. The task of this course is to expose you to the reasons why good strategic management nearly always produces good company performance and to instruct you in the methods of crafting a well-conceived strategy and then successfully executing it.

During the course, you can expect to learn what the role and tasks of the strategy-maker are. You will grapple with what strategy means and with all the ramifications of figuring out which strategy is best in light of a company's over-all situation. You will get a workout in sizing up a variety of industry and competitive situations, in using the tools of strategic analysis, in considering the pros and cons of strategic alternatives, and in crafting an attractive strategic plan. You will learn about the principal managerial tasks associated with implementing the chosen strategy successfully. You will become more skilled as a strategic thinker and you will develop your powers of business judgment. The excitement comes from the extra savvy you will pick up about playing the game of business and from the blossoming of your entrepreneurial and competitive instincts.

In the midst of all this, another purpose is accomplished: to help you integrate and apply what you've learned in prior courses. Strategic management is a big-picture course. It deals with the grand sweep of how to manage. Unlike your other business courses where the subject matter was narrowly aimed at a particular function or piece of the business—accounting, finance, marketing, production, human resources, or information systems—this course deals with the company's entire makeup and situation both inside and outside. Nothing is ignored or assumed away. The task is to arrive at solid judgments about how all the relevant factors add up. This makes strategic management an integrative, capstone course in which you reach back to use concepts and techniques covered in previous courses. For perhaps the first time you'll see how the various pieces of the business puzzle fit together and why the different parts of a business need to be managed in strategic harmony for the organization to operate in winning fashion.

No matter what your major is, the content of this course has all the ingredients to be the best course you've taken—best in the sense of learning a lot about business and holding your interest from beginning to end. Dig in, get involved, and make the most of what the course has to offer. As you tackle the subject matter, ponder Ralph Waldo Emerson's observation, "Commerce is a game of skill which many people play, but which few play well." What we've put between these covers is aimed squarely at helping you become a wiser, shrewder player. Good luck!

A.A.T.
A.J.S.

P.S. We've created an easy-to-use, PC-based software package called STRAT-ANALYST to assist you in analyzing the cases included in this edition. Its features and capabilities are fully described on p. xiv of the Preface. If your instructor has elected to make use of STRAT-ANALYST optional and no copies are on the bookstore shelf, your bookstore can order a copy for you from the publisher. Instructions for booting the disk come with the software; all other instructions are provided directly on the screens. Should you misplace the instructions for booting the disk, your instructor can provide you with a replacement instruction sheet.

CONTENTS

## PART ONE

THE CONCEPTS AND TECHNIQUES OF STRATEGIC MANAGEMENT

## CHAPTER ONE

THE STRATEGIC MANAGEMENT PROCESS
AN OVERVIEW

"Cheshire Puss," she [Alice] began . . . *"would you please tell me which way I ought to go from here?"*
"That depends on where you want to get to," said the cat.

Lewis Carroll

My job is to make sure the company has a strategy and that everybody follows it.

Kenneth H. Olsen
Former CEO, Digital Equipment Corporation

A strategy is a commitment to undertake one set of actions rather than another.

Sharon M. Oster
Professor, Yale University

This book is about the managerial tasks of crafting, implementing, and executing company strategies. Strategy is grounded in the array of competitive moves and business approaches management depends on to produce successful performance. Strategy, in effect, is management's game plan for strengthening the organization's position, pleasing customers, and achieving performance targets. Managers devise strategies to guide *how* the company's business will be conducted and to help them make reasoned, cohesive choices among alternative courses of action. The strategy managers decide on indicates that "among all the paths and actions we could have chosen, we decided to follow this route and conduct our business in this manner." Without a strategy, a manager has no thought-out course to follow, no roadmap to manage by, no unified action program to produce the intended results.

Management's game plan involves every major function and department—purchasing, production, finance, marketing, human resources, R&D. Each has a role in the strategy. The strategy-making challenge is to mold business decisions and competitive actions taken across the company into a cohesive *pattern*. The prevailing pattern of moves and approaches indicates what the current strategy is; new moves and approaches under consideration signal how the current strategy may be embellished or recast.

Crafting and implementing strategy are core management functions. Among all the things managers do, few affect company performance more fundamentally than how well its management team charts the company's long-term direction, develops competitively effective strategic moves and business approaches, and executes the strategy in ways that produce the targeted results. Indeed, *good strategy and good strategy execution are the most trustworthy signs of good management.*

There's a strong case for linking "good management" to how well managers craft and execute strategy. Some managers design shrewd strategies but fail to carry them out well. Others design mediocre strategies but execute them competently. Both situations open the door to shortfalls in performance. Managers must combine good strategy-making with good strategy execution for company performance to approach maximum potential. The better conceived a company's strategy and the more proficient its execution, the greater the chance the company will be a solid performer. Powerful execution of a powerful strategy is not only a proven recipe for business success but also the best test of excellent management.

Granted, good strategy combined with good strategy execution doesn't *guarantee* that a company will avoid periods of weak or ho-hum performance. On occasion it takes time for management's efforts to show good results. And even well-managed organizations can face adverse and unforeseen conditions. But neither the "we need more time" reason nor the bad luck of adverse events excuses mediocre performance year after year. It is management's responsibility to adjust to unexpectedly tough conditions by undertaking strategic defenses and business approaches that can overcome adversity. Indeed, the essence of good strategy-making is to build a market position strong enough and an organization capable enough to produce successful performance despite unforeseeable events, potent competition, and internal problems.

> To qualify as excellently managed, an organization must exhibit excellent execution of an excellent strategy.

THE FIVE TASKS OF STRATEGIC MANAGEMENT

The strategy-making, strategy-implementing process consists of five interrelated managerial tasks:

1. Deciding what business the company will be in and forming a strategic vision of where the organization needs to be headed—in effect, infusing the organization with a sense of purpose, providing long-term direction, and establishing a clear mission to be accomplished.
2. Converting the strategic vision and mission into measurable objectives and performance targets.
3. Crafting a strategy to achieve the desired results.
4. Implementing and executing the chosen strategy efficiently and effectively.
5. Evaluating performance, reviewing new developments, and initiating corrective adjustments in long-term direction, objectives, strategy, or implementation in light of actual experience, changing conditions, new ideas, and new opportunities.

Figure 1–1 illustrates this process. Together, these five components define what we

FIGURE 1–1 | **The Five Tasks of Strategic Management**

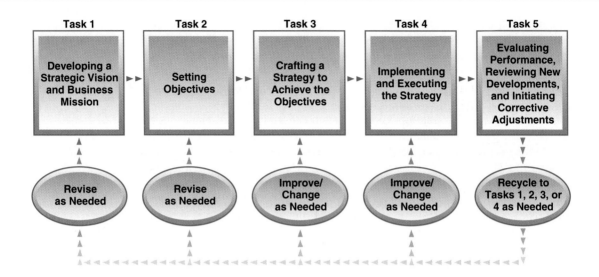

mean by the term strategic management. Let's explore this framework in more detail to set the stage for all that follows.

DEVELOPING A STRATEGIC VISION AND BUSINESS MISSION

The foremost direction-setting question senior managers need to ask is "What is our vision for the company—what are we trying to do and to become?" Developing a carefully reasoned answer to this question pushes managers to consider what the company's business character is and should be and to develop a clear picture of where the company needs to be headed over the next 5 to 10 years. Management's answer to "who we are, what we do, and where we're headed" charts a course for the organization to take and helps establish a strong organizational identity. What a company seeks to do and to become is commonly termed the company's mission. A mission statement defines a company's business and provides a clear view of what the company is trying to accomplish for its customers. But managers also have to think strategically about where they are trying to take the company. Management's concept of the business needs to be supplemented with a concept of the company's future business makeup and long-term direction. Management's view of the kind of company it is trying to create and its intent to stake out a particular business position represent a *strategic vision* for the company. By developing and communicating a business mission and strategic vision, management infuses the workforce with a sense of purpose and a persuasive rationale for the company's future direction. Some examples of company mission and vision statements are presented in Illustration Capsule 1.

A well-conceived strategic vision prepares a company for the future, establishes long-term direction, and indicates the company's intent to stake out a particular business position.

SETTING OBJECTIVES

The purpose of setting objectives is to convert managerial statements of business mission and company direction into specific performance targets, something the organization's progress can be measured by. Objective-setting implies challenge, establishing performance targets that require stretch and disciplined effort. The chal-

ILLUSTRATION CAPSULE 1

EXAMPLES OF COMPANY MISSION AND VISION STATEMENTS

Otis Elevator

Our mission is to provide any customer a means of moving people and things up, down, and sideways over short distances with higher reliability than any similar enterprise in the world.

Avis Rent-a-Car

Our business is renting cars. Our mission is total customer satisfaction.

McCormick & Company

The primary mission of McCormick & Company is to expand our worldwide leadership position in the spice, seasoning, and flavoring markets.

The Saturn Division of General Motors

To market vehicles developed and manufactured in the United States that are world leaders in quality, cost, and customer satisfaction through the integration of people, technology, and business systems and to transfer knowledge, technology, and experience throughout General Motors.

Public Service Company of New Mexico

Our mission is to work for the success of people we serve by providing our customers reliable electric service, energy information, and energy options that best satisfy their needs.

American Red Cross

The mission of the American Red Cross is to improve the quality of human life; to enhance self-reliance and concern for others; and to help people avoid, prepare for, and cope with emergencies.

Eastman Kodak

To be the world's best in chemical and electronic imaging.

McCaw Cellular Communications

Develop a reliable wireless network that empowers people with the freedom to travel anywhere—across the hall or across the continent—and communicate effortlessly.

Compaq Computer

To be the leading supplier of PCs and PC servers in all customer segments.

Long John Silver's

To be America's best quick service restaurant chain. We will provide each guest great tasting, healthful, reasonably priced fish, seafood, and chicken in a fast, friendly manner on every visit.

Source: Company annual reports.

lenge of trying to close the gap between actual and desired performance pushes an organization to be more inventive, to exhibit some urgency in improving both its financial performance and its business position, and to be more intentional and focused in its actions. Setting challenging but achievable objectives thus helps guard against complacency, drift, internal confusion over what to accomplish, and status quo organizational performance. As Mitchell Leibovitz, CEO of Pep Boys—Manny, Moe, and Jack, puts it, "If you want to have ho-hum results, have ho-hum objectives."

Objectives are yardsticks for tracking an organization's performance and progress.

The objectives managers establish should ideally include both short-range and long-range performance targets. Short-range objectives spell out the immediate improvements and outcomes management desires. Long-range objectives prompt managers to consider what to do *now* to position the company to perform well over the longer term. As a rule, when tradeoffs have to be made between achieving long-run objectives and achieving short-run objectives, long-run objectives should take precedence. Rarely does a company prosper from repeated management actions that sacrifice better long-run performance for better short-term performance.

Objective-setting is required of *all* managers. Every unit in a company needs concrete, measurable performance targets that contribute meaningfully toward achieving company objectives. When companywide objectives are broken down into specific targets for each organizational unit and lower-level managers are held accountable for achieving them, a results-oriented climate builds throughout the enterprise. The ideal situation is a team effort where each organizational unit is striving hard to produce results in its area of responsibility that will help the company reach its performance targets and achieve its strategic vision.

From a companywide perspective, two types of performance yardsticks are called for: financial objectives and strategic objectives. *Financial objectives* are important because without acceptable financial performance an organization risks being denied the resources it needs to grow and prosper. *Strategic objectives* are needed to prompt managerial efforts to strengthen a company's overall business and competitive position. Financial objectives typically relate to such measures as earnings growth, return on investment, borrowing power, cash flow, and shareholder returns. Strategic objectives, however, concern a company's competitiveness and long-term business position in its markets: growing faster than the industry average, overtaking key competitors on product quality or customer service or market share, achieving lower overall costs than rivals, boosting the company's reputation with customers, winning a stronger foothold in international markets, exercising technological leadership, gaining a sustainable competitive advantage, and capturing attractive growth opportunities. Strategic objectives serve notice that management not only intends to deliver good financial performance but also to improve the organization's competitive strength and long-range business prospects.

Examples of the kinds of strategic and financial objectives companies set are shown in Illustration Capsule 2.

Companies need both financial objectives and strategic objectives.

CRAFTING A STRATEGY

Strategy-making brings into play the critical managerial issue of *how* to achieve the targeted results in light of the organization's situation and prospects. Objectives are the "ends," and strategy is the "means" of achieving them. In effect, strategy is the pattern of actions managers employ to achieve strategic and financial performance targets. The task of crafting a strategy starts with solid diagnosis of the company's internal and external situation. Only when armed with hard analysis of the big picture are managers prepared to devise a sound strategy to achieve targeted strategic and financial results. Why? Because misdiagnosis of the situation greatly raises the risk of pursuing ill-conceived strategic actions.

An organization's strategy consists of the actions and business approaches management employs to achieve the targeted organizational performance.

A company's strategy is typically a blend of (1) deliberate and purposeful actions and (2) as-needed reactions to unanticipated developments and fresh competitive pressures. As illustrated in Figure 1–2, strategy is more than what managers have carefully plotted out in advance and *intend* to do as part of some grand strategic plan. New circumstances always emerge, whether important technological developments, rivals' successful new product introductions, newly enacted government regulations and policies, widening consumer interest in different kinds of performance features, or whatever. There's always enough uncertainty about the future that managers cannot plan every strategic action in advance and pursue their *intended strategy* without alteration. Company strategies end up, therefore, being a composite of planned actions (intended strategy) and as-needed reactions to unforeseen conditions ("unplanned" strategy responses). Consequently, *strategy is best conceived as a combination of planned actions and on-the-spot adaptive reactions to fresh develop-*

Strategy is both proactive (intended) and reactive (adaptive).

ILLUSTRATION CAPSULE 2

STRATEGIC AND FINANCIAL OBJECTIVES OF WELL-KNOWN CORPORATIONS

NationsBank

To build the premier financial services company in the U.S.

Ford Motor Company

To satisfy our customers by providing quality cars and trucks, developing new products, reducing the time it takes to bring new vehicles to market, improving the efficiency of all our plants and processes, and building on our teamwork with employees, unions, dealers, and suppliers.

Exxon

To provide shareholders a secure investment with a superior return.

Alcan Aluminum

To be the lowest-cost producer of aluminum and to out-

perform the average return on equity of the Standard and Poor's industrial stock index.

General Electric

To become the most competitive enterprise in the world by being number one or number two in market share in every business the company is in.

Apple Computer

To offer the best possible personal computing technology, and to put that technology in the hands of as many people as possible.

Atlas Corporation

To become a low-cost, medium-size gold producer, producing in excess of 125,000 ounces of gold a year and building gold reserves of 1,500,000 ounces.

Quaker Oats Company

To achieve return on equity at 20% or above, "real" earnings growth averaging 5% or better over time; to be a leading marketer of strong consumer brands; and to improve the profitability of low-return businesses or divest them.

Source: Company annual reports.

ing industry and competitive events. The strategy-making task involves developing a game plan, or intended strategy, and then adapting it as events unfold. A company's actual strategy is something managers must craft as events transpire outside and inside the company.

Strategy and Entrepreneurship Crafting strategy is an exercise in entrepreneurship and outside-in strategic thinking. The challenge is for company managers to keep their strategies closely matched to such outside drivers as changing buyer preferences, the latest actions of rivals, market opportunities and threats, and newly appearing business conditions. Company strategies can't be responsive to changes in the business environment unless managers exhibit entrepreneurship in studying market trends, listening to customers, enhancing the company's competitiveness, and steering company activities in new directions in a timely manner. Good strategy-making is therefore inseparable from good business entrepreneurship. One cannot exist without the other.

A company encounters two dangers when its managers fail to exercise strategy-making entrepreneurship. One is a stale strategy. The faster a company's business environment is changing, the more critical it becomes for its managers to be good entrepreneurs in diagnosing shifting conditions and instituting strategic adjustments. Coasting along with a status quo strategy tends to be riskier than making modifications. Strategies that are increasingly out of touch with market realities make a company a good candidate for a performance crisis.

Strategy-making is fundamentally a market-driven entrepreneurial activity—risk-taking, venturesomeness, business creativity, and an eye for spotting emerging market opportunities are all involved in crafting a strategic action plan.

FIGURE 1–2 | **A Company's Actual Strategy Is Partly Planned and Partly Reactive to Changing Circumstances**

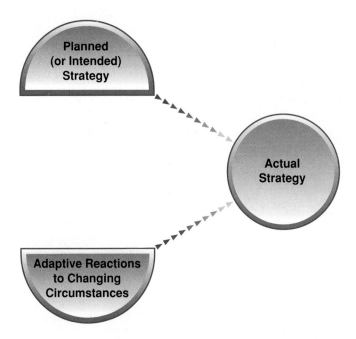

The second danger is inside-out strategic thinking. Managers with weak entrepreneurial skills are usually risk-averse and hesitant to embark on a new strategic course so long as the present strategy produces acceptable results. They pay only perfunctory attention to market trends and listen to customers infrequently. Often, they either dismiss new outside developments as unimportant ("we don't think it will really affect us") or else study them to death before taking actions. Being comfortable with the present strategy, they focus their energy and attention inward on internal problem-solving, organizational processes and procedures, reports and deadlines, company politics, and the administrative demands of their jobs. Consequently the strategic actions they initiate tend to be inside-out and governed by the company's traditional approaches, what is acceptable to various internal political coalitions, what is philosophically comfortable, and what is safe, both organizationally and careerwise. Inside-out strategies, while not disconnected from industry and competitive conditions, stop short of being market-driven and customer-driven. Rather, outside considerations end up being compromised to accommodate internal considerations. The weaker a manager's entrepreneurial instincts and capabilities, the greater a manager's propensity to engage in inside-out strategizing, an outcome that raises the potential for reduced competitiveness and weakened organizational commitment to total customer satisfaction.

Good strategy-making is more outside-in than inside-out.

How boldly managers embrace new strategic opportunities, how much they emphasize out-innovating the competition, and how often they lead actions to improve organizational performance are good barometers of their entrepreneurial spirit. Entrepreneurial strategy-makers are inclined to be first-movers, responding quickly and opportunistically to new developments. They are willing to take prudent risks and initiate trailblazing strategies. In contrast, reluctant entrepreneurs are risk-averse; they tend to be late-movers, hopeful about their chances of soon catching up and alert to how they can avoid whatever "mistakes" they believe first-movers have made. They prefer incremental strategic change over bold and sweeping strategic moves.

In strategy-making, all managers, not just senior executives, must take prudent risks and exercise entrepreneurship. Entrepreneurship is involved when a district customer service manager, as part of a company's commitment to better customer service, crafts a strategy to speed the response time on service calls by 25 percent and commits $15,000 to equip all service trucks with mobile telephones. Entrepreneurship is involved when a warehousing manager contributes to a company's strategic emphasis on total quality by figuring out how to reduce the error frequency on filling customer orders from one error every 100 orders to one error every 100,000. A sales manager exercises strategic entrepreneurship by deciding to run a special promotion and cut sales prices by 5 percent to wrest market share away from rivals. A manufacturing manager exercises strategic entrepreneurship in deciding, as part of a companywide emphasis on greater cost competitiveness, to source an important component from a lower-priced South Korean supplier instead of making it in-house. Company strategies can't be truly market- and customer-driven unless the strategy-related activities of managers all across the company have an outside-in entrepreneurial character and contribute to boosting customer satisfaction and achieving sustainable competitive advantage.

Why Company Strategies Evolve Frequent finetuning and tweaking of a company's strategy, first in one department or functional area and then in another, are quite normal. On occasion, quantum changes in strategy are called for—when a competitor makes a dramatic move, when technological breakthroughs occur, or when crisis strikes and managers are forced to make radical strategy alterations very quickly. Because strategic moves and new action approaches are ongoing across the business, an organization's strategy forms over a period of time and then reforms as the number of changes begin to mount. Current strategy is typically a blend of holdover approaches, fresh actions and reactions, and potential moves in the planning stage. Except for crisis situations (where many strategic moves are often made quickly to produce a substantially new strategy almost overnight) and new company start-ups (where strategy exists mostly in the form of plans and intended actions), it is common for key elements of a company's strategy to emerge in bits and pieces as the business develops.

> A company's strategy is dynamic, emerging in bits and pieces as the enterprise develops, always subject to revision whenever managers see avenues for improvement or a need to adapt business approaches to changing conditions.

Rarely is a company's strategy so well-conceived and durable that it can withstand the test of time. Even the best-laid business plans must be adapted to shifting market conditions, altered customer needs and preferences, the strategic maneuvering of rival firms, the experience of what is working and what isn't, emerging opportunities and threats, unforeseen events, and fresh thinking about how to improve the strategy. This is why strategy-making is a dynamic process and why a manager must reevaluate strategy regularly, refining and recasting it as needed.

However, when strategy changes so fast and so fundamentally that the game plan undergoes major overhaul every few months, managers are almost certainly guilty of poor strategic analysis, erratic decision-making, and weak "strategizing." Quantum changes in strategy are needed occasionally, especially in crisis situations, but they cannot be made too often without creating undue organizational confusion and disrupting performance. Well-crafted strategies normally have a life of at least several years, requiring only minor tweaking to keep them in tune with changing circumstances.

What Does a Company's Strategy Consist Of?   Company strategies concern *how:* how to grow the business, how to satisfy customers, how to outcompete rivals, how to respond to changing market conditions, how to manage each functional piece of the business, how to achieve strategic and financial objectives. The hows of strategy tend to be company-specific, customized to a company's own situation and performance objectives. In the business world, companies have a wide degree of strategic freedom. They can diversify broadly or narrowly, into related or unrelated industries, via acquisition, joint venture, strategic alliances, or internal start-up. Even when a company elects to concentrate on a single business, prevailing market conditions usually offer enough strategy-making latitude that close competitors can easily avoid carbon-copy strategies—some pursue low-cost leadership, others stress various combinations of product/service attributes, and still others elect to cater to the special needs and preferences of narrow buyer segments. Hence, descriptions of the content of company strategy necessarily have to be suggestive rather than definitive.

Figure 1–3 depicts the kinds of actions and approaches that reflect a company's overall strategy. Because many are visible to outside observers, most of a company's strategy can be deduced from its actions and public pronouncements. Yet, there's an unrevealed portion of strategy outsiders can only speculate about—the actions and moves company managers are considering. Managers often, for good reason, choose not to reveal certain elements of their strategy until the time is right.

To get a better understanding of the content of company strategies, see the overview of McDonald's strategy in Illustration Capsule 3 on page 12.

Company strategies are partly visible and partly hidden to outside view.

FIGURE 1–3 | **Understanding a Company's Strategy—What to Look For**

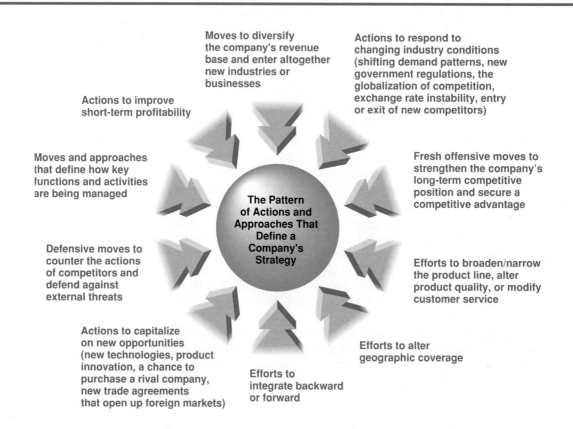

Strategy and Strategic Plans Developing a strategic vision and mission, establishing objectives, and deciding on a strategy are basic direction-setting tasks. They map out where the organization is headed, its short-range and long-range performance targets, and the competitive moves and internal action approaches to be used in achieving the targeted results. Together, they constitute a *strategic plan.* In some companies, especially large corporations committed to regular strategy reviews and formal strategic planning, a document describing the upcoming year's strategic plan is prepared and circulated to managers and employees (although parts of the plan may be omitted or expressed in general terms if they are too sensitive to reveal before they are actually undertaken). In other companies, the strategic plan is not put in writing for widespread distribution but rather exists in the form of consensus and commitments among managers about where to head, what to accomplish, and how to proceed. Organizational objectives are the part of the strategic plan most often spelled out explicitly and communicated to managers and employees.

However, annual strategic plans seldom anticipate all the strategically relevant events that will transpire in the next 12 months. Unforeseen events, unexpected opportunities or threats, plus the constant bubbling up of new proposals encourage managers to modify planned actions and forge "unplanned" reactions. Postponing the recrafting of strategy until it's time to work on next year's strategic plan is both foolish and unnecessary. Managers who confine their strategizing to the company's regularly scheduled planning cycle (when they can't avoid turning something in) have a wrongheaded concept of what their strategy-making responsibilities are. Once-a-year strategizing under "have to" conditions is not a prescription for managerial success.

STRATEGY IMPLEMENTATION AND EXECUTION

The strategy-implementing function consists of seeing what it will take to make the strategy work and to reach the targeted performance on schedule—the skill here is being good at figuring out what must be done to put the strategy in place, execute it proficiently, and produce good results. The job of implementing strategy is primarily a hands-on, close-to-the-scene administrative task that includes the following principal aspects:

- Building an organization capable of carrying out the strategy successfully.
- Developing budgets that steer resources into those internal activities critical to strategic success.
- Establishing strategy-supportive policies.
- Motivating people in ways that induce them to pursue the target objectives energetically and, if need be, modifying their duties and job behavior to better fit the requirements of successful strategy execution.
- Tying the reward structure to the achievement of targeted results.
- Creating a company culture and work climate conducive to successful strategy implementation.
- Installing internal support systems that enable company personnel to carry out their strategic roles effectively day in and day out.
- Instituting best practices and programs for continuous improvement.
- Exerting the internal leadership needed to drive implementation forward and to keep improving on how the strategy is being executed.

The administrative aim is to create "fits" between the way things are done and what it takes for effective strategy execution. The stronger the fits, the better the execution of

ILLUSTRATION CAPSULE 3

A STRATEGY EXAMPLE: MCDONALD'S

In 1993 McDonald's was the leading food service retailer in the global consumer marketplace, with a strong brand name and systemwide restaurant sales exceeding $22 billion. Two-thirds of its 13,000 restaurants were franchised to 3,750 owner/operators around the world. Sales had grown an average of 8 percent in the U.S. and 20 percent outside the U.S. over the past 10 years.

The company-pioneered food quality specifications, equipment technology, marketing and training programs, operating systems, and supply systems were considered industry standards throughout the world. The Company's strategic priorities were continued growth, providing exceptional customer care, remaining an efficient and quality producer, offering high value, and effectively marketing McDonald's brand on a global scale. McDonald's strategy had the following core elements:

Growth Strategy

- Add 700 to 900 restaurants annually, some company-owned and some franchised, with about two-thirds outside the United States.
- Promote more frequent customer visits via the addition of breakfast and dinner menu items, low-price specials, and Extra Value Meals.

Franchising Strategy

- Be highly selective in granting franchises. (McDonald's approach was to recruit only highly motivated, talented entrepreneurs with integrity and

business experience and train them to become active, on-premise owners of McDonald's; no franchises were granted to corporations, partnerships, or passive investors.)

Store Location and Construction Strategy

- Locate restaurants only on sites that offer convenience to customers and afford long-term sales growth potential. (The company utilized sophisticated site selection techniques to obtain premier locations. In the U.S., the company supplemented its traditional suburban and urban locations with outlets in food courts, major airports, hospitals, and universities; outside the U.S., the strategy was to establish an initial presence in center cities, then open freestanding units with drive-thrus outside center cities. Where site ownership was not practical, McDonald's secured long-term leases.)
- Reduce site costs and building costs by using standardized, cost-efficient store designs and consolidating purchases of equipment and materials via a global sourcing system. (One of the company's four approved designs was half the size of a traditional restaurant, required a smaller parcel of land, was about 25% cheaper, and could accommodate nearly the same volume.)
- Utilize store and site designs that are attractive and pleasing inside and out, and where feasible provide drive-thru service and play areas for children.

Product Line Strategy

- Offer a limited menu.

(continued)

strategy. The most important fits are between strategy and organizational capabilities, between strategy and the reward structure, between strategy and internal support systems, and between strategy and the organization's culture (the latter emerges from the values and beliefs shared by organizational members, the company's approach to people management, and ingrained behaviors, work practices, and ways of thinking). Fitting the ways the organization does things internally to what it takes for effective strategy execution helps unite the organization behind the accomplishment of strategy.

The strategy-implementing task is easily the most complicated and time-consuming part of strategic management. It cuts across virtually all facets of managing and must be initiated from many points inside the organization. The strategy-implementer's

ILLUSTRATION CAPSULE 3

(concluded)

- Expand product offerings into new categories of fast food (chicken, Mexican, pizza, and so on) and include more items for health-conscious customers.
- Do extensive testing to ensure consistent high quality and ample customer appeal before rolling out new menu items systemwide.

Store Operations

- Establish stringent product standards, strictly enforce restaurant operating procedures (especially as concerns food preparation, store cleanliness and friendly, courteous counter service), and build close working relationships with suppliers to assure that food is safe and of the highest quality. (Generally, McDonald's does not supply food, paper products, or equipment to restaurants; instead, it approves suppliers from whom these items can be purchased.)
- Develop new equipment and production systems that improve the ability to serve hotter, better-tasting food, faster and with greater accuracy.

Sales Promotion, Marketing, and Merchandising

- Enhance the McDonald's image of quality, service, cleanliness, and value globally via heavy media advertising and in-store merchandise promotions funded with fees tied to a percent of sales revenues at each restaurant.
- Continue to use value pricing and Extra Value Meals to build customer traffic.
- Use Ronald McDonald to create greater brand

awareness among children and the Mc prefix to reinforce the connection of menu items and McDonald's.

Human Resources and Training

- Offer wage rates that are equitable and nondiscriminatory in every location; teach job skills; reward both individual accomplishments and teamwork; offer career opportunities.
- Hire restaurant crews with good work habits and courteous attitudes and train them to act in ways that will impress customers.
- Provide proper training on delivering customer satisfaction and running a fast-food business to franchisees, restaurant managers, and assistant managers. (Instructors at four Hamburger University campuses in Illinois, Germany, England, and Japan in 1992 trained over 3,000 students in 20 languages.)

Social Responsibility

- Operate in a socially responsible manner by supporting educational programs for student employees, Ronald McDonald Houses (at year-end 1992, there were 150 houses in nine countries providing a home-away-from-home for families of seriously ill children receiving treatment at nearby hospitals), workforce diversity and voluntary affirmative action, minority-owned franchises (McDonald's franchises included the largest and most successful group of minority entrepreneurs in the U.S.), recycling (McDonald's McRecycle USA program has won national awards), and by providing nutritional information on McDonald's products to customers.

Source: Company annual reports.

agenda for action emerges from careful assessment of what the organization must do differently and better to carry out the strategic plan proficiently. Each manager has to think through the answer to "What has to be done in my area to carry out my piece of the strategic plan, and how can I best get it done?" How much internal change is needed to put the strategy into effect depends on the degree of strategic change, how much internal practices deviate from what the strategy requires, and how well strategy and organizational culture already match. As needed changes and actions are identified, management must supervise all the details of implementation and apply enough pressure on the organization to convert objectives into results. Depending on the amount of internal change involved, full implementation can take several months to several years.

Strategy implementation is fundamentally an action-oriented, make-it-happen activity—organizing, budgeting, policy-making, motivating, culture-building, and leading are all part of achieving the target results.

EVALUATING PERFORMANCE, REVIEWING NEW DEVELOPMENTS, AND INITIATING CORRECTIVE ADJUSTMENTS

None of the previous four tasks are one-time exercises. New circumstances call for corrective adjustments. Long-term direction may need to be altered, the business redefined, and management's vision of the organization's future course narrowed or broadened. Performance targets may need raising or lowering in light of past experience and future prospects. Strategy may need to be modified because of shifts in long-term direction, because new objectives have been set, or because of changing conditions in the environment.

The search for ever better strategy execution is also continuous. Sometimes an aspect of implementation does not go as well as intended and changes have to be made. Progress is typically uneven—faster in some areas and slower in others. Some tasks get done easily; others prove nettlesome. Implementation has to be thought of as a process, not an event. It occurs through the pooling effect of many managerial decisions and many incremental actions on the part of work groups and individuals across the organization. Budget revisions, policy changes, reorganization, personnel changes, reengineered activities and work processes, culture-changing actions, and revised compensation practices are typical actions managers take to make a strategy work better.

> A company's mission, objectives, strategy, and approach to implementation are never final; evaluating performance, reviewing changes in the surrounding environment, and making adjustments are normal and necessary parts of the strategic management process.

WHY STRATEGIC MANAGEMENT IS AN ONGOING PROCESS

Because each one of the five tasks of strategic management requires constant evaluation and a decision whether to continue or change, a manager cannot afford distractions. Nothing about the strategic management process is final—all prior actions are subject to modification as conditions in the surrounding environment change and ideas for improvement emerge. Strategic management is a process filled with motion. Changes in the organization's situation, either from the inside or outside or both, fuel the need for strategic adjustments. This is why, in Figure 1–1, we highlight the recycling feature inherent in the strategic management process.

The task of evaluating performance and initiating corrective adjustments is both the end and the beginning of the strategic management cycle. The march of external and internal events guarantees that revisions in mission, objectives, strategy, and implementation will be needed sooner or later. It is always incumbent on management to push for better performance—to find ways to improve the existing strategy and how it is being executed. Changing external conditions add further impetus to the need for periodic revisions in a company's mission, performance objectives, strategy, and approaches to strategy execution. Adjustments usually involve fine-tuning, but occasions for major strategic reorientation do arise—sometimes prompted by significant external developments and sometimes by sharply sliding financial performance. Strategy managers must stay close enough to the situation to detect when changing conditions require a strategic response and when they don't. It is their job to sense the winds of change, recognize significant changes early, and initiate adjustments.

CHARACTERISTICS OF THE PROCESS

Although developing a mission, setting objectives, forming a strategy, implementing and executing the strategic plan, and evaluating performance portray what strategic management involves, actually performing these five tasks is not so cleanly divided into separate, neatly sequenced compartments. There is much interplay among the five tasks. For example, considering what strategic actions to take raises issues about whether and how the strategy can be satisfactorily implemented. Deciding on a company mission shades into setting objectives (both involve directional priorities). To establish challenging but achievable objectives, managers must consider both current performance and the strategy options available to improve performance. Deciding on a strategy is entangled with decisions about long-term direction and whether objectives have been set too high or too low. Clearly, the direction-setting tasks of developing a mission, setting objectives, and crafting strategy need to be integrated and done as a package, not individually.

Second, the five strategic management tasks are not done in isolation from a manager's other job responsibilities—supervising day-to-day operations, dealing with crises, going to meetings, preparing reports, handling people problems, and taking on special assignments and civic duties. Thus, while the job of managing strategy is the most important managerial function insofar as organizational success or failure is concerned, it isn't all managers must do or be concerned about.

Third, crafting and implementing strategy make erratic demands on a manager's time. Change does not happen in an orderly or predictable way. Events can build quickly or gradually; they can emerge singly or in rapid-fire succession; and their implications for strategic change can be easy or hard to diagnose. Hence the task of reviewing and adjusting the strategic game plan can take up big chunks of management time in some months and little time in other months. As a practical matter, there is as much skill in knowing *when* to institute strategic changes as there is in knowing *what* to do.

Last, the big day in, day out time-consuming aspect of strategic management involves trying to get the best strategy-supportive performance out of every individual and trying to perfect the current strategy by refining its content and execution. Managers usually spend most of their efforts improving bits and pieces of the current strategy rather than developing and instituting radical changes. Excessive changes in strategy can be disruptive to employees and confusing to customers, and they are usually unnecessary. Most of the time, there's more to be gained from improving execution of the present strategy. Persistence in making a sound strategy work better is often the key to managing the strategy to success.

> Strategic management is a process; the boundaries between the five tasks are conceptual, not real.

WHO PERFORMS THE FIVE TASKS OF STRATEGIC MANAGEMENT?

An organization's chief executive officer, as captain of the ship, is the most visible and important strategy manager. The title of CEO carries with it the mantles of chief direction-setter, chief objective-setter, chief strategy-maker, and chief strategy-implementer for the total enterprise. Ultimate responsibility for leading the tasks of formulating and implementing a strategic plan for the whole organization rests with the CEO, even though many other managers normally have a hand in the process. What the CEO views as strategically important usually is reflected in the company's strategy, and the CEO customarily puts a personal stamp of approval on big strategic decisions and actions.

Vice presidents for production, marketing, finance, human resources, and other functional departments have important strategy-making and strategy-implementing responsibilities as well. Normally, the production VP has a lead role in developing the company's production strategy; the marketing VP oversees the marketing strategy effort; the financial VP is in charge of devising an appropriate financial strategy; and so on. Usually, functional vice presidents are also involved in proposing key elements of the overall company strategy and developing major new strategic initiatives, working closely with the CEO to hammer out a consensus and coordinate various aspects of the strategy more effectively. Only in the smallest, owner-managed companies is the strategy-making, strategy-implementing task small enough for a single manager to handle.

But managerial positions with strategy-making and strategy-implementing responsibility are by no means restricted to CEOs, vice presidents, and owner-entrepreneurs. Every major organizational unit in a company—business unit, division, staff support group, plant, or district office—normally has a leading or supporting role in the company's strategic game plan. And the manager in charge of that organizational unit, with guidance from superiors, usually ends up doing some or most of the strategy-making for the unit and deciding how to implement whatever strategic choices are made. While managers farther down in the managerial hierarchy obviously have a narrower, more specific strategy-making/strategy-implementing role than managers closer to the top, every manager is a strategy-maker and strategy-implementer for the area he/she supervises.

One of the primary reasons why middle- and lower-echelon managers are part of the strategy-making/strategy-implementing team is that the more geographically scattered and diversified an organization's operations are, the more unwieldy it becomes for senior executives to craft and implement all the necessary actions and programs. Managers in the corporate office seldom know enough about the situation in every geographic area and operating unit to direct every move made in the field. It is common practice for top-level managers to grant some strategy-making responsibility to managerial subordinates who head the organizational subunits where specific strategic results must be achieved. Delegating a strategy-making role to on-the-scene managers charged with implementing whatever strategic moves are made in their areas fixes accountability for strategic success or failure. When the managers who implement the strategy are also its architects, it is hard for them to shift blame or make excuses if they don't achieve the target results. And since they have participated in developing the strategy they are trying to implement and execute, they ought to have strong buy-in and support for the strategy, an essential condition for effective strategy execution.

In diversified companies where the strategies of several different businesses have to be managed, there are usually four distinct levels of strategy managers:

- The chief executive officer and other senior corporation-level executives who have primary responsibility and personal authority for big strategic decisions affecting the total enterprise and the collection of individual businesses the enterprise has diversified into.

- Managers who have profit-and-loss responsibility for one specific business unit and who are delegated a major leadership role in formulating and implementing strategy for that unit.

- Functional area managers within a given business unit who have direct authority over a major piece of the business (manufacturing, marketing and sales, finance, R&D, personnel) and whose role it is to support the business unit's overall strategy with strategic actions in their own areas.

- Managers of major operating units (plants, sales districts, local offices) who have on-the-scene responsibility for developing the details of strategic efforts in their areas and for implementing and executing the overall strategic plan at the grassroots level.

All managers are involved in the strategy-making and strategy-implementing process.

Single-business enterprises need no more than three of these levels (a business-level strategy manager, functional area strategy managers, and operating-level strategy managers). In a large single-business company, the team of strategy managers consists of the chief executive, who functions as chief strategist with final authority over both strategy and its implementation; the vice presidents in charge of key functions (R&D, production, marketing, finance, human resources, and so on); plus as many operating-unit managers of the various plants, sales offices, distribution centers, and staff support departments as it takes to handle the company's scope of operations. Proprietorships, partnerships, and owner-managed enterprises, however, typically have only one or two strategy managers since in small-scale enterprises the whole strategy-making/strategy-implementing function can be handled by just a few key people.

Managerial jobs involving strategy formulation and implementation abound in not-for-profit organizations as well. In federal and state government, heads of local, district, and regional offices function as strategy managers in their efforts to respond to the needs and situations of the areas they serve (a district manager in Portland may need a slightly different strategy than a district manager in Orlando). In municipal government, the heads of various departments (fire, police, water and sewer, parks and recreation, health, and so on) are strategy managers because they have line authority for the operations of their departments and thus can influence departmental objectives, the formation of a strategy to achieve these objectives, and how the strategy is implemented.

Managerial jobs with strategy-making/strategy-implementing roles are thus the norm rather than the exception. The job of crafting and implementing strategy touches virtually every managerial job in one way or another, at one time or another. Strategic management is basic to the task of managing; it is not something just top-level managers deal with.

THE ROLE AND TASKS OF STRATEGIC PLANNERS

If senior and middle managers have the lead roles in strategy-making and strategy-implementing in their areas of responsibility, what should strategic planners do? Is there a legitimate place in big companies for a strategic planning department staffed with specialists in planning and strategic analysis? The answer is yes. But the planning department's role and tasks should consist chiefly of helping to gather and organize information that strategy-makers need, establishing and administering an annual strategy review cycle whereby managers reconsider and refine their strategic plans, and coordinating the process of reviewing and approving the strategic plans developed for all the various parts of the company. Strategic planners can help managers at all levels crystallize the strategic issues that ought to be addressed; in addition, they can provide data, help analyze industry and competitive conditions, and distribute information on the company's strategic performance. But strategic planners should not make strategic decisions, prepare strategic plans (for someone else to implement), or make strategic action recommendations that usurp the strategy-making responsibilities of managers in charge of major operating units.

When strategic planners are asked to go beyond providing staff assistance and actually prepare a strategic plan for management's consideration, either of two adverse consequences may occur. First, some managers will gladly toss their tough strategic problems onto the desks of strategic planners and let the planners do their strategic thinking for them. The planners, not knowing as much about the situation as managers do, are in a weaker position to design a workable action plan. And they can't be held responsible for implementing what they recommend. Giving planners responsibility for strategy-making and line managers responsibility for implementation makes it hard to fix accountability for poor results. It also deludes line managers into thinking they shouldn't be held responsible for crafting a strategy for their own organizational unit or for devising solutions to strategic problems in their area of responsibility. The hard truth is that strategy-making is not a staff function, nor is it something that can be handed off to an advisory committee of lower-ranking managers. Second, when line managers have no ownership stake in or personal commitment to the strategic agenda proposed by the planners, they give it lip service, perhaps make a few token implementation efforts, and quickly get back to business as usual, knowing that the formal written plan concocted by the planners carries little weight in shaping their own action agenda and decisions. Unless the planners' written strategic plan has visible, credible top-management support, it quickly collects dust on managers' shelves. Absent belief in and commitment to the actions recommended by the planners, few managers will take the work of the strategic planning staff seriously enough to pursue implementation—strategic planning then comes to be seen as just another bureaucratic exercise.

Either consequence renders formal strategic planning efforts ineffective and opens the door for a strategy-making vacuum conducive to organizational drift or to fragmented, uncoordinated strategic decisions. The odds are that the organization will have no strong strategic rudder and insufficient top-down direction. Having staffers or advisory committees formulate strategies for areas they do not directly manage is therefore flawed in two respects: (1) they can't be held accountable if their recommendations don't produce the desired results since they don't have authority for directing implementation, and (2) there's a strong chance that what they recommend won't be well accepted or enthusiastically implemented by those who "have to sing the song the planners have written"—lukewarm buy-in is a guaranteed plan-killer.

On the other hand, when line managers are expected to be the chief strategy-makers and strategy-implementers for the areas they head, their own strategy and implementation end up being put to the test. As a consequence, their buy-in becomes a given, and they usually commit the time and resources to make the plan work (their annual performance reviews and perhaps even their future careers with the organization are at risk if the plan fails and they fail to achieve the target results!). When those who craft strategy are also those who must implement strategy, there's no question who is accountable for results. Moreover, when authority for crafting and implementing the strategy of an organizational unit is placed on the shoulders of the unit manager, it's easy to fix accountability for results and it pushes strategic decisions down to the manager closest to the action who *should* know what to do. Unit managers who consistently prove incapable of crafting and implementing good strategies and achieving target results have to be moved to less responsible positions.

THE STRATEGIC ROLE OF THE BOARD OF DIRECTORS

Since lead responsibility for crafting and implementing strategy falls to key managers, the chief strategic role of an organization's board of directors is to see that the overall task of managing strategy is adequately done. Boards of directors normally review important strategic moves and officially approve the strategic plans submitted by senior management—a procedure that makes the board ultimately responsible for the strategic actions taken. But directors rarely can or should play a direct role in for-

---

Strategic Management Principle
Strategy-making is not a proper task for strategic planners.

Strategic Management Principle
A board of directors' role in the strategic management process is to critically appraise and ultimately approve strategic action plans but rarely, if ever, to develop the details.

mulating strategy. The immediate task of directors is to ensure that all proposals have been adequately analyzed and considered and that the proposed strategic actions are superior to available alternatives; flawed proposals are customarily withdrawn for revision by management.

The longer-range task of directors is to evaluate the caliber of senior executives' strategy-making and strategy-implementing skills. The board must determine whether the current CEO is doing a good job of strategic management (as a basis for awarding salary increases and bonuses and deciding on retention or removal) and evaluate the strategic skills of other senior executives in line to succeed the CEO. In recent years, at General Motors, IBM, American Express, Goodyear, and Compaq Computer, company directors concluded that executives were not adapting their company's strategy fast enough and fully enough to the changes sweeping their markets. They pressured the CEOs to resign, and installed new leadership to provide the impetus for strategic renewal. Boards who fail to review the strategy-making, strategy-implementing skills of senior executives face embarrassment or even lawsuits when an out-dated strategy sours company performance and management fails to come up with a promising turnaround strategy.

THE BENEFITS OF A "STRATEGIC APPROACH" TO MANAGING

The message of this book is that doing a good job of managing inherently requires good strategic thinking and good strategic management. Today's managers have to think strategically about their company's position and about the impact of changing conditions. They have to monitor the external situation closely enough to know when to institute strategy change. They have to know the business well enough to know what kinds of strategic changes to initiate. Simply said, the fundamentals of strategic management need to drive the whole approach to managing organizations. The chief executive officer of one successful company put it well when he said:

> In the main, our competitors are acquainted with the same fundamental concepts and techniques and approaches that we follow, and they are as free to pursue them as we are. More often than not, the difference between their level of success and ours lies in the relative thoroughness and self-discipline with which we and they develop and execute our strategies for the future.

The advantages of first-rate strategic thinking and conscious strategy management (as opposed to freewheeling improvisation, gut feel, and drifting along) include (1) providing better guidance to the entire organization on the crucial point of "what it is we are trying to do and to achieve," (2) making managers more alert to the winds of change, new opportunities, and threatening developments, (3) providing managers with a rationale for evaluating competing budget requests for investment capital and new staff—a rationale that argues strongly for steering resources into strategy-supportive, results-producing areas, (4) helping to unify the numerous strategy-related decisions by managers across the organization, and (5) creating a more proactive management posture and counteracting tendencies for decisions to be reactive and defensive.

The advantage of being proactive is that trailblazing strategies can be the key to better long-term performance. Business history shows that high-performing enterprises often initiate and lead, not just react and defend. They launch strategic offensives to out-innovate and out-maneuver rivals and secure sustainable competitive advantage, then use their market edge to achieve superior financial performance. Aggressive pursuit of a creative, opportunistic strategy can propel a firm into a leadership position, paving the way for its products/services to become the industry standard.

TERMS TO REMEMBER

In the chapters to come, we'll be using some key phrases and terms again and again. You'll find the following definitional listing helpful.

Strategic vision—a view of an organization's future direction and business course; a guiding concept for what the organization is trying to do and to become.

Organization mission—management's customized answer to the question "What is our business and what are we trying to accomplish on behalf of our customers?" A mission statement broadly outlines the organization's activities and business makeup.

Financial objectives—the targets management has established for the organization's financial performance.

Strategic objectives—the targets management has established for strengthening the organization's overall business position and competitive vitality.

Long-range objectives—the results to be achieved either within the next three to five years or else on an ongoing basis year after year.

Short-range objectives—the organization's near-term performance targets; the amount of short-term improvement signals how fast management is trying to achieve the long-range objectives.

Strategy—the pattern of actions managers employ to achieve organizational objectives; a company's actual strategy is partly planned and partly reactive to changing circumstances.

Strategic plan—a statement outlining an organization's mission and future direction, near-term and long-term performance targets, and strategy.

Strategy formulation—the entire direction-setting management function of conceptualizing an organization's mission, setting performance objectives, and crafting a strategy. The end product of strategy formulation is a strategic plan.

Strategy implementation—the full range of managerial activities associated with putting the chosen strategy into place, supervising its pursuit, and achieving the targeted results.

On the following pages, we will probe the strategy-related tasks of managers and the methods of strategic analysis much more intensively. When you get to the end of the book, we think you will see that two factors separate the best-managed organizations from the rest: (1) superior strategy-making and entrepreneurship, and (2) competent implementation and execution of the chosen strategy. There's no escaping the fact that the quality of managerial strategy-making and strategy-implementing has a significant impact on organization performance. A company that lacks clear-cut direction, has vague or undemanding objectives, has a muddled or flawed strategy, or can't seem to execute plans competently is a company whose performance is probably suffering, whose business is at long-term risk, and whose management is less than capable.

SUGGESTED READINGS

Andrews, Kenneth R. *The Concept of Corporate Strategy.* 3rd ed. Homewood, Ill.: Richard D. Irwin, 1987, chap. 1.

Gluck, Frederick W. "A Fresh Look at Strategic Management." *Journal of Business Strategy* 6 no. 2 (Fall 1985), pp. 4–21.

Hax, Arnoldo C., and Nicolas S. Majluf. *The Strategy Concept and Process: A Pragmatic Approach.* Englewood Cliffs, N.J.: Prentice-Hall, 1991, chaps. 1 and 2.

Kelley, C. Aaron. "The Three Planning Questions: A Fable." *Business Horizons* 26, no. 2 (March–April 1983), pp. 46–48.

Mintzberg, Henry. "The Strategy Concept: Five Ps for Strategy." *California Management Review* 30, no. 1 (Fall 1987), pp. 11–24.

———. "The Strategy Concept: Another Look at Why Organizations Need Strategies." *California Management Review* 30, no. 1 (Fall 1987), pp. 25–32.

———. "Crafting Strategy." *Harvard Business Review* 65, no. 4 (July–August 1987), pp. 66–75.

Quinn, James B. *Strategies for Change: Logical Incrementalism.* Homewood, Ill.: Richard D. Irwin, 1980, chaps. 2 and 3.

Ramanujam, V., and N. Venkatraman. "Planning and Performance: A New Look at an Old Question." *Business Horizons* 30, no. 3 (May–June 1987), pp. 19–25.

Yip, George S. *Total Global Strategy: Managing for Worldwide Competitive Advantage.* Englewood Cliffs, N.J.: Prentice-Hall, 1992, chap. 1.

## CHAPTER TWO

THE THREE STRATEGY-MAKING TASKS
DEVELOPING A STRATEGIC VISION, SETTING OBJECTIVES, AND CRAFTING A STRATEGY

How can you lead if you don't know where you are going?

George Newman
The Conference Board

Management's job is not to see the company as it is . . . but as it can become.

John W. Teets
CEO, Greyhound Corporation

Once your direction becomes clear to you and fully visible to others, all the elements of winning—attitude, performance, teamwork, and competition—begin to come together.

Dennis Conner

Without a strategy the organization is like a ship without a rudder, going around in circles. It's like a tramp; it has no place to go.

Joel Ross and Michael Kami

In this chapter, we provide a more in-depth look at each of the three strategy-making tasks: developing a strategic vision and business mission, setting performance objectives, and crafting a strategy to produce the desired results. We also examine the kinds of strategic decisions made at each management level, the major determinants of a company's strategy, and four frequently used managerial approaches to forming a strategic plan.

DEVELOPING A STRATEGIC VISION AND MISSION: THE FIRST DIRECTION-SETTING TASK

Management's views about what activities the organization intends to pursue and the long-term course it charts for the future constitute a *strategic vision*. A strategic vision provides a big picture perspective of "who *we* are, what *we* do, and where *we* are headed." It leaves no doubt about the company's long-term direction and where management intends to take the company. A well-conceived strategic vision is a prerequisite to effective strategic leadership. A manager cannot function effectively as either leader or strategy-maker without a sound concept of the business, what activities to pursue, what not to pursue, and what kind of long-term competitive position to build vis-à-vis both customers and competitors.

Although we use the following terms interchangeably, we like *strategic vision* better than the more common term *business mission* or *mission statement*. Missions tend to be more concerned with the present ("What is our business?") than with the bigger issue of long-term direction (where are we headed, what new things do we intend to pursue, what will our business makeup be in 5 to 10 years, what kind of company are we trying to become, and what sort of long-term market position do we aspire to achieve?).

Strategic visions and company mission statements are always highly personalized. Generic statements, applicable to any company or to any industry, have no managerial value. A strategic vision/mission statement sets an organization apart from others in its industry and gives it its own special identity, business emphasis, and path for development. For example, the mission of a globally active New York bank like Citicorp has little in common with that of a locally owned small-town bank even though both are in the banking industry. Compaq Computer is not on the same strategic path as IBM, even though both sell personal computers. General Electric is not on the same long-term strategic course as Whirlpool Corp., even though both are leaders in the major home appliance business; while Whirlpool's business is concentrated in appliances, GE has major business positions in aircraft engines, defense electronics, engineering plastics, electric power generation equipment, factory automation, locomotives, lighting, medical diagnostic imaging, and TV broadcasting (it owns NBC). Similarly, there are important differences between the long-term strategic direction of such fierce business rivals as Intel and Motorola, Philips and Matsushita, Eastman Kodak and Fuji Photo Film Co., Michelin and Bridgestone/Firestone, Procter & Gamble and Unilever, and British Telecom and AT&T. Illustration Capsule 4 describes Delta Airlines' strategic vision.

Sometimes companies mistakenly couch their mission in terms of making a profit. However, profit is more correctly an *objective* and a *result* of what the company does. The desire to make a profit says nothing about the business arena in which profits are to be sought. Missions based on making a profit are incapable of distinguishing one type of profit-seeking enterprise from another—the business and long-term direction of Sears are plainly different from the business and long-term direction of Toyota, even though both endeavor to earn a profit. A company that says its mission is to make a profit begs the question "What will we do to make a profit?" To know anything useful about a company's business mission, we must know management's answer to "make a profit doing what and for whom?"

There are three distinct aspects involved in forming a well-conceived strategic vision and expressing it in a company mission statement:

- Understanding what business a company is really in.
- Communicating the vision and mission in ways that are clear, exciting, and inspiring.
- Deciding when to alter the company's strategic course and change its business mission.

Effective strategy-making begins with a concept of what the organization should and should not do and a vision of where the organization needs to be headed.

Visionless companies are unsure what business position they are trying to stake out.

ILLUSTRATION CAPSULE 4

DELTA AIRLINES' STRATEGIC VISION

In late 1993, Ronald W. Allen, Delta's chief executive officer, described the company's vision and business mission in the following way:

. . . we want Delta to be the **Worldwide Airline of Choice.**

　Worldwide, because we are and intend to remain an innovative, aggressive, ethical, and successful competitor that offers access to the world at the highest standards of customer service. We will continue to look for opportunities to extend our reach through new routes and creative global alliances.

Airline, because we intend to stay in the business we know best—air transportation and related services. We won't stray from our roots. We believe in the long-term prospects for profitable growth in the airline industry, and we will continue to focus time, attention, and investment on enhancing our place in that business environment.

Of Choice, because we value the loyalty of our customers, employees, and investors. For passengers and shippers, we will continue to provide the best service and value. For our personnel, we will continue to offer an ever more challenging, rewarding, and result-oriented workplace that recognizes and appreciates their contributions. For our shareholders, we will earn a consistent, superior financial return.

Source: Sky Magazine, December 1993, p. 10.

UNDERSTANDING AND DEFINING THE BUSINESS

Deciding what business an organization is in is neither obvious nor easy. Is IBM in the computer business (a product-oriented definition) or the information and data processing business (a customer service or customer needs type of definition) or the advanced electronics business (a technology-based definition)? Is Coca-Cola in the soft-drink business (in which case its strategic vision can be trained narrowly on the actions of Pepsi, 7UP, Dr Pepper, Canada Dry, and Schweppes)? Or is it in the beverage industry (in which case management must think strategically about positioning Coca-Cola products in a market that includes fruit juices, alcoholic drinks, milk, bottled water, coffee, and tea)? This is not a trivial question for Coca-Cola. Many young adults get their morning caffeine fix by drinking cola instead of coffee; with a beverage industry perspective as opposed to a soft-drink industry perspective, Coca-Cola management is more likely to perceive a long-term growth opportunity in winning youthful coffee drinkers over to its colas.

　Arriving at a good business definition usually requires taking three factors into account:[1]

> A company's business is defined by what needs it is trying to satisfy, by which customer groups it is targeting, and by the technologies it will use and the functions it will perform in serving the target market.

1. Customer needs, or *what* is being satisfied.
2. Customer groups, or *who* is being satisfied.
3. The technologies used and functions performed—*how* customers' needs are satisfied.

Defining a business in terms of what to satisfy, who to satisfy, and how the organization will go about producing the satisfaction makes a complete definition. It takes all three. Just knowing what products or services a firm provides is never enough. Products or services *per se* are not important to customers; a product or service becomes a

---

[1]Derek F. Abell, *Defining the Business: The Starting Point of Strategic Planning* (Englewood Cliffs, N.J.: Prentice-Hall, 1980), p. 169.

business when it satisfies a need or want. Without the need or want there is no business. Customer groups are relevant because they indicate the market to be served—the geographic domain to be covered and the types of buyers the firm is going after.

Technology and functions performed are important because they indicate *how* the company will satisfy the customers' needs and how much of the industry's production-distribution chain its activities will span. For instance, a firm's business can be *specialized,* concentrated in just one stage of an industry's total production-distribution chain, or *fully integrated,* spanning all parts of the industry chain. Wal-Mart, Home Depot, Toys-R-Us, and The Limited are essentially one-stage firms. Their operations focus on the retail end of the consumer goods business; they don't manufacture the items they sell. Delta Airlines is a one-stage enterprise; it doesn't manufacture the airplanes it flies, and it doesn't operate the airports where it lands. Delta made a conscious decision to limit its business mission to moving travelers from one location to another via commercial jet aircraft. Major international oil companies like Exxon, Mobil, and Chevron, however, are fully integrated. They lease drilling sites, drill wells, pump oil, transport crude oil in their own ships and pipelines to their own refineries, and sell gasoline and other refined products through their own networks of branded distributors and service station outlets. Because of the disparity in functions performed and technology employed, the business of a retailer like Lands' End or Wal-Mart is much narrower and quite different than that of a fully integrated enterprise like Exxon.

Between these two extremes, firms can stake out *partially integrated* positions, participating only in selected stages of the industry. Goodyear, for instance, both manufactures tires and operates a chain of company-owned retail tire stores, but it has not integrated backward into rubber plantations and other tire-making components. General Motors, the world's most integrated manufacturer of cars and trucks, makes between 60 and 70 percent of the parts and components used in assembling GM vehicles. But GM is moving to outsource a greater fraction of its parts and systems components, and it relies totally on a network of independent, franchised dealers to handle sales and service functions.

So one way of distinguishing a firm's business, especially among firms in the same industry, is by looking at which functions it performs in the production-distribution chain and how far its scope of operation extends across all the business activities involved in getting products to end-users.

One good example of a business definition that incorporates all three components—needs served, target market, and functions performed— is Polaroid's business definition during the early 1970s: "perfecting and marketing instant photography to satisfy the needs of more affluent U.S. and West European families for affection, friendship, fond memories, and humor." McDonald's mission is focused on "serving a limited menu of hot, tasty food quickly in a clean, friendly restaurant for a good value" to a broad base of fast-food customers worldwide (McDonald's serves approximately 25 million customers daily at some 13,000 restaurants in over 65 countries). The concepts that McDonald's uses to define its business are a limited menu, good-tasting fast-food products of consistent quality, value pricing, exceptional customer care, convenient locations, and global market coverage.

Trying to identify needs served, target market, and functions performed in a single, snappy sentence is a challenge, and many firms' mission statements fail to illuminate all three bases explicitly. The mission statements of some companies are thus better than others in terms of how they cut to the chase of what the enterprise is really about.

A Broad or Narrow Business Definition?　A small Hong Kong printing company that defines its business broadly as "Asian-language communications" gains no practical guidance in making direction-setting decisions. With such a definition the company could pursue limitless courses, many well beyond its scope and capability. To have managerial value, strategic visions, business definitions, and mission statements must be narrow enough to pin down the company's real arena of business interest. Consider the following definitions based on broad-narrow scope:

Broad Definition	Narrow Definition
• Beverages	• Soft drinks
• Footwear	• Athletic footwear
• Furniture	• Wrought iron lawn furniture
• Global mail delivery	• Overnight package delivery
• Travel and tourism	• Ship cruises in the Caribbean

Broad-narrow definitions are relative, of course. Being in "the furniture business" is probably too broad a concept for a company intent on being the largest manufacturer of wrought-iron lawn furniture in North America. On the other hand, "soft drinks" has proved too narrow a scope for a growth-oriented company like Coca-Cola, which, with its beverage-industry perspective, acquired Minute-Maid and Hi-C (to capitalize on growing consumer interest in fruit-juice products) and Taylor Wine Company (using the California Cellars brand to establish a foothold in wines).[2] The U.S. Postal Service operates with a broad definition, providing global mail-delivery services to all types of senders. Federal Express, however, operates with a narrow business definition based on handling overnight package delivery for customers who have unplanned emergencies and tight deadlines.

Diversified firms have more sweeping business definitions than do single-business enterprises. Their mission statements typically are phrased narrowly enough to pinpoint their current customer-market-technology arenas but are open-ended and adaptable enough to incorporate expansion into new businesses. Alcan, Canada's leading aluminum company, used broad, inclusive words in expressing its strategic vision and mission:

Diversified companies have broader missions and business definitions than single-business enterprises.

> Alcan is determined to be the most innovative diversified aluminum company in the world. To achieve this position, Alcan will be one, global, customer-oriented enterprise committed to excellence and lowest cost in its chosen aluminum businesses, with significant resources devoted to building an array of new businesses with superior growth and profit potential.

Thermo Electron Corp., a substantially more diversified enterprise, used simultaneous broad-narrow terms to define its arenas of business interest:

> Thermo Electron Corporation develops, manufactures, and markets environmental, analytical, and test instruments, alternative-energy power plants, low-emission combustion systems, paper- and waste-recycling equipment, and biomedical products. The company also operates power plants and provides services in environmental sciences and

---

[2]Coca-Cola's foray into wines was not viewed as successful enough to warrant continuation; the division was divested about five years after initial acquisition.

analysis, thermal waste treatment, and specialty metals fabrication and processing, as well as research and product development in unconventional imaging, laser technology, and direct-energy conversion.

Times Mirror Corp., also a diversified enterprise, describes its business scope in broad but still fairly explicit terminology:

Times Mirror is a media and information company principally engaged in newspaper publishing; book, magazine and other publishing; and cable and broadcast television.

John Hancock's mission statement communicates a shift from its long-standing base in insurance to a broader mission in insurance, banking, and diversified financial services:

At John Hancock, we are determined not just to compete but to advance, building our market share by offering individuals and institutions the broadest possible range of products and services. Apart from insurance, John Hancock encompasses banking products, full brokerage services and institutional investment, to cite only a few of our diversified activities. We believe these new directions constitute the right moves . . . the steps that will drive our growth throughout the remainder of this century.

Mission Statements for Functional Departments   There's also a place for mission statements for key functions (R&D, marketing, finance) and support units (human resources, training, information systems). Every department can benefit from a consensus statement spelling out its contribution to the company mission, its principal role and activities, and the direction it needs to be moving. Functional and departmental managers who think through and debate with subordinates and higher-ups what their unit needs to focus on and do have a clearer view of how to lead the unit. Three examples from actual companies indicate how a functional mission statement puts the spotlight on a unit's organizational *role* and *scope:*

- The mission of the human resources department is to contribute to organizational success by developing effective leaders, creating high-performance teams, and maximizing the potential of individuals.
- The mission of the corporate claims department is to minimize the overall cost of liability, workers compensation, and property damage claims through competitive cost containment techniques and loss prevention and control programs.
- The mission of corporate security is to provide services for the protection of corporate personnel and assets through preventive measures and investigations.

COMMUNICATING THE STRATEGIC VISION

How to describe the strategic vision, word it in the form of a mission statement, and communicate it down the line to lower-level managers and employees is almost as important as the strategic soundness of the organization's business concept and long-term direction. A vision and mission couched in words that inspire and challenge help build committed effort from employees and serve as powerful motivational tools. Bland language, platitudes, and motherhood-and-apple-pie-style verbiage must be scrupulously avoided—they can be a turn-off rather than a turn-on. Managers need to communicate the vision in words that arouse a strong sense of organizational purpose, build pride, and induce employee buy-in. People are proud to be associated with a company that has a worthwhile mission and is trying to be the world's best at something competitively significant. Having an exciting mission or cause brings the workforce together, galvanizes people to act, stimulates extra effort, and causes people to live the business instead of just coming to work.[3] In organizations with freshly changed missions, executives need to provide a compelling rationale for the new direction and why things must be done differently. Unless people understand how a company's business environment is changing and why a new direction is needed, a new mission statement does little to win employees' commitment or alter work practices—outcomes that can open up a trust gap and make it harder to move the organization down the chosen path.

The best-worded mission statements are simple and concise; they speak loudly and clearly, generate enthusiasm for the firm's future course, and elicit personal effort and dedication from everyone in the organization. They have to be presented and then repeated over and over as a worthy organizational challenge, one capable of benefiting customers in a valuable and meaningful way—indeed it is crucial that the mission stress the payoff for customers and not the payoff for stockholders. It goes *without saying* that the company intends to profit shareholders from its efforts to provide real value to its customers. A crisp, clear, often-repeated, inspiring strategic vision has the power to turn heads in the intended direction and begin a new organizational march. When this occurs, the first step in organizational direction-setting is successfully completed. Illustration Capsule 5 is a good example of an inspiration-oriented company vision and mission.

WHEN TO CHANGE THE MISSION— WHERE ENTREPRENEURSHIP COMES IN

A member of Maytag's board of directors summed it up well when commenting on why the company acquired a European appliance-maker and expanded its arena of business into international markets: "Times change, conditions change." The march of new events and altered circumstances make it incumbent on managers to continually reassess their company's position and prospects, always checking for *when* it's time to steer a new course and adjust the mission. The key strategic question here is "What new directions should we be moving in *now* to get ready for the changes we see coming in our business?"

Repositioning an enterprise in light of emerging developments and changes on the horizon lessens the chances of getting trapped in a stagnant or declining core business or letting attractive new growth opportunities slip away because of inaction. Good entrepreneurs have a sharp eye for shifting customer wants and needs, emerging technological capabilities, changing international trade conditions, and other important signs of growing or shrinking business opportunity. They attend quickly to users' problems and complaints with the industry's current products and services. They listen intently when a customer says, "If only . . ." Such clues and information tidbits stimulate them to think creatively and strategically about ways to break new ground. Appraising new customer-market-technology opportunities ultimately leads to entrepreneurial judgments about which fork in the road to take. It is the strategy-

A well-worded mission statement creates enthusiasm for the future course management has charted; the motivational goal in communicating the mission is to pose a challenge that inspires and engages everyone in the organization.

The entrepreneurial challenge in developing a mission is to recognize when emerging opportunities and threats in the surrounding environment makes it desirable to revise the organization's long-term direction.

---

[3]Tom Peters, *Thriving on Chaos* (New York: Harper & Row, Perennial Library Edition, 1988), pp. 486–487; and Andrall E. Pearson, "Corporate Redemption and The Seven Deadly Sins," *Harvard Business Review* 70, no. 3 (May–June 1992), pp. 66–68.

ILLUSTRATION CAPSULE 5

NOVACARE'S BUSINESS MISSION

NovaCare is a fast-growing health care company specializing in providing patient rehabilitation services on a contract basis to nursing homes. Rehabilitation therapy is a $10 billion industry, of which 35 percent is provided contractually; the contract segment is highly fragmented with over 1,000 competitors. In 1990 NovaCare was a $100 million company, with a goal of being a $300 million business in 1994. The company stated its business mission and vision as follows:

NovaCare is people committed to making a difference . . . enhancing the future of all patients . . . breaking new ground in our professions . . . achieving excellence . . . advancing human capability . . . changing the world in which we live.

We lead the way with our enthusiasm, optimism, patience, drive, and commitment.

We work together to enhance the quality of our patients' lives by reshaping lost abilities and teaching new skills. We heighten expectations for the patient and family. We rebuild hope, confidence, self-respect, and a desire to continue.

We apply our clinical expertise to benefit our patients through creative and progressive tech-

niques. Our ethical and performance standards require us to expend every effort to achieve the best possible results.

Our customers are national and local health care providers who share our goal of enhancing the patients' quality of life. In each community, our customers consider us a partner in providing the best possible care. Our reputation is based on our responsiveness, high standards, and effective systems of quality assurance. Our relationship is open and proactive.

We are advocates of our professions and patients through active participation in the professional, regulatory, educational, and research communities at national, state, and local levels.

Our approach to health care fulfills our responsibility to provide investors with a high rate of return through consistent growth and profitability.

Our people are our most valuable asset. We are committed to the personal, professional, and career development of each individual employee. We are proud of what we do and dedicated to our Company. We foster teamwork and create an environment conducive to productive communication among all disciplines.

NovaCare is a company of people in pursuit of this Vision.

Source: Company annual report.

maker's job to evaluate the risks and prospects of alternative paths and make direction-setting decisions to position the enterprise for success in the years ahead. *A well-chosen mission prepares a company for the future.*

Many companies in consumer electronics and telecommunications believe their future products will incorporate microprocessors and other elements of computer technology. So they are broadening their vision about industry boundaries and establishing new business positions through acquisitions, alliances, and joint ventures to gain better access to cutting-edge technology. Cable TV companies and telephone companies are in a strategic race to install fiber optics technology and position themselves to market a whole new array of services—pay-per-view TV, home shopping, electronic mail, electronic banking, home security systems, energy management systems, information services, and high-speed data transfer—to households and businesses. Numerous companies in manufacturing, seeing the collapse of trade barriers and the swing to a world economy, are broadening their strategic vision from serving domestic markets to serving global markets. Coca-Cola, Kentucky Fried Chicken, and McDonald's are pursuing market opportunities in China, Europe, Japan, and Russia. Japanese automobile companies are working to establish a much bigger presence in the European car market. CNN, Turner Broadcasting's very successful all-news cable channel, is fast winning its way into more and more homes the world over, solidifying its position as the first global all-news channel, a major shift from 10 years ago when its mission was to build a loyal U.S. audience. A company's mission has a finite life, one subject to change whenever top management concludes that the present mission is no longer adequate.

A well-conceived, well-worded mission statement has real managerial value: (1) it crystalizes senior executives' own views about the firm's long-term direction and business makeup, (2) it reduces the risk of visionless management and rudderless decision-making, (3) it conveys an organizational purpose and identity that motivate employees to go all out and do their very best work, (4) it provides a beacon lower-level managers can use to form departmental missions, set departmental objectives, and craft functional and departmental strategies that are in sync with the company's direction and strategy, and (5) it helps an organization prepare for the future.

SETTING OBJECTIVES: THE SECOND DIRECTION-SETTING TASK

Objectives represent a managerial commitment to achieving specific performance targets by a certain time.

Setting objectives converts the strategic vision and directional course into target outcomes and performance milestones. Objectives represent a managerial commitment to producing specified results in a specified time frame. They spell out *how much* of *what kind* of performance *by when.* They direct attention and energy to what needs to be accomplished.

THE MANAGERIAL VALUE OF SETTING OBJECTIVES

Unless an organization's long-term direction and business mission are translated into *measurable* performance targets and managers are pressured to show progress in reaching these targets, statements about direction and mission will end up as nice words, window dressing, and unrealized dreams of accomplishment. The experiences of countless companies and managers teach that *companies whose managers set objectives for each key result area and then aggressively pursue actions calculated to achieve their performance targets typically outperform companies whose managers have good intentions, try hard, and hope for success.*

For performance objectives to have value as a management tool, they must be stated in *quantifiable* or measurable terms and they must contain a *deadline for achievement.* This means avoiding generalities like "maximize profits," "reduce costs," "become more efficient," or "increase sales," which specify neither how much or when. Objective-setting is a call for action—what to achieve, when to achieve it, and who is responsible. As Bill Hewlett, co-founder of Hewlett-Packard, once observed, "You cannot manage what you cannot measure . . . And what gets measured gets done."[4] Spelling out organization objectives in measurable terms and then holding managers accountable for reaching their assigned targets within a specified time frame (1) substitutes purposeful strategic decision-making for aimless actions and confusion over what to accomplish and (2) provides a set of benchmarks for judging the organization's performance.

---

[4]As quoted in Charles H. House and Raymond L. Price, "The Return Map: Tracking Product Teams," Harvard Business Review 60, no. 1 (January–February 1991), p. 93.

WHAT KINDS OF OBJECTIVES TO SET

Objectives are needed for each *key result* managers deem important to success.[5] Two types of key result areas stand out: those relating to *financial performance* and those relating to *strategic performance*. Achieving acceptable financial performance is a must; otherwise the organization's survival ends up at risk. Achieving acceptable strategic performance is essential to sustaining and improving the company's long-term market position and competitiveness. Specific kinds of financial and strategic performance objectives are shown below:

Strategic Management Principle
Every company needs both strategic objectives and financial objectives.

Financial Objectives	Strategic Objectives
• Faster revenue growth	• A bigger market share
• Faster earnings growth	• A higher, more secure industry rank
• Higher dividends	• Higher product quality
• Wider profit margins	• Lower costs relative to key competitors
• Higher returns on invested capital	• Broader or more attractive product line
• Stronger bond and credit ratings	• A stronger reputation with customers
• Bigger cash flows	• Superior customer service
• A rising stock price	• Recognition as a leader in technology and/or product innovation
• Recognition as a "blue chip" company	• Increased ability to compete in international markets
• A more diversified revenue base	• Expanded growth opportunities
• Stable earnings during recessionary periods	• Total customer satisfaction

Illustration Capsule 6 provides a sampling of the strategic and financial objectives of three well-known enterprises.

Strategic Objectives versus Financial Objectives: Which Take Precedence? Both financial and strategic objectives carry top priority. However, sometimes companies under pressure to improve near-term financial performance elect to kill or postpone strategic moves that hold promise for strengthening the enterprise's business and competi-

---

[5]The literature of management is filled with references to *goals* and *objectives*. These terms are used in a variety of ways, many of them conflicting. Some writers use the term goals to refer to the long-run results an organization seeks to achieve and the term objectives to refer to immediate, short-run performance targets. Some writers reverse the usage, referring to objectives as the desired long-run results and goals as the desired short-run results. Others use the terms interchangeably. And still others use the term goals to refer to broad organizationwide performance targets and the term objectives to designate specific targets set by subordinate managers in response to the broader, more inclusive goals of the whole organization. In our view, little is gained from semantic distinctions between goals and objectives. The important thing is to recognize that the results an enterprise seeks to attain vary both in scope and in time perspective. Nearly always, organizations need to have broad and narrow performance targets for both the near-term and long-term. It is inconsequential which targets are called goals and which objectives. To avoid a semantic jungle, we use the single term *objectives* to refer to the performance targets and results an organization seeks to attain. We use the adjectives *long-range* (or long-run) and *short-range* (or short-run) to identify the relevant time frame, and we try to describe objectives in words that indicate their intended scope and level in the organization.

ILLUSTRATION CAPSULE 6

EXAMPLES OF CORPORATE OBJECTIVES: MCDONALD'S, RUBBERMAID, AND MCCORMICK & COMPANY

McDonald's

- To achieve 100 percent total customer satisfaction . . . everyday . . . in every restaurant . . . for every customer.

Rubbermaid

- To increase annual sales from $1 billion to $2 billion in five years.
- To enter a new market every 18 to 24 months.
- To have 30 percent of sales each year come from products not in the company's product line five years earlier.
- To be the lowest cost, highest quality producer in the household products industry.

- To achieve a 15 percent average annual growth in sales, profits, and earnings per share.

McCormick & Company

- To achieve a 20 percent return on equity.
- To achieve a net sales growth rate of 10 percent per year.
- To maintain an average earnings per share growth rate of 15 percent per year.
- To maintain total debt-to-total capital at 40 percent or less.
- To pay out 25 percent to 35 percent of net income in dividends.
- To make selective acquisitions which complement our current businesses and can enhance our overall returns.
- To dispose of those parts of our business which do not or cannot generate adequate returns or do not fit our business strategy.

Source: Company annual reports.

Strategic objectives need to be competitor-focused, usually aiming at unseating a competitor considered to be the industry's best in a particular category.

tive position for the long haul. The pressures on managers to opt for better near-term financial performance and to sacrifice at least some strategic moves aimed at building a stronger competitive position are especially pronounced when (1) an enterprise is struggling financially, (2) the resource commitments for strategically beneficial moves will materially detract from the bottom line for several years, and (3) the proposed strategic moves are risky and have an uncertain market and competitive payoff.

Yet, there are dangers in management's succumbing time and again to the lure of immediate gains in margins and return on investment when it means paring or forgoing strategic moves that would build a stronger business position. A company that consistently passes up opportunities to strengthen its long-term competitive position in order to realize better near-term financial gains risks diluting its competitiveness, losing momentum in its markets, and impairing its ability to stave off market challenges from ambitious rivals. The business landscape is littered with ex–market leaders who put more emphasis on boosting next quarter's profit than strengthening long-term market position. The danger of trading off long-term gains in market position for near-term gains in bottom-line performance is greatest when a profit-conscious market leader has competitors who invest relentlessly in gaining market share in preparation for the time when they will be big and strong enough to outcompete the leader in a head-to-head market battle. One need look no further than Japanese companies' patient and persistent strategic efforts to gain market ground on their more profit-centered American and European rivals to appreciate the pitfall of letting

Strategic Management Principle
Building a stronger long-term competitive position benefits shareholders more lastingly than improving short-term profitability.

short-term financial objectives dominate. The surest path to protecting and sustaining a company's profitability quarter after quarter and year after year is to pursue strategic actions that strengthen its competitiveness and business position.

The Concept of Strategic Intent   A company's strategic objectives are important for another reason—they indicate *strategic intent* to stake out a particular business position.[6] The strategic intent of a large company may be industry leadership on a national or global scale. The strategic intent of a small company may be to dominate a market niche. The strategic intent of an up-and-coming enterprise may be to overtake the market leaders. The strategic intent of a technologically innovative company may be to pioneer a promising discovery and open a whole new vista of products and market opportunities—as did Xerox, Apple Computer, Microsoft, Merck, and Sony.

> **Basic Concept**
> A company exhibits *strategic intent* when it relentlessly pursues a certain long-term strategic objective and concentrates its strategic actions on achieving that objective.

The time horizon underlying a company's strategic intent is long-term. Companies that rise to prominence in their markets almost invariably begin with strategic intents that are out of proportion to their immediate capabilities and market positions. But they set ambitious long-term strategic objectives and then pursue them relentlessly, sometimes even obsessively, over a 10 - to 20-year period. In the 1960s, Komatsu, Japan's leading earth-moving equipment company, was less than one-third the size of Caterpillar, had little market presence outside Japan, and depended on its small bulldozers for most of its revenue. Komatsu's strategic intent was to "encircle Caterpillar" with a broader product line and then compete globally against Caterpillar. By the late 1980s, Komatsu was the industry's second-ranking company, with a strong sales presence in North America, Europe, and Asia plus a product line that included industrial robots and semiconductors as well as a broad array of earth-moving equipment.

Often, a company's strategic intent takes on a heroic character, serving as a rallying cry for managers and employees alike to go all out and do their very best. Canon's strategic intent in copying equipment was to "Beat Xerox." Komatsu's motivating battle cry was "Beat Caterpillar." The strategic intent of the U.S. government's Apollo space program was to land a person on the moon ahead of the Soviet Union. Throughout the 1980s, Wal-Mart's strategic intent was to "overtake Sears" as the largest U.S. retailer (a feat accomplished in 1991). In such instances, strategic intent signals a deep-seated commitment to winning—unseating the industry leader, remaining the industry leader (and becoming more dominant in the process), or otherwise beating long odds to gain a significantly stronger business position. A capably managed enterprise whose strategic objectives exceed its present reach and resources can be a more formidable competitor than a company with modest strategic intent.

Long-Range versus Short-Range Objectives   An organization needs both long-range and short-range objectives. Long-range objectives serve two purposes. First, setting performance targets five or more years ahead pushes managers to take actions *now* in order to achieve the targeted long-range performance *later* (a company that has an objective of doubling its sales within five years can't wait until the third or fourth year of its five-year strategic plan to begin growing its sales and customer base!). Second, having explicit long-range objectives prompts managers to weigh the impact

---

[6]The concept of strategic intent is described in more detail in Gary Hamel and C. K. Pralahad, "Strategic Intent," *Harvard Business Review* 89, no. 3 (May–June 1989), pp. 63–76. This section draws upon their pioneering discussion.

of today's decisions on longer-range performance. Without the pressure to make progress in meeting long-range performance targets, it is human nature to base decisions on what is most expedient and worry about the future later. The problem with short-sighted decisions, of course, is that they put a company's long-term business position at greater risk.

Short-range objectives spell out the immediate and near-term results to be achieved. They indicate the *speed* at which management wants the organization to progress as well as the *level of performance* being aimed for over the next two or three periods. Short-range objectives can be identical to long-range objectives anytime an organization is already performing at the targeted long-term level. For instance, if a company has an ongoing objective of 15 percent profit growth every year and is currently achieving this objective, then the company's long-range and short-range profit objectives coincide. The most important situation where short-range objectives differ from long-range objectives occurs when managers are trying to elevate organizational performance and cannot reach the long-range/ongoing target in just one year. Short-range objectives then serve as stairsteps or milestones.

THE "CHALLENGING BUT ACHIEVABLE" TEST

Objectives should not represent whatever levels of achievement management decides would be "nice." Wishful thinking has no place in objective-setting. For objectives to serve as a tool for *stretching* an organization to reach its full potential, they must be *challenging but achievable.* Satisfying this criterion means setting objectives in light of several important "inside-outside" considerations:

- What performance levels will industry and competitive conditions realistically allow?
- What results will it take for the organization to be a successful performer?
- What performance is the organization capable of *when pushed?*

To set challenging but achievable objectives, managers must judge what performance is possible in light of external conditions against what performance the organization is capable of achieving. The tasks of objective-setting and strategy-making often become intertwined at this point. Strategic choices, for example, cannot be made in a financial vacuum; the money has to be there to execute them. Consequently, decisions about strategy are contingent on setting the organization's financial performance objectives high enough to (1) execute the chosen strategy, (2) fund other needed actions, and (3) please investors and the financial community. Objectives and strategy also intertwine when it comes to matching the means (strategy) with the ends (objectives). If a company can't achieve established objectives (because the objectives are set unrealistically high or the present strategy can't deliver the desired performance), the objectives or the strategy need adjustment to produce a better fit.

THE NEED FOR OBJECTIVES AT ALL MANAGEMENT LEVELS

For strategic thinking and strategy-driven decision-making to permeate organization behavior, performance targets must be established not only for the organization as a whole but also for each of the organization's separate businesses, product lines, functional areas, and departments.[7] Only when every manager, from the CEO to the lowest-

---

[7]Peter F. Drucker, *Management: Tasks, Responsibilities, Practices* (New York: Harper & Row, 1974), p. 100. See also Charles H. Granger, "The Hierarchy of Objectives," *Harvard Business Review* 42, no. 3 (May–June 1963), pp. 63–74.

Company performance targets should be challenging but achievable.

level manager, is held accountable for achieving specific results and when each unit's objectives support achievement of company objectives is the objective-setting process complete enough to ensure that the whole organization is headed down the chosen path and that each part of the organization knows what it needs to accomplish.

The objective-setting process is more top-down than bottom-up. To see why strategic objectives at one managerial level tend to drive objectives and strategies at the next level down, consider the following example. Suppose the senior executives of a diversified corporation establish a corporate profit objective of $5 million for next year. Suppose further, after discussion between corporate management and the general managers of the firm's five different businesses, each business is given the challenging but achievable profit objective of $1 million by year-end (i.e., if the five business divisions contribute $1 million each in profit, the corporation can reach its $5 million profit objective). A concrete result has thus been agreed on and translated into measurable action commitments at two levels in the managerial hierarchy. Next, suppose the general manager of business unit X, after some analysis and discussion with functional area managers, concludes that reaching the $1 million profit objective will require selling 100,000 units at an average price of $50 and producing them at an average cost of $40 (a $10 profit margin times 100,000 units equals $1 million profit). Consequently, the general manager and the manufacturing manager settle on a production objective of 100,000 units at a unit cost of $40; and the general manager and the marketing manager agree on a sales objective of 100,000 units and a target selling price of $50. In turn, the marketing manager breaks the sales objective of 100,000 units into unit sales targets for each sales territory, each item in the product line, and each salesperson.

A top-down process of establishing performance targets for strategy-critical activities, business processes, and departmental units is a logical way of breaking down companywide targets into pieces that lower-level units and managers are responsible for achieving. Such an approach also provides a valuable degree of *unity* and *cohesion* to objective-setting and strategy-making in different parts of the organization. Generally speaking, organizationwide objectives and strategy need to be established first so they can *guide* objective-setting and strategy-making at lower levels. Top-down objective-setting and strategizing steer lower-level units toward objectives and strategies that take their cues from those of the total enterprise. When objective-setting and strategy-making begin at the bottom levels of an organization and organizationwide objectives and strategies reflect the aggregate of what has bubbled up from below, the resulting strategic action plan is likely to be inconsistent, fragmented, or uncoordinated. Bottom-up objective-setting, with no guidance from above, nearly always signals an absence of strategic leadership on the part of senior executives.

> **Strategic Management Principle**
> Objective-setting needs to be more of a top-down than a bottom-up process in order to guide lower-level managers and organizational units toward outcomes that support the achievement of overall business and company objectives.

CRAFTING A STRATEGY: THE THIRD DIRECTION-SETTING TASK

Organizations need strategies to guide *how* to achieve objectives and *how* to pursue the organization's mission. Strategy-making is all about *how*—how to reach performance targets, how to outcompete rivals, how to achieve sustainable competitive advantage, how to strengthen the enterprise's long-term business position, how to make management's strategic vision for the company a reality. A strategy is needed for the company as a whole, for each business the company is in, and for each functional piece of each business—R&D, purchasing, production, sales and marketing, finance, human resources, and so on. An organization's overall strategy and

> **Basic Concept**
> An organization's *strategy* is all about *how* to get the company from where it is to where it wants to go—it is the means to achieving the desired end results.

managerial game plan emerge from the *pattern* of actions already initiated and the plans managers have for fresh moves. In forming a strategy out of the many feasible options, a manager acts as a forger of responses to market change, a seeker of new opportunities, and a synthesizer of the different moves and approaches taken at various times in various parts of the organization.[8]

The strategy-making spotlight, however, needs to be kept trained on the important facets of management's game plan for running the enterprise—those actions that determine what market position the company is trying to stake out and that underpin whether the company will succeed. Low-priority issues (whether to increase the advertising budget, raise the dividend, locate a new plant in country X or country Y) and routine managerial housekeeping (whether to own or lease company vehicles, how to reduce sales force turnover) are not basic to the strategy, even though they must be dealt with. Strategy is inherently action-oriented; it concerns what to do, when to do it, and who should be involved. Unless there is action, unless something happens, unless somebody does something, strategic thinking and planning simply go to waste and, in the end, amount to nothing.

An organization's strategy evolves over time. It's seldom possible to plan all the bits and pieces of a company's strategy in advance and then go for long periods without change. Reacting and responding to happenings either inside the company or in the surrounding environment is a normal part of the strategy-making process. The dynamic and partly unpredictable character of competition, budding trends in buyer needs and expectations, unplanned increases or decreases in costs, mergers and acquisitions among major industry players, new regulations, the raising or lowering of trade barriers, and countless other events can make parts of the strategy obsolete. There is always something new to react to and some new strategic window opening up. This is why the task of crafting strategy is never ending. And it is why a company's actual strategy turns out to be a blend of its intended or planned strategy and its unplanned reactions to fresh developments.

THE STRATEGY-MAKING PYRAMID

As we emphasized in the opening chapter, strategy-making is not just a task for senior executives. In large enterprises, decisions about what approaches to take and what new moves to initiate involve senior executives in the corporate office, heads of business units and product divisions, the heads of major functional areas within a business or division (manufacturing, marketing and sales, finance, human resources, and the like), plant managers, product managers, district and regional sales managers, and lower-level supervisors. In diversified enterprises, strategies are initiated at four distinct organization levels. There's a strategy for the company and all of its businesses as a whole *(corporate strategy)*. There's a strategy for each separate business the company has diversified into *(business strategy)*. Then there is a strategy for each specific functional unit within a business *(functional strategy)*—each business usually has a production strategy, a marketing strategy, a finance strategy, and so on. And, finally, there are still narrower strategies for basic operating units—plants, sales districts and regions, and departments within functional areas *(operating strategy)*. Figure 2–1 shows the strategy-making pyramid for a diversified company. In single-business enterprises, there are only three levels of strategy-making (business strategy, functional strategy, and operating strategy) unless diversification into other businesses becomes an active

---

[8]Henry Mintzberg, "The Strategy Concept II: Another Look at Why Organizations Need Strategies," California Management Review 30, no. 1 (Fall 1987), pp. 25–32.

FIGURE 2-1 | **The Strategy-Making Pyramid**

A DIVERSIFIED COMPANY

Responsibility of corporate-level managers ◄◄◄ → **Corporate Strategy**

Two-Way Influence

Responsibility of business-level general managers ◄◄◄ → **Business Strategies**

Two-Way Influence

Responsibility of heads of major functional areas within a business unit or division ◄◄◄ → **Functional Strategies (R & D, manufacturing, marketing, finance, human resources, etc.)**

Two-Way Influence

Responsibility of plant managers, geograghic unit managers, and lower-level supervisors ◄◄◄ → **Operating Strategies (regions and districts, plants, departments with functional areas)**

A SINGLE - BUSINESS COMPANY

Responsibility of executive-level managers ◄◄◄ → **Business Strategy**

Two-Way Influence

Responsibility of heads of major functional areas within a business ◄◄◄ → **Functional Strategies (R & D, manufacturing, marketing, finance, human resources, etc.)**

Two-Way Influence

Responsibility of plant managers, geograghic unit managers, and lower-level supervisors ◄◄◄ → **Operating Strategies (regions and districts, plants, departments with functional areas)**

T A B L E 2–1 | **How the Strategy-Making Task Tends to Be Shared**

Strategy Level	Lead Responsibility	Primary Strategy-Making Concerns at Each Managerial Level
• Corporate strategy	• CEO, other key executives (decisions are typically reviewed/approved by boards of directors)	• Building and managing a high-performing portfolio of business units (making acquisitions, strengthening existing business positions, divesting businesses that no longer fit into management's plans) • Capturing the synergy among related business units and turning it into competitive advantage • Establishing investment priorities and steering corporate resources into businesses with the most attractive opportunities • Reviewing/revising/unifying the major strategic approaches and moves proposed by business-unit managers
• Business strategies	• General manager/head of business unit (decisions are typically reviewed/approved by a senior executive or a board of directors)	• Devising moves and approaches to compete successfully and to secure a competitive advantage • Forming responses to changing external conditions • Uniting the strategic initiatives of key functional departments • Taking action to address company-specific issues and operating problems
• Functional strategies	• Functional managers (decisions are typically reviewed/approved by business-unit head)	• Crafting moves and approaches to support business strategy and to achieve functional/departmental performance objectives • Reviewing/revising/unifying strategy-related moves and approaches proposed by lower-level managers
• Operating strategies	• Field-unit heads/lower-level managers within functional areas (decisions are reviewed/approved by functional area head/department head)	• Crafting still narrower and more specific approaches/moves aimed at supporting functional and business strategies and at achieving operating-unit objectives

consideration. Table 2–1 highlights the kinds of strategic actions that distinguish each of the four strategy-making levels.

CORPORATE STRATEGY

Corporate strategy is the overall managerial game plan for a diversified company. Corporate strategy extends companywide—an umbrella over all a diversified company's businesses. It consists of the moves made to establish business positions in different industries and the approaches used to manage the company's group of businesses. Figure 2–2 depicts the core elements that identify a diversified company's corporate strategy. Crafting corporate strategy for a diversified company involves four kinds of initiatives:

1. *Making the moves to accomplish diversification.* The first concern in diversification is what the company's portfolio of businesses should consist of—specifically, what industries to diversify into, and whether to enter the industries by starting a new business or acquiring another company (an established leader, an up-and-coming company, or a troubled company with

Basic Concept
Corporate strategy concerns how a diversified company intends to establish business positions in different industries and the actions and approaches employed to improve the performance of the group of businesses the company has diversified into.

F I G U R E 2-2 | **Identifying the Corporate Strategy of a Diversified Company**

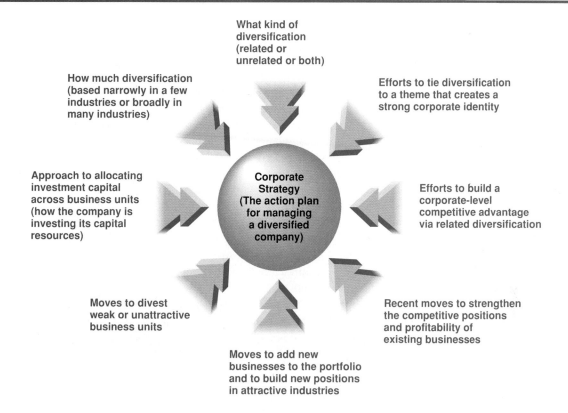

turnaround potential). This piece of corporate strategy establishes whether diversification is based narrowly in a few industries or broadly in many industries, and it shapes how the company will be positioned in each of the target industries.

2. *Initiating actions to boost the combined performance of the businesses the firm has diversified into.* As positions are created in the chosen industries, corporate strategy-making concentrates on ways to get better performance out of the business-unit portfolio. Decisions must be reached about how to strengthen the long-term competitive positions and profitabilities of the businesses the firm has invested in. Corporate parents can help their business subsidiaries be more successful by financing additional capacity and efficiency improvements, by supplying missing skills and managerial know-how, by acquiring another company in the same industry and merging the two operations into a stronger business, and/or by acquiring new businesses that strongly complement existing businesses. The overall plan for managing a group of diversified businesses usually involves pursuing rapid-growth strategies in the most promising businesses, keeping the other core businesses healthy, initiating turnaround efforts in weak-performing businesses with potential, and divesting businesses that are no longer attractive or that don't fit into management's long-range plans.

3. *Finding ways to capture the synergy among related business units and turn it into competitive advantage.* When a company diversifies into businesses with

related technologies, similar operating characteristics, the same distribution channels, common customers, or some other synergistic relationship, it gains competitive advantage potential not open to a company that diversifies into totally unrelated businesses. Related diversification presents opportunities to transfer skills, share expertise, or share facilities, thereby reducing overall costs, strengthening the competitiveness of some of the company's products, or enhancing the capabilities of particular business units—any of which can represent a significant source of competitive advantage. The greater the relatedness among the businesses of a diversified company, the greater the opportunities for skills transfer and/or sharing across businesses and the bigger the window for creating competitive advantage. Indeed, what makes related diversification so attractive is the synergistic *strategic fit* across related business units that allows company resources to be leveraged into a combined performance *greater* than the units could achieve operating independently. The $2 + 2 = 5$ aspect of strategic fit makes related diversification a very appealing strategy for boosting corporate performance and shareholder value.

4. *Establishing investment priorities and steering corporate resources into the most attractive business units.* A diversified company's different businesses are usually not equally attractive from the standpoint of investing additional funds. This facet of corporate strategy-making involves deciding on the priorities— i.e., investing more capital in some of the businesses and channeling resources into areas where earnings potentials are higher and away from areas where they are lower. Corporate strategy may include divesting business units that are chronically poor performers or those in an increasingly unattractive industry. Divestiture frees up unproductive investments for redeployment to promising business units or for financing attractive new acquisitions.

Corporate strategy is crafted at the highest levels of management. Senior corporate executives normally have lead responsibility for devising corporate strategy and for choosing among whatever recommended actions bubble up from lower-level managers. Key business-unit heads may also be influential, especially in strategic decisions affecting the businesses they head. Major strategic decisions are usually reviewed and approved by the company's board of directors.

BUSINESS STRATEGY

Basic Concept
Business strategy concerns the actions and the approaches crafted by management to produce successful performance in one specific line of business; the central business strategy issue is *how* to build a stronger long-term competitive position.

The term *business strategy* (or business-level strategy) refers to the managerial game plan for a single business. It is mirrored in the pattern of approaches and moves crafted by management to produce successful performance in *one specific line of business*. The core elements of business strategy are illustrated in Figure 2–3. For a stand-alone single-business company, corporate strategy and business strategy are one and the same since there is only one business to form a strategy for. The distinction between corporate strategy and business strategy is relevant only for diversified firms.

The central thrust of business strategy is how to build and strengthen the company's long-term competitive position in the marketplace. Toward this end, business strategy is concerned principally with (1) forming responses to changes under way in the industry, the economy at large, the regulatory and political arena, and other relevant areas, (2) crafting competitive moves and market approaches that can lead to sustainable competitive advantage, (3) uniting the strategic initiatives of functional departments, and (4) addressing specific strategic issues facing the company's business.

Clearly, business strategy encompasses whatever moves and new approaches managers deem prudent in light of market forces, economic trends and developments, buyer needs and demographics, new legislation and regulatory requirements, and other such broad external factors. A good strategy is well-matched to the external situation; as the external environment changes in significant ways, then adjustments in strategy are made on an as-needed basis. Whether a company's response to external change is quick or slow tends to be a function of how long events must unfold before managers can assess their implications and how much longer it then takes to form a strategic response. Some external changes, of course, require little or no response, while others call for significant strategy alterations. On occasion, external factors change in ways that pose a formidable strategic hurdle—for example, cigarette manufacturers face a tough challenge holding their own against the mounting antismoking campaign.

What separates a powerful business strategy from a weak one is the strategist's ability *to forge a series of moves and approaches capable of producing sustainable competitive advantage.* With a competitive advantage, a company has good prospects for above-average profitability and success in the industry. Without competitive advantage, a company risks being outcompeted by stronger rivals and locked into

FIGURE 2-3 | **Identifying Strategy for a Single-Business Company**

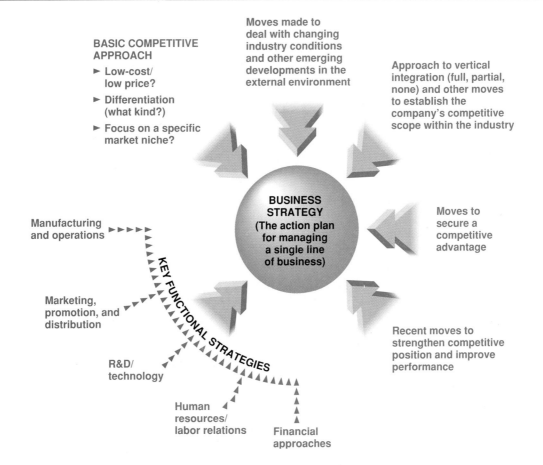

A business strategy is powerful if it produces a sizable and sustainable competitive advantage; it is weak if it results in competitive disadvantage.

mediocre performance. Crafting a business strategy that yields sustainable competitive advantage has three facets: (1) deciding where a firm has the best chance to win a competitive edge, (2) developing product/service attributes that have strong buyer appeal and set the company apart from rivals, and (3) neutralizing the competitive moves of rival companies.

A company's strategy for competing is typically both offensive and defensive—some actions are aggressive and amount to direct challenges to competitors' market positions; others counter fresh moves made by rivals. Three of the most frequently used competitive approaches are (1) striving to be the industry's low-cost producer (thereby aiming for a cost-based competitive advantage over rivals), (2) pursuing differentiation based on such advantages as quality, performance, service, styling, technological superiority, or unusually good value, and (3) focusing on a narrow market niche and winning a competitive edge by doing a better job than rivals of serving the special needs and tastes of its buyers.

Internally, business strategy involves taking actions to develop the skills and capabilities needed to achieve competitive advantage. Successful business strategies usually aim at building the company's competence in one or more core activities crucial to strategic success and then using the core competence as a basis for winning a competitive edge over rivals. A *core competence* is something a firm does especially well in comparison to rival companies. It thus represents a source of competitive strength. Core competencies can relate to R&D, mastery of a technological process, manufacturing capability, sales and distribution, customer service, or anything else that is a competitively important aspect of creating, producing, or marketing the company's product or service. *A core competence is a basis for competitive advantage because it represents specialized expertise that rivals don't have and cannot readily match.*

On a broader internal front, business strategy must also aim at uniting strategic initiatives in the various functional areas of business (purchasing, production, R&D, finance, human resources, sales and marketing, and distribution). Strategic actions are needed in each functional area to *support* the company's competitive approach and overall business strategy. Strategic unity and coordination across the various functional areas add power to the business strategy.

Business strategy also extends to action plans for addressing any special strategy-related issues unique to the company's competitive position and internal situation (such as whether to add new capacity, replace an obsolete plant, increase R&D funding for a promising technology, or reduce burdensome interest expenses). Such custom tailoring of strategy to fit a company's specific situation is one of the reasons why every company in an industry has a different business strategy.

Lead responsibility for business strategy falls in the lap of the manager in charge of the business. Even if the business head does not personally wield a heavy hand in the business strategy-making process, preferring to delegate much of the task to others, he or she is still accountable for the strategy and the results it produces. The business head, as chief strategist for the business, has at least two other responsibilities. The first is seeing that supporting strategies in each of the major functional areas of the business are well-conceived and consistent with each other. The second is getting major strategic moves approved by higher authority (the board of directors and/or corporate-level officers) if needed and keeping them informed of important new developments, deviations from plan, and potential strategy revisions. In diversified companies, business-unit heads may have the additional obligation of making sure business-level objectives and strategy conform to corporate-level objectives and strategy themes.

FUNCTIONAL STRATEGY

The term *functional strategy* refers to the managerial game plan for a particular department or key functional activity within a business. A company's marketing strategy, for example, represents the managerial game plan for running the marketing part of the business. A company needs a functional strategy for every major departmental unit and piece of the business—for R&D, production, marketing, customer service, distribution, finance, human resources, and so on. Functional strategies, while narrower in scope than business strategy, add relevant detail to the overall business game plan by setting out the actions, approaches, and practices to be employed in managing a particular department or business function. The primary role of a functional strategy is to *support* the company's overall business strategy and competitive approach. A related role is to create a managerial roadmap for achieving the functional area's objectives and mission. Thus, functional strategy in the production/manufacturing area represents the game plan for *how* manufacturing activities will be managed to support business strategy and achieve the manufacturing department's objectives and mission. Functional strategy in the finance area consists of *how* financial activities will be managed in supporting business strategy and achieving the finance department's objectives and mission.

Lead responsibility for strategy-making in the functional areas of a business is normally delegated to the respective functional department heads unless the business-unit head decides to exert a strong influence. In crafting strategy, a functional department head ideally works closely with key subordinates and touches base with the heads of other functional areas and the business head often. If functional heads plot strategy independent of each other or the business head they open the door for uncoordinated or conflicting strategies. Compatible, mutually reinforcing functional strategies are essential for the overall business strategy to have maximum impact. Plainly, a business's marketing strategy, production strategy, finance strategy, and human resources strategy should be in sync rather than serving their own narrower purposes. Coordination across functional area strategies is best accomplished during the deliberation stage. If inconsistent functional strategies are sent up the line for final approval, the business head must spot the conflicts and get them resolved.

Basic Concept
Functional strategy concerns the managerial game plan for running a major functional activity within a business—R&D, production, marketing, customer service, distribution, finance, human resources, and so on; a business needs as many functional strategies as it has major activities.

OPERATING STRATEGY

Operating strategies concern the even narrower strategic initiatives and approaches for managing key operating units (plants, sales districts, distribution centers) and for handling daily operating tasks with strategic significance (advertising campaigns, materials purchasing, inventory control, maintenance, shipping). Operating strategies, while of lesser scope, add further detail and completeness to functional strategies and to the overall business plan. Lead responsibility for operating strategies is usually delegated to front-line managers, subject to review and approval by higher-ranking managers.

Even though operating strategy is at the bottom of the strategy-making pyramid, its importance should not be downplayed. For example, a major plant that fails in its strategy to achieve production volume, unit cost, and quality targets can undercut the achievement of company sales and profit objectives and wreak havoc with the whole company's strategic efforts to build a quality image with customers. One cannot reliably judge the importance of a given strategic move by the organizational or managerial level where it is initiated.

Basic Concept
Operating strategies concern how to manage key organizational units within a business (plants, sales districts, distribution centers) and how to perform strategically significant operating tasks (materials purchasing, inventory control, maintenance, shipping, advertising campaigns).

Frontline managers are part of an organization's strategy-making team because many operating units have strategy-critical performance targets and need to have strategic action plans in place to achieve them. A regional manager needs a strategy customized to the region's particular situation and objectives. A plant manager needs a strategy for accomplishing the plant's objectives, carrying out the plant's part of the company's overall manufacturing game plan, and dealing with any strategy-related problems that exist at the plant. A company's advertising manager needs a strategy for getting maximum audience exposure and sales impact from the ad budget. The following two examples illustrate how operating strategy supports higher-level strategies:

- A company with a low-price, high-volume business strategy and a need to achieve low manufacturing costs launches a companywide effort to boost worker productivity by 10 percent. To contribute to the productivity-boosting objective: (1) the manager of employee recruiting develops a strategy for interviewing and testing job applicants that is thorough enough to weed out all but the most highly motivated, best-qualified candidates; (2) the manager of information systems devises a way to use office technology to boost the productivity of office workers; (3) the employee benefits manager devises an improved incentive-compensation plan to reward increased output by manufacturing employees; and (4) the purchasing manager launches a program to obtain new efficiency-increasing tools and equipment in quicker, less costly fashion.
- A distributor of plumbing equipment emphasizes quick delivery and accurate order-filling as keystones of its customer service approach. To support this strategy, the warehouse manager (1) develops an inventory stocking strategy that allows 99 percent of all orders to be completely filled without back ordering any item and (2) institutes a warehouse staffing strategy that allows any order to be shipped within 24 hours.

UNITING THE STRATEGY-MAKING EFFORT

The previous discussion underscores that *a company's strategic plan is a collection of strategies* devised by different managers at different levels in the organizational hierarchy. The larger the enterprise, the more points of strategic initiative it has. Management's direction-setting effort is not complete until the separate layers of strategy are unified into a coherent, supportive pattern. Ideally the pieces and layers of strategy should fit together like the pieces of a picture puzzle. Unified objectives and strategies don't emerge from an undirected process where managers at each level set objectives and craft strategies independently. Indeed, functional and operating-level managers have a duty to set performance targets and invent strategic actions that will help achieve business objectives and make business strategy more effective.

Harmonizing objectives and strategies piece by piece and level by level can be tedious and frustrating, requiring numerous consultations and meetings, annual strategy review and approval processes, the experience of trial and error, and months (sometimes years) of consensus building. The politics of gaining strategic consensus and the battle of trying to keep all managers and departments focused on what's best for the total enterprise (as opposed to what's best for their departments or careers) are often big obstacles in unifying the layers of objectives and strategies.[9] Broad consen-

Objectives and strategies that are unified from an organization's top-management levels to its bottom-management levels do not come from an undirected process where managers at each level have objective-setting and strategy-making autonomy.

---

[9] Functional managers are sometimes more interested in doing what is best for their own areas, building their own empires, and consolidating their personal power and organizational influence than they are in cooperating with other functional managers to unify behind the overall business strategy. As a result, it's easy for functional area support strategies to conflict, thereby forcing the business-level general manager to spend time and energy refereeing functional strategy conflicts and building support for a more unified approach.

sus is particularly difficult when there is ample room for opposing views and disagreement. Managerial discussions about an organization's mission, basic direction, objectives and strategies often provoke heated debate and strong differences of opinion.

Figure 2–4 portrays the networking of objectives and strategies through the managerial hierarchy. The two-way arrows indicate that there are simultaneous bottom-up and top-down influences on missions, objectives, and strategies at each level. These vertical linkages, if managed in a way that promotes coordination, can help unify the direction-setting and strategy-making activities of many managers into a mutually reinforcing pattern. The tighter that coordination is enforced, the tighter the linkages in the missions, objectives, and strategies of the various organizational units. Tight linkages safeguard against organizational units straying from the company's charted strategic course.

As a practical matter, however, corporate and business missions, objectives, and strategies need to be clearly outlined and communicated down the line before much progress can be made in direction-setting and strategy-making at the functional and operating levels. Direction and guidance need to flow from the corporate level to the business level and from the business level to the functional and operating levels. The strategic disarray that occurs in an organization when senior managers don't exercise strong top-down direction-setting and strategic leadership is akin to what would happen to a football team's offensive performance if the quarterback decided not to call a play for the team, but instead let each player pick whatever play he thought would work best at his respective position. In business, as in sports, all the strategy-makers in a company are on the same team. They are obligated to perform their strategy-making tasks in a manner that benefits the whole company, not in a manner that suits personal or departmental interests. A company's strategy is at full power only when its many pieces are united. This means that the strategizing process proceeds more from the top down than from the bottom up. Lower-level managers cannot do good strategy-making without understanding the company's long-term direction and higher-level strategies.

> Consistency between business strategy and functional/operating strategies comes from organizationwide allegiance to business objectives; functional and operating-level managers have a duty to set performance targets and invent strategic actions that will help achieve business objectives and improve the execution of business strategy.

THE FACTORS THAT SHAPE A COMPANY'S STRATEGY

Many situational considerations enter into crafting strategy. Figure 2–5 depicts the primary factors that shape a company's strategic approaches. The interplay of these factors and the influence that each has on the strategy-making process vary from company to company. No two strategic choices are made in exactly the same context; even in the same industry situational factors differ enough from company to company that each company ends up pursuing a customized strategy. This is why carefully sizing up all the various situational factors, both external and internal, is the starting point in crafting strategy.

SOCIETAL, POLITICAL, REGULATORY, AND CITIZENSHIP CONSIDERATIONS

What an enterprise can and cannot do strategywise is always constrained by what is legal, by what complies with government policies and regulatory requirements, by what is socially acceptable, and by what constitutes community citizenship. Outside pressures also come from other sources—special interest groups, the glare of investigative reporting, a fear of unwanted political action, and the stigma of negative

> Societal, political, regulatory, and citizenship factors limit the strategic actions a company can or should take.

FIGURE 2-4 | The Networking of Missions, Objectives, and Strategies in the Strategy-Making Pyramid

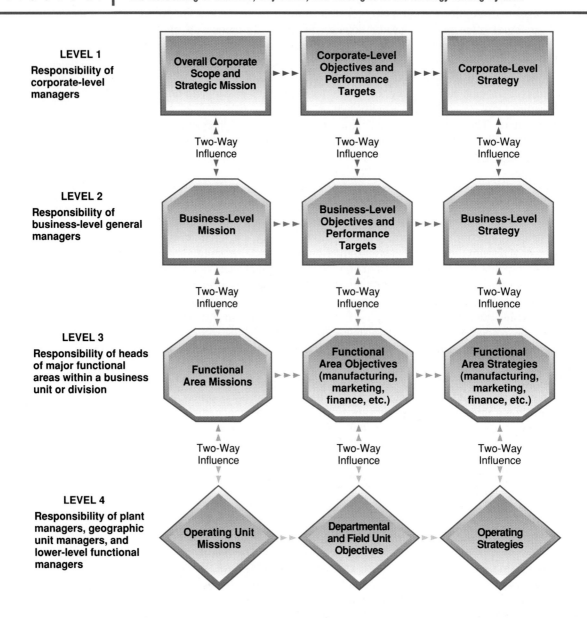

opinion. Societal concerns over health and nutrition, alcohol and drug abuse, hazardous waste disposal, sexual harassment, and the impact of plant closings on local communities affect the strategies of many companies. American concerns over the size of foreign imports and political debate over whether to impose tariffs to cure the chronic U.S. trade deficit are driving forces in the strategic decisions of Japanese and European companies to locate plants in the United States. Heightened awareness of the dangers of cholesterol have prompted most food products companies to phase out high-fat ingredients and substitute low-fat ingredients, despite the extra costs.

Factoring in societal values and priorities, community concerns, and the potential

FIGURE 2-5 | Factors Shaping the Choice of Company Strategy

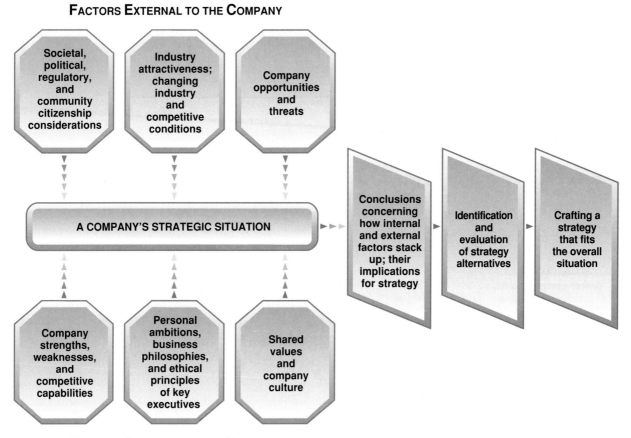

for onerous legislation and regulatory requirements is a regular part of external situation analysis at more and more companies. Intense public pressure and adverse media coverage make such a practice prudent. The task of making an organization's strategy socially responsible means (1) conducting organizational activities within the bounds of what is considered ethical and in the general public interest; (2) responding positively to emerging societal priorities and expectations; (3) demonstrating a willingness to take action ahead of regulatory confrontation; (4) balancing stockholder interests against the larger interests of society as a whole; and (5) being a good citizen in the community.

Corporate social responsibility is showing up in company mission statements. John Hancock, for example, concludes its mission statement with the following sentence:

In pursuit of this mission, we will strive to exemplify the highest standards of business ethics and personal integrity; and shall recognize our corporate obligation to the social and economic well-being of our community.

At Union Electric, a St. Louis–based utility company, the following statement is official corporate policy:

> As a private enterprise entrusted with an essential public service, we recognize our civic responsibility in the communities we serve. We shall strive to advance the growth and welfare of these communities and shall participate in civic activities which fulfill that goal—for we believe this is both good citizenship and good business.

INDUSTRY ATTRACTIVENESS AND COMPETITIVE CONDITIONS

Industry attractiveness and competitive conditions are big strategy-determining factors. A company's assessment of the industry and competitive environment has a direct bearing on how it should try to position itself in the industry and on its basic competitive strategy approach. When competitive conditions intensify significantly, a company must respond with strategic actions to protect its position. Fresh moves on the part of rival companies, changes in the industry's price-cost-profit economics, and new technological developments can alter the requirements for competitive success and mandate reconsideration of strategy. When a firm concludes its industry environment has grown unattractive and it is better off investing company resources elsewhere, it may begin a strategy of disinvestment and eventual abandonment. A strategist, therefore, has to be a student of industry and competitive conditions.

SPECIFIC MARKET OPPORTUNITIES AND THREATS

The particular business opportunities open to a company and the threatening external developments that it faces are key influences on strategy. They both point to the need for strategic action. A company's strategy needs to be deliberately aimed at capturing its best growth opportunities, especially the ones that hold the most promise for building sustainable competitive advantage and enhancing profitability. Likewise, strategy should be geared to providing a defense against external threats to the company's well-being and future performance. For strategy to be successful, it has to be well-matched to market opportunities and threatening external developments; this usually means crafting offensive moves to capitalize on the company's most promising market opportunities and crafting defensive moves to protect the company's competitive position and long-term profitability.

ORGANIZATIONAL STRENGTHS, WEAKNESSES, AND COMPETITIVE CAPABILITIES

Experience shows management should build strategy around what the company does well and avoid strategies whose success depends on something the company does poorly or has never done at all. In short, *strategy must be well-matched to company strengths, weaknesses, and competitive capabilities*. Pursuing an opportunity without the organizational competencies and resources to capture it is foolish. An organization's strengths make some opportunities and strategies attractive; likewise its internal weaknesses and its present competitive market position make certain strategies risky or even out of the question.

One of the most pivotal strategy-shaping internal considerations is whether a company has or can build the core strengths or competencies needed to execute a strategy proficiently. An organization's core strengths—the things it does especially well—are an important strategy-making consideration because of (1) the skills and capabilities they provide in capitalizing on a particular opportunity, (2) the competitive edge they

Strategic Management Principle
A company's strategy ought to be closely matched to industry and competitive conditions.

Strategic Management Principle
A well-conceived strategy aims at capturing a company's best growth opportunities and defending against external threats to its well-being and future performance.

Strategic Management Principle
A company's strategy ought to be grounded in what it is good at doing (i.e., its organizational strengths and competitive capabilities); it is perilous for success to depend on what it is not so good at doing (i.e., its organizational and competitive weaknesses).

may give a firm in the marketplace, and (3) the potential they have for becoming a cornerstone of strategy. The best path to competitive advantage is found where a firm has core strengths in one or more of the key requirements for market success, where rivals do not have matching or offsetting competencies, and where rivals can't develop comparable strengths except at high cost and/or over an extended period of time.[10]

Even if an organization has no outstanding core competencies (and many do not), it still must shape its strategy to suit its particular skills and available resources. It never makes sense to develop a strategic plan that cannot be executed with the skills and resources a firm is able to muster.

THE PERSONAL AMBITIONS, BUSINESS PHILOSOPHIES, AND ETHICAL BELIEFS OF MANAGERS

Managers do not dispassionately assess what strategic course to steer. Their choices are often influenced by their own vision of how to compete and how to position the enterprise and by what image and standing they want the company to have. Both casual observation and formal studies indicate that managers' ambitions, values, business philosophies, attitudes toward risk, and ethical beliefs have important influences on strategy.[11] Sometimes the influence of a manager's personal values, experiences, and emotions is conscious and deliberate; at other times it may be unconscious. As one expert noted in explaining the relevance of personal factors to strategy, "People have to have their hearts in it."[12]

The personal ambitions, business philosophies, and ethical beliefs of managers are usually stamped on the strategies they craft.

Several examples of how business philosophies and personal values enter into strategy-making are particularly noteworthy. Japanese managers are strong proponents of strategies that take a long-term view and that aim at building market share and competitive position. In contrast, some U.S. corporate executives and Wall Street financiers draw criticism for overemphasizing short-term profits at the expense of long-term competitive positioning and for being more attracted to strategies involving a financial play on assets (leveraged buyouts and stock buybacks) rather than using corporate resources to make long-term strategic investments. Japanese companies also display a quite different philosophy regarding the role of suppliers. Their preferred supplier strategy is to enter into long-term partnership arrangements with key suppliers because they believe that working closely with the same supplier year after year improves the quality and reliability of component parts, permits just-in-time delivery, and reduces inventory carrying costs. In U.S. and European companies, the traditional strategic approach has been to play suppliers off against one another, doing business on a short-term basis with whoever offers the best price and promises acceptable quality.

Attitudes toward risk also have a big influence on strategy. Risk-avoiders are inclined toward "conservative" strategies that minimize downside risk, have a quick payback, and produce sure short-term profits. Risk-takers lean more toward oppor-

---

[10]David T. Kollat, Roger D. Blackwell, and James F. Robeson, *Strategic Marketing* (New York: Holt, Rinehart & Winston, 1972), p. 24.

[11]See, for instance, William D. Guth and Renato Tagiuri, "Personal Values and Corporate Strategy," *Harvard Business Review* 43, no. 5 (September–October 1965), pp. 123–32; Kenneth R. Andrews, *The Concept of Corporate Strategy,* 3rd ed. (Homewood, Ill.: Richard D. Irwin, 1987), chap. 4; and Richard F. Vancil, "Strategy Formulation in Complex Organizations," *Sloan Management Review* 17, no. 2 (Winter 1986), pp. 4–5.

[12]Andrews, *The Concept of Corporate Strategy,* p. 63.

tunistic strategies where visionary moves can produce a big payoff over the long term. Risk-takers prefer innovation to imitation and bold strategic offensives to defensive moves to protect the status quo.

Managerial values also shape the ethical quality of a firm's strategy. Managers with strong ethical convictions take pains to see that their companies observe a strict code of ethics in all aspects of the business. They expressly forbid such practices as accepting or giving kickbacks, badmouthing rivals' products, and buying political influence with political contributions. Instances where a company's strategic actions run afoul of high ethical standards include charging excessive interest rates on credit card balances, employing bait-and-switch sales tactics, continuing to market products suspected of having safety problems, and using ingredients that are known health hazards.

THE INFLUENCE OF SHARED VALUES AND COMPANY CULTURE ON STRATEGY

An organization's policies, practices, traditions, philosophical beliefs, and ways of doing things combine to give it a distinctive culture. A company's strategic actions typically reflect its cultural traits and managerial values. In some cases a company's core beliefs and culture even dominate the choice of strategic moves. This is because culture-related values and beliefs become so embedded in management's strategic thinking and actions that they condition how the enterprise responds to external events. Such firms have a culture-driven bias about how to handle strategic issues and what kinds of strategic moves it will consider or reject. Strong cultural influences partly account for why companies gain reputations for such strategic traits as technological leadership, product innovation, dedication to superior craftsmanship, a proclivity for financial wheeling and dealing, a desire to grow rapidly by acquiring other companies, a strong people-orientation, or unusual emphasis on customer service and total customer satisfaction.

A company's values and culture can dominate the kinds of strategic moves it considers or rejects.

In recent years, more companies began to articulate the core beliefs and values underlying their business approaches. One company expressed its core beliefs and values like this:

> We are market-driven. We believe that functional excellence, combined with teamwork across functions and profit centers, is essential to achieving superb execution. We believe that people are central to everything we will accomplish. We believe that honesty, integrity, and fairness should be the cornerstone of our relationships with consumers, customers, suppliers, stockholders, and employees.

Wal-Mart's founder, Sam Walton, was a fervent believer in frugality, hard work, constant improvement, dedication to customers, and genuine care for employees. The company's commitment to these values is deeply ingrained in its strategy of low prices, good values, friendly service, productivity through the intelligent use of technology, and hard-nosed bargaining with suppliers.[13] At Hewlett-Packard, the company's basic values, known internally as "the HP Way," include sharing the company's success with employees, showing trust and respect for employees, providing customers with products and services of the greatest value, being genuinely interested in

---

[13]Sam Walton with John Huey, *Sam Walton: Made in America* (New York: Doubleday, 1992); and John P. Kotter and James L. Heskett, *Corporate Culture and Performance* (New York: Free Press, 1992), pp. 17 and 36.

providing customers with effective solutions to their problems, making profit a high stockholder priority, avoiding the use of long-term debt to finance growth, individual initiative and creativity, teamwork, and being a good corporate citizen.[14] At both Wal-Mart and Hewlett-Packard, the value systems are deeply ingrained and widely shared by managers and employees. Whenever this happens, values and beliefs are more than an expression of nice platitudes; they become a way of life within the company.[15]

LINKING STRATEGY WITH ETHICS

Strategy ought to be ethical. It should involve rightful actions, not wrongful ones; otherwise it won't pass the test of moral scrutiny. This means more than conforming to what is legal. Ethical and moral standards go beyond the prohibitions of law and the language of "thou shalt not" to the issues of *duty* and the language of "should do and should not do." Ethics concerns human duty and the principles on which this duty rests.[16]

Every business has an ethical duty to each of five constituencies: owners/shareholders, employees, customers, suppliers, and the community at large. Each of these constituencies affects the organization and is affected by it. Each is a stakeholder in the enterprise, with certain expectations as to what the enterprise should do and how it should do it.[17] Owners/shareholders, for instance, rightly expect a return on their investment. Even though investors may individually differ in their preferences for profits now versus profits later, their tolerances for greater risk, and their enthusiasm for exercising social responsibility, business executives have a moral duty to pursue profitable management of the owners' investment.

A company's duty to employees arises out of respect for the worth and dignity of individuals who devote their energies to the business and who depend on the business for their economic well-being. Principled strategy-making requires that employee-related decisions be made equitably and compassionately, with concern for due process and for the impact that strategic change has on employees' lives. At best, the chosen strategy should promote employee interests as concerns wage and salary levels, career opportunities, job security, and overall working conditions. At worst, the chosen strategy should not disadvantage employees. Even in crisis situations where adverse employee impact cannot be avoided, businesses have an ethical duty to minimize whatever hardships have to be imposed in the form of workforce reductions, plant closings, job transfers, relocations, retraining, and loss of income.

The duty to the customer arises out of expectations that attend the purchase of a good or service. Inadequate appreciation of this duty led to product liability laws and a host of regulatory agencies to protect consumers. All kinds of strategy-related ethical issues still arise here, however. Should a seller inform consumers *fully* about the contents of its product, especially if it contains ingredients that, though officially approved for use, are suspected of having potentially harmful effects? Is it ethical for the makers of alcoholic beverages to sponsor college events, given that many college

Every strategic action a company takes should be ethical.

A company has ethical duties to owners, employees, customers, suppliers, the communities where it operates, and the public at large.

---

[14]Kotter and Heskett, *Corporate Culture and Performance,* pp. 60–61.

[15]For another example of the impact of values and beliefs, see Richard T. Pascale, "Perspectives on Strategy: The Real Story behind Honda's Success," in Glenn Carroll and David Vogel, *Strategy and Organization: A West Coast Perspective* (Marshfield, Mass.: Pitman Publishing, 1984), p. 60.

[16]Harry Downs, "Business Ethics: The Stewardship of Power," working paper provided to the authors.

[17]Ibid.

students are under 21? Is it ethical for cigarette manufacturers to advertise at all (even though it is legal)? Is it ethical for manufacturers to produce and sell products they know have faulty parts or defective designs that may not become apparent until after the warranty expires?

A company's ethical duty to its suppliers arises out of the market relationship that exists between them. They are both partners and adversaries. They are partners in the sense that the quality of suppliers' parts affects the quality of a firm's own product. They are adversaries in the sense that the supplier wants the highest price and profit it can get while the buyer wants a cheaper price, better quality, and speedier service. A company confronts several ethical issues in its supplier relationships. Is it ethical to threaten to cease doing business with a supplier unless the supplier agrees not to do business with key competitors? Is it ethical to reveal one supplier's price quote to a rival supplier? Is it ethical to accept gifts from suppliers? Is it ethical to pay a supplier in cash?

A company's ethical duty to the community at large stems from its status as a citizen of the community and as an institution of society. Communities and society are reasonable in expecting businesses to be good citizens—to pay their fair share of taxes for fire and police protection, waste removal, streets and highways, and so on, and to exercise care in the impact their activities have on the environment and on the communities in which they operate. The community and public interest should be accorded the same recognition and attention as the other four constituencies. Whether a company is a good community citizen is ultimately demonstrated by the way it supports community activities, encourages employees to participate in community activities, handles the health and safety aspects of its operations, accepts responsibility for overcoming environmental pollution, relates to regulatory bodies and employee unions, and exhibits high ethical standards.

Carrying Out Ethical Responsibilities   Management, not constituent groups, is responsible for managing the enterprise. Thus, it is management's perceptions of its ethical duties and of constituents' claims that drive whether and how strategy is linked to ethical behavior. Ideally, managers weigh strategic decisions from each constituent's point of view and, where conflicts arise, strike a rational, objective, and equitable balance among the interests of all five constituencies. If any of the five constituencies conclude that management is not doing its duty, they have their own avenues for recourse. Concerned investors can act through the annual shareholders' meeting, by appealing to the board of directors, or by selling their stock. Concerned employees can unionize and bargain collectively, or they can seek employment elsewhere. Customers can switch to competitors. Suppliers can find other buyers or pursue other market alternatives. The community and society can do anything from staging protest marches to stimulating political and governmental action.[18]

A management that truly cares about business ethics and corporate social responsibility is proactive rather than reactive in linking strategic action and ethics. It steers away from ethically or morally questionable business opportunities. It won't do business with suppliers that engage in activities the company does not condone. It produces products that are safe for its customers to use. It operates a workplace environment that is safe for employees. It recruits and hires employees whose values and behavior match the company's principles and ethical standards. It acts to reduce any environmental pollution it causes. It cares about *how* it does business and whether its

---

[18]Ibid.

ILLUSTRATION CAPSULE 7

HARRIS CORPORATION'S COMMITMENTS TO ITS STAKEHOLDERS

Harris Corporation is a major supplier of information, communication, and semiconductor products, systems, and services to commercial and governmental customers throughout the world. The company utilizes advanced technologies to provide innovative and cost-effective solutions for processing and communicating data, voice, text, and video information. The company's sales exceed $2 billion, and it employs nearly 23,000 people. In a recent annual report, the company set forth its commitment to satisfying the expectations of its stakeholders:

Customers—For customers, our objective is to achieve ever-increasing levels of satisfaction by providing quality products and services with distinctive benefits on a timely and continuing basis worldwide. Our relationships with customers will be forthright and ethical, and will be conducted in a manner to build trust and confidence.

Shareholders—For shareholders, the owners of our company, our objective is to achieve sustained growth in earnings-per-share. The resulting stock-price appreciation combined with dividends should provide our shareholders with a total return on investment that is competitive with similar investment opportunities.

Employees—The people of Harris are our company's most valuable asset, and our objective is for every employee to be personally involved in and share the success of the business. The company is committed to providing an environment which encourages all employees to make full use of their creativity and unique talents; to providing equitable compensation, good working conditions, and the opportunity for personal development and growth which is limited only by individual ability and desire.

Suppliers—Suppliers are a vital part of our resources. Our objective is to develop and maintain mutually beneficial partnerships with suppliers who share our commitment to achieving increasing levels of customer satisfaction through continuing improvements in quality, service, timeliness, and cost. Our relationships with suppliers will be sincere, ethical, and will embrace the highest principles of purchasing practice.

Communities—Our objective is to be a responsible corporate citizen. This includes support of appropriate civic, educational, and business activities, respect for the environment, and the encouragement of Harris employees to practice good citizenship and support community programs. Our greatest contribution to our communities is to be successful so that we can maintain stable employment and create new jobs.

Source: 1988 Annual Report.

actions reflect integrity and high ethical standards. Illustration Capsule 7 describes Harris Corporation's ethical commitments to its stakeholders.

TESTS OF A WINNING STRATEGY

What are the criteria for weeding out candidate strategies? How can a manager judge which strategic option is best for the company? What are the standards for determining whether a strategy is successful or not? Three tests can be used to evaluate the merits of one strategy over another and to gauge how good a strategy is:

The Goodness of Fit Test—A good strategy is well-matched to the company's internal and external situation—without situational fit, a strategy's appropriateness is suspect.

The Competitive Advantage Test—A good strategy leads to sustainable competitive advantage. The bigger the competitive edge that a strategy helps build, the more powerful and effective it is.

The Performance Test—A good strategy boosts company performance. Two kinds of performance improvements are the most telling: gains in profitability and gains in the company's long-term business strength and competitive position.

Strategic options judged to have low potential on one or more of these criteria are candidates to be dropped from further consideration. The strategic option judged to have the highest potential on all three counts can be regarded as the best or most attractive strategic alternative. Once a strategic commitment is made and enough time elapses to see results, these same tests can be used to assess how well a company's current strategy is performing. The bigger the margins by which a strategy satisfies all three criteria when put to test in the marketplace, the more it qualifies as a winning strategy.

There are, of course, some additional criteria for judging the merits of a particular strategy: clarity, internal consistency among all the pieces of strategy, timeliness, match to the personal values and ambitions of key executives, the degree of risk involved, and flexibility. Whenever appropriate, these can be used to supplement the three tests posed above.

Strategic Management Principle
A strategy is not a true winner unless it ts the enterprise's situation, builds sustainable competitive advantage, and improves company performance.

APPROACHES TO PERFORMING THE STRATEGY-MAKING TASK

Companies and managers perform the strategy-making task differently. In small, owner-managed companies strategy-making is developed informally. Often the strategy is never reduced to writing but exists mainly in the entrepreneur's own mind and in oral understandings with key subordinates. Large companies, however, tend to develop their plans via an annual strategic planning cycle (complete with prescribed procedures, forms, and timetables) that includes broad management participation, lots of studies, and multiple meetings to probe and question. The larger and more diverse an enterprise, the more managers feel it is better to have a structured annual process with written plans, management scrutiny, and official approval at each level.

Along with variations in the organizational process of formulating strategy are variations in how managers personally participate in analyzing the company's situation and deliberating what strategy to pursue. The four basic strategy-making styles managers use are:[19]

The Master Strategist Approach—Here the manager functions as chief strategist and chief entrepreneur, exercising *strong* influence over assessments of the situation, over the strategy alternatives that are explored, and over the details of strategy. This does not mean that the manager personally does all the work; it means that the manager personally becomes the chief architect of strategy and wields a proactive hand in shaping some or all of the major pieces of strategy. The manager acts as strategy commander and has a big ownership stake in the chosen strategy.

The Delegate-It-to-Others Approach—Here the manager in charge delegates the exercise of strategy-making to others, perhaps a strategic planning staff or a task force of trusted subordinates. The manager then personally stays off to the side,

---

[19]This discussion is based on David R. Brodwin and L. J. Bourgeois, "Five Steps to Strategic Action," in Glenn Carroll and David Vogel, *Strategy and Organization: A West Coast Perspective* (Marshfield, Mass.: Pitman Publishing, 1984), pp. 168-78.

keeps in touch with how things are progressing via reports and oral conversations, offers guidance if need be, smiles or frowns as trial balloon recommendations are informally run by him/her for reaction, then puts a stamp of approval on the strategic plan after it has been formally presented and discussed and a consensus emerges. But the manager rarely has much ownership in the recommendations and, privately, may not see much urgency in pushing *hard* to implement some or much of what has been stated in writing in the company's "official strategic plan." Also, it is generally understood that "of course, we may have to proceed a bit differently if conditions change"—which gives the manager flexibility to go slow or ignore those approaches/moves that "on further reflection may not be the thing to do at this time." This strategy-making style has the advantage of letting the manager pick and chose from the smorgasbord of strategic ideas that bubble up from below, and it allows room for broad participation and input from many managers and areas. The weakness is that a manager can end up so detached from the process of formal strategy-making that no real strategic leadership is exercised—indeed, subordinates are likely to conclude that strategic planning isn't important enough to warrant a big claim on the boss's personal time and attention. The stage is then set for rudderless direction-setting. Often the strategy-making that does occur is short-run oriented and reactive; it says more about today's problems than positioning the enterprise to capture tomorrow's opportunities.

The Collaborative Approach—This is a middle approach whereby the manager enlists the help of key subordinates in hammering out a consensus strategy that all the key players will back and do their best to implement successfully. The biggest strength of this strategy-making style is that those who are charged with crafting the strategy also are charged with implementing it. Giving subordinate managers such a clear-cut ownership stake in the strategy they must implement enhances commitment to successful execution. And when subordinates have had a hand in proposing their part of the overall strategy, they can be held accountable for making it work—the "I told you it was a bad idea" alibi won't fly.

The Champion Approach—In this style, the manager is interested neither in a big personal stake in the details of strategy nor in the time-consuming tedium of leading others through participative brainstorming or a collaborative "group wisdom" exercise. Rather, the idea is to encourage subordinate managers to develop, champion, and implement sound strategies. Here strategy moves upward from the "doers" and the "fast-trackers." Executives serve as judges, evaluating the strategy proposals reaching their desks. This approach works best in large diversified corporations where the CEO cannot personally orchestrate strategy-making in each of many business divisions. For headquarters executives to capitalize on having people in the enterprise who can see strategic opportunities that they cannot, they must delegate the initiative for strategy-making to managers at the business-unit level. Corporate executives may well articulate general strategic themes as organizationwide guidelines for strategic thinking, but the key to good strategy-making is stimulating and rewarding new strategic initiatives conceived by a champion who believes in the opportunity and badly wants the blessing to go after it. With this approach, the total strategy ends up being the sum of the championed initiatives that get approved.

These four basic managerial approaches to forming a strategy illuminate several aspects about how strategy emerges. In situations where the manager in charge personally functions as the chief architect of strategy, the choice of what strategic course to steer is a product of his/her own vision about how to position the enterprise and of the manager's ambitions, values, business philosophies, and sense of what moves to make next. Highly centralized strategy-making works fine when the manager in charge has a powerful, insightful vision of what needs to be done and how to do it. The primary weakness of the master strategist approach is that the caliber of the strategy depends so heavily on one person's strategy-making skills. It also breaks down in large enterprises where many strategic initiatives are needed and the strategy-making task is too complex for one person to handle alone.

Of the four basic approaches managers can use in crafting strategy, none is inherently superior—each has strengths and weaknesses.

On the other hand, the group approach to strategy-making has its risks too. Sometimes, the strategy that emerges is a middle-of-the-road compromise, void of bold, creative initiative. Other times, it represents political consensus, with the outcome shaped by influential subordinates, by powerful functional departments, or by majority coalitions that have a common interest in promoting their particular version of what the strategy ought to be. Politics and the exercise of power are most likely to come into play in situations where there is no strong consensus on what strategy to adopt; this opens the door for a political solution to emerge. The collaborative approach is conducive to political strategic choices as well, since powerful departments and individuals have ample opportunity to try to build a consensus for their favored strategic approach. However, the big danger of a delegate-it-to-others approach is a serious lack of top-down direction and strategic leadership.

The strength of the champion approach is also its weakness. The value of championing is that it encourages people at lower organizational levels to make suggestions and propose innovative ideas. Individuals with attractive strategic proposals are given the latitude and resources to try them out, thus helping keep strategy fresh and renewing an organization's capacity for innovation. On the other hand, the championed actions, because they come from many places in the organization, are not likely to form a coherent pattern or promote clear strategic direction. With championing, the chief executive has to work at ensuring that what is championed adds power to the overall organization strategy; otherwise, strategic initiatives may be launched in directions that have no integrating links or overarching rationale.

All four styles of handling the strategy-making task thus have strengths and weaknesses. All four can succeed or fail depending on how well the approach is managed and depending on the strategy-making skills and judgments of the individuals involved.

KEY POINTS

Management's direction-setting task involves developing a mission, setting objectives, and forming a strategy. Early on in the direction-setting process, managers need to form a vision of where to lead the organization and to answer the question, "What is our business and what will it be?" A well-conceived mission statement helps channel organizational efforts along the course management has charted and builds a strong sense of organizational identity. Effective visions are clear, challenging, and inspiring; they prepare a firm for the future, and they make sense in the marketplace. A well-conceived, well-said mission statement serves as a beacon of long-term direction and creates employee buy-in.

The second direction-setting step is to establish strategic and financial objectives for the organization to achieve. Objectives convert the mission statement into specific performance targets. The agreed-on objectives need to be challenging but achievable, and they need to spell out precisely how much by when. In other words, objectives should be measurable and should involve deadlines for achievement. Objectives are needed at all organizational levels.

The third direction-setting step entails forming strategies to achieve the objectives set in each area of the organization. A corporate strategy is needed to achieve corporate-level objectives; business strategies are needed to achieve business-unit performance objectives; functional strategies are needed to achieve the performance targets set for each functional department; and operating-level strategies are needed to achieve the objectives set in each operating and geographic unit. In effect, an organization's strategic plan is a collection of unified and interlocking strategies. As shown in Table 2–1, different strategic issues are addressed at each level of managerial strategy-making. Typically, the strategy-making task is more top-down than bottom-up. Lower-level strategy supports and complements higher-level strategy and contributes to the achievement of higher-level, companywide objectives.

Strategy is shaped by both outside and inside considerations. The major external considerations are societal, political, regulatory, and community factors; industry attractiveness; and the company's market opportunities and threats. The primary internal considerations are company strengths, weaknesses, and competitive capabilities; managers' personal ambitions, philosophies, and ethics; and the company's culture and shared values. A good strategy must be well matched to all these situational considerations. In addition, a good strategy must lead to sustainable competitive advantage and improved company performance.

There are essentially four basic ways to manage the strategy formation process in an organization: the master strategist approach where the manager in charge personally functions as the chief architect of strategy, the delegate-it-to-others approach, the collaborative approach, and the champion approach. All four have strengths and weaknesses. All four can succeed or fail depending on how well the approach is managed and depending on the strategy-making skills and judgments of the individuals involved.

SUGGESTED READINGS

Andrews, Kenneth R. *The Concept of Corporate Strategy.* 3rd ed. Homewood, Ill.: Dow Jones Irwin, 1987, chaps. 2, 3, 4, and 5.

Campbell, Andrew, and Laura Nash. *A Sense of Mission: Defining Direction for the Large Corporation.* Reading, Mass.: Addison-Wesley, 1993.

Foster, Lawrence W. "From Darwin to Now: The Evolution of Organizational Strategies." *Journal of Business Strategy* 5, no. 4 (Spring 1985), pp. 94–98.

Hamel, Gary, and C. K. Prahalad. "Strategic Intent." *Harvard Business Review* 89, no. 3 (May–June 1989), pp. 63–76.

———. "Strategy as Stretch and Leverage." *Harvard Business Review* 71, no. 2 (March–April 1993), pp. 75–84.

Hammer, Michael, and James Champy. *Reengineering the Corporation.* New York: Harper Business, 1993, chap. 9.

Hax, Arnaldo C., and Nicolas S. Majluf. *The Strategy Concept and Process: A Pragmatic Approach.* Englewood Cliffs, N.J.: Prentice-Hall, 1991, chaps. 3, 4, 8, and 9.

Ireland, R. Duane, and Michael A. Hitt. "Mission Statements: Importance, Challenge, and Recommendations for Development." *Business Horizons* (May–June 1992), pp. 34–42.

Morris, Elinor. "Vision and Strategy: A Focus for the Future." *Journal of Business Strategy* 8, no. 2 (Fall 1987), pp. 51–58.

Mintzberg, Henry. "Crafting Strategy." *Harvard Business Review* 65, no. 4 (July–August 1987), pp. 66–77.

Porter, Michael E. "Toward a Dynamic Theory of Strategy." *Strategic Management Journal* 12 (1991), pp. 95–118.

Quinn, James Brian. *Strategies for Change: Logical Incrementalism.* Homewood, Ill.: Richard D. Irwin, 1980, chaps. 2 and 4.

## CHAPTER THREE

INDUSTRY AND COMPETITIVE ANALYSIS

Analysis is the critical starting point of strategic thinking.

Kenichi Ohmae

Awareness of the environment is not a special project to be undertaken only when warning of change becomes deafening . . .

Kenneth R. Andrews

Crafting strategy is an analysis-driven exercise, not an activity where managers can succeed through good intentions and creativity. Judgments about what strategy to pursue have to be grounded in a probing assessment of a company's external environment and internal situation. Unless a company's strategy is well-matched to both external and internal circumstances, its suitability is suspect. The two biggest situational considerations are (1) industry and competitive conditions (these are the heart of a single-business company's "external environment") and (2) a company's own internal situation and competitive position. This chapter examines the techniques of *industry and competitive analysis,* the term commonly used to refer to external situation analysis of a single-business company. In the next chapter, we'll cover the tools of *company situation analysis.* Industry and competitive analysis looks broadly at a company's external *macroenvironment;* company situation analysis concerns a firm's immediate *microenvironment.*

Figure 3–1 illustrates the kinds of strategic thinking managers need to do to diagnose a company's situation. Note the logical flow from scrutiny of the company's external and internal situation to evaluation of alternatives to choice of strategy. Managers must have a keen grasp of the strategic aspects of a company's macro- and microenvironments to do a good job of establishing a strategic vision, setting objectives, and crafting a winning strategy. Absent such understanding, the door is wide open for managers to be seduced into a strategic game plan that doesn't fit the situation

FIGURE 3–1 | How Strategic Thinking and Strategic Analysis Lead to Good Strategic Choices

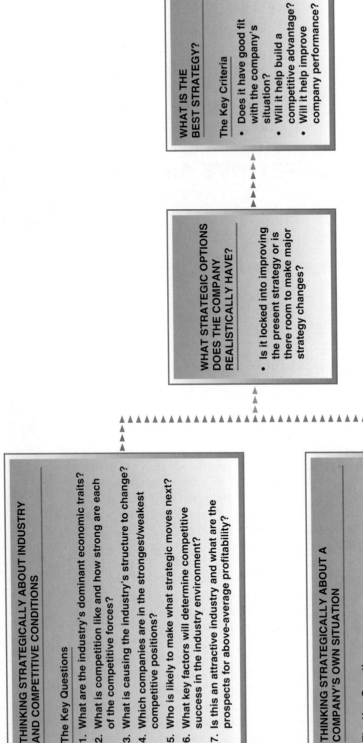

THINKING STRATEGICALLY ABOUT INDUSTRY AND COMPETITIVE CONDITIONS

The Key Questions

1. What are the industry's dominant economic traits?
2. What is competition like and how strong are each of the competitive forces?
3. What is causing the industry's structure to change?
4. Which companies are in the strongest/weakest competitive positions?
5. Who is likely to make what strategic moves next?
6. What key factors will determine competitive success in the industry environment?
7. Is this an attractive industry and what are the prospects for above-average profitability?

THINKING STRATEGICALLY ABOUT A COMPANY'S OWN SITUATION

The Key Questions

1. How well is the company's present strategy working?
2. What are the company's strengths, weaknesses, opportunities, and threats?
3. Are the company's costs competitive with rivals?
4. How strong is the company's competitive position?
5. What strategic problems need to be addressed?

WHAT STRATEGIC OPTIONS DOES THE COMPANY REALISTICALLY HAVE?

- Is it locked into improving the present strategy or is there room to make major strategy changes?

WHAT IS THE BEST STRATEGY?

The Key Criteria

- Does it have good fit with the company's situation?
- Will it help build a competitive advantage?
- Will it help improve company performance?

well, that holds little prospect for building competitive advantage, and that is unlikely to boost company performance.

THE METHODS OF INDUSTRY AND COMPETITIVE ANALYSIS

Industries differ widely in their economic characteristics, competitive situations, and future outlooks. The pace of technological change can range from fast to slow. Capital requirements can vary from big to small. The market can extend from local to worldwide. Sellers' products can be standardized or highly differentiated. Competitive forces can be strong or weak and can reflect varying degrees of emphasis on price, product performance, service, promotion, and so on. Buyer demand can be rising briskly or declining. Industry conditions differ so much that leading companies in unattractive industries can find it hard to earn respectable profits, while even weak companies in attractive industries can turn in good performances. Moreover, industry conditions change continuously as one or more aspects grow or diminish in influence.

Industry and competitive analysis utilizes a toolkit of concepts and techniques to get a clear fix on changing industry conditions and on the nature and strength of competitive forces. This tool kit provides a way of thinking strategically about any industry's overall situation and drawing conclusions about whether the industry represents an attractive investment for company funds. Industry and competitive analysis aims at developing probing answers to seven questions:

1. What are the industry's dominant economic traits?
2. What competitive forces are at work in the industry and how strong are they?
3. What are the drivers of change in the industry and what impact will they have?
4. Which companies are in the strongest/weakest competitive positions?
5. Who's likely to make what competitive moves next?
6. What key factors will determine competitive success or failure?
7. How attractive is the industry in terms of its prospects for above-average profitability?

The answers to these questions build understanding of a firm's surrounding environment and, collectively, form the basis for matching its strategy to changing industry conditions and competitive realities.

QUESTION 1: WHAT ARE THE INDUSTRY'S DOMINANT ECONOMIC TRAITS?

Because industries differ significantly in their basic character and structure, industry and competitive analysis begins with an overview of the industry's dominant economic traits. As a working definition, we use the word *industry* to mean a group of firms whose products have so many of the same attributes that they compete for the same buyers. The factors to consider in profiling an industry's economic features are fairly standard:

- Market size.
- Scope of competitive rivalry (local, regional, national, international, or global).
- Market growth rate and where the industry is in the growth cycle (early development, rapid growth and takeoff, early maturity, late maturity and saturation, stagnant and aging, decline and decay).

Managers are ill-prepared for the task of choosing a direction for the company to head or a strategy to get it there without first analyzing the company's present situation—what external conditions it faces and what its capabilities are.

- Number of rivals and their relative sizes—is the industry fragmented with many small companies or concentrated and dominated by a few large companies?
- The number of buyers and their relative sizes.
- The prevalence of backward and forward integration.
- Ease of entry and exit.
- The pace of technological change in both production process innovation and new product introductions.
- Whether the product(s)/service(s) of rival firms are highly differentiated, weakly differentiated, or essentially identical.
- Whether companies can realize scale economies in purchasing, manufacturing, transportation, marketing, or advertising.
- Whether high rates of capacity utilization are crucial to achieving low-cost production efficiency.
- Whether the industry has a strong learning and experience curve such that average unit cost declines as *cumulative* output (and thus the experience of "learning by doing") builds up.
- Capital requirements.
- Whether industry profitability is above/below par.

An industry's economic characteristics impose boundaries on the kinds of strategic approaches a company can pursue.

Table 3–1 provides a sample profile of the economic character of the sulfuric acid industry.

An industry's economic characteristics are important because of the implications they have for strategy. For example, in capital-intensive industries where investment

T A B L E 3–1 | **A Sample Profile of the Dominant Economic Characteristics of the Sulfuric Acid Industry**

Market Size: $400-$500 million annual revenues; 4 million tons total volume.

Scope of Competitive Rivalry: Primarily regional; producers rarely sell outside a 250-mile radius of plant due to high cost of shipping long distances.

Market Growth Rate: 2–3 percent annually. **Stage in Life Cycle:** Mature.

Number of Companies in Industry: About 30 companies with 110 plant locations and capacity of 4.5 million tons. Market shares range from a low of 3 percent to a high of 21 percent.

Customers: About 2,000 buyers; most are industrial chemical firms.

Degree of Vertical Integration: Mixed; 5 of the 10 largest companies are integrated backward into mining operations and also forward in that sister industrial chemical divisions buy over 50 percent of the output of their plants; all other companies are engaged solely in manufacturing.

Ease of Entry/Exit: Moderate entry barriers exist in the form of capital requirements to construct a new plant of minimum efficient size (cost equals $10 million) and ability to build a customer base inside a 250-mile radius of plant.

Technology/Innovation: Production technology is standard and changes have been slow; biggest changes are occurring in products—1–2 newly formulated specialty chemicals products are being introduced annually, accounting for nearly all of industry growth.

Product Characteristics: Highly standardized; the brands of different producers are essentially identical (buyers perceive little real difference from seller to seller).

Scale Economies: Moderate; all companies have virtually equal manufacturing costs but scale economies exist in shipping in multiple carloads to same customer and in purchasing large quantities of raw materials.

Experience Curve Effects: Not a factor in this industry.

Capacity Utilization: Manufacturing efficiency is highest between 90–100 percent of rated capacity; below 90 percent utilization, unit costs run significantly higher.

Industry Profitability: Subpar to average; the commodity nature of the industry's product results in intense price-cutting when demand slackens, but prices firm up during periods of strong demand. Profits track the strength of demand for the industry's products.

in a single plant can run several hundred million dollars, a firm can spread the burden of high fixed costs by pursuing a strategy that promotes high utilization of fixed assets and generates more revenue per dollar of fixed-asset investment. Thus commercial airlines employ strategies to boost the revenue productivity of their multimillion dollar jets by cutting ground time at airport gates (to get in more flights per day with the same plane) and by using multi-tiered price discounts to fill up otherwise empty seats on each flight. In industries characterized by one product advance after another, companies must spend enough time and money on R&D to keep their technical prowess and innovative capability abreast of competitors—a strategy of continuous product innovation becomes a condition of survival.

In industries like semiconductors, the presence of a *learning/experience* curve effect in manufacturing causes unit costs to decline about 20 percent each time *cumulative* production volume doubles. With a 20 percent experience curve effect, if the first 1 million chips cost $100 each, by a production volume of 2 million the unit cost would be $80 (80 percent of $100), by a production volume of 4 million the unit cost would be $64 (80 percent of $80), and so on. When an industry is characterized by a strong experience curve effect in its manufacturing operations, a company that moves first to initiate production of a new-style product and develops a strategy to capture the largest market share can win the competitive advantage of being the low-cost producer. The bigger the experience curve effect, the bigger the cost advantage of the company with the largest *cumulative* production volume, as shown in Figure 3–2.

Table 3–2 presents some additional examples of how an industry's economic traits are relevant to managerial strategy-making.

Basic Concept
When a strong learning/experience curve effect causes unit costs to decline substantially as cumulative production volume builds, a strategy to become the largest-volume manufacturer can offer the competitive advantage of being the industry's lowest-cost producer.

QUESTION 2: WHAT IS COMPETITION LIKE AND HOW STRONG ARE EACH OF THE COMPETITIVE FORCES?

One important component of industry and competitive analysis involves delving into the industry's competitive process to discover the main sources of competitive pressure and how strong each competitive force is. This analytical step is essential because managers cannot devise a successful strategy without in-depth understanding of the industry's competitive character.

FIGURE 3–2 | **Comparison of Experience Curve Effects for 10 Percent, 20 Percent, and 30 Percent Cost Reductions for Each Doubling of Cumulative Production Volume**

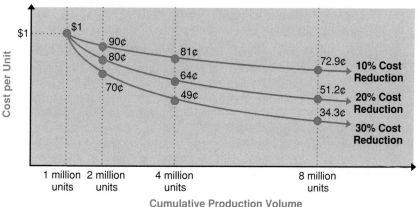

T A B L E 3–2 | **Examples of the Strategic Importance of an Industry's Key Economic Characteristics**

Factor/Characteristic	Strategic Importance
• Market size	• Small markets don't tend to attract big/new competitors; large markets often draw the interest of companies looking to acquire competitors with established positions in attractive industries.
• Market growth rate	• Fast growth breeds new entry; growth slowdowns spawn increased rivalry and a shake-out of weak competitors.
• Capacity surpluses or shortages	• Surpluses push prices and profit margins down; shortages pull them up.
• Industry profitability	• High-profit industries attract new entrants; depressed conditions encourage exit.
• Entry/exit barriers	• High barriers protect positions and profits of existing firms; low barriers make existing firms vulnerable to entry.
• Product is a big-ticket item for buyers	• More buyers will shop for lowest price.
• Standardized products	• Buyers have more power because it is easier to switch from seller to seller.
• Rapid technological change	• Raises risk factor; investments in technology facilities/equipment may become obsolete before they wear out.
• Capital requirements	• Big requirements make investment decisions critical; timing becomes important; creates a barrier to entry and exit.
• Vertical integration	• Raises capital requirements; often creates competitive differences and cost differences among fully versus partially versus nonintegrated firms.
• Economies of scale	• Increases volume and market share needed to be cost competitive.
• Rapid product innovation	• Shortens product life cycle; increases risk because of opportunities for leapfrogging.

The Five-Forces Model of Competition Even though competitive pressures in various industries are never precisely the same, the competitive process works similarly enough to use a common analytical framework in gauging the nature and intensity of competitive forces. As Professor Michael Porter of the Harvard Business School has convincingly demonstrated, *the state of competition in an industry is a composite of five competitive forces:*[1]

1. The rivalry among competing sellers in the industry.
2. The market attempts of companies in other industries to win customers over to their own *substitute* products.
3. The potential entry of new competitors.
4. The bargaining power and leverage exercisable by suppliers of inputs.
5. The bargaining power and leverage exercisable by buyers of the product.

Porter's *five-forces model,* as depicted in Figure 3–3, is a powerful tool for systematically diagnosing the principal competitive pressures in a market and assessing how strong and important each one is. Not only is it the most widely used technique of competition analysis, but it is also relatively easy to use.

The Rivalry among Competing Sellers The strongest of the five competitive forces is *usually* the jockeying for position and buyer favor that goes on among rival firms. Rivalry emerges because one or more competitors sees an opportunity to better meet

---

[1]For a thoroughgoing treatment of the five-forces model by its originator, see Michael E. Porter, *Competitive Strategy: Techniques for Analyzing Industries and Competitors* (New York: Free Press, 1980), chapter 1.

FIGURE 3-3 | The "Five-Forces" Model of Competition: A Key Analytical Tool

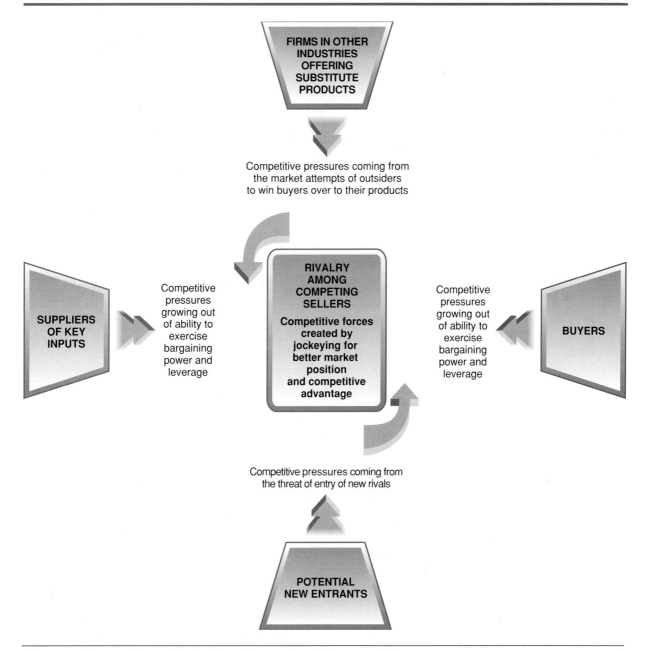

Source: Adapted from Michael E. Porter, "How Competitive Forces Shape Strategy," *Harvard Business Review 57*, no. 2 (March–April 1979), pp. 137–45.

customer needs or is under pressure to improve its performance. The intensity of rivalry among competing sellers is reflected by how vigorously they employ such competitive tactics as lower prices, snazzier features, increased customer services, longer warranties, special promotions, and new product introductions. Rivalry can range from friendly to cutthroat, depending on how frequently and how aggressively companies undertake fresh moves that threaten rivals' profitability. Ordinarily, rivals are clever at adding new wrinkles to their product offerings that enhance buyer appeal, and they persist in trying to exploit weaknesses in each other's market approaches.

Irrespective of whether rivalry is lukewarm or heated, every company is challenged to craft a successful strategy for competing—ideally, one that *produces a competitive edge over rivals* and strengthens its position with buyers. The big complication in most industries is that the success of any one firm's strategy hinges on what strategies its rivals employ and the resources rivals are willing and able to put behind their strategic efforts. The "best" strategy for one firm in its maneuvering for competitive advantage depends, in other words, on the competitive capabilities and strategies of rival companies. Such mutual interdependence means that whenever one firm makes a strategic move, its rivals often retaliate with offensive or defensive countermoves. This pattern of action and reaction makes competitive rivalry a "war-games" type of contest that is conducted in a market setting according to the rules of fair competition. Indeed, from a strategy-making perspective, *competitive markets are economic battlefields.*

Not only do competitive contests among rival sellers assume different intensities but the kinds of competitive pressures that emerge from cross-company rivalry also vary over time. The relative emphasis that rival companies put on price, quality, performance features, customer service, warranties, advertising, dealer networks, new product innovation, and so on shifts as they try different tactics to catch buyers' attention and as competitors initiate fresh offensive and defensive maneuvers. Rivalry is thus dynamic; the current competitive scene is ever-changing as companies act and react, sometimes in rapid-fire order and sometimes methodically, and as their strategic emphasis swings from one mix of competitive tactics to another.

Two facets of competitive rivalry stand out: (1) the launch of a powerful competitive strategy by one company intensifies the competitive pressures on the remaining companies and (2) the manner in which rivals employ various competitive weapons to try to outmaneuver one another shapes "the rules of competition" in the industry and determines the requirements for competitive success. Once an industry's prevailing rules of competitive rivalry are understood, managers can determine whether competitive rivalry is fierce, moderate, or attractively weak and whether it is likely to increase or diminish in strength.

Regardless of the industry, several common factors seem to influence the tempo of rivalry among competing sellers:[2]

1. *Rivalry intensifies as the number of competitors increases and as competitors become more equal in size and capability.* Up to a point, the greater the number of competitors, the greater the probability of fresh, creative strategic initiatives. In addition, when rivals are more equal in size and capability, they can usually compete on a fairly even footing, making it harder for one or two firms to "win" the competitive battle and dominate the market.

2. *Rivalry is usually stronger when demand for the product is growing slowly.* In a rapidly expanding market, there tends to be enough business for everybody to grow. Indeed, it may take all of a firm's financial and managerial resources just to keep abreast of the growth in buyer demand, much less steal rivals' customers. But when growth slows or when market demand drops

---

Principle of Competitive Markets

Competitive jockeying among rival firms is a dynamic, everchanging process as firms initiate new offensive and defensive moves and emphasis swings from one mix of competitive weapons to another.

---

[2]These indicators of what to look for in evaluating the intensity of intercompany rivalry are based on Porter, *Competitive Strategy,* pp. 17–21.

unexpectedly, expansion-minded firms and/or firms with excess capacity often cut prices and deploy other sales-increasing tactics, thereby igniting a battle for market share that can result in a shake-out of the weak and less efficient firms. The industry then consolidates into a smaller, but individually stronger, number of sellers.

3. *Rivalry is more intense when industry conditions tempt competitors to use price cuts or other competitive weapons to boost unit volume.* Whenever fixed costs account for a large fraction of total cost, unit costs tend to be lowest at or near full capacity since fixed costs can be spread over more units of production. Unused capacity imposes a significant cost-increasing penalty because there are fewer units carrying the fixed cost burden. In such cases, if market demand weakens and capacity utilization begins to fall off, the pressure of rising unit costs pushes rival firms into secret price concessions, special discounts, rebates, and other sales-increasing tactics, thus heightening competition. Likewise, when a product is perishable, seasonal, or costly to hold in inventory, competitive pressures build quickly anytime one or more firms decide to dump excess supplies on the market.

4. *Rivalry is stronger when customers' costs to switch brands are low.* The lower the costs of switching, the easier it is for rival sellers to raid one another's customers. On the other hand, high switching costs give a seller some protection against the efforts of rivals to raid its customers.

5. *Rivalry is stronger when one or more competitors is dissatisfied with its market position and launches moves to bolster its standing at the expense of rivals.* Firms that are losing ground or in financial trouble often react aggressively by acquiring smaller rivals, introducing new products, boosting advertising, discounting prices, and so on. Such actions can trigger a new round of competitive maneuvering and a hotly contested battle for market share.

6. *Rivalry increases in proportion to the size of the payoff from a successful strategic move.* The more rewarding an opportunity, the more likely some firm will aggressively pursue a strategy to capture it. The size of the strategic payoff varies partly with the speed of retaliation. When competitors respond slowly (or not at all), the initiator of a fresh competitive strategy can reap benefits in the intervening period and perhaps gain a first-mover advantage that is not easily surmounted. The greater the benefits of moving first, the more likely some firm will accept the risk and try it.

7. *Rivalry tends to be more vigorous when it costs more to get out of a business than to stay in and compete.* The higher the exit barriers (and thus the more costly it is to abandon a market), the stronger the incentive for firms to remain and compete as best they can, even though they may be earning low profits or even incurring losses.

8. *Rivalry becomes more volatile and unpredictable the more diverse competitors are in terms of their strategies, personalities, corporate priorities, resources, and countries of origin.* A diverse group of sellers often contains one or more mavericks willing to rock the boat with unconventional moves and market approaches, thus generating a livelier and less predictable competitive environment. Attempts by cross-border rivals to gain stronger footholds in each other's domestic markets is a surefire factor in boosting the intensity of rivalry, especially when foreign rivals have lower costs.

9. *Rivalry increases when strong companies outside the industry acquire weak firms in the industry and launch aggressive, well-funded moves to transform their newly acquired competitors into major market contenders.* A classic example of this occurred when Philip Morris, a leading cigarette firm with excellent marketing know-how, shook up the U.S. beer industry's approach to marketing by acquiring stodgy Miller Brewing Company in the late 1960s. In short order, Philip Morris revamped the marketing of Miller High Life and pushed it to the number two best-selling brand. PM also pioneered low-calorie beers with the introduction of Miller Lite—a move that made light beer the fastest-growing segment in the beer industry.

In sizing up the competitive pressures created by rivalry among existing competitors, the strategist's job is to identify what the current weapons of competitive rivalry are, to stay on top of how the game is being played, and to judge how much pressure cross-company rivalry is going to put on profitability. Competitive rivalry is considered intense when the actions of competitors are driving down industry profits, moderate when most companies can earn acceptable profits, and weak when most companies in the industry can earn above-average returns on investment. Chronic outbreaks of cutthroat competition among rival sellers make an industry brutally competitive.

The Competitive Force of Potential Entry New entrants to a market bring new production capacity, the desire to establish a secure place in the market, and sometimes substantial resources with which to compete.[3] Just how serious the competitive threat of entry is in a particular market depends on two classes of factors: *barriers to entry* and the *expected reaction of incumbent firms to new entry.* A barrier to entry exists whenever it is hard for a newcomer to break into the market and/or economic factors put a potential entrant at a disadvantage relative to its competitors. There are several types of entry barriers:[4]

- *Economies of scale*—Scale economies deter entry because they force potential competitors either to enter on a large-scale basis (a costly and perhaps risky move) or to accept a cost disadvantage (and consequently lower profitability). Large-scale entry is a difficult barrier to hurdle because it can create chronic overcapacity problems in the industry and it can so threaten the market shares of existing firms that they retaliate aggressively (with price cuts, increased advertising and sales promotion, and similar blocking actions) to maintain their positions. Either way, a potential entrant is discouraged by the prospect of lower profits. Entrants may encounter scale-related barriers not just in production, but in advertising, marketing and distribution, financing, after-sale customer service, raw materials purchasing, and R&D as well.

- *Inability to gain access to technology and specialized know-how*—Many industries require technological capability and skills not readily available to a new entrant. Key patents can effectively bar entry as can lack of technically skilled personnel and an inability to execute complicated manufacturing techniques. Existing firms often carefully guard know-how that gives them an

---

[3]Michael E. Porter, "How Competitive Forces Shape Strategy," *Harvard Business Review* 57, no. 2 (March–April 1979), p. 138.
[4]Porter, *Competitive Strategy,* pp. 7–17.

edge in technology and manufacturing capability. Unless new entrants can gain access to such proprietary knowledge, they will lack the technical capability to compete on a level playing field.

- *The existence of learning and experience curve effects*—When lower unit costs are partly or mostly a result of experience in producing the product and other learning curve benefits, new entrants face a cost disadvantage competing against existing firms with more accumulated know-how.

- *Brand preferences and customer loyalty*—Buyers are often attached to established brands. European consumers, for example, are fiercely loyal to European brands of major household appliances. High brand loyalty means that a potential entrant must be prepared to spend enough money on advertising and sales promotion to overcome customer loyalties and build its own clientele. Substantial time and money can be involved. In addition, if it is difficult or costly for a customer to switch to a new brand, a new entrant must persuade buyers that its brand is worth the switching costs. To overcome the switching cost barrier, new entrants may have to offer buyers a discounted price or an extra margin of quality or service. All this can mean lower expected profit margins for new entrants—something that increases the risk to start-up companies dependent on sizable, early profits to support their new investments.

- *Capital requirements*—The larger the total dollar investment needed to enter the market successfully, the more limited the pool of potential entrants. The most obvious capital requirements are associated with manufacturing plant and equipment, working capital to finance inventories and customer credit, introductory advertising and sales promotion to establish a clientele, and cash reserves to cover start-up losses.

- *Cost disadvantages independent of size*—Existing firms may have cost advantages not available to potential entrants regardless of the entrant's size. These advantages can include access to the best and cheapest raw materials, possession of patents and proprietary technology, the benefits of learning and experience curve effects, existing plants built and equipped years earlier at lower costs, favorable locations, and lower borrowing costs.

- *Access to distribution channels*—In the case of consumer goods, a potential entrant may face the barrier of gaining adequate access to distribution channels. Wholesale distributors may be reluctant to take on a product that lacks buyer recognition. A network of retail dealers may have to be set up from scratch. Retailers have to be convinced to give a new brand ample display space and an adequate trial period. The more existing producers tie up present distribution channels, the tougher entry will be. To overcome this barrier, potential entrants may have to "buy" distribution access by offering better margins to dealers and distributors or by giving advertising allowances and other promotional incentives. As a consequence, a potential entrant's profits may be squeezed unless and until its product gains enough acceptance that distributors and retailers want to carry it.

- *Regulatory policies*—Government agencies can limit or even bar entry by requiring licenses and permits. Regulated industries like cable TV, electric and gas utilities, radio and television broadcasting, liquor retailing, and railroads feature government-controlled entry. In international markets, host governments commonly limit foreign entry and must approve all foreign investment applications. Stringent government-mandated safety regulations and environmental pollution standards are entry barriers because they raise entry costs.

- *Tariffs and international trade restrictions*—National governments commonly use tariffs and trade restrictions (antidumping rules, local content requirements, and quotas) to raise entry barriers for foreign firms. In 1988, due to tariffs imposed by the South Korean government, a Ford Taurus cost South Korean car buyers over $40,000. European governments require that certain Asian products, from electronic typewriters to copying machines, contain European-made parts and labor equal to 40 percent of selling price. And to protect European chipmakers from low-cost Asian competition, European governments instituted a rigid formula for calculating floor prices for computer memory chips.

Even if a potential entrant is willing to tackle the problems of entry barriers, it still faces the issue of how existing firms will react.[5] Will incumbent firms offer only passive resistance, or will they aggressively defend their market positions using price cuts, increased advertising, new product improvements, and whatever else is calculated to give a new entrant (as well as other rivals) a hard time? A potential entrant can have second thoughts when financially strong incumbent firms send clear signals that they will stoutly defend their market positions against entry. A potential entrant may also turn away when incumbent firms can use leverage with distributors and customers to keep their business.

The best test of whether potential entry is a strong or weak competitive force is to ask if the industry's growth and profit prospects are attractive enough to induce additional entry. When the answer is no, potential entry is not a source of competitive pressure. When the answer is yes (as in industries where lower-cost foreign competitors are exploring new markets), then potential entry is a strong force. The stronger the threat of entry, the greater the motivation of incumbent firms to fortify their positions against newcomers to make entry more costly or difficult.

One additional point: the threat of entry changes as the industry's prospects grow brighter or dimmer and as entry barriers rise or fall. For example, the expiration of a key patent can greatly increase the threat of entry. A technological discovery can create an economy of scale advantage where none existed before. New actions by incumbent firms to increase advertising, strengthen distributor-dealer relations, step up R&D, or improve product quality can raise the roadblocks to entry. In international markets, entry barriers for foreign-based firms fall as tariffs are lowered, as domestic wholesalers and dealers seek out lower-cost foreign-made goods, and as domestic buyers become more willing to purchase foreign brands.

Principle of Competitive Markets
The competitive threat that outsiders will enter the market is stronger when entry barriers are low, when incumbent firms are not inclined to fight vigorously to prevent a newcomer from gaining a market foothold, and when a newcomer can expect to earn attractive profits.

Competitive Pressures from Substitute Products   Firms in one industry are, quite often, in close competition with firms in another industry because their respective products are good substitutes. The producers of eyeglasses compete with the makers of contact lenses. The producers of wood stoves compete with such substitutes as kerosene heaters and portable electric heaters. The sugar industry competes with companies that produce artificial sweeteners. The producers of plastic containers confront strong competition from manufacturers of glass bottles and jars, paperboard cartons, and tin cans and aluminum cans. Aspirin manufacturers must consider how their product compares with other pain relievers and headache remedies.

---

[5]Porter, "How Competitive Forces Shape Strategy," p. 140, and Porter, *Competitive Strategy*, pp. 14–15.

Competitive pressures from substitute products operate in several ways. First, the presence of readily available and competitively priced substitutes places a ceiling on the prices an industry can afford to charge for its product without giving customers an incentive to switch to substitutes and risking sales erosion.[6] This price ceiling, at the same time, puts a lid on the profits that industry members can earn unless they find ways to cut costs. When substitutes are cheaper than an industry's product, industry members come under heavy competitive pressure to reduce their prices and find ways to absorb the price cuts with cost reductions. Second, the availability of substitutes inevitably invites customers to compare quality and performance as well as price. For example, firms that buy glass bottles and jars from glassware manufacturers monitor whether they can just as effectively and economically package their products in plastic containers, paper cartons, or tin cans. Competitive pressures from substitute products thus push industry participants to convince customers their product is more advantageous than substitutes. Usually this requires devising a competitive strategy to differentiate the industry's product from substitute products via some combination of lower price, better quality, better service, and more desirable performance features.

Another determinant of whether substitutes are a strong or weak competitive force is how difficult or costly it is for the industry's customers to switch to substitute products.[7] Typical switching costs include employee retraining costs, the purchase costs of any additional equipment, payments for technical help in making the changeover, the time and cost in testing the quality and reliability of the substitute, and the psychic costs of severing old supplier relationships and establishing new ones. If switching costs are high, sellers of substitutes must offer a major cost or performance benefit in order to steal the industry's customers away. When switching costs are low, it's much easier for sellers of substitutes to convince buyers to change over to their products.

Principle of Competitive Markets
The competitive threat posed by substitute products is strong when prices of substitutes are attractive, buyers' switching costs are low, and buyers believe substitutes have equal or better features.

As a rule, then, the lower the price of substitutes, the higher their quality and performance, and the lower the user's switching costs, the more intense the competitive pressures posed by substitute products. The best indicators of the competitive strength of substitute products are the rate at which their sales are growing, the market inroads they are making, their plans for expanding production capacity, and the size of their profits.

The Power of Suppliers   Whether the suppliers to an industry are a weak or strong competitive force depends on market conditions in the supplier industry and the significance of the item they supply.[8] The competitive force of suppliers is greatly diminished whenever the item they provide is a standard commodity available on the open market from a large number of suppliers with ample capability to fill orders. Then it is relatively simple to obtain whatever is needed from a list of capable suppliers, dividing purchases among several to promote lively competition for orders. In such cases, suppliers have market power only when supplies become tight and users are so anxious to secure what they need that they agree to terms more favorable to suppliers. Suppliers are likewise in a weak bargaining position whenever there are good substitute inputs and switching is neither costly nor difficult. For example, soft drink bottlers can effectively check the power of aluminum can suppliers by using more plastic containers and glass bottles.

---

[6]Porter, "How Competitive Forces Shape Strategy," p. 142, and Porter, *Competitive Strategy,* pp. 23–24.
[7]Porter, *Competitive Strategy,* p. 10.
[8]Ibid., pp. 27–28.

Suppliers also have less leverage when the industry they are supplying is a *major* customer. In this case, the well-being of suppliers becomes closely tied to the well-being of their major customers. Suppliers then have a big incentive to protect the customer industry via reasonable prices, improved quality, and the development of new products and services that might enhance their customers' competitive positions, sales, and profits. When industry members form close working relationships with major suppliers, they may gain substantial benefit in the form of better quality components, just-in-time deliveries, and reduced inventory costs.

On the other hand, when the item suppliers provide accounts for a sizable fraction of the costs of an industry's product, is crucial to the industry's production process, and/or significantly affects the quality of the industry's product, suppliers have considerable influence on the competitive process. This is particularly true when a few large companies control most of the available supplies and have pricing leverage. Likewise, a supplier (or group of suppliers) possesses bargaining leverage the more difficult or costly it is for users to switch to alternate suppliers. Big suppliers with good reputations and growing demand for their output are harder to wring concessions from than struggling suppliers striving to broaden their customer base or more fully utilize their production capacity.

Principle of Competitive Markets
The suppliers to a group of rival firms are a strong competitive force whenever they have sufficient bargaining power to put certain rivals at a competitive disadvantage based on the prices they can command, the quality and performance of the items they supply, or the reliability of their deliveries.

Suppliers are also more powerful when they can supply a component more cheaply than industry members can make it themselves. For instance, most producers of outdoor power equipment (lawnmowers, rotary tillers, snowblowers, and so on) find it cheaper to source the small engines they need from outside manufacturers rather than make their own because the quantity they need is too little to justify the investment and master the process. Specialists in small-engine manufacture, by supplying many kinds of engines to the whole power equipment industry, obtain a big enough sales volume to capture scale economies, become proficient in all the manufacturing techniques, and keep costs well below what power equipment firms could realize on their own. Small-engine suppliers then are in a position to price the item below what it would cost the user to self-manufacture but far enough above their own costs to generate an attractive profit margin. In such situations, the bargaining position of suppliers is strong *until* the volume of parts a user needs becomes large enough for the user to justify backward integration. Then the balance of power shifts from suppliers to users. The more credible the threat of backward integration into the suppliers' business becomes, the more leverage users have in negotiating favorable terms with suppliers.

A final instance in which an industry's suppliers play an important competitive role is when suppliers, for one reason or another, do not have the capability or the incentive to provide items of high or consistent quality. For example, if a manufacturer's suppliers provide components that have a relatively high defect rate or that fail prematurely, they can so increase the warranty and defective goods costs of the manufacturer that its profits, reputation, and competitive position are seriously impaired.

The Power of Buyers   Just as with suppliers, the competitive strength of buyers can range from strong to weak. Buyers have substantial bargaining leverage in a number of situations.[9] The most obvious is when buyers are large and purchase a sizable percentage of the industry's output. The bigger buyers are and the larger the quantities

---

[9]Ibid., pp. 24–27.

they purchase, the more clout they have in negotiating with sellers. Often, purchasing in large quantities gives a buyer enough leverage to obtain price concessions and other favorable terms. Buyers also gain power when the costs of switching to competing brands or substitutes are relatively low. Any time buyers have the flexibility to fill their needs by sourcing from several sellers rather than having to use just one brand, they have added room to negotiate with sellers. When sellers' products are virtually identical, it is relatively easy for buyers to switch from seller to seller at little or no cost. However, if sellers' products are strongly differentiated, buyers are less able to switch without incurring sizable changeover costs.

One last point: all buyers are not likely to possess equal degrees of bargaining power with sellers, and some may be less sensitive than others to price, quality, or service. For example, in the apparel industry, major manufacturers confront significant customer power when selling to retail chains like Wal-Mart or Sears. But they can get much better prices selling to the small owner-managed apparel boutiques.

Strategic Implications of the Five Competitive Forces The value of the five-forces model is the assist it provides in exposing the makeup of competitive forces. *To analyze the competitive environment, managers must assess the strength of each one of the five competitive forces.* The collective impact of these forces determines what competition is like in a given market. As a rule, the stronger competitive forces are, the lower is the collective profitability of participant firms. The most brutally competitive situation occurs when the five forces create market conditions tough enough to impose prolonged subpar profitability or even losses on most or all firms. The competitive structure of an industry is clearly "unattractive" from a profit-making standpoint if rivalry among sellers is very strong, entry barriers are low, competition from substitutes is strong, and both suppliers and customers are able to exercise considerable bargaining leverage. On the other hand, when competitive forces are not collectively strong, the competitive structure of the industry is "favorable" or "attractive" from the standpoint of earning superior profits. The "ideal" competitive environment from a profit-making perspective is where both suppliers and customers are in weak bargaining positions, there are no good substitutes, entry barriers are relatively high, and rivalry among present sellers is only moderate. However, even when some of the five competitive forces are strong, an industry can be competitively attractive to those firms whose market position and strategy provide a good enough defense against competitive pressures to preserve their ability to earn above-average profits.

To deal successfully with competitive forces, managers must craft strategies that (1) insulate the firm as much as possible from the five competitive forces, (2) influence the industry's competitive rules in the company's favor, and (3) provide a strong, secure position of advantage from which to "play the game" of competition as it unfolds in the industry. Managers cannot do this task well without a perceptive understanding of the industry's whole competitive picture. The five-forces model is a tool for gaining this understanding.

QUESTION 3: WHAT IS CAUSING THE INDUSTRY'S COMPETITIVE STRUCTURE AND BUSINESS ENVIRONMENT TO CHANGE?

An industry's economic features and competitive structure say a lot about the basic nature of the industry environment but very little about the ways in which the environment may be changing. All industries are characterized by trends and new developments that either gradually or speedily produce changes important enough to

Principle of Competitive Markets
Buyers become a stronger competitive force the more they are able to exercise bargaining leverage over price, quality, service, or other terms of sale.

A company's competitive strategy is increasingly effective the more it provides good defenses against the five competitive forces, influences the industry's competitive rules in the company's favor, and helps create sustainable competitive advantage.

require a strategic response from participating firms. The popular hypothesis about industries going through evolutionary phases or life-cycle stages helps explain industry change but is still incomplete.[10] The life-cycle stages are strongly keyed to the overall industry growth rate (which is why such terms as rapid growth, early maturity, saturation, and decline are used to describe the stages). Yet there are more causes of industry change than an industry's position on the growth curve.

The Concept of Driving Forces   While it is important to judge what growth stage an industry is in, there's more analytical value in identifying the specific factors causing fundamental industry and competitive adjustments. Industry and competitive conditions change *because forces are in motion that create incentives or pressures for change*.[11] The most dominant forces are called *driving forces* because they have the biggest influence on what kinds of changes will take place in the industry's structure and competitive environment. Driving forces analysis has two steps: identifying what the driving forces are and assessing the impact they will have on the industry.

The Most Common Driving Forces   Many events can affect an industry powerfully enough to qualify as driving forces. Some are one of a kind, but most fall into one of several basic categories.[12]

- *Changes in the long-term industry growth rate*—Shifts in industry growth up or down are a force for industry change because they affect the balance between industry supply and buyer demand, entry and exit, and how hard it will be for a firm to capture additional sales. An upsurge in long-term demand frequently attracts new entrants to the market and encourages established firms to invest in additional capacity. A shrinking market can cause some companies to exit the industry and induce those remaining to close their least efficient plants and retrench to a smaller production base.

- *Changes in who buys the product and how they use it*—Shifts in buyer composition and new ways of using the product can force adjustments in customer service offerings (credit, technical assistance, maintenance and repair), open the way to market the industry's product through a different mix of dealers and retail outlets, prompt producers to broaden/narrow their product lines, increase/decrease capital requirements, and change sales and promotion approaches. The development of new cable-converter boxes is now allowing home computer service firms like Prodigy, CompuServe, and America Online to sign up cable companies to deliver their games, bulletin boards, data services, and electronic shopping services to home subscribers via cable television. Consumer enthusiasm for cordless and cellular telephones has opened a major new buyer segment for telephone equipment manufacturers.

- *Product innovation*—Product innovation can broaden an industry's customer base, rejuvenate industry growth, and widen the degree of product differentiation among rival sellers. Successful new product introductions strengthen the market position of the innovating companies, usually at the

Industry conditions change because important forces are driving industry participants (competitors, customers, or suppliers) to alter their actions; the *driving forces* in an industry are the *major underlying causes* of changing industry and competitive conditions.

---

[10]For a more extended discussion of the problems with the life-cycle hypothesis, see Porter, *Competitive Strategy,* pp. 157–62.

[11]Porter, *Competitive Strategy,* p. 162.

[12]What follows draws on the discussion in Porter, *Competitive Strategy,* pp. 164–83.

expense of companies who stick with their old products or are slow to follow with their own versions of the new product. Industries where product innovation has been a key driving force include copying equipment, cameras and photographic equipment, computers, electronic video games, toys, prescription drugs, frozen foods, and personal computer software.

- *Technological change*—Advances in technology can dramatically alter an industry's landscape, making it possible to produce new and/or better products at lower cost and opening up whole new industry frontiers. Technological developments can also produce changes in capital requirements, minimum efficient plant sizes, vertical integration benefits, and learning or experience curve effects.

- *Marketing innovation*—When firms are successful in introducing new ways to market their products, they can spark a burst of buyer interest, widen industry demand, increase product differentiation, and/or lower unit costs—any or all of which can alter the competitive positions of rival firms and force strategy revisions.

- *Entry or exit of major firms*—The entry of one or more foreign companies into a market once dominated by domestic firms nearly always shakes up competitive conditions. Likewise, when an established domestic firm from another industry attempts entry either by acquisition or by launching its own start-up venture, it usually applies its skills and resources in some innovative fashion that introduces a new element to competition. Entry by a major firm often produces a "new ballgame" not only with new key players but also with new rules for competing. Similarly, exit of a major firm changes competitive structure by reducing the number of market leaders (perhaps increasing the dominance of the leaders who remain) and causing a rush to capture the exiting firm's customers.

- *Diffusion of technical know-how*—As knowledge about how to perform a particular activity or execute a particular manufacturing technology spreads, any technically based competitive advantage held by firms originally possessing this know-how erodes. The diffusion of such know-how can occur through scientific journals, trade publications, on-site plant tours, word-of-mouth among suppliers and customers, and the hiring away of knowledgeable employees. It can also occur when the possessors of technological know-how license others to use it for a royalty fee or team up with a company interested in turning the technology into a new business venture. Quite often, technological know-how can be acquired by simply buying a company that has the wanted skills, patents, or manufacturing capabilities. In recent years technology transfer across national boundaries has emerged as one of the most important driving forces in globalizing markets and competition. As companies in more countries gain access to technical know-how, they upgrade their manufacturing capabilities in a long-term effort to compete head-on against established companies. Examples of where technology transfer has turned a largely domestic industry into an increasingly global one include automobiles, tires, consumer electronics, telecommunications, and computers.

- *Increasing globalization of the industry*—Industries move toward globalization for any of several reasons. One or more nationally prominent firms may launch aggressive long-term strategies to win a globally dominant market position. Demand for the industry's product may pop up in more and more countries.

Trade barriers may drop. Technology transfer may open the door for more companies in more countries to enter the industry arena on a major scale. Significant labor cost differences among countries may create a strong reason to locate plants for labor-intensive products in low-wage countries (wages in South Korea, Taiwan, and Singapore, for example, are about one-fourth those in the U.S.). Significant cost economies may accrue to firms with world-scale volumes as opposed to national-scale volumes. Multinational companies with the ability to transfer their production, marketing, and management know-how from country to country at very low cost can sometimes gain a significant competitive advantage over domestic-only competitors. As a consequence, global competition usually shifts the pattern of competition among an industry's key players, favoring some and disadvantaging others. Such occurrences make globalization a driving force. Globalization is most likely to be a driving force in industries *(a)* based on natural resources (supplies of crude oil, copper, and cotton, for example, are geographically scattered all over the globe), *(b)* where low-cost production is a critical consideration (making it imperative to locate plant facilities in countries where the lowest costs can be achieved), and *(c)* where one or more growth-oriented, market-seeking companies are pushing hard to gain a significant competitive position in as many attractive country markets as they can.

- *Changes in cost and efficiency*—In industries where new economies of scale are emerging or where strong learning curve effects allow firms with the most production experience to undercut rivals' prices, large market share becomes such a distinct advantage that all firms must shift to volume-building strategies—triggering a "race for growth." Likewise, sharply rising costs for a key input (either raw materials or labor) can cause a scramble to either *(a)* line up reliable supplies of the input at affordable prices or *(b)* search out lower-cost substitute inputs. Any time important changes in cost or efficiency take place in an industry, widening or shrinking cost differences among key competitors can dramatically alter the state of competition.

- *Emerging buyer preferences for differentiated products instead of a commodity product (or for a more standardized product instead of strongly differentiated products)*—Sometimes growing numbers of buyers decide that a standard "one size fits all" product with a bargain price meets their needs as effectively as premium-priced brands with snappy features and options. Such a development tends to shift patronage away from sellers of more expensive differentiated products to sellers of cheaper commodity products and create a price-competitive market environment. Pronounced shifts toward greater product standardization can so dominate a market that the strategic freedom of rival producers is limited to driving costs out of the business and competing hard on price. On the other hand, a shift away from standardized products occurs when sellers are able to win a bigger and more loyal buyer following by introducing new features, making style changes, offering options and accessories, and creating image differences via advertising and packaging. Then the driver of change is the contest among rivals to cleverly outdifferentiate one another. Industries evolve differently depending on whether the market forces in motion are acting to increase or decrease the emphasis on product differentiation.

- *Regulatory influences and government policy changes*—Regulatory and governmental actions can often force significant changes in industry practices and strategic approaches. Deregulation has been a big driving force in the airline, banking, natural gas, and telecommunications industries. President Clinton's proposal for universal health insurance recently became a driving force in the health care industry. In international markets, host governments can open up their domestic markets to foreign participation or close them off to protect domestic companies, thus shaping whether the competitive struggle occurs on a level playing field or favors domestic firms (owing to government protectionism).

- *Changing societal concerns, attitudes, and lifestyles*—Emerging social issues and changing attitudes and lifestyles can be powerful instigators of industry change. Consumer concerns about salt, sugar, chemical additives, cholesterol, and nutrition have forced food producers to reexamine food processing techniques, redirect R&D efforts into the use of healthier ingredients, and engage in contests to come up with healthier products that also taste good. Safety concerns are now altering the competitive emphasis in the automobile, toy, and outdoor power equipment industries, to mention a few. Increased interest in physical fitness has spawned whole new industries to supply exercise equipment, jogging clothes and shoes, and medically supervised diet programs. Social concerns about air and water pollution are major forces in industries that discharge waste products. Growing antismoking sentiment has emerged as the major driver of change in the tobacco industry.

- *Reductions in uncertainty and business risk*—A young, emerging industry is typically characterized by an unproven cost structure and much uncertainty over potential market size, how much time and money will be needed to surmount technological problems, and what distribution channels to emphasize in accessing potential buyers. Emerging industries tend to attract only risk-taking entrepreneurial companies. Over time, however, if pioneering firms succeed and uncertainty about the industry's viability fades, more conservative firms are usually enticed to enter the industry. Often, these later entrants are larger, financially strong firms looking to invest in attractive growth industries. In international markets, conservatism is prevalent in the early stages of globalization. Firms guard against risk by relying initially on exporting, licensing, and joint ventures to enter foreign markets. Then, as experience accumulates and perceived risk levels decline, companies move more quickly and aggressively to form wholly owned subsidiaries and to pursue full-scale, multicountry competitive strategies.

The foregoing list of *potential* driving forces in an industry indicates why it is too simplistic to view industry change only in terms of the growth stages model and why it is essential to probe for the *causes* underlying the emergence of new competitive conditions.

However, while many forces of change may be at work in a given industry, no more than three or four are likely to qualify as *driving* forces in the sense that they will act as *the major determinants* of how the industry evolves and operates. Thus, strategic analysts must resist the temptation to label everything they see changing as driving forces; the analytical task is to evaluate the forces of industry and competitive change carefully enough to separate major factors from minor ones.

Sound analysis of an industry's driving forces is a prerequisite to sound strategy-making. Without keen awareness of what external factors will have the greatest effect

The task of driving forces analysis is to separate the major causes of industry change from the minor ones; usually no more than three or four factors qualify as driving forces.

on the company's business over the next one to three years, managers are ill-prepared to craft a strategy tightly matched to changing external conditions. Similarly, if managers are uncertain about the implications of each driving force or if their views are incomplete or off-base, it's difficult for them to craft a strategy that is responsive to the driving forces and their consequences for the industry. So driving forces analysis is not something to take lightly; it has practical strategy-making value and is basic to the task of thinking strategically about the business.

Environmental Scanning Techniques   One way to get a jump on which driving forces are likely to emerge is to utilize environmental scanning techniques for early detection of new straws in the wind. *Environmental scanning* involves studying and interpreting the sweep of social, political, economic, ecological, and technological events in an effort to spot budding trends and conditions that could eventually impact the industry. Environmental scanning involves time frames well beyond the next one to three years—for example, it could involve judgments about the demand for energy in the year 2010, what kinds of household appliances will be in the "house of the future," what people will be doing with computers 20 years from now, or what will happen to our forests in the 21st century if the demand for paper continues to grow at its present rate. Environmental scanning thus attempts to spot first-of-a-kind happenings and new ideas and approaches that are catching on and to extrapolate their possible implications 5 to 20 years into the future. The purpose and value of environmental scanning is to raise the consciousness of managers about potential developments that could have an important impact on industry conditions or pose new opportunities and threats.

Environmental scanning can be accomplished by systematically monitoring and studying current events, constructing scenarios, and employing the Delphi method (a technique for finding consensus among a group of knowledgeable experts). Environmental scanning methods are highly qualitative and subjective. The appeal of environmental scanning, notwithstanding its speculative nature, is that it helps managers lengthen their planning horizon, translate vague inklings of future opportunities or threats into clearer strategic issues (for which they can begin to develop strategic answers), and think strategically about future developments in the surrounding environment.[13] Companies that undertake formal environmental scanning on a fairly continuous and comprehensive level include General Electric, AT&T, Coca-Cola, Ford, General Motors, Du Pont, and Shell Oil.

QUESTION 4: WHICH COMPANIES ARE IN THE STRONGEST/WEAKEST POSITIONS?

The next step in examining the industry's competitive structure is to study the market positions of rival companies. One technique for revealing the competitive positions of industry participants is *strategic group mapping*.[14] This analytical tool is a bridge

Margin notes:

Managers can use *environmental scanning* to spot budding trends and clues of change that could develop into new driving forces.

Strategic group mapping is a technique for displaying the different competitive positions that rival firms occupy in the industry.

---

[13]For further discussion of the nature and use of environmental scanning, see Roy Amara and Andrew J. Lipinski, *Business Planning for an Uncertain Future: Scenarios and Strategies* (New York: Pergamon Press, 1983); Harold E. Klein and Robert U. Linneman, "Environmental Assessment: An International Study of Corporate Practice," *Journal of Business Strategy* 5, no. 1 (Summer 1984), pp. 55–75; and Arnoldo C. Hax and Nicolas S. Majluf, *The Strategy Concept and Process* (Englewood Cliffs, N.J.: Prentice-Hall, 1991), chapters 5 and 8.

[14]Porter, *Competitive Strategy,* chapter 7.

between looking at the industry as a whole and considering the standing of each firm separately. It is most useful when an industry has so many competitors that it is not practical to examine each one in depth.

Using Strategic Group Maps to Assess the Competitive Positions of Rival Firms A strategic group consists of those rival firms with similar competitive approaches and positions in the market.[15] Companies in the same strategic group can resemble one another in any of several ways: they may have comparable product line breadth, use the same kinds of distribution channels, be vertically integrated to much the same degree, offer buyers similar services and technical assistance, use essentially the same product attributes to appeal to similar types of buyers, emphasize the same distribution channels, depend on identical technological approaches, and/or sell in the same price/quality range. An industry contains only one strategic group when all sellers approach the market with essentially identical strategies. At the other extreme, there are as many strategic groups as there are competitors when each rival pursues a distinctively different competitive approach and occupies a substantially different competitive position in the marketplace.

The procedure for constructing a strategic group map and deciding which firms belong in which strategic group is straightforward:

- Identify the competitive characteristics that differentiate firms in the industry— typical variables are price/quality range (high, medium, low), geographic coverage (local, regional, national, global), degree of vertical integration (none, partial, full), product line breadth (wide, narrow), use of distribution channels (one, some, all), and degree of service offered (no-frills, limited, full service).
- Plot the firms on a two-variable map using pairs of these differentiating characteristics.
- Assign firms that fall in about the same strategy space to the same strategic group.
- Draw circles around each strategic group, making the circles proportional to the size of the group's respective share of total industry sales revenues.

This produces a two-dimensional *strategic group map* such as the one for the retail jewelry industry portrayed in Illustration Capsule 8.

To map the positions of strategic groups accurately in the industry's overall strategy space, several guidelines need to be observed.[16] First, the two variables selected as axes for the map should *not* be highly correlated; if they are, the circles on the map will fall along a diagonal and strategy-makers will learn nothing more about the relative positions of competitors than they would by considering just one of the variables. For instance, if companies with broad product lines use multiple distribution channels while companies with narrow lines use a single distribution channel, then one of the variables is redundant. Looking at broad versus narrow product lines reveals just as much about who is positioned where as adding single versus multiple distribution channels. Second, the variables chosen as axes for the map should expose big differences in how rivals position themselves to compete in the marketplace. This, of course, means analysts must identify the characteristics that differentiate rival firms and use these differences as variables for the axes and as

---

[15]Ibid., pp. 129–30.
[16]Ibid., pp. 152–54.

ILLUSTRATION CAPSULE 8

STRATEGIC GROUP MAP OF COMPETITORS IN THE RETAIL JEWELRY INDUSTRY

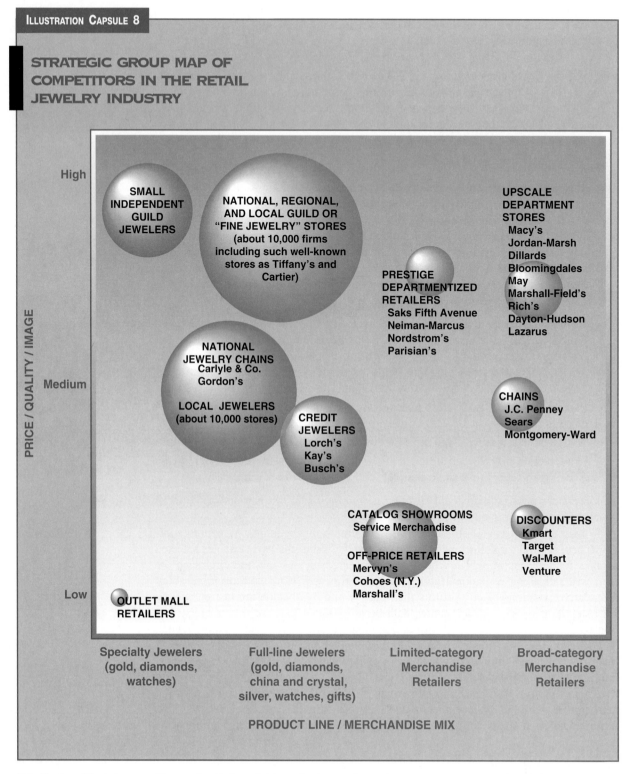

Note: The sizes of the circles are roughly proportional to the market shares of each group of competitors

the basis for deciding which firm belongs in which strategic group. Third, the variables used as axes don't have to be either quantitative or continuous; rather, they can be discrete variables or defined in terms of distinct classes and combinations. Fourth, drawing the sizes of the circles on the map proportional to the combined sales of the firms in each strategic group allows the map to reflect the relative sizes of each strategic group. Fifth, if more than two good competitive variables can be used as axes for the map, several maps can be drawn to give different exposures to the competitive positioning relationships present in the industry's structure. Because there is not necessarily one best map for portraying how competing firms are positioned in the market, it is advisable to experiment with different pairs of competitive variables.

Strategic group analysis helps deepen management understanding of competitive rivalry.[17] To begin with, *driving forces and competitive pressures often favor some strategic groups and hurt others*. Firms in adversely affected strategic groups may try to shift to a more favorably situated group; how hard such a move proves to be depends on whether entry barriers into the target strategic group are high or low. Attempts by rival firms to enter a new strategic group nearly always increase competitive pressures. If certain firms are known to be trying to change their competitive positions on the map, then attaching arrows to the circles showing the targeted direction helps clarify the picture of competitive jockeying among rivals.

A second thing to look for is whether *the profit potential of different strategic groups varies due to the strengths and weaknesses in each group's market position*. Differences in profitability can occur because of differing degrees of bargaining leverage with suppliers or customers and differing degrees of exposure to competition from substitute products outside the industry.

Generally speaking, *the closer strategic groups are to each other on the map, the stronger competitive rivalry among member firms tends to be*. Although firms in the same strategic group are the closest rivals, the next closest rivals are in the immediately adjacent groups. Often, firms in strategic groups that are far apart on the map hardly compete at all. For instance, Tiffany's and Wal-Mart both sell gold and silver jewelry, but the prices and perceived qualities of their products are much too different to generate any real competition between them. For the same reason, Timex is not a meaningful competitive rival of Rolex, and Subaru is not a close competitor of Lincoln or Mercedes-Benz.

> Some strategic groups are usually more favorably positioned than other strategic groups because driving forces and competitive pressures do not affect each group evenly and because profit prospects vary among groups based on the relative attractiveness of their market positions.

QUESTION 5: WHAT STRATEGIC MOVES ARE RIVALS LIKELY TO MAKE NEXT?

Studying the actions and behavior of one's closest competitors is essential. Unless a company pays attention to what competitors are doing, it ends up flying blind into competitive battle. A company can't expect to outmaneuver its rivals without monitoring their actions and anticipating what moves they are likely to make next. As in sports, a good scouting report is invaluable. The strategies rivals are using and the actions they are likely to take next have direct bearing on a company's own best strategic moves—whether it needs to defend against specific actions taken by rivals or whether rivals' moves provide an opening for a new offensive thrust.

> Successful strategists take great pains in scouting competitors—understanding their strategies, watching their actions, sizing up their strengths and weaknesses, and trying to anticipate what moves they will make next.

---

[17]Ibid., pp. 130, 132–38, and 154–55.

Identifying Competitors' Strategies   A quick profile of key competitors can be obtained by studying where they are in the industry, their strategic objectives as revealed by actions recently taken, and their basic competitive approaches. Table 3–3 provides an easy-to-use scheme for categorizing the objectives and strategies of rival companies. Such a summary, along with a strategic group map, usually suffices to diagnose the competitive intent of rivals.

Evaluating Who the Industry's Major Players Are Going to Be   It's usually obvious who the *current* major contenders are, but these same firms are not necessarily positioned strongly for the future. Some may be losing ground or be ill-equipped to compete on the industry's future battleground. Smaller companies may be moving into contention and poised for an offensive against larger but vulnerable rivals. Long-standing market leaders sometimes slide quickly down the industry's ranks; others end up being acquired. Today's industry leaders don't automatically become tomorrow's.

In deciding whether a competitor is favorably or unfavorably positioned to gain market ground, attention needs to center on why there is potential for it to do better or worse than other rivals. Usually, how securely a company holds its present market share is a function of its vulnerability to driving forces and competitive pressures, whether it has a competitive advantage or disadvantage, and whether it is the likely target of offensive attack from other industry participants. Pinpointing which rivals are poised to gain market position and which rivals seem destined to lose market share helps a strategist anticipate what kinds of moves they are likely to make next.

Predicting Competitors' Next Moves   This is the hardest yet most useful part of competitor analysis. Good clues about what moves a specific company may make next come from studying its situation—understanding its strategic intent, monitoring how well it is faring in the marketplace, and determining how much pressure it is under to improve its financial performance. Aggressive rivals on the move are strong candidates for some type of new strategic initiative. Content rivals are likely to continue their present strategy with only minor fine-tuning. Ailing rivals can be performing so poorly that fresh strategic moves, either offensive or defensive, are virtually certain. Since managers generally operate from assumptions about the industry's future and beliefs about their own firm's situation, insights into their strategic thinking can be gleaned from their public pronouncements about where the industry is headed and what it will take to be successful, what they are saying about their firm's situation, information from the grapevine about what they are doing, and their past actions and leadership styles. Another thing to consider is whether a rival has the flexibility to make major strategic changes or whether it is locked into pursuing its same basic strategy with minor adjustments.

To succeed in predicting a competitor's next moves, one has to have a good feel for the rival's situation, how its managers think, and what its options are. Doing the necessary detective work can be tedious and time-consuming since the information comes in bits and pieces from many sources. But scouting competitors well enough to anticipate their next moves allows managers to prepare effective countermoves (perhaps even beat a rival to the punch!) and to take rivals' probable actions into account in designing the best course of action.

Managers who fail to study competitors closely risk being blindsided by "surprise" actions on the part of rivals.

T A B L E 3-3 | Categorizing the Objectives and Strategies of Competitors

Competitive Scope	Strategic Intent	Market Share Objective	Competitive Position/Situation	Strategic Posture	Competitive Strategy
• Local • Regional • National • Multicountry • Global	• Be the dominant leader • Overtake the present industry leader • Be among the industry leaders (top 5) • Move into the top 10 • Move up a notch or two in the industry rankings • Overtake a particular rival (not necessarily the leader) • Maintain position • Just survive	• Aggressive expansion via both acquisition and internal growth • Expansion via internal growth (boost market share at the expense of rival firms) • Expansion via acquisition • Hold on to present share (by growing at a rate equal to the industry average) • Give up share if necessary to achieve short-term profit objectives (stress profitability, not volume)	• Getting stronger; on the move • Well-entrenched; able to maintain its present position • Stuck in the middle of the pack • Going after a different market position (trying to move from a weaker to a stronger position) • Struggling; losing ground • Retrenching to a position that can be defended	• Mostly offensive • Mostly defensive • A combination of offense and defense • Aggressive risk-taker • Conservative follower	• Striving for low cost leadership • Mostly focusing on a market niche —High end —Low end —Geographic —Buyers with special needs —Other • Pursuing differentiation based on —Quality —Service —Technological superiority —Breadth of product line —Image and reputation —More value for the money —Other attributes

Note: Since a focus strategy can be aimed at any of several market niches and a differentiation strategy can be keyed to any of several attributes, it is best to be explicit about what kind of focus strategy or differentiation strategy a given firm is pursuing. All focusers do not pursue the same market niche, and all differentiators do not pursue the same differentiating attributes.

QUESTION 6: WHAT ARE THE KEY FACTORS FOR COMPETITIVE SUCCESS?

An industry's *key success factors* (KSFs) are the strategy-related action approaches, competitive capabilities, and business outcomes that every firm must be competent at doing or must concentrate on achieving in order to be competitively and financially successful. KSFs are business aspects all firms in the industry must pay close attention to—the specific outcomes crucial to market success (or failure) and the competencies and competitive capabilities with the most direct bearing on company profitability. In the beer industry, the KSFs are full utilization of brewing capacity (to keep manufacturing costs low), a strong network of wholesale distributors (to gain access to as many retail outlets as possible), and clever advertising (to induce beer drinkers to buy a particular brand and thereby pull beer sales through the established wholesale/retail channels). In apparel manufacturing, the KSFs are appealing designs and color combinations (to create buyer interest) and low-cost manufacturing efficiency (to permit attractive retail pricing and ample profit margins). In tin and aluminum cans, where the cost of shipping empty cans is substantial, one of the keys is having plants located close to end-use customers so that the plant's output can be marketed within economical shipping distances (regional market share is far more crucial than national share).

Determining the industry's key success factors, in light of prevailing and anticipated industry and competitive conditions, is a top-priority analytical consideration. At the very least, managers need to know the industry well enough to conclude what is more important to competitive success and what is less important. Company managers who misdiagnose what factors are truly crucial to long-term competitive success are prone to employ ill-conceived strategies or to pursue less important competitive targets. Frequently, a company with perceptive understanding of industry KSFs can gain sustainable competitive advantage by training its strategy on industry KSFs and devoting its energies to being distinctively better than rivals at succeeding on these factors. Indeed, using one or more of the industry's KSFs as *cornerstones* for the company's strategy is often a wise approach to crafting a winning managerial game plan.

Key success factors vary from industry to industry and even from time to time within the same industry as driving forces and competitive conditions change. Table 3–4 provides a shopping list of the most common types of key success factors. Only rarely does an industry have more than three or four key success factors at any one time. And even among these three or four, one or two usually outrank the others in importance. Managers, therefore, have to resist the temptation to include factors that have only minor importance on their list of key success factors—the purpose of identifying KSFs is to make judgments about what things are more important to competitive success and what things are less important. To compile a list of every factor that matters even a little bit defeats the purpose of concentrating management attention on the factors truly crucial to long-term competitive success.

QUESTION 7: IS THE INDUSTRY ATTRACTIVE AND WHAT ARE ITS PROSPECTS FOR ABOVE-AVERAGE PROFITABILITY?

The final step of industry and competitive analysis is to review the overall industry situation and develop reasoned conclusions about the relative attractiveness or unattractiveness of the industry, both near-term and long-term. An assessment that the industry is fundamentally attractive typically suggests using an aggressive grow-and-build strategy, expanding sales efforts and investing in additional facilities and equipment as needed to strengthen the firm's long-term competitive position in the

An industry's key success factors spell the difference between profit and loss and, ultimately, between competitive success and failure.

Strategic Management Principle
A sound strategy incorporates industry key success factors.

TABLE 3-4 | Types of Key Success Factors

Technology-Related KSFs
- Scientific research expertise (important in such fields as pharmaceuticals, medicine, space exploration, other "high-tech" industries)
- Production process innovation capability
- Product innovation capability
- Expertise in a given technology

Manufacturing-Related KSFs
- Low-cost production efficiency (achieve scale economies, capture experience curve effects)
- Quality of manufacture (fewer defects, less need for repairs)
- High utilization of fixed assets (important in capital intensive/high fixed-cost industries)
- Low-cost plant locations
- Access to adequate supplies of skilled labor
- High labor productivity (important for items with high labor content)
- Low-cost product design and engineering (reduces manufacturing costs)
- Flexibility to manufacture a range of models and sizes/take care of custom orders

Distribution-Related KSFs
- A strong network of wholesale distributors/dealers
- Gaining ample space on retailer shelves
- Having company-owned retail outlets
- Low distribution costs
- Fast delivery

Marketing-Related KSFs
- A well-trained, effective sales force
- Available, dependable service and technical assistance
- Accurate filling of buyer orders (few back orders or mistakes)
- Breadth of product line and product selection
- Merchandising skills
- Attractive styling/packaging
- Customer guarantees and warranties (important in mail-order retailing, big ticket purchases, new product introductions)

Skills-Related KSFs
- Superior talent (important in professional services)
- Quality control know-how
- Design expertise (important in fashion and apparel industries)
- Expertise in a particular technology
- Ability to come up with clever, catchy ads
- Ability to get newly developed products out of the R&D phase and into the market very quickly

Organizational Capability
- Superior information systems (important in airline travel, car rental, credit card, and lodging industries)
- Ability to respond quickly to shifting market conditions (streamlined decision-making, short lead times to bring new products to market)
- More experience and managerial know-how

Other Types of KSFs
- Favorable image/reputation with buyers
- Overall low cost (not just in manufacturing)
- Convenient locations (important in many retailing businesses)
- Pleasant, courteous employees
- Access to financial capital (important in newly emerging industries with high degrees of business risk and in capital-intensive industries)
- Patent protection

business. If the industry and competitive situation is judged relatively unattractive, more successful industry participants may choose to invest cautiously, look for ways to protect their long-term competitiveness and profitability, and perhaps acquire smaller firms if the price is right. Weaker companies may consider leaving the industry or merging with a rival. Stronger companies may consider diversification into more attractive businesses. Outsiders considering entry may decide against investing in the business and look elsewhere for opportunities.

Important factors for company managers to consider in drawing conclusions about whether the industry is a good business to be in include

- The industry's growth potential.
- Whether the industry will be favorably or unfavorably impacted by the prevailing driving forces.
- The potential for the entry/exit of major firms (probable entry reduces attractiveness to existing firms; the exit of a major firm or several weak firms opens up market share growth opportunities for the remaining firms).
- The stability/dependability of demand (as affected by seasonality, the business cycle, the volatility of consumer preferences, inroads from substitutes, and the like).
- Whether competitive forces will become stronger or weaker.
- The severity of problems/issues confronting the industry as a whole.
- The degrees of risk and uncertainty in the industry's future.
- Whether competitive conditions and driving forces are conducive to rising or falling industry profitability.

As a general proposition, if an industry's overall profit prospects are above average, the industry can be considered attractive. If its profit prospects are below average, it is unattractive. However, it is a mistake to think of industries as being attractive or unattractive in an absolute sense. Attractiveness is relative, not absolute, and conclusions one way or the other are in the eye of the beholder. Companies on the outside may look at an industry's environment and conclude that it is an unattractive business for them to get into; they may see more profitable opportunities elsewhere. But a favorably positioned company already in the industry may survey the very same business environment and conclude that the industry is attractive because it has the resources and competitive capabilities to exploit the vulnerabilities of its weaker rivals, gain market share, build a strong leadership position, and grow its revenues and profits at a rapid clip. Hence industry attractiveness *always* has to be appraised from the standpoint of a particular company. Industries unattractive to outsiders may be attractive to insiders. Industry environments unattractive to weak competitors may be attractive to strong competitors.

> A company that is uniquely well-situated in an otherwise unattractive industry can, under certain circumstances, still earn unusually good profits.

While companies contemplating entry into an industry can rely on the above list of factors, along with the answers to the first six questions, to draw conclusions about industry attractiveness, companies already in the industry need to consider the following additional aspects:

- The company's competitive position in the industry and whether its position is likely to grow stronger or weaker (being a well-entrenched leader in an otherwise lackluster industry can still produce good profitability).
- The company's potential to capitalize on the vulnerabilities of weaker rivals (thereby converting an unattractive *industry* situation into a potentially rewarding *company* opportunity).

- Whether the company is insulated from, or able to defend against, the factors that make the industry unattractive.
- Whether continued participation in this industry adds importantly to the firm's ability to be successful in other industries in which it has business interests.

ACTUALLY DOING AN INDUSTRY AND COMPETITIVE ANALYSIS

Table 3–5 provides a *format* for reporting the pertinent facts and conclusions of industry and competitive analysis. It pulls the relevant concepts and considerations together in systematic fashion and makes it easier to do a concise, understandable analysis of the industry and competitive environment.

Two things should be kept in mind in doing industry and competitive analysis. One, the task of analyzing a company's external situation cannot be reduced to a mechanical, formula-like exercise in which facts and data are plugged in and definitive conclusions come pouring out. There can be several appealing scenarios about how an industry will evolve and what future competitive conditions will be like. For this reason, strategic analysis always leaves room for differences of opinion about how all the factors add up and how industry and competitive conditions will change. However, while no strategy analysis methodology can guarantee a single conclusive diagnosis, it doesn't make sense to shortcut strategic analysis and rely on opinion and casual observation. Managers become better strategists when they know what analytical questions to pose, can use situation analysis techniques to find answers, and have the skills to read clues about which way the winds of industry and competitive change are blowing. This is why we concentrated on suggesting the right questions to ask, explaining concepts and analytical approaches, and indicating the kinds of things to look for.

Two, sweeping industry and competitive analyses need to be done every one to

T A B L E 3-5 | **Industry and Competitive Analysis Summary Profile**

1. Dominant Economic Characteristics of the Industry Environment (market growth, geographic scope, industry structure, scale economies, experience curve effects, capital requirements, and so on)

2. Competition Analysis

- Rivalry among competing sellers (a strong, moderate, or weak force/weapons of competition)
- Threat of potential entry (a strong, moderate, or weak force/assessment of entry barriers)
- Competition from substitutes (a strong, moderate, or weak force/why)
- Power of suppliers (a strong, moderate, or weak force/why)
- Power of customers (a strong, moderate, or weak force/why)

3. Driving Forces

4. Competitive Position of Major Companies/ Strategic Groups

- Favorably positioned/why
- Unfavorably positioned/why

5. Competitor Analysis

- Strategic approaches/predicted moves of key competitors
- Whom to watch and why

6. Key Success Factors

7. Industry Prospects and Overall Attractiveness

- Factors making the industry attractive
- Factors making the industry unattractive
- Special industry issues/problems
- Profit outlook (favorable/unfavorable)

three years; in the interim, managers are obliged to continually update and reexamine their thinking as events unfold. There's no substitute for being a good student of industry and competitive conditions and staying on the cutting edge of what's happening in the industry. Anything else leaves a manager unprepared to initiate shrewd and timely strategic adjustments.

KEY POINTS

Thinking strategically about a company's external situation involves probing for answers to the following seven questions:

1. *What are the industry's dominant economic traits?* Industries differ significantly on such factors as market size and growth rate, the scope of competitive rivalry, the number and relative sizes of both buyers and sellers, ease of entry and exit, whether sellers are vertically integrated, how fast basic technology is changing, the extent of scale economies and experience curve effects, whether the products of rival sellers are standardized or differentiated, and overall profitability. An industry's economic characteristics are important because of the implications they have for crafting strategy.

2. *What is competition like and how strong are each of the five competitive forces?* The strength of competition is a composite of five forces: the rivalry among competing sellers, the presence of attractive substitutes, the potential for new entry, the leverage major suppliers have, and the bargaining power of customers. The task of competition analysis is to assess each force, determine whether it produces strong or weak competitive pressures, and then think strategically about what sort of competitive strategy, given the "rules" of competition in the industry, the company will need to employ to *(a)* insulate the firm as much as possible from the five competitive forces, *(b)* influence the industry's competitive rules in the company's favor, and *(c)* gain a competitive edge.

3. *What is causing the industry's competitive structure and business environment to change?* Industry and competitive conditions change because forces are in motion that create incentives or pressures for change. The most common driving forces are changes in the long-term industry growth rate, changes in buyer composition, product innovation, entry or exit of major firms, globalization, changes in cost and efficiency, changing buyer preferences for standardized versus differentiated products or services, regulatory influences and government policy changes, changing societal and lifestyle factors, and reductions in uncertainty and business risk. Sound analysis of driving forces and their implications for the industry is a prerequisite to sound strategy-making.

4. *Which companies are in the strongest/weakest competitive positions?* Strategic group mapping is a valuable, if not necessary, tool for understanding the similarities, differences, strengths, and weaknesses inherent in the market positions of rival companies. Rivals in the same or nearby strategic group(s) are close competitors whereas companies in distant strategic groups usually pose little or no immediate threat.

5. *What strategic moves are rivals likely to make next?* This analytical step involves identifying competitors' strategies, deciding which rivals are likely to be strong contenders and which weak contenders, evaluating their

competitive options, and predicting what moves they are likely to make next. Scouting competitors well enough to anticipate their actions helps prepare effective countermoves (perhaps even beat a rival to the punch) and allows managers to take rivals' probable actions into account in designing their own company's best course of action. Managers who fail to study competitors closely risk being blindsided by "surprise" actions on the part of rivals. A company can't expect to outmaneuver its rivals without monitoring their actions and anticipating what moves they may make next.

6. *What are the key factors for competitive success?* Key success factors are the strategy-related action approaches, competitive capabilities, and business outcomes which all firms in an industry must be competent at doing or must concentrate on achieving in order to be competitively and financially successful. Determining the industry's key success factors, in light of industry and competitive conditions, is a top-priority analytical consideration. Frequently, a company can gain sustainable competitive advantage by training its strategy on industry KSFs and devoting its energies to being distinctively better than rivals at succeeding on these factors. Companies that only dimly perceive what factors are truly crucial to long-term competitive success are less likely to have winning strategies.

7. *Is the industry attractive and what are its prospects for above-average profitability?* The answer to this question is a major driver of company strategy. An assessment that the industry and competitive environment is fundamentally attractive typically suggests employing an aggressive strategy to build a strong competitive position in the business, expanding sales efforts and investing in additional facilities and equipment as needed. If the industry is relatively unattractive, outsiders considering entry may decide against it and look elsewhere for opportunities, weak companies in the industry may merge with or be acquired by a rival, and strong companies may restrict further investments and employ cost-reduction strategies and/or product innovation strategies to boost long-term competitiveness and protect their profitability. On occasion, an industry that is unattractive overall is still very attractive to a favorably situated company with the skills and resources to take business away from weaker rivals.

Good industry and competitive analysis is crucial to good strategy-making. A competently done industry and competitive analysis provides the keen understanding of a company's macroenvironment managers need to craft a strategy that fits the company's external situation well.

SUGGESTED READINGS

D'Aveni, Richard A. *Hypercompetition.* New York: Free Press, 1994, chaps. 5 and 6.

Ghemawat, Pankaj. "Building Strategy on the Experience Curve." *Harvard Business Review* 64, no. 2 (March–April 1985), pp. 143–49.

Linneman, Robert E., and Harold E. Klein. "Using Scenarios in Strategic Decision Making." *Business Horizons* 28, no. 1 (January–February 1985), pp. 64–74.

Ohmae, Kenichi. *The Mind of the Strategist.* New York: Penguin Books, 1983, chaps. 3, 6, 7, and 13.

Porter, Michael E. "How Competitive Forces Shape Strategy." *Harvard Business Review* 57, no. 2 (March–April 1979), pp. 137–45.

————. *Competitive Strategy: Techniques for Analyzing Industries and Competitors.* New York: Free Press, 1980, chap. 1.

————. *Competitive Advantage.* New York: Free Press, 1985, chap. 2.

Yip, George S. *Total Global Strategy: Managing for Worldwide Competitive Advantage.* Englewood Cliffs, N.J.: Prentice-Hall, 1992, chap. 10.

Zahra, Shaker A. and Sherry S. Chaples. "Blind Spots in Competitive Analysis." *Academy of Management Executives* 7, no. 2 (May 1993), pp. 7–28.

## CHAPTER FOUR

COMPANY SITUATION ANALYSIS

Understand what really makes a company "tick."

Charles R. Scott
CEO, Intermark Corporation

The secret of success is to be ready for opportunity when it comes.

Benjamin Disraeli

If a company is not "best in world" at a critical activity, it is sacrificing competitive advantage by performing that activity with its existing technique.

James Brian Quinn

In the previous chapter we described how to use the tools of industry and competitive analysis to think strategically about a company's external situation. In this chapter we discuss how to size up a company's strategic position in that environment. Company situation analysis centers on five questions:

1. How well is the present strategy working?
2. What are the company's strengths, weaknesses, opportunities, and threats?
3. Are the company's prices and costs competitive?
4. How strong is the company's competitive position?
5. What strategic issues does the company face?

To explore these questions, four new analytical techniques need to be mastered: SWOT analysis, value chain analysis, strategic cost analysis, and competitive strength assessment. These techniques are basic strategic management tools because they expose the pluses and minuses of a company's situation, the strength of its competitive position, and whether the present strategy needs to be modified.

QUESTION 1: HOW WELL IS THE PRESENT STRATEGY WORKING?

In evaluating how well a company's present strategy is working, a manager has to start with what the strategy is (see Figure 2–3 in Chapter 2 to refresh your recollection of the key components of business strategy) and what the company's strategic and financial objectives are. The first thing to pin down is the company's competitive approach—whether it is (1) striving to be a low-cost leader, (2) stressing ways to differentiate its product offering from rivals, or (3) concentrating its efforts on a narrow market niche. Another strategy-defining consideration is the firm's competitive scope within the industry—how many stages of the industry's production-distribution chain it operates in (one, several, or all), the size and diversity of its geographic market coverage, and the size and diversity of its customer base. The company's functional strategies in production, marketing, finance, human resources, and so on further characterize company strategy. In addition, the company may have initiated some recent strategic moves (for instance, a price cut, stepped-up advertising, entry into a new geographic area, or merger with a competitor) that are integral to its strategy and that aim at securing a particular competitive advantage and/or improved competitive position. Reviewing the rationale for each piece of the strategy—for each competitive move and each functional approach—clarifies what the present strategy is.

While there's merit in evaluating the strategy from a qualitative standpoint (its completeness, internal consistency, rationale, and suitability to the situation), the best evidence of how well a company's strategy is working comes from studying the company's recent strategic and financial performance and seeing what story the numbers tell about the results the strategy is producing. Obvious indicators of strategic and financial performance include (1) the firm's market share ranking in the industry, (2) whether the firm's profit margins are increasing or decreasing and how large they are relative to rival firms' margins, (3) trends in the firm's net profits and return on investment, (4) the company's credit rating, (5) whether the firm's sales are growing faster or slower than the market as a whole, (6) the firm's image and reputation with its customers, and (7) whether the company is regarded as a leader in technology, product innovation, product quality, customer service, and the like. The stronger a company's current overall performance, the less likely the need for radical changes in strategy. The weaker a company's strategic and financial performance, the more its current strategy must be questioned. Weak performance is usually a sign of weak strategy or weak execution or both.

The stronger a company's strategic and financial performance, the more likely it has a well-conceived, well-executed strategy.

QUESTION 2: WHAT ARE THE COMPANY'S STRENGTHS, WEAKNESSES, OPPORTUNITIES, AND THREATS?

Sizing up a firm's internal strengths and weaknesses and its external opportunities and threats is commonly known as *SWOT analysis*. It is an easy-to-use technique for getting a quick *overview* of a firm's strategic situation. SWOT analysis underscores the basic principle that strategy must produce a good fit between a company's internal capability (its strengths and weaknesses) and its external situation (reflected in part by its opportunities and threats).

IDENTIFYING INTERNAL STRENGTHS AND WEAKNESSES

A *strength* is something a company is good at doing or a characteristic that gives it an important capability. A strength can be a skill, important expertise, a valuable organizational resource or competitive capability, or an achievement that puts the company in a position of market advantage (like having a better product, stronger name recognition, superior technology, or better customer service). A strength can also result from alliances or cooperative ventures with a partner having expertise or capabilities that enhance a company's competitiveness.

A *weakness* is something a company lacks or does poorly (in comparison to others) or a condition that puts it at a disadvantage. A weakness may or may not make a company competitively vulnerable, depending on how much the weakness matters in the marketplace. Table 4–1 indicates the kinds of factors managers should consider in determining a company's internal strengths and weaknesses.

Once managers identify a company's internal strengths and weaknesses, the two compilations need to be carefully evaluated from a strategy-making perspective. Some strengths are more important than others because they matter more in determining performance, in competing successfully, and in forming a powerful strategy. Likewise, some internal weaknesses can prove fatal, while others are inconsequential or easily remedied. Sizing up a company's strengths and weaknesses is akin to constructing a *strategic balance sheet* where strengths represent *competitive assets* and weaknesses represent *competitive liabilities*. The strategic issues are whether the company's strengths/assets adequately overcome its weaknesses/liabilities (50-50 balance is definitely not the desired condition!), how to meld company strengths into an effective strategy, and whether management actions are needed to tilt the company's strategic balance more toward strengths/assets and away from weaknesses/liabilities.

> **Basic Concept**
> A company's internal strengths usually represent competitive assets; its internal weaknesses usually represent competitive liabilities.

From a strategy-making perspective, a company's strengths are significant because they can form the cornerstones of strategy and the basis for creating competitive advantage. If a company doesn't have strong capabilities and competitive assets around which to craft an attractive strategy, managers need to take decisive remedial action to develop organizational strengths and competencies that can underpin a sound strategy. At the same time, managers have to correct competitive weaknesses that make the company vulnerable, hurt its strategic performance, or disqualify it from pursuing an attractive opportunity. The strategy-making principle here is simple: *a company's strategy should be well-suited to its strengths, weaknesses, and competitive capabilities*. It is foolhardy to pursue a strategic plan that cannot be competently executed with the skills and resources a company can marshal or that can be undermined by company weaknesses. As a rule, managers should build their strategies around what the company does best and avoid strategies that place heavy demands on areas where the company is weakest or has unproven ability.

> **Strategic Management Principle**
> Successful strategists seek to capitalize on what a company does best—its expertise, strengths, core competencies, and strongest competitive capabilities.

Core Competencies   One of the "trade secrets" of first-rate strategic management is consolidating a company's technological, production, and marketing know-how into core competencies that enhance its competitiveness. *A core competence is something a company does especially well in comparison to its competitors.* In practice, there

---

[1]For a fuller discussion of the core competence concept, see C. K. Prahalad and Gary Hamel, "The Core Competence of the Corporation," *Harvard Business Review* 90, no. 3 (May–June 1990), pp. 79–93.

TABLE 4-1 | **SWOT Analysis—What to Look for in Sizing Up a Company's Strengths, Weaknesses, Opportunities, and Threats**

Potential Internal Strengths

- Core competencies in key areas
- Adequate financial resources
- Well-thought-of by buyers
- An acknowledged market leader
- Well-conceived functional area strategies
- Access to economies of scale
- Insulated (at least somewhat) from strong competitive pressures
- Proprietary technology
- Cost advantages
- Better advertising campaigns
- Product innovation skills
- Proven management
- Ahead on experience curve
- Better manufacturing capability
- Superior technological skills
- Other?

Potential External Opportunities

- Ability to serve additional customer groups or expand into new markets or segments
- Ways to expand product line to meet broader range of customer needs
- Ability to transfer skills or technological know-how to new products or businesses
- Integrating forward or backward
- Falling trade barriers in attractive foreign markets
- Complacency among rival firms
- Ability to grow rapidly because of strong increases in market demand
- Emerging new technologies

Potential Internal Weaknesses

- No clear strategic direction
- Obsolete facilities
- Subpar profitability because . . .
- Lack of managerial depth and talent
- Missing some key skills or competencies
- Poor track record in implementing strategy
- Plagued with internal operating problems
- Falling behind in R&D
- Too narrow a product line
- Weak market image
- Weak distribution network
- Below-average marketing skills
- Unable to finance needed changes in strategy
- Higher overall unit costs relative to key competitors
- Other?

Potential External Threats

- Entry of lower-cost foreign competitors
- Rising sales of substitute products
- Slower market growth
- Adverse shifts in foreign exchange rates and trade policies of foreign governments
- Costly regulatory requirements
- Vulnerability to recession and business cycle
- Growing bargaining power of customers or suppliers
- Changing buyer needs and tastes
- Adverse demographic changes
- Other?

are many possible types of core competencies: excellent skills in manufacturing a high quality product, know-how in creating and operating a system for filling customer orders accurately and swiftly, the capability to provide better after-sale service, a unique formula for selecting good retail locations, unusual innovativeness in developing new products, better skills in merchandising and product display, superior mastery of an important technology, a carefully crafted process for researching customer needs and tastes and spotting new market trends, an unusually effective sales force, outstanding skills in working with customers on new applications and uses of the product, and expertise in integrating multiple technologies to create whole families of new products. Typically, a core competence relates to a set of skills, expertise in performing particular activities, or a company's scope and depth of technological know-how; it resides in a company's people, not in assets on the balance sheet.

The importance of a core competence to strategy-making rests with (1) the added capability it gives a company in going after a particular market opportunity, (2) the competitive edge it can yield in the marketplace, and (3) its potential for being a cornerstone of strategy. It is always easier to build competitive advantage when a firm has a core competence in performing activities important to market success, when rival companies do not have offsetting competencies, and when it is costly and time-consuming for rivals to match the competence. Core competencies are thus valuable competitive assets, capable of being the mainsprings of a company's success.

Strategic Management Principle
Core competencies empower a company to build competitive advantage.

IDENTIFYING EXTERNAL OPPORTUNITIES AND THREATS

Market opportunity is a big factor in shaping a company's strategy. Indeed, managers can't match strategy to the company's situation without first identifying each industry opportunity and appraising the growth and profit potential each one holds. Depending on industry conditions, opportunities can be plentiful or scarce and can range from wildly attractive (an absolute "must" to pursue) to marginally interesting (low on the company's list of strategic priorities).

In appraising industry opportunities and ranking their attractiveness, managers have to guard against equating industry opportunities with company opportunities. Not every company in an industry is well-positioned to pursue each opportunity that exists in the industry—some companies are more competitively situated than others and a few may be hopelessly out of contention or at least limited to a minor role. A company's strengths, weaknesses, and competitive capabilities make it better suited to pursuing some industry opportunities than others. *The industry opportunities most relevant to a particular company are those that offer important avenues for profitable growth, those where a company has the most potential for competitive advantage, and those which the company has the financial resources to pursue.* An industry opportunity that a company doesn't have the capability to capture is an illusion.

Often, certain factors in a company's external environment pose *threats* to its well-being. Threats can stem from the emergence of cheaper technologies, rivals' introduction of new or better products, the entry of low-cost foreign competitors into a company's market stronghold, new regulations that are more burdensome to a company than to its competitors, vulnerability to a rise in interest rates, the potential of a hostile takeover, unfavorable demographic shifts, adverse changes in foreign exchange rates, political upheaval in a foreign country where the company has facilities, and the like. Table 4–1 also presents a checklist of things to be alert for in identifying a company's external opportunities and threats.

Opportunities and threats not only affect the attractiveness of a company's situation but point to the need for strategic action. To be adequately matched to a company's situation, strategy must (1) be aimed at pursuing opportunities well-suited to the company's capabilities and (2) provide a defense against external threats. SWOT analysis is therefore more than an exercise in making four lists. The important part of SWOT analysis involves *evaluating* a company's strengths, weaknesses, opportunities, and threats and *drawing conclusions* about the attractiveness of the company's situation and the possible need for strategic action. Some of the pertinent strategy-making questions to consider, once the SWOT listings have been compiled, are:

Strategic Management Principle
Successful strategists aim at capturing a company's best growth opportunities and creating defenses against threats to its competitive position and future performance.

- Does the company have any internal strengths or core competencies an attractive strategy can be built around?
- Do the company's weaknesses make it competitively vulnerable and/or do they disqualify the company from pursuing certain industry opportunities? Which weaknesses does strategy need to correct?
- Which industry opportunities does the company have the skills and resources to pursue with a real chance of success? Which industry opportunities are "best" from the company's standpoint? (*Remember:* Opportunity without the means to capture it is an illusion.)
- What external threats should management be worried most about and what strategic moves should be considered in crafting a good defense?

Unless management is acutely aware of the company's internal strengths and weaknesses and its external opportunities and threats, it is ill-prepared to craft a strategy tightly matched to the company's situation. SWOT analysis is therefore an essential component of thinking strategically about a company's situation.

QUESTION 3: ARE THE COMPANY'S PRICES AND COSTS COMPETITIVE?

Assessing whether a company's costs are competitive with those of its close rivals is a necessary and crucial part of company situation analysis.

Company managers are often stunned when a competitor cuts price to "unbelievably low" levels or when a new market entrant comes on strong with a very low price. The competitor may not, however, be "dumping," buying market share, or waging a desperate move to gain sales; it may simply have substantially lower costs. One of the most telling signs of whether a company's market position is strong or precarious is whether its prices and costs are competitive with industry rivals. Price-cost comparisons are especially critical in a commodity-product industry where the value provided to buyers is the same from seller to seller, price competition is typically the ruling market force, and lower-cost companies have the upper hand. But even in industries where products are differentiated and competition centers around the different attributes of competing brands as much as around price, rival companies have to keep their costs *in line* and make sure that any added costs they incur and price premiums they charge create ample buyer value.

Competitors usually don't incur the same costs in supplying their products to end-users. The cost disparities can range from trivial to competitively significant and can arise from any of several factors:

- Differences in the prices paid for raw materials, components parts, energy, and other items purchased from suppliers.
- Differences in basic technology and the age of plants and equipment. (Because rival companies usually invest in plants and key pieces of equipment at different times, their facilities have somewhat different technological efficiencies and different fixed costs. Older facilities are typically less efficient, but if they were less expensive to construct or were acquired at bargain prices, they *may* still be reasonably cost competitive with modern facilities.)
- Differences in internal operating costs due to economies of scale associated with different-size plants, learning and experience curve effects, different wage rates, different productivity levels, different operating practices, different organization structures and staffing levels, different tax rates, and the like.

- Differences in rival firms' exposure to inflation rates and changes in foreign exchange rates (as can occur in global industries where competitors have plants located in different nations).
- Differences in marketing costs, sales and promotion expenditures, and advertising expenses.
- Differences in inbound transportation costs and outbound shipping costs.
- Differences in forward channel distribution costs (the costs and markups of distributors, wholesalers, and retailers associated with getting the product from the point of manufacture into the hands of end users).

For a company to be competitively successful, its costs must be in line with those of close rivals. While some cost disparity is justified so long as the products or services of closely competing companies are sufficiently differentiated, a high-cost firm's market position becomes increasingly vulnerable the more its costs exceed those of close rivals.

Principle of Competitive Markets
The higher a company's costs are above those of close rivals, the more competitively vulnerable it becomes.

STRATEGIC COST ANALYSIS AND VALUE CHAINS

Given the numerous opportunities for cost disparities, a company must thus be alert to how its costs compare with rivals'. This is where *strategic cost analysis* comes in. *Strategic cost analysis focuses on a firm's cost position relative to its rivals'.*

Basic Concept
Strategic cost analysis involves comparing a company's cost position relative to key competitors activity by activity all the way from raw materials purchase to the price paid by ultimate customers.

The Value Chain Concept The primary analytical tool of strategic cost analysis is a *value chain* identifying the activities, functions, and business processes that have to be performed in designing, producing, marketing, delivering, and supporting a product or service.[2] The chain of value-creating activities starts with raw materials supply and continues on through parts and components production, manufacturing and assembly, wholesale distribution, and retailing to the ultimate end-user of the product or service.

A *company's* value chain shows the linked set of activities and functions it performs internally (see Figure 4–1). The chain includes a profit margin because a markup over the cost of performing the firm's value-creating activities is customarily part of the price (or total cost) borne by buyers—creating value that exceeds the cost of doing so is a fundamental objective of business.

By disaggregating a company's operations into strategically relevant activities and business processes, it is possible to better understand the company's cost structure and to see where the major cost elements are. Each activity in the value chain incurs costs and ties up assets; assigning the company's operating costs and assets to each individual activity in the chain provides cost estimates for each activity. The costs a company incurs in performing each activity can be driven up or down by two types of factors: *structural drivers* (scale economies, experience curve effects, technology requirements, capital intensity, and product line complexity) and *executional drivers* (how committed the work force is to continuous improvement, employee attitudes and organizational capabilities regarding product quality and process quality, cycle time in getting newly developed products to market, utilization of existing capacity,

Basic Concept
A company's value chain identifies the primary activities that create value for customers and the related support activities; value chains are a tool for thinking strategically about the relationships among activities performed inside and outside the firm—which ones are strategy-critical and how core competencies can be developed.

---

[2]Value chains and strategic cost analysis are described at greater length in Michael E. Porter, *Competitive Advantage* (New York: Free Press, 1985), chapters 2 and 3; Robin Cooper and Robert S. Kaplan, "Measure Costs Right: Make the Right Decisions," *Harvard Business Review* 66, no. 5 (September–October, 1988), pp. 96–103; and John K. Shank and Vijay Govindarajan, *Strategic Cost Management* (New York: Free Press, 1993), especially chapters 2–6 and 10.

FIGURE 4-1 | **Representative Company Value Chain**

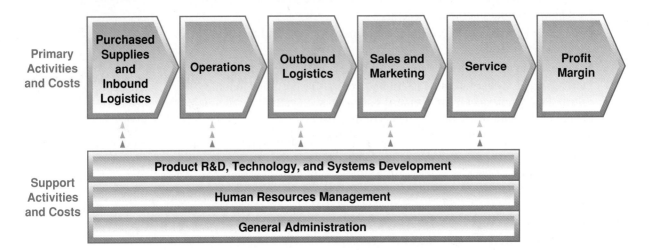

Primary Activities
- **Purchased Supplies and Inbound Logistics**—Activities, costs, and assets associated with purchasing fuel, energy, raw materials, parts components, merchandise, and consumable items from vendors; receiving, storing, and disseminating inputs from suppliers; inspection; and inventory management.
- **Operations**—Activities, costs, and assets associated with converting inputs into final product form (production, assembly, packaging, equipment maintenance, facilities, operations, quality assurance, environmental protection).
- **Outbound Logistics**—Activities, costs, and assets dealing with physically distributing the product to buyers (finished goods warehousing, order processing, order picking and packing, shipping, delivery vehicle operations).
- **Sales and Marketing**—Activities, costs, and assets related to sales force efforts, advertising and promotion, market research and planning, and dealer/distributor support.
- **Service**—Activities, costs, and assets associated with providing assistance to buyers, such as installation, spare parts delivery, maintenance and repair, technical assistance, buyer inquiries, and complaints.

Support Activities
- **Research, Technology, and Systems Development**—Activities, costs, and assets relating to product R&D, process R&D, process design improvement, equipment design, computer software development, telecommunications systems, computer-assisted design and engineering, new database capabilities, and development of computerized support systems.
- **Human Resources Management**—Activities, costs, and assets associated with the recruitment, hiring, training, development, and compensation of all types of personnel; labor relations activities; development of knowledge-based skills.
- **General Administration**—Activities, costs, and assets relating to general management, accounting and finance, legal and regulatory affairs, safety and security, management information systems, and other "overhead" functions.

Source: Adapted from Michael E. Porter, *Competitive Advantage* (New York: The Free Press, 1985), pp. 37–43.

whether internal business processes are efficiently designed and executed, and how effectively the firm works with suppliers and/or customers to reduce the costs of performing its activities). Understanding a company's cost structure means understanding

- Whether it is trying to achieve a competitive advantage based on (1) lower costs (in which case managerial efforts to lower costs along the company's value chain should be highly visible) or (2) differentiation (in which case managers may deliberately spend more performing those activities responsible for creating the differentiating attributes).

- Cost behavior in each activity in the value chain and how the costs of one activity spill over to affect the costs of others.
- Whether the linkages among activities in the company's value chain present opportunities for cost reduction (for example, Japanese VCR producers were able to reduce prices from $1,300 in 1977 to under $300 in 1984 by spotting the impact of an early step in the value chain, product design, on a later step, production, and deciding to drastically reduce the number of parts).[3]

Value chains are also a tool for understanding the firm's cost structure and how costs are driven up or down within activities and across activities.

However, there's more to strategic cost analysis and a company's cost competitiveness than just comparing the costs of activities comprising rivals' value chains. Competing companies often differ in their degrees of vertical integration. Comparing the value chain for a partially integrated rival against a fully integrated rival requires adjusting for differences in scope of activities performed. Moreover, uncompetitive prices can have their origins in activities performed by suppliers or by forward channel allies involved in getting the product to end-users. Suppliers or forward channel allies may have excessively high cost structures or profit margins that jeopardize a company's cost competitiveness even though its costs for internally performed activities are competitive.

For example, when determining Michelin's cost competitiveness vis-à-vis Goodyear and Bridgestone in supplying replacement tires to vehicle owners, one has to look at more than whether Michelin's tire manufacturing costs are above or below Goodyear's and Bridgestone's. If a buyer has to pay $400 for a set of Michelin tires and only $350 for comparable sets of Goodyear or Bridgestone tires, Michelin's $50 price disadvantage in the replacement tire marketplace can stem not only from higher manufacturing costs (reflecting, *perhaps,* the added costs of Michelin's strategic efforts to build a better quality tire with more performance features) but also from (1) differences in what the three tiremakers pay their suppliers for materials and tire-making components and (2) differences in the operating efficiencies, costs, and markups of Michelin's wholesale-retail dealer outlets versus those of Goodyear and Bridgestone. Thus, determining whether a company's prices and costs are competitive from an end-user's standpoint requires looking at the activities and costs of competitively relevant suppliers and forward allies, as well as the costs of internally performed activities.

As the tire industry example makes clear, a company's value chain is embedded in a larger system of activities that includes the value chains of its upstream suppliers and downstream customers or allies engaged in getting its product/service to end-users.[4] Accurately assessing a company's competitiveness in end-use markets requires that company managers understand the entire value delivery system, not just the company's own value chain; at the very least, this means considering the value chains of suppliers and forward channel allies (if any)—as shown in Figure 4-2. Suppliers' value chains are relevant because suppliers perform activities and incur costs in creating and delivering the purchased inputs used in a company's own value chain; the cost and

A company's cost competitiveness depends not only on the costs of internally performed activities (its own value chain) but also on costs in the value chains of suppliers and forward channel allies.

---

[3]M. Hegert and D. Morris, "Accounting Data for Value Chain Analysis," *Strategic Management Journal* 10 (1989), p. 183.
[4]Porter, *Competitive Advantage,* p. 34.

FIGURE 4-2 | **The Value Chain System**

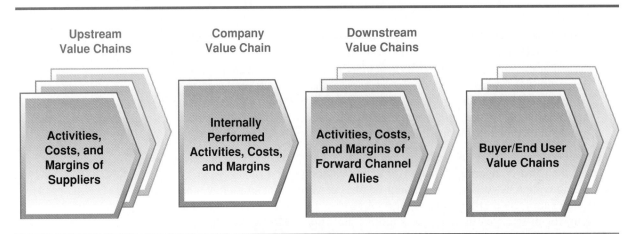

Source: Adapted from Michael E. Porter, *Competitive Advantage* (New York: The Free Press, 1985), p. 35.

quality of these inputs influence the company's cost and/or differentiation capabilities. Anything a company can do to reduce its suppliers' costs or improve suppliers' effectiveness can enhance its own competitiveness. Forward channel value chains are relevant because (1) the costs and margins of downstream companies are part of the price the ultimate end-user pays and (2) the activities forward channel allies perform affect the end-user's satisfaction. Furthermore, a company can often enhance its competitiveness by undertaking activities that have a beneficial impact on its customers' value chains. For instance, some aluminum can producers constructed plants next to beer breweries and delivered cans on overhead conveyors directly to brewers' can-filling lines. This resulted in significant savings in production scheduling, shipping, and inventory costs for both container producers and breweries.[5]

Although the value chains in Figures 4–1 and 4–2 are typical, the nature of the chains and the relative importance of the activities within them vary by industry and by company position in the value chain system. The value chain for the pulp and paper industry (timber farming, logging, pulp mills, papermaking, printing, and publishing) differs from the chain for the home appliance industry (parts and components manufacture, assembly, wholesale distribution, retail sales). The value chain for the soft drink industry (processing of basic ingredients, syrup manufacture, bottling and can filling, wholesale distribution, retailing) differs from the chain for the computer software industry (programming, disk loading, marketing, distribution). A producer of bathroom and kitchen faucets depends heavily on the activities of wholesale distributors and building supply retailers to represent its products to homebuilders and do-it-yourselfers; a producer of small gasoline engines markets directly to the makers of lawn and garden equipment. A wholesaler's most important activities and costs deal with purchased goods, inbound logistics, and outbound logistics. A hotel's most important activities and costs are in operations—check-in and check-out, maintenance and housekeeping, dining and room service, conventions and meetings, and accounting. A global public accounting firm's most important activities and costs revolve around customer service

[5]Hegert and Morris, "Accounting Data for Value Chain Analysis," p. 180.

and human resources management (recruiting and training a highly competent professional staff). Outbound logistics is a crucial activity at Domino's Pizza but comparatively insignificant at Blockbuster. Sales and marketing are dominant activities at Coca-Cola but only minor activities at electric and gas utilities. Consequently, generic value chains like those in Figures 4–1 and 4–2 are illustrative, not absolute, and may require adaptation to fit a particular company's circumstances.

Developing the Data for Strategic Cost Analysis   The data requirements for value chain analysis can be formidable. Typically, the analyst must break down a firm's departmental cost accounting data into the costs of performing specific activities.[6] The appropriate degree of disaggregation depends on the economics of the activities and how valuable it is to develop cross-company cost comparisons for narrowly defined activities as opposed to broadly defined activities. A good guideline is to develop separate cost estimates for activities having different economics and for activities representing a significant or growing proportion of cost.[7]

Traditional accounting identifies costs according to broad categories of expenses—wages and salaries, employee benefits, supplies, travel, depreciation, R&D, and other fixed charges. *Activity-based costing* entails assigning these broad categories of costs to the specific tasks and activities being performed, as shown in Table 4–2.[8] It also entails developing cost estimates for activities performed in the competitively relevant portions of suppliers' and downstream customers' value chains. To benchmark the firm's cost position against rivals, costs for the same activities for each rival must be estimated—an advanced art in competitive intelligence. But despite the tediousness of developing cost estimates activity by activity and the imprecision of some of the estimates, the payoff in exposing the costs of particular internal tasks and functions and the cost competitiveness of one's position vis-à-vis rivals makes activity-based costing a valuable strategic management tool. Despite the calculation problems, every company's managers should attempt to estimate the value chain for their business.[9] Illustration Capsule 9 shows a simplified value chain comparison for two prominent brewers of beer—Anheuser-Busch (the U.S. industry leader) and Adolph Coors (the third-ranking brewer).

The most important application of value chain analysis is to expose how a particular firm's cost position compares with the cost positions of its rivals. What is needed is competitor versus competitor cost estimates for supplying a product or service to a well-defined customer group or market segment. The size of a company's cost advantage/disadvantage can vary from item to item in the product line, from customer group to customer group (if different distribution channels are used), and from geographic market to geographic market (if cost factors vary across geographic regions).

BENCHMARKING THE COSTS OF KEY ACTIVITIES

Many companies today are benchmarking the costs of performing a given activity against competitors' costs (and/or against the costs of a noncompetitor in another

---

[6]For discussions of the accounting challenges in calculating the costs of value chain activities, see Shank and Govindarajan, *Strategic Cost Management,* pp. 62–72 and chapter 5, and Hegert and Morris, "Accounting Data for Value Chain Analysis," pp. 175–88.

[7]Porter, *Competitive Advantage,* p. 45.

[8]For a discussion of activity-based cost accounting, see Cooper and Kaplan, "Measure Costs Right: Make the Right Decisions," pp. 96–103; Shank and Govindarajan, *Strategic Cost Management,* Chapter 11; and Terence P. Paré, "A New Tool for Managing Costs," *Fortune,* June 14, 1993, pp. 124–29.

[9]Shank and Govindarajan, *Strategic Cost Management,* p. 62.

TABLE 4-2 | **The Difference between Traditional Cost Accounting and Activity-Based Cost Accounting**

Traditional Cost Accounting Categories in Departmental Budget		Cost of Performing Specific Departmental Activities Using Activity-Based Cost Accounting	
Wages and salaries	$350,000	Evaluate supplier capabilities	$135,750
Employee benefits	115,000	Process purchase orders	82,100
Supplies	6,500	Expedite supplier deliveries	23,500
Travel	2,400	Expedite internal processing	15,840
Depreciation	17,000	Check quality of items purchased	94,300
Other fixed charges	124,000	Check incoming deliveries against purchase orders	48,450
Miscellaneous operating expenses	25,250	Resolve problems	110,000
		Internal administration	130,210
	$640,150		$640,150

Source: Adapted from information in Terence P. Paré, "A New Tool for Managing Costs," *Fortune,* June 14, 1993, pp. 124–29.

industry that efficiently and effectively performs much the same activity or business process). Benchmarking focuses on cross-company comparisons of how well basic functions and processes in the value chain are performed—how materials are purchased, how suppliers are paid, how inventories are managed, how employees are trained, how payrolls are processed, how fast the company can get new products to market, how the quality control function is performed, how customer orders are filled and shipped, and how maintenance is performed.[10] The ultimate objective is to understand the best practices in performing an activity, to learn how lower costs are actually achieved, and to take action to improve a company's cost competitiveness whenever benchmarking reveals that the costs of performing an activity are out of line with what other companies (competitors or noncompetitors) have been able to achieve successfully.

In 1979, Xerox became an early pioneer in the use of benchmarking when Japanese manufacturers began selling mid-size copiers in the U.S. for $9,600 each—less than Xerox's production costs.[11] Although Xerox management suspected its Japanese competitors were dumping, it sent a team of line managers to Japan, including the head of manufacturing, to study competitors' business processes and costs. Fortunately, Xerox's joint venture partner in Japan, Fuji-Xerox, knew the competitors well. The team found that Xerox's costs were excessive due to gross inefficiencies in its manufacturing processes and business practices; the study proved instrumental in Xerox's efforts to become cost competitive and prompted Xerox to embark on a long-term program to benchmark 67 of its key work processes against companies identified as having the "best practices" in performing these processes. Xerox quickly decided not to restrict its benchmarking efforts to its office equipment rivals but to extend them to any company regarded as "world class" in performing an activity relevant to Xerox's business. Illustration Capsule 10 describes one of Ford Motor's benchmarking experiences.

Benchmarking the performance of company activities against rivals and other best-practice companies provides hard evidence of a company's cost competitiveness.

---

[10]For more details, see Gregory H. Watson, *Strategic Benchmarking: How to Rate Your Company's Performance Against the World's Best* (New York: John Wiley, 1993) and Robert C. Camp, *Benchmarking: The Search for Industry Best Practices That Lead to Superior Performance* (Milwaukee:ASQC Quality Press, 1989). See also Alexandra Biesada, "Strategic Benchmarking," *Financial World,* September 29, 1992, pp. 30–38.

[11]Jeremy Main, "How to Steal the Best Ideas Around," *Fortune,* October 19, 1992, pp. 102–3.

ILLUSTRATION CAPSULE 9

VALUE CHAINS FOR ANHEUSER-BUSCH AND ADOLPH COORS BEERS

In the table below are average cost estimates for the combined brands of beer produced by Anheuser-Busch and Coors. The example shows raw material costs, other manufacturing costs, and forward channel distribution costs. The data are for 1982.

Value Chain Activities and Costs	Estimated Average Cost Breakdown for Combined Anheuser-Busch Brands		Estimated Average Cost Breakdown for Combined Adolph Coors Brands	
	Per 6-Pack of 12-oz Cans	Per Barrel Equivalent	Per 6-Pack of 12-oz Cans	Per Barrel Equivalent
1. Manufacturing costs:				
Direct production costs:				
Raw material ingredients	$0.1384	$ 7.63	$0.1082	$ 5.96
Direct labor	0.1557	8.58	0.1257	6.93
Salaries for nonunionized personnel	0.0800	4.41	0.0568	3.13
Packaging	0.5055	27.86	0.4663	25.70
Depreciation on plant and equipment	0.0410	2.26	0.0826	4.55
Subtotal	0.9206	50.74	0.8396	46.27
Other expenses:				
Advertising	0.0477	2.63	0.0338	1.86
Other marketing costs and general administrative expenses	0.1096	6.04	0.1989	10.96
Interest	0.0147	0.81	0.0033	0.18
Research and development	0.0277	1.53	0.0195	1.07
Total manufacturing costs	$1.1203	$61.75	$1.0951	$60.34
2. Manufacturer's operating profit	0.1424	7.85	0.0709	3.91
3. Net selling price	1.2627	69.60	1.1660	64.25
4. Plus federal and state excise taxes paid by brewer	0.1873	10.32	0.1782	9.82
5. Gross manufacturer's selling price to distributor/wholesaler	1.4500	79.92	1.3442	74.07
6. Average margin over manufacturer's cost	0.5500	30.31	0.5158	28.43
7. Average wholesale price charged to retailer (inclusive of taxes in item 4 above but exclusive of other taxes)	$2.00	$110.23	$1.86	$102.50
8. Plus other assorted state and local taxes levied on wholesale and retail sales (this varies from locality to locality)	0.60		0.60	
9. Average 20% retail markup over wholesale cost	0.40		0.38	
10. Average price to consumer at retail	$3.00		$2.84	

Note: The difference in the average cost structures for Anheuser-Busch and Adolph Coors is, to a substantial extent, due to A-B's higher proportion of super-premium beer sales. A-B's super-premium brand, Michelob, was the bestseller in its category and somewhat more costly to brew than premium and popular-priced beers.

Source: Compiled by Tom McLean, Elsa Wischkaemper, and Arthur A. Thompson, Jr., from a wide variety of documents and field interviews.

ILLUSTRATION CAPSULE 10

FORD MOTOR COMPANY'S BENCHMARKING OF ITS ACCOUNTS PAYABLE ACTIVITY

In the 1980s Ford's North American accounts payable department employed more than 500 people. Clerks spent the majority of their time straightening out the relatively few situations where three documents—the purchase order issued by the purchasing department, the receiving document prepared by clerks at the receiving dock, and the invoice sent by the vendor/supplier to accounts payable—did not match. Sometimes resolving the discrepancies took weeks of time and the efforts of many people. Ford managers believed that by

using computers to automate some functions performed manually, head count could be reduced to 400. Before proceeding, Ford managers decided to visit Mazda—a company in which Ford had recently acquired a 25 percent ownership interest. To their astonishment, Mazda handled its accounts payable function with only five people. Following Mazda's lead, Ford benchmarkers created an invoiceless system where payments to suppliers were triggered automatically when the goods were received. The reengineered system allowed Ford to reduce its accounts payable staff to under 200, a lot more than Mazda but much better than would have resulted without benchmarking the accounts payable activity.

Sources: Michael Hammer and James Champy, *Reengineering the Corporation* (New York: HarperBusiness, 1993), pp. 39–43, and Jeremy Main, "How to Steal the Best Ideas Around," *Fortune,* October 19, 1992, p. 106.

Sometimes cost benchmarking can be accomplished by collecting information from published reports, trade groups, and industry research firms and by talking to knowledgeable industry analysts, customers, and suppliers (customers, suppliers, and joint-venture partners often make willing benchmarking allies). Usually, though, benchmarking requires field trips to the facilities of competing or noncompeting companies to observe how things are done, ask questions, compare practices and processes, and perhaps exchange data on productivity, staffing levels, time requirements, and other cost components. However, benchmarking involves competitively sensitive information about how lower costs are achieved, and close rivals can't be expected to be completely open, even if they agree to host facilities tours and answer questions. But the explosive interest of companies in benchmarking costs and identifying best practices has prompted consulting organizations (for example, Andersen Consulting, A. T. Kearney, Best Practices Benchmarking & Consulting, and Towers Perrin) and several newly formed councils and associations (the International Benchmarking Clearinghouse and the Strategic Planning Institute's Council on Benchmarking) to gather benchmarking data, do benchmarking studies, and distribute information about best practices and the costs of performing activities to clients/members without identifying the sources. The ethical dimension of benchmarking is discussed in Illustration Capsule 11. Over 80 percent of *Fortune 500* companies now engage in some form of benchmarking.

Benchmarking is a manager's best tool for determining whether the company is performing particular functions and activities efficiently, whether its costs are in line with competitors, and which internal activities and business processes need to be improved. It is a way of learning which companies are best at performing certain activities and functions and then imitating—or, better still, improving on—their techniques. Toyota managers got their idea for just-in-time inventory deliveries by studying how U.S. supermarkets replenished their shelves. Southwest Airlines reduced the turnaround time of its aircraft at each scheduled stop by studying pit crews on the auto racing circuit.

ILLUSTRATION CAPSULE 11

BENCHMARKING AND ETHICAL CONDUCT

Because actions between benchmarking partners can involve competitively sensitive data and discussions, conceivably raising questions about possible restraint of trade or improper business conduct, the SPI Council on Benchmarking and The International Benchmarking Clearinghouse urge all individuals and organizations involved in benchmarking to abide by a code of conduct grounded in ethical business behavior. The code is based on the following principles and guidelines:

- In benchmarking with competitors, establish specific ground rules up front, e.g., "We don't want to talk about those things that will give either of us a competitive advantage; rather, we want to see where we both can mutually improve or gain benefit." Do not discuss costs with competitors if costs are an element of pricing.

- Do not ask competitors for sensitive data or cause the benchmarking partner to feel that sensitive data must be provided to keep the process going. Be prepared to provide the same level of information that you request. Do not share proprietary information without

prior approval from the proper authorities of both parties.

- Use an ethical third party to assemble and blind competitive data, with inputs from legal counsel, for direct competitor comparisons.

- Consult with legal counsel if any information gathering procedure is in doubt, e.g., before contacting a direct competitor.

- Any information obtained from a benchmarking partner should be treated as internal, privileged information. Any external use must have the partner's permission.

- Do not:
  - Disparage a competitor's business or operations to a third party.
  - Attempt to limit competition or gain business through the benchmarking relationship.
  - Misrepresent oneself as working for another employer.

- Demonstrate commitment to the efficiency and effectiveness of the process by being adequately prepared at each step, particularly at initial contact. Be professional, honest, and courteous. Adhere to the agenda—maintain focus on benchmarking issues.

Sources: The SPI Council on Benchmarking, The International Benchmarking Clearinghouse, and conference presentation of AT&T Benchmarking Group, Des Moines, Iowa, October 1993.

STRATEGIC OPTIONS FOR ACHIEVING COST COMPETITIVENESS

Value chain analysis can reveal a great deal about a firm's cost competitiveness. One of the fundamental insights of strategic cost analysis is that a company's competitiveness depends on how well it manages its value chain relative to how well competitors manage theirs.[12] Examining the makeup of a company's own value chain and comparing it to rivals' indicates who has how much of a cost advantage/disadvantage and which cost components are responsible. Such information is vital in crafting strategies to eliminate a cost disadvantage or create a cost advantage.

Looking again at Figure 4–2, observe that there are three main areas in a company's overall value chain where important differences in the costs of competing firms can occur: in the suppliers' part of the industry value chain, in a company's own activity segments, or in the forward channel portion of the industry chain. If a firm's lack of cost competitiveness lies either in the backward (upstream) or forward (downstream) sections of the value chain, then reestablishing cost competitiveness

Strategic actions to eliminate a cost disadvantage need to be linked to the location in the value chain where the cost differences originate.

[12]Shank and Govindarajan, *Strategic Cost Management*, p. 50.

may have to extend beyond the firm's own in-house operations. When a firm's cost disadvantage is principally associated with the costs of items purchased from suppliers (the upstream end of the industry chain), company managers can pursue any of several strategic actions to correct the problem:[13]

- Negotiate more favorable prices with suppliers.
- Work with suppliers to help them achieve lower costs.
- Integrate backward to gain control over the costs of purchased items.
- Try to use lower-priced substitute inputs.
- Do a better job of managing the linkages between suppliers' value chains and the company's own chain; for example, close coordination between a company and its suppliers can permit just-in-time deliveries that lower a company's inventory and internal logistics costs and that may also allow its suppliers to economize on their warehousing, shipping, and production scheduling costs—a win-win outcome for both (instead of a zero-sum game where a company's gains match supplier concessions).
- Try to make up the difference by cutting costs elsewhere in the chain.

A company's strategic options for eliminating cost disadvantages in the forward end of the value chain system include[14]

- Pushing distributors and other forward channel allies to reduce their markups.
- Working closely with forward channel allies/customers to identify win-win opportunities to reduce costs. A chocolate manufacturer learned that by shipping its bulk chocolate in liquid form in tank cars instead of 10-pound molded bars, it saved its candy bar manufacturing customers the cost of unpacking and melting, and it eliminated its own costs of molding bars and packing them.
- Changing to a more economical distribution strategy, including the possibility of forward integration.
- Trying to make up the difference by cutting costs earlier in the cost chain.

When the source of a firm's cost disadvantage is internal, managers can use any of nine strategic approaches to restore cost parity:[15]

1. Initiate internal budget reductions and streamline operations.
2. Reengineer business processes and work practices (to boost employee productivity, improve the efficiency of key activities, increase the utilization of company assets, and otherwise do a better job of managing the cost drivers).
3. Try to eliminate some cost-producing activities altogether by revamping the value chain system (for example, shifting to a radically different technological approach or maybe bypassing the value chains of forward channel allies and marketing directly to end-users).

---

[13]Porter, *Competitive Advantage,* chapter 3.
[14]Ibid.
[15]Ibid.

4. Relocate high-cost activities to geographic areas where they can be performed more cheaply.
5. See if certain activities can be outsourced from vendors or performed by contractors more cheaply than they can be done internally.
6. Invest in cost-saving technological improvements (automation, robotics, flexible manufacturing techniques, computerized controls).
7. Innovate around the troublesome cost components as new investments are made in plant and equipment.
8. Simplify the product design so that it can be manufactured more economically.
9. Try to make up the internal cost disadvantage by achieving savings in the backward and forward portions of the value chain system.

VALUE CHAIN ANALYSIS, CORE COMPETENCIES, AND COMPETITIVE ADVANTAGE

How well a company manages its value chain activities relative to competitors is a key to building valuable core competencies and leveraging them into sustainable competitive advantage. With rare exceptions, a firm's products or services are not a basis for sustainable competitive advantage—it is too easy for a resourceful company to clone, improve on, or find an effective substitute for them.[16] Rather, a company's competitive edge is usually grounded in its skills and capabilities relative to rivals' and, more specifically, in the scope and depth of its ability to perform competitively crucial activities along the value chain better than rivals.

Core competencies emerge from a company's experience, learned skills, and focused efforts in performing one or more related value chain components. Merck and Glaxo, two of the world's most competitively capable pharmaceutical companies, built their strategic positions around expert performance of a few key activities: extensive R&D to achieve first discovery of new drugs, a carefully constructed approach to patenting, skill in gaining rapid and thorough clinical clearance through regulatory bodies, and unusually strong distribution and sales force capabilities.[17] To arrive at a sound diagnosis of a company's true competitive capabilities, managers need to do four things:

> Value chain analysis is a powerful managerial tool for identifying which activities in the chain have competitive advantage potential.

1. Construct a value chain of company activities.
2. Examine the linkages among internally performed activities and the linkages with suppliers' and customers' chains.
3. Identify the activities and competencies critical to customer satisfaction and market success.
4. Make appropriate internal and external benchmarking comparisons to determine how well the company performs activities (which activities represent core competencies and which ones are better performed by outsiders?) and how its cost structure compares with competitors.

The strategy-making lesson of value chain analysis is that increased company competitiveness hinges on managerial efforts to concentrate company resources and talent on those skills and activities where the company can gain dominating expertise to serve its target customers.

---

[16]James Brian Quinn, *Intelligent Enterprise* (New York: Free Press, 1993), p. 54.
[17]Quinn, *Intelligent Enterprise,* p. 34.

QUESTION 4: HOW STRONG IS THE COMPANY'S COMPETITIVE POSITION?

Systematic assessment of whether a company's competitive position is strong or weak *relative to close rivals* is an essential step in company situation analysis.

Using value chain concepts and the other tools of strategic cost analysis to determine a company's cost competitiveness is necessary but not sufficient. A more broad-ranging assessment needs to be made of a company's competitive position and competitive strength. Particular elements to single out for evaluation are (1) how strongly the firm holds its present competitive position, (2) whether the firm's position can be expected to improve or deteriorate if the present strategy is continued (allowing for fine-tuning), (3) how the firm ranks *relative to key rivals* on each important measure of competitive strength and industry key success factors, (4) whether the firm enjoys a competitive advantage or is currently at a disadvantage, and (5) the firm's ability to defend its position in light of industry driving forces, competitive pressures, and the anticipated moves of rivals.

Table 4–3 lists some indicators of whether a firm's competitive position is improving or slipping. But company managers need to do more than just identify the areas of competitive improvement or slippage. They have to judge whether the company has a net competitive advantage or disadvantage vis-à-vis key competitors and whether the company's market position and performance can be expected to improve or deteriorate under the current strategy.

Managers can begin the task of evaluating the company's competitive strength by using benchmarking techniques to compare the company against industry rivals not just on cost but also on such competitively important measures as product quality, customer service, customer satisfaction, financial strength, technological skills, and product cycle time (how quickly new products can be taken from idea to design to market). It is not enough to benchmark the costs of activities and identify best practices; a company should benchmark itself against competitors on all strategically and competitively important aspects of its business.

T A B L E 4–3 | The Signs of Strength and Weakness in a Company's Competitive Position

Signs of Competitive Strength	Signs of Competitive Weakness
• Important core competencies	• Confronted with competitive disadvantages
• Strong market share (or a leading market share)	• Losing ground to rival firms
• A pacesetting or distinctive strategy	• Below-average growth in revenues
• Growing customer base and customer loyalty	• Short on financial resources
• Above-average market visibility	• A slipping reputation with customers
• In a favorably situated strategic group	• Trailing in product development
• Concentrating on fastest-growing market segments	• In a strategic group destined to lose ground
• Strongly differentiated products	• Weak in areas where there is the most market potential
• Cost advantages	• A higher-cost producer
• Above-average profit margins	• Too small to be a major factor in the marketplace
• Above-average technological and innovational capability	• Not in good position to deal with emerging threats
• A creative, entrepreneurially alert management	• Weak product quality
• In position to capitalize on opportunities	• Lacking skills and capabilities in key areas

COMPETITIVE STRENGTH ASSESSMENTS

The most telling way to determine how strongly a company holds its competitive position is to quantitatively assess whether the company is stronger or weaker than close rivals on each key success factor and each important indicator of competitive strength. Much of the information for competitive position assessment comes from previous analyses. Industry and competitive analysis reveals the key success factors and competitive measures that separate industry winners from losers. Competitor analysis and benchmarking data provide a basis for judging the strengths and capabilities of key rivals.

Step one is to make a list of the industry's key success factors and most telling measures of competitive strength or weakness (6 to 10 measures usually suffice). Step two is to rate the firm and its key rivals on each factor. Rating scales from 1 to 10 are best to use although ratings of stronger (+), weaker (–), and about equal (=) may be appropriate when information is scanty and assigning numerical scores conveys false precision. Step three is to sum the individual strength ratings to get an overall measure of competitive strength for each competitor. Step four is to draw conclusions about the size and extent of the company's net competitive advantage or disadvantage and to take specific note of areas where the company's competitive position is strongest and weakest.

Table 4–4 provides two examples of competitive strength assessment. The first one employs an *unweighted rating scale;* with unweighted ratings each key success factor/competitive strength measure is assumed to be equally important. Whichever company has the highest strength rating on a given measure has an implied competitive edge on that factor; the size of its edge is mirrored in the margin of difference between its rating and the ratings assigned to rivals. Summing a company's strength ratings on all the measures produces an overall strength rating. The higher a company's overall strength rating, the stronger its competitive position. The bigger the margin of difference between a company's overall rating and the scores of lower-rated rivals, the greater its implied net competitive advantage. Thus, ABC's total score of 61 (see the top half of Table 4–4) signals a greater net competitive advantage over Rival 4 (with a score of 32) than over Rival 1 (with a score of 58).

However, it is better methodology to use a weighted rating system because the different measures of competitive strength are unlikely to be equally important. In a commodity-product industry, for instance, having low unit costs relative to rivals is nearly always the most important determinant of competitive strength. In an industry with strong product differentiation the most significant measures of competitive strength may be brand awareness, amount of advertising, reputation for quality, and distribution capability. In a *weighted rating system* each measure of competitive strength is assigned a weight based on its perceived importance in shaping competitive success. The largest weight could be as high as .75 (maybe even higher) in situations where one particular competitive variable is overwhelmingly decisive or as low as .20 when two or three strength measures are more important than the rest. Lesser competitive strength indicators can carry weights of .05 or .10. No matter whether the differences between the weights are big or little, *the sum of the weights must add up to 1.0.*

Weighted strength ratings are calculated by deciding how a company stacks up on each strength measure (using the 1 to 10 rating scale) and multiplying the assigned rating by the assigned weight (a rating score of 4 times a weight of .20 gives a weighted rating of .80). Again, the company with the highest rating on a

High competitive strength ratings signal a strong competitive position and possession of competitive advantage; low ratings signal a weak position and competitive disadvantage.

A weighted competitive strength analysis is conceptually stronger than an unweighted analysis because of the inherent weakness in assuming that all the strength measures are equally important.

TABLE 4–4 | **Illustrations of Unweighted and Weighted Competitive Strength Assessments**

A. Sample of an Unweighted Competitive Strength Assessment
Rating scale: 1 = Very weak; 10 = Very strong

Key Success Factor/Strength Measure	ABC Co.	Rival 1	Rival 2	Rival 3	Rival 4
Quality/product performance	8	5	10	1	6
Reputation/image	8	7	10	1	6
Manufacturing capability	2	10	4	5	1
Technological skills	10	1	7	3	8
Dealer network	9	4	10	5	1
Marketing/advertising	9	4	10	5	1
Financial strength	5	10	7	3	1
Relative cost position	5	10	3	1	4
Customer service	5	7	10	1	4
Unweighted overall strength rating	61	58	71	25	32

B. Sample of a Weighted Competitive Strength Assessment
Rating scale: 1 = Very weak; 10 = Very strong

Key Success Factor/Strength Measure	Weight	ABC Co.	Rival 1	Rival 2	Rival 3	Rival 4
Quality/product performance	0.10	8/0.80	5/0.50	10/1.00	1/0.10	6/0.60
Reputation/image	0.10	8/0.80	7/0.70	10/1.00	1/0.10	6/0.60
Manufacturing capability	0.10	2/0.20	10/1.00	4/0.40	5/0.50	1/0.10
Technological skills	0.05	10/0.50	1/0.05	7/0.35	3/0.15	8/0.40
Dealer network	0.05	9/0.45	4/0.20	10/0.50	5/0.25	1/0.05
Marketing/advertising	0.05	9/0.45	4/0.20	10/0.50	5/0.25	1/0.05
Financial strength	0.10	5/0.50	10/1.00	7/0.70	3/0.30	1/0.10
Relative cost position	0.35	5/1.75	10/3.50	3/1.05	1/0.35	4/1.40
Customer service	0.15	5/0.75	7/1.05	10/1.50	1/0.15	4/1.60
Sum of weights	1.00					
Weighted overall strength rating		6.20	8.20	7.00	2.10	2.90

given measure has an implied competitive edge on that measure, with the size of its edge reflected in the difference between its rating and rivals' ratings. The weight attached to the measure indicates how important the edge is. Summing a company's weighted strength ratings for all the measures yields an overall strength rating. Comparisons of the weighted overall strength scores indicate which competitors are in the strongest and weakest competitive positions and who has how big a net competitive advantage over whom.

The bottom half of Table 4–4 shows a sample competitive strength assessment for ABC Company using a weighted rating system. Note that the unweighted and weighted rating schemes produce a different ordering of the companies. In the weighted system, ABC Company dropped from second to third in strength, and Rival 1 jumped from third into first because of its high strength ratings on the two most important factors. Weighting the importance of the strength measures can thus make a significant difference in the outcome of the assessment.

Competitive strength assessments provide useful conclusions about a company's competitive situation. The ratings show how a company compares against rivals, factor by factor or measure by measure, thus revealing where it is strongest and weakest and against whom. Moreover, the overall competitive strength scores indicate whether the company is at a net competitive advantage or disadvantage against each rival. The firm with the largest overall competitive strength rating can be said to have a net competitive advantage over each rival.

Knowing where a company is competitively strong and where it is weak is essential in crafting a strategy to strengthen its long-term competitive position. As a general rule, a company should try to convert its competitive strengths into sustainable competitive advantage and take strategic actions to protect against its competitive weaknesses. At the same time, competitive strength ratings point to which rival companies may be vulnerable to competitive attack and the areas where they are weakest. When a company has important competitive strengths in areas where one or more rivals are weak, it makes sense to consider offensive moves to exploit rivals' competitive weaknesses.

Competitive strengths and competitive advantages enable a company to improve its long-term market position.

QUESTION 5: WHAT STRATEGIC ISSUES DOES THE COMPANY FACE?

The final analytical task is to home in on the strategic issues management needs to address in forming an effective strategic action plan. Here, managers need to draw upon all the prior analysis, put the company's overall situation into perspective, and get a lock on exactly where they need to focus their strategic attention. This step should not be taken lightly. Without a precise fix on what the issues are, managers are not prepared to start crafting a strategy—a good strategy must offer a plan for dealing with all the strategic issues that need to be addressed.

Effective strategy-making requires thorough understanding of the strategic issues a company faces.

To pinpoint issues for the company's strategic action agenda, managers ought to consider the following:

- Whether the present strategy is adequate in light of driving forces at work in the industry.
- How closely the present strategy matches the industry's *future* key success factors.
- How good a defense the present strategy offers against the five competitive forces—particularly those that are expected to intensify in strength.
- In what ways the present strategy may not adequately protect the company against external threats and internal weaknesses.
- Where and how the company may be vulnerable to the competitive efforts of one or more rivals.
- Whether the company has competitive advantage or must work to offset competitive disadvantage.
- Where the strong spots and weak spots are in the present strategy.
- Whether additional actions are needed to improve the company's cost position, capitalize on emerging opportunities, and strengthen the company's competitive position.

These considerations should indicate whether the company can continue the same basic strategy with minor adjustments or whether major overhaul is called for.

The better matched a company's strategy is to its external environment and internal situation, the less need there is to contemplate big shifts in strategy. On the other hand, when the present strategy is not well-suited for the road ahead, managers need to give top priority to the task of crafting a new strategy.

Table 4–5 provides a format for doing company situation analysis. It incorporates the concepts and analytical techniques discussed in this chapter and provides a way of reporting the results of company situation analysis in a systematic, concise manner.

T A B L E 4-5 | **Company Situation Analysis**

1. Strategic Performance Indicators

Performance Indicator	19—	19—	19—	19—	19—
Market share	—	—	—	—	—
Sales growth	—	—	—	—	—
Net profit margin	—	—	—	—	—
Return on equity investment	—	—	—	—	—
Other?	—	—	—	—	—

2. Internal Strengths

Internal Weaknesses

External Opportunities

External Threats

3. Competitive Strength Assessment
　　Rating scale: 1 = Very weak; 10 = Very strong.

Key Success Factor/ Competitive Variable	Weight	Firm A	Firm B	Firm C	Firm D	Firm E
Quality/product performance						
Reputation/image						
Manufacturing capability						
Technological skills						
Dealer network						
Marketing/advertising						
Financial strength						
Relative cost position						
Customer service						
Other?						
Overall strength rating						

4. Conclusions Concerning Competitive Position
　　(Improving/slipping? Competitive advantages/disadvantages?)

5. Major Strategic Issues/Problems the Company Must Address

KEY POINTS

There are five key questions to consider in performing company situation analysis:

1. *How well is the present strategy working?* This involves evaluating the strategy from a qualitative standpoint (completeness, internal consistency, rationale, and suitability to the situation) and also from a quantitative standpoint (the strategic and financial results the strategy is producing). The stronger a company's current overall performance, the less likely the need for radical strategy changes. The weaker a company's performance and/or the faster the changes in its external situation (which can be gleaned from industry and competitive analysis), the more its current strategy must be questioned.

2. *What are the company's strengths, weaknesses, opportunities, and threats?* A SWOT analysis provides an overview of a firm's situation and is an essential component of crafting a strategy tightly matched to the company's situation. A company's strengths, especially its core competencies, are important because they can serve as major building blocks for strategy; company weaknesses are important because they may represent vulnerabilities that need correction. External opportunities and threats come into play because a good strategy necessarily aims at capturing attractive opportunities and at defending against threats to the company's well-being.

3. *Are the company's prices and costs competitive?* One telling sign of whether a company's situation is strong or precarious is whether its prices and costs are competitive with industry rivals. Strategic cost analysis and value chain analysis are essential tools in benchmarking a company's prices and costs against rivals, determining whether the company is performing particular functions and activities cost effectively, learning whether its costs are in line with competitors, and deciding which internal activities and business processes need to be scrutinized for improvement. Value chain analysis teaches that how competently a company manages its value chain activities relative to rivals is a key to building valuable core competencies and leveraging them into sustainable competitive advantage.

4. *How strong is the company's competitive position?* The key appraisals here involve whether the company's position is likely to improve or deteriorate if the present strategy is continued, how the company matches up against key rivals on industry KSFs and other chief determinants of competitive success, and whether and why the company has a competitive advantage or disadvantage. Quantitative competitive strength assessments, using the methodology presented in Table 4–4, indicate where a company is competitively strong and weak and provide insight into the company's ability to defend or enhance its market position. As a rule a company's competitive strategy should be built on its competitive strengths and attempt to shore up areas where it is competitively vulnerable. Also, the areas where company strengths match up against competitor weaknesses represent the best potential for new offensive initiatives.

5. *What strategic issues does the company face?* The purpose of this analytical step is to develop a complete strategy-making agenda using the results of both company situation analysis and industry and competitive analysis. The emphasis here is on drawing conclusions about the strengths and weaknesses

of a company's strategy and framing the issues that strategy-makers need to consider.

Good company situation analysis, like good industry and competitive analysis, is crucial to good strategy-making. A competently done company situation analysis exposes strong and weak points in the present strategy, company capabilities and vulnerabilities, and the company's ability to protect or improve its competitive position in light of driving forces, competitive pressures, and the competitive strength of rivals. Managers need such understanding to craft a strategy that fits the company's situation well.

SUGGESTED READINGS

Abell, Derek F. *Managing with Dual Strategies.* New York: Free Press, 1993, chaps. 9 and 10.

Andrews, Kenneth R. *The Concept of Corporate Strategy.* 3rd ed. Homewood, Ill.: Richard D. Irwin, 1987, chap. 3.

Fahey, Liam, and H. Kurt Christensen. "Building Distinctive Competencies into Competitive Advantages." Reprinted in Liam Fahey, *The Strategic Planning Management Reader,* Englewood Cliffs, N.J.: Prentice-Hall, 1989, pp. 113–18.

Hax, Arnoldo C., and Nicolas S. Majluf. *Strategic Management: An Integrative Perspective.* Englewood Cliffs, N.J.: Prentice-Hall, 1984, chap. 15.

Henry, Harold W. "Appraising a Company's Strengths and Weaknesses." *Managerial Planning,* July–August 1980, pp. 31–36.

Paine, Frank T., and Leonard J. Tischler. "Evaluating Your Costs Strategically." Reprinted in Liam Fahey, *The Strategic Planning Management Reader,* Englewood Cliffs, N.J.: Prentice-Hall, 1989, pp. 118–23.

Prahalad, C. K., and Gary Hamel. "The Core Competence of the Corporation." *Harvard Business Review* 90, no. 3 (May–June 1990), pp. 79–93.

Shank, John K., and Vijay Govindarajan. *Strategic Cost Management: The New Tool for Competitive Advantage.* New York: Free Press, 1993.

Stalk, George, Philip Evans, and Lawrence E. Shulman. "Competing on Capabilities: The New Rules of Corporate Strategy." *Harvard Business Review* 70, no. 2 (March–April 1992), pp. 57–69.

Watson, Gregory H. *Strategic Benchmarking: How to Rate Your Company's Performance Against the World's Best.* New York: John Wiley & Sons, 1993.

## CHAPTER FIVE

STRATEGY AND COMPETITIVE ADVANTAGE

Competing in the marketplace is like war. You have injuries and casualties, and the best strategy wins.

John Collins

The essence of strategy lies in creating tomorrow's competitive advantages faster than competitors mimic the ones you possess today.

Gary Hamel and C. K. Prahalad

You've got to come up with a plan. You can't wish things will get better.

John F. Welch
CEO, General Electric

Winning business strategies are grounded in sustainable competitive advantage. A company has *competitive advantage* whenever it has an edge over rivals in attracting customers and defending against competitive forces. There are many sources of competitive advantage: having the best-made product on the market, delivering superior customer service, achieving lower costs than rivals, being in a more convenient geographic location, proprietary technology, features and styling with more buyer appeal, shorter lead times in developing and testing new products, a well-known brand name and reputation, and providing buyers more value for the money (a combination of good quality, good service, and acceptable price). Essentially, though, to succeed in building a competitive advantage, a company's strategy must aim at providing buyers with what they perceive as superior value—a good product at a lower price or a better product that is worth paying more for.

This chapter focuses on how a company can achieve or defend a competitive advantage.[1] We begin by describing the basic types of competitive strategies and then

---

[1]The definitive work on this subject is Michael E. Porter, *Competitive Advantage* (New York: Free Press, 1985). The treatment in this chapter draws heavily on Porter's pioneering contribution.

Investing aggressively in creating sustainable competitive advantage is a company's singlemost dependable contributor to above-average ROI.

examine how these approaches rely on offensive moves to build competitive advantage and on defensive moves to protect competitive advantage. In the concluding two sections we survey the pros and cons of a vertical integration strategy and look at the competitive importance of timing strategic moves—when it is advantageous to be a first-mover and when it is better to be a late-mover.

THE FIVE GENERIC COMPETITIVE STRATEGIES

A company's competitive strategy consists of the business approaches and initiatives it takes to attract customers, withstand competitive pressures, and strengthen its market position. The objective, quite simply, is to knock the socks off rival companies ethically and honorably, earn a competitive advantage in the marketplace, and cultivate a clientele of loyal customers. A company's strategy for competing typically contains both offensive and defensive actions, with emphasis shifting from one to the other as market conditions warrant. And it includes short-lived tactical maneuvers designed to deal with immediate conditions, as well as actions calculated to have lasting impact on the firm's long-term competitive capabilities and market position.

Competitive strategy has a narrower scope than business strategy. Business strategy not only concerns the issue of how to compete but also embraces functional area strategies, how management plans to respond to changing industry conditions of all kinds (not just those that are competition-related), and how management intends to address the full range of strategic issues confronting the business. Competitive strategy deals exclusively with management's action plan for competing successfully and providing superior value to customers.

Companies the world over try every conceivable approach to attracting customers, earning their loyalty on repeat sales, outcompeting rivals, and winning an edge in the marketplace. And since managers tailor short-run tactics and long-term maneuvers to fit their company's specific situation and market environment, there are countless strategy variations and nuances. In this sense, there are as many competitive strategies as there are competitors. However, beneath the subtleties and superficial differences are impressive similarities when one considers (1) the company's market target and (2) the type of competitive advantage the company is trying to achieve. Five categories of competitive strategy approaches stand out:[2]

1. *A low-cost leadership strategy*—Striving to be the overall low-cost provider of a product or service that appeals to a broad range of customers.

2. *A broad differentiation strategy*—Seeking to differentiate the company's product offering from rivals' in ways that will appeal to a broad range of buyers.

3. *A best-cost provider strategy*—Giving customers more value for the money by combining an emphasis on low cost with an emphasis on upscale differentiation; the target is to have the best (lowest) costs and prices relative to producers of products with comparable quality and features.

---

[2]The classification scheme is an adaptation of one presented in Michael E. Porter, *Competitive Strategy: Techniques for Analyzing Industries and Competitors* (New York: Free Press, 1980), chapter 2 and especially pp. 35–39 and 44–46.

FIGURE 5-1 | The Five Generic Competitive Strategies

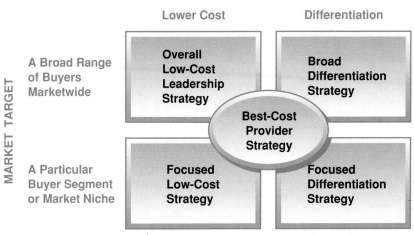

Source: Adapted from Michael E. Porter, Competitive Strategy (New York: Free Press, 1980), pp. 35–40

4. *A focused or market niche strategy based on lower cost*—Concentrating on a narrow buyer segment and outcompeting rivals on the basis of lower cost.

5. *A focused or market niche strategy based on differentiation*—Offering niche members a product or service customized to their tastes and requirements.

The five generic competitive approaches are shown in Figure 5–1; each stakes out a different market position and involves fundamentally different approaches to managing the business. Table 5–1 highlights the distinctive features of these generic competitive strategies (for simplicity, the two strains of focused strategies are combined under one heading since they differ only on one feature—the basis of competitive advantage).

LOW-COST PROVIDER STRATEGIES

Striving to be the industry's overall low-cost provider is a powerful competitive approach in markets where many buyers are price-sensitive. The aim is to open up a sustainable cost advantage over competitors and then use the company's lower-cost edge as a basis for either underpricing competitors and gaining market share at their expense or earning a higher profit margin selling at the going market price. A cost advantage generates superior profitability unless it is used up in aggressive price-cutting efforts to win sales from rivals. Achieving low-cost leadership typically means making low cost *relative to competitors* the theme of the firm's entire business strategy—though low cost cannot be pursued so zealously that a firm's offering ends up being too spartan and frills-free to generate buyer appeal. Illustration Capsule 12 describes ACX Technologies' strategy for gaining low-cost leadership in aluminum cans.

A low-cost leader's basis for competitive advantage is lower overall costs than competitors. Successful low-cost leaders are exceptionally good at finding ways to drive costs out of their businesses.

TABLE 5-1 | Distinctive Features of the Generic Competitive Strategies

Type of Feature	Low-Cost Leadership	Broad Differentiation	Best-Cost Provider	Focused Low-Cost and Focused Differentiation
Strategic target	• A broad cross-section of the market.	• A broad cross-section of the market.	• Value-conscious buyers.	• A narrow market niche where buyer needs and preferences are distinctively different from the rest of the market.
Basis of competitive advantage	• Lower costs than competitors.	• An ability to offer buyers something different from competitors.	• Give customers more value for the money	• Lower cost in serving the niche or an ability to offer niche buyers something customized to their requirements and tastes.
Product line	• A good basic product with few frills (acceptable quality and limited selection).	• Many product variations, wide selection, strong emphasis on the chosen differentiating features.	• Good-to-excellent attributes, several-to-many upscale features.	• Customized to fit the specialized needs of the target segment.
Production emphasis	• A continuous search for cost reduction without sacrificing acceptable quality and essential features.	• Invent ways to create value for buyers; strive for product superiority.	• Incorporate upscale features and attributes at low cost.	• Tailor-made for the niche.
Marketing emphasis	• Try to make a virtue out of product features that lead to low cost.	• Build in whatever features buyers are willing to pay for. • Charge a premium price to cover the extra costs of differentiating features.	• Underprice rival brands with comparable features.	• Communicate the focuser's unique ability to satisfy the buyer's specialized requirements.
Sustaining the strategy	• Economical prices/ good value. • All elements of strategy aim at contributing to a sustainable cost advantage—the key is to manage costs down, year after year, in every area of the business.	• Communicate the points of difference in credible ways. • Stress constant improvement and use innovation to stay ahead of imitative competitors. • Concentrate on a few key differentiating features; tout them to create a reputation and brand image.	• Unique expertise in managing costs down and product/ service caliber up simultaneously.	• Remain totally dedicated to serving the niche better than other competitors; don't blunt the firm's image and efforts by entering other segments or adding other product categories to widen market appeal.

118

ILLUSTRATION CAPSULE 12

ACX TECHNOLOGIES' STRATEGY TO BECOME A LOW-COST PRODUCER OF ALUMINUM CANS

ACX Technologies began as an idea of William Coors, CEO of Adolph Coors beer company, to recycle more used aluminum cans back into new cans. Typical aluminum can–making operations involved producing thick aluminum slabs from a smelter using bauxite ore combined with as much as 50% scrap aluminum, including used aluminum beverage cans; the slabs of aluminum ingot were fed into a rolling mill to achieve the required thickness. Cans were then formed by stamping pieces of thin aluminum sheet into a seamless can with the top open for filling.

Coor's idea was to produce aluminum-can sheet from 95% recycled cans. He began by purchasing rights to technology that his company had helped develop in Europe; the technology used lower-cost electric arc furnaces to melt aluminum scrap directly, short-cutting the smelter process, which required heavy capital investment and big production volumes to be competitive. Coors then built a plant in Colorado that could grind and melt used cans and pour hot aluminum through a continuous caster to make aluminum sheet suitable for the tops and tabs of beverage cans. It took seven years to develop alloys with the desired attributes and to fine-tune the process—Coors originally believed it could be done in less than two years.

In mid-1991 Coors announced it would build a new $200 million mill in Texas to make sheet aluminum for the body of the can—the product with the most exacting specifications but also the number one end use for aluminum in the United States. Production was expected to begin by mid-1992, but problems and delays soon pushed the start-up date into fall 1993. The new plant's low-cost advantages stemmed from several factors:

- Lower capital investment.
- Use of 95% recycled aluminum cans as feedstock—reducing raw material costs in producing aluminum sheet by 10 to 15%.
- Lower electricity requirements—electric arc technology used only about one-fifth of the electricity of bauxite-smelter technology.

- Comparatively low electric rates at the Texas location.
- Reduced labor costs as compared to bauxite-smelter technology.

Overall, production costs were expected to be anywhere from 20 to 35% below the costs of aluminum can producers using traditionally produced aluminum sheet, depending on the prevailing market prices for aluminum ingot and scrap aluminum. In addition, the mill had greater flexibility than traditional producers to vary its alloy mixes to meet different customer specifications.

Meanwhile, in December 1992 during construction of the Texas plant, Coors decided to spin off all aluminum can operations (along with a paper-packaging operation making patented polyethylene cartons with high quality metallic graphics—packaging for Cascade boxes and Lever 2000 soapbars are examples; a ceramics unit making materials for high-tech applications; and several developmental businesses) into a new publicly-owned company called ACX Technologies. The new company had 1992 revenues of $570 million, about 28% of which were sales to Coors. The breakdown of revenues in 1992 was aluminum for cans 17%, graphics packaging 37%, ceramics materials 32%, and developmental businesses 14% (including corn wet milling, biotechnology, defense electronics, and biodegradable polymers).

In summer 1993, the Texas plant was in start-up and can makers began testing the quality of its aluminum sheet. Coors was the first to qualify ACX's output for use; at year-end 1993 four other can users were testing the suitability of the plant's output for their products. ACX expected the plant to ship close to 50 million pounds of aluminum by year-end 1993 and 100 million pounds or more in 1994 as new customers placed orders. Analysts believed that ACX, given its cost advantage, could grow its annual volume to 1.0 to 1.5 billion pounds in 10 years as it perfected the process and gained acceptance for the quality of its output.

The company's new shares were issued at $10.75 in December 1992 when it went public. In the first 20 days of trading the price climbed to $21.75. Later in 1993, shares traded as high as $46. In May 1994 they were trading in the mid-$30s.

Sources: Based on information published by The Robinson-Humphrey Company and on Marc Charlier, "ACX Strives to Become Aluminum's Low-Cost Producer," *The Wall Street Journal,* September 29, 1993, p. B2.

Opening Up a Cost Advantage   To achieve a cost advantage, a firm's cumulative costs across its value chain must be lower than competitors' cumulative costs. There are two ways to accomplish this:[3]

- Do a better job than rivals of performing internal value chain activities efficiently and of managing the factors that drive the costs of value chain activities.
- Revamp the firm's value chain to bypass some cost-producing activities altogether.

Let's look at each of the two avenues for gaining a cost advantage.

Controlling the Cost Drivers   A firm's cost position is the result of the behavior of costs in each activity in its total value chain. The major cost drivers which come into play in determining a company's costs in each activity segment of the chain fall into two categories: (1) structural determinants of cost that depend on the fundamental economic nature of the business; and (2) executional cost determinants that stem directly from how well internal activities are managed.[4]

Structural Cost Drivers

1. *Economies or diseconomies of scale*. Economies and diseconomies of scale can be found or created in virtually every segment of the value chain. For example, manufacturing economies can sometimes be achieved by simplifying the product line and scheduling longer production runs for fewer models. A geographically organized sales force can realize economies as regional sales volume grows because a salesperson can write larger orders at each sales call and/or because of reduced travel time between calls; on the other hand, a sales force organized by product line can encounter travel-related diseconomies if salespersons have to spend disproportionately more travel time calling on distantly spaced customers. In global industries, modifying products by country instead of selling a standard product worldwide tends to boost unit costs because of lost time in model changeover, shorter production runs, and inability to reach the most economic scale of production for each model. Boosting local or regional market share can lower sales and marketing costs per unit, whereas opting for a bigger national share by entering new regions can create scale diseconomies unless and until market penetration in the newly entered regions reaches efficient proportions.

2. *Learning and experience curve effects*. Experience-based cost savings can come from improved layout, gains in labor efficiency, debugging of technology, product design modifications that enhance manufacturing efficiency, redesign of machinery and equipment to gain increased operating speed, getting samples of a rival's products and having design engineers study how they are made, and tips from suppliers, consultants, and ex-employees of rival firms. Learning tends to vary with the amount of management attention devoted to capturing the benefits of experience of both the firm and outsiders. Learning benefits can be kept proprietary by building or modifying production equipment in-house, retaining key

---

[3]Michael E. Porter, *Competitive Advantage* (New York: Free Press, 1985), p. 97.
[4]The list and explanations are condensed from Porter, *Competitive Advantage*, pp. 70–107.

employees, limiting the dissemination of information through employee publications, and enforcing strict nondisclosure provisions in employment contracts.

3. *Linkages with other activities in the chain.* When the cost of one activity is affected by how other activities are performed, companies can lower costs of linked activities through superior coordination and/or joint optimization. Linkages with suppliers tend to center on suppliers' product-design characteristics, quality-assurance procedures, delivery and service policies, and the manner in which the supplier's product is furnished (for example, nails delivered in prepackaged 1-lb., 5-lb., and 10-lb. assortments instead of 100-lb. bulk cartons can reduce a hardware dealer's labor costs in filling individual customer orders). The easiest supplier linkages to exploit are those where both a supplier's and firm's costs fall because of coordination and/or joint optimization. Linkages with forward channels tend to center on location of warehouses, materials handling, outbound shipping, and packaging.

4. *Sharing opportunities with other business units within the enterprise.* Activities shared with a sister unit can create significant cost savings. Cost sharing can help achieve scale economies, shorten the learning curve in mastering a new technology, and/or achieve fuller capacity utilization. Sometimes the know-how gained in one division can be used to help lower costs in another; sharing know-how is significant when the activities are similar and know-how can be readily transferred from one unit to another.

5. *The benefits of vertical integration versus outsourcing.* Partially or fully integrating into the activities of either suppliers or forward channel allies can allow an enterprise to detour suppliers or buyers with considerable bargaining power. Vertical integration can also result in cost savings when it is feasible to coordinate or merge adjacent activities in the value chain. On the other hand, it is sometimes cheaper to outsource certain functions and activities to outside specialists, who by virtue of their expertise and volume can perform the activity/function more cheaply.

6. *Locational variables.* Locations differ in their prevailing wage levels, tax rates, energy costs, inbound and outbound shipping and freight costs, and so on. Opportunities may exist for reducing costs by relocating plants, field offices, warehousing, or headquarters operations. Moreover, whether sister facilities are nearby or far apart affects the costs of shipping intrafirm inventory, outbound freight on goods shipped to customers, and coordination.

Executional Cost Drivers

1. *Timing considerations associated with first-mover advantages and disadvantages.* Sometimes the first major brand in the market is able to establish and maintain its brand name at a lower cost than later brand arrivals—being a first-mover turns out to be cheaper than being a late-mover. On other occasions, such as when technology is developing fast, late-purchasers can benefit from waiting to install second- or third-generation equipment that is both cheaper and more efficient; first-generation users often incur added costs associated with debugging and learning how to use an immature and unperfected technology. Likewise, companies that follow rather

than lead new product development efforts sometimes avoid many of the costs that pioneers incur in performing pathbreaking R&D and opening up new markets.

2. *The percentage of capacity utilization.* High fixed costs as a percentage of total costs create a stiff unit-cost penalty for underutilization of existing capacity. Increased capacity utilization spreads indirect and overhead costs over a larger unit volume and enhances the efficiency of fixed assets. The more capital-intensive the business, the more important this cost driver becomes. Finding ways to minimize the ups and downs in seasonal capacity utilization can be an important source of cost advantage.[5]

3. *Strategic choices and operating decisions.* Managers at various levels affect a firm's costs through the decisions they make:

- Increasing/decreasing the number of products offered.
- Adding/cutting the services provided to buyers.
- Incorporating more/fewer performance and quality features into the product.
- Paying higher/lower wages and fringes to employees relative to rivals and firms in other industries.
- Increasing/decreasing the number of different forward channels utilized in distributing the firm's product.
- Raising/lowering the levels of R&D support relative to rivals.
- Putting more/less emphasis on higher productivity and efficiency as compared to rivals.
- Raising/lowering the specifications for purchased materials.

Managers intent on achieving low-cost leader status have to understand which structural and executional factors drive the costs of each activity in the firm's total value chain. Then they have to use their knowledge about the cost drivers to reduce costs for every activity where cost savings can be identified. The task of continuously coming up with ways to drive costs out of the business (and ways to avoid incurring some costs at all) is seldom simple or painless; rather, it is a task that managers have to attack with ingenuity and single-minded toughness.

Revamping the Makeup of the Value Chain Dramatic cost advantages can emerge from finding innovative ways to restructure processes and tasks, cut out frills, and provide the basics more economically. The primary ways companies can achieve a cost advantage by reconfiguring their value chains include:

- Simplifying the product design.
- Stripping away the extras and offering only a basic, no-frills product or service, thereby cutting out activities and costs associated with multiple features and options.

---

[5]A firm can improve its capacity utilization by *(a)* serving a mix of accounts with peak volumes spread throughout the year, *(b)* finding off-season uses for its products, *(c)* serving private-label customers that can intermittently use the excess capacity, *(d)* selecting buyers with stable demands or demands that are counter to the normal peak/valley cycle, *(e)* letting competitors serve the buyer segments whose demands fluctuate the most, and *(f)* sharing capacity with sister units having a different pattern of needs.

- Reengineering core business processes to cut out needless work steps and low-value-added activities.
- Shifting to a simpler, less capital-intensive, or more streamlined technological process.
- Finding ways to bypass the use of high-cost raw materials or component parts.
- Using direct-to-end-user sales and marketing approaches that cut out the often large costs and margins of wholesalers and retailers (costs and margins in the wholesale-retail portions of the value chain often represent 50 percent of the price paid by final consumers).
- Relocating facilities closer to suppliers, customers, or both to curtail inbound and outbound logistics costs.
- Achieving a more economical degree of forward or backward vertical integration relative to competitors.
- Dropping the "something for everyone" approach and focusing on a limited product/service to meet a special, but important, need of the target buyer, thereby eliminating activities and costs associated with numerous product versions.

Successful low-cost producers usually achieve their cost advantages by exhaustively pursuing cost savings throughout the value chain. All avenues are used and no area of potential is overlooked. Normally, low-cost producers have a very cost-conscious corporate culture symbolically reinforced with spartan facilities, limited perks and frills for executives, intolerance of waste, intensive screening of budget requests, and broad employee participation in cost-control efforts. But while low-cost providers are champions of frugality, they are usually aggressive in committing funds to projects that promise to drive costs out of the business.

The Keys to Success Managers intent on pursuing a low-cost-provider strategy have to scrutinize each cost-creating activity and identify what drives its cost. Then they have to use their knowledge about the cost drivers to manage the costs of each activity down further year after year. They have to be proactive in redesigning business processes, eliminating nonessential work steps, and reengineering the value chain. By totally revamping how activities are performed and coordinated, companies have been able to achieve savings of 30 to 70 percent, compared to the 5 to 10 percent possible with creative tinkering and adjusting. As the two examples in Illustration Capsule 13 indicate, companies can sometimes achieve dramatic cost advantages from restructuring their value chains and slicing out a number of cost-producing activities that produce little value added insofar as customers are concerned.

Companies that employ low-cost leadership strategies include Lincoln Electric in arc welding equipment, Briggs and Stratton in small gasoline engines, BIC in ball-point pens, Black and Decker in power tools, Stride Rite in footwear, Beaird-Poulan in chain saws, Ford in heavy-duty trucks, General Electric in major home appliances, Wal-Mart in discount retailing, and Southwest Airlines in commercial airline travel.

The Competitive Defenses of Low-Cost Leadership Being the low-cost provider in an industry provides some attractive defenses against the five competitive forces.
- In meeting the challenges of *rival competitors,* the low-cost company is in the best position to compete offensively on the basis of price, to defend against price war conditions, to use the appeal of lower price to grab sales (and market share) from rivals, and to earn above-average profits (based on bigger profit

ILLUSTRATION CAPSULE 13

WINNING A COST ADVANTAGE: IOWA BEEF PACKERS AND FEDERAL EXPRESS

Iowa Beef Packers and Federal Express have been able to win strong competitive positions by restructuring the traditional value chains in their industries. In beef packing, the traditional cost chain involved raising cattle on scattered farms and ranches, shipping them live to labor-intensive, unionized slaughtering plants, and then transporting whole sides of beef to grocery retailers whose butcher departments cut them into smaller pieces and package them for sale to grocery shoppers.

Iowa Beef Packers revamped the traditional chain with a radically different strategy—large automated plants employing nonunion labor were built near economically transportable supplies of cattle, and the meat was partially butchered at the processing plant into smaller high-yield cuts (sometimes sealed in plastic casing ready for purchase), boxed, and shipped to retailers. IBP's inbound cattle transportation expenses, traditionally a major cost item, were cut significantly by avoiding the weight losses that occurred when live animals were shipped long distances; major outbound shipping cost savings were achieved by not having to ship whole sides of beef with their high waste factor.

Iowa Beef's strategy was so successful that it was, in 1985, the largest U.S. meatpacker, surpassing the former industry leaders, Swift, Wilson, and Armour.

Federal Express innovatively redefined the value chain for rapid delivery of small parcels. Traditional firms like Emery and Airborne Express operated by collecting freight packages of varying sizes, shipping them to their destination points via air freight and commercial airlines, and then delivering them to the addressee. Federal Express opted to focus only on the market for overnight delivery of small packages and documents. These were collected at local drop points during the late afternoon hours and flown on company-owned planes during early evening hours to a central hub in Memphis where from 11 PM to 3 AM each night all parcels were sorted, then reloaded on company planes, and flown during the early morning hours to their destination points, where they were delivered the next morning by company personnel using company trucks. The cost structure so achieved by Federal Express was low enough to permit it to guarantee overnight delivery of a small parcel anywhere in the United States for a price as low as $11. In 1986, Federal Express had a 58 percent market share of the air-express package delivery market versus a 15 percent share for UPS, 11 percent for Airborne Express, and 10 percent for Emery/Purolator.

Source: Based on information in Michael E. Porter, *Competitive Advantage* (New York: Free Press, 1985), p. 109.

margins or greater sales volume). Low cost is a powerful defense in markets where price competition thrives.

- In defending against the power of *buyers,* low costs provide a company with partial profit-margin protection, since powerful customers are rarely able to bargain price down past the survival level of the next most cost-efficient seller.
- In countering the bargaining leverage of *suppliers,* the low-cost producer is more insulated than competitors from powerful suppliers *if* the primary source of its cost advantage is greater internal efficiency. (A low-cost provider whose cost advantage stems from being able to buy components at favorable prices from outside suppliers could be vulnerable to the actions of powerful suppliers.)
- As concerns *potential entrants,* the low-cost leader can use price-cutting to make it harder for a new rival to win customers; the pricing power of the low-cost provider acts as a barrier for new entrants.
- In competing against *substitutes,* a low-cost leader is better positioned to use low price as a defense against companies trying to gain market inroads with a substitute product or service.

A low-cost company's ability to set the industry's price floor and still earn a profit erects barriers around its market position. Anytime price competition becomes a major market force, less efficient rivals get squeezed the most. Firms in a low-cost position relative to rivals have a competitive edge in meeting the demands of buyers who want low price.

A low-cost leader is in the strongest position to set the floor on market price.

When a Low-Cost Provider Strategy Works Best A competitive strategy predicated on low-cost leadership is particularly powerful when

1. Price competition among rival sellers is especially vigorous.
2. The industry's product is essentially standardized or a commodity readily available from a host of sellers (a condition that allows buyers to shop for the best price).
3. There are few ways to achieve product differentiation that have value to buyers (put another way, the differences between brands do not matter much to buyers), thereby making buyers very sensitive to price differences.
4. Most buyers utilize the product in the same ways—with common user requirements, a standardized product can satisfy the needs of buyers, in which case low selling price, not features or quality, becomes the dominant factor in causing buyers to choose one seller's product over another's.
5. Buyers incur low switching costs in changing from one seller to another, thus giving them the flexibility to switch readily to lower-priced sellers having equally good products.
6. Buyers are large and have significant power to bargain down prices.

As a rule, the more price sensitive buyers are and the more inclined they are to base their purchasing decisions on which seller offers the best price, the more appealing a low-cost strategy becomes. In markets where rivals compete mainly on price, low cost relative to competitors is the only competitive advantage that matters.

The Risks of a Low-Cost Provider Strategy A low-cost competitive approach has its drawbacks though. Technological breakthroughs can open up cost reductions for rivals that nullify a low-cost leader's past investments and hard-won gains in efficiency. Rival firms may find it easy and/or inexpensive to imitate the leader's low-cost methods, thus making any advantage short-lived. A company driving zealously to push its costs down can become so fixated on cost reduction that it fails to react to subtle but significant market swings—like growing buyer interest in added features or service, new developments in related products that start to alter how buyers use the product, or declining buyer sensitivity to price. The low-cost zealot risks getting left behind as buyers opt for enhanced quality, innovative performance features, faster service, and other differentiating features. Again, heavy investments in cost reduction can lock a firm into both its present technology and present strategy, leaving it vulnerable to new technologies and to growing customer interest in something other than a cheaper price.

To avoid the risks and pitfalls of a low-cost leadership strategy, managers must understand that the strategic target is *low cost relative to competitors,* not absolute low cost. In pursuing low-cost leadership, managers must take care not to strip away features and services that buyers consider essential. Furthermore, from a competitive strategy perspective, the value of a cost advantage depends on its sustainability. Sustainability, in turn, hinges on whether the company achieves its cost advantage in ways difficult for rivals to copy or match.

DIFFERENTIATION STRATEGIES

The essence of a differentiation strategy is to be unique in ways that are valuable to customers and that can be sustained.

Differentiation strategies become an attractive competitive approach whenever buyers' needs and preferences are too diverse to be fully satisfied by a standardized product. To be successful with a differentiation strategy, a company has to study buyers' needs and behavior carefully to learn what buyers consider important, what they think has value, and what they are willing to pay for. Then the company has to incorporate one, or maybe several, attributes and features with buyer appeal into its product/service offering—enough to set its offering visibly and distinctively apart. Competitive advantage results once a sufficient number of buyers become strongly attached to the differentiated attributes and features. The stronger the buyer appeal of the differentiated features, the stronger the company's competitive advantage.

Successful differentiation allows a firm to

- Command a premium price for its product, and/or
- Increase unit sales (because additional buyers are won over by the differentiating features), and/or
- Gain buyer loyalty to its brand (because some buyers are strongly attracted to the differentiating features).

Differentiation enhances profitability whenever the extra price the product commands outweighs the added costs of achieving the differentiation. Company differentiation strategies fail when buyers don't value the brand's uniqueness enough to buy it instead of rivals' brands and/or when a company's approach to differentiation is easily copied or matched by its rivals.

Types of Differentiation Themes Companies can pursue differentiation from many angles: a different taste (Dr Pepper and Listerine), special features (Jenn Air's indoor-cooking tops with a vented built-in grill for barbecuing), superior service (Federal Express in overnight package delivery), spare parts availability (Caterpillar guarantees 48-hour spare parts delivery to any customer anywhere in the world or else the part is furnished free), more for the money (McDonald's and Wal-Mart), engineering design and performance (Mercedes in automobiles), prestige and distinctiveness (Rolex in watches), product reliability (Johnson & Johnson in baby products), quality manufacture (Karastan in carpets and Honda in automobiles), technological leadership (3M Corporation in bonding and coating products), a full range of services (Merrill Lynch), a complete line of products (Campbell's soups), and top-of-the-line image and reputation (Brooks Brothers and Ralph Lauren in menswear, Kitchen Aid in dishwashers, and Cross in writing instruments).

Activities Where Differentiation Opportunities Exist Differentiation is not something hatched in marketing and advertising departments, nor is it limited to the catchalls of quality and service. The possibilities for successful differentiation exist in activities performed anywhere in the industry's value chain. The most common places in the chain where differentiation opportunities exist include:

1. *Purchasing and procurement activities* that ultimately spill over to affect the performance or quality of the company's end product. (McDonald's gets high ratings on its french fries partly because it has very strict specifications on the potatoes purchased from suppliers.)

2. *Product-oriented R&D activities* that hold potential for improved designs and performance features, expanded end uses and applications, wider product

variety, shorter lead times in developing new models, more frequent first-on-the-market victories, added user safety, greater recycling capability, and enhanced environmental protection.

3. *Production process–oriented R&D activities* that allow custom-order manufacture, environmentally safe production methods, and improved product quality, reliability, or appearance.

4. *Manufacturing activities* that can reduce product defects, prevent premature product failure, extend product life, allow better warranty coverages, improve economy of use, result in more end-user convenience, and enhance product appearance. (The quality edge enjoyed by Japanese automakers stems from their superior performance of manufacturing and assembly-line activities.)

5. *Outbound logistics and distribution activities* that allow for faster delivery, more accurate order filling, and fewer warehouse and on-the-shelf stockouts.

6. *Marketing, sales, and customer service activities* that can result in such differentiating attributes as superior technical assistance to buyers, faster maintenance and repair services, more and better product information provided to customers, more and better training materials for end users, better credit terms, quicker order processing, more frequent sales calls, and greater customer convenience. (IBM boosts buyer value by providing its mainframe computer customers with extensive technical support and round-the-clock operating maintenance.)

Managers need a full understanding of the sources of differentiation and the activities that drive uniqueness to devise a sound differentiation strategy and evaluate various differentiation approaches.[6]

Achieving a Differentiation-Based Competitive Advantage   One key to a successful differentiation strategy is to create buyer value in ways unmatched by rivals. There are three approaches to creating buyer value. One is to incorporate product attributes and user features that lower the buyer's overall costs of using the company's product—Illustration Capsule 14 lists options for making a company's product more economical to use. A second approach is to incorporate features that raise the performance a buyer gets out of the product—Illustration Capsule 15 contains differentiation avenues that enhance product performance and buyer value.

A differentiator's basis for competitive advantage is a product whose attributes differ significantly from the products of rivals.

A third approach is to incorporate features that enhance buyer satisfaction in noneconomic or intangible ways. Goodyear's new Aquatread tire design appeals to safety-conscious motorists wary of slick roads in rainy weather. Wal-Mart's campaign to feature products "Made in America" appeals to customers concerned about the loss of American jobs to foreign manufacturers. Rolex, Jaguar, Cartier, Ritz-Carlton, and Gucci have differentiation-based competitive advantages linked to buyer desires for status, image, prestige, upscale fashion, superior craftsmanship, and the finer things in life. L. L. Bean makes its mail-order customers feel secure in their purchases by providing an unconditional guarantee with no time limit: "All of our products are guaranteed to give 100 percent satisfaction in every way. Return anything purchased from us at anytime if it proves otherwise. We will replace it, refund your purchase price, or credit your credit card, as you wish."

[6]Porter, *Competitive Advantage,* p. 124.

ILLUSTRATION CAPSULE 14

DIFFERENTIATING FEATURES THAT LOWER BUYER COSTS

A company doesn't have to lower price to make it cheaper for a buyer to use its product. An alternative is to incorporate features and attributes into the company's product/service package that

- Reduce the buyer's scrap and raw materials waste. Example of differentiating feature: cut-to-size components.
- Lower the buyer's labor costs (less time, less training, lower skill requirements). Examples of differentiating features: snap-on assembly features, modular replacement of worn-out components.
- Cut the buyer's downtime or idle time. Examples of differentiating features: greater product reliability, ready spare parts availability, or less frequent maintenance requirements.
- Reduce the buyer's inventory costs. Example of differentiating feature: just-in-time delivery.
- Reduce the buyer's pollution control costs or waste disposal costs. Example of differentiating feature: scrap pickup for use in recycling.
- Reduce the buyer's procurement and order-processing costs. Example of differentiating

feature: computerized on-line ordering and billing procedures.
- Lower the buyer's maintenance and repair costs. Example of differentiating feature: superior product reliability.
- Lower the buyer's installation, delivery, or financing costs. Example of differentiating feature: 90-day payment same as cash.
- Reduce the buyer's need for other inputs (energy, safety equipment, security personnel, inspection personnel, other tools and machinery). Example of differentiating feature: fuel-efficient power equipment.
- Raise the trade-in value of used models.
- Lower the buyer's replacement or repair costs if the product unexpectedly fails later. Example of differentiating feature: longer warranty coverage.
- Lower the buyer's need for technical personnel. Example of differentiating feature: free technical support and assistance.
- Boost the efficiency of the buyer's production process. Examples of differentiating features: faster processing speeds, better interface with ancillary equipment.

Source: Adapted from Michael E. Porter, *Competitive Advantage* (New York: Free Press, 1985), pp. 135–37.

A firm whose differentiation strategy delivers only modest extra value but clearly signals that extra value may command a higher price than a firm that actually delivers higher value but signals it poorly.

Real Value, Perceived Value, and Signals of Value Buyers seldom pay for value they don't perceive, no matter how real the unique extras may be.[7] Thus the price premium that a differentiation strategy commands reflects *the value actually delivered* to the buyer and *the value perceived* by the buyer (even if not actually delivered). Actual and perceived value can differ whenever buyers have trouble assessing what their experience with the product will be. Incomplete knowledge on the part of buyers often causes them to judge value based on such *signals* as price (where price connotes quality), attractive packaging, extensive ad campaigns (i.e., how well-known the product is), ad content and image, the quality of brochures and sales presentations, the seller's facilities, the seller's list of customers, the firm's market share, length of time the firm has been in business, and the professionalism, appearance, and personality of the seller's employees. Such signals of value may be as important as actual value (1) when the nature of differentiation is subjective or hard to quantify, (2) when buyers are making a first-time purchase, (3) when repurchase is infrequent, and (4) when buyers are unsophisticated.

[7]This discussion draws from Porter, *Competitive Advantage*, pp. 138–42. Porter's insights here are particularly important to formulating differentiating strategies because they highlight the relevance of "intangibles" and "signals."

ILLUSTRATION CAPSULE 15

DIFFERENTIATING FEATURES THAT RAISE THE PERFORMANCE A USER GETS

To enhance the performance a buyer gets from using its product/service, a company can incorporate features and attributes that

- Provide buyers greater reliability, durability, convenience, or ease of use.
- Make the company's product/service cleaner, safer, quieter, or more maintenance-free than rival brands.

- Exceed environmental or regulatory standards.
- Meet the buyer's needs and requirements more completely, compared to competitors' offerings.
- Give buyers the option to add on or to upgrade later as new product versions come on the market.
- Give buyers more flexibility to tailor their own products to the needs of their customers.
- Do a better job of meeting the buyer's future growth and expansion requirements.

Source: Adapted from Michael E. Porter, *Competitive Advantage,* (New York: Free Press, 1985), pp. 135–38.

Keeping the Cost of Differentiation in Line Once company managers identify what approach to creating buyer value and establishing a differentiation-based competitive advantage makes the most sense given the nature of the company's product/service and competitive situation, they must build the value-creating attributes into the product at an acceptable cost. Attempts to achieve differentiation usually raise costs. The trick to profitable differentiation is either to keep the costs of achieving differentiation below the price premium the differentiating attributes can command in the marketplace (thus increasing the profit margin per unit sold) or offset thinner profit margins with enough added volume to increase total profits (larger volume can make up for smaller margins provided differentiation adds enough extra sales). It usually makes sense to add extra differentiating features that are not costly but add to buyer satisfaction—fine restaurants typically provide such extras as a slice of lemon in the water glass, valet parking, and complimentary after-dinner mints. The overriding condition in pursuing differentiation is that a firm must be careful not to get its unit costs so far out of line with competitors' that it has to charge a higher price than buyers are willing to pay.

What Makes a Differentiation Strategy Attractive Differentiation offers a buffer against the strategies of rivals when it results in enhanced buyer loyalty to a company's brand or model and greater willingness to pay a little (perhaps a lot!) more for it. In addition, successful differentiation (1) erects entry barriers in the form of customer loyalty and uniqueness that newcomers find hard to hurdle, (2) mitigates buyers' bargaining power since the products of alternative sellers are less attractive to them, and (3) helps a firm fend off threats from substitutes not having comparable features or attributes. To the extent that differentiation allows a company to charge a higher price and have bigger profit margins, it is in a stronger position to withstand the efforts of powerful vendors to get a higher price for the items they supply. Thus, as with cost leadership, successful differentiation creates lines of defense for dealing with the five competitive forces.

For the most part, differentiation strategies work best in markets where (1) there are many ways to differentiate the product or service and many buyers perceive these differences as having value, (2) buyer needs and uses of the item or service are diverse, and (3) few rival firms are following a similar differentiation approach.

The most appealing approaches to differentiation are those that are hard or expensive for rivals to duplicate. Easy-to-copy differentiating features cannot produce sustainable competitive advantage. Indeed, resourceful competitors can, in time, clone almost any product. This is why sustainable differentiation usually has to be linked to unique internal skills and core competencies. When a company has skills and capabilities that competitors cannot readily match and when its expertise can be used to perform activities in the value chain where differentiation potential exists, then it has a strong basis for sustainable differentiation. As a rule, differentiation yields a longer-lasting and more profitable competitive edge when it is based on

- Technical superiority.
- Product quality.
- Comprehensive customer service.

Such differentiating attributes are widely perceived by buyers as having value; moreover, the skills and expertise required to produce them tend to be tougher for rivals to copy or overcome profitably.

The Risks of a Differentiation Strategy   There are, of course, no guarantees that differentiation will produce a meaningful competitive advantage. If buyers see little value in uniqueness (i.e., a standard item meets their needs), then a low-cost strategy can easily defeat a differentiation strategy. In addition, differentiation can be defeated if competitors can quickly copy most or all of the appealing product attributes a company comes up with. Rapid imitation means that a firm never achieves real differentiation since competing brands keep changing in like ways each time a company makes a new move to set its offering apart from rivals'. Thus, to be successful at differentiation a firm must search out lasting sources of uniqueness that are burdensome for rivals to overcome. Aside from these considerations, other common pitfalls in pursuing differentiation include[8]

> A low-cost producer strategy can defeat a differentiation strategy when buyers are satisfied with a basic product and don't think "extra" attributes are worth a higher price.

- Trying to differentiate on the basis of something that does not lower a buyer's cost or enhance a buyer's well-being, as perceived by the buyer.
- Overdifferentiating so that price is too high relative to competitors, or product quality or service levels exceed buyers' needs.
- Trying to charge too high a price premium (the bigger the price differential the harder it is to keep buyers from switching to lower-priced competitors).
- Ignoring the need to signal value and depending only on intrinsic product attributes to achieve differentiation.
- Not understanding or identifying what buyers consider as value.

THE STRATEGY OF BEING A BEST-COST PROVIDER

This strategy aims at giving customers *more value for the money.* It combines a strategic emphasis on low cost with a strategic emphasis on *more than minimally acceptable* quality, service, features, and performance. The idea is to create superior

---

[8]Porter, *Competitive Advantage,* pp. 160–62.

value by meeting or exceeding buyers' expectations on quality-service-features-performance attributes and by beating their expectations on price. The strategic objective is to become the low-cost provider of a product or service with *good-to-excellent* attributes, then use the cost advantage to underprice brands with comparable attributes. Such a competitive approach is termed a *best-cost provider strategy* because the producer has the best (lowest) cost relative to producers whose brands are comparably positioned on the quality-service-features-performance scale.

The competitive advantage of a best-cost provider comes from matching close rivals on key quality-service-features-performance dimensions and beating them on cost. To become a best-cost provider, a company must match quality at a lower cost than rivals, match features at a lower cost than rivals, match product performance at a lower cost than rivals, and so on. What distinguishes a successful best-cost provider is expertise in incorporating upscale product or service attributes at a low cost, or, to put it a bit differently, an ability to contain the costs of providing customers with a better product. The most successful best-cost producers have the skills to simultaneously manage unit costs down and product calibre up—see Illustration Capsule 16.

A best-cost provider strategy has great appeal from the standpoint of competitive positioning. It produces superior customer value by balancing a strategic emphasis on low cost against a strategic emphasis on differentiation. In effect, it is a *hybrid* strategy that allows a company to combine the competitive advantage of both low cost and differentiation to arrive at superior buyer value. In markets where buyer diversity makes product differentiation the norm and many buyers are price and value sensitive, a best-cost producer strategy can be more advantageous than either a pure low-cost producer strategy or a pure differentiation strategy keyed to product superiority. This is because a best-cost provider can position itself near the middle of the market with either a medium-quality product at a below-average price or a very good product at a medium price. Often the majority of buyers prefer a mid-range product rather than the cheap, basic product of a low-cost producer or the expensive product of a top-of-the-line differentiator.

The most powerful competitive approach a company can pursue is to strive relentlessly to become a lower-and-lower-cost producer of a higher-and-higher-caliber product, with the intention of eventually becoming the industry's absolute lowest-cost producer and, simultaneously, the producer of the industry's overall best product.

FOCUSED OR MARKET NICHE STRATEGIES

What sets focused strategies apart from low-cost or differentiation strategies is concentrated attention on a narrow piece of the total market. The target segment or niche can be defined by geographic uniqueness, by specialized requirements in using the product, or by special product attributes that appeal only to niche members. The objective is to do a better job of serving buyers in the target market niche than rival competitors. *A focuser's basis for competitive advantage is either (1) lower costs than competitors in serving the market niche or (2) an ability to offer niche members something different from other competitors.* A focused strategy based on low cost depends on there being a buyer segment whose requirements are less costly to satisfy compared to the rest of the market. A focused strategy based on differentiation depends on there being a buyer segment that demands unique product attributes.

Examples of firms employing some version of a focused strategy include Tandem Computers (a specialist in "nonstop" computers for customers who need a "fail-safe" system), Rolls Royce (in super luxury automobiles), Cannondale (in top-of-the-line mountain bikes), Fort Howard Paper (specializing in paper products for industrial and commercial enterprises only), commuter airlines like Horizon and Atlantic Southeast (specializing in low-traffic, short-haul flights linking major airports with

ILLUSTRATION CAPSULE 16

TOYOTA'S BEST-COST PRODUCER STRATEGY FOR ITS LEXUS LINE

Toyota Motor Co. is widely regarded as the leading low-cost producer among the world's motor vehicle manufacturers. Despite its emphasis on product quality, Toyota has achieved absolute low-cost leadership because of its considerable skills in efficient manufacturing techniques and because its models are positioned in the low-to-medium end of the price spectrum where high production volumes are conducive to low unit costs. But when Toyota decided to introduce its new Lexus models to compete in the luxury-car market, it employed a classic best-cost producer strategy. Toyota's Lexus strategy had three features:

- Transferring its expertise in making high-quality Toyota models at low cost to making premium quality luxury cars at costs below other luxury-car makers, especially Mercedes and BMW. Toyota executives reasoned that Toyota's manufacturing skills should allow it to incorporate high-tech performance features and upscale quality into Lexus models at less cost than other luxury-car manufacturers.

- Using its relatively lower manufacturing costs to underprice Mercedes and BMW, both of which had models selling in the $40,000 to $75,000 range (and some even higher). Toyota believed that with its cost advantage it could price

attractively equipped Lexus models in the $38,000 to $42,000 range, drawing price-conscious buyers away from Mercedes and BMW and perhaps inducing quality-conscious Lincoln and Cadillac owners to trade up to a Lexus.

- Establishing a new network of Lexus dealers, separate from Toyota dealers, dedicated to providing a level of personalized, attentive customer service unmatched in the industry.

In the 1993–94 model years, the Lexus 400 series models were priced in the $40,000 to $45,000 range and competed against Mercedes's 300/400E series, BMW's 525i/535i series, Nissan's Infiniti Q45, Cadillac Seville, Jaguar, and Lincoln's Continental Mark VIII series. The lower-priced Lexus 300 series, priced in the $30,000 to $38,000 range, competed against Cadillac Eldorado, Acura Legend, Infiniti J30, Buick Park Avenue, Mercedes's new C-Class series, BMW's 315 series, and Oldsmobile's new Aurora line.

Lexus's best-cost producer strategy was so successful that Mercedes, plagued by sagging sales and concerns about overpricing, reduced its prices significantly on its 1994 models and introduced a new C-Class series, priced in the $30,000 to $35,000 range, to become more competitive. The Lexus LS 400 models and the Lexus SC 300/400 models ranked first and second, respectively, in the widely watched J. D. Power & Associates quality survey for 1993 cars; the entry-level Lexus ES 300 model ranked eighth.

smaller cities 50 to 250 miles away), and Bandag (a specialist in truck tire recapping that promotes its recaps aggressively at over 1,000 truck stops). Illustration Capsule 17 describes Motel 6's focused low-cost strategy and Ritz-Carlton's focused differentiation strategy.

Using a focused strategy to compete on the basis of low cost is a fairly common business approach. Producers of private-label goods have lowered their marketing, distribution, and advertising costs by concentrating on direct sales to retailers and chain discounters who stock a no-frills house brand to sell at discount to name brand merchandise. Discount stock brokerage houses have lowered costs by focusing on customers who are willing to forgo the investment research, advice, and financial services offered by full-service firms like Merrill Lynch in return for 30 percent or more commission savings on their buy-sell transactions. Pursuing a cost advantage via focusing works well when a firm can find ways to lower costs significantly by limiting its customer base to a well-defined buyer segment.

At the other end of the market spectrum, companies like Ritz-Carlton, Tiffany's, Porsche, Haagen-Dazs, and W. L. Gore (the maker of Gore-tex) crafted successful differentiation-based focused strategies targeted at upscale buyers wanting

ILLUSTRATION CAPSULE 17

FOCUSED STRATEGIES IN THE LODGING INDUSTRY: MOTEL 6 AND RITZ-CARLTON

Motel 6 and Ritz-Carlton compete at opposite ends of the lodging industry. Motel 6 employs a focused strategy keyed to low cost; Ritz-Carlton employs a focused strategy based on differentiation.

Motel 6 caters to price-conscious travelers who want a clean, no-frills place to spend the night. To be a low-cost provider of overnight lodging, Motel 6 (1) selects relatively inexpensive sites on which to construct its units—usually near interstate exits and high traffic locations but far enough away to avoid paying prime site prices; (2) builds only basic facilities—no restaurant or bar and only rarely a swimming pool; (3) relies on standard architectural designs that incorporate inexpensive materials and low-cost construction techniques; and (4) has simple room furnishings and decorations. These approaches lower both investment costs and operating costs. Without restaurants, bars, and all kinds of guest services, a Motel 6 unit can be operated with just front desk personnel, room cleanup crews, and skeleton building-and-grounds maintenance. To promote the Motel 6 concept with travelers who have simple overnight requirements, the chain uses unique, rec-ognizable radio ads done by nationally syndicated radio personality Tom Bodett; the ads describe Motel 6's clean rooms, no-frills facilities, friendly atmosphere, and dependably low rates (usually under $30 per night).

In contrast, the Ritz-Carlton caters to discriminating travelers and vacationers willing and able to pay for top-of-the-line accommodations and world-class personal service. Ritz-Carlton hotels feature (1) prime locations and scenic views from many rooms, (2) custom architectural designs, (3) fine dining restaurants with gourmet menus prepared by accomplished chefs, (4) elegantly appointed lobbies and bar lounges, (5) swimming pools, exercise facilities, and leisure time options, (6) upscale room accommodations, (7) an array of guest services and recreation opportunities appropriate to the location, and (8) large, well-trained professional staffs who do their utmost to make each guest's stay an enjoyable experience.

Both companies concentrate their attention on a narrow piece of the total market. Motel 6's basis for competitive advantage is lower costs than competitors in providing basic, economical overnight accommodations to price-constrained travelers. Ritz-Carlton's advantage is its capability to provide superior accommodations and unmatched personal service for a well-to-do clientele. Each is able to succeed, despite polar opposite strategies, because the market for lodging consists of diverse buyer segments with diverse preferences and abilities to pay.

products/services with world-class attributes. Indeed, most markets contain a buyer segment willing to pay a big price premium for the very finest items available, thus opening the strategic window for some competitors to employ differentiation-based focused strategies aimed at the very top of the market pyramid.

When Focusing Is Attractive A focused strategy based either on low cost or differentiation becomes increasingly attractive as more of the following conditions are met:

- The segment is big enough to be profitable.
- The segment has good growth potential.
- The segment is not crucial to the success of major competitors.
- The focusing firm has the skills and resources to serve the segment effectively.
- The focuser can defend itself against challengers based on the customer goodwill it has built up and its superior ability to serve buyers in the segment.

A focuser's specialized skills in serving the target market niche provide a basis for defending against the five competitive forces. Multisegment rivals may not have the same competitive capability to serve the focused firm's target clientele. The focused firm's competence in serving the market niche raises entry barriers, thus making it harder for companies outside the niche to enter. A focuser's unique capabilities in serving the niche also present a hurdle that makers of substitute products must overcome. The bargaining leverage of powerful customers is blunted somewhat by their own unwillingness to shift their business to rival companies less capable of meeting their expectations.

Focusing works best (1) when it is costly or difficult for multisegment competitors to meet the specialized needs of the target market niche, (2) when no other rival is attempting to specialize in the same target segment, (3) when a firm doesn't have the resources to go after a wider part of the total market, and (4) when the industry has many different segments, thereby allowing a focuser to pick an attractive segment suited to its strengths and capabilities.

The Risks of a Focused Strategy   Focusing carries several risks. One is the chance that competitors will find effective ways to match the focused firm in serving the narrow target market. A second is the potential for the niche buyer's preferences and needs to shift toward the product attributes desired by the market as a whole. An erosion of the differences across buyer segments lowers entry barriers into a focuser's market niche and provides an open invitation for rivals in adjacent segments to begin competing for the focuser's customers. A third risk is that the segment becomes so attractive it is soon inundated with competitors, causing segment profits to be splintered.

USING OFFENSIVE STRATEGIES TO SECURE COMPETITIVE ADVANTAGE

Competitive advantage is nearly always achieved by successful offensive strategic moves; defensive strategies can protect competitive advantage but rarely are the basis for achieving competitive advantage. How long it takes for a successful offensive to create an edge is a function of the industry's competitive characteristics.[9] The *buildup period,* shown in Figure 5–2, can be short, as in service businesses that need little in the way of equipment and distribution system support to implement a new offensive move. Or the buildup can take much longer, as in capital intensive and technologically sophisticated industries where firms may need several years to debug a new technology, bring new capacity on-line, and win consumer acceptance of a new product. Ideally, an offensive move builds competitive advantage quickly; the longer it takes, the more likely rivals will spot the move, see its potential, and begin a counter-response. The size of the advantage (indicated on the vertical scale in Figure 5–2) can be large (as in pharmaceuticals where patents on an important new drug produce a substantial advantage) or small (as in apparel where popular new designs can be imitated quickly).

Following a successful competitive offensive is a *benefit period* during which the fruits of competitive advantage can be enjoyed. The length of the benefit period depends on how much time it takes rivals to launch counteroffensives and begin closing the competitive gap. A lengthy benefit period gives a firm valuable time to earn above-average profits and recoup the investment made in creating the advantage. The best strategic offensives produce big competitive advantages and long benefit periods.

> Competitive advantage is usually acquired by employing a creative offensive strategy that isn't easily thwarted by rivals.

---

[9]Ian C. MacMillan, "How Long Can You Sustain a Competitive Advantage?" reprinted in Liam Fahey, *The Strategic Planning Management Reader* (Englewood Cliffs, N.J.: Prentice-Hall, 1989), pp. 23–24.

F I G U R E 5–2 | **The Building and Eroding of Competitive Advantage**

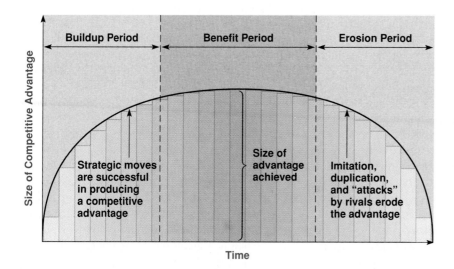

As competitors respond with serious counteroffensives to attack the advantage, the *erosion period* begins. Any competitive advantage a firm currently holds will eventually be eroded by the actions of competent, resourceful competitors.[10] Thus, to sustain an initially won advantage, a firm must devise a second strategic offensive. The groundwork for the second offensive needs to be laid during the benefit period so that everything is ready for launch when competitors mount efforts to cut into the leader's advantage. To successfully sustain a competitive advantage, a company must stay a step ahead of rivals by initiating one creative strategic offensive after another to improve its market position and retain customer favor.

There are six basic types of strategic offensives:[11]

- Initiatives to match or exceed competitor strengths.
- Initiatives to capitalize on competitor weaknesses.
- Simultaneous initiatives on many fronts.
- End-run offensives.
- Guerrilla offensives.
- Preemptive strikes.

INITIATIVES TO MATCH OR EXCEED COMPETITOR STRENGTHS

There are two good reasons to go head-to-head against rival companies, pitting one's own strengths against theirs, price for price, model for model, promotion tactic for promotion tactic, and geographic area by geographic area. The first is to try to gain market share by outcompeting weaker rivals. Challenging weaker rivals where they

[10]Ian C. MacMillan, "Controlling Competitive Dynamics by Taking Strategic Initiative," *The Academy of Management Executive* 2, no. 2 (May 1988), p. 111.

[11]Philip Kotler and Ravi Singh, "Marketing Warfare in the 1980s," *The Journal of Business Strategy* 1, no. 3 (Winter 1981), pp. 30–41; Philip Kotler, *Marketing Management,* 5th ed. (Englewood Cliffs, N.J.: Prentice-Hall, 1984), pp. 401–6; and Ian MacMillan, "Preemptive Strategies," *Journal of Business Strategy* 14, no. 2 (Fall 1983), pp. 16–26.

are strongest is attractive whenever a firm has a superior product offering and the organizational capabilities to win profitable sales and market share away from less competent and less resourceful competitors. The other reason is to whittle away at a strong rival's competitive advantage. Here success is measured by how much the competitive gap is narrowed. The merits of a strength-against-strength offensive challenge, of course, depend on how much the offensive costs compared to its competitive benefits. To succeed, the initiator needs enough competitive strength and resources to take at least some market share from the targeted rivals. Absent good prospects for long-term competitive gains and added profitability, such an offensive is ill-advised.

> One of the most powerful offensive strategies is to challenge rivals with an equally good or better product at a lower price.

Attacking a competitor's strengths can involve initiatives on any of several fronts—price-cutting, running comparison ads, adding new features that appeal to the rival's customers, constructing major new plant capacity in the rival's backyard, or bringing out new models to match the rival model for model. In one classic ploy, the aggressor challenges the targeted rival with an equally good offering at a lower price.[12] This can produce market share gains if the targeted rival has strong reasons for not resorting to price cuts of its own and if the challenger convinces buyers that its product is just as good. However, such a strategy increases profits only if volume gains offset the impact of thinner margins per unit sold.

> Challenging larger, entrenched competitors with aggressive price-cutting is foolhardy unless the aggressor has either a cost advantage or greater financial strength.

Another way to mount a price-aggressive challenge is to first achieve a cost advantage and then hit competitors with a lower price.[13] Price-cutting supported by a cost advantage is perhaps the strongest basis for launching and sustaining a price-aggressive offensive. Without a cost advantage, price-cutting works only if the aggressor has more financial resources and can outlast its rivals in a war of attrition.

INITIATIVES TO CAPITALIZE ON COMPETITOR WEAKNESSES

In this offensive approach, a company tries to gain market inroads by directing its competitive attention to the weaknesses of rivals. There are a number of ways to achieve competitive gains at the expense of rivals' weaknesses:

- Concentrate on geographic regions where a rival has a weak market share or is exerting less competitive effort.
- Pay special attention to buyer segments that a rival is neglecting or is weakly equipped to serve.
- Go after the customers of those rivals whose products lag on quality, features, or product performance; in such cases, a challenger with a better product can often convince the most performance-conscious customers to switch to its brand.
- Make special sales pitches to the customers of those rivals who provide subpar customer service—it may be relatively easy for a service-oriented challenger to win a rival's disenchanted customers.
- Try to move in on rivals that have weak advertising and weak brand recognition—a challenger with strong marketing skills and a recognized brand name can often win customers away from lesser-known rivals.
- Introduce new models or product versions that exploit gaps in the product lines of key rivals; sometimes "gap fillers" turn out to be a market hit and develop

---

[12]Kotler, *Marketing Management,* p. 402.
[13]Kotler, *Marketing Management,* p. 403.

into new growth segments—witness Chrysler's success in minivans. This initiative works well when new product versions satisfy certain buyer needs that heretofore have been ignored or neglected.

As a rule, initiatives that exploit competitor weaknesses stand a better chance of succeeding than do those that challenge competitor strengths, especially if the weaknesses represent important vulnerabilities and the rival is caught by surprise with no ready defense.[14]

SIMULTANEOUS INITIATIVES ON MANY FRONTS

On occasion a company may see merit in launching a grand competitive offensive involving multiple initiatives (price cuts, increased advertising, new product introductions, free samples, coupons, in-store promotions, rebates) across a wide geographic and competitive front. Such all-out campaigns can throw a rival off-balance, diverting its attention in many directions and forcing it to protect many pieces of its customer base simultaneously. Hunt's ketchup tried such an offensive several years ago in an attempt to wrest market share away from Heinz. The attack began when Hunt's introduced two new ketchup flavors (pizza and hickory) to disrupt consumers' taste preferences, create new flavor segments, and capture more shelf space in retail stores. Simultaneously, Hunt's lowered its price to 70 percent of Heinz's price, offered sizable trade allowances to retailers, and raised its advertising budget to over twice the level of Heinz's.[15] The offensive failed because not enough Heinz users tried the Hunt's brands, and many of those who did soon switched back to Heinz. Wide-scale offensives have their best chance of success when a challenger with an attractive product or service also has the financial resources to outspend rivals in courting customers; then it may be able to blitz the market with an array of promotional offers sufficient to entice large numbers of buyers to switch their brand allegiance.

END-RUN OFFENSIVES

End-run offensives seek to avoid head-on challenges tied to aggressive price-cutting, escalated advertising, or costly efforts to outdifferentiate rivals. Instead the idea is to maneuver *around* competitors and be the first to enter unoccupied market territory. Examples of end-run offensives include moving aggressively into geographic areas where close rivals have little or no market presence, trying to create new segments by introducing products with different attributes and performance features to better meet the needs of selected buyers, and leapfrogging into next-generation technologies to supplant existing products and/or production processes. With an end-run offensive, a company can gain a significant first-mover advantage in a new arena and force competitors to play catch-up. The most successful end-runs change the rules of the competitive game in the aggressor's favor.

GUERRILLA OFFENSIVES

Guerrilla offensives are particularly well-suited to small challengers who have neither the resources nor the market visibility to mount a full-fledged attack on industry leaders. A guerrilla offensive uses the hit-and-run principle, selectively attacking

---

[14]For a discussion of the use of surprise, see William E. Rothschild, "Surprise and the Competitive Advantage," *Journal of Business Strategy* 4, no. 3 (Winter 1984), pp. 10–18.

[15]As cited in Kotler, *Marketing Management,* p. 404.

where and when an underdog can temporarily exploit the situation to its own advantage. There are several ways to wage a guerrilla offensive:[16]

1. Go after buyer groups that are not important to major rivals.

2. Go after buyers whose loyalty to rival brands is weakest.

3. Focus on areas where rivals are overextended and have spread their resources most thinly (possibilities include going after selected customers located in isolated geographic areas, enhancing delivery schedules at times when competitors' deliveries are running behind, adding to quality when rivals have quality control problems, and boosting technical services when buyers are confused by competitors' proliferation of models and optional features).

4. Make small, scattered, random raids on the leaders' customers with such tactics as occasional lowballing on price (to win a big order or steal a key account).

5. Surprise key rivals with sporadic but intense bursts of promotional activity to pick off buyers who might otherwise have selected rival brands.

6. If rivals employ unfair or unethical competitive tactics and the situation merits it, file legal actions charging antitrust violations, patent infringement, or unfair advertising.

PREEMPTIVE STRIKES

Preemptive strategies involve moving first to secure an advantageous position that rivals are foreclosed or discouraged from duplicating. There are several ways to win a prime strategic position with preemptive moves:[17]

- Expand production capacity well ahead of market demand in hopes of discouraging rivals from following with expansions of their own. When rivals are "bluffed" out of adding capacity for fear of creating long-term excess supply and having to struggle with the bad profit economics of underutilized plants, the preemptor stands to win a bigger market share as market demand grows and it has the production capacity to take on new orders.

- Tie up the best (or the most) raw material sources and/or the most reliable, high-quality suppliers via long-term contracts or backward vertical integration. This move can relegate rivals to struggling for second-best supply positions.

- Secure the best geographic locations. An attractive first-mover advantage can often be locked up by moving to obtain the most favorable site along a heavily traveled thoroughfare, at a new interchange or intersection, in a new shopping mall, in a natural beauty spot, close to cheap transportation or raw material supplies or market outlets, and so on.

- Obtain the business of prestigious customers.

- Build a "psychological" image in the minds of consumers that is unique and hard to copy and that establishes a compelling appeal and rallying cry. Examples include Avis's well-known "We try harder" theme; Frito-Lay's guarantee to

---

[16]For more details, see Ian MacMillan "How Business Strategists Can Use Guerrilla Warfare Tactics," *Journal of Business Strategy* 1, no. 2 (Fall 1980), pp. 63–65; Kathryn R. Harrigan, *Strategic Flexibility* (Lexington, Mass.: Lexington Books, 1985), pp. 30–45; and Liam Fahey, "Guerrilla Strategy: The Hit-and-Run Attack," in Fahey, *The Strategic Management Planning Reader,* pp. 194–97.

[17]The use of preemptive moves is treated comprehensively in Ian MacMillan, "Preemptive Strategies," *Journal of Business Strategy,* pp. 16–26. What follows in this section is based on MacMillan's article.

retailers of "99.5% service"; Holiday Inn's assurance of "no surprises"; and Prudential's "piece of the rock" image of safety and permanence.

- Secure exclusive or dominant access to the best distributors in an area.

General Mills's Red Lobster restaurant chain succeeded in tying up access to excellent seafood suppliers. DeBeers became the dominant world distributor of diamonds by buying up the production of most of the important diamond mines. DuPont's aggressive capacity expansions in titanium dioxide, while not blocking all competitors from expanding, did discourage enough to give it a leadership position in the titanium dioxide industry. Fox's stunning $6.2 billion preemptive bid over CBS to televise NFL games is widely regarded as a strategic move to catapult Fox into the ranks of the major TV networks alongside ABC, CBS, and NBC.

To be successful, a preemptive move doesn't have to totally block rivals from following or copying; it merely needs to give a firm a "prime" position. A prime position is one that puts rivals at a competitive disadvantage and is not easily circumvented.

CHOOSING WHO TO ATTACK

Aggressor firms need to analyze which of their rivals to challenge as well as how to outcompete them. Four types of firms make good targets:[18]

1. *Market leaders.* Waging an offensive against strong leaders risks squandering valuable resources in a futile effort and perhaps even precipitating a fierce and profitless industrywide battle for market share—caution is well advised. Offensive attacks on a major competitor make the best sense when the leader in terms of size and market share is not a "true leader" in terms of serving the market well. Signs of leader vulnerability include unhappy buyers, sliding profits, strong emotional commitment to a technology the leader has pioneered, outdated plants and equipment, a preoccupation with diversification into other industries, a product line that is clearly not superior to what several rivals have, and a competitive strategy that lacks real strength based on low-cost leadership or differentiation. Attacks on leaders can also succeed when the challenger is able to revamp its value chain or innovate to gain a fresh cost-based or differentiation-based competitive advantage.[19] Attacks on leaders need not have the objective of making the aggressor the new leader, however; a challenger may "win" by simply wresting enough sales from the leader to make the aggressor a stronger runner-up.

2. *Runner-up firms.* Launching offensives against weaker runner-up firms whose positions are vulnerable entails relatively low risk. This is an especially attractive option when a challenger's competitive strengths match the runner-up's weaknesses.

3. *Struggling enterprises that are on the verge of going under.* Challenging a hard-pressed rival in ways that further sap its financial strength and competitive position can weaken its resolve and hasten its exit from the market.

4. *Small local and regional firms.* Because these firms typically have limited expertise, a challenger with broader capabilities is well-positioned to raid their biggest and best customers—particularly those who are growing rapidly, have increasingly sophisticated requirements, and may already be thinking about switching to a supplier with more full-service capability.

---

[18]Kotler, *Marketing Management,* p. 400.
[19]Porter, *Competitive Advantage,* p. 518.

As we have said, successful strategies are grounded in competitive advantage. This goes for offensive strategies too. The kinds of competitive advantages that usually offer the strongest basis for a strategic offensive include:[20]

- Having a lower-cost product design.
- Having lower-cost production capability.
- Having product features that deliver superior performance to buyers or that lower user costs.
- An ability to give buyers more responsive after-sale support.
- Having the resources to escalate the marketing effort in an undermarketed industry.
- Pioneering a new distribution channel.
- Having the capability to bypass wholesale distributors and sell direct to the end user.

Almost always, a strategic offensive should be tied to what a firm does best—its competitive strengths and capabilities. As a rule, these strengths should take the form of a *key skill* (cost reduction capabilities, customer service skills, technical expertise) a uniquely *strong functional competence* (engineering and product design, manufacturing expertise, advertising and promotion, marketing know-how) or *superior ability to perform key activities* in the value chain that lower cost or enhance differentiation.[21]

USING DEFENSIVE STRATEGIES TO PROTECT COMPETITIVE ADVANTAGE

The foremost purpose of defensive strategy is to protect competitive advantage and fortify the firm's competitive position.

In a competitive market, all firms are subject to challenges from rivals. Market offensives can come both from new entrants in the industry and from established firms seeking to improve their market positions. The purpose of defensive strategy is to lower the risk of being attacked, weaken the impact of any attack that occurs, and influence challengers to aim their efforts at other rivals. While defensive strategy usually doesn't enhance a firm's competitive advantage, it helps fortify a firm's competitive position and sustain whatever competitive advantage it does have.

There are several basic ways for a company to protect its competitive position. One approach involves trying to block the avenues challengers can take in mounting an offensive; the options include[22]

- Broadening the firm's product line to close off vacant niches and gaps to would-be challengers.
- Introducing models or brands that match the characteristics challengers' models already have or might have.
- Keeping prices low on models that most closely match competitors' offerings.
- Signing exclusive agreements with dealers and distributors to keep competitors from using the same ones.
- Granting dealers and distributors sizable volume discounts to discourage them from experimenting with other suppliers.

[20]Ibid., pp. 520–22.
[21]For more details, see MacMillan, "Controlling Competitive Dynamics," pp. 112–16.
[22]Porter, *Competitive Advantage,* pp. 489–94.

- Offering free or low-cost training to product users.
- Making it harder for competitors to get buyers to try their brands by (1) giving special price discounts to buyers who are considering trial use of rival brands, (2) resorting to high levels of couponing and sample giveaways to buyers most prone to experiment, and (3) making early announcements about impending new products or price changes to induce potential buyers to postpone switching.
- Raising the amount of financing provided to dealers and/or to buyers.
- Reducing delivery times for spare parts.
- Increasing warranty coverages.
- Patenting alternative technologies.
- Maintaining a participation in alternative technologies.
- Protecting proprietary know-how in product design, production technologies, and other strategy-critical value chain activities.
- Signing exclusive contracts with the best suppliers to block access of aggressive rivals.
- Purchasing natural resource reserves ahead of present needs to keep them from competitors.
- Avoiding suppliers that also serve competitors.
- Challenging rivals' products or practices in regulatory proceedings.

Moves such as these not only buttress a firm's present position, they also present competitors with a moving target. Protecting the status quo isn't enough. A good defense entails adjusting quickly to changing industry conditions and, on occasion, being a first-mover to block or preempt moves by would-be aggressors. A mobile defense is preferable to a stationary defense.

A second approach to defensive strategy entails signaling challengers that there is a real threat of strong retaliation if a challenger attacks. The goal is to dissuade challengers from attacking at all (by raising their expectations that the resulting battle will be more costly to the challenger than it is worth) or at least divert them to options that are less threatening to the defender. Would-be challengers can be signaled by[23]

- Publicly announcing management's commitment to maintain the firm's present market share.
- Publicly announcing plans to construct adequate production capacity to meet and possibly surpass the forecasted growth in industry volume.
- Giving out advance information about a new product, technology breakthrough, or the planned introduction of important new brands or models in hopes that challengers will be induced to delay moves of their own until they see if the announced actions actually are forthcoming.
- Publicly committing the company to a policy of matching competitors' terms or prices.
- Maintaining a war chest of cash and marketable securities.
- Making an occasional strong counter-response to the moves of weak competitors to enhance the firm's image as a tough defender.

Another way to dissuade rivals is to try to lower the profit inducement for challengers to launch an offensive. When a firm's or industry's profitability is enticingly high,

---

[23]Ibid., pp. 495–97. The listing here is selective; Porter offers a greater number of options.

challengers are more willing to tackle high defensive barriers and combat strong retaliation. A defender can deflect attacks, especially from new entrants, by deliberately forgoing some short-run profits and using accounting methods that obscure profitability.

VERTICAL INTEGRATION STRATEGIES AND COMPETITIVE ADVANTAGE

Vertical integration extends a firm's competitive scope within the same industry. It involves expanding the firm's range of activities backward into sources of supply and/or forward toward end users of the final product. Thus, if a manufacturer elects to build a new plant to make certain component parts rather than purchase them from outside suppliers, it remains in essentially the same industry as before. The only change is that it has business units in two production stages in the industry's value chain system. Similarly, if a personal computer manufacturer elects to integrate forward by opening 100 retail stores to market its brands directly to users, it remains in the personal computer business even though its competitive scope extends further forward in the industry chain.

Vertical integration strategies can aim at *full integration* (participating in all stages of the industry value chain) or *partial integration* (building positions in just some stages of the industry's total value chain). A firm can accomplish vertical integration by starting its own operations in other stages in the industry's activity chain or by acquiring a company already performing the activities it wants to bring in-house.

THE STRATEGIC ADVANTAGES OF VERTICAL INTEGRATION

The only good reason for investing company resources in vertical integration is to strengthen the firm's competitive position.[24] Unless vertical integration produces sufficient cost savings to justify the extra investment or yields a competitive advantage, it has no real payoff profitwise or strategywise.

Integrating backward generates cost savings only when the volume needed is big enough to capture the same scale economies suppliers have and when suppliers' production efficiency can be matched or exceeded. Backward integration is most advantageous when suppliers have sizable profit margins, when the item being supplied is a major cost component, and when the needed technological skills are easily mastered. Backward vertical integration can produce a differentiation-based competitive advantage when a company, by performing in-house activities that were previously outsourced, ends up with a better-quality product/service offering, improves the calibre of its customer service, or in other ways enhances the performance of its final product. On occasion, integrating into more stages along the value chain can add to a company's differentiation capabilities by allowing it to build or strengthen its core competencies, better master key skills or strategy-critical technologies, or add features that deliver greater customer value.

Backward integration can also spare a company the uncertainty of being dependent on suppliers of crucial components or support services, and it can lessen a com-

> A vertical integration strategy has appeal
> *only* if it significantly strengthens a firm's competitive position.

---

[24]See Kathryn R. Harrigan, "Matching Vertical Integration Strategies to Competitive Conditions," *Strategic Management Journal* 7, no. 6 (November–December 1986), pp. 535–56; for a discussion of the advantages and disadvantages of vertical integration, see John Stuckey and David White, "When and When *Not* to Vertically Integrate," *Sloan Management Review* (Spring 1993), pp. 71–83.

pany's vulnerability to powerful suppliers that raise prices at every opportunity. Stockpiling, fixed-price contracts, multiple-sourcing, long-term cooperative partnerships, or the use of substitute inputs are not always attractive ways for dealing with uncertain supply conditions or with economically powerful suppliers. Companies that are low on a key supplier's customer priority list can find themselves waiting on shipments every time supplies get tight. If this occurs often and wreaks havoc in a company's own production and customer relations activities, backward integration can be an advantageous strategic solution.

The strategic impetus for forward integration has much the same roots. In many industries, independent sales agents, wholesalers, and retailers handle competing brands of the same product; they have no allegiance to any one company's brand and tend to push "what sells" and earns them the biggest profits. Undependable sales and distribution channels can give rise to costly inventory pileups and frequent underutilization of capacity, thereby undermining the economies of a steady, near-capacity production operation. In such cases, it can be advantageous for a manufacturer to integrate forward into wholesaling and/or retailing in order to build a committed group of dealers and outlets representing its products to end users. Sometimes even a small increase in the average rate of capacity utilization can boost manufacturing margins enough so a firm really profits from company-owned distributorships, franchised dealer networks, and/or a chain of retail stores. On other occasions, integrating forward into the activity of selling directly to end users can result in a relative cost advantage and lower selling prices to end users by eliminating many of the costs of using regular wholesale-retail channels.

For a raw materials producer, integrating forward into manufacturing may permit greater product differentiation and provide an avenue of escape from the price-oriented competition of a commodity business. Often, in the early phases of an industry's value chain, intermediate goods are commodities in the sense that they have essentially identical technical specifications irrespective of producer (as is the case with crude oil, poultry, sheet steel, cement, and textile fibers). Competition in the markets for commodity or commoditylike products is usually fiercely price competitive, with the shifting balance between supply and demand giving rise to volatile profits. However, the closer the activities in the chain get to the ultimate consumer, the greater the opportunities for a firm to break out of a commoditylike competitive environment and differentiate its end product via design, service, quality features, packaging, promotion, and so on. Product differentiation often reduces the importance of price compared to other value-creating activities and allows for improved profit margins.

THE STRATEGIC DISADVANTAGES OF VERTICAL INTEGRATION

Vertical integration has some substantial drawbacks, however. It boosts a firm's capital investment in the industry, increasing business risk (what if the industry goes sour?) and perhaps denying financial resources to more worthwhile pursuits. A vertically integrated firm has vested interests in protecting its present investments in technology and production facilities even if they are becoming obsolete. Because of the high costs of abandoning such investments before they are worn out, fully integrated firms tend to adopt new technologies slower than partially integrated or nonintegrated firms. Second, integrating forward or backward locks a firm into relying on its own in-house activities and sources of supply (that later may prove more costly than outsourcing) and potentially results in less flexibility in accommodating buyer demand for greater product variety.

The big disadvantage of vertical integration is that it locks a firm deeper into the industry; unless operating across more stages in the industry's value chain builds competitive advantage, it is a questionable strategic move.

Third, vertical integration can pose problems of balancing capacity at each stage in the value chain. The most efficient scale of operation at each activity link in the value chain can vary substantially. Exact self-sufficiency at each interface is the exception not the rule. Where internal capacity is deficient to supply the next stage, the difference has to be bought externally. Where internal capacity is excessive, customers need to be found for the surplus. And if by-products are generated, they require arrangements for disposal.

Fourth, integration forward or backward often calls for radically different skills and business capabilities. Manufacturing, wholesale distribution, and retailing are different businesses with different key success factors, even though the physical products are the same. Managers of a manufacturing company should consider carefully whether it makes good business sense to invest time and money in developing the expertise and merchandising skills to integrate forward into wholesaling or retailing. Many manufacturers learn the hard way that owning and operating wholesale-retail networks present many headaches, fit poorly with what they do best, and don't always add the kind of value to their core business they thought they would. Integrating backward into parts and components manufacture isn't as simple or profitable as it sometimes sounds either. Personal computer makers, for example, frequently have trouble getting timely deliveries of the latest semiconductor chips at favorable prices, but most don't come close to having the resources or capabilities to integrate backward into chip manufacture; the semiconductor business is technologically sophisticated and entails heavy capital requirements and ongoing R&D effort, and mastering the manufacturing process takes a long time.

Fifth, backward vertical integration into the production of parts and components can reduce a company's manufacturing flexibility, lengthening the time it takes to make design and model changes and to bring new products to market. Companies that alter designs and models frequently in response to shifting buyer preferences often find vertical integration into parts and components burdensome because of constant retooling and redesign costs and the time it takes to implement coordinated changes throughout the value chain. Outsourcing is often quicker and cheaper than vertical integration, allowing a company to be more flexible and more nimble in adapting its product offering to fast-changing buyer preferences. Most of the world's automakers, despite their expertise in automotive technology and manufacturing, have concluded that they are better off from the standpoints of quality, cost, and design flexibility purchasing many of their key parts and components from manufacturing specialists rather than integrating backward to supply their own needs.

Unbundling and Outsourcing Strategies   In recent years, some vertically integrated companies have found vertical integration to be so competitively burdensome that they have adopted vertical deintegration (or unbundling) strategies. Deintegration involves withdrawing from certain stages/activities in the value chain system and relying on outside vendors to supply the needed products, support services, or functional activities. Outsourcing pieces of the value chain formerly performed in-house makes strategic sense whenever

- An activity can be performed better or more cheaply by outside specialists.
- The activity is not crucial to the firm's ability to achieve sustainable competitive advantage and won't hollow out its core competencies, essential skills, or technical know-how.
- It reduces the company's risk exposure to changing technology and/or changing buyer preferences.

- It streamlines company operations in ways that improve organizational flexibility, cut cycle time, speed decision-making, and reduce coordination costs.
- It allows a company to concentrate on its core business and do what it does best.

Often, many of the advantages of vertical integration can be captured and many of the disadvantages avoided via long-term cooperative partnerships with key suppliers.

All in all, therefore, a strategy of vertical integration can have both important strengths and weaknesses. Which direction the scales tip on vertical integration depends on (1) whether it can enhance the performance of strategy-critical activities in ways that lower cost or increase differentiation, (2) its impact on investment costs, flexibility and response times, and administrative overheads associated with coordinating operations across more stages, and (3) whether it creates competitive advantage. Absent solid benefits, vertical integration is not likely to be an attractive competitive strategy option.

FIRST-MOVER ADVANTAGES AND DISADVANTAGES

When to make a strategic move is often as crucial as *what* move to make. Timing is especially important when *first-mover advantages* or *disadvantages* exist.[25] Being first to initiate a strategic move can have a high payoff when (1) pioneering helps build a firm's image and reputation with buyers, (2) early commitments to supplies of raw materials, new technologies, distribution channels, and so on can produce an absolute cost advantage over rivals, (3) first-time customers remain strongly loyal to pioneering firms in making repeat purchases, and (4) moving first constitutes a pre-emptive strike, making imitation extra hard or unlikely. The bigger the first-mover advantages, the more attractive that making the first move becomes.

However, a wait-and-see approach doesn't always carry a competitive penalty. Being a first-mover may entail greater risks than being a late-mover. First-mover disadvantages (or late-mover advantages) arise when (1) pioneering leadership is much more costly than followership and only negligible experience curve effects accrue to the leader, (2) technological change is so rapid that early investments are soon rendered obsolete (thus allowing following firms to gain the advantages of next-generation products and more efficient processes), (3) it is easy for latecomers to crack the market because customer loyalty to pioneering firms is weak, and (4) the hard-earned skills and know-how developed by the market leaders during the early competitive phase are easily copied or even surpassed by late-movers. Good timing, therefore, is an important ingredient in deciding whether to be aggressive or cautious in pursuing a particular move.

> Because of first-mover advantages and disadvantages, competitive advantage is often attached to *when* a move is made as well as to *what* move is made.

KEY POINTS

The challenge of competitive strategy—whether it be overall low-cost, broad differentiation, best-cost, focused low-cost, or focused differentiation—is to create a competitive advantage for the firm. Competitive advantage comes from positioning a firm in the marketplace so it has an edge in coping with competitive forces and in attracting buyers.

[25]Porter, *Competitive Strategy,* pp. 232–33.

A strategy of trying to be the low-cost provider works well in situations where

- The industry's product is essentially the same from seller to seller (brand differences are minor).
- Many buyers are price-sensitive and shop for the lowest price.
- There are only a few ways to achieve product differentiation that have much value to buyers.
- Most buyers use the product in the same ways and thus have common user requirements.
- Buyers' costs in switching from one seller or brand to another are low (or even zero).
- Buyers are large and have significant power to negotiate pricing terms.

To achieve a low-cost advantage, a company must become more skilled than rivals in controlling structural and executional cost drivers and/or it must find innovative cost-saving ways to revamp its value chain. Successful low-cost providers usually achieve their cost advantages by imaginatively and persistently ferreting out cost savings throughout the value chain. They are good at finding ways to drive costs out of their businesses.

Differentiation strategies seek to produce a competitive edge by incorporating attributes and features into a company's product/service offering that rivals don't have. Anything a firm can do to create buyer value represents a potential basis for differentiation. Successful differentiation is usually keyed to lowering the buyer's cost of using the item, raising the performance the buyer gets, or boosting a buyer's psychological satisfaction. To be sustainable, differentiation usually has to be linked to unique internal skills and core competencies that give a company capabilities its rivals can't easily match. Differentiation tied just to unique physical features seldom is lasting because resourceful competitors are adept at cloning, improving on, or finding substitutes for almost any feature or trait that appeals to buyers.

Best-cost provider strategies combine a strategic emphasis on low cost with a strategic emphasis on more than minimal quality, service, features, or performance. The aim is to create competitive advantage by giving buyers more value for the money; this is done by matching close rivals on key quality-service-features-performance attributes and beating them on the costs of incorporating such attributes into the product or service. To be successful with a best-cost provider strategy, a company must have unique expertise in incorporating upscale product or service attributes at a lower cost than rivals; its core competencies must revolve around an ability to manage unit costs down and product/service calibre up simultaneously.

The competitive advantage of focusing is earned either by achieving lower costs in serving the target market niche or by developing an ability to offer niche buyers something different from rival competitors—in other words, it is either *cost-based* or *differentiation-based*. Focusing works best when

- Buyer needs or uses of the item are diverse.
- No other rival is attempting to specialize in the same target segment.
- A firm lacks the capability to go after a wider part of the total market.
- Buyer segments differ widely in size, growth rate, profitability, and intensity in the five competitive forces, making some segments more attractive than others.

A variety of offensive strategic moves can be used to secure a competitive advantage. Strategic offensives can be aimed either at competitors' strengths or at their weaknesses; they can involve end-runs or grand offensives on many fronts; they can be designed as guerrilla actions or as preemptive strikes; and the target of the offensive can be a market leader, a runner-up firm, or the smallest and/or weakest firms in the industry.

The strategic approaches to defending a company's position usually take the form of (1) making moves that fortify the company's present position, (2) presenting competitors with a moving target to avoid "out of date" vulnerability, and (3) dissuading rivals from even trying to attack.

Vertically integrating forward or backward makes strategic sense only if it strengthens a company's position via either cost reduction or creation of a differentiation-based advantage. Otherwise, the drawbacks of vertical integration (increased investment, greater business risk, increased vulnerability to technological changes, and less flexibility in making product changes) outweigh the advantages (better coordination of production flows and technological know-how from stage to stage, more specialized use of technology, greater internal control over operations, greater scale economies, and matching production with sales and marketing). There are ways to achieve the advantages of vertical integration without encountering the drawbacks.

The timing of strategic moves is important. First-movers sometimes gain strategic advantage; at other times, such as when technology is developing fast, it is cheaper and easier to be a follower than a leader.

SUGGESTED READINGS

Aaker, David A. "Managing Assets and Skills: The Key to a Sustainable Competitive Advantage." *California Management Review* 31, no. 2 (Winter 1989), pp. 91–106.

Cohen, William A. "War in the Marketplace." *Business Horizons* 29, no. 2 (March–April 1986), pp. 10–20.

Coyne, Kevin P. "Sustainable Competitive Advantage—What It Is, What It Isn't." *Business Horizons* 29, no. 1 (January–February 1986), pp. 54–61.

D'Aveni, Richard A. *Hypercompetition: The Dynamics of Strategic Maneuvering* (New York: Free Press, 1994), chaps. 1, 2, 3, and 4.

Harrigan, Kathryn R. "Guerrilla Strategies of Underdog Competitors." *Planning Review* 14, no. 16 (November 1986), pp. 4–11.

———. "Formulating Vertical Integration Strategies." *Academy of Management Review* 9, no. 4 (October 1984), pp. 638–52.

Hout, Thomas, Michael E. Porter, and Eileen Rudden. "How Global Companies Win Out." *Harvard Business Review* 60, no. 5 (September–October 1982), pp. 98–108.

MacMillan, Ian C. "Preemptive Strategies." *Journal of Business Strategy* 14, no. 2 (Fall 1983), pp. 16–26.

———. "Controlling Competitive Dynamics by Taking Strategic Initiative." *The Academy of Management Executive* 2, no. 2 (May 1988), pp. 111–18.

Porter, Michael E. *Competitive Advantage* (New York: Free Press, 1985), chaps. 3, 4, 5, 7, 14, and 15.

Rothschild, William E. "Surprise and the Competitive Advantage." *Journal of Business Strategy* 4, no. 3 (Winter 1984), pp. 10–18.

Stuckey, John and David White, "When and When *Not* to Vertically Integrate," *Sloan Management Review* (Spring 1993), pp. 71–83.

Venkatesan, Ravi. "Strategic Outsourcing: To Make or Not to Make." *Harvard Business Review* 7, no. 6 (November–December 1992), pp. 98–107.

## CHAPTER SIX

MATCHING STRATEGY TO A COMPANY'S SITUATION

Strategy isn't something you can nail together in slapdash fashion by sitting around a conference table . . .

Terry Haller

The essence of formulating competitive strategy is relating a company to its environment . . . the best strategy for a given firm is ultimately a unique construction reflecting its particular circumstances.

Michael E. Porter

You do not choose to become global. The market chooses for you; it forces your hand.

Alain Gomez
CEO, Thomson, S.A.

The task of matching strategy to a company's situation is complicated because of the many external and internal factors managers have to weigh. However, while the number and variety of considerations is necessarily lengthy, the most important drivers shaping a company's strategic options fall into two broad categories:

- The nature of industry and competitive conditions.
- The firm's own competitive capabilities, market position, and best opportunities.

The dominant strategy-shaping industry and competitive conditions revolve around what stage in the life-cycle the industry is in (emerging, rapid growth, mature, declining), the industry's structure (fragmented versus concentrated), the nature and relative strength of the five competitive forces, and the scope of competitive rivalry (particularly whether the company's market is globally competitive). The pivotal company-specific considerations hinge on (1) whether the company is an industry leader, an up-and-coming challenger, a content runner-up, or an also-ran struggling to survive, and (2) the company's particular set of strengths, weaknesses, opportunities, and threats. But even these few categories occur in too many combinations to cover here. However, we can demonstrate what the task of matching strategy to the situation involves by considering five classic types of industry environments:

1. Competing in emerging and rapidly growing industries.
2. Competing in maturing industries.
3. Competing in stagnant or declining industries.
4. Competing in fragmented industries.
5. Competing in international markets.

and three classic types of company situations:

1. Firms in industry leadership positions.
2. Firms in runner-up positions.
3. Firms that are competitively weak or crisis-ridden.

STRATEGIES FOR COMPETING IN EMERGING INDUSTRIES

An emerging industry is one in the early, formative stage. Most companies in an emerging industry are in a start-up mode, adding people, acquiring or constructing facilities, gearing up production, trying to broaden distribution and gain buyer acceptance. Often, there are important product design problems and technological problems to be worked out as well. Emerging industries present managers with some unique strategy-making challenges:[1]

- Because the market is new and unproven, there are many uncertainties about how it will function, how fast it will grow, and how big it will get; the little historical data available is virtually useless in projecting future trends.
- Much of the technological know-how tends to be proprietary and closely guarded, having been developed in-house by pioneering firms; some firms may file patents in an effort to secure competitive advantage.
- Often, there is no consensus regarding which of several competing production technologies will win out or which product attributes will gain the most buyer favor. Until market forces sort these things out, wide differences in product quality and performance are typical and rivalry centers around each firm's efforts to get the market to ratify its own strategic approach to technology, product design, marketing, and distribution.
- Entry barriers tend to be relatively low, even for entrepreneurial start-up companies; well-financed, opportunity-seeking outsiders are likely to enter if the industry has promise for explosive growth.
- Experience curve effects often permit significant cost reductions as volume builds.
- Firms have little hard information about competitors, how fast products are gaining buyer acceptance, and users' experiences with the product; there are no trade associations gathering and distributing information.

---

[1]Michael E. Porter, *Competitive Strategy* (New York: Free Press, 1980), pp. 216–23.

- Since all buyers are first-time users, the marketing task is to induce initial purchase and to overcome customer concerns about product features, performance reliability, and conflicting claims of rival firms.
- Many potential buyers expect first-generation products to be rapidly improved, so they delay purchase until technology and product design mature.
- Often, firms have trouble securing ample supplies of raw materials and components (until suppliers gear up to meet the industry's needs).
- Many companies, finding themselves short of funds to support needed R&D and get through several lean years until the product catches on, end up merging with competitors or being acquired by outsiders looking to invest in a growth market.

The two critical strategic issues confronting firms in an emerging industry are (1) how to finance the start-up phase and (2) what market segments and competitive advantages to go after in trying to secure a leading industry position.[2] Competitive strategies keyed either to low cost or differentiation are usually viable. Focusing should be considered when financial resources are limited and the industry has too many technological frontiers to pursue at once; one option for financially constrained enterprises is to form a strategic alliance or joint venture with another company to gain access to needed skills and resources. Because an emerging industry has no established "rules of the game" and industry participants employ widely varying strategic approaches, a well-financed firm with a powerful strategy can shape the rules and become a recognized industry leader.

Dealing with all the risks and opportunities of an emerging industry is one of the most challenging business strategy problems. To be successful in an emerging industry, companies usually have to pursue one or more of the following strategic avenues:[3]

1. Try to win the early race for industry leadership with risk-taking entrepreneurship and a bold, creative strategy. Broad or focused differentiation strategies keyed to product superiority typically offer the best chance for early competitive advantage.

2. Push to perfect the technology, to improve product quality, and to develop attractive performance features.

3. Try to capture any first-mover advantages associated with more models, better styling, early commitments to technologies and raw materials suppliers, experience curve effects, and new distribution channels.

4. Search out new customer groups, new geographical areas to enter, and new user applications. Make it easier and cheaper for first-time buyers to try the industry's first-generation product.

5. Gradually shift the advertising emphasis from building product awareness to increasing frequency of use and creating brand loyalty.

6. As technological uncertainty clears and a dominant technology emerges, adopt it quickly. While there's merit in trying to pioneer the "dominant design" approach, such a strategy carries high risk when there are many competing

Strategic success in an emerging industry calls for bold entrepreneurship, a willingness to pioneer and take risks, an intuitive feel for what buyers will like, quick response to new developments, and opportunistic strategy-making.

---

[2] Charles W. Hofer and Dan Schendel, *Strategy Formulation: Analytical Concepts* (St. Paul, Minn.: West Publishing, 1978), pp. 164–65.

[3] Phillip Kotler, *Marketing Management,* 5th ed. (Englewood Cliffs, N.J.: Prentice-Hall, 1984), p. 366, and Porter, *Competitive Strategy,* chapter 10.

technologies, R&D is costly, and rapidly moving technological developments quickly make early investments obsolete.

7. Use price cuts to attract the next layer of price-sensitive buyers into the market.

8. Expect well-financed outsiders to move in with aggressive strategies as industry sales start to take off and the perceived risk of investing in the industry lessens. Try to prepare for the entry of powerful competitors by forecasting *(a)* who the probable entrants will be (based on present and future entry barriers) and *(b)* the types of strategies they are likely to employ.

The short-term value of winning the early race for growth and market share leadership has to be balanced against the longer-range need to build a durable competitive edge and a defendable market position.[4] New entrants, attracted by the growth and profit potential, may crowd the market. Aggressive newcomers, aspiring to industry leadership, can quickly become major players by acquiring and merging the operations of weaker competitors. Young companies in fast-growing markets face three strategic hurdles: (1) managing their own rapid expansion, (2) defending against competitors trying to horn in on their success, and (3) building a competitive position extending beyond their initial product or market. Such companies can help their cause by selecting knowledgeable members for their boards of directors, by hiring entrepreneurial managers with experience in guiding young businesses through the start-up and takeoff stages, by concentrating on out-innovating the competition, and perhaps by merging with or acquiring another firm to gain added expertise and a stronger resource base.

STRATEGIES FOR COMPETING IN MATURING INDUSTRIES

The rapid-growth environment of a young industry cannot go on forever. However, the transition to a slower-growth, maturing industry environment does not begin on an easily predicted schedule, and the transition can be forestalled by a steady stream of technological advances, product innovations, or other driving forces that keep rejuvenating market demand. Nonetheless, when growth rates do slacken, the transition to market maturity usually produces fundamental changes in the industry's competitive environment:[5]

1. *Slowing growth in buyer demand generates more head-to-head competition for market share.* Firms that want to continue on a rapid-growth track start looking for ways to take customers away from competitors. Outbreaks of price-cutting, increased advertising, and other aggressive tactics are common.

2. *Buyers become more sophisticated, often driving a harder bargain on repeat purchases.* Since buyers have experience with the product and are familiar with competing brands, they are better able to evaluate different brands and can use their knowledge to negotiate a better deal with sellers.

3. *Competition often produces a greater emphasis on cost and service.* As sellers all begin to offer the product attributes buyers prefer, buyer choices increasingly depend on which seller offers the best combination of price and service.

---

[4]Hofer and Schendel, *Strategy Formulation,* pp. 164–65.
[5]Porter, *Competitive Strategy,* pp. 238–40.

4. *Firms have a "topping out" problem in adding production capacity.* Slower rates of industry growth mean slowdowns in capacity expansion. Each firm has to monitor rivals' expansion plans and time its own capacity additions to minimize oversupply conditions in the industry. With slower industry growth, the mistake of adding too much capacity too soon can adversely affect company profits well into the future.

5. *Product innovation and new end-use applications are harder to come by.* Producers find it increasingly difficult to create new product features, find further uses for the product, and sustain buyer excitement.

6. *International competition increases.* Growth-minded domestic firms start to seek out sales opportunities in foreign markets. Some companies, looking for ways to cut costs, relocate plants to countries with lower wage rates. Greater product standardization and diffusion of technological know-how reduce entry barriers and make it possible for enterprising foreign companies to become serious market contenders in more countries. Industry leadership passes to companies that succeed in building strong competitive positions in most of the world's major geographic markets and in winning the biggest global market shares.

7. *Industry profitability falls temporarily or permanently.* Slower growth, increased competition, more sophisticated buyers, and occasional periods of overcapacity put pressure on industry profit margins. Weaker, less-efficient firms are usually the hardest hit.

8. *Stiffening competition induces a number of mergers and acquisitions among former competitors, drives the weakest firms out of the industry, and, in general, produces industry consolidation.* Inefficient firms and firms with weak competitive strategies can survive in a fast-growing industry with booming sales. But the intensifying competition that accompanies industry maturity exposes competitive weakness and throws second- and third-tier competitors into a survival-of-the-fittest contest.

As industry maturity begins to hit full force, and changes in the competitive environment set in, several strategic moves can strengthen firms' competitive positions.[6]

In a maturing industry, strategic emphasis needs to be on efficiency-increasing, profit-preserving measures: pruning the product line, improving production methods, reducing costs, accelerating sales promotion efforts, expanding internationally, and acquiring distressed competitors.

Pruning the Product Line A wide selection of models, features, and product options has competitive value during the growth stage when buyers' needs are still evolving. But such variety can become too costly as price competition stiffens and profit margins are squeezed. Maintaining too many product versions prevents firms from achieving the economies of long production runs. In addition, the prices of slow-selling versions may not cover their true costs. Pruning marginal products from the line lowers costs and permits more concentration on items whose margins are highest and/or where the firm has a competitive advantage.

More Emphasis on Process Innovations Efforts to "reinvent" the manufacturing process can have a fourfold payoff: lower costs, better production quality, greater capability to turn out multiple product versions, and shorter design-to-market cycles. Process innovation can involve mechanizing high-cost activities, revamping production lines

---

[6]The following discussion draws on Porter, *Competitive Strategy*, pp. 241–46.

to improve labor efficiency, creating self-directed work teams, reengineering the manufacturing portion of the value chain, and increasing use of advanced technology (robotics, computerized controls, and automatic guided vehicles). Japanese firms have become remarkably adept at using manufacturing process innovation to become lower-cost producers of higher-quality products.

A Stronger Focus on Cost Reduction Stiffening price competition gives firms extra incentive to reduce unit costs. Such efforts can cover a broad front: companies can push suppliers for better prices, switch to lower-priced components, develop more economical product designs, cut low-value activities out of the value chain, streamline distribution channels, and reengineer internal processes.

Increasing Sales to Present Customers In a mature market, growing by taking customers away from rivals may not be as appealing as expanding sales to existing customers. Strategies to increase purchases by existing customers can involve providing complementary items and ancillary services, and finding more ways for customers to use the product. Convenience food stores, for example, have boosted average sales per customer by adding video rentals, automatic bank tellers, and deli counters.

Purchasing Rival Firms at Bargain Prices Sometimes the facilities and assets of distressed rivals can be acquired cheaply. Bargain-priced acquisitions can help create a low-cost position if they also present opportunities for greater operating efficiency. In addition, an acquired firm's customer base can provide expanded market coverage. The most desirable acquisitions are those that will significantly enhance the acquiring firm's competitive strength.

Expanding Internationally As its domestic market matures, a firm may seek to enter foreign markets where attractive growth potential still exists and competitive pressures are not so strong. Several manufacturers in highly industrialized nations found international expansion attractive because equipment no longer suitable for domestic operations could be used in plants in less-developed foreign markets (a condition that lowered entry costs). Such possibilities arise when (1) foreign buyers have less sophisticated needs and have simpler, old-fashioned, end-use applications, and (2) foreign competitors are smaller, less formidable, and do not employ the latest production technology. Strategies to expand internationally also make sense when a domestic firm's skills, reputation, and product are readily transferable to foreign markets. Even though the U.S. market for soft drinks is mature, Coca-Cola has remained a growth company by upping its efforts to penetrate foreign markets where soft-drink sales are expanding rapidly.

STRATEGIC PITFALLS

Perhaps the biggest strategic mistake a company can make as an industry matures is steering a middle course between low cost, differentiation, and focusing. Such strategic compromises guarantee that a firm will end up stuck in the middle with a fuzzy strategy, a lack of commitment to winning a competitive advantage based on either low cost or differentiation, an average image with buyers, and little chance of springing into the ranks of the industry leaders. Other strategic pitfalls include sacrificing long-term competitive position for short-term profit, waiting too long to respond to

One of the greatest strategic mistakes a firm can make in a maturing industry is pursuing a compromise between low-cost, differentiation, and focusing such that it ends up "stuck in the middle" with a fuzzy strategy, an average image, an ill-defined market identity, no competitive advantage, and little prospect of becoming an industry leader.

price-cutting, getting caught with too much capacity as growth slows, overspending on marketing efforts to boost sales growth, and failing to pursue cost reduction soon enough and aggressively enough.

STRATEGIES FOR FIRMS IN STAGNANT OR DECLINING INDUSTRIES

Many firms operate in industries where demand is growing more slowly than the economywide average or is even declining. Although harvesting the business to obtain the greatest cash flow, selling out, or closing down are obvious end-game strategies for uncommitted competitors with dim long-term prospects, strong competitors may be able to achieve good performance in a stagnant market environment.[7] Stagnant demand by itself is not enough to make an industry unattractive. Selling out may or may not be practical, and closing operations is always a last resort.

Businesses competing in slow-growth/declining industries have to accept the difficult realities of an environment of continuing stagnation, and they must resign themselves to performance targets consistent with available market opportunities. Cash flow and return-on-investment criteria are more appropriate than growth-oriented performance measures, but sales and market share growth are by no means ruled out. Strong competitors may be able to take sales from weaker rivals, and the acquisition or exit of weaker firms creates opportunities for the remaining companies to capture greater market share.

In general, companies that succeed in stagnant industries rely heavily on one of the following three strategic themes:[8]

> Achieving competitive advantage in stagnant or declining industries usually requires pursuing one of three competitive approaches: focusing on growing market segments within the industry, differentiating on the basis of better quality and frequent product innovation, or becoming a lower cost producer.

1. *Pursue a focused strategy by identifying, creating, and exploiting the growth segments within the industry.* Stagnant or declining markets, like other markets, are composed of numerous segments or niches. Frequently, one or more of these segments is growing rapidly, despite stagnation in the industry as a whole. An astute competitor who is first to concentrate on the attractive growth segments can escape stagnating sales and profits and possibly achieve competitive advantage in the target segments.

2. *Stress differentiation based on quality improvement and product innovation.* Either enhanced quality or innovation can rejuvenate demand by creating important new growth segments or inducing buyers to trade up. Successful product innovation opens up an avenue for competing besides meeting or beating rivals' prices. Differentiation based on successful innovation has the additional advantage of being difficult and expensive for rival firms to imitate.

3. *Work diligently and persistently to drive costs down.* When increases in sales cannot be counted on to generate increases in earnings, companies can improve profit margins and return on investment by continuous productivity improvement and cost reduction year after year. Potential cost-saving actions include (a) outsourcing functions and activities that can be performed more

---

[7]R. G. Hamermesh and S. B. Silk, "How to Compete in Stagnant Industries," *Harvard Business Review* 57, no. 5 (September–October 1979), p. 161.
[8]Ibid., p. 162.

ILLUSTRATION CAPSULE 18

YAMAHA'S STRATEGY IN THE PIANO INDUSTRY

For some years now, worldwide demand for pianos has been declining—in the mid-1980s the decline was 10% annually. Modern-day parents have not put the same stress on music lessons for their children as prior generations of parents did. In an effort to see if it could revitalize its piano business, Yamaha conducted a market research survey to learn what use was being made of pianos in households that owned one. The survey revealed that the overwhelming majority of the 40 million pianos in American, European, and Japanese households were seldom used. In most cases, the reasons the piano had been purchased no longer applied. Children had either stopped taking piano lessons or were grown and had left the household; adult household members played their pianos sparingly, if at all—only a small percentage were accomplished piano players. Most pianos were serving as a piece of fine furniture and were in good condition despite not being tuned regularly. The survey also confirmed that the income levels of piano owners were well above average.

Yamaha's piano strategists saw the idle pianos in these upscale households as a potential market opportunity. The strategy that emerged entailed marketing an attachment that would convert the piano into an old-fashioned automatic player piano capable of playing a wide number of selections recorded on $3\frac{1}{2}$-inch floppy disks (the same kind used to store computer data). The player piano conversion attachment carried a $2,500 price tag. Concurrently, Yamaha introduced Disklavier, an upright acoustic player piano model that could play *and record* performances up to 90 minutes long; the Disklavier retailed for $8,000. At year-end 1988 Yamaha offered 30 prerecorded disks for $29.95 each and planned to release a continuing stream of new selections. Yamaha believed that these new high-tech products held potential to reverse the downtrend in piano sales.

cheaply by outsiders, (b) completely redesigning internal business processes, (c) consolidating underutilized production facilities, (d) adding more distribution channels to ensure the unit volume needed for low-cost production, (e) closing low-volume, high-cost distribution outlets, and (f) cutting marginally beneficial activities out of the value chain.

These three strategic themes are not mutually exclusive.[9] Introducing new, innovative versions of a product can *create* a fast-growing market segment. Similarly, relentless pursuit of greater operating efficiencies permits price reductions that create price-conscious growth segments. Note that all three themes are spinoffs of the generic competitive strategies, adjusted to fit the circumstances of a tough industry environment.

The most attractive declining industries are those in which sales are eroding only slowly, there is large built-in demand, and some profitable niches remain. The most common strategic mistakes companies make in stagnating or declining markets are (1) getting trapped in a profitless war of attrition, (2) diverting too much cash out of the business too quickly (thus accelerating a company's demise), and (3) being overly optimistic about the industry's future and waiting complacently for things to get better.

Illustration Capsule 18 describes the creative approach taken by Yamaha to reverse declining market demand for pianos.

---

[9]Ibid., p. 165.

STRATEGIES FOR COMPETING IN FRAGMENTED INDUSTRIES

A number of industries are populated by hundreds, even thousands, of small and medium-sized companies, many privately held and none with a substantial share of total industry sales.[10] The standout competitive feature of a fragmented industry is the absence of market leaders with king-sized market shares or widespread buyer recognition. Examples of fragmented industries include book publishing, landscaping and plant nurseries, kitchen cabinets, oil tanker shipping, auto repair, restaurants and fast-food, public accounting, women's dresses, metal foundries, meat packing, paperboard boxes, log homes, hotels and motels, and furniture.

Any of several reasons can account for why the supply side of an industry is fragmented:

- Low entry barriers allow small firms to enter quickly and cheaply.
- An absence of large-scale production economies permits small companies to compete on an equal cost footing with larger firms.
- Buyers require relatively small quantities of customized products (as in business forms, interior design, and advertising); because demand for any particular product version is small, sales volumes are not adequate to support producing, distributing, or marketing on a scale that yields advantages to a large firm.
- The market for the industry's product/service is local (dry cleaning, residential construction, medical services, automotive repair), giving competitive advantage to local businesses familiar with local buyers and local market conditions.
- Market demand is so large and so diverse that it takes very large numbers of firms to accommodate buyer requirements (restaurants, energy, apparel).
- High transportation costs limit the radius a plant can economically service—as in concrete blocks, mobile homes, milk, and gravel.
- Local regulations make each geographic area somewhat unique.
- The industry is so new that no firms have yet developed the skills and resources to command a significant market share.

In fragmented industries competitors usually have the strategic latitude (1) to compete broadly or to focus and (2) to pursue either a low-cost or a differentiation-based competitive advantage.

Some fragmented industries consolidate naturally as they mature. The stiffer competition that accompanies slower growth produces a shake-out of weak, inefficient firms and a greater concentration of larger, more visible sellers. Other fragmented industries remain atomistically competitive because it is inherent in the nature of their businesses. And still others remain stuck in a fragmented state because existing firms lack the resources or ingenuity to employ a strategy powerful enough to drive industry consolidation.

Competitive rivalry in fragmented industries can vary from moderately strong to fierce. Low barriers make entry of new competitors an ongoing threat. Competition from substitutes may or may not be a major factor. The relatively small size of companies in fragmented industries puts them in a weak position to bargain with powerful suppliers and buyers, although sometimes they can become members of a

[10]This section is summarized from Porter, *Competitive Strategy,* chapter 9.

cooperative formed for the purpose of using their combined leverage to negotiate better sales and purchase terms. In such an environment, the best a firm can expect is to cultivate a loyal customer base and grow a bit faster than the industry average. Competitive strategies based either on low cost or product differentiation are viable unless the industry's product is highly standardized. Focusing on a well-defined market niche or buyer segment usually offers more competitive advantage potential than striving for broad market appeal. Suitable competitive strategy options in a fragmented industry include

- **Constructing and operating "formula" facilities**—This strategic approach is frequently employed in restaurant and retailing businesses operating at multiple locations. It involves constructing standardized outlets in favorable locations at minimum cost and then polishing to a science how to operate all outlets in a superefficient manner. McDonald's, Home Depot, and 7-Eleven have pursued this strategy to perfection, earning excellent profits in their respective industries.

- **Becoming a low-cost operator**—When price competition is intense and profit margins are under constant pressure, companies can stress no-frills operations featuring low overhead, high-productivity/low-cost labor, lean capital budgets, and dedicated pursuit of total operating efficiency. Successful low-cost producers in a fragmented industry can play the price-cutting game and still earn profits above the industry average.

- **Increasing customer value through integration**—Backward or forward integration may contain opportunities to lower costs or enhance the value provided to customers. Examples include assembling components before shipment to customers, providing technical advice, or opening regional distribution centers.

- **Specializing by product type**—When a fragmented industry's products include a range of styles or services, a strategy to focus on one product/service category can be very effective. Some firms in the furniture industry specialize in only one furniture type such as brass beds, rattan and wicker, lawn and garden, or early American. In auto repair, companies specialize in transmission repair, body work, or speedy oil changes.

- **Specialization by customer type**—A firm can cope with the intense competition of a fragmented industry by catering to those customers (1) who have the least bargaining leverage (because they are small in size or purchase small amounts), (2) who are the least price sensitive, or (3) who are interested in unique product attributes, a customized product/service, or other "extras."

- **Focusing on a limited geographic area**—Even though a firm in a fragmented industry can't win a big share of total industrywide sales, it can still try to dominate a local/regional geographic area. Concentrating company efforts on a limited territory can produce greater operating efficiency, speed delivery and customer services, promote strong brand awareness, and permit saturation advertising, while avoiding the diseconomies of stretching operations out over a much wider area. Supermarkets, banks, and sporting goods retailers successfully operate multiple locations within a limited geographic area.

In fragmented industries, firms generally have the strategic freedom to pursue broad or narrow market targets and low-cost or differentiation-based competitive advantages. Many different strategic approaches can exist side by side.

STRATEGIES FOR COMPETING IN INTERNATIONAL MARKETS

Companies are motivated to expand into international markets for any of three basic reasons: a desire to seek out new markets, a competitive need to achieve lower costs, or a desire to access natural resource deposits in other countries. Whatever the reason, an international strategy has to be situation-driven. Special attention has to be paid to how national markets differ in buyer needs and habits, distribution channels, long-run growth potential, driving forces, and competitive pressures. In addition to the basic market differences from country to country, there are four other situational considerations unique to international operations: cost variations among countries, fluctuating exchange rates, host government trade policies, and the pattern of international competition.

Competing in international markets poses a bigger strategy-making challenge than competing in only the company's home market.

Country-to-Country Cost Variations   Differences in wage rates, worker productivity, inflation rates, energy costs, tax rates, government regulations, and the like create sizable variations in manufacturing costs from country to country. Plants in some countries have major manufacturing cost advantages because of lower input costs (especially labor), relaxed government regulations, or unique natural resources. In such cases, the low-cost countries become principal production sites, and most of the output is exported to markets in other parts of the world. Companies with facilities in these locations (or that source their products from contract manufacturers in these countries) have a competitive advantage. The competitive role of low manufacturing costs is most evident in low-wage countries like Taiwan, South Korea, Mexico, and Brazil, which have become production havens for goods with high labor content.

Another important manufacturing cost consideration in international competition is the concept of *manufacturing share* as distinct from brand share or market share. For example, although less than 40 percent of all the video recorders sold in the United States carry a Japanese brand, Japanese companies do 100 percent of the manufacturing—all sellers source their video recorders from Japanese manufacturers.[11] In microwave ovens, Japanese brands have less than a 50 percent share of the U.S. market, but the manufacturing share of Japanese companies is over 85 percent. *Manufacturing share is significant because it is a better indicator than market share of the industry's low-cost producer.* In a globally competitive industry where some competitors are intent on global dominance, being the worldwide low-cost producer is a powerful competitive advantage. Achieving low-cost producer status often requires a company to have the largest worldwide manufacturing share, with production centralized in one or a few superefficient plants. However, important marketing and distribution economies associated with multinational operations can also yield low-cost leadership.

Fluctuating Exchange Rates   The volatility of exchange rates greatly complicates the issue of geographic cost advantages. Exchange rates often fluctuate as much as 20 to 40 percent annually. Changes of this magnitude can totally wipe out a country's low-cost advantage or transform a former high-cost location into a competitive-cost location. A strong U.S. dollar makes it more attractive for U.S. companies to manufacture

---

[11]C. K. Prahalad and Yves L. Doz, *The Multinational Mission* (New York: Free Press, 1987), p. 60.

in foreign countries. Declines in the value of the dollar against foreign currencies can eliminate much of the cost advantage that foreign manufacturers have over U.S. manufacturers and can even prompt foreign companies to establish production plants in the United States.

Host Government Trade Policies   National governments enact all kinds of measures affecting international trade and the operation of foreign companies in their markets. Host governments may impose import tariffs and quotas, set local content requirements on goods made inside their borders by foreign-based companies, and regulate the prices of imported goods. In addition, outsiders may face a web of regulations regarding technical standards, product certification, prior approval of capital spending projects, withdrawal of funds from the country, and minority (sometimes majority) ownership by local citizens. Some governments also provide subsidies and low-interest loans to domestic companies to help them compete against foreign-based companies. Other governments, anxious to obtain new plants and jobs, offer foreign companies a helping hand in the form of subsidies, privileged market access, and technical assistance.

MULTICOUNTRY COMPETITION VERSUS GLOBAL COMPETITION

There are important differences in the patterns of international competition from industry to industry.[12] At one extreme, competition can be termed *multicountry* or *multidomestic* because it takes place country by country; competition in each national market is essentially independent of competition in other national markets. For example, there is a banking industry in France, one in Brazil, and one in Japan, but competitive conditions in banking differ markedly in all three countries. Moreover, a bank's reputation, customer base, and competitive position in one nation have little or no bearing on its ability to compete successfully in another. In industries where multicountry competition prevails, the power of a company's strategy in any one nation and any competitive advantage it yields are largely confined to that nation and do not spill over to other countries where it operates. With multicountry competition there is no "international market," just a collection of self-contained country markets. Industries characterized by multicountry competition include beer, life insurance, apparel, metals fabrication, many types of food products (coffee, cereals, canned goods, frozen foods), and many types of retailing.

Multicountry (or *multidomestic*) *competition* exists when competition in one national market is independent of competition in another national market—there is no "international market," just a collection of self-contained country markets.

At the other extreme is *global competition* where prices and competitive conditions across country markets are strongly linked together and the term international or global market has true meaning. In a globally competitive industry, a company's competitive position in one country both affects and is affected by its position in other countries. Rival companies compete against each other in many different countries, but especially so in countries where sales volumes are large and where having a competitive presence is strategically important to building a strong global position in the industry. In global competition, a firm's overall competitive advantage grows out of its entire worldwide operations; the competitive advantage it creates at its home base is supplemented by advantages growing out of its operations in other countries (having plants in low-wage countries, a capability to serve customers with multinational operations of their own, and a brand reputation that is transferable from

Global competition exists when competitive conditions across national markets are linked strongly enough to form a true international market and when leading competitors compete head-to-head in many different countries.

---

[12]Michael E. Porter, *The Competitive Advantage of Nations* (New York: Free Press, 1990), pp. 53–54.

country to country). *A global competitor's market strength is directly proportional to its portfolio of country-based competitive advantages.* Global competition exists in automobiles, television sets, tires, telecommunications equipment, copiers, watches, and commercial aircraft.

An industry can have segments that are globally competitive and segments where competition is country by country.[13] In the hotel-motel industry, for example, the low- and medium-priced segments are characterized by multicountry competition because competitors mainly serve travelers within the same country. In the business and luxury segments, however, competition is more globalized. Companies like Nikki, Marriott, Sheraton, and Hilton have hotels at many international locations and use worldwide reservation systems and common quality and service standards to gain marketing advantages in serving businesspeople and travelers who make frequent international trips.

In lubricants, the marine engine segment is globally competitive because ships move from port to port and require the same oil everywhere they stop. Brand reputations have a global scope, and successful marine engine lubricant producers (Exxon, British Petroleum, and Shell) operate globally. In automotive motor oil, however, multicountry competition dominates. Countries have different weather conditions and driving patterns, production is subject to limited scale economies and shipping costs are high, and retail distribution channels differ markedly from country to country. Thus domestic firms, like Quaker State and Pennzoil in the U.S. and Castrol in Great Britain, can be leaders in their home markets without competing globally.

All these situational considerations, along with the obvious cultural and political differences between countries, shape a company's strategic approach in international markets.

> In multicountry competition, rival firms vie for national market leadership. In globally competitive industries, rival firms vie for worldwide leadership.

TYPES OF INTERNATIONAL STRATEGIES

There are six distinct strategic options for a company participating in international markets. It can

1. *License foreign firms to use the company's technology or produce and distribute the company's products* (in which case international revenues will equal the royalty income from the licensing agreement).

2. *Maintain a national (one-country) production base and export goods to foreign markets* using either company-owned or foreign-controlled forward distribution channels.

3. *Follow a multicountry strategy* whereby a company's international strategy is crafted country by country to be responsive to buyer needs and competitive conditions in each country where it operates. Strategic moves in one country are made independent of actions taken in another country; strategy coordination across countries is secondary to matching company strategy to individual country conditions.

4. *Follow a global low-cost strategy* where the company strives to be a low-cost supplier to buyers in most or all strategically important markets of the world. The company's strategic efforts are coordinated worldwide to achieve a low-cost position relative to all competitors.

---

[13] Ibid., p. 61.

5. *Follow a global differentiation strategy* whereby a firm differentiates its product on the same attributes in all countries to create a globally consistent image and a consistent competitive theme. The firm's strategic moves are coordinated across countries to achieve consistent differentiation worldwide.

6. *Follow a global focus strategy* where company strategy is aimed at serving the same identifiable niche in each of many strategically important country markets. Strategic actions are coordinated globally to achieve a consistent low-cost or differentiation-based competitive approach in the target niche worldwide.

Licensing makes sense when a firm with valuable technical know-how or a unique patented product has neither the internal organizational capability nor the resources in foreign markets. By licensing the technology or the production rights to foreign-based firms, the firm at least realizes income from royalties.

Using domestic plants as a production base for exporting goods to foreign markets is an excellent initial strategy for pursuing international sales. It minimizes both risk and capital requirements, and it is a conservative way to test the international waters. With an export strategy, a manufacturer can limit its involvement in foreign markets by contracting with foreign wholesalers experienced in importing to handle the entire distribution and marketing function in their countries or regions of the world. If it is more advantageous to maintain control over these functions, a manufacturer can establish its own distribution and sales organizations in some or all of the target foreign markets. Either way, a firm minimizes its direct investments in foreign countries because of its home-based production and export strategy. Such strategies are commonly favored by Korean and Italian companies—products are designed and manufactured at home and only marketing activities are performed abroad. Whether such a strategy can be pursued successfully over the long run hinges on the relative cost competitiveness of a home-country production base. In some industries, firms gain additional scale economies and experience curve benefits from centralizing production in one or several giant plants whose output capability exceeds demand in any one country market; obviously, to capture such economies a company must export to markets in other countries. However, this strategy is vulnerable when manufacturing costs in the home country are substantially higher than in foreign countries where rivals have plants.

The pros and cons of a multicountry strategy versus a global strategy are a bit more complex.

A MULTICOUNTRY STRATEGY OR A GLOBAL STRATEGY?

The need for a multicountry strategy derives from the sometimes vast differences in cultural, economic, political, and competitive conditions in different countries. The more diverse national market conditions are, the stronger the case for a *multicountry strategy* where the company tailors its strategic approach to fit each host country's market situation. In such cases, the company's overall international strategy is a collection of its individual country strategies.

While multicountry strategies are best suited for industries where multicountry competition dominates, global strategies are best suited for globally competitive industries. A *global strategy* is one where the company's strategy for competing is mostly the same in all countries. Although *minor* country-to-country differences in strategy do exist to accommodate specific competitive conditions in host countries, the company's fundamental competitive approach (low-cost, differentiation, or

A multicountry strategy is appropriate for industries where multicountry competition dominates, but a global strategy works best in markets that are globally competitive or beginning to globalize.

focused) remains the same worldwide. Moreover, a global strategy involves (1) integrating and coordinating the company's strategic moves worldwide and (2) selling in many if not all nations where there is significant buyer demand. Table 6–1 provides a point-by-point comparison of multicountry versus global strategies. The question of which of these two strategies to pursue is the foremost strategic issue firms face when they compete in international markets.

The strength of a multicountry strategy is that it matches the company's competitive approach to host country circumstances. A multicountry strategy is essential when there are significant country-to-country differences in customers' needs and buying habits (see Illustration Capsule 19), when buyers in a country insist on special-order or highly customized products, when buyer demand for the product exists in comparatively few national markets, when host governments enact regulations requiring that products sold locally meet strict manufacturing specifications or performance standards, and when the trade restrictions of host governments are so diverse and complicated they preclude a uniform, coordinated worldwide market approach. However, a multicountry strategy has two big drawbacks: it entails very

TABLE 6–1 | *Differences between Multicountry and Global Strategies*

	Multicountry Strategy	Global Strategy
Strategic Arena	• Selected target countries and trading areas.	• Most countries which constitute critical markets for the product, at least North America, the European Community, and the Pacific Rim (Australia, Japan, South Korea, and Southeast Asia).
Business Strategy	• Custom strategies to fit the circumstances of each host country situation; little or no strategy coordination across countries.	• Same basic strategy worldwide; minor country-by-country variations where essential.
Product-line Strategy	• Adapted to local needs.	• Mostly standardized products sold worldwide.
Production Strategy	• Plants scattered across many host countries.	• Plants located on the basis of maximum competitive advantage (in low-cost countries, close to major markets, geographically scattered to minimize shipping costs, or use of a few world-scale plants to maximize economies of scale—as most appropriate).
Source of Supply for Raw Materials and Components	• Suppliers in host country preferred (local facilities meeting local buyer needs; some local sourcing may be required by host government).	• Attractive suppliers from anywhere in the world.
Marketing and Distribution	• Adapted to practices and culture of each host country.	• Much more worldwide coordination; minor adaptation to host country situations if required.
Company Organization	• Form subsidiary companies to handle operations in each host country; each subsidiary operates more or less autonomously to fit host country conditions.	• All major strategic decisions are closely coordinated at global headquarters; a global organizational structure is used to unify the operations in each country.

ILLUSTRATION CAPSULE 19

NESTLÉ'S MULTICOUNTRY STRATEGY IN INSTANT COFFEE

Nestlé is the world's largest food company with over $33 billion in revenues, market penetration on all major continents, and plants in over 60 countries. The star performer in Nestlé's food products lineup is coffee, with sales of over $5 billion and operating profits of $600 million. Nestlé is the world's largest producer of coffee. It is also the world's market leader in mineral water (Perrier), condensed milk, frozen food, candies, and infant food.

In 1992 the company's Nescafé brand was the leader in the instant coffee segment in virtually every national market but the U.S., where it ranked number two behind Maxwell House. Nestlé produced 200 types of instant coffee, from lighter blends for the U.S. market to dark espressos for Latin America. To keep its instant coffees matched to consumer tastes in different coun-

tries (and areas within some countries), Nestlé operated four coffee research labs, with a combined budget of $50 million annually, to experiment with new blends in aroma, flavor, and color. The strategy was to match the blends marketed in each country to the tastes and preferences of coffee drinkers in that country, introducing new blends to develop new segments when opportunities appeared and altering blends as needed to respond to changing tastes and buyer habits.

Although instant coffee sales were declining worldwide due to the introduction of new style automatic coffeemakers, sales were rising in two tea-drinking countries, Britain and Japan. In Britain, Nescafé was promoted extensively to build a wider base of instant coffee drinkers. In Japan, where Nescafé was considered a luxury item, the company made its Japanese blends available in fancy containers suitable for gift-giving. In 1993 Nestlé began introducing Nescafé instant coffee and Coffee-Mate creamer in several large cities in China.

Sources: Shawn Tully, "Nestlé Shows How to Gobble Markets," *Fortune,* January 16, 1989, pp. 74–78; "Nestlé: A Giant in a Hurry," *Business Week,* March 22, 1993, pp. 50–54; and company annual reports.

little strategic coordination across country boundaries, and it is not tied tightly to competitive advantage. The primary orientation of a multicountry strategy is responsiveness to local country conditions, not building a multinational competitive advantage over other international competitors and the domestic companies of host countries.

A global strategy, because it is more uniform from country to country, can concentrate on securing a sustainable low-cost or differentiation-based competitive advantage over both international and domestic rivals. Whenever country-to-country differences are small enough to be accommodated within the framework of a global strategy, a global strategy is preferable to a multicountry strategy because of the value of uniting a company's competitive efforts worldwide to pursue lower cost or differentiation.

GLOBAL STRATEGY AND COMPETITIVE ADVANTAGE

There are two ways in which a firm can gain competitive advantage (or offset domestic disadvantages) with a global strategy.[14] One way exploits a global competitor's ability to deploy R&D, parts manufacture, assembly, distribution centers, sales and marketing, customer service centers and other activities among nations in a manner that lowers costs or achieves greater product differentiation; the other way draws on a global competitor's ability to coordinate its dispersed activities in ways that a domestic-only competitor cannot.

---

[14]Ibid., p. 54.

A global strategy enables a firm to pursue sustainable competitive advantage by locating activities in the most advantageous nations and coordinating its strategic actions worldwide; a domestic-only competitor forfeits such opportunities.

Locating Activities   To use location to build competitive advantage, a global firm must consider two issues: (1) whether to concentrate each activity it performs in one or two countries or to disperse performance of the activity to many nations and (2) in which countries to locate particular activities. Activities tend to be concentrated in one or two locations when there are significant economies of scale in performing an activity, when there are advantages in locating related activities in the same area to achieve better coordination, and when there is a steep learning or experience curve associated with performing an activity in a single location. Thus in some industries scale economies in parts manufacture or assembly are so great that a company establishes one large plant from which it serves the world market. Where just-in-time inventory practices yield big cost savings and/or where the assembly firm has long-term partnering arrangements with its key suppliers, parts manufacturing plants may be clustered around final assembly plants.

On the other hand, dispersing activities is more advantageous than concentrating them in several instances. Buyer-related activities—such as distribution to dealers, sales and advertising, and after-sale service—usually must take place close to buyers. This means physically locating the capability to perform such activities in every country market where a global firm has major customers (unless buyers in several adjoining countries can be served quickly from a nearby central location). For example, firms that make mining and oil drilling equipment maintain operations in many international locations to support customers' needs for speedy equipment repair and technical assistance. Large public accounting firms have numerous international offices to service the foreign operations of their multinational corporate clients. A global competitor that effectively disperses its buyer-related activities can gain a service-based competitive edge in world markets over rivals whose buyer-related activities are more concentrated—this is one reason the Big Six public accounting firms have been so successful relative to second-tier firms. Dispersing activities to many locations is also competitively advantageous when high transportation costs, diseconomies of large size, and trade barriers make it too expensive to operate from a central location. Many companies distribute their products from multiple locations to shorten delivery times to customers. In addition, it is strategically advantageous to disperse activities to hedge against the risks of fluctuating exchange rates, supply interruptions (due to strikes, mechanical failures, and transportation delays), and adverse political developments. Such risks are greater when activities are concentrated in a single location.

The classic reason for locating an activity in a particular country is lower costs.[15] Even though a global firm has strong reason to disperse buyer-related activities to many international locations, such activities as materials procurement, parts manufacture, finished goods assembly, technology research, and new-product development can frequently be decoupled from buyer locations and performed wherever advantage lies. Components can be made in Mexico, technology research done in Frankfurt, new products developed and tested in Phoenix, and assembly plants located in Spain, Brazil, Taiwan, and South Carolina. Capital can be raised in whatever country it is available on the best terms.

Low front-end cost is not the only locational consideration, however. A research unit may be situated in a particular nation because of its pool of technically trained

---

[15]Ibid., p. 57.

personnel. A customer service center or sales office may be opened in a particular country to help develop strong relationships with pivotal customers. An assembly plant may be located in a country in return for the host government's allowing freer import of components from large-scale, centralized parts plants located elsewhere.

Coordinating Activities and Strategic Moves Aligning and coordinating company activities located in different countries contributes to sustainable competitive advantage in several different ways. If a firm learns how to assemble its product more efficiently at its Brazilian plant, the accumulated knowledge and expertise can be transferred to its assembly plant in Spain. Knowledge gained in marketing a company's product in Great Britain can be used to introduce the product in New Zealand and Australia. A company can shift production from one country to another to take advantage of exchange rate fluctuations, to enhance its leverage with host country governments, and to respond to changing wage rates, energy costs, or trade restrictions. A company can enhance its brand reputation by consistently incorporating the same differentiating attributes in its products in all worldwide markets where it competes. The reputation for quality that Honda established worldwide first in motorcycles and then in automobiles gave it competitive advantage in positioning Honda lawnmowers at the upper end of the market—the Honda name gave the company instant credibility with buyers.

A global competitor can choose where and how to challenge rivals. It may decide to retaliate against aggressive rivals in the country market where the rival has its biggest sales volume or its best profit margins in order to reduce the rival's financial resources for competing in other country markets. It may decide to wage a price-cutting offensive against weak rivals in their home markets, capturing greater market share and subsidizing any short-term losses with profits earned in other country markets.

A company that competes only in its home country has access to none of the competitive advantage opportunities associated with international locations or coordination. By shifting from a domestic strategy to a global strategy, a domestic company that finds itself at a competitive disadvantage against global companies can begin to restore its competitiveness.

STRATEGIC ALLIANCES

Strategic alliances are cooperative agreements between firms that go beyond normal company-to-company dealings but that fall short of merger or full partnership.[16] An alliance can involve joint research efforts, technology sharing, joint use of production facilities, marketing one another's products, or joining forces to manufacture components or assemble finished products. Strategic alliances are a means for firms in the same industry yet based in different countries to compete on a more global scale while still preserving their independence. Historically, export minded firms in industrialized nations sought alliances with firms in less-developed countries to import and market their products locally—such arrangements were often necessary to gain access to the less-developed country's market. More recently, leading companies from different parts of the world have formed strategic alliances to strengthen their

Strategic alliances can help companies in globally competitive industries strengthen their competitive positions while still preserving their independence.

---

[16]Ibid., p. 65. See also Kenichi Ohmae, "The Global Logic of Strategic Alliances," *Harvard Business Review* 89, no. 2 (March–April 1989), pp. 143–54.

mutual ability to serve whole continental areas and move toward more global market participation. Both Japanese and American companies are actively forming alliances with European companies to strengthen their ability to compete in the 12-nation European Community and to capitalize on the opening up of Eastern European markets. Illustration Capsule 20 describes Toshiba's successful use of strategic alliances and joint ventures to pursue related technologies and product markets.

Companies enter into alliances for several strategically beneficial reasons.[17] The three most important are to gain economies of scale in production and/or marketing, to fill gaps in their technical and manufacturing expertise, and to acquire market access. By joining forces in producing components, assembling models, and marketing their products, companies can realize cost savings not achievable with their own small volumes. Allies learn much from one another in performing joint research, sharing technological know-how, and studying one another's manufacturing methods. Alliances are often used by outsiders to meet governmental requirements for local ownership, and allies can share distribution facilities and dealer networks, thus mutually strengthening their access to buyers. In addition, alliances affect competition; not only can alliances offset competitive disadvantages but they also can result in the allied companies' directing their competitive energies more toward mutual rivals and less toward one another. Many runner-up companies, wanting to preserve their independence, resort to alliances rather than merger to try to close the competitive gap on leading companies.

Alliances have their pitfalls, however. Achieving effective coordination between independent companies, each with different motives and perhaps conflicting objectives, is a challenging task. It requires many meetings of many people over a period of time to iron out what is to be shared, what is to remain proprietary, and how the cooperative arrangements will work. Allies may have to overcome language and cultural barriers as well. The communication, trust-building, and coordination costs are high in terms of management time. Often, once the bloom is off the rose, partners discover they have deep differences of opinion about how to proceed and conflicting objectives and strategies. Tensions build up, working relationships cool, and the hoped-for benefits never materialize.[18] Many times, allies find it difficult to collaborate effectively in competitively sensitive areas, thus raising questions about mutual trust and forthright exchanges of information and expertise. There can also be clashes of egos and company cultures. The key people on whom success or failure depends may have little personal chemistry, be unable to work closely together or form a partnership, or be unable to come to consensus.

> Strategic alliances are more effective in combating competitive disadvantage than in gaining competitive advantage.

Most important, though, is the danger of depending on another company for essential expertise and capabilities over the long term. To be a serious market contender, a company must ultimately develop internal capabilities in all areas important to strengthening its competitive position and building a sustainable competitive advantage. Where this is not feasible, merger is a better solution than strategic alliance. Strategic alliances are best used as a transitional way to combat competitive disadvantage in international markets; rarely if ever can they be relied on as a means for creating competitive advantage. Illustration Capsule 21 relates the experiences of companies with strategic alliances.

---

[17]Porter, *The Competitive Advantage of Nations,* p. 66; see also Jeremy Main, "Making Global Alliances Work," *Fortune,* December 17, 1990, pp. 121–26.

[18]Jeremy Main, "Making Global Alliances Work," p. 125.

ILLUSTRATION CAPSULE 20

TOSHIBA'S USE OF STRATEGIC ALLIANCES AND JOINT VENTURES

Toshiba, Japan's oldest and third largest electronics company (after Hitachi and Matsushita), over the years has made technology licensing agreements, joint ventures, and strategic alliances cornerstones of its corporate strategy. Using such partnerships to complement its own manufacturing and product innovation capabilities, it has become a $37 billion maker of electrical and electronics products—from home appliances to computer memory chips to telecommunications equipment to electric power generation equipment.

Fumio Sato, Toshiba's CEO, contends that joint ventures and strategic alliances are a necessary component of strategy for a high-tech electronics company with global ambitions:

> It is no longer an era in which a single company can dominate any technology or business by itself. The technology has become so advanced, and the markets so complex, that you simply can't expect to be the best at the whole process any longer.

Among Toshiba's two dozen major joint ventures and strategic alliances are

- A five-year-old joint venture with Motorola to design and make dynamic random access memory chips (DRAMs) for Toshiba and microprocessors for Motorola. Initially the two partners invested $125 million apiece in the venture and have since invested another $480 million each.
- A joint venture with IBM to make flat-panel liquid crystal displays in color for portable computers.
- Two other joint ventures with IBM to develop computer memory chips (one a "flash" memory chip that remembers data even after the power is turned off).
- An alliance with Sweden-based Ericsson, one of the world's biggest telecommunications manufacturers, to develop new mobile telecommunications equipment.

- A partnership with Sun Microsystems, the leading maker of microprocessor-based workstations, to provide portable versions of the workstations to Sun and to incorporate Sun's equipment in Toshiba products to control power plants, route highway traffic, and monitor automated manufacturing processes.
- A $1 billion strategic alliance with IBM and Siemens to develop and produce the next-generation DRAM—a single chip capable of holding 256 million bits of information (approximately 8,000 typewritten pages).
- An alliance with Apple Computer to develop CD-ROM-based multimedia players that plug into a TV set.
- A joint project with the entertainment division of Time Warner to design advanced interactive cable television technology.

Other alliances and joint ventures with General Electric, United Technologies, National Semiconductor, Samsung (Korea), LSI Logic (Canada), and European companies like Olivetti, SCS-Thomson, Rhone-Poulenc, Thomson Consumer Electronics, and GEC Alstholm are turning out such products as fax machines, copiers, medical equipment, computers, rechargeable batteries, home appliances, and nuclear and steam power generating equipment.

So far, none of Toshiba's relationships with partners have gone sour despite potential conflicts among related projects with competitors (Toshiba has partnerships with nine other chip makers to develop or produce semiconductors). Toshiba attributes this to its approach to alliances: choosing partners carefully, being open about Toshiba's connections with other companies, carefully defining the role and rights of each partner in the original pact (including who gets what if the alliance doesn't work out), and cultivating easy relations and good friendships with each partner. Toshiba's management believes that strategic alliances and joint ventures are an effective way for the company to move into new businesses quickly, share the design and development costs of ambitious new products with competent partners, and achieve greater access to important geographic markets outside Japan.

Source: Based on Brenton R. Schlender, "How Toshiba Makes Alliances Work," *Fortune,* October 4, 1993, pp. 116–20.

ILLUSTRATION CAPSULE 21

COMPANY EXPERIENCES WITH STRATEGIC ALLIANCES

As the chairman of British Aerospace recently observed, a strategic alliance with a foreign company is "one of the quickest and cheapest ways to develop a global strategy." AT&T formed joint ventures with many of the world's largest telephone and electronics companies. Boeing, the world's premier manufacturer of commercial aircraft, partnered with Kawasaki, Mitsubishi, and Fuji to produce a long-range, wide-body jet for delivery in 1995. General Electric and Snecma, a French maker of jet engines, have a 50-50 partnership to make jet engines to power aircraft made by Boeing, McDonnell-Douglas, and Airbus Industrie (Airbus, the leading European maker of commercial aircraft, was formed by an alliance of aerospace companies from Britain, Spain, Germany, and France). The GE/Snecma alliance is regarded as a model because it existed for 17 years and it produced orders for 10,300 engines, totaling $38 billion.

Since the early 1980s, hundreds of strategic alliances have been formed in the motor vehicle industry as car and truck manufacturers and automotive parts suppliers moved aggressively to get in stronger position to compete globally. Not only have there been alliances between automakers strong in one region of the world and automakers strong in another region but there have also been strategic alliances between vehicle makers and key parts suppliers (especially those with high-quality parts and strong technological capabilities). General Motors and Toyota in 1984 formed a 50-50 partnership called New United Motor Manufacturing Inc. (NUMMI) to produce cars for both companies at an old GM plant in Fremont, California. The strategic value of the GM-Toyota alliance was that Toyota would learn how to deal with suppliers and workers in the

U.S. (as a prelude to building its own plants in the U.S.) while GM would learn about Toyota's approaches to manufacturing and management. Each company sent managers to the NUMMI plant to work for two or three years to learn and absorb all they could, then transferred their NUMMI "graduates" to jobs where they could be instrumental in helping their companies apply what they learned. Toyota moved quickly to capitalize on its experiences at NUMMI. By 1991 Toyota had opened two plants on its own in North America, was constructing a third plant, and was producing 50% of the vehicles it sold in North America in its North American plants. While General Motors incorporated much of its NUMMI learning into the management practices and manufacturing methods it was using at its newly opened Saturn plant in Tennessee, it proceeded more slowly than Toyota. American and European companies are generally regarded as less skilled than the Japanese in transferring the learning from strategic alliances into their own operations.

Many alliances fail or are terminated when one partner ends up acquiring the other. A 1990 survey of 150 companies involved in terminated alliances found that three-fourths of the alliances had been taken over by Japanese partners. A nine-year alliance between Fujitsu and International Computers, Ltd., a British manufacturer, ended when Fujitsu acquired 80% of ICL. According to one observer, Fujitsu deliberately maneuvered ICL into a position of having no better choice than to sell out to its partner. Fujitsu began as a supplier of components for ICL's mainframe computers, then expanded its role over the next nine years to the point where it was ICL's only source of new technology. When ICL's parent, a large British electronics firm, saw the mainframe computer business starting to decline and decided to sell, Fujitsu was the only buyer it could find.

Source: Jeremy Main, "Making Global Alliances Work," *Fortune*, December 17, 1990, pp. 121–26.

To realize the most from strategic alliance, companies should observe five guidelines:[19]

1. Pick a compatible partner; take the time to build strong bridges of communication and trust and don't expect immediate payoffs.

2. Choose an ally whose products and market strongholds *complement* rather than compete directly with the company's own products and customer base.

---

[19]Ibid.

3. Learn thoroughly and rapidly about a partner's technology and management; transfer valuable ideas and practices into one's own operations promptly.

4. Be careful not to divulge competitively sensitive information to a partner.

5. View the alliance as temporary (5 to 10 years); continue longer if it's beneficial but don't hesitate to terminate the alliance and go it alone when the payoffs run out.

STRATEGIC INTENT, PROFIT SANCTUARIES, AND CROSS-SUBSIDIZATION

Competitors in international markets can be distinguished not only by their strategies but also by their long-term strategic objectives and strategic intent. Four types of competitors stand out:[20]

- Firms whose strategic intent is *global dominance* or, at least, high rank among the global market leaders; such firms pursue some form of global strategy.

- Firms whose primary strategic objective is *defending domestic dominance* in their home market, even though they derive some of their sales internationally (usually under 20 percent) and have operations in several or many foreign markets.

- Firms who aspire to a growing share of worldwide sales and whose primary strategic orientation is *host country responsiveness;* such firms have a multicountry strategy and may already derive a large fraction of their revenues from foreign operations.

- *Domestic-only firms* whose strategic intent does not extend beyond building a strong competitive position in their home country market; such firms base their competitive strategies on domestic market conditions and watch events in the international market only for their impact on the domestic situation.

The types of firms are *not* equally well-positioned to be successful in markets where they compete head-on. Consider the case of a purely domestic U.S. company in competition with a Japanese company operating in many country markets and aspiring to global dominance. The Japanese company can cut its prices in the U.S. market to gain market share at the expense of the U.S. company, subsidizing any losses with profits earned in its home sanctuary and in other foreign markets. The U.S. company has no effective way to retaliate. It is vulnerable even if it is the U.S. market leader. However, if the U.S. company is a multinational competitor and operates in Japan as well as elsewhere, it can counter Japanese pricing in the United States with retaliatory price cuts in its competitor's main profit sanctuary, Japan, and in other countries where it competes against the same Japanese company.

Thus, a domestic-only competitor is not on a level playing field in competing against a multinational rival. When aggressive global competitors enter a domestic-only company's market, one of the domestic-only competitor's best strategic defenses is to switch to a multinational or global strategy to give it the same cross-subsidizing capabilities the aggressors have.

Profit Sanctuaries and Critical Markets *Profit sanctuaries* are country markets where a company has a strong or protected market position and derives substantial profits.

---

[20]Prahalad and Doz, *The Multinational Mission*, p. 52.

Japan, for example, is a profit sanctuary for most Japanese companies because trade barriers erected around Japanese industries by the Japanese government effectively block foreign companies from competing for a large share of Japanese sales. Protected from the threat of foreign competition in their home market, Japanese companies can safely charge somewhat higher prices to their Japanese customers and thus earn attractively large profits on sales made in Japan. In most cases, a company's biggest and most strategically crucial profit sanctuary is its home market, but multinational companies also have profit sanctuaries in those country markets where they have strong competitive positions, big sales volumes, and attractive profit margins.

> A particular nation is a company's *profit sanctuary* when the company, either because of its strong competitive position or protective governmental trade policies, derives a substantial part of its total profits from sales in that nation.

Profit sanctuaries are valuable competitive assets in global industries. Companies with large, protected profit sanctuaries have competitive advantage over companies that don't have a dependable sanctuary. Companies with multiple profit sanctuaries are more favorably positioned than companies with a single sanctuary. Normally, a global competitor with multiple profit sanctuaries can successfully attack and beat a domestic competitor whose only profit sanctuary is its home market.

To defend against global competitors, companies don't have to compete in all or even most foreign markets, but they do have to compete in all critical markets. *Critical markets* are markets in countries

- That are the profit sanctuaries of key competitors.
- That have big sales volumes.
- That contain prestigious customers whose business it is strategically important to have.
- That offer exceptionally good profit margins due to weak competitive pressures.[21]

The more critical markets a company participates in, the greater its ability to use cross-subsidization as a defense against competitors intent on global dominance.

The Competitive Power of Cross-Subsidization   Cross-subsidization is a powerful competitive weapon. It involves using profits earned in one or more country markets to support a competitive offensive against key rivals or to gain increased penetration of a critical market. A typical offensive involves matching (or nearly matching) rivals on product quality and service, then charging a low enough price to draw customers away from rivals. While price-cutting may result in a challenger's earning lower profits (or even incurring losses) in the critical market it is attacking, it may still realize acceptable overall profits when the above-average earnings from its profit sanctuaries are added in.

> A competent global competitor with multiple profit sanctuaries can wage and generally win a competitive offensive against a domestic competitor whose only profit sanctuary is its home market.

Cross-subsidization is most powerful when a global firm with multiple profit sanctuaries is aggressively intent on achieving global market dominance over the long term. Both a domestic-only competitor and a multicountry competitor with no strategic coordination between its locally responsive country strategies are vulnerable to competition from rivals intent on global dominance. A global strategy can defeat a domestic-only strategy because a one-country competitor cannot effectively defend its market share over the long term against a global competitor with cross-subsidization capability. The global company can use lower prices to siphon off the domestic company's customers, all the while gaining market share, building name recognition, and supporting its strategic offensive with profits earned in its other critical markets.

---

[21]Ibid., p. 61.

It can adjust the depth of its price-cutting to move in and capture market share quickly, or it can shave prices slightly to make gradual market inroads over a decade or more so as not to threaten domestic firms precipitously and perhaps trigger protectionist government actions. When attacked in this manner, a domestic company's best short-term hope is to pursue immediate and perhaps dramatic cost reduction and, if the situation warrants, to seek government protection in the form of tariff barriers, import quotas, and antidumping penalties. In the long term, the domestic company has to find ways to compete on a more equal footing—a difficult task when it must charge a price to cover full unit costs plus a margin for profit while the global competitor can charge a price only high enough to cover the incremental costs of selling in the domestic company's profit sanctuary. The best long-term strategic defenses for a domestic company are to enter into strategic alliances with foreign firms or to adopt a global approach to strategy and compete on an international scale, although sometimes it is possible to drive enough costs out of the business over the long term to survive with a domestic-only strategy. As a rule, however, competing only domestically is a perilous strategy in an industry populated with global competitors.

To defend against aggressive international competitors intent on global dominance, a domestic-only competitor usually has to abandon its domestic focus, become a multinational competitor, and craft a multinational competitive strategy.

While a company with a multicountry strategy has some cross-subsidy defense against a company with a global strategy, its vulnerability comes from a lack of competitive advantage and a probable cost disadvantage. A global competitor with a big manufacturing share and world-scale state-of-the-art plants is almost certain to be a lower-cost producer than a multicountry strategist with many small plants and short production runs turning out specialized products country by country. Companies pursuing a multicountry strategy thus need differentiation and focus-based advantages keyed to local responsiveness in order to defend against a global competitor. Such a defense is adequate in industries with significant enough national differences to impede use of a global strategy. But if an international rival can accommodate necessary local needs within a global strategy and still retain a cost edge, then a global strategy can defeat a multicountry strategy.

STRATEGIES FOR INDUSTRY LEADERS

The competitive positions of industry leaders normally range from stronger-than-average to powerful. Leaders typically are well-known, and strongly entrenched leaders have proven strategies (keyed either to low-cost leadership or to differentiation). Some of the best-known industry leaders are Anheuser-Busch (beer), IBM (mainframe computers), McDonald's (fast-food), Gillette (razor blades), Campbell's Soup (canned soups), Gerber (baby food), AT&T (long-distance telephone service), Eastman Kodak (camera film), and Levi Strauss (jeans). The main strategic concern for a leader revolves around how to sustain a leadership position, perhaps becoming the *dominant* leader as opposed to *a* leader. However, the pursuit of industry leadership and large market share per se is primarily important because of the competitive advantage and profitability that accrue to being the industry's biggest company.

Three contrasting strategic postures are open to industry leaders and dominant firms:[22]

---

[22]Kotler, *Marketing Management,* chapter 23; Michael E. Porter, *Competitive Advantage* (New York: Free Press, 1985), chapter 14; and Ian C. MacMillan, "Seizing Competitive Initiative," *The Journal of Business Strategy* 2, no. 4 (Spring 1982), pp. 43–57.

1. **Stay-on-the-offensive strategy**—This strategy rests on the principle that the best defense is a good offense. Offensive-minded leaders stress being first-movers to sustain their competitive advantage (lower cost or differentiation) and to reinforce their reputation as *the* leader. A low-cost provider aggressively pursues cost reduction, and a differentiator constantly tries new ways to set its product apart from rivals' brands. The theme of a stay-on-the-offensive strategy is relentless pursuit of continuous improvement and innovation. Striving to be first with new products, better performance features, quality enhancements, improved customer services, or ways to cut production costs not only helps a leader avoid complacency but it also keeps rivals on the defensive scrambling to keep up. The array of offensive options can also include initiatives to expand overall industry demand—discovering new uses for the product, attracting new users of the product, and promoting more frequent use. In addition, a clever offensive leader stays alert for ways to make it easier and less costly for potential customers to switch their purchases from runner-up firms to its own products. Unless a leader's market share is already so dominant that it presents a threat of antitrust action (a market share under 60 percent is usually "safe"), a stay-on-the-offensive strategy means trying to grow *faster* than the industry as a whole and wrest market share from rivals. A leader whose growth does not equal or outpace the industry average is losing ground to competitors.

2. **Fortify-and-defend strategy**—The essence of "fortify and defend" is to make it harder for new firms to enter and for challengers to gain ground. The goals of a strong defense are to hold onto the present market share, strengthen current market position, and protect whatever competitive advantage the firm has. Specific defensive actions can include

   - Attempting to raise the competitive ante for challengers and new entrants via increased spending for advertising, higher levels of customer service, and bigger R&D outlays.
   - Introducing more of the company's own brands to match the product attributes that challenger brands have or could employ.
   - Adding personalized services and other "extras" that boost customer loyalty and make it harder or more costly for customers to switch to rival products.
   - Broadening the product line to close off possible vacant niches for competitors to slip into.
   - Keeping prices reasonable and quality attractive.
   - Building new capacity ahead of market demand to try to block the market expansion potential of smaller competitors.
   - Investing enough to remain cost competitive and technologically progressive.
   - Patenting the feasible alternative technologies.
   - Signing exclusive contracts with the best suppliers and dealer distributors.

   A fortify-and-defend strategy best suits firms that have already achieved industry dominance and don't wish to risk antitrust action. It is also well-suited to situations where a firm wishes to milk its present position for profits and cash flow because the industry's prospects for growth are low or because further gains in market share do not appear profitable enough to go after. But the fortify-and-defend strategy always entails trying to grow as fast as the

Industry leaders can strengthen their long-term competitive positions with strategies keyed to aggressive offense, aggressive defense, or muscling smaller rivals into a follow-the-leader role.

market as a whole (to stave off market share slippage) and requires reinvesting enough capital in the business to protect the leader's ability to compete.

3. **Follow-the-leader strategy**—Here the leader's strategic posture involves using its competitive muscle (ethically and fairly!) to encourage runner-up firms to be content followers rather than aggressive challengers. The leader plays competitive hardball when smaller rivals rock the boat with price cuts or mount new market offensives that directly threaten its position. Specific responses can include quickly matching and perhaps exceeding challengers' price cuts, using large promotional campaigns to counter challengers' moves to gain market share, and offering better deals to the major customers of maverick firms. Leaders can also court distributors assiduously to dissuade them from carrying rivals' products, provide salespersons with documented information about the weaknesses of an aggressor's products, or try to fill any vacant positions in their own firms by making attractive offers to the better executives of rivals that "get out of line." When a leader consistently meets any moves to cut into its business with strong retaliatory tactics, it sends clear signals that offensive attacks on the leader's position will be met head-on and probably won't pay off. However, leaders pursuing this strategic approach should choose their battles. It may be more strategically productive to assume a hands-off posture and not respond in hardball fashion when smaller rivals attack each other's customer base in ways that don't affect its own.

STRATEGIES FOR RUNNER-UP FIRMS

Runner-up firms occupy weaker market positions than the industry leader(s). Some runner-up firms are up-and-coming *market challengers,* employing offensive strategies to gain market share and a stronger market position. Others behave as *content followers,* willing to coast along in their current positions because profits are adequate. Follower firms have no urgent strategic issue to confront beyond "What kinds of strategic changes are the leaders initiating and what do we need to do to follow along?"

A challenger firm interested in improving its market standing needs a strategy aimed at building a competitive advantage of its own. *Rarely can a runner-up firm improve its competitive position by imitating the strategies of leading firms. A cardinal rule in offensive strategy is to avoid attacking a leader head-on with an imitative strategy, regardless of the resources and staying power an underdog may have.*[23] Moreover, if a challenger has a 5 percent market share and needs a 20 percent share to earn attractive returns, it needs a more creative approach to competing than just "try harder."

In industries where large size yields significantly lower unit costs and gives large-share competitors an important cost advantage, small-share firms have only two viable strategic options: try to increase their market share (and achieve cost parity with larger rivals) or withdraw from the business (gradually or quickly). The competitive strategies most underdogs use to build market share are based on (1) becoming a lower-cost producer and using lower price to win customers from weak, higher-cost rivals and (2) using differentiation strategies based on quality, technological superiority, better customer service, best cost, or innovation. Achieving low-cost leadership is

> Rarely can a runner-up firm successfully challenge an industry leader with a copycat strategy.

[23]Porter, *Competitive Advantage,* p. 514.

usually open to an underdog only when one of the market leaders is not already solidly positioned as the industry's low-cost producer. But a small-share firm may still be able to reduce its cost disadvantage by merging with or acquiring smaller firms; the combined market shares may provide the needed access to size-related economies. Other options include revamping its value chain to produce the needed cost savings and finding ways to better manage executional cost drivers.

In situations where scale economies or experience curve effects are small and a large market share produces no cost advantage, runner-up companies have more strategic flexibility and can consider any of the following six approaches:[24]

1. **Vacant-niche strategy**—This version of a focused strategy involves concentrating on customer or end-use applications that market leaders have bypassed or neglected. An ideal vacant niche is of sufficient size and scope to be profitable, has some growth potential, is well-suited to a firm's own capabilities and skills, and for one reason or another is not interesting to leading firms. Two examples where vacant-niche strategies worked successfully are regional commuter airlines serving cities with too few passengers to attract the interest of major airlines and health foods producers (like Health Valley, Hain, and Tree of Life) that cater to local health food stores—a market segment traditionally ignored by Pillsbury, Kraft General Foods, Heinz, Nabisco, Campbell's Soup, and other leading food products firms.

2. **Specialist strategy**—A specialist firm trains its competitive effort on one market segment: a single product, a particular end use, or buyers with special needs. The aim is to build competitive advantage through product uniqueness, expertise in special-purpose products, or specialized customer services. Smaller companies that successfully use a specialist focused strategy include Formby's (a specialist in stains and finishes for wood furniture, especially refinishing), Liquid Paper Co. (a leader in correction fluid for writers and typists), Canada Dry (known for its ginger ale, tonic water, and carbonated soda water), and American Tobacco (a leader in chewing tobacco and snuff).

3. **Ours-is-better-than-theirs strategy**—The approach here is to use a differentiation-based focused strategy keyed to superior product quality or unique attributes. Sales and marketing efforts are aimed directly at quality-conscious and performance-oriented buyers. Fine craftsmanship, prestige quality, frequent product innovations, and/or close contact with customers to solicit their input in developing a better product usually undergird this "superior product" approach. Some examples include Beefeater and Tanqueray in gin, Tiffany in diamonds and jewelry, Chicago Cutlery in premium-quality kitchen knives, Baccarat in fine crystal, Cannondale in mountain bikes, Bally in shoes, and Patagonia in apparel for outdoor recreation enthusiasts.

4. **Content-follower strategy**—Follower firms deliberately refrain from initiating trendsetting strategic moves and from aggressive attempts to steal customers away from the leaders. Followers prefer approaches that will not provoke competitive retaliation, often opting for focus and differentiation strategies that keep them out of the leaders' paths. They react and respond

---

[24]For more details, see Kotler, *Marketing Management,* pp. 397–412; R. G. Hamermesh, M. J. Anderson, Jr., and J. E. Harris, "Strategies for Low Market Share Businesses," *Harvard Business Review* 56, no. 3 (May–June 1978), pp. 95–102; and Porter, *Competitive Advantage,* chapter 15.

rather than initiate and challenge. They prefer defense to offense. And they rarely get out of line with the leaders on price. Union Camp (in paper products) has been a successful market follower by consciously concentrating on selected product uses and applications for specific customer groups, focused R&D, profits rather than market share, and cautious but efficient management.

5. **Growth-via-acquisition strategy**—One way to strengthen a company's position is to merge with or acquire weaker rivals to form an enterprise that has more competitive strength and a larger share of the market. Commercial airline companies such as Northwest, USAir, and Delta owe their market share growth during the past decade to acquisition of smaller, regional airlines. Likewise, the Big Six public accounting firms enhanced their national and international coverage by merging or forming alliances with smaller CPA firms at home and abroad.

6. **Distinctive-image strategy**—Some runner-up companies build their strategies around ways to make themselves stand out from competitors. A variety of strategic approaches can be used: creating a reputation for charging the lowest prices, providing prestige quality at a good price, going all out to give superior customer service, designing unique product attributes, being a leader in new product introduction, or devising unusually creative advertising. Examples include Dr Pepper's strategy in calling attention to its distinctive taste, Apple Computer's making it easier and more interesting for people to use a personal computer, and Mary Kay Cosmetics' distinctive use of the color pink.

In industries where big size is definitely a key success factor, firms with low market shares have some obstacles to overcome: (1) less access to economies of scale in manufacturing, distribution, or sales promotion; (2) difficulty in gaining customer recognition; (3) an inability to afford mass media advertising on a grand scale; and (4) difficulty in funding capital requirements.[25] But *it is erroneous to view runner-up firms as inherently less profitable or unable to hold their own against the biggest firms*. Many firms with small market shares earn healthy profits and enjoy good reputations with customers. Often, the handicaps of smaller size can be surmounted and a profitable competitive position established by (1) focusing on a few market segments where the company's strengths can yield a competitive edge; (2) developing technical expertise that will be highly valued by customers; (3) aggressively pursuing the development of new products for customers in the target market segments; and (4) using innovative/"dare to be different"/"beat the odds" entrepreneurial approaches to outmanage stodgy, slow-to-change market leaders. Runner-up companies have a golden opportunity to gain market share if they make a leapfrog technological breakthrough, if the leaders stumble or become complacent, or if they have the patience to nibble away at the leaders and build up their customer base over a long period of time.

STRATEGIES FOR WEAK BUSINESSES

A firm in an also-ran or declining competitive position has four basic strategic options. If it has the financial resources, it can launch an *offensive turnaround strat-*

---

[25]Hamermesh, Anderson, and Harris, "Strategies for Low Market Share Businesses," p. 102.

The strategic options for a competitively weak company include waging a modest offensive to improve its position, defending its present position, being acquired by another company, or employing a harvest strategy.

egy keyed either to low-cost or "new" differentiation themes, pouring enough money and talent into the effort to move up a notch or two in the industry rankings and become a respectable market contender within five years or so. It can employ a *fortify-and-defend* strategy, using variations of its present strategy and fighting hard to keep sales, market share, profitability, and competitive position at current levels. It can opt for an *immediate abandonment strategy* and get out of the business, either by selling out to another firm or by closing down operations if a buyer cannot be found. Or it can employ a *harvest strategy,* keeping reinvestment to a bare-bones minimum and taking actions to maximize short-term cash flows in preparation for an orderly market exit. The gist of the first three options is self-explanatory. The fourth merits more discussion.

A *harvest strategy* steers a middle course between preserving the status quo and exiting as soon as possible. Harvesting is a phasing down or endgame strategy that involves sacrificing market position in return for improved cash flows or short-term profitability. The overriding financial objective is to reap the greatest possible harvest of cash to deploy to other business endeavors.

The measures taken in a harvest strategy are fairly clear-cut. The operating budget is chopped to a rock-bottom level; reinvestment in the business is held to a bare minimum. Capital expenditures for new equipment are put on hold or given low financial priority (unless replacement needs are unusually urgent); instead, efforts are made to stretch the life of existing equipment and make do with present facilities as long as possible. Price may be raised gradually, promotional expenses slowly cut, quality reduced in not-so-visible ways, nonessential customer services curtailed, and the like. Although harvesting results in shrinking sales and market share, if cash expenses can be cut even faster, then after-tax cash flows may rise (at least temporarily) and the company's profits will erode slowly rather than rapidly.

Harvesting is a reasonable strategic option for a weak business in the following circumstances:[26]

1. When the industry's long-term prospects are unattractive.
2. When rejuvenating the business would be too costly or at best marginally profitable.
3. When the firm's market share is becoming increasingly costly to maintain or defend.
4. When reduced levels of competitive effort will not trigger an immediate or rapid falloff in sales.
5. When the enterprise can redeploy the freed resources in higher opportunity areas.
6. When the business is *not* a crucial or core component of a diversified company's portfolio of business interests (harvesting a noncore business is strategically preferable to harvesting a core business).
7. When the business does not contribute other desired features (sales stability, prestige, a well-rounded product line) to a company's overall business portfolio.

The more of these seven conditions present, the more ideal the business is for harvesting.

---

[26]Phillip Kotler, "Harvesting Strategies for Weak Products," *Business Horizons* 21, no. 5 (August 1978), pp. 17–18.

Harvesting strategies make the most sense for diversified companies that have sideline or noncore business units in weak competitive positions or in unattractive industries. Such companies can take the cash flows from harvesting unattractive, noncore business units and reallocate them to business units with greater profit potential or to the acquisition of new businesses.

TURNAROUND STRATEGIES FOR BUSINESSES IN CRISIS

Turnaround strategies are needed when a business worth rescuing goes into crisis; the objective is to arrest and reverse the sources of competitive and financial weakness as quickly as possible. Management's first task in formulating a suitable turnaround strategy is to diagnose what lies at the root of poor performance. Is it an unexpected downturn in sales brought on by a weak economy? An ill-chosen competitive strategy? Poor execution of an otherwise workable strategy? An overload of debt? Can the business be saved, or is the situation hopeless? Understanding what is wrong with the business and how serious its strategic problems are is essential because different diagnoses lead to different turnaround strategies.

Some of the most common causes of business trouble are taking on too much debt, overestimating the potential for sales growth, ignoring the profit-depressing effects of an overly aggressive effort to "buy" market share with deep price-cuts, being burdened with heavy fixed costs because of an inability to utilize plant capacity, betting on R&D efforts to boost competitive position and profitability and failing to come up with effective innovations, betting on technological long shots, being too optimistic about the ability to penetrate new markets, making frequent changes in strategy (because the previous strategy didn't work out), and being overpowered by the competitive advantages enjoyed by more successful rivals. Curing these kinds of problems and achieving a successful business turnaround can involve any of the following actions:

- Revising the existing strategy.
- Launching efforts to boost revenues.
- Pursuing cost reduction.
- Selling off assets to raise cash to save the remaining part of the business.
- Using a combination of these efforts.

Strategy Revision When weak performance is caused by bad strategy, the task of strategy overhaul can proceed along any of several paths: (1) shifting to a new competitive approach to rebuild the firm's market position; (2) overhauling internal operations and functional area strategies to better support the same overall business strategy; (3) merging with another firm in the industry and forging a new strategy keyed to the newly merged firm's strengths; and (4) retrenching into a reduced core of products and customers more closely matched to the firm's strengths. The most appealing path depends on prevailing industry conditions, the firm's particular strengths and weaknesses, its competitive capabilities vis-à-vis rival firms, and the severity of the crisis. Situation analysis of the industry, major competitors, and the firm's own competitive position and its skills and resources are prerequisites for action. As a rule, successful strategy revision must be tied to the ailing firm's strengths and near-term competitive capabilities and directed at its best market opportunities.

Boosting Revenues Revenue-increasing turnaround efforts aim at generating increased sales volume. There are a number of revenue-building options: price cuts, increased promotion, a bigger sales force, added customer services, and quickly achieved product improvements. Attempts to increase revenues and sales volumes are necessary (1) when there is little or no room in the operating budget to cut expenses and still break even and (2) when the key to restoring profitability is increased utilization of existing capacity. If buyer demand is not especially price sensitive because of differentiating features, the quickest way to boost short-term revenues may be to raise prices rather than opt for volume-building price cuts.

Cutting Costs Cost-reducing turnaround strategies work best when an ailing firm's value chain and cost structure are flexible enough to permit radical surgery, when operating inefficiencies are identifiable and readily correctable, when the firm's costs are obviously bloated and there are many places where savings can be quickly achieved, and when the firm is relatively close to its break-even point. Accompanying a general belt-tightening can be an increased emphasis on paring administrative overheads, elimination of nonessential and low value-added activities in the firm's value chain, modernization of existing plant and equipment to gain greater productivity, delay of nonessential capital expenditures, and debt restructuring to reduce interest costs and stretch out repayments.

Selling Off Assets Assets reduction/retrenchment strategies are essential when cash flow is a critical consideration and when the most practical ways to generate cash are (1) through sale of some of the firm's assets (plant and equipment, land, patents, inventories, or profitable subsidiaries) and (2) through retrenchment (pruning of marginal products from the product line, closing or selling older plants, reducing the workforce, withdrawing from outlying markets, cutting back customer service, and the like). Sometimes crisis-ridden companies sell off assets not so much to unload losing operations and to stem cash drains as to raise funds to save and strengthen the remaining business activities. In such cases, the choice is usually to dispose of non-core business assets to support strategy renewal in the firm's core business(es).

Combination Efforts Combination turnaround strategies are usually essential in grim situations that require fast action on a broad front. Likewise, combination actions frequently come into play when new managers are brought in and given a free hand to make whatever changes they see fit. The tougher the problems, the more likely the solutions will involve multiple strategic initiatives.

Turnaround efforts tend to be high-risk undertakings, and they often fail. A landmark study of 64 companies found no successful turnarounds among the most troubled companies in eight basic industries.[27] Many of the troubled businesses waited too long to begin a turnaround. Others found themselves short of both the cash and entrepreneurial talent needed to compete in a slow-growth industry characterized by a fierce battle for market share. Better-positioned rivals simply proved too strong to defeat in a long, head-to-head contest. Even when successful, many troubled companies go through a series of turnaround attempts and management changes before long-term competitive viability and profitability are finally restored.

---

[27]William K. Hall, "Survival Strategies in a Hostile Environment," *Harvard Business Review* 58, no. 5 (September–October 1980), pp. 75–85. See also Frederick M. Zimmerman, *The Turnaround Experience: Real-World Lessons in Revitalizing Corporations* (New York: McGraw-Hill, 1991), and Gary J. Castrogiovanni, B. R. Baliga, and Roland E. Kidwell, "Curing Sick Businesses: Changing CEOs in Turnaround Efforts," *Academy of Management Executive* 6, no. 3 (August 1992), pp. 26–41.

THIRTEEN COMMANDMENTS FOR CRAFTING SUCCESSFUL BUSINESS STRATEGIES

Business experiences over the years prove again and again that disastrous courses of action can be avoided by adhering to good strategy-making principles. The wisdom gained from these past experiences can be distilled into 13 commandments which, if faithfully observed, can help strategists craft better strategic action plans.

1. *Place top priority on crafting and executing strategic moves that enhance the company's competitive position for the long term.* An ever stronger competitive position pays off year after year, but the glory of meeting one quarter's and one year's financial performance targets quickly fades. Shareholders are never well-served by managers who let short-term financial performance considerations rule out strategic initiatives that will meaningfully bolster the company's long-term competitive position and competitive strength. The best way to protect a company's long-term profitability is with a strategy that strengthens the company's long-term competitiveness.

2. *Understand that a clear, consistent competitive strategy, when well-crafted and well-executed, builds reputation and recognizable industry position; a frequently changed strategy aimed at capturing momentary market opportunities yields fleeting benefits.* Short-run financial opportunism, absent any long-term strategic consistency, tends to produce the worst kind of profits: one-shot rewards that are unrepeatable. Over the long haul, a company that has a well-conceived, consistent competitive strategy aimed at securing an ever stronger market position will outperform and defeat a rival whose strategic decisions are driven by a desire to meet Wall Street's short-term financial performance expectations. In an ongoing enterprise, the game of competition ought to be played for the long term, not the short term.

3. *Avoid "stuck in the middle" strategies that represent compromises between lower costs and greater differentiation and between broad and narrow market appeal.* Compromise strategies rarely produce sustainable competitive advantage or a distinctive competitive position—well-executed best-cost producer strategies are the only exception where a compromise between low cost and differentiation succeeds. Usually, companies with compromise or middle-of-the-road strategies end up with average costs, average differentiation, an average image and reputation, a middle-of-the-pack industry ranking, and little prospect of climbing into the ranks of the industry leaders.

4. *Invest in creating a sustainable competitive advantage.* It is the single most dependable contributor to above-average profitability.

5. *Play aggressive offense to build competitive advantage and aggressive defense to protect it.*

6. *Avoid strategies capable of succeeding only in the most optimistic circumstances.* Expect competitors to employ countermeasures and expect times of unfavorable market conditions.

7. *Be cautious in pursuing a rigid or inflexible strategy that locks the company in for the long term with little room to maneuver—inflexible strategies can be made obsolete by changing market conditions.* Strategies to achieve top quality or lowest cost should be interpreted as *relative to competitors'* and/or customers' needs rather than based on arbitrary management absolutes. While

long-term strategic consistency is usually a virtue, strategic absolutes and constants are usually flaws—some adapting to changing circumstances and some discovery of ways to improve are normal and necessary.

8. *Don't underestimate the reactions and the commitment of rival firms.* Rivals are most dangerous when they are pushed into a corner and their well-being is threatened.

9. *Be wary of attacking strong, resourceful rivals without solid competitive advantage and ample financial strength.*

10. *Consider that attacking competitive weakness is usually more profitable than attacking competitive strength.*

11. *Be judicious in cutting prices without an established cost advantage.* Only a low-cost producer can win at price-cutting over the long term.

12. *Be aware that aggressive moves to wrest market share away from rivals often provoke aggressive retaliation in the form of a marketing "arms race" and/or price wars*—to the detriment of everyone's profits. Aggressive moves to capture a bigger market share invite cutthroat competition, particularly when the market is plagued with high inventories and excess production capacity.

13. *Strive to open up very meaningful gaps in quality or service or performance features when pursuing a differentiation strategy.* Tiny differences between rivals' product offerings may not be visible or important to buyers.

KEY POINTS

It is not enough to understand that a company's basic competitive strategy options are overall low-cost leadership, broad differentiation, best cost, focused low cost, and focused differentiation and that there are a variety of offensive, defensive, first-mover, and late-mover initiatives and actions to choose from. Managers must also understand that the array of strategic options is narrowed and shaped by (1) the nature of industry and competitive conditions and (2) a firm's own competitive capabilities, market position, and best opportunities. Some strategic options are better suited to certain specific industry and competitive environments than others. Some strategic options are better suited to certain specific company situations than others. This chapter portrays the multifaceted task of matching strategy to a firm's external and internal situations by considering five classic types of industry environments and three classic types of company situations.

Rather than try to summarize the main points we made about choosing strategies for these eight sets of circumstances (the relevant principles can't really be encapsulated in three or four sentences each), we think it more useful to conclude by outlining a broader framework for matching strategy to *any* industry and company situation. Table 6–2 provides a summary checklist of the most important situational considerations and strategic options. Matching strategy to the situation starts with an overview of the industry environment and the firm's competitive standing in the industry (columns 1 and 2 in Table 6–2):

1. What basic type of industry environment does the company operate in (emerging, rapid growth, mature, fragmented, global, commodity-product)? What strategic options and strategic postures are usually best suited to this generic type of environment?

T A B L E 6-2 | Matching Strategy to the Situation (A checklist of optional strategies and generic situations)

Industry Environments

- Young, emerging industry
- Rapid growth
- Consolidating to a smaller group of competitors
- Mature/slow growth
- Aging/declining
- Fragmented
- International/global
- Commodity product orientation
- High technology/rapid changes

Company Positions/ Situations

- Dominant leader
  — Global
  — National
  — Regional
  — Local
- Leader
- Aggressive challenger
- Content follower
- Weak/distressed candidate for turnaround or exit
- "Stuck in the middle"/no clear strategy or market image

Situational Considerations

- External
  — Driving forces
  — Competitive pressures
  — Anticipated moves of key rivals
  — Key success factors
  — Industry attractiveness
- Internal
  — Current company performance
  — Strengths and weaknesses
  — Opportunities and threats
  — Cost position
  — Competitive strength
  — Strategic issues and problems

Market Share and Investment Options

- Grow and build
  — Capture a bigger market share by growing faster than industry as a whole
  — Invest heavily to capture growth potential
- Fortify and defend
  — Protect market share; grow at least as fast as whole industry
  — Invest enough resources to maintain competitive strength and market position
- Retrench and retreat
  — Surrender weakly held positions when forced to, but fight hard to defend core markets/customer base
  — Maximize short-term cash flow
  — Minimize reinvestment of capital in the business
- Overhaul and reposition
  — Pursue a turnaround
- Abandon/liquidate
  — Sell out
  — Close down

Strategy Options

- Competitive approach
  — Overall low-cost
  — Differentiation
  — Best-cost
  — Focused low-cost
  — Focused differentiation
- Offensive initiatives
  — Competitor strengths
  — Competitor weaknesses
  — End run
  — Guerrilla warfare
  — Preemptive strikes
- Defensive initiatives
  — Fortify/protect
  — Retaliatory
  — Harvest
- International initiatives
  — Licensing
  — Export
  — Multicountry
  — Global
- Vertical integration initiatives
  — Forward
  — Backward

2. What position does the firm have in the industry (strong vs. weak vs. crisis-ridden; leader vs. runner-up vs. also-ran)? How does the firm's standing influence its strategic options given the stage of the industry's development—in particular, which options have to be ruled out?

Next, strategists need to factor in the primary external and internal situational considerations (column 3) and decide how all the factors add up. This should narrow the firm's basic market share and investment options (column 4) and strategic options (column 5).

The final step is to custom-tailor the chosen generic strategic approaches (columns 4 and 5) to fit *both* the industry environment and the firm's standing vis-à-vis competitors. Here, it is important to be sure that (1) the customized aspects of the proposed strategy are well-matched to the firm's competencies and competitive capabilities and (2) the strategy addresses all strategic issues the firm confronts.

In weeding out weak strategies and weighing the pros and cons of the most attractive ones, the answers to the following questions often indicate the way to go:

- What kind of competitive edge can the company realistically hope to have and what strategic moves/approaches will it need take to secure this edge?
- Does the company have the organizational capabilities and financial resources to succeed in these moves and approaches? If not, can they be acquired?
- Once built, how can the competitive advantage be protected? What defensive strategies need to be employed? Will rivals counterattack? What will it take to blunt their efforts?
- Are any rivals particularly vulnerable? Should the firm mount an offensive to capitalize on these vulnerabilities? What offensive moves need to be employed?
- What additional strategic moves are needed to deal with driving forces in the industry, specific threats and weaknesses, and any other issues/problems unique to the firm?

As the choice of strategic initiatives is developed, there are several pitfalls to avoid:

- Designing an overly ambitious strategic plan—one that calls for a lot of different strategic moves and/or that overtaxes the company's resources and capabilities.
- Selecting a strategy that represents a radical departure from or abandonment of the cornerstones of the company's prior success—a radical strategy change need not be rejected automatically, but it should be pursued only after careful risk assessment.
- Choosing a strategy that goes against the grain of the organization's culture or that conflicts with the values and philosophies of the most senior executives.
- Being unwilling to make a decisive *choice* about how to compete. Trying to achieve competitive advantage through several means simultaneously often produces so many compromises and inconsistent actions that the company fails to achieve any of them and ends up stuck in the middle.

Table 6–3 suggests a generic format for presenting a strategic action plan for a single-business enterprise.

TABLE 6-3 | **Sample Format for a Strategic Action Plan**

1. Strategic Vision and Mission

2. Strategic Objectives
   - Short term
   - Long term

3. Financial Objectives
   - Short term
   - Long term

4. Overall Business Strategy

5. Supporting Functional Strategies
   - Production
   - Marketing/sales
   - Finance
   - Personnel/human resources
   - Other

6. Recommended Actions
   - Immediate
   - Longer-range

SUGGESTED READINGS

Bleeke, Joel A. "Strategic Choices for Newly Opened Markets." *Harvard Business Review* 68, no. 5 (September–October 1990), pp. 158–65.

Bolt, James F. "Global Competitors: Some Criteria for Success." *Business Horizons* 31, no. 1 (January–February 1988), pp. 34–41.

Cooper, Arnold C., and Clayton G. Smith. "How Established Firms Respond to Threatening Technologies." *Academy of Management Executive* 6, no. 2 (May 1992), pp. 55–57.

D'Aveni, Richard A. *Hypercompetition: Managing the Dynamics of Strategic Maneuvering.* New York: Free Press, 1994, chaps. 3 and 4.

Feldman, Lawrence P., and Albert L. Page. "Harvesting: The Misunderstood Market Exit Strategy." *Journal of Business Strategy* 5, no. 4 (Spring 1985), pp. 79–85.

Finkin, Eugene F. "Company Turnaround." *Journal of Business Strategy* 5, no. 4 (Spring 1985), pp. 14–25.

Gordon, Geoffrey L., Roger J. Calantrone, and C. Anthony di Benedetto. "Mature Markets and Revitalization Strategies: An American Fable." *Business Horizons* (May–June 1991), pp. 39–50.

Hall, William K. "Survival Strategies in a Hostile Environment." *Harvard Business Review* 58, no. 5 (September–October 1980), pp. 75–85.

Hamermesh, R. G., and S. B. Silk. "How to Compete in Stagnant Industries." *Harvard Business Review* 57, no. 5 (September–October 1979), pp. 161–68.

Heany, Donald F. "Businesses in Profit Trouble." *Journal of Business Strategy* 5, no. 4 (Spring 1985), pp. 4–13.

Hofer, Charles W. "Turnaround Strategies." *Journal of Business Strategy* 1, no. 1 (Summer 1980), pp. 19–31.

Lei, David. "Strategies for Global Competition." *Long Range Planning* 22, no. 1 (February 1989), pp. 102–9.

Mayer, Robert J. "Winning Strategies for Manufacturers in Mature Industries." *Journal of Business Strategy* 8, no. 2 (Fall 1987), pp. 23–31.

Ohmae, Kenichi. "The Global Logic of Strategic Alliances." *Harvard Business Review* 67, no. 2 (March–April 1989), pp. 143–54.

Porter, Michael E. *Competitive Strategy: Techniques for Analyzing Industries and Competitors.* New York: Free Press, 1980, chaps. 9–13.

Porter, Michael E. *The Competitive Advantage of Nations.* New York: Free Press, 1990, chap. 2.

Sugiura, Hideo, "How Honda Localizes Its Global Strategy." *Sloan Management Review* 33 (Fall 1990), pp. 77–82.

Yip, George S. *Total Global Strategy.* Englewood Cliffs, N.J.: Prentice-Hall, 1992, chaps. 1, 2, 3, 5, and 7.

Zimmerman, Frederick M. *The Turnaround Experience: Real-World Lessons in Revitalizing Corporations.* New York: McGraw-Hill, 1991.

## CHAPTER SEVEN

CORPORATE DIVERSIFICATION STRATEGIES

. . . to acquire or not to acquire: that is the question.

Robert J. Terry

Strategy is a deliberate search for a plan of action that will develop a business's competitive advantage and compound it.

Bruce D. Henderson

In this chapter and the next, we move up one level in the strategy-making hierarchy. Attention shifts from formulating strategy for a single-business enterprise to formulating strategy for a diversified enterprise. Because a diversified company is a collection of individual businesses, corporate strategy-making is a bigger-picture exercise than crafting line-of-business strategy. In a single-business enterprise, management has to contend with only one industry environment and the question of how to compete successfully in it. But in a diversified company corporate managers have to craft a multibusiness, multi-industry strategic action plan for a number of different business divisions competing in diverse industry environments.

As explained in Chapter 2, the task of crafting corporate strategy for a diversified company concerns

1. Deciding on moves to position the company in the industries chosen for diversification (the basic strategic options here are to acquire a company in the target industry, form a joint venture with another company to enter the target industry, or start a new company internally and try to grow it from the ground up).

2. Devising actions to improve the long-term performance of the corporation's portfolio of businesses once diversification is achieved (helping to strengthen the competitive positions of existing businesses, divesting businesses that no

longer fit into management's long-range plans, and adding new businesses to the portfolio).

3. Trying to capture whatever strategic-fit benefits exist within the portfolio of businesses and turn them into competitive advantage.

4. Evaluating the profit prospects of each business unit and steering corporate resources into the most attractive strategic opportunities.

These four tasks are sufficiently time-consuming and demanding that corporate-level decision-makers generally refrain from becoming immersed in the details of crafting and implementing business-level strategies, preferring instead to delegate lead responsibility for business strategy to the heads of each business unit.

In this chapter we survey the generic types of corporate diversification strategies and describe how a company can use diversification to create or compound competitive advantage for its business units. In Chapter 8 we will examine the techniques and procedures for assessing the strategic attractiveness of a diversified company's business portfolio.

FROM SINGLE-BUSINESS CONCENTRATION TO DIVERSIFICATION

Most companies begin as small single-business enterprises serving a local or regional market. During a company's early years, its product line tends to be limited, its capital base thin, and its competitive position vulnerable. Usually, a young company's strategic emphasis is on increasing sales volume, boosting market share, and cultivating a loyal clientele. Profits are reinvested and new debt is taken on to grow the business as fast as conditions permit. Price, quality, service, and promotion are tailored more precisely to customer needs. As soon as practical, the product line is broadened to meet variations in customer wants and to capture sales opportunities in related end-use applications.

Opportunities for geographic market expansion are normally pursued next. The natural sequence of geographic expansion proceeds from local to regional to national to international markets, though the degree of penetration may be uneven from area to area because of varying profit potentials. Geographic expansion may, of course, stop well short of global or even national proportions because of intense competition, lack of resources, or the unattractiveness of further market coverage.

Somewhere along the way, the potential of vertical integration, either backward to sources of supply or forward to the ultimate consumer, may become a strategic consideration. Generally, vertical integration makes strategic sense only if it significantly enhances a company's profitability and competitive strength.

So long as the company has its hands full trying to capitalize on profitable growth opportunities in its present industry, there is no urgency to pursue diversification. But when company growth potential starts to wane, the strategic options are either to become more aggressive in taking market share away from rivals or to pursue diversification into other lines of businesses. A decision to diversify raises the question "What kind and how much diversification?" The strategic possibilities are wide open. A company can diversify into closely related businesses or into totally unrelated businesses. It can diversify to a small extent (less than 10 percent of total revenues and profits) or to a large extent (up to 50 percent of revenues and profits). It can move into one or two large new businesses or a greater number of small ones. And once

Diversification doesn't need to become a strategic priority until a company begins to run out of growth opportunities in its core business.

once diversification is achieved, the time may come when management has to consider divesting or liquidating businesses that are no longer attractive.

WHY A SINGLE-BUSINESS STRATEGY IS ATTRACTIVE

Companies that concentrate on a single business can achieve enviable success over many decades without relying upon diversification to sustain their growth. McDonald's, Delta Airlines, Coca-Cola, Domino's Pizza, Apple Computer, Wal-Mart, Federal Express, Timex, Campbell's Soup, Anheuser-Busch, Xerox, Gerber, and Polaroid all won their reputations in a single business. In the nonprofit sector, continued emphasis on a single activity has proved successful for the Red Cross, Salvation Army, Christian Children's Fund, Girl Scouts, Phi Beta Kappa, and American Civil Liberties Union.

Concentrating on a single line of business (totally or with a small dose of diversification) has some useful organizational and managerial advantages. First, single-business concentration entails less ambiguity about "who we are and what we do." The energies of the *total* organization are directed down *one* business path. There is less chance that senior management's time or limited organizational resources will be stretched too thin over too many diverse activities. Entrepreneurial efforts can be trained exclusively on keeping the firm's business strategy and competitive approach responsive to industry change and fine-tuned to customer needs. All the firm's managers, especially top executives, can have hands-on contact with the core business and in-depth knowledge of operations. Most senior officers will usually have risen through the ranks and possess firsthand experience in field operations. (In broadly diversified enterprises, corporate managers seldom have had the opportunity to work in more than one or two of the company's businesses.) Furthermore, concentrating on one business carries a heftier built-in incentive for managers to direct the company toward capturing a stronger long-term competitive position in the industry rather than pursuing the fleeting benefits of juggling corporate assets to produce higher short-term profits. The company can devote the full force of its organizational resources to becoming better at what it does. Important competencies and competitive skills are more likely to emerge. With management's attention focused exclusively on one business, the probability is higher that good ideas will emerge on how to improve production technology, better meet customer needs with innovative new product features, and enhance efficiencies or differentiation capabilities along the value chain. The more successful a single-business enterprise is, the more able it is to parlay its accumulated experience and distinctive expertise into a sustainable competitive advantage and a prominent leadership position in its industry.

There are important organizational and managerial advantages to concentrating on just one business.

THE RISK OF A SINGLE-BUSINESS STRATEGY

The big risk of single-business concentration is putting all of a firm's eggs in one industry basket. If the industry stagnates or becomes competitively unattractive, company prospects dim, and superior profit performance is much harder to achieve. At times, changing customer needs, technological innovation, or new substitute products can undermine or wipe out a single-business firm—consider, for example, what the word processing capabilities of personal computers have done to the electric typewriter business and what compact disk technology is doing to the market for cassette tapes and records. For this reason most single-business companies turn their strategic attention to diversification when their business starts to show signs of peaking out.

WHEN DIVERSIFICATION STARTS TO MAKE SENSE

To analyze when diversification makes the most strategic sense, consider Figure 7–1 where the variable of competitive position is plotted against various rates of market growth to create four distinct strategic situations that might be occupied by an undiversified company.[1] Firms that fall into the rapid market growth/strong competitive position box have several logical strategy options, the strongest of which in the near term may be continuing to pursue single-business concentration. Given the industry's high growth rate (and implicit long-term attractiveness), it makes sense for firms in this position to push hard to maintain or increase their market shares, further develop core competencies, and make whatever capital investments are necessary to continue in a strong industry position. At some juncture, a company in this box may contemplate vertical integration if this would add to its competitive strength. Later, when market growth starts to slow, it can consider a diversification strategy to spread business risk and transfer the skills or expertise the company has built up into closely *related* businesses.

When to diversify depends partly on a company's growth opportunities in its present industry and partly on its competitive position.

Firms in the rapid growth/weak position category should first address the questions of (1) why their current approach to the market has resulted in a weak competitive position and (2) what it will take to become an effective competitor. Second they should consider their options for rejuvenating their present competitive strategy (given the high rate of market growth). In a rapidly expanding market, even weak firms should be able to improve their performance and make headway in building a stronger market position. If the firm is young and struggling to develop, it usually has a better chance for survival in a growing market where plenty of new business is up for grabs than in a stable or declining industry. However, if a weakly positioned company in a rapid-growth market lacks the resources and skills to hold its own, its best option is merger either with another company in the industry that has the missing pieces or with an outsider having the cash and resources to support the firm's development. Vertical integration, either forward or backward or both, is an option for a weakly positioned firm whenever it can materially strengthen the firm's competitive position. A third option is diversification into related or unrelated businesses (if adequate financing can be found). If all else fails, abandonment—divestiture in the case of a multibusiness firm or liquidation in the case of a single-business firm—has to become an active strategic option. While abandonment may seem extreme because of the high growth potential, a company unable to make a profit in a booming market probably does not have the ability to make a profit at all—particularly if competition stiffens or industry conditions sour.

Companies with a weak competitive position in a relatively slow-growth market should look at (1) initiating actions to create a more attractive competitive position, (2) merging with or being acquired by a rival to build a stronger base for competing, (3) diversifying into related or unrelated areas if ample financial resources are available, (4) integrating forward or backward if such actions will boost profits and long-term competitive strength, (5) employing a harvest-then-divest strategy, and (6) liquidating their position in the business by either selling out to another firm or closing down operations.

Companies that are strongly positioned in a slow-growth industry should consider taking the excess cash flow from their existing business to finance a diversification

---

[1] C. Roland Christensen, Norman A. Berg, and Malcolm S. Salter, *Policy Formulation and Administration,* 7th ed. (Homewood, Ill.: Richard D. Irwin, 1976), pp. 16–18.

FIGURE 7-1 | **Matching Corporate Strategy Alternatives to Fit an Undiversified Firm's Situation**

COMPETITIVE POSITION

	WEAK	STRONG
RAPID	**STRATEGY OPTIONS** (in probable order of attractiveness) • **Reformulate single-business concentration strategy (to achieve turnaround).** • **Acquire another firm in the same business (to strengthen competitive position).** • **Vertical integration (forward or backward if it strengthens competitive position).** • **Diversification.** • **Be acquired by/sell out to a stronger rival.** • **Abandonment (a last resort in the event all else fails).**	**STRATEGY OPTIONS** (in probable order of attractiveness) • **Continue single-business concentration –International expansion (if market opportunities exist).** • **Vertical integration (if it strengthens the firm's competitive position).** • **Related diversification (to transfer skills and expertise built up in the company's core business to adjacent businesses).**
SLOW	**STRATEGY OPTIONS** (in probable order of attractiveness) • **Reformulate single-business concentration strategy (to achieve turnaround).** • **Merger with a rival firm (to strengthen competitive position).** • **Vertical integration (only if it strengthens competitive position substantially).** • **Diversification.** • **Harvest/divest.** • **Liquidation (a last resort in the event all else fails).**	**STRATEGY OPTIONS** (in probable order of attractiveness) • **International expansion (if market opportunities exist).** • **Related diversification.** • **Unrelated diversification.** • **Joint ventures into new areas.** • **Vertical integration (if it strengthens competitive position).** • **Continue single-business concentration (achieve growth by taking market share from weaker rivals).**

MARKET GROWTH RATE

strategy. Diversification into businesses where a firm can leverage its core competencies and competitive strengths is usually the best strategy. But diversification into totally unrelated businesses has to be considered if none of its related business opportunities offer attractive profit prospects. Joint ventures with other organizations into new fields of endeavor are another logical possibility. Vertical integration should be a last resort (since it provides no escape from the industry's slow-growth condition) and makes strategic sense only if a firm can expect sizable profit gains. Unless it sees important growth *segments* within the industry that merit further invest-and-build actions, a strong company in a slow-growth industry usually needs to curtail new investment in its present business to free cash for new endeavors.

Companies with strong competitive positions in slow-growth industries are prime candidates for diversifying into new businesses.

When to diversify is therefore partly a function of a firm's competitive position and partly a function of the remaining opportunities in its home-base industry. There really is no well-defined point at which companies in the same industry should diversify. Indeed, companies in the same industry can rationally choose different diversification approaches and launch them at different times.

BUILDING SHAREHOLDER VALUE: THE ULTIMATE JUSTIFICATION FOR DIVERSIFYING

The overriding purpose of corporate diversification is to build shareholder value. For diversification to enhance shareholder value, corporate strategy must do more than simply diversify the company's business risk by investing in more than one industry. Shareholders can achieve the same risk diversification on their own by purchasing stock in companies in different industries. Strictly speaking, *diversification does not create shareholder value unless a diversified group of businesses perform better under a single corporate umbrella than they would perform operating as independent, stand-alone businesses.* For example, if company A diversifies by purchasing company B and if A and B's consolidated profits in the years to come prove no greater than what each would have earned on its own, then A's diversification into business B won't provide its shareholders with added value. Company A's shareholders could have achieved the same 2 + 2 = 4 result on their own accord by purchasing stock in company B. Shareholder value is not *created* by diversification unless it produces a 2 + 2 = 5 effect where sister businesses perform better together as part of the same firm than they could have performed as independent companies.

To create shareholder value, a diversifying company must get into businesses that can perform better under common management than they could perform as stand-alone enterprises.

THREE TESTS FOR JUDGING A DIVERSIFICATION MOVE

The problem with such a strict benchmark of whether diversification has enhanced shareholder value is that it requires speculative judgments about how well a diversified company's businesses would have performed on their own. Comparisons of actual performance against the hypothetical of what performance might have been under other circumstances are never very satisfactory and, besides, they represent after-the-fact assessments. Strategists have to base diversification decisions on future expectations. Attempts to gauge the impact of particular diversification moves on shareholder value do not have to be abandoned, however. Corporate strategists can make before-the-fact assessments of whether a particular diversification move is capable of increasing shareholder value by using three tests:[2]

1. **The attractiveness test:** The industry chosen for diversification must be attractive enough to yield consistently good returns on investment. Whether an industry is attractive depends chiefly on the presence of favorable competitive conditions and a market environment conducive to long-term profitability. Such indicators as rapid growth or a sexy product are unreliable proxies of attractiveness.

2. **The cost-of-entry test:** The cost to enter the target industry must not be so high as to erode the potential for good profitability. A catch-22 situation can

---

[2]Michael E. Porter, "From Competitive Advantage to Corporate Strategy," *Harvard Business Review* 45, no. 3 (May–June 1987), pp. 46–49.

prevail here, however. The more attractive the industry, the more expensive it can be to get into. Entry barriers for start-up companies are nearly always high—were barriers low, a rush of new entrants would soon erode the potential for high profitability. And buying a company already in the business typically entails a high acquisition cost because of the industry's strong appeal. Costly entry undermines the potential for enhancing shareholder value.

3. **The better-off test:** The diversifying company must bring some potential for competitive advantage to the new business it enters, or the new business must offer added competitive advantage potential to the company's present businesses. The opportunity to create sustainable competitive advantage where none existed before means there is also opportunity for added profitability and shareholder value.

Diversification moves that satisfy all three tests have the greatest potential to build shareholder value over the long term. Diversification moves that can pass only one or two tests are suspect.

DIVERSIFICATION STRATEGIES

Once the decision is made to pursue diversification, any of several different paths can be taken. There is plenty of room for varied strategic approaches. Figure 7–2 shows the paths a company can take in moving from a single-business enterprise to a diversified enterprise. Vertical integration strategies may or may not enter the picture depending on the extent to which forward or backward integration strengthens a firm's competitive position or helps it secure a competitive advantage. When diversification becomes a serious strategic option, a choice must be made whether to pursue related diversification, unrelated diversification, or some mix of both. Once diversification is accomplished, management's task is to figure out how to manage the collection of businesses the company has invested in—the six fundamental strategic options are shown in the last box of Figure 7–2.

We can better understand the strategic issues corporate managers face in creating and managing a diversified group of businesses by looking at six diversification-related strategies:

1. Strategies for entering new industries—acquisition, start-up, and joint ventures.
2. Related diversification strategies.
3. Unrelated diversification strategies.
4. Divestiture and liquidation strategies.
5. Corporate turnaround, retrenchment, and restructuring strategies.
6. Multinational diversification strategies.

The first three are ways to diversify; the last three are strategies to strengthen the positions and performance of companies that have already diversified.

STRATEGIES FOR ENTERING NEW BUSINESSES

Entry into new businesses can take any of three forms: acquisition, internal start-up, and joint ventures. *Acquisition of an existing business* is the most popular means of diversifying into another industry and has the advantage of much quicker entry into

FIGURE 7–2 | **Corporate Strategy Alternatives**

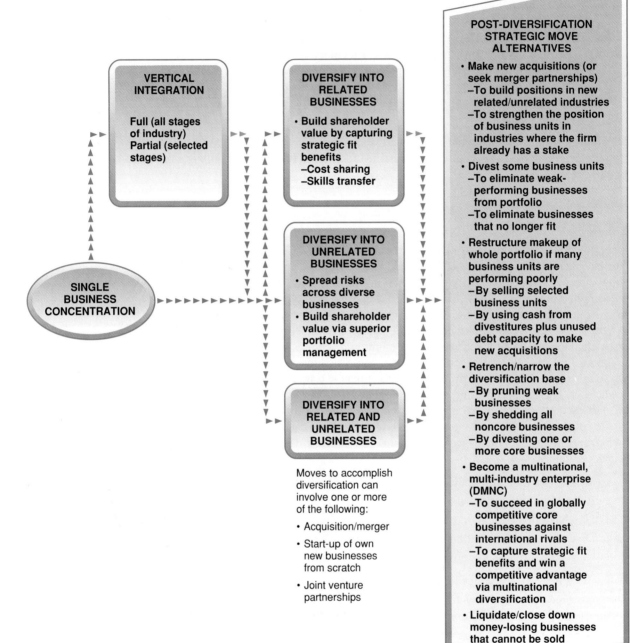

the target market.[3] At the same time, it helps a diversifier overcome such entry barriers as acquiring technological experience, establishing supplier relationships, becoming big enough to match rivals' efficiency and unit costs, having to spend large sums on introductory advertising and promotions to gain market visibility and brand recognition, and getting adequate distribution. In many industries, going the internal start-up route and trying to develop the knowledge, resources, scale of operation, and market reputation necessary to become an effective competitor can take years and entail all the problems of getting a brand new company off the ground and operating.

However, finding the right kind of company to acquire sometimes presents a challenge.[4] The big dilemma an acquisition-minded firm faces is whether to buy a successful company at a high price or a struggling company at a bargain price. If the buying firm has little knowledge of the industry but ample capital, it is often better off purchasing a capable, strongly positioned firm—unless the acquisition price is unreasonably high. On the other hand, when the acquirer sees promising ways to transform a weak firm into a strong one and has the money, the know-how, and the patience to do it, a struggling company can be the better long-term investment.

The cost-of-entry test requires that the expected profit stream of an acquired business provide an attractive return on the total acquisition cost and on any new capital investment needed to sustain or expand its operations. A high acquisition price can make meeting that test improbable or difficult. For instance, suppose that the price to purchase a company is $3 million and that the business is earning after-tax profits of $200,000 on an equity investment of $1 million (a 20 percent annual return). Simple arithmetic requires that the acquired business's profits be tripled for the purchaser to earn the same 20 percent return on the $3 million acquisition price that the previous owners were getting on their $1 million equity investment. Building the acquired firm's earnings from $200,000 to $600,000 annually could take several years—and require additional investment on which the purchaser would also have to earn a 20 percent return. Since the owners of a successful and growing company usually demand a price that reflects their business's future profit prospects, it's easy for such an acquisition to flunk the cost-of-entry test. A would-be diversifier can't count on being able to acquire a desirable company in an appealing industry at a price that still permits attractive returns on investment.

Achieving diversification through *internal start-up* involves creating a new company under the corporate umbrella to compete in the desired industry. A newly formed organization not only has to overcome entry barriers, it also has to invest in new production capacity, develop sources of supply, hire and train employees, build channels of distribution, grow a customer base, and so on. Generally, forming a start-up company to enter a new industry is more attractive when (1) there is ample time to launch the business from the ground up, (2) incumbent firms are likely to be slow or ineffective in responding to a new entrant's efforts to crack the market, (3) internal entry has lower costs than entry via acquisition, (4) the company already has in-house most or all of the skills it needs to compete effectively, (5) adding new production capacity will not adversely impact the supply-demand balance in the industry,

One of the big stumbling blocks to entering attractive industries by acquisition is the difficulty of finding a suitable company at a price that satisfies the cost-of-entry test.

The biggest drawbacks to entering an industry by forming a start-up company internally are the costs of overcoming entry barriers and the extra time it takes to build a strong and profitable competitive position.

---

[3]In recent years, hostile takeovers have become a hotly debated and sometimes abused approach to acquisition. The term *takeover* refers to the attempt (often sprung as a surprise) of one firm to acquire ownership or control over another firm against the wishes of the latter's management (and perhaps some of its stockholders).

[4]Michael E. Porter, *Competitive Strategy: Techniques for Analyzing Industries and Competitors* (New York: Free Press, 1980), p. 354–55.

and (6) the targeted industry is populated with many relatively small firms so the new start-up does not have to compete head-to-head against larger, more powerful rivals.[5]

Joint ventures are a useful way to gain access to a new business in at least three types of situations.[6] First, a joint venture is a good way to do something that is uneconomical or risky for an organization to do alone. Second, joint ventures make sense when pooling the resources and competencies of two or more independent organizations produces an organization with more of the skills needed to be a strong competitor. In such cases, each partner brings special talents or resources that the other doesn't have and that are important for success. Third, joint ventures with foreign partners are sometimes the only or best way to surmount import quotas, tariffs, nationalistic political interests, and cultural roadblocks. The economic, competitive, and political realities of nationalism often require a foreign company to team up with a domestic partner in order to gain access to the national market in which the domestic partner is located. Domestic partners offer outside companies the benefits of local knowledge, managerial and marketing personnel, and access to distribution channels. However, such joint ventures often pose complicated questions about how to divide efforts among the partners and about who has effective control.[7] Conflicts between foreign and domestic partners can arise over whether to use local sourcing of components, how much production to export, whether operating procedures should conform to the foreign company's standards or to local preferences, who has control of cash flows, and how to distribute profits.

RELATED DIVERSIFICATION STRATEGIES

In choosing which industries to diversify into, the two basic options are to pick industries *related* to or *unrelated* to the organization's core business and what the organization already does. A related diversification strategy involves diversifying into businesses that possess some kind of "strategic fit." *Strategic fit* exists when different businesses have sufficiently related value chains that there are important opportunities for (1) transferring skills and expertise from one business to another or (2) combining the related activities of separate businesses into a single operation and reducing costs.[8] *A diversified firm that exploits these value-chain interrelationships and captures the benefits of strategic fit achieves a consolidated performance greater than the sum of what the businesses can earn pursuing independent strategies.* The presence of strategic fit within a diversified firm's business portfolio, together with corporate management's deftness and skill in capturing the benefits of the interrelationships, makes related diversification a 2 + 2 = 5 phenomenon and becomes a basis for competitive advantage. The bigger the strategic-fit benefits, the bigger the competitive advantage of related diversification and the more that related diversification satisfies the better-off test for building shareholder value.

Related diversification involves diversifying into businesses whose value chains have appealing strategic fits.

---

[5]Ibid., pp. 344–45.

[6]Peter Drucker, *Management: Tasks, Responsibilities, Practices* (New York: Harper & Row, 1974), pp. 720–24. Strategic alliances offer much the same benefits as joint ventures, but represent a weaker commitment to entering a new business.

[7]Porter, *Competitive Strategy,* p. 340.

[8]Michael E. Porter, *Competitive Advantage* (New York: Free Press, 1985), pp. 318–19 and pp. 337–53; Kenichi Ohmae, *The Mind of the Strategist* (New York: Penguin Books, 1983), pp. 121–24; and Porter, "From Competitive Advantage to Corporate Strategy," pp. 53–57.

Strategic-fit relationships can arise out of the opportunity for technology sharing, the existence of common labor skills and requirements, use of common suppliers and raw materials sources, the potential for joint manufacture of parts and components, the presence of similar operating methods and similar managerial know-how, reliance on the same types of marketing and merchandising skills, the possibility of sharing a common sales force and using the same wholesale distributors or retail dealers, the potential for combining after-sale service activities, or the advantages and synergistic effects of a common brand name. The fit or relatedness can occur anywhere along the businesses' respective value chains. Strategic-fit relationships are important because they represent opportunities for cost-saving efficiencies, technology or skills transfers, added differentiation, or brand name advantages, all of which are avenues for gaining competitive advantages over business rivals that have not diversified or that have diversified but not in ways that give them access to such strategic-fit benefits.

Some of the most commonly used approaches to related diversification are

- Entering businesses where sales force, advertising, and distribution activities can be shared (a bread bakery buying a maker of crackers and salty snack foods).

- Exploiting closely related technologies (a marketer of agricultural seeds and fertilizers diversifying into chemicals for insect and plant disease control).

- Transferring know-how and expertise from one business to another (a successful operator of hamburger outlets acquiring a chain specializing in Mexican fast-foods).

- Transferring the organization's brand name and reputation with consumers to a new product/service (a tire manufacturer diversifying into automotive repair centers).

- Acquiring new businesses that will uniquely help the firm's position in its existing businesses (a cable TV broadcaster purchasing a sports team or purchasing a movie production company to provide original programming).

Examples of related diversification abound. BIC Pen, which pioneered inexpensive disposable ballpoint pens, used its core competencies in low-cost manufacturing and mass merchandising as its basis for diversifying into disposable cigarette lighters and disposable razors—both of which required low-cost production know-how and skilled consumer marketing for success. Tandy Corp. practiced related diversification when its chain of Radio Shack outlets, which originally handled mostly radio and stereo equipment, added telephones, intercoms, calculators, clocks, electronic and scientific toys, personal computers, and peripheral computer equipment. The Tandy strategy was to use the marketing access provided by its thousands of Radio Shack locations to become one of the world's leading retailers of electronic technology to individual consumers. Philip Morris, a leading cigarette manufacturer, employed a marketing-related diversification strategy when it purchased Miller Brewing, General Foods, and Kraft and transferred its skills in cigarette marketing to the marketing of beer and food products. Lockheed pursued a customer needs-based diversification strategy in creating business units to supply the Department of Defense with missiles, rocket engines, aircraft, electronic equipment, ships, and contract R&D for weapons. Procter & Gamble's lineup of products includes Jif peanut butter, Duncan Hines cake mixes, Folger's coffee, Tide laundry detergent, Crisco vegetable oil, Crest toothpaste, Ivory soap, Charmin toilet tissue, and Head and Shoulders shampoo—all different businesses with different competi-

What makes related diversification attractive is the opportunity to turn strategic fits into competitive advantage.

ILLUSTRATION CAPSULE 22

EXAMPLES OF COMPANIES WITH RELATED BUSINESS PORTFOLIOS

Presented below are the business portfolios of four companies that have pursued some form of related diversification:

Gillette

- Blades and razors
- Toiletries (Right Guard, Silkience, Foamy, Dry Idea, Soft & Dry, Oral-B toothbrushes, White Rain, Toni)
- Writing instruments and stationery products (Paper Mate pens, Liquid Paper correction fluids, Waterman pens)
- Braun shavers, cordless curlers, coffeemakers, alarm clocks, and electric toothbrushes

PepsiCo

- Soft drinks (Pepsi, Mountain Dew, Slice)
- Kentucky Fried Chicken
- Pizza Hut
- Taco Bell
- Frito-Lay
- 7UP International (non-US sales of 7UP)

Philip Morris Companies

- Cigarettes (Marlboro, Virginia Slims, Benson & Hedges, and Merit)
- Miller Brewing Company
- Kraft General Foods (Maxwell House, Sanka, Oscar Mayer, Kool-Aid, Jell-O, Post cereals, Birds-Eye frozen foods, Kraft cheeses, Sealtest dairy products, Breyer's ice cream)
- Mission Viejo Realty

Johnson & Johnson

- Baby products (powder, shampoo, oil, lotion)
- Disposable diapers
- Band-Aids and wound care products
- Stayfree, Carefree, Sure & Natural, and Modess feminine hygiene products
- Tylenol
- Prescription drugs
- Surgical and hospital products
- Dental products
- Oral contraceptives
- Veterinary and animal health products

Source: Company annual reports.

Strategic fits among related businesses offer the competitive advantage potential of *(a)* lower costs, *(b)* efficient transfer of key skills, technological expertise, or managerial know-how from one business to another, or *(c)* ability to share a common brand name.

tors and different production requirements. But P&G's products still represent related diversification because they all move through the same wholesale distribution systems, are sold in common retail settings to the same shoppers, are advertised and promoted in the same ways, and utilize the same marketing and merchandising skills. Illustration Capsule 22 shows the business portfolios of several companies that have pursued a strategy of related diversification.

STRATEGIC FIT, ECONOMIES OF SCOPE, AND COMPETITIVE ADVANTAGE

A related diversification strategy clearly has considerable appeal. It allows a firm to preserve a degree of unity in its business activities, reap the competitive advantage benefits of skills transfer or lower costs, and still spread investor risks over a broader business base.

Diversifying into businesses where technology, facilities, functional activities, or distribution channels can be shared can lead to lower costs because of economies of scope. *Economies of scope* exist whenever it is less costly for two or more businesses to be operated under centralized management than to function as independent businesses. The economies of operating over a wider range of businesses or product lines can arise from cost-saving opportunities to share resources or combine activities anywhere along the respective value chains of the businesses and from shared use of an established brand name. The greater the economies of scope associated with the particular businesses a company has diversified into, the greater the potential for creating a competitive advantage based on lower costs.

Both skills transfer and activity sharing enable the diversifier to earn greater profits from its businesses than the businesses could earn operating independently. Thus the economies of scope. The key to activity sharing and skills transfer opportunities and thus to cost saving is diversification into businesses with strategic fit. While strategic-fit relationships can occur throughout the value chain, most fall into one of three broad categories.

Economies of scope arise from the ability to eliminate costs by operating two or more businesses under the same corporate umbrella; the cost-saving opportunities can stem from interrelationships anywhere along the businesses' value chains.

Market-Related Fit   When the value chains of different businesses overlap such that the products are used by the same customers, distributed through common dealers and retailers, or marketed and promoted in similar ways, then the businesses enjoy *market-related strategic fit*. A variety of cost-saving opportunities (or economies of scope) spring from market-related strategic fit: using a single sales force for all related products rather than having separate sales forces for each business, advertising the related products in the same ads and brochures, using the same brand names, coordinating delivery and shipping, combining after-sale service and repair organizations, coordinating order processing and billing, using common promotional tie-ins (cents-off couponing, free samples and trial offers, seasonal specials, and the like), and combining dealer networks. Such market-related strategic fits usually allow a firm to economize on its marketing, selling, and distribution costs.

In addition to economies of scope, market-related fit can generate opportunities to transfer selling skills, promotional skills, advertising skills, and product differentiation skills from one business to another. Moreover, a company's brand name and reputation in one product can often be transferred to other products. Honda's name in motorcycles and automobiles gave it instant credibility and recognition in entering the lawnmower business without spending large sums on advertising. Canon's reputation in photographic equipment was a competitive asset that facilitated the company's diversification into copying equipment. Panasonic's name in consumer electronics (radios, TVs) was readily transferred to microwave ovens, making it easier and cheaper for Panasonic to diversify into the microwave oven market.

Operating Fit   Different businesses have *operating fit* when there is potential for activity sharing or skills transfer in procuring materials, conducting R&D, mastering a new technology, manufacturing components, assembling finished goods, or performing administrative support functions. Sharing-related operating fits usually present cost-saving opportunities; some derive from the economies of combining activities into a larger-scale operation *(economies of scale),* and some derive from the ability to eliminate costs by performing activities together rather than independently *(economies of scope).* The bigger the proportion of cost that a shared activity represents, the more significant the shared cost savings become and the bigger the cost advantage that can result. With operating fit, the most important skills transfer opportunities usually relate to situations where technological or manufacturing expertise in one business has beneficial applications in another.

Management Fit   This type of fit emerges when different business units have comparable types of entrepreneurial, administrative, or operating problems, thereby allowing managerial know-how in one line of business to be transferred to another. Transfers of managerial expertise can occur anywhere in the value chain. Ford transferred its automobile financing and credit management know-how to the savings and loan industry when it acquired some failing savings and loan associations during the 1989 bailout of the crisis-ridden S&L industry. Emerson Electric transferred its skills in low-cost manufacture to its newly acquired Beaird-Poulan chain saw business division; the transfer of management know-how drove Beaird-Poulan's new strategy, changed the way its chain saws were designed and manufactured, and paved the way for new pricing and distribution emphasis.

Capturing Strategic-Fit Benefits   It is one thing to diversify into industries with strategic fit and another to actually realize the benefits. To capture the benefits of activity sharing, related activities must be merged into a single functional unit and coordinated; then the cost savings (or differentiation advantages) must be squeezed out. Merged functions and coordination can entail reorganization costs, and management must determine that the benefit of *some* centralized strategic control is great enough to warrant sacrifice of business-unit autonomy. Likewise, where skills transfer is the cornerstone of strategic fit, managers must find a way to make the transfer effective without stripping too many skilled personnel from the business with the expertise. The more a company's diversification strategy is tied to skills transfer, the more it has to develop a big enough and talented enough pool of specialized personnel not only to supply new businesses with the skill but also to master the skill sufficiently to create competitive advantage.

> Competitive advantage achieved through strategic fits among related businesses adds to the performance potential of the firm's individual businesses; this extra source of competitive advantage allows related diversification to have a 2 + 2 = 5 effect on shareholder value.

UNRELATED DIVERSIFICATION STRATEGIES

Despite the strategic-fit benefits associated with related diversification, a number of companies opt for unrelated diversification strategies—they exhibit a willingness to diversify into *any industry* with a good profit opportunity. Corporate managers exert no deliberate effort to seek out businesses having strategic fit with the firm's other businesses. While companies pursuing unrelated diversification may try to make certain their diversification targets meet the industry-attractiveness and cost-of-entry tests, the conditions needed for the better-off test are either disregarded or relegated to secondary status. Decisions to diversify into one industry versus another are the product of an opportunistic search for "good" companies to acquire—*the basic premise of unrelated diversification is that any company that can be acquired on good financial terms and that has satisfactory profit prospects represents a good business to diversify into.* Much time and effort goes into finding and screening acquisition candidates. Typically, corporate strategists screen candidate companies using such criteria as

> A strategy of unrelated diversification involves diversifying into whatever industries and businesses hold promise for attractive financial gain; exploiting strategic-fit relationships is secondary.

- Whether the business can meet corporate targets for profitability and return on investment.
- Whether the new business will require substantial infusions of capital to replace fixed assets, fund expansion, and provide working capital.
- Whether the business is in an industry with significant growth potential.
- Whether the business is big enough to contribute significantly to the parent firm's bottom line.

- Whether there is a potential for union difficulties or adverse government regulations concerning product safety or the environment.
- Whether there is industry vulnerability to recession, inflation, high interest rates, or shifts in government policy.

Sometimes, companies with unrelated diversification strategies concentrate on identifying acquisition candidates that offer quick opportunities for financial gain because of their "special situation." Three types of businesses may hold such attraction:

- *Companies whose assets are undervalued*—opportunities may exist to acquire such companies for less than full market value and make substantial capital gains by reselling their assets and businesses for more than their acquired costs.
- *Companies that are financially distressed*—such businesses can often be purchased at a bargain price, their operations turned around with the aid of the parent companies' financial resources and managerial know-how, and then either held as long-term investments in the acquirers' business portfolios (because of their strong earnings or cash flow potential) or sold at a profit, whichever is more attractive.
- *Companies that have bright growth prospects but are short on investment capital*—capital-poor, opportunity-rich companies are usually coveted diversification candidates for a financially strong, opportunity-seeking firm.

Companies that pursue unrelated diversification nearly always enter new businesses by acquiring an established company rather than by forming a start-up subsidiary within their own corporate structures. Their premise is that growth by acquisition translates into enhanced shareholder value. Suspending application of the better-off test is seen as justifiable so long as unrelated diversification results in sustained growth in corporate revenues and earnings and so long as none of the acquired businesses end up performing badly.

Illustration Capsule 23 shows the business portfolios of several companies that have pursued unrelated diversification. Such companies are frequently labeled *conglomerates* because there is no strategic theme in their diversification makeup and because their business interests range broadly across diverse industries.

THE PROS AND CONS OF UNRELATED DIVERSIFICATION

Unrelated or conglomerate diversification has appeal from several financial angles:

1. Business risk is scattered over a variety of industries, making the company less dependent on any one business. While the same can be said for related diversification, unrelated diversification places no restraint on how risk is spread. An argument can be made that unrelated diversification is a superior way to diversify financial risk as compared to related diversification because the company's investments can span a bigger variety of totally different businesses.

2. Capital resources can be invested in whatever industries offer the best profit prospects; cash flows from company businesses with lower profit prospects can be diverted to acquiring and expanding business units with higher growth and profit potentials. Corporate financial resources are thus employed to maximum advantage.

ILLUSTRATION CAPSULE 23

DIVERSIFIED COMPANIES WITH UNRELATED BUSINESS PORTFOLIOS

Union Pacific Corporation

- Railroad operations (Union Pacific Railroad Company)
- Oil and gas exploration
- Mining
- Microwave and fiber optic transportation information and control systems
- Hazardous waste management disposal
- Trucking (Overnite Transportation Company)
- Oil refining
- Real estate

United Technologies, Inc.

- Pratt & Whitney aircraft engines
- Carrier heating and air-conditioning equipment
- Otis elevators
- Sikorsky helicopters
- Essex wire and cable products
- Norden defense systems)
- Hamilton Standard controls
- Space transportation systems
- Automotive components

Westinghouse Electric Corporation

- Electric utility power generation equipment
- Nuclear fuel
- Electric transmission and distribution products
- Commercial and residential real estate financing
- Equipment leasing
- Receivables and fixed asset financing
- Radio and television broadcasting
- Longines-Wittnauer Watch Co.
- Beverage bottling
- Elevators and escalators
- Defense electronic systems (missile launch equipment, marine propulsion)
- Commercial furniture
- Community land development

Textron, Inc.

- Bell helicopters
- Paul Revere Insurance
- Missile reentry systems
- Lycoming gas turbine engines and jet propulsion systems
- E-Z-Go golf carts
- Homelite chain saws and lawn and garden equipment
- Davidson automotive parts and trims
- Specialty fasteners
- Avco Financial Services
- Jacobsen turf care equipment
- Tanks and armored vehicles

Source: Company annual reports.

3. Company profitability is somewhat more stable because hard times in one industry may be partially offset by good times in another—ideally, cyclical downswings in some of the company's businesses are counterbalanced by cyclical upswings in other businesses the company has diversified into.

4. To the extent that corporate managers are exceptionally astute at spotting bargain-priced companies with big upside profit potential, shareholder wealth can be enhanced.

While entry into an unrelated business can often pass the attractiveness and the cost-of-entry tests (and sometimes even the better-off test), a strategy of unrelated diversification has drawbacks. One Achilles' heel of conglomerate diversification is the big demand it places on corporate-level management to make sound decisions regarding fundamentally different businesses operating in fundamentally different industry and competitive environments. The greater the number of businesses a company is in and the more diverse they are, the harder it is for corporate managers to oversee each subsidiary and spot problems early, to have real expertise in evaluating the attractiveness of each business's industry and competitive environment, and to judge the calibre of strategic actions and plans proposed by business-level managers. As one president of a diversified firm expressed it:

> . . . we've got to make sure that our core businesses are properly managed for solid, long-term earnings. We can't just sit back and watch the numbers. We've got to know what the real issues are out there in the profit centers. Otherwise, we're not even in a position to check out our managers on the big decisions.[9]

With broad diversification, corporate managers have to be shrewd and talented enough to (1) discern a good acquisition from a bad acquisition, (2) select capable managers to run each of many different businesses, (3) discern when the major strategic proposals of business-unit managers are sound, and (4) know what to do if a business unit stumbles. Because every business tends to encounter rough sledding, a good way to gauge the risk of diversifying into new unrelated areas is to ask, "If the new business got into trouble, would we know how to bail it out?" When the answer is no, unrelated diversification can pose significant financial risk and the business's profit prospects are more chancy.[10] As the former chairman of a Fortune 500 company advised, "Never acquire a business you don't know how to run." It takes only one or two big strategic mistakes (misjudging industry attractiveness, encountering unexpected problems in a newly acquired business, or being too optimistic about how hard it will be to turn a struggling subsidiary around) to cause a precipitous drop in corporate earnings and crash the parent company's stock price.

Second, without the competitive advantage potential of strategic fit, consolidated performance of an unrelated multibusiness portfolio tends to be no better than the sum of what the individual business units could achieve if they were independent, and it may be worse to the extent that corporate managers meddle unwisely in business-unit operations or hamstring them with corporate policies. Except, perhaps, for the added financial backing that a cash-rich corporate parent can provide, a strategy of unrelated diversification does nothing for the competitive strength of the individual business units. Each business is on its own in trying to build a competitive edge—the unrelated nature of sister businesses offers no basis for cost reduction, skills transfer, or technology sharing. In a widely diversified firm, the value added by corporate managers depends primarily on how good they are at deciding what new businesses to add, which ones to get rid of, how best to deploy available financial resources to build a higher-performing collection of businesses, and the quality of the decision-making guidance they give to the general managers of their business subsidiaries.

Third, although in theory unrelated diversification offers the potential for greater sales-profit stability over the course of the business cycle, in practice attempts at countercyclical diversification fall short of the mark. Few attractive businesses have

The two biggest drawbacks to unrelated diversification are the difficulties of competently managing many different businesses and being without the added source of competitive advantage that strategic fit provides.

---

[9]Carter F. Bales, "Strategic Control: The President's Paradox," *Business Horizons* 20, no. 4 (August 1977), p. 17.
[10]Of course, management may be willing to assume the risk that trouble will not strike before it has had time to learn the business well enough to bail it out of almost any difficulty. See Peter Drucker, *Management: Tasks, Responsibilities, Practices,* p. 709.

opposite up-and-down cycles; the great majority of businesses are similarly affected by economic good times and hard times. There's no convincing evidence that the consolidated profits of broadly diversified firms are more stable or less subject to reversal in periods of recession and economic stress than the profits of less diversified firms.[11]

Despite these drawbacks, unrelated diversification can sometimes be a desirable corporate strategy. It certainly merits consideration when a firm needs to diversify away from an endangered or unattractive industry and has no distinctive skills it can transfer to an adjacent industry. There's also a rationale for pure diversification to the extent owners have a strong preference for investing in several unrelated businesses instead of a family of related ones. Otherwise, the argument for unrelated diversification hinges on the case-by-case prospects for financial gain.

A key issue in unrelated diversification is how wide a net to cast in building the business portfolio. In other words, should the corporate portfolio contain few or many unrelated businesses? How much business diversity can corporate executives successfully manage? A reasonable way to resolve the issue of how much diversification comes from answering two questions: "What is the least diversification it will take to achieve acceptable growth and profitability?" and "What is the most diversification that can be managed given the complexity it adds?"[12] The optimal amount of diversification usually lies between these two extremes.

UNRELATED DIVERSIFICATION AND SHAREHOLDER VALUE

Unrelated diversification is fundamentally a finance-driven approach to creating shareholder value whereas related diversification is fundamentally strategy-driven. *Related diversification represents a strategic approach to building shareholder value* because it is predicated on exploiting the linkages between the value chains of different businesses to lower costs, transfer skills and technological expertise across businesses, and gain other strategic-fit benefits. The objective is to convert the strategic fits among the firm's businesses into an extra measure of competitive advantage that goes beyond what business subsidiaries are able to achieve on their own. The added competitive advantage a firm achieves through related diversification is the driver for building greater shareholder value.

In contrast, *unrelated diversification is principally a financial approach to creating shareholder value* because it is predicated on astute deployment of corporate financial resources and executive skill in spotting financially attractive business opportunities. Since unrelated diversification produces no strategic-fit opportunities of consequence, corporate strategists can't build shareholder value by acquiring companies that create or compound competitive advantage for its business subsidiaries—in a conglomerate, competitive advantage doesn't go beyond what each business subsidiary can achieve independently through its own competitive strategy. Consequently, for unrelated diversification to result in enhanced shareholder value (above the 2 + 2 = 4 effect that the subsidiary businesses could produce through independent operations and that shareholders could obtain by purchasing ownership interests in a variety of businesses to spread investment risk on their own behalf),

> Unrelated diversification is a financial approach to creating shareholder value; related diversification, in contrast, represents a strategic approach.

> For corporate strategists to build shareholder value in some way other than through strategic fits and competitive advantage, they must be smart enough to produce financial results from a group of businesses that exceed what business-level managers can produce.

---

[11]Ibid., p. 767. Research studies in the interval since 1974, when Drucker made his observation, uphold his conclusion—on the whole, broadly diversified firms do not outperform less diversified firms over the course of the business cycle.

[12]Ibid., pp. 692–93.

corporate strategists must exhibit superior skills in creating and managing a portfolio of diversified business interests. This specifically means

- Doing a superior job of diversifying into new businesses that can produce consistently good returns on investment (satisfying the attractiveness test).
- Doing an excellent job of negotiating favorable acquisition prices (satisfying the cost-of-entry test).
- Making astute moves to sell previously acquired business subsidiaries at their peak and getting premium prices (this requires skills in discerning when a business subsidiary is on the verge of confronting adverse industry and competitive conditions and probable declines in long-term profitability).
- Being shrewd in shifting corporate financial resources out of businesses where profit opportunities are dim and into businesses where rapid earnings growth and high returns on investment are occurring.
- Doing such a good job overseeing the firm's business subsidiaries and contributing to how they are managed (by providing expert problem-solving skills, creative strategy suggestions, and decision-making guidance to business-level managers) that the businesses perform at a higher level than they would otherwise be able to do (a possible way to satisfy the better-off test).

To the extent that corporate executives are able to craft and execute a strategy of unrelated diversification that produces enough of the above outcomes for an enterprise to consistently outperform other firms in generating dividends and capital gains for stockholders, then a case can be made that shareholder value has truly been enhanced. Achieving such results consistently requires supertalented corporate executives, however. Without them, unrelated diversification is a very dubious and unreliable way to try to build shareholder value—there are far more who have tried it and failed than who have tried and succeeded.

DIVESTITURE AND LIQUIDATION STRATEGIES

Even a shrewd corporate diversification strategy can result in the acquisition of business units that, down the road, just do not work out. Misfits or partial fits cannot be completely avoided because it is impossible to predict precisely how getting into a new line of business will actually work out. In addition, long-term industry attractiveness changes with the times; what was once a good diversification move into an attractive industry may later turn sour. Subpar performance by some business units is bound to occur, thereby raising questions of whether to keep them or divest them. Other business units, despite adequate financial performance, may not mesh as well with the rest of the firm as was originally thought.

A business needs to be considered for divestiture when corporate strategists conclude it no longer fits or is an attractive investment.

Sometimes, a diversification move that seems sensible from a strategic-fit standpoint turns out to lack the compatibility of values essential to a *cultural fit*.[13] Several pharmaceutical companies had just this experience. When they diversified into cosmetics and perfume, they discovered their personnel had little respect for the "frivolous" nature of such products compared to the far nobler task of developing miracle drugs to cure the ill. The absence of shared values and cultural compatibility between the medical research and chemical-compounding expertise of the pharmaceutical

---

[13]Ibid., p. 709.

companies and the fashion-marketing orientation of the cosmetics business was the undoing of what otherwise was diversification into businesses with technology-sharing potential, product-development fit, and some overlap in distribution channels.

When a particular line of business loses its appeal, the most attractive solution usually is to sell it. Normally such businesses should be divested as fast as is practical. To drag things out serves no purpose unless time is needed to get it into better shape to sell. The more business units in a diversified firm's portfolio, the more likely that it will have occasion to divest poor performers, "dogs," and misfits. A useful guide to determine if and when to divest a business subsidiary is to ask the question, "If we were not in this business today, would we want to get into it now?"[14] When the answer is no or probably not, divestiture should be considered.

Divestiture can take either of two forms. The parent can spin off a business as a financially and managerially independent company in which the parent company may or may not retain partial ownership. Or the parent may sell the unit outright, in which case a buyer needs to be found. As a rule, divestiture should not be approached from the angle of "Who can we pawn this business off on and what is the most we can get for it?"[15] Instead, it is wiser to ask "For what sort of organization would this business be a good fit, and under what conditions would it be viewed as a good deal?" Organizations for which the business is a good fit are likely to pay the highest price.

Of all the strategic alternatives, liquidation is the most unpleasant and painful, especially for a single-business enterprise where it means the organization ceases to exist. For a multi-industry, multibusiness firm to liquidate one of its lines of business is less traumatic. The hardships of job eliminations, plant closings, and so on, while not to be minimized, still leave an ongoing organization, perhaps one that is healthier after its pruning. In hopeless situations, an early liquidation effort usually serves owner-stockholder interests better than an inevitable bankruptcy. Prolonging the pursuit of a lost cause exhausts an organization's resources and leaves less to liquidate; it can also mar reputations and ruin management careers. Unfortunately, it is seldom simple for management to differentiate between when a turnaround is achievable and when it isn't. This is particularly true when emotions and pride overcome sound business judgment—as often they do.

CORPORATE TURNAROUND, RETRENCHMENT, AND PORTFOLIO RESTRUCTURING STRATEGIES

Turnaround, retrenchment, and portfolio restructuring strategies come into play when corporate management has to restore an ailing business portfolio to good health. Poor performance can be caused by large losses in one or more business units that pull the corporation's overall financial performance down, a disproportionate number of businesses in unattractive industries, a bad economy adversely impacting many of the firm's business units, an excessive debt burden, or ill-chosen acquisitions that haven't lived up to expectations.

Corporate turnaround strategies focus on efforts to restore money-losing businesses to profitability instead of divesting them. The intent is to get the whole company back in the black by curing the problems of those businesses in the portfolio

---

[14]Ibid., p. 94.
[15]Ibid., p. 719.

that are most responsible for pulling overall performance down. Turnaround strategies are most appropriate in situations where the reasons for poor performance are short-term, the ailing businesses are in attractive industries, and divesting the money-losers does not make long-term strategic sense.

Corporate retrenchment strategies involve reducing the scope of diversification to a smaller number of businesses. Retrenchment is usually undertaken when corporate management concludes that the company is in too many businesses and needs to concentrate its efforts on a few core businesses. Sometimes diversified firms retrench because they can't make certain businesses profitable after several frustrating years of trying or because they lack funds to support the investment needs of all of their business subsidiaries. More commonly, however, corporate executives conclude that the firm's diversification efforts have ranged too far afield and that the key to improved long-term performance lies in concentrating on building strong positions in a smaller number of businesses. Retrenchment is usually accomplished by divesting businesses that are too small to make a sizable contribution to earnings or that have little or no strategic fit with the company's core businesses. Divesting such businesses frees resources that can be used to reduce debt or support expansion of the company's core businesses.

Portfolio restructuring strategies involve radical surgery on the mix and percentage makeup of the types of businesses in the portfolio. For instance, one company over a two-year period divested 4 business units, closed down the operations of 4 others, and added 25 new lines of business to its portfolio, 16 through acquisition and 9 through internal start-up. Restructuring can be prompted by any of several conditions: (1) when a strategy review reveals that the firm's long-term performance prospects have become unattractive because the portfolio contains too many slow-growth, declining, or competitively weak business units; (2) when one or more of the firm's core businesses fall prey to hard times; (3) when a new CEO takes over and decides to redirect where the company is headed; (4) when "wave of the future" technologies or products emerge and a major shakeup of the portfolio is needed to build a position in a potentially big new industry; (5) when the firm has a unique opportunity to make an acquisition so big that it has to sell several existing business units to finance the new acquisition; or (6) when major businesses in the portfolio have become more and more unattractive, forcing a shakeup in the portfolio in order to produce satisfactory long-term corporate performance.

Portfolio restructuring involves bold strategic action to revamp the diversified company's business makeup through a series of divestitures and new acquisitions.

Portfolio restructuring typically involves both divestitures and new acquisitions. Candidates for divestiture include not only weak or up-and-down performers or those in unattractive industries, but also those that no longer fit (even though they may be profitable and in attractive-enough industries). Many broadly diversified companies, disenchanted with the performance of some acquisitions and having only mixed success in overseeing so many unrelated business units, restructure their business portfolios to a narrower core of activities. Business units incompatible with newly established related diversification criteria are divested, the remaining units regrouped and aligned to capture more strategic fit benefits, and new acquisitions made to strengthen the parent company's business position in the industries it has chosen to emphasize.

The recent trend among broadly diversified companies to demerge and deconglomerate is being driven by a growing preference for building diversification around the creation of strong competitive positions in a few, well-selected industries. Indeed, in response to investor disenchantment with the conglomerate approach to diversification (evident in the fact that conglomerates often have *lower* price-earnings ratios than companies with related diversification strategies), some conglomerates have undertaken portfolio restructuring and retrenchment in a deliberate effort to escape being regarded as a conglomerate.

MULTINATIONAL DIVERSIFICATION STRATEGIES

The distinguishing characteristics of a multinational diversification strategy are a *diversity of businesses* and a *diversity of national markets*.[16] Here, corporate managers have to conceive and execute a substantial number of strategies—at least one for each industry, with as many multinational variations as is appropriate for the situation. At the same time, managers of diversified multinational corporations (DMNCs) need to be alert for beneficial ways to coordinate their firms' strategic actions across industries and countries. The goal of strategic coordination at the headquarters level is to bring the full force of corporate resources and capabilities to the task of securing sustainable competitive advantages in each business and national market.[17]

THE EMERGENCE OF MULTINATIONAL DIVERSIFICATION

Until the 1960s, multinational companies (MNCs) operated fairly autonomous subsidiaries in each host country, each catering to the special requirements of its own national market.[18] Management tasks at company headquarters primarily involved finance functions, technology transfer, and export coordination. In pursuing a national responsiveness strategy, the primary competitive advantage of an MNC was grounded in its ability to transfer technology, manufacturing know-how, brand name identification, and marketing and management skills from country to country quite efficiently, allowing them to beat out smaller host country competitors on price, quality, and management know-how. Standardized administrative procedures helped minimize overhead costs, and once an initial organization for managing foreign subsidiaries was put in place, entry into additional national markets could be accomplished at low incremental costs. Frequently, an MNC's presence and market position in a country was negotiated with the host government rather than driven by international competition.

During the 1970s, however, multicountry strategies based on national responsiveness began to lose their effectiveness. Competition broke out on a global scale in more and more industries as Japanese, European, and U.S. companies pursued international expansion in the wake of trade liberalization and the opening up of market opportunities in both industrialized and less-developed countries.[19] The relevant market arena in many industries shifted from national to global principally because the strategies of global competitors, most notably the Japanese companies, involved gaining a market foothold in host country markets via lower-priced, higher-quality offerings than established companies. To fend off global competitors, traditional MNCs were driven to integrate their operations across national borders in a quest for better efficiencies and lower manufacturing costs. Instead of separately manufacturing a complete product range in each country, plants became more specialized in their production operations to gain the economies of longer production runs, to per-

---

[16]C. K. Prahalad and Yves L. Doz, *The Multinational Mission* (New York: Free Press, 1987), p. 2.
[17]Ibid., p. 15.
[18]Yves L. Doz, *Strategic Management in Multinational Companies* (New York: Pergamon Press, 1985), p. 1.
[19]Ibid., pp. 2–3.

mit use of faster automated equipment, and to capture experience curve effects. Country subsidiaries obtained the rest of the product range they needed from sister plants in other countries. Gains in manufacturing efficiencies from converting to state-of-the-art, world-scale manufacturing plants more than offset increased international shipping costs, especially in light of the other advantages globalized strategies offered. With a global strategy, an MNC could locate plants in countries with low labor costs—a key consideration in industries whose products have high labor content. With a global strategy, an MNC could also exploit differences in tax rates, setting transfer prices in its integrated operations to produce higher profits in low-tax countries and lower profits in high-tax countries. Global strategic coordination also gave MNCs increased ability to take advantage of country-to-country differences in interest rates, exchange rates, credit terms, government subsidies, and export guarantees. As a consequence of these advantages, it became increasingly difficult for a company that produced and sold its product in only one country to succeed in an industry populated with aggressive competitors intent on achieving global dominance.

During the 1980s another source of competitive advantage began to emerge: using the strategic fit advantages of related diversification to build stronger competitive positions in several related global industries simultaneously. Being a diversified MNC (DMNC) became competitively superior to being a single-business MNC in cases where strategic fits existed across global industries. Related diversification is most capable of producing competitive advantage for a multinational company where expertise in a core technology can be applied in different industries (at least one of which is global) and where there are important economies of scope and brand name advantages to being in a family of related businesses.[20] Illustration Capsule 24 indicates Honda's strategy in exploiting gasoline engine technology and its well-known name by diversifying into a variety of products with engines.

> A multinational corporation can gain competitive advantage by diversifying into global industries having related technologies.

SOURCES OF COMPETITIVE ADVANTAGE FOR A DMNC

When a multinational company has expertise in a core technology and has diversified into a series of related products and businesses to exploit that core, a centralized R&D effort coordinated at the headquarters level holds real potential for competitive advantage. By channeling corporate resources directly into a strategically coordinated R&D/technology effort, as opposed to letting each business unit perform its own R&D function, the DMNC can launch a world-class, global-scale assault to advance the core technology, generate technology-based manufacturing economies within and across product/business lines, make across-the-board product improvements, and develop complementary products—all significant advantages in a globally competitive marketplace. In the absence of centralized coordination, R&D/technology investments are likely to be scaled down to match each business's product-market perspective, setting the stage for lost opportunity as the strategic-fit benefits of coordinated technology management slip through the cracks and go uncaptured.[21]

The second source of competitive advantage for a DMNC concerns the distribution and brand name advantages that can accrue from diversifying into related global industries. Consider, for instance, the competitive strength of such Japanese DMNCs

---

[20]Pralahad and Doz, *The Multinational Mission,* pp. 62–63.
[21]Ibid.

ILLUSTRATION CAPSULE 24

HONDA'S COMPETITIVE ADVANTAGE
THE TECHNOLOGY OF ENGINES

At first blush anyone looking at Honda's lineup of products—cars, motorcycles, lawn mowers, power generators, outboard motors, snowmobiles, snowblowers, and garden tillers—might conclude that Honda has pursued unrelated diversification. But underlying the obvious product diversity is a common core: the technology of engines.

The basic Honda strategy is to exploit the company's expertise in engine technology and manufacturing and to capitalize on its brand recognition. One Honda ad teases consumers with the question, "How do you put six Hondas in a two-car garage?" It then shows a garage containing a Honda car, a Honda motorcycle, a Honda snowmobile, a Honda lawnmower, a Honda power generator, and a Honda outboard motor.

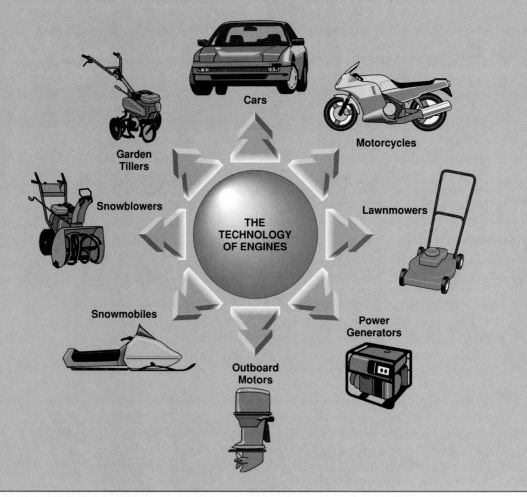

Source: Adapted from C. K. Prahalad and Yves L. Doz, *The Multinational Mission* (New York: Free Press, 1987), p. 62.

as Sanyo and Matsushita. Both have diversified into a range of globally competitive consumer goods industries—TVs, stereo equipment, radios, VCRs, small domestic appliances (microwave ovens, for example), and personal computers. By widening their scope of operations in products marketed through similar distribution channels, Sanyo and Matsushita have not only exploited related technologies but also built stronger distribution capabilities, captured logistical and distribution-related economies, and established greater brand awareness for their products.[22] Such competitive advantages are not available to a domestic-only company pursuing single-business concentration. Moreover, with a well-diversified product line and a multinational market base, a DMNC can enter new country markets or new product markets and gain market share via below-market pricing (and below-average cost pricing if need be), subsidizing the entry with earnings from one or more of its country market profit sanctuaries and/or earnings in other businesses.

> A multinational corporation can also gain competitive advantage by diversifying into related global industries where the strategic fits produce economies of scope and the benefits of brand name transfer.

Both a one-business multinational company and a one-business domestic company are weakly positioned to defend their market positions against a determined DMNC willing to accept lower short-term profits in order to win long-term competitive position in a desirable new market. A one-business domestic company has only one profit sanctuary—its home market. A one-business multinational company may have profit sanctuaries in several country markets but all are in the same business. Each is vulnerable to a DMNC that launches a major strategic offensive in their profit sanctuaries and low-balls its prices to win market share at their expense. A DMNC's ability to keep hammering away at competitors with low-ball prices year after year may reflect either a cost advantage growing out of its related diversification strategy or a willingness to cross-subsidize low profits or even losses with earnings from its profit sanctuaries in other country markets and/or its earnings from other businesses. Sanyo, for example, by pursuing related diversification keyed to product-distribution-technology strategic fit and managing its product families on a global scale, has the ability to encircle domestic companies like Zenith (which manufactures TVs and small computer systems) and Maytag (which manufactures home appliances) and put them under serious competitive pressure. In Zenith's case, Sanyo can peck away at Zenith's market share in TVs and in the process weaken the loyalty of TV retailers to the Zenith brand. In Maytag's case, Sanyo can diversify into large home appliances (by acquiring an established appliance maker or manufacturing on its own) and cross-subsidize a low-priced market entry against Maytag and other less-diversified home appliance firms with earnings from its many other business and product lines. If Sanyo chooses, it can keep its prices low for several years to gain market share at the expense of domestic rivals, turning its attention to profits after the battle for market share and competitive position is won.[23] Some additional aspects of the competitive power of broadly diversified enterprises is described in Illustration Capsule 25.

> A multinational corporation that diversifies into related global industries is well-positioned to outcompete both a one-business domestic company and a one-business multinational company.

The competitive principle is clear: A DMNC has a strategic arsenal capable of defeating both a single-business MNC and a single-business domestic company over the long term. The competitive advantages of a DMNC, however, depend on employing a related diversification strategy in industries that are already globally competitive or are on the verge of becoming so. Then the related businesses have to be managed so as to capture strategic-fit benefits. DMNCs have the biggest competitive advantage potential in industries with technology-sharing and

> A DMNC's most potent advantages usually derive from technology sharing, economies of scope, shared brand names, and its potential to employ cross-subsidization tactics.

---

[22]Ibid., p. 64.
[23]Ibid.

ILLUSTRATION CAPSULE 25

MITSUBISHI: THE COMPETITIVE POWER OF A KEIRETSU

Mitsubishi is Japan's largest *keiretsu*—a family of affiliated companies. With combined 1992 sales of $175 billion, the Mitsubishi keiretsu consists of 28 core companies: Mitsubishi Corp. (the trading company), Mitsubishi Heavy Industries (the group's biggest manufacturer—shipbuilding, air conditioners, forklifts, robots, gas turbines), Mitsubishi Motors, Mitsubishi Steel, Mitsubishi Aluminum, Mitsubishi Oil, Mitsubishi Petrochemical, Mitsubishi Gas Chemical, Mitsubishi Plastics, Mitsubishi Cable, Mitsubishi Electric, Mitsubishi Construction, Mitsubishi Paper Mills, Mitsubishi Mining and Cement, Mitsubishi Rayon, Nikon, Asahi Glass, Kirin Brewery, Mitsubishi Bank (the world's fifth largest bank and the lead bank for family companies), Tokio Marine and Fire Insurance (one of the world's largest insurance companies), and eight others. Beyond this core group are hundreds of other Mitsubishi-related subsidiaries and affiliates.

The 28 core companies of the Mitsubishi keiretsu are bound together by cross-ownership of each other's stock (the percentage of shares of each core company owned by other members ranges from 17% to 100%, with an average of 27%), by interlocking directorships (it is standard for officers of one company to sit on the boards of other keiretsu members), joint ventures, and long-term business relationships. They use each other's products and services in many instances—among the suppliers to Mitsubishi Motor's Diamond Star plant in Bloomington, Illinois, are 25 Mitsubishi and Mitsubishi-related suppliers. It is common for them to join forces to make acquisitions—five Mitsubishi companies teamed to buy a cement plant in California; Mitsubishi Corp. bought an $880 million chemical company in Pittsburgh with financial assistance from Mitsubishi Bank and Mitsubishi Trust, then sold pieces to Mitsubishi Gas Chemical, Mitsubishi Rayon, Mitsubishi Petrochemical, and Mitsubishi Kasei. Mitsubishi Bank and occasionally other Mitsubishi financial enterprises serve as a primary financing source for new ventures and as a financial safety net if keiretsu members encounter tough market conditions or have financial problems.

Despite these links, there's no grand Mitsubishi strategy. Each company operates independently, pursuing its own strategy and markets. On occasion, group members find themselves going after the same markets competing with each other. Nor do member companies usually get sweetheart deals from other members; for example, Mitsubishi Heavy Industries lost out to Siemens in competing to supply gas turbines to a new power plant that Mitsubishi Corp.'s wholly owned Diamond Energy subsidiary constructed in Virginia. But operating independence does not prevent them from recognizing their mutual interests, cooperating voluntarily without formal controls, or turning inward to

(continued)

technology-transfer opportunities and where there are important economies of scope and brand name benefits associated with competing in related product families.

A DMNC also has important cross-subsidization potential for winning its way into attractive new markets. However, while DMNCs have significant cross-subsidization powers, they rarely use them in the extreme. It is one thing to use a *portion* of the profits and cash flows from existing businesses to cover reasonable short-term losses to gain entry to a new business or a new country market; it is quite another to drain corporate profits indiscriminately (and thus impair overall company performance) to support either deep price discounting and quick market penetration in the short term or continuing losses over the longer term. At some juncture, every business and every market entered has to make a profit contribution or become a candidate for abandonment. Moreover, the company has to wring consistently acceptable overall performance from the whole business portfolio. So there are limits to cross-subsidization. As a general rule, cross-subsidization is justified only if there is a good chance that short-term losses can be amply recouped in some way over the long term.

ILLUSTRATION CAPSULE 25

(concluded)

keiretsu members for business partnerships on ventures perceived as strategically important.

A President's Council, consisting of 49 chairmen and presidents, meets monthly, usually the second Friday of the month. While the formal agenda typically includes a discussion of joint philanthropical and public relations projects and a lecture by an expert on some current topic, participants report instances where strategic problems or opportunities affecting several group members are discussed and major decisions made. It is common for a Mitsubishi company involved in a major undertaking (initiating its first foray into the U.S. or European markets or developing a new technology) to ask for support from other members. In such cases, group members who can take business actions that contribute to solutions are expected to do so. The President's Council meetings also serve to cement personal ties, exchange information, identify mutual interests, and set up follow-on actions by subordinates. Other ways that Mitsubishi uses to foster an active informal network of contacts, information sharing, cooperation, and business relationships among member companies include regular get-togethers of Mitsubishi-America and Mitsubishi-Europe executives and even a matchmaking club where member company employees can meet prospective spouses.

In recent years, Mitsubishi companies introduced a number of consumer products in the U.S. and elsewhere, all branded with a three-diamond logo derived from the crest of the founding samurai family—cars and trucks made by Mitsubishi Motors, big-screen TVs and mobile phones made by Mitsubishi Electric, and air conditioners produced by Mitsubishi Heavy Industries. Mitsubishi executives believe common logo usage has produced added brand awareness; for example, in the U.S. Mitsubishi Motors' efforts to advertise and market its cars and trucks helped boost brand awareness of Mitsubishi TVs. In several product categories one or more Mitsubishi companies operate in stages all along the industry value chain—from components production to assembly to shipping, warehousing, and distribution.

Similar practices exist in the other five of the six largest Japanese keiretsu: Dai-Ichi Kangin with 47 core companies, Mitsui Group with 24 core companies (including Toyota and Toshiba), Sanwa with 44 core companies, Sumitomo with 20 core companies (including NEC, a maker of telecommunications equipment and personal computers), and Fuyo with 29 core companies (including Nissan and Canon). Most observers agree that Japan's keiretsu model gives Japanese companies major competitive advantages in international markets. According to a Japanese economics professor at Osaka University, "Using group power, they can engage in cutthroat competition."

Source: Based on information in "Mighty Mitsubishi Is on the Move" and "Hands across America: The Rise of Mitsubishi," *Business Week,* September 24, 1990, pp. 98–107.

COMBINATION DIVERSIFICATION STRATEGIES

The six corporate diversification approaches described above are not mutually exclusive. They can be pursued in combination and in varying sequences, allowing ample room for companies to customize their diversification strategies to fit their own circumstances. The most common business portfolios created by corporate diversification strategies are

- A dominant-business enterprise with sales concentrated in one major core business but with a modestly diversified portfolio of either related or unrelated businesses (amounting to one-third or less of total corporatewide sales).
- A narrowly diversified enterprise having a *few* (two to five) *related core* business units.
- A broadly diversified enterprise made up of *many* mostly *related* business units.
- A narrowly diversified enterprise composed of a *few* (two to five) *core* business units in *unrelated* industries.

- A broadly diversified enterprise having *many* business units in mostly *unrelated* industries.
- A multibusiness enterprise that has diversified into unrelated areas but that has a portfolio of related businesses within each area—thus giving it *several unrelated groups of related businesses.*

In each case, the geographic markets of individual businesses within the portfolio can range from local to regional to national to multinational to global. Thus, a company can be competing locally in some businesses, nationally in others, and globally in still others.

KEY POINTS

Most companies have their business roots in a single industry. Even though they may have since diversified into other industries, a substantial part of their revenues and profits still usually comes from the original or core business. Diversification becomes an attractive strategy when a company runs out of profitable growth opportunities in its core business (including any opportunities to integrate backward or forward to strengthen its competitive position). The purpose of diversification is to build shareholder value. Diversification builds shareholder value when a diversified group of businesses can perform better under the auspices of a single corporate parent than they would as independent, stand-alone businesses. Whether a particular diversification move is capable of increasing shareholder value hinges on the attractiveness test, the cost-of-entry test, and the better-off test.

There are two fundamental approaches to diversification—into related businesses and into unrelated businesses. The rationale for related diversification is *strategic:* diversify into businesses with strategic fit, capitalize on strategic-fit relationships to gain competitive advantage, then use competitive advantage to achieve the desired 2 + 2 = 5 impact on shareholder value. Businesses have strategic fit when their value chains offer potential (1) for realizing economies of scope or cost-saving efficiencies associated with sharing technology, facilities, functional activities, distribution outlets, or brand names; (2) for skills transfers or technology transfers; and/or (3) for added differentiation. Such competitive advantage potentials can exist anywhere along the value chains of related businesses.

The basic premise of unrelated diversification is that any business that has good profit prospects and can be acquired on good financial terms is a good business to diversify into. Unrelated diversification is basically a *financial* approach to diversification; strategic fit is a secondary consideration compared to the expectation of financial gain. Unrelated diversification surrenders the competitive advantage potential of strategic fit in return for such advantages as (1) spreading business risk over a variety of industries and (2) gaining opportunities for quick financial gain (if candidate acquisitions have undervalued assets, are bargain-priced and have good upside potential given the right management, or need the backing of a financially strong parent to capitalize on attractive opportunities). In theory, unrelated diversification also offers greater earnings stability over the business cycle, a third advantage. However, achieving these three outcomes consistently requires corporate executives who are smart enough to avoid the considerable disadvantages of unrelated diversification. The greater the number of businesses a conglomerate company is in and the more diverse these businesses are, the more that corporate executives are stretched to know enough about each business to distinguish a good acquisition from a risky one, select capable managers to run each business, know when the major strategic proposals of business units are sound, or wisely decide what to do when a business unit stumbles. Unless corporate managers are exceptionally shrewd and talented, unrelated diversification is a dubious and unreliable approach to building shareholder value when compared to related diversification.

Once diversification is accomplished, corporate management's task is to manage the firm's business portfolio for maximum long-term performance. There are six different strategic options for improving a diversified company's performance: (1) make new acquisitions, (2) divest weak-performing business units or those that no longer fit, (3) restructure the makeup of the portfolio when overall performance is poor and future prospects are bleak, (4) retrench to a narrower diversification base, (5) pursue multinational diversification, and (6) liquidate money-losing businesses with poor turnaround potential.

The most popular option for getting out of a business that is unattractive or doesn't fit is to sell it—ideally to a buyer for whom the business has attractive fit. Sometimes a business can be divested by spinning it off as a financially and managerially independent enterprise in which the parent company may or may not retain an ownership interest.

Corporate turnaround, retrenchment, and restructuring strategies are used when corporate management has to restore an ailing business portfolio to good health. Poor performance can be caused by large losses in one or more businesses that pull overall corporate performance down, by too many business units in unattractive industries, by an excessive debt burden, or by ill-chosen acquisitions that haven't lived up to expectations. Corporate turnaround strategies aim at restoring money-losing businesses to profitability instead of divesting them. Retrenchment involves reducing the scope of diversification to a smaller number of businesses by divesting those that are too small to make a sizable contribution to corporate earnings or those that don't fit with the narrower business base on which corporate management wants to concentrate company resources and energies. Restructuring strategies involve radical portfolio shakeups, divestiture of some businesses and acquisition of others to create a group of businesses with much improved performance potential.

Multinational diversification strategies feature a diversity of businesses and a diversity of national markets. Despite the complexity of having to devise and manage so many strategies (at least one for each industry, with as many variations for country markets as may be needed), multinational diversification can be a competitively advantageous strategy. DMNCs can use the strategic-fit advantages of related diversification (economies of scope, skills transfer, and shared brand names) to build competitively strong positions in several related global industries simultaneously. Such advantages, if competently exploited, can allow a DMNC to outcompete a one-business domestic rival or a one-business multinational rival over time. A one-business domestic company has only one profit sanctuary—its home market. A single-business multinational company may have profit sanctuaries in several countries, but all are in the same business. Both are vulnerable to a DMNC that launches offensive campaigns in their profit sanctuaries. The DMNC can use its lower-cost advantage growing out of its economies of scope to underprice rivals and gain market share at their expense. Even without a cost advantage, the DMNC can decide to underprice such rivals and subsidize its lower profit margins (or even losses) with the profits earned in its other businesses. A well-financed and competently managed DMNC can sap the financial and competitive strength of one-business domestic-only and multinational rivals. DMNCs have the biggest competitive advantage potential in industries with significant economies of scope, shared brand name benefits, and technology-sharing opportunities.

SUGGESTED READINGS

Buzzell, Robert D. "Is Vertical Integration Profitable?" *Harvard Business Review* 61, no. 1 (January–February 1983), pp. 92–102.

Goold, Michael, and Kathleen Luchs. "Why Diversify? Four Decades of Management Thinking." *Academy of Management Executive* 7, no. 3 (August 1993), pp. 7–25.

Harrigan, Kathryn R. "Matching Vertical Integration Strategies to Competitive Conditions." *Strategic Management Journal* 7, no. 6 (November–December 1986), pp. 535–56.

Hax, Arnoldo, and Nicolas S. Majluf. *The Strategy Concept and Process.* Englewood Cliffs, N.J.: Prentice-Hall, 1991, chaps. 9, 11, and 15.

Hofer, Charles W. "Turnaround Strategies." *Journal of Business Strategy* 1, no. 1 (Summer 1980), pp. 19–31.

Hoffman, Richard C. "Strategies for Corporate Turnarounds: What Do We Know about Them?" *Journal of General Management* 14, no. 3 (Spring 1989), pp. 46–66.

Kumpe, Ted, and Piet T. Bolwijn. "Manufacturing: The New Case for Vertical Integration." *Harvard Business Review* 88, no. 2 (March–April 1988), pp. 75–82.

Ohmae, Kenichi. *The Mind of the Strategist.* New York: Penguin Books, 1983, chaps. 10 and 12.

Prahalad, C. K., and Yves L. Doz. *The Multinational Mission.* New York: Free Press, 1987, chaps. 1 and 2.

## CHAPTER EIGHT

STRATEGIC ANALYSIS OF DIVERSIFIED COMPANIES

If we can know where we are and something about how we got there, we might see where we are trending—and if the outcomes which lie naturally in our course are unacceptable, to make timely change.

Abraham Lincoln

No company can afford everything it would like to do. Resources have to be allocated. The essence of strategic planning is to allocate resources to those areas that have the greatest future potential.

Reginald Jones

Once a company diversifies, three strategic issues emerge to challenge corporate strategy-makers:

- How attractive is the group of businesses the company is in?
- Assuming the company sticks with its present lineup of businesses, how good is its performance outlook in the years ahead?
- If the previous two answers are not satisfactory, what should the company do to get out of some businesses, strengthen the positions of remaining businesses, and get into new businesses to boost the performance prospects of its business portfolio?

Crafting and implementing action plans to improve the attractiveness and competitive strength of a company's business-unit portfolio is the heart of corporate-level strategic management.

Strategic analysis of diversified companies builds on the concepts and methods used for single-business companies. But there are also new aspects to consider and additional analytical approaches to master. To evaluate the strategy of a diversified company, assess the caliber and potential of its businesses, and decide what strategic actions to take next, managers need to adhere closely to the following eight-step procedure:

1. Identify the present corporate strategy.
2. Construct one or more business portfolio matrices to reveal the character of the company's business portfolio.
3. Compare the long-term attractiveness of each industry the company is in.
4. Compare the competitive strength of the company's business units to see which ones are strong contenders in their respective industries.
5. Rate each business unit on the basis of its historical performance and future prospects.
6. Assess each business unit's compatibility with corporate strategy and determine the value of any strategic-fit relationships among existing business units.
7. Rank the business units in terms of priority for new capital investment and decide whether the strategic posture for each business unit should be aggressive expansion, fortify and defend, overhaul and reposition, or harvest/divest. (The task of initiating *specific* business-unit strategies to improve the business unit's competitive position is usually delegated to business-level managers, with corporate-level managers offering suggestions and having authority for final approval.)
8. Craft new strategic moves to improve overall corporate performance—change the makeup of the portfolio via acquisitions and divestitures, improve coordination among the activities of related business units to achieve greater cost-sharing and skills-transfer benefits, and steer corporate resources into the areas of greatest opportunity.

The rest of this chapter describes this eight-step process and introduces analytical techniques needed to arrive at sound corporate strategy appraisals.

IDENTIFYING THE PRESENT CORPORATE STRATEGY

Strategic analysis of a diversified company starts by probing the organization's present strategy and business makeup. Recall from Figure 2–2 in Chapter 2 that a good overall perspective of a diversified company's corporate strategy comes from looking at

Evaluating a diversified firm's business portfolio needs to begin with a clear identification of the firm's diversification strategy.

- The extent to which the firm is diversified (as measured by the proportion of total sales and operating profits contributed by each business unit and by whether the diversification base is broad or narrow).
- Whether the firm's portfolio is keyed to related or unrelated diversification, or a mixture of both.
- Whether the scope of company operations is mostly domestic, increasingly multinational, or global.
- The nature of recent moves to boost performance of key business units and/or strengthen existing business positions.
- Any moves to add new businesses to the portfolio and build positions in new industries.
- Any moves to divest weak or unattractive business units.
- Management efforts to realize the benefits of strategic-fit relationships and use diversification to create competitive advantage.
- The proportion of capital expenditures going to each business unit.

Getting a clear fix on the current corporate strategy and its rationale sets the stage for a thorough strategy analysis and, subsequently, for making whatever refinements or major alterations management deems appropriate.

MATRIX TECHNIQUES FOR EVALUATING DIVERSIFIED PORTFOLIOS

One of the most-used techniques for assessing the quality of a diversified company's businesses is portfolio matrix analysis. *A business portfolio matrix* is a two-dimensional display comparing the strategic positions of each business a diversified company is in. Matrices can be constructed using any pair of strategic position indicators. The most revealing indicators are industry growth rate, market share, long-term industry attractiveness, competitive strength, and stage of product/market evolution. Usually one dimension of the matrix relates to the attractiveness of the industry environment and the other to the strength of a business within the industry. Three types of business portfolio matrices are used most frequently—the growth-share matrix developed by the Boston Consulting Group, the industry attractiveness–business strength matrix pioneered at General Electric, and the Hofer–A. D. Little industry life-cycle matrix.

A business portfolio matrix is a two-dimensional display comparing the strategic positions of every business a diversified company is in.

THE GROWTH-SHARE MATRIX

The first business portfolio matrix to receive widespread use was a four-square grid devised by the Boston Consulting Group (BCG), a leading management consulting firm.[1] Figure 8–1 illustrates a BCG-type matrix. The matrix is formed using *industry growth rate* and *relative market share* as the axes. Each business unit in the corporate portfolio appears as a "bubble" on the four-cell matrix, with the size of each bubble or circle scaled to the percent of revenues it represents in the overall corporate portfolio.

The BCG portfolio matrix compares a diversified company's businesses on the basis of industry growth rate and relative market share.

Early BCG methodology arbitrarily placed the dividing line between "high" and "low" industry growth rates at around twice the real GNP growth rate plus inflation, but the boundary can be set at any percentage (5 percent, 10 percent, or whatever) managers consider appropriate. Business units in industries growing faster than the economy as a whole should end up in the "high-growth" cells and those in industries growing slower in the "low-growth" cells ("low-growth" industries are those that are mature, aging, stagnant, or declining). Rarely does it make sense to put the dividing line between high growth and low growth at less than 5 percent.

Relative market share is the ratio of a business's market share to the market share held by the largest rival firm in the industry, with market share measured in unit volume, not dollars. For instance, if business A has a 15 percent share of its industry's total volume and A's largest rival has 30 percent, A's relative market share is 0.5. If business B has a market-leading share of 40 percent and its largest rival has 30 percent, B's relative market share is 1.33. Given this definition, only business units that are market share leaders in their respective industries will have relative market shares

[1]The original presentation is Bruce D. Henderson, "The Experience Curve—Reviewed. IV. The Growth Share Matrix of the Product Portfolio" (Boston: The Boston Consulting Group, 1973), Perspectives No. 135. For an excellent chapter-length treatment of the use of the BCG growth-share matrix in strategic portfolio analysis, see Arnoldo C. Hax and Nicolas S. Majluf, *Strategic Management: An Integrative Perspective* (Englewood Cliffs, N.J.: Prentice-Hall, 1984), chapter 7.

FIGURE 8-1 | **The BCG Growth-Share Business Portfolio Matrix**

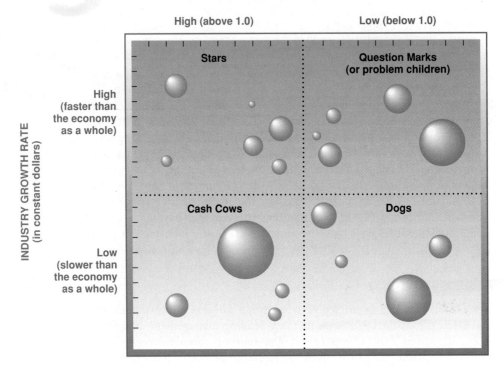

Note: *Relative* market share is defined by the ratio of a company's own market share to the market share held by its largest rival. When the vertical dividing line is set at 1.0, the only way a firm can achieve a star or cash cow position in the growth-share matrix is to have the largest market share in the industry. Since this is a very stringent criterion, it may be "fairer" and more revealing to locate the vertical dividing line in the matrix at about 0.75 or 0.80.

greater than 1.0. Business units that trail rivals in market share will have ratios below 1.0.

BCG's original standard put the border between "high" and "low" relative market share at 1.0, as shown in Figure 8–1. When the boundary is set at 1.0, circles in the two left-side cells of the matrix represent businesses that are market share leaders in their industries. Circles in the two right-side cells identify businesses that are runners-up in their industries. The degree to which they trail is indicated by the size of the relative market share ratio. A ratio of .10 indicates that the business has a market share only one-tenth that of the largest firm in the market; a ratio of .80 indicates a market share four-fifths or 80 percent as big as the leading firm's. Many portfolio analysts think that putting the boundary between high and low relative market share at 1.0 is unreasonably stringent because only businesses with the largest market share in their industry qualify for the two left-side cells of the matrix. They advocate putting the boundary at about 0.75 or 0.80 so businesses to the left have *strong* or above-average market positions (even though they are not *the* leader) and businesses to the right are clearly in underdog or below-average positions.

Using *relative* market share instead of *actual* market share to construct the growth-share matrix is analytically superior because the former measure is a better indicator of comparative market strength and competitive position. A 10 percent market share is much stronger if the leader's share is 12 percent than if it is 50 percent; the use of relative market share captures this difference. Equally important, relative market share is likely to reflect relative cost based on experience in producing the product and economies of large-scale production. Large businesses may be able to operate at lower unit costs than smaller firms because of technological and efficiency gains that attach to larger size. But the Boston Consulting Group accumulated evidence that the phenomenon of lower unit costs went beyond just the effects of scale economies; they found that, as the cumulative volume of production increased, the knowledge gained from the firm's growing production experience often led to the discovery of additional efficiencies and ways to reduce costs even further. BCG labeled the relationship between *cumulative production volume* and lower unit costs *the experience curve effect* (for more details, see Figure 3–1 in Chapter 3). A sizable experience curve effect in an industry's value chain places a strategic premium on market share: the competitor that gains the largest market share tends to realize important cost advantages which, in turn, can be used to lower prices and gain still additional customers, sales, market share, and profit. The stronger the experience curve effect in a business, the more dominant its role in strategy-making.[2]

> Relative market share is a better indicator of a business's competitive strength and market position than a simple percentage measure of market share.

With these features of the BCG growth-share matrix in mind, we are ready to explore the portfolio implications for businesses in each cell of the matrix in Figure 8–1.

Question Marks and Problem Children Business units in the upper-right quadrant of the growth-share matrix were labeled by BCG as "question marks" or "problem children." Rapid market growth makes such business units attractive from an industry standpoint. But their low relative market share (and thus reduced access to experience curve effects) raises a question about whether they have the strength to compete successfully against larger, more cost-efficient rivals—hence, the question mark or problem child designation. Question mark businesses, moreover, are typically "cash hogs"—so labeled because their cash needs are high (owing to the large investment needed to finance rapid growth and new product development) and their internal cash generation is low (owing to low market share, less access to experience curve effects and scale economies, and consequently thinner profit margins). A question mark/cash hog business in a fast-growing industry may require large infusions of cash just to keep up with rapid market growth—and even bigger cash infusions if it must outgrow the market and gain enough market share to become an industry leader. The corporate parent of a cash hog/question mark has to decide whether it is worthwhile to fund the perhaps considerable investment requirements of such a business.

> A "cash hog" business is one whose internal cash flows are inadequate to fully fund its needs for working capital and new capital investment.

BCG has argued that the two best strategic options for a question mark business are (1) an aggressive invest-and-expand strategy to capitalize on the industry's rapid-growth opportunities or (2) divestiture, in the event that the costs of expanding capacity and building market share outweigh the potential payoff and financial risk. Pursuit of a fast-growth strategy is imperative any time an attractive question mark business is in an industry characterized by a strong experience curve effect; in such

[2] For two insightful discussions of the strategic importance of the experience curve, see Pankoy Ghemawat, "Building Strategy on the Experience Curve," *Harvard Business Review* 64, no. 2 (March–April 1985), pp. 143–49, and Bruce D. Henderson, "The Application and Misapplication of the Experience Curve," *Journal of Business Strategy* 4, no. 3 (Winter 1984), pp. 3–9.

cases it takes major gains in market share to begin to match the lower costs of firms with greater cumulative production experience and bigger market shares. The stronger the experience curve effect, the more potent the cost advantages of rivals with larger relative market shares. Consequently, so the BCG thesis goes, unless a question mark/problem child business can successfully pursue a fast-growth strategy and win major market share gains, it cannot hope to become cost competitive with large-volume firms that are further down the experience curve. Divestiture then becomes the only other viable long-run alternative. BCG's corporate strategy prescriptions for question mark/problem child businesses are straightforward: divest those that are weaker and have less chance to catch the leaders on the experience curve; invest heavily in high-potential question marks and groom them to become tomorrow's "stars."

Stars   Businesses with high relative market share positions in high-growth markets rank as stars in the BCG grid because they offer excellent profit and growth opportunities. They are the business units an enterprise depends on to boost overall performance of the total portfolio.

Given their dominant market-share position and rapid growth environment, stars typically require large cash investments to expand production facilities and meet working capital needs. But they also tend to generate their own large internal cash flows due to the low-cost advantage of scale economies and cumulative production experience. Star businesses vary as to their cash hog status. Some can cover their investment needs with self-generated cash flows; others require capital infusions from their corporate parents to stay abreast of rapid industry growth. Normally, strongly positioned star businesses in industries where growth is beginning to slow tend to be self-sustaining in terms of cash flow and make little claim on the corporate parent's treasury. Young stars, however, typically require substantial investment capital *beyond what they can generate on their own* and are thus cash hogs.

Cash Cows   Businesses with a high relative market share in a low growth market are designated "cash cows" in the BCG scheme. A *cash cow business* generates substantial cash surpluses over what is needed for reinvestment and growth. There are two reasons why a business in this box tends to be a cash cow. Because of the business's high relative market share and industry leadership position, it has the sales volumes and reputation to earn attractive profits. Because it is in a slow-growth industry, cash flows from current operations typically exceed what is needed for capital reinvestment and competitive maneuvers to sustain its present market position.

Many of today's cash cows are yesterday's stars, having gradually moved down on the vertical scale (dropping from the top cell into the bottom cell) as industry demand matured. Cash cows, though less attractive from a growth standpoint, are valuable businesses. The surplus cash flows they generate can be used to pay corporate dividends, finance acquisitions, and provide funds for investing in emerging stars and problem children being groomed as future stars. Every effort should be made to keep strong cash cow businesses in healthy condition to preserve their cash-generating capability over the long term. The goal should be to fortify and defend a cash cow's market position while efficiently generating dollars to redeploy elsewhere. Weakening cash cows (those drifting toward the lower right corner of the cash cow cell) may become candidates for harvesting and eventual divestiture if stiffer competition or increased capital requirements (stemming from new technology) cause cash flow surpluses to dry up or, in the worst case, become negative.

Margin notes:

The standard strategy prescriptions for a "question mark" business are to either invest aggressively and grow it into a star performer or else divest it and shift resources to businesses with better prospects.

"Star" businesses have strong competitive positions in rapidly growing industries, are major contributors to corporate revenue and profit growth, and may or may not be cash hogs.

A "cash cow" business is a valuable part of a diversified company's business portfolio because it generates cash for financing new acquisitions, funding the capital requirements of cash hog businesses, and paying dividends.

Dogs Businesses with a low relative market share in a slow-growth industry are called "dogs" because of their dim growth prospects, their trailing market position, and the squeeze that trailing the experience curve leaders puts on their profit margins. Weak dog businesses (those positioned in the lower right corner of the dog cell) often cannot generate attractive long-term cash flows. Sometimes they cannot produce enough cash to support a rear-guard fortify-and-defend strategy—especially if competition is brutal and profit margins are chronically thin. Consequently, except in unusual cases, BCG prescribes that weaker-performing dog businesses be harvested, divested, or liquidated, depending on which alternative yields the most cash.

Weaker "dog" businesses should be harvested, divested, or liquidated; stronger dogs can be retained as long as their profits and cash flows remain acceptable.

Implications for Corporate Strategy The chief contribution of the BCG growth-share matrix is the attention it draws to the cash flow and investment characteristics of various types of businesses and how corporate financial resources can be shifted between business subsidiaries to optimize the performance of the whole corporate portfolio. According to BCG analysis, a sound, long-term corporate strategy should utilize the excess cash generated by cash cow business units to finance market share increases for cash hog businesses—the young stars unable to finance their own growth internally and problem children with the best potential to grow into stars. If successful, the cash hogs eventually become self-supporting stars. Then, when stars' markets begin to mature and their growth slows, they become cash cows. The "success sequence" is thus problem child/question mark to young star (but perhaps still a cash hog) to self-supporting star to cash cow.

The BCG growth-share matrix highlights the cash flow, investment, and profitability characteristics of various types of businesses and the benefits of shifting a diversified company's financial resources between them to optimize the whole portfolio's performance.

Weaker, less-attractive question mark businesses unworthy of a long-term invest-and-expand strategy are often a liability to a diversified company because of the high cost economics associated with their low relative market share and because their cash hog nature typically requires the corporate parent to keep pumping more capital into the business to keep abreast of fast-paced market growth. According to BCG prescriptions, weaker question marks should be prime divestiture candidates *unless* (1) they can be kept profitable and viable with their own internally generated funds or (2) the capital infusions needed from the corporate parent are quite modest.

Not every question mark business is a cash hog or a disadvantaged competitor, however. Those in industries with small capital requirements, few scale economies, and weak experience curve effects can often compete ably against larger industry leaders and contribute enough to corporate earnings and return on investment to justify retention. Clearly, though, weaker question marks still have a low-priority claim on corporate resources and a tenuous role in the portfolio. Question mark businesses unable to become stars are destined to drift vertically downward in the matrix, becoming dogs as their industry growth slows and market demand matures.

Dogs should be retained only as long as they contribute adequately to overall company performance. Strong dogs may produce a positive cash flow and show average profitability. But the further a dog business moves toward the bottom right corner of the BCG matrix, the more likely it is tying up assets that could be redeployed more profitably elsewhere. BCG recommends harvesting a weakening or already weak dog. When a harvesting strategy is no longer attractive, a weak dog should be eliminated from the portfolio.

There are two "disaster sequences" in the BCG scheme of things: (1) when a star's position in the matrix erodes over time to that of a problem child and then is dragged by slowing industry growth into the dog category and (2) when a cash cow loses market leadership to the point where it becomes a dog on the decline. Other strategic mistakes include overinvesting in a safe cash cow; underinvesting in a high-potential question mark so instead of moving into the star category it tumbles into a dog; and scattering resources thinly over many question marks rather than concentrating on the best question marks to boost their chances of becoming stars.

The growth-share matrix has significant shortcomings.

Strengths and Weaknesses in the Growth-Share Matrix Approach The BCG business portfolio matrix makes a definite contribution to the corporate strategist's toolkit when it comes to evaluating the attractiveness of a diversified company's businesses and devising general prescriptions for strategy and direction for each business unit in the portfolio. Viewing a diversified group of businesses as a collection of cash flows and cash requirements (present and future) is a major step forward in understanding the financial aspects of corporate strategy. The BCG matrix highlights the financial interaction within a corporate portfolio, shows the kinds of financial considerations that must be dealt with, and explains why priorities for corporate resource allocation can differ from business to business. It also provides good rationalizations for both invest-and-expand strategies and divestiture. Yet, it is analytically incomplete and potentially misleading:

1. A four-cell matrix based on high-low classifications hides the fact that many businesses (the majority?) are in markets with an average growth rate and have relative market shares that are neither high nor low but in between or intermediate. In which cells do these average businesses belong?

2. While viewing businesses as stars, cash cows, dogs, or question marks does have communicative appeal, it is a misleading simplification to classify all businesses into one of four categories. Some market-share leaders are never really stars in terms of profitability. All businesses with low relative market shares are not dogs or question marks—in many cases, runner-up firms have proven track records in terms of growth, profitability, and competitive ability, even gaining on the so-called leaders. Hence, a key characteristic to assess is the *trend* in a firm's relative market share. Is it gaining ground or losing ground and why? This weakness of the matrix can be solved by placing directional arrows on each of the circles in the matrix—see Figure 8–2.

3. The BCG matrix is not a reliable indicator of relative investment opportunities across business units.[3] For example, investing in a star is not necessarily more attractive than investing in a lucrative cash cow. The matrix doesn't indicate if a question mark business is a potential winner or a likely loser. It says nothing about whether shrewd investment can turn a strong dog into a cash cow.

4. Being a market leader in a slow-growth industry does not guarantee cash cow status because *(a)* the investment requirements of a fortify-and-defend strategy, given the impact of inflation and changing technology on the costs of replacing worn-out facilities and equipment, can soak up much or all of the available internal cash flows and *(b)* as markets mature, competitive forces often stiffen and the ensuing vigorous battle for volume and market share can shrink profit margins and wipe out any surplus cash flows.

5. To thoroughly assess the relative long-term attractiveness of a group of businesses, corporate strategists need to examine more than just industry growth and relative market share—as our discussion in Chapter 3 clearly indicated.

[3]Derek F. Abell and John S. Hammond, *Strategic Market Planning* (Englewood Cliffs, N.J.: Prentice-Hall, 1979), p. 212.

F I G U R E 8–2 | **Present versus Future Positions in the Portfolio Matrix**

6. The connection between relative market share and profitability is not as tight as the experience curve effect implies. The importance of cumulative production experience in lowering unit costs varies from industry to industry. Sometimes, a larger market share translates into a unit-cost advantage; sometimes it doesn't. Hence, it is wise to be cautious when prescribing strategy based on the assumption that experience curve effects are strong enough and cost differences among competitors big enough to totally drive competitive advantage (there are more sources of competitive advantage than just experience curve economics).

THE INDUSTRY ATTRACTIVENESS–BUSINESS STRENGTH MATRIX

An alternative approach that avoids some of the shortcomings of the BCG growth-share matrix was pioneered by General Electric with help from the consulting firm of McKinsey and Company. GE's effort to analyze its broadly diversified portfolio produced a nine-cell matrix based on the two dimensions of long-term industry attractiveness and business strength/competitive position (see Figure 8–3).[4] Both dimensions of

In the attractiveness-strength matrix, each business's location is plotted using quantitative measures of long-term industry attractiveness and business strength/competitive position.

---

[4]For an expanded treatment, see Michael G. Allen, "Diagramming GE's Planning for What's WATT," in *Corporate Planning: Techniques and Applications,* ed. Robert J. Allio and Malcolm W. Pennington (New York: AMACOM, 1979), and Hax and Majluf, *Strategic Management: An Integrative Perspective,* chapter 8.

FIGURE 8–3 | General Electric's Industry Attractiveness–Business Strength Matrix

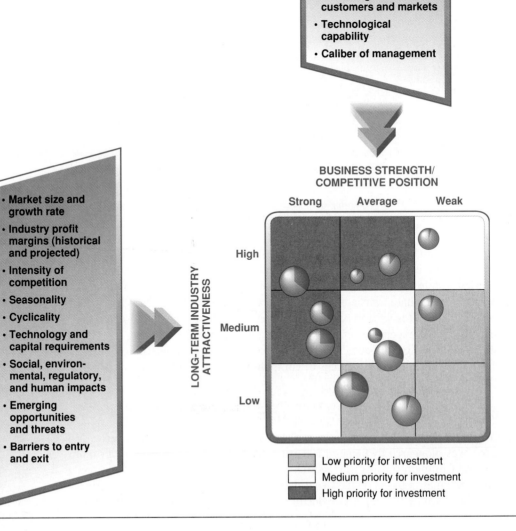

the matrix are a composite of several factors as opposed to a single factor. The criteria for determining long-term industry attractiveness include market size and growth rate; technological requirements; the intensity of competition; entry and exit barriers; seasonality and cyclical influences; capital requirements; emerging industry threats and opportunities; historical and projected industry profitability; and social, environmental, and regulatory influences. To arrive at a formal, quantitative measure of long-term industry attractiveness, the chosen measures are assigned weights based on their importance to corporate management and their role in the diversification strategy. The sum of the weights must add up to 1.0. Weighted attractiveness ratings are calculated by multiplying the industry's rating on each factor (using a 1 to 5 or 1 to 10 rating scale) by the factor's weight. For example, a rating score of 8 times a weight of .25 gives a weighted rating of 2.0. The sum of weighted ratings for all the attractiveness factors yields the industry's long-term attractiveness. The procedure is shown below:

Industry Attractiveness Factor	Weight	Rating	Weighted Industry Rating
Market size and projected growth	.15	5	0.75
Seasonality and cyclical influences	.10	8	0.80
Technological considerations	.10	1	0.10
Intensity of competition	.25	4	1.00
Emerging opportunities and threats	.15	1	0.15
Capital requirements	.05	2	0.10
Industry profitability	.10	3	0.30
Social, political, regulatory, and environmental factors	.10	7	0.70
Industry Attractiveness Rating	1.00		3.90

Attractiveness ratings are calculated for each industry represented in the corporate portfolio. Each industry's attractiveness score determines its position on the vertical scale in Figure 8–3.

To arrive at a quantitative measure of business strength/competitive position, each business in the corporate portfolio is rated using the same kind of approach as for industry attractiveness. The factors used to assess business strength/competitive position include such criteria as market share, relative cost position, ability to match rival firms on product quality, knowledge of customers and markets, possession of desirable core competencies, adequacy of technological know-how, caliber of management, and profitability relative to competitors (as specified in the box in Figure 8–3). Analysts have a choice between rating each business unit on the same generic factors (which strengthens the basis for interindustry comparisons) or rating each business unit's strength on the factors most pertinent to its industry (which gives a sharper measure of competitive position than a generic set of factors). Each business's strength/position rating determines its position along the horizontal axis of the matrix—that is, whether it merits a strong, average, or weak designation.[5]

---

[5]Essentially the same procedure is used in company situation analysis to do a competitive strength assessment (see Table 4–3 in Chapter 4). The only difference is that in the GE methodology the same set of competitive strength factors is used for every industry to provide a common benchmark for making comparisons across industries. In strategic analysis at the business level, the strength measures are *always* industry specific, never generic generalizations.

The industry attractiveness and business strength scores provide the basis for locating a business in one of the nine cells of the matrix. In the GE attractiveness-strength matrix, the area of the circles is proportional to the size of the industry, and the pie slices within the circle reflect the business's market share.

Corporate Strategy Implications   The most important strategic implications from the attractiveness-strength matrix concern the assignment of investment priorities to each of the company's business units. Businesses in the three cells at the upper left, where long-term industry attractiveness and business strength/competitive position are favorable, are accorded top investment priority. The strategic prescription for businesses falling in these three cells is "grow and build," with businesses in the high-strong cell having the highest claim on investment funds. Next in priority come businesses positioned in the three diagonal cells stretching from the lower left to the upper right. These businesses are usually given medium priority. They merit steady reinvestment to maintain and protect their industry positions; however, if such a business has an unusually attractive opportunity, it can win a higher investment priority and be given the go-ahead to employ a more aggressive strategic approach. The strategy prescription for businesses in the three cells in the lower right corner of the matrix is typically harvest or divest (in exceptional cases where good turnaround potential exists, it can be "overhaul and reposition" using some type of turnaround approach).[6]

The nine-cell attractiveness-strength approach has three desirable attributes. First, it allows for intermediate rankings between high and low and between strong and weak. Second, it incorporates explicit consideration of a much wider variety of strategically relevant variables. The BCG matrix is based on only two considerations—industry growth rate and relative market share; the nine-cell GE matrix takes many factors into account to determine long-term industry attractiveness and business strength/competitive position. Third, and most important, the nine-cell matrix stresses the channeling of corporate resources to businesses with the greatest probability of achieving competitive advantage and superior performance. It is hard to argue against the logic of concentrating resources in those businesses that enjoy a higher degree of attractiveness and competitive strength, being very selective in making investments in businesses with intermediate positions, and withdrawing resources from businesses that are lower in attractiveness and strength unless they offer exceptional turnaround potential.

However, the nine-cell GE matrix, like the four-cell growth-share matrix, provides no real guidance on the specifics of business strategy; the most that can be concluded from the GE matrix analysis is what *general* strategic posture to take: aggressive expansion, fortify and defend, or harvest-divest. Such prescriptions, though valuable from an overall portfolio management perspective, ignore the issue of strategic coordination across related businesses as well as the issue of what specific competitive approaches and strategic actions to take at the business-unit level. Another weakness is that the attractiveness-strength matrix effectively hides businesses that are about to emerge as winners because their industries are entering the takeoff stage.[7]

The nine-cell attractiveness-strength matrix has a stronger conceptual basis than the four-cell growth-share matrix.

---

[6]At General Electric, each business actually ended up in one of five types of categories: (1) *high-growth potential* businesses deserving top investment priority, (2) *stable base* businesses deserving steady reinvestment to maintain position, (3) *support* businesses deserving periodic investment funding, (4) *selective pruning or rejuvenation* businesses deserving reduced investment funding, and (5) *venture* businesses deserving heavy R&D investment.

[7]Charles W. Hofer and Dan Schendel, *Strategy Formulation: Analytical Concepts* (St. Paul, Minn.: West Publishing, 1978), p. 33.

FIGURE 8–4 | The Life-Cycle Portfolio Matrix

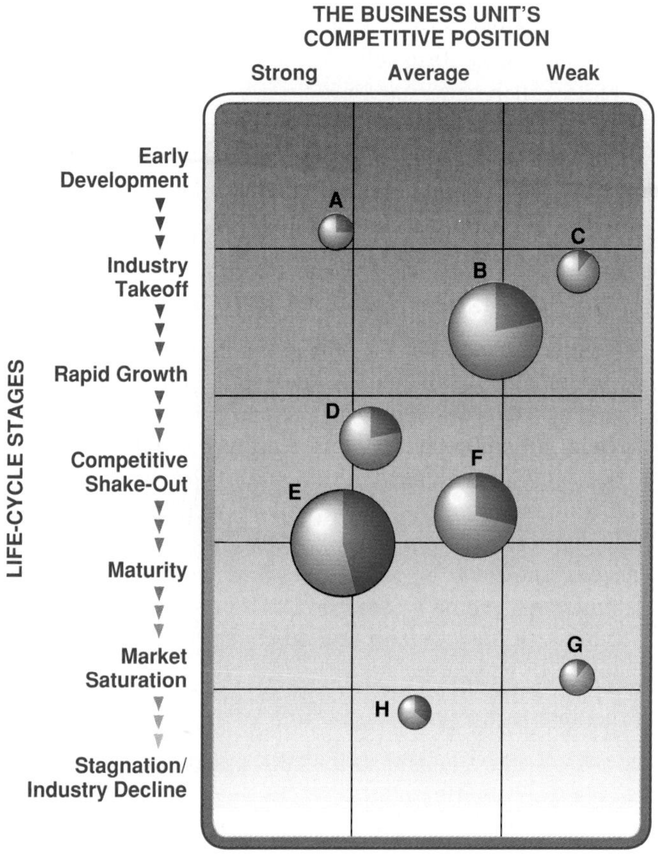

THE BUSINESS UNIT'S
COMPETITIVE POSITION

Strong   Average   Weak

LIFE-CYCLE STAGES

Early Development
Industry Takeoff
Rapid Growth
Competitive Shake-Out
Maturity
Market Saturation
Stagnation/ Industry Decline

THE LIFE-CYCLE MATRIX

To better identify a *developing winner* business, analysts can use a 15-cell matrix where business units are plotted based on stage of industry evolution and strength of competitive position, as shown in Figure 8–4.[8] Again, the circles represent the sizes of the industries involved, and pie wedges denote the business's market share. In Figure 8–4, business A could be labeled a *developing winner;* business C a *potential loser,* business E an *established winner,* business F a cash cow, and business G a loser or a dog. The power of the life-cycle matrix is the story it tells about the distribution of a diversified company's businesses across the stages of industry evolution.

The life-cycle matrix highlights how a diversified firm's businesses are distributed across the stages of the industry life-cycle.

DECIDING WHICH PORTFOLIO MATRIX TO CONSTRUCT

Restricting portfolio analysis to just one type of matrix is unwise. Each matrix has its pros and cons, and each tells a different story about the portfolio's strengths and weaknesses. Provided adequate data is available, all three matrices should be con-

[8]Ibid., p. 34. This approach to business portfolio analysis was reportedly first used in actual practice by consultants at Arthur D. Little, Inc. For a full-scale review of this portfolio matrix approach, see Hax and Majluf, *Strategic Management: An Integrative Perspective,* chapter 9.

structed since there's merit in assessing the company's business portfolio from different perspectives. Corporate managers need to understand the mix of industries represented in the portfolio, the strategic position each business has in its industry, the portfolio's performance potential, and the kinds of financial and resource allocation considerations that have to be dealt with. Using all three matrices to view a diversified portfolio enhances such understanding.

COMPARING INDUSTRY ATTRACTIVENESS

The more attractive the industries that a company has diversified into, the better its performance prospects.

A principal consideration in evaluating a diversified company's strategy is the attractiveness of the industries it has diversified into. The more attractive these industries, the better the company's long-term profit prospects. Industry attractiveness needs to be evaluated from three perspectives:

1. *The attractiveness of each industry represented in the business portfolio.* The relevant question is "Is this a good industry for the company to be in?" Ideally, each industry the firm has diversified into can pass the attractiveness test.
2. *Each industry's attractiveness relative to the others.* The question to answer here is "Which industries in the portfolio are the most attractive and which are the least attractive?" Ranking the industries from most attractive to least attractive is a prerequisite for deciding how to allocate corporate resources.
3. *The attractiveness of all the industries as a group.* The question here is "How appealing is the mix of industries?" A company whose revenues and profits come chiefly from businesses in unattractive industries probably needs to consider restructuring its business portfolio.

All the industry attractiveness considerations discussed in Chapter 3 have application in this analytical phase.

An industry attractiveness-business strength portfolio matrix provides a strong, systematic basis for judging which business units are in the most attractive industries. If such a matrix has not been constructed, quantitative rankings of industry attractiveness can be developed using the same procedure described earlier for the nine-cell GE portfolio matrix. As a rule, all the industries represented in the business portfolio should, at minimum, be judged on the following attractiveness factors:

- *Market size and projected growth rate*—faster-growing industries tend to be more attractive than slow-growing industries, other things being equal.
- *The intensity of competition*—industries where competitive pressures are relatively weak are more attractive than industries where competitive pressures are strong.
- *Technological and production skills required*—industries where the skill requirements are closely matched to company capabilities are more attractive than industries where the company's technical and/or manufacturing know-how is limited.
- *Capital requirements*—industries with low capital requirements (or amounts within the company's reach) are relatively more attractive than industries where investment requirements could strain corporate financial resources.
- *Seasonal and cyclical factors*—industries where demand is relatively stable and dependable are more attractive than industries where there are wide swings in buyer demand.

- *Industry profitability*—industries with healthy profit margins and high rates of return on investment are generally more attractive than industries where profits have historically been low or where the business risks are high.
- *Social, political, regulatory, and environmental factors*—industries with significant problems in these areas are less attractive than industries where such problems are no worse than most businesses encounter.
- *Strategic fits with other industries the firm has diversified into*—an industry can be attractive simply because it has valuable strategic-fit relationships with other industries represented in the portfolio.

Calculation of industry attractiveness ratings for all industries in the corporate portfolio provides a basis for ranking the industries from most to least attractive. If formal industry attractiveness ratings seem too cumbersome or tedious to calculate, corporate managers can rely on their knowledge of conditions in each industry to classify individual industries as having "high," "medium," or "low" attractiveness. However, the validity of such subjective assessments depends on whether management has probed industry conditions sufficiently to make dependable judgments.

For a diversified company to be a strong performer, a substantial portion of its revenues and profits must come from business units judged to be in attractive industries. It is particularly important that core businesses be in industries with a good outlook for growth and above-average profitability. Business units in the least attractive industries may be divestiture candidates, unless they are positioned strongly enough to overcome the adverse industry environment or they are a strategically important component of the portfolio.

COMPARING BUSINESS-UNIT STRENGTH

Doing an appraisal of each business unit's strength and competitive position in its industry helps corporate managers judge a business unit's chances for success. The task here is to evaluate whether the business is well-positioned in its industry and the extent to which it already is or can become a strong market contender. The two most revealing techniques for evaluating a business's position in its industry are SWOT analysis and competitive strength assessment. Quantitative rankings of the strength/position of the various business units in the corporate portfolio can be calculated using either the procedure described in constructing the attractiveness-strength matrix or the procedure presented in Chapter 4. Assessments of how a diversified company's business subsidiaries compare in competitive strength should be based on such factors as

- *Relative market share*—business units with higher relative market shares normally have greater competitive strength than those with lower shares.
- *Ability to compete on price and/or quality*—business units that are very cost competitive and/or have established brand names and reputations for excellent product quality tend to be more strongly positioned in their industries than business units struggling to establish recognized names or to achieve cost parity with major rivals.
- *Technology and innovation capabilities*—business units recognized for their technological leadership and track record in innovation are usually strong competitors in their industry.

- *How well the business unit's skills and competences match industry key success factors*—the more a business unit's strengths match the industry's key success factors, the stronger its competitive position tends to be.
- *Profitability relative to competitors*—business units that consistently earn above-average returns on investment and have bigger profit margins than their rivals usually have stronger competitive positions than business units with below-average profitability for their industry. Moreover, above-average profitability signals competitive advantage while below-average profitability usually denotes competitive disadvantage.

Other competitive strength indicators that can be employed include knowledge of customers and markets, production capabilities, marketing skills, reputation and brand name awareness, and the caliber of management.

Calculation of competitive strength ratings for each business unit provides a basis for judging which ones are in strong positions in their industries and which are in weak positions. If analysts lack sufficient data, they can rely on their knowledge of each business unit's competitive situation to classify it as being in a "strong," "average," or "weak" competitive position. If trustworthy, such subjective assessments of business-unit strength can substitute for quantitative measures.

Managerial evaluations of which businesses in the portfolio enjoy the strongest competitive positions add further rationale and justification for corporate resource allocation. A company may earn larger profits over the long term by investing in a business with a competitively strong position in a moderately attractive industry than by investing in a weak business in a glamour industry. This is why a diversified company needs to consider *both* industry attractiveness and business strength in deciding where to steer resources.

> Shareholder interests are generally best served by concentrating corporate resources on businesses that can contend for market leadership in their industries.

Many diversified companies concentrate their resources on industries where they can be strong market contenders and divest businesses that are not good candidates for becoming leaders. At General Electric, the whole thrust of corporate strategy and corporate resource allocation is to put GE's businesses into a number one or two position in both the United States and globally—see Illustration Capsule 26.

COMPARING BUSINESS-UNIT PERFORMANCE

Once each business subsidiary is rated on the basis of industry attractiveness and competitive strength, the next step is to evaluate which businesses have the best performance prospects and which ones the worst. The most important considerations in judging business-unit performance are sales growth, profit growth, contribution to company earnings, and the return on capital invested in the business; sometimes, cash flow generation is a big consideration, especially for cash cow businesses or businesses with potential for harvesting. Information on each business's past performance can be gleaned from financial records. While past performance is not necessarily a good predictor of future performance, it does signal which businesses have been strong performers and which have been weak performers. The industry attractiveness-business strength evaluations should provide a solid basis for judging future prospects. Normally, strong business units in attractive industries have significantly better prospects than weak businesses in unattractive industries.

The growth and profit outlooks for the company's core businesses generally determine whether the portfolio as a whole will turn in a strong or weak performance. Noncore businesses with subpar track records and little expectation for improvement

ILLUSTRATION CAPSULE 26

PORTFOLIO MANAGEMENT AT GENERAL ELECTRIC

When Jack Welch became CEO of General Electric in 1981, he launched a corporate strategy effort to reshape the company's diversified business portfolio. Early on he issued a challenge to GE's business-unit managers to become number one or number two in their industry; failing that, the business units either had to capture a

Sears), and Kidder Peabody (a Wall Street investment banking firm). Internally, many of the company's smaller business operations were put under the direction of larger "strategic business units." But, most significantly, in 1989, 12 of GE's 14 strategic business units were market leaders in the United States and globally (the company's financial services and communications units served markets too fragmented to rank).

In 1989, having divested most of the weak businesses and having built existing businesses into leading

GE Strategic Business Units	Market Standing in the United States	Market Standing in the World
Aircraft engines	First	First
Broadcasting (NBC)	First	Not applicable
Circuit breakers	Tied for first with two others	Tied for first with three others
Defense electronics	Second	Second
Electric motors	First	First
Engineering plastics	First	First
Factory automation	Second	Third
Industrial and power systems	First	First
Lighting	First	Second
Locomotives	First	Tied for first
Major home appliances	First	Tied for second
Medical diagnostic imaging	First	First

decided technological advantage translatable into a competitive edge or face possible divestiture.

By 1989, GE was a different company. Under Welch's prodding, GE divested operations worth $9 billion—TV operations, small appliances, a mining business, and computer chips. It spent a total of $24 billion acquiring new businesses, most notably RCA, Roper (a maker of major appliances whose biggest customer was

contenders, Welch launched a new initiative within GE to dramatically boost productivity and reduce the size of GE's bureaucracy. Welch argued that for GE to continue to be successful in a global marketplace, the company had to press hard for continuous cost reduction in each of its businesses and cut through bureaucratic procedures to shorten response times to changing market conditions.

Source: Developed from information in Stratford P. Sherman, "Inside the Mind of Jack Welch," *Fortune,* March 27, 1989, pp. 39–50.

are logical candidates for divestiture. Business subsidiaries with the brightest profit and growth prospects generally should head the list for capital investment.

STRATEGIC-FIT ANALYSIS

The next analytical step is to determine how well each business unit fits into the company's overall business picture. Fit needs to be looked at from two angles: (1) whether a business unit has valuable strategic fit with other businesses the firm has diversified into (or has an opportunity to diversify into) and (2) whether the business unit meshes well with corporate strategy or adds a beneficial dimension to the corporate portfolio. A business is more attractive *strategically* when it has activity-sharing, skills transfer, or brand-name transfer opportunities that enhance competitive advantage, and when it fits in with the firm's strategic direction. A business is more valuable *financially* when it is capable of contributing heavily to corporate performance objectives (sales growth, profit growth, above-average return on investment, and so on) and when it materially enhances the company's overall worth. Just as businesses with poor profit prospects ought to become divestiture candidates, so should businesses that don't fit strategically into the company's overall business picture. Firms that emphasize related diversification probably should divest businesses with little or no strategic fit unless such businesses are unusually good financial performers or offer superior growth opportunities.

Business subsidiaries that don't fit strategically should be considered for divestiture unless their financial performance is outstanding.

RANKING THE BUSINESS UNITS ON INVESTMENT PRIORITY

Using the information and results of the preceding evaluation steps, corporate strategists can rank business units in terms of priority for new capital investment and decide on a general strategic direction for each business unit. The task is to determine where the corporation should be investing its financial resources. Which business units should have top priority for new capital investment and financial support? Which business units should carry the lowest priority for new investment? The ranking process should clarify management thinking about what the basic strategic approach for each business unit should be—invest-and-grow (aggressive expansion), fortify-and-defend (protect current position with new investments as needed), overhaul-and-reposition (try to move the business into a more desirable industry position and to a better spot in the business portfolio matrix), or harvest-divest. In deciding whether to divest a business unit, corporate managers should rely on a number of evaluating criteria: industry attractiveness, competitive strength, strategic fit with other businesses, performance potential (profit, return on capital employed, contribution to cash flow), compatibility with corporate priorities, capital requirements, and value to the overall portfolio.

In ranking the business units on investment priority, consideration needs to be given to whether and how corporate resources and skills can be used to enhance the competitive standing of particular business units.[9] The potential for skills transfer and infusion of new capital becomes especially important when the firm has business units in less than desirable competitive positions and/or where improvement in some key success area could make a big difference to the business unit's performance. It is also important when corporate strategy is predicated on strategic fits that involve transferring corporate skills to recently acquired business units to strengthen their competitive capabilities.[10]

Improving a diversified company's long-term financial performance entails concentrating company resources on businesses with good to excellent prospects and investing minimally, if at all, in businesses with subpar prospects.

CRAFTING A CORPORATE STRATEGY

The preceding analysis sets the stage for crafting strategic moves to improve a diversified company's overall performance. The basic issue of "what to do" hinges on the

---

[9]Hofer and Schendel, *Strategy Formulation: Analytical Concepts,* p. 80.
[10]Michael E. Porter, *Competitive Advantage* (New York: Free Press, 1985), chapter 9.

conclusions drawn about the overall *mix* of businesses in the portfolio.[11] Key considerations here are: Does the portfolio contain enough businesses in very attractive industries? Does the portfolio contain too many marginal businesses or question marks? Is the proportion of mature or declining businesses so great that corporate growth will be sluggish? Does the firm have enough cash cows to finance the stars and emerging winners? Can the company's core businesses be counted on to generate dependable profits and/or cash flow? Is the portfolio overly vulnerable to seasonal or recessionary influences? Does the portfolio contain businesses that the company really doesn't need to be in? Is the firm burdened with too many businesses in average-to-weak competitive positions? Does the makeup of the business portfolio put the company in good position for the future? Answers to these questions indicate whether corporate strategists should consider divesting certain businesses, making new acquisitions, or restructuring the makeup of the portfolio.

THE PERFORMANCE TEST

A good test of the strategic and financial attractiveness of a diversified firm's business portfolio is whether the company can attain its performance objectives with its current lineup of businesses. If so, no major corporate strategy changes are indicated. However, if a performance shortfall is probable, corporate strategists can take any of several actions to close the gap:[12]

1. *Alter the strategic plans for some (or all) of the businesses in the portfolio.* This option involves renewed corporate efforts to get better performance out of its present business units. Corporate managers can push business-level managers for better business-unit performance. However, pursuing better short-term performance, if done too zealously, can impair a business's potential for performing better over the long term. Cancelling expenditures that will bolster a business's long-term competitive position in order to squeeze out better short-term financial performance is a perilous strategy. In any case there are limits on how much extra performance can be squeezed out to reach established targets.

2. *Add new business units to the corporate portfolio.* Boosting overall performance by making new acquisitions and/or starting new businesses internally raises some new strategy issues. Expanding the corporate portfolio means taking a close look at *(a)* whether to acquire related or unrelated businesses, *(b)* what size acquisition(s) to make, *(c)* how the new unit(s) will fit into the present corporate structure, *(d)* what specific features to look for in an acquisition candidate, and *(e)* whether acquisitions can be financed without shortchanging present business units on their new investment requirements. Nonetheless, adding new businesses is a major strategic option, one frequently used by diversified companies to escape sluggish earnings performance.

3. *Divest weak-performing or money-losing businesses.* The most likely candidates for divestiture are businesses in a weak competitive position, in a relatively unattractive industry, or in an industry that does not "fit." Funds from

[11]Barry Hedley, "Strategy and the Business Portfolio," *Long Range Planning* 10, no. 1 (February 1977), p. 13; and Hofer and Schendel, *Strategy Formulation,* pp. 82–86.
[12]Hofer and Schendel, *Strategy Formulation: Analytical Concepts,* pp. 93–100.

divestitures can, of course, be used to finance new acquisitions, pay down corporate debt, or fund new strategic thrusts in the remaining businesses.

4. *Form alliances to try to alter conditions responsible for subpar performance potentials.* In some situations, alliances with domestic or foreign firms, trade associations, suppliers, customers, or special interest groups may help ameliorate adverse performance prospects.[13] Forming or supporting a political action group may be an effective way of lobbying for solutions to import-export problems, tax disincentives, and onerous regulatory requirements.

5. *Lower corporate performance objectives.* Adverse market circumstances or declining fortunes in one or more core business units can render companywide performance targets unreachable. So can overly ambitious objective-setting. Closing the gap between actual and desired performance may then require revision of corporate objectives to bring them more in line with reality. Lowering performance objectives is usually a "last resort" option, used only after other options come up short.

FINDING ADDITIONAL DIVERSIFICATION OPPORTUNITIES

One of the major corporate strategy-making concerns in a diversified company is whether to pursue further diversification and, if so, how to identify the "right" kinds of industries and businesses to get into. For firms pursuing unrelated diversification, the issue of where to diversify next always remains wide open—the search for acquisition candidates is based more on financial criteria than on industry or strategic criteria. Decisions to add unrelated businesses to the firm's portfolio are usually based on such considerations as whether the firm has the financial ability to make another acquisition, whether new acquisitions are badly needed to boost overall corporate performance, whether one or more acquisition opportunities have to be acted on before they are purchased by other firms, and whether the timing is right for another acquisition (corporate management may have its hands full dealing with the current portfolio of businesses).

Firms with unrelated diversification strategies hunt for businesses that offer attractive financial returns—regardless of what industry they're in.

With a related diversification strategy, however, the search for new industries is aimed at identifying industries whose value chains have fits with the value chains of one or more businesses represented in the company's business portfolio.[14] The interrelationships can concern (1) product or process R&D, (2) opportunities for joint manufacturing and assembly, (3) marketing, distribution channel, or common brand-name usage, (4) customer overlaps, (5) opportunities for joint after-sale service, or (6) common managerial know-how requirements—essentially any area where market-related, operating, or management fits can occur.

Firms with related diversification strategies look for an attractive industry with good strategic fit.

Once strategic-fit opportunities outside a diversified firm's related business portfolio are identified, corporate strategists have to distinguish between opportunities where important competitive advantage potential exists (through cost savings, skill transfers, and so on) and those where the strategic-fit benefits are minor. The size of the competitive advantage potential depends on whether the strategic-fit benefits are competitively significant, how much it will cost to capture the benefits, and how

---

[13]For an excellent discussion of the benefits of alliances among competitors in global industries, see Kenichi Ohmae, "The Global Logic of Strategic Alliances," *Harvard Business Review* 67, no. 2 (March–April 1989), pp. 143–54.

[14]Porter, *Competitive Advantage,* pp. 370–371.

difficult it will be to merge or coordinate the business unit interrelationships.[15] Often, careful analysis reveals that while there are many actual and potential business unit interrelationships and linkages, only a few have enough strategic importance to generate meaningful competitive advantage.

DEPLOYING CORPORATE RESOURCES

To get ever-higher levels of performance out of a diversified company's business portfolio, corporate managers also have to do an effective job of allocating corporate resources. They have to steer resources out of low-opportunity areas into high-opportunity areas. Divesting marginal businesses is one of the best ways of freeing unproductive assets for redeployment. Surplus funds from cash cow businesses and businesses being harvested also add to the corporate treasury. Options for allocating these funds include (1) investing in ways to strengthen or expand existing businesses, (2) making acquisitions to establish positions in new industries, (3) funding long-range R&D ventures, (4) paying off existing long-term debt, (5) increasing dividends, and (6) repurchasing the company's stock. The first three are *strategic* actions; the last three are *financial* moves. Ideally, a company will have enough funds to serve both its strategic and financial purposes. If not, strategic uses of corporate resources should take precedence over financial uses except in unusual and compelling circumstances.

GUIDELINES FOR MANAGING THE PROCESS OF CRAFTING CORPORATE STRATEGY

Although formal analysis and entrepreneurial brainstorming normally undergird the corporate strategy-making process, there is more to where corporate strategy comes from and how it evolves. Rarely is there an all-inclusive grand formulation of the total corporate strategy. Instead, corporate strategy in major enterprises emerges incrementally from the unfolding of many different internal and external events, the result of probing the future, experimenting, gathering more information, sensing problems, building awareness of the various options, spotting new opportunities, developing ad hoc responses to unexpected crises, communicating consensus as it emerges, and acquiring a feel for all the strategically relevant factors, their importance, and their interrelationships.[16]

Strategic analysis is not something that the executives of diversified companies do all at once in comprehensive fashion. Such big reviews are sometimes scheduled, but research indicates that major strategic decisions emerge gradually rather than from periodic, full-scale analysis followed by prompt decision. Typically, top executives approach major strategic decisions a step at a time, often starting from broad, intuitive conceptions and then embellishing, fine-tuning, and modifying their original thinking as more information is gathered, as formal analysis confirms or modifies their judgments about the situation, and as confidence and consensus build for what strategic moves need to be made. Often attention and resources are concentrated on a few critical strategic thrusts that illuminate and integrate corporate direction, objectives, and strategies.

[15]Ibid., pp. 371–72.
[16]Ibid., pp. 58 and 196.

KEY POINTS

Strategic analysis in diversified companies is an eight-step process:

Step 1: *Get a clear fix on the present strategy*—whether the emphasis is on related or unrelated diversification; whether the scope of company operations is mostly domestic, increasingly multinational, or global; recent moves to add new businesses and build positions in new industries; recent divestitures; any efforts to capture strategic fits and create competitive advantage based on economies of scope, skills transfer, or shared brand name; and how much capital is being invested in each business. This step sets the stage for thorough evaluation of the need for strategy changes.

Step 2: *Construct a four-cell growth-share matrix, a nine-cell attractiveness-business strength matrix, and/or a life-cycle matrix to expose the strategic quality of the company's portfolio and the relative positions of its different businesses.* The nine-cell attractiveness-business strength matrix is conceptually and methodologically superior to the four-cell growth-share matrix, mainly because it incorporates consideration of a richer variety of strategically relevant considerations.

Step 3: *Evaluate the relative attractiveness of each industry represented in the company's portfolio.* If a nine-cell industry attractiveness-business strength matrix was constructed in Step 2, then the information is already available. Quantitative ratings of industry attractiveness, using the methodology described, are more systematic and reliable than qualitative subjective judgments.

Step 4: *Evaluate the relative competitive positions and business strength of each of the company's business units.* Again, this is a simple step if a nine-cell industry attractiveness-business strength matrix has been constructed. As always, quantitative ratings of competitive strength, using the same methodology as for industry attractiveness or the methodology presented in Table 4–4 in Chapter 4, are preferable to subjective judgments.

Step 5: *Rank the past performance of different business units from best to worst and rank their future performance prospects from best to worst.* Normally, strong business units in attractive industries have significantly better prospects than weak businesses or businesses in unattractive industries. This step provides a basis for concluding how well the portfolio as a whole should perform in the future.

Step 6: *Determine which businesses have important strategic fits with other businesses in the portfolio and how well each business fits in with the parent company's direction and strategy.* A business is more attractive *strategically* if it contributes economies of scope, skills transfer opportunities, and shared brand-name opportunities and if it is a business the parent company should be in for the foreseeable future. A business is more attractive *financially* if it is capable of contributing heavily to the firm's future financial performance.

Step 7: *Rank the business units from highest to lowest in investment priority,* thereby determining where the parent company should concentrate new capital investments. Also, determine a general strategic direction for each business unit (invest-and-expand, fortify-and-defend, overhaul-and-reposition, harvest, or divest).

Step 8: *Use the preceding analysis to craft a series of moves to improve overall corporate performance.* The most advantageous actions include

- Making acquisitions, starting new businesses from within, and divesting marginal businesses or businesses that no longer match the corporate direction and strategy.
- Devising moves to strengthen the long-term competitive positions of the company's core businesses.
- Acting to create strategic-fit opportunities and turn them into long-term competitive advantage.
- Steering corporate resources out of low-opportunity areas into high-opportunity areas.

SUGGESTED READINGS

Bettis, Richard A., and William K. Hall. "Strategic Portfolio Management in the Multibusiness Firm." *California Management Review* 24 (Fall 1981), pp. 23–38.

_____. "The Business Portfolio Approach—Where It Falls Down in Practice." *Long Range Planning* 16, no. 2 (April 1983), pp. 95–104.

Christensen, H. Kurt, Arnold C. Cooper, and Cornelius A. Dekluyuer. "The Dog Business: A Reexamination." *Business Horizons* 25, no. 6 (November–December 1982), pp. 12–18.

Haspeslagh, Phillippe. "Portfolio Planning: Uses and Limits." *Harvard Business Review* 60, no. 1 (January–February 1982), pp. 58–73.

Haspeslagh, Phillippe C., and David B. Jamison. *Managing Acquisitions: Creating Value through Corporate Renewal.* New York: Free Press, 1991.

Hax, Arnoldo, and Nicolas S. Majluf. *Strategic Management: An Integrative Perspective.* Englewood Cliffs, N.J.: Prentice-Hall, 1984, chaps. 7–9.

_____. *The Strategy Concept and Process.* Englewood Cliffs, N.J.: Prentice-Hall, 1991, chaps. 8–11 and 15.

Henderson, Bruce D. "The Application and Misapplication of the Experience Curve." *Journal of Business Strategy* 4, no. 3 (Winter 1984), pp. 3–9.

Naugle, David G., and Garret A. Davies. "Strategic-Skill Pools and Competitive Advantage." *Business Horizons* 30, no. 6 (November–December 1987), pp. 35–42.

Porter, Michael E. *Competitive Advantage.* New York: Free Press, 1985, chaps. 9–11.

_____. "From Competitive Advantage to Corporate Strategy." *Harvard Business Review* 65, no. 3 (May–June 1987), pp. 43–59.

## CHAPTER NINE

IMPLEMENTING STRATEGY: CORE COMPETENCIES, REENGINEERING, AND STRUCTURE

We strategize beautifully, we implement pathetically.

An auto-parts firm executive

Just being able to conceive bold new strategies is not enough. The general manager must also be able to translate his or her strategic vision into concrete steps that "get things done."

Richard G. Hamermesh

Organizing is what you do before you do something, so that when you do it, it is not all mixed up.

A. A. Milne

Once managers have decided on a strategy, the next step is to convert it into actions and good results. Putting a strategy into place and getting the organization to execute it well call for a different set of managerial tasks and skills. Whereas crafting strategy is largely a market-driven entrepreneurial activity, implementing strategy is primarily an operations-driven activity revolving around the management of people and business processes. Whereas successful strategy-making depends on business vision, shrewd industry and competitive analysis, and entrepreneurial creativity, successful strategy implementation depends on leading, motivating, and working with and through others to create strong "fits" between how the organization performs its core business activities and the requirements for good strategy execution. Implementing strategy is an action-oriented, make-things-happen task that tests a manager's ability to direct organizational change, design and supervise business processes, motivate people, and achieve performance targets.

Experienced managers, savvy in strategy-making and strategy-implementing, are emphatic in declaring that it is a whole lot easier to develop a sound strategic plan than it is to make it happen. According to one executive, "It's been rather easy for us to decide where we wanted to go. The hard part is to get the organization to act on the new priorities."[1] What makes strategy implementation a tougher, more time-consuming management challenge than crafting strategy is the wide array of managerial activities that have to be attended to, the many ways managers can proceed, the demanding people-management skills required, the perseverance it takes to get a variety of initiatives launched and moving, the number of bedeviling issues that must be worked out, and the resistance to change that must be overcome. *Just because managers announce a new strategy doesn't mean that subordinates will agree with it or cooperate in implementing it.* Some may be skeptical about the merits of the strategy, seeing it as contrary to the organization's best interests, unlikely to succeed, or threatening to their own careers. Moreover, company personnel may interpret the new strategy differently, be uncertain about how their departments will fare, and have different ideas about the internal changes the new strategy will entail. Long-standing attitudes, vested interests, inertia, and ingrained organizational practices don't melt away when managers decide on a new strategy and start to implement it. It takes adept managerial leadership to overcome pockets of doubt and disagreement, build consensus for how to proceed, secure the commitment and cooperation of concerned parties, and get all the implementation pieces into place. Depending on how much consensus building and organizational change is involved, the implementation process can take several months to several years.

> The strategy-implementer's task is to convert the strategic plan into action and get on with what needs to be done to achieve the targeted strategic and financial objectives.

A FRAMEWORK FOR IMPLEMENTING STRATEGY

Implementing strategy entails converting the organization's strategic plan into action and then into results. Like crafting strategy, it's a job for the whole management team, not a few senior managers. While an organization's chief executive officer and the heads of major organizational units (business divisions, functional departments, and key operating units) are ultimately responsible for seeing that strategy is implemented successfully, the implementation process typically impacts every part of the organizational structure, from the biggest operating unit to the smallest frontline work group. Every manager has to think through the answer to "What has to be done in my area to implement our part of the strategic plan, and what should I do to get these things accomplished?" In this sense, all managers become strategy-implementers in their areas of authority and responsibility, and all employees are participants. One of the keys to successful implementation is communication. Management must present the case for organizational change so clearly and persuasively that there is determined commitment throughout the ranks to carry out the strategy and meet performance targets. Ideally, managers turn the implementation process into a companywide crusade. When they achieve the strategic objectives and financial and operating performance targets, they can consider the implementation successful.

> Companies don't implement strategies, people do.

> Every manager has an active role in the process of implementing and executing the firm's strategic plan.

Unfortunately, there are no 10-step checklists, no proven paths, and few concrete guidelines for tackling the job—strategy implementation is the least charted, most open-ended part of strategic management. The best evidence on do's and don'ts comes from personal experiences, anecdotal reports, and case studies—and the wisdom they yield is inconsistent. What's worked well for some managers has been tried by others and found lacking. The reasons are understandable. Not only are some managers more effective than others in employing this or that recommended

> Managing strategy implementation is more art than science.

---

[1]As quoted in Steven W. Floyd and Bill Wooldridge, "Managing Strategic Consensus: The Foundation of Effective Implementation," *Academy of Management Executive* 6, no. 4 (November 1992), p. 27.

approach to organizational change but each instance of strategy implementation takes place in a different organizational context. Different business practices and competitive circumstances, different work environments and cultures, different policies, different compensation incentives, and different mixes of personalities and organizational histories require a customized approach to strategy implementation—one based on individual situations and circumstances, the strategy-implementer's best judgment, and the implementer's ability to use particular change techniques adeptly.

THE PRINCIPAL TASKS

While managers' approaches should be tailor-made for the situation, certain bases have to be covered no matter what the organization's circumstances; these include

- Building an organization capable of carrying out the strategy successfully.
- Developing budgets to steer ample resources into those value-chain activities critical to strategic success.
- Establishing strategically appropriate policies and procedures.
- Instituting best practices and mechanisms for continuous improvement.
- Installing support systems that enable company personnel to carry out their strategic roles successfully day in and day out.
- Tying rewards and incentives to the achievement of performance objectives and good strategy execution.
- Creating a strategy-supportive work environment and corporate culture.
- Exerting the internal leadership needed to drive implementation forward and to keep improving on how the strategy is being executed.

These managerial tasks crop up repeatedly in the strategy implementation process, no matter what the specifics of the situation, and drive the priorities on the strategy-implementer's agenda—as depicted in Figure 9–1. One or two of these tasks usually end up being more crucial or time-consuming than others, depending on the organization's financial condition and competitive capabilities, the nature and extent of the strategic change involved, the requirements for creating sustainable competitive advantage, the strength of ingrained behavior patterns that have to be changed, whether there are important weaknesses to correct or new competencies to develop, the configuration of personal and organizational relationships in the firm's history, any pressures for quick results and near-term financial improvements, and all other relevant factors.

In devising an action agenda, strategy-implementers should begin with a probing assessment of what the organization must do differently and better to carry out the strategy successfully, then consider how to make the necessary internal changes as rapidly as practical. The strategy-implementer's action priorities should concentrate on fitting how the organization performs its value-chain activities and conducts its internal business to what it takes for first-rate strategy execution. A series of "fits" are needed. Organizational skills and capabilities must be carefully matched to the requirements of strategy—especially if the chosen strategy is predicated on a competence-based competitive advantage. Resources must be allocated in a manner calculated to provide departments with the people and operating budgets needed to execute their strategic roles effectively. The company's reward structure, policies, information systems, and operating practices need to push for strategy execution, rather than playing a merely passive role or, even worse, acting as obstacles. Equally important, is the need for managers to do things in a manner and style that create and nurture a strategy-supportive work environment and corporate culture. The stronger such fits, the better the chances for successful strategy implementation. Systematic management

FIGURE 9-1 | **The Eight Big Managerial Components of Implementing Strategy**

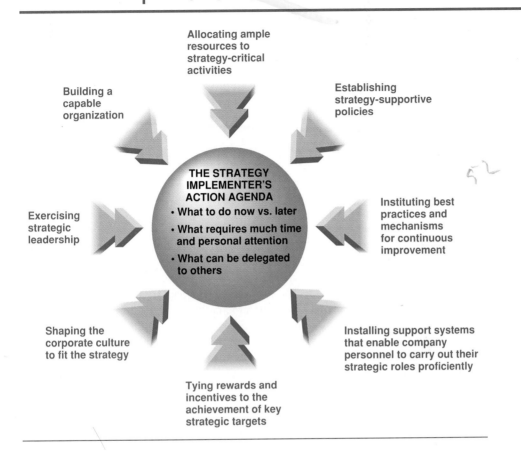

efforts to match how the organization goes about its business with the needs of good strategy execution help unite the organization in a team effort to achieve the intended performance outcomes. Successful strategy-implementers have a knack for diagnosing what their organizations need to do to execute the chosen strategy well, and they are creative in finding ways to perform key value-chain activities effectively.

LEADING THE IMPLEMENTATION PROCESS

One make-or-break determinant of successful strategy implementation is how well management leads the process. Managers can exercise leadership in many ways. They can play an active, visible role or a low-key, behind-the-scenes one. They can make decisions authoritatively or on the basis of consensus; delegate much or little; be personally involved in the details of implementation or stand on the sidelines and coach others; proceed swiftly (launching implementation initiatives on many fronts) or deliberately (remaining content with gradual progress over a long time frame). How managers lead the implementation task tends to be a function of (1) their experience and knowledge about the business; (2) whether they are new to the job or veterans; (3) their network of personal relationships with others in the organization; (4) their own diagnostic, administrative, interpersonal, and problem-solving skills; (5) the authority they've been given; (6) the leadership style they're comfortable with; and (7) their view of the role they need to play to get things done.

Although major initiatives to implement corporate and business strategies usually have to be led by the CEO and other senior officers, top-level managers still have to rely on the active support and cooperation of middle and lower managers to push strategy changes into functional areas and operating units and to carry out the strategy effectively on a daily basis. Middle- and lower-level managers not only are responsible for initiating and supervising the implementation process in their areas of authority but they also are instrumental in seeing that performance targets are met and in working closely with employees to improve strategy execution on the front lines where key value-chain activities are performed.

The action agenda of senior-level strategy-implementers, especially in big organizations with geographically scattered operating units, mostly involves communicating the case for change to others, building consensus for how to proceed, installing strong allies in positions where they can push implementation along in key organizational units, urging and empowering subordinates to get the process moving, establishing measures of progress and deadlines, recognizing and rewarding those who achieve implementation milestones, reallocating resources, and personally presiding over the strategic change process. Thus, the bigger the organization, the more the success of the chief strategy-implementer depends on the cooperation and implementing skills of operating managers who can push needed changes at the lowest organizational levels. In small organizations, the chief strategy-implementer doesn't have to work through middle managers and can deal directly with frontline managers and employees, personally orchestrating the action steps and implementation sequence, observing firsthand how implementation is progressing, and deciding how hard and how fast to push the process along. Irrespective of organization size and whether implementation involves sweeping or minor changes, the most important leadership trait is a strong, confident sense of "what to do" to achieve the desired results. Knowing "what to do" comes from a savvy understanding of the business and the organization's circumstances.

> The real strategy-implementing skill is being good at figuring out what it will take to execute the strategy proficiently.

In the remainder of this chapter and the next two chapters, we survey the ins and outs of the manager's role as chief strategy-implementer. The discussion is framed around the eight managerial components of the strategy implementation process and the most often-encountered issues associated with each. This chapter explores the management tasks of building a capable organization. Chapter 10 looks at budget allocations, policies, best practices, internal support systems, and strategically appropriate reward structures. Chapter 11 deals with creating a strategy-supportive corporate culture and exercising strategic leadership.

BUILDING A CAPABLE ORGANIZATION

Proficient strategy execution depends heavily on competent personnel, better-than-adequate skills and competitive capabilities, and effective internal organization. Building a capable organization is thus always a top strategy-implementing priority. Three types of organization-building actions are paramount:

1. Selecting able people for key positions.
2. Making certain that the organization has the skills, core competencies, managerial talents, technical know-how, and competitive capabilities it needs.
3. Organizing business processes and decision-making in a manner that is conducive to successful strategy execution.

SELECTING PEOPLE FOR KEY POSITIONS

Assembling a capable management team is one of the first cornerstones of the organization-building task. Strategy-implementers must determine the kind of core management team they need to execute the strategy successfully and then find the right people to fill each slot. Sometimes the existing management team is suitable; sometimes it needs to be strengthened and/or expanded by promoting qualified people from within or by bringing in outsiders whose backgrounds, ways of thinking, and leadership styles suit the situation. In turnaround and rapid-growth situations, and in instances when a company doesn't have insiders with the requisite experience and management know-how, filling key management slots from the outside is a fairly standard organization-building approach.

The important skill in assembling a core executive group is discerning what mix of backgrounds, experiences, know-how, values, beliefs, management styles, and personalities will reinforce and contribute to successful strategy execution. As with any kind of team-building exercise, it is important to put together a compatible group of managers who possess the full set of skills to get things done. The personal chemistry needs to be right, and the talent base needs to be appropriate for the chosen strategy. Picking a solid management team is an essential organization-building function—often the first strategy implementation step to take.[2] Until key slots are filled with able people, it is hard for strategy implementation to proceed at full speed.

> Putting together a strong management team with the right personal chemistry and mix of skills is one of the first strategy-implementing steps.

BUILDING CORE COMPETENCIES

An equally important organization-building concern is that of staffing operating units with the specialized talents, skills, and technical expertise needed to give the firm a competitive edge over rivals in performing one or more critical activities in the value chain. When it is difficult or impossible to outstrategize rivals (beat them on the basis of a superior strategy), the other main avenue to industry leadership is to outexecute them (beat them with superior strategy implementation). Superior strategy execution is essential in situations where rival firms have very similar strategies and can readily imitate one another's strategic maneuvers. Building core competencies and organizational capabilities that rivals can't match is one of the best ways to outexecute them. This is why one of management's most important strategy-implementing tasks is to guide the building of core competencies in competitively advantageous ways.

> **Strategic Management Principle**
> Building core competencies and organizational capabilities that rivals can't match is a sound foundation for sustainable competitive advantage.

Core competencies can relate to any strategically relevant factor: greater proficiency in product development, better manufacturing know-how, the capability to provide customers better after-sale services, faster response to changing customer requirements, superior performance in minimizing costs, the capacity to reengineer and redesign products faster than rivals, superior inventory management systems, strong marketing and merchandising skills, specialized depth in unique technologies, or greater effectiveness in promoting union-management cooperation. Honda's core competence is its depth of expertise in gasoline engine technology and small engine design. Intel's is in the design of complex chips for personal computers. Procter & Gamble's core competencies reside in its superb marketing-distribution skills and its R&D capabilities in five core technologies—fats, oils, skin chemistry, surfactants, and emulsifiers.[3] Sony's core competencies are its expertise in electronic technology and its ability to translate that expertise into innovative products (miniaturized radios and video cameras, TVs and VCRs with unique features). Most often, a company's core competencies emerge incrementally as it moves either to bolster skills that contributed to earlier successes or to respond to customer problems, new tech-

---

[2]For an analytical framework in top-management team analysis, see Donald C. Hambrick, "The Top Management Team: Key to Strategic Success," *California Management Review* 30, no. 1 (Fall 1987), pp. 88–108.

[3]James Brian Quinn, *Intelligent Enterprise* (New York: Free Press, 1992), p. 76.

technological and market opportunities, and the competitive maneuverings of rivals.[4] Occasionally, company managers may foresee coming changes in customer-market requirements and proactively build up new sets of competencies that offer a competitive edge.

Four traits concerning core competencies are important to a strategy-implementer's organization-building task:[5]

- Core competencies rarely consist of narrow skills or the work efforts of a single department. Rather, they are composites of skills and activities performed at different locations in the firm's value chain that, when linked, create unique organizational capability.

- Because core competencies typically originate in the combined efforts of different work groups and departments, individual supervisors and department heads can't be expected to see building the overall corporation's core competencies as their responsibility.

- The key to leveraging a company's core competencies into long-term competitive advantage is concentrating more effort and more talent than rivals on deepening and strengthening these competencies.

- Because customers' needs change in often unpredictable ways and the specific skills needed for competitive success cannot always be accurately forecasted, a company's selected bases of competence need to be broad enough and flexible enough to respond to an unknown future.

The multiskill, multiactivity character of core competencies makes building and strengthening them an exercise in (1) managing human skills, knowledge bases, and intellect and (2) coordinating and networking the efforts of different work groups and departments at every related place in the value chain. It's an exercise best orchestrated by senior managers who understand how the organization's core competencies are created and who can enforce the necessary networking and cooperation among functional departments and managers protective of their turf. Moreover, organization builders have to concentrate enough resources and management attention on core competence-related activities to achieve the *dominating depth* needed for competitive advantage.[6] This does not necessarily mean spending more money on competence-related activities than present or potential competitors. It does mean consciously focusing more talent on them and making appropriate internal and external benchmarking comparisons to move toward best-in-industry, if not best-in-world, status. To achieve dominance on lean financial resources, companies like Cray in large computers, Lotus in software, and Honda in small engines leveraged the expertise of their talent pool by frequently re-forming high-intensity teams and reusing key people on special projects.[7] In leveraging internal knowledge and skills rather than physical assets or market position, it is superior selection, training, powerful cultural influences, cooperative networking, motivation, empowerment, attractive incentives, organizational flexibility, short deadlines, and good databases—not big operating budgets—that are the usual keys to success.[8]

> Core competencies don't come into being or reach strategic fruition without conscious management attention.

---

[4]Ibid.

[5]Quinn, *Intelligent Enterprise,* pp. 52–53, 55, 73, and 76.

[6]Ibid., p. 73.

[7]Ibid.

[8]Ibid., pp. 73–74.

Strategy-implementers can't afford to become complacent once core competencies are in place and functioning. It's a constant organization-building challenge to broaden, deepen, or modify them in response to ongoing customer-market changes. But it's a task worth pursuing. Core competencies that are finely honed and kept current with shifting circumstances can provide a big executional advantage. Distinctive core competencies and organizational capabilities are not easily duplicated by rival firms; thus any competitive advantage that results from them is likely to be sustainable, paving the way for above-average organizational performance. Dedicated management attention to the task of building strategically relevant internal skills and capabilities is always one of the keys to of effective strategy implementation.

Employee Training   Training and retraining are important parts of the strategy implementation process when a company shifts to a strategy requiring different skills, managerial approaches, and operating methods. Training is also strategically important in organizational efforts to build skills-based competencies. And it is a key activity in businesses where technical know-how is changing so rapidly that a company loses its ability to compete unless its skilled people have cutting-edge knowledge and expertise. Successful strategy-implementers see that the training function is adequately funded and that effective training programs are in place. If the chosen strategy calls for new skills or different know-how, training should be placed near the top of the action agenda because it needs to be done early in the strategy implementation process.

MATCHING ORGANIZATION STRUCTURE TO STRATEGY

There are few hard-and-fast rules for organizing the work effort in a strategy-supportive fashion. Every firm's organization chart is idiosyncratic, reflecting prior organizational patterns, executive judgments about how best to arrange reporting relationships, the politics of who to give which assignments, and varying internal circumstances. Moreover, every strategy is grounded in its own set of key success factors and value-chain activities. So a customized organization structure is appropriate. The following four guidelines can be helpful in fitting structure to strategy:

1. Pinpoint the primary activities and key tasks in the value chain that are pivotal to successful strategy execution and make them the main building blocks in the organization structure.

2. If all facets of a strategy-related activity cannot, for some reason, be placed under the authority of a single manager, establish ways to bridge departmental lines and achieve the necessary coordination.

3. Determine the degrees of authority needed to manage each organizational unit, endeavoring to strike an effective balance between capturing the advantages of both centralization and decentralization.

4. Determine whether noncritical activities can be outsourced more efficiently or effectively than they can be performed internally.

Pinpointing Strategy-Critical Activities   In any business, some activities in the value chain are always more critical to strategic success than others. From a strategy perspective, a certain portion of an organization's work involves routine administrative housekeeping (doing the payroll, managing cash flows, handling grievances and the usual assortment of people problems, providing corporate security, managing stockholder relations, maintaining fleet vehicles, and complying with regulations). Other activities are support functions (data processing, accounting, training, public relations, market research, legal and legislative affairs, and purchasing). Among the primary value-chain activities are certain crucial business processes that have to be performed exceedingly well for the strategy succeed. For instance, hotel/motel enterprises have to be good at fast check in/check out, room maintenance, food service, and creating a pleasant ambiance. A manufacturer of chocolate bars must be skilled in purchasing quality cocoa beans at low prices, efficient production (a fraction of a cent in cost savings per bar can mean seven-figure improvement in the bottom line), merchandising, and promotional activities. In discount stock brokerage, the strategy-critical activities are fast access to information, accurate order execution, efficient record-keeping and transactions processing, and good customer service. In specialty chemicals, the critical activities are R&D, product innovation, getting new products onto the market quickly, effective marketing, and expertise in assisting customers. Strategy-critical activities vary according to the particulars of a firm's strategy, value-chain makeup, and competitive requirements.

Two questions help identify what an organization's strategy-critical activities are: "What functions have to be performed extra well or in timely fashion to achieve sustainable competitive advantage?" and "In what value-chain activities would malperformance seriously endanger strategic success?"[9] The answers generally point to the crucial activities and organizational areas on which to concentrate organization-building efforts.

The rationale for making strategy-critical activities the main building blocks in the organization structure is compelling: if activities crucial to strategic success are to get the attention and organizational support they merit, they have to be centerpieces in the organizational scheme. When key business units and strategy-critical functions are put on a par with or, worse, superseded by less important activities, they usually end up with fewer resources and less clout in the organization's power structure than they deserve. On the other hand, when the primary value-creating activities form the core of a company's organization structure and their managers hold key positions on the organization chart, their role and power is ingrained in daily operations and decision-making. Senior executives seldom send a stronger signal about what is strategically important than by making key business units and critical activities prominent organizational building blocks and, further, giving the managers of these units a visible, influential position in the organizational pecking order. In many cases, there is merit in operating each of these main organizational units as profit centers.

In deciding how to graft routine and staff support activities onto the basic building block structure, company managers must understand the strategic relationships among the primary and support functions that make up its value chain. Activities can be related by the flow of work along the value chain, by the type of customer served, by the distribution channels used, by the technical skills and know-how needed to perform them, by their contribution to building a core competence, by their role in a work process that spans traditional departmental lines, by their role in how customer value is created, by their sequence in the value chain, by the skills-transfer opportunities they present, and by the potential for combining or coordinating them in a manner that will reduce total costs, to mention some of the most obvious. Such relationships are important because one or more such linkages usually signal how to

Strategic Management Principle
Matching structure to strategy requires making strategy-critical activities and strategy-critical organizational units the main building blocks in the organization structure.

---

[9]Peter F. Drucker, *Management: Tasks, Responsibilities, Practices* (New York: Harper & Row, 1974), pp. 530, 535.

structure reporting relationships and where there's a need for close cross-functional coordination. If the needs of successful strategy execution are to drive organization design, then the relationships to look for are those that (1) link one work unit's performance to another and (2) can be melded into a core competence.

Managers need to be particularly alert to the fact that in traditional functionally organized structures, pieces of strategically relevant activities are often scattered across many departments. The process of filling customer orders accurately and promptly is a case in point. The order fulfillment process begins when a customer places an order, ends when the goods are delivered, and typically includes a dozen or so steps performed by different people in different departments.[10] Someone in customer service receives the order, logs it in, and checks it for accuracy and completeness. It may then go to the finance department, where someone runs a credit check on the customer. Another person may be needed to approve credit terms or special financing. Someone in sales calculates or verifies the correct pricing. When the order gets to inventory control, someone has to determine if the goods are in stock. If not, a back order may be issued or the order routed to production planning so that it can be factored into the production schedule. When the goods are ready, warehouse operations prepares a shipment schedule. Personnel in the traffic department determine the shipment method (rail, truck, air, water) and choose the route and carrier. Product handling picks the product from the warehouse, verifies the picking against the order, and packages the goods for shipment. Traffic releases the goods to the carrier, which takes responsibility for delivery to the customer. Each handoff from one department to the next entails queues and wait times. Although such organization incorporates Adam Smith's division of labor principle (every person involved has specific responsibility for performing one simple task) and allows for tight management control (everyone in the process is accountable to a manager for efficiency and adherence to procedures), *no one oversees the whole process and its result.*[11] Accurate, timely order fulfillment, despite its relevance to effective strategy execution, ends up being neither a single person's job nor the job of any one functional department.[12]

> Functional specialization can result in the pieces of strategically relevant activities being scattered across many different departments.

Managers have to guard against organization designs that unduly fragment strategically relevant activities. Parceling strategy-critical work efforts across many specialized departments contributes to an obsession with activity (performing the assigned tasks in the prescribed manner) rather than result (customer satisfaction, competitive advantage, lower costs). So many handoffs lengthen completion time and frequently drive up overhead costs since coordinating the fragmented pieces can soak up hours of effort on the parts of many people. Nonetheless, some fragmentation is necessary, even desirable, in the case of support activities like finance and accounting, human resource management, engineering, technology development, and information systems where functional centralization works to good advantage. The key in weaving support activities into the organization design is to establish reporting and coordinating arrangements that

- Maximize how support activities contribute to enhanced performance of the primary, strategy-critical tasks in the firm's value chain.
- Contain the costs of support activities and minimize the time and energy internal units have to spend doing business with each other.

---

[10]Michael Hammer and James Champy, *Reengineering the Corporation* (New York: HarperBusiness, 1993), pp. 26–27.
[11]Ibid.
[12]Ibid., pp. 27–28.

Without such arrangements, the cost of transacting business internally becomes excessive, and functional managers, forever diligent in guarding their turf and protecting their prerogatives to run their areas as they see fit, can weaken the strategy execution effort and become part of the strategy-implementing problem rather than part of the solution.

Reporting Relationships and Cross-Functional Coordination   The classic way to coordinate the activities of organizational units is to position them in the hierarchy so that those most closely related report to a single person. Managers higher up in the pecking order generally have authority over more organizational units and thus the clout to coordinate, integrate, and arrange for the cooperation of units under their supervision. In such structures, the chief executive officer, chief operating officer, and business-level managers end up as central points of coordination because of their positions of authority over the whole unit. When a firm is pursuing a related diversification strategy, coordinating the related activities of independent business units often requires the centralizing authority of a single corporate-level officer. Also, companies with either related or unrelated diversification strategies commonly centralize such staff support functions as public relations, finance and accounting, employee benefits, and data processing at the corporate level.

But, as the customer order fulfillment example illustrates, it isn't always feasible to position closely related value-chain activities and/or organizational units vertically under the coordinating authority of a single executive. Formal reporting relationships have to be supplemented. Options for unifying the strategic efforts of interrelated organizational units include the use of coordinating teams, cross-functional task forces, dual reporting relationships, informal organizational networking, voluntary cooperation, incentive compensation tied to group performance measures, and strong executive-level insistence on teamwork and interdepartmental cooperation (including removal of recalcitrant managers who stonewall cooperative efforts).

Determining the Degree of Authority and Independence to Give Each Unit   Companies must decide how much authority and decision-making latitude to give managers of each organization unit, especially the heads of business subsidiaries and functional departments. In a highly centralized organization structure, top executives retain authority for most strategic and operating decisions and keep a tight rein on business-unit heads and department heads; comparatively little discretionary authority is granted to subordinate managers. The weakness of centralized organization is that its vertical, hierarchical character tends to foster excessive bureaucracy and stall decision-making until the review-approval process runs its course through the management layers. In a highly decentralized organization, managers (and, increasingly, many nonmanagerial employees) are empowered to act on their own in their areas of responsibility. In a diversified company operating on the principle of decentralized decision-making, for example, business unit heads have broad authority to run the subsidiary with comparatively little interference from corporate headquarters. Moreover, the business head gives functional department heads considerable decision-making latitude. Employees with customer contact are empowered to do what it takes to please customers.

Delegating greater authority to subordinate managers and employees creates a more horizontal organization structure with fewer management layers. Whereas in a centralized vertical structure managers and workers have to go up the ladder of

Resolving which decisions to centralize and which to decentralize is always a big issue in organization design.

authority for an answer, in a decentralized horizontal structure they develop their own answers and action plans—making decisions and being accountable for results is part of their job. Streamlining the decision-making process usually shortens the time it takes to respond to competitors' actions, changing customer preferences, and other market developments. And it spurs new ideas, creative thinking, innovation, and greater involvement on the part of subordinate managers and employees.

In recent years, there's been a decided shift from authoritarian, multilayered hierarchical structures to flatter, more decentralized structures that stress employee empowerment. The new preference for leaner management structures and empowered employees is grounded in two tenets. (1) Decision-making authority should be pushed down to the lowest organizational level capable of making timely, informed, competent decisions—those people (managers or nonmanagers) nearest the scene who are knowledgeable about the issues and trained to weigh all the factors. Insofar as strategic management is concerned, decentralization means that the managers of each organizational unit should not only lead the crafting of their unit's strategy but also lead the decision-making on how to implement it. Decentralization thus requires selecting strong managers to head each organizational unit and holding them accountable for crafting and executing appropriate strategies for their units. Managers who consistently produce unsatisfactory results and have poor track records in strategy-making and strategy-implementing have to be weeded out. (2) Employees below the management ranks should be empowered to exercise judgement on matters pertaining to their jobs. The case for empowering employees to make decisions and be accountable for their performance is based on the belief that a company that draws on the combined brainpower of all its employees can outperform a company where the approach to people management consists of transferring ideas from the heads of bosses into the actions of workers-doers. To ensure that the decisions of empowered people are as well-informed as possible, great pains have to be taken to put accurate, timely data into everyone's hands and make sure they understand the links between their performance and company performance. Delayered corporate hierarchies and rapid diffusion of information technologies make greater empowerment feasible. It's possible now to create "a wired company" where people have direct electronic access to data and other employees and managers, allowing them to access information quickly, check with superiors as needed and take responsible action. Typically, there are genuine morale gains when people are well-informed and allowed to operate in a self-directed way.

One of the biggest exceptions to decentralizing strategy-related decisions and giving lower-level managers more operating rein arises in diversified companies with related businesses. In such cases, strategic-fit benefits are often best captured by either centralizing decision-making authority or enforcing close cooperation and shared decision-making. For example, if businesses with overlapping process and product technologies have their own independent R&D departments, each pursuing their own priorities, projects, and strategic agendas, it's hard for the corporate parent to prevent duplication of effort, capture either economies of scale or economies of scope, or broaden the vision of the company's R&D efforts to include new technological pathways, product families, end-use applications, and customer groups. Likewise, centralizing control over the related activities of separate businesses makes sense when there are opportunities to share a common sales force, utilize common distribution channels, rely upon a common field service organization to handle customer requests for technical assistance or provide maintenance and repair services, and so on. And for reasons previously discussed, limits also have to be placed on the

Centralizing strategy-implementing authority at the corporate level has merit when the related activities of related businesses need to be tightly coordinated.

independence of functional managers when pieces of strategy-critical processes are located in different organizational units and require close coordination for maximum effectiveness.

Reasons to Consider Outsourcing Noncritical Activities   Each supporting activity in a firm's value chain and within its traditional staff groups can be considered a "service."[13] Most overheads, for example, are just services the company chooses to produce internally. Often, such services can be readily purchased from outside vendors. An outsider, by concentrating specialists and technology in its area of expertise, can sometimes perform these services better or more cheaply than a company that performs the activities only for itself. Outsourcing activities not crucial to its strategy allows a company to concentrate its own energies and resources on those value-chain activities where it can create unique value, where it can be best in the industry (or, better still, best in the world), and where it needs strategic control to build core competencies, achieve competitive advantage, and manage key customer-supplier relationships.[14] Managers too often spend inordinate amounts of time, psychic energy, and resources wrestling with functional support groups and other internal bureaucracies, diverting attention from the company's strategy-critical activities. Approached from a strategic point of view, outsourcing noncrucial support activities (and maybe a few selected primary activities in the value chain if they are not a basis for competitive advantage) can decrease internal bureaucracies, flatten the organization structure, provide the company with heightened strategic focus, and increase competitive responsiveness.[15]

Critics contend that extensive outsourcing can hollow out a company, leaving it at the mercy of outside suppliers and barren of the skills and organizational capabilities needed to be master of its own destiny.[16] However, a number of companies have successfully relied on outside components suppliers, product designers, distribution channels, advertising agencies, and financial services firms. For years Polaroid Corporation bought its film medium from Eastman Kodak, its electronics from Texas Instruments, and its cameras from Timex and others, while it concentrated on producing its unique self-developing film packets and designing its next generation of cameras and films. Nike concentrates on design, marketing, and distribution to retailers, while outsourcing virtually all production of its shoes and sporting apparel. Many mining companies outsource geological work, assaying, and drilling. Ernest and Julio Gallo Winery outsources 95 percent of its grape production, letting farmers take on the weather and other grape-growing risks while it concentrates on wine production and the marketing-sales function.[17] The major airlines outsource their in-flight meals even though food quality is important to travelers' perception of overall service quality. Eastman Kodak, Ford, Exxon, Merrill Lynch, and Chevron have outsourced their data processing activities to computer service firms, believing that outside specialists can perform the needed services at lower costs and equal or better quality. Outsourcing certain value-chain activities makes strategic sense whenever outsiders can perform them at lower cost and/or with higher value-added than the buyer company can perform them internally.[18]

Outsourcing noncritical activities has many advantages.

---

[13]Quinn, *Intelligent Enterprise,* p. 32.
[14]Ibid., p. 37.
[15]Ibid., pp. 33 and 89.
[16]Ibid., pp. 39–40.
[17]Ibid., p. 43.
[18]Ibid., p. 47.

WHY STRUCTURE FOLLOWS STRATEGY

Research confirms the merits of matching organization design and structure to the particular needs of strategy. A landmark study by Alfred Chandler found that changes in an organization's strategy bring about new administrative problems which, in turn, require a new or refashioned structure for the new strategy to be successfully implemented.[19] Chandler's study of 70 large corporations revealed that structure tends to follow the growth strategy of the firm—but often not until inefficiency and internal operating problems provoke a structural adjustment. The experiences of these firms followed a consistent sequential pattern: new strategy creation, emergence of new administrative problems, a decline in profitability and performance, a shift to a more appropriate organizational structure, and then recovery to more profitable levels and improved strategy execution. That managers should reassess their company's internal organization whenever strategy changes is pretty much common sense. A new strategy is likely to entail new or different skills and key activities; if these go unrecognized, the resulting mismatch between strategy and structure can open the door to implementation and performance problems.

Strategic Management Principle
Attempting to carry out a new strategy with an old organizational structure is usually unwise.

How Structure Evolves as Strategy Evolves   As firms develop from small, single-business companies into more complex enterprises employing vertical integration, geographic expansion, and diversification strategies, their organizational structures tend to evolve from one-person management to functional departments to divisions to decentralized business units. Single-business companies are usually organized around functional departments. In vertically integrated firms, the major building blocks are divisional units, each of which performs one (or more) of the major processing steps along the value chain (raw materials production, components manufacture, assembly, wholesale distribution, retail store operations); each division in the value-chain sequence may operate as a profit center for performance measurement purposes. Companies with broad geographic coverage typically are divided into regional operating units, each of which has profit-loss responsibility for its assigned geographic area. The typical building blocks of a diversified company are its individual businesses; the authority for business-unit decisions is delegated to business-level managers. Each business unit operates as an independent profit center, with corporate headquarters performing assorted support functions for all the businesses.

THE STRATEGIC ADVANTAGES AND DISADVANTAGES OF DIFFERENT ORGANIZATIONAL STRUCTURES

There are five formal approaches to matching structure to strategy: (1) functional specialization, (2) geographic organization, (3) decentralized business divisions, (4) strategic business units, and (5) matrix structures featuring dual lines of authority and strategic priority. Each has strategic advantages and disadvantages, and each usually needs to be supplemented with formal or informal organizational arrangements to fully coordinate the work effort.

---

[19]Alfred Chandler, *Strategy and Structure* (Cambridge, Mass.: MIT Press, 1962). Although the stress here is on matching structure to strategy, it is worth noting that structure can and does influence the choice of strategy. A good strategy must be doable. When an organization's present structure is so far out of line with the requirements of a particular strategy that the organization would have to be turned upside down to implement it, the strategy may not be doable and should not be given further consideration. In such cases, structure shapes the choice of strategy. The point here, however, is that once strategy is chosen, structure must be modified to fit the strategy if, in fact, an approximate fit does not already exist. Any influences of structure on strategy should, logically, come before the point of strategy selection rather than after it.

Functional Organization Structures   Organizational structures anchored around functionally specialized departments are far and away the most popular form for matching structure to strategy in single-business enterprises. However, just what form the functional specialization takes varies according to customer-product-technology considerations. For instance, a technical instruments manufacturer may be organized around research and development, engineering, production, technical services, quality control, marketing, personnel, and finance and accounting. A hotel may have an organization based on front-desk operations, housekeeping, building maintenance, food service, convention services and special events, guest services, personnel and training, and accounting. A discount retailer may divide its organizational units into purchasing, warehousing and distribution, store operations, advertising, merchandising and promotion, and corporate administrative services. Two types of functional organizational approaches are diagrammed in Figure 9–2.

Making specialized functions the main organizational building blocks works best when a firm's value chain consists of a series of discipline-specific activities, each requiring a fairly extensive set of specialized skills, experience, and know-how. In such instances, departmental units staffed with experts in every facet of the activity is an attractive way (1) to exploit any learning/experience curve benefits or economy-of-scale opportunities associated with division of labor and the use of specialized technology and equipment and (2) to develop deep expertise in an important business function. When dominating depth in one or more functional specialties enhances operating efficiency and/or organizational know-how, it becomes a basis for competitive advantage (lower cost or unique capability). Functional structures work quite satisfactorily so long as strategy-critical activities closely match functional specialties, there's minimal need for interdepartmental cooperation, and top-level management is able to short-circuit departmental rivalries and create a spirit of teamwork, trust, and interdepartmental cooperation.

A functional structure has two Achilles' heels: excessive functional myopia and fragmentation of strategy-critical business processes across traditional departmental lines. It's tough to achieve tight strategic coordination across strongly entrenched functional bureaucracies that don't "talk the same language" and that prefer to do their own thing without outside interference. Functional specialists are prone to focus inward on departmental matters and upward at their boss's priorities but not outward on the business, the customer, or the industry.[20] Members of functional departments usually have strong departmental loyalties and are protective of departmental interests. There's a natural tendency for each functional department to push for solutions and decisions that advance its well-being and organizational influence (despite the lip service given to cooperation and "what's best for the company"). All this creates an organizational environment where functional departments operate as vertical silos, or stovepipes, and a breeding ground for departmental bureaucracies, excessive layers of management, authoritarian decision-making, and narrow perspectives. In addition, functionally dominated structures, because of preoccupation with developing deeper expertise and improving functional performance, have tunnel vision when it comes to devising entrepreneurially creative responses to major customer-market-technological changes. They are quick to kill ideas or discard alternatives that aren't compatible with the present functional structure. Classical functional structures also exacerbate the problems of process fragmentation whenever a firm's value chain includes strat-

Functional departments develop strong functional mindsets and are prone to approach strategic issues more from a functional than a business perspective.

---

[20]Hammer and Champy, *Reengineering the Corporation,* p. 28.

FIGURE 9-2 | **Functional Organizational Structures**

A. The Building Blocks of a "Typical" Functional Organizational Structure

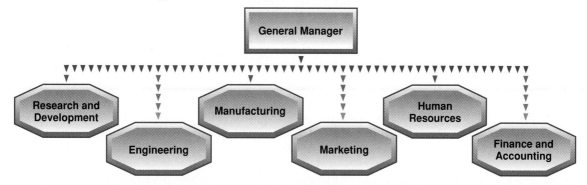

B. The Building Blocks of a Process-Oriented Functional Structure

STRATEGIC ADVANTAGES	STRATEGIC DISADVANTAGES
• Centralized control of strategic results.	• Excessive fragmentation of strategy-critical processes.
• Very well suited for structuring a single business.	• Can lead to interfunctional rivalry and conflict, rather than team-play and cooperation—GM must referee functional politics.
• Structure is linked tightly to strategy by designating key activities as functional departments.	
• Promotes in-depth functional expertise.	• Multilayered management bureaucracies and centralized decision-making slow response times.
• Well suited to developing functional skills and functional-based competencies.	• Hinders development of managers with cross-functional experience because the ladder of advancement is up the ranks within the same functional area.
• Conducive to exploiting learning/experience curve effects associated with functional specialization.	• Forces profit responsibility to the top.
• Enhances operating efficiency where tasks are routine and repetitive.	• Functional specialists often attach more importance to what's best for the functional area than to what's best for the whole business—can lead to functional empire-building.
	• Functional myopia often works against creative entrepreneurship, adapting to change, and attempts to create cross-functional core competencies.

egy-critical activities that, by their very nature, are cross-functional rather than discipline specific. Process fragmentation not only complicates the problems of achieving interdepartmental coordination but also poses serious hurdles to developing cross-functional core competencies.

Interdepartmental politics, functional empire-building, functional myopia, and process fragmentation can impose a time-consuming administrative burden on the general manager, who is the only person on the organization chart with authority to resolve cross-functional differences and to enforce interdepartmental cooperation. In a functional structure, much of a GM's time and energy is spent opening lines of communication across departments, tempering departmental rivalries, convincing stovepipe thinkers of the merits of broader solutions, devising ways to secure cooperation, and working to mold desirable cross-functional core competencies. To be successful, a GM has to be tough and uncompromising in insisting that department heads be team players and that functional specialists work together closely as needed; failure to cooperate fully has to carry negative consequences (specifically, a lower job performance evaluation and maybe even reassignment).

To strike a good balance between being function-driven and team-driven, the formal functional structure has to be supplemented with coordinating mechanisms—frequent use of interdisciplinary task forces to work out procedures for coordinating fragmented processes and strategy-critical activities, incentive compensation schemes tied to joint performance measures, empowerment of cross-functional teams that possess all the skills needed to perform strategy-critical processes in a unified, timely manner, and the formation of interdisciplinary teams charged with building the internal organizational bridges needed to create cross-functional organizational capabilities. On occasion, rather than continuing to scatter related pieces of a business process across several functional departments and scrambling to integrate their efforts, it may be better to reengineer the work effort and create *process* departments by pulling the people who performed the pieces in functional departments into a group that works together to perform the whole process.[21] Bell Atlantic did so in cutting through its bureaucratic procedures for connecting a telephone customer to its long-distance carrier.[22] In Bell Atlantic's functional structure, when a business customer requested a connection between its telephone system and a long-distance carrier for data services, the request traveled from department to department, taking two to four weeks to complete all the internal processing steps. In reengineering that process, Bell Atlantic pulled workers doing the pieces of the process from the many functional departments and put them on teams that, working together, could handle most customer requests in a matter of days and sometimes hours. Because the work was recurring—similar customer requests had to be processed daily—the teams were permanently grouped into a "process department."

A geographic organization structure is well-suited to firms pursuing different strategies in different geographic regions.

Geographic Forms of Organization   Organizing on the basis of geographic areas or territories is a common structural form for enterprises operating in diverse geographic markets or serving an expansive geographic area. As indicated in Figure 9–3, geographic organization has advantages and disadvantages, but the chief reason for its popularity is that it promotes improved performance.

---

[21]Ibid., p. 66.
[22]Ibid., pp. 66–67.

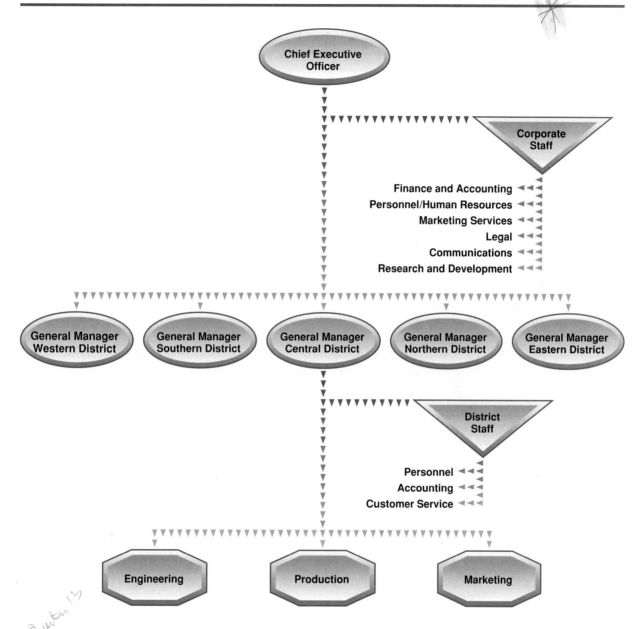

Chief Executive Officer

Corporate Staff
Finance and Accounting
Personnel/Human Resources
Marketing Services
Legal
Communications
Research and Development

General Manager Western District **General Manager Southern District** **General Manager Central District** **General Manager Northern District** **General Manager Eastern District**

District Staff
Personnel
Accounting
Customer Service

Engineering **Production** **Marketing**

STRATEGIC ADVANTAGES

- Allows tailoring of strategy to needs of each geographical market.
- Delegates profit/loss responsibility to lowest strategic level.
- Improves functional coordination within the target market.
- Takes advantage of economies of local operations.
- Area units make an excellent training ground for higher-level general managers.

STRATEGIC DISADVANTAGES

- Poses a problem of how much geographic uniformity headquarters should impose versus how much geographic diversity should be allowed.
- Greater difficulty in maintaining consistent company image/reputation from area to area when area managers exercise much strategic freedom.
- Adds another layer of management to run the geographic units.
- Can result in duplication of staff services at headquarters and district levels, creating a cost disadvantage.

In the private sector, a territorial structure is typically utilized by discount retailers, power companies, cement firms, restaurant chains, and dairy products enterprises. In the public sector, such organizations as the Internal Revenue Service, the Social Security Administration, the federal courts, the U.S. Postal Service, state troopers, and the Red Cross have adopted territorial structures in order to be directly accessible to geographically dispersed clienteles. Multinational enterprises use geographic structures to manage the diversity they encounter operating across national boundaries.

Raymond Corey and Steven Star cite Pfizer International as a good example of a company whose strategic requirements made geographic decentralization advantageous:

> Pfizer International operated plants in 27 countries and marketed in more than 100 countries. Its product lines included pharmaceuticals (antibiotics and other ethical prescription drugs), agricultural and veterinary products (such as animal feed supplements and vaccines and pesticides), chemicals (fine chemicals, bulk pharmaceuticals, petrochemicals, and plastics), and consumer products (cosmetics and toiletries).
>
> Ten geographic Area Managers reported directly to the President of Pfizer International and exercised line supervision over Country Managers. According to a company position description, it was "the responsibility of each Area Manager to plan, develop, and carry out Pfizer International's business in the assigned foreign area in keeping with company policies and goals."
>
> Country Managers had profit responsibility. In most cases a single Country Manager managed all Pfizer activities in his country. In some of the larger, well-developed countries of Europe there were separate Country Managers for pharmaceutical and agricultural products and for consumer lines.
>
> Except for the fact that New York headquarters exercised control over the to-the-market prices of certain products, especially prices of widely used pharmaceuticals, Area and Country Managers had considerable autonomy in planning and managing the Pfizer International business in their respective geographic areas. This was appropriate because each area, and some countries within areas, provided unique market and regulatory environments. In the case of pharmaceuticals and agricultural and veterinary products (Pfizer International's most important lines), national laws affected formulations, dosages, labeling, distribution, and often price. Trade restrictions affected the flow of bulk pharmaceuticals and chemicals and packaged products, and might in effect require the establishment of manufacturing plants to supply local markets. Competition, too, varied significantly from area to area.[23]

Decentralized Business Units   Grouping activities along business and product lines has been a favored organizing device among diversified enterprises for the past 70 years, beginning with the pioneering efforts of DuPont and General Motors in the 1920s. Separate business/product divisions emerged because diversification made a functionally specialized manager's job incredibly complex. Imagine the problems a manufacturing executive and his/her staff would have if put in charge of, say, 50 different plants using 20 different technologies to produce 30 different products in eight different businesses/industries. In a multibusiness enterprise, the practical organizational sequence is corporate to business to functional area within a business rather than corporate to functional area (aggregated for all businesses).

---

[23]Raymond Corey and Steven H. Star, *Organization Strategy: A Marketing Approach* (Boston: Harvard Business School, 1971), pp. 23–24.

Thus while functional departments and geographic divisions are the standard organizational building blocks in a single-business enterprise, in a multibusiness corporation the basic building blocks are the individual businesses. Authority over each business unit is typically delegated to a business-level manager. The approach is to put entrepreneurial general managers in charge of each business unit, give them authority to formulate and implement a business strategy, motivate them with performance-based incentives, and hold them accountable for results. Each business unit then operates as a stand-alone profit center and is organized around whatever functional departments and geographic units suit the business's strategy, key activities, and operating requirements.

Fully independent business units, however, pose an organizational obstacle to companies pursuing related diversification: *there is no mechanism for coordinating related activities across business units.* It can be tough to get autonomy-conscious business-unit managers to coordinate and share related activities. They are prone to argue about turf and about being held accountable for activities outside their control. To capture strategic-fit benefits in a diversified company, corporate headquarters must devise some internal organizational means for achieving strategic coordination across related business-unit activities. One option is to centralize related functions at the corporate level—e.g., maintaining a corporate R&D department if there are technology and product development fits, creating a special corporate sales force to call on customers who purchase from several of the company's business units, combining the dealer networks and sales force organizations of closely related businesses, merging the order processing and shipping functions of businesses with common customers, and consolidating the production of related components and products into fewer, more efficient plants. Alternatively, corporate officers can develop bonus arrangements that give business-unit managers strong incentives to work together to achieve the full benefits of strategic fit. If the strategic-fit relationships involve skills or technology transfers across businesses, corporate headquarters can arrange to transfer people with the requisite skills and know-how from one business to another and can create interbusiness teams to open the flow of proprietary technology, managerial know-how, and related skills between businesses.

A typical line-of-business organization structure is shown in Figure 9–4, along with the strategy-related pros and cons of this organizational form.

Strategic Business Units   In broadly diversified companies, the number of decentralized business units can be so great that the span of control is too much for a single chief executive. Then it may be useful to group related businesses and to delegate authority over them to a senior executive who reports directly to the chief executive officer. While this imposes a layer of management between business-level managers and the chief executive, it may nonetheless improve strategic planning and top-management coordination of diverse business interests. This explains both the popularity of the group vice president concept among multibusiness companies and the creation of strategic business units.

A *strategic business unit* (SBU) is a grouping of business subsidiaries based on some important strategic elements common to all. The elements can be an overlapping set of competitors, closely related value-chain activities, a common need to compete globally, emphasis on the same kind of competitive advantage (low cost or differentiation), common key success factors, or technologically related growth opportunities. At General Electric, a pioneer in the concept of SBUs, 190 businesses

In a diversified firm, the basic organizational building blocks are its business units; each business is operated as a stand-alone profit center.

Strategic Management Principle
A decentralized business-unit structure can block success of a related diversification strategy unless specific organizational arrangements are devised to coordinate the related activities of related businesses.

FIGURE 9-4 | **A Decentralized Line-of-Business Organization Structure**

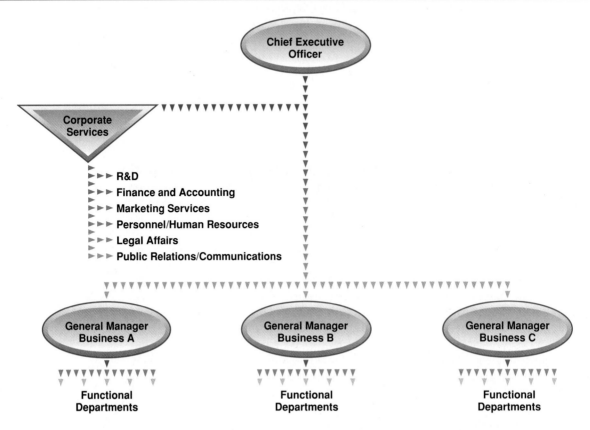

STRATEGIC ADVANTAGES

- Offers a logical and workable means of decentralizing responsibility and delegating authority in diversified organizations.
- Puts responsibility for business strategy in closer proximity to each business's unique environment.
- Allows each business unit to organize around its own value chain system, key activities and functional requirements.
- Frees CEO to handle corporate strategy issues.
- Puts clear profit/loss accountability on shoulders of business-unit managers.

STRATEGIC DISADVANTAGES

- May lead to costly duplication of staff functions at corporate and business-unit levels, thus raising administrative overhead costs.
- Poses a problem of what decisions to centralize and what decisions to decentralize (business managers need enough authority to get the job done, but not so much that corporate management loses control of key business-level decisions).
- May lead to excessive division rivalry for corporate resources and attention.
- Business/division autonomy works against achieving coordination of related activities in different business units, thus blocking to some extent the capture of strategic-fit benefits.
- Corporate management becomes heavily dependent on business-unit managers.
- Corporate managers can lose touch with business-unit situations, end up surprised when problems arise, and not know much about how to fix such problems.

were grouped into 43 SBUs and then aggregated further into six "sectors."[24] At Union Carbide, 15 groups and divisions were decomposed into 150 "strategic planning units" and then regrouped and combined into 9 new "aggregate planning units." At General Foods, SBUs were originally defined on a product-line basis but were later redefined according to menu segments (breakfast foods, beverages, main meal products, desserts, and pet foods). SBUs make headquarters' reviews of the strategies of lower-level units less imposing (there is no practical way for a CEO to conduct in-depth reviews of a hundred or more different businesses). A CEO can, however, effectively review the strategic plans of a lesser number of SBUs, leaving detailed business strategy reviews and direct supervision of individual businesses to the SBU heads. Figure 9–5 illustrates the SBU form of organization, along with its strategy-related pros and cons.

> **Basic Concept**
> A strategic business unit (SBU) is a grouping of related businesses under the supervision of a senior executive.

The SBU concept provides broadly diversified companies with a way to rationalize the organization of many different businesses and a management arrangement for capturing strategic-fit benefits and streamlining strategic planning and budgeting processes. The strategic function of the group vice president is to provide the SBU with some cohesive direction, enforce strategic coordination across related businesses, and keep an eye out for trouble at the business-unit level, providing counsel and additional corporate support as needed. The group vice president, as strategic coordinator for all businesses in the SBU, can facilitate resource sharing and skills transfers where appropriate and unify the strategic decisions and actions of businesses in the SBU. The SBU, in effect, becomes a strategy-making, strategy-implementing unit with a wider field of vision and operations than a single business unit. It serves as a diversified company's organizational mechanism for capturing strategic-fit benefits across businesses and adding to the competitive advantage that each business in the SBU is able to build on its own. Moreover, it affords opportunity to "cross-pollinate" the activities of separate businesses, ideally creating enough new capability to stretch a company's strategic reach into adjacent products, technologies, and markets. Aggressive pursuit of resource-sharing, skills-transfer, and cross-pollination opportunities is one of the best avenues companies can use to develop the internal capabilities needed to enter new business areas.

> SBU structures are a means for managing broad diversification and enforcing strategic coordination across related businesses.

Matrix Forms of Organization   A matrix organization is a structure with two (or more) channels of command, two lines of budget authority, and two sources of performance and reward. The key feature of the matrix is that authority for a business/product/project/venture and authority for a function or business process are overlaid (to form a matrix or grid), and decision-making responsibility in each unit/cell of the matrix is shared between the business/project/venture team manager and the functional/process manager—as shown in Figure 9–6. In a matrix structure, subordinates have a continuing dual assignment: to the business/project/process/venture and to their home-base function. The outcome is a compromise between functional specialization (engineering, R&D, manufacturing, marketing, finance) and product line, project, process, line-of-business or special venture divisions (where all of the specialized talent needed for the product line/project/line-of-business/venture are assigned to the same divisional or departmental unit).

> Matrix structures, although complex to manage and sometimes unwieldy, allow a firm to be organized in two different strategy-supportive ways at the same time.

---

[24]William K. Hall, "SBUs: Hot, New Topic in the Management of Diversification," *Business Horizons* 21, no. 1 (February 1978), p. 19. For an excellent discussion of the problems of implementing the SBU concept at 13 companies, see Richard A. Bettis and William K. Hall, "The Business Portfolio Approach—Where It Falls Down in Practice," *Long Range Planning* 16, no. 2 (April 1983), pp. 95–104.

F I G U R E 9–5 | **An SBU Organization Structure**

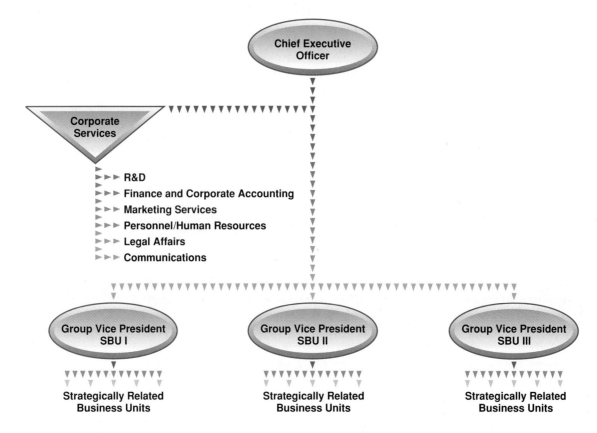

STRATEGIC ADVANTAGES

- Provides a strategically relevant way to organize the business-unit portfolio of a broadly diversified company.

- Facilitates the coordination of related activities within an SBU, thus helping to capture the benefits of strategic fits in the SBU.

- Promotes more cohesiveness among the new initiatives of separate but related businesses.

- Allows strategic planning to be done at the most relevant level within the total enterprise.

- Makes the task of strategic review by top executives more objective and more effective.

- Helps allocate corporate resources to areas with greatest growth opportunities.

STRATEGIC DISADVANTAGES

- It is easy for the definition and grouping of businesses into SBUs to be so arbitrary that the SBU serves no other purpose than administrative convenience. If the criteria for defining SBUs are rationalizations and have little to do with the nitty-gritty of strategy coordination, then the groupings lose real strategic significance.

- The SBUs can still be myopic in charting their future direction.

- Adds another layer to top management.

- The roles and authority of the CEO, the group vice president, and the business-unit manager have to be carefully worked out or the group vice president gets trapped in the middle with ill-defined authority.

- Unless the SBU head is strong willed, very little strategy coordination is likely to occur across business units in the SBU.

- Performance recognition gets blurred; credit for successful business units tends to go to corporate CEO, then to business-unit head, last to group vice president.

FIGURE 9-6 | **A Matrix Organization Structure***

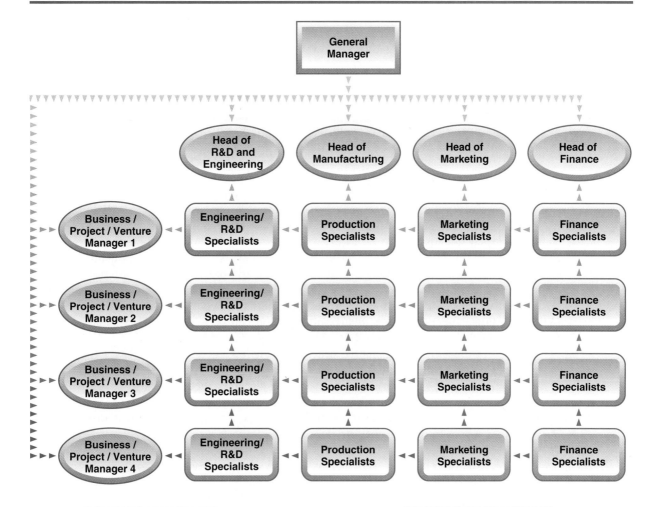

STRATEGIC ADVANTAGES

- Gives formal attention to each dimension of strategic priority.
- Creates checks and balances among competing viewpoints.
- Facilitates capture of functionally based strategic fits in diversified companies.
- Promotes making trade-off decisions on the basis of "what's best for the organization as a whole."
- Encourages cooperation, consensus-building, conflict resolution, and coordination of related activities.

STRATEGIC DISADVANTAGES

- Very complex to manage.
- Hard to maintain "balance" between the two lines of authority.
- So much shared authority can result in a transactions logjam and disproportionate amounts of time being spent on communications.
- It is hard to move quickly and decisively without getting clearance from many other people.
- Promotes an organizational bureaucracy and hamstrings creative entrepreneurship.

*Arrows indicate reporting channels.

A matrix-type organization is a genuinely different structural form and represents a "new way of life." It breaks the unity-of-command principle; two reporting channels, two bosses, and shared authority create a new kind of organizational climate. In essence, the matrix is a conflict resolution system through which strategic and operating priorities are negotiated, power is shared, and resources are allocated internally on the basis of "strongest case for what is best overall for the unit.[25]

The impetus for matrix organizations stems from growing use of strategies that create a simultaneous need for process teams, special project managers, product managers, functional managers, geographic area managers, new-venture managers, and business-level managers—all of whom have important strategic responsibilities. When at least two of several variables (product, customer, technology, geography, functional area, business process, and market segment) have roughly equal strategic priorities, a matrix organization can be an effective structural form. A matrix structure promotes internal checks and balances among competing viewpoints and perspectives, with separate managers for different dimensions of strategic initiative. A matrix arrangement thus allows each of several strategic considerations to be managed directly and to be formally represented in the organization structure. In this sense, it helps middle managers make trade-off decisions from an organizationwide perspective.[26] The other big advantage of matrix organization is that it can serve as a mechanism for capturing strategic fit. When the strategic fits in a diversified company are related to a specific functional area (R&D, technology, marketing), or cross traditional functional lines, matrix organization can be a reasonable structural arrangement for coordinating activity sharing and skills transfer.

Companies using matrix structures include General Electric, Texas Instruments, Citibank, Shell Oil, TRW, Bechtel, Boeing, and Dow Chemical. Illustration Capsule 27 on p. 264–265 describes how one broadly diversified company with global strategies in each of its businesses developed a matrix-type structure to manage its operations worldwide. However, in most companies, use of matrix organization is confined to a portion of what the firm does (certain important functions) rather than its whole organizing scheme.

Many companies and managers shun matrix organization because of its chief weaknesses.[27] It is a complex structure to manage; people end up confused or frustrated over who to report to for what. Moreover, because the matrix signals a need for communication and consensus, a "transactions logjam" can result. People in one area are pushed into transacting business with people in another area and networking their way through internal bureaucracies. Action turns into paralysis since, with shared authority, it is hard to move decisively without first checking with other people and getting clearance. Much time and psychic energy get eaten up in meetings and communicating back and forth. Sizable transactions costs and longer decision times can result with little value-added work accomplished. Even so, in some situations the benefits of conflict resolution, consensus building, and coordination outweigh these weaknesses, as the ABB example in Illustration Capsule 27 indicates.

---

[25]For two excellent critiques of matrix organizations, see Stanley M. Davis and Paul R. Lawrence, "Problems of Matrix Organizations," *Harvard Business Review* 56, no. 3 (May–June 1978), pp. 131–42, and Erik W. Larson and David H. Gobeli, "Matrix Management: Contradictions and Insights," *California Management Review* 29, no. 4 (Summer 1987), pp. 126–38.

[26]Davis and Lawrence, "Problems of Matrix Organizations," p. 132.

[27]Thomas J. Peters and Robert H. Waterman, Jr., *In Search of Excellence* (New York: Harper & Row, 1982), pp. 306–7.

Supplementing the Basic Organization Structure None of the basic structural designs is wholly adequate for organizing the total work effort in strategy-supportive ways. Some weaknesses can be corrected by using two or more of the structural designs simultaneously—many companies are large enough and diverse enough to have SBUs, functionally organized business units, geographic organizational structures in one or more businesses, units employing matrix principles, and several functionally specialized departments. But in many companies strategy-supportive organization requires supplementing the formal structure with special coordinating mechanisms and "creative disorganization"—cross-functional task forces, project teams, venture teams, self-sufficient work teams to perform whole processes, and special empowerment of key individuals to cut through red tape and get things done quickly when necessary. Six of the most frequently used devices for supplementing the formal organization structure are:

1. *Special project teams*—creating a separate, largely self-sufficient work group to oversee the completion of a special activity (setting up a new technological process, bringing out a new product, starting up a new venture, consummating a merger with another company, seeing through the completion of a government contract, supervising the construction and opening of a new plant). Project teams are especially suitable for one-of-a-kind situations with a finite life expectancy when the normal organization is not equipped to achieve the same results in addition to regular duties.

2. *Cross-functional task forces*—bringing a number of top-level executives and/or specialists together to solve problems requiring specialized expertise from several parts of the organization, coordinating strategy-related activities that span departmental boundaries, or exploring ways to leverage the skills of different functional specialists into broader core competencies. Task forces seem to be most effective when they have less than 10 members, membership is voluntary, the seniority of the members is proportional to the importance of the problem, the task force moves swiftly to deal with its assignment, they are used sparingly—only on an as-needed basis, no staff is assigned, and documentation is scant.[28] Companies that have used task forces successfully form them to solve pressing problems, produce some solutions efficiently, and then disband them.

3. *Venture teams*—forming a group of individuals to manage the launch of a new product, entry into a new geographic market, or creation of a specific new business. Dow, General Mills, Westinghouse, General Electric, and Monsanto used the venture-team approach to regenerate an entrepreneurial spirit. The difficulties with venture teams include deciding who the venture manager should report to; whether funding for ventures should come from corporate, business, or departmental budgets; how to keep the venture clear of bureaucratic and vested interests; and how to coordinate large numbers of different ventures.

4. *Self-contained work teams*—forming a group of people drawn from different disciplines who work together on a semipermanent basis to continuously improve organizational performance in specific strategy-related areas—shortening the lab-to-market cycle time, boosting product quality, improving

---

[28]Ibid., pp. 127–32.

ILLUSTRATION CAPSULE 27

MATRIX ORGANIZATION IN A DIVERSIFIED GLOBAL COMPANY
THE CASE OF ASEA BROWN BOVERI

Asea Brown Boveri (ABB) is a diversified multinational corporation headquartered in Zurich, Switzerland. ABB was formed in 1987 through the merger of Asea, one of Sweden's largest industrial enterprises, and Brown Boveri, a major Swiss company. Both companies manufactured electrical products and equipment. Following the merger, ABB acquired or took minority positions in 60 companies, mostly outside Europe. In 1991 ABB had annual revenues of $25 billion and employed 240,000 people around the world, including 150,000 in Western Europe, 40,000 in North America, 10,000 in South America, and 10,000 in India. The company was a world leader in the global markets for electrical products, electrical installations and service, and power-generation equipment and was the dominant European producer. European sales accounted for 60% of revenues, while North America accounted for 30% and Asia 15%.

To manage its global operations, ABB had devised a matrix organization that leveraged its core competencies in electrical-power technologies and its ability to achieve global economies of scale while, at the same time, maximizing its national market visibility and responsiveness. At the top of ABB's corporate organi-

zation structure was an executive committee composed of the CEO, Percy Barnevik, and 12 colleagues; the committee consisted of Swedes, Swiss, Germans, and Americans, several of whom were based outside Switzerland. The group, which met every three weeks at various locations around the world, was responsible for ABB's corporate strategy and performance.

Along one dimension of ABB's global matrix were 50 or so business areas (BAs), each representing a closely related set of products and services. The BAs were grouped into eight "business segments"; each segment was supervised by a different member of the executive committee. Each BA had a leader charged with responsibility for (1) devising and championing a global strategy, (2) setting quality and cost standards for the BA's factories worldwide, (3) deciding which factories would export to which country markets, (4) rotating people across borders to share technical expertise, create mixed-nationality teams to solve BA problems, and build a culture of trust and communication, and (5) pooling expertise and research funds for the benefit of the BA worldwide. BA leaders worked out of whatever world location made the most sense for their BA. For example, the BA leader for power transformers, who had responsibility for 25 factories in 16 countries, was a Swede who worked out of Mannheim, Germany; the BA leader for electric metering was an American based in North Carolina.

(continued)

customer service, cutting delivery times, eliminating stockouts, reducing the costs of purchased materials and components, increasing assembly-line productivity, trimming equipment downtime and maintenance expenses, or designing new models. American Express cut out three layers of hierarchy when it developed self-managed teams to handle all types of customer inquiries in a single-call, quick-resolution manner.[29]

5. *Process teams*—putting functional specialists who perform pieces of a business process together on a team instead of assigning them to their home-base functional department. Such teams can be empowered to reengineer the process, held accountable for results, and rewarded on the basis of how well the process is performed. Much of Chrysler's revitalization is due to dramatically revamping its new-model development process using "platform teams."[30] Each platform team consists of members from engineering, design, finance, purchasing, and marketing. The team is responsible for the car's design from beginning to end, has broad decision-making power, and is held

---

[29]Quinn, *Intelligent Enterprise,* p. 163.
[30]"Can Jack Smith Fix GM?" *Business Week,* November 1, 1993, pp. 130–31.

ILLUSTRATION CAPSULE 27

(concluded)

Along the other dimension of the matrix was a group of national enterprises with presidents, boards of directors, financial statements, and career ladders. The presidents of ABB's national enterprises had responsibility for maximizing the performance and effectiveness of all ABB activities within their country's borders. Country presidents worked closely with the BA leaders to evaluate and improve what was happening in ABB's business areas in their countries.

Inside the matrix were 1,200 "local" ABB companies with an average of 200 employees, each headed by a president. The local company president reported both to the national president in whose country the local company operated and to the leader of the BA to which its products/services were assigned. Each local company was a subsidiary of the ABB national enterprise where it was located. Thus, all of ABB's local companies in Norway were subsidiaries of ABB Norway, the national company for Norway; all ABB operations in Portugal were subsidiaries of ABB Portugal, and so on. The 1,200 presidents of ABB's local companies were expected to be excellent profit center managers, able to answer to two bosses effectively. The local president's

global boss was the BA manager who established the local company's role in ABB's global strategy and, also, the rules a local company had to observe in supporting this strategy. The local president's country boss was the national CEO, with whom it was necessary to cooperate on local issues.

ABB believed that its matrix structure allowed it to optimize its pursuit of global business strategies and, at the same time, maximize its performance in every country market where it operated. The matrix was a way of being global and big strategically, yet small and local operationally. Decision-making was decentralized (to BA leaders, country presidents, and local company presidents), but reporting and control was centralized (through the BA leaders, the country presidents, and the executive committee). ABB saw itself as a federation of national companies with a global coordination center.

Only 100 professionals were located in ABB's corporate headquarters in Zurich. A management information system collected data on all profit centers monthly, comparing actual performance against budgets and forecasts. Data was collected in local currencies but translated into U.S. dollars to allow for cross-border analysis. ABB's corporate financial statements were reported in U.S. dollars, and English was ABB's official language. All high-level meetings were conducted in English.

Source: Compiled from information in William Taylor, "The Logic of Global Business: An Interview with ABB's Percy Barnevik," *Harvard Business Review* 69, no. 2 (March–April 1991), pp. 90–105.

accountable for the success or failure of their design. Teams coordinate their designs with manufacturing so that the models will be easier to build and consult regularly with purchasing agents regarding parts quality. In one case Chrysler purchasing agents elected to pay 30 percent more for a better part because the engineer on the platform team believed the added cost would be offset by the time saved during assembly.

6. *Contact managers*—providing a single point of contact for customers when the steps of a process either are so complex or are dispersed in such a way that integrating them for a single person or team to perform is impractical.[31] Acting as a buffer between internal processes and the customer, the contact person endeavors to answer customer questions and solve customer problems as if he or she were responsible for performing the called-for activities. To perform this role, contact persons need access to all the information systems that the persons actually performing the process use and the ability to contact those people with questions and requests for further assistance when necessary. The

---

[31]Hammer and Champy, *Reengineering the Corporation*, pp. 62–63.

best results are achieved when contact persons are empowered to use their own judgment to get things done in a manner that will please customers. Duke Power, a Charlotte-based electric utility, uses empowered customer service representatives to resolve the problems of residential customers while shielding them from whatever goes on "behind the scenes" to produce solutions.

PERSPECTIVES ON ORGANIZING THE WORK EFFORT

There's no perfect or ideal organization structure. All the basic designs have their strategy-related strengths and weaknesses. To do a good job of matching structure to strategy, strategy-implementers have to pick a basic design, modify it as needed to fit the company's particular business makeup, and then supplement it with whatever coordinating mechanisms and communication arrangements it takes to support effective execution of the firm's strategy. While practical realities often dictate giving some consideration to existing reporting relationships, to the personalities involved, to internal politics, and to other situational idiosyncrasies, strategy-structure factors have to predominate.

Peter Drucker, one of the foremost authorities on managing, sums up the intricacies of organization design:

> The simplest organization structure that will do the job is the best one. What makes an organization structure "good" is the problems it does not create. The simpler the structure, the less that can go wrong.
>
> Some design principles are more difficult and problematic than others. But none is without difficulties and problems. None is primarily people-focused rather than task-focused; none is more "creative," "free," or "democratic." Design principles are tools; and tools are neither good nor bad in themselves. They can be used properly or improperly; and that is all. To obtain both the greatest possible simplicity and the greatest "fit," organization design has to start out with a clear focus on *key activities* needed to produce *key results.* They have to be structured and positioned in the simplest possible design. Above all, the architect of organization needs to keep in mind the purpose of the structure he is designing.[32]

Current Organizational Trends Many of today's companies are remodeling their traditional hierarchical structures built around functional specialization and centralized authority. Such structures make good strategic and organizational sense so long as (1) activities can be divided into simple, repeatable tasks that can be mastered quickly and then efficiently performed in mass quantity, (2) there are important benefits to deep functional expertise in each managerial discipline, and (3) customer needs are sufficiently standardized that it is easy to prescribe procedures for satisfying them. But traditional hierarchies become a liability in businesses where customer preferences are shifting from standardized products to custom orders and special features, product life-cycles are growing shorter, flexible manufacturing methods are replacing mass production techniques, customers want to be treated as individuals, the pace of technological change is accelerating, and market conditions are fluid. Multilayered management hierarchies and functionalized bureaucracies that require people to look upward in the organizational structure for answers tend to bog down in such environments. They can't deliver responsive customer service or adapt fast enough to changing conditions. Functional silos, task-oriented work, process fragmentation, layered

---

[32]Drucker, *Management: Tasks, Responsibilities, Practices,* pp. 601–2.

management hierarchies, centralized decision-making, growing functional and middle-management bureaucracies, lots of checks and controls, and long response times can undermine competitive success in fluid or volatile business environments. Success in fast-changing markets depends on strategies featuring important organizational capabilities: quick response to shifting customer preferences, short design-to-market cycles, make-it-right-the-first-time quality, custom-order and multiversion production, expedited delivery, personalized customer service, accurate order filling, rapid assimilation of new technologies, creativity and innovativeness, and speedy reactions to external competitive developments.

These new components of business strategy are driving a revolution in corporate organization.[33] Much of the corporate downsizing movement is aimed at busting up functional and middle management bureaucracies and recasting authoritarian pyramidal organizational structures into flatter, decentralized structures. The latest organizational designs for matching structure to strategy feature fewer layers of management authority, small-scale business units, reengineered work processes to cut back on fragmentation across functional department lines, creation of process teams and interdisciplinary work groups, lean staffing of corporate support functions, partnerships with key suppliers, empowerment of firstline supervisors and nonmanagement employees, open communications vertically and laterally, computers and telecommunications technologies to provide fast access to and dissemination of information, and accountability for results rather than emphasis on activity. The new organizational themes are lean, flat, responsive, and innovative. The new tools of organizational design are managers and workers empowered to act on their own judgments, reengineered work processes, and self-directed work teams.

The command-and-control paradigm of vertically layered structures assumes that the people actually performing work have neither the time nor the inclination to monitor and control it and that they lack the knowledge to make informed decisions about how best to do it; hence, the need for prescribed procedures, close supervision, and managerial control of decision-making. In flat, decentralized structures, these assumptions are discarded. Jobs are defined more broadly; several tasks are integrated into a single job where possible. People operate in a more self-directed fashion, armed with the information they need to get things done. Fewer managers are needed because deciding how to do things becomes part of each person's or team's job.

Reengineering Can Promote Better Implementation Reengineering strategy-critical business processes to reduce fragmentation across traditional departmental lines and cut bureaucratic overheads has proven to be a legitimate organization design tool. It's not a passing fad or another management program of the month. Process organization is every bit as valid an organizing principle as functional specialization. Strategy execution is improved when the pieces of strategy-critical activities and core business processes performed by different departments are properly integrated and coordinated.

Companies that have reengineered some of their business processes have ended up compressing formerly separate steps and tasks into jobs performed by a single person and integrating jobs into team activities. Reorganization then follows, a natural consequence of task synthesis and job redesign. The experiences of companies that have successfully reengineered and restructured their operations in strategy-supportive

---

[33]Evidence to this effect is contained in the scores of examples reported in Tom Peters, *Liberation Management* (New York: Alfred A. Knopf, 1992); Quinn, *Intelligent Enterprise;* and Hammer and Champy, *Reengineering the Corporation.*

ways suggest attacking process fragmentation and overhead reduction in the following fashion:[34]

- Develop a flow chart of the total business process, including its interfaces with other value-chain activities.
- Try to simplify the process first, eliminating tasks and steps where possible and analyzing how to streamline the performance of what remains.
- Determine which parts of the process can be automated (usually those that are repetitive, time-consuming, and require little thought or decision); consider introducing advanced technologies that can be upgraded to achieve next-generation capability and provide a basis for further productivity gains down the road.
- Evaluate each activity in the process to determine whether it is strategy-critical or not. Strategy-critical activities are candidates for benchmarking to achieve best-in-industry or best-in-world performance status.
- Weigh the pros and cons of outsourcing activities that are noncritical or that contribute little to organizational capabilities and core competencies.
- Design a structure for performing the activities that remain; reorganize the personnel and groups who perform these activities into the new structure.

Reengineer, then reorganize.

Reengineering can produce dramatic gains in productivity and organizational capability when done properly. In the order-processing section of General Electric's circuit breaker division, elapsed time from order receipt to delivery was cut from three weeks to three days by consolidating six production units into one, reducing a variety of former inventory and handling steps, automating the design system to replace a human custom-design process, and cutting the organizational layers between managers and workers from three to one.[35] Productivity rose 20 percent in one year, and unit manufacturing costs dropped 30 percent.

There's no escaping the conclusion that reengineering, in concert with advanced office technologies, empowerment, and the use of self-directed work teams, provides company managers with important new organization design options. Organizational hierarchies can be flattened and middle-management layers removed. Responsibility and decision-making authority can be pushed downward and outward to those places in the organization where customer contacts are made. Strategy-critical processes can be unified, performed more quickly and at lower cost, and made more responsive to changing customer preferences and expectations. Used properly, these new design approaches can trigger big gains in organizational creativity and employee productivity.

Illustration Capsule 28 reports the results of a study of trends in organizational arrangements in multinational and global companies.

KEY POINTS

The job of strategy implementation is to convert strategic plans into actions and good results. The test of successful strategy implementation is whether actual organization performance matches or exceeds the targets spelled out in the strategic plan. Shortfalls in performance signal weak strategy, weak implementation, or both.

---

[34]Quinn, *Intelligent Enterprise,* p. 162.

[35]T. Stuart, "GE Keeps Those Ideas Coming," *Fortune,* August 12, 1991. For other examples, see Gene Hall, Jim Rosenthal, and Judy Wade, "How to Make Reengineering Really Work," *Harvard Business Review* 71, no. 6 (November–December 1993), pp. 119–31.

ILLUSTRATION CAPSULE 28

ORGANIZATIONAL APPROACHES FOR INTERNATIONAL AND GLOBAL MARKETS

A 1993 study of 43 large U.S.-based consumer products companies conducted by McKinsey & Co., a leading management consulting firm, identified internal organizational actions with the strongest and weakest links to rapidly growing sales and profits in international and global markets.

Organizational Actions Strongly Linked to International Success

- Centralizing international decision-making in every area except new product development.
- Having a worldwide management development program and more foreigners in senior management posts.
- Requiring international experience for advancement into top management.
- Linking global managers with video-conferencing and electronic mail.
- Having product managers of foreign subsidiaries report to a country general manager.
- Using local executives to head operations in foreign

countries (however, this is rapidly ceasing to distinguish successful companies because nearly everyone has implemented such a practice).

Organizational Actions Weakly Linked to International Success

- Creating global divisions.
- Forming international strategic business units.
- Establishing centers of excellence (where a single company facility takes global responsibility for a key product or emerging technology (too new to evaluate pro or con).
- Using cross-border task forces to resolve problems and issues.
- Creating globally-integrated management information systems.

However, the lists of organizational do's and don'ts are far from decisive. In general, the study found that internal organizational structure "doesn't matter that much" as compared to having products with attractive prices and features. It is wrong to expect good results just because of good organization. Moreover, certain organizational arrangements, such as centers of excellence, are too new to determine whether they positively affect sales and profit growth.

Source: Based on information reported by Joann S. Lublin, "Study Sees U.S. Businesses Stumbling on the Road to Globalization," *The Wall Street Journal,* March 22, 1993, p. B4B.

In deciding how to implement strategy, managers have to determine what internal conditions are needed to execute the strategic plan successfully. Then they must create these conditions as rapidly as practical. The process involves creating a series of tight fits:

- Between strategy and the organization's skills, competencies, and structure.
- Between strategy and budgetary allocations.
- Between strategy and policy.
- Between strategy and internal support systems.
- Between strategy and the reward structure.
- Between strategy and the corporate culture.

The tighter the fits, the more powerful strategy execution becomes and the more likely targeted performance can actually be achieved.

Implementing strategy is not just a top-management function; it is a job for the whole management team. All managers function as strategy-implementers in their respective areas of authority and responsibility. All managers have to consider what actions to take in their areas to achieve the intended results—they each need an *action agenda.*

The three major organization-building actions are (1) filling key positions with able people, (2) seeing that the organization has the skills, know-how, core competencies, and internal capabilities needed to perform its value-chain activities proficiently, and (3) structuring the work effort and deciding what the organization chart should look like. Selecting able people for key positions tends to be one of the earliest strategy implementation steps because it takes a full complement of capable managers to get changes in place and functioning smoothly.

Building strategy-critical core competencies is one of the best ways to outexecute rivals with similar strategies. Core competencies emerge from skills and activities performed at different points in the value chain that, when linked, create unique organizational capability. The key to leveraging a company's core competencies into long-term competitive advantage is to concentrate more effort and more talent than rivals do on strengthening and deepening these competencies. The multiskill, multiactivity character of core competencies makes achieving dominating depth an exercise in (1) managing human skills, knowledge bases, and intellect and (2) coordinating and networking the efforts of different work groups and departments at every place in the value chain related to such competencies.

Matching structure to strategy centers around making strategy-critical activities the main organizational building blocks and finding effective ways to bridge organizational lines of authority and coordinate the related efforts of separate units and individuals. Other big considerations include what decisions to centralize and what decisions to decentralize and whether noncritical activities can be outsourced more effectively or efficiently than they can be performed internally.

All organization structures have strategic advantages and disadvantages; there is no one best way to organize. Functionally specialized organization structures have traditionally been the most popular way to organize single-business companies. Functional organization works well where strategy-critical activities closely match discipline-specific activities and minimal interdepartmental cooperation is needed. But it has significant drawbacks: functional myopia and empire-building, interdepartmental rivalries, excessive process fragmentation, and vertically layered management hierarchies.

Geographic organization structures are favored by enterprises operating in diverse geographic markets or across expansive geographic areas. SBU structures are well-suited to companies pursuing related diversification. Decentralized business-unit structures are well-suited to companies pursuing unrelated diversification. Matrix structures work well for companies that need separate lines of authority and managers for each of several strategic dimensions (products, buyer segments, functional departments, projects or ventures, technologies, core business processes, geographic areas) yet also need close cooperation between these managers to coordinate related value-chain activities, share or transfer skills, and perform certain related activities jointly.

Whatever formal organization structure is chosen, it usually has to be supplemented with interdisciplinary task forces, incentive compensation schemes tied to measures of joint performance, empowerment of cross-functional teams to perform and unify fragmented processes and strategy-critical activities, special project and venture teams, self-contained work teams, and contact managers.

New strategic priorities like short design-to-market cycles, multiversion production, and personalized customer service are promoting a revolution in organization-building featuring lean, flat, horizontal structures that are responsive and innovative. Such designs for matching structure to strategy involve fewer layers of management authority, small-scale business units, reengineering work processes to reduce fragmentation across departmental lines, the creation of process teams and cross-functional work groups, managers and workers empowered to act on their own judgments, partnerships with key suppliers and increased outsourcing of noncritical activities, lean staffing of internal support functions, and use of computers and telecommunications technologies to provide fast access to and information.

SUGGESTED READINGS

Aaker, David A. "Managing Assets and Skills: The Key to a Sustainable Competitive Advantage." *California Management Review* 31 (Winter 1989), pp. 91–106.

Bartlett, Christopher A., and Sumantra Ghoshal. "Matrix Management: Not a Structure, a Frame of Mind." *Harvard Business Review* 68, no. 4 (July–August 1990), pp. 138–45.

Bettis, Richard A., and William K. Hall. "The Business Portfolio Approach—Where It Falls Down in Practice." *Long Range Planning* 16, no. 2 (April 1983), pp. 95–104.

Chandler, Alfred D. *Strategy and Structure*. Cambridge, Mass.: MIT Press, 1962.

Hall, Gene, Jim Rosenthal, and Judy Wade. "How to Make Reengineering Really Work." *Harvard Business Review* 71, no. 6 (November–December 1993), pp. 119–31.

Hambrick, Donald C. "The Top Management Team: Key to Strategic Success." *California Management Review* 30, no. 1 (Fall 1987), pp. 88–108.

Hammer, Michael, and James Champy. *Reengineering the Corporation*. New York: HarperBusiness, 1993, chaps. 2 and 3.

Howard, Robert. "The CEO as Organizational Architect: An Interview with Xerox's Paul Allaire." *Harvard Business Review* 70, no. 5 (September–October 1992), pp. 107–19.

Katzenbach, Jon R., and Douglas K. Smith. "The Discipline of Teams." *Harvard Business Review* 71, no. 2 (March–April 1993), pp. 111–24.

Larson, Erik W., and David H. Gobeli. "Matrix Management: Contradictions and Insights." *California Management Review* 29, no. 4 (Summer 1987), pp. 126–27.

Powell, Walter W. "Hybrid Organizational Arrangements: New Form or Transitional Development?" *California Management Review* 30, no. 1 (Fall 1987), pp. 67–87.

Prahalad, C. K., and Gary Hamel. "The Core Competence of the Corporation." *Harvard Business Review* 68 (May–June 1990), pp. 79–93.

Quinn, James Brian. *Intelligent Enterprise*. New York: Free Press, 1992, chaps. 2 and 3.

Stalk, George, Philip Evans, and Lawrence E. Shulman. "Competing on Capabilities: The New Rules of Corporate Strategy." *Harvard Business Review* 70, no. 2 (March–April 1992), pp. 57–69.

Yip, George S. *Total Global Strategy: Managing for Worldwide Competitive Advantage*. Englewood Cliffs, N.J.: Prentice-Hall, 1992, chap. 8.

IMPLEMENTING STRATEGY: BUDGETS, POLICIES, BEST PRACTICES, SUPPORT SYSTEMS, AND REWARDS

If you talk about change but don't change the reward and recognition system, nothing changes.

Paul Allaire
CEO, Xerox Corporation

. . . Winning companies know how to do their work better.

Michael Hammer and James Champy

. . . While a corporation can come up with a plan for the future, it takes everybody's help—and commitment—to implement it.

Ronald W. Allen
CEO, Delta Airlines

In the previous chapter we emphasized the importance of building an organization capable of performing strategy-critical activities in a coordinated and highly competent manner. In this chapter we discuss five additional strategy-implementing tasks:

1. Reallocating resources to match the budgetary and staffing requirements of the new strategy.
2. Establishing strategy-supportive policies.
3. Instituting best practices and mechanisms for continuous improvement.
4. Installing support systems that enable company personnel to carry out their strategic roles proficiently day in and day out.
5. Employing motivational practices and incentive compensation methods that enhance organizationwide commitment to good strategy execution.

LINKING BUDGETS TO STRATEGY

Implementing strategy forces a manager into the budget-making process. Organizational units need enough resources to carry out their parts of the strategic plan. This includes having enough of the right kinds of people and having sufficient operating funds for organizational units to do their work successfully. Strategy-implementers must screen subordinates' requests for new capital projects and bigger operating budgets, distinguishing between what would be nice and what can make a cost-justified contribution to strategy execution. Moreover, implementers have to make a persuasive, documented case to superiors on what additional resources, if any, it will take to execute their assigned pieces of company strategy.

How well a strategy-implementer links budget allocations to the needs of strategy can either promote or impede the implementation process. Too little funding slows progress and impedes the ability of organizational units to execute their pieces of the strategic plan proficiently. Too much funding wastes organizational resources and reduces financial performance. Both outcomes argue for the strategy-implementer to be deeply involved in the budgeting process, closely reviewing the programs and budget proposals of strategy-critical organization units.

Implementers must also be willing to shift resources from one area to another to support new strategic initiatives and priorities. A change in strategy nearly always calls for budget reallocations. Units important in the old strategy may now be oversized and overfunded. Units that now have a bigger and more critical strategic role may need more people, new equipment, additional facilities, and above-average increases in their operating budgets. Strategy-implementers need to be active and forceful in shifting resources, downsizing some areas, upsizing others, and amply funding activities with a critical role in the new strategy. They have to exercise their power to allocate resources to make things happen and make the tough decisions to kill projects and activities that are no longer justified. The essential condition is that the funding requirements of the new strategy must drive how capital allocations are made and the size of each unit's operating budgets. Underfunding organizational units and activities pivotal to strategic success can defeat the whole implementation process.

Aggressive resource reallocation can have a positive strategic payoff. For example, at Harris Corporation where the strategy was to diffuse research ideas into areas that were commercially viable, top management regularly shifted groups of engineers out of government projects and moved them (as a group) into new commercial venture divisions. Boeing used a similar approach to reallocating ideas and talent; according to one Boeing officer, "We can do it (create a big new unit) in two weeks. We couldn't do it in two years at International Harvester."[1] Forceful actions to reallocate operating funds and move people into new organizational units signal a strong commitment to implementing strategic change and are frequently needed to catalyze the implementation process and give it credibility.

Fine-tuning the implementation of a company's existing strategy seldom requires big movements of people and money from one area to another. The desired improvements can usually be accomplished through above-average budget increases to organizational units where new initiatives are contemplated and below-average increases

Strategic Management Principle
Depriving strategy-critical groups of the funds needed to execute their pieces of the strategy can undermine the implementation process.

New strategies usually call for significant budget reallocations.

---

[1] Thomas J. Peters and Robert H. Waterman, Jr., *In Search of Excellence* (New York: Harper & Row, 1980), p. 125.

(or even small cuts) for the remaining organizational units. The chief exception occurs where a prime ingredient of corporate/business strategy is to generate fresh, new products and business opportunities within the existing budget. Then, as proposals and business plans worth pursuing bubble up from below, decisions have to be made regarding where the needed capital expenditures, operating budgets, and personnel will come from. Companies like 3M, GE, and Boeing shift resources and people from area to area on an as-needed basis to support the launch of new products and new business ventures. They empower "product champions" and small bands of would-be entrepreneurs by giving them financial and technical support and by setting up organizational units and programs to help new ventures blossom more quickly.

CREATING STRATEGY-SUPPORTIVE POLICIES AND PROCEDURES

Changes in strategy generally call for some changes in work practices and how internal operations are conducted. Asking people to alter established procedures and behavior always upsets the internal order of things. It is normal for pockets of resistance to develop and for people to exhibit some degree of stress and anxiety about how the changes will affect them, especially when the changes may eliminate jobs. Questions are also likely to arise over what needs to be done in like fashion and where there ought to be leeway for independent action.

Prescribing policies and operating procedures aids the task of implementing strategy in several ways:

1. New or freshly revised policies and procedures provide top-down guidance to operating managers, supervisory personnel, and employees regarding how certain things now need to be done and what behavior is expected, thus establishing some degree of regularity, stability, and dependability in how management has decided to try to execute the strategy and operate the business on a daily basis.

2. Policies and procedures help align actions and behavior with strategy throughout the organization, placing limits on independent action and channeling individual and group efforts along the intended path. Policies and procedures counteract tendencies for some people to resist or reject common approaches—most people refrain from violating company policy or ignoring established practices without first gaining clearance or having strong justification.

3. Policies and standardized operating procedures help enforce needed consistency in how particular strategy-critical activities are performed in geographically scattered operating units (different plants, sales regions, customer service centers, or the individual outlets in a chain operation). Eliminating significant differences in the operating practices and procedures of organizational units performing common functions is necessary to avoid sending mixed messages to internal personnel and to customers who do business with the company at multiple locations.

4. Because dismantling old policies and procedures and instituting new ones invariably alter the character of the internal work climate, strategy-implementers can use the policy-changing process as a powerful lever for changing the corporate culture in ways that produce a stronger fit with the new strategy.

ILLUSTRATION CAPSULE 29

NIKE'S MANUFACTURING POLICIES AND PRACTICES

When Nike decided on a strategy of outsourcing 100% of its athletic footwear from independent manufacturers (all of which turned out, for reasons of low cost, to be located in Taiwan, South Korea, Thailand, Indonesia, and China), it developed a series of policies and production practices to govern its working relationships with its "production partners" (a term Nike carefully nurtured because it implied joint responsibilities):

- Nike personnel were stationed on-site at all key manufacturing facilities; each Nike representative tended to stay at the same factory site for several years to get to know the partner's people and processes in detail. They functioned as liaisons with Nike headquarters, working to match Nike's R&D and new product design efforts with factory capabilities and to keep monthly orders for new production in line with the latest sales forecasts.

- Nike instituted a quality assurance program at each factory site to enforce up-to-date and effective quality management practices.

- Nike endeavored to minimize ups and downs in monthly production orders at factory sites making Nike's premium-priced top-of-the-line models (volumes typically ran 20,000 to 25,000 pairs daily); the policy was to keep month-to-month variations in order quantity under 20%. These factories made Nike footwear exclusively and were expected to codevelop new models and to coinvest in new technologies.

- Factory sites that made mid-to-low-end Nike products in large quantities (usually 70,000 to 85,000 pairs per day), known as "volume producers," were expected to handle most ups and downs in monthly orders themselves; these factories usually produced shoes for five to eight other buyers, giving them the flexibility to juggle orders and stabilize their production.

- It was strict Nike policy to pay its bills from production partners on time, providing them with predictable cash flows.

Source: Based on information in James Brian Quinn, *Intelligent Enterprise* (New York: Free Press, 1992), pp. 60–64.

From a strategy implementation perspective, therefore, company managers need to be inventive in devising policies and practices that can provide vital support to effective strategy implementation. McDonald's policy manual, in an attempt to steer "crew members" into stronger quality and service behavior patterns, spells out such detailed procedures as "Cooks must turn, never flip, hamburgers. If they haven't been purchased, Big Macs must be discarded in 10 minutes after being cooked and french fries in 7 minutes. Cashiers must make eye contact with and smile at every customer." At Delta Airlines, it is corporate policy to test the aptitudes of all applicants for flight attendants' positions for friendliness, cooperativeness, and teamwork. Caterpillar Tractor has a policy of guaranteeing its customers 24-hour parts delivery anywhere in the world; if it fails to fulfill the promise, it supplies the part free. Hewlett-Packard requires R&D people to make regular visits to customers to learn about their problems, talk about new product applications, and, in general, keep the company's R&D programs customer-oriented. Illustration Capsule 29 describes Nike's manufacturing policies and practices in some detail.

Thus there is a definite role for new and revised policies and procedures in the strategy implementation process. Wisely constructed policies and procedures help enforce strategy implementation by channeling actions, behavior, decisions, and practices in directions that improve strategy execution. When policies and practices aren't strategy-supportive, they become a barrier to the kinds of attitudinal and behavioral changes strategy-implementers are trying to promote. Often, people opposed to certain elements of the strategy or certain implementation approaches will

Well-conceived policies and procedures aid implementation; out-of-sync policies are barriers.

hide behind or vigorously defend long-standing policies and operating procedures in an effort to stall implementation or divert the approach to implementation along a different route. Any time a company alters its strategy, managers should review existing policies and operating procedures, proactively revise or discard those that are out of sync, and formulate new ones to facilitate execution of new strategic initiatives.

None of this implies that companies need huge policy manuals. Too much policy can be as stifling as wrong policy or as chaotic as no policy. Sometimes, the best policy for implementing strategy is a willingness to empower subordinates and let them do it any way they want if it makes sense and works. A little "structured chaos" can be a good thing when individual creativity and initiative are more essential to good strategy execution than standardization and strict conformity. When Rene McPherson became CEO at Dana Corp., he dramatically threw out 22½ inches of policy manuals and replaced them with a one-page statement of philosophy focusing on "productive people."[2] Creating a strong supportive fit between strategy and policy can mean more policies, less policies, or different policies. It can mean policies that require things to be done a certain way or policies that give employees leeway to do activities the way they think best.

INSTITUTING BEST PRACTICES AND A COMMITMENT TO CONTINUOUS IMPROVEMENT

Identifying and implementing best practices is a journey not a destination.

If value-chain activities are to be performed as effectively and efficiently as possible, each department and organizational unit needs to benchmark how it performs specific tasks and activities against best-in-industry or best-in-world performers. A strong commitment to searching out and adopting best practices is integral to effective strategy implementation—especially for strategy-critical and big-dollar activities where better quality performance or lower costs can translate into a sizable bottom-line impact.

The benchmarking movement to search out, study, and implement best practices has spawned a number of spinoff efforts—reengineering (the redesign of business processes), continuous improvement programs, and total quality management (TQM). A 1991 survey by The Conference Board showed 93 percent of manufacturing companies and 69 percent of service companies have implemented some form of quality improvement program.[3] Another survey found that 55 percent of American executives and 70 percent of Japanese executives used quality improvement information at least monthly as part of their assessment of overall business performance.[4] Indeed, quality improvement processes have now become part of the fabric of implementing strategies keyed to defect-free manufacture, superior product quality, superior customer service, and total customer satisfaction.

Management interest in quality improvement programs typically originates in a company's production areas—fabrication and assembly in manufacturing enterprises, teller transactions in banks, order picking and shipping at catalog firms, or customer-

---

[2]Ibid., p. 65.
[3]Judy D. Olian and Sara L. Rynes, "Making Total Quality Work: Aligning Organizational Processes, Performance Measures, and Stakeholders," *Human Resource Management* 30, no. 3 (Fall 1991), p. 303.
[4]Ibid.

contact interfaces in service organizations. Other times, initial interest begins with executives who hear TQM presentations, read about TQM, or talk to people in other companies that have benefited from total quality programs. Usually, interested managers have quality and customer-satisfaction problems they are struggling to solve.

While TQM concentrates on the production of quality goods and the delivery of excellent customer service, to succeed it must extend organizationwide to employee efforts in all departments—HR, billing, R&D, engineering, accounting and records, and information systems—that may lack less-pressing customer-driven incentives to improve. This is because the institution of best practices and continuous improvement programs involves reforming the corporate culture and shifting to a total quality/continuous improvement business philosophy that permeates every facet of the organization. TQM aims at instilling enthusiasm and commitment to doing things right from top to bottom of the organization. It entails a restless search for continuing improvement, the little steps forward each day that the Japanese call *kaizen*. TQM is a race without a finish. The managerial objective is to kindle an innate, burning desire in people to use their ingenuity and initiative to progressively improve on how tasks and value-chain activities are performed. TQM preaches that there's no such thing as good enough and that everyone has a responsibility to participate in continuous improvement—see Illustration Capsule 30 describing Motorola's approach to involving employees in the TQM effort.

Best practices, reengineering, and continuous improvement efforts like TQM all aim at improved efficiency and reduced costs, better product quality, and greater customer satisfaction. The essential difference between reengineering and TQM is that reengineering aims at quantum gains on the order of 30 to 50 percent or more whereas total quality programs stress incremental progress, striving for inch-by-inch gains again and again in a never-ending stream. The two approaches to improved performance of value-chain activities are not mutually exclusive; it makes sense to use them in tandem. Reengineering can be used first to produce a good basic design that yields dramatic improvements in performing a business process. Total quality programs can then be used as a follow-on to work out bugs, perfect the process, and gradually improve both efficiency and effectiveness. Such a two-pronged approach to implementing organizational change is like a marathon race where you run the first four laps as fast as you can, then gradually pick up speed the remainder of the way.

Surveys indicate that some companies benefit from reengineering and TQM and some do not.[5] Usually, the biggest beneficiaries are companies that view such programs not as ends in themselves but as tools for implementing and executing company strategy more effectively. The skimpiest payoffs from best practices, TQM, and reengineering occur when company managers seize them as something worth trying, novel ideas that could improve things; in most such instances, they result in strategy-blind efforts to simply manage better. There's an important lesson here. Best practices, TQM, and reengineering all need to be seen and used as part of a bigger-picture effort to execute strategy proficiently. Only strategy can point to which activities matter and what performance targets make the most sense. Absent a strategic framework, managers lack the context in which to fix things that really matter to business-unit performance and competitive success.

TQM entails creating a total quality culture bent on continuously improving the performance of every task and value-chain activity.

Reengineering seeks one-time quantum improvement; TQM seeks ongoing incremental improvement.

When best practices, reengineering, and TQM are not part of a wider-scale effort to improve strategy execution and business performance, they deteriorate into strategy-blind efforts to manage better.

---

[5]See, for example, Gene Hall, Jim Rosenthal, and Judy Wade, "How to Make Reengineering Really Work," *Harvard Business Review* 71, no. 6 (November–December 1993), pp. 119–31.

ILLUSTRATION CAPSULE 30

MOTOROLA'S APPROACH TO TQM AND TEAMWORK

Motorola is rated as one of the best companies in measuring performance against its strategic targets and in promoting total quality practices that lead to continuous improvement. Motorola was selected in 1988 as one of the first winners of the Malcolm Baldrige Quality Award and has since improved on its own award-winning efforts. In 1993, the company estimated it was saving about $2.2 billion annually from its team-oriented approach to TQM and continuous improvement.

A central feature of Motorola's approach is a year-long contest highlighting the successes of employee teams from around the world in improving internal company practices, making better products, saving money, pleasing customers, and sharing best practices with other Motorola groups. The contest, known as the Total Customer Satisfaction Team Competition, in 1992 attracted entries from nearly 4,000 teams involving nearly 40,000 of Motorola's 107,000 employees. Preliminary judging eventually reduced the 1992 finalists to 24 teams from around the world, all of which were invited to Chicago in January 1993 to make a 12-minute presentation to a panel of 15 senior executives, including the CEO. Twelve teams were awarded gold medals and 12 silver medals. The gold medalists are listed below.

Motorola does not track the costs of the contest because "the benefits are so overwhelming." It has sent hundreds of videos about the contests to other companies wanting details. However, TQM consultants are skeptical whether other companies have progressed far enough in establishing a team-based quality culture to benefit from a companywide contest. The downsides to such elaborate contests, they say, are the added costs (preparation, travel, presentation, and judging) and the risks to the morale of those who don't win.

Gold Medal Teams	Work Location	Achievement
B.E.A.P. Goes On	Florida	Removed bottleneck in testing pagers by using robots.
The Expedition	Malaysia	Designed and delivered a new chip for Apple Computer in six months.
Operation Paging Storm	Singapore	Eliminated component alignment defect in papers.
ET/EV=1	Illinois	Streamlined order process for auto electronics.
The Mission	Arizona	Developed quality system for design of iridium satellites.
Class Act	Illinois	Cut training program from 5 years to 2 with better results.
Dyna-Attackers	Dublin	Cut production time and defect rate on new battery part.
Orient Express	Malaysia	Cut response time on tooling orders from 23 days to 4.
The Dandles	Japan	Improved efficiency of boiler operations.
Cool Blue Racers	Arizona	Cut product development time in half to win IBM contract.
IO Plastics Misload	Manila	Eliminated resin seepage in modulator assembly.

Source: Based on information reported in Barnaby J. Feder, "At Motorola, Quality Is a Team Sport," *New York Times,* January 21, 1993, pp. C1 and C6.

To get the most from benchmarking, best practices, reengineering, TQM, and related tools for enhancing organizational competence in executing strategy, managers have to start with a clear fix on the indicators of successful strategy execution—defect-free manufacture, on-time delivery, low overall costs, exceeding customers' expectations, faster cycle time, increased product innovation, or some other specific performance measure. Benchmarking best-in-industry and best-in-world performance of most or all value-chain activities provides a realistic basis for setting internal performance milestones and longer-range targets.

Then comes the managerial task of building a total quality culture and instilling the necessary commitment to achieving the targets and performance measures that the strategy requires. The action steps managers can take include[6]

- Visible, unequivocal, and unyielding commitment to total quality and continuous improvement, including a quality vision and specific, measurable quality goals.
- Nudging people toward TQ-supportive behaviors by initiating such organizational programs as

  - Screening job applicants rigorously and hiring only those with attitudes and aptitudes right for quality-based performance.
  - Quality training for most employees.
  - Using teams and team-building exercises to reinforce and nurture individual effort (expansion of a TQ culture is facilitated when teams become more cross-functional, multitask, and increasingly self-managed).
  - Recognizing and rewarding individual and team efforts regularly and systematically.
  - Stressing prevention (doing it right the first time) not inspection (instituting ways to correct mistakes).

- Empowering employees so that authority for delivering great service or improving products is in the hands of the doers rather than the overseers.
- Providing quick electronic information access to doers so that real-time data can drive actions and decisions and feedback can continuously improve value-chain activities.
- Preaching that performance can, and must, be improved because competitors are not resting on past laurels and customers are always looking for something better.

If the targeted performance measures are appropriate to the strategy and if all organizational members (top executives, middle managers, professional staff, and line employees) buy into the process of continuous improvement, then the work climate will be conducive to proficient strategy execution and good bottom-line business performance.

INSTALLING SUPPORT SYSTEMS

Company strategies can't be implemented or executed well without a number of support systems for business operations. American, United, Delta, and other major airlines cannot hope to provide world-class passenger service without a computerized reservation system, an accurate and expeditious baggage handling system, and a strong aircraft maintenance program. Federal Express has a computerized parcel-tracking system that can instantly report the location of any given package in its transit-delivery process; it has communication systems that allow it to coordinate its 21,000 vans nationwide to make an average of 720,000 stops per day to pick up customer packages; and it has leading-edge flight operations systems that allow a single controller to direct as many as 200 FedEx aircraft simultaneously, overriding their

---

[6]Olian and Rynes, "Making Total Quality Work," pp. 305–6 and 310–11.

flight plans should weather or special emergencies arise—all these operations essential to FedEx's strategy of next-day delivery of a package that "absolutely, positively has to be there."[7]

Otis Elevator has a sophisticated support system called OtisLine to coordinate its maintenance efforts nationwide.[8] Trained operators take all trouble calls, input critical information on a computer screen, and dispatch people directly via a beeper system to the local trouble spot. From the trouble-call inputs, problem patterns can be identified nationally and the information communicated to design and manufacturing personnel, allowing them to quickly alter design specifications or manufacturing procedures when needed to correct recurring problems. Also, much of the information needed for repairs is provided directly from faulty elevators through internally installed microcomputer monitors, further lowering outage time.

Procter & Gamble codes the more than 900,000 call-in inquiries it receives annually on its toll-free 800 number to obtain early warning signals of product problems and changing tastes.[9] Domino's Pizza has computerized systems at each outlet to facilitate ordering, inventory, payroll, cash flow, and work control functions, thereby freeing managers to spend more time on supervision, customer service, and business development activities.[10] Most telephone companies, electric utilities, and TV broadcasting systems have on-line monitoring systems to spot transmission problems within seconds and increase the reliability of their services. At Mrs. Fields' Cookies, systems can monitor sales at 15-minute intervals and suggest product mix changes, promotional tactics, or operating adjustments to improve customer response—see Illustration Capsule 31.

Well-conceived, state-of-the art support systems not only facilitate better strategy execution, they also can strengthen organizational capabilities enough to provide a competitive edge over rivals. For example, a company with a differentiation strategy based on superior quality needs systems for training personnel in quality techniques, tracking product quality at each production step, and ensuring that all goods shipped meet quality standards. A company striving to be a low-cost provider needs systems that exploit opportunities to drive costs out of the business. Fast-growing companies need employee recruiting systems to attract and hire qualified employees in large numbers. In businesses such as public accounting and management consulting where large numbers of professional staffers need cutting-edge technical know-how, companies have to install systems to train and retrain employees regularly and keep them supplied with up-to-date information.

INSTITUTING FORMAL REPORTING OF STRATEGIC INFORMATION

Accurate information is an essential guide to action. Every organization needs systems for gathering and reporting strategy-critical information and tracking key performance measures over time. Telephone companies have elaborate information systems to measure signal quality, connection times, interrupts, wrong connections, billing errors, and other measures of reliability. To track and manage the quality of passenger service, airlines have information systems to monitor gate delays, on-time

---

Strategic Management Principle

Innovative, state-of-the-art support systems can be a basis for competitive advantage if they give a firm capabilities that rivals can't match.

Accurate, timely information allows organizational members to monitor progress and take corrective action promptly.

---

[7]James Brian Quinn, *Intelligent Enterprise* (New York: Free Press, 1992) pp. 114–15.
[8]Ibid., p. 181.
[9]Ibid., p. 186.
[10]Ibid., p. 111.

ILLUSTRATION CAPSULE 31

OPERATING PRACTICES AND SUPPORT SYSTEMS AT MRS. FIELDS' COOKIES, INC.

Mrs. Fields' Cookies is one of the best known specialty foods companies in the United States with over 500 outlets in operation in malls, airports, and other high pedestrian-traffic locations; the company also has over 250 outlets retailing other bakery and cookie products. Debbi Fields, age 37, is the company's founder and CEO. Her business concept for Mrs. Fields' Cookies is "to serve absolutely fresh, warm cookies as though you'd stopped by my house and caught me just taking a batch from the oven." Cookies not sold within two hours are removed from the case and given to charity. The company's major form of advertising is sampling; store employees walk around the shopping mall giving away cookie samples. People are hired for store crews on the basis of warmth, friendliness, and the ability to have a good time giving away samples, baking fresh batches, and talking to customers during the course of a sale.

To implement its strategy, the company developed several novel practices and a customized computer support system. One key practice is giving each store an *hourly* sales quota. Another is for Fields to make unannounced visits to her stores, where she masquerades as a casual shopper to test the enthusiasm and sales techniques of store crews, sample the quality of the cookies they are baking, and observe customer reactions.

Debbi's husband Randy developed a software program that keeps headquarters and stores in close contact. Via the computer network, each store manager receives a daily sales goal (broken down by the hour) based on the store's recent performance history and on such special factors as special promotions, mall activities, weekdays vs. weekends, holiday shopping patterns, and the weather forecast. With the hourly sales quotas also comes a schedule of the number of cookies to bake and when to bake them. As the day progresses, store managers type in actual hourly sales figures and customer counts. If customer counts are up but sales are lagging, the computer is programmed to recommend more aggressive sampling or more suggestive selling. If it becomes obvious the day is going to be a bust for the store, the computer automatically revises the sales projections for the day, reducing hourly quotas and instructing how much to cut back cookie baking. To facilitate crew scheduling by the store manager, sales projections are also provided for two weeks in advance. All job applicants must sit at the store's terminal and answer a computerized set of questions as part of the interview process.

In addition, the computer software contains a menu giving store staff immediate access to company personnel policies, maintenance schedules for store equipment, and repair instructions. If a store manager has a specific problem, it can be entered on the system and routed to the appropriate person. Messages can be sent directly to Debbi Fields via the computer; even if she is on a store inspection trip, her promise is to respond to all inquiries within 48 hours.

The computerized information support system serves several objectives: (1) it gives store managers more time to work with their crews and achieve sales quotas as opposed to handling administrative chores and (2) it gives headquarters instantaneous information on store performance and a means of controlling store operations. Debbi Fields sees the system as a tool for projecting her influence and enthusiasm into more stores more frequently than she could otherwise reach.

Source: Developed from information in Mike Korologos, "Debbi Fields," *Sky Magazine,* July 1988, pp. 42–50.

departures and arrivals, baggage handling times, lost baggage complaints, stockouts on meals and drinks, overbookings, and maintenance delays and failures. Many companies have provided customer-contact personnel with instant electronic access to customer databases so that they can respond effectively to customer inquiries and personalize customer services.

To properly oversee strategy implementation, company managers need prompt feedback on implementation initiatives to steer them to a successful conclusion in case early steps don't produce the expected progress or things seem to be drifting off course. Such monitoring (1) allows managers to detect problems early and adjust either the strategy or how it is being implemented and (2) provides some assurance that things are moving ahead as planned.[11] Early experiences are sometimes difficult to assess, but they yield the first hard data and should be closely scrutinized as a basis for corrective action.

Information systems need to cover four broad areas: (1) customer data, (2) operations data, (3) employee data, and (4) financial performance data. All key strategic performance indicators have to be measured as often as practical. Many retail companies generate daily sales reports for each store and maintain up-to-the-minute inventory and sales records on each item. Manufacturing plants typically generate daily production reports and track labor productivity on every shift. Monthly profit-and-loss statements are common, as are monthly statistical summaries.

In designing formal reports to monitor strategic progress, five guidelines should be observed:[12]

1. Information and reporting systems should involve no more data and reporting than is needed to give a reliable picture. The data gathered should emphasize strategically meaningful outcomes and symptoms of potentially significant developments. Temptations to supplement "what managers need to know" with other "interesting" but marginally useful information should be avoided.

2. Reports and statistical data-gathering have to be timely—not too late to take corrective action or so often as to overburden.

3. The flow of information and statistics should be kept simple. Complicated reports confound readers and divert attention to methodological issues; long or overly-detailed reports run the risk of going unread; and too many reports consume unnecessary amounts of managerial time.

4. Information and reporting systems should aim at "no surprises"; i.e., they should point out early warning signs rather than just produce information. It is debatable whether reports should receive wide distribution ("for your information"); but they should always be provided to managers who are in a position to act when trouble signs appear.

5. Statistical reports should flag exceptions and big or unusual variances from plan, thus directing management attention to significant departures from targeted performance.

Statistical information gives the strategy-implementer a feel for the numbers; reports and meetings provide a feel for new developments and problems; and personal contacts add a feel for the people dimension. All are good barometers of overall performance and good indicators of which things are on and off track. Managers have to identify problem areas and deviations from plan before they can take actions either to improve implementation or fine-tune strategy.

DESIGNING STRATEGY-SUPPORTIVE REWARD SYSTEMS

It is important for organizational subunits and for individuals to be committed to implementing strategy and achieving performance targets. Company managers typi-

[11]Boris Yavitz and William H. Newman, *Strategy in Action* (New York: Free Press, 1982), pp. 209–10.

[12]Peter F. Drucker, *Management: Tasks, Responsibilities, Practices* (New York: Harper & Row, 1974), pp. 498–504; Harold Koontz, "Management Control: A Suggested Formulation of Principles," *California Management Review* 2, no. 2 (Winter 1959), pp. 50–55; and William H. Sihler, "Toward Better Management Control Systems," *California Management Review* 14, no. 2 (Winter 1971), pp. 33–39.

cally try to enlist organizationwide commitment to carrying out the strategic plan by motivating people and rewarding them for good performance. The range of options includes offering people the chance to be part of something exciting, giving them an opportunity for greater personal satisfaction, challenging them with ambitious performance targets for them, using the carrot of promotion and the stick of being "sidelined" in a routine or dead-end job, giving praise, recognition, constructive criticism, more (or less) responsibility, increased (or decreased) job control and decision-making autonomy, offering a better shot at assignments in attractive locations, the intangible bonds of group acceptance, greater job security, and the promise of sizable financial rewards (salary increases, performance bonuses, stock options, and retirement packages). But motivational techniques and rewards have to be used *creatively* and linked tightly to the factors and targets necessary for good strategy execution.

MOTIVATIONAL PRACTICES

Successful strategy-implementers inspire and challenge employees to do their best. They get employees to buy into the strategy and commit to making it work. They allow employees to participate in making decisions about how to perform their jobs, and they try to make jobs interesting and satisfying. As Frederick Herzberg said, "If you want people motivated to do a good job, give them a good job to do." They structure individual efforts into teams and work groups in order to facilitate an exchange of ideas and a climate of support. They devise strategy-supportive motivational approaches and use them effectively. Consider some actual examples:[13]

One of the biggest strategy-implementing challenges is to employ motivational techniques that build whole-hearted commitment and winning attitudes among employees.

- At Mars Inc. (best known for its candy bars), every employee, including the president, gets a weekly 10 percent bonus by coming to work on time each day that week. This on-time incentive is designed to minimize absenteeism and tardiness and to boost worker productivity in order to produce the greatest number of candy bars during each available minute of machine time.
- In a number of Japanese companies, employees meet regularly to hear inspirational speeches, sing company songs, and chant the corporate litany. In the United States, Tupperware conducts a weekly Monday night rally to honor, applaud, and fire up its salespeople who conduct Tupperware parties. Amway and Mary Kay Cosmetics hold similar inspirational get-togethers for their sales force organizations.
- A San Diego area company assembles its 2,000 employees at its six plants the first thing every workday to listen to a management talk about the state of the company. Then they engage in brisk calisthenics. This company's management believes "that by doing one thing together each day, it reinforces the unity of the company. It's also fun. It gets the blood up." Managers take turns making the presentations. Many of the speeches "are very personal and emotional, not approved beforehand or screened by anybody."
- Texas Instruments and Dana Corp. insist that teams and divisions set their own goals and have regular peer reviews.
- Procter & Gamble's brand managers are asked to compete fiercely against each other; the official policy is "a free-for-all among brands with no holds barred." P&G's system of purposeful internal competition breeds people who love to

---

[13]Alfie Kohn, "Rethinking Rewards," *Harvard Business Review* 71, no. 6 (November–December 1993), p. 49.

compete and excel. Those who win become corporate heroes, and around them emerges a folklore of war stories of valiant brand managers who waged uphill struggles against great odds and made market successes out of their brands.

These motivational approaches accentuate the positive; others blend positive and negative features. Consider the way Harold Geneen, former president and chief executive officer of ITT, allegedly combined the use of money, tension, and fear:

> Geneen provides his managers with enough incentives to make them tolerate the system. Salaries all the way through ITT are higher than average—Geneen reckons 10 percent higher—so that few people can leave without taking a drop. As one employee put it: "We're all paid just a bit more than we think we're worth." At the very top, where the demands are greatest, the salaries and stock options are sufficient to compensate for the rigors. As someone said, "He's got them by their limousines."
>
> Having bound his [managers] to him with chains of gold, Geneen can induce the tension that drives the machine. "The key to the system," one of his [managers] explains, "is the profit forecast. Once the forecast has been gone over, revised, and agreed on, the managing director has a personal commitment to Geneen to carry it out. That's how he produces the tension on which the success depends." The tension goes through the company, inducing ambition, perhaps exhilaration, but always with some sense of fear: what happens if the target is missed?[14]

If a strategy-implementer's motivational approach and reward structure induces too much stress, internal competitiveness, and job insecurity, the results can be counterproductive. For a healthy work environment, positive reinforcement needs to outweigh negative reinforcement. Yet it is unwise to completely eliminate pressure for performance and the anxiety it evokes. There is no evidence that a no-pressure work environment leads to superior strategy execution or sustained high performance. As the CEO of a major bank put it, "There's a deliberate policy here to create a level of anxiety. Winners usually play like they're one touchdown behind."[15] High-performing organizations need a cadre of ambitious people who relish the opportunity to climb the ladder of success, love a challenge, thrive in a performance-oriented environment, and find some competition and pressure useful to satisfy their own drives for personal recognition, accomplishment, and self-satisfaction. Unless meaningful incentive and career consequences are associated with successfully implementing strategic initiatives and hitting strategic performance targets, few people will attach much significance to the company's strategic plan.

Positive motivational approaches generally work better than negative ones.

REWARDS AND INCENTIVES

The conventional view is that a manager's push for strategy implementation should incorporate more positive than negative motivational elements because when cooperation is positively enlisted and rewarded, rather than strong-armed by a boss's orders, people tend to respond with more enthusiasm and more effort. Nevertheless, how much of which incentives to use depends on how hard the task of strategy implementation will be. A manager has to do more than just talk to everyone about how important new strategic practices and performance targets are to the organization's future well-being. No matter how inspiring, talk seldom commands people's best efforts for

---

[14]Anthony Sampson, *The Sovereign State of ITT* (New York: Stein and Day, 1973), p. 132.

[15]As quoted in John P. Kotter and James L. Heskett, *Corporate Culture and Performance* (New York: Free Press, 1992), p. 91.

long. To get employees' sustained, energetic commitment, management has to be resourceful in designing and using motivational incentives—both monetary and non-monetary. The more a manager understands what motivates subordinates and the more he or she relies on motivational incentives as a tool for implementing strategy, the greater will be employees' commitment to good day in, day out execution of their roles in the company's strategic plan.

Linking Work Assignments to Performance Targets The first step in creating a strategy-supportive system of rewards and incentives is to define jobs and assignments in terms of the *results to be accomplished,* not the duties and functions to be performed. Focusing the jobholder's attention and energy on what to *achieve* as opposed to what activities to perform boosts the chances of reaching agreed-on outcomes. It is flawed thinking to stress duties and activities in job descriptions in hopes that the by-products will be the desired kinds of accomplishments. In any job, performing assigned tasks is not equivalent to achieving intended outcomes. Working hard, staying busy, and diligently attending to assigned duties do not guarantee results. Stressing "what to accomplish" instead of "what to do" is an important difference. As any student knows, just because an instructor teaches doesn't mean students are learning. Teaching and learning are different things—the first is an activity and the second is a result.

Emphasizing what to accomplish—that is, performance targets for individual jobs, work groups, departments, businesses, and the entire company—has the larger purpose of making the work environment results-oriented. Without target objectives, individuals and work groups can become so engrossed in the details of performing assigned functions on schedule that they lose sight of what the tasks are intended to accomplish. By regularly tracking actual achievement versus targeted performance (monthly, weekly, or daily if need be), managers can proactively concentrate on making the right things happen rather than supervising people closely in hopes that the right outcomes will materialize if every activity is performed according to the book. Making the right things happen is what results-oriented management is all about.

To create a tight fit between carrying out work assignments and accomplishing the strategic plan, managers must use strategic and financial objectives as the basis for incentive compensation. If the details of strategy have been fleshed out thoroughly from the corporate level down to the operating level, appropriate measures of performance either exist or can be developed for the whole company, for each business unit, for each functional department, for each operating unit, and for each work group. These become the targets that strategy-implementers aim at achieving, and they form the basis for deciding on the necessary jobs, skills, expertise, funding, and time frame.

Usually a number of performance measures are needed at each level. At the corporate and line-of-business levels, performance objectives typically revolve around measures of profitability (total profit, return on equity investment, return on total assets, return on sales, operating profit, and so on), sales and earnings growth, market share, product quality, customer satisfaction, and other hard measures that market position, overall competitiveness, and future prospects have improved. In the manufacturing area, the strategy-relevant performance measures may focus on unit manufacturing costs, employee productivity, on-time production and shipping, defect rates, the number and extent of work stoppages due to labor disagreements and equipment breakdowns, and so on. In the marketing area, measures may include unit selling costs, dollar sales and unit volume, sales penetration of each target customer group, market share, the fate of newly introduced products, the frequency of customer

> Job assignments should stress the results to be achieved rather than the duties and activities to be performed.

complaints, the number of new accounts acquired, and customer satisfaction surveys. While most performance measures are quantitative, several may have elements of subjectivity—the state of labor-management relations, employee morale, the effectiveness of advertising campaigns, and how far the firm is ahead of or behind rivals on quality, service, and technological capability.

Rewarding Performance   The most dependable way to keep people focused on the objectives laid out in the strategic plan and to make achieving these objectives a way of life up and down the organization is to generously reward individuals and groups who achieve their assigned targets and deny rewards to those who don't. For strategy-implementers, doing a good job needs to mean one thing: achieving the agreed-on performance targets. Any other standard undermines implementation of the strategic plan and condones the diversion of time and energy into activities that don't much matter (if such activities are really important, they deserve a place in the strategic plan). The pressure to achieve the targeted strategic performance should be unrelenting. A "no excuses" standard has to prevail.[16]

> **Strategic Management Principle**
>
> The strategy-implementer's standard for judging whether individuals and organizational units have done a good job must be whether they achieved their performance targets.

With the pressure to perform must come deserving and meaningful rewards. Without an ample payoff, the system breaks down, and the strategy-implementer is left with the unworkable option of barking orders and pleading for compliance. Some of the best performing companies—Wal-Mart, Nucor Steel, Lincoln Electric, Electronic Data Systems, Remington Products, and Mary Kay Cosmetics—owe much of their success to a set of incentives and rewards that induce people to do the things needed to hit performance targets and execute strategy well enough for the companies to become leaders in their industries.

Nucor's strategy was (and is) to be *the* low-cost producer of steel products. Because labor costs are a significant fraction of total cost in the steel business, successful implementation of Nucor's low-cost strategy requires achieving lower labor costs per ton of steel than competitors'. To drive its labor costs per ton below rivals', Nucor management utilizes production incentives that give workers bonuses roughly equal to their regular wages if their production teams meet or exceed weekly production targets; the regular wage scale is set at levels comparable to wages for similar manufacturing jobs in the local areas where Nucor has plants. Bonuses are paid every two weeks based on the prior weeks' actual production levels measured against the targets. The results of Nucor's piece-rate incentive plan are impressive. Nucor's labor productivity (in output per worker) runs over 50% above the average of the unionized workforces of the industry's major producers. Nucor enjoys about a $50 to $75 per ton cost advantage over large, integrated steel producers like U.S. Steel and Bethlehem Steel (a substantial part of which comes from its labor cost advantage), and Nucor workers are the highest-paid workers in the steel industry.

At Remington Products, only 65 percent of factory workers' paychecks is salary; the rest is based on piece-work incentives. The company conducts 100 percent inspections of products, and rejected items are counted against incentive pay for the responsible worker. Top-level managers earn more from bonuses than from their salaries. During the first four years of Remington's incentive program, productivity rose 17 percent.

---

[16]Tom Peters and Nancy Austin, *A Passion for Excellence* (New York: Random House, 1985), p. xix.

These and other experiences demonstrate some important lessons about designing rewards and incentives:

1. *The performance payoff must be a major, not minor, piece of the total compensation package.* Incentives that amount to 20 percent or more of total compensation are big attention-getters and are capable of driving individual effort.

2. *The incentive plan should extend to all managers and all workers,* not just be restricted to top management. It is a gross miscalculation to expect that lower-level managers and employees will work their tails off to hit performance targets just so a few senior executives can get lucrative rewards!

3. *The reward system must be administered with scrupulous care and fairness.* If performance standards are set unrealistically high or if individual performance evaluations are not accurate and well-documented, dissatisfaction and disgruntlement with the system will overcome any positive benefits.

4. *The incentives must be tightly linked to achieving only those performance targets spelled out in the strategic plan* and not to any other factors that get thrown in because they are thought to be nice occurrences. Performance evaluation based on factors not related to the strategy signal that either the strategic plan is incomplete (because important performance targets were left out) or management's real agenda is something other than what was stated in the strategic plan.

5. *The performance targets each individual is expected to achieve should involve outcomes that the individual can personally affect.* The role of incentives is to enhance individual commitment and channel behavior in beneficial directions. This role is not well-served when the performance measures an individual is judged by are outside his/her arena of influence.

Aside from these general guidelines it is hard to prescribe what kinds of incentives and rewards to develop except to say that the payoff must be directly attached to performance measures that indicate the strategy is working and implementation is on track. If the company's strategy is to be a low-cost provider, the incentive system must reward performance that lowers costs. If the company has a differentiation strategy predicated on superior quality and service, the incentive system must reward such outcomes as zero defects, infrequent need for product repair, low numbers of customer complaints, and speedy order processing and delivery. If a company's growth is predicated on a strategy of new product innovation, incentives should be tied to factors such as the percentages of revenues and profits coming from newly introduced products.

WHY THE PERFORMANCE-REWARD LINK IS IMPORTANT

The use of incentives and rewards is the single most powerful tool management has to win strong employee commitment to carrying out the strategic plan. Failure to use this tool wisely and powerfully will weaken the entire implementation process. *Decisions on salary increases, incentive compensation, promotions, who gets which key assignments, and the ways and means of awarding praise and recognition are the strategy-implementer's foremost attention-getting, commitment-generating devices.* How a company's incentives are structured signals what sorts of behavior and

Strategic Management Principle
The reward structure is management's most powerful strategy-implementing tool.

performance management wants; how managers parcel out raises, promotions, and praise says more about who is considered to be doing a good job than any other factor. Such matters seldom escape the closest employee scrutiny. A company's system of incentives and rewards thus ends up being the vehicle by which its strategy is emotionally ratified in the form of real commitment. Incentives make it in employees' self-interest to do what is needed to achieve the performance targets spelled out in the strategic plan.

MAKING PERFORMANCE-DRIVEN COMPENSATION WORK

Creating a tight fit between strategy and the reward structure is generally best accomplished by agreeing on strategy-critical performance objectives, fixing responsibility and deadlines for achieving them, and treating their achievement as a pay-for-performance *contract*. From a strategy-implementation perspective, the key is to make strategically relevant measures of performance the dominating basis for designing incentives, evaluating individual efforts, and handing out rewards. Every organizational unit, every manager, every team or work group, and ideally every employee needs to have clearly defined performance targets to aim at that reflect measurable progress in implementing the strategic game plan, and then they must be held accountable for achieving them. For example, at Banc One, the fifth largest U.S. bank and the second most profitable bank in the world (based on return on assets), a high level of customer satisfaction is a key performance objective. To enhance employee commitment to the task of pleasing customers, Banc One ties the pay scales in each branch office to that branch's customer satisfaction rating—the higher the branch's ratings, the higher that branch's pay scales. By shifting from a theme of equal pay for equal work to one of equal pay for equal performance, Banc One has focused the attention of branch employees on the task of pleasing, even delighting, their customers.

To prevent undermining and undoing pay-for-performance approaches to strategy implementation, companies must be scrupulously fair in comparing actual performance against agreed-on performance targets. Everybody needs to understand how their incentive compensation is calculated and how their individual performance targets contribute to organizational performance targets. The reasons for anyone's failure or deviations from targets have to be explored fully to determine whether the causes are attributable to poor individual performance or to circumstances beyond the individual's control. Skirting the system to find ways to reward nonperformers must be absolutely avoided. It is debatable whether exceptions should be made for people who've tried hard, gone the extra mile, yet still come up short because of circumstances beyond their control—a good case can be made either way. The problem with making exceptions for unknowable, uncontrollable, or unforeseeable circumstances is that once "good" excuses start to creep into justifying rewards for nonperformers, the door is open for all kinds of "legitimate" reasons why actual performance failed to match targeted performance. In short, people at all levels have to be held accountable for carrying out their assigned parts of the strategic plan, and they have to know their rewards are based on the caliber of their strategic accomplishments.

KEY POINTS

A change in strategy nearly always calls for budget reallocations. Reworking the budget to make it more strategy-supportive is a crucial part of the implementation process because every organization unit needs to have the people, equipment, facilities, and other resources to carry out its part of the strategic plan (but no *more* than what it really needs!). Implementing a new strategy often entails shifting resources from one area to another—downsizing units that are overstaffed and overfunded, upsizing those more critical to strategic success, and killing projects and activities that are no longer justified.

Anytime a company alters its strategy, company managers are well-advised to review existing policies and operating procedures, revising those that are out of sync and devising new ones. Prescribing new or freshly revised policies and operating procedures aids the task of implementation (1) by providing top-down guidance to operating managers, supervisory personnel, and employees regarding how certain things now need to be done and what behavior is expected; (2) by placing limits on independent actions and decisions; (3) by enforcing needed consistency in how particular strategy-critical activities are performed in geographically scattered operating units; and (4) by helping to create a strategy-supportive work climate and corporate culture. Huge policy manuals are uncalled for. Indeed, when individual creativity and initiative are more essential to good execution than standardization and conformity, it is often wise to give people the freedom to do things however they see fit and hold them accountable for good results. Hence, creating a supportive fit between strategy and policy can mean more policies, fewer policies, or different policies.

Competent strategy execution entails visible, unyielding managerial commitment to best practices and continuous improvement. Benchmarking, instituting best practices, reengineering core business processes, and total quality management programs all aim at improved efficiency, lower costs, better product quality, and greater customer satisfaction. All these techniques are important tools for learning how to execute a strategy more proficiently. Benchmarking provides a realistic basis for setting performance targets. Instituting "best-in-industry" or "best-in-world" operating practices in most or all value-chain activities is essential to create a total quality, high-performance work environment. Reengineering is a way to make quantum progress in being world class while TQM instills a commitment to continuous improvement. Typically, such techniques involve organizing the work effort around cross-functional, multitask teams and work groups that are self-directed and/or self-managed.

Company strategies can't be implemented or executed well without a number of support systems to carry on business operations. Well-conceived, state-of-the-art support systems not only facilitate better strategy execution, they can also strengthen organizational capabilities enough to provide a competitive edge over rivals. In an age of computers, computerized monitoring and control systems, and expanding communications capabilities, companies can't hope to outexecute their competitors without elaborate information systems and technologically sophisticated operating capabilities that allow people to perform their jobs effectively and efficiently.

Strategy-supportive motivational practices and reward systems are powerful management tools for gaining employee buy-in and commitment. Positive motivational practices generally work better than negative ones, but there is a place for both. There's also a place for both monetary and nonmonetary incentives. For monetary incentives to work well (1) the monetary payoff should be a major percentage of the compensation package, (2) the incentive plan should extend to all managers and workers, (3) the system should be administered with care and fairness, (4) the incentives should be linked to performance targets spelled out in the strategic plan, and (5) each individual's performance targets should involve outcomes the person can personally affect.

SUGGESTED READINGS

Grant, Robert M., Rami Shani, and R. Krishnan, "TQM's Challenge to Management Theory and Practice." *Sloan Management Review* (Winter 1994), pp. 25–35.

Herzberg, Frederick. "One More Time: How Do You Motivate Employees?" *Harvard Business Review* 65, no. 4 (September–October 1987), pp. 109–20.

Johnson, H. Thomas. *Relevance Regained*. New York: Free Press, 1992.

Kiernan, Matthew J. "The New Strategic Architecture: Learning to Compete in the Twenty-First Century." *Academy of Management Executive* 7, no. 1 (February 1993), pp. 7–21.

Kohn, Alfie. "Why Incentive Plans Cannot Work." *Harvard Business Review* 71, no. 5 (September–October 1993), pp. 54–63.

Olian, Judy D. and Sara L. Rynes, "Making Total Quality Work: Aligning Organizational Processes, Performance Measures, and Stakeholders," *Human Resource Management* 30, no. 3 (Fall 1991), pp. 303–333.

Wiley, Carolyn. "Incentive Plan Pushes Production." *Personnel Journal* (August 1993), pp. 86–91.

Quinn, James Brian. *Intelligent Enterprise*. New York: Free Press, 1992, chap. 4.

Shetty, Y. K. "Aiming High: Competitive Benchmarking for Superior Performance." *Long-Range Planning* 26, no. 1 (February 1993), pp. 39–44.

## CHAPTER ELEVEN

IMPLEMENTING STRATEGY: CULTURE AND LEADERSHIP

Weak leadership can wreck the soundest strategy; forceful execution of even a poor plan can often bring victory.

Sun Zi

Effective leaders do not just reward achievement, they celebrate it.

Shelley A. Kirkpatrick and Edwin A. Locke

Ethics is the moral courage to do what we know is right, and not to do what we know is wrong.

C. J. Silas
CEO, Philips Petroleum

. . . A leader lives in the field with his troops.

H. Ross Perot

In the previous two chapters we examined six of the strategy-implementer's tasks—building a capable organization, steering ample resources into strategy-critical activities and operating units, establishing strategy-supportive policies, instituting best practices and programs for continuous improvement, creating internal support systems to enable better execution, and employing appropriate motivational practices and compensation incentives. In this chapter we explore the two remaining implementation tasks: creating a strategy-supportive corporate culture and exerting the internal leadership needed to drive implementation forward.

BUILDING A STRATEGY-SUPPORTIVE CORPORATE CULTURE

Every company has a unique organizational culture. Each has its own business philosophy and principles, its own ways of approaching problems and making decisions, its own embedded patterns of "how we do things around here," its own lore (stories

THE CULTURE AT NORDSTROM

The culture at Nordstrom, a department store retailer noted for exceptional commitment to its customers, revolves around the company's motto: "Respond to Unreasonable Customer Requests." Living up to the company's motto is so strongly ingrained in behavior that employees learn to relish the challenges that some customer requests pose. Usually, meeting customer demands in pleasing fashion entails little more than gracious compliance and a little extra personal attention. But occasionally it means paying a customer's parking ticket when in-store gift wrapping takes longer than normal or hand delivering items purchased by phone to the airport for a customer with an emergency need.

At Nordstrom, each out-of-the-ordinary customer request is seen as an opportunity for a "heroic" act by an employee and a way to build the company's reputation for great service. Nordstrom encourages these acts by promoting employees noted for outstanding service, keeping scrapbooks of "heroic" acts, and paying its salespeople entirely on commission (it is not unusual for good salespeople at Nordstrom to earn double what they would at other department store retailers). For go-getters who truly enjoy retail selling and pleasing customers, Nordstrom is a great company to work for. But the culture weeds out those who can't meet Nordstrom's demanding standards and rewards those who are prepared to be what Nordstrom stands for.

Source: Based on information in Tracy Goss, Richard Pascale, and Anthony Athos, "Risking the Present for a Powerful Future," *Harvard Business Review* 71, no. 6 (November–December 1993), pp. 101–2.

told over and over to illustrate company values and what they mean to employees), its own taboos and political don'ts—in other words, its own ingrained beliefs, behavior and thought patterns, business practices, and personality. The bedrock of Wal-Mart's culture is dedication to customer satisfaction, zealous pursuit of low costs, a strong work ethic, Sam Walton's legendary frugality, the ritualistic Saturday morning headquarters meetings to exchange ideas and review problems, and company executives' commitment to visiting stores, talking to customers, and soliciting suggestions from employees. At Frito-Lay, stories abound of potato chip route salesmen slogging through mud and snow to uphold the company's 99.5 percent service level. At McDonald's the constant message from management is the overriding importance of quality, service, cleanliness, and value; employees are drilled over and over on the need for attention to detail and perfection in every fundamental of the business. Illustration Capsule 32 describes the culture of Nordstrom's.

Corporate culture refers to a company's values, beliefs, traditions, operating style, and internal work environment.

WHERE DOES CORPORATE CULTURE COME FROM?

The taproot of corporate culture is the organization's beliefs and philosophy about how its affairs ought to be conducted—the reasons why it does things the way it does. A company's culture is manifested in the values and business principles that management preaches and practices, in its ethical standards and official policies, in its stakeholder relationships (especially its dealings with employees, unions, stockholders, vendors, and the communities in which it operates), in the traditions the organization maintains, in its supervisory practices, in employees' attitudes and behavior, in the legends people repeat about happenings in the organization, in the peer pressures that exist, in the organization's politics, and in the "chemistry" and the "vibrations" that permeate the work environment. All these sociological forces, some of which operate quite subtly, combine to define an organization's culture.

Beliefs and practices that become embedded in a company's culture can originate anywhere: from one influential individual, work group, department, or division, from the bottom of the organizational hierarchy or the top.[1] Very often, many components of the culture are associated with a founder or other early leaders who articulated them as a company philosophy, a set of principles which the organization should rigidly adhere to, company policies, a vision, a business strategy, or a combination of these. Over time, these cultural underpinnings come to be shared by company managers and employees and then persist as new employees are encouraged to adopt and follow the professed values and practices. A company's culture is a product of internal social forces; it represents an interdependent set of values and behavioral norms that prevail across the organization.

Once established, company cultures can be perpetuated by continuity of leadership, by screening and selecting new group members according to how well their values and behavior fit in, by systematic indoctrination of new members in the culture's fundamentals, by the efforts of senior group members to reiterate core values in daily conversations and pronouncements, by the telling and retelling of company legends, by regular ceremonies honoring members who display cultural ideals, and by visibly rewarding those who follow cultural norms and penalizing those who don't.[2] However, even stable cultures aren't static. Crises and new challenges evolve into new ways of doing things. Arrival of new leaders and turnover of key members often spawn new or different values and practices that alter the culture. Diversification into new businesses, expansion into different geographical areas, and rapid growth that adds new employees can all cause a culture to evolve.

Although it is common to speak about corporate culture in the singular, companies typically have multiple cultures (or subcultures).[3] Values, beliefs, and practices can vary significantly by department, geographic location, division, or business unit. A company's subcultures can clash, or at least not mesh well, if recently acquired business units have not yet been assimilated or if different organizational units have conflicting managerial styles, business philosophies, and operating approaches.

THE POWER OF CULTURE

Most managers, as a consequence of their own experiences and of reading case studies in the business press, accept that an organization's culture is an important contributor (or obstacle) to successful strategy execution. Thomas Watson, Jr., who succeeded his father as CEO at IBM, stated the case for a culture-performance link eloquently in a 1962 speech at Columbia University:

> The basic philosophy, spirit, and desire of an organization have far more to do with its relative achievements than do technological or economic resources, organization structure, innovation, and timing. All these things weigh heavily on success. But they are, I think, transcended by how strongly the people in the organization believe in its basic precepts and how faithfully they carry them out.[4]

The beliefs, goals, and practices called for in a strategy may be compatible with a firm's culture or they may not. When they are not, a company usually finds it difficult to implement the strategy successfully.[5] A close culture-strategy match that energizes people throughout the company to do their jobs in a strategy-supportive manner adds

---

[1] John P. Kotter and James L. Heskett, *Corporate Culture and Performance* (New York: Free Press, 1992), p. 7.

[2] Ibid., pp. 7–8.

[3] Ibid., p. 5.

[4] "A Business and Its Beliefs," McKinsey Foundation Lecture (New York: McGraw-Hill, 1963), as quoted in Kotter and Heskett, *Corporate Culture and Performance,* p. 17.

[5] Kotter and Heskett, *Corporate Culture and Performance,* p. 5.

significantly to the power and effectiveness of strategy execution. Strong cultures promote good long-term performance when there's fit and hurt performance when there's little fit. When a company's culture is out of sync with what is needed for strategic success, the culture has to be changed as rapidly as can be managed; the more entrenched the culture, the greater the difficulty of implementing new or different strategies. A sizable and prolonged strategy-culture conflict weakens and may even defeat managerial efforts to make the strategy work.

A tight culture-strategy alignment is a powerful lever for channeling behavior and helping employees do their jobs in a more strategy-supportive manner; this occurs in two ways:[6]

- *A work environment where the culture matches well with the conditions for good strategy execution provides a system of informal rules and peer pressures regarding how to conduct business internally and how to go about doing one's job.* Culturally approved behavior thrives, while culturally disapproved behavior gets squashed and often penalized. In a company where strategy and culture are misaligned, ingrained values and operating philosophies don't cultivate strategy-supportive work habits; often, the very kinds of behavior needed to execute strategy successfully run afoul of the culture and attract negative recognition rather than praise and reward.

- *A strong strategy-supportive culture nurtures and motivates people to their best; it provides structure, standards, and a value system in which to operate; and it promotes strong company identification among employees.* All this makes employees feel genuinely better about their jobs and work environment and, more often than not, stimulates them to perform closer to the best of their abilities.

This says something important about the task of leading strategy implementation: *anything so fundamental as implementing a strategic plan involves moving the organization's culture into close alignment with the requirements for proficient strategy execution.* The optimal condition is a work environment that enlists and encourages people to perform strategy-critical activities in superior fashion. As one observer noted:

> It has not been just strategy that led to big Japanese wins in the American auto market. It is a culture that enspirits workers to excel at fits and finishes, to produce moldings that match and doors that don't sag. It is a culture in which Toyota can use that most sophisticated of management tools, the suggestion box, and in two years increase the number of worker suggestions from under 10,000 to over 1 million with resultant savings of $250 million.[7]

Strong versus Weak Cultures

Company cultures vary widely in the degree to which they are embedded in company practices and behavioral norms. A company's culture can be weak and fragmented in the sense that many subcultures exist, few values and behavioral norms are widely shared, and there are few traditions. In such cases, organizational members typically have no deeply felt sense of company identity; they view their company as merely a place to work and their job only as a way to make a living. While they may have some feelings of loyalty toward their department, their colleagues, their union, or their boss, they usually have no strong emotional allegiance to the company or its

---

[6]Ibid., pp. 15–16.
[7]Robert H. Waterman, Jr., "The Seven Elements of Strategic Fit," *Journal of Business Strategy* 2, no. 3 (Winter 1982), p. 70.

business mission. On the other hand, a company's culture can be strong and cohesive in the sense that the company conducts its business according to a clear and explicit set of principles and values, that management devotes considerable time to communicating these principles and values to organizational members and explaining how they relate to its business environment, and that the values are shared widely across the company—by senior executives and rank-and-file employees alike.[8] Strong-culture companies typically have creeds or values statements, and executives regularly stress the importance of using these values and principles as the basis for decisions and actions taken throughout the organization. In strong culture companies values and behavioral norms are so deeply rooted that they don't change much when a new CEO takes over—although they can erode over time if the CEO ceases to nurture them.

> A strong culture is a valuable asset when it matches strategy and a dreaded liability when it doesn't.

Three factors contribute to the development of strategically supportive strong cultures: (1) a founder or strong leader who establishes values, principles, and practices that are consistent and sensible in light of customer needs, competitive conditions, and strategic requirements; (2) a sincere, long-standing company commitment to operating the business according to these established traditions, thereby creating an internal environment that supports decision-making based on cultural norms; and (3) a genuine concern for the well-being of the organization's three biggest constituencies—customers, employees, and shareholders. Continuity of leadership, small group size, stable group membership, geographic concentration, and considerable success all contribute to the emergence of a strong culture.[9]

Low-Performance or Unhealthy Cultures

There are a number of unhealthy cultural characteristics that can undermine a company's business performance.[10] One unhealthy organizational trait is a politicized internal environment that allows influential managers to operate their fiefdoms autonomously and resist needed change. In politically dominated cultures, many issues get resolved on the basis of turf, vocal support or opposition by powerful executives, personal lobbying by a key executive, and coalitions among individuals or departments with vested interests in a particular outcome. What's best for the company plays second fiddle to personal aggrandizement.

A second unhealthy cultural trait, one that can plague companies suddenly confronted with fast-changing business conditions, is hostility to change and to people who champion new ways of doing things. Executives who don't value managers or employees with initiative or new ideas put a damper on experimentation and on efforts to improve the status quo. Avoiding risks and not screwing up become more important to a person's career advancement than entrepreneurial successes and innovative accomplishments. This trait is most often found in companies with multilayered management bureaucracies that have enjoyed considerable market success and whose business environments have been hit with accelerating change. General Motors, IBM, Sears, and Eastman Kodak are classic examples; all four gradually became burdened by a stifling bureaucracy that rejected innovation. Now, they are struggling to reinvent the cultural approaches that caused them to succeed in the first place.

A third unhealthy characteristc is promoting managers who understand structures, systems, budgets, and controls better than they understand vision, strategies, inspiration, and culture-building. While the former are adept at solving internal organiza-

---

[8]Terrence E. Deal and Allen A. Kennedy, *Corporate Cultures* (Reading, Mass.: Addison-Wesley, 1982), p. 22.
[9]Vijay Sathe, *Culture and Related Corporate Realities* (Homewood, Ill.: Richard D. Irwin, 1985).
[10]Kotter and Heskett, *Corporate Culture and Performance,* chapter 6.

tional challenges, if they ascend to senior executive positions, the company can find itself short on the entrepreneurial skills and leadership needed to manage strategic change—a condition that ultimately erodes long-term performance.

A fourth characteristic of low-performance cultures is an aversion to looking outside the company for superior practices and approaches. Sometimes a company enjoys such great market success and reigns as an industry leader for so long that its management becomes inbred and arrogant. It believes it has all the answers or can develop them on its own. Insular thinking, inward-looking solutions, and a must-be-invented-here syndrome often precede a decline in company performance. Kotter and Heskett cite Avon, BankAmerica, Citicorp, Coors, Ford, General Motors, Kmart, Kroger, Sears, Texaco, and Xerox as examples of companies that had low-performance cultures during the late 1970s and early 1980s.[11]

Changing problem cultures is very difficult because of the heavy anchor of deeply held values, habits, and the emotional clinging of people to the old and familiar. Sometimes executives succeed in changing the values and behaviors of small groups of managers and even whole departments or divisions, only to find the changes eroded over time by the actions of the rest of the organization. What is communicated, praised, supported, and penalized by the entrenched majority undermines the new emergent culture and halts its progress. Executives can revamp formal organization charts, announce new strategies, bring in managers from the outside, introduce new technologies, and open new plants, yet fail at altering embedded cultural traits and behaviors because of skepticism about the new directions and covert resistance to altering traditional methods.

ADAPTIVE CULTURES

In fast-changing business environments, the capacity to introduce new strategies and organizational practices is a necessity if a company is to achieve superior performance over long periods of time.[12] This requires a culture that *helps* the company adapt to environmental change rather than a culture that has to be coaxed and cajoled to change. The hallmarks of an adaptive culture are: (1) leaders who have a greater commitment to timeless business principles and to organizational stakeholders—customers, employees, shareowners, suppliers, and the communities where the company operates—than to any specific business strategy or operating practice; and (2) group members who are receptive to risk-taking, experimentation, innovation, and changing strategies and practices whenever necessary to satisfy the legitimate interests of stakeholders.

In adaptive cultures, members share a feeling of confidence that the organization can deal with whatever threats and opportunities come down the pike. Hence, members willingly embrace a proactive approach to identifying issues, evaluating the implications and options, and implementing workable solutions—there's a spirit of doing what's necessary to ensure long-term organizational success *provided core values and business principles are upheld in the process.* Managers habitually fund product development initiatives, evaluate new ideas openly, and take prudent risks to create new business positions. Entrepreneurship is encouraged and rewarded. Strategies and traditional operating practices are modified as needed to adjust to or take advantage of changes in the business environment. The leaders of adaptive cultures

Adaptive cultures are a strategy-implementer's best ally.

---

[11]Ibid., p. 68.
[12]This section draws heavily from Kotter and Heskett, *Corporate Culture and Performance,* chapter 4.

are adept at changing the right things in the right ways, not changing for the sake of change and not compromising core values or business principles. Adaptive cultures are very supportive of managers and employees at all ranks who propose or help initiate useful change; indeed, executives consciously seek, train, and promote individuals who display these leadership traits.

In adaptive cultures, top management genuinely cares about the well-being of all key constituencies—customers, employees, stockholders, major suppliers, and the communities where the company operates—and tries to satisfy all their legitimate interests simultaneously. No group is ignored, and fairness to all constituencies is a decision-making principle—a commitment often described as "doing the right thing."[13] In less-adaptive cultures where resistance to change is the norm, managers often behave conservatively and politically to protect or advance their own careers, the interests of their immediate work groups, or their pet projects. They avoid risk-taking and prefer following to leading when it comes to technological change and new product innovation.[14]

CREATING THE FIT BETWEEN STRATEGY AND CULTURE

It is the *strategy-maker's* responsibility to select a strategy compatible with the "sacred" or unchangeable parts of prevailing corporate culture. It is the *strategy-implementer's* task, once strategy is chosen, to change whatever facets of the corporate culture hinder effective execution.

Changing a company's culture and aligning it with strategy are among the toughest management tasks—easier to talk about than do. The first step is to diagnose which facets of the present culture are strategy-supportive and which are not. Then, managers have to talk openly and forthrightly to all concerned about those aspects of the culture that have to be changed. The talk has to be followed swiftly by visible, forceful actions to modify the culture—actions that everyone will understand are intended to establish a new culture more in tune with the strategy.

Symbolic Actions and Substantive Actions Managerial actions to tighten the culture-strategy fit need to be both symbolic and substantive. Symbolic actions are valuable for the signals they send about the kinds of behavior and performance strategy-implementers wish to encourage. The most important symbolic actions are those that top executives take to serve as role models—leading cost reduction efforts by curtailing executive perks; emphasizing the importance of responding to customers' needs by requiring *all* officers and executives to spend a significant portion of each week talking with customers and understanding their requirements; and initiating efforts to alter policies and practices identified as hindrances in executing the new strategy. Another category of symbolic actions includes the events organizations hold to designate and honor people whose actions and performance exemplify what is called for in the new culture. Many universities give outstanding teacher awards each year to symbolize their commitment to and esteem for instructors who display exceptional classroom talents. Numerous businesses have employee-of-the-month awards. The military has a long-standing custom of awarding ribbons and medals for exemplary actions. Mary Kay Cosmetics awards an array of prizes—from ribbons to pink automobiles—to its beauty consultants for reaching various sales plateaus.

---

[13]Ibid., p. 52.
[14]Ibid., p. 50.

The best companies and the best executives expertly use symbols, role models, ceremonial occasions, and group gatherings to tighten the strategy-culture fit. Low-cost leaders like Wal-Mart and Nucor are renowned for their Spartan facilities, executive frugality, intolerance of waste, and zealous control of costs. Executives sensitive to their role in promoting strategy-culture fits make a habit of appearing at ceremonial functions to praise individuals and groups that "get with the program." They honor individuals who exhibit cultural norms and reward those who achieve strategic milestones. They participate in employee training programs to stress strategic priorities, values, ethical principles, and cultural norms. Every group gathering is seen as an opportunity to implant values, praise good deeds, reinforce cultural norms, and promote changes that assist strategy implementation. Sensitive executives make sure that current decisions and policy changes will be construed by organizational members as consistent with and supportive of the company's new strategic direction.[15]

In addition to being out front personally and symbolically leading the push for new behaviors and communicating the reasons for new approaches, strategy-implementers have to convince all those concerned that the effort is more than cosmetic. Talk and plans have to be complemented by substantive actions and real movement. The actions taken have to be credible, highly visible, and unmistakably indicative of the seriousness of management's commitment to new strategic initiatives and the associated cultural changes. There are several ways to accomplish this. One is to engineer some quick successes that highlight the benefits of strategy-culture changes, thus making enthusiasm for the changes contagious. However, instant results are usually not as important as having the will and patience to create a solid, competent team psychologically committed to pursuing the strategy in a superior fashion. The strongest signs that management is truly committed to creating a new culture include: replacing old-culture traditionalist managers with "new breed" managers, changing long-standing policies and operating practices that are dysfunctional or that impede new initiatives, undertaking major reorganizational moves that bring structure into better alignment with strategy, tying compensation incentives directly to the new measures of strategic performance, and making major budgetary reallocations that shift substantial resources from old-strategy projects and programs to new-strategy projects and programs.

At the same time, chief strategy-implementers must be careful to *lead by example*. For instance, if the organization's strategy involves a drive to become the industry's low-cost producer, senior managers must display frugality in their own actions and decisions: Spartan decorations in the executive suite, conservative expense accounts and entertainment allowances, a lean staff in the corporate office, scrutiny of budget requests, and so on. The CEO of SAS Airlines, Jan Carlzon, symbolically reinforced the primacy of quality service for business customers by flying coach instead of first class and by giving up his seat to waitlisted travelers.[16]

Implanting the needed culture-building values and behavior depends on a sincere, sustained commitment by the chief executive coupled with extraordinary persistence in reinforcing the culture at every opportunity through both word and deed. Neither charisma nor personal magnetism are essential. However, personally talking to many departmental groups about the reasons for change *is* essential; organizational changes are seldom accomplished successfully from an office. Moreover, creating and sustaining a strategy-supportive culture is a job for the whole management team. Major

Awards ceremonies, role models, and symbols are a fundamental part of a strategy-implementer's culture-shaping effort.

Senior executives must personally lead efforts to align culture with strategy.

---

[15]Judy D. Olian and Sara L. Rynes, "Making Total Quality Work: Aligning Organizational Processes, Performance Measures, and Stakeholders," *Human Resource Management* 30, no. 3 (Fall 1991), p. 324.
[16]Ibid.

cultural change requires many initiatives from many people. Senior officers, department heads, and middle managers have to reiterate values, "walk the talk," and translate the organization's philosophy into everyday practice. In addition, for the culture-building effort to be successful, strategy-implementers must enlist the support of firstline supervisors and employee opinion-leaders, convincing them of the merits of practicing and enforcing cultural norms at the lowest levels in the organization. Until a big majority of employees join the new culture and share an emotional commitment to its basic values and behavioral norms, there's considerably more work to be done in both instilling the culture and tightening the culture-strategy fit.

The task of making culture supportive of strategy is not a short-term exercise. It takes time for a new culture to emerge and prevail; it's unrealistic to expect an overnight transformation. The bigger the organization and the greater the cultural shift needed to produce a culture-strategy fit, the longer it takes. In large companies, changing the corporate culture in significant ways can take three to five years at minimum. In fact, it is usually tougher to reshape a deeply ingrained culture that is not strategy-supportive than it is to instill a strategy-supportive culture from scratch in a brand new organization.

ESTABLISHING ETHICAL STANDARDS AND VALUES

A strong corporate culture founded on ethical business principles and moral values is a vital driving force behind continued strategic success. Many executives are convinced that a company must care about *how* it does business; otherwise a company's reputation, and ultimately its performance, is put at risk. Corporate ethics and values programs are not window dressing; they are undertaken to create an environment of strongly held values and convictions and to make ethical conduct a way of life. Morally upstanding values and high ethical standards nurture the corporate culture in a very positive way—they connote integrity, "doing the right thing," and genuine concern for stakeholders.

> An ethical corporate culture has a positive impact on a company's long-term strategic success; an unethical culture can undermine it.

Companies establish values and ethical standards in a number of different ways.[17] Companies steeped in tradition with a rich folklore to draw on rely on word-of-mouth indoctrination and the power of tradition to instill values and enforce ethical conduct. But many companies today set forth their values and codes of ethics in written documents. Table 11–1 indicates the kinds of topics such statements cover. Written statements have the advantage of explicitly stating what the company intends and expects, and they serve as benchmarks for judging both company policies and actions and individual conduct. They put a stake in the ground and define the company's position. Value statements serve as a cornerstone for culture-building; a code of ethics serves as a cornerstone for developing a corporate conscience. Illustration Capsule 33 presents the Johnson & Johnson Credo, the most publicized and celebrated code of ethics and values among U.S. companies. J&J's CEO calls the credo "the unifying force for our corporation." Illustration Capsule 34 presents the pledge that Bristol-Myers Squibb makes to all of its stakeholders.

> Values and ethical standards must not only be explicitly stated but they must also be ingrained into the corporate culture.

Once values and ethical standards have been formally set forth, they must be institutionalized and ingrained in the company's policies, practices, and actual conduct. Implementing the values and code of ethics entails several actions:

- Incorporation of the statement of values and the code of ethics into employee training and educational programs.

---

[17]The Business Roundtable, *Corporate Ethics: A Prime Asset,* February 1988, pp. 4–10.

TABLE 11–1   **Topics Generally Covered in Value Statements and Codes of Ethics**

Topics Covered in Values Statements	Topics Covered in Codes of Ethics
• Importance of customers and customer service	• Honesty and observance of the law
• Commitment to quality	• Conflicts of interest
• Commitment to innovation	• Fairness in selling and marketing practices
• Respect for the individual employee and the duty the company has to employees	• Using inside information and securities trading
• Importance of honesty, integrity, and ethical standards	• Supplier relationships and purchasing practices
• Duty to stockholders	• Payments to obtain business/Foreign Corrupt Practices Act
• Duty to suppliers	• Acquiring and using information about others
• Corporate citizenship	• Political activities
• Importance of protecting the environment	• Use of company assets, resources, and property
	• Protection of proprietary information
	• Pricing, contracting, and billing

ILLUSTRATION CAPSULE 33

THE JOHNSON & JOHNSON CREDO

- We believe our first responsibility is to the doctors, nurses, and patients, to mothers and all others who use our products and services.
- In meeting their needs everything we do must be of high quality.
- We must constantly strive to reduce our costs in order to maintain reasonable prices.
- Customers' orders must be serviced promptly and accurately.
- Our suppliers and distributors must have an opportunity to make a fair profit.
- We are responsible to our employees, the men and women who work with us throughout the world.
- Everyone must be considered as an individual.
- We must respect their dignity and recognize their merit.
- They must have a sense of security in their jobs.
- Compensation must be fair and adequate, and working conditions clean, orderly, and safe.
- Employees must feel free to make suggestions and complaints.

- There must be equal opportunity for employment, development, and advancement for those qualified.
- We must provide competent management, and their actions must be just and ethical.
- We are responsible to the communities in which we live and work and to the world community as well.
- We must be good citizens—support good works and charities and bear our fair share of taxes.
- We must encourage civic improvements and better health and education.
- We must maintain in good order the property we are privileged to use, protecting the environment and natural resources.
- Our final responsibility is to our stockholders.
- Business must make a sound profit.
- We must experiment with new ideas.
- Research must be carried on, innovative programs developed, and mistakes paid for.
- New equipment must be purchased, new facilities provided, and new products launched.
- Reserves must be created to provide for adverse times.
- When we operate according to these principles, the stockholders should realize a fair return.

Source: 1982 Annual Report.

ILLUSTRATION CAPSULE 34

THE BRISTOL-MYERS SQUIBB PLEDGE

To those who use our products . . .
We affirm Bristol-Myers Squibb's commitment to the highest standards of excellence, safety, and reliability in everything we make. We pledge to offer products of the highest quality and to work diligently to keep improving them.

To our employees and those who may join us . . .
We pledge personal respect, fair compensation, and equal treatment. We acknowledge our obligation to provide able and humane leadership throughout the organization, within a clean and safe working environment. To all who qualify for advancement, we will make every effort to provide opportunity.

To our suppliers and customers . . .
We pledge an open door, courteous, efficient, and ethical dealing, and appreciation for their right to a fair profit.

To our shareholders . . .
We pledge a companywide dedication to continued profitable growth, sustained by strong finances, a high level of research and development, and facilities second to none.

To the communities where we have plants and offices . . .
We pledge conscientious citizenship, a helping hand for worthwhile causes, and constructive action in support of civic and environmental progress.

To the countries where we do business . . .
We pledge ourselves to be a good citizen and to show full consideration for the rights of others while reserving the right to stand up for our own.

Above all, to the world we live in . . .
We pledge Bristol-Myers Squibb to policies and practices which fully embody the responsibility, integrity, and decency required of free enterprise if it is to merit and maintain the confidence of our society.

Source: 1990 Annual Report.

- Explicit attention to values and ethics in recruiting and hiring to screen out applicants who do not exhibit compatible character traits.
- Communication of the values and ethics code to all employees and explaining compliance procedures.
- Management involvement and oversight, from the CEO down to firstline supervisors.
- Strong endorsements by the CEO.
- Word-of-mouth indoctrination.

In the case of codes of ethics, special attention must be given to sections of the company that are particularly sensitive and vulnerable—purchasing, sales, and political lobbying.[18] Employees who deal with external parties are in ethically sensitive positions and often are drawn into compromising situations. Procedures for enforcing ethical standards and handling potential violations have to be developed.

The compliance effort must permeate the company, extending into every organizational unit. The attitudes, character, and work history of prospective employees must be scrutinized. Every employee must receive adequate training. Line managers at all levels must give serious and continuous attention to the task of explaining how the values and ethical code apply in their areas. In addition, they must insist that company values and ethical standards become a way of life. In general, instilling values and insisting on ethical conduct must be looked on as a continuous culture-building,

[18]Ibid, p. 7.

culture-nurturing exercise. Whether the effort succeeds or fails depends largely on how well corporate values and ethical standards are visibly integrated into company policies, managerial practices, and actions at all levels.

BUILDING A SPIRIT OF HIGH PERFORMANCE INTO THE CULTURE

An ability to instill strong individual commitment to strategic success and to create an atmosphere in which there is constructive pressure to perform is one of the most valuable strategy-implementing skills. When an organization performs consistently at or near peak capability, the outcome is not only improved strategic success but also an organizational culture permeated with a spirit of high performance. Such a spirit of performance should not be confused with whether employees are "happy" or "satisfied" or whether they "get along well together." An organization with a spirit of high performance emphasizes achievement and excellence. Its culture is results-oriented, and its management pursues policies and practices that inspire people to do their best.

A results-oriented culture that inspires people to do their best is conducive to superior strategy execution.

Companies with a spirit of high performance typically are intensely people-oriented, and they reinforce their concern for individual employees on every conceivable occasion in every conceivable way. They treat employees with dignity and respect, train each employee thoroughly, encourage employees to use their own initiative and creativity in performing their work, set reasonable and clear performance expectations, utilize the full range of rewards and punishment to enforce high-performance standards, hold managers at every level responsible for developing the people who report to them, and grant employees enough autonomy to stand out, excel, and contribute. To create a results-oriented organizational culture, a company must make champions out of the people who turn in winning performances:[19]

- At Boeing, General Electric, and 3M Corporation, top executives make a point of ceremoniously honoring individuals who believe so strongly in their ideas that they take it on themselves to hurdle the bureaucracy, maneuver their projects through the system, and turn them into improved services, new products, or even new businesses. In these companies, "product champions" are given high visibility, room to push their ideas, and strong executive support. Champions whose ideas prove out are usually handsomely rewarded; those whose ideas don't pan out still have secure jobs and are given chances to try again.

- The manager of a New York area sales office rented the Meadowlands Stadium (home field of the New York Giants) for an evening. After work, the salespeople were all assembled at the stadium and asked to run one at a time through the players' tunnel onto the field. As each one emerged, the electronic scoreboard flashed the person's name to those gathered in the stands—executives from corporate headquarters, employees from the office, family, and friends. Their role was to cheer loudly in honor of the individual's sales accomplishments. The company involved was IBM. The occasion for this action was to reaffirm IBM's commitment to satisfy an individual's need to be part of something great and to reiterate IBM's concern for championing individual accomplishment.

- Some companies upgrade the importance and status of individual employees by referring to them as Cast Members (Disney), crew members (McDonald's), or

---

[19]Thomas J. Peters and Robert H. Waterman, Jr., *In Search of Excellence* (New York: Harper & Row, 1982), pp. xviii, 240, and 269, and Thomas J. Peters and Nancy Austin, *A Passion for Excellence* (New York: Random House, 1985), pp. 304–7.

associates (Wal-Mart and J. C. Penney). Companies like Mary Kay Cosmetics, Tupperware, and McDonald's actively seek out reasons and opportunities to give pins, buttons, badges, and medals for good showings by average performers—the idea being to express appreciation and give a motivational boost to people who stand out doing "ordinary" jobs.

- McDonald's has a contest to determine the best hamburger cooker in its entire chain. It begins with a competition to determine the best hamburger cooker in each store. Store winners go on to compete in regional championships, and regional winners go on to the "All-American" contest. The winners get trophies and an All-American patch to wear on their shirts.

- Milliken & Co. holds Corporate Sharing Rallies once every three months; teams come from all over the company to swap success stories and ideas. A hundred or more teams make five-minute presentations over a two-day period. Each rally has a major theme—quality, cost reduction, and so on. No criticisms and negatives are allowed, and there is no such thing as a big idea or a small one. Quantitative measures of success are used to gauge improvement. All those present vote on the best presentation and several ascending grades of awards are handed out. Everyone, however, receives a framed certificate for participating.

What makes a spirit of high performance come alive is a complex network of practices, words, symbols, styles, values, and policies pulling together that produces extraordinary results with ordinary people. The drivers of the system are a belief in the worth of the individual, strong company commitment to job security and promotion from within, managerial practices that encourage employees to exercise individual initiative and creativity in doing their jobs, and pride in doing the "itty-bitty, teeny-tiny things" right. A company that treats its employees well generally benefits from increased teamwork, higher morale, and greater employee loyalty.

While emphasizing a spirit of high performance nearly always accentuates the positive, there are negative reinforcers too. Managers whose units consistently perform poorly have to be removed. Aside from the organizational benefits, weak-performing managers should be reassigned for their own good—people who find themselves in a job they cannot handle are usually frustrated, anxiety-ridden, harassed, and unhappy.[20] Moreover, subordinates have a right to be managed with competence, dedication, and achievement. Unless their boss performs well, they themselves cannot perform well. In addition, weak-performing workers and people who reject the cultural emphasis on dedication and high performance have to be weeded out. Recruitment practices need to aim at selecting highly motivated, ambitious applicants whose attitudes and work habits mesh well with a results-oriented corporate culture.

EXERTING STRATEGIC LEADERSHIP

The litany of good strategic management is simple enough: formulate a sound strategic plan, implement it, execute it to the fullest, win! But it's easier said than done. Exerting take-charge leadership, being a "spark plug," ramrodding things through, and getting things done by coaching others to do them are difficult tasks. Moreover, a strategy manager has many different leadership roles to play: chief entrepreneur and strategist, chief administrator and strategy-implementer, culture builder, supervisor,

---

[20] Peter Drucker, *Management: Tasks, Responsibilities, Practices* (New York: Harper & Row, 1974), p. 457.

crisis solver, taskmaster, spokesperson, resource allocator, negotiator, motivator, adviser, arbitrator, consensus builder, policymaker, policy enforcer, mentor, and head cheerleader. Sometimes it is useful to be authoritarian and hardnosed; sometimes it is best to be a perceptive listener and a compromising decision-maker; and sometimes a strongly participative, collegial approach works best. Many occasions call for a highly visible role and extensive time commitments, while others entail a brief ceremonial performance with the details delegated to subordinates.

In general, the problem of strategic leadership is one of diagnosing the situation and choosing from any of several ways to handle it. Six leadership roles dominate the strategy-implementer's action agenda:

1. Staying on top of what is happening and how well things are going.
2. Promoting a culture in which the organization is "energized" to accomplish strategy and perform at a high level.
3. Keeping the organization responsive to changing conditions, alert for new opportunities, and bubbling with innovative ideas.
4. Building consensus, containing "power struggles," and dealing with the politics of crafting and implementing strategy.
5. Enforcing ethical standards.
6. Pushing corrective actions to improve strategy execution and overall strategic performance.

MANAGING BY WALKING AROUND (MBWA)

To stay on top of how well the implementation process is going, a manager needs to develop a broad network of contacts and sources of information, both formal and informal. The regular channels include talking with key subordinates, reviewing reports and the latest operating results, talking to customers, watching the competitive reactions of rival firms, tapping into the grapevine, listening to rank-and-file employees, and observing the situation firsthand. However, some information tends to be more trustworthy than the rest. Written reports may represent "the truth but not the whole truth." Bad news may be covered up, minimized, or not reported at all. Sometimes subordinates delay conveying failures and problems in hopes that more time will give them room to turn things around. As information flows up an organization, there is a tendency for it to get censored and sterilized to the point that it may fail to reveal strategy-critical information. Hence, there is reason for strategy managers to guard against major surprises by making sure that they have accurate information and a "feel" for the existing situation. The chief way this is done is by regular visits "to the field" and talking with many different people at many different levels. The technique of *managing by walking around* (MBWA) is practiced in a variety of styles:[21]

MBWA is one of the techniques effective leaders use.

- At Hewlett-Packard, there are weekly beer busts in each division, attended by both executives and employees, to create a regular opportunity to keep in touch. Tidbits of information flow freely between down-the-line employees and executives—facilitated in part because "the HP Way" is for people at all ranks to be addressed by their first names. Bill Hewlett, one of HP's cofounders, had a companywide reputation for getting out of his office and "wandering around" the plant greeting people, listening to what was on their minds, and asking questions. He found this so valuable that he made MBWA a standard practice

---

[21]Ibid., pp. xx, 15, 120–23, 191, 242–43, 246–47, 287–90. For an extensive report on the benefits of MBWA, see Peters and Austin, *A Passion for Excellence,* chapters 2, 3, and 19.

for all HP managers. Furthermore, ad hoc meetings of people from different departments spontaneously arise; they gather in rooms with blackboards and work out solutions informally.

- McDonald's founder Ray Kroc regularly visited store units and did his own personal inspection on Q.S.C.&V. (Quality, Service, Cleanliness, and Value)— the themes he preached regularly. There are stories of his pulling into a unit's parking lot, seeing litter lying on the pavement, getting out of his limousine to pick it up himself, and then lecturing the store staff at length on the subject of cleanliness.

- The CEO of a small manufacturing company spends much of his time riding around the factory in a golf cart, waving to and joking with workers, listening to them, and calling all 2,000 employees by their first names. In addition, he spends a lot of time with union officials, inviting them to meetings and keeping them well-informed about what is going on.

- Wal-Mart executives have had a long-standing practice of spending two to three days every week visiting Wal-Mart's stores and talking with store managers and employees. Sam Walton, Wal-Mart's founder, insisted "The key is to get out into the store and listen to what the associates have to say. Our best ideas come from clerks and stockboys."

- When Ed Carlson became CEO of United Airlines, he traveled about 200,000 miles a year talking with United's employees. He observed, "I wanted these people to identify me and to feel sufficiently comfortable to make suggestions or even argue with me if that's what they felt like doing . . . Whenever I picked up some information, I would call the senior officer of the division and say that I had just gotten back from visiting Oakland, Reno, and Las Vegas, and here is what I found."

- At Marriott Corp. Bill Marriott personally inspects Marriott hotels. He also invites all Marriott guests to send him their evaluations of Marriott's facilities and services; he personally reads every customer complaint and has been known to telephone hotel managers about them.

Managers at many companies attach great importance to informal communications. They report that it is essential to have a "feel" for situations and to have the ability to gain quick, easy access to information. When executives stay in their offices, they tend to become isolated and often surround themselves with people who are not likely to offer criticism and different perspectives. The information they get is secondhand, screened and filtered, and sometimes dated.

FOSTERING A STRATEGY-SUPPORTIVE CLIMATE AND CULTURE

Strategy-implementers have to be out front in promoting a strategy-supportive organizational climate and culture. When major strategic changes are being implemented, a manager's time is best spent personally leading the changes and promoting needed cultural adjustments. In general, organizational cultures need major overhaul every 5 to 25 years, depending on how fast events in the company's business environment move.[22] When only strategic fine-tuning is being implemented, it takes less time and effort to bring values and culture into alignment with strategy, but there is still a lead role for the manager to play in pushing ahead and prodding for continuous improve-

---

[22]Kotter and Heskett, *Corporate Culture and Performance,* p. 91.

ments. Successful strategy leaders recognize it is their responsibility to convince people that the chosen strategy is right and that implementing it to the best of the organization's ability is top priority.

The single most visible factor that distinguishes successful culture-change efforts from failed attempts is competent leadership at the top. Effective management action to match culture and strategy has several attributes:[23]

- A stakeholders-are-king philosophy that links the need to change to the need to serve the long-term best interests of all key constituencies.

- An openness to new ideas.

- Challenging the status quo with very basic questions: Are we giving customers what they really need and want? How can we be more competitive on cost? Why can't design-to-market cycle time be halved? How can we grow the company instead of downsizing it? Where will the company be five years from now if it sticks with just its present business?

- Persuading individuals and groups to commit themselves to the new direction and energizing individuals and departments sufficiently to make it happen despite the obstacles.

- Repeating the new messages again and again, explaining the rationale for change, and convincing skeptics that all is not well and things must be changed.

- Recognizing and generously rewarding those who exhibit new cultural norms and who lead successful change efforts—this helps cultivate expansion of the coalition for change.

- Creating events where everyone in management is forced to listen to angry customers, dissatisfied stockholders, and alienated employees to keep management informed and to help them realistically assess organizational strengths and weaknesses.

Only top management has the power to bring about major cultural change.

Great power is needed to force major cultural change—to overcome the springback resistance of entrenched cultures—and great power normally resides only at the top. Moreover, the interdependence of values, strategies, practices, and behaviors inside organizations makes it difficult to change anything fundamental without simultaneously undertaking wider-scale changes. Usually the people with the power to effect change of that scope are those at the top.

Both words and deeds play a part in strategic leadership. Words inspire people, infuse spirit and drive, define strategy-supportive cultural norms and values, articulate the reasons for strategic and organizational change, legitimize new viewpoints and new priorities, urge and reinforce commitment, and arouse confidence in the new strategy. Deeds add credibility to the words, create strategy-supportive symbols, set examples, give meaning and content to the language, and teach the organization what sort of behavior is needed and expected.

Highly visible symbols and imagery are needed to complement substantive actions. One General Motors manager explained how symbolism and managerial style accounted for the striking difference in performance between two large plants:[24]

At the poorly performing plant, the plant manager probably ventured out on the floor once a week, always in a suit. His comments were distant and perfunctory. At South

---

[23]Ibid., pp. 84, 144, and 148.
[24]As quoted in Peters and Waterman, *In Search of Excellence,* p. 262.

Gate, the better plant, the plant manager was on the floor all the time. He wore a baseball cap and a UAW jacket. By the way, whose plant do you think was spotless? Whose looked like a junkyard?

As a rule, the greater the degree of strategic change being implemented and/or the greater the shift in cultural norms needed to accommodate a new strategy, the more visible and unequivocal the strategy-implementer's words and deeds need to be. Lessons from well-managed companies show that what the strategy leader says and does has a significant bearing on down-the-line strategy implementation and execution.[25] According to one view, "It is not so much the articulation . . . about what an [organization] should be doing that creates new practice. It's the imagery that creates the understanding, the compelling moral necessity that the new way is right."[26] Moreover, the actions and images, both substantive and symbolic, have to be hammered out regularly, not just restricted to ceremonial speeches and special occasions. This is where a high profile and "managing by walking around" come into play. As a Hewlett-Packard official expresses it in the company publication *The HP Way:*

> Once a division or department has developed a plan of its own—a set of working objectives—it's important for managers and supervisors to keep it in operating condition. This is where observation, measurement, feedback, and guidance come in. It's our "management by wandering around." That's how you find out whether you're on track and heading at the right speed and in the right direction. If you don't constantly monitor how people are operating, not only will they tend to wander off track but also they will begin to believe you weren't serious about the plan in the first place. It has the extra benefit of getting you off your chair and moving around your area. By wandering around, I literally mean moving around and talking to people. It's all done on a very informal and spontaneous basis, but it's important in the course of time to cover the whole territory. You start out by being accessible and approachable, but the main thing is to realize you're there to listen. The second reason for MBWA is that it is vital to keep people informed about what's going on in the company, especially those things that are important to them. The third reason for doing this is because it is just plain fun.

Such contacts give the manager a "feel" for how things are progressing, and they provide opportunity to speak with encouragement, lift spirits, shift attention from the old to the new priorities, create some excitement, and project an atmosphere of informality and fun—all of which drive implementation in a positive fashion and intensify the organizational energy behind strategy execution. John Welch of General Electric sums up the hands-on role and motivational approach well: "I'm here every day, or out into a factory, smelling it, feeling it, touching it, challenging the people."[27]

The vast majority of companies probably don't have strong, adaptive cultures capable of producing excellent long-term performance in a fast-paced market and competitive environment. In such companies, managers have to do more than show incremental progress. Conservative incrementalism seldom leads to major cultural adaptations; more usually, gradualism is defeated by the resilience of entrenched cultures and the ability of vested interests to thwart or minimize the impact of piecemeal change. Only with bold leadership and concerted action on many fronts can a company succeed in tackling so large and difficult a task as major cultural change.

---

[25]Ibid., chapter 9.

[26]Warren Bennis, *The Unconscious Conspiracy: Why Leaders Can't Lead* (New York: AMACOM, 1987), p. 93.

[27]As quoted in Ann M. Morrison, "Trying to Bring GE to Life," *Fortune,* January 25, 1982, p. 52.

KEEPING THE INTERNAL ORGANIZATION RESPONSIVE AND INNOVATIVE

While formulating and implementing strategy is a manager's responsibility, the task of generating fresh ideas, identifying new opportunities, and being responsive to changing conditions cannot be accomplished by a single person. It is an organization-wide task, particularly in large corporations. One of the toughest parts of exerting strategic leadership is generating a dependable supply of fresh ideas from the rank and file, managers and employees alike, and promoting an entrepreneurial, opportunistic spirit that permits continuous adaptation to changing conditions. A flexible, responsive, innovative internal environment is critical in fast-moving high-technology industries, in businesses where products have short life-cycles and growth depends on new product innovation, in companies with widely diversified business portfolios (where opportunities are varied and scattered), in markets where successful product differentiation depends on out-innovating the competition, and in situations where low-cost leadership hinges on continuous improvement and new ways to drive costs out of the business. Managers cannot mandate such an environment by simply exhorting people to "be creative."

One useful leadership approach is to take special pains to foster, nourish, and support people who are willing to champion new ideas, better services, new products, and new product applications and are eager for a chance to try turning their ideas into new divisions, new businesses, and even new industries. When Texas Instruments reviewed 50 or so successful and unsuccessful new product introductions, one factor marked every failure: "Without exception we found we hadn't had a volunteer champion. There was someone we had cajoled into taking on the task."[28] The rule seems to be that an idea either finds a champion or dies. The best champions are persistent, competitive, tenacious, committed, and fanatic about the idea and seeing it through to success.

Empowering Champions In order to promote an organizational climate where champion innovators can blossom and thrive, strategy managers need to do several things. First, individuals and groups have to be encouraged to bring their ideas forward, be creative, and exercise initiative. The culture has to nurture, even celebrate, experimentation and innovation. Everybody must be expected to contribute ideas and seek out continuous improvement. The trick is to keep a sense of urgency alive in the business so that people see change and innovation as a necessity. Second, the champion's maverick style has to be tolerated and given room to operate. People's imaginations need to be encouraged to fly in all directions. Freedom to experiment and a practice of informal brainstorming sessions need to become ingrained. Above all, people with creative ideas must not be looked on as disruptive or troublesome. Third, managers have to induce and promote lots of "tries" and be willing to tolerate mistakes and failures. Most ideas don't pan out, but the organization learns from a good attempt even when it fails. Fourth, strategy managers should be willing to use all kinds of ad hoc organizational forms to support ideas and experimentation—venture teams, task forces, "performance shootouts" among different groups working on competing approaches, informal "bootlegged" projects composed of volunteers, and so on. Fifth, strategy managers have to see that the rewards for successful champions are large and visible and that people who champion an unsuccessful idea are encouraged to try again rather than punished or sidelined. In effect, the leadership task is to create an adaptive, innovative culture that embraces organizational responses to

High-performance cultures make champions out of people who excel.

The faster a company's business environment changes, the more attention managers must pay to keeping the organization innovative and responsive.

---

[28]As quoted in Peters and Waterman, *In Search of Excellence,* pp. 203–4.

changing conditions rather than fearing the new conditions or seeking to minimize them. Companies with conspicuously innovative cultures include Sony, 3M, Motorola, and Levi Strauss. All four inspire their employees with strategic visions to excel and be world-class at what they do.

DEALING WITH COMPANY POLITICS

A manager can't effectively formulate and implement strategy without being perceptive about company politics and being adept at political maneuvering.[29] Politics virtually always comes into play in formulating the strategic plan. Inevitably, key individuals and groups form coalitions, and each group presses the benefits and potential of its own ideas and vested interests. Political considerations enter into decisions about which objectives take precedence and which lines of business in the corporate portfolio have top priority in resource allocation. Internal politics is a factor in building a consensus for one strategic option over another.

As a rule, there is even more politics in implementing strategy than in formulating it. Typically, internal political considerations affect practical issues such as whose areas of responsibility get reorganized, who reports to whom, who has how much authority over subunits, what individuals should fill key positions and head strategy-critical activities, and which organizational units will get the biggest budget increases. As a case in point, Quinn cites a situation where three strong managers who fought each other constantly formed a potent coalition to resist a reorganization scheme that would have coordinated the very things that caused their friction.[30]

_32_

Company politics presents strategy leaders with the challenge of building consensus for the strategy and how to implement it.

In short, political considerations and the forming of individual and group alliances are integral parts of building organizationwide support for the strategic plan and gaining consensus on how to implement it. Political skills are a definite, maybe even necessary, asset for managers in orchestrating the whole strategic process.

A strategy manager must understand how an organization's power structure works, who wields influence in the executive ranks, which groups and individuals are "activists" and which are defenders of the status quo, who can be helpful and who may not be in a showdown on key decisions, and which direction the political winds are blowing on a given issue. When major decisions have to be made, strategy managers need to be especially sensitive to the politics of managing coalitions and reaching consensus. As the chairman of a major British corporation expressed it:

> I've never taken a major decision without consulting my colleagues. It would be unimaginable to me, unimaginable. First, they help me make a better decision in most cases. Second, if they know about it and agree with it, they'll back it. Otherwise, they might challenge it, not openly, but subconsciously.[31]

The politics of strategy centers chiefly around stimulating options, nurturing support for strong proposals and killing weak ones, guiding the formation of coalitions on particular issues, and achieving consensus and commitment. A recent study of strategy management in nine large corporations showed that successful executives relied upon the following political tactics:[32]

---

[29]For further discussion of this point see Abraham Zaleznik, "Power and Politics in Organizational Life," _Harvard Business Review_ 48, no. 3 (May–June 1970), pp. 47–60; R. M. Cyert, H. A. Simon, and D. B. Trow, "Observation of a Business Decision," _Journal of Business,_ October 1956, pp. 237–48; and James Brian Quinn, _Strategies for Change: Logical Incrementalism_ (Homewood, Ill.: Richard D. Irwin, 1980).

[30]Quinn, _Strategies for Change,_ p. 68.

[31]Ibid., p. 65. This statement was made by Sir Alastair Pilkington, Chairman, Pilkington Brothers, Ltd.

[32]Ibid., pp. 128–45.

- Letting weakly supported ideas and proposals die through inaction.
- Establishing additional hurdles or tests for strongly supported ideas that the manager views as unacceptable but that are best not opposed openly.
- Keeping a low political profile on unacceptable proposals by getting subordinate managers to say no.
- Letting most negative decisions come from a group consensus that the manager merely confirms, thereby reserving personal veto for big issues and crucial moments.
- Leading the strategy but not dictating it—giving few orders, announcing few decisions, depending heavily on informal questioning, and seeking to probe and clarify until a consensus emerges.
- Staying alert to the symbolic impact of one's actions and statements lest a false signal stimulate proposals and movements in unwanted directions.
- Ensuring that all major power bases within the organization have representation in or access to top management.
- Injecting new faces and new views into considerations of major changes to preclude those involved from coming to see the world the same way and then acting as systematic screens against other views.
- Minimizing political exposure on issues that are highly controversial and in circumstances where opposition from major power centers can trigger a "shootout."

The politics of strategy implementation is especially critical when it comes to introducing a new strategy against the resistance of those who support the old one. Except for crisis situations where the old strategy is plainly revealed as out-of-date, it is usually bad politics to push the new strategy via attacks on the old one.[33] Bad-mouthing old strategy can easily be interpreted as an attack on those who formulated it and those who supported it. The old strategy and the judgments behind it may have been well-suited to the organization's earlier circumstances, and the people who made these judgments may still be influential.

In addition, the new strategy and/or the plans for implementing it may not have been the first choices of others, and lingering doubts may remain. Good arguments may exist for pursuing other actions. Consequently, in trying to surmount resistance, nothing is gained by knocking the arguments for alternative approaches. Such attacks often produce alienation instead of cooperation.

In short, to bring the full force of an organization behind a strategic plan, the strategy manager must assess and deal with the most important centers of potential support for and opposition to new strategic thrusts.[34] He or she needs to secure the support of key people, co-opt or neutralize serious opposition and resistance when and where necessary, learn where the zones of indifference are, and build as much consensus as possible.

ENFORCING ETHICAL BEHAVIOR

For an organization to display consistently high ethical standards, the CEO and those around the CEO must be openly and unequivocally committed to ethical and moral conduct.[35] In companies that strive hard to make high ethical standards a reality, top

---

[33]Ibid., pp. 118–19.
[34]Ibid., p. 205.
[35]The Business Roundtable, *Corporate Ethics,* pp. 4–10.

management communicates its commitment in a code of ethics, in speeches and company publications, in policies concerning the consequences of unethical behavior, in the deeds of senior executives, and in the actions taken to ensure compliance. Senior management iterates and reiterates to employees that it is not only their duty to observe ethical codes but also to report ethical violations. While such companies have provisions for disciplining violators, the main purpose of enforcement is to encourage compliance rather than administer punishment. Although the CEO leads the enforcement process, all managers are expected to make a personal contribution by stressing ethical conduct with their subordinates and by involving themselves in the process of monitoring compliance with the code of ethics. "Gray areas" must be identified and openly discussed with employees, and procedures created for offering guidance when issues arise, for investigating possible violations, and for resolving individual cases. The lesson from these companies is that it is never enough to assume activities are being conducted ethically, nor can it be assumed that employees understand they are expected to act with integrity.

High ethical standards cannot be enforced without the open and unequivocal commitment of the chief executive.

There are several concrete things managers can do to exercise ethics leadership.[36] First and foremost, they must set an excellent ethical example in their own behavior and establish a tradition of integrity. Company decisions have to be seen as ethical—"actions speak louder than words." Second, managers and employees have to be educated about what is ethical and what is not; ethics training programs may have to be established and gray areas pointed out and discussed. Everyone must be encouraged to raise issues with ethical dimensions, and such discussions should be treated as a legitimate topic. Third, top management should regularly reiterate its unequivocal support of the company's ethical code and take a strong stand on ethical issues. Fourth, top management must be prepared to act as the final arbiter on hard calls; this means removing people from a key position or terminating them when they are guilty of a violation. It also means reprimanding those who have been lax in monitoring and enforcing ethical compliance. Failure to act swiftly and decisively in punishing ethical misconduct is interpreted as a lack of real commitment.

A well-developed program to ensure compliance with ethical standards typically includes (1) an oversight committee of the board of directors, usually made up of outside directors; (2) a committee of senior managers to direct ongoing training, implementation, and compliance; (3) an annual audit of each manager's efforts to uphold ethical standards and formal reports on the actions taken by managers to remedy deficient conduct; and (4) periodically requiring people to sign documents certifying compliance with ethical standards.[37]

LEADING THE PROCESS OF MAKING CORRECTIVE ADJUSTMENTS

No strategic plan and no scheme for strategy implementation can foresee all the events and problems that will arise. Making adjustments and mid-course corrections is a normal and necessary part of strategic management.

When responding to new conditions involving either the strategy or its implementation, prompt action is often needed. In a crisis, the typical approach is to push key subordinates to gather information and formulate recommendations, personally preside over extended discussions of the proposed responses, and try to build a quick consensus among members of the executive inner circle. If no consensus emerges or

Corrective adjustments in the company's approach to strategy implementation should be made on an as-needed basis.

---

[36]Ibid.
[37]Ibid.

if several key subordinates remain divided, the burden falls on the strategy manager to choose the response and urge its support.

When time permits a full-fledged evaluation, strategy managers seem to prefer a process of incrementally solidifying commitment to a response.[38] The approach involves

1. Staying flexible and keeping a number of options open.
2. Asking a lot of questions.
3. Gaining in-depth information from specialists.
4. Encouraging subordinates to participate in developing alternatives and proposing solutions.
5. Getting the reactions of many different people to proposed solutions to test their potential and political acceptability.
6. Seeking to build commitment to a response by gradually moving toward a consensus solution.

The governing principle seems to be to make a final decision as late as possible to (1) bring as much information to bear as needed, (2) let the situation clarify enough to know what to do, and (3) allow the various political constituencies and power bases within the organization to move toward a consensus solution. Executives are often wary of committing themselves to a major change too soon because it limits the time for further fact-finding and analysis, discourages others from asking questions that need to be raised, and precludes thorough airing of all the options.

Corrective adjustments to strategy need not be just reactive, however. Proactive adjustments can improve the strategy or its implementation. The distinctive feature of a proactive adjustment is that it arises from management initiatives rather than from forced reactions. Successful strategy managers employ a variety of proactive tactics:[39]

Strategy leaders should be proactive as well as reactive in reshaping strategy and how it is implemented.

1. Commissioning studies to explore and amplify areas where they have a "gut feeling" or sense a need exists.
2. Shopping ideas among trusted colleagues and putting forth trial concepts.
3. Teaming people with different skills, interests, and experiences and letting them push and tug on interesting ideas to expand the variety of approaches considered.
4. Contacting a variety of people inside and outside the organization to sample viewpoints, probe, and listen, thereby deliberating short-circuiting all the careful screens of information flowing up from below.
5. Stimulating proposals for improvement from lower levels, encouraging the development of competing ideas and approaches, and letting the momentum for change come from below, with final choices postponed until it is apparent which option best matches the organization's situation.
6. Seeking new options and solutions that go beyond extrapolations from the status quo.
7. Accepting and committing to partial steps forward as a way of building comfort levels before going on ahead.
8. Managing the politics of change to promote managerial consensus and solidify management's commitment to whatever course of action is chosen.

---

[38]Quinn, *Strategies for Change,* pp. 20–22.
[39]Ibid., chapter 4.

The process leaders go through in deciding on corrective adjustments is essentially the same for both proactive and reactive changes; they sense needs, gather information, amplify understanding and awareness, put forth trial concepts, develop options, explore the pros and cons, test proposals, generate partial (comfort-level) solutions, empower champions, build a managerial consensus, and finally formally adopt an agreed-on course of action.[40] The ultimate managerial prescription may have been given by Rene McPherson, former CEO at Dana Corporation. Speaking to a class of students at Stanford University, he said, "You just keep pushing. You just keep pushing. I made every mistake that could be made. But I just kept pushing."[41]

All this, once again, highlights the fundamental nature of strategic management: the job of formulating and implementing strategy is not one of steering a clear-cut, linear course while carrying out the original strategy intact according to some preconceived and highly detailed implementation plan. Rather, it is one of creatively (1) adapting and reshaping strategy to unfolding events and (2) drawing upon whatever managerial techniques are needed to align internal activities and behaviors with strategy. The process is interactive, with much looping and recycling to fine-tune and adjust visions, objectives, strategies, implementation approaches, and cultures to one another in a continuously evolving process where the conceptually separate acts of crafting and implementing strategy blur and join together.

KEY POINTS

Building a strategy-supportive corporate culture is important to successful implementation because it produces a work climate and organizational esprit de corps that thrive on meeting performance targets and being part of a winning effort. An organization's culture emerges from why and how it does things the way it does, the values and beliefs that senior managers espouse, the ethical standards expected of all, the tone and philosophy underlying key policies, and the traditions the organization maintains. Culture thus concerns the atmosphere and "feeling" a company has and the style in which it gets things done.

Very often, the elements of company culture originate with a founder or other early influential leaders who articulate certain values, beliefs, and principles the company should adhere to, which then get incorporated into company policies, a creed or values statement, strategies, and operating practices. Over time, these values and practices become shared by company employees and managers. Cultures are perpetuated as new leaders act to reinforce them, as new employees are encouraged to adopt and follow them, as legendary stories that exemplify them are told and retold, and as organizational members are honored and rewarded for displaying the cultural norms.

Company cultures vary widely in strength and in makeup. Some cultures are strongly embedded, while others are weak and fragmented in the sense that many subcultures exist, few values and behavioral norms are shared companywide, and there are few strong traditions. Some cultures are unhealthy, dominated by self-serving politics, resistant to change, and too inwardly focused; such cultural traits are often precursors to declining company performance. In fast-changing business environments, adaptive cultures are best because the internal environment is receptive to change, experimentation, innovation, new strategies, and new operating practices needed to respond to changing stakeholder requirements. One significant defining

---

[40]Ibid., p. 146.
[41]As quoted in Peters and Waterman, *In Search of Excellence,* p. 319.

trait of adaptive cultures is that top management genuinely cares about the well-being of all key constituencies—customers, employees, stockholders, major suppliers, and the communities where it operates—and tries to satisfy all their legitimate interests simultaneously.

The philosophy, goals, and practices implicit or explicit in a new strategy may or may not be compatible with a firm's culture. A close strategy-culture alignment promotes implementation and good execution; a mismatch poses real obstacles. Changing a company's culture, especially a strong one with traits that don't fit a new strategy's requirements, is one of the toughest management challenges. Changing a culture requires competent leadership at the top. It requires symbolic actions (leading by example) and substantive actions that unmistakably indicate top management is seriously committed. The stronger the fit between culture and strategy, the less managers have to depend on policies, rules, procedures, and supervision to enforce what people should and should not do; rather, cultural norms are so well-observed that they automatically guide behavior.

Healthy corporate cultures are also grounded in ethical business principles and moral values. Such standards connote integrity, "doing the right thing," and genuine concern for stakeholders and for how the company does business. To be effective, corporate ethics and values programs have to become a way of life through training, strict compliance and enforcement procedures, and reiterated management endorsements.

Successful strategy-implementers exercise an important leadership role. They stay on top of how well things are going by spending considerable time outside their offices, wandering around the organization, listening, coaching, cheerleading, picking up important information, and keeping their fingers on the organization's pulse. They take pains to reinforce the corporate culture through the things they say and do. They encourage people to be creative and innovative in order to keep the organization responsive to changing conditions, alert to new opportunities, and anxious to pursue fresh initiatives. They support "champions" of new approaches or ideas who are willing to stick their necks out and try something innovative. They work hard at building consensus on how to proceed, on what to change and what not to change. They enforce high ethical standards. And they push corrective action to improve strategy execution and overall strategic performance.

A manager's action agenda for implementing and executing strategy is thus expansive and creative. As we indicated at the beginning of our discussion of strategy implementation (Chapter 9), eight bases need to be covered:

1. Building an organization capable of carrying out the strategy successfully.
2. Developing budgets to steer ample resources into those value-chain activities critical to strategic success.
3. Establishing strategically appropriate policies and procedures.
4. Instituting best practices and mechanisms for continuous improvement.
5. Installing support systems that enable company personnel to carry out their strategic roles successfully day in and day out.
6. Tying rewards and incentives tightly to the achievement of performance objectives and good strategy execution.
7. Creating a strategy-supportive work environment and corporate culture.
8. Leading and monitoring the process of driving implementation forward and improving on how the strategy is being executed.

Making progress on these eight tasks sweeps broadly across virtually every aspect of administrative and managerial work.

Because each instance of strategy implementation occurs under different organizational circumstances, a strategy-implementer's action agenda always needs to be situation specific—there's no neat generic procedure to follow. And, as we said at the beginning, implementing strategy is an action-oriented, make-the-right-things-happen task that challenges a manager's ability to lead and direct organizational change, create or reinvent business processes, manage and motivate people, and achieve performance targets. If you now better understand the nature of the challenge, the range of available approaches, and the issues that need to be considered, we will look upon our discussion in these last three chapter as a success.

SUGGESTED READINGS

Bettinger, Cass. "Use Corporate Culture to Trigger High Performance." *Journal of Business Strategy* 10, no. 2 (March–April 1989), pp. 38–42.

Bower, Joseph L., and Martha W. Weinberg. "Statecraft, Strategy, and Corporate Leadership." *California Management Review* 30, no. 2 (Winter 1988), pp. 39–56.

Deal, Terrence E., and Allen A. Kennedy. *Corporate Cultures*. Reading, Mass.: Addison-Wesley, 1982, especially chaps. 1 and 2.

Eccles, Robert G. "The Performance Measurement Manifesto." *Harvard Business Review* 69 (January–February 1991), pp. 131–37.

Floyd, Steven W., and Bill Wooldridge. "Managing Strategic Consensus: The Foundation of Effective Implementation." *Academy of Management Executive* 6, no. 4 (November 1992), pp. 27–39.

Freeman, R. Edward, and Daniel R. Gilbert, Jr. *Corporate Strategy and the Search for Ethics.* Englewood Cliffs, N.J.: Prentice-Hall, 1988.

Gabarro, J. J. "When a New Manager Takes Charge." *Harvard Business Review* 64, no. 3 (May–June 1985), pp. 110–23.

Ginsburg, Lee and Neil Miller, "Value-Driven Management," *Business Horizons* (May–June 1992), pp. 25–27.

Green, Sebastian. "Strategy, Organizational Culture, and Symbolism." *Long Range Planning* 21, no. 4 (August 1988), pp. 121–29.

Kirkpatrick, Shelley A., and Edwin A. Locke. "Leadership: Do Traits Matter?" *Academy of Management Executive* 5, no. 2 (May 1991), pp. 48–60.

Kotter, John P. "What Leaders Really Do." *Harvard Business Review* 68 (May–June 1990), pp. 103–11.

——————, and James L. Heskett. *Corporate Culture and Performance.* New York: Free Press, 1992.

O'Toole, James. "Employee Practices at the Best-Managed Companies." *California Management Review* 28, no. 1 (Fall 1985), pp. 35–66.

Paine, Lynn Sharp. "Managing for Organizational Integrity." *Harvard Business Review* 72, no. 2 (March–April 1994), pp. 106–117.

Pascale, Richard. "The Paradox of 'Corporate Culture': Reconciling Ourselves to Socialization." *California Management Review* 27, no. 2 (Winter 1985), pp. 26–41.

Quinn, James Brian. *Strategies for Change: Logical Incrementalism.* Homewood, Ill.: Richard D. Irwin, 1980, chap. 4.

———. "Managing Innovation: Controlled Chaos." *Harvard Business Review* 64, no. 3 (May–June 1985), pp. 73–84.

Reimann, Bernard C., and Yoash Wiener. "Corporate Culture: Avoiding the Elitest Trap." *Business Horizons* 31, no. 2 (March–April 1988), pp. 36–44.

Scholz, Christian. "Corporate Culture and Strategy—The Problem of Strategic Fit." *Long Range Planning* 20 (August 1987), pp. 78–87.

## PART TWO

CASES IN STRATEGIC MANAGEMENT

A GUIDE TO CASE ANALYSIS

I keep six honest serving men
(They taught me all I knew);
Their names are What and Why and When;
And How and Where and Who.

Rudyard Kipling

In most courses in strategic management, students practice at being strategy managers via case analysis. A case sets forth, in a factual manner, the events and organizational circumstances surrounding a particular managerial situation. It puts readers at the scene of the action and familiarizes them with all the relevant circumstances. A case on strategic management can concern a whole industry, a single organization, or some part of an organization; the organization involved can be either profit seeking or not-for-profit. The essence of the student's role in case analysis is to *diagnose* and *size up* the situation described in the case and then to recommend appropriate action steps.

WHY USE CASES TO PRACTICE STRATEGIC MANAGEMENT

A student of business with tact
Absorbed many answers he lacked.
But acquiring a job,
He said with a sob,
"How does one fit answer to fact?"

The foregoing limerick was used some years ago by Professor Charles Gragg to characterize the plight of business students who had no exposure to cases.[1] Gragg observed that the mere act of listening to lectures and sound advice about managing does little for anyone's management skills and that the accumulated managerial wisdom cannot effectively be passed on by lectures and assigned readings alone. Gragg suggested that if anything had been learned about the practice of management, it is that a storehouse of ready-made textbook answers does not exist. Each managerial situation has unique aspects, requiring its own diagnosis, judgement, and tailor-made actions. Cases provide would-be managers with a valuable way to practice wrestling with the actual problems of actual managers in actual companies.

The case approach to strategic analysis is, first and foremost, an exercise in learning by doing. Because cases provide you with detailed information about conditions and problems of different industries and companies, your task of analyzing company after company and situation after situation has the twin benefit of boosting your analytical skills and exposing you to the ways companies and managers actually do things. Most college students have limited managerial backgrounds and only fragmented knowledge about different companies and real-life strategic situations. Cases help substitute for actual on-the-job experience by (1) giving you broader exposure to a variety of industries, organizations, and strategic problems; (2) forcing you to assume a managerial role (as opposed to that of just an onlooker); (3) providing a test of how to apply the tools and techniques of strategic management; and (4) asking you to come up with pragmatic managerial action plans to deal with the issues at hand.

OBJECTIVES OF CASE ANALYSIS

Using cases to learn about the practice of strategic management is a powerful way for you to accomplish five things:[2]

1. Increase your understanding of what managers should and should not do in guiding a business to success.
2. Build your skills in conducting strategic analysis in a variety of industries, competitive situations, and company circumstances.
3. Get valuable practice in diagnosing strategic issues, evaluating strategic alternatives, and formulating workable plans of action.
4. Enhance your sense of business judgment, as opposed to uncritically accepting the authoritative crutch of the professor or "back-of-the-book" answers.
5. Gaining in-depth exposure to different industries and companies, thereby gaining something close to actual business experience.

If you understand that these are the objectives of case analysis, you are less likely to be consumed with curiosity about "the answer to the case." Students who have grown comfortable with and accustomed to textbook statements of fact and definitive lecture notes are often frustrated when discussions about a case do not produce concrete answers. Usually, case discussions produce good arguments for more than one

---

[1]Charles I. Gragg, "Because Wisdom Can't Be Told," in *The Case Method at the Harvard Business School,* ed. M. P. McNair (New York: McGraw-Hill, 1954), p. 11.
[2]Ibid., pp. 12–14; and D. R. Schoen and Philip A. Sprague, "What Is the Case Method?" in *The Case Method at the Harvard Business School,* ed. M. P. McNair, pp. 78–79.

course of action. Differences of opinion nearly always exist. Thus, should a class discussion conclude without a strong, unambiguous consensus on what do to, don't grumble too much when you are *not* told what the answer is or what the company actually did. Just remember that in the business world answers don't come in conclusive black-and-white terms. There are nearly always several feasible courses of action and approaches, each of which may work out satisfactorily. Moreover, in the business world, when one elects a particular course of action, there is no peeking at the back of a book to see if you have chosen the best thing to do and no one to turn to for a provably correct answer. The only valid test of management action is *results*. If the results of an action turn out to be "good," the decision to take it may be presumed "right." If not, then the action chosen was "wrong" in the sense that it didn't work out.

Hence, the important thing for a student to understand in case analysis is that the managerial exercise of identifying, diagnosing, and recommending builds your skills; discovering the right answer or finding out what actually happened is no more than frosting on the cake. Even if you learn what the company did, you can't conclude that it was necessarily right or best. All that can be said is "here is what they did. . . ."

The point is this: *The purpose of giving you a case assignment is not to cause you to run to the library to look up what the company actually did but, rather, to enhance your skills in sizing up situations and developing your managerial judgment about what needs to be done and how to do it.* The aim of case analysis is for *you* to bear the strains of thinking actively, of offering your analysis, of proposing action plans, and of explaining and defending your assessments—this is how cases provide you with meaningful practice at being a manager.

PREPARING A CASE FOR CLASS DISCUSSION

If this is your first experience with the case method, you may have to reorient your study habits. Unlike lecture courses where you can get by without preparing intensively for each class and where you have latitude to work assigned readings and reviews of lecture notes into your schedule, a case assignment requires conscientious preparation before class. You will not get much out of hearing the class discuss a case you haven't read, and you certainly won't be able to contribute anything yourself to the discussion. What you have got to do to get ready for class discussion of a case is to study the case, reflect carefully on the situation presented, and develop some reasoned thoughts. Your goal in preparing the case should be to end up with what you think is a sound, well-supported analysis of the situation and a sound, defensible set of recommendations about which managerial actions need to be taken.

To prepare a case for class discussion, we suggest the following approach:

1. *Read the case through rather quickly for familiarity.* The initial reading should give you the general flavor of the situation and indicate which issue or issues are involved. If your instructor has provided you with study questions for the case, now is the time to read them carefully.

2. *Read the case a second time.* On this reading, try to gain full command of the facts. Begin to develop some tentative answers to the study questions your instructor has provided. If your instructor has elected not to give you assignment questions, then start forming your own picture of the overall situation being described.

3. *Study all the exhibits carefully.* Often, the real story is in the numbers contained in the exhibits. Expect the information in the case exhibits to be crucial enough to materially affect your diagnosis of the situation.

4. *Decide what the strategic issues are.* Until you have identified the strategic issues and problems in the case, you don't know what to analyze, which tools and analytical techniques are called for, or otherwise how to proceed. At times the strategic issues are clear—either being stated in the case or else obvious from reading the case. At other times you will have to dig them out from all the information given.

5. *Start your analysis of the issues with some number crunching.* A big majority of strategy cases call for some kind of number crunching on your part. This means calculating assorted financial ratios to check out the company's financial condition and recent performance, calculating growth rates of sales or profits or unit volume, checking out profit margins and the makeup of the cost structure, and understanding whatever revenue-cost-profit relationships are present. See Table 1 for a summary of key financial ratios, how they are calculated, and what they show.

6. *Use whichever tools and techniques of strategic analysis are called for.* Strategic analysis is not just a collection of opinions; rather, it entails application of a growing number of powerful tools and techniques that cut beneath the surface and produce important insight and understanding of strategic situations. Every case assigned is strategy related and contains an opportunity to usefully apply the weapons of strategic analysis. Your instructor is looking for you to demonstrate that you know *how* and *when* to use the strategic management concepts presented earlier in the course. Furthermore, expect to have to draw regularly on what you have learned in your finance, economics, production, marketing, and human resources management courses.

7. *Check out conflicting opinions and make some judgments about the validity of all the data and information provided.* Many times cases report views and contradictory opinions (after all, people don't always agree on things, and different people see the same things in different ways). Forcing you to evaluate the data and information presented in the case helps you develop your powers of inference and judgment. Asking you to resolve conflicting information "comes with the territory" because a great many managerial situations entail opposing points of view, conflicting trends, and sketchy information.

8. *Support your diagnosis and opinions with reasons and evidence.* The most important things to prepare for are your answers to the question "Why?" For instance, if after studying the case you are of the opinion that the company's managers are doing a poor job, then it is your answer to "Why?" that establishes just how good your analysis of the situation is. If your instructor has provided you with specific study questions for the case, by all means prepare answers that include all the reasons and number-crunching evidence you can muster to support your diagnosis. *Generate at least two pages of notes!*

9. *Develop an appropriate action plan and set of recommendations.* Diagnosis divorced from corrective action is sterile. The test of a manager is always to convert sound analysis into sound actions—actions that will produce the desired results. Hence, the final and most telling step in preparing a case is to develop an action agenda for management that lays out a set of specific

T A B L E 1 | **A Summary of Key Financial Ratios, How They Are Calculated, and What They Show**

Ratio	How Calculated	What It Shows
Profitability Ratios		
1. Gross profit margin	$\dfrac{\text{Sales} - \text{Cost of goods sold}}{\text{Sales}}$	An indication of the total margin available to cover operating expenses and yield a profit.
2. Operating profit margin (or return on sales)	$\dfrac{\text{Profits before taxes and before interest}}{\text{Sales}}$	An indication of the firm's profitability from current operations without regard to the interest charges accruing from the capital structure.
3. Net profit margin (or net return on sales)	$\dfrac{\text{Profits after taxes}}{\text{Sales}}$	Shows after tax profits per dollar of sales. Subpar profit margins indicate that the firm's sales prices are relatively low or that costs are relatively high, or both.
4. Return on total assets	$\dfrac{\text{Profits after taxes}}{\text{Total assets}}$ or $\dfrac{\text{Profits after taxes} + \text{interest}}{\text{Total assets}}$	A measure of the return on total investment in the enterprise. It is sometimes desirable to add interest to aftertax profits to form the numerator of the ratio since total assets are financed by creditors as well as by stockholders; hence, it is accurate to measure the productivity of assets by the returns provided to both classes of investors.
5. Return on stockholder's equity (or return on net worth)	$\dfrac{\text{Profits after taxes}}{\text{Total stockholders' equity}}$	A measure of the rate of return on stockholders' investment in the enterprise.
6. Return on common equity	$\dfrac{\text{Profits after taxes} - \text{Preferred stock dividends}}{\text{Total stockholders' equity} - \text{Par value of preferred stock}}$	A measure of the rate of return on the investment which the owners of the common stock have made in the enterprise.
7. Earnings per share	$\dfrac{\text{Profits after taxes} - \text{Preferred stock dividends}}{\text{Number of shares of common stock outstanding}}$	Shows the earnings available to the owners of each share of common stock.
Liquidity Ratios		
1. Current ratio	$\dfrac{\text{Current assets}}{\text{Current liabilities}}$	Indicates the extent to which the claims of short-term creditors are covered by assets that are expected to be converted to cash in a period roughly corresponding to the maturity of the liabilities.
2. Quick ratio (or acid-test ratio)	$\dfrac{\text{Current assets} - \text{Inventory}}{\text{Current liabilities}}$	A measure of the firm's ability to pay off short-term obligations without relying on the sale of its inventories
3. Inventory to net working capital	$\dfrac{\text{Inventory}}{\text{Current assets} - \text{Current liabilities}}$	A measure of the extent to which the firm's working capital is tied up in inventory.
Leverage Ratios		
1. Debt-to-assets ratio	$\dfrac{\text{Total debt}}{\text{Total assets}}$	Measures the extent to which borrowed funds have been used to finance the firm's operations.
2. Debt-to-equity ratio	$\dfrac{\text{Total debt}}{\text{Total stockholders' equity}}$	Provides another measure of the funds provided by creditors versus the funds provided by owners.

TABLE 1 | **A Summary of Key Financial Ratios, How They Are Calculated, and What They Show (*cont.*)**

Ratio	How Calculated	What It Shows
Leverage Ratios (*cont.*)		
3. Long-term debt-to equity ratio	$\dfrac{\text{Long-term debt}}{\text{Total shareholders' equity}}$	A widely used measure of the balance between debt and equity in the firm's long-term capital structure.
4. Times-interest-earned (or coverage) ratio	$\dfrac{\text{Profits before interest and taxes}}{\text{Total interest charges}}$	Measures the extent to which earnings can decline without the firm becoming unable to meet its annual interest costs.
5. Fixed-charge coverage	$\dfrac{\text{Profits before taxes and interest} + \text{Lease obligations}}{\text{Total interest charges} + \text{Lease obligations}}$	A more inclusive indication of the firm's ability to meet all of its fixed-charge obligations.
Activity Ratios		
1. Inventory turnover	$\dfrac{\text{Sales}}{\text{Inventory of finished goods}}$	When compared to industry averages, it provides an indication of whether a company has excessive or perhaps inadequate finished goods inventory.
2. Fixed assets turnover	$\dfrac{\text{Sales}}{\text{Fixed Assets}}$	A measure of the sales productivity and utilization of plant and equipment.
3. Total assets turnover	$\dfrac{\text{Sales}}{\text{Total Assets}}$	A measure of the utilization of all the firm's assets; a ratio below the industry average indicates the company is not generating a sufficient volume of business, given the size of its asset investment.
4. Accounts receivable turnover	$\dfrac{\text{Annual credit sales}}{\text{Accounts receivable}}$	A measure of the average length of time it takes the firm to collect the sales made on credit.
5. Average collection period	$\dfrac{\text{Accounts receivable}}{\text{Total sales} \div 365}$ or $\dfrac{\text{Accounts receivable}}{\text{Average daily sales}}$	Indicates the average length of time the firm must wait after making a sale before it receives payment.
Other Ratios		
1. Dividend yield on common stock	$\dfrac{\text{Annual dividends per share}}{\text{Current market price per share}}$	A measure of the return to owners received in the form of dividends.
2. Price-earnings ratio	$\dfrac{\text{Current market price per share}}{\text{After tax earnings per share}}$	Faster-growing or less-risky firms tend to have higher price-earnings ratios than slower-growing or more-risky firms.
3. Dividend payout ratio	$\dfrac{\text{Annual dividends per share}}{\text{After tax earnings per share}}$	Indicates the percentage of profits paid out as dividends.
4. Cash flow per share	$\dfrac{\text{After tax profits} + \text{Depreciation}}{\text{Number of common shares outstanding}}$	A measure of the discretionary funds over and above expenses that are available for use by the firm.

Note: Industry-average ratios against which a particular company's ratios may be judged are available in *Modern Industry* and *Dun's Reviews* published by Dun & Bradstreet (14 ratios for 125 lines of business activities), Robert Morris Associates' *Annual Statement Studies* (11 ratios for 156 lines of business), and the FTC-SEC's *Quarterly Financial Report* for manufacturing corporations.

develop an action agenda for management that lays out a set of specific recommendations on what to do. Bear in mind that proposing realistic, workable solutions is far preferable to casually tossing out off-the-top-of-your-head suggestions. Be prepared to argue why your recommendations are more attractive than other courses of action that are open.

As long as you are conscientious in preparing your analysis and recommendations, and as long as you have ample reasons, evidence, and arguments to support your views, you shouldn't fret unduly about whether what you've prepared is the right answer to the case. In case analysis there is rarely just one right approach or one right set of recommendations. Managing companies and devising and implementing strategies are not such exact sciences that there exists a single provably correct analysis and action plan for each strategic situation. Of course, some analyses and action plans are better than others; but, in truth, there's nearly always more than one good way to analyze a situation and more than one good plan of action. So, if you have done a careful and thoughtful job of preparing the case, don't lose confidence in the correctness of your work and judgement.

PARTICIPATING IN CLASS DISCUSSION OF A CASE

Classroom discussions of cases are sharply different from attending a lecture class. In a case class students do most of the talking. The instructor's role is to solicit student participation, keep the discussion on track, ask "Why?" often, offer alternative views, play the devil's advocate (if no students jump in to offer opposing views), and otherwise lead the discussion. The students in the class carry the burden for analyzing the situation and for being prepared to present and defend their diagnoses and recommendations. Expect a classroom environment, therefore, that calls for *your* size-up of the situation, *your* analysis, what actions *you* would take, and why *you* would take them. Do not be dismayed if, as the class discussion unfolds, some insightful things are said by your fellow classmates that you did not think of. It is normal for views and analyses to differ and for the comments of others in the class to expand your own thinking about the case. As the old adage goes, "Two heads are better than one." So it is to be expected that the class as a whole will do a more penetrating and searching job of case analysis than will any one person working alone. This is the power of group effort, and its virtues are that it will help you see more analytical applications, let you test your analyses and judgments against those of your peers, and force you to wrestle with differences of opinion and approaches.

To orient you to the classroom environment on the days a case discussion is scheduled, we compiled the following list of things to expect:

1. Expect students to dominate the discussion and do most of the talking. The case method enlists a maximum of individual participation in class discussion. It is not enough to be present as a silent observer; if every student took this approach, there would be no discussion. (Thus, expect a portion of your grade to be based on your participation in case discussions.)

2. Expect the instructor to assume the role of extensive questioner and listener.

3. Be prepared for the instructor to probe for reasons and supporting analysis.

4. Expect and tolerate challenges to the views expressed. All students have to be willing to submit their conclusions for scrutiny and rebuttal. Each student needs to learn to state his or her views without fear of disapproval and to overcome the hesitation of speaking out. Learning respect for the views and approaches of others is an integral part of case analysis exercises. But there are times when it is OK to swim against the tide of majority opinion. In the practice of management, there is always room for originality and unorthodox

approaches. So while discussion of a case is a group process, there is no compulsion for you or anyone else to cave in and conform to group opinions and group consensus.

5. Don't be surprised if you change your mind about some things as the discussion unfolds. Be alert to how these changes affect your analysis and recommendations (in the event you get called on).

6. Expect to learn a lot from each case discussion; use what you learned to be better prepared for the next case discussion.

There are several things you can do on your own to be good and look good as a participant in class discussions:

- Although you should do your own independent work and independent thinking, don't hesitate before (and after) class to discuss the case with other students. In real life, managers often discuss the company's problems and situation with other people to refine their own thinking.

- In participating in the discussion, make a conscious effort to contribute, rather than just talk. There is a big difference between saying something that builds the discussion and offering a long-winded, off-the-cuff remark that leaves the class wondering what the point was.

- Avoid the use of "I think," "I believe," and "I feel"; instead, say, "My analysis shows . . ." and "The company should do . . . because . . ." Always give supporting reasons and evidence for your views; then your instructor won't have to ask you "Why?" every time you make a comment.

- In making your points, assume that everyone has read the case and knows what it says; avoid reciting and rehashing information in the case—instead, use the data and information to explain your assessment of the situation and to support your position.

- Always prepare good notes (usually two or three pages' worth) for each case and use them extensively when you speak. There's no way you can remember everything off the top of your head—especially the results of your number crunching. To reel off the numbers or to present all five reasons why, instead of one, you will need good notes. When you have prepared good notes to the study questions and use them as the basis for your comments, *everybody* in the room will know you are well prepared, and your contribution to the case discussion will stand out.

PREPARING A WRITTEN CASE ANALYSIS

Preparing a written case analysis is much like preparing a case for class discussion, except that your analysis must be more complete and reduced to writing. Unfortunately, though, there is no ironclad procedure for doing a written case analysis. All we can offer are some general guidelines and words of wisdom—this is because company situations and management problems are so diverse that no one mechanical way to approach a written case assignment always works.

Your instructor may assign you a specific topic around which to prepare your written report. Or, alternatively, you may be asked to do a comprehensive written case analysis, where the expectation is that you will (1) *identify* all the pertinent issues that management needs to address, (2) perform whatever *analysis* and *evaluation* is appropriate, and (3) propose an *action plan* and *set of recommendations* addressing the issues you have identified. In going through the exercise of identify, evaluate, and recommend, keep the following pointers in mind.[3]

Identification   It is essential early on in your paper that you provide a sharply focused diagnosis of strategic issues and key problems and that you demonstrate a good grasp of the company's present situation. Make sure you can identify the firm's strategy (use the concepts and tools in Chapters 1–8 as diagnostic aids) and that you can pinpoint whatever strategy implementation issues may exist (again, consult the material in Chapters 9 and 10 for diagnostic help). Consult the key points we have provided at the end of each chapter for further diagnostic suggestions. Consider beginning your paper by sizing up the company's situation, its strategy, and the significant problems and issues that confront management. State problems/issues as clearly and precisely as you can. Unless it is necessary to do so for emphasis, avoid recounting facts and history about the company (assume your professor has read the case and is familiar with the organization).

Analysis and Evaluation   This is usually the hardest part of the report. Analysis is hard work! Check out the firm's financial ratios, its profit margins and rates of return, and its capital structure, and decide how strong the firm is financially. Table 1 contains a summary of various financial ratios and how they are calculated. Use it to assist in your financial diagnosis. Similarly, look at marketing, production, managerial competence, and other factors underlying the organization's strategic successes and failures. Decide whether the firm has core skills and competencies and, if so, whether it is capitalizing on them.

Check to see if the firm's strategy is producing satisfactory results and determine the reasons why or why not. Probe the nature and strength of the competitive forces confronting the company. Decide whether and why the firm's competitive position is getting stronger or weaker. Use the tools and concepts you have learned about to perform whatever analysis and evaluation is appropriate.

In writing your analysis and evaluation, bear in mind four things:

1. You are obliged to offer analysis and evidence to back up your conclusions. Do not rely on unsupported opinions, over-generalizations, and platitudes as a substitute for tight, logical argument backed up with facts and figures.

2. If your analysis involves some important quantitative calculations, use tables and charts to present the calculations clearly and efficiently. Don't just tack the exhibits on at the end of your report and let the reader figure out what they mean and why they were included. Instead, in the body of your report cite some of the key numbers, highlight the conclusions to be drawn from the exhibits, and refer the reader to your charts and exhibits for more details.

3. Demonstrate that you have command of the strategic concepts and analytical tools to which you have been exposed. Use them in your report.

4. Your interpretation of the evidence should be reasonable and objective. Be wary of preparing a one-sided argument that omits all aspects not favorable to your conclusions. Likewise, try not to exaggerate or overdramatize. Endeavor

[3]For some additional ideas and viewpoints, you may wish to consult Thomas J. Raymond, "Written Analysis of Cases," in *The Case Method at the Harvard Business School,* ed. M. P. McNair, pp. 139–63. Raymond's article includes an actual case, a sample analysis of the case, and a sample of a student's written report on the case.

to inject balance into your analysis and to avoid emotional rhetoric. Strike phrases such as "I think," "I feel," and "I believe" when you edit your first draft and write in "My analysis shows," instead.

Recommendations The final section of the written case analysis should consist of a set of definite recommendations and a plan of action. Your set of recommendations should address all of the problems/issues you identified and analyzed. If the recommendations come as a surprise or do not follow logically from the analysis, the effect is to weaken greatly your suggestions of what to do. Obviously, your recommendations for actions should offer a reasonable prospect of success. High-risk, bet-the-company recommendations should be made with caution. State how your recommendations will solve the problems you identified. Be sure the company is financially able to carry out what you recommend; also check to see if your recommendations are workable in terms of acceptance by the persons involved, the organization's competence to implement them, and prevailing market and environmental constraints. Try not to hedge or weasel on the actions you believe should be taken.

By all means state your recommendations in sufficient detail to be meaningful—get down to some definite nitty-gritty specifics. Avoid such unhelpful statements as "the organization should do more planning" or "the company should be more aggressive in marketing its product." For instance, do not simply say "the firm should improve its market position" but state exactly how you think this should be done. Offer a definite agenda for action, stipulating a timetable and sequence for initiating actions, indicating priorities, and suggesting who should be responsible for doing what.

In proposing an action plan, remember there is a great deal of difference between, on the one hand, being responsible, for a decision that may be costly if it proves in error and, on the other hand, casually suggesting courses of action that might be taken when you do not have to bear the responsibility for any of the consequences. A good rule to follow in making your recommendations is: *Avoid recommending anything you would not yourself be willing to do if you were in management's shoes.* The importance of learning to develop good judgment in a managerial situation is indicated by the fact that, even though the same information and operating data may be available to every manager or executive in an organization, the quality of the judgments about what the information means and which actions need to be taken does vary from person to person.[4]

It goes without saying that your report should be well organized and well written. Great ideas amount to little unless others can be convinced of their merit—this takes tight logic, the presentation of convincing evidence, and persuasively written arguments.

THE TEN COMMANDMENTS OF CASE ANALYSIS

As a way of summarizing our suggestions about how to approach the task of case analysis, we have compiled what we like to call "The Ten Commandments of Case Analysis." They are shown in Table 2. If you observe all or even most of these commandments faithfully as you prepare a case either for class discussion or for a written report, your chances of doing a good job on the assigned cases will be much improved. Hang in there, give it your best shot, and have some fun exploring what the real world of strategic management is all about.

---

[4]Gragg, "Because Wisdom Can't Be Told," p. 10.

TABLE 2 | **The Ten Commandments of Case Analysis**

To be observed in written reports and oral presentations, and while participating in class discussions.

1. Read the case twice, once for an overview and once to gain full command of the facts; then take care to explore every one of the exhibits.
2. Make a list of the problems and issues that have to be confronted.
3. Do enough number crunching to discover the story told by the data presented in the case. (To help you comply with this commandment, consult Table 1 to guide your probing of a company's financial condition and financial performance.)
4. Look for opportunities to use the concepts and analytical tools you have learned earlier.
5. Be thorough in your diagnosis of the situation and make at least a one- or two-page outline of your assessment.
6. Support any and all opinions with well-reasoned arguments and numerical evidence; don't stop until you can purge "I think" and "I feel" from your assessment and, instead, are able to rely completely on "My analysis shows."
7. Develop charts, tables, and graphs to expose more clearly the main points of your analysis.
8. Prioritize your recommendations and make sure they can be carried out in an acceptable time frame with the available skills and financial resources.
9. Review your recommended action plan to see if it addresses all of the problems and issues you identified.
10. Avoid recommending any course of action that could have disastrous consequences if it doesn't work out as planned; therefore, be as alert to the downside risks of your recommendations as you are to their upside potential and appeal.

THE MANAGER AS CHIEF STRATEGY-MAKER AND STRATEGY-IMPLEMENTER

CAMPUS DESIGNS, INC.

Barbara J. Allison, University of Alabama
A. J. Strickland, University of Alabama

Campus Designs, Inc. (CDI), a small vendor of collegiate licensed products located in Tuscaloosa, Alabama, was started in the spring of 1986 by four University of Alabama fraternity brothers, Seth Chapman, Billy and Tom Pittman, and David Gross, with an investment of $200 apiece. The fourth member, David Gross, was soon bought out by the other three because he was not contributing to the enterprise. Seth Chapman, who grew up in Ridgewood, New Jersey, and graduated from the University of Alabama with a major in marketing, described how Campus Designs got started:

> Noticing that [there were] a lot of T-shirts out on the market, I came up with an idea of my own design, and since I have no artistic ability I went to two fraternity brothers who used to do all our fraternity T-shirts . . . and I asked them if it was feasible to do this wraparound design that I had for a shirt. So, they got together, did a design, and we had it printed up.

Billy Pittman, who graduated from the University of Alabama in May 1984 with a double major in graphic design and communications, and his younger brother Tom, who planned to graduate in December 1990 with a bachelor of arts in advertising, were responsible for that first design, which featured banner-clad red and white elephants jovially parading around the bottom of a white T-shirt.

In the spring of 1986, Seth and Tom set up a credit account with a Tuscaloosa screen printing company, Promotional Pullovers, and had 25 of these original T-shirts printed up, which they sold out of a bedroom in their fraternity house. According to Seth, the shirts sold "pretty well," and it wasn't long until their fraternity brothers were wanting more shirts. Their fraternity's enthusiasm for the design inspired them to consider taking their imprinted T-shirts to local bookstores. Tom commented that

> We experienced a great deal of success with local bookstores, and that success eventually inspired us to turn the whole thing into a full-time business venture.

By 1989, Campus Designs had grown from a supplier of a single trademarked collegiate design, bearing a trademarked logo and design of the University of Alabama, which was only available in an adult-size T-shirt, to a supplier of (1) two trademarked collegiate designs, bearing the trademarked logos and designs of over 35 colleges and universities around the country; (2) a full line of fraternity and sorority designs; (3) "gameday" designs for the University of Alabama; and (4) custom designs for local organizations, made available in adult T-shirts, sweatshirts, and tank tops.

At the start of 1990, Seth, Billy, and Tom set some objectives that would help them focus better on how to grow their young company to its full potential. These objectives centered around the development of additional trademarked designs for more colleges and universities and the extension of their product line to include a line of children's clothing and additional adult-size apparel items. At the close of 1989, a review of Campus Designs' financial position revealed a healthy growth in sales for the year (see Exhibits 1 and 2). CDI's sales had increased from $10,000 in 1986 to $329,548 in 1989.

E X H I B I T 1 | Income Statement for Campus Designs, Inc., 1988 and 1989

	1989	1988
Sales	$329,548	$225,857
Cost of sales		
Purchases	130,139	102,565
Freight in	2,783	3,891
Printing	54,474	33.480
Total cost of sales	187,396	139,936
Gross profit	142,152	85,921
General and administrative expenses		
Accounting and legal fees	9,085	1,244
Advertising	9,237	4,686
Commissions	20,101	3,119
Depreciation	1,847	882
Dues and subscriptions	1,079	2,528
Insurance—liability	2,661	3,317
Interest	5,731	7,218
Market expense	9,438	3,989
Office supplies	2,808	1,422
Postage and freight	8,303	6,923
Rent	5,883	3,021
Royalties	14,582	9,323
Salaries—officers	27,277	1,891
Supplies	3,420	1,387
Taxes and licenses	4,884	1,141
Telephone	4,907	6,016
Travel and entertainment	5,952	6,328
Utilities	1,934	533
Collection cost	2,815	-0-
Miscellaneous	227	-0-
Total general and administrative expenses	142,171	64,968
Income (Loss) from operations	(19)	20,953
Income taxes	-0-	2,637
Net income (Loss)	$ (19)	$ 18,316

Source: Campus Designs, Inc.

EXHIBIT 2 | Balance Sheet for Campus Designs, Inc., 1988 and 1989

	1989	1988
ASSETS		
Current assets		
Cash	$ 793	$ 6,331
Accounts receivable—net	50,511	42,292
Inventory	23,809	17,279
Total current assets	75,113	65,902
Property, plant, and equipment		
Furniture and fixtures	9,236	6,003
Less: accumulated depreciation	2,730	882
Net property, plant, and equipment	6,506	5,121
Total assets	$81,125	$71,023
LIABILITIES AND STOCKHOLDERS' EQUITY		
Current liabilities		
Accounts payable	$15,590	$ 6,382
Accrued interest and taxes	5,708	2,798
Notes payable	5,798	2,655
Current portion—long-term debt	10,134	10,134
Total current liabilities	37,230	21,969
Long-term liabilities		
Notes payable	43,043	47,681
Less: current portion	10,134	10,134
Total long-term liabilities	32,909	37,547
Total liabilities	70,139	59,516
Stockholders' equity		
Common stock	840	840
Treasury stock	(2,520)	(2,520)
Retained earnings	12,666	13,187
Total stockholders' equity	10,986	11,507
Total liabilities and stockholders' equity	$81,125	$71,023

Source: Campus Designs, Inc.

The success of 1989 led the management team at CDI to refer to it as a "springboard" year and one that would bring with it major company changes, including an increased effort to boost company sales in the coming year. In order to facilitate their movement toward successful company growth, the three young men had purchased display space at a large athletic industry trade show where they could market their company's products to a wide buyer audience and also see how their product line stacked up against competitors'. The three young co-owners of CDI had attended the trade show for the past three years and had found the vibrant environment, daily industry seminars, and lectures that it offered to be extremely rewarding.

Each February, thousands of manufacturers, distributors, retailers, and curious spectators converged upon the World Congress Center in downtown Atlanta to participate in one of the largest athletic goods conventions in the world. Atlanta's World Congress Center was a fabulous convention facility that lent itself to major trade shows for buyers of all types of products. With several exhibit halls and thousands of square feet of exhibition space, the World Congress Center was capable of bringing several hundred vendors together to create extravagant displays of goods for distributors and retailers to consider carrying in their lines. The athletic goods convention, christened the Super Show, was a four-day showcase of the wares of nearly 2,000 companies involved in the production of athletic-related products, including exercise equipment, bowling balls, athletic shoes, sports posters, athletic apparel, and an array of objects embellished with sports themes. The Super Show was so large that attendees described it as a comprehensive "show-and-tell" assembly where one could learn a lot about what competitors were doing, gain a perspective of what was happening marketwide, and see what kinds of new products and styles were coming into the marketplace.

THE 1990 SUPER SHOW

Stepping into the Super Show arena, the casewriter was immediately struck by the bustle of activity—suavely dressed businessmen and businesswomen darted past; large groups of adolescent internationals fidgeted in registration lines; and muscle-bound males and Lycra-clad females strolled deliberately through the crowd.

From a nearby exhibit a thunderous roar of rock-and-roll music exploded above the din of the market floor. Simultaneously, clouds of smoke filled the air above a raised platform as a spectrum of stage lights blinked off and on in a continuous, unsynchronized pattern while strobe lights projected their glimmering rays in all directions. Human figures, outfitted in vendor apparel, could be detected sauntering across the elevated stage and the luminous blue letters A-D-I-D-A-S appeared overhead as the blanket of smoke slowly disappeared. The familiar crack of a bat making direct contact with a ball created a startling echo that vibrated through the air as a vendor demonstrated the attributes of his newest batting machine model to curious onlookers. Concurrently, the buzzers and bells of video games sounded in the background, and from the far end of the exhibit hall Converse answered the Adidas extravaganza with a deafening spectacle of its own. The enthusiasm, professionalism, and competitive spirit demonstrated by these sports vendors gave heightened meaning to the popular Nike aphorism "Just do it." Nestled among all this activity was the unpretentious exhibit of Campus Designs.

At one point, Tom Pittman moved along the seemingly endless rows of exhibitors of collegiate licensed products and reflected on the past days' events, especially the seminar he had attended concerning ways in which companies involved in the production of apparel items could integrate forward into screen printing their own designs onto the garments they supplied. CDI had not made a decision to put their own Campus Designs' label in the garments it vended (the company bought garments from Fruit of the Loom) nor to screen print its designs on the garments it sold. As an active step toward greater product control and reduced manufacturing costs, Seth, Billy, and Tom had been seriously considering doing the screen printing for their merchandise. While Tom made his way further along the aisles of competitors, he noticed that many of the vendors had modest exhibits comparable to CDI's. However, some of the larger, better-known suppliers, like Artex, had erected semipermanent two-story structures equipped with wet bars, upholstered seating areas, and elaborate audiovisual displays. The sight of these exhibits roused Tom's imagination and he envisioned the day when CDI might have such an exhibitor display.

Tom and his co-managers had been contemplating the future direction of CDI and what actions they would have to take in order to prepare their company to compete more effectively with these larger suppliers. Tom felt certain that the marketing ideas learned at the Super Show could be put to good use over the next few months in developing improved production, marketing, and management strategies for CDI.

THE COLLEGIATE LICENSING INDUSTRY

The collegiate licensing industry, an industry that consists of *any* object embellished with the trademarked logos, designs, and emblems of a collegiate institution, flourished in the 1980s (see Exhibit 3 for the trademarks of the University of Alabama). Initially, licensed products consisted mostly of apparel items such as T-shirts, sweats, caps, and jackets, but as the industry grew, so did the types of collegiate products available to consumers. In 1989, for example, diehard alumni of most major universities would have had little difficulty in purchasing a toilet seat with the likeness of the university's mascot adorning it. Other licensed products that became available to consumers over the years were auto accessories, calendars, blankets, fishing lures, license plates, furniture, jewelry, and insulated beverage holders.

Collegiate licensing was a neophyte industry in 1981, when Bill and Pat Battle (father and son) organized a centralized licensing agency, Collegiate Concepts International (CCI). Bill Battle was formerly the head football coach at the University of Tennessee and had won All-American honors playing for Paul "Bear" Bryant's 1961 national championship team at the University of Alabama. Some of the primary rea-

EXHIBIT 3 | **Trademarks of the University of Alabama**

The University of Alabama restricts the manner in which its official seal can be utilized. Therefore, written consent from the University of Alabama must be obtained prior to the manufacture of any sample or prototype of a product for review by the University of Alabama Licensing Advisory Committee.

WORDING　　　　　　　　　　　　　　　　　　**GRAPHICS**

University of Alabama ®
U of A ®
ALABAMA ®

BAMA ®
CRIMSON TIDE ®
ROLL TIDE ®

Source: The University of Alabama.

sons the Battles decided to form CCI were, among other things, to relieve university officials from the various formalities associated with licensing, to aid suppliers in obtaining licensing agreements, and to furnish retailers with the names of suppliers of "officially licensed collegiate products." Officially licensed collegiate products could be easily identified by the red, white, and blue hang-tag, or label, which was attached to every item approved by the consortium (see Exhibit 4). Over the next nine years, the market for collegiate licensed products grew from a $1 million-a-year industry in 1981 to a $1 billion-a-year industry in 1989, based on retail sales. The sales of collegiate licensed products had expanded at an average rate of 83 percent per year since 1985.[1]

In August 1983, CCI merged with International Collegiate Enterprises and formed a consortium called CCI/ICE (referred to as either CCI/ICE or CCI). By 1989 the consortium had generated licensing agreements with approximately 1,500 suppliers (200 national and the remaining 1,300 providing regional, state, or local service), and

EXHIBIT 4 | **Hang-Tags for Officially Licensed Collegiate Products**

**Hang-Tag for Officially Licensed
Collegiate Products Bearing the
Trademarks of CCI/ICE -
Represented Institutions**

Source: *The Sporting Goods Dealer,* August 1989, front cover.

**Hang-Tag for Officially Licensed
Collegiate Products Bearing the
Trademarks of Independent
(Non-CCI/ICE-Represented)
Institutions**

Source: Pat Battle, CCI/ICE.

---

[1]*The Sporting Goods Dealer,* August 1989, p. L-6.

was the exclusive agent for 108 major universities, 10 football bowl games, and the Southeastern Conference. In 1989 the retail sales of products bearing the trademarks of CCI/ICE–represented universities topped the $300 million mark (see Exhibit 5). CCI believed it was the agent for 34 percent of the retail sales in the collegiate licensing industry.

CCI was not an agent for transactions involving its licensed suppliers and some institutions that preferred to handle their own licensing directly—most notably, Notre Dame, the University of Michigan, and the University of Miami (FL). Officials from these independent universities had recently held an informal meeting at which they developed their own official collegiate licensing hang-tag (see Exhibit 4). It was not unusual for independent universities to require special fees of companies wanting to manufacture or distribute items imprinted with their official trademarks. For instance,

EXHIBIT 5 | **Retail Sales of Products Bearing the Trademarks of CCI/ICE-Represented Institutions**

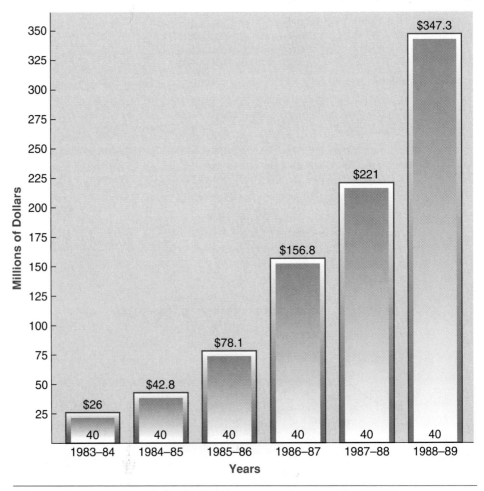

*The remaining $652,700,000 of the $1,000,000,000 were retail sales not involving CCI/ICE.

†Projected sales.

Source: *The Sporting Goods Dealer,* August 1989, p. L-2.

licensing agreements with UCLA required the supplier to provide the university with a $1,000 cash advance on sales.[2]

Once a licensing agreement was established between CCI/ICE and a supplier, it was CCI/ICE's responsibility to act as a liaison between that supplier and the consortium's member institutions. The licensing committees for individual universities reserved the right to allow suppliers to produce and sell products bearing the logos and trademarks of their institutions or to refuse suppliers that privilege. At the present time, a supplier had to pay a university a standard royalty fee of 6.5 percent of the net wholesale price of each item sold for the use of its trademarked logos, designs, and emblems. The various suppliers sent the dollar amounts they owed institutions, based on this royalty fee, directly to CCI/ICE for further processing.

According to Dr. Finus Gaston, associate director of business services and purchasing manager at the University of Alabama:

> Traditionally for the past six years universities have charged [suppliers] a 6.5 percent [sometimes 7.5 percent] royalty fee of their net wholesale price [to retailers]. As of January 1990, that's going to change a bit because about 35 to 45 percent of the universities have decided that they need to be more in line with the royalty rates charged by the National Football League, Major League Baseball, the National Hockey League, and the National Basketball Association. Their royalty fees run anywhere from 9 to 11 percent.

Insuring that member institutions received these royalty fees was one of the major services provided by the CCI/ICE consortium. CCI-affiliated suppliers were required to mail the royalty fees they owed member institutions directly to CCI/ICE headquarters. CCI then retained a percentage of the gross royalties owed to its member institutions as compensation for services rendered. The basic fee CCI charged an institution was based on the wholesale dollar amount of licensed products bearing the trademarked logos, designs, and emblems of that institution that were sold by the various CCI/ICE-affiliated suppliers to retailers. As a rule, the greater the dollar volume, the smaller the percentage fee, but the service was negotiable and could vary based on other factors. According to CCI's Pat Battle:

> The overhead fee charged by CCI is based on the individual relationships we have with any given university and the university always receives a majority of the royalties it has earned.

Without revealing specific fee numbers, Battle indicated that CCI's standard fee schedule was stair-stepped downward as sales volume rose: the highest percentage fee applied to the first $50,000 of licensed products sold by the various CCI/ICE-affiliated suppliers to retailers; the service fee decreased at each of the next three $50,000 intervals of licensed products sold; on all sales over $200,000 the fee became a level fixed percentage.

In 1989 CCI/ICE paid out $8,000,000 in royalty fees. Of the $550,000 in gross royalties generated by the University of Alabama in 1989, $32,000 went to CCI/ICE in the form of a basic overhead fee. University of Alabama officials allocated the university's $518,000 in net royalties to the athletic department budget, a program supporting graduate scholarships, and to the university's internal administrative overhead account. Likewise, Ohio State University set aside $100,000 of its royalties for scholarships.[3]

---

[2]Interview with Billy Pittman.
[3]Candyce Meherani and Rachel Orr, "Be True to Your School," *Nation's Business* 75 (June 1987), pp. 46, 48.

Approximately 80 to 85 percent of the royalties received by CCI/ICE member institutions came from suppliers' sales of apparel items; the remainder came from suppliers' sale of hard goods, such as chairs, clocks, glassware, bumper stickers, car tags, pennants, and watches.[4] Of CCI/ICE's 1,500 suppliers, 300 handled only the so-called hard-goods items. The remaining 1,200 supplied only soft goods or both soft and hard goods.

PRODUCTS/SUPPLIERS

Many licensed suppliers of collegiate products were not only engaged in the production or vending of collegiate apparel items, but the production or vending of other licensed products, such as "huggers," key chains, sunglasses, blankets, and Frisbees. The Game, one of the larger suppliers, for example, offered a wide range of apparel items, including T-shirts, sweatpants, caps, scarves, and gloves, while at the same time providing a host of other products such as team pennants and souvenirs. Many of the smaller suppliers carried only T-shirts, tank tops, and sweatshirts, while larger suppliers, such as Champion Products, Inc., carried larger garment selections consisting of athletic uniforms, recreational and leisure wear, cycling clothes, Lycra workout outfits, and athletic shoes. The various types of suppliers in the collegiate licensing industry are shown in Exhibit 6.

Exhibit 7 contains the names of the top 50 CCI/ICE–affiliated suppliers, based on 1989 sales volume. The sales and market shares of the top 10 CCI/ICE-affiliated suppliers are shown in Exhibit 8.

The major players in this industry had adopted various production methods that they believed to be conducive to the implementation of effective and efficient business operations. Russell Athletic, for example, was a fully integrated national supplier. Its operations spanned the entire manufacturing process: spinning the yarn from cotton and synthetic fibers such as polyester; producing woven and knit fabrics; dying, bleaching, screen printing, and otherwise finishing those fabrics; and manufacturing finished apparel in various cutting and sewing operations. Russell had over 5,000,000 square feet of office, manufacturing, and warehousing space.[5] The com-

EXHIBIT 6 | **Types of Suppliers of Collegiate Licensed Products**

Types of Supplier	Percentage of Suppliers
Fully integrated manufacturer (makes own garments, does own designs, does own screen printing, and may have own in-house sales force)	Less than 1%
Does own designs and own screen printing (or contracts screen printing to outsiders) on garments having the supplier's private label	5%
Does own designs and screen printing on garments having the manufacturer's label	75%
Design only; purchases garments from manufacturer and contracts out screen printing	Approximately 19%

Source: Pat Battle, CCI/ICE.

---

[4]Interview with Pat Battle, CCI/ICE.
[5]Russell Corporation, Annual Report, 1988.

EXHIBIT 7 | **Top 50 CCI/ICE-Affiliated Suppliers of Collegiated Licensed Products**

1. Champion Products, Inc.	26. PM Enterprises
2. Galt Sand	27. Ebert Sportswear, Inc.
3. Nutmeg Mills	28. Bike Athletic
4. Game Sports Novelties	29. H. H. Cutler
5. Artex	30. Fieldcrest Cannon
6. Logo 7	31. Touchdown Sportswear
7. Russell Athletic	32. Sports Specialties
8. H. Wolf & Sons, Inc.	33. Hutch Sporting Goods
9. Rah-Rah Sales, Inc.	34. Name Droppers Int.
10. Chalk Line	35. Trau & Loenver, Inc.
11. Starter Sportswear	36. Gamemaster Athletic
12. Velva Sheen	37. Javelin
13. M. J. Soffe Co.	38. Athletic Distributors
14. Desert Sportswear	39. Rella Corp.
15. Jansport / Downers	40. P. & K. Products
16. College Concepts	41. Custom T's
17. Winning Ways/Gear	42. Ram Graphics
18. National Screenprint	43. R. C. Sportswear
19. Gulf Coast Sportswear	44. MVP Corp.
20. Robby's Sporting Goods	45. Ross Sportswear
21. Sports Products of America	46. American Screen Printing Co.
22. Custom Silk Screen	47. J & M Sportswear
23. Dodger Manufacturing	48. Imprinted Products Corp.
24. Swingster	49. Third Street Sportswear
25. Tultex	50. Carolina Connection

Source: *The Sporting Goods Dealer,* August 1989, p. L-14.

pany employed a staff of individuals specifically responsible for the development of graphic designs imprinted on apparel items. The majority of these designs were for officially licensed products of universities and professional sports teams. The manufacturing processes that Russell Athletic utilized for its imprinted sportswear were both automated and manual. According to Terrie Lashley, Russell Athletic's Eastern sales manager, manual processes were reserved for smaller or extremely intricate screen printing jobs. Ms. Lashley also stated:

> Russell's direct participation in the entire manufacturing process allows us to maintain greater control over our supply of materials, the fabric content of our products, the quality of our products, and basic apparel design, and, even more important than these, it allows us to keep production costs down.

Ms. Lashley observed that Russell's relatively low production costs gave the company a competitive advantage over suppliers with less integrated operations who obtained their goods in small lots from sewing contractors or who obtained their garments in bulk lots and farmed out the screen printing function.

Russell was also involved in providing branded and private label apparel items to other suppliers, many of whom it was in direct competition with. Russell's branded apparel items bore the Jerzees™ label, recognized as a sign of quality by both retailers and consumers. Private-label garments provided by Russell contained a label with whatever name and logo the purchaser specified.

Large national suppliers such as The Game and Artex purchased private-label goods from apparel makers and did their own screen printing. Such an arrangement

EXHIBIT 8 | **Top 10 CCI/ICE Suppliers: Market Share, Sales, and Production Method**

Company	Market Share	Sales to Retailers	Type of Supplier
Champion Products, Inc.	8.0%	$13,892,000	Fully integrated manufacturer using own brand in garment
Galt Sand	5.0	8,682,500	Uses own private label in garments supplied by outside manufacturer
Nutmeg Mills	4.7	8,161,550	Uses own private label in garments supplied by outside manufacturer
The Game	3.4	5,904,100	Uses own private label in garments supplied by outside manufacturer
Artex	3.3	5,730,450	Uses own private label in garments supplied by outside manufacturer
Logo 7	3.1	5,383,150	Uses own private label in garments supplied by outside manufacturer
Russell Athletic	2.9	5,035,850	Fully integrated manufacturer using own brand in garment
H. Wolf & Sons, Inc.	2.75	4,775,375	Uses own private label in garments supplied by outside manufacturer
Rah-Rah Sales, Inc.	2.1	3,646,650	Uses garments carrying outside manufacturer's brand
Chalk Line	1.9	3,299,350	Uses own private label in garments supplied by outside manufacturer

Source: Pat Battle, CCI/ICE.

allowed these companies to retain responsibility for graphics and design and the quality of their print work while relying on the services of such apparel manufacturers as Fuentes and Badger for their supply of blank apparel items.

According to Davey Solomon, vice president of finance and materials management, The Game is not involved in the production of "blanks" (the name given to apparel items that have not yet been imprinted) because the production process can be very capital- and labor-intensive. Buying blanks in bulk, imprinted with The Game's private label, allowed the company to achieve brand identity and concentrate all its resources on marketing and distribution without having to invest scarce dollars in the manufacturing process. The Game, which was not in the collegiate licensing business five years ago, had wholesale sales of $25,000,000 annually (equal to $50 million at retail), much of which came from the sale of collegiate licensed products. Solomon indicated that while The Game had established sound relationships with its private-label suppliers, it did not have a lot of buying leverage insofar as being able to negotiate lower prices on its garment purchases. According to Mr. Solomon, this was true of all companies who bought blanks imprinted with their private labels.

Rah-Rah Sales, Inc., which for the past four years had utilized private-label blanks and done its screen printing in-house, was switching to branded blanks from private-label blanks. The company was also closing a company-operated cut-and-sew facility used to make fleece shorts, shimmel shirts, and T-shirts. The major reason for the company's move away from the use of private-label merchandise was a marked loss of business from major department stores. Many department store shoppers were discerning enough to recognize that they could purchase a shirt, even if it was not of the same design, with a Rah-Rah label in it from a discount store for 20 to 25 percent less than if they purchased it from a leading department store. Rah-Rah Sales felt that switching to apparel items carrying the brands of well-known manufacturers would allow the company to preserve its profitable relationship with department stores. By sourcing garments for its department store customers from suppliers such as Hanes, Fruit of the Loom, or Russell Athletic and sourcing blanks for its own private-label garments from its present supplier, H. L. Miller, Rah-Rah's management hoped to move the company toward differentiation of its products strictly by design.

DISTRIBUTION / MARKETING

In the early 1980s between 30 and 40 percent of collegiate licensed products were sold at campus bookstores, college athletic events, and off-campus bookstores. By 1990, however, the suppliers of collegiate licensed products had expanded their distribution channels to include J.C. Penney, Wal-Mart, Sears, sporting goods stores, and upscale and specialty apparel stores, driving the market share of campus-related retailers down to under 5 percent. Even so, the volume of collegiate licensed products being sold at campus bookstores, college athletic events, and off-campus bookstores was greater than ever due to mushrooming sales industrywide.[6]

The suppliers of collegiate products used various distribution channels. Exhibits 9 and 10 outline the distribution systems utilized by Champion Products and Russell Athletic, respectively. While both of these companies utilized the services of independent manufacturers' representatives on occasion (both Champion Products and Russell Athletic had their own in-house sales forces as well), they used sales agents that did not represent competing lines.

The Game utilized 70 independent sales representatives geographically scattered across the United States; these sales reps, although handling lines other than collegiate licensed products, were exclusive agents for The Game's line of collegiate products and did not handle competing lines of collegiate items.

For the most part, suppliers with broad geographic coverage and wide product lines had a competitive advantage over narrow-line and local suppliers because of the quality of service they offered retailers, the larger selection of merchandise they carried, and the relatively lower prices they could offer due to scaled economies.

Pat Battle commented that CCI/ICE picked up about 30 new suppliers per month and lost about 10 suppliers per month. The chief reason suppliers withdrew was their poorly developed distribution system and inability to generate a profitable volume of orders from retail outlets. Battle cited instances where mediocre products thrived in the industry because companies had succeeded in convincing retailers to carry their line while potential gold mine products failed miserably because suppliers were

---

[6]Interview with Finus Gaston, associate director of business services and purchasing manager, University of Alabama.

EXHIBIT 9 | **Marketing and Distribution Approaches of Champion Products, Inc.**

Distribution Channels	Products	Sales Approach	Commission	Consumer Segments
Athletic/ institutional	Athletic uniforms (custom and standardized)	Company sales force of approximately 90 persons—sell direct to consumer	7%	Coaches, equipment managers, end users
Bookstore	Imprinted athletic and recreational wear	Same as athletic/ institutional market	7%	Independent and university-affiliated bookstores and leased store operations
Retail	Imprinted athletic and recreational wear, including those bearing the "Champion" and "C" logos; Lycra workout outfits; cycling clothes; athletic shoe line	Company sales force of approximately 50 persons (separate from that of the athletic/institutional market)	5%	Major department stores, specialty stores, athletic retailers, the military
Special markets	Products centered around corporate premium promotions, sales to theme parks and resorts, specialty catalog sales	Special promotions done by the company		Corporations, theme parks, resorts, and mail-order catalog sales
Factory outlet stores	Discontinued styles, overruns, manufacturing seconds, customer returns	Sold directly through 23 factory outlet stores		General public
International	"Champion"-branded products	Licensees in foreign countries		Foreign countries including: Austria, Belgium, Canada, England, Finland, Germany, Greece, Italy, Japan, Netherlands, Norway, Spain, Sweden, and Switzerland

*Company hopes that the growth of this market will help them develop a private label business.
Source: Champion Products, Inc., Annual Report, 1988.

unable to secure adequate wholesale or retail distribution. It was common for the larger suppliers to market their collegiate licensed products internationally as well as nationally and several advertised their licensed products in popular men's and women's fashion and sports magazines and trade journals. A few suppliers had developed point-of-sale displays for in-store use by retailers carrying their lines; this was more common for hard-goods items than for apparel wear.

INDUSTRY GROWTH

The growth of the collegiate licensing industry was traceable to a number of factors. During the 1980s comfortable, loose-fitting apparel items were seen as the perfect answer for the more active and casual life-styles that were emerging. Movies such as *Flashdance,* with their sportswear-clad starlets, maneuvered activewear items out of the gym and into the classroom, grocery store, and the workplace. Apparel items with the trademarks of universities, which previously were worn primarily by university students, gained popularity not only among this initial segment but with other consumer segments as a result.

E X H I B I T 1 0 | **Marketing and Distribution Approaches Used by Russell Athletic Corp.**

Distribution Channels	Products	Sales Approach	Consumer Segments
Athletic division	Athletic uniforms—sold under the Russell Athletic label (custom and standardized)—and activewear	Company salesmen and six independent sales agents who maintain offices in 12 locations throughout the United States and Canada	Sporting goods dealers, college bookstores, sports specialty shops, department stores
Knit apparel division	Wide variety of knitted apparel under the company's Jerzees™ brand and private labels	Company salesmen out of offices located in New York, Chicago, Atlanta, and Alexander City	Mass merchandisers, wholesalers, discounters, chain stores, screen printers
Fabrics division	Woven fabrics in a wide variety of patterns	Company's own marketing staff from offices located in New York, Atlanta, and Alexander City; sales representatives located in Dallas, Denver, Los Angeles, Miami, Philadelphia, Montreal, and Toronto	Other manufacturers of apparel
Quality mills	Knit products under the Cross Creek label including placket shirts, rugby styled shirts, and turtlenecks	Company-employed sales force with offices in Mt. Airy, Los Angeles, and New York and outside agents	Golf shops, department stores, and specialty shops

Source: Russell Athletic, Annual Report, 1988.

Also, the creative spirit exhibited by suppliers of collegiate licensed products helped fuel industry growth. Imaginative and unique designs began to pour into the marketplace. Garments exhibiting a simple, classic university emblem or traditional mascot design were complemented with all kinds of individualistic, unique, one-of-a-kind, and special-occasion designs. People who wanted something that was different from what the person sitting next to them had on or something that was a reflection of the individual's personality or disposition could find items to their liking. There were items for almost every taste and price range. Designers displayed university mascots and emblems in a variety of ways. Consumers were given an assortment of themes to choose from: happy, sad, and even provocative mascots; designs with hearts, bears, happy faces, and cartoon characters on them; and the names of universities presented in block lettering or script.

Other reasons for the rapid growth in the sales of collegiate licensed products included

- A rise in the number of televised collegiate athletic events.
- Increased regional fan support for college athletic programs.
- Growing popularity of universities with successful athletic programs.

As one licensing specialist put it, "The ties to alma maters are so strong that people want to wear them (licensed goods) even if you're living in Los Angeles and you went to Bates College in Maine." Rising enrollments and the growing number of alumni a university had also played a vital part in the popularity of its licensed merchandise (see Exhibit 11).

EXHIBIT 11 | **Top Royalty Recipients**

Ranked below are the top CCI/ICE member institutions in order of royalty receipts for 1988–89. Large enrollments and total alumni play a major part in the popularity of merchandise with a respective college's license. Success in the athletic arena is another key factor in licensed products' demand.

Rank	School	Enrollment	Total Alumni
1.	Michigan	32,432	323,025
2.	North Carolina	20,300	174,000
3.	Indiana	32,550	290,267
4.	Alabama	16,000	150,000
5.	Georgia	26,000	170,000
6.	Kentucky	21,500	76,967
7.	Georgetown	11,967	70,000
8.	Florida State	22,550	140,479
9.	Tennessee	25,842	180,000
10.	Auburn	19,000	115,217
11.	Nebraska	22,730	204,000
12.	Purdue	32,243	235,000
13.	Illinois	34,854	391,652
14.	Arizona State	41,470	115,000
15.	Arizona	23,943	117,778
16.	Clemson	13,062	N.A.
17.	South Carolina	22,685	174,000
18.	North Carolina St.	24,558	N.A.
19.	Kansas	26,500	185,000
20.	Yale	5,151	115,000
21.	Duke	5,100	80,000
22.	Virginia	17,629	110,000
23.	Louisville	21,087	68,000
24.	Maryland	32,528	300,000
25.	Wisconsin	44,584	226,159
26.	UNLV	13,500	17,500
27.	Georgia Tech	11,500	77,805
28.	Hawaii	19,700	N.A.
29.	Oklahoma St.	21,000	N.A.
30.	Mississippi	10,840	56,000
31.	Boston College	14,561	165,000
32.	Connecticut	17,085	85,000
33.	Vanderbilt	8,968	77,000
34.	Kansas St.	19,301	N.A.
35.	Delaware	13,400	N.A.

N.A. Not Available.

Source: *The Sporting Goods Dealer,* August 1989, p. L-4.

LICENSING ISSUES

The collegiate licensing industry was plagued by the existence of unlicensed collegiate goods in the marketplace. The sale of such goods was illegal. Therefore, CCI/ICE had taken steps to enforce its exclusive right to license the trademarked logos, designs, and emblems of those entities it represented. The consortium's present course of action when dealing with a supplier or retailer of unlicensed goods was first to ask the company to discontinue the unauthorized use of the university's trademarked logos, designs, and emblems; follow the initial request with a cease-and-desist letter, personal visits, and telephone calls; and, as a last resort, to proceed with litigation. Litigation required that a university whose trademarked logos, designs, and emblems were being infringed upon initiate legal action. CCI/ICE guided the process, and CCI/ICE attorneys prosecuted the case if the university so desired.

CCI/ICE representatives had banded together with various city officials to try to bring a speedy halt to the selling of unlicensed goods. Many cities had implemented infringement ordinances that supplemented existing trademark laws. These ordinances were carried out by enforcement teams, usually consisting of university representatives, CCI/ICE members, and individuals from the city's police department and legal office. These enforcement teams visited stadium vendors who sold their products to sporting fans as they approached sporting events and retailers to check for unlicensed products. If unlicensed products were found, a number of things could happen to the merchant: (1) the merchant could be asked to remove all unlicensed products from sale, (2) the business could be closed down, (3) the merchant could be arrested. In many instances retailers were not even aware of the licensing programs that were in effect. CCI/ICE believed that it was imperative to take aggressive action in stopping the sale of unlicensed products. The consortium saw its best long-run strategy being continued enforcement of the universal use of the "officially licensed collegiate products" hang-tag.

Another issue confronting the collegiate licensing industry was that of copyright infringement. In order to combat the problem of competitors' pirating their designs, many suppliers copyrighted their designs. Suppliers who did not have their designs copyrighted were at the mercy of suppliers who did "knock-offs" of their designs.

The collegiate licensing industry as a whole did not endorse the selling of products imprinted with offensive language, derogatory messages, inappropriate graphics, or messages that reflected adversely upon a university institution. CCI/ICE, along with university officials, had been stepping up measures to insure that knock-offs and offensive products were kept out of the marketplace. This was not an easy task and, according to one licensing official, "The consumer needs to be educated about licensed goods . . . they should be cautioned to buy only those items bearing collegiate markings that have the 'officially licensed collegiate products' hang-tag." The "officially licensed collegiate products" hang-tag did not, however, guarantee a quality product; rather it signified only that a product had been manufactured under legal, university-sanctioned conditions.

Because of the rapid growth of collegiate and sports team licensing, industry observers had speculated that apparel companies such as Fruit of the Loom and Hanes would get in on the action through some form of forward integration. In early 1989, Hanes, a subsidiary of Sara Lee Corp., did so by acquiring Champion Products. Although the acquisition was not solely for the purpose of Champion's extensive licensing business (Champion was in other market segments that were of strategic interest to Sara Lee), Champion's licensing business was seen as both lucrative and having excellent growth potential.

TRENDS

One of the major trends taking place in the collegiate licensing industry was the subtle modification of basic garment designs. Oversized T-shirts were especially popular among adolescent girls and young adult females, doubling as both daywear and sleepwear and, according to their users, being extremely comfortable. Another trend involved cross-licensing of cartoon and animated characters (such as Snoopy, Bugs Bunny, and Elmer Fudd) with collegiate and or professional sports teams; this expanded design possibilities. Several companies, including Nutmeg Mills, Artex, and Chalk Line, had acquired licensing rights to various cartoon and animated characters. David Mitchell, director of retail licensing for NFL Properties, explained the synergism created when cartoon and sport licenses teamed up:

> People who might not think of buying a Snoopy garment by itself would consider buying it if it had the NFL [or college] logo on it . . . The reverse is also true. Someone who wouldn't buy an NFL [or college] licensed item by itself, like a grandmother buying for a grandchild, would buy it if it had Snoopy on it because of the element of cuteness.

In addition, there were growing numbers of hard-goods and soft-goods products embellished with the trademarked logos, designs, and emblems of universities—rear window brake lights in cars, telephones, underwear, towels, beanbag chairs, and jewelry. Suppliers were endeavoring to differentiate their designs through the use of metallic and neon ink and screen printing processes that made their designs resemble newsprint or appear to be three dimensional. A trend, popular among college students, was the gameday T-shirt displaying the date, location, and the names of the competing teams in a multicolored design; smaller companies were more likely to provide such specialized products than were larger companies, mainly because of the small production runs and localized markets.

CAMPUS DESIGNS, INC.

When we started selling to the bookstores the T-shirts were selling well . . . that's when we kind of had an idea in our head[s] that it might be something a little bit more than making a little extra money to buy beer or whatever on.

Seth Chapman
Cofounder of Campus Designs

When Campus Designs was first getting started, the three cofounders wanted to make sure that the product they were marketing, which was embellished with a trademarked logo and design of the University of Alabama, was legal. This led them to Finus Gaston. By June 1986, a licensing agreement had been signed between the University of Alabama and Campus Designs. Gaston asked the cofounders to get in contact with CCI/ICE for assistance with any licensing opportunities that might become available in the future. Campus Designs signed on with CCI/ICE shortly thereafter and began marketing its product more aggressively, especially in Alabama. Seth pointed out:

> We then went to a sporting goods store to find out if we could sell through the chain, and they were interested, and [bookstores] as well as other people [we were selling to] started asking for shirts imprinted with logos and designs for other schools besides Alabama.

With this increased interest in their product, Tom and Billy began developing designs for three other universities in the Southeastern Conference—Auburn, Georgia, and Florida. By the fall of 1986, CDI had severed its ties with its original screen printer, Promotional Pullovers, and was utilizing the services of a newly established screen printing operation—Art Works. Art Works' management team consisted of three individuals: Brian Johnson, owner; Mark Gambel, office manager; and Tom LaBee, production manager. All were former employees of Promotional Pullovers.

During the spring and summer of 1986, Campus Designs ran its business out of Tom's bedroom at the fraternity house and a rented house where Seth was living. T-shirt shipments were received at the rented house, while Tom's room functioned as storage space for the T-shirts and the address for important business mail. As sales began to grow, so did the need for a more functional place of business. In the fall of 1986 the cofounders transferred their operations to a rented apartment where Tom and Seth had begun living. This arrangement remained until the spring of 1988. According to Seth:

> We moved into an apartment about a mile away, fairly close to campus, and that got really bad because I ended up sleeping with sweatshirts. My apartment, when Tom was living with me, was just covered with sweatshirts and T-shirts and paper. We had salesmen coming in there, so it was really a tight scene. And then we realized that we needed to move our office somewhere where we would just do our office work so we'd have a place to sleep and be able to live comfortably and get away from things.

In early 1988, the company decided to share an office in downtown Tuscaloosa with Art Works; the rent was split 50–50.

By mid-1988, CDI was starting to prosper. Tom and Seth had set up a joint account at Central Bank of Tuscaloosa, through which business operations were handled. As the business continued to grow, so did their need for working capital to finance inventories and accounts receivable. They found it necessary, as Seth put it, to start "hitting our parents up for money." Their parents agreed to cosign a loan. The bank loan gave Campus Designs the financial flexibility needed to foster its growth. The company was able to purchase blanks in greater volume, cover screen printing costs, and expand geographic market coverage to other southeastern universities.

Before long CDI began to outgrow the office space that it shared with Art Works; office space adjacent to Art Works was rented, providing 1,400 square feet of storage, drafting, and office space for Campus Designs to operate in. By early 1990, the business had grown to the point where more space was needed and the owners were looking for a location that would provide them with more room.

CAMPUS DESIGN'S PRODUCT LINE

Products offered by CDI in 1989 consisted of two trademarked lines of apparel, Campus Rapp™ and Circle-M™, a complete line of fraternity and sorority designs, gameday shirts, and custom designs for special events sponsored by local organizations. Apparel items were limited to T-shirts, sweatshirts, and tank tops available in adult sizes only. In 1989, Campus Designs experienced a drastic falloff in demand for its tank tops; sales of the once-popular garment type were not expected to rise in the coming year. All production requirements, other than design, were contracted out to other organizations.

CAMPUS DESIGN'S SUPPLIERS OF BLANKS

Originally, Promotional Pullovers supplied Campus Designs with all its manufacturing needs, from supplying blank apparel items to performing the screen printing process. Promotional Pullovers charged CDI the normal screen printing price for their services. However, as CDI's sales grew, the owners began to look for ways to lower costs. Their search for lower-cost suppliers was complicated by the fact that the industry was undergoing a cotton shortage—prices were high and supplies of all-cotton garments were limited. The agreements Campus Designs had with its blanks suppliers left the company subject to late deliveries and expensive COD charges.

In the summer of 1987, Campus Designs investigated the possibility of establishing an account with Hanes, Inc., to supply blanks, but found the asking prices too high. A few months later the company decided to use Fruit of the Loom as its principal supplier. Accounts with several other wholesalers were maintained as backups in case Fruit of the Loom was unable to fill the company's orders on a timely basis.

In late 1989, Fruit of the Loom announced price increases for the coming year that were substantial enough for CDI to consider changing suppliers. In shopping the market for alternative sources of supply, Campus Designs learned that blank apparel items could be obtained from Hanes at prices comparable to the new prices being charged by Fruit of the Loom. However, the three owners concluded that the business relationship they had established with Fruit of the Loom, considering their dependable service and quality products, justified continuation with the company's present supplier.

The following is a schedule of the prices CDI paid for blank apparel items in 1989:

Item	Price
Tanks	$2.00
T-shirts	2.40
Sweatshirts:	
Raglan	4.42
Set-in	5.04

SCREEN PRINTING

The ties the co-owners had established with Promotional Pullovers had paid off when Brian Johnson, a former Promotional Pullovers employee, had established Art Works. Brian, along with Mark Gambel and Tom LaBee, had broken with Promotional Pullovers because of conflicts with its management. CDI began using the screen printing services of Art Works as soon as it was operational early in the fall of 1986.

CDI's relationship with Art Works had evolved over the last few years. Initially, Campus Designs relied on Art Works for the entire screen printing process. Beginning in mid-1988, Campus Designs began supplying film positives to Art Works, significantly reducing screen printing costs. The prices Art Works charged Campus Designs for their services in 1989 were as follows:

Campus Designs became concerned when Art Works announced new screen print-

Screen charge with film positive provided by Art Works*	$18 per screen
Screen charge with film positive provided by customer	14 per screen
Screen printing charge per garment—regular design	0.46 each
Screen printing charge per garment—wraparound design	0.82 each
10% surcharge on rush jobs	

*Designs can require up to six or more screens per garment depending on the number of colors in the design.

Source: Campus Designs.

Campus Designs became concerned when Art Works announced new screen printing prices starting in 1990. Charges for small orders, the majority of orders placed by CDI, were scheduled to go up more than 30 percent, and in some cases as much as 200 percent, plus the surcharge on rush orders was to be increased from 10 to 20 percent. With this news and on the advice of their accountant, the owners of CDI began actively seeking alternative screen printing options. It was Campus Designs' practice to have a design screen printed as orders for the design were placed. This had resulted in CDI placing small monthly screen printing orders, for the same designs, with Art Works, creating high setup costs for Art Works. The following is a summary of the size of screen printing orders CDI usually placed with Art Works:

Order Size	Approximate Number of Units	As a Percentage of Orders
Small	30–70	75.0%
Medium	71–359	12.5
Large	360–600+	12.5

THE SCREEN PRINTING PROCESS

Tom LaBee, who oversaw the majority of Art Works' screen printing processes, and Mark Gambel described for the casewriter what is involved in screen printing apparel items. Two distinct processes can be utilized for screen printing materials—a manual process and an automated process. Art Works employed a manual process. Film positives of the design to be screen printed are shot onto screens of clear plastic acetate. Separate film positives are taken for the various parts of the designs that are to appear in different colors.

The individual screens, with their black images, are then exposed to ultraviolet light. The ultraviolet light exposes emulsions on the screen, resulting in a nonporous surface. When the screens have been exposed to the ultraviolet light for the proper amount of time, anywhere from 15 to 20 minutes, they are removed and rinsed down with tap water. The black images on the screens create porous surfaces through which the inks used in screen printing can flow. Next, the screens are clamped securely into place in a manual screen printing apparatus with a revolving base. The apparatus can hold up to six screens at one time. The arms of the apparatus onto which the screens are clamped have an area above them into which colors of ink, corresponding to the design on the screen, are poured. The ink used in screen printing is an ink plastisol, which is the same material, in liquid form, out of which the plastic handles of many pliers and other hardware tools are made.

The individual pieces of clothing to be printed are stretched smooth over a stationary base onto which the various arms of the manual screen printing apparatus are lowered. A squeegee is then pulled across the encasement of ink plastisol, dispersing ink through the porous sections of the individual screens and onto the pieces of clothing. This process is done one screen at a time and one piece of clothing at a time. When the design is complete, the piece of clothing is removed from the stationary base and placed on a conveyor belt which carries it through a large dryer set at 270 degrees Fahrenheit. The drying process utilized by Art Works took two and a half minutes to complete.

In automated processes the articles of clothing are sent along a conveyor belt, which is driven by a hydraulic timing chain. The screens with their various designs and ink colors are hydraulically lowered onto the various pieces of clothing. When the design is complete, the printed items are sent through a dryer. In automated screen printing, the process has to be done under supervision and the changing of screens has to be done manually.

Mark Gambel noted that a major difference between manual and automated screen printing is that machines can work for hours on end, where manual screen printing is strenuous and the workers need to take periodic breaks. He commented further, however, that for a company the size of Art Works, doing relatively small print jobs, a manual process is actually more economical and faster than an automated process would be. Another difference between manual and automated processes is the price of the machinery involved. Automated machinery could cost anywhere from $3,000 to $100,000, while manual equipment ranges from $200 to $2,000. Comparative prices for manual and automatic screen printing equipment in 1989 were as follows:

Equipment	Manual Price	Automated
2–4 arm screen printer	$ 200–500	
4–6 arm screen printer	500–1,200	$20,000–40,000
6–8 arm screen printer	1,200–2,000	40,000–100,000
Very small dryer		3,000
Small dryer		6,000–10,000
Medium dryer		10,000–20,000
Large dryer		20,000–30,000

Source: Campus Designs, Inc.

Graphic Designs Billy, who along with his brother Tom, was responsible for most of the company's artwork, explained his start with Campus Designs:

> [I] got started with Campus Designs in a roundabout way. We started out selling the designs locally and to a few other universities, and I was doing the artwork in Huntsville while working a full-time job. It developed into a full-time effort on my part in 1987 and 1988 when we really started getting the business going.

The company's first design was a wraparound front and back print design, which was given the name Campus Rapp. Tom and Billy used their creative talents and came up with a version of this design for 39 colleges and universities. In 1989, they created a second design, trademarked as Circle-M, which Billy explained was

> [an adaptation] of a design that was popular at the University of Alabama, and involves a front-pocket area print and a large bold print on the back.

Exhibit 12 shows the colleges and universities for which these two designs were available.

EXHIBIT 12 | **Universities Represented in Campus Designs' Product Line**

Circle-M™ Designs*		Campus Rapp™ Designs	
Alabama	Maryland	Alabama	Michigan
Auburn	Miami	Arizona	Michigan State
Duke	Michigan	Auburn	Minnesota
Florida	Michigan State	Baylor	Nebraska
Florida State	North Carolina	Duke	North Carolina
Georgetown	North Carolina State	Florida	North Carolina State
Georgia	Ohio State	Florida State	Ohio State
Georgia Tech	Penn State	Georgia	Oregon State
Indiana	Pittsburgh	Georgetown	Penn State
Kentucky	Syracuse	Georgia Tech	Pittsburgh
LSU	UNC Charlotte	Illinois State	Purdue
Louisville		Indiana	Seton Hall
		Kansas	South Carolina
		Kansas State	Syracuse
		Kentucky	Tennessee
		LSU	Texas
		Louisville	UNLV
		Maryland	Washington
		Miami	West Virginia

*CIRCLE-M™ designs are not available on tank tops.
Source: Campus Designs, Inc.

Because of the growth in licensed products, Billy Pittman believed that it was very important for CDI to develop designs which were distinctive enough to set Campus Designs apart from bigger companies. Unique designs were critical because Campus Designs could not compete with large-scale suppliers on price, quantity, and quality.

Apart from design uniqueness, Campus Designs believed it had a competitive edge over many of its competitors, especially larger rivals, because the owners were personally tuned into the university scene. Tom Pittman elaborated:

> Because we're so young still, we're not very far removed from the university market itself, especially since we live here in Tuscaloosa. It's kind of hard to become that far removed from it . . . We can stay in touch with what the students like and I think we can be a little more responsive to the types of designs that the students will like. Likewise we can pick up on what's on students' minds, what's happening on campus, what students like and don't like because we talk to them all the time and we spend a lot of our time on campuses. This puts us in position to respond quicker than some big gigantic company . . . even though we're small.

The owners' personal experiences allowed them to spot opportunities and trends that larger suppliers had not or could not react to. For instance, Campus Designs had the ability to supply the increasingly popular gameday shirts for all University of Alabama athletic events, a market niche that larger suppliers such as Russell Athletic found uneconomical to pursue.

In order to stay on the cutting edge of design technology, Campus Designs had begun using computer graphics to enhance the speed, quality, and creativeness of the designs it turned out. The company was monitoring the costs and capabilities of software programs that could perform such tasks as typesetting, a very time-consuming and expensive process if done without the aid of computers. These software programs were expensive and usually required that the user have a special computer system (costing approximately $10,000) in order to utilize the software package effectively. In 1989 Campus Designs had its typesetting done by an outside source at a cost of $20 to $30 per design. Billy summed up CDI's design strategy in this way:

> In the future, for the newer lines of designs that we come up with, we're going to have to be very creative . . . use our minds and work on something that not really sets a trend but is in step with what the larger companies are doing—but maybe just half a step beyond what they are doing, so that we can retain our little niche in the marketplace.

DISTRIBUTION AND MARKETING

CDI wanted to market its designs to as many schools as possible. It had therefore undertaken a major commitment to do anything new. Billy expounded, stating:

> Our rep groups, who have done very well for us in the South, in the Northeast . . . need new things constantly. If we can supply those designs, something that's a little bit different, then we'll remain competitive . . . and be able to increase our volume and that's our goal—to constantly be building the volume and getting the new product out.

A disadvantage that CDI had in gaining wider distribution was its practice of charging buyers the full wholesale price. Larger suppliers generally had three pricing advantages available to them that were unavailable to Campus Designs and other small suppliers: (1) scale economies, (2) purchase discounts, such as 2 percent for payment within 30 days, and (3) price breaks on big volume orders. Although larger companies provided price breaks, Tom believed that CDI's customer service was superior:

> Larger companies can have . . . hundreds of people working in a customer service department. Well, we are the customer service department, so we can be a little more responsive to something. [Since] there are only three of us working, our customers know us all by first name.

Distribution   CDI distributed its products through independent manufacturers' representative groups; the reps called on bookstores, wholesalers, and retailers who stocked collegiate apparel. The various rep groups were generally obtained through contacts made at industry trade shows. The first rep group that CDI used was Rupp Bookmeier, who serviced Michigan and Ohio. The relationship between CDI and Rupp Bookmeier had since been dissolved and Campus Designs had begun looking for another rep group to secure orders in those two states. The manufacturers' reps CDI used were independent contractors and handled several lines of apparel. CDI had no guarantee that its reps would push CDI's line harder than any other line they handled. Since reps worked totally on commission, they tended to be loyal to whatever products were selling the best. See Exhibit 13 for an outline of CDI's system of distribution in 1989.

Tom Pittman believed that CDI's system of distribution needed some improvements. Their distribution force was small and many of their current rep groups simply were not as reliable as they needed to be.

CDI gameday T-shirts for University of Alabama athletic events were sold exclusively through an account with The Supe Store, the University of Alabama's on-campus bookstore. Campus Designs' fraternity and sorority shirts were sold mostly

EXHIBIT 13 | Manufacturers' Representatives Handling Campus Designs' Products, 1990

Manufacturers' Representatives	Geographic Coverage	Products	Commission
Cole-Harris	Alabama, Mississippi, Georgia, Tennessee, North and South Carolina	Circle-M, Campus Rapp	10%
Earl Williams	Florida	Circle-M, Campus Rapp	10
Pat and Dan O'Connell	Eastern Pennsylvania, Delaware, Virginia, D.C., Maryland	Circle-M, Campus Rapp	10
Bonnie Ross	Upstate New York, Syracuse	Circle-M, Campus Rapp, Greek Shirts	10
Herman, Thompson and Wells	New York City	Circle-M, Campus Rapp	10

Source: Campus Designs, Inc.

at industry trade shows and by one independent manufacturers' representative, Jack Kirch. In 1989 Campus Designs was looking for a manufacturers' rep that could give its fraternity and sorority designs wider market exposure.

In addition to the efforts of its independent sales reps, Campus Designs' marketing efforts in 1989 included a direct mail campaign to retailers who had either inquired about the company or who were believed to be potential customers. The company also did limited advertising in trade journals such as *Sports Trends* and *Impressions.*

In 1989, the percentages of Campus Designs' sales accounted for by the various retail outlets were as follows:

Retailers	Spring 1989	Fall 1989
Sporting goods retailers	45%	35%
Campus bookstores	35	45
Department stores	15	15
Specialty/gift stores	5	5

Source: Campus Designs, Inc.

Tom and Billy pointed out that many times retailers would simply say no to their products; the two most significant reasons were that (1) CDI did not offer price breaks on quantity orders as did larger suppliers and (2) CDI supplied branded apparel items as opposed to supplying apparel items with Campus Designs' own private label. A third reason buyers sometimes gave was that they were already stocking a similar design. Billy related an instance where a buyer claimed that CDI's Alabama Campus Rapp design was almost identical to a design she was already carrying. Billy later found out that the existing design she was referring to consisted of the name of the university screen printed onto the T-shirt in a wraparound pattern. Billy used such episodes as a reminder that CDI must constantly strive to come up with new and creative designs.

It was standard procedure for retailers to mark up collegiate licensed products 100 percent—that is, an item costing the retailer $5 was sold for $10. Parisian, an Alabama-based department store retailer, marked up the collegiate licensed products it merchandised 100 percent plus $2.

CDI's wholesale prices to retailers in 1989 were:

Garment	Wholesale Price	Percentage of 1989 Sales
Tanks	$ 6.00	5%
T-shirts	6.75	75
Sweatshirts:		
Raglan	11.00	20
Set-in	11.50	

Source: Campus Designs, Inc.

DEALING WITH KNOCK-OFFS OF CDI'S DESIGNS

"Copying is the highest form of flattery and the lowest form of doing business," noted Billy Pittman following three incidents in which other companies had copied CDI's designs. In one incident in the fall of 1987, Artex, a leading supplier, developed a knock-off of CDI's University of North Carolina Tarheels Campus Rapp design. CDI contacted CCI/ICE, who turned the matter over to university officials. Artex's penalty for copying the CDI design consisted of a small monetary fine and a mandate to destroy their screens of the design.

Other CDI designs that had been copied were its University of Alabama Campus Rapp design and the Syracuse University Circle-M design. These incidents provoked CDI to institute legal action, but as Tom put it:

As we continue to grow, it's going to continue to happen. Taking legal action against a company that does it is very expensive but it's something we feel we have to do. We can't be seen as a company that lets others get by with knocking off our designs. We're small and we're fresh meat out there for all those sharks.

CDI had trademarked its Campus Rapp and Circle-M designs. Trademarks lasted for 21 years and cost $500 each. It had also copyrighted the individual designs within those product trademarks, such as the specific designs for the University of Tennessee, Florida State University, and Wake Forest. The cost of copyrighting designs was $10 each. See Exhibit 14 for examples of CDI's copyrighted designs.

COMPANY ORGANIZATION

Campus Designs' owners did not want to become locked into a particular job function. Decisions were made by group consensus. All three were familiar with every aspect of company operations and functioned as coequals. Seth commented on the assignment of job titles and the philosophy behind their rotation of job titles:

The job titles are basically meaningless; they are just assigned for outside business purposes. We rotate jobs so that everyone can get a better feel for the various responsibilities involved in running a company . . . but as I said earlier the titles really don't mean anything to us. Everyone is responsible for any business situation that might come up whether they're the secretary, the vice president, or the president—it doesn't matter.

EXHIBIT 14 | **A Sample of CDI's Copyrighted Designs**

THE FUTURE

At the beginning of 1990, the three co-owners were in the process of developing a line of children's designs based on the Circle-M design. They planned to test this line in a market consisting of the three major universities in Florida, the two major universities in Alabama, and Syracuse University. They were also in the process of developing another design for a number of schools called The Big Play. This design was to be an action sports photo containing (1) either a basketball player, football player, baseball player, or lacrosse player, (2) the name of the institution, and (3) the institution's key logo (see Exhibit 14). At schools where all four sports were popular, all four designs would be developed; where only three of the four sports were popular, then just those three would be developed. This design was showcased at the Super Show in February 1990.

When the casewriter asked, "Where do you see the company being in five years?" the three men responded in the following ways:

Seth: I see us having top-quality facilities. I also see all aspects of our business, such as production, marketing, and designing being top-notch. I believe that we will be involved in the production of other licensed products like professionally licensed products and maybe even some other fashion type things.

Tom: In five years I see us having our own private label, a better system of distribution, and a larger staff. Hopefully, we will be working fewer hours and not having to pull all-nighters. I also see Campus Designs having better name recognition.

Billy: I see us being more in control of the various facets of the business—not relying so much on outside sources—internalizing more of the aspects of the business. I also see us responding quicker to market opportunities—getting out new designs faster. I also hope to see all three of us become more skilled in the management and training side of the business.

The casewriter also asked whether they were having fun at what they were doing:

Seth: I don't know if you'd call it fun . . . but there is just something here that keeps you going. A business of your own allows you to come and go as you please—I like that. I also like the people I am working with.

Tom: I wouldn't be doing it if it wasn't fun. It is nice to be in a position where you are responsible for everything. The success of Campus Designs depends on us and there is always room for improvement. I find that to be an exciting challenge.

Billy: I'd rather be doing this than anything else.

THE BOSTON YWCA

Donna M. Gallo, The University of Massachusetts
Barbara Gottfried, Bentley College
Alan N. Hoffman, Bentley College

In the summer of 1991, Mary Kinsell, controller and chief financial officer for the Boston YWCA, briefed her successor, Carolyn Rosen, and Marti Wilson-Taylor, the YWCA's new executive director. Deeply aware of the organization's financial crisis, Kinsell noted that the past 20 years had created many difficulties for the once strong and prominent Boston YWCA. Especially pressing was the need to seek out new sources of funding because of significant cuts in federal funding to nonprofit organizations, increased demand and competition in the fitness and day care industries, and rising operating costs. In addition, the YWCA faced questions about how to deal with several aging YWCA buildings, located in prime neighborhoods of Boston, but unmodernized and slowly deteriorating. Ms. Kinsell warned, "The Boston YWCA is like a dowager from an old Boston family who has seen better days. It is 'building rich' and 'cash poor.' Leveraging equity from its buildings is difficult and making operations generate enough cash flow to maintain the buildings seems almost impossible." The Boston YWCA had to meet these challenges or be forced to cut back its activities; even bankruptcy was not out of the question. Exhibits 1 and 2 provide recent financial statements.

THE FIRST 100 YEARS

The Young Women's Christian Association (YWCA) is a nonprofit organization whose original mission was "To provide for the physical, moral, and spiritual welfare of young women in Boston," where it was founded. For more than 12 decades it had done just that, meeting the changing needs of women in the community by providing services, opportunities, and support in an environment of shared sisterhood.

In 1866, a group of affluent women formed the Boston Young Women's Christian Association to rent rooms to women and children whom the industrial revolution had forced to leave failing farms for work in city factories. Not only working conditions but living conditions for such women were deplorable in the city's

EXHIBIT 1 | The Boston YWCA's Balance Sheet, June 30, 1991 (With Comparative Totals as of June 30, 1990)

Assets	Current Fund	Plant Fund	Endowment Fund	June 30, 1991 Totals	June 30, 1990 Totals
Current assets:					
Cash	$ 137,469	$ 66,292	—	$ 203,761	$ 110,684
Cash in escrow and security deposits	40,642	—	—	40,642	37,932
Accounts receivable (less allowance for doubtful accounts of $3,500 in 1991 and $2,687 in 1990)	102,334	—	—	102,334	166,245
Supplies and prepaid expenses	54,452	—	—	54,452	73,613
Total current assets	334,897	66,292	—	401,189	388,474
Pooled investments	1,793,198	—	$3,180,303	4,973,501	4,775,252
Land, buildings and equipment, net	—	2,147,155	—	2,147,155	1,869,963
Deferred charges	—	349,638	—	349,638	349,638
	1,793,198	2,496,793	3,180,303	7,470,294	6,994,853
	$2,128,095	$2,563,085	$3,180,303	$7,871,483	$7,383,327
Liabilities and Fund Balances (Deficit)					
Current liabilities:					
Current maturities of long-term notes payable	—	$ 18,979	—	$ 18,979	$ 17,524
Accounts payable and accrued expenses	$ 254,757	—	—	254,757	201,581
Deferred revenue	182,073	—	—	182,073	202,717
Total current liabilities	436,830	18,979	—	455,809	421,822
Long-term notes payable, less current maturities	—	1,196,746	—	1,196,746	910,443
Loan payable to endowment fund	—	—	—	—	143,841
Total liabilities	436,830	1,215,725	—	1,652,555	1,476,106
Fund balances (deficit):					
Unrestricted:					
Designated by governing board to function as endowment	1,507,135	—	—	1,507,135	1,453,867
Undesignated	(101,933)	—	—	(101,933)	(354,084)
	1,405,202	—	—	1,405,202	1,099,783
Restricted—nonexpendable	286,063	223,798	$3,180,303	3,690,164	3,545,183
Net investment in plant	—	1,123,562	—	1,123,562	1,262,255
Total fund balances	1,691,265	1,347,360	3,180,303	6,218,928	5,907,221
	$2,128,095	$2,563,085	$3,180,303	$7,871,483	$7,383,327

slums. The Boston YWCA offered a clean, safe housing alternative, as well as recreation, companionship, and an employment referral network for women. The success of the facility led to the opening of the Berkeley Residence (40 Berkeley Street, Boston) in 1884 with accommodations for 200 residents and an employment and training bureau. The Berkeley Residence also housed the first YWCA gymnasium in America. A crucial part of the YWCA's mission was to "empower women through fitness, health care, and independent employment opportunities." At this early date in the YWCA's history, most of the funding for the Boston YWCA's facilities and services was raised by wealthy women patrons through their family connections and from their friends and acquaintances. From its inception, unlike the larger, more well-known, and more aggressive Boston YMCA, which easily garnered bank loans and donations, the Boston YWCA had to struggle to fund its projects.

E X H I B I T 2 | **The Boston YWCA's Statement of Support and Revenue, Expenses, Capital Additions, and Changes in Fund Balances, Year Ended June 30, 1991** *(With comparative totals for the year ended June 30, 1990)*

	Current	Plant	Endowment	June 30, 1991	June 30, 1990
Support:					
United Way	$ 703,643	—	—	$ 703,643	$ 713,500
Contributions and grants	233,264	—	—	233,264	197,700
Legacies and bequests	150,386	—	—	150,386	537,540
	1,087,293	—	—	1,087,293	1,448,740
Operating revenue:					
Program fees	320,611	—	—	320,611	355,170
Government-sponsored programs	471,615	—	—	471,615	411,050
Membership	45,674	—	—	45,674	71,579
Housing and food service	1,589,587	—	—	1,589,587	1,586,553
	2,427,487	—	—	2,427,487	2,424,352
Nonoperating revenue:					
Rental income	302,641	—	—	302,641	298,036
Investment income	278,982	—	—	278,982	244,224
Net realized gain on investments	41,392	—	—	41,392	2,308
Other revenue	7,967	—	—	7,967	43,790
	630,982	—	—	630,982	588,358
Total support and revenue	$4,145,762	—	—	$4,145,762	$4,461,450
Expenses					
Program services:					
Aswalos House	$ 250,621	$ 14,782	—	$ 265,403	$ 384,776
Berkeley Residence	1,053,131	86,465	—	1,139,596	1,054,106
Cass Branch	1,216,544	128,673	—	1,345,217	1,394,075
Childcare	422,411	2,030	—	424,441	344,011
Harvard	6,132	—	—	6,132	—
	2,948,839	231,950	—	3,180,789	3,176,968
Supporting services:					
General and administration	632,657	15,364	—	648,021	793,861
Fundraising	287,448	6,981	—	294,429	135,978
	920,105	22,345	—	942,450	929,839
Total expenses	3,868,944	254,295	—	4,123,239	4,106,807
Excess (deficiency) of support and revenue over expenses before capital additions	$ 276,818	$ (254,295)	—	$ 22,523	$ 354,643
Capital Additions					
Grants and gifts	$ 106,495	$ 38,985	—	$ 145,480	$ 314,798
Investment income	—	5,529	$ 65,598	71,127	68,018
Net realized gain on investment transactions	—	—	72,577	72,577	63,874
Write-off of deferred charges	—	—	—	—	(305,312)
Loss on sale of asset	—	—	—	—	(11,856)
Total capital additions	106,495	44,514	138,175	289,184	129,522
Excess (deficiency) of support and revenue over expenses after capital additions	383,313	(209,781)	138,175	311,707	484,165
Fund balances, beginning of year	1,379,040	1,486,053	3,042,128	5,907,221	5,423,056
Transfers between funds:					
Plant acquisition	(274,155)	274,155	—	—	—
Principal repayment on loan payable to endowment fund	(143,841)	143,841	—	—	—
Permanent fund transfer	346,908	(346,908)	—	—	—
	(71,088)	71,088	—	—	—
Fund balances, end of year	$1,691,265	$1,347,360	$3,180,303	$6,218,928	$5,907,221

In the ensuing decades, the Boston YWCA opened The School of Domestic Science to train women as institutional housekeepers and managers, and started a secretarial training program and other training and educational programs for women. In 1911, the Boston YWCA became affiliated with the other YWCAs in the United States. By this time, the YWCA was no longer purely a philanthropic association run by wealthy women for poor women, but an association of working women meeting the needs of other working women in the home and marketplace. Nevertheless, the support of wealthy patrons continued to be crucial to the YWCA's viability as a community resource.

In the early 1920s, to raise funds for yet another new building, the "Y" initiated a capital campaign under the slogan "Every Girl Needs the YWCA." Over $1 million was contributed by middle-class as well as wealthy donors, and in 1927 ground was broken at the corner of Clarendon and Stuart Streets for the Boston YWCA's new headquarters. The new building, with recreational facilities, a swimming pool, classrooms, meeting rooms, and offices for the staff, was dedicated in 1929 and has served as headquarters for the association ever since.

During World War II, the YWCA contributed to the war effort by sponsoring educational lectures and forums such as "Fix-It-Yourself" for the wives of servicemen, offering housing to women doing war work, and providing recreation and entertainment to men and women in the armed services. As always, the YWCA continued to be managed and funded primarily by women, for women.

After the war, YWCA activity expanded in new directions. YWCA administrators made a concerted effort to reach out to immigrant women. And an interracial charter was adopted at the national convention calling for racial integration and the participation of minority groups in every aspect of the association, the community, and the nation. In addition, rapid postwar population growth in the suburbs west of Boston led to the opening in 1964 of the West Suburban Branch of the "Y" in Natick, Massachusetts, 20 miles west of Boston. The Natick "Y" focused its energies on the needs and wants of suburban women and their children. Finally, advocates formed a lobbying group, the YWCA Public Affairs Committee, to address housing and family planning issues and to call attention to the needs of women, especially mothers, that were not being met by traditional social service organizations.

Throughout its first 100 years, the Boston YWCA, staffed and funded almost entirely by women, worked to assist women to take charge of their lives, plan for their futures, and become economically independent and self-supporting.

RECENT HISTORY AND THE CHANGING ENVIRONMENT

In 1866, the Boston YWCA became the first YWCA in the nation. Today we are part of the oldest and largest women's organization in the world, serving all people regardless of sex, race, religion, or income. Our One Imperative is the elimination of racism.

Mary L. Reed
Former Executive Director, 1986

The 1960s were a time of social and cultural upheaval, especially with regard to civil rights and equal treatment for people of all races. In support of the civil rights movement, the YWCA made a commitment to fight racism and to integrate its own programs and services at every level, initiating a special two-year action plan in 1963 with this goal. The operating budget for the plan provided for two staff members and support services to become more involved with other community groups working in the areas of fair housing, voter registration, and literacy programs. In 1967, the YWCA's first black president, Mrs. Robert W. Clayton, was elected at the National Convention. In 1968 the Boston YWCA opened Aswalos House in Dorchester, Massachusetts, especially to meet the needs of women in the inner city. As a fitting end to the 1960s, the One Imperative "To eliminate racism wherever it exists and by any means necessary" was adopted and added to the YWCA's statement of purpose as a philosophical basis for the YWCA in coming years.

Although fighting racism remained an important focus, in the 1970s the YWCA shifted its attention to issues raised by the changing roles of women in American society. The 1960s and 1970s were decades of revival and growth in the feminist movement in the United States and throughout the world. The social and political arenas in which the Boston and other YWCAs were operating were changing rapidly. More and more women had begun working outside the home, while raising children. The number of women living at or near the poverty level had increased. Classes and programs at the YWCA were redesigned to meet the changing times. YWCAs started offering instruction in survival skills for urban living; in 1977, because nontraditional jobs for women were on the rise, the "Y" launched its first nontraditional training program, funded by the federal government, to train women to work in the construction industry.

Starting in the 1960s and increasingly in the 1970s, federal, state, and local governments became more heavily involved in social welfare programs, gradually replacing private charitable and voluntary organizations as the primary funding source for people in need and the organizations that helped them. At the same time that the YWCA began to rely more on government funding and less on private donations, the makeup of the YWCA's Board of Directors in the 1960s and 1970s changed to reflect the racial and class diversity of the women in the communities the YWCA served. While the new Board members helped the YWCA respond effectively to the immediate needs of the inner city community, they lost touch with the monied constituency that had formerly been the YWCA's base of support, and that monied constituency in turn shifted its attention and support to other causes.

The late 1970s saw a dramatic rise in the number of unwed mothers, teen pregnancies, and teen parents. With more state and federal funds available for social programs, many nonprofit social organizations directed their energies to establishing themselves as vendors or service providers to win government contracts. The Boston YWCA became a major vendor in the areas of child care, employment training, teen services, and domestic abuse programming. As a result of the YWCA's strong advocacy efforts, major federal and state contracts were awarded to the YWCA to study issues related to teen pregnancy. The YWCA's redirecting its efforts in this fashion toward securing government funding was a factor that significantly eroded its traditional base of private support among well-to-do women who had for generations been the primary source of funds for the YWCA in Boston.

As the 1970s came to a close, the financial outlook for the Boston YWCA began to appear critical. Given the community's growing need for services and the "Y's" aging facilities, the management team of the Boston YWCA realized it had to make some tough decisions about allocating scarce funds. If management decided to approve new programs or purchase new facilities, it would have to pull funds from existing programs and services. If management continued to allocate funds for services and programs while making only minimal allocations for facility maintenance, it risked incurring the cost of major repairs further down the line or else allowing the Boston YWCA's facilities to gradually deteriorate. Though the management team did not want to lose sight of the YWCA's immediate commitment to the women and children in the community, it believed the "Y's" financial crisis would require foresight, careful planning, and some hard choices.

THE ECONOMIC CRUNCH

In the early 1980s when a growing number of nonprofit organizations thus found themselves competing for public funding for social programs, the Reagan administration tightened funding at the federal level and many nonprofit organizations were forced to go back to raising funds in the traditional way through private donations, grants, bequests, and the United Way. The mid-1980s, however, were prosperous years, especially in the Boston area, and so a growing crisis was postponed. Individuals and companies gave more generously than in past years to nonprofits, and to compete for this pool of private funding as well as the limited federal funds available during the Reagan era, nonprofit organizations expanded their reach into everything from homeless shelters and food pantries to drug and alcohol rehabilitation centers and actually increased the number of programs.

However, the economic downturn in late 1987 immediately cut into private funding, and frugal corporations and the general public became more reluctant and discerning about where they directed their charitable contributions. A funding crisis for the YWCA started to loom. It became increasingly difficult to raise the funds necessary to keep up "Y" facilities and to fund ongoing programs at needed levels. As the economy in the Northeast worsened, the need for services increased proportionally and at a more rapid rate than the Boston YWCA had ever witnessed. To make matters worse, the Boston YWCA had to contend with its old, somewhat stodgy, mainstream image (as compared to the proliferation of new-wave homeless shelters and battered women's shelters or safe houses) and also with a growing misperception of the YWCA as an organization run primarily by women of color for women of color.

The banking industry climate in Boston during the late 1980s also entered a crisis period. Many Northeastern banks were in financial trouble and those that had lent freely in the mid-1980s now scrutinized closely every loan request and rejected a large majority. Loans for capital improvements and construction were not looked upon favorably by most Boston area banks, and money to fund new projects and large renovations for charitable organizations became hard to obtain. The negative outlook for increased funding of charitable causes had not improved in the Boston area as of 1991, when Mary Kinsell found herself briefing new Chief Financial Officer Carolyn Rosen and new Executive Director Marti Wilson-Taylor about the hard decisions the Boston YWCA faced regarding what to do about its shrinking resources.

SOURCES OF FUNDING

The revenues for the Boston YWCA came from three sources:

1. *Support funds*—funds from the United Way of Massachusetts Bay, from contributions, grants, legacies, and bequests.
2. *Operating revenue*—money from program fees, government-sponsored programs, membership dues, housing fees, and food services.

3. *Nonoperating revenue*—income from leasing of office space to outside concerns, investment income, and net realized gain on investments.

The table below shows the percentage each source of revenue has contributed to the Boston YWCA's total revenues for the past six years.

Source	1985	1986	1987	1988	1989	1990
Support funds	22%	22%	23%	21%	24%	33%
Operating revenue	67	66	65	67	63	54
Nonoperating revenue	11	12	12	12	13	13
	100%	100%	100%	100%	100%	100%

From 1985 to 1989 the United Way accounted for 70 to 80 percent of the Boston YWCA's support funds revenue. But the national headquarters of the United Way had recently come under fire for certain lavish expenditures and, like all nonprofit social service organizations in the late 1980s, the United Way found itself in a fiercely competitive fund-raising environment. The United Way of Massachusetts Bay anticipated a 30 percent drop in pledges for 1991 which would affect all the agencies it funded, including the Boston YWCA. At the same time, operating revenues for the YWCA had dropped off in 1990 as well so that more, rather than less, support funding was needed to continue present programs. Since support funding was expected to continue to decrease over the next three to five years, the Boston YWCA had to develop new sources of funding to maintain its services and cover operating expenses. Exhibit 3 presents a detailed breakdown of the Boston YWCA's revenue sources in 1991.

FACILITIES

In 1987, the Boston YWCA was operating from four facilities in the neighborhoods of Boston and one in a western suburb of the city. During 1987, the Boston Redevelopment Authority, a commission which oversaw all real estate development in the

EXHIBIT 3 | **The Boston YWCA's Revenue Sources, 1991**

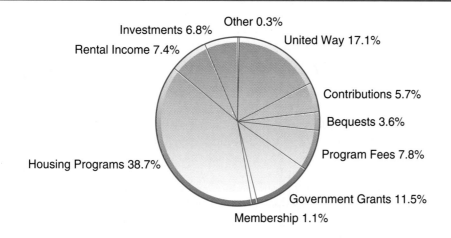

city, awarded a parcel of land to the YWCA for $1 on which to build a new facility as part of the city's redevelopment plan. The new facility (never in fact constructed) would replace the old Dorchester YWCA, Aswalos House, which in turn a grant would convert to transitional housing for unwed mothers and their children. Since the YWCA also had other existing facilities in need of maintenance and repair, the management team embarked on a three-year study to analyze its programs, services, and properties. Early during the study period, management won approval from the Boston YWCA's governing board for an aggressive renovation program to modernize all facilities and protect the value of the YWCA's major assets, its buildings.

As part of this renovation, repair, and maintenance program, the "Y's" management team was asked to perform a thorough review of its programs and services. The most beneficial programs in terms of revenue and those the community had the greatest need for had to be assessed in terms of expected growth and space requirements. Allowance also had to be made for accommodating new programs. Those programs that were no longer financially feasible or in demand were to be eliminated. The management team planned to complete its research and decision-making prior to implementing any expansion or renovation of the buildings.

A current organization chart showing facilities, programs, and management structure is presented in Exhibit 4.

WEST SUBURBAN PROGRAM CENTER

When the YWCA expanded, and opened a branch in Natick, Massachusetts, in 1964, it bought a building that quickly became inadequate to the YWCA's needs, and in 1981 the Natick center moved to a new facility. The resources for women at this branch were designed to serve a suburban constituency, and included programs for women reentering the job market after years of parenting, training programs for displaced workers, spousal and family abuse programs, divorce support groups, and counseling for women suffering from breast cancer. However, in 1988, after much research and years of restructuring the services offered at the West Suburban Program Center, its inability to support itself financially through its operations led to a decision to close down the facility.

ASWALOS HOUSE

Aswalos House, located in Dorchester, Massachusetts, an urban center within the jurisdiction of the City of Boston, was originally opened in 1968. Until 1989, it housed an After School Enrichment Program and a Teen Development Program, which offered training for word processing and clerical work, and GED preparation courses. Later, Aswalos House added a program for teen mothers.

In 1989, a $100,000 HUD grant transformed Aswalos House into transitional housing for teenage mothers and their children, and existing programs were transferred to other facilities. Originally the programs were to be transferred to the new Dorchester Branch planned for the parcel acquired from the City of Boston. However, that parcel was never developed because development costs were estimated at $1.5 to $2 million; when the YWCA was able to raise only $300,000, the parcel of land was returned to the City of Boston.

The new Aswalos House for teen mothers opened in October, 1990, and provided transitional housing for ten mothers and their children. Prospective occupants had to be between 16 and 20 years old and demonstrate severe financial need. Counseling services were provided, and a staff case worker arranged for schooling and job train-

EXHIBIT 4 | Table of Organization for the Boston YWCA, 1991

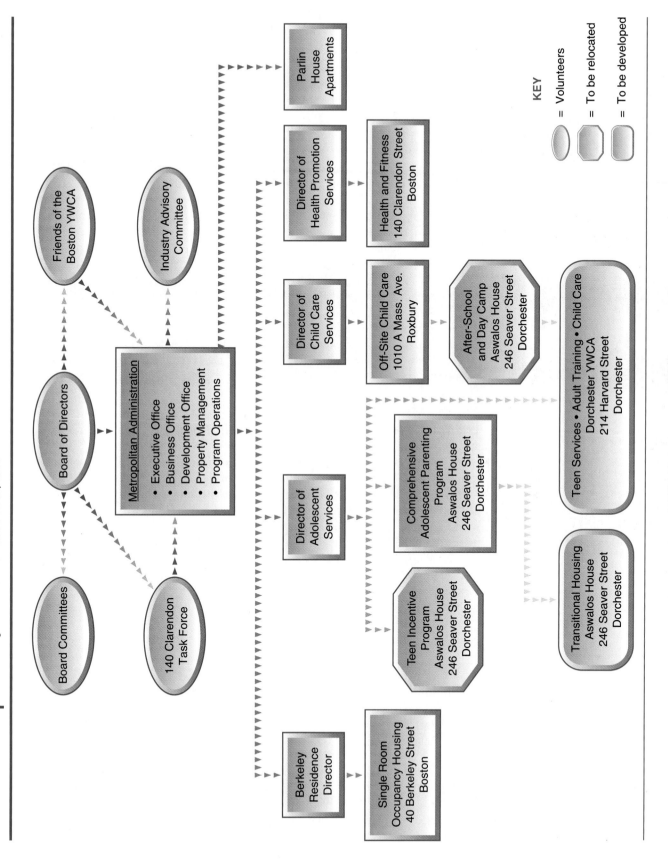

KEY

= Volunteers

= To be relocated

= To be developed

ing for the teenagers. In addition, a staff housing advocate coordinated permanent housing for the mothers and their children.

Half the expense of running the facility was covered by a federal grant to the Boston YWCA. The remaining half was made up by fees paid by the teen mothers from their welfare income, contributions from the United Way, and private donations.

YWCA CHILD CARE CENTER

The YWCA Child Care Center was rather inconveniently located in downtown Boston on the fringe of the commercial district, and was rented rather than owned by the YWCA. To be licensed as a day care center in the Commonwealth of Massachusetts, it had to undergo extensive renovations. The owner of the property contributed a substantial portion of the cost of the renovation work, and the balance of the expense was covered by a private grant so that no loans were necessary to complete the project.

The center, a licensed preschool, provided day care for 50 children at fees of $110 a week per toddler and $150 a week per child for children under the age of three. Some scholarships were available for families who were unable to pay. When the center first opened, many of its clients were on state-funded day care vouchers. Participation had dropped considerably, however, because a significant percentage of state-funded day care vouchers were cut from the state budget. To compensate for the loss of clients, the center went into the infant care business, caring for children from six months to two years of age, but it continued to run at less than capacity.

THE BERKELEY RESIDENCE

The Berkeley Residence was opened in 1884 in downtown Boston to serve as housing for women of all ages. Originally there was housing for 100 residents, an employment and training bureau, and a gymnasium, the first in the country for women. In 1907, 35 rooms and a meeting hall were added to the facility.

In 1985 the Berkeley Residence was cited by Boston's Building Code Department because it did not meet current safety and fire codes of the city or the Commonwealth. Major repairs and renovations estimated at $1 million were necessary to bring the building up to healthy, safe, and legal standards. In 1986, a construction loan for the full amount was secured at 10 percent interest amortized over 25 years. Once the project was completed, payments would come to approximately $100,000 annually. Work began in 1988. Repairs that were needed to the infrastructure of the building included a conversion from oil heat to gas, a sprinkler system and smoke detector system wired throughout the building, and new elevators, as well as many other lesser repairs and other maintenance work. Tenants were not displaced during construction, a major concern at the beginning of the project's planning stage.

After completion of the renovation in the spring of 1991, the facility had 215 rooms, which were rented on a long-term or short-term basis to women of all ages. The Berkeley Residence offered inexpensive rent and meals, an answering service, and maid service. Other services at the facility included a referral network for jobs and services, social services, tourist information, and emergency services. The building was open and staffed 24 hours a day, 7 days a week, and provided safe, secure housing at reasonable rates for single women in the city.

BOSTON YWCA HEADQUARTERS AT 140 CLARENDON STREET

Constructed between 1927 and 1929, the headquarters for the Boston YWCA was advantageously located at the corner of Clarendon and Stuart Streets on the edge of one of the city's most prestigious retail districts, Newbury and Boylston Streets and Copley Place in the heart of Boston's Back Bay business district. The area offered the finest in upscale retail stores and desirable office space, including the John Hancock Building and the Prudential Center. The Clarendon Headquarters, a 13-story brick and steel building, sat on approximately 13,860 square feet of land and included approximately 167,400 square feet of space. It currently housed the YWCA administration offices, the Parlin House Apartments, the Melnea Cass Branch of the YWCA, and several commercial tenants. The Melnea Cass Branch operated health and fitness facilities (including a swimming pool) and employment training programs. The Parlin Apartments occupied floors 9 to 13 and consisted of studio and one- and two-bedroom apartments rented at market rates.

The building had not been significantly renovated since its completion in 1929, and no longer complied with city and state building codes. In 1987, the elevators desperately needed repairs at an estimated cost of $270,000. The building also needed a new sprinkler system to ensure the safety of its residents and tenants and to bring the building up to code. The Parlin Apartments needed major renovations to achieve acceptable standards of safety, appearance, and comfort. At present, the apartments all shared a common electric meter; rewiring was required to enable separate metering and allow tenants to pay their own electricity costs. The YWCA's administrative offices were also in need of improvements and repairs.

The health and fitness facilities had old, dreary locker rooms that were unattractive to current and potential members, and a larger men's locker room was needed to accommodate male members. To keep up with new trends in the fitness industry, the YWCA needed to refurbish its space for aerobics classes and purchase new weight training equipment. The YWCA had also been forced to close the pool for repairs, and the pool building itself needed significant exterior work. Cost estimates for the work on the pool and pool building were in excess of $200,000. At the same time, declining interest in the area's health and fitness clubs and increasing competition in both day care and health and fitness had had a negative impact on revenues at the headquarters' facility.

Because the YWCA's Clarendon headquarters was in disrepair, it had become very costly to maintain and operate the building. In years past, the Board of Directors had chosen to funnel resources into the YWCA's programs rather than into general repairs and maintenance of the facilities; but despite the emphasis on supporting revenue-producing programs at the headquarters building, the facility was currently running at a net loss in excess of $200,000 a year.

In 1988 a certified appraiser valued the Clarendon property at $16 million. The Boston YWCA's Board of Directors then sought a $7 million loan for the proposed renovations from several major Boston area banking and financial institutions, but most of these institutions did not respond favorably to the loan request. The banks raised serious questions about whether the YWCA's existing and potential cash flows could meet the debt-service obligation. While there were several other reasons for the banks' refusing to loan the YWCA the funds necessary for the renovations, including the YWCA's own uncertainty about how the changes would impact revenues, some Board members and managers believed that the YWCA's status as a women's organization without connections in the old-boy network of the banking establishment contributed to the YWCA's lack of financial credibility. Finally, in 1991, commercial real estate values in the Boston area had declined significantly since the 1988 appraisal and it was unlikely that the 140 Clarendon Street headquarters facility could be sold for close to its 1988 appraisal of $16 million.

The executive committee of the Boston YWCA was considering several options for the Clarendon headquarters:

1. Sell the building with a guaranteed lease-back for its facilities and offices.
2. Sell the building to an interested local insurance company and rent space for the administrative offices in a nearby office building.
3. Bring in an equity partner to fund the renovations for a percentage of ownership in the facility.
4. Continue with minimal renovations and little change in operations or programs.

INCREASING COMPETITION IN FITNESS SERVICES

In 1989, the management team of the Boston YWCA hired a consulting firm to review the Health Promotion Services division, housed at 140 Clarendon Street, one of the YWCA's primary sources of both operating revenue and expense, and to propose ways to enhance this branch of the YWCA's services. The consultants surveyed current, former, and potential members about the strengths and weaknesses of the YWCA's Health Promotion Services including appearance, cleanliness, scheduling, products (e.g., equipment, classes, swimming pool), and overall management of the facility. This study revealed considerable competition from 13 health and fitness providers located in the areas served by the Boston YWCA:

1. Bally's Holiday Fitness Centers.
2. Healthworks.
3. Fitcorp.
4. BostonSports.
5. SkyClub.
6. The Mount Auburn Club.
7. Nautilus Plus.
8. Fitness International.
9. Fitness First.
10. The Club at Charles River Park.
11. Mike's Gym.
12. Fitness Unlimited.
13. Gold's Gym.

These businesses provided fairly standardized products and services: basketball and racquetball courts, exercise and weight equipment, exercise and aerobics classes, hot tubs and steam rooms, locker rooms, and showers with towels available. Several of these facilities were new and had had elaborate grand openings and extensive advertising campaigns to attract new members. However, the consultants noted that the Boston YWCA occupied a unique niche that was affordable, emphasized fitness in a noncompetitive and noncommercial environment, catered to a diverse cross-section of people, and had conveniently located facilities. Other clubs were perceived as more commercial and competitive than the YWCA, with a greater emphasis on social interaction and amenities such as saunas, raquetball and squash courts, and eating facilities. A comparison of the YWCA's Health Promotion Services to other health clubs in the city showed the YWCA to be in a price range somewhere between the commercial clubs and the no-frills gymnasiums. Fees at commercial clubs ranged from $800 to $1200 a year, plus a one-time initiation fee of $100 to $1200; user fees at no-frills gymnasiums ranged from $300 to $400 per year. Facilities fees at the Boston YWCA were between $420 and $600 a year, plus an annual membership fee of $35.

The YWCA had health and fitness facilities comparable in size to competitors, but its space was not as well laid out and, unlike other clubs, its facilities were not air-conditioned. The YWCA's health and fitness membership dropped significantly during the summer months; at most other clubs summer was the peak season. The YWCA also ranked behind the top four clubs in cleanliness, and members noted that its dreary atmosphere contributed to their sense of its uncleanliness. The YWCA's weightlifting equipment and weight machines were not quite up to the standards of competitors and the YWCA lacked the staffing and supervision other clubs provided. On the other hand, the YWCA had a swimming pool, an indoor track, and day care. Only one other club had a pool close in size to the YWCA's and only two other clubs had indoor tracks or provided day care.

According to the consultants' study, current users of the YWCA's Health Promotion Services joined because the YWCA was convenient, provided a caring environment that encouraged participation and involvement, and was relatively inexpensive. A current user profile revealed that members were generally seeking a health and fitness experience for themselves as individuals rather than a social atmosphere and that what mattered to them was convenient class schedules, adequate staffing, communication with the members, timely information, affordable pricing, an atmosphere without pressure, and an open, caring, and diverse environment. The complaint most often cited among current users was the lack of communication with members regarding schedule changes for classes, changes in the hours of operation, class cancellations, pool closings, and changes in procedures and policies of the club. Other factors that concerned current members were lack of cleanliness, dreary appearance, the small size of the men's locker room, poor management of the staff, poor management of class capacity, inadequate maintenance of equipment, unpopular scheduling of classes, the unsatisfactory layout of the facility, and the lack of public relations and advertising to attract new members.

Former members were also surveyed to determine why they did not renew. Their reasons mirrored the complaints of current members:

- Poor communications with members.
- Equipment breakdowns.
- Untimely equipment repairs.
- Poor upkeep/cleanliness.
- Poor ventilation.
- Dreary appearance.
- Dissatisfaction with staff (no personal attention).
- Rigid schedules.
- Lack of air conditioning.
- Overall deterioration of the facility.

The study also concluded that marketing and promotion of the programs and services offered by the Health Promotion Services division were minimal, with little effort put into attracting new members. Much of what the Boston YWCA did in terms of programs and service offerings was nearly invisible in the community.

THE BOSTON YWCA's FUTURE

Marti Wilson-Taylor, the new executive director, and Carolyn Rosen, the new chief financial officer, realized that several major decisions concerning the YWCA's physical facilities and programs and services had to be made. They also knew it was largely up to them to recommend a strategic direction for the Boston YWCA for the remainder of the 1990s and to gain the Board's approval of their proposed strategic action plan.

NEWTECH INSTRUMENTS LIMITED

Michael Skipton, Memorial University, Newfoundland, Canada

In March 1992, Don Nickerson, president of NewTech Instruments Limited, a six-year-old electronics manufacturing company based in St. John's, Newfoundland, was sitting at his desk watching as the snow flurry outside gradually turned to rain. He was considering the decision that the management group had to make by the end of the week.

NewTech had grown fairly steadily under Nickerson's leadership since its establishment in 1986. Sales figures had shown fairly consistent growth and sales projections for the future were assuming continuation of this growth. However, NewTech was running out of manufacturing space and currently was renting additional storage space in order to fulfill recent contracts. NewTech seemed to have finally outgrown its present facilities, leaving two major options: expand in their present location through leasing more space, or move to another larger facility elsewhere.

However, Nickerson was reluctant to incur significant financial commitments and then see sales decline in the future. This was a possibility as there were general concerns that the industrial recession would continue for some time and that any economic recovery would be slow. NewTech was operating in some of the world's most dynamic and competitive markets and the company had learned by experience not to count its contracts before they were signed, and sometimes not even if they were. There was no guarantee that sales projections for the future would actually materialize. As Don Nickerson considered the decision that must be made, he reviewed the events that had brought NewTech to this point.

COMPANY HISTORY AND BACKGROUND

NewTech was established in October 1986 to manufacture and market the Hydroball—an innovative current profiling system for ocean, lake, and river applications. The Hydroball technology was unique in the world. It was based on the con-

---

This case was prepared with the assistance of Craig Pollett, BComm ('91) for the Atlantic Entrepreneurial Institute. Copyright © 1993, the Atlantic Entrepreneurial Institute.

cept that if an object, that is, a Hydroball probe, was dropped into water it would move horizontally as it sank. The horizontal movement depended on the speed and direction of any currents at the different depths in the water through which it was sinking. As the Hydroball probe transmitted a signal its movement could be followed using a ship-mounted signal receiver. The current profile of the water column through which the Hydroball was sinking could then be calculated. The Hydroball probes were single-use items, as after use a Hydroball would come to rest on the bottom of the ocean, river, or lake and could not be recovered. Hydroball was the only current profiling system that worked in salt and fresh water (further technical details are given in Exhibit 1). In 1987, the Hydroball system received a Canada Award for Invention under the federal government's Canada Awards for Business Excellence Program.

NewTech was initially capitalized at $3 million as a 50-50 joint venture between the inventor of the Hydroball technology and NewTel Enterprises Ltd. The inventor had developed prototype technology for the Hydroball, as well as the ship-mounted signal receiver, and this technology was deemed to be worth $1.5 million. NewTel contributed $1.5 million in long-term and working capital and management personnel to enable marketing and manufacturing. NewTel Enterprises Ltd. was a financial holding company owning as its major asset Newfoundland Telephone Company Ltd. An important objective of NewTel was to invest in developing businesses in Newfoundland. For this reason, NewTech was established as a company that had a primary objective to become a Newfoundland-based electronics manufacturer. At the time of its establishment there was no electronics company in St. John's having significant manufacturing capability.

Don Nickerson was formerly employed by Newfoundland Telephone and started as president of NewTech in December 1986 with two other managers also from Newfoundland Telephone, and a secretary. One of these managers came to establish and manage production, and the other to establish and manage quality assurance. Three production employees and two electronics technicians were recruited in early 1987, and a vice president of marketing was hired in March 1987.

NewTech was established in space leased in the St. John's regional office and manufacturing/distribution facility of Northern Telecom Ltd. NewTech's manufacturing space was approximately 4,200 square feet and office space was 2,680 square feet. Approximately $300,000 was spent on equipment in the production facility. From the start, NewTech made a strategic decision to deliver a high level of product quality, and accordingly invested in the necessary quality assurance system and procedures.

THE HYDROBALL SYSTEM

The Hydroball probes and the signal receiver contained a circuit board and electrical components. While sophisticated systems and test equipment were a large part of quality assurance, good housekeeping was also important. It was necessary to be free from static electricity and to minimize the amount of dust that could cause bad connections and short circuits. The NewTech manufacturing facility was deliberately planned to be bright, shiny, and an attractive place to work. Employees were encouraged to keep it clean and looking good.

THE HYDROBALL EXPERIENCE

Hydroball development was aimed to be completed by the inventor in early 1987, at which time it would be turned over to NewTech to manufacture and market the

EXHIBIT 1 | **The Hydroball Current Profiling System**

Products

HYDROBALL
Current Profiling System
(XCP/XBT/XCTD)

The product is used to measure ocean current speed, direction and temperature profiles. Operating to depths of 500 metres, the system uses an acoustic link to transmit data as the expendable probe drifts to the sea floor. The data is captured by an ultrashort baseline phased array hydrophone,

processed, and the resulting profile displayed on a colour monitor. This easy to use system offers significant advantages when current profiles must be taken from moving vessels, and when speed and efficiency are critical to an offshore operation.

LPM
Copper Telecommunications
Cable Splice Closure Product

Low pressure molding (LPM) is a patented method of

transporting molten polyethylene to a job site and using it to mold a closure around a prepared splice bundle. The application is for non pressurized copper cables in the buried and underground Outside Plant environments. It enjoys a significant cost advantage over conventional closure systems.

Electronic Crustacean Stimulator

A device designed for use in the shell fish processing industry. The unit enables the processor to determine the condition of the crustacean and therefore its suitability for processing.

In-House Facilities
- Anti-static climate controlled room
- Potting shop for acoustic transducers
- Electronic test equipment
- Hydrostatic test equipment

Associated Facilities
- Acoustic tank
- Seakeeping (wave) tank
- Tow tank

Capabilities
- Build to print
  - circuit board assemblies
  - wire harnesses
  - mechanical assemblies
  - special assemblies
- Circuit board repairs
- Specialized test equipment design and manufacture
- Product design, development, and manufacture

Quality Standards
Quality Assurance/Quality Control procedures equivalent to NATO's AQAP-4.

NewTech's HYDROBALL, the world's first absolute profiling system using a disposable hydroacoustic profiler.

system, including Hydroball probes and the ship-mounted signal receiver. The first three manufactured units were produced by NewTech in the spring of 1987, and sea trials were carried out in early June. Although the manufacturing specifications were achieved, it was found that the overall performance of the system in use required improvement, involving development and redesign work in a number of significant areas. Further development work involving sea trials was then undertaken from June 1987 to February 1988.

This development work was funded by the joint venture partners, and used up financial resources that had originally been earmarked for manufacturing and marketing purposes. However, in the last set of trials, potential customers were taken out to sea off Cape Spear lighthouse near St. John's and the working system was demonstrated to them. This resulted in NewTech's first sale of the system. By June 1988, a marketing strategy had been formulated and marketing efforts were under way worldwide. Advertising in the marine survey instruments and systems trade press was being carried out, and 12 distributors covering most of the world, except for the then communist bloc, had been found. However, by late summer, NewTech had become very concerned about the lack of sales of systems and disposable Hydroball probes. A consultant was retained to study the problem.

By October 1988, the consultant reported that NewTech's marketing efforts were as good as anything he could think of, but that their expectations of market size and rate of penetration must be radically scaled down. It seemed that the market was not as big as indicated in a previous market study commissioned by the inventor, prior to NewTech's being established. Most of the potential customers listed in that original study were not considering the product. NewTech was finding that purchasers of marine hydrographic survey equipment were very cautious and conservative and did not make purchases in response to advertisements or trade shows. A lot of time, money, or even one's reputation could be lost if a ship got to a survey site but the measuring equipment did not work. Most potential purchasers preferred to wait until someone else had used new equipment in the field and then to ask them about their experience with it. In any case, in the northern hemisphere the summer was not the time to be trying to contact buyers of marine hydrographic survey instruments as most of them were out surveying. Between 1988 and 1990, NewTech continued to refine the system. In particular, the ship-mounted hydrophone signal receiver was further developed to make it easier to attach to the outside of a vessel hull. Originally this hydrophone was 14 inches in diameter and 18 inches high, but new developments in electronics design and assembly enabled the size to be reduced to 3.5 inches in diameter and 20 inches high.

Sales of Hydroball systems and probes continued to be slow and erratic. During 1988, 2 systems and 60 probes, worth $129,000, were sold. In 1989, 4 systems and 324 probes, worth $380,000, were sold. Since then, there had been no further sales of systems and few sales of probes. As things turned out, the amount of current profiling work carried out in the world during 1988 and 1989 was at a historic low. By early 1992, NewTech had received over 1,000 inquiries concerning the Hydroball system, but had only sold 6 systems and approximately 750 probes.

THE DECISION TO CARRY ON

By summer 1988, NewTech managers and the Board of Directors were aware that the real potential market size for the Hydroball system was considerably smaller than originally estimated, and that the likely rate of market penetration would be much slower. Newly estimated sales and profitability projections, based on Hydroball systems and probes alone, were insufficient to sustain the company.

The key strategic decision was made by the shareholders in NewTech that even though sales of the Hydroball systems could not be expected to sustain the company, they would carry on. The shareholders believed that NewTech would be able to develop other businesses. Although one of the shareholders, NewTel Enterprises Ltd., had the financial resources to be able to take a longer-term view, the inventor was unable to put in additional funds to assist NewTech to find these other products/services and markets. (As things turned out, the inventor had other projects and businesses that he owned which required funding. He sold his 50 percent shareholding in NewTech to NewTel Enterprises Ltd. in March 1989.)

NewTech's shareholders then directed the company to pursue a mission of becoming a Newfoundland-based electronics manufacturing company, with the aims of being profitable within three to five years, creating employment in Newfoundland, and utilizing the technical institutional infrastructure in St. John's. This infrastructure included the Memorial University Faculties of Science, Engineering and Applied Science, and Business Administration, the Centre for Cold Ocean Resources Engineering, and the Ocean Sciences Centre, the Marine Institute, and the National Research Council of Canada's Institute for Marine Dynamics—a $60 million research facility established on the university campus.

NEWTECH'S EXPANSION INTO OTHER BUSINESSES

NewTech management began to search for other products or services opportunities where the company had the internal resources to be competitive. Since then, NewTech had followed a path largely defined by an increasing variety of contract and build-to-print work. A key element of this strategy was to invest in a formal quality assurance system.

REPAIR OF PRINTED CIRCUIT BOARDS

Each Hydroball probe had a circuit board which was brought in and assembled by NewTech. In addition, every signal receiver had a number of complicated circuit boards that went inside it. NewTech managers identified their investment and expertise in building and testing printed circuit boards as a possible foundation for business development.

By early fall 1988, NewTech had decided that it could offer a repair service for printed circuit boards and, as the company had an urgent requirement for positive cash flow, management decided to try to find customers as quickly as possible. Fortunately, NewTech already had contacts with Newfoundland Telephone Company Ltd. and became aware of its requirements for repair of printed circuit boards.

The potential customer department had a number of circuit boards in various pieces of communications equipment that were expected to fail for one reason or another after a certain length of service. Replacement boards were inserted into the equipment and the faulty boards were then repaired. There was enough equipment, and therefore failing boards, to generate a constant need for replacement and repair. Up until this time, boards needing repair had been sent out of Newfoundland. The repair price was relatively high, shipping charges were being incurred, and the turn-around time was at least one month.

NewTech was able to offer to repair the boards with a one-week turnaround, with no shipping charges, and a somewhat lower price. One individual from NewTech was therefore assigned to "go down to the telephone company and convince them that we have the capabilities to repair their boards." While this might seem an easy sell it definitely was not. There was considerable customer concern over the ability of NewTech to carry out high quality repairs and to reliably assure this high level of quality. However, NewTech obtained an initial contract and, based on its quality work, was able to obtain continuation of this business after the initial batches had been repaired.

While this new business provided some steady income for NewTech, it was by itself insufficient to sustain the firm. Nor were there large growth prospects for the supply of failing or otherwise defective printed circuit boards in Newfoundland.

QUALITY ASSURANCE SYSTEM

In fall 1988, NewTech decided to invest in the highest quality specifications and assurance systems as the basis for seeking electronics manufacturing opportunities. Further funding assistance was obtained from ACOA through another of its assistance programs. ACOA funded approximately 70 percent of the consultants' fees, and about 50 percent of the total $100,000 cost of the additional measuring and testing equipment that was needed. NewTech had, since early 1989, been working to the NATO AQAP-4 quality standard, and had met the quality requirements of such companies as Northern Radar and General Motors.

CABLES FOR NORTHERN TELECOM

In spring 1989, Northern Telecom's Belleville, Ontario, plant approached NewTech with a request to produce a ribbon cable for use in some of their products. (A ribbon cable was made up of a number of individual strands of wire running side by side and embedded in a plastic coating, and looked like a ribbon, with connectors at each end.) NewTech began the initial production run of cables in mid-1989 and had sold 24,000 of them to Northern Telecom by the end of 1990 for sales of $549,913. During 1991, NewTech produced another 23,000 of the ribbon cables, generating sales of $527,000. During the first quarter of 1992, sales of ribbon cables were $175,000.

Also, in mid-1991, NewTech began production of five other types of cables for Northern Telecom. Sales of these cables totalled 5,000 units or about $100,000 by the end of 1991. During the first quarter of 1992 sales of these cables were $87,500.

BUILD-TO-PRINT CONTRACTS

Build-to-print was where a customer required a certain product built to its design and specifications, by a certain time, and usually according to a specified delivery schedule and price. Build-to-print could involve some original design work. Much of the build-to-print business in Canada originated with Canadian government defense spending, aerospace contracts, or related research and development projects.

Beginning late in the fall of 1988, NewTech began to bid on build-to-print contracts. It was unsuccessful until, in mid-1989, the company was informed by ACOA that General Motors of Canada Ltd. had been awarded a Canadian government contract to supply 200 Light Armored Vehicles (LAVs). It was a condition of the contract that GM seek out qualified suppliers in Canada, and they had approached ACOA, in its supplier development/advocacy role, for a list of possible Newfoundland subcontractors.

LIGHT ARMORED VEHICLE DRIVER'S INSTRUMENT PANEL

NewTech managers met with GM representatives and persuaded them to inspect

NewTech's manufacturing and design facilities. GM representatives were naturally skeptical that an unknown electronics manufacturing company situated in Newfoundland would be able to meet its production and quality requirements and do so reliably. It was crucial that NewTech was able to show that best practices were in place and were being used in design, production, and quality assurance processes. Following the GM inspection, NewTech was asked to quote on the contract for the driver's instrument panel for the LAV.

On January 10, 1990, NewTech and GM held a news conference to announce the awarding of a contract, worth approximately $870,000, to NewTech. This contract called for NewTech to provide 200 panels at a proposed rate of 10 per month for 20 months. Production got under way in March 1990, and by November 1991 NewTech had filled the entire order, four months earlier than the March 1992 deadline. GM was very impressed with the quality and service provided by NewTech. None of the panels had to be returned or even altered on-site as NewTech had gone to great lengths to ensure that they were thoroughly inspected and tested before they left the plant.

Since NewTech had demonstrated that it could provide a high level of quality on a consistent basis, it was successful in bidding for a further instrument panel contract with GM in early 1991, as GM had won a further contract to supply more LAVs. Unfortunately, political changes led to the cancellation of the entire order and consequently NewTech's subcontract. However, GM Canada was marketing the LAV internationally and was hopeful of obtaining orders for at least 1,100 units worldwide by 1995.

Light Armored Vehicle Fuel Tank Sensor

Late in 1989, GM suggested that NewTech might be able to design a circuit to solve a problem that GM had with the sensor in the LAV fuel tank and its indicator light on the driver's instrument panel. NewTech developed a prototype circuit design and sent it to GM. NewTech managers were pleasantly surprised when, in spring 1990, GM gave NewTech a NATO part number and placed an order for 200 sets of wired circuits for the initial batch of LAVs. Again, this fuel tank sensor could be installed on all LAVs sold internationally.

Light Armored Vehicle Alarm Annunciator Panel

In summer 1991, as a result of involvement with GM Canada's LAV contract, NewTech found out that GM was not happy with the LAV Alarm Annunciator Panel, another of the driver's instruments. It was based on outdated technology, was not as reliable as ideally required, was not repairable in the field, and cost $2,200 per unit. As a result of their associations with Newfoundland Telephone, NewTech personnel had experience in alarm technology and they decided to speculatively design a more modern unit and offer this design to GM. They were able to design a panel that incorporated vehicle alarm indicator lights, for example, low oil pressure and handbrake on, and battlefield alarm indicator lights, for example, fire or gas attack. A prototype was demonstrated to GM in September 1991, and a manufacturing contact was obtained in early fall 1991. The NewTech unit was more functional, more robust, repairable in the field, and had a lower price. At least 1,100 units, at a price of $1,500 per unit, were expected to be sold by NewTech over five years.

Light Armored Vehicle Driver's Head-Up Display

Also in summer 1991, as a result of involvement with GM Canada's LAV contract,

NewTech found out that GM had a requirement for a digital, electronic, externally mounted head-up display (HUD) for the LAV driver. This HUD would be used by the driver when the vehicle was moving unsealed and the armored hatch cover over the driver's head was open. NewTech was successful in being able to design a 6"x1"x1" HUD, readable in bright sunshine and incorporating on its long side facing the driver a digital speedometer and simplified vehicle and battlefield alarm indicator lights. In fall 1991, GM placed orders for this unit. At least 1,100 units at a price of $410 each were expected to be sold by NewTech over five years.

COPPER TELECOMMUNICATIONS CABLE SPLICE CLOSURE PRODUCT

The copper telecommunications cable splice closure product was a patented method of transporting molten polyethylene to a job site and using it in a low-pressure molding process to mold a closure around a prepared cable splice bundle. The application was for nonpressurized cables in the buried and underground outside-plant environments. It enjoyed a significant cost advantage over conventional closure systems. The rights to this technology were purchased from Northern Telecom in late 1988. Sales were expected to be approximately $140,000 over the three years 1992 to 1995. Potential customers included Newfoundland Telephone and other companies that were laying communications and control cabling.

SALINITY METER

In February 1988, NewTech was contacted by a St. John's scientist who had independently originated a design for an underwater salinity meter. Since that time NewTech and the scientist had collaborated in developing a working prototype device. Efforts were under way to market the device to other manufacturers of hydrographic measuring equipment with the aim of persuading them to incorporate the salinity meter into their products or product ranges. When a manufacturer decided to include the salinity meter in its offerings, the form of the prototype would be redesigned to meet that manufacturer's particular specifications and NewTech would aim to build it.

CRAB TESTER

As part of its strategy to develop additional business opportunities, NewTech also sought contract research and development projects from government departments. In mid-1989, NewTech became involved with the crustacean tester concept through taking part in a design competition sponsored by the provincial Department of Fisheries.

When crabs were processed, only live crabs could be used. The standard method for inspecting crabs coming into the processing plant to find out whether they were alive or dead was to take a crab, pull its shell off as fast as possible, and pull open its flesh to see if its heart was beating. Needless to say, this was somewhat injurious to the crab and this shock treatment could itself cause a crab's heart to stop beating, thus leading to rejection of what was in fact a live crab. In any case, this treatment caused a consequent reduction in product quality.

The Department of Fisheries had the idea that a better method would be to stimulate the crab's nervous system with a small electric shock, and if the crab was alive its legs would move. The Department had carried out trials of this testing method and was convinced that it did work to select only live crabs. (Perhaps, if the crab were more intelligent, it would try not to move in the hope that it would be perceived as dead and be thrown back into the sea. However, even more intelligent crabs are presumably unable to keep their legs from moving when given an electric shock.)

NewTech won the Department's design competition for an easy-to-use portable unit and six were built in 1989. Fisherpersons now picked up a crab and held it by its back, put the two prongs of NewTech's test instrument on the crab, pressed a button, and a light flashed to confirm that a current had gone through the crab—and if the crab twitched it was alive.

This product would never be a large money maker, but it was bringing in an income and it had begun to build NewTech's reputation with provincial government departments.

ADNATECH MANUFACTURING CORPORATION

In September 1989, NewTech was approached by Adnatech, a St. John's company, to manufacture the Rodent Guard. When the device was screwed into a light socket, it generated a pulsating high frequency ultrasonic sound barrier that specifically irritated the auditory nerves of rodents, forcing them to leave the area covered by the Rodent Guard. Areas that contained materials upon which rodents could potentially feed, or areas from which rodents had to be especially excluded, could be protected. An initial batch of 5,000 units at $75 each were produced by NewTech. Further units would be produced in the future depending on orders from Adnatech.

EJE TRANS-LITE INC.

In early 1990, NewTech was approached by representatives of EJE, which had developed a small but powerful light that was activated by contact with water. Its main market was as an attachment for lifevests used on cruise ships. Pending legislation would make such lights mandatory for the cruise industry worldwide. Production began in late 1990, and during 1991 NewTech produced 155,000 lights for EJE, worth about $1,250,000. The lights had a projected life of 8 to 10 years, although the legislation required replacement every 5 years.

The initial production run was taken up by ship operators in fulfilling the legislative requirements. The market had then dropped to a level determined by replacements and by sales to operators of ships where the light was not mandatory. However, EJE expected that regulations similar to those in the cruise industry would be introduced in the airline industry, a much larger potential market.

TELEPHONE REFURBISHMENT

In April 1991, NewTech won a six-week contract to refurbish used telephone sets as Newfoundland Telephone Company's contribution to helping the environment through recycling. Even though at the time NewTech did not have sufficient manufacturing facilities to carry out this contract on top of ongoing work, Don Nickerson believed that it could lead to similar more substantial contracts in the future. With this in mind, he rearranged the manufacturing area and hired two trailers to provide temporary storage space so that NewTech could carry out the contract. Once again, NewTech and its employees delivered on time and with superior quality. By the end of 1991, NewTech had won several more short-term refurbishing contracts and had added seven new workbenches to handle the extra production.

In February 1992, NewTech was advised that it would likely be awarded a contract to do all the telephone refurbishing for a year. The contract would be worth approximately $1,000,000 and production would be approximately 550 sets per week, based on the demand estimates from Newfoundland Telephone.

WHALE ALERTER

In recent years there had been increasing concern over the sad fate of whales that became trapped in fishing nets around Newfoundland and Labrador. The Memorial University Whale Research Centre and Centre for Cold Ocean Resources Engineering (C-CORE) had for some time been jointly working on developing an "alerter" in the form of a buoy that could be attached to the fishing nets. This device gave out an intermittent and loud ultrasonic signal that, it was hoped, would alert whales and cause them to avoid the nets.

In February 1991, NewTech was approached by the Whale Research Centre and C-CORE with a prototype and was asked to carry out further development work and produce a batch of alerters for more extensive sea trials. NewTech carried out design-for-manufacture and in doing this it was also able to enhance the performance of the alerter units, so that battery life was extended from 3 to 40 days. Two hundred alerters were sold to C-CORE in 1991. Further development work and sales were dependent on the field trials now under way. If successful, these alerters might have worldwide sales potential.

RADIO SIGNAL RECEPTOR

In mid-1991, NewTech commenced negotiations with a firm in the United Kingdom for the worldwide manufacturing and marketing rights to a radio signal receptor which that firm had developed. The receptor was a small, pen-sized unit that could replace any traditional radio antenna and actually amplify the signal for better reception. One major potential market was the automobile industry which could use it to replace radio antennas on vehicles. Nickerson himself had one of the units installed in his own vehicle and experienced its effectiveness (not only in producing a clear signal, but also in reducing the annoying noise caused by wind drag on a traditional antenna).

In fall 1991, the negotiations were successfully completed. NewTech had secured the services of a North American distributor and it was expected that the receptor would go into full production in spring 1992. Market forecasts suggested an initial sales level of 5,000 units per month

CONTRACT WITH NORCONTROL, LTD.

During 1990, NewTech was involved with Norcontrol Ltd. in its efforts to obtain a contract to supply and install a ship simulator at the Marine Institute in St. John's. As things turned out NewTech did not obtain work from this contract, but received instead a manufacturing contract from Norcontrol for other products. This arrangement was preferable to both companies. Fifty "signal acquisition units" were to be produced for Norcontrol during 1992, and, if these were satisfactory, orders for up to 500 further units were likely over the following four years. NewTech's selling price would be $725 per unit.

NEWTECH'S ORGANIZATION AND OPERATIONS

In March 1992, NewTech employed 39 people. Sales had grown from $129,600 in 1988 to $3.3 million in 1991 (Exhibit 2). However, it was only in 1991 that the company began to make a profit.

EXHIBIT 2 | **NewTech Instruments' Income Statements, 1988–91 (In thousands of Canadian dollars)**

	1988	1989	1990	1991
Sales	$129.6	$589.0	$1,052.2	$3,345.4
Cost of sales	89.1	321.7	694.7	2,527.5
Gross profit	40.5	267.3	357.5	817.9
Other income	13.3	1.8	26.1	51.5
Expenses				
Salaries (administrative)	260.1	268.4	282.4	338.2
Rent	22.2	22.2	14.6	14.6
Professional fees	49.1	13.7	4.2	9.5
Travel	24.6	13.7	12.4	24.5
Office expenses	9.2	9.5	12.9	12.7
Pension and benefits	29.4	29.8	34.5	46.7
Telephone	21.7	22.2	24.9	21.9
Miscellaneous	31.2	28.5	121.7	36.3
Marketing	148.0	151.2	167.1	130.9
Depreciation	6.7	9.2	10.1	11.3
Accounting	13.8	17.4	9.9	6.2
R&D amortization	201.2	345.2	1,254.4	0.0
Insurance	2.4	0.3	0.6	1.0
Municipal taxes	3.4	4.6	2.4	4.3
Research and development	62.8	26.7	9.9	34.3
Bank charges	1.6	1.3	2.0	3.2
	887.4	963.9	1,964.0	695.6
Interest expense	29.3	97.5	183.4	150.7
	916.7	1,061.4	2,147.4	846.3
Income (loss) before income taxes	(862.9)	(792.3)	(1,763.8)	23.1
Income tax	27.5	288.9	(394.6)	10.5
Net income	$(890.4)	$(1,081.2)	$(1,369.2)	$ 12.6

Source: Company records.

NewTech's offices and manufacturing facilities were located in space leased in the Northern Telecom provincial head office/manufacturing and distribution building in St. John's. The front section of NewTech's space, 2,680 square feet, was taken up by the office area, and the rear section, 4,200 square feet, by the manufacturing area. This manufacturing area included the actual work area, a storage area, a hazardous materials storage area, and the mechanical workshop. For most of 1991 and into 1992, NewTech had been fully utilizing its manufacturing space. During 1991, the company had to rent two trailers as storage space in order to be able to complete the telephone refurbishing contracts.

All production work was done at workbenches. Each bench was an independent production area in itself, providing all the tools necessary to manufacture intricate electronic component assemblies. In March 1992, NewTech was operating with 24 workbenches, 7 of which had been added to cope with the extra production requirements since mid-1991.

Don Nickerson was also aware of other considerations related to the pressures on manufacturing space. The provincial Department of Health was applying pressure concerning the small size of the women's washroom relative to the number of women employees. It was also becoming apparent that with the increasing number of employees, the staff lunch room, which often served as a storage area, could no longer be used to store materials. More recently it had become clear that there was an increasing requirement for additional hazardous material storage space, which must be constructed according to all fire and safety regulations.

MANAGEMENT ISSUES AND FUTURE OUTLOOK

Projections of sales revenues, operating expenses, and overheads for 1992 to 1996 are given in Exhibit 3. As the manufacturing facilities were already insufficient, it looked as if more space was needed, and soon. Fortunately, there was no similar pressure on the office space and obtaining further office space was not envisaged.

The management group had been uncertain about how much manufacturing space to accommodate additional workbenches, and so on, was required. They did know, however, that with their present square footage of manufacturing space, including storage areas and washrooms and excluding the temporary trailer storage, they could handle the work needed to support an estimated maximum sales revenue of $3 million.

If they decided to go ahead, NewTech could expand its manufacturing facilities in several ways. The first option was to expand the existing facility; the second was to lease another existing building; the third was to buy another existing building; and the fourth option was to construct a new building of their own. If the company was to move, the one-time cost to move furnishings, fittings, and all manufacturing equipment and supplies, including setup costs in the new location, would be $120,000.

OPTION 1: EXPAND EXISTING FACILITY

Through negotiations with the Northern Telecom manager and landlord, Don Nickerson had secured an agreement to allow NewTech to lease an additional 3,000 square feet in the rear of the building. However, he was concerned whether this amount of space would be sufficient to accommodate the required increased workspace and the other additions to storage areas and washrooms that were becoming needed. The rental cost of existing space in the Northern Telecom building was $9.60 per square foot per year and Don Nickerson believed that this rate would be charged for any new space.

OPTION 2: LEASE ANOTHER EXISTING BUILDING

The second option was to lease a building in Donovan's Industrial Park in the adjoining city of Mount Pearl. As it happened, there was only one available building that could possibly house NewTech's type of operation. This warehouse-type of facility had more than adequate total square footage, but the relatively large office area would have to be reduced in order to be able to establish the manufacturing area at the required size. As well, changes in the ventilation and waste disposal systems would be required to meet NewTech's stringent quality assurance standards. The lease itself would cost $22 per square foot per year for the square footage that NewTech required, and building modifications would be at NewTech's expense.

OPTION 3: PURCHASE ANOTHER EXISTING BUILDING

Very close to NewTech's present facility was a building in reasonable condition

EXHIBIT 3 | **NewTech Instruments Financial Projections, 1992-96 (In thousands of Canadian dollars)**

	1992	1993	1994	1995	1996
Sales revenues					
Refurbishing services	$ 977.2	$1,050.0	$1,310.0	$1,512.0	$1,814.0
Northern	998.9	1,600.7	1,728.8	1,867.0	2,016.4
Translite	606.9	828.0	900.0	1,112.0	1,200.0
General Motors	219.0	1,490.8	1,907.0	2,323.0	2,323.0
Norcontrol	231.3	783.0	797.5	797.5	203.0
Contract work	1,509.1	296.5	352.0	407.0	462.0
Receptor	476.8	1,104.0	1,242.0	1,380.0	1,380.0
New projects	0	674.0	552.7	1,391.5	3,391.6
Miscellaneous projects	197.4	173.0	210.0	210.0	210.0
Total sales revenues	$5,216.6	$8,000.0	$9,000.0	$11,000.0	$13,000.0
Plant overheads					
Plant depreciation	$ 63.6	$ 97.0	$106.2	$113.2	$120.2
Municipal taxes	3.5	4.0	4.1	4.3	4.4
Cleaning and garbage	9.9	13.2	14.0	14.6	15.0
Other costs	3.9	4.2	4.7	5.0	5.4
Labor	19.3	19.2	20.0	21.0	22.0
Equipment maintenance	12.1	12.7	13.1	13.0	13.0
Total plant overheads	$112.3	$150.3	$162.1	$171.1	$180.0
Operating expenses					
Salaries (administrative)	$266.9	$411.6	$466.1	$ 484.7	$ 504.1
Professional fees	0	6.0	6.0	6.0	6.0
Travel	19.7	25.0	25.0	25.0	25.0
Office expenses	12.9	13.0	13.7	14.3	15.0
Pension and benefits	82.6	87.0	90.5	94.1	97.9
Health and education tax	0	0	0	0	0
Telephone	21.8	22.0	22.0	22.0	22.0
Miscellaneous	17.5	19.0	20.0	20.9	22.0
Marketing	152.5	249.2	254.8	306.5	327.1
Depreciation	14.5	23.8	26.9	29.7	32.5
Accounting	8.5	11.5	11.5	11.5	11.5
R&D amortization	0	0	0	0	0
Insurance	1.2	1.4	1.4	1.4	1.4
Municipal taxes	4.3	4.7	4.8	4.9	5.0
Research & development	4.1	30.0	30.0	30.0	30.0
Bank charges	3.2	4.0	4.0	4.0	4.0
Total operating expenses	$609.7	$908.2	$976.7	$1,055.0	$1,103.5

Note: Rent or mortgage costs for manufacturing space must be added to the projections for plant overheads.
Note: Rent or mortgage costs for the office area must be added to the operating expense projections.
Source: Company records.

which had been recently vacated by a St. John's printing and publishing company. This building, which had contained their printing plant and offices, was for sale. It included front offices and a large rear production area (now empty) with large loading doors and loading dock. The cost to buy the land and building was estimated to be around $75 per square foot, for approximately 12,000 square feet.

However, the building required significant capital expenditure in the form of improvements such as repairs to a sagging roof. It would also require the same types of improvements and modifications as the other buildings under consideration in order to meet quality assurance standards. A further concern was that the floor in the plant area had been reinforced in places to enable the installation of very large printing presses. The reinforcement had been made by pouring extra concrete so that the floor was now on two levels. This concrete would be costly to remove and if left in place would complicate the arrangement of the manufacturing space and the work flows. The total cost of the required improvements and modifications to this building was estimated at $250,000.

OPTION 4: CONSTRUCT A NEW BUILDING

NewTech had used the services of a contractor to estimate the cost of constructing a new building. The contractor had provided a quote of $60 per square foot to construct the kind of facility that NewTech needed. However, NewTech managers knew that they had more than construction costs to consider. For example, there were the problems of where the building would be located, where land must be bought, and the building and activity permissions required. Also, utilities and services would need to be paid for, employees would have to travel, and assorted other expenses would arise.

CINEPLEX ODEON

Joseph Lampel, New York University
Jamal Shamsie, McGill University

Garth Drabinsky, chairman and CEO of Cineplex Odeon, has never been known to shy away from a fight. On June 30, 1989, he was true to his reputation as he faced a group of unsettled shareholders at the company's annual meeting in a downtown Toronto theater. Drabinsky had burly guards posted at the entrances and exits, instructed his public relations staff to keep their lips sealed, and did not allow reporters to bring in any electronic equipment.

The firm stance reflected a hardball approach to business that had earned Drabinsky the nickname Darth, after the screen supervillain Darth Vader. But this reputation was based on more than just an aura of toughness and a knack for brilliant deals. It was founded on significant accomplishments in the movie industry. Through a combination of innovative theater formats, bold acquisitions, and strong financial alliances, Drabinsky had developed Cineplex Odeon into the second largest theater chain in North America (see Exhibit 1). In the process, Drabinsky had single-handedly changed the face of film exhibition, rejuvenating what had become a stagnant part of the industry.

As long as Drabinsky continued to pile success upon success, his aggressive style and disregard for conventions were tolerated. His dominance over all aspects of Cineplex Odeon had been deemed necessary for the pursuit of his unique and ambitious vision. But now, with doubts being raised about the financial health of Cineplex Odeon (see Exhibits 2 and 3), Drabinsky's reputation as a brilliant strategist was being subjected to increased scrutiny. Drabinsky was also facing strong resistance, and had suffered serious setbacks in his recent attempts to gain a controlling interest in his company. All of these developments had created an unusually high level of anxiety and anticipation among the audience that had gathered for the company's annual meeting.

The authors wish to acknowledge the assistance of Xavier Gonzalez-Sanfeliu. Copyright © 1990 by the authors.

EXHIBIT 1 | Leading Movie Theater Chains in North America, 1984–88

	1984		1985		1986		1987		1988	
	Screens	Locations	Screens	Locations	Screens	Locations	Screens	Locations	Screens	Locations
United Artists	1,063	344	1,124	329	1,595	437	2,048	485	2,677	686
Cineplex Odeon	439	170	1,117	394	1,510	495	1,644	492	1,832	502
American Multi-Cinema	800	156	956	182	1,336	263	1,528	277	1,614	278
General Cinema	1,083	331	1,163	333	1,275	342	1,358	332	1,400	321
Loews	215	66	232	66	300	85	310	87	822	221
Carmike	432	182	435	168	674	236	669	220	701	213
Hoyts	105	25	103	22	240	52	275	55	550	120
National Amusements	314	84	345	84	393	88	404	77	552	91
Mann	325	98	350	110	456	126	447	110	456	109
Famous Players	466	199	469	196	466	176	427	147	448	148

Source: *Variety.*

EXHIBIT 2 | Cineplex Odeon's Income Statements, 1984–88 (In millions of dollars for the year ended December)

	1984	1985	1986	1987	1988
Revenues					
Admissions	$42.7	$ 85.0	$230.3	$322.4	$355.6
Concessions	12.3	24.9	71.4	101.6	114.6
Distribution and other	9.3	7.8	30.8	61.2	156.4§
Sales of properties*	2.8	6.6	24.4	35.0	69.2
	$67.1	$124.3	$356.9	$520.2	695.8^\parallel$
Expenses					
Operating expenses	$48.7	$ 89.5	$258.3	$371.9	$464.3
Cost of concessions	3.7	6.0	13.7	18.8	21.6
Cost of sold properties	0.9	2.7	11.7	21.6	61.8
General and administrative	3.5	5.7	15.3	18.0	26.6
Depreciation and amortization†	2.1	3.7	14.3	24.0	38.1
	$58.9	$107.6	$313.3	$454.3	$612.4
Other income	0.1	0.3	—	—	3.6
Interest expenses‡	2.5	4.0	16.2	27.0	42.9
Income taxes	2.2	5.0	6.3	4.3	3.7
Extraordinary items	5.6	2.3	1.4	—	—
Net income	$ 9.2	$ 10.3	$ 22.5	$ 34.6	$ 40.4

*Shown as part of operating revenue.
†Depreciation schedule changed from 1986 to lower this charge.
‡Excludes interest costs that have been capitalized.
§Includes proceeds from sale of 49 percent interest in Film House.
$^\parallel$Later changed to $648 million to exclude proceeds from sale of Film House.
Source: Cineplex Odeon annual reports.

But the mounting pressure could hardly mute Drabinsky's forceful style. He ruled the meeting with an iron hand, disdainfully rejecting any attacks from the audience, and defiantly reaffirming his faith in the future of Cineplex Odeon. "I am completely sanguine," he remarked, "that the company will continue to grow."[1] As far as Drabinsky was concerned, this was not the first time he had found himself in a tight corner.

THE EARLY YEARS

A CONSUMING PASSION

Garth Drabinsky's determination to beat the odds began early in life. Stricken by polio at the age of three, he spent most of his childhood checking in and out of hospitals. After a long period of infirmity he was able to walk without a brace, although he has a pronounced limp to this day. The same willpower and concentration that Drabinsky used to confront his illness were later applied to other parts of his life. Although he excelled in a wide variety of activities, it was the silver screen that truly captured his passion.

---

[1] "The Perils of Drabinsky," *Report on Business Magazine,* July 1989.

EXHIBIT 3 | **Cineplex Odeon's Balance Sheets, 1984–88 (In millions of dollars for the year ended December)**

	1984	1985	1986	1987	1988
Assets					
Current assets					
Cash and receivables	$ 5.2	$ 10.0	$ 20.1	$ 42.3	$ 151.5
Distribution advances	3.8	5.3	9.0	21.3	36.9
Inventories and prepaid expenses	3.0	4.6	11.0	13.3	13.0
Property investments	—	—	16.6	22.7	25.6
Fixed assets					
Properties and equipment	49.2	53.3	208.9	261.5	296.7
Leaseholds	17.4	26.9	324.1	490.2	594.4
Accumulated depreciation*	4.3	7.2	19.6	40.2	66.3
Other assets					
Long-term investments	2.7	6.2	14.3	50.0	130.3
Goodwill†	0.6	0.6	40.9	52.6	54.0
Deferred charges	0.8	1.7	6.6	12.0	27.1
	$78.4	$101.4	$631.9	$925.7	$1,263.2
Liabilities and Equity					
Current liabilities					
Bank loans	—	$ 4.8	$ 0.1	$ 20.7	$ 21.7
Payables and accruals	$10.0	13.5	47.7	74.9	129.5
Income taxes	—	0.4	1.9	4.6	5.7
Matured long-term debt	2.1	1.1	6.3	6.0	10.8
Long-term debt	36.1	40.7	317.6	449.7	663.8
Other liabilities					
Lease obligations	—	—	15.9	14.6	14.9
Deferred income taxes	0.8	4.2	11.1	13.3	10.4
Pension obligations	—	—	3.7	4.0	6.3
Minority interest	—	—	—	—	25.1
Shareholders' equity					
Capital stock	39.5	37.1	212.1	289.2	283.7
Translation adjustment	—	—	(3.6)	1.9	13.4
Retained earnings	(10.1)	(0.4)	19.1	46.8	77.9
	$78.4	$101.4	$631.9	$925.7	$1,263.2

*As of 1986, depreciation rates were reduced to 2.5 percent from 5.0 percent straight-line for buildings and to 6.7 percent from 10.0 percent straight-line for equipment.

†As of 1986, goodwill is being amortized over 40 years instead of over 20 years.

Source: Cineplex Odeon annual reports.

Beginning with his law studies at the University of Toronto in the early 1970s, Drabinsky began to make movies his life's work. He took a keen interest in the emerging field of entertainment law, and later wrote a textbook on the subject that became a standard reference source. His studies, however, did not prevent him from producing a half-hour TV show starring William Shatner, and launching a movie magazine that was given away free at cinemas.

In 1976, Drabinsky made a foray into movie production. His first film featured Donald Sutherland but it was never completed. The following year, he teamed up with producer Joel Michaels to form a film production company that remained active for several years. Among the movies that the company produced were *The Silent Partner* with Christopher Plummer, *The Changeling* with George C. Scott, and *Tribute* with Jack Lemmon. Although acclaimed critically, none of these films did well at the box office.

A MULTIPLEX STRATEGY

In 1979, Garth Drabinsky joined forces with Nathan Taylor, an industry veteran who had long believed in the concept of theaters with multiple screens. Drabinsky found the idea appealing, and together the two formed Cineplex. Their first multiplex theater was located in Toronto's Eaton Centre, a newly developed shopping center. It contained 18 screens, with seating capacity ranging from 60 to 150 people per screen.

Cineplex saw itself as a niche player. It countered the trend in the industry that saw exhibitors using their large theaters to get the potentially lucrative releases from the Hollywood distributors (see Appendix to this case). Instead, the newly developed multiplex chain used its small screens to show specialty movies, in particular foreign films and art films that could not be shown profitably in large theaters. As Taylor put it, Cineplex was not out to challenge the major chains, but to complement them:

> We are seeking to develop a market that to some extent doesn't exist. We are taking specialized markets and filling their needs. It's a latent market and a different niche than the major chains go after.[2]

In addition, Cineplex sought to obtain successful U.S. films after they had completed their run with the larger theater chains. It was industry practice for the share of the box office receipts accruing to the distributor to decrease with the run of the movie. Although this allowed exhibitors to keep more of the revenues, the inevitable decline in attendance ordinarily forced large theaters to discontinue exhibition once the number of empty seats exceeded a certain level. It was at this point that Cineplex could pick up the films, and by virtue of its small theaters keep most of the seats full.

The advantages of the multiplex concept were primarily due to a carefully planned use of shared facilities. All the theaters in a location were served by a single box office and a single concession stand. The use of advanced projection technology made it possible for one or two projectionists in a centralized projection booth to handle all screening duties in a multiplex theater. Show times were staggered in order to avoid congestion. Even advertising costs were lowered by using a single ad for all the films playing at a particular location.

The success of the multiplex concept spurred Cineplex to expand its operations across Canada. The company also made an entry into the large U.S. market with the development of a 14-screen theater complex in the Beverly Hills section of Los Angeles. By the end of 1982, the company was operating almost 150 screens in 20 different locations.

A CLOSE BRUSH WITH BANKRUPTCY

The rapid rate of expansion brought Cineplex face to face with financial and market realities that its owners had not anticipated. During its expansion the company had amassed $21 million in debt, mostly in high and floating interest rates. This came in

---

[2]"Cineplex Getting the Big Picture," *Financial Post,* June 14, 1980.

the midst of an economic recession that cut deeply into the company's earnings. To make matters worse, U.S. distributors were increasingly reluctant to supply Cineplex with the hit films for fear of alienating the two large Canadian exhibition chains, Famous Players and Canadian Odeon. Without the revenues of major U.S. releases the company's future was bleak.

To avert imminent bankruptcy, Cineplex took steps throughout 1983 to reduce its debt and improve its cash flow by selling off some of the company's assets, raising funds through the public offering of more shares, and persuading the banks to extend further credit. But these measures did not address the company's blocked access to major releases. To break through the barrier, Drabinsky sought government intervention. Using his legal training, he marshaled the evidence and managed to convince the Canadian government that strong grounds existed for launching an investigation into the existence of a conspiracy aimed at depriving Cineplex of access to major releases.

In the face of government investigation, and possible sanctions, the U.S. distributors modified their stand and agreed to a system of competitive bidding that would ensure all had equal access to their films. With this hurdle surmounted Drabinsky was able to secure financial backing from institutional investors. A large investment came from Claridge, a holding company owned by the Bronfmans, one of Canada's most powerful business families.

To Drabinsky, the close brush with bankruptcy had also revealed a basic flaw in his company's position. He became acutely aware that his small theaters generated insufficient revenues to bid for early runs of the most lucrative U.S. films. So when the principal owner of Canadian Odeon passed away, Drabinsky saw an opportunity that was not to be missed. Canadian Odeon had been greatly weakened by the new bidding system that Drabinsky had helped to bring about. Alarmed by Odeon's poor performance, the heirs finally accepted Drabinsky's offer of a little over $22 million for the entire chain.

The acquisition of Canadian Odeon in the spring of 1984, at what many viewed as a bargain-basement price, ended a remarkable turnaround for a company that just two years earlier had faced bankruptcy. Now, with over 450 screens in as many as 170 different locations, Cineplex was a major player in the industry. Drabinsky relished his comeback, and was not above taking a passing shot at his detractors: "A lot of people who were waiting for me to go under were disappointed. Well, they didn't get their jollies."[3]

CINEPLEX ODEON'S STRATEGY

The formation of Cineplex Odeon crowned Drabinsky's comeback from the verge of bankruptcy, but he was not content to rest on his laurels. Now that he controlled one of North America's major theater chains he set out to transform the moviegoing experience itself. With the advent of pay-television channels and prerecorded videocassettes, it was becoming increasingly difficult to lure moviegoers from the comfort of their homes.

Drabinsky aimed to change the public's perceptions by renovating the theaters, beginning with the physical format. Cineplex Odeon discarded the uniformly drab design common in most theater chains in favor of artwork in the lobbies, lush woolen

---

[3]"Upwardly Mogul," *Report on Business Magazine,* December 1985.

carpets spread over marble floors, and coral and peach color-coordinated walls. The screening auditoriums featured scientifically contoured seats, digital background music, and state-of-the-art projection systems. As a final touch, the company reintroduced real buttered popcorn in the concession stands, and cafes that offered freshly made cappucino.

The metamorphosis was completed with the unveiling of a new company logo in the form of a curved bowl that was reminiscent of a Greek amphitheater. Furthermore, in choosing colors for the logo, Drabinsky decided on a combination of imperial purple and fuchsia. For him, the logo was no mere representation; it was intended to make people sit up and take notice. As Drabinsky put it, "I felt that this would be more of a bravado kind of statement. I don't think anyone was ready for that."[4]

Cineplex Odeon's new format differed sharply from the prevailing industry response to the threat posed by pay television and take-home videocassettes. Most theater chains were trying to cut their fixed costs by slicing old movie palaces into tiny cinemas and eliminating many services that were deemed inessential. Drabinsky, on the other hand, believed that the moviegoing experience was not confined to what was shown on the screen. When patrons entered the theater, Drabinsky wanted them to leave behind a mundane existence and gradually move into a different reality. In the words of Drabinsky:

> We are determined to give back to our patrons the rush and excitement and anticipation and curiosity that should be theirs when they leave the techno-regimented world of their daily lives for the fantasy world of escape that is the movies.[5]

MANAGING COSTS

Drabinsky's strategy, however, proved costly. Cineplex Odeon found itself spending almost $3 million on a typical six-screen multiplex, a third more than the average for the industry. But as far as Drabinsky was concerned, the additional investment bore fruit not only at the box office, but at the concession counter as well. The classier upscale atmosphere was meant to entice customers into spending more time in the theaters before and after the movie, resulting in higher sales at the concession counter. Indeed, the concessions at Cineplex Odeon's theaters usually generated almost $2 per moviegoer, an amount close to twice the industry average.

Still, the additional revenues generated by higher concession sales covered only a fraction of the fixed costs of a typical Cineplex Odeon theater. In an effort to reduce costs, Drabinsky had imposed stringent cost controls throughout his organization. Odeon's management was Drabinsky's first target. Upon acquisition, Drabinsky dismissed about two-thirds of Odeon's head office staff, and cut the pay of the remaining personnel by 10 percent. He also canceled their company credit cards as an incentive to frugality. As he put it at the time, "When you make people use their own money they think hard about the justification they'll have to provide when filing their expense claims."[6] The cost-cutting campaign did not leave any facet of the company's operations untouched. Even the traditional cardboard containers used to sell popcorn were replaced with bags, a move that saved Cineplex Odeon close to $1 million per year.

---

[4]"King of the Silver Screen," *Macleans,* September 28, 1987.
[5]"Big Money at the Movies," *Macleans,* July 28, 1986.
[6]"Upwardly Mogul."

In spite of these measures, Drabinsky was forced to search for other sources of revenue. He raised admission fees well above the competition in most markets, and began to show commercials before the screening of the main feature. Both moves were highly unpopular. Irate patrons expressed their anger in a number of cities, sometimes by protesting outside Cineplex Odeon's theaters. The most publicized of these protests occurred in New York City, where Mayor Ed Koch joined picketers in a call for a boycott of the chain because of its price increase.

The criticisms against Drabinsky were tempered by his use of promotional gimmicks. Most significant among these was the tactic of offering lower admission prices on Tuesdays. Attendance at Cineplex theaters had climbed substantially for these Tuesdays, generating additional revenues as well as restoring some measure of goodwill among customers.

A POWERFUL COMPETITOR

With Drabinsky at the helm, Cineplex Odeon now launched a major expansion into North America's main movie markets. By and large, this expansion was based on a series of acquisitions in the United States (see Exhibit 4). In an industry known for tough negotiators and agile deal makers, Garth Drabinsky gained a reputation as a tenacious and abrasive businessman. He used his stamina and his adversarial style of bargaining to wear opponents down. His biggest acquisition involved the Plitt theater chain, which had almost 600 screens in over 200 locations.

EXHIBIT 4 | **Cineplex Odeon's Acquisitions of U.S. Theaters, 1985–87**

1985	Plitt Theaters Los Angeles, California 574 screens / 209 locations
1986	Septum Cinemas Atlanta, Georgia 48 screens / 12 locations
1986	Essaness Theaters Chicago, Illinois 41 screens / 13 locations
1986	RKO Century Warner Theaters New York, New York 97 screens / 42 locations
1986	Neighborhood Theaters Richmond, Virginia 76 screens / 25 locations
1986	SRO Theaters Seattle, Washington 99 screens / 33 locations
1987	Walter Reade Organization New York, New York 11 screens / 8 locations
1987	Circle Theaters Washington, D.C. 80 screens / 22 locations

Source: Cineplex Odeon.

In every market he entered Drabinsky used all the means at his disposal to gain market share and keep the competition on the defensive. He pursued Famous Players, his long-standing rival in Canada, with special vengeance. In 1986 Drabinsky seized an opportunity to lease part of a building in Toronto that housed the Imperial Theatre, a six-theater complex operated by Famous Players. Since his part of the building contained the main entrance to all of the theaters in the complex, Drabinsky exercised the right to deny Famous Players public access. He used barbed wire and security guards with Doberman pinschers to enforce the blockade. Ultimately, Famous Players was forced to close down and sell this key location to Cineplex Odeon, but not before it extracted a public apology from Drabinsky, and a commitment that the facility would never be used to show motion pictures.

Drabinsky also tried to use the size of his chain to obtain added clout with film studios and distributors. He consistently used Cineplex Odeon's size to bargain hard to obtain potential hits on more favorable terms, but his insistence on having his way created friction in his relationships with suppliers. The tensions erupted into the open in 1987 when Columbia Pictures rejected Drabinsky's demand that Bernardo Bertolucci's epic *The Last Emperor* be made available for wide release during the Christmas period. In retaliation, Drabinsky refused to exhibit another of the studio's films that was slated for Christmas release. The episode led to more of Columbia's films being diverted to other chains, such as Famous Players, Drabinsky's major Canadian competitor.

Drabinsky's readiness to challenge industry conventions had upset many who felt that he did not play by the rules. Walter Senior, the president of Famous Players, considered Drabinsky's tactics ultimately destructive. As he put it in the aftermath of the Imperial Theatre affair: "We all learn in school that when you set out to destroy someone, it becomes a weakness."[7] Myron Gottlieb, Cineplex Odeon's chief administrative officer, believed that much of the harsh treatment meted out to Drabinsky in the press reflected his impact on the industry rather than simply his style:

> There's been a lot of press about Garth, and some of it's been negative up until now. Some of it has been because of his aggressiveness, but more of it is because of the antagonism to the waves he's created in the industry.[8]

VERTICAL MOVES

In 1982, at a time when Cineplex was still a small company screening foreign and art films, Drabinsky moved to consolidate and expand the company's other film-related activities. These consisted mainly of a film-making subsidiary originally started by Nathan Taylor and a film distribution arm launched by Drabinsky in 1979.

The film-making subsidiary was one of Canada's largest and was located just north of Toronto. Its facilities were rented out to various groups for film and television production. These included two sound stages, dressing and wardrobe rooms, a carpentry mill, a plaster shop, and editing and screening rooms. The distribution arm had been originally created by Drabinsky to provide foreign and art films to the newly developed Cineplex chain. It quickly developed into one of the largest distribution companies in Canada, acquiring the right to distribute films to theaters and on videocassettes, as well as for use on network and pay television.

---

[7]"King of the Silver Screen."
[8]"A Czar Is Born," *Canadian Business,* October 1984.

In 1986, Drabinsky increased the involvement of his company in film making through the acquisition of the Film House. The Toronto-based facility consisted of a large film-processing laboratory, and a fully equipped postproduction sound studio. Following its purchase, Cineplex Odeon increased the capacity of the film laboratory and constructed new upgraded sound facilities.

Meanwhile, Drabinsky expanded the film production and distribution activities of his company into the United States. With the move into this larger market, Cineplex Odeon was able to step up its level of participation in film making. It began to contribute toward the production of small-budget films such as Paul Newman's *The Glass Menagerie* and Prince's rock concert film, *Sign o' the Times.*

Finally, Drabinsky entered into a collaborative venture with MCA, a large U.S. entertainment conglomerate. The two companies agreed to jointly develop and operate a large film studio and theme park in Orlando, Florida, that would compete with Disney World. The move reflected Drabinsky's determination to make Cineplex Odeon into a corporation that spanned every part of the movie industry. As he put it:

> It's an amalgamated company with revenue from theaters, distribution, production, the studio, and, down the road, live theater. People aren't buying a share in this company just to have a share in a motion picture. They're getting a share in a vertically integrated entertainment corporation.[9]

A ONE-MAN SHOW

Cineplex Odeon was firmly under the control of Drabinsky, who had concentrated power in his hands over the years. He became president of the company in 1980, added the title of chief executive officer in 1982, and was confirmed as chairman of the board in 1986. The titles symbolized Drabinsky's total involvement with the company and it was well known that no one else was allowed to speak on behalf of the company.

In both deed and word Drabinsky attempted to communicate to his employees the total commitment that was expected of them. The managers who worked in close proximity to Drabinsky found his driving energy both exhilarating and exhausting. Lynda Friendly, vice president of marketing and communications since 1982, sat in on all of Drabinsky's interviews with the press and was inspired by his stamina and drive:

> Garth is so bloody energetic. I don't know how he does it. It's mind over matter. He stretches people to their absolute limit. He is a teacher, a mentor—a leader.[10]

Other officers, however, found Drabinsky's energy difficult to emulate. They did not appreciate the midnight phone calls they regularly received from Drabinsky, nor did they agree that they must be ready to sacrifice all to their work. As a former Cineplex Odeon executive described it, the pressure Drabinsky put on managers was relentless:

> He works seven days a week and doesn't believe in holidays. Holidays are a disloyalty to the corporation and he *is* the corporation. He is tireless and he expects the same amount of dedication and effort from everyone else.[11]

---

[9] "Movie Mogul," *Business Journal,* October 1982.
[10] "King of the Silver Screen."
[11] "Tough Bosses," *Report on Business Magazine,* December 1987.

Some of Drabinsky's immediate subordinates found his drive for total control unacceptable. His consolidation of power had been accompanied by a significant turnover among the top executives of the company. Several of the present executive officers had been appointed since 1986 (see Exhibit 5). Those who had survived the transition were for the most part people with close personal ties to Drabinsky. Lynda Friendly, for example, had known Drabinsky since they attended synagogue together as teenagers. One of the most important loyalists was Myron Gottlieb, who had financially supported Drabinsky since the starting days of the company. Gottlieb's career in Cineplex Odeon closely dovetailed that of Drabinsky. He became the vice chairman of the board in 1982, and was appointed to the position of chief administrative officer in 1985.

OPERATING PHILOSOPHY

By January 1, 1989, Cineplex Odeon was the second largest motion picture exhibitor in North America with just over 1,800 screens in 500 different locations (Exhibit 1). Almost two-thirds of the company's screens were located in the United States and were spread out over 20 different states. The remaining one-third of these screens were situated in six different Canadian provinces. Cineplex Odeon theaters could be found in virtually all major population centers, from New York to Los Angeles in the United States, and from Toronto to Vancouver in Canada. Close to 90 percent of the chain's theaters, however, were located in leased premises, with rent calculated as a percentage of box office receipts, subject to a minimum.

As of early 1989, the company had close to 13,000 employees. These included film projectionists, cashiers, concession workers, ushers, and ticket takers. However, the bulk of these employees were hired on a part-time basis during seasons of high demand, and they were paid the minimum wage. Only about 15 percent of the employees were represented by unions. For each theater, the information obtained from its computerized box office terminals was used to schedule the minimal amount of staff for any given show. In addition to staff employed to operate the theater, Cineplex Odeon employed as many as 100 full-time architects, engineers, and draftsmen, all used for the design and renovation of theaters.

The Cineplex Odeon chain of theaters was divided into districts, with each district under the control of a supervisor. The task of a district supervisor was to ensure that all theaters followed guidelines set by the head office. He or she also regularly inspected theaters and reported the results to the head office. This report was contrasted with information provided by an independent agency whose representatives visited each theater on a random basis. In addition to this information, the head office relied on weekly reports supplied by the theater's manager detailing market conditions, competitors' activities, and audience response to advanced screening.

The centralization of information was matched by a consistent effort to centralize purchasing and accounting. All supplies and services were purchased centrally in order to maximize economies and reduce spoilage and waste. The computerized box office allowed the company to monitor ticket sales, as well as exercise stringent controls on the handling of cash.

Cineplex Odeon put a great deal of emphasis on a set of standards and practices set forth in staff orientation and training manuals. These standards were often drafted by Drabinsky, who went to great lengths to ensure that they were followed to the letter. He visited theaters regularly, often dropping by unannounced to talk with cashiers or ushers. He also phoned or saw 20 or 25 theater managers a week.

E X H I B I T 5 | **Profile of Cineplex Odeon's Senior Executives, 1989**

	G. I. Drabinsky	M. I. Gottlieb	J. M. Banks	A. Karp	L. Friendly	C. Bruner	E. Jacob
Title(s)	Chairman of board; president; chief executive officer	Vice chairman of board; chief administrative officer	Senior executive vice president, corporate affairs	Senior executive vice president	Executive vice president, marketing and communications	Senior vice president; treasurer	Senior vice president; chief financial officer
Age	40	45	57	48	39	31	35
Previous positions	Director since 1978	Director since 1980	Director 1983–86	—	Senior vice president, marketing and communications	Assistant treasurer	Vice president and corporate controller
Year of entry	1980	1985	1987	1986	1982	1985	1987
Previous employment	Law firm	Investment firm	Law firm	Law firm	Not available	Public accounting firm	Electronics firm

Source: Cineplex Odeon, Form 10-K.

All of this reflected Drabinsky's conviction that he had to know everything that went on in his theaters and constantly be on the lookout for problems that needed correcting. He was known to deliver a silent but none-too-subtle reprimand to ushers by bending down in front of them to pick up a single piece of spilled popcorn. An employee who had observed Drabinsky in action commented: "Anything that is not absolutely perfect drives him crazy. He leaves people with a lasting impression when they screw up."[12]

FINANCIAL STRUCTURE

As of January 1, 1989, Cineplex Odeon had 23.9 million common shares and 23.6 subordinate restricted voting shares outstanding. The company made the transition from private to public financing in 1982 when it was listed on the Toronto Stock Exchange. The total value of its equity was estimated at $375 million (Exhibit 3).

A large block of shares, representing just over 30 percent of the company's total equity, was in the hands of Claridge, a holding company. For the most part, Claridge handled the investments of the Bronfman family, owners of the Seagram liquor business. The investment was made in 1983 to help Cineplex out of its early difficulties. Claridge had backed the development of the Eaton Centre, in the basement of which Cineplex had opened its first theaters.

In a subsequent deal Drabinsky sold a large block of shares to MCA, a U.S. entertainment conglomerate that owns Universal Studios. The deal allowed MCA to purchase up to 50 percent of the company's outstanding shares. However, MCA's control of Cineplex Odeon was restricted to 33 percent by Canadian law, which limits voting shares by foreign companies.

In 1987 Cineplex Odeon consummated its first offering of shares in the United States and was listed on the New York Stock Exchange. In spite of this substantial enlargement of the company's equity base, most of the financing during 1987 and 1988 was through the use of debt. Not surprisingly, the price of Cineplex Odeon's shares had fluctuated. It reached a high around the time of the MCA purchase, but had dropped considerably since then. In spite of the decline, Drabinsky continued to defend the company's low gross margins and insisted that his chain had the highest return on equity among major exhibition chains. The fault, Drabinsky claimed on one occasion, was in the brokerage industry, and not in the performance of Cineplex Odeon:

> The brokerage industry is just full of people who like to hear themselves speak, but there's not a lot of substance there. This company is complete substance from top to bottom.[13]

FUTURE HORIZONS

RELENTLESS GROWTH

In spite of growing financial constraints, Cineplex Odeon had not slowed the pace of its expansion. The company continued to construct new theaters, and to refurbish existing ones. Cineplex Odeon had about 2,100 screens in North America alone in 1992. For Drabinsky the expansion had a dual purpose. First, he wanted to surge past his competitors and capture an increasing share of the North American market.

---

[12]"A New Hollywood Legend Called—Garth Drabinsky?" *Business Week,* September 23, 1985.
[13]"Drabinsky's Movie Machine," *Financial Times,* August 26, 1985.

Second, Drabinsky believed that only a larger Cineplex Odeon could force the major distributors to give the chain the big-budget movies at more favorable terms.

But several other large exhibition chains that competed with Cineplex Odeon were also on the move, building new multiscreen theaters and acquiring smaller chains (see Exhibit 1). Many in the industry feared that the proliferation of screens would not be matched by a corresponding increase in movie attendance. A major recession could aggravate the situation.

Drabinsky's critics contended that costly acquisitions and expensive theaters were making Cineplex Odeon especially vulnerable to an industry slowdown. For his part, Drabinsky had sought to allay the fears of shareholders by insisting that the growth of Cineplex Odeon was neither haphazard nor reckless:

> I want you to appreciate that everything we do is part of a thoroughly studied, painstakingly thought-out game plan. We're not expanding for the sake of expanding.[14]

Plans for the expansion of theaters were not confined to the North American continent. Drabinsky had unveiled plans to spend around $100 million to develop over 100 screens in the United Kingdom by the end of 1990. He believed that better theaters and a faster release of major U.S. films could reverse the decline in attendance and reinvigorate the British market.

In addition to theater expansion, Drabinsky had been getting his company increasingly involved in film production since it had the capacity to both distribute and exhibit movies. During 1988, Cineplex Odeon helped to finance and distribute movies by such noted directors as John Schlesinger and Oliver Stone. The company had also negotiated a joint production agreement with small production companies headed by Robert Redford and Taylor Hackford. But Drabinsky had frequently stated that Cineplex Odeon would restrict itself to making a few low-budget films and not become involved in the risky business of producing big-budget movies.

Drabinsky had also extended his production activities to other entertainment areas. Cineplex Odeon financed the run of some lavish Broadway musicals in Toronto during 1988. The company converted the Toronto theater it wrested from the Famous Players chain into a 2,100-seat center for the performing arts. The theater, a vaudeville palace in its previous incarnation, now restored to its former glory, was used to stage the Canadian production of Andrew Lloyd Webber's *The Phantom of the Opera* in 1989, with an initial production cost over $6.5 million.

A PERFORMANCE UNDER SCRUTINY

Drabinsky's unrelenting drive for growth put pressure on the company's finances. During 1988, Cineplex Odeon asked the banks to boost its line of credit by another $175 million to $750 million. More recently, the company sold off 50 percent of the Film House, its film production operation in Toronto, and most of its share in the Florida theme park to a British entertainment firm. The company also raised capital by selling off some of its theaters, then leasing them back.

In the opinion of a number of industry observers, the true financial position of Cineplex Odeon was masked by the company's accounting practices (see the footnotes to Exhibits 2 and 3). In 1986, the company extended the period over which it would depreciate its properties and its goodwill, resulting in inflated asset values and understated costs. The company's operating profits were also believed to be overstated because one-time sales of assets were included as part of operating revenue.

---

[14]"Market Apathy the Real Culprit, Drabinsky Says," *Toronto Globe and Mail,* May 13, 1988.

The financial uncertainty created apprehension among the company's stockholders, who still recalled the narrow escape from bankruptcy six years earlier. Drabinsky, however, denied that he was undermining Cineplex Odeon by involving the company in activities it could ill afford. He frequently reiterated his conviction that he must at all times be ready to take advantage of emerging opportunities. When asked in a recent interview to predict the company's future development, he had this to say:

> If you asked me five years ago what Cineplex would look like today, I wouldn't have predicted what we have today. So when you ask me today what Cineplex will look like in five years, I can't tell you exactly.[15]

Publicly, Drabinsky rebuffed his critics and sought to allay shareholders' fears. In private, he and his close associates sought to gain control of Cineplex Odeon by making an offer to buy the 30 percent stake held by Bronfman's holding company. Taken together with the 8 percent stake that was already owned by Drabinsky and Gottlieb, they would have had enough shares to outvote and outflank MCA, which was restricted to a 33 percent limit on voting rights.

But MCA moved swiftly to obtain an injunction preventing the deal from going through, even as Drabinsky and Gottlieb were putting on the finishing touches. A financial analyst attempted to explain the reasons for MCA's reaction:

> No one understands what Drabinsky and Gottlieb are up to. They pulled out of the Florida deal, they sold off Film House, they are taking bigger risks in film production, and now the Bronfmans are getting out. From MCA's point of view there are probably lots of reasons to stop Garth from getting control.[16]

MCA eventually managed to get the court to rule that the offer that had been made by Drabinsky and his associates should be extended to all of Cineplex Odeon's outstanding shareholders. This forced Drabinsky to scramble for over $1 billion of financing in order to back such an offer. It was widely speculated that if he was not able to raise this required amount, he could be forced out of the company that he had always considered to be his own.

APPENDIX: THE MOVIE INDUSTRY

SUPPLY OF MOVIES

The number of movies available for exhibition had grown significantly over the past few years. Most of this growth in supply resulted from the increased activities of smaller independent distribution companies. The numbers of feature-length films released over the last five years were as follows:

	1984	1985	1986	1987	1988
Major distributors	169	149	142	133	159
Smaller distributors	210	271	296	354	330
Total	379	420	438	487	489

Source: *Variety.*

---

[15] "Darth' Plays Movie Hardball—and Wins," *Financial Times,* December 28, 1987.
[16] "Clash of the Movie Titans," *Financial Post,* April 22–24, 1989.

In spite of the growing number of suppliers, the bulk of the revenues still came from the films distributed by the nine major companies that had dominated the industry for more than 50 years. Based in Hollywood, these companies include Paramount, Warner Brothers, Disney, Universal, and Columbia. In 1988, the 159 films that were released by these firms accounted for more than 90 percent of the box office dollars in the United States and Canada.

The relative success of the major distributors stems in large part from their greater supply of capital. The typical Hollywood studio spent, on the average, almost $16 million for each of the films produced during 1988. Another $4 to $6 million was usually spent to market or advertise the movie and up to $2 million can be spent on making sufficient copies of the film so that it can be released to a wide number of theaters.

The movies of the smaller distributors are usually budgeted at under $5 million and frequently lack the major stars or production values that can increase their chances of striking it rich at the box office. In fact, an industry publication recently reported that more than half of the movies that are offered by the smaller distributors do not ever play in theaters, but are released directly into the videocassette market.

Although the major distributors continue to dominate the industry, they have long abandoned their practice of binding the most attractive movie directors and stars to long-term employment contracts. Most of the Hollywood movies are now typically made through contractual arrangements with thousands of smaller production outfits. The major distributor may either fund a movie from start to finish or provide a portion of the financing in return for a share of the subsequent box office receipts.

As a result of lackluster financial results, some of the smaller distributors have either folded their operations or merged with other distributors. Even some of the major distributors have merged together, such as the amalgamation of MGM with United Artists. These trends indicate that in the future, fewer major distributors will control the total number of movies available to theaters for exhibition.

EXHIBITION OF MOVIES

Recent surveys have indicated that a large segment of the population—up to 45 percent in recent years—has stopped going out to see movies. Consequently, there has been a growing emphasis upon improving the quality of theaters to entice more people into visiting them. This has resulted in large-scale renovations of existing theaters as well as the construction of new ones. During this process, hundreds of smaller independent theaters have been forced to sell out to the larger chains that could more easily afford to make the necessary investments.

Industry estimates indicate that there were over 23,000 screens in the United States and Canada by the end of 1988. Almost 50 percent of these were collectively held by the top 10 exhibition chains. During the 80s, some of the major movie distributors had also begun to buy up theater chains. These distribution companies argued that by owning theaters they could guarantee the public a higher-quality presentation of their movies.

The major distributors had been forced to divest themselves of their theaters at the peak of the growth of the movie industry. In the late 1940s, the U.S. Justice Department ruled that the same companies could not make, as well as show, movies. The legislation was a result of allegations that the movie distributors were restricting their movies to their own theaters and engaging in fixing prices. However, the attitudes toward restrictions on the ownership of movie theaters had become more relaxed in recent years. In part, this had been made possible by clearer and more stringent laws that provided fairer access to movies by all exhibitors.

REVENUES FROM THEATERS

There is widespread debate about the effects of recessions on movie attendance. Some financial analysts have recently shown that box office receipts decreased during the early 1930s and during the early 1970s. In fact, ticket sales in 1971 dipped to 820 million admissions before picking up again.

For the most part, however, annual ticket sales had been relatively stable at around one billion admissions per year for almost 30 years. The audience for movies in theaters was heavily dominated by younger individuals, particularly below 30 years of age. But recent evidence suggested that the traditional drop in attendance after the age of 30 had been lessening.

Box office receipts had risen considerably over the years, largely as a result of increases in the prices of tickets. There was considerable variation in ticket sales over the year, with almost half of the sales coming between late May and early September as well as between late November and early January. The box office totals for the United States over the past five years were as follows:

1984	$4.0 billion
1985	$3.8 billion
1986	$3.7 billion
1987	$4.2 billion
1988	$4.4 billion

Source: *Variety.*

The average ticket price had risen to $4.11 in 1988, up from $3.36 in 1984. Theater owners were generally reluctant to raise ticket prices more rapidly than inflation for fear of losing viewers. Increasingly, however, they had come to rely upon the lobby concession stand to make their profits. Once inside the theaters, moviegoers became a captive market for popcorn, soft drinks, and candy sold at inflated prices. Recent surveys indicate that exhibition chains derive as much as 20 percent of their revenues from high-profit items sold at their concessions.

SPLITTING OF REVENUES

There was considerable wrangling between the distributors and exhibitors over the distribution of box office revenues. The distributors had tried to use their new sources of revenue from videocassettes and pay TV to reduce their dependence on the theaters.

In spite of the growing availability of these new channels, distribution companies reached more people through exhibiting their movies in theaters. More significantly, the values of their movies on videocassettes and pay TV were heavily dependent upon a respectable theatrical run. A successful movie will create more demand for pay TV as well as for videocassette rentals.

In recent years, the exhibitors had been able to use the increased supply of movies to negotiate a larger share of the box office receipts. But the observed increase in the total number of screens across the continent was expected to allow the distributors to regain the advantage. Several growing exhibition chains may have to compete with

B I T   6 | **Revenue Sources for Movie Productions, 1980 and 1988**

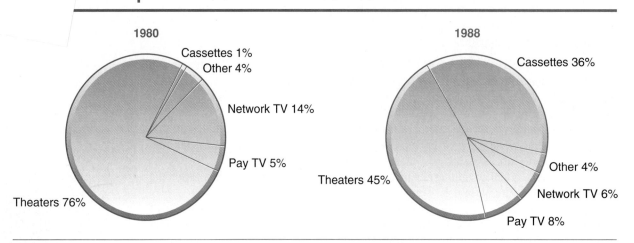

1980

Cassettes 1%
Other 4%
Network TV 14%
Pay TV 5%
Theaters 76%

1988

Cassettes 36%
Other 4%
Network TV 6%
Pay TV 8%
Theaters 45%

Source: *Variety.*

each other to get the potential hit movies, which still tend to come from a few large Hollywood studios.

Typically, the distributor and the exhibitor split the box office revenue equally with each other. The distributor eventually passes on to the producers and investors about 20 percent of the revenue of a movie. The remainder is retained by the distributor to cover internal operating and advertising costs.

CRAFTING STRATEGY IN SINGLE-BUSINESS COMPANIES

FLUENT MACHINES, INC. (A)

Raymond M. Kinnunen, Northeastern University
John A. Seeger, Bentley College
James F. Molloy, Northeastern University

For a start-up to succeed you really need three things. First is extraordinary, talented people. Second, you need a good idea; and third, you need money. All three things are getting scarcer and scarcer. I've lived through two successful high-tech start-ups. I never really thought I'd find a classy situation for a third one.

Neil Ferris, cofounder of Fluent Machines, Inc., reflected in January of 1990 on his experiences with start-up companies. Ferris had joined Data General Corporation when it split off from Digital Equipment Corp. Data General became a thriving manufacturer of minicomputers. He and others left Data General to design and build the first graphics workstations, in a new company called Apollo Computers. Apollo's legendary success (sales went from $0 in 1980 to $216 million four years later) made millionaires of 60 of its employees. Ferris left his Apollo vice presidency in 1986, when the company reached $250 million in revenues. "I took a reprieve, and did some fly fishing," he said. In 1989, with revenues of $700 million per year, Apollo sold out to Hewlett-Packard. The value of the sale was $476 million.

In June of 1989 Ferris teamed with David Nelson for a third start-up, a company they called Fluent Machines, Inc. "We've each been through two of these," said Ferris. "Now here we are, subjecting ourselves to the same torment again." (Exhibit 1 gives the backgrounds of Ferris and Nelson.) Ferris commented:

David Nelson is extraordinarily gifted. He is everything I'm not. He's a world class EE designer. I tend to be more an operating person. I'm his complement when it comes to driving the day-to-day business issues of the company. David has a strategic view of how the future will be changed by technology and can translate those ideas into useful products. He knows what our product will look like, even if he can't say when it will be ready to show a prospect.

Copyright © 1992 by R. M. Kinnunen. Reprinted from *Entrepreneurship: Theory and Practice,* Fall 1993. Used with permission.

EXHIBIT 1 | **Fluent Machines' Top Management Team**

Dr. David Nelson, Founder and President
Prior to founding Fluent Machines, Dr. Nelson was vice president and chief technical officer at Apollo Computer, a company which he cofounded in 1980. At Apollo, Dr. Nelson played an instrumental role in defining the overall architecture of the modern engineering workstation. His areas of expertise include systems engineering, user interfaces, and software development tools. Before founding Apollo, Dr. Nelson was Director of Research at Prime Computer, and Manager of the Architectural Research Division at Digital Equipment Corporation. He received his Ph.D. degree in electrical engineering from the University of Maryland.

Cornelius Ferris, Vice President for Operations and Chief Financial Officer
Prior to joining Fluent in 1989, Neil Ferris held senior manufacturing and operations planning positions at several high-growth computer companies. He was one of the first employees at both Apollo Computer and Data General Corporation. At Apollo he became vice president for Massachusetts manufacturing. At Data General he was corporate director of manufacturing and planning. Before joining Data General, Mr. Ferris served as senior procurement manager at Honeywell. He received his MBA and BA degrees from Northeastern University.

THE COMPANY AND ITS PRODUCT

Dr. Nelson observed an increasing demand for moving images and sound in a broad range of desktop computer applications. He saw an opportunity for a new company to solve the challenging technical problems associated with integrating full-motion video and audio into networked computing environments. Dr. Nelson assembled an experienced engineering team. The team consisted of graduates of the MIT Media Laboratory, the world's leading digital audio/video research facility, and hardware and software designers experienced in digital video, systems, and networks.

The company's 1989 business plan defined a "fluent machine" as a device that "naturally integrates the types and forms of information that people deal with (including text, graphs, spreadsheets, sound, pictures, and motion video)." Neither television nor computer systems fit this definition, since each dealt exclusively with a subset of these forms. A fluent machine, then, was a new concept that would combine advantages of both television and computers—a so-called multimedia machine.

The business plan stated that Fluent Machines, Inc., would become a leading supplier of technology to *enable* standard computer systems to become *fluent*—that is, be able to deal with sound and motion video as seamlessly as they did with text, data, and graphics. Fluent Machines, according to Neil Ferris, would be a technology company, generating ideas and encapsulating them in

some kind of a product offering . . . Basically it's the ability to take video and convert it into digital processing capability in real time. You can plug a videotape into the side of your computer, which will now have in it a couple of our printed circuit boards. Now you can store the pictures and stereo audio from the VCR directly onto the hard disk and then retrieve that information and pop it up on the screen whenever you want.

Other products may bring pictures and text together, but they rely on patchworks of hardware like videoplayers. They aren't "natural" or "seamless." Our technology will store the images directly in digital form, for instant access.

The company intended to develop OEM relationships with major computer systems vendors who would license, resell, or manufacture Fluent's software and hardware products. Fluent also aimed to market its own products with standard PC componentry, selling multimedia systems to value-added resellers (VARs) focusing on specific vertical markets and sophisticated end users.

Fluent had already had preliminary discussions with a number of major computer systems vendors. The founders intended to market technological expertise in several areas as a basis for forming broad joint agreements for development, manufacturing, and distribution (Exhibit 2 lists companies that had been targeted for a variety of technical applications). David Nelson clearly believed that the environment of the 90s was very different from that of the 80s:

Times have really changed. We can envision how this system is going to work in five years, but we don't know who is going to put all the pieces together. It literally is a tech-

EXHIBIT 2 | **Technology Market Opportunities**

Discussions with one major computer company have yielded interest in the following, in rough order of priority:

1. Licensing OS/2 system and device drivers from DVI (Digital Video Interactive).
2. Jointly defining multimedia data exchange standards (data link libraries).
3. Licensing the CenterStage development environment.
4. Licensing hierarchical sub-band audio/visual compression algorithms to run on IBM-developed hardware.
5. Licensing/funding a Microchannel Architecture (MCA)-based AVOC.
6. Licensing/funding an MCA-based CODEDC.
7. Collaborating on a low-cost VLSI chip implementation of Fluent's compression technology.

Other prospects include companies who have committed to DVI, have an interest in multimedia, are focused on IBM compatibility/competitiveness, seek technology leadership, wish to maintain geographic distribution influence, or are searching for technologies to sustain growth and enhance margins. Companies with whom Fluent has already initiated serious discussions include

Company	Strategy/Interest
Bull/Zenith Data	Develop leadership in multimedia imaging.
Compaq	Use multimedia to promote technology leadership and enhance margins.
Fujitsu	License CenterStage as development environment for FM Towns Machine.
Intel	License OS/2 drivers, CenterStage to promote DVI.
NEC	Follow IBM (e.g., support DVI and enhancements).
Olivetti	License/OEM all Fluent products to enhance DVI.
Philips	Support development environment capability for CD-I; find nonthreatening ways to support multimedia (e.g. VDI) on PC product line.
Samsung	Support Fluent technology under Unix/enhance margins.

Fluent has had discussions with and will target other PC workstation vendors and consumer products companies over time. For those that Fluent has presented to, discussions have been too preliminary to indicate specific interests. These include

Acer	Everex	Northgate
Amstrad	HP	Ricoh
Apple	HCL	Siemens/Nixdorf
AST Research	Hitachi	Silicon Graphics
AT&T	ICL	Sony
Canon	Matsushita	Sun Microsystems
Dell Computer	NCR	Toshiba

Source: Company documents.

nology food chain. So many people playing, but you haven't the foggiest idea who is going to buy from whom.

Even though Fluent had already done a substantial amount of work on marketing and sales, it was a very difficult area to define. Ferris noted:

> It's an emerging market. It has an uncertain size. Nobody quite knows the timing of it. It's more timing than size. How much money do you have to spend to stay in this game until the market emerges? You have to finance the company under a high degree of uncertainty, as compared to apple pie and shoes where there is a built-in marketplace. We have to bet that the technology and the market emerge at the same time. And if the market does show up, will the technology really do all the things it says it does?

Some observers noted there was uncertainty about whether the market would appear at all. The fluent machine concept might catch on as successfully as the facsimile transmitter, or it might find no takers at all. Other advanced concepts had failed: William Poduska's Stardent Computers had invested $180 million in the "super-workstation" concept, whose market never materialized. Three global consortia—led by RCA, MCA, and Matsushita—had spent nearly $1 billion developing the high-fidelity videodisk for home entertainment; the market never materialized. Early development of voice-mail technology was slowed because venture capitalists thought nobody would talk to machines. Outcomes for technology adoption in the marketplace seemed impossible to predict.

Because of these uncertainties, the development of Fluent Machines was quite different from the course of events Ferris and Nelson had experienced in their two previous start-ups. At Apollo Computers, the technology appeared just as computer-aided design software became popular, and demand exploded. David Nelson explained:

> Apollo was like a rocket launch, with solid rocket boosters and no throttle control. You lit it and it cleared the tower; it was either going into orbit or going into the ocean. One or the other, but you had no control over it.
>
> Fluent is much more like a lumbering airplane on a long runway. We are constantly wondering just how hard we should pull up on the stick. We are going to go up a hundred feet and look around and then climb very slowly, because the times are very different now.

Nelson also had his own view of a major threat facing start-up companies—the possibility that established competitors could copy the start-up's new technology and exploit it before the newcomer could capitalize on the opportunity. He elaborated:

> One of my beliefs about start-ups—and this is shocking to a venture capital person—is that you have to build a nearly useless product. If you are going to own market share as a start-up, then that market has to be diddley. It has to be so minuscule that nobody else is interested. To do that, you've got to develop something that's nearly useless.
>
> My rule of thumb is develop the first product so there are probably only a couple of hundred people in the world that would buy it. Then sell it to half of those people and use that to finance your next product. Your next product should be slightly less useless.
>
> Apollo's first workstation was a $40,000 box that had a green display and no applications. It was nearly useless; you couldn't do anything on it. That was perfect, because we knew DEC wouldn't build one of them.

Fluent did not intend to manufacture products directly. Circuit-board-level products were to be manufactured by one or more qualified suppliers, and system-level products would be assembled by an existing assembly company, or be supplied by one or more of Fluent's OEM companies. Thus, Ferris and Nelson intended to utilize the assets and capabilities of many external suppliers, minimizing the need for facilities and direct labor and operating at the lowest absolute overhead required to ship high-volume, quality products.

Initially, the core technology of Fluent Machines focused on two specific areas. The first was a combination of proprietary hardware and software, designed to compress and decompress full motion video in real time and then to render the video onto multiple concurrent windows on the display. Compressed color video required 15 megabytes of storage per minute of recorded material.

The second area of focus was a high-level application environment called "Center-Stage," based on extensive use of object-oriented technology. This user environment would integrate several advanced software technologies into a coherent set designed for rapid prototyping, development, and execution of multimedia applications. Connecting these two areas would be standard hardware componentry like Intel 80386/486 processors, Windows 3.0, OS/2 Presentation Manager, and a wide range of standard utility programs.

FINANCING

In January of 1990, management was seeking the company's first round of external funding, at the level of $5 million. If financing was secured by March, management felt that further funds would not be required until the first quarter of 1991. Ferris commented:

> We invested—David predominantly—well in excess of a million dollars as seed money. That's kind of unheard of, putting your own money into one of these things. But we felt it would do two things: one, bring us a better valuation from the venture capitalists, although it's an expensive way of doing it; and two, it should lower the absolute percentage of the business we have to give up to the external investors, at least in the first round.

In January of 1990, Fluent Machines was targeting a small group of venture capital firms for their first external round of funding. The funding would be necessary in order to meet the goal of the first product rollouts from August to December of 1990. Exhibit 3 shows the complete list of financial assumptions and projections contained in Fluent's 1989 business plan.

Ideally, the investors selected in 1989 would provide more than just new capital. They would also add value through marketing and management expertise and/or access to corporate strategic relationships. Ferris explained:

> Different venture capital firms are known for their own investment concepts. Some want to invest in communications firms, for example, and have lots of contacts there. Others are strong in computer technology, or software. You have to select the investors you think are going to be applicable, and you have to look at industry names. You want somebody who has a reputation, who has deep pockets, who has competent management, who can pull that second round off with you.
>
> There are basically two ways of taking money now, besides loans. You can go with the traditional venture capitalists, like Applied Technologies, which goes out and gets money from five to ten other companies, builds a fund of $30 million, and invests it in your company (up to a maximum of ten percent of your equity). The other way is to do your funding with a major corporation, like Olivetti, that has its own venture capital fund. Generally, corporate partners will give a higher valuation of the company than

EXHIBIT 3 | **Fluent Machines' Financial Projections for 1990-1992** *(As contained in 1989 Business Plan)*

Assumptions

1. First product ship in Q3, 1990.
2. First OEM revenue realized in 1991.
3. Receivables collected 60 days prior to shipment.
4. Material purchase/payment 60 days prior to ship date.
5. Payroll and expense payments in month incurred.
6. Systems assembly and test to be done on a third-party subcontract basis.
7. All indirect operations/manufacturing expenses included in Operations.
8. Subchapter S election made for 1989 and 1990 prior to external investor funding.

Financial Plan Summary	1990	1991	1992
Net cash out (in $ millions)—year	$4.3	$ 5.7	$ 3.1
—cumulative	5.0	10.7	13.8
Revenue	0.5	4.4	18.1
Headcount	37	54	73

you will get from a traditional venture capitalist. All of them are more cautious now than they were ten years ago.

What you really have to do in the first round of financing is to be thinking about your second round. It is critically important that your first-round investors have the strength and capability to pull you into the second round too. They all have the right to invest in the second round by contract, and you need them to pull others into the deal. In the final analysis, however, company management has to lead, manage, and close the deal.

REFERENCES

Bell, G. *High-Tech Ventures: The Guide for Entrepreneurial Success.* Reading, Mass.: Addison-Wesley, 1991.

"The Sons of Apollo May Outshine the Original." *Business Week,* February 18, 1991, pp. 124–25.

"Videodiscs: A Three-Way Race for a Billion-Dollar Jackpot." *Business Week,* July 7, 1980, pp. 72–82.

FLUENT MACHINES, INC. (B)

Raymond M. Kinnunen, Northeastern University
John A. Seeger, Bentley College
James F. Molloy, Northeastern University

By June of 1990 Fluent had raised a total of $4.75 million from the founders, venture capitalists, and corporate investors. Investors included three leading venture capital firms—Harvard Management, Applied Technology Investors, and FIP Investors—all with extensive contacts in the high-technology environment, and three major corporations in electronics and communications—Olivetti (Italy), NYNEX, and ASCII Corporation (Japan). All the money raised was in return for equity. (See Exhibits 1 and 2 for 1990 year-end financial data.)

Fluent began product rollouts in the fall of 1990. (Exhibit 3 shows excerpts from Fluent literature describing potential product applications.) By the end of the year they had placed seven machines, valued at approximately $30,000 each, at "beta test" sites, where the customers would share their experience with Fluent. Compaq Computer, FCB Leber Kats Partners (an advertising agency), Lotus Development, NYNEX, and the University of Lowell were among these key accounts. Fluent was highly selective in its choice of customers since management wanted high-visibility accounts that would have credibility as references in future marketing efforts.

The goal was to sell 25 to 30 machines and then do a product revision that, among other things, would reduce the price of the product. As part of the marketing effort, David Nelson was on the road selling to the major strategic companies that Fluent wanted to do business with worldwide. Ferris explained:

> We need to create a "pull" environment. Everybody knows there is a market out there. The question is, when will it emerge? What color will it be? What shape will it be? There are lots of studies but nobody will stake their life on it.
>
> That gets back to the whole financing thing. We have to do an impedance match between the burn rate of the company and when the market takes off. If we burn too much fuel and the market is not ready, we are going to drive down our valuations in the second round. So we have to manage the cash exceptionally well.

Copyright © 1992 by R. M. Kinnunen. Reprinted from *Entrepreneurship: Theory and Practice,* Fall 1993. Used with permission.

EXHIBIT 1 | **Fluent Machines, Inc., Statement of Earnings, Year Ended December 31, 1990** *(Unaudited)*

	Actual	Planned
Revenue		
System sales	$ 224,737	$ 286,000
Cost of sales		
Systems at standard cost	97,820	144,512
Gross profit	126,917	141,488
Costs and expenses		
Salaries and wages	1,365,165	1,298,598
Fringe expenses	204,882	239,929
Research and development	548,701	405,084
Employee hiring	75,985	53,010
Travel, meals, and entertainment	185,355	167,456
Contract labor and consultants	323,326	220,890
Audit and legal	93,857	57,363
Office supplies	17,035	10,729
Other office expense	38,514	39,858
Promotion	67,467	138,449
Royalties (nonrefundable)	55,500	130,000
Marketing expense	17,433	26,817
Depreciation	44,580	10,540
Equipment rental and repairs	39,114	82,453
Facilities expense	119,733	120,590
Telephone	31,550	22,898
Insurance expense	7,898	6,687
Miscellaneous expense	24,625	37,178
Budget variance—1990	(45,000)	55,645
Total expenses	3,215,720	3,124,174
Earnings (Loss) from operations	(3,088,803)	(2,982,686)
Other income and expense		
Interest income	31,423	3,575
Interest expense	12,425	5,384
Prior year adjustment	117,692	0
Net income (Loss) before taxes	(2,952,113)	(2,984,495)
Provision for income taxes		
Federal and state income tax	0	0
Net earnings (Loss)	($2,952,113)	($2,984,495)

We have to stay very flexible. We have to put a lot of oars in a lot of different waters right now, talk to a lot of different people.

The big win, to me, is in the strategic deals. I'm afraid there will be a great temptation to do short-term revenue. But if you want to be an enabling technology company, you must have well-established relationships with the major players that will draw you along in the future.

Management began work on the second round of financing in September of 1990, with the expectation that they would close the second round in March or April of 1991. Ferris and Nelson had underestimated the length of time necessary to secure

EXHIBIT 2 | **Fluent Machines, Inc., Balance Sheet, December 31, 1990** *(Unaudited)*

Assets	
Current assets	
Cash and marketable securities	$ 979,982
Accounts receivable	183,241
Tax refunds receivable	204
Inventory	123,061
Prepaid assets	30,327
Total current assets	1,316,815
Long-term assets	
Land and leaseholds	1,896
Equipment and tooling	30,135
Computers	263,230
Software	11,899
Accumulated depreciation	(57,371)
Organization costs	2,857
Total assets	$ 1,569,461
Liabilities and Shareholders' Equity	
Current liabilities	
Accounts payable	$ 283,182
Withheld payroll taxes	605
Accrued benefits	29,084
Accrued legal/auditing/consulting	13,769
Other accrued taxes	908
Total current liabilities	327,548
Long-term liabilities	0
Shareholders' equity	
Common stock	24,005
Preferred stock	37,500
Capital in excess of par value	4,748,474
Retained earnings, current year	(2,952,096)
Retained earnings, prior year	(615,970)
Total shareholders' equity	1,241,913
Total liabilities and equity	$ 1,569,462

the first round, which took a solid six months after three months of thinking, travelling around, and talking to people informally. Nelson elaborated further:

Finding investors you can be comfortable with, who understand what you are doing, is a long, drawn-out process. We had some problems in that area because we are in such a complex space that relatively few potential investors could understand what we were doing or accept the ambiguity.

Probably 30 percent of the problem was that they didn't understand what the product was, or what it was we were doing. The other 70 percent of the problem was that *we* didn't know what we were doing, either, but we were asking somebody to bet on us anyway.

David Nelson believed that the environment of the 90s would be very different from that of the 80s. One dimension of the difference, in his view, was that companies were not "doing it alone" anymore. Some form of relationship with other companies seemed to be the trend. Nelson commented in relation to Fluent:

> Somehow we are going to have these relationships, but we don't have the foggiest idea yet of the relative players in the value chain. However, over the next year we *are* going to form some business relationships, and they *are* going to provide some revenue. We will have certain expectations from that, and that's going to accelerate our growth.

MANAGEMENT AND THE FUTURE

The management team at Fluent had extensive experience in running high-growth, high-technology companies. By the end of 1990, the firm employed 22 people with an average age of 29. Fluent's senior executives were supported by a skilled senior staff with experience in dozens of high-technology companies (see Exhibit 4). Still, the company's small size and limited resources placed considerable pressure on the management team. Neil Ferris commented:

> You've got to be very creative, to maximize literally every hour of every day. You've got to time-share. I'm the operations guy by title, but I'll spend time on finance, or on the marketing side. I spend half my time with engineering.
>
> The biggest difficulty is we just don't have enough hands on deck. There's just not enough hours. It isn't a question of competence, because we really have competent people. But you need your Saturdays and Sundays at the office to do the things you couldn't do on Mondays and Fridays. It's really classic start-up stuff.

A major issue facing management was how to tell the market about the products and technologies they had already developed. Ferris commented on the problem:

> You want to go and prove the concept to the key shakers and movers of the world, but at the same time you have to do these OEM deals. In addition, there are strategic deals and technology relationships. Each eats up a tremendous portion of your management time.

Another issue was financing. Nelson estimated that in the second round of financing they would be looking for $6 to $10 million. (Exhibit 5 shows financial projections for 1991 and 1992.) He explained:

> There's no magic number there. It's just that the lower your cash goes, the sooner you have to go out again. It's what the market will bear. There are a lot of funny parameters. The question is, how much money do you need to make enough technical or market progress to justify a large step increase in the company's value?
>
> I put a million bucks into this thing, thinking that a million bucks would get us up to 20 people and into product development and therefore show investors a real company. Not true. What I found was that I had a certain valuation I could command. That valuation was the same whether I was alone in my living room the second day out of Apollo, or sitting here with 20 engineers working.

In addition to funding, Ferris and Nelson were also trying to round out the management team. For example, they had only recently hired the vice presidents of sales, marketing, and technology. Neil Ferris had strengths in operations, as Nelson did in technology. Nelson described his own management style:

> I envision myself running for the bow of the ship to see what is coming, and then running way back to the stern to tug on the tiller. At all costs I avoid the boiler room,

EXHIBIT 3 | **Literature Describing Potential Product Applications**

Shakespeare Was Right

You're on stage every day . . .

Communicating to your sales force.

Training your field service group.

Selling to potential customers.

We communicate using the full range of human senses. Information can be conveyed in a variety of ways: Video. Text. Sight. Sound. But personal computers fall short of communicating in an intuitive way. Until now.

Fluent Machines has created a desktop computer unlike any other you've ever seen. Lifelike video displayed in one or more windows on your screen. Stereo sound with audio quality on par with your CD player. And . . . spreadsheets, word processing files, or any other OS/2 application. As a business tool, it will increase your firm's competitive advantage *and* bottom line in ways you never thought possible: Training applications that show and describe complex procedures. Sales presentations with the impact of video.

Let's see how a Fluent Machine can be put to work for your organization. Today.

"I've Never Seen a Spreadsheet Do That!"

Imagine a financial statement for a clothing manufacturer that communicates visually. As you scan the statement, you notice strong year-to-year revenue growth. Clicking our mouse on "1989 Sales," a video window appears in the corner of the screen. Models are shown at a fashion show in New York displaying the company's new line of casual wear. The accompanying audio explains that this new line of clothes was the primary contributor to a 16% growth in sales. Click on "Cost of Goods Sold," and the company's CEO appears, explaining that margins increased by 5% due to a decrease in the cost of cotton fabric.

Science fiction? Not with *Fluent* Multimedia. You can easily extend the capabilities of OS/2 applications by linking them to video & audio. Using the Dynamic Data Exchange (DDE) protocol, off-the-shelf applications such as EXCEL, AutoCad, or Word Perfect are instantly enabled with multimedia.

For example, load EXCEL and an AUDIO/VIDEO bar automatically appears as one of the pulldown menus. Linking a cell to a video clip is a simple process. In the case of the financial statement for the clothing manufacturer, by utilizing the Fluent NAVIGATOR query application, a user might look for the appropriate clip by searching through the video archive. Using the BROWSER, you can view several clips in a separate window. Once the right clip is found, click the LINK command to tie the video segment to the cell.

"Where's That Clip of Video?"

You work in a video production studio of an advertising agency and archive hundreds of reels of stock footage. Managing it is a nightmare, but high throughput and rapid prototyping of concepts are essential elements of your business.

because the boiler room is for operational people to sort out. At Apollo, I used to nicely flip back and forth from the front to the back of the ship.

The problem with most people is they get stuck in the middle, running the company. I'm not particularly good at that and I don't particularly enjoy it. Neil is the type of guy who can do that a lot better than I can. That's the trick, trying to get the right complement of people.

The two founders were also looking for a chief operating officer, one with a marketing focus. Nelson commented:

Over time we will shift from being a technology company to a marketing company— probably in our second, third, or fourth year. At that point, I am not the guy to run the company. My ideal scenario is to bring in not just a COO, but an heir-apparent CEO.

When the technology is stable enough that you can do a two-year engineering plan, and you know who your competitors are, and you know what the revenue streams are, then it's much better to give the job up to a market-oriented CEO. I would step aside to be chairman, CTO, whatever. I'm not particularly enamored with running companies.

EXHIBIT 3 | **Literature Describing Potential Product Applications (*continued*)**

A creative director, pitching to a prospective account, wants to quickly piece together a prototype ad to show the client. She needs all clips of sports cars snaking down a windy road. You know you have several of them, but getting to them quickly is impossible. Putting together the prototype ad is expensive and time consuming. Your meeting with the client is tomorrow at 10:00 AM.

With *Fluent* Multimedia, you can handle these tasks in minutes, not days. Video and audio are easily sorted and retrieved using a powerful object-oriented database that supports advance search techniques. In seconds you determine that you have 15 shots. Viewing each clip, you choose the most appropriate and combine it with other pieces of stock footage. You overlay audio and titles, then compile it to a VCR tape. Production time: 1 hour.

A Video Editing Suite on Your Desk

Whether communicating with your sales force or potential customers, no medium matches the impact of videotape. However, video is expensive to produce and edit. Once created, it's difficult to revise and reuse. *Fluent* Multimedia puts video editing tools on your desktop, radically reducing production time and cost.

With the ability to capture video "on-the-fly" users can instantly access and manipulate videotape, live broadcast feeds, or input from a video camera. Whether it's an NTSC or PAL input, the *Fluent* architecture can handle it. Once captured, video is easily edited using the CenterStage user environment. Cut and paste video segments. Clip in text or graphics. Update with revisions. Then compile the content to a new videotape. All on your desk.

What desktop publishing was to the 1980s, desktop video will be in the 1990s . . . with *Fluent* Multimedia.

Viewing the World from a Different Angle

To harness the true potential of multimedia, *Fluent's* architecture allows users to create applications with a virtually unlimited number of concurrent video windows. In a sales training simulation, the prospect appears in a video window asking the sales trainee a question. The trainee's response is captured live via a video camera. His image appears in a separate window beside the buyer. The response is stored and reviewed at a later date by the trainee and his instructor. An aircraft manufacturer creates a multimedia maintenance manual. The top and side views of installing a wing flap are displayed concurrently. In a video editing application, 15 video icons are displayed simultaneously, each representing a separate video segment.

With the ability to display up to 256 concurrent video windows, *Fluent* Multimedia adds a new dimension to the impact of applications. With NTSC output capability, you also have the added flexibility of displaying via a large monitor, overhead projector, or closed-circuit TV network.

Source: Company literature.

EXHIBIT 4 | **Fluent Machines' Key Staff Members, December 1990**

Paul Patterson, Vice President, Sales
Years experience: 25
Previous positions:
    Tricord. Vice president, marketing and sales
    Edge Computers. Vice president, marketing and sales
    Apollo Computer. District operations manager
Education: BA, MacAlester College

Larry Pape, Vice President, Marketing
Years experience: 20
Previous positions:
    Microtechnology Sources. Vice president, sales and marketing
    Apple Computer. Director, North American sales operations
    Control Data. General manager, education technology center
    Boulder Valley State Education Center. Director
    IBM. Marketing representative
Education: BS, Applied Mathematics. BS, Music

Dr. Prem Uppaluru, Vice President, Technology
Fields of expertise:
    Network computing, object-oriented systems, operating systems, databases, parallel processing,
        computer architecture
Previous Positions:
    Samsung Software America. Vice president, engineering
    Bellcore.
    Bell Laboratories.
Education: PhD in computer science and engineering, University of Texas at Austin

Dr. David Backer, Vice President, Video Application
Fields of Expertise:
    Multimedia, computer-aided learning
Previous Positions:
    Mirror Systems (Times Mirror Co.). Founder and director
    Consultant to:
        WGBH Television
        Gerber Systems Technology
        Pratt Center for Computer Graphics in Design
        Hoffman-LaRoche Pharmaceutical
Education: PhD, Media Laboratory, M.I.T.

EXHIBIT 5 | **Fluent Machines' Projected Income Statement, 1991 and 1992**

	1991	1992
Revenues	$3,050	$11,707
Cost of goods sold	1,491	1,505
Gross profit	1,559	6,202
R and D expense	1,854	2,254
Marketing expense	626	904
Sales expense	491	836
Operating expense	351	692
Administrative expense	790	1,008
	4,112	5,694
Profit before Taxes	($2,553)	$ 508

Source: Company Documents, December, 1990.

SUSAN'S SPECIAL LAWNS

David C. Snook-Luther, University of Wyoming
Grant L. Lindstrom, University of Wyoming

Susan's Special Lawns was the inspiration of Susan Jensen. The business started in 1989 selling wildflower seeds. Its early success attracted her husband David's interest. Together they expanded the business to include some landscape design and irrigation equipment installation. By 1992 the Jensens established a market for custom wildflower seed sales and plantings and had completed a few significant landscape jobs successfully. They saw the next step as deciding on a strategy for the future.

HOW SUSAN'S SPECIAL LAWNS BEGAN

Susan had been an avid gardener and flower lover all her life. Having previously lived in prime growing areas on the West Coast and in the South, Susan had recently moved to the ruggedly beautiful but very different growing region of the high Rocky Mountains. Over the last few years, she had learned how to adapt her gardening experience and know-how to the growing climate of her new home in a moderate-sized university town. In the spring of 1988, she decided to remove the sod on part of her lawn that bordered the sidewalk and plant naturally growing wildflowers. By early summer the flowers were in full bloom.

The response to her flowered border was quite gratifying. As she was working in her flower beds, people would often stop to tell her how beautiful they thought her yard looked. Many people asked her where she had gotten her seed. She told them they could find wildflower seeds in just about any major retail outlet store such as Kmart, Target, or May's.

The case authors would like to recognize Craig Grenvik, Savyasachi Gupta, and Trent Kaufman for their help in data collection and compiling company information. Management cooperated in the field research for this case. All events and incidents are real, but all names and financial information have been disguised at the organization's request. This version of the case was presented at a meeting of the North American Case Research Association, November 1992; a different version appears under the same name in the *Case Research Journal*. Copyright © by David C. Snook-Luther.

The following spring 1989, she wanted to try something different. Since she was quite familiar with the individual species, Susan wanted to create a personalized garden where she could plant different flowers in different areas to achieve a color and size contrast. This was virtually impossible when buying seed from the major retailers because they sold seed only in generic mixes. She located the Applewood Seed Co., a wholesaler that sold individual species of wildflower seeds, and obtained the individual varieties she wanted.

The response to her new flower beds was even greater than the previous year. Several people noticed flowers in her beds that they had never seen before. Susan explained which species she had in her beds, the blooming cycles of each, and the special planting and watering requirements. It was clear to Susan many people had a deeper interest in these special flowers than just looking at their brilliant colors and she began selling seed packets of her own as a sideline.

1990

The following spring, Susan decided to try to sell wildflowers as both individual species and in custom mixes. She spent $300 on seeds and another $100 on containers. She rationalized that even if she didn't make money, she would be introducing more people to her world of special flowers.

The seed sales exceeded her wildest expectations. People not only bought for themselves, they purchased seeds as gifts for friends and relatives. Soon Susan had to order more seed. By the end of May 1990, Susan had sold $3,260 worth on $850 investment in seeds and packaging. The amount of seed sold in two months was enough to plant nearly one and a half acres of flowers.

As people began to learn about Susan and her business, they started seeking her advice on many aspects of gardening. She began to do custom flower beds for residences. In late April the owners of a local bank building requested her services to revitalize the lawn and flower beds on the premises. Susan soon found she had too much business to handle on just a part-time basis and decided to take incompletes on her course work at the university where she was pursuing a master's degree in physics to devote all her time to the business.

In the beginning, Susan's husband David was less than enthusiastic about the seed business, thinking it would be a sure flop. To keep peace in the household he agreed to the venture. David had done quite well with his degree in statistics and had a job working about 40 hours a week as a research associate in the university statistics department; the geology department wanted to hire him for another 30 hours a week if he was willing to do both jobs.

David had worked for a commercial landscaping company that specialized in golf course construction while he was in school. As Susan's customers' requests for help in landscaping grew, he realized the seed sales could act as a springboard into the lucrative landscaping business. His interest in and support for the business grew. His thorough knowledge of irrigation systems and landscape design added another dimension to the business.

By mid-June, the Jensens had diversified into small-scale landscaping projects including planting small trees and shrubs, laying sod, laying flagstone for walkways and patios, and shrub and small tree pruning. David prepared for expansion into irrigation systems. In late July, Susan's Special Lawns was asked to do a complete landscaping job for a residence, starting from scratch. The job included the landscape design, a sprinkler system, laying sod for the lawn, tree and shrub plantings, and, of course, wildflower seed plantings. Within two days of starting the project, the

Jensens realized they were going to need help to finish the project on time and hired their first part-time employee, Gerald Green, an MBA student at the university.

During the fall of 1990, the company continued to sell wildflower seeds and do small landscaping projects. The seed sales entered a new era when Susan decided to try to sell her seeds through local retail dealers. A large local drug store and a popular local gift shop agreed to sell her seed. At first, Susan used the same packaging as she had during the year. There were two types of packaging. Individual species were sold in small test tubes and mixes were sold in small plastic bags containing Susan's business card.

To spur sales during the Christmas holiday season, Susan tried two other packaging ideas. The first consisted of putting five individual species in a wooden crate where the seeds were clearly visible. The process of building these crates was quite tedious and reaction to them was mixed. The second technique was quite successful. Susan bent glass tubing into the shape of a candy cane, melted one end creating a seal, and filled the cane with wildflower seeds.

Reaction to the candy canes was excellent. Both of her retailers rapidly ran out stock. With her last production run of the season, Susan was able to create and fill 20 canes an hour. At a wholesale price of $2.50, an hour of work a day was quite satisfactory. By year's end the initial $400 gamble had produced $10,621 in revenues.

1991

The Jensens had high hopes for Susan's Special Lawns in 1991. They found new suppliers for landscaping and irrigation products and, in anticipation of larger projects to come, they acquired a computer-assisted-design (CAD) software package, two 40 megabyte hard drives, a laser printer for the computer system to create high-resolution drawings and blueprints, a professional composting device, and two vintage trucks to haul the larger loads of equipment and waste materials. The balance sheet and income statements shown in Exhibits 1 and 2 show this expansion and the substantial business loan used to finance it. Both Susan and David considered this rapid expansion of assets necessary to grow Susan's Special Lawns into a viable landscaping business. They were so sure of their decision, they were willing to commit their personal assets, including their house, to secure the loan.

The Jensens valued Gerald Green's opinion and often discussed their business plans with him. One evening late in the summer after an especially difficult week of long days to successfully meet a deadline on a large irrigation system installation, David reflected on how things had gone and spoke about his thoughts for the future.

> This has been a year for experience. We have done a lot of work, but we haven't made much money for all our effort. We estimate jobs and put in competitive bids, but something always happens that makes the job take 20 to 40 percent longer than I planned. This means Susan and I have to work longer hours and we don't have time to do the planning and preparation we should be doing. I have learned a lot about planning a job and what I have to do to keep projects on schedule. I'm just glad we didn't get the contract for one of those really big jobs we bid on. We could have lost the business before we even got started with all the extra labor we would have had to hire and the equipment we would have had to rent. But now we're ready to make a move and we have plenty of opportunities.
>
> We must make a move! I can't continue to do all of my research work and keep up with the current demands of this business too. We need to make the business large enough to support us comfortably without other sources of income.
>
> I have three ideas about where the business should go. First, we can expand the number of retail outlets for the wildflower seed business. Susan has some good ideas for

EXHIBIT 1 | **Balance Sheet, Susan's Special Lawns, 1990–91**

	As of 12-31-90	As of 3-31-91	As of 6-30-91
Assets			
Current assets			
Cash	$ 775	$ 275	$ 275
Accounts receivable	830	781	4,947
Office supplies	225	268	356
Operating supplies	198	256	512
Prepaid expenses	918	550	1,378
Inventory	2,830	3,053	5,819
Total current assets	$ 5,776	$ 5,183	$13,287
Fixed assets			
Office furniture	$ 100	$ 100	$ 100
Office electronic equipment	1,861	1,861	2,955
Library	1,089	1,195	1,245
Machinery and equipment	2,284	2,300	3,847
Vehicles	5,700	5,700	7,485
Accumulated depreciation	–4,193	–5,074	–6,208
Total fixed assets	6,841	6,082	9,424
Total assets	$12,617	$11,265	$22,711
Liabilities and Owner's Equity			
Current liabilities			
Accounts payable	$ 66	$ 0	$ 2,006
Notes payable	7,848	9,511	14,808
Payroll taxes payable	41	3	1,062
Sales tax payable	168	21	308
Total current liabilities	$ 8,123	$ 9,535	$18,184
Long-term liabilities			
Total long-term liabilities	0	0	0
Total liabilities	$ 8,123	$ 9,535	$18,184
Equity			
Jensen capital	7,671	8,345	9,582
Jensen drawing	–9,767	–12,063	–12,063
Retained earnings	1,868	6,590	5,448
Current earnings	4,722	–1,142	1,560
Total equity	4,494	1,730	4,527
Total liabilities and equity	$12,617	$11,265	$22,711

promotions throughout the year. Valentine's, Easter, Thanksgiving, and Memorial Day are potentially as good as Christmas for seed promotions. With the right promotion we should be able to dramatically expand the number of retail outlets we have. Providing seeds and promotional materials to fund-raising groups should also be a good outlet.

Second, we can do a lot more with landscape planning too. With the CAD software and the new computer equipment, we can make very attractive diagrams and elevations of custom landscape plans for people. Coupled with the attractive color photographs of our landscapes, people can get a clear idea of the dramatic effect the right use of wild-flowers with other plantings has on outdoor spaces.

Finally, we have a terrific opportunity in designing and selling do-it-yourself irrigation systems. One of the regional distributors is so interested in the idea they gave me the CAD system developed by one of the major manufacturers. I am integrating the manufacturer's CAD system with our own CAD and accounting systems to provide a higher level of service to do-it-yourself customers than anything currently available. Combined with the

EXHIBIT 2 | **Income Statement, Susan's Special Lawns, 1990–91**

	Jan. 1990 through Dec. 1990	Jan. 1991 through Mar. 1991	April 1991 through June 1991
Income			
Seed sales	$10,621	$ 838	$ 2,893
Irrigation system sales	3,468	0	7,045
Landscaping services	12,763	500	8,523
Net sales	$26,852	$ 1,338	$18,461
Cost of goods sold			
Seeds	2,658	54	1,124
Irrigation materials	1,214	0	2,466
Landscaping supplies	3,620	10	3,426
Total cost of goods sold	7,492	64	7,016
Gross profit	$19,360	$ 1,274	$11,445
Expenses			
Owners' salaries	$ 1,250	$ 80	$ 3,750
Contracted services	1,285	23	328
Payroll taxes	156	10	412
Advertising	1,130	130	701
Mortgage for home office	1,009	275	325
Auto expense	1,012	181	961
Depreciation	4,193	881	1,134
Insurance	578	225	299
Research and development	84	0	0
Licenses	342	0	50
Office expense	517	120	129
Equipment rental	163	17	412
Telephone	268	92	48
Utilities	143	72	42
Total expenses	$12,130	$ 2,106	$ 8,591
Net operating income	7,230	-832	2,854
Interest expense	671	310	687
Income before taxes	6,559	-1,142	2,167
Taxes	1,837	0	607
Net income	$ 4,722	$ -1,142	$ 1,560

laser printer we can quickly show potential customers a high quality drawing of an overall irrigation system plan, a summary list of parts and prices, equipment required for the installation, and estimates of the installation time required. If they choose to buy the plans, we also would give them detailed construction plans, complete parts lists with current prices, and the specific skills, equipment, permits, and licenses required at different points of the installation. We can even incorporate a detailed landscape design showing the specific plantings set in locations with the proper light and water requirements. Then, depending on their interests and abilities, customers can contract with us for any part of the job from parts, seed, sod and plants, to consulting advice or a turnkey installation. We should be able to handle a fairly large geographic area with such a service.

Gerald was excited by David's vision, but also apprehensive for his friend. There were several points he felt David might not have considered adequately.

David I think these are great ideas with a lot of potential. However, there are a few things that worry me. First, seed sales have not increased significantly since the first year. Second, our time is so tight that every time one of our big jobs takes longer, not only do we lose money on that job, but it forces Susan to delay some of the smaller jobs which provide a steady stream of income. Any misstep that substantially changes the planned time allocations for these moves could be very serious. Finally, I'm just not sure what the market potential for seeds, landscaping, and irrigation systems is in this geographic market, and how our competition is likely to respond to our moves.

David thought for a moment and said:

You are right, but I don't have time to answer these questions—if they can be answered. Right now I'm doing well just to get the things done I have to do. But we have to do something to generate enough profits to service the debt we have taken on. Can you help?

Gerald paused while he contemplated the work it would take, then replied:

This is an interesting problem and not that difficult to deal with. It would be fun to try out some of the things I have been learning, and I have some friends in the MBA program that may be willing to help do part of the research for the experience. Let me see what we can do. I should be able to give you a fairly complete report in about four weeks.

GERALD'S REPORT

As promised, four weeks later Gerald gave David the report he had promised him. What follows is the text of that report.

REGIONAL AND LOCAL ANALYSIS

The central front range of the Rocky Mountains is dominated by one large metropolitan area, Denver, and several cities of approximately 100,000 people. The economy is diversified and growing at a moderate rate even through a recession in the U.S. economy.

The population of our town is about 26,000 people. The population in the trade area is about 50,000 people. It is at least 70 miles to a major city. The town is characterized mainly by its service economy, with the two largest employers being a state university and the hospital. The town also gets significant revenues from agriculture, light manufacturing, and extractive industries. The extractive industry has produced boom and bust periods in the past. Most profits were used for substantial personal, business, and government capital projects. Having survived a severe recession caused by a bust in the petroleum and uranium industries, the economy has grown at a modest inflation-adjusted annual rate of about 3 percent for the last five years. Business formations have been slightly above the rate of business closings. New housing construction is moribund, but sales of existing housing and remodeling are fairly brisk.

LOCAL INDUSTRY ANALYSIS

Residential Sprinklers A survey of local sprinkler-system installers indicated that about 40 sprinkler systems were installed during the year. This number has grown from about 25 systems installed four years ago. With the average residential sprinkler system costing $3,500, the size of the current market is about $140,000. It is expected that this market will grow at about the same rate over the next four years to about 65 systems and $227,500 in current dollars. Unlike some areas of the region and country that are severely affected by drought, water supplies and water costs in the city are not expected to be affected over this period.

Typical customers in the city fall into four groups: (1) convenience-minded home owners, (2) price-sensitive home owners, (3) real estate owners that do not occupy the premises, and (4) large commercial projects. I interviewed 10 people who fall into one of the first three groups, who had shopped for average residential sprinkler systems, and who decided not to purchase one. Eight people said they would have purchased the system if the price had been $2,800. Additionally, four people said that they would be interested in installing part, or all, of their own system if there was a significant savings.

My selling experience with these systems is a ratio of one sale for every three qualified prospects (prospects who expressed a serious interest in a system). If 80 percent of the two-thirds of the prospects who don't buy systems would buy a comparable system for $2,800, then the market could be increased from 40 to 96. Assuming the average sale at $2,800 rather than $3,500, I estimate the current market would increase from $140,000 to $268,800, or about 48 percent. However, it seems likely that about 30 premium systems could be sold for an average price of about $3,500. If so, the total current market would be closer to $290,000. Clearly, there are significant opportunities and profits if we can achieve significant savings in system costs.

Costs for residential sprinkler parts and materials run about 30 percent of the retail price. Exhibit 3 shows a typical cost chain for firms in the city for the average sprinkler installation. The competitive bidding procedures used for commercial installations result in high revenue contracts at much lower profits. Larger contractors use volume discounts on large purchases to lower parts and material costs, and use costly, sophisticated equipment to achieve substantially lower labor costs in bidding for commercial installations.

The availability of low-cost, high-quality, part-time labor provided by the university students fits well with the highly seasonal nature of the business. This labor force also establishes an effective barrier to competition in residential sprinkler system installations from firms outside the city. Large outside contractors can successfully bid on large commercial projects in the area, but they cannot compete profitably in the residential sprinkler market. Also, given the presence of several

EXHIBIT 3 | **Estimated Cost Chain for Typical Sprinkler System**

Material	+	Parts	+	Labor	+	Marketing	+	Overhead	+	Margin	=	Price
$300		$735		$1,300		$105		$280		$780		$3,500

Material: After volume discounts, materials costs for pipe, etc., range from $175 to $325.

Parts: Parts cost from $640 to $800, with volume purchase discounts ranging from 2.5% to 15%. There's a wide diversity in the volume purchased and the quality of parts used; the $735 figure is based on a total cost of $790 and a 7% discount.

Labor: Labor costs using labor-intensive technologies are about 40% of the selling price. Only one of the firms uses much labor-saving technology to install sprinkler systems. The $1,300 figure assumes the typical labor cost in this market averages 37% of sales price.

Marketing: Marketing costs are typically about 3% of sales price.

Overhead: Overhead ranges from 6% to 11% of sales, depending on the kind of equipment used. Most of the firms in this market do not have the costs of maintaining a lot of specialized equipment. The $280 figure is based on average overhead of 8% of sales price.

Margin: The margin is derived from the rest the numbers.

Price: The average residential sprinkler system retails for about $3,500.

good local firms, the potential market is not great enough to attract large firms to make a substantial equipment investment in a local branch. Exhibits 4 and 5 show estimated cost chains for local competitors and for a do-it-yourself system.

Landscaping This industry segment includes landscape design, mowing and fertilizing, sodding and planting, tree trimming and spraying, and a corollary market for landscaping byproducts in composting. It has been very difficult to estimate the size of the local market. The total sales of the leading firm in mowing and fertilizing are $200,000. They estimate their share of this market segment at 70 percent. Judging by the number of people employed by other firms doing some aspect of landscaping in the area, I estimate that the market is between $450,000 and $600,000. The market has been growing moderately over the last five years, with firms adding one or two workers or a piece of major equipment each year.

EXHIBIT 4 | **Estimated Cost Chains for Local Sprinkler Competitors**

	Material	+	Parts	+	Labor	+	Marketing	+	Overhead	+	Margin	=	Price
Jack's	$175		$575		$ 520		$100		$400		$1,405		$3,200
Green Lawn	230		625		1,400		100		200		945		3,500
Pasque Flower	325		700		1,440		100		200		835		3,600
Shaklee's	250		640		1,400		100		200		910		3,500
Susan's	350		780		1,400		150		200		620		3,500

Materials: Jack's uses the lowest-cost materials (one-half the cost of PVC) and gets higher discounts than other firms.
Green Lawn uses the lowest-cost materials, but only qualifies for mid-volume discounts.
Pasque Flower uses the highest-quality materials and qualifies for a higher discount.
Shaklee's uses the lowest-quality materials and qualifies only for low-volume discounts.
Susan's Special Lawns uses high-quality materials and only qualifies for the lowest volume discount.
Parts: Jack's uses the lowest-cost parts and qualifies for close to the highest discounts available on low-quality parts.
Green Lawn uses the lowest-cost parts but only qualities for mid-volume discounts on these parts.
Pasque Flower uses the highest-quality parts and qualifies for one of the higher discounts available for quality parts.
Shaklee's uses the lowest-quality parts and qualifies only for low-volume discounts.
Susan's Special Lawns uses high-quality parts and since they have the smallest market share, they only qualify for the lowest volume discount.
Labor: Jack's uses a line puller to install his pipe; such technology can reduce labor costs to 16% of sales.
Green Lawn not only does not use labor-saving technology, they also must hire independent plumbers and electricians to complete the installation, substantially increasing labor costs.
The materials Pasque Flower uses cannot be used with the labor-saving technologies employed by some other firms.
Shaklee's is one of the least efficient firms in the market.
Susan's Special Lawns does not use any labor-saving equipment, and has hired an MBA student to help them in all phases of their business including installations.
Marketing: Assumes that all firms exert about the same marketing effort as a percentage of sales except for Susan's Special Lawns. Because of its small size, Susan's spends fewer dollars, but a higher percentage.
Overhead: Assumes that everyone's overhead is approximately the same, except for Jack's who must maintain additional equipment.
Margin: Margins are derived from the other numbers.
Price: Prices are based on survey data.

EXHIBIT 5 | **Estimated Cost Chain for Do-It-Yourself Sprinkler Systems**

	Material	+	Parts	+	Labor	+	Marketing	+	Overhead	+	Margin	=	Price
Susan's Special Lawns	$300		$700		$0		$100		$100		$1,200		$2,400

Material: Assumes Susan's will sell the highest-quality materials since it is better suited to do-it-yourself installation and will not require special equipment. Susan's should be able to realize significant volume discounts as the market develops.

Parts: Susan's can give buyers a choice in the quality of parts they wish to purchase. This cost chain shows costs for high-quality parts and a high-volume discount.

Labor: Labor costs will be absorbed directly by the purchaser and are not reflected in the sales price.

Marketing: Although the total marketing effort will increase, marketing costs/unit will remain the same.

Overhead: Overhead will be reduced. Minimal inventory is required since parts and materials will be ordered after the contract is signed. Maintenance will decrease since less equipment will be required to support sales.

Margin: The margin is derived from the numbers. Eight nonpurchasers were interviewed who said that they would have purchased a system if it had cost $2,800. Four of these nonpurchasers would have been interested in a do-it-yourself system if the savings were great enough.

Price: The $2,400 price is used because it is less than the $2,800 they said they would pay for a completely installed system, and it is a $1,100 savings over the current price of an installed system.

Our telephone survey did not reveal any major shifts in consumer tastes in the city. Xeriscaping using nonliving ground cover such as rocks and wood chips along with hardy species of flora is growing at an average rate of 250% in the desert Southwest and southern California. With adequate rain and low water costs in the city, local residents will not benefit greatly by changing to this landscape. Although there will be some opportunities for market growth from yards switching to xeriscaping for aesthetic reasons, the growth will be moderate. Likewise, opportunities for growth from composting will be moderate since local landfills have plenty of space and trash removal is cheap.

Economies of size are important in this market. A firm must achieve a minimum size before it can justify major equipment purchases such as bucket trucks for tree trimming and power spraying equipment. Given the limited market size due partly to the short growing season, there are opportunities to use a preemptive strategy. The city market can support one firm with a major piece of equipment well, but support for two firms would be marginal at best.

Labor costs in landscaping range from about 60 percent for sodding to over 98 percent for landscape design. Although the numbers can vary substantially depending on the specific type of work the firm does, Exhibit 6 presents an average cost chain for a firm doing general lawn care.

Wildflower Seeds Wildflower seed planting is increasing significantly. However, Susan estimates that the maximum potential for local wildflower seed sales is about $12,000. Although wildflower seed sales are highly seasonal with peak sales in the spring, significant markets exist at other times of the year. For example, Susan has found that a significant gift market for wildflower seeds exists at Christmas. No one knows how large other specialized markets for wildflower seeds may be.

Profit margins on seeds exclusive of packaging are very high, about 150 percent. Packaging costs can be negligible to several times the cost of the seeds for special

EXHIBIT 6 | Estimated Cost Chain for General Lawn Maintenance

Material	+	Labor	+	Marketing	+	Overhead	+	Margin	=	Price
$15		$75		$10		$25		$125		$250

Material: Assumes that materials are 6% of the selling price.
Labor: Assumes that labor is 30% of the selling price.
Marketing: Assumes that marketing is 2% to 4% of the selling price.
Overhead: Overhead is estimated from the rest of the numbers.
Margin: Assumes that gross margin is about 50%.
Price: Based on a typical price of $250.

EXHIBIT 7 | Estimated Cost Chain for Wildflower Seeds (*Candy cane gift*)

	Seeds	+	Packaging	+	Labor	+	Marketing	+	Overhead	+	Margin	=	Price
Susan's Special Lawns	$0.55		$0.20		$0.30		$0.10		$0.05		$1.30		$2.50

Seeds: Assumes seeds costs are about 22% of the wholesale price.
Packaging: Packaging typically is about 4% of the wholesale price; the candy-cane package was about double the cost of typical packaging as a percentage of the wholesale price.
Labor: Susan can make 20 canes an hour. Assuming that Susan would have to pay someone else at least $6/hr., the direct labor cost/cane would be $0.30. Other costs, such as delivery, are included in overhead.
Marketing: Assumes that marketing is 4% of the wholesale price.
Overhead: Assumes that overhead is 2% of the wholesale price.
Margin: Margin is derived from the other numbers.
Price: The wholesale price for the canes was $2.50.

gift packages. Unit sales revenue is from $2 to $10, depending on the number of seeds in the package and the type of package. The small unit sales price is the reason larger seed companies using inexpensive mass market distribution channels dominate the industry. Their control of the bulk of seed production and the mass marketing channels reduces the threat of large new entrants in the wildflower seed industry. Exhibit 7 shows a cost chain for wildflower seed sales.

Outdoor Lighting Our cost/revenue estimates for this market are about as poor as our estimates for lawn-sprinkler systems are good. The only residential systems in town have been installed by the occupants. All of these systems used simple do-it-yourself packages.

Residential lighting systems range from about $2,000 to over $10,000. Roughly, 40 percent of the selling price is labor, and parts and material are 30 percent. One article we found said that a respectable gross margin is about 18 percent. In this geographic area, it is likely that once the business gets going, marketing costs will be about 3 percent. See Exhibit 8 for an estimated cost chain.

COMPETITOR ANALYSIS

Residential Sprinklers There are five firms in addition to Susan's Special Lawns that could sell and install residential sprinkler systems in the city: Green Lawn, Jack's,

EXHIBIT 8 | **Estimated Cost Chain for Outdoor Lighting**

Material	+	Labor	+	Marketing	+	Overhead	+	Margin	=	Price
$1,500		$2,000		$150		$450		$900		$5,000

Material: Assumes that parts and materials are about 30% of the cost of the system.
Labor: Assumes that labor is about 40% of the selling price.
Marketing: Assumes that marketing will be about 3% of the selling price.
Overhead: Overhead costs are derived from the rest of the numbers.
Margin: A respectable gross margin on these systems is about 18%.
Price: Residential lighting systems run from about $2,000 to $10,000; the typical system Susan's would install is assumed to be about $5,000.

Aries, Pasque Flower, and Shaklee's. Retail stores such as Kmart, Wal-Mart, United Builders Co., Tru-Value and others sell lawn hose, the accompanying sprinklers, and battery operated spigot timers that can substitute for underground systems.

Competitive rivalry for residential sprinklers in the city is moderate. Because of the short installation season and the relatively small market, most of the residential firms use labor-intensive installation procedures supported by light equipment. When a job is large enough, or enough jobs are waiting to warrant it, they rent heavier equipment from out-of-town suppliers. This means that none of the firms have significant excess capacity and all of them seem to be content with the status quo.

Green Lawn will try to build on its existing base of loyal lawn care customers who depend on them for mowing, fertilization, tree spraying, and sod laying. They probably will continue to focus only on the high margin residential market and avoid the lower margin commercial market. In part, this is because Green Lawn does not have the necessary licenses to do its own wiring and plumbing work. The cost of contracting with a licensed plumber and electrician is significant. Also, the company lacks the experience and expertise to design commercial projects that require detailed flow analyses such as water pound, pressure drop, and triangulation to calculate equivalent precipitation accumulation.

Green Lawn sells the second-most-expensive systems in the area, typically about $3,500, while using the poorest quality parts, materials, and designs. They compensate for the high price and low quality by selling to loyal customers who want the extensive service the company provides. Their marketing reflects this approach. Green Lawn places only a few small ads in the local newspaper in the spring and a small ad in the Yellow Pages. Their primary marketing is through two newsletters sent to all of their current customers and customers from the previous year, and word-of-mouth referrals. The first newsletter is in early spring announcing the services they will offer, their unit prices, and special rates for season contracts. This helps them keep a tight rein on past customers. A large percentage of their new customers are neighbors of existing customers who see the outstanding results the company delivers. Green Lawn will go to great lengths to protect its customer base from competitor advances.

Pasque Flower has extensive experience installing systems in the city and has earned a reputation for excellent systems at somewhat higher prices, about $3,600 for the typical system. They use the highest-quality parts, and pay about $325 for pipe and related materials after their discount which is as much as $150/job more than some high-volume competitors pay for lower-quality pipe. Because of their choice of materials and labor-intensive installation methods, Pasque Flower's labor costs are higher than those of other competitors. The owner has a degree in civil engineering, designs and supervises all installations, and has all the licenses required to install residential and commercial irrigation systems.

Pasque Flower has installed a number of systems for businesses and shopping centers in the community. However, for some reason they did not participate in the bidding for the two largest commercial contracts this year—two new schools and a medium-size amusement park.

The firm does little advertising, but their retail location is on the most heavily traveled street in the city and a few blocks from Wal-Mart and several fast-food stores. This gives their logo excellent exposure and their lawn shows people the benefits of their services. In addition to irrigation systems, which represent about 40 percent of their revenue, Pasque Flower does landscape design and tree planting and trimming.

Jack's specializes in sprinkler installations and completes more systems each year than any other firm in the city. The company also has more labor-saving irrigation installation equipment than any other local firm, and runs two crews while other firms run only one. They use lower-quality irrigation system components, but the price of the systems is attractive to customers, typically about $3,200.

Jack's has the experience and all the necessary licenses to complete an installation. In addition it owns a line-pulling machine that uses polyethylene pipe, which costs about half as much as the polyvinylchloride (PVC) pipe used by most of the other firms. Also, the line puller can install the pipe at a fraction of the cost of digging when laying the pipe through existing grass. The line puller makes a slit in the grass and lays a continuous length of flexible polyethylene pipe in a narrow groove in the soil. In addition to being faster, it also avoids having to replace sod, which is necessary with the trench method. This gives Jack's a significant cost advantage over the other firms. Jack's can be expected to vigorously protect its position in sprinkler installations.

Aries is a general contractor for commercial buildings and houses. They bid aggressively on commercial irrigation projects and currently do not accept residential jobs. In past recessions they occasionally have taken residential work.

Shaklee's may be going out of business. The founder died in 1989 and left a big vacuum in the organization. His children are trying to keep the business alive, but are struggling. It would be wise to watch further developments with this company. Some useful assets may become available.

Exhibit 9 summarizes the competitive environment in a strategic group map. Firms are classified by the relative cost of the systems they install and by the quality/service associated with the systems.

Landscaping Three local companies do limited residential landscaping: Shaklee's, Pasque Flower, and Green Lawn. Services included in this market segment are sod laying, tree/shrub planting, flagstone walkways, and lawn maintenance services. A number of substitute sources of competition exist. Local nurseries and mass merchandisers sell flora directly to homeowners who do their own landscaping. A local community college offers courses in landscape design and lawn care, and the university does soil analysis for a fee.

EXHIBIT 9 | **Strategic Group Map for Irrigation System Installations**

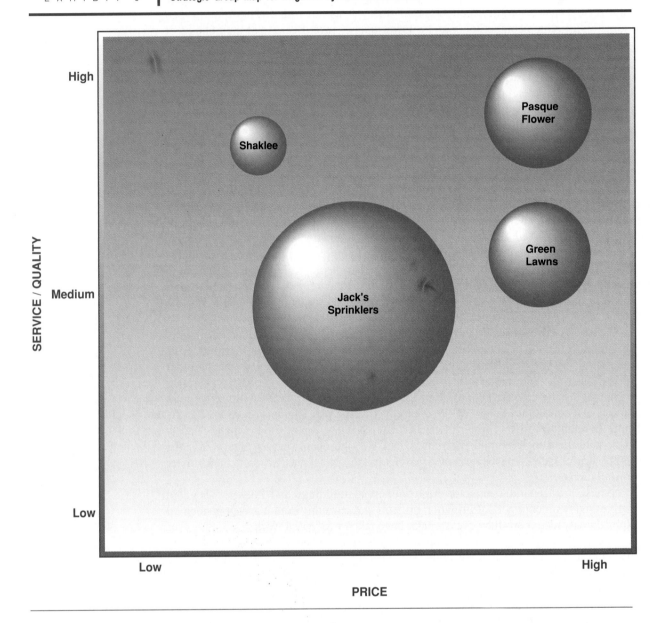

There does appear to be one significant opportunity in landscaping. No one in the city or in the region advertises landscape design that includes outdoor lighting. In fact, the Small Business Administration office does not list a single landscaping company in the region that advertises outdoor lighting as a service. Currently electricians are the only listed source for outdoor lighting installations. Installers of outdoor lighting must obtain a license by passing the state low-voltage electrical test, which serves as a barrier to most landscape firms. Susan's Special Lawns does possess such a license.

Green Lawn has the strongest market position in the lawn maintenance segment. As noted earlier, they are recognized for their extensive, high-quality service in lawn maintenance, which includes about 70 percent of the market in power raking, mowing, and lawn and tree spraying. They also have a large share of the market for sod laying.

Green Lawn's strategy is to retain and monopolize their existing customers by providing every lawn care service that the customer could ask for. In return for this high level of service, they also charge the highest price in town for every service they provide. Green Lawn provides their customers with extensive advice, but their ability to provide customers with detailed plans for a design is extremely limited. One of their strengths is that they suggest plans their customers can use to improve their yards over several years, and then follow up by reminding the customers about what improvements they were going to do for that year.

Pasque Flower's primary landscape market is in tree planting and trimming. They have equipment that can handle the planting of trees of almost any size including mature trees. Pasque Flower also owns a bucket truck that allows them to efficiently trim large mature trees. The firm has about 80 percent of this market. They also do a substantial amount of sod laying. Most of Pasque Flower's landscape designs are developed for commercial projects.

Shaklee's participation in the landscape market currently is limited to some sod laying. It is not clear whether they will continue in this business.

Wildflower Seeds There are two large national suppliers of wildflower seeds who sell significant amounts of seed in the city. Burpee sells several wildflower mixes primarily through mail-order channels. High Altitude Gardens sells standard mixes through nurseries and major retailers such as Wal-Mart, Kmart, and Target. Susan's has a strong name recognition in the local area and sells through gift shops, and recently has started selling through nurseries and flower shops.

Green Lawn attempted to preempt Susan's venture into wildflower landscaping by advertising seed sales and providing the service to its customers in 1989. They also filed a complaint with the city charging the Jensens with a zoning violation for placing a sign in their front yard advertising the name of the business. Susan was forced to remove the sign and subsequently suffered a substantial reduction in the number of customers that came to her house to purchase seeds. Green Lawn has since reduced its effort and sells only wildflower mixes as part of its landscaping projects.

Currently there is little local competition. However, the remaining growth potential is limited. Susan will have to look beyond the city, possibly beyond the region, to find growth opportunities. The problem is that this could place her in head-to-head competition with the national seed companies. It appears, however, that a number of promotional niches exist for wildflower seed sales. In addition to gifts, it may be that wildflower seeds can be used by various nonprofit and not-for-profit organizations for promotional fund-raising. Other niche opportunities may exist for mail-order sales by advertising and promotion in special interest publications. It is difficult to tell how large such markets may be, but many of these markets can be explored with minimal cost. Early successes can be used to support more market tests. At least for the short run, such efforts are unlikely to attract much attention or response from the national seed companies.

Some cash-flow projections for sprinklers, outdoor lighting, and seed sales are shown in Exhibits 10, 11, and 12.

EXHIBIT 10 | **Projected Cash Flows for Do-It-Yourself Sprinklers, 1992–93**

	1992	1993 Pessimistic	Optimistic
Sources of cash			
From operations			
Revenues (20 jobs at $2,400 each)	$48,000	$48,000	$84,000
Adjustments to convert to cash			
Decrease/increase in acct receivable	–9,600	0	–7,200
Cash generated from revenue	38,400	48,000	76,800
Expenses	24,000	24,000	42,000
Adjustments to convert to cash			
Decrease/increase in inventory	500	1,000	2,000
Depreciation expense	–600	–600	–600
Cash dispursed for expenses	23,900	24,400	43,400
Cash generated from operations	$14,500	$23,600	$33,400
Uses of cash			
Labor to develop CAD system	$ 4,000	$ 2,000	$ 2,000
Interest expense	300	300	600
Taxes paid	6,720	6,720	12,000
Total uses of cash	11,020	9,020	14,600
Other sources of cash			
Salary invested back in company	4,000	0	0
Net increase in cash	$ 7,480	$14,580	$18,800

EXHIBIT 11 | **Projected Cash Flows from Outdoor Lighting Sales, 1992–93**

	1992	1993
Sources of cash		
From operations		
Revenues	$17,500	$28,000
Adjustments to convert to cash		
Decrease/increase in accounts receivable	–3,000	–1,000
Cash generated from revenue	14,500	27,000
Expenses	13,000	20,800
Adjustments to convert to cash		
Decrease/increase in inventory	2,000	0
Depreciation expense	–1,000	–1,000
Cash dispursed for expenses	14,000	19,800
Cash generated from operations	$ 500	$ 7,200
Uses of cash		
Lighting equipment	$ 1,000	$ 500
Interest expense	300	300
Taxes paid	1,150	1,875
Total uses of cash	2,450	2,675
Net increase in cash	$ –1,950	$ 4,525

EXHIBIT 12 | **Projected Cash Flows From Seed Sales, 1992–93**

	1992	1993
Sources of cash		
From operations		
Revenues (from local market)	$11,000	$12,000
Revenues (regional sales)	10,000	20,000
Adjustments to convert to cash		
Decrease/increase in accounts receivable	–2,000	–2,000
Cash generated from revenue	19,000	30,000
Expenses	13,020	19,840
Adjustments to convert to cash		
Decrease/increase in inventory	1,000	1,000
Depreciation expense	–300	–300
Cash dispursed for expenses	13,720	20,540
Cash generated from operations	$ 5,280	$ 9,460
Uses of cash		
Travel to fund-raising conventions	$ 2,000	$ 3,000
Promotional literature	500	750
Interest expense	300	300
Taxes paid	1,450	2,280
Total uses of cash	4,250	6,330
Net increase in cash	$ 1,030	$ 3,130

TIME TO DEVELOP A STRATEGY

The Jensens read this report by Gerald Green with great interest. They talked with each other about it at length, but had trouble arriving at any decisions regarding what to do. Susan commented

> I am impressed with how much information Gerald has been able to collect in such a short time, yet I'm not sure what to make of it. Besides, I have a business to run. All of the landscape and sprinkler-system work we have been doing lately has put me behind on preparing for the upcoming gift season. The drug store called yesterday to say that their seed display is getting low. I seriously doubt that we are prepared to handle any more than we are doing now.

David said he would talk to Gerald. The next day after Gerald and David finished up what they thought would be the last landscaping job for the season, David spoke briefly with Gerald:

> Gerald, your report is very impressive. Susan and I thought that it contained a lot of good information but we've had a hard time digesting what it means for the business. Susan and I agree we need to make some decisions very soon or it will be too late to do anything this year. However, before we go any further, Susan and I want to hear your recommendations. Let's get together after lunch Saturday, talk about your recommended actions, and try to come up with a plan.

Gerald agreed to meet with the Jensens at 1:30 PM on Saturday afternoon. On his way home, Gerald started thinking how he could put all the material he had been learning in his strategic management course to good use in helping the Jensens decide on a strategic plan for Susan's Special Lawns.

HICKORY RIDGE GOLF CLUB

Harold Valentine, University of South Carolina
Allen C. Amason, University of South Carolina
James J. Chrisman, Louisiana State University

Greg Hamilton, owner and manager of Hickory Ridge Golf Club (HRGC), a modest nine-hole golf course in Columbia, South Carolina, nursed his first cup of coffee of the day lost in thought. Normally, Hamilton would have been bustling around the course, preparing for the day's business. Play was generally brisk in the mornings of warm, June days, and the morning of June 1, 1989, promised to be no exception. In spite of this, Hamilton knew he had to make several decisions that could have an important short- and long-term impact on the profitability, and perhaps even the survival, of his business.

In 1988, its first year of business, Hickory Ridge generated revenues in excess of $116,000. However, the firm lost over $17,000. Exhibit 1 provides the 1988 profit and loss statement for HRGC. Exhibit 2 provides HRGC's common size balance sheet for 1988. As seen in Exhibit 3, greens fees accounted for the largest single portion of the revenues, followed by cart rentals.

The facilities at Hickory Ridge also needed improvement. The course needed restoration, the clubhouse needed extensive work, and much of the equipment was inadequate. In addition, the club's fleet of nine electric carts had not been sufficient to meet 1988 demand, much less the increase in cart usage expected for the remainder of 1989. The current fleet of carts was old and required frequent repair; this further aggravated the profit situation. Hamilton knew a decision was needed on whether or not to purchase or lease new carts, and if so, from whom. He was also aware that to supply the money for all the improvements to the facilities, revenues would have to increase substantially.

Unfortunately, several unanswered questions complicated the decision-making process. How much revenue had previously been lost due to the inadequate cart fleet? How much could be gained by improving the course or the clubhouse? More

*This is a revised version of a case prepared by Harold Valentine and Allen C. Amason under the direction of James J. Chrisman while an assistant professor of management at the University of South Carolina. Copyright © 1991 by James J. Chrisman. Reprinted with permission from *Entrepreneurship: Theory and Practice,* Summer 1992.

EXHIBIT 1 | Hickory Ridge Golf Club: Profit and Loss Statement, 1988 *(From IRS Schedule C)*

Sales	$116,270
Cost of goods sold	−21,079
Gross profit	95,191
Salaries and administrative expenses	
Wages and salaries	36,327
Repairs	7,532
Supplies	13,885
Utilities and telephone	7,549
Advertising	900
Car and truck expenses	2,353
Insurance	6,411
Dues and publications	693
Rent on business property	1,338
Taxes	4,905
Interest expense	13,459
Depreciation	13,590
Other	3,859
Net profit	−$ 17,610

EXHIBIT 2 | Hickory Ridge Golf Club: Common Size Balance Sheet Compared to Industry Averages

	Hickory Ridge	Industry*
Assets		
Current assets	10.0%	18.9%
Cash and equivalents	4.0	7.4
Inventory	2.2	10.9
Other current	3.8	0.6
Fixed assets	78.0	73.3
Intangibles and other noncurrent assets	12.0	7.8
Total assets	100.0%	100.0%
Liabilities		
Short-term payables	4.8%	9.1%
Other payables	10.0	15.9
Long-term debt	80.0	44.5
Equity	5.2	30.5
Total liabilities and equity	100.0%	100.0%

*SIC #7992, Public golf courses with sales of less than $500,000.

Industry Source: Robert Morris Associates, '90 Annual Statement Studies, 1990.

EXHIBIT 3 | Hickory Ridge Golf Club Revenues, 1988–89

	Greens Fees	Golf Carts	Pull Carts	Snack Bar Pro Shop	Beer	Total Revenues
1988						
January	$ 1,069	$ 290	$ 38	$ 280	$ 800	$ 2,476
February	2,906	833	92	360	1,920	6,110
March	4,601	1,728	127	997	2,400	9,852
April	7,713	2,773	271	2,337	1,380	14,474
May	6,463	2,236	252	1,443	1,960	12,354
June	5,193	1,866	210	1,116	1,880	10,264
July	5,665	2,436	204	1,691	2,000	11,996
August	5,811	2,657	188	1,242	1,900	11,798
September	5,616	2,382	204	465	1,800	10,467
October	5,024	1,943	201	864	1,100	9,132
November	4,969	1,762	190	883	1,000	8,804
December	4,925	1,664	210	748	996	8,543
Total	$59,954	$22,569	$2,186	$12,426	$19,136	$116,270
1989						
January	$ 5,497	$ 1,803	$ 206	$ 665	$ 1,680	$ 9,851
February	3,700	1,023	163	853	800	6,539
March	7,472	2,404	338	1,347	2,040	13,601
April	10,531	3,297	509	2,511	2,080	18,928
May	11,056	4,209	566	2,404	2,000	20,235
Total	$38,256	$12,736	$1,782	$ 7,780	$ 8,600	$ 69,154

important, Hamilton wondered how any decision, on the carts or other matters, would affect revenues in 1989. To further complicate the situation, Hamilton was unsure whether his course was positioned to attract the influx of new golfers and the large base of experienced golf enthusiasts in the area. To formulate a strategy, Hamilton knew he would have to rely on his own knowledge and experience as well as the advice of the course architect and mechanic, Harold Valentine. As he finished his coffee, Hamilton vowed to bring up the subject with Valentine that afternoon.

HAMILTON'S BACKGROUND

For Hamilton, the purchase of Hickory Ridge was an important step in fulfilling a lifelong dream—to own and run a public golf course. Born on May 18, 1950, and raised in Columbus, Ohio, Hamilton was introduced to golf by Arnold Adams, owner of Possum Run Golf and Swim Club. Adams, who gave Hamilton his first job, was far more than just an employer. He passed on to Hamilton his love of golf, and his conviction that golf should be a game easily accessible to the general public. For several years Hamilton spent nearly every spare moment of his time on the course with Adams.

Marriage at age 21 brought many changes to Hamilton's life, including three children, but his dream to own a golf course remained unchanged. His wife, Dr. Cynthia Hamilton, supported Hamilton emotionally and financially through her psychiatry practice. In 1978, the couple moved to Columbia, South Carolina, where Hamilton took the position of assistant pro at a local golf club, Linrick Golf Course. While there, Hamilton earned his PGA assistant's license and hoped to eventually earn his PGA professional's license.

BACKGROUND OF HICKORY RIDGE GOLF CLUB

HRGC opened in 1957 as an 18-hole, par-71 golf course. It was built on a modest budget by the Williams family, who owned the land. The Williams family operated the course for less than a decade before selling it in 1964. Following several owner-ship changes over the next 15 years, the McAllister family bought the course in 1978. Almost immediately, the McAllisters, who were in the construction business, cut the golf course to nine holes and built a housing development on what had been the "back nine." The McAllisters invested minimal amounts of money in maintaining the course, and gradually it fell into the dilapidated state in which Hamilton found it in 1988.

CONDITIONS AT PURCHASE

At the time of Hamilton's purchase, there was little reason to believe that HRGC had ever been a pleasant, well-kept golf course. The clubhouse and the equipment shed had accumulated an abundance of garbage over the years. What little equipment remained was virtually unusable. One old tractor was the only piece of heavy equip-ment available and had to be jump-started before being used. The gang and greens mowers were almost beyond repair and were unable to perform the functions for which they had been designed. There was no mechanical sand trap rake, necessitating hand raking of all the bunkers. There was an ancient fairway aerator and a fleet of 14 vintage-1976 E-Z-GO carts. Of these, only 6 carts worked at all, and they were extremely dangerous to use; some did not have brakes or a reverse gear.

The condition of the course was not much better. The grounds were overgrown, and the encroaching bushes, weeds, and trees gave the course an air of abandonment. There was a significant amount of grass in the sand traps, and sand that had escaped discouraged grass from growing where it was needed. The greens were receding from lack of care and were being eaten away by fungus and weeds. The tees were eroding noticeably due to improper cart path management and design. Inadequate aeration produced ground that was hard, making it difficult for the grass to infiltrate the top-soil and grow properly. Finally, the pond on the course was an eyesore. The pond was overgrown and full of garbage; there was less than three feet of water at its deepest point, making it unsuitable for irrigation.

IMPROVEMENTS AND CHANGES

Needless to say, Hamilton's refurbishing encompassed the course's buildings, equip-ment, and grounds. Hoping to keep the transition of ownership smooth, Hamilton sought to retain the employees who had worked at the course under the McAllisters. Poor communication and personal conflicts, however, led to frequent disagreements between these workers and Hamilton in the early months of HRGC's development. By July 1988, the course superintendent had been fired and most of the other person-nel problems were resolved. Johnny Clayton was hired as greenskeeper and Harold Valentine as architect/mechanic.

Because the clubhouse and shop areas were nearly inaccessible, the trash that had accumulated was removed, clearing the way for several improvements. Hamilton's original office was a 50-square-foot closet which he unwillingly shared with the pesticides and herbicides. To solve this problem, Hamilton had a larger office built on the back of the clubhouse. He installed a pro shop and, from scratch, built up its inventory to be able to provide golfers with some basic supplies and accessories. He also improved the snack bar, buying some new tables and chairs, a refrigerator, and a hot dog machine.

In addition, there were improvements to the equipment. Hamilton was able to repair the gang mower but the other pieces of equipment, including the greens mower and the tractor, had to be replaced. In May 1988, in an effort to bolster the pathetic cart fleet, HRGC purchased 12 1984-model Club Car electric carts. Two of the older carts were then junked, giving HRGC a total of 16 usable carts.

Another major capital expenditure was the purchase of a new irrigation system, an absolute necessity in maintaining a quality golf course. The irrigation system was installed on all greens and tees, and on five of the nine fairways. A submersible pump in a newly dug quartz-aquifer well kept the reservoir pond filled. A new 30 horsepower pump was installed to provide pressure for the system. To help reduce algae and aquatic weed growth, the pond was stocked with fish.

The holes in the course required a great deal of attention. Eroded areas were filled and the turf grass and greens revamped. Fairways were aerated and brush was cut away from the roughs to widen the holes. New tee markers and flags were purchased and areas that might be damaged by the carts were roped off. Additionally, cables were installed along the road to prevent damage from vandals who had previously driven cars on the fairways and greens.

Hamilton also made a move to ensure that the course met the needs and preferences of its customers. Acting on a marketing research project completed in April 1989, Hamilton decided to change the price structure of the course and restrict alcohol use to that which was purchased on the course.

INDUSTRY ENVIRONMENT

By 1988, golf had become a booming business that was expected to grow rapidly in the 1990s. Nearly every authority agreed that the number of players and the volume of revenues they brought in were steadily increasing. According to *Golf Market Today* (1989), there were approximately 11.2 million golfers in the United States in 1970. At the beginning of 1989, that figure had nearly doubled to 21.7 million. Also important was that the rate of growth had accelerated over each of the past four years. Researchers from the National Golf Foundation estimated that over 30 million people would be golfing in the United States by the year 2000.

This explosive growth was largely attributed to increased interest among women, the elderly, and the "baby boomers" (*PGA Magazine,* 1989). Of particular importance was the impact women were likely to have on the future of the game. In 1989, women represented around 25 percent of all golfers yet accounted for 40 percent of all new players. Like their male counterparts, many had careers and found golf an excellent way to relax and conduct business (*Savvy,* 1989).

The growth of golf also caught the attention of the business world. *Business Week* (1989) called golf "a global phenomenon" and a "$20 billion industry with a growth rate that is nothing short of phenomenal." The golf boom had been felt in the stock market too, with many corporations—such as Emhart Industries, a maker of club shafts, and American Brands, a maker of golf shoes—seeing significant changes in their stock prices (*Research Recommendations,* 1989). This growth had also led to increased corporate sponsorship on the PGA tour, as well as higher purses at PGA events (*Golf Digest,* 1989).

The possibilities for growth seemed limitless, and it appeared unlikely that supply could keep up with demand, even though both the number of courses opened and under construction rose from 1987 to 1988 (*Golf Market Today,* 1989; *Golf Digest,* 1989). In 1987, there were 145 new courses opened and 513 under construction or in the planning stage; in 1988, 211 courses opened and 662 were being constructed or planned. Nevertheless, overcrowded courses were becoming more common and the situation in some areas was becoming serious (*Business Week,* 1989). Even planning for 50 percent growth over the next decade—some believed this growth would be closer to 100 percent (*Golf Digest,* 1989)—the golf industry estimated that 4,000 new facilities, or an average in excess of one course opening per day, would be necessary over the next 10 years (*Golf Market Today,* 1989).

The Golf Course Superintendents Association singled out the lack of public golf courses as the major contributor to the overall facility shortage (*Golf Course Management,* 1989). Over 80 percent of all golfers used public courses, and this figure was expected to increase. For this reason *Golf Market Today* estimated that at least 60 percent of all new courses needed to be public.

KEYS TO SUCCESS

Despite the rapid growth, the keys to running a successful course had not changed much; for example, it was important to have a clean, well-maintained course and polite, well-trained employees. However, by 1989 golf was becoming a game played by people of diverse incomes, social backgrounds, and ages. It had become increasingly important for golf course owners to understand the needs and habits of a changing and growing clientele. For instance, some courses in Florida sought to lure in the seniors with special senior citizens discount packages, failing to consider the fact that most of their golfers were already seniors. Owners of these courses sometimes went bankrupt because they did not understand the market and were unable to keep costs in line with revenues.

Diversity was a watchword within the industry. Experienced golfers were fascinated with high-tech equipment: the newer, the more innovative, the more original, the better. Therefore, pro shops were stocking more high-performance equipment and golfing extras. Moreover, golfers desired courses with a variety of views and shots; a course layout that lacked variety bored the average golfer.

LOCAL ENVIRONMENT

HRGC was located in Columbia, South Carolina, a city with a metropolitan population of approximately 465,000. Between 1980 and 1988, the city had grown by about 13.5 percent. With an unemployment rate of only 3.9 percent, the area was generally considered to be prosperous. The average per capita income of the area was $13,795 in 1987. Exhibit 4 provides selected demographic data on the area.

The majority of the existing population was distributed in the areas north, west, and east of downtown, extending in each direction about 15 miles. New retail and residential developments were concentrated primarily in the northeast and northwest quadrants of the city as a large portion of the area's future growth was expected to be centered in these two regions.

Furthermore, in 1987 there were approximately 34,000 students enrolled in the nine colleges and universities in the area. A single state university, located in the mid-

EXHIBIT 4 | **Demographic Characteristics of the Columbia, South Carolina, Metropolitan Area**

	Population Estimates (in 000s)		Estimated Average Household Effective Buying Income		Estimated Retail Sales per Household	
	1988	1993	1988	1993	1988	1993
Lexington County	180.5	203.6	$31,251	$44,888	$12,532	$17,729
Columbia Metro Area	465.8	498.3	32,602	46,758	17,026	24,153
South Carolina	3511.0	3712.0	27,058	38,954	15,932	22,761
South Atlantic region	42921.5	46127.2	31,915	45,074	18,252	25,918
United States	247920.3	259268.5	33,198	46,997	17,745	24,989

Source: "Survey of Buying Power: Part II," *Sales & Marketing Management,* November 13, 1989, pp. 81, 102.

POPULATION BREAKDOWNS BY AGE, SEX, AND RACE

	Total	<5 years	5–17 years	18–64 years	≥65 years	Median Age	Percent Male	Percent White
Columbia Metro Area								
1980 actual	410,088	28,510	86,026	265,429	30,123	27.3	49.2%	69.9%
1990 projected	472,800	34,570	82,820	312,570	42,890	31.0	NA	NA
South Carolina								
1980 actual	3,121,820	238,516	703,450	1,892,526	287,328	28.0	48.6	68.8
1990 projected	3,622,000	272,600	619,200	2,248,700	409,500	32.0	NA	NA

Source: *South Carolina Statistical Abstract 1989,* South Carolina Budget and Control Board, pp. 288–89, 297.

EXHIBIT 5 | **College and University Enrollments in Columbia, South Carolina**

	1987	1988	1989	1990	1992 (est)
University of South Carolina	23,946	26,435	25,692	25,613	26,625
Other area colleges	10,540	10,986	11,654	12,768	13,604
Total enrollments	34,486	37,421	37,346	38,381	40,229

middle of downtown, represented the majority of the student population. Exhibit 5 provides information on college and university enrollments in the Columbia area.

LOCAL GOLF INDUSTRY

The local golf scene was changing and growing with the community. The southeastern by-pass was expected to be completed by late 1990. This by-pass would complete the interstate's encirclement of the metropolitan area, making most public golf courses in the region accessible to local golfers (within a 30-minute drive). There also was the possibility of new competition in the local industry. Four syndicates, two from Florida, and one each from Texas and California, were analyzing the potential profitability of constructing major 27- to 36-hole golf complexes in the area. Other local groups had received approval to build additional holes, the local government was seeking to obtain grants to build an 18- or 27-hole course southeast of town, and a country club on the west side of town was considering the construction

EXHIBIT 6 | The Columbia Public Golfer: Market Survey Results, 1989

The survey summarized below was based on the responses of 210 individuals in the Columbia Metro Area

- 68% of the respondents were from 20 to 40 years old.
- 56% of the respondents drove between 5 and 15 miles to play golf.
- 38% of the respondents' income was below $10,000; 28% of the respondents' income was between $20,000 and $30,000.
- 83% of the respondents located new golf courses through word-of-mouth.
- 51% of the respondents would play more golf if lower green fees were available.
- 65% of the respondents played golf more than 15 times per year.
- 62% of the respondents that were pro shop customers said that their most frequent purchase was golf balls.
- 57% of the respondents said that they would prefer food items such as hot dogs and hot sandwiches offered in the clubhouse.
- 72% of the respondents preferred to play 18 holes of golf per outing.
- 87% of the respondents preferred to ride in a cart or walk with a pull cart while golfing.
- 62% of the respondents said that the primary determinant in the selection of a golf course was the condition of the fairways and greens.
- 60% of the respondents said that they expected to pay between $4 and $6 per round.
- 97% of the respondents preferred to play with a friend or a foursome.
- 27% of the respondents preferred to play on Saturdays.
- 80% of the respondents were male.
- 34% of the respondents were college students; 49% were in the workforce.

Source: Postich, Miller, and Valentine, 1989.

of nine additional holes to complement the nine holes it had recently completed. If it did so, this club would be able to offer its customers a total of 27 holes of golf. Generally, there was a regional trend toward clubs offering a combination of memberships and pay-for-play options. Golf was also becoming more accessible to the public because prices were rising more slowly than the cost of living.

A 1989 marketing study conducted for Hickory Ridge Golf Club helped explain local conditions. This study targeted 210 golfers, both familiar and unfamiliar with HRGC, and had a margin of error of plus or minus two percentage points (see Exhibit 6). The following summarizes the findings of the study:

Hickory Ridge Golf Club, as well as other area public golf courses, have [sic] a clientele that consists mainly of 20-to-40-year-old males who prefer to play 18 holes of golf per day. These individuals play more than 15 times per year. Of these players almost 43 percent are college students. We believe that the level of college play can be increased by sponsoring a student/professor day early during each semester. It is our finding that lower green fees coupled with good greens and fairways are the most important factors to the public golfer. Financial records revealed that weekdays hold the greatest opportunity for increased profitability. This may be accomplished by increasing league play. It should be noted that in order to avoid simply shifting weekend play to weekday play, courses should refrain from lowering weekday rates.

Our study has determined that the public golfer seeks a greater selection of golf balls and hot food. While riding carts are most preferred, a ratio of 7 pull carts to 10 riding carts should be maintained in future purchases. Word-of-mouth is by far the most prevalent manner in which golfers learn about new courses. Therefore road signs should be used for directional purposes only, keeping all forms of advertising within a 15-mile radius. By following these recommendations, Hickory Ridge Golf Club should continue to have a substantial increase in play.

EXHIBIT 7 | **Columbia Area Golf Courses: May 1989**

Private	Location and Miles from Downtown	
1. Coldstream Country Club Inc., Irmo, SC	Northwest	16
2. Columbia Country Club, Columbia, SC	Northeast	20
3. Crickentree Golf Club, Columbia, SC	Northeast	25
4. Forest Lake Country Club, Columbia, SC	Northeast	5
5. Golden Hills Golf and Country Club, Lexington, SC	West	20
6. Mid Carolina Club Inc., Prosperity, SC	Northwest	30
7. Timberlake Plantation, Chapin, SC	Northwest	35
8. Wild Wood Country Club, Columbia, SC	Northeast	15
9. The Windermere Club, Blythwood, SC	Northeast	20
10. Woodlands Country Club, Columbia, SC	Northeast	17
Public		
11. Charwood Country Club, West Columbia, SC	Southwest	12
12. Coopers Creek Golf Club, Pelion, SC	Southwest	20
13. Hickory Ridge Golf Club, Columbia, SC	Southeast	10
14. Hidden Valley Country Club, West Columbia, SC	South	15
15. Lake Marion Golf Club, Santee, SC	South	40
16. Linrick Golf Course, Columbia, SC	North	15
17. Paw Paw Country Club, Bamberg, SC	Southwest	40
18. Persimmon Hill Golf Club, Johnston, SC	Southwest	30
19. Pineland Plantation Golf Club, Sumter, SC	East	30
20. Sedgewood Country Club, Hopkins, SC	Southeast	15
21. White Pines Country Club, Camden, SC	East	40

COMPETITORS

In 1989 HRGC had 20 competitors in the area. Of these, 10 were public and 10 were private (see Exhibit 7). Only one course, Sedgewood Golf Course, was located within five miles of HRGC. Exhibits 8 through 10 provide information on the characteristics of each golf course in the area.

Sedgewood Golf Course   Sedgewood Golf Course, HRGC's nearest competitor, was very different in significant ways. Sedgewood was an 18-hole, 6810-yard, par-72 public course with restricted tee times on weekends and holidays. Besides the fact that Sedgewood was a regulation, 18-hole course, the most noticeable difference was in the price structure. A round of 9 holes cost $7 to $11, depending on the day it was played, and a round of 18 holes cost $11 to $13. A riding cart cost an additional $9 per person for 9 holes and $18 per person for 18 holes. In comparison, on weekdays HRGC charged $4.50 for 9 holes, $7 for 18, and $8 for the entire day; its rates were $1.50 higher on weekends and holidays. Furthermore, at HRGC it cost only $6.50 per 9 holes per cart regardless of the time of week. One notable similarity between the two courses, however, was a lack of adequate course maintenance.

Other Facilities   Also noteworthy were the facilities of other competitors. All area courses had pro shops on the premises, and there were a total of 29 pro shops in the area. These ranged from broad-based discount shops, such as Nevada Bob's, to

EXHIBIT 8 | **Characteristics of Columbia Area Golf Courses: Dues, Greens Fees, and Hours**

Private Courses				
# from Exhibit 7	Dues/Fees	Open Hours	Closed	Tee Time
1.	$77/month, $210 initiation	7:30 AM–6:00 PM	Thanksgiving and Christmas	8 AM
2.	NA	NA	NA	NA
3.	$9,500 equity	8:30 AM–dark	Monday	NA
4.	$2,500 equity	8:00 AM–6:30 PM		9 AM
5.	$75/month, $2,187 initiation	8:00 AM–6:30 PM	Monday, Thanksgiving, Christmas, and New Year's	8 AM
6.	$30/month, $750 initiation	8:00 AM–8:00 PM	Christmas	8 AM
7.	$90/month, $2,500 initiation*	8:00 AM–7:00 PM	Christmas	9 AM
8.	$100/month, $7,500 initiation	7:30 AM–8:00 PM	Christmas and New Year's	8 AM
9.	$100/month, $2,500 initiation	8:00 AM–8:00 PM	Monday, Thursday, Friday, Thanksgiving Christmas, and New Year's	10 AM
10.	$105/month, $2,000 initiation	8:00 AM–7:00 PM		8 AM

Public Courses				
# from Exhibit 7	Dues/Fees Weekdays, Weekends (9/18)	Open Hours	Closed	Tee Time
11.	$6.00/10.00, $8.00/12.00	7:30 AM–9:30 PM		8 AM
12.	$9.00/11.00, $9.00/11.00	7:00 AM–dark		10 AM
13.**	$4.50/7.00, $6.00/8.50	8:00 AM–dark		Open
14.	$6.00/8.00, $12.00/12.00	8:00 AM–dark		8 AM
15.	$15.00/25.00, $15.00/25.00	Daylight–dark		7 AM
16.	$5.50/8.50, $6.50/10.50	7:30 AM–dark	Christmas	8 AM
17.	$10.50/16.80, $13.65/21.00	8:00 AM–dark	Christmas	10 AM
18.	$5.50/11.00, $8.00/16.000	8:00 AM–7:00 PM	Christmas	8 AM
19.	$5.00/10.00, $8.00/12.00	7:00 AM–dark	Christmas	8 AM
20.	$7.00/11.00, $11.00/13.00	7:30 AM–dark	Christmas	10 AM
21.	$8.00/8.00, $10.00/10.00	7:30 AM–dark		Open

Note: NA = not available.
*Property ownership required.
**Nine-hole course.

extremely exclusive shops at some of the finer country clubs, most of which were run by sales representatives. The majority of shop revenues tended to come from club repair and the sale of clubs, golf balls, tees, and golf gloves. The average shop was likely to stock around 30 sets of clubs, although the biggest volume local shops were known to stock in excess of 100 sets. In addition, most shops stocked golf clothing such as socks, shoes, and hats, and many also carried shirts and pants. Certain pro shops, particularly those in country clubs, stocked extremely large inventories of clothing items. Often, the inventory of the pro shop was related to the exclusivity of the club and the wealth of the club's clientele. It was difficult for the pro shops to compete with the discount stores when the customers were price sensitive.

Only three courses offered full restaurants and all of these were private courses. The remaining private courses had limited dining facilities. Most clubs operated

EXHIBIT 9 | **Characteristics of Columbia Area Golf Courses: Amenities and Special Rates**

			Private Courses			
# from Exhibit 7	Pro Shop	Senior Rate (9/18)	Student Rate (9/18)	Restaurant	Snack Bar	Lockers
1.	Yes	No	No	Yes	No	No
2.	NA	NA	NA	NA	NA	NA
3.	Yes	No	No	Grill	Yes	Yes
4.	Yes	No	No	Yes	Yes	Yes
5.	Yes	No	No	Yes	Yes	Yes
6.	Yes	No	No	Yes	Yes	Yes
7.	Yes	No	No	Grill	No	Yes
8.	Yes	No	No	Grill	No	Yes
9.	Yes	No	No	Yes	Yes	Yes
10.	Yes	No	No	Yes	Yes	Yes
			Public Courses			
# from Exhibit 7	Pro Shop	Senior Rate (9/18)	Student Rate (9/18)	Restaurant	Snack Bar	Lockers
11.	Yes	$5.00/6.00	$5.00/6.00	No	Yes	No
12.	Yes	No	No	No	Yes	Yes
13.*	Yes	$4.50 weekday	$4.50 weekday	No	Yes	Yes
14.	Yes	$6.00	$6.00	No	Yes	No
15.	Yes	No	No	No	Yes	No
16.	Yes	$4.50/6.00	$4.50/6.00	No	Yes	No
17.	Yes	No	No	No	Yes	No
18.	Yes	No	No	Yes	No	No
19.	Yes	Varies	No	No	Yes	No
20.	Yes	$1 off	$1 off	No	Yes	No
21.	Yes	Varies	No	Yes	Yes	Yes

*Nine-hole course.

snack bars. Generally, the operators of public courses felt the profit potential of a restaurant was limited. Only two had grills. These offered hot sandwiches, hamburgers, and so forth, as well as drinks and snacks, and were open during lunch and dinner hours. Almost all of the public courses had simple snack bar facilities, however, offering hot dogs, cold drinks, chips, and candy.

Another thing many public courses lacked were locker areas and shower facilities. These were potentially appealing to the blue-collar workers, who would often golf on the way to or from work. Although 8 of the 10 private courses offered locker areas, only 2 of the 11 public courses did so.

CURRENT OPERATIONS

In practical terms, Hamilton believed that HRGC was without close competition because of its distinctive characteristics. It was the only nine-hole golf course in the area. It was unusually level and short (2,807 yards, compared to the local average of

EXHIBIT 10 | **Characteristics of Columbia Area Golf Courses: Course and Cart Information**

	Private Courses		
# from Exhibit 7	Yardage	Par	Cart Fees (9/18)
1.	6,155	71	$4.75/8.40 person
2.	NA	NA	NA
3.	6,471	72	$8.00/16.00 per cart
4.	6,450	72	$2.50/5.00 per person
5.	6,461	71	$5.00/8.00 per person
6.	6,600	72	$3.50/7.00 per person
7.	6,703	72	$4.75/8.50 per person
8.	6,726	72	$9.05 + tax per person for 18 holes
9.	6,900	72	$5.25/10.50 per person
10.	6,786	72	$4.00/8.00 per person
	Public Courses		
# from Exhibit 7	Yardage	Par	Cart Fees (9/18)
11.	6,100	72	$4.00/8.00 per person
12.	6,550	72	$4.00/8.00 per person
13.*	2,807	35	$6.50 per cart
14.	6,700	72	$4.00/8.00 per person
15.	6,615	72	Included in greens fee
16.	7,080	73	$6.00/12.00 per cart
17.	6,700	72	Included in greens fee
18.	7,050	72	$4.50/9.00 per person
19.	7,084	72	$4.00/8.00 per person
20.	6,810	72	$9.00/18.00 per cart
21.	6,400	72	$4.00/8.00 per person

*Nine-hole course.

3,313 yards for nine holes) for a par-35, nine-hole course, making it especially suitable for elderly and young players. Its length, the absence of hills, and the lack of water, which came directly into play on only one hole, made HRGC a good course for the beginning golfer or the experienced golfer who wanted to walk the course or wanted a safe course on which to practice (see Exhibit 11 for course layout). Besides Hickory Ridge, only six of the other area courses were open 365 days per year, and only one of them had entirely unrestricted tee times. Overall, these factors attracted many beginners, senior citizens, students, women, and blue-collar customers to HRGC.

As noted earlier, these customers represented a rapidly growing segment of the golfing public. Golf had traditionally been a sport of affluent, middle-aged males. However, the growing popularity of golf was being driven by groups of people who had not been especially interested in the game in the past. Hamilton believed that the other courses in the area were not designed to serve these newer, more diverse customer groups. He believed that Hickory Ridge could exploit a great opportunity by

EXHIBIT 11 | **Hickory Ridge Golf Club: Course Layout**

Hole	Length	Par	Features
1	324 yards	4	Straight, narrow, next to road
2	328 yards	4	Straight, next to road, bordered by water
3	313 yards	4	Straight, next to road, water barrier
4	360 yards	4	Dog leg right, wooded obstruction
5	214 yards	3	Straight, narrow, close trees
6	282 yards	4	Straight, narrow, close trees
7	166 yards	3	Straight, open
8	382 yards	4	Straight, open
9	438 yards	5	Straight, open

focusing its facility and efforts on the needs of the new golfer. Hamilton knew, however, that it would be unwise to alienate traditional golfers.

SALES

Sales were broken down into five areas: greens fees, cart rentals, snack bar and pro shop sales, beer sales, and pull cart rentals (see Exhibit 3). During the first five months of 1989, course revenues from greens fees, golf carts, and pull carts amounted to $52,774.

In addition to course revenues, HRGC stocked golf balls, a moderate selection of golf clubs (as well as some rentals), golf gloves, and other complementary items such as socks. The shop did not carry golf shoes or clothes. HRGC usually kept six sets of golf clubs in stock, at a value of approximately $2,000. After a round of golf, players could also relax with a chili dog and a cold drink at the snack bar and watch the PGA tour or a ballgame on television before making the trip back home. Through May, snack bar, beer, and pro shop sales had contributed $16,380 to revenues in 1989.

FEES AND TEE TIMES

The marketing survey Hamilton commissioned provided the impetus for changes in pricing and advertising. For weekdays, greens fees were raised by 50 cents across-the-board to $4.50 for 9 holes, $7.00 for 18 holes, and $8.00 for the entire day. Weekend and holiday rates were increased by $1.50 to $6.00 for 9 holes, $8.50 for 18 holes, and $9.50 for the entire day. The cart rates were raised from $6.00 to $6.50 per nine holes and senior citizen and student discount fees were restricted to weekdays.

The new fee structure was designed with two purposes in mind. It was intended to underprice the competition while still allowing an acceptable profit margin (between 2.5 and 4 percent). It was also intended to make golf accessible to as many residents of the area as possible, many of whom were new to the sport and were very conscious of price.

Hamilton made no change in tee times, however, keeping them open and making the course available on a first-come-first-served basis 365 days a year. His reason for this was to allow the greatest number of people to tee off in the shortest amount of time possible, while providing the maximum number of tee-off hours; he did not want any unnecessary restrictions on the golfers.

ADVERTISING

The market survey had also recommended targeting certain groups that might find HRGC appealing, such as elderly and student golfers. As a result, Hamilton formulated an advertising strategy designed to entice a greater number of college students to HRGC. In hopes of catching the eye of new students, Hamilton concentrated his advertising efforts at the beginning of each semester, reducing his efforts as final exams neared. He advertised in the local paper, and planned to advertise in the university paper. The local paper, a statewide publication, charged $85.50 for a one-weekend advertisement. The university newspaper, which was published during the spring and fall semesters, charged $25.00 per week for advertisements. Billboards were also employed along the main roads to provide directions as well as to bring in golfers who might not otherwise have known about HRGC. In addition, because the survey indicated that the vast majority of golfers (more than four-fifths) try out new courses as a result of word-of-mouth, Hamilton concentrated on promoting a friendly atmosphere at HRGC and rejected both radio and television advertising, which he had previously been considering.

MAINTENANCE AND FACILITIES

To make the course more appealing and playable, Hamilton continued his efforts to clean up the course and the clubhouse, and the existing facilities had taken on a markedly different and improved appearance as a consequence. Despite the improvements, HRGC still suffered from problems with erosion at the tee areas and inconsistent conditions on the greens. Conditions were steadily improving, though, because the newer equipment led to more efficient and productive course maintenance. Nevertheless, HRGC's facilities had not changed much since Hamilton bought the course. The only additions were the office built in the clubhouse and the pumphouse constructed near the pond.

EMPLOYEES

Hamilton continued to employ Jim Alsing and Pete Peterson to operate the counter. Their work consisted of collecting greens and cart fees, controlling cart usage, managing the snack bar and pro shop, keeping the area clean, and some miscellaneous administrative duties.

Hamilton had hired Johnny Clayton to be the course greenskeeper, and Harold Valentine as course architect and mechanic. The bulk of the maintenance work fell upon these two individuals. Clayton's primary duties were to maintain the greens, fairways, and roughs, along with a host of other special projects. His devotion to the golf business was largely due to his father who had previously been an employee at the course. Valentine, along with being the course agronomist and chemical specialist, worked as part-time mechanic. He had ten years of experience as a mechanic with the Navy, as well as years of agricultural experience growing up on his father's farm in Tennessee. Valentine also worked on a variety of miscellaneous projects as schedules required.

STRATEGIC ISSUES

Hamilton owned a 15-acre, pie-shaped plot of ground adjacent to the golf course. He was considering adding a nine-hole, par-27 course there; however, construction costs would be $75,000 at the minimum, money that would have to be borrowed. Hamilton also wondered whether the lot would be sufficient to support a quality nine-hole course.

Another potential use for the land would be to add a driving range. A driving range could be completed at a significantly lower cost and might appeal to Hickory Ridge's customers. Hamilton estimated that a driving range could be built for $30,000. However, there was a new driving range currently being developed less than two miles away. The new range was not, however, connected to any area golf course.

OPERATING ISSUES

Besides his long-range concerns, Hamilton had many pressing operating issues that had to be resolved before his goals for HRGC could be attained.

COURSE EQUIPMENT

Improvement of the course was a top priority. Unfortunately, Hickory Ridge's equipment was barely sufficient for maintenance, much less improvement. With no mower for the rough, Hamilton was trying to use the fairway mower. This, however, did not work well on the higher, thicker rough grass. A new mower would cost $1,150.

A new rotivator would allow HRGC to use more efficient aeration techniques. A rotivator cuts thin slices in the ground and can be used the entire year. The old aerator made large holes in the turf and was only used once a year to minimize interference with play. Rotivators cost $3,000.

In addition, the sand traps had to be raked by hand, a slow and tedious job that was not done as often as it should have been. A mechanical trap rake would allow for daily maintenance of the bunkers but would cost around $1,200.

The irrigation system reached all tees and greens, but only five of the nine fairways. Although quality irrigation was a necessity on any golf course, it was especially important in the South where long, hot, dry summers could destroy good turf. Unfortunately, expanding the irrigation system would involve digging on the affected fairways. In spite of the interruption in play that this would cause, Hamilton wanted to extend the irrigation system to the other four fairways. Expanding the irrigation system would cost approximately $6,000.

CLUBHOUSE AND SNACK BAR IMPROVEMENTS

The clubhouse was in need of significant renovation; the ceiling leaked and the paneling was generally unattractive. Hamilton's desire to renovate became more earnest as the ratio of revenues from clubhouse activities (pro shop and snack bar) to revenues from the golf course increased. Renovation costs were expected to be approximately $8,000.

In addition to the clubhouse, new equipment was also needed for the snack bar. The most immediate concern was the cooler. When Hamilton bought HRGC, the only cooler in the snack bar was a whiskey barrel filled with ice. Although adequate, it was inefficient. Each time a drink was ordered the attendant had to reach down into the ice to find the desired brand. The attendant also had to keep track of how much of each brand was on ice to be sure that he did not run out of any one drink. The cost of replacing the cooler was estimated at $1,585.

CART FLEET REPLACEMENT

Hamilton's cart fleet was sorely depleted. Out of the original 14 E-Z-GO carts, only 2 were still running. The brakes on one of those were irreparably damaged and unlikely to last much longer. Nine of the 12 recently acquired Club Car carts were usable. The other three had been rendered completely useless by cracks in the transaxles and main drive gears. The 9 that were still in use suffered from various mechanical problems, however. The fusible links on two of the carts, parts that normally last for years, were burning out about every two weeks. On a third cart the rear support bracket for one of the shock absorbers had broken. Because the frame to which the bracket was attached was constructed of aluminum, it required a special type of welding not available at a reasonable cost.

There were other problems that pointed to the general deterioration of the fleet. Hamilton was beginning to recognize that extensive body damage could occur to fiberglass carts on a heavily wooded course such as HRGC, and that fiberglass repairs were extremely expensive. On several carts, the batteries were no longer holding their charges all day, and tires were beginning to lose air overnight. Both of these problems were becoming progressively worse. Furthermore, 3 of the 12 battery chargers had suffered failures in the power supply units, rendering them completely useless. Since none of the replacement parts ordered from Club Car had arrived, it was necessary to cannibalize parts from the three useless carts to keep the fleet operational.

These mechanical problems were causing trouble for Hamilton. For one thing, he had contracted to supply 15 carts for a golf league of 30 people. On any given day he could be certain of only 6 to 9 working carts. Even more significant was the fact that the proportion of golfers at HRGC who desired to use riding carts (the cart rental ratio) had increased from 26 to 31 percent. Likewise, while the level of play had increased by 36 percent over the previous year, the number of cart rentals had increased by 42 percent over the same period. More than ever, Hamilton's customers wanted to use carts but fewer and fewer were available. New carts would cost between $2,580 and $3,500 apiece.

WORKSHOP ADDITION

A temperature-controlled workshop was also needed adjacent to the clubhouse. Because of extremely high temperatures in the metal cart shed in the summer, repair work there was almost impossible. If a new fleet of carts was bought or rented, or if the old fleet was repaired, this workshop improvement would be mandatory. A workshop would cost at least $1,000.

HAMILTON'S DECISION

All these issues weighed upon Hamilton's mind. He knew that he would need to spend money in order to turn Hickory Ridge into the kind of facility he wanted it to be. However, his limited budget meant that he had to prioritize his efforts; he realized he could not possibly do everything at once since there were so many areas that needed attention.

Because of carts' ability to contribute revenue directly and to enhance the perception of the course, Hamilton believed that before he did anything else he would have to replace his aging cart fleet. The expanded cart fleet could provide a source of increased revenue, which could then be invested in new equipment for the course.

The problem was that Hamilton was not sure how he should proceed in solving the cart dilemma. If he repaired the current fleet, he might risk continued problems. On the other hand, leasing and purchasing both involved long-term commitments and large amounts of money. He could not, however, ignore the problem. Every day he waited meant lost revenues and lost golfers. A frustrated golfer who decided to go somewhere else to play might never come back. Hamilton and Valentine had investigated various options available to alleviate the cart crisis. There were several options, each with its own set of questions to consider.

ALTERNATIVES

The first alternative considered was to repair the current fleet with borrowed funds. Following this plan meant that the cost of repairs and the remaining life of the used carts would be important. Valentine believed that repairing the current fleet would provide no more than four years of extended operation and would provide a minimum amount of visible improvement in the overall situation.

A second alternative was to purchase an entirely different fleet or a fleet of used carts, as they had in 1988. Either option would require borrowed funds. With the prime rate at 11.5 percent, HRGC's ability to obtain and repay such a loan was open to debate.

A third alternative was to lease a fleet, which would require no additional borrowing. If this alternative was selected, Hamilton would need to decide whether or not to purchase a maintenance agreement along with the leased fleet. Under a lease agreement, Hamilton would control the number of carts to be maintained by the course, but not how they could be used. For example, some leases prohibit the use of carts to do maintenance work.

There were several other factors that Hamilton and Valentine needed to consider. First, they had to consider what types of options would be necessary to meet the expectations of the customers. Do customers want sun roofs, full cart enclosures for winter golf, and sweater baskets? Second, they needed to decide if they wanted to use three-wheel or four-wheel carts. Although more expensive, four-wheelers caused less turf damage and had a lower insurance cost because of their greater riding stability. They also had to decide if they wanted gas or electric carts. Gas-powered carts required the purchase of fuel and oil, and needed more daily maintenance. They were also noisier, gave off fumes, and did not ride smoothly. Electric-powered carts were heavier, caused greater soil compaction and grass deterioration, but provided a smoother ride. Because they ran on electricity, they required the purchase of battery packs, which had to be replaced every three years. Finally, they had to determine how many carts would be needed.

To help make the correct decision, four regional cart companies were investigated: Melex, Yamaha, Club Car, and E-Z-GO. Each of these companies was well established and provided carts for lease or purchase. Valentine visited each of these firms, seeking information on purchase prices and on four-year lease agreements without a maintenance contract. Exhibit 12 provides the specific information Valentine obtained from each vendor.

Certainly, the cart situation was one of many critical issues and Hamilton's decision on its resolution would affect business at the club for a long time. However, Hamilton could not help but wonder what impact addressing the cart fleet first would have on the rest of his plans. Clearly, he could not do everything at once. The market was expanding but so was the competition. He knew he had to quickly formulate and implement a strategy that could adequately address these matters and place Hickory Ridge in a position that would lead to a long-term competitive advantage with respect to its customers and competitors.

EXHIBIT 12 | **Golf Cart Vendor Comparisons**

	Melex	Yamaha	Club Car	E-Z-GO
Purchase price				
Gas	$2,800	$3,500	$3,250	$2,900
Electric	2,580	3,200	2,800	2,680
Lease price				
Monthly	$ 59	$ 72	$ 71	$ 59
Residual value	675	1,400	450	675
Location				
Service	Raleigh, NC	Newnan, GA	Augusta, GA	Augusta, GA
Manufacturing plant	Yugoslavia	Japan	U.S.	U.S.
Industry experience in U.S.	10 years	8 years	30 years	35 years
Company products and services				
Cart quality	good	average	average	excellent
Appearance	good	average	good	good
Service	good	below average	good	good
Parts availability	average	average	below average	good
Cart body	metal	fiberglass	fiberglass	metal

Source: Harold Valentine's perceptions and factual data collected from visits to each company.

VAIL ASSOCIATES, INC.

Herman L. Boschken, San Jose State University

In 1962, Earl Eaton and Pete Seibert along with several associates opened the Vail Ski Resort. Prior to this, the Vail Valley had been home to numerous ranchers and sheepherders. Drawn by ideal mountain conditions and a proposed interstate freeway, Eaton and Seibert formed Vail Associates (VA) and embarked on a mission of making Vail a world-class ski resort. By the 1980s, that status was achieved; by the 1993 season, the resort had held the ski industry's number one ranking for attracting the most skiers for six consecutive years.

But, in many ways, Vail was approaching a strategic crossroads. The industry had been changing—an aging population was shrinking demand for skiing and newer resorts, like Whistler in Canada, were winning a growing share of the market. Internally, the firm Eaton and Seibert had created had experienced ownership problems for some time. The firm had been sold first to Texas oilman Harry Bass in 1976 and then to Denver businessman George Gillett in 1985. Gillett, who previously had owned the Harlem Globetrotters, had invested heavily in new ski facilities. In 1991, however, Vail Associates' corporate parent, Gillett Enterprises, ran into serious financial difficulties and in 1992, a New York investment firm led by Leon Black gained control of Gillett's empire. Gillett, however, stayed on as Vail Associates' board chairman and Andy Daly, a seasoned Vail professional manager, was brought in as CEO. And Daly saw the transition to new ownership as a time to ponder Vail's future and to consider strategy alternatives that would keep it a profitable, world-class resort.

VAIL: THE FACILITIES

The resort had opened in 1962 with a gondola, a mid-mountain chairlift, a Back Bowls chairlift, and a $5 lift ticket. Accommodations were minimal. By the 1980s, Vail had become its own town of 6,000 permanent residents, mountain facilities were vast, lift tickets were $40 a day, and VA had built a second resort nearby at Beaver Creek, originally for the 1976 Olympics. See Exhibits 1 and 2 for details of the two facilities in 1994; Exhibits 3 and 4 show trail maps for the two ski areas.

EXHIBIT 1 | **Vail Mountain Fact Sheet, Winter 1993–94**

Location
100 miles/160 km west of Denver on Interstate 70—140 miles/224 km east of Grand Junction on Interstate 70—35 miles/56 km east of Vail's
Eagle County Airport—surrounded by 1.2 million acres of the White River National Forest—Eagle County, Colorado

The Village
Nestled below the ski slopes of Vail Mountain, Vail is a pedestrian village with two centers: Vail Village and Lionshead. From East Vail to West
Vail and between Vail Village and Lionshead, a complimentary intra-resort bus system runs from approximately 6 to 2 AM seven days a week.

Permanent Population: 6,000   Bed Base: 32,100; 41,305 Valley Wide (East Vail to Edwards)

Bars and Restaurants: 108   Shops: 258

Mountain Information
Ski Season: November 13, 1993, through April 17, 1994

Hours of Operation: 8:30 AM to 3:30 PM daily, MST.

Mountain Statistics				**Trail classification:**	
Base elevation:	8,200 feet	2,500 meters		Front side:	32% Beginner
Mid-Vail elevation:	10,300 feet	3,140 meters		(1,258 acres/509 hectares)	36% Intermediate
Top elevation:	11,250 feet	3,491 meters			32% Advanced
Vertical rise:	3,250 feet	991 meters		Back side:*	36% Intermediate
Snowmaking:	332 acres	134.4 hectares		(2,734 acres/1,107 hectares)	64% Advanced
Average snowfall:	335 inches	8.50 meters			
Total developed trails:	4,014 acres	1,625 hectares			
Total named trails:	121 trails				
Longest run:	4.5 miles	7.2 km			

*The Back Bowls include Sun Down, Sun Up, Tea Cup, China, Siberia, and Mongolia bowls. Terrain classification in the bowls varies according to weather conditions.

Mountain Statistics:
Base elevation: 8,200 feet / 2,500 meters
Mid-Vail elevation: 10,300 feet / 3,140 meters
Top elevation: 11,250 feet / 3,491 meters
Vertical rise: 3,250 feet / 991 meters
Snowmaking: 332 acres / 134.4 hectares
Average snowfall: 335 inches / 8.50 meters
Total developed trails: 4,014 acres / 1,625 hectares
Total named trails: 121 trails
Longest run: 4.5 miles / 7.2 km
("Flapjack" to "Riva Ridge")
Expanse: 7 miles / 11.3 km
(The Mongolia Surface Lift in the east to the Cascade Lift in the west.)
TOTAL PERMIT AREA: 12,500 acres / 5,058 hectares
Vail is the largest single-mountain ski area in North America.

Total number of lifts: 25

Lifts include: 1 Vista Bahn Express (high-speed detachable enclosed quad);

7 high-speed quads, 2 fixed-grip quads, 1 gondola, 3 triple chairlifts, 6 double chairlifts, 5 surface lifts.

Total uphill capacity: 41,855 skiers per hour

Vail has more high-speed detachable quad chairlifts than any other ski area in the world—8 total.

Lift Ticket Prices

Adults		**Children**	
Adult Full-Day	$45	Child Full-Day	$32
Adult Half-Day	$39	Child Half-Day	$26
Adult 2-Day	$90	Child 2-Day	$64
Adult 3-Day	$135	Child 3-Day	$96
Adult 4-Day	$168	Child 4-Day	$128
Adult 5-Day	$210	Child 5-Day	$160
Adult 6-Day	$240	Child 6-Day	$192
Adult 7-Day	$280	Child 7-Day	$224
Senior Citizens		**Foot Passenger**	
65–69 years of age	$36	Adult	$15
70 years or older	Free	Children	$10

Premier Passport, the joint Aspen and Vail lift ticket designed for international guests offers a minimum 10 out of 12 day lift ticket and a
maximum 18 out of 21 day lift ticket, at a rate of $38 per day, including a one-way ground transfer between the two resorts.

®Registered trademarks of Vail Associates, Inc.

EXHIBIT 1 | **Vail Mountain Fact Sheet, Winter 1993–94 (Continued)**

Skier Service Information

Snow watch: For a daily update on Vail and Beaver Creek Resort snow conditions call: (303) 476-4888. In Denver: (303) 296-3155

TV8 on cable television continuously updates skiers on weather conditions, recently opened trails and upcoming events. The station features a daily morning show with ski tips and helpful hints and is available in most lodge rooms throughout the valley.

Lift status signs are located at major decision points on the mountain, advising skiers of lifts in operation and approximate waiting times.

Complimentary *Meet the Mountain* tours are offered at 1 PM on Sundays, Mondays and Tuesdays. Tours begin at Wildwood Shelter.

Grooming information is posted at Golden Peak, Vail Village, Lionshead and most lift boards. Vail currently has 16 grooming snowcats.

Ski Corral offers overnight ski storage at Golden Peak, Vail Village and Lionshead.

Skier services personnel, wearing red and purple uniforms, answer questions and assist skiers on the mountain.

Lost and found is located in the Lionshead Gondola building, open 8 AM–6 PM daily, (303) 479-2059.

Sunday services are offered at 12:30 PM each Sunday at Two Elk, Mid-Vail, and Eagle's Nest. (nondenominational)

Dining on the Mountain

When dining on Vail Mountain, we suggest you eat early or eat late and ski through the lunch hour. Vail has six cafeterias, two restaurants and three trailside snack bars.

Two Elk Restaurant overlooks China Bowl and specializes in Southwest, Oriental, and American cruisine. A full salad bar, a baked potato bar and a pasta bar are also offered. The restaurant was so successful during its first season (1991-1992) that 200 seats were added to total 700 indoor seats. There are also 500 seats at the full-service, outdoor barbecue.

Cook Shack is a favorite restaurant on Vail Mountain featuring eclectic, American cuisine. The Cook Shack is a sit-down, full-service restaurant. Reservations are recommended at (303) 479-2030.

Dog Haus Express, located at the base of the Avanti Express, is a gourmet hot dog, ski-by stand featuring several different gourmet hot dogs with assorted savory mustards. Beer, wine, soft drinks and snacks are also available.

Eagle's Nest, located at the top of the Lionshead Gondola, has one of the most panoramic views found on Vail Mountain. The menu selection ranges from salads and taco bars to soups and burgers. A full yogurt bar complete with all imaginable toppings is also available.

Golden Peak Restaurant offers breakfast specials, burgers, soups, sandwiches, and salads. Après-ski at Golden Peak is casual in the upstairs bar.

Mid-Vail, where the mountain meets at noon, is the largest facility on Vail Mountain. With two cafeterias on different levels, a full deli, pizzeria, and outdoor barbecue, Mid-Vail is located at the top of the Vista Bahn and near the base of chairs 3 and 4.

Pronto's Porch, located at the base of the Northwoods Express, is a vending-machine express for hot sandwiches, burritos, soft drinks and more. Quarters and dollar bills only are accepted. Microwaves are available for heating selections.

Trail's End, located in the Lionshead Gondola building, opens for breakfast at 7:30 AM with daily specials. Lunch menu selections includes soups, sandwiches and daily specials. Lively après-ski entertainment is offered daily.

Wildwood Shelter, located at the top of chair 3, offers daily health-food specials. This small Italian-theme restaurant's specialties include lasagna, meatball sandwiches, vegetarian pita bread sandwiches and a potato bar.

Wine Stube is a small, intimate restaurant featuring popular ethnic dishes sure to warm the hungry skier. The restaurant is located at the top of the gondola and reservations are recommended at (303) 479-2034.

Wok 'n' Roll Express offers skiers a quick lunch at the base of the Orient Express lift in China Bowl. This ski-by pagoda specializes in fried rice and "Yakitori" (Chinese chicken).

Ski Equipment Rentals

Vail Associates has rental shops at Golden Peak and Lionshead which offer the finest equipment from beginner to high-performance, featuring Rossignol skis, Salomon boots and Scott poles. A standard rental package of boots, skis and poles is $14 per day. Snowboards and monoskis are available. Reservations are suggested and may be made by calling (303) 479-2050. Both shops offer free slopeside overnight ski storage with their rentals.

Recreational Ski Racing

Vail offers recreational racers both NASTAR and pay-to-race programs. Skiers of all ability levels compete in NASTAR competition against a pacesetter time set by the U.S. Ski Team's fastest skier. Individuals with top-placing times earn one of several medals awarded daily. Race fees are $5 for the first run and $1 for each additional run. NASTAR is held on "Race Track" daily from 12:30 PM to 2 PM. Group NASTAR races may be arranged by calling (303) 476-5601, ext. 4050.

Pay-to-race is a self-timing course open daily from 10 AM to 3 PM on Swingsville and is $1.00 per run. Season passes are available for $25. The Vail and Beaver Creek Ski School offers several racing clinics.

EXHIBIT 1 | **Vail Mountain Fact Sheet, Winter 1993–94 (Continued)**

Children's Programs

The popular *Family Night Out* is a dinner theater show and offers the perfect photo opportunity with Disney's Sport Goofy. It takes place on Tuesday nights starting in December. Call the Activities Desk™ at (303) 949-9090 for information and reservations.

The Western characters Sourdough Pete, Jackrabbit Joe, Buckaroo Bob, and Mirabelle can be seen skiing around Ft. Whippersnapper and Gitchegumee Gulch. They are joined by their other Western friends for the *Kid's Night Out Goes Western* dinner theater show on Thursday nights beginning December 23 through March 31. This is a fun, western evening for kids in kindergarten through sixth grade.

During Christmas and Spring vacation weeks, Beaver Creek Resort hosts a Friday night *Kid's Night Out Goes Hollywood.* This is a pizza and make your own video evening for kids 10 through 14. Teens will also have their evening for broomball and snowshoeing. For prices, reservations and more information please call the Activities Desk™ at (303) 949-9090.

Sport Goofy, Disney's ambassador of fun, fitness and skiing, also entertains the kids and is available for photo opportunities and après-ski hot chocolate at the Children's Centers weekly through the winter. Call (303) 479-2040 for his schedule.

Hot Winter Nights will be back for its fourth season beginning in December. Featuring the Vail and Beaver Creek Ski School Demonstration Team and a fireworks display, this extravaganza showcases the many forms of skiing.

Call the Activities Desk™ at (303) 949-9090 for information, prices and reservations for any of these programs. Also, for a weekly recorded update on family programs, call our Family Activities Hotline at (303) 479-2048.

Children's Ski School

Vail has two Children's Skiing centers at Lionshead and Golden Peak. The Small World Play School Nursery is located at Golden Peak. The Children's Skiing Center opens at 8 AM seven days a week.

Small World (Non-ski)

8 AM–4:30 PM

Toddlers and Preschoolers have snow play

- 2–18 months infant care — $55
- Toddlers, 18–30 months, infant care — 55
- Preschoolers 2 1/2–6 years, includes lunch — 55

Reservations required: Golden Peak 479-5044

Children's Skiing Center

3–6 Year Olds

10 AM–3 PM (register by 9:45 AM)

- Mini Mice, willing, potty-trained 3-year olds (nap available) Lesson/Lunch — $70
- Mogul Mice (can't stop on their own) ages 4–6, Lesson/Lunch/Lift — 70

- Super Stars (mountain skier) All-Day Lesson/Lunch/Lift — $70

6–12 Year Olds

9:30 AM–3:45 PM (register by 9:15 AM)

Class Lesson, All Levels

Lesson/Lift — $70

Specific program descriptions may be found in the Vail and Beaver Creek Ski School brochure. Children's trail maps are available at all children's ski school locations. All children's ski school programs include a lift ticket. For more information, call 479-4450 or 479-4440.

Adult Ski School

The Vail/Beaver Creek Ski School has three base locations in Vail–Golden Peak, Vail Village and Lionshead– and three on-mountain locations–Two Elk, Mid–Vail and Eagle's Nest. Programs available at each location vary; for specifics, please stop by any location or call (303) 476-3239. Ski School is definitely a fun way to enhance your vacation!

All Day Programs (including a lunch break with your instructor)

One Day

- "Discover Skiing" (level 1 & 2) — Lesson/Lift — $ 75
- Advanced Beginner (levels 3 & 4) — Lesson/Lift — 100
- Intermediate/Advanced (level 5-9) — Lesson/Lift — 100
- All levels (1-9) — Lesson only — 55

Three Day

- "Discover Skiing" (level 1 & 2), — Lesson/Lift/Rental — $210
- Advanced Beginner-Advanced (levels 3-9)

  Lesson/Lift/Rental — $285
- "Breakthrough" (levels 5-8) Mon.-Wed.,

  Lesson/Lift — $300

  Lesson only — 200

Half-Day Afternoon Programs

- "Discover Skiing" (level 1 & 2) — Lesson/Lift — $ 60
- Advanced Beginner (levels 3 & 4) — Lesson/Lift — 60
- Intermediate/Advanced (levels 5-9) — Lesson only — 48
- All levels (1-9) — Lesson only — 48

E X H I B I T   1 | **Vail Mountain Fact Sheet, Winter 1993–94   (Continued)**

Snowboard Programs (ages 8 and above)

All Day Programs (including a lunch break with your instructor)

One-Day

- "Discover Boarding" (level 1 & 2)   Lesson/Lift $ 75
- Advanced Beginner (levels 3 & 4)   Lesson/Lift   100
- Intermediate-Advanced (levels 5-9)   Lesson/Lift   100
- All levels (1-9)   Lesson only   55

Half-Day Afternoon Programs

- "Discover Boarding" (levels 1 & 2)   Lesson/Lift $ 60
- Advanced Beginner (levels 3 & 4)   Lesson/Lift   60

Cross-Country Programs

In Vail, there are two Cross-Country locations: Golden Peak and Vail Golf Course. Availablity of programs varies. Please call (303) 845-5313 or stop by any ski school location.

All-Day

- Lesson and Tour $51
- Tour   51
- Gourmet Lunch Tour 65
- Telemark Festival
  (with lift ticket)   55
  (no lift ticket)   35

Half-Day

- Lesson or Tour $34
- Two half days   60
- Snowshoe tour   34

Three Day

- Lessons and/or
  Tour $135

Rentals available at both locations. One day of your multiday lift ticket may be exchanged for a half day cross-country lesson with rental equipment.

Private Instruction

Is available for all ages, interests and abilities. Reservations are recommended (303) 476-3239

All Day (1-5 persons) $370   Two Hour (1-5 persons) $180

Half Day Morning or Afternoon (1-5 persons)   255   One hour (1-5 persons) upon availability   90

Value Packages

Are available in three- or five-day package formats and include lift, lesson, and rental. For specifics, stop by any ski school location or Vail Assiciates' rental outlet, or call (303) 476-3239.

Accommodations

Vail has a bed base of 32,100 ranging from hotels and ski lodges to bed and breakfasts and condominiums. Most lodges are located on the free shuttle bus route or have private shuttle services. For reservations and information, contact:

Vail/Beaver Creek Reservations, P.O. Box 7, Vail, Colorado 81658   (303) 949-5750

Nationwide: 1-800-525-2257   **Travel Agent Hotline:** 1-800-237-0643   **FAX:** (303) 845-5729

Transportation

Air: New this year, **Northwest Airlines** will be offering daily nonstop 757 jet service from Minneapolis/St. Paul to Vail/Eagle County Airport beginning December 17, 1993.

Airport: Vail's Eagle County Airport is 35 miles west of Vail.

Airlines: **All airlines serve Vail/Eagle County Airport.**
American Airlines: nonstop 757 service from Chicago, Dallas, New York and Miami with connections from more than 130 cities worldwide.
Delta Air Lines: convenient connecting service via Salt Lake City from Los Angeles, Phoenix, San Diego, San Francisco, Seattle and more than 40 cities throughout the West.
Northwest Airlines: daily nonstop 757 jet service from Minneapolis/St. Paul.
United Airlines: daily service from Denver.

Reservations: For flight reservation information, lodging packages including lift tickets and ground transfers, call Vail/Beaver Creek Reservations at 1-800-525-2257.

Shuttle services: Scheduled nonstop door-to-door service between Denver and the Vail Valley.

Vans to Vail	(303) 476-4467	Colorado Mountain Express	(303) 949-4227
Vail Valley Taxi	(303) 476-TAXI	Airport Transportation Service	(303) 476-7576

Rental Cars: Rental cars are available at Denver Stapleton Airport, Vail and Beaver Creek Resort, and Eagle County Airport.

Budget	800-527-0700–*(303) 949-6012	Thrifty	1-800-367-2277–*(303) 949-7787
Hertz**	800-654-3131–*(303) 524-7177	National	1-800-328-4567–*(303) 476-6634

*Rental car agency phone numbers in the Vail Valley Dollar Rent A Car**1-800-421-6868
**Hertz and Dollar Rent A Car have car rentals available on site at Eagle County Airport.

EXHIBIT 1 | **Vail Mountain Fact Sheet, Winter 1993–94 (Concluded)**

Winter Activities

The Activities Desk of Vail can help arrange nonskiing activities and may be reached at (303) 476-9090. Winter activities available in the Vail Valley include:

Art Galleries	Cross-Country Ski Tours	Ice Skating–indoor/outdoor	Snowmobiling
Athletic Clubs and Spas	Dogsledding	Movie Theaters	Snowcat Tours and Skiing
Bobsledding	Fine Dining	Parasailing	Snowshoeing
Colorado Heritage Center	Hot-Air Balloon Rides	Shopping	
Cross-Country Hut System	Ice Hockey	Sleighrides	

Vail Bobsled: Skiers enjoy the 2,900-foot-long course, with speeds sometimes reaching 50 mph. It is located just below Mid-Vail near Short Cut run. The ride lasts approximately one minute and costs $12 per ride per person.

Snowmobile Tours: Situated at 9,500 feet, Piney River Ranch offers three snowmobile tours daily—lunch, afternoon, and dinner. Call (303) 476-3941 for reservations and information.

Resort Information

Vail Associates, Inc., P. O. Box 7, Vail, Colorado 81658
Corporate Offices—(303) 476-5601   Snow Reports—(303) 476-4888 or 476-4889

CONTACTS:

Public Relations:	Ross Palmer, Director of Public Relations	(303) 845-5721
	Paul Witt, Media Relations Manager	(303) 845-5720
Sales:	Steve Shanley, Director of Sales and Advertising	(303) 845-5709
	Spencer Butts, Director Vail/Beaver Creek Reservations	(303) 845-5736
Marketing:	Bob Kunkel, Vice President	(303) 845-5884
	Mia Vlaar, International Marketing Manager	(303) 845-5712
Advertising:	Chris Jarnot, Advertising Manager	(303) 845-5718
Photography:	Jack Affleck, Photographer	(303) 845-5749
Conference Facilities:	Leslie Southworth, Group Sales Manager	(303) 845-5702
Conventions:	Stacey Swank, Convention Sales Manager	(303) 845-5751

Source: Vail Associates.

Vail and Beaver Creek were located in Eagle County, Colorado, about 100 miles west of Denver on Interstate 70. Air transportation was available through Denver Stapleton International Airport and the Eagle County Jetport (winter only). Ground transportation was provided by car rental agencies, Greyhound Bus, and several van operators. The ride up from Denver was two hours; the ride from the Eagle Jetport was about 45 minutes.

Vail was the largest single-mountain ski area in North America with 12,500 acres under U.S. Forest Service permit. Skiing was provided on both sides of a seven-mile ridge paralleling the interstate. Within its boundaries, it sported 120 trails, 20 lifts efficiently laid out, and uphill capacity for 35,820 skiers per hour. Vertical rise was 3,250 feet and the longest run was four and a half miles. Snow was reliable and averaged 334.5 inches annually. Its vast size and variable terrain offered the most variety of any resort in North America. In a week's stay, few visitors were able to explore all its opportunities.

Located behind a tiny valley 10 miles west of Vail, the mountain at Beaver Creek, which opened in 1980, was smaller and the facilities were more exclusive. Within its 5,600 acre ski area, Beaver Creek had 59 trails, 11 lifts, and uphill capacity of 19,075 skiers per hour. Vertical rise was 3,340 feet and the longest run was 2.75 miles. Like Vail, it was known for its family skiing, but until its Grouse Mountain area opened in 1991, it was not known for a broad selection of advanced runs. Besides downhill, it was the location of VA's principal cross-country facility.

EXHIBIT 2 | Beaver Creek® Mountain Fact Sheet, Winter 1993–94

Location

110 miles/176 km west of Denver on Interstate 70—130 miles/208 km east of Grand Junction on Interstate 70—25 miles/40 km east of Eagle County Airport. Surrounded by 1.2 million acres of the White River National Forest—Eagle County, Colorado.

The Resort

Beaver Creek Resort is America's most elegant ski destination and winner of Snow County's overall resort design and slopes and trails awards. Emphasis at the resort is on superior service and first-class accommodations, and dining facilities and family programs.

Permanent Population: 150	Bed Base: 4,700 (Beaver Creek Resort)
Bars and Restaurants: 22	4,000 (Avon)
	41,305 (Valley Wide: East Vail to Edwards)

Mountain Information

Ski season:	November 20, 1993, to April 17, 1994
Hours of Operation:	8:30 AM to 3:30 PM daily, MST.

Mountain Statistics

Base elevation:	8,100 feet	2,469 meters	Longest run: (Centennial Run)	2.75 miles 4.4 km
Spruce Saddle elevation:	10,200 feet	3,110 meters	Trail Classification:	18% Beginner
Summit elevation:	11,440 feet	3,488 meters		39% Intermediate
Vertical rise:	3,340 feet	1,018 meters		43% Advanced
Snowmaking:	361 acres	146 hectares	Total number of lifts:	10
Average snowfall:	330 inches	8.38 meters	Lifts include:	2 high-speed detachable quad chairlifts
Total developed trails:	1,125 acres	455 hectares		4 triple chairlifts
Total named trails:	61 trails			4 double chairlifts (15 planned for buildout)
Total permit area:	5,600 acres	2,266 hectares	Total uphill capacity:	17,228 skiers per hour

McCoy Park Cross-Country Track System

The Beaver Creek Cross-Country Ski Center is located in Strawberry Park at the base of chair 12 and offers lessons and equipment rentals. The track system includes 32 km of groomed double-set track with a skating lane, 19 scenic trails at the top of the mountain and 5 km of snowshoe trails. A recreational biathlon course is open two days a week.

Lift Ticket Prices

Adults		**Children**	
Adult Full-Day	$45	Child Full-Day	$32
Adult Half-Day	$39	Child Half-Day	$26
Adult 2-Day	$90	Child 2-Day	$64
Adult 3-Day	$135	Child 3-Day	$96
Adult 4-Day	$168	Child 4-Day	$128
Adult 5-Day	$210	Child 5-Day	$160
Adult 6-Day	$240	Child 6-Day	$192
Adult 7-Day	$280	Child 7-Day	$224
Senior Citizens		**Foot Passenger**	
65–69 years of age	$36	Adult	$15
70 years or older	Free	Children	$10

Premier Passport, the joint Aspen and Vail lift ticket designed for international guests offers a minimum 10 out of 12 day lift ticker and a maximum 18 out of 21 day lift ticket, at a rate of $38 per day, including a one-way ground transfer between the two resorts.

®Registered trademarks of Vail Associates, Inc.

EXHIBIT 2 | **Beaver Creek® Mountain Fact Sheet, Winter 1993–94 (Continued)**

Skier Service Information

Snow watch: For a daily update on Vail and Beaver Creek Resort snow conditions call: (303) 476-4888. In Denver: (303) 296-3155.

TV8 updates skiers on weather conditions, recently opened trails, and upcoming events. The station features The Beaver Creek Resort Report with ski tips and helpful hints. It is available on channel 8 in most lodge rooms throughout the valley.

Complimentary *Meet the Mountain* tours are offered at 1 PM on Mondays and Wednesdays. Tours begin at Spruce Saddle.

Grooming information is posted at the Centennial Express Lift as well as most lift boards. Beaver Creek Mountain currently has 10 grooming snowcats.

Ski Corral offers overnight ski storage at the base of the Centennial Express lift. Complimentary ski storage is offered to guests using rental equipment.

Lost and found is located at the Ski Corral at the base of the Centennial Express Lift. Hours are from 8 AM–5 PM daily.

Sunday religious services are offered at 12:30 PM each Sunday at Spruce Saddle (non-denominational).

Skier service personnel, wearing red and purple uniforms, answer questions and assist skiers on the mountain.

Dining on the Mountain

In addition to a variety of cafes and restaurants in Beaver Creek Village, there are five on-mountain restaurants and cafeterias.

Beano's Cabin: This elegant log cabin is set in Larkspur Bowl in the midst of the White River National Forest. It is open only to Beaver Creek Club members during lunch. In the evening, Beano's offers the public a sleigh ride and gourmet dinner. Dinner selections vary. Nine sleigh departures to Beano's Cabin leave nightly from Rendezvous Cabin starting at 4:45 and ending at 9:00 PM. The Beano's sleigh-ride dinner is a must during a vacation at Vail and Beaver Creek Resort. Reservations are required and may be made by calling (303) 949-9090. Prices are $69 per person, $46 for children under 12 and include transportation, six-course gourmet meal, and tax. Alcohol and gratuity not included.

McCoy's Bar and Restaurant: Managed by the Hyatt Regency Beaver Creek. Cafeteria-style breakfasts and lunch, après-ski cocktails, hors d'oeurves, and entertainment are available daily.

Rafter's: Located at Spruce Saddle, this table-service restaurant provides leisurely lunches with spectacular views of the Gore Range and the Eagle Valley. Pasta, soups, sandwiches and pizza are some of the items offered. Reservations are recommended and may be made by calling (303) 949-6050.

Red Tail Camp: Located at the base of chairs 9 and 11, this small warming hut offers fast food. There is an outdoor barbecue during springtime and restrooms are available.

Spruce Saddle Restaurant: Located mid-mountain, Spruce Saddle Restaurant had been completely renovated for the 1993–'94 season. The restaurant now seats 800 people and has an enlarged outdoor deck, as well as a special 120-seat lunch room for the Beaver Creek Ski School children's programs. Spruce Saddle offers cafeteria-style dining, storage lockers and convenience facilities.

Ski Equipment Rentals

Beaver Creek Sports in two locations in the Village Hall building offers complete rental and retail services for adults and children. A standard package of Rossignol, K2 skis, Salomon boots, and Scott poles is $14 per day. High-performance equipment and snowboards are also available. Reservations are suggested and may be made by calling (303) 949-2310. Both shops offer free slopeside ski storage with their rentals.

Recreational Ski Racing

Beaver Creek Mountain offers recreational racers both NASTAR and pay-to-race programs. Skiers of all ability levels compete in NASTAR competition against a pacesetter time set by the U.S. Ski Team's fastest skier. Individuals with top-placing times earn one of several medals awarded daily. Race fees are $5 for the first run and $1 for each additional run. NASTAR is held on Bear Trap, Wednesday through Sunday, from 11 AM–2 PM Group NASTAR races may be arranged by calling (303) 479-4050.

Pay-to-race is a self-timing course open daily on Bear Trap and is $1.00 per run. The course is open from 10 AM–3 PM.

Season passes are available for $25. For information on racing clinics offered by the Vail and Beaver Creek Ski School, call (303) 476-3239.

Children's Programs

Sport Goofy, Disney's ambassador of fun, fitness, health and skiing loves to visit Beaver Creek Resort, joining families at weekly aprés ski hot chocolate parties. Call (303) 479-2040 for Sport Goofy's schedule.

The popular *Family Night Out* is a dinner theater show and offers the perfect photo opportunity with Disney's Sport Goofy. It takes place on selected Wednesday nights starting in December.

The Western characters Sourdough Pete, Jackrabbit Joe, Buckaroo Bob and Mirabelle can be seen skiing around Tombstone Territory or telling stories at the Sheriff's office. They are joined by their other Western friends for the *Kid's Night Out Goes Western* dinner theater show on selected Tuesday nights beginning in December. This is a fun, western evening for kids in kindergarten through sixth grade.

During Christmas and Spring vacation weeks, Beaver Creek Resort hosts a Friday night *Kid's Night Out Goes Hollywood.* This is a pizza and make your own video evening for kids 10 through 14. Teens will also have their own evenings for broomball and snowshoeing.

E X H I B I T 2 | **Beaver Creek® Mountain Fact Sheet, Winter 1993–94 (Continued)**

Children's Programs (Continued)

On Thursday nights, the whole family is invited to the free Thursday Night Lights ski down on Haymeadow, and intermediate and above skiers are welcome to take part.

Call the Activities Desk™ at (303) 949-9090 for information, prices and reservations for any of these programs. Also, for a weekly recorded update on family programs, call our Family Activities Hotline at (303) 479-2048.

Children's Ski School

Beaver Creek Resort has a Children's Adventure Center™ in Village Hall which includes tickets sales, program areas, a full service rental shop, boot fitting rooms and a lunch area. The Children's Skiing Center opens at 8:00 AM seven days a week. The Small World Play School™ Nursery is located creekside below the Activites Desk.

Small World (Non-ski):

8 AM–4:30 PM

Toddlers and preschoolers have snow play

- 2–18 months infant care — $55
- Toddlers, 18–30 months, infant care — 55
- Preschoolers 2 1/2–6 years, includes lunch — 55

Reservations required: Small World Play School 845-5325

Specific program descriptions may be found in the Vail and Beaver Creek Ski School brochure. Children's adventure mountain maps are available at all children's ski school locations.

All children's ski school programs include a lift ticket. Ski Week and Family Value Packages available. For more information call (303) 845-5464.

3–6 Year Olds

10:15 AM–3 PM (register by 9:45 AM)

- Mini Mice, willing, potty-trained 3-year olds
  (nap available) Lesson/Lunch/Lift — $70
- Mogul Mice (can't stop on their own)
  ages 4–6, Lesson/Lunch/Lift — 70
- Super Stars (mountain skier)
  All-Day Lesson/Lunch/Lift — 70

6–12 Year Olds

9:30 AM–3:45 PM (register by 9:00 AM)

  Specially Grouped, All Levels Lesson — $70

Adult Ski School

At Beaver Creek Resort, the Vail/Beaver Creek Ski School has its base location in Village Hall and on-mountain location inside Spruce Saddle. For program specifics, please stop by any ski school location or call (303) 476-3239. Ski School is definitely a fun way to enhance your vacation!

All-Day Programs (including a lunch break with your instructor)

One Day

- "Discover Skiing" (levels 1 & 2) — Lesson/Lift — $ 75
- Advanced Beginner (levels 3 & 4) — Lesson/Lift — 100
- Intermediate–Advanced (levels 5–9) — Lesson/Lift — 100
- All levels (1–9) — Lesson only — 55

Three Day

- "Discover Skiing" (levels 1 & 2), — Lesson/Lift/Rental — $ 210
- Advanced Beginner–Advanced (levels 3–9)
  — Lesson/Lift/Rental — 285
- "Breakthrough" (levels 5–8) Mon.-Wed.,
  — Lesson/Lift — 300
  — Lesson only — 200

Half-Day Afternoon Programs

- "Discover Skiing" (levels 1 & 2) — Lesson/Lift — $60
- Advanced Beginner (levels 3 & 4) — Lesson/Lift — 60
- Intermediate/Advanced (levels 5–9) — Lesson only — 48
- All levels (1–9) — Lesson only — 48
- Semi-Private (levels 1–9) — Lesson only — 75

Snowboard Programs (ages 8 and above)

All Day Programs (including lunch break with instructor)

One Day

- "Discover Boarding" (levels 1 & 2) — Lesson/Lift — $ 75
- Advanced Beginner (levels 3 & 4) — Lesson/Lift — 100
- Intermediate–Advanced (levels 5–9) — Lesson/Lift — 100
- All levels (1–9) — Lesson only — 55

Half-Day Afternoon Programs

- "Discover Boarding" (levels 1 & 2) — Lesson/Lift — $60
- Advanced Beginner (levels 3 & 4) — Lesson/Lift — 60

EXHIBIT 2 | **Beaver Creek® Mountain Fact Sheet, Winter 1993–94 (Continued)**

Cross-Country Programs

At Beaver Creek Resort, the Cross-Country Center is located in Strawberry Park, adjacent to the Strawberry Park chairlift (#12). A wide range of programs are available, and unique to Beaver Creek Resort is the 32K set track at the top of the mountain. For program specifics, stop by any ski school location or please call (303) 845-5313.

All Day
- Lesson and Tour $51
- Tour 51
- Telemark Festival
  (with lift ticket) 55
  (no lift ticket) 35

Half Day
- Lesson or Tour $34
- Two half days 60
- Snowshoe Tour 34

Rentals available at both locations. One day of your multi-day lift ticket may be exchanged for a half-day cross-country lesson with rental equipment.

McCoy Park Track Access
- Adult All-Day $15
- Child All-Day 7
- Adult Afternoon Half Day 12
- Child Afternoon Half Day 5
- Track Multi-Day (per day) 13

Three Day
- Lessons and/or Tour $135

Private Instruction is available for all ages, interests and abilities. Reservations are recommended (303) 476-3239

All Day (1–5 persons)	$370	Two Hour (1–5 persons)	$180
Half Day Morning or Afternoon (1–5 persons)	255	One Hour (1–5 persons) upon availability	90

Value Packages are available in three- or five-day formats and include lift, lesson and rental. For specifics, stop by any ski school location or Vail Associates' rental outlet, or call (303) 476-3239.

Accommodations

Beaver Creek Resort has a bed base of 4,700 ranging from elegant lodges to deluxe condominiums. A free Dial-A-Ride shuttle service is extended to all resort guests and may be reached by calling (303) 949-1938. Trapper's Cabin, a four-diamond mountaintop retreat, offers guests personalized service in a relaxing atmosphere. For reservations and lodging information contact:
Vail/Beaver Creek Reservations, P. O. Box 7, Vail, Colorado 81658   (303) 949-5750
Nationwide: 1-800-622-3131   **Travel Agent Hotline:** 1-800-237-0643   FAX: (303) 845-5729

Transportation

Air: New this year, **Northwest Airlines** will be offering daily nonstop 757 jet service from Minneapolis/St. Paul to Vail/Eagle County Airport beginning December 17, 1993.

Airport: Vail's Eagle County Airport is 25 miles west of Beaver Creek Resort.

Airlines: All airlines serve Vail/Eagle County Airport.

American Airlines: nonstop 757 service from Chicago, Dallas, New York and Miami with connections from more than 130 cities worldwide.

Delta Air Lines: convienient connecting service via Salt Lake City from Los Angeles, Pheonix, San Diego, San Francisco, Seattle and more than 40 cities throughout the West.

Northwest Airlines: daily nonstop 757 jet service from Minneapolis/St. Paul.

United Airlines: daily service from Denver.

Reservations: For flight reservation information, lodging packages including lift tickets and ground transfers, call Vail/Beaver Creek Reservations at 1-800-622-3131.

Shuttle services: Scheduled nonstop door-to-door service between Denver and the Vail Valley.

Vans to Vail	(303) 476-4467	Colorado Mountain Express	(303) 949-4227
Vail Valley Taxi	(303) 476-TAXI	Airport Transportation Service	(303) 476-7576

Rental Cars: Rental cars are available at Denver Stapleton Airport, Vail and Beaver Creek Resort, and Eagle County Airport.

Budget	800-527-0700–*(303) 949-6012	Thrifty	1-800-367-2277–*(303) 949-7787
Hertz**	800-654-3131–*(303) 524-7177	National	1-800-328-4567–*(303) 476-6634

*Rental car agency phone numbers in the Vail Valley Dollar Rent A Car**   1-800-421-6868
**Hertz and Dollar Rent A Car have car rentals available on site at Eagle County Airport.

EXHIBIT 2 | Beaver Creek® Mountain Fact Sheet, Winter 1993–94 (Concluded)

Winter Activities

The Activities Desk at Beaver Creek can help arrange nonskiing activities and may be reached at (303) 949-9090. Winter activities available in the Vail Valley include:

Art Galleries	Cross-Country Ski Tours	Ice Hockey	Sleighrides
Athletic Clubs and Spas	Dogsledding	Ice Skating–indoor/outdoor	Snowmobiling
Bobsledding	Fine Dining	Movie Theaters	Snowcat Tours and Skiing
Colorado Heritge Center	Hot-Air Balloon Rides	Shopping	Snowshoeing
Cross-Country Hut System			

Resort Information

Vail Associates, Inc., P. O. Box 7, Vail, Colorado 81658

Corporate Offices—(303)476-5601   Snow Reports—(303)476-4888

CONTACTS:

Public Relations:	Ross Palmer, Director of Public Relations	(303)845-5721
	Paul Witt, Media Relations Manager	(303)845-5720
Sales:	Steve Shanley, Director of Sales and Advertising	(303)845-5709
	Spencer Butts, Director of Sales for Vail/Beaver Creek Reservations	(303)845-5736
Marketing:	Bob Kunkel, Vice President Marketing	(303)845-5884
	Mai Vlaar, International Marketing Manager	(303)845-5712
Advertising:	Chris Jarnot, Advertising Manager	(303)845-5718
Photography:	Jack Affleck, Photographer	(303)845-5749
Conference Facilities:	Lesile Southworth, Group Sales Manager	(303)845-5702
Conventions:	Stacey Swank, Convention Sales Manager	(303)845-5751

Source: Vail Associates.

Adjacent to these ski areas were the villages of Vail and Beaver Creek. Vail was an elongated eight-mile town nestled between the interstate and the mountain. It had two pedestrian-only village centers, which were connected to each other and the town's outlying areas by a complimentary bus system. Built like a quaint European resort, Vail had 115 restaurants and bars, 120 shops, and accommodations for 32,000 people. It was the full- and part-time residence of numerous celebrities, including Ross Perot and Thomas Watson, and was the Western White House during the Ford Administration.

Beaver Creek was an Alpine-style village built in a tiny valley three miles uphill from Avon, a town along the interstate which housed many of the employees for the two resorts. As Colorado's bid for the 1976 winter Olympics, Beaver Creek was planned and designed by a state-of-the-art CAD computer system. Emphasizing elegance, exclusivity, and first-class accommodations, it had 22 restaurants, 20 shops, and overnight capacity for 4,700 people. It was connected to Avon and Vail by a scheduled shuttle. Gerald Ford, Jack Nicklaus, and several other well-known personalities had vacation homes in Beaver Creek.

During the 1980s, Vail Associates enlarged its strategy by implementing an all-seasons resort plan. Vail and Beaver Creek were surrounded by 1.2 million acres of the White River National Forest, which provided numerous opportunities for summer recreation including boating, white-water rafting, backpacking, horseback riding, fishing, and hunting. Within the two resorts, summer facilities included mountain biking on the ski slopes, horse stables, and an 18-hole golf course at Beaver Creek. At its newly acquired Piney River Ranch (located 12 miles from Vail), VA had a

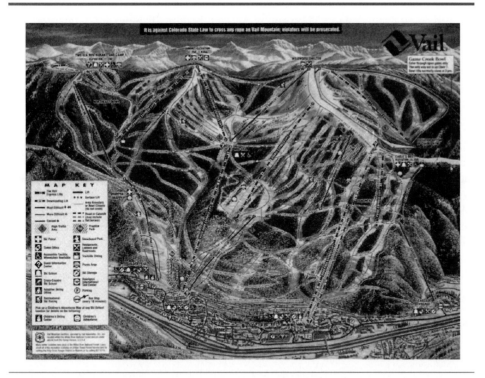

superb day lodge, stables, a shop and restaurant, boating, fishing, and wilderness hiking. The towns of Vail and Avon sponsored a variety of arts and a concert series; golf and tennis facilities were available throughout the area. See Exhibit 5 for a description of summer recreation opportunities in the area.

THE RESORT/RECREATION INDUSTRY

The outdoor resort industry had no exact boundaries. It overlapped the vacation resort industry and the amusement/recreation industry. The preferences, expectations, and pocketbooks of vacationers and outdoor recreation enthusiasts varied enormously, creating a fragmented and highly diverse range of business opportunities. Within this vast and evolving industry, Vail competed with both day-use ski slopes having few accommodations on-site and "destination" resorts, like itself, providing a full complement of winter and summer activities and accommodations. With destination resorts having the most market reach, Colorado claimed a number of the best known because of its location in the rugged Rockies centered between the east and west coasts. In the state, Vail competed with Summit County resorts (Breckenridge, Keystone, Arapahoe Basin, and Copper), the Aspen/Snowmass area, Steamboat Springs, Winter Park, and Telluride.

EXHIBIT 5 | **Promotional Description of Summer Activities in the Vail–Beaver Creek Area, 1992**

Dry mild days, cool nights, and an unsurpassed natural setting have helped make the Vail Valley the perfect summer resort community. The quality of amenities, activities, and services is surpassed only by the quantity.

Golfers are challenged by five championship courses within a 15-mile stretch. Tennis buffs have over 40 courts from which to choose. And in the rarefied air at 8,200 feet, golf and tennis balls fly 10 to 20 percent farther than back home.

But there is more. The White River National Forest, in which Vail is located, offers hikers, campers, mountain bikers, horseback riders, climbers, and other adventurous souls the experience of a lifetime.

You don't have to stay on the ground, either. A morning balloon ride high above the Rockies may be the ultimate way to begin a day.

Many rivers, including the mighty Colorado, challenge expert and novice white-water enthusiasts. Sailboarding and boating are popular sports, and fishermen find solace along the bountiful streams, rivers, lakes, and ponds of the region.

Of course, you don't have to head for the hills for a moment of serenity. Sunbathing by a pool, picnicking along a nearby creek, or taking a quiet gondola ride to a mountaintop barbecue offer the relaxation so important to a complete vacation.

In mid-summer, the Jerry Ford Invitational Golf Tournament brings out the stars and the pros. Bob Hope, Clint Eastwood, Dinah Shore, Tip O'Neill, and Jack Nicklaus are a few who regularly compete—and perform—in this pro-am charity benefit.

In September, Vailfest shines as brightly as the golden aspen leaves. This local version of Munich's Oktoberfest has the same vitality as the original, and its own beer gardens.

The arts are alive and well in Vail, too. Bravo! Colorado presents concerts, recitals, and dance programs at the Gerald R. Ford Amphitheater and other venues. During the year, a community theater group entertains with a variety of musicals, comedies, and dramas. The Eagle Valley Arts Council sponsors a series of art shows in Vail and Beaver Creek; and the World Forum, hosted by President Ford, and the Vail Symposium feature distinguished guests.

In addition, there remain the numerous amenities that can be enjoyed year-round. Fine restaurants, exciting nightlife, superb accommodations, and fabulous shopping do not change with the weather.

Source: Vail Associates' promotional materials.

Beyond Colorado, VA competed with Utah resorts (notably Park City and Deer Valley), California resorts (Mammoth and Heavenly Valley), and Canadian resorts (Whistler/Blackcomb and Banff). Exhibit 6 provides a summary comparison of facilities provided by Vail and its principal competitors.

From a consumer standpoint, Vail was often the top-rated ski resort in ski magazine surveys, and had held the leading single-mountain market share for several years running. A comparison of the volume of skiers for Vail/Beaver Creek and other competitors is shown for the 1991 season in Exhibit 7. Much of Vail's success was attributable to the fact that Vail Associates was the only firm in the industry able to exert functional control over all aspects of the destination environment (mountain activities and accommodations).

The ski industry, however, had not been healthy since the late 1980s. An aging population had shrunk consumer demand, especially in the category of young singles and childless married couples. Many former skiers and some who would otherwise have been inclined to ski had shifted to other segments of the vacation industry. As shown in Exhibit 8, a *Better Homes & Gardens* survey found ski vacations ranked 8th out of a field of 10 and accounted for only 12 percent of vacation intentions in 1992.

VAIL ASSOCIATES: ORGANIZATION AND ADMINISTRATION

Vail Associates was a medium-sized business enterprise. As shown in Exhibit 9, the firm had assets of $311.8 million, of which about $185 million was in property and plant and equipment. These included lift structures, mountain lodges, grooming and snowmaking equipment, vehicles, some employee housing, administrative and commercial buildings, an 18-hole golf course and clubhouse at Beaver Creek, Piney River Ranch, and development properties. VA did not own the mountains, but leased the land from the U.S. Forest Service. The Vail mountain lease expires in 2030 and the lease on Beaver Creek expires in 2010.

EXHIBIT 6 | **Comparative Statistics for Destination Ski Resort Facilities, 1992**

Resort Name	Location	Lift Ticket Price	Skiable Acreage	Vertical Rise (ft.)	Number of Lifts	Number of Trails	Lift Capacity (skiers/hr.)
Ski the Summit (Breckenridge, Keystone, Copper)	Colorado	$37	4,874	3,750	60	358	90,000
Vail/Beaver Creek	Colorado	40	18,100	3,340	33	179	54,895
Aspen/Snowmass	Colorado	40	3,125	4,028	24	147	31,310
Steamboat Springs	Colorado	39	2,500	3,600	20	106	30,000
Winter Park	Colorado	36	1,301	3,060	20	112	30,600
Telluride	Colorado	39	1,050	3,522	10	62	10,836
Taos	New Mexico	35	1,092	2,612	11	72	13,500
Park City	Utah	40	2,200	3,100	13	83	19,700
Deer Valley	Utah	43	1,000	2,200	11	58	13,500
Mammoth/June	California	37	4,000	3,100	38	185	43,000
Whistler/Blackcomb	British Columbia	43	6,998	5,280	28	200	26,350

EXHIBIT 7 | **Millions of Skier Days at Selected Destination Ski Resorts, 1991**

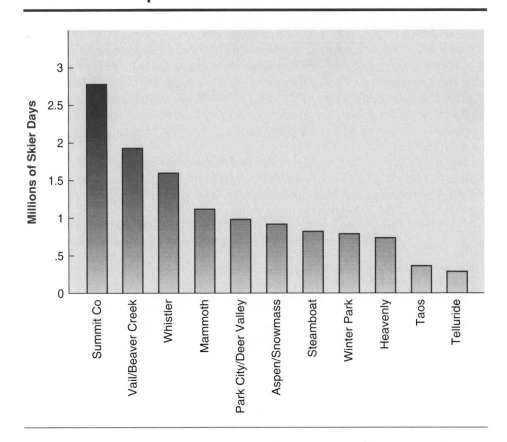

With these facilities, Vail Associates generated annual revenues of about $100 million (see Exhibit 10). Revenues were highly seasonal, mostly coming during the four months December through March. With 1.5 million annual skier days, about $60 million was generated from lift ticket sales. The rest came from food services, commercial leases, central reservation services, summer activities, real estate development and sales, and hospitality management contracts with local hotels and condominium complexes.

The organization had about 800 permanent employees, mostly in mountain operations (supervision staff, maintenance, and construction) and general administration (finance, human resources, information systems, etc.). Of these, about 175 held managerial and supervisory positions. During the ski season, employment peaked at 3,600 with the hiring of over 2,700 seasonal employees to run lift, ski school, food service, and retail operations. Because of seasonality, the firm experienced a 40 percent new hire rate each winter. The remaining 60 percent were returning employees that came back for two or more seasons. The employees were split about two-thirds to Vail and one-third to Beaver Creek.

VA managed a wide array of resort activities. To do this, it used a "mixed" organization structure. As shown on Vail's organization chart in Exhibit 11, the corporate-level functions consisted of general administration, finance, business development (managed TV 8 Vail Productions), legal counsel, and marketing. Marketing was a dominant corporate function and contained VA's international multimedia network,

EXHIBIT 8 | **Survey of Intentions of Vacationers, 1991-92**

Why They Go

Travelers whose most recent vacation trip in the past years was with children cited these as very important motivations:

Being together as a family	92%
Getting away from stress of home and work	82%
Finding rest and relaxation	73%
Excitement and new experiences	43%
Visiting friends/relatives	42%
Learning about new places and people	35%
Being physically active	31%
Pampering, indulging in luxury	18%

Where They Go

Family vacationers who intend to travel this year with children are planning these activities:

Ocean/beach vacation	60%
Visit historical sites	51%
Visit theme parks/attractions	49%
Visit a lake	41%
Adventure vacation (camping, hiking, etc.)	40%
City vacation, resort vacation	33%
Overseas vacation, Canadian vacation	13%
Skiing vacation	12%
Cruise vacation	11%
Mexican vacation	10%
Other	7%

Source: Survey by the U.S. Travel Data Center for *Better Homes and Gardens,* January 1992

EXHIBIT 9 | **Statement of Assets, September 1992 (*in $millions*)**

Current assets:	
Cash	$ 5.7
Accounts receivable	1.8
Short-term securities	2.5
Long-term assets:	
Plant and equipment	168.3
Real estate property	16.5
Other (mostly intangibles, including goodwill)	117.0
Total assets	$311.8

EXHIBIT 10 | **Operating Income Summary, Fiscal Year Ending September 30, 1989-92 (*in $millions*)**

	1992	1991	1990	1989
Net revenues	$113.6	$104.6	$110.6	$91.1
Operating costs	78.7	77.5	86.4	73.0
Income from operations	$ 34.9	$ 27.1	$ 24.2	$18.1
Gross operating margin	30.7%	25.9%	21.8%	19.9%

EXHIBIT 11 | Vail Associates' Organization Chart, 1991

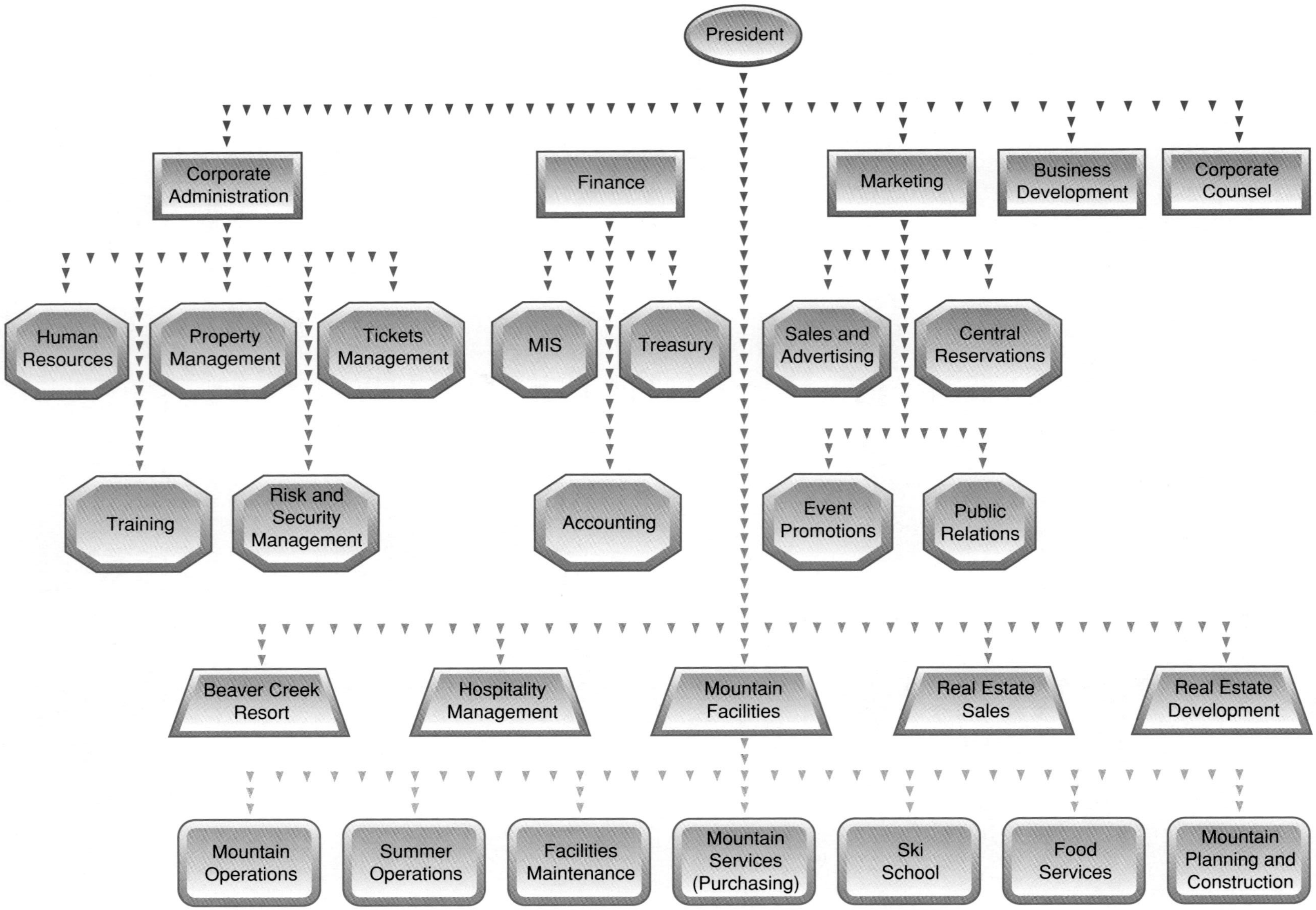

which had achieved major successes in New York, Boston, and Chicago markets as well as in Britain, Germany, Australia, and Mexico. In addition to its corporate functions, marketing operated the firm's central reservation and travel agency services. Although some competition existed, VA handled the vast majority of individual and travel agent bookings for the Vail Valley.

At the operating level Vail Associates was organized around five product-line divisions. The largest division was mountain facilities, which handled most of the resort activities, including ski operations (lifts, ski patrol, trail grooming, and snowmaking), summer operations, facilities maintenance, mountain services (mainly purchasing), ski school, food services, and mountain planning and construction. Most of the division's employees were seasonal.

The second largest product division was Beaver Creek, which operated as a miniature of the overall organization and had its own corporate functions and product units. Its various components were responsible not only to the head of the Beaver Creek division but also to their respective functions in the larger VA organization.

VA's smallest divisions included its two realty activities. The resorts contained a variety of properties not owned by VA including hotels, condominiums, retail and commercial buildings, and restaurants. Through these divisions, VA was the principal real estate agent in Vail Valley for these properties. A third realty division, hospitality management, contracted to manage a number of the privately owned hotels and condominiums.

Although Vail Valley functioned much like a corporate town, it was not managed by Vail Associates alone. Beaver Creek was a planned unit development operated by a homeowners' association, which VA currently controlled with a majority of the board. The town of Vail was incorporated as a city in 1966 and its public administration operated a variety of community services including police and fire, public transit, streets, sewers and water, and public facilities (skating rink, library, and common grounds). The Town of Avon, at the entrance to Beaver Creek, operated the usual array of municipal services but did not provide services to Beaver Creek except emergency services and transit. Also important were other public agencies including the U.S. Forest Service, various state agencies, a school district, and Eagle County government.

Vail and Beaver Creek had a strong, well-organized business community made up of retailers, hotel people, other developers, and property associations. As an organized group, they managed their respective properties, helped sponsor cultural, humanitarian, and sports events, and participated in developing covenants and restrictions regulating impacts on village character and the valley generally.

Combined, these public agencies and private groups interacted with VA to plan and control the operation of facilities, giving the appearance of a fully integrated delivery system of resort services. Although not free of conflict over VA's sometimes heavy hand, Vail's success was in large part due to the spirit of cooperation and goodwill that prevailed among the Vail Valley's network of public officials, governing groups, businesses, and residents.

Andy Daly's challenge, as president of Vail Associates, was to develop a strategy to ensure that his company and the Vail Valley would continue to attract skiers and vacationers in growing numbers. He wondered what action steps he could take to improve on what had been achieved so far.

THE PHOTOVOLTAICS INDUSTRY IN 1992:
A U.S. PERSPECTIVE
Murray Silverman, San Francisco State University

In 1992, the global photovoltaics industry had the potential to become a $100 billion per year industry within 20 years. When and whether this potential would be realized depended on the extent to which the costs of generating electricity with photovoltaic technology could be reduced and on the rate at which markets could be developed. A number of major corporations and small entrepreneurial firms were betting on the large market potential of PV technology. Companies with photovoltaic subsidiaries included Amoco, Texas Instruments, Mobil, Canon, British Petroleum, and Siemens Industries; other major corporations were sitting on the sidelines prepared to enter the industry. In the shadow of these corporate giants, smaller entrepreneurial firms were jockeying for position and assessing which technological paths and business strategies would ultimately lead to success.

Photovoltaics (PV) is a technology based on the direct conversion of sunlight into electricity using thin semiconductor layers. PV devices produce electricity in proportion to the amount of sunlight reaching them and they do so with no moving parts and no emissions. Photovoltaic panels are different from solar thermal panels that also are mounted on rooftops but contain pipes that circulate water heated by the sun. Solar thermal panels supply hot water while photovoltaic panels supply electricity. In 1992 PV technology was used to generate the electricity for most communication satellites and remote telecommunication repeaters and respondors. PV technology was also used to power handheld calculators, watches, and other electronic devices; in such products it represented a convenient and economically sound option to batteries. In remote geographic areas where residences and vacation cabins did not have access to electric utility suppliers, or in isolated Third-World villages, PV panels were used to power lights, pumps, refrigerators, and other important appliances. PV

The case author acknowledges the assistance and suggestions provided by Ken Zweibel, PhD, at the National Renewable Energy Laboratories in Golden, Colorado, and Robert Johnson at Strategies Unlimited in Mountain View, California, as well as the editorial efforts of Susan Worthman, MBA, San Francisco State University.

companies believed a significant amount of the electricity in homes and businesses could eventually be generated economically with PV technology.

The PV industry was being pioneered by companies in the U.S., Japan, and a few European countries. Rapid advances were being made in the development and manufacturing of PV devices, spawning a fast growing global market. Industry revenues at the manufacturing level were an estimated $350 million in 1992. Industry and governmental experts believed that R&D, improved manufacturing processes, and economies of scale would reduce the cost of PV-generated electricity to make it competitive with conventional electricity costs. However, there was considerable uncertainty regarding the rate at which PV system costs would decline. In the meantime, most PV manufacturers were operating at a loss as they continued to invest in R&D.

U.S. PV firms had been playing a leading role in basic R&D and in developing more efficient manufacturing processes. They maintained a one-third global market share between 1985 and 1991. However, several events raised questions about whether the U.S. would maintain a dominant global role in PV technology. U.S. firms had not been supported by the government to the same extent as firms in other countries. One prominent U.S. PV company, Chronar, filed for Chapter 11 in 1990 due to a shortage of capital and doubts about the long-term viability of its technological approach. ARCO Solar, a subsidiary of Atlantic Richfield and the largest U.S. PV manufacturer, was acquired in 1990 by Siemens, a German firm that was one of the world's largest manufacturers of power generation equipment. General Electric and Westinghouse, the two biggest U.S. manufacturers of electric power generation equipment, were not, as yet, major players in the PV industry.

The principal barrier to widespread utilization of PV in 1992 was that the current cost of PV-generated electricity was two to four times greater than electricity supplied by electric utilities using conventional central station technologies. Despite the high costs, PV technology was a viable electricity source in a number of specialized situations and end-use applications. The primary alternative to PV in remote areas was small diesel generators. These generators required the constant hauling of diesel fuel and access to technical assistance for maintenance and repair. Because PV panels required no fuel and little or no maintenance, they were much more convenient. PV panels were an economic and virtually necessary power source for satellites, unattended communication systems on mountain tops or on buoys at sea, remote residences and vacation homes, and remote lighting applications where conventional electricity sources, batteries, or diesel generators were impractical, unreliable, inconvenient, or too costly. Moreover, the declining cost of PV-generated electricity was slowly and steadily diminishing the economic advantage of diesel generators.

Another advantage of PV technology was its modularity: the ability to add generating capacity in increments matched to equivalent increases in electricity usage. This was a significant comparative benefit in certain instances since central station power plants generally had to be relatively large to be cost effective.

Finally, as a renewable energy technology, PV generation had important environmental benefits. Renewable energy technologies were those that converted the earth's recurring natural resources, such as sunlight, wind, falling water, crops (biomass), tides, and geothermal heat deep beneath the earth's crust into usable energy. Conventional power plants burned nonrenewable fossil fuels: oil, coal, and natural gas. Continued global population growth and industrial development was projected to deplete the world's nonrenewable fossil fuels at an ever faster pace, making the development of renewable energy sources attractive. However, whether and when severe shortages in fossil fuel supplies would become a market reality were uncertain.

While burning fossil fuels caused air pollution and, according to some scientists, contributed to global warming, renewable energy technologies had little or no impact on the earth's atmosphere. The burning of fossil fuels produced sizable carbon dioxide emissions, said to be a major cause of global warming. Other emissions consisted of sulfur dioxides and various nitrous oxides that had been linked to acid rain that destroyed forests and polluted rivers and lakes. Fossil fuel emissions also contributed to air quality problems in major cities worldwide. Renewable technologies (excluding biomass), on the other hand, had no emissions, and were thus considered to be pollution-free sources of electric energy. While nuclear generation of electricity did not contribute to any of the atmospheric problems associated with fossil fuels, it posed a different set of major environmental threats: nuclear waste disposal, the potential for nuclear accidents and radiation leakages, and nuclear proliferation.

Global awareness and concern regarding fossil fuel's environmental problems were accelerating. The Earth Summit Conference in Rio de Janeiro in 1991 demonstrated the willingness of most countries to work together in addressing these environmental issues. As worldwide energy markets began to place greater value on the environmental benefits of renewable energy sources, industry participants expected their usage to increase dramatically. The demand for each renewable technology was expected to depend on its relative cost, accessibility, and other specific characteristics that made it more or less attractive to buyers. Exhibit 1 shows historical and projected cost trends for various renewable and nonrenewable energy generating technologies.

HISTORY OF THE PHOTOVOLTAICS INDUSTRY

Although many people believed the conversion of sunlight into electricity was a recent development, it predated Edison's electric bulb by 40 years. In 1839, Edmond Becquerel, a French physicist, first recognized the phenomenon when he placed one of two metal electrodes in a conductive fluid, exposed it to sunlight, and registered a small voltage. The first solar cells were developed in the late 1800s, but their low efficiencies and extremely high manufacturing costs rendered them little more than curiosities.

In the 1950s, researchers began to experiment with different semiconductor materials as part of their efforts to reduce costs and improve the efficiencies of solar cells. However, the cells developed in the 1950s were still prohibitively expensive. In the 1960s the U.S. space program rescued photovoltaics, as solar cells had the potential to meet the need for a lightweight, longlasting power source for satellites and space exploration. Large government contracts sponsored both research and manufacturing, resulting in cost reductions and increases in solar cell efficiencies. Solar cells came to be the almost exclusive power source for satellites and space exploration devices.

The R&D efforts spawned by the space program took off in the 1970s due to the oil crisis and public concern about environmental issues. As the cost of PV-generated electricity began to decline and performance reliability was documented, viable terrestrial applications began to emerge. The initial market for PV products was applications in remote areas where photovoltaics was the only practical generating technology. During the 1970s and early 1980s government demonstration projects for energy conservation emerged as another major market. In the 1980s, photovoltaic technology progressed to the point where it could be used to power such consumer products as calculators and watches. In 1992 the largest market was to provide electric power to homes in remote geographical areas where it was too expensive to extend power

E X H I B I T　1　|　**Comparative Cost Estimates of Alternative Generating Technologies**

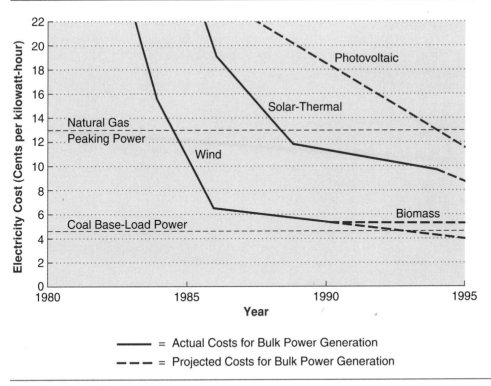

- = Actual Costs for Bulk Power Generation
- - - = Projected Costs for Bulk Power Generation

Source: *Scientific American*, 1990.

lines. However, if the cost of PV-generated electricity could be brought down under 6 cents per kilowatt-hour, then PV technology could compete with conventional fossil fuel and nuclear generation as a primary source for generating electricity.

CAPITAL REQUIREMENTS

The significant technological progress in PV research over the past decades had consumed considerable investment capital. The cash flows companies generated through product sales had so far been exceeded by the investment requirements in R&D and manufacturing facilities. And of course, the considerable uncertainty regarding the future of photovoltaics had made investments in PV business ventures extremely risky. Had the U.S. government not underwritten PV research in both university and private sector settings during the 1960s and 1970s, commercial applications of PV technology might never have occurred.

During the 1970s and 1980s, the U.S. government had funded close to $1 billion in PV R&D and demonstration projects. Private investment had exceeded $2 billion. The 1978 Solar Photovoltaic Energy Research, Development, and Demonstration Act established a goal of "production of electricity from photovoltaic systems cost-competitive with utility-generated electricity from conventional sources." The U.S. Department of Energy (DOE) was actively involved in programs aimed at realizing this goal. However, the DOE PV budget peaked in 1980 at $155 million, and support for PV had averaged only $40 million annually through 1992. Low governmental funding for renewable energy technologies was attributed to relatively low oil and natural gas prices and the low priority given to the impact of fossil-fuel-related environmental problems by the Reagan and Bush Administrations. In contrast to the minimal support for PV in the U.S., the Japanese and German governments had pushed hard to help their domestic PV companies succeed in the global marketplace. In the late 1980s, Germany's PV budget was 65 percent larger than the U.S. budget and Japan's was 40 percent greater.

While national governments had supported the development of PV technology, over $2 billion has been invested by the private sector. Oil companies, flush with cash from the windfall created by rising crude oil prices in the 1974–82 period, had initially been the heaviest investors in solar technology; they viewed PV as an opportunity to diversify into another energy business, potentially reducing risks associated with heavy dependence on oil and natural gas. By 1983, eight U.S. and four foreign oil companies had invested in PV. By 1988, four of the seven U.S. firms manufacturing photovoltaics were subsidiaries of U.S. oil companies. As of 1992, one of the largest U.S. PV producers was Solarex, a subsidiary of Amoco. More recently, electric utilities, union pension funds, and electronics companies had been investing in the industry. Data for 1988 showed that private investment totaled $200 million compared to government investments of $150 million.

THE COSTS OF PHOTOVOLTAIC GENERATION

The cost economics of photovoltaic generation of electricity was entirely different from steam and nuclear generation technologies. In conventional power plants that ran on fuel oil, natural gas, or coal, fuel costs averaged 30 to 50 percent of total generating costs, other operating and maintenance expenses averaged 20 to 40 percent, and capital costs averaged 10 to 30 percent. In nuclear plants, total generating costs consisted of fuel (10 to 25 percent), other operating and maintenance expenses (10 to 35 percent), and capital costs (60 to 80 percent). The cost of PV-generated electricity consisted of 50 to 70 percent capital (for equipment) and 30 to 50 percent for all other costs; fuel costs were zero. The relatively high upfront investment costs in a PV system were a major barrier for potential users; many were unwilling or unable to finance these systems. The life span of a PV module depended on the base technology used to produce it. The most mature technology, flat plate crystalline, had been proven to have very low maintenance costs over a useful life exceeding 20 years.

PV costs consisted of two primary components: (1) the cost of the modules, which included the PV cells, wiring, and the encapsulation necessary to seal the cells for protection from moisture and dust; and (2) all other costs, referred to as the balance of system (BOS) costs. The BOS cost categories included system design and installation, land, support structures, maintenance, power conditioning equipment and, when necessary, storage systems and storage costs. Power conditioning equipment was necessary if the direct current (DC) generated by the PV module had to be converted to alternating current (AC)—necessary for most applications and electricity-using devices. (Some users were able to purchase equipment driven by DC current.) Storage costs related to rechargeable batteries that stored the electricity generated during sunlight hours, to be used at the convenience of the consumer. If the PV system was linked to the distribution lines of an electric utility, there was no need for storage since all electricity produced could either be used at the time it was generated or dispatched directly into an electric utility's distribution system. Federal law required that public utilities purchase excess electricity produced by certain qualified independently owned and operated power generating systems. In most current applications, BOS costs were approximately half of total system costs.

The cost of generating electricity through PV or other power generation technologies was typically expressed in cents per kilowatt-hour (1 kilowatt-hour or kwh equaled the use of 1,000 watts of electricity for 1 hour). Residential utility customers in the U.S. paid an average of 8 cents/kwh for electricity (since 1 kilowatt equaled 1,000 watts, a 100-watt light bulb burning for 10 hours cost the average residential customer 8 cents for the electricity used); however, depending on the geographic area, residential rates ranged from as low as 5 cents per kwh to a high of 14 cents per kwh. Average residential usage was about 9,000 kwhs annually, with a range of 3,000 to 30,000 kwhs. Rates for commercial and industrial customers in the U.S. averaged 5 to 8 cents per kwh, with usage averaging 50,000 kwhs annually for commercial customers and about 1,000,000 kwhs annually for industrial customers. In Germany and Japan, residential users paid on the order of 15 cents/kwh.

PV prices have been declining continuously since their application in satellites—see Exhibit 2. By 1992, a PV system tied into the electric utility grid could supply electricity for approximately 30 to 40 cents/kwh. For a stand-alone system, the cost was slightly higher due to the added expense of storage for night-time usage.

MARKETS FOR PHOTOVOLTAIC GENERATING SYSTEMS

The basic product sold by a PV manufacturer was a module capable of producing a few hundred watts of electricity under ideal sunlight conditions. Multiple modules could be linked to increase the amount of power supplied by the system. Ten panels, each capable of producing 100 watts of electricity, could supply 1 kilowatt (kw) of capacity; one thousand 1-kw systems could, if linked, supply 1000 kilowatts or 1 megawatt (mw) of capacity. Residences typically required 3 to 10 kw of capacity, depending on the amount of electricity-using devices in operation simultaneously and if electric heating or air-conditioning was utilized. Commercial customers could require up to 3 to 5 mw of capacity (but the average was under 1 mw); industrial customers could require anywhere from 1 mw to over 100 mw of capacity. Individual

EXHIBIT 2 | **Cost of Electricity Generation from Photovoltaic Modules**

Year	Modules ($/kwh)	Worldwide mw Shipped
1973	$7.50	–
1975	3.50	–
1977	1.75	–
1979	1.00	–
1981	.75	5
1983	.60	15
1985	.50	23
1987	.40	29
1989	.35	40
1991	.30	55

Source: K. Zweibel, "PV Technology Rationale," NREL, Colorado, September 1990.

electricity-using devices typically required less than 1 kw of capacity and often less than .5 kw—a 40-watt light bulb, for example, required only .04 kw of generating capability.

In 1991, PV producers worldwide shipped modules equal to 55 mw of generating capacity and realized combined revenues of $350 million. Considering that a single, medium-sized coal-fired power plant could produce 800 mw, that the largest investor-owned electric utility in the U.S., the Southern Company, had an installed capacity of over 30,000 mw, and that the installed capacity of all electricity producers in the U.S. exceeded 725,000 mw, the total amount of generating capacity produced by the PV industry was tiny. On the other hand, 55 mw of photovoltaic generating capacity produced manufacturing revenues of $350 million—an amount sufficient to encourage further development of the industry. Industry participants were buoyed by several factors:

- Current sales levels were high enough to stimulate growing buyer awareness.
- Sales demonstrated that there was a viable market for PV applications even at present price levels and that additional end-use markets could be penetrated as costs were driven down further and further.
- The growing base of installed PV devices provided needed information regarding reliability, actual operating experience, maintenance costs, and user acceptance.
- Growing demand justified capacity increases, the accumulation of manufacturing experience, and further capital investment.
- Current revenues and cash flows were big enough to help defray a portion of R&D costs.

Furthermore, industry observers believed the future potential of photovoltaics was demonstrated by its double-digit growth during the 1970s and 1980s.

MARKET SEGMENTS

In 1992 the distinct niche markets for PV products included remote commercial/industrial and household applications, consumer electronics, and electric utilities.

Industrial and Commercial Applications This segment included applications that in many cases replaced battery driven systems. Virtually all were truly cost competitive for the customer, although other benefits—such as low maintenance requirements—sometimes contributed to the PV purchase decision. The size of these markets increased significantly as the cost of PV-generated electricity declined. The major end-use applications were

- *PV-powered communications systems* for transmitting telephone, radio, or TV signals in remote or hard-to-access locations—such systems were durable and reliable as compared to transmitters powered by batteries that required periodic replacement.
- *Warning signal devices* for navigation and aircraft beacons, highway signs, and railroads. Buyers of such devices included the military, Coast Guard, oil companies, railway companies, and highway departments. The Coast Guard had already purchased 10,000 PV-powered systems to replace more costly battery-powered systems.

- *Remote monitoring systems* to measure weather and climate, pollution levels, highway conditions, and seismic movements—over 20,000 such systems had been sold worldwide.
- *Lighting* for remote bus shelters, billboards, security devices, and campground restrooms.

Off-Grid Household Applications Remote habitation applications, such as lighting, appliances, and water pumping for isolated residences and village power, represented the largest and fastest growing segment of PV demand—about 45 percent of annual global sales in 1992. In the U.S. in 1992, there were over 17,000 remote residences and vacation cabins powered by PV systems; many had a diesel generator to serve as a backup or to supplement needs beyond those supplied by the PV system. As of 1990, 20,000 PV-powered water pumping systems had been installed worldwide for remote residences, crop irrigation, and drinking water for campgrounds or grazing cattle.

Industry experts believed the time would come when the cost of PV systems would be competitive with and perhaps even lower than the rates charged by electric utilities—especially those whose rates exceeded 12 cents per kwh. They speculated that as the costs of PV generation fell below 15 cents per kwh, homeowners could economically supplement utility-supplied electricity with power from modules on their roofs. Some analysts envisioned new roofing materials where the top layer would be covered with photovoltaic cells. The cost of the PV system would then be partially offset by its substituting as a roofing material.

Village power represented a huge potential market for PV. Isolated villages in underdeveloped nations needed refrigeration for vaccines and power for medical emergencies, lighting, community phones, radio, and TV, all of which provided an introduction into the modern world. It was estimated that there were 5 million villages worldwide that could use PV systems. In India alone, there were an estimated 300,000 villages with no electricity. Off the coast of Korea, there were 3,000 islands using diesel generators for electric power; they were subject to frequent outages, required constant mechanical maintenance (parts and skilled labor), and had to be resupplied with diesel fuel on an ongoing basis via a costly shipping network.

Consumer Products Consumer products powered by PV were an innovation that came about primarily as a result of the development of amorphous silicon (A-Si) in the 1980s. This new technology resulted in low-cost, lightweight cells that could be used to power calculators, watches, radios, and a variety of small toys. Approximately 15 percent of worldwide PV shipments in 1991 were solar cells for consumer products.

Electric Utilities The largest potential market for photovoltaics involved electric utilities' generating electricity from PV systems tied directly into their existing distribution lines. One approach would involve vast arrays of PV modules covering acres of land, serving in effect as central power-generating sources for utility customers. For this alternative to be economical, the cost of PV-generated electricity would have to decline below 6 cents per kwh or else environmental restrictions on fossil-fuel power plants would have to become so stringent as to make renewable technologies like PV or windpower a necessary generating source. Industry analysts believed that PV systems could become an economical way for utilities to meet daytime peak loads for electricity; this could involve installing their own large PV "solar farms" or installing small-scale PV systems directly on residential or commercial customers' sites as a supplemental electricity source to be used during the utility's daytime peak load periods. Also, some utilities were expected to enter the business of selling, installing, and maintaining PV systems for remote residences or even urban customers who wanted their own on-site generating capability.

Utility executives and power generation personnel were, however, reluctant to rely on unproven generating technologies, given that utility customers expected power to be instantly available at all times. Photovoltaic generating systems presented reliability challenges for utility engineers because PV systems could not produce electricity except during daylight hours and because the amount of electricity generated varied according to light quality. This introduced new load-balancing and capacity-planning challenges for utilities and their customers. Still, several electric utilities, including California's two largest companies—Pacific Gas & Electric (PG&E) and Southern California Edison—had made significant investments in photovoltaics R&D and experimental PV systems, citing such benefits as diversification of generating resources, concern about adverse environmental impacts of fossil-fuel generation, and the ease of adding PV modules on an as-needed basis. One strategy PV companies were using to convince utilities of the merits and reliability of PV was to persuade them to use PV for their own remote power equipment needs, such as special transmission line switches and water level sensors. By 1992 over 20 utilities were using PV devices in such applications; PG&E had over 700 such installations.

Another important initiative in developing the utility market for PV was a public/private partnership called the Photovoltaics for Utility-Scale Applications (PVUSA) Project. The U.S. Department of Energy (DOE), California Energy Commission, Electric Power Research Institute, and PG&E were the major sponsors of PVUSA. Various PV systems using different technologies were being tested at a site in Davis, California. The project was dedicated to proving that photovoltaic technology could play a major role as a future national energy source and be a viable alternative for utility-scale power generation.

DISTRIBUTION CHANNELS

In the early years of the industry's development, firms like Solarex and Arco Solar not only built PV modules but also marketed them directly to end users and provided technical assistance to users in integrating them into their power supply systems. This assistance was critical to building greater acceptance of PV products, serving to both educate and reassure first-time buyers. Potential buyers were unaware of PV products, their benefits, or how to combine them with other system components. They often needed technical expertise to design a system matched to their specific needs. Many buyers also required installation assistance and were reluctant to purchase without assurance that service follow-up would be available. With the direct involvement of PV manufacturers, who could best demonstrate product uses and benefits, install systems, and offer after-sale service, these buyer concerns were gradually overcome.

As use of PV devices became more widespread, distributors and retailers of electrical equipment and electric supplies began to assume a bigger role in serving end users' needs. In 1992 the primary selling channels were through distributor-integrators, retail outlets, and manufacturers' direct sales to end users. Distributor-integrators, as well as many retailers, performed selling, engineering, and after-sales service functions. They purchased the components that completed the system powered by the

PV modules (pumps, inverters, batteries, and so on) and sold the complete system to end users. Their technical staffs assisted in the design specifications and installation of the systems. Sales through distributor-integrators provided the broadest geographic and end-market representation. Large distributor-integrators sold both direct and through other dealers. Photocomm, one of the largest distributors in the U.S., sold approximately 60 percent through other dealers and the remaining 40 percent directly to end users. PV manufacturers could sell to either the large distributors or the small dealers. Smaller dealers either carried a full line of PV systems or decided to specialize in certain end-use applications—for example, remote communication systems or remote residential systems. Establishing and maintaining relationships with smaller dealers was a more costly marketing approach for manufacturers. However, it was a way for smaller manufacturers to enter the market and establish sales for their products. For manufacturers to sell direct to end users involved high selling costs and only made sense for sizable projects. For example, Solec International made a direct sale to a California transportation agency for PV-powered phones placed along major highways.

Distributors did not establish exclusive relationships with a single manufacturer. This reduced the risk of not having modules available for shipment on demand as a result of production shortages by any one PV manufacturer. In some instances, distributors might have one-year contracts with manufacturers to purchase a specific volume of modules. Distributors were also extremely price sensitive, viewing the modules of reputable manufacturers as essentially identical commodity items.

ALTERNATIVE PV TECHNOLOGIES

Solar cells differed by both semiconductor material and base technology. The most common semiconductor material used in solar cells was silicon, although a number of other materials (copper indium diselenide, cadmium telluride, and gallium arsenide) had been tried and tested. The competing base technology paths included (1) *thin film*—cells made from very thin films of semiconductor materials; (2) *concentrators*—an approach that used concentrating lenses to increase the amount of sunlight reaching each cell, rather than allowing sunlight to strike the cells directly; and (3) *non-thin film*—the initial PV technology. These three approaches involved different trade-offs relative to cell efficiencies, module production costs, and system costs.

Thin films had comparatively lower sunlight-to-electricity conversion efficiencies than non-thin film, but possessed the greatest potential for reduced production costs. Thin films were usually made by vacuum deposition of semiconductor material onto a solid substrate (metal or glass). This type of continuous manufacturing process lent itself to mass-production economies that probably could not be obtained with non-thin film technologies.

Concentrator systems had extremely high cell efficiencies, allowing them to generate more power than an equivalent-size system using the other technologies. However, their balance of system costs (mirrors, lenses, trackers, and so on) were much higher than those for the other two PV technologies.

In 1992 none of the three base technologies had emerged as more promising than the others. From an industrywide standpoint, there were reasons to continue pursuing R&D for all three approaches. But it was costly for a company to pursue more than one technological approach. Each technology path had to be supported by an R&D infrastructure and manufacturing process that was distinct from the others and each R&D

panies were acutely aware of the risks of investing heavily in what might ultimately prove to be the wrong technology and then being unprepared or unable to switch to whichever PV technology turned out to be the most cost effective and reliable.

CRYSTALLINE AND POLYCRYSTALLINE SILICON

The early years of PV research were dominated by non thin-film silicon, either crystalline or polycrystalline, produced in a variety of ways. Crystalline silicon cells were made from pure silicon, which was melted at a high temperature and then slowly drawn to form a large crystal. The original (and still predominant) method used to make this crystal was the Czochralski (CZ) process, which resulted in a crystal about 15 cm in diameter and one meter in length. The crystal was cut into thin wafers with a diamond saw. Half of the silicon crystal, now worth hundreds of dollars per kilogram, was turned into useless sawdust in the slicing process. Commercial crystalline solar modules typically converted 11 to 14 percent of the sunlight that struck them into electricity. As of 1992, laboratory cell efficiencies of 22 percent had been reached. Single cell efficiencies achieved in the lab were always higher than what could be achieved in a commercially manufactured module.

Other non-thin film processes based on silicon included (1) *ribbon-growth techniques,* which involved forming a relatively thin, flat ribbon of crystalline silicon that did not have to be sliced; (2) *polycrystalline cells* produced by casting ingots of molten silicon—polycrystalline cells had slightly lower conversion efficiencies but were cheaper to manufacture because the casting process was less expensive; and (3) *other polycrystalline technologies.*

Worldwide shipments of photovoltaics were dominated by crystalline cells and polycrystalline cells, each with approximately one-third market share. Siemens Solar Industries was the largest PV manufacturer in the world, and its output was dominated by CZ crystalline cells. Solarex, the largest U.S. producer in 1992, used a polycrystalline cast-ingot technology in its modules. Mobil Solar and Westinghouse had both made substantial investments in different ribbon-growth technologies and were in the process of setting up manufacturing capability. A number of other U.S. firms, including Astropower, Texas Instruments, and Global PV Specialists, were actively involved in developing polycrystalline technologies, but had not yet geared up for commercial production and application.

THIN FILM TECHNOLOGY

In 1974, David Carlson, a physicist at RCA Laboratories, demonstrated the commercial viability of a thin-film PV device using silicon, hoping to create an inexpensive solar cell. During the 1980s considerable progress was made in developing ultra-thin silicon cells from amorphous silicon (A-Si). Initially, researchers did not believe that amorphous silicon could sustain an appreciable photovoltaic effect, but laboratory cell efficiencies over 14 percent were achieved. However, manufactured modules typically had initial efficiencies of only 6 to 7 percent and showed a degradation in efficiency on the order of 20 percent during use. A-Si thin films were still promising, in spite of these shortcomings, because considerably less of the expensive pure silicon was used to make them and because they could be manufactured via a cheaper process. Progress was being made in solving the efficiency degradation problem. In 1992 Texas Instruments announced it had discovered a way to make ultra-thin cells from regular commercial-grade silicon instead of pure silicon, thereby reducing its material costs for silicon by 83 percent.

The area of greatest promise in A-Si was considered to be in multijunction cells. In this approach, more than one layer of semiconductor thin film was deposited on the substrate. Each layer was designed with different sunlight absorption properties and could capture a larger portion of the solar radiation spectrum than a single thin-film layer. Theorists predicted efficiencies for tandem cells could reach 35 to 40 percent.

Up until the late 1980s, Arco Solar and Chronar were among the world leaders in thin-film amorphous silicon technology. A number of Japanese firms, including Sanyo Electric, Kaneka, and Kyocera, were well positioned in A-Si; several Japanese electronics manufacturers purchased their modules and used them as a power source in their consumer products.

A few other thin-film materials had attracted considerable R&D investment dollars. The most promising of these were cadmium telluride (CdTe) and copper indium diselenide (CIS). Both CIS and CdTe were attractive because they had achieved higher conversion efficiencies than cells made of A-Si and their efficiency did not appear to deteriorate after extended use; it also appeared that they could be manufactured less expensively. On the other hand, CdTe and CIS were still in the experimental stage; technical data were sketchy and testing of the cells in actual operating situations was still under way. As of 1992, neither CdTe or CIS technologies had been commercialized. It was possible, however, that one of them could displace A-Si and even crystalline technologies, depending on the progress that was made in the lab and in developing manufacturing processes.

One critical roadblock for PV cells made from CdTe and CIS, besides being years behind A-Si on the learning curve, was environmental concerns. Both CdTe and CIS utilized cadmium, which was considered a hazardous pollutant in water supplies. While the amounts of cadmium involved were extremely small, and the likelihood of cadmium wastes leaching into streams and rivers was very low, the mere presence of cadmium could trigger a sensitive alarm button among environmentalists.

CONCENTRATOR TECHNOLOGIES

Another PV technology being actively pursued involved the use of concentrators, a method that dramatically increased the efficiency of solar cells. In this approach, optical systems using mirrors and lenses concentrated sunlight on crystalline or thin-film gallium arsenide (GaAs) PV cells. The modules and concentrators were automatically rotated to track the sun's movement. Efficiencies of over 30 percent had been achieved with this method. The cost of the optical elements and rotation devices was offset by the higher conversion efficiencies.

About 15 small U.S. companies saw long-term potential in the concentrator technology and had committed their R&D efforts to it. But to succeed they had to resolve several technological issues: (1) finding ways to increase the already high cell efficiencies; (2) improving the ability to dissipate heat from the cells and prevent degradation in efficiency; and (3) reducing the costs associated with the optical and tracking systems.

Despite the fact that concentrator technology was proven and reliable, its commercial potential was limited because it was best suited to large-scale applications. The cost and minimum size requirements for the mirrors, lenses, and trackers made the system uneconomical for small applications, such as remote habitation, water pumping, and transmitters, that constituted the bulk of the current demand for PV products. Commercial and industrial interest in concentrating systems was much smaller than that involved with thin film and other flat-plate alternatives. Most sales of concentrator systems were for larger demonstration projects funded by utilities or governments.

THE GLOBAL PV INDUSTRY

The PV industry in 1992 consisted of (1) R&D laboratories, (2) manufacturers of solar cells, modules, and panels, (3) systems integrators-distributors, and (4) retail outlets. Some R&D labs had not yet commercialized their research efforts, while all the manufacturers were engaged in R&D activities. The core of the industry consisted of R&D labs and the manufacturers. There were about 40 PV manufacturers worldwide. However, many of the industry's players, R&D based start-ups or R&D labs being incubated by large corporations, had not yet produced any commercial products. The number of organizations conducting R&D was estimated to be over 100. Systems integrators-distributors and retail outlets had the capability to provide installation and field-support services. Distributor-integrators sold to both smaller retail electric supply houses and direct to end users. The global infrastructure to distribute and market PV products to end users was still developing. In the U.S., the geographical coverage, technical expertise, and marketing capabilities of distributors-retailers was more evolved than in other countries. In addition to these primary PV industry activities, another group of firms was involved in supplying the industry with raw materials, PV system components, and manufacturing equipment.

INDUSTRY SIZE, GROWTH, AND STRUCTURE

The worldwide PV industry shipped 55.3 mw of modules in 1991 representing approximately $500 million in retail sales. Manufacturing output had doubled since 1985.

Exhibit 3 shows PV module shipments by world region. U.S. producers' share of worldwide shipments slipped from 65 percent in 1981 to its current level of 31 percent. In 1991, Japanese producers' market share was 36 percent and European producers held 24 percent. European producers had tripled their shipments between 1986 and 1991. Europe's strong growth was attributed to environmental concerns triggered by the Chernobyl nuclear accident and to strong governmental support of the efforts of European companies to develop PV products. European interest in pho-

EXHIBIT 3 | **Worldwide Shipments of PV Modules to Commercial and Consumer Users, 1986–91** *(In megawatts)*

Producing Region	Megawatts Shipped					
	1986	1987	1988	1989	1990	1991
United States	7.1	8.7	11.3	14.1	14.8	17.1
Japan	12.6	13.2	12.8	14.2	16.8	19.9
Europe	4.0	4.5	6.7	7.9	10.2	13.4
Rest of world	2.3	2.8	3.0	4.0	4.7	5.0
Total	26.0	29.2	33.8	40.2	46.5	55.3

Source: Paul D. Maycock, *PV News,* 1992.

photovoltaics had led some industry experts to predict that their production of PV would overtake the U.S. and Japan by 1995.

Exhibit 4 lists the major PV manufacturers worldwide (as of 1991) and their technology base. The market was dominated by Siemens Solar (U.S./Germany), Solarex (U.S.), Sanyo (Japan), Kyocera (Japan), and Kaneka (Japan), who together accounted for more than half the world module shipments.

Modules were bought and sold based on their rated generating capacity. A typical module might be rated at 25 or 50 watts. This power rating was the peak amount of electricity the module was capable of generating under prespecified sunlight conditions. In 1992, prices for larger modules from manufacturer to distributor averaged $4.50 per peak watt. Thus, a 50-watt module produced $225 in sales revenue for the manufacturer. Manufacturers typically offered ten-year warranties with their modules. Kyocera offered a 12-year warranty. Because there were few differences between equivalently rated modules, competition between manufacturers was based primarily on price.

Despite the industry's rapid growth, only one or two firms in the industry made a profit in the 1980s and early 1990s. Most were sustaining substantial losses according to Strategies Unlimited, a market research firm that closely followed the industry. Pricing strategies were a major reason for these losses. The larger PV firms set prices based on the costs of manufacturing and marketing the products, and prices generally did not reflect the firm's R&D costs and long-term investments to develop the market for PV products. The larger firms had been sustaining annual losses in the $5 to $20 million range.

EXHIBIT 4 | **Leading Photovoltaic Manufacturers in 1991**

Company	Technology	Country	Production (mw)
Siemens Solar	Single crystal/CIS	U.S./Germany	9.0
Sanyo	Amorphous/poly	Japan	6.0
Kyocera	Polycrystal/A-Si	Japan	5.8
Solarex	Amorphous/poly	U.S.	5.6
Kaneka	Amorphous	Japan	3.1
BP Solar Systems	Single/poly crystal	U.K./Spain	2.2
Telefunken	Single/poly crystal	Germany	2.1
Photowatt	Polycrystal	France	1.8
Taiyo Yuden	Amorphous	Japan	1.6
Helios	Single/poly	Italy	1.5
ItalSolar	Single/poly	Italy	1.5
Solec International	Single crystal	U.S.	1.2
NAPS–France	A-Si	France	1.0
Sharp	Single crystal	Japan	1.0
Hoxan	Single crystal	Japan	0.8
Matsushita	CdTe	Japan	0.8
Siemens Solar	Single crystal	Germany	0.8
Isofoton	Single crystal	Spain	0.5
RES	Single/poly	Netherlands	0.5
Astropower	Polycrystal	U.S.	0.45

Source: Paul D. Maycock, *PV News*, 1992.

Prices and sales volumes in 1992 were somewhat more favorable for the manufacturers than in the late 1980s. Some firms were targeting break-even, including coverage of longer term investments in R&D and marketing, within the next one to three years.

TECHNOLOGY AND MANUFACTURING STRATEGIES

There was considerable uncertainty as to which technology would first become competitive in the market for large-scale electricity generation. Both basic R&D and manufacturing-process technology offered opportunities for significant cost reductions. Firms had to decide the extent to which they would pursue these two avenues, each of which required sizable investments. The stakes were high since utility industry projections called for construction of about 800,000 mw of new generating capacity worldwide by the year 2005, resulting in a potential market for power generation equipment of $20 billion to $30 billion annually. Exhibit 5 shows worldwide shipments of modules based on the different technologies in 1991. The market was dominated by single-crystal and polycrystalline technologies, which together accounted for two-thirds of world shipments. Thin films accounted for almost another third. Japan dominated in thin films, due to sales to Japanese manufacturers of solar calculators and consumer electronics products.

Several larger manufacturers—Siemens Solar, BP Solar, Solarex, Kyocera, and Sharp—had made commitments to both thin film and either crystalline or polycrystalline non-thin film technologies—see Exhibit 4. BP Solar produced both crystalline and polycrystalline modules as well as CdTe cells. Siemens Solar was pursuing three R&D tracks: crystalline silicon, A-Si, and CIS. The small number of firms with multiple R&D tracks reflected the large capital and technical resource investments required to participate in a specific technological approach. Most of the companies that had pursued more than one technology were subsidiaries of multibillion dollar corporations with the ability to absorb short-term losses and fund a competitive R&D effort.

Whereas during the 1970s and 1980s, the primary R&D thrust was on improving cell efficiency, by 1990 ways to reduce manufacturing costs were also receiving significant attention. Potential sources of cost reduction included economies of scale, experience curve effects, and improved process technologies. Many of the existing production lines were set up to produce about 1 mw of annual capacity, a size that

EXHIBIT 5 | **Shipments of PV Modules by Technology Type, 1991** *(In megawatts)*

Cell Type	Total Shipments	Percent of Total
Amorphous silicon (indoor)	8.34 mw	15.1%
Amorphous silicon (terrestrial)	5.40	9.8
Amorphous silicon (total)	13.74	24.9
Single crystal	19.70	35.6
Polycrystal	20.90	37.8
Cadmium telluride	0.80	1.4
Ribbon	0.20	0.3
Concentrator	0.035	—
Total	55.375 mw	100%

Source: Paul D. Maycock, *PV News*, 1992.

was considered suboptimal. Industry executives believed a 5 to 10 mw per year thin-film plant would result in significant scale economies. Building a plant of this size required an investment in the $5 to $20 million range. The equipment for these plants was similar to that used in the semiconductor and glass industries and was readily available. The real difficulty in making such plants operational, especially for thin-film technologies, was the complex process engineering required to obtain the targeted efficiencies and yields. Typically, it took several years to achieve a smooth-running process with acceptable yields. Prices and availabilities of silicon, cadmium, tellerium, indium, and selenium were not currently an issue as needed quantities could be readily obtained from several suppliers. Even if PV sales grew rapidly, producers believed materials suppliers could expand fast enough to keep abreast of the raw materials needs. The one exception was uncertainty regarding the price of indium under rapid growth conditions.

Solarex had plans for a 10 mw plant for thin films, but the construction go-ahead awaited further cost estimates and market developments. Solarex executives hoped to produce thin films for $1.30/watt, leaving $1.20/watt to cover balance of system (BOS) costs, thus meeting targeted $2.50/watt installed-system costs. The $1.20/watt BOS costs were considered feasible based on studies by two independent engineering and research firms. Such costs would mean users could generate electricity for 12 to 15 cents/kwh, a range competitive with utility costs for peaking power and with retail electric rates charged by some utilities. Experience curve effects were considered to be a major contributor to achieving progressively lower costs in manufacturing thin-film PV modules.

The U.S. Department of Energy initiated the five-year Photovoltaic Manufacturing Technology Project (PVMaT) in 1990, based on its assessment that process technology was the primary area in need of attention and investment. A key element of this project was to identify manufacturing problems requiring R&D solutions and to commit resources to resolve problem areas in manufacturing.

LONG-TERM DEMAND SCENARIOS

Future PV demand and industry growth hinged on a variety of technological, political, economic, and institutional factors. In order to assess the future of renewable energy technologies in the United States, including photovoltaics, biomass, geothermal, wind, hydropower and solar thermal, a task force composed of scientists and engineers working under the auspices of the U.S. Department of Energy developed a report entitled "The Potential of Renewable Energy." Using a time frame of four decades (1990–2030), three scenarios relating to the U.S. energy supply mix were considered. The business-as-usual (BAU) Scenario assumed that U.S. government R&D expenditures would continue at the present levels and that energy policy would remain unchanged. In this scenario, renewables would supply 15 percent of total energy requirements by 2030, up from 8 percent in 1990. In the research, development, and demonstration-intensification scenario (RD&D), federal funding for PV energy projects was expanded by a factor of 2 or 3 times its current level to about $3 billion over the next two decades. In this scenario, technology potentials were accelerated, and renewables supplied 28 percent of total energy requirements. In the national premiums scenario, a market pull approach was assumed. This scenario assumed that the environmental benefits of renewable energy sources would result in environmental regulations that effectively reduced the cost of renewable energy or else provided market incentives for using it. Under this scenario, renewables would

EXHIBIT 6 | **Estimated Amount of Electric Energy Obtainable from Photovoltaic Sources: Three Scenarios for the 1990–2030 Period**

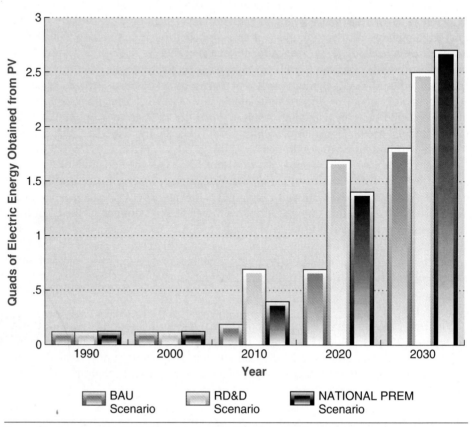

Source: "The Potential of Renewable Energy," *An Interlaboratory White Page,* NREL, Colorado, March 1990.

supply 22 percent of total energy needs by 2030. Growth in the size of the PV market in the U.S. for each of these scenarios is portrayed in Exhibit 6. Although all three scenarios forecast the development of a substantial market for PV, the BAU scenario was the most pessimistic in outlook. Significant market size was not reached under any scenario until after the year 2000, when the cost of generating electricity through PV was expected to reach $0.10/kwh.

THE PV INDUSTRY IN THE UNITED STATES

The U.S. photovoltaics industry was composed of approximately 40 firms engaged in PV R&D or in both PV R&D and manufacturing. These firms employed close to 1,500 employees; U.S. producers shipped approximately 17 mw of modules in 1991. In addition, the industry supported an evolving infrastructure of systems integrators-distributors and a variety of suppliers of raw materials, capital equipment, and components. Exhibits 7 and 8 show U.S. module shipments by company and market sector, respectively. (Note: In the discussion that follows, Siemens Solar is referred to as a U.S. firm because it was headquartered in the U.S. and had its labs and facilities here; however, it was a wholly owned subsidiary of Siemens, a German corporation.)

EXHIBIT 7 | **Shipments of PV Modules by U.S.-Based Producers, 1986–91** (*In megawatts*)

Company	1986	1987	1988	1989	1990	1991	R&D Base	Form of Organization
Siemens Solar	4.0 mw	4.2 mw	5.5 mw	6.5 mw	7.0 mw	9.0 mw	Crystalline Si, CIS, and A-Si	Subsidiary of Siemens Industries of Germany
Solarex	1.9	2.9	3.2	5.0	5.4	5.6	Crystalline Si and CIS	Subsidiary of Amoco, a U.S. oil company
APS	0.3	0.7	1.0	0.5	0.3	0.2	A-Si	
Solec International	0.3	0.3	0.6	0.9	0.9	1.2	Crystalline Si	Small entrepreneurial firm
USSC	0.1	0.3	0.4	0.5	0.6	0.2	A-Si	Joint venture between a smaller U.S. corporation and Canon, Inc., of Japan
Entech	—	—	0.2	0.3	0.03	0.03	Crystalline Si (concentrators)	Small entrepreneurial firm
Mobil Solar	0.2	0.05	0.1	0.05	0.05	0.2	Crystalline Si (ribbon silicon)	Subsidiary of Mobil Corp., a U.S. oil company
Astropower	—	—	0.1	0.2	0.4	0.45	Crystalline Si (silicon firm)	Small entrepreneurial firm
All others	0.3	0.2	0.2	0.15	0.12	0.2		
Total	7.1 mw	8.65 mw	11.3 mw	14.1 mw	14.8 mw	17.1 mw		

Source: Paul D. Maycock, *PV News*, 1992.

INDUSTRY STRUCTURE

The U.S. industry was dominated by Siemens Solar and Solarex, who between them accounted for 85 percent of U.S. industry shipments in 1991. Other U.S. firms were in the position of either having only small-scale module output, trying to develop a manufacturing process, or performing basic R&D. Recent exits, acquisitions, divestitures, and strategic alliances had changed the industry's makeup in significant ways:

- Chronar, a major producer of A-Si, filed for Chapter 11 in 1990. Its assets and personnel were reorganized into a new company, Advanced Photovoltaic Systems.
- Glasstech Solar left the industry when its efforts in A-Si did not develop as anticipated. However, a successor company—Solar Cells, Inc.—was formed prior to Glasstech Solar's demise in order to pursue the CdTe technology.
- In 1992, Coors Corporation bought Photon Energy, a small entrepreneurial PV firm involved in CdTe.
- ARCO Solar was sold to Siemens Solar in 1990.
- United Solar Systems, a leader in A-Si, was formed in 1991 as a joint venture between Energy Conversion Devices (a preexisting PV firm) and Canon (a Japanese firm).

The various industry players also represented different corporate structures. Several were subsidiaries of large corporations, while others were privately held entrepreneurial ventures (Exhibit 7).

EXHIBIT 8 | **U.S. Shipments of PV Modules by Market Category, 1986–91** (*In megawatts*)

Application/Market Category	1986	1987	1988	1989	1990	1991
Connected to electric utility grid	0.5 mw	0.2 mw	0.6 mw	0.4 mw	0.4 mw	0.2 mw
Central station power plants (1 mw or more)	—	—	—	—	—	—
Exports	3.8	4.7	5.5	5.9	6.4	9.0*
Off-grid residential	0.6	1.5	2.2	2.5	2.8	2.6
Government projects	0.3	0.05	0.2	0.5	0.5	0.5
Off-grid industrial and commercial	1.4	1.6	2.0	2.3	2.5	2.4
Consumer products (less than 10w)	0.5	0.6	0.8	2.5	2.2	2.4
Total	7.1 mw	8.65 mw	11.3 mw	14.1 mw	14.8 mw	17.1 mw

*Includes 2 mw shipped as cells.

Source: Paul D. Maycock, *PV News,* 1992.

U.S. COMPETITIVENESS

U.S. PV firms had lost ground to the Europeans and the Japanese during the 1980s. The U.S. industry had managed to sustain its competitive edge in many areas, however, despite moderate governmental support. While crystalline and polycrystalline silicon technologies were relatively well-researched, and global competitors had achieved similar levels of technical competence, numerous technological innovations were being spearheaded by U.S. firms. Chief among these were Mobil and Westinghouse's ribbon-growth technologies, Astropower's polycrystalline silicon film, and Texas Instrument's spheral solar technology. U.S. firms also remained in the forefront of technology development in thin films. In amorphous silicon, research on multi-junction cells by Solarex, United Solar Systems (USSC), and several universities was considered to be the most advanced in the world. In thin-film cadmium telluride and thin-film copper indium diselenide, U.S. firms had a significantly larger infrastructure supporting basic research activities. U.S. firms also led global competitors in developing thin-film process technologies. Significant advances were being made by PV firms through the funding support of the Department of Energy's Photovoltaic Manufacturing Technology Project.

The U.S. led other countries in the development of a distribution infrastructure. This was primarily due to an earlier start for U.S. PV firms as a result of their dominance during the 1970s and early 1980s. However, distribution channels were developing quickly in Japan, Europe, and the Third-World countries.

PROFILES OF U.S. COMPETITORS

The following are brief profiles of the two dominant U.S. players, Solarex and Siemens Solar, and of a representative sampling of other competitors with different technology paths.

Siemens Solar Industries   Siemens Solar was the largest U.S. producer of PV modules, accounting for 58 percent of total U.S. production (Exhibit 7). Formerly Arco Solar, the business had been acquired from Atlantic Richfield in 1990. The company's corporate parent was Germany's second largest industrial corporation, with 1992 sales of $50 billion and after-tax profits of $1.3 billion. Siemens Solar had a U.S. manufacturing facility for single-crystal silicon in Camarillo, California, and a new facility, designed to add 6 to 8 mw of capacity in single-crystal technology, in Vancouver, Washington. Siemens also had a facility in Munich, Germany. Its 1991 output of 9 mw was from single-crystal Cz silicon; however, it was actively involved in research on thin-film CIS. The company had a pilot manufacturing facility to try to commercialize its CIS technology. Until recently, a large portion of Siemens Solar output was sold through Photocomm, a large U.S. distributor-integrator. However, Kyocera offered Photocomm a better price and the company switched a significant number of its purchases to Kyocera. Siemens Solar was able to ship a considerable portion of its output to the European market, avoiding a loss of sales.

Solarex   This company, a subsidiary of Amoco, was the second largest PV manufacturer in the U.S.; Amoco had 1992 sales of $40 billion and after-tax profits of $600 million. Headquartered in Maryland, Solarex had a sales office in Italy to serve Europe, Africa, and the Middle East and a sales office in Hong Kong and a manufacturing plant in Australia to serve Asia. The company produced polycrystalline silicon, thin-film amorphous silicon, and was engaged in research in copper indium diselenide. Most of its 1991 shipments of 5.6 mw were cast polycrystalline silicon. Solarex's thin-film division, located in Newtown, Pennsylvania, could produce about 1 mw of amorphous silicon PV products. Most of its A-Si products involved small specialty applications, for fence chargers, gate openers, and recreational vehicles. Solarex had concentrated its R&D effort on multijunction A-Si and was currently developing prototype equipment for manufacturing multijunction A-Si products. The firm was researching CIS technology in laboratory experiments but had no immediate plans to begin commercialization.

Other Competitors   Several U.S. companies were active in single-crystal or polycrystalline silicon, including two smaller firms—Solec International and Crystal Systems. Mobil Solar, Westinghouse, Texas Instruments, and Astropower were all engaged in R&D related to non-thin film silicon technology.

Other U.S. companies, besides Solarex, pursuing the multijunction amorphous silicon technology included the Utility Power Group and USSC. The latter was a 1991 joint venture between Energy Conversion Devices and Canon, Inc. ECD entered the PV industry in the late 1970s but needed a financially strong partner like Canon to take its technology to large-scale production.

In addition to Solarex and Siemens Solar, the active CIS pursuers included a smaller company, ISET, and a relatively new entrant, Martin Marrietta—a major defense contractor and aerospace products firm. Boeing Aerospace was involved during the 1980s, but had since dropped out. In 1992 there were no competitors outside the U.S. pursuing CIS technology.

The pursuit of the cadmium telluride thin-film technology in the U.S. was limited to two firms: Solar Cells, Inc., a small entrepreneurial firm, and Golden Photon, Inc. (formerly Photon Energy), which had been acquired by Coors Corporation. A larger firm, Ametek, dropped out in 1989. In fact, the pursuit of CdTe was limited to a few global players. Internationally, only two companies, BP Solar (a subsidiary of oil giant British Petroleum) and Matsushita (Japan's largest electronics firm) were currently involved in CdTe R&D.

Solar Cells, Inc., of Toledo, Ohio, was an example of a small privately held, entrepreneurial firm operating in the PV industry without the deep pocket support of a large corporate parent. Solar Cells was targeting its efforts on the bulk power utility market and Third-World village electrification. Solar Cells had designed a new state-of-the-art semiconductor manufacturing facility to produce large area panels. The production line was intended to have an annual capacity of 200,000 solar panels, equal to 10 mw of generating capacity. The facility would have a continuous, high throughput, computer-controlled manufacturing system. Solar Cells had developed a proprietary technique which it believed would yield a cost advantage over other thin-film products provided it could operate its high throughput, continuous manufacturing process at close to full capacity. To sell its 10 mw of generating capability Solar Cell's management believed the company needed to focus on the utility market which had the required volume of demand and the purchasing resources to match. Solar Cells was trying to complete development of the manufacturing process and anticipated that construction of a 20 mw facility could begin in mid-1993.

VIDEO CONCEPTS, INC.

John Dunkelberg, Wake Forest University
Tom Goho, Wake Forest University

As Chad Rowan, the owner of Video Concepts, looked over his monthly income statement, he could only shake his head about how everything might have been so much different. In many ways he was a successful entrepreneur, having started and grown a profitable business. In other ways, he felt trapped in a long-term no-win situation. The question now was what actions to take given the business predicament he faced. Basically, Chad had a profitable business. But the profits were relatively small, and had stopped growing since a strong competitor, Blockbuster Video, had moved into town. They were not enough to pay off his long-term debts and provide him with any more than a subsistence living. In addition, the chances of selling his business for enough to pay off his debts, and then start another business, were not good.

In reflecting on what might have been, Chad commented:

I had really hoped to expand Video Concepts into several similar-sized towns within a couple of hours driving distance from here. The financial projections, which had been fairly accurate until Blockbuster arrived, indicated expansion was possible. I thought I was growing fast and had put about as much capital into the business as I could afford. I had even hoped to get a partner to go into this business with me, and one was very interested. Right now, however, I do not feel that I'm getting a very good return on my time and capital.

I guess I'm getting a taste of my own medicine. As I grew, several local businesses went out of business, but the good news is that the total market has grown since Blockbuster opened its store. Their marketing clout has brought more people into the market.

[To compete with Blockbuster] I've tried everything I can think of to get market share. The only way to increase revenues seems to be to raise the rental price, but my lower price is the best marketing strategy I have. If I raise the price, I'm afraid I will lose a lot of market share.

CHAD ROWAN'S BUSINESS BACKGROUND

Chad Rowan had been interested in having his own business since he had started and operated a lawn service business in high school. Chad had started in the ninth grade mowing lawns for his neighbors using his family's lawn mower. By the time he had graduated from high school, his lawn service clientele was big enough to support the purchase of a riding mower, two smaller mowers, two blowers, a lawn aerator, an edger, and a trimmer; he also had to employ three of his high school friends to keep abreast of demand for his services. The profits from the lawn service business were enough to pay Chad's tuition to college and he continued to operate the business throughout his four college years.

Chad majored in business and took the only two courses that were available in entrepreneurship and small business management. During his senior year he began to look into the video rental business, which at that time was a relatively new industry. His investigation resulted in a research paper on the video rental business. The paper included a business plan for the start-up of a small video rental store with an inventory of about 500 videotapes. By the middle of his senior year, Chad knew he wanted to start a video rental business and had identified a site, a vacant retail store in the downtown business district of his hometown.

VIDEO CONCEPTS: THE FIRST THREE YEARS

After graduation in 1987, Chad opened Video Concepts, a video rental store with 200 square feet of retail space and a 500-tape rental library in Lexington, North Carolina, a town of about 28,000 people. Video Concepts started slowly but was profitable within six months. Chad tried several innovative marketing techniques including home delivery, a free rental after ten rentals, and selling soft drinks and popcorn both at the store and with the delivered videos. To help reduce the expense of the start-up business, Chad lived at home with his parents and took only $500 a month for his own wages. Revenues that first year were $64,000 with all surplus cash flows being used to buy additional videotapes. At the end of the first year's operation, Chad decided to expand and open a second, larger store.

A one-thousand-square-foot retail store was available in a small shopping center that served a major neighborhood area. Chad borrowed $80,000 from his banker to open the second store, using the value of some corporate stocks that he owned as collateral. The loan was a seven-year note with only interest due during the term of the loan and the entire principal due in seven years. The new store had 3,000 video tapes. Chad purchased all his new releases through Major Video, one of the top three wholesale distributors in the United States. To increase the size of his video library, he purchased over 2,000 used tapes from a firm that bought up tapes from bankrupt firms for resale. Over the next two years, Video Concepts' revenues continued to grow rapidly and operations remained profitable. Chad, however, continued to reinvest all profits in purchasing additional tapes. Revenues during the second year increased to $173,000, and then in the third year to $278,000.

GROWTH CONTINUES

The chance to open a third store became a reality when a furniture retail store located in Lexington's busiest shopping district decided to move to its own, larger building on the outskirts of town. The store contained 3,000 square feet of space, enough to hold over 12,000 tapes on display. Chad obtained a three-year lease on the store and opened his third video rental store in the fall of 1990. Video Concepts now had stores in the three main shopping areas of Lexington.

The new Video Concepts store used open display racks for the videotapes and customers could quickly and easily locate the type of movies they wanted by going to the appropriate section (marked new releases, horror, science fiction, action, classical, and so on) and walking down the aisle. Checking out was quick and easy, thanks to a new computer software program that reduced checkout time to less than 30 seconds per customer. In addition, the software program provided a management information capability that allowed Chad to keep track of the number of times each tape was rented, how many tapes each customer rented, and who had past-due tapes. The system also allowed Chad to easily track sales on a daily, weekly, or monthly basis. The third store and the more efficient operating practices enabled Video Concepts to become a growing and fairly profitable business.

During the next year, growth in rental volume at the three Video Concept stores continued, with the majority of the gains coming from the new store. Chad continued the policy of a free rental after ten rentals, reduced the price per rental to $1.99 per night, and introduced some advertising centered primarily on local high school promotional events. The original two stores experienced little revenue growth but remained profitable.

Video Concepts' aggressive expansion and rising market share forced weaker video rental outlets in Lexington to go out of business. By the summer of 1991, only 6 of Chad's original 17 competitors were still operating. Chad thought his aggressive pricing strategy, high quality service, and good selection of new releases were factors in the demise of some of his smaller competitors. The six remaining competitors had an average inventory of less than 1,000 videotapes and none had more than 1,600 tapes. Chad estimated that combined annual revenues from video rentals in all stores in Lexington was about $600,000 in early 1991.

The increase in video rental chain stores nationally had not gone unnoticed by Chad, and he had visited several competitors' stores in nearby cities. During his visits, Chad had primarily tried to see what other video rental businesses were doing and learn what he could do to be more efficient and stay competitive. Although he had visited Blockbuster Video stores in several nearby cities, Chad estimated that Blockbuster outlets would require annual revenues of at least $600,000 to be profitable. For this reason Chad believed that Lexington was too small to attract a major video rental chain store. He also believed that his three-store Video Concepts operation was as well stocked and efficiently operated as any of the national chains, including Blockbuster.

Believing that Video Concepts' market position in Lexington was secure, he began paying himself a modest annual salary of $15,000. In addition, he decided to start paying off the second loan of $200,000 that he had taken out to open the third store. To obtain this last loan, Chad had used all the assets that he owned as collateral because he believed that these stores were an excellent investment. In the summer of 1991, with sales increasing every month, Chad had reason to think that Video Concepts represented a very good investment.

SERIOUS COMPETITION ARRIVES

In August, Blockbuster Entertainment announced that it would open a store in Lexington. Blockbuster, although a very young corporation, was the largest video rental chain store in the United States. Blockbuster had grown from 19 stores in 1986 to

2,829 stores (1,805 company-owned and 1,024 franchises) in 1991 and had total revenues of about $1.2 billion. The typical Blockbuster store carried 8,000 to 14,000 tapes and the stores ranged in size from 4,000 to 10,000 square feet. In 1991 the 1,248 company-owned Blockbuster stores that had been in operation for more than a year were averaging monthly revenues of $75,000.

Although the growth in the United States in consumer spending on video rentals seemed to have slowed, Blockbuster Video believed it had the opportunity to take market share away from the smaller competitors through its strategy of building large stores with a greater selection of tapes than most of its competitors. As the largest video rental chain in the United States, Blockbuster also had advantages in marketing and in the purchase of inventory. Blockbuster Video's standard pricing was $3.50 per tape for two nights, but local stores had some pricing discretion.

In the fall of 1991, Blockbuster built a new store almost across the street from Chad's main Video Concepts store. It purchased a vacant lot for $310,000 and then leased a 6,400-square-foot building, which was built to their specifications, under a long-term lease agreement for $8.50 per square foot for the first three years. The cost of completely furnishing the building, including the videotapes, was about $375,000, and Blockbuster spent over $150,000 on the grand opening promotions. Altogether, Blockbuster spent about $835,000 to open its Lexington store compared to the just over $200,000 that Video Concepts had spent to open its similar-sized store. Blockbuster's operating costs were comparable to Video Concepts' since the computer checkout equipment was similar and both firms had approximately the same personnel costs. Both firms depreciated their tapes over 12 months.

BLOCKBUSTER'S IMPACT ON VIDEO CONCEPTS

Chad decided not to try to meet the grand opening blitz by Blockbuster with an advertising promotion of his own, but he did start including brochures on Video Concepts with each rental. The brochure noted that the rental fee at Video Concepts was lower than Blockbuster's, that Video Concepts had a new game section where Nintendo games were available, that Video Concepts was a family entertainment store (no X-rated videos), and that Video Concepts was a locally owned store that supported local school events. Chad felt his past reputation for low prices ($1.99 versus $3.50 at Blockbuster), his hometown ownership, and courteous service were the appropriate strategic response to a well-financed competitor. He did not believe that he should even attempt to match Blockbuster's advertising budget and that he should not try to beat Blockbuster at its game. That is, he must continue to do what he did best and not try to match Blockbuster's marketing strategy. He did, however, increase the number of tapes purchased for each new release.

With the opening of the new Blockbuster store and its attendant grand opening marketing campaign, Video Concept's revenues dropped about 25 percent for two months and then started slowly climbing back to their previous levels. During this two-month period, Chad had worked even harder to provide excellent customer service through brief training sessions for his employees. He had always had employee training sessions, but these emphasized the competitive threat from Blockbuster and the need to provide the best customer service possible. The primary points of these sessions were directed toward informing customers, as they checked out, of how many rentals they had to go before they would obtain a free rental, the customers' ability to reserve videos, and Video Concepts' willingness to deliver videos to customers' homes at no extra charge. (These were all services that Blockbuster did not offer.)

Nonetheless, Video Concepts' revenues hit a plateau of just under $40,000 per month and stayed there, with the normal minor seasonal variations, for the next 12 months. During this time, Chad attempted several marketing promotions including rent-one-get-one-free on the normally slow nights (Mondays, Tuesdays, and Wednesdays), and he mailed brochures to all of Video Concepts customers that included a brief highlighting of the advantages of shopping Video Concepts over Blockbuster (lower price and the extra services), and a free rental coupon.

The promotions seemed to help Video Concepts maintain its current revenue level, but they were costly and resulted in lower profitability for the three-store operation. To try to improve Video Concepts' profitability, Chad examined his operation for ways of further improving efficiency. By studying the hour-by-hour sales patterns, he was able to more efficiently schedule his employees. He also used the information provided by the software program to determine when the rentals of "hit" and/or new releases had peaked.

Hit videos presented two big problems. One concerned how many tapes to purchase. There seemed to be little correlation between a hit at the box office and a hit from rentals. When a movie was first released for video rental, Chad would buy 40 to 50 videotapes at a cost of about $60 each. The demand for these videos would be very high for about six weeks to three months, after which the demand would drop significantly. The second problem was to determine when and how many of the tapes to sell before the demand dropped to the level of non-hit videos. Once a hit video rental had peaked, Chad had learned that there was a fairly good market for used tapes for a short period of time and, if the tape was not sold during this time, he would end up with a tape that had very little rental demand and little resell value. Chad believed that he had solved the second problem by carefully watching the sales figures for the tapes. Analysis of this information helped to minimize his investment in tape inventory and marginally improved cash flow.

THE DILEMMA

Two years after Blockbuster had opened its store, Chad carefully analyzed the financial statements for Video Concepts—see Exhibits 1 and 2. The company was profitable and had been able to maintain revenues. Chad estimated that the arrival of Blockbuster had increased the demand for video rentals in Lexington to about $1,300,000 a year. He believed Blockbuster's share was about $700,000 a year and that the few remaining independents had around $100,000 a year in revenues.

Chad saw the current competitive situation as being fairly straightforward. Video Concepts had a store that was comparable to Blockbuster's in tape selection, personnel costs, and efficiency of operation. Video Concepts had a cost advantage in having lower store leasing costs ($3.50 per square foot versus $8.50) but Blockbuster had a bigger advantage in being able to use its purchasing power to purchase videotapes at a much lower cost. Video Concepts' major marketing strength was its lower rental price ($1.99 versus $3.00) but Blockbuster utilized a much larger advertising budget to attract customers. (All the Blockbuster stores in that region of North Carolina charged $3.50 rental except the one in Lexington.)

As had happened nationwide, the growth of video rental revenue leveled off in the

EXHIBIT 1 | **Video Concepts' Income Statement, 12 Months Ending June 30, 1993**

Revenues	$465,958
Cost of goods*	192,204
Gross profit	273,754
Expenses	
Salaries**	108,532
Payroll taxes	11,544
Utilities	20,443
Rent	23,028
Office expenses	26,717
Maintenance	6,205
Advertising expenses	4,290
Interest expenses	27,395
Total expenses	228,154
Income before taxes	45,600
Taxes	10,944
Net Income	$ 34,656

*Cost of goods = purchase price minus market value of tapes. This method is used because most of the tapes purchased are depreciated over a 12-month period.

**Salaries include Chad's salary of $15,000.

Lexington area starting in 1992. Nationwide in 1992, sales increased only 4.7 percent for Blockbuster stores that had been in operation more than one year. Future industry growth did not look bright as there were signs of market maturity and, more importantly, telecommunications companies were accelerating efforts to create an information superhighway to households using fiber optics technology that permitted in-home viewing of movies on a pay-per-view basis. This technology, however, was still in developmental stages and its spread to small towns was years away. Nonetheless, it was becoming more apparent every day that the long-term threat of fiber optics technology to render video rentals obsolete was real.

Looking to the future, Chad felt that for all his efforts, the net income from the Video Concepts operation would not provide him as high a return on his time and his capital as he had expected. He was still paying only the interest on his long-term loans, and current cash flows were not big enough to pay down his bank loans very quickly. Chad was considering several options. One alternative was to raise the price of an overnight rental to $2.49 to make the business more profitable; but Chad was afraid of what the consequences of such a move might be. He also was thinking about hiring someone to manage the business so that he could find another job for himself. He had had offers of corporate jobs in the past and was considering exploring this option again. Another alternative was to try to sell the business. As Chad pondered these alternatives, he tried to think of a solution that he might have overlooked. What he was sure of, however, was that he did not wish to keep working 12-hour days at a business that did not seem to have a bright future.

EXHIBIT 2 | **Video Concepts' Balance Sheet, 12 Months Ending June 30, 1993**

Assets	
Cash	$ 15,274
Inventory	4,162
Prepaid expenses	1,390
Total current assets	20,826
Office equipment	48,409
Furniture and fixtures	53,400
Videocassette tapes	303,131
Leasehold improvements	39,800
Accumulated depreciation*	(151,981)
Total assets	$313,585
Liabilities and Stockholders' Equity	
Accounts payable	$15,429
Sales taxes payable	2,415
Payroll taxes payable	3,270
Total current liabilities	21,114
Bank term loan	247,518
Common stock	20,800
Retained earnings	24,153
Total liabilities and equity	$313,585

*Includes the depreciation of tapes.

REFERENCES

"Blockbuster Idea Might Work for Computer Industry," *MacWeek,* May 24, 1993, p. 62.

"Blockbuster, IBM Plans Set Retailers Spinning," *Variety,* May 17, 1993, p. 117.

"Blockbuster Sizes Up PPV Potential: Talks Home Delivery with Bell Atlantic," *Billboard,* January 30, 1993, p. 11.

"Blockbuster Goes After a Bigger, Tougher Rep," *Variety,* January 25, 1993, p. 151.

"Changes in Distribution Landscape Have Players Scouting Claims," *Billboard,* May 16, 1993, p. 52.

"Oscar Noms Mean Gold for Video Industry," *Variety,* February 24, 1992, p. 79.

"Play It Again and Again Sam," *Newsweek,* December 16, 1991, p. 57.

"Recording Industry Hits Blockbuster," *Advertising Age,* May 17, 1993, p. 46.

"Record Store of Near Future: Computers Replace the Racks", *The New York Times,* May 12, 1993, p. A1.

"Stretching the Tape," *The New York Times,* April 22, 1993, p. B5.

"Video and Laser Hot Sheet," *Rolling Stone,* March 4, 1993, p. 72.

"VSDA Regaining Its Sense of Direction", *Variety,* June 8, 1992, p. 19.

RYKÄ, INC.: LIGHTWEIGHT ATHLETIC SHOES FOR WOMEN

Valerie J. Porciello, Bentley College
Alan N. Hoffman, Bentley College
Barbara Gottfried, Bentley College

Rykä has a great story to tell. We are the only athletic footwear company that is exclusively for women, by women, and now supporting women.

Sheri Poe

On the day after Christmas 1990, Sheri Poe, president and chief executive officer of Rykä, Inc., knew she was on the verge of the marketing break she'd been waiting for. During the past year, Poe had sent several free pairs of Rykä athletic shoes to Oprah Winfrey, and today Poe was featured as a successful female entrepreneur on Winfrey's popular talk show with a television viewing audience numbering in the 10s of millions—almost entirely women. Rykä's new line of Ultra-Lite aerobic shoes (see Exhibit 1) had just begun to penetrate the retail market. Poe could not have planned a better advertising spot than Winfrey tossing pairs of Rykä shoes into the studio audience exclaiming, "Can you believe how light these are?"

Indeed, after the Oprah broadcast, the Ultra-Lite line became an overnight success. Lady Footlocker immediately put the Ultra-Lite shoe line in 200 stores, up from the 50 that had been carrying Rykä's regular line of athletic shoes. Retailers received thousands of requests for Rykä products from consumers, and the sharp upturn in demand quickly exhausted the company's inventories. It took Rykä over three months to catch up with the orders. Industry analysts believed that the shot in the arm provided by the Ultra-Lite sales literally saved the company.

Rykä, Inc., designed, developed, and marketed athletic footwear for women, including aerobic, aerobic/step, cross-training, walk-run, and walking shoes. The company's products were sold all over the world in sporting goods stores, athletic-footwear specialty stores, and department stores.

The authors would like to thank Jeffrey Shuman, Holly Fowler, Maura Riley, Liliana Prado, Christine Forkus, and Mary Fandel for their valuable contributions to this case.

THE ULTIMATE LIGHTWEIGHT SHOE FOR THE ACTIVE WOMAN

Rykä shoes are made for top performance. You'll find that Rykä shoes will help you look good and feel great, no matter how demanding your fitness program.

Rykä shoes are designed, engineered, and manufactured by women for women. Because a woman's needs in a comfortable, attractive, high performance athletic shoe are different from a man's.

As you lace up for your first workout in your new Rykä shoes, you'll feel the difference. With every pair of Rykä shoes goes the positive energy of women who believe in other women.

Step forward with confidence, and be your best.

Sheri Poe

Sheri Poe
Founder and President

Specially designed for stepping, the RYKA STEP shoe has special flex channels placed in the forefoot providing the flexibility necessary for stepping while still maintaining excellent forefoot cushioning for aerobics.

Whether it's high impact, low impact, or step aerobics, RYKA's STEP shoes are superior in cushioning, shock absorption, stability and performance.

RYKA's STEP shoes are made with the highest performance midsole and outsole materials available - Nitorgen Ultra-Lite.

© 1994 RYKA, INC.

As a new entrant into the highly competitive athletic-footwear industry, an industry dominated by well-known giants with sales in the billions, the fledgling Rykä Corporation had had no choice but to rely on low-budget, guerrilla-marketing tactics such as the Oprah show appearance. After that time, however, Rykä marketing turned to radio and glossy magazine advertising. Rykä print ads appeared regularly in *City Sports, Shape, American Fitness, Elle,* and *IDEA Today,* magazines that particularly targeted women aged 21 to 35, who cared seriously not just about how they looked, but about physical fitness.

COMPANY BACKGROUND

Rykä was first organized in 1986 as ABE Corporation, but changed its name to Rykä in February 1987 when it commenced operations. The company was cofounded by Martin P. Birrittella and his wife, Sheri Poe. Prior to founding Rykä, Birrittella had worked at Matrix International Industries as a vice president of sales and marketing from 1980 to 1986. At Matrix he was responsible for developing and marketing footwear and health and fitness products, and had two patents pending for shoe designs that were assigned to Matrix. From 1982 to 1985, Sheri Poe was national sales manager for Matrix. She then moved to TMC Group, a $15-million giftware maker based in New Hampshire, where she was national accounts manager from May 1986 to June 1987.

Sheri Poe, Rykä's current president and chief executive officer, was one of only two female corporate CEOs in the state of Massachusetts. Poe, an exercise fanatic, admitted to really knowing nothing about making athletic shoes when she cofounded Rykä. In 1986 Poe had injured her back in an aerobics class and was convinced that the injury had been caused by her shoes, which had never fit properly. After an exhaustive search for footwear that would not cause her body stress, it occurred to Poe that many other women were probably having the same trouble she was finding a shoe that really fit, and she decided to start her own women's athletic-footwear company. As she conceived it, what would make Rykä distinctive was that rather than adapting men's athletic shoes for women, Rykä would design athletic shoes especially suited for women's feet and bodies. Rykä introduced its first two styles of athletic shoes in September 1987 and began shipping the shoes in March 1988.

Poe overcame considerable difficulty obtaining venture capital to finance Rykä's start-up. Potential investors questioned her ability to compete with industry leaders such as Nike and Reebok, given that she had no money and no retail experience. They turned down her requests for loans. Some of these same venture capitalists later called Poe to ask how they could get in on her $8 million business.

Since she couldn't get financing from venture capitalists, Poe mortgaged her own house and turned to family and friends to help finance the company. She also continued to search for willing investors and eventually discovered a Denver investment banker who agreed to do an initial public offering of common stock. Poe got a $250,000 bridge loan before the initial public offering—which happened to be about the time the stock market crashed in October 1987. Nevertheless, Rykä went public on April 15, 1988, and despite the unstable market, 4,000,000 shares in the company were sold at $1 per share in less than a week. The Denver firm completed a second offering before going out of business. Poe then turned to Paulson Capital Corporation in Oregon for a third offering in mid-1990.

SHERI POE

Sheri Poe believed that her status as Rykä's president inspired other women to buy the company's products. As she pointed out, "We're the only company that can tell women that the person running the company is a woman who works out every day." Poe's image and profile were the most critical components in Rykä's marketing strategy. Rather than using professional models, Rykä's print advertisements featured Poe working out; and in the company's recent venture into television advertising spots, Poe was the company spokesperson. The caption on a 1992 ad for Rykä's Series 900 aerobic shoe read, "Our president knows that if you huff and puff, jump up and down, and throw your weight around, you eventually get what you want." The ad evoked images of Poe's own determination to succeed, and endeavored to include her audience as co-conspirators who knew how hard it was for a woman to make it in the business world because they had "been there" themselves.

As part of Rykä's unique marketing strategy, Poe appeared on regional television and radio shows throughout the country and had been interviewed by numerous magazines and newspapers. Feature articles on Poe and Rykä had appeared in *Entrepreneurial Woman, Executive Female,* and *Working Woman.* Poe had successfully worked the female angle: she appealed to contemporary working women because, while being something of a celebrity, she came across as a down-to-earth woman who just happened to be a successful executive, and was a [divorced and now remarried] mother too. A *Boston Business Journal* article described her as a CEO whose title "does not cramp [her] style . . . she eschews power suits for miniskirts and jeans, drives herself to work, and lets calls from her kids interrupt her meetings."

THE ATHLETIC FOOTWEAR INDUSTRY

The $11-billion athletic-footwear industry was highly competitive. Three major firms dominated the market: Nike, Reebok, and L.A. Gear. Second-tier competitors included Adidas, Avia, Asics, and Converse. All these companies had greater financial strength and more resources than Rykä. While Rykä's sales were $12.1 million in 1992, Nike's were $3.4 billion, Reebok's $3.0 billion, and L.A. Gear's $430 million.

In 1987, the industry as a whole grew at a rate of 20 percent; but by 1991 the annual growth rate in sales had shrunk to approximately 4 percent. The athletic-footwear market was considered a mature market in 1993. Despite the subdued growth characteristics of the overall industry, however, a number of segments were rapidly expanding because of high specialization, technological innovation, and image and fashion appeal.

PRODUCT SPECIALIZATION

The athletic footwear industry was divided into various submarkets by end-use specialization: basketball, tennis, running, aerobic, cross-training, walking, and so on. Rykä competed in only three segments: aerobic, walking, and cross-training shoes.

Aerobic Segment   The aerobic segment of the athletic-shoe industry accounted for approximately $500 million in annual sales. Reebok pioneered the segment and continued to be the industry leader. The market was primarily made up of women and had grown rapidly in recent years. Rykä's number one market was aerobics; in 1991, 80 percent of Rykä's sales came from the Ultra-Lite and step aerobic lines.

Walking Segment   The second major market Rykä competed in was the walking segment. This high-growth market was the fourth largest product category in the athletic shoe industry. In 1991, 70 million people walked for exercise and sales reached $1.7 billion. Reebok led this segment and was concentrating its marketing efforts on young women. Nevertheless, while the male and younger female walking markets had experienced some growth, the walking segment was primarily focused on women 45 to 55 years old. Ten percent of Rykä's sales came from its Series 500 walking shoe and the company expected the walking shoe segment to be its greatest growth category.

Cross-Training Segment   Ryka also competed in the cross-training segment of the athletic-shoe market. Cross-training shoes were popular because they could be used for a variety of activities. Nike created this segment, and maintained the lead in market share. Overall sales for the segment were currently at $1.2 billion and growth was strong. Rykä derived 10 percent of its revenues from cross-training shoes.

TECHNOLOGICAL INNOVATION

Reebok and Nike were fast moving toward the goal of being identified as the most technologically advanced producers of performance shoes. Rykä understood that it had to keep up with research and development to survive. In October 1988, Ryka introduced its nitrogen footwear system, Nitrogen/ES (the ES stood for Energy Spheres). The system was developed over a two-year period by a design team with over 35 patents in shoe design and state-of-the-art composite plastics. The ES ambient air compression spheres contained nitrogen microballoons that provided significantly more energy return than the systems of any of Rykä's major competitors. Consumer response to the Nitrogen/ES shoe was overwhelming, and in 1989 Rykä discontinued sales of a number of models that did not include this special feature. Two patents were filed for the Nitrogen/ES System. One had been granted; the other was pending. Rykä was concerned that it would be easy for Reebok or Nike to adopt Rykä's technology with little risk of an infringement suit. Rykä's limited financial resources would make it burdensome to enforce its rights in a lengthy court battle.

FASHION

Rykä had focused on performance rather than fashion because Poe believed that fashion-athletic footwear was susceptible to trends and to the economy whereas the demand for performance shoes was based on the ongoing need of women to protect their physical well-being. Nevertheless, a large segment of athletic-footwear consumers purchased footwear products based on looks rather than function. In fact, fashion and styling trends were a mainstay among Rykä's major competitors, especially Reebok, the originator of the fashion aerobic-shoe market; 80 to 90 percent of fashion aerobic-shoe buyers did not participate in aerobics but wore the shoes for casual use and other recreational purposes.

Although Rykä shoes were as technologically advanced as Reebok, Nike, or L.A. Gear's, they were often overlooked by fashion-conscious footwear shoppers unfamiliar with the Rykä name. Despite the fact that Rykä's sales had grown even during the most recent economic downturn, many retail shoe dealers didn't carry Rykä shoes, opting instead to stock brands that were well known and widely advertised. The lack of a nationally recognized name was a serious market obstacle for any footwear company. All manufacturers of branded footwear products, including Rykä, spent a substantial fraction of their revenues for advertising campaigns and marketing initiatives to expand their dealer networks and get their names before prospective buyers.

A ROCKY START AND A NEW DIRECTION

Given the saturation of the athletic-footwear market, athletic-shoe companies had to have more than a good product to stay alive; they needed to pull customers to their products with advertising and celebrity endorsements and to push their brands through retail outlets, most of which stocked several brands. Rykä concentrated much of its energies on marketing. As a new manufacturer in an already crowded industry, Poe understood the possibility of being marketed right out of business by big competitors like Nike and Reebok with millions to spend on advertising and marketing. Rykä's approach was to offer similar products, but focus on the most cost-effective ways to reach its narrow target market, thus carving out a niche that the industry leaders wouldn't see as worth their time and attention.

Sheri Poe had learned the importance of focusing on a vacant market niche the hard way. When the company was first founded, it tried unsuccessfully to challenge the brand name manufacturers in all product categories, including running, tennis, aerobics, walking, and cross-training shoes. However, given its limited capital and the huge advertising budgets of Reebok, Nike, and L.A. Gear, Rykä quickly learned it could not compete in all these different markets at once. Rykä cut back on its product line and began to focus primarily on aerobic shoes and secondarily on walking shoes. Equally important, it decided to design shoes especially for women who wanted a lightweight, high-performance shoe that was attractive, comfortable, and well-suited for exercise and physical fitness programs. Poe did not believe that Rykä had to become an industry giant to succeed.

In the already crowded athletic-footwear industry, the various competitors were continually jockeying for a better market position and a competitive edge. Currently, athletic footwear for women was the fastest growing segment of the athletic-footwear market. Women's athletic footwear accounted for 55 percent of Reebok's sales, 60 percent of Avia's sales, 45 percent of L.A. Gear's sales, and 17 percent of Nike's $2.2 billion in domestic sales. In recent years, Reebok and Nike had fought for the number one spot in the women's market; so far, Reebok had prevailed, but in each of the past two years, Nike had posted 30 percent growth in its sales of women's shoes. Continued growth in the women's athletic-footwear market was the most important trend in the sporting goods industry in 1993 and it was on this segment that Rykä had staked its future. Rykä believed it was taking the product in a truly new direction.

Rykä strategy was to design and manufacture shoes specifically for women, while the women's shoe lines of the big-name shoe companies were typically smaller sizes of men's shoes made on men's lasts. Ryka had developed a fitness shoe crafted specifically for women's feet that incorporated a patented design for better shock absorption and durability. None of the other companies in the athletic-shoe industry could boast of having designed their shoes exclusively for the physical characteristics and needs of women; all other contenders had broader lines or different target markets. However, it was the Ultra-Lite mid-sole, Rykä's most significant and successful product advancement, that put Rykä on a par with or perhaps ahead of competitors in terms of product attributes. The Rykä Ultra-Lite aerobics shoe weighed 7.7 ounces, roughly 30 percent of the weight of a regular aerobic shoe. Within two months of its introduction in December 1990 (and Poe's appearance on Oprah), the company had sold all its Ultra-Lites (the suggested retail price was $70 a pair). It took Rykä three months to begin filling additional shoe orders from retailers; this created concerns that Rykä might not be able to capitalize on the success of its new line. Both Nike and Reebok quickly came out with a line of lightweight aerobic shoes. Despite the competition, however, Rykä's Ultra-Lite line continued to attract buyers, accounting for close to 90 percent of its $8.8 million in gross sales for 1991.

Having established a sales base and clientele in the aerobics category, Rykä sought to further differentiate its products from competitors. Its current product line included a Series 900 aerobic/step shoe, a Series 700 aerobic shoe, a Series 800 cross-training shoe, and a Series 500 walking shoe. To make sure its shoe designs were not perceived as too specialized, Rykä had developed the Aerobic Step 50/50 model and a lightweight version of it, the Step-Lite 50/50 model; these two product versions could be worn for both high-impact and step aerobics. Included in the Series 500 walking shoe line was a dual purpose walk/run shoe, the 570, for women who complemented their walking routine with running, but didn't want to buy different shoes for each separate activity. Rykä was considering a special new series for people with foot problems or back problems because an increasing number of podiatrists and chiropractors were recommending Rykä walking shoes to their patients.

THE RYKÄ ROSE FOUNDATION

The Rykä ROSE (Regaining One's Self-Esteem) Foundation was a not-for-profit organization created by Sheri Poe to help women who had been the victims of violent crimes. The foundation was launched in September 1992, and Poe herself personally pledged $250,000. Poe founded the ROSE Foundation because she was raped at age 19. The trauma resulting from the rape led to further suffering from bulimia. She saw herself as a survivor who needed to do something to help fellow victims. "For me, having a company that just made a product was not enough. I wanted to do something more."

Rykä had made a commitment to donate 7% of its pre-tax profits to the foundation and to sponsor special fundraising events to help strengthen community prevention and treatment programs for women who were victims of violent crimes. Rykä included information on the foundation in brochures that were packaged with each box of shoes. For Poe, this was more than a marketing ploy to win customers' approval of the company's social conscience and boost their loyalty to the company's products. She considered Rykä's financial commitment to the ROSE Foundation a natural extension of the company's commitment to women.

The foundation had created alliances with health clubs, nonprofit organizations, and corporations in an effort to reach women directly with educational materials and programs. In addition, the ROSE Foundation funded a $25,000 grants program to encourage organizations to develop creative solutions to the widespread problem of violence against women. One of the foundation's beneficiaries, the National Victim Center, received an award of $10,000 to set up a toll-free (800) telephone number for victims and their families through which they could obtain immediate information, referrals, and other types of assistance.

Poe hoped that the foundation would act as a catalyst for coalition-building to help stop violence against women. But she also saw the foundation as a means of involving retailers in marketing socially responsible programs directly to women. Lady

Foot Locker was the first retailer to join forces with the ROSE Foundation. In October 1993, Lady Foot Locker conducted a two-week promotional campaign in its 550 U.S. stores, distributing free education brochures and holding a special sweepstakes contest to raise awareness about violence against women. Customer response was overwhelmingly positive, and Lady Foot Locker was considering a future partnership with the ROSE Foundation. Foot Locker, Champs, and Athletic X-press had also expressed interest in the foundation. MVP Sports, a New England retailer that operated eight stores in the New England area, had recently sponsored a two-week information-based campaign featuring Sheri Poe that included radio, TV, and newspaper advertisements. Doug Barron, president of MVP Sports, was so impressed with the concept and progressive thinking of the Rykä ROSE Foundation that he decided his company would donate $2 to the foundation for each pair of Rykä athletic shoes sold during the 1992 holiday season.

Poe considered Rykä and its foundation unique. As she saw it, the company had a great story to tell. Not only was it the only athletic-footwear company that was exclusively for women, it supported women. It was "the first athletic shoe with a soul." She believed that the foundation would appeal to Rykä customers who appreciated the idea that their buying power was helping less fortunate women. But Poe's choice to make Rykä a socially responsible company right from the beginning did not enjoy unanimous approval. Critics had suggested that Rykä would be better off funneling any extra cash back into the company until it was financially strong and well established in the marketplace. Supporters, however, claimed that the reputation Rykä had garnered as an ethical company, one as concerned about social issues as about the bottom line, effectively appealed to socially concerned women consumers; they argued that the ROSE Foundation was worth in good press whatever it cost the company in actual dollars, because the company had effectively carved out a niche that spoke on many different levels to both women's societal concerns and their lifestyles.

MARKETING

Rykä's promotional strategy was aimed at creating both brand awareness and sales at the retail level. In 1988, Rykä entered into a six-figure, eight-year licensing agreement with the U.S. Ski Team that permitted Rykä to market its products as the team's official training shoes. Also in 1988, the American Aerobics Association International boosted Rykä's brand name recognition when it chose Rykä to replace Avia as the association's preferred brand of aerobics shoes. In 1989 *Shape* magazine named Rykä number one in its aerobic shoe category.

Most recently, Rykä had begun sponsoring aerobics teams and aerobics competitions. In July 1992, 25 countries competed in the World Aerobic championships in Las Vegas, Nevada; the Canadian team was sponsored by Rykä Athletic Footwear. In September 1992, Rykä was the premier sponsor and the official shoe of the Canadian National Aerobic championship held in Vancouver, B.C. To ensure the success of the event and build awareness for the sport of competitive aerobics, Rykä successfully promoted the Canadian nationals through retailers, athletic clubs, and individuals. Given that virtually every previous aerobics competition worldwide had been sponsored by Reebok, Canada's selection of Rykä as official sponsor was a significant milestone for Rykä, as well as marking Rykä's international recognition as a core brand in the women's athletic market.

THE RYKÄ TRAINING BODY

Early on, Sheri Poe determined that the most effective way to reach the female aerobics niche was by promoting Rykä shoes to aerobics instructors. Rykä spent almost as much as the industry leaders on print advertisements in aerobics instructors' magazines, and very little on print advertising elsewhere. Unlike its big competitors, Rykä did not use celebrity endorsements to sell its products; the company's marketing theory was that women cared more about what felt good on their feet than about what any particular celebrity had to say.

Beyond advertising in aerobics magazines, Rykä had successfully used direct-mail marketing techniques to convince aerobics instructors to become participants in the Rykä Training Body. In 1993 this group comprised more than 40,000 women employed as fitness instructors and personal trainers throughout the country. They were sent Rykä product information four to six times per year and given discounts on Rykä shoes. Rykä also had a group of these instructors tied in with designated local retailers; the role of these instructors was to direct students to those retailers, who then offered discounts on Rykä shoes to the students. From time to time, Rykä-affiliated instructors put on demonstrations to educate consumers about what to look for in an aerobics shoe.

In addition to increasing sales and promoting the Rykä name, the relationship between Rykä and the aerobics profession had led to significant product design innovations. Aerobic instructors' suggestions, based on their own experience as well as on feedback from students in their classes, had led to such improvements as more effective cushioning and better arch support. Also, instructor feedback helped Rykä become the first manufacturer to respond to the new step-aerobics trend by developing and marketing lightweight shoes specifically designed to support up-and-down step motions.

DEALER RELATIONS, PROMOTIONS, AND ADVERTISING

Rykä's marketing efforts were also aimed at the retail dealers who sold Rykä products. In Rykä's early days, Poe and her advertising manager, Laurie Ruddy, personally visited retail stores to meet salespeople and sell them on Rykä products. In 1993, the vice president of sales and marketing had responsibility for maintaining contact with retailers and developing incentive programs, giveaways, and small monetary bonuses to keep salespeople excited. The company also provided premiums, such as fanny packs or water bottles, for customers.

Given the highly competitive nature of the athletic-footwear industry, Rykä management believed effective advertising was crucial in promoting the features of Rykä shoes and creating buyer preference for the Rykä brand. As a two-year old company in 1989, Rykä had found itself strapped for cash to invest in promotional efforts to penetrate the athletic-shoe market; its $3.5 million loss that year was largely attributable to advertising expenditures of approximately $2.5 million—an amount that was huge for Rykä but small compared to the more than $100 million spent on advertising during the same period by the combination of Nike, Reebok, and L.A. Gear.

Recently, Rykä had begun to advertise beyond trade publications. Because of ads appearing in *Shape, City Sports, American Fitness, ELLE,* and *Idea Today* magazines in 1993, Rykä's brand recognition was considerably higher, even though Rykä's advertising and marketing budget was only about nine percent of sales. However, Poe attributed Rykä's marketing success primarily to its direct marketing techniques, especially its targeting of certified aerobic instructors to wear Rykä shoes. In October

1992, after three successive quarters of record sales and little profitability, Poe announced that Rykä was going to expand its direct marketing to consumers, even if it required increased spending to penetrate the marketplace beyond aerobics instructors. At the time, Rykä's total advertising budget was approximately $1.5 million. By way of comparison, Nike had spent $20 million on a 1991 pan-European campaign to launch a single new model and Reebok was in the midst of a $28 million ad campaign that specifically targeted women.

OPERATIONS

As was common in the athletic-footwear industry, Rykä shoes were made by independent manufacturers in Europe and the Far East, including South Korea and Taiwan, according to Rykä product specifications. Rykä's troubles in its first three years were made the worse by the poor quality of products provided by its manufacturer in Taiwan. By 1992–93, however, the shoes were being sourced from Korean manufacturers and strict quality-control measures were in effect. The company relied on a Far Eastern buying agent, under Rykä's direction, for the selection of suppliers, inspection of goods prior to shipment, and shipment of finished goods.

Rykä's management believed that outsourcing its footwear products minimized company investment in fixed assets and lowered costs and business risk. Because there was underutilized factory manufacturing capacity in countries outside South Korea and Taiwan, Rykä's management believed that alternative sources of product manufacturing were readily available should the company need them. Because of volatile exchange rates, the potential for trade disputes and tariff adjustments, the risks of foreign political upheaval, and a strong desire to avoid heavy dependence on one supplier, Rykä preferred to remain free of any long-term contract with manufacturers, relying instead on short-term purchases. Orders were placed on a volume basis through its agent and Rykä received finished products within 120 days of an order. When necessary, Rykä paid a premium to reduce the time required to deliver finished goods from the factory to meet customer demand.

The principal raw materials in Rykä shoes were leather, rubber, ethylvinyl acetate, polyurethane, cambrelle, and pigskin, all of which were readily obtainable from numerous suppliers in the United States and abroad. Nevertheless, even though Rykä or its contract manufacturers could locate new sources of raw materials within a relatively short period of time if needed, Rykä's outsourcing strategy of placing orders as needed with whichever contract manufacturers had the best price made it vulnerable to any unexpected difficulties in manufacturing or shipment. Rykä did not maintain large stockpiles of inventory to buffer any delays in deliveries from producers.

DISTRIBUTION

Rykä products were sold in sporting goods stores, athletic footwear stores, selected high-end department stores (Nordstrom's), and sport-specialty retailers including Foot Locker, Lady Foot Locker, Athlete's Foot Store, Foot Action, U.S. Athletics, and Oshman's.

Rykä's biggest retail dealer was Lady Foot Locker, which had 476 stores in the United States and 250 stores in Canada. In November 1992, Rykä announced that starting in early 1993, 400 Lady Foot Locker stores would display permanent Rykä signage, identifying Rykä as a brand especially promoted by Foot Locker. During the spring of 1992, FOOTACTION USA, a division of the Melville Corporation, and the second largest specialty-footwear retailer in the country, began selling Rykä athletic shoes on a trial basis in 40 stores. The trial was so successful that FOOTACTION agreed to purchase five styles of Rykä shoes for its stores; in September 1992, Rykä announced that 150 FOOTACTION stores would begin to carry its products nationally.

In late 1992, Rykä received orders from three large retail sporting goods chains, adding well over 200 store outlets to its distribution network. The 12th largest sporting goods retailer in the country, MC Sporting Goods, based in Grand Rapids, Michigan, decided to carry five styles of Rykä athletic shoes in each of its 73 stores. Tampa-based Sports and Recreation started selling four styles of Rykä athletic shoes in its 23 sporting goods stores; Charlie Burks, head footwear buyer for Sports and Recreation, based his decision to stock Rykä shoes on his belief that the chain's customers were looking for new, exciting styles of athletic shoes at affordable prices and that Rykä delivered on performance, fashion, and value. Athletic Express, with 135 stores, was Rykä's third new account.

In 1989, Lady Foot Locker and Foot Locker retailers accounted for 13 percent of Rykä's net sales. As of 1993, Rykä had expanded its dealer base to the point where no single retail chain or group under common control accounted for more than 10 percent of its total revenue.

KEY PERSONNEL

When Rykä was in its initial start-up mode, Sheri Poe used industry-standard salaries, stock options, and the opportunity for significant input into the day-to-day operations of the company to attract four top executives from Reebok for positions in sales, advertising, and public relations. Even though the new executive team was able to double sales between Rykä's first and second years, the compensation burden for four high-powered executives was too much for the young company. Three of the four Reebok veterans had since left the company. In 1988, Rykä had only 4 employees. In 1993, Rykä employed 22 people at its Norwood headquarters and 35 sales representatives across the country. Rykä's small size permitted agility and flexibility, enabling the company to implement changes quickly. The company's outsourcing strategy allowed it to get new designs into stores fast, sometimes within 120 days, and to respond promptly to increases or decreases in the sales of particular models.

In November 1992, Rykä appointed Roy S. Kelvin, a former New York investment banker, to be vice president and chief financial officer. Poe expected Kelvin's background would be valuable in helping Rykä raise capital to finance the company's growing operating requirements. Some people also believed Kelvin's appointment was an acknowledgment on Poe's part that Rykä was competing for funds in an old boys' network and that it was extremely valuable to have a former member of the network to make contacts with the investment community and give the company financial credibility. Kelvin's other priorities were to find ways to trim operating expenses and improve profit margins.

FINANCIAL INFORMATION

So far Rykä had financed its operations principally through public stock offerings, warrants to purchase additional common shares, and private sales of its common stock; the company had netted approximately $7.2 million from stock sales. As of

EXHIBIT 2 | **Rykä's Stock Price Performance, 1991–92**

Calendar Period	1992		1991	
	High	Low	High	Low
First quarter	$2.31	$0.53	$1.06	$0.22
Second quarter	2.44	1.19	0.87	0.50
Third quarter	1.69	1.19	0.90	0.56
Fourth quarter	1.89	0.97	0.78	0.56

Note: Rykä's common stock was traded on NASDAQ.

The company did not pay dividends to its stockholders and did not plan to pay dividends in the forseeable future.

Source: 1992 annual report.

mid-1992, private investors owned 65 percent of Rykä's common stock and Sheri Poe controlled most of the remaining 35 percent. In September 1992, the company was engaged in raising additional financial capital. Rykä had extended the date for redemption of its outstanding common stock purchase warrants issued in the company's 1990 public offering another two weeks. Poe was very pleased with the response to the warrant solicitation and agreed to the extension to allow the maximum number of shareholders to exercise their warrants. If all public and underwriter warrants were exercised, the company expected to receive approximately $6.3 million in gross proceeds. Stock price data is shown in Exhibit 2. Exhibits 3 and 4 present recent financial data.

In 1991, Rykä had negotiated an agreement with its Korean trading company to increase its line of credit from $2.5 million to $3.5 million. Additional working capital was available from a letter of credit financing agreement and an accounts receivable line of credit.

Rykä's product costs were higher than those of larger companies for several reasons. Rykä's small sales volumes (under 500,000 pairs annually) made it difficult to take advantage of volume production discounts offered by contract manufacturers. Moreover, the company had opted to pay somewhat higher prices for its products in order to achieve and maintain higher quality. Also, Rykä's inventory financing arrangement with its Korean trading company included financing costs, commissions, and fees, adding further to Rykä's overall cost per pair.

THE FUTURE

While Sheri Poe was proud of what Rykä had accomplished over the past six years, she knew the company's market position was far from secure. Competition in athletic footwear was fierce. Nike and Reebok were formidable rivals. For Rykä to be successful over the long term, the company would need both a sound strategy and ample capital.

REFERENCES

Colter, Gene. "On Target: Athletics Shoes Just for Women; Women's Awareness of Athletic Shoes; Special Super Show Athletics Issue." *Footwear News,* Feb 18, 1991.

Dutter, Greg. "Making Strides." *Sporting Goods Business,* March 1992, p. 34.

EXHIBIT 3 | **Financial Summary for Rykä, Inc., 1991–92**

	Year Ended December 31		Percent Change
	1992	1991 (1)	
Gross sales	$13,329,777	$8,838,911	50.8%
Discounts, returns, and allowances	1,136,134	860,986	32.0
Net sales	12,193,643	7,977,925	52.8
Cost of goods sold	8,867,375	5,231,346	69.5
Gross profit	3,326,268	2,746,579	21.1
Operating expenses			
General and administrative	1,239,245 (2)	1,287,925	-3.8
Marketing	1,722,618	1,396,769	23.3
Research and development	148,958	155,576	-4.3
Total operating expenses	3,110,821	2,840,270	9.5
Operating income (loss)	215,447	(93,691)	
Other (income) expense:			
Interest expense	516,455	418,469	23.4
Interest income	(4,196)	(12,648)	-66.8
Total other (income) expense	512,259	405,821	26.2
Net loss	$ (296,812)	$ (499,512)	-40.6
Net loss per share	($0.01)	($0.03)	
Weighted average shares outstanding	19,847,283	18,110,923	
Cash and cash equivalents	$ 1,029,161	$ 166,030	519.9%
Current assets	8,199,411	4,367,255	87.7
Total assets	8,306,262	4,498,021	84.7
Current liabilities	4,134,974	3,623,668	14.1
Stockholders' equity	4,153,410	834,902	397.5

Note 1: To provide comparability with the current year presentation, $410,000 of 1991 product financing expenses has been reclassified from cost of goods sold to interest expense.

Note 2: General and administrative expense includes a charge of $138,000 for reserves against a receivable relating to the liquidation of the company's licensed distributor in the U.K.

Source: Company annual report.

Fucini, Suzy. "A Women's Game: Women Have Become the Hottest Focus of Today's Marketing." *Sporting Goods Dealer,* Aug. 1992, p. 34.

Goodman, Doug. "Reebok Chief Looks Beyond Nike." *Advertising Age,* January 29, 1990, p. 57.

Grimm, Matthew. "Nike Targets Women with Print Campaign." *Adweek's Marketing Week,* Dec. 10, 1990, p. 12.

Hower, Wendy. "Gender Gap: The Executive Suite is Still Wilderness for Women." *Boston Business Journal,* July 27, 1992, sec2 p. 5.

Kelly, Craig T. "Fashion Sells Aerobics Shoes." January 1990, p. 39.

Lee, Sharon; McAllister, Robert; Rooney, Ellen; Tedeschi, Mark. "Community Ties Nourish Growth of Aerobic Sales; Aerobic Programs Boost Sales of Aerobic Shoes." *Footwear News,* Oct. 7, 1991, p. 17.

Magiera, Marcy. "Nike Again Registers No. 1 Performance." *Advertising Age,* May 7, 1990, p. 4.

Magiera, Marcy. "Nike Again Registers No. 1 Performance," *Advertising Age,* January 29, 1990, p. 16.

E X H I B I T 4 | **Rykä's Financial Performance, 1988–92**

	Year Ended December 31				
	1992	**1991**	**1990**	**1989**	**1988**
Statement of Operations Data					
Net sales	$12,193,643	$7,977,925	$ 4,701,538	$ 4,916,542	$991,684
Gross profit before inventory write-down	3,326,268	2,746,579	1,013,445	1,364,340	308,901
Inventory write-down to lower of cost or market			906,557		
Gross profit	3,326,288	2,746,579	106,888	1,364,340	308,901
Costs and expenses	3,110,821	2,840,270	3,598,728	4,368,774	1,687,806
Operating income (loss)	215,447	(93,691)	(3,491,840)	(3,004,434)	(1,378,905)
Interest expense, net	512,260	405,821	218,817	548,149	148,485
Expenses incurred in connection with termination of merger agreement			377,855		
Net loss	$ (296,813)	$ (499,512)	$(4,088,512)	$(3,522,583)	$(1,527,390)
Net loss per share	$(0.01)	$(0.03)	$(0.27)	$(0.31)	$(0.16)
Weighted average shares outstanding	19,847,283	18,110,923	15,336,074	11,616,088	9,397,360
Number of common shares outstanding	23,101,948	18,136,142	18,005,142	13,242,500	10,252,500
Balance Sheet Data					
Total assets	$ 8,319,229	$4,498,021	$2,711,713	$3,553,000	$2,073,058
Total debt	410,673	68,258	88,149	974,521	247,340
Net working capital	4,077,404	743,587	1,097,827	1,643,352	1,140,173
Stockholders' equity	4,166,377	834,902	1,299,264	1,848,059	1,341,858

Source: Company annual report.

"New England Retailer Joins Rykä in Fight Against Domestic Violence." *Business Wire,* Nov 13, 1990.

"Nike Takes Reebok's Edge; Advertising Expenditures of Top Sports Shoes Manufacturers." Nexis "mrktng," April 16, 1992, p. 10.

Poe, Sheri. "To Compete with Giants, Choose Your Niche." *Nation's Business,* July 1992, p. 6.

Powell, Robert J. "Ryka Is Off and Running." *Boston Business Journal,* Feb. 29, 1988, p. 3.

"Rykä Adds 100 Stores to Distribution Network." *Business Wire,* Nov. 3, 1992.

"Rykä Announces Extension for Warrant Redemption." *Business Wire,* Sept. 11, 1992.

"Rykä Announces Record First Quarter 1991 Results." *Business Wire,* April 24, 1991.

"Rykä Completes $4.7 Million Offering." *Business Wire,* July 24, 1990.

"Rykä Introduces New Nitrogen System." *Business Wire,* Oct. 20, 1988.

"Rykä Launches ROSE Foundation to Help Stop Violence Against Women." Rykä, Inc., News Release, Sept. 28, 1992.

Rykä 1991 in Review, Annual Report, Rykä, Inc.

"A Rykä Rose: Sheri Poe on Career, Family, and Purpose." *Sporting Goods Dealer,* Sept. 1992.

"Rykä to expand its presence in Foot Locker Stores," *Business Wire,* Jun 4, 1992.

"Rykä Vaults to $8M in Its Lightweight Sneaks." *Boston Business Journal,* March 30, 1992, p. 9.

Simon, Ruth. "The No-P/E stocks." *Forbes,* Oct. 2, 1989, p. 40.

Touby, Laurel Allison. "Creativity vs. Cash." *Working Woman,* Nov. 1991, p. 73.

Witt, Louise. "Rykä Turns to Aerobics for Toehold in Market," *Boston Business Journal,* April 1, 1991, p. 6.

Wolfensberger, Beth. "Shoe Marketers Have Itch to Enter Niche Markets." *Boston Business Journal,* March 19, 1990, p. 7.

THE WORLD AUTOMOTIVE INDUSTRY IN 1994

Arthur A. Thompson, Jr., The University of Alabama
John E. Gamble, Auburn University at Montgomery

In 1994, there were more than 150 motor vehicle companies in the world producing roughly 50 million passenger cars, vans, light trucks, heavy-duty trucks, buses, and assorted other commercial vehicles annually. Motor vehicle production was the world's biggest industrial activity, accounting for 2 percent of total world output and $825 to $875 billion in revenues. Motor vehicle producers ranged from obscure Third World companies making less than 50,000 vehicles for their own home country market to such well-known global competitors as General Motors, Toyota, Ford, Nissan, Honda, and Volkswagen-Audi that produced millions of vehicles and that had a presence in most of the world's major geographic markets. The 30 largest manufacturers (see Exhibit 1) accounted for over 90 percent of total production in 1992. Competition was fierce among the major U.S., European, and Japanese producers, with three Korean companies positioning themselves to join the fray.

THE INDUSTRY CLIMATE

For the past 20 years, Japanese automakers had reigned as the acknowledged masters of high-quality, low-cost manufacture. Until the 1980s, the Japanese automakers' strategy was to build world-scale production facilities in Japan, take advantage of Japanese trade restrictions to capture their own growing home market at very profitable prices, and then export the balance of their production to world markets at aggressive prices calculated to gain market share over the long term. Starting in the 1980s, the Japanese companies had expanded their strategy to include building production bases in North America and Europe and adding luxury cars, minivans, trucks, and sports-utility vehicles to their traditional small-vehicle lineup. Led by Toyota, Nissan, and Honda, Japanese producers in 1994 were engaged in building strong competitive positions in all major geographic markets and had a collective strategic

Copyright © 1994 by Arthur A. Thompson, Jr.

EXHIBIT 1 | **The World 30 Largest Motor Vehicle Producers, 1992**

Rank by units produced 1992	Maker/Country	Major Nameplates	1992 Units Produced		1992 Revenues		1992 Profits	
			Thousands	% change from 1991	$ Millions	% change from 1991	$ Millions	% change from 1991
1	General Motors (U.S.)	Chevrolet, Buick, Opel, Pontiac, Oldsmobile, Cadillac, Saturn, GMC	7,146	1.9%	$132,775	7.3%	($23,498)	—
2	Ford Motor (U.S.)	Ford, Lincoln, Jaguar, Mercury	5,764	7.6%	$100,786	13.3%	($7,385)	—
3	Toyota Motor (Japan)[1]	Toyota, Lexus	4,249	(2.2%)	$79,114	1.3%	$1,813	(42.4%)
4	Volkswagen (Germany)	Volkswagen, Audi, SEAT	3,500	8.1%	$56,734	23.2%	$50	(92.5%)
5	Nissan Motor (Japan)[2]	Nissan, Infiniti	2,963	(4.0%)	$50,248	2.8%	($449)	(159.0%)[4]
6	Chrysler (U.S.)	Plymouth, Dodge, Chrysler, Jeep, Eagle	2,175	16.6%	$36,897	25.6%	$723	—
7	Peugeot (France)	Peugeot, Citroën, Talbot	2,050	(0.6%)	$29,387	3.5%	$637	(35.0%)
8	Renault (France)	Renault	2,042	14.0%	$33,885	15.1%	$1,073	96.5%
9	Honda Motor (Japan)[2]	Honda, Acura	1,852	(7.2%)	$33,370	0.9%	$307	(37.0%)
10	Mitsubishi Motors (Japan)[2]	Mitsubishi	1,832	(1.1%)	$25,482	8.2%	$207	(6.6%)
11	Fiat (Italy)	Fiat, Lancia, Alfa Romeo	1,830	6.8%	$47,929	2.4%	$447	(50.3%)
12	Suzuki Motor (Japan)[2]	Suzuki	1,381	1.0%	$10,153	6.3%	$153	2.7%
13	Mazda Motor (Japan)[2]	Mazda	1,248	(9.6%)	$20,867	1.5%	$10	(85.3%)
14	Daihatsu Motor (Japan)[2]	Daihatsu	836	(5.4%)	$7,043	6.3%	($35)	(297.4%)[4]
15	Hyundai Motor (South Korea)	Hyundai	702	9.5%	$8,606	2.6%	$62	(17.9%)
16	VAZ (Volzhky) (Russia)	Lada, Zhiguli	674[E]	(0.1%)	N.A.	—	N.A.	—
17	Fuji Heavy Industries (Japan)[2]	Subaru	648	1.9%	$8,460	7.2%	($218)	—
18	BMW (Germany)	BMW	598	8.1%	$20,611	11.2%	$465	0.8%
19	Daimler-Benz (Germany)	Mercedes-Benz	529	(8.5%)	$63,340	10.5%	$929	(17.8%)
20	Kia Motors (South Korea)	Kia	479	20.0%	$4,385	11.8%	$19	(11.0%)
21	Isuzu Motors (Japan)[3]	Isuzu	473	0.4%	$12,459	9.1%	($227)	—
22	British Aerospace (Britain)	Rover, Land Rover	405	(3.6%)	$17,839	(6.0%)	($1,567)	—
23	Volvo (Sweden)	Volvo	304	9.3%	$14,921	11.5%	($792)	(687.0%)[4]
24	Daewoo (South Korea)	Daewoo	283	39.4%	$28,334	11.7%	$384	—
25	FSM (Poland)	Fiat 126, Cinquecento	143[E]	10.8%	N.A.	—	N.A.	—
26	Tofas (Turkey)	Tofas	142	32.5%	$1,103	12.7%	$134	277.1%
27	ZAZ (Zaporojetz) (Ukraine)	Tavria	133[E]	(4.3%)	N.A.	—	N.A.	—
28	Maruti Udyog (India)[2]	Zen, Omni, Gypsy	128	5.8%	$761	(6.3%)	$13	7.2%
29	Proton (Malaysia)[2]	Saga	103	(1.9%)	$900	12.1%	$104	9.5%
30	AZLK (Moskovsky) (Russia)	Moskvitch	102[E]	(2.9%)	N.A.	—	N.A.	—

*Revenues and profits represent figures for entire corporation, not just auto business. N.A. Not available. [E]Estimate. [1]Figures are for fiscal year ended June 30, 1992. [2]Fiscal year ended March 31, 1993. [3]Fiscal year ended October 31, 1992. [4]Percentage decrease in excess of 100% represents a swing from profit to loss.
Source: *Fortune*, October 4, 1993, p. 74.

strategic intent to globally dominate the industry. Going into 1994, the Japanese makers of cars and trucks commanded market shares of 96 percent in Japan, 22 percent in North America, 12 percent in Western Europe, 55 percent in Australia and New Zealand, 30 percent in South Africa, 53 percent in Taiwan, and 10 percent in South Korea. Japanese companies were also a factor in the car and truck markets of Central America, Chile, Venezuela, the Middle East, Pakistan, China, Thailand, Hong Kong, and Singapore. Worldwide, the Japanese producers had a combined market share approaching 30 percent and had their sights set on increasing it to 35 to 40 percent by the late 1990s. Exhibits 2a and 2b depict the sales success of Japanese producers at home and abroad.

THE JAPANESE PRODUCERS' CLIMB TO INDUSTRY PROMINENCE

Since World War II, Japanese companies had boosted annual production from 10,000 vehicles to a peak of 13.5 million vehicles at Japan-based plants and had worldwide capacity approaching 17 million vehicles. Despite the cyclical nature of the industry, Japanese automakers had achieved sales gains in 39 of the past 44 years. By way of comparison, over the same time frame U.S. manufacturers had increased production less than threefold, fallen behind Japan in total production, and been able to boost sales volume in only 24 of the past 44 years.

In moving into contention for leadership of the world automotive industry, Japan's automakers had progressed through four distinct phases. The first phase entailed importing the technology needed for manufacturing (mostly from the U.S.), building the requisite labor and managerial skills, and developing a larger home market for Japanese-made vehicles. Japan's initial success reflected (1) low-cost skilled labor and cheap steel, (2) home demand conditions (narrow roads and streets, short-driving distances, and high gasoline prices) that led manufacturers to focus on small-car production, (3) an emphasis on quality ("fit and finish") to satisfy appearance-conscious Japanese buyers, and (4) strong competitive rivalry among Japanese producers that honed their manufacturing skills and marketing savvy.

The second phase was marked by a strong emphasis on exports and development of a world market for Japanese-made vehicles. The first Japanese cars introduced in the U.S. in the late 1950s were very small, slow, and underpowered, rendering them unsatisfactory on American highways. But Japanese engineers learned from their mistakes and designed the next generation of Japanese vehicles to be suitable for both Japanese and American driving conditions. By 1971 Toyota was the second-largest foreign seller in the U.S. market, behind Volkswagen, and Japanese-made vehicles passed European-made vehicles in sales in the American market. Japanese automakers succeeded in penetrating the markets in many other countries as well, and Japan became the world's leading exporter of vehicles by the end of the 1970s.

Much of the Japanese success during this second phase stemmed from Japanese automakers' ability to achieve large gains in labor productivity via manufacturing process improvements. Between 1965 and 1975, Japanese car output rose 300 percent, yet the number of workers grew by just 50 percent. In addition, Japanese companies invested aggressively in large modern plants to capture scale economies. To secure worker cooperation in the productivity-enhancing effort, Japanese automakers guaranteed their employees lifetime employment and often provided such other benefits as promotion by seniority, corporate recreational facilities, subsidized housing, semiannual bonuses based on productivity gains and company profitability, and retirement plans. Japanese unions accepted productivity-enhancing technological

EXHIBIT 2A | **The Success of Japanese Producers in Penetrating World Markets for Motor Vehicles, 1960–92**

Total Production of Motor Vehicles in Japan

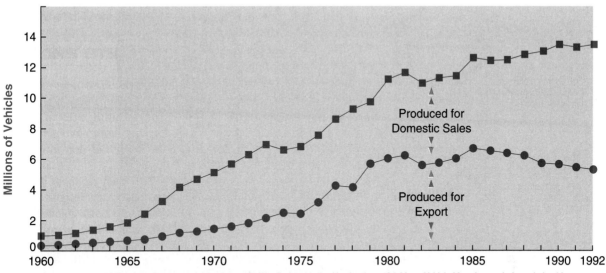

Sources: *Automotive News,* 1989 Market Data Book Issue, p. 3; *1989 Ward's Automotive Yearbook,* p. 104; Motor Vehicle Manufacturer's Association Motor Vehicle Data, 1983 edition, p. 79; *Automotive News,* 1993 Market Data Book, p. 3; *Automotive News,* 1991 Market Data Book, p. 3.

EXHIBIT 2B | **Japanese Passenger Car Import Penetration— Selected Countries, 1978–92** *(As a percent of domestic new car registrations)*

	1978	1984	1988	1992
Australia	33.3%	47.4%	46.5%	50.1%
Austria	7.0	27.0	33.0	31.5
Belgium	17.9	20.1	21.3	21.3
Denmark	13.7	32.7	32.8	42.3
Finland	20.4	37.9	41.4	36.6
France	1.8	3.0	2.9	4.1
Germany, West	3.7	12.0	15.2	13.4
Greece	13.8	30.9	38.9	29.6
Ireland	23.9	27.4	44.0	41.8
Italy	0.1	0.2	1.0	3.2
The Netherlands	19.0	22.0	27.7	27.0
New Zealand	33.5	65.2	58.2	66.6
Norway	20.4	33.5	39.3	50.1
Portugal	17.6	8.5	7.8	n.a.
Spain	0.0	0.6	0.9	3.7
Sweden	9.7	15.0	25.5	24.5
Switzerland	12.6	24.5	31.1	29.8
United Kingdom	11.0	11.1	9.4	10.4
United States	12.0	18.3	19.9	30.1

Sources: Motor Vehicle Manufacturers Association, *World Motor Vehicle Data,* 1990 edition, p. 29; *Ward's Automotive Yearbook, 1993,* pp. 70, 81.

change in exchange for long-term employment guarantees. Unions maintained a cooperative relationship with manufacturers, and manufacturers went to great lengths to cultivate worker loyalty and keep enthusiasm at a high pitch. Employee turnover was low and unexcused absenteeism averaged less than 1 percent. The culture in Japanese plants encouraged assembly-line workers to maintain their equipment, take pride in the quality of their work, and suggest ways to improve their work methods.

At the same time that the Japanese were making an all-out effort to reduce the labor-cost content in their cars and capture scale economies, they pursued quality improvement. In effect, Japanese automakers patterned their strategy after the example set by West Germany's Volkswagen—make small, fuel-efficient, reliable, and affordable cars (during the 1960s and early 1970s, the VW Beetle was the most popular imported car in the U.S. and was regarded as the world's best high-quality, inexpensive small car).

The third phase in Japan's climb to prominence came during the early and mid-1980s. Prodded by rises in the value of the Japanese yen (which tended to boost the prices of Japanese cars sold in foreign markets), Japanese automakers put new meaning into the term efficient manufacturing. They developed their now-famous just-in-time supply procedures, redesigned parts to allow greater production efficiency, made use of robots during assembly, and instituted a host of other quality control and productivity practices. They stressed continuous improvement, zealously ferreting out ways to cut costs and boost quality. And they invested heavily in flexible manufacturing systems and shortening their design cycles. The outcomes were better vehicle quality, better repair records, and better customer satisfaction ratings than their foreign competitors'. Steps were also taken to establish production bases in North America and Europe to circumvent the continuing rise in the yen against U.S. and European currencies, to deflect union protests about the job-depressing effect of Japanese car imports and politicians' concerns over vehicle-related trade deficits, and to buffer the effects of European trade restrictions on car imports. As of 1994, Hondas were being made in Ohio, Canada, and Great Britain; Toyotas in Kentucky, California, Canada, and Great Britain; Nissans in Tennessee, Mexico, and Great Britain; Mazdas in Michigan and Spain; Mitsubishis in Illinois; Subarus and Isuzus in Indiana; and Suzukis in Canada. Nissan had doubled its assembly capability in Mexico from 100,000 vehicles to 200,000 vehicles and had a Mexican plant that turned out engines, transaxles, and some stamped parts. All told, Japanese automakers in 1993 had the capacity to make 1.7 million vehicles at 8 wholly or partly owned U.S. assembly plants, and they had plans in place to expand their North American production capability to nearly 3 million units by the late 1990s. As of 1994, the Japanese had 11 assembly plants in North America and 4 in Europe.

The fourth phase in the Japanese strategy to dominate the world automotive industry involved the introduction of premium-priced luxury cars to compete head-on against the most prestigious names in passenger cars—Cadillac, Lincoln, Mercedes-Benz, BMW, Volvo, Porsche, and Jaguar. Honda was the first Japanese maker to enter the luxury-car field, introducing the Acura Legend (sticker prices of about $30,000) in 1986; the company sold 71,000 Legends in the U.S. in 1987; since then, Acura had been the third-best-selling luxury car in the U.S. In fall 1989 Toyota introduced its 1990 Lexus models and Nissan introduced the Infiniti; both were priced in the $35,000 to $45,000 range. Mazda and Mitsubishi introduced upscale vehicles in 1992 and 1993. The addition of luxury cars gave the leading Japanese companies passenger-car lines ranging from low-priced subcompacts and compacts to top-of-line cars equipped with a variety of advanced engineering and technology features (plus minivans, sports-utility models, and truck lines). Luxury-car sales accounted for almost 10 percent of total passenger-car volume in the U.S. and Europe; the $50 billion luxury segment was attractive to both manufacturers and dealers because of the wider profit margins built into the prices of luxury models.

THE DECLINING MARKET SHARES OF GM, FORD, AND CHRYSLER IN THE U.S. MARKET

While the Japanese producers forged their long-term global strategic offensive, U.S. producers struggled unsuccessfully to ward off rising sales of foreign imports in their strategically important U.S. home market. Five factors had kept General Motors, Ford, and Chrysler on the defensive between the mid-1970s and the early 1990s:

- When U.S. gasoline prices spiraled to as much as $1.75 per gallon in the late 1970s, buyer preferences shifted strongly toward smaller, fuel-efficient cars. Sales of foreign-made compacts getting over 25 miles per gallon rose. Sales of U.S.-made models—long, roomy, six-passenger cars with heavy bodies and powerful V-8 engines that delivered only 10 to 14 miles per gallon—fell. General Motors, Ford, and Chrysler launched crash programs to downsize their lineup of big-car models and introduce a host of compact and subcompact models. But this put them on the horns of a short-term profit dilemma: the profit margins on small cars were much smaller than on large cars. To moderate the profit erosion, all three U.S. producers elected not to put the same look and feel of quality and the same calibre of technological features into their low-priced small cars as they put into their middle and upper-end models. Until GM introduced its Saturn models in 1990, no U.S. producer exhibited a long-term commitment to build a truly high-quality "import-fighter" that could be produced and marketed at a profit.
- Escalating prices for new vehicles prompted buyers to stretch out their car payments and buy a new vehicle less frequently, putting a damper on new-vehicle sales in the U.S.
- Stricter government regulations regarding fuel economy, safety, and pollution emissions forced U.S. companies to make further costly design changes in all their models, contributed to higher sticker prices, and kept Detroit auto executives busy wrangling with politicians and regulators over what the new standards should be and when they should take effect.
- Preoccupied with their scramble to comply with government regulations, revamp their product lines, and protect short-term profits, U.S. manufacturers paid insufficient attention to assembly-line "fits and finishes" and to quality control in parts manufacture during the late 1970s and early 1980s. Buyers of U.S. makes complained of an inordinately large number of new-car defects. Even though U.S. manufacturers had made major progress since 1985 in narrowing the quality gap, in 1994 they were still trying to overcome widespread buyer perception that American vehicles were not as well made as Japanese vehicles.
- Meanwhile, throughout the 1980s, the Japanese companies did a better job of reading the market and learning what customers liked; they upgraded interior trim and comfort, added features, and improved engines and transmissions. When certain models failed to sell well, they quickly restyled them and also introduced new models to respond to changing buyer preferences. U.S. auto executives consistently underestimated the competitive prowess of the Japanese companies in styling, engines, and transmissions.

During the 1982–92 period, General Motors, Ford, and Chrysler closed 54 assembly, engine, and parts plants; since 1980, the United Automobile Workers union had lost 500,000 members to job cutbacks across the U.S. automotive industry, an amount equal to one-third of the UAW's membership. Despite all the plant closings, an overcapacity situation still prevailed in North America in 1994 and Detroit's Big Three had scheduled further plant shutdowns since it was they who had older, less-efficient, less-adaptable, and underutilized facilities—see Exhibit 3 for statistics showing the manufacturing decline of the U.S. producers and the rising North American output of foreign, mostly Japanese, producers.

THE SITUATION IN EUROPE

European vehicle producers had recently consolidated into a smaller number of stronger companies and were bracing for renewed Japanese and U.S. attempts to penetrate the European market. Japanese success in Europe had been restricted by protectionist trade practices—as of 1992, vehicles imported from Japan were limited to 11 percent of the market in Britain, to 3 percent in France, to 1 percent in Spain, and to 2,500 vehicles in Italy. However, the Japanese had circumvented these restrictions by building four assembly plants in Europe in the 1990s; in 1994 they were using

EXHIBIT 3 | **Comparative North American Assembly Plant Statistics, 1978, 1988, and 1992, with Projections for 1996**

	GM	Ford	Chrysler	All Other Producers	Total
1978					
Assembly plants	41	24	11	2	78
Vehicle output	8,314,000	4,420,000	1,871,000	48,000	14,653,000
Output per plant	202,780	184,167	170,091	24,000	187,859
Output share (%)	56.7	30.2	12.8	0.3	100.0
1988					
Assembly plants	36	19	13	10	78
Vehicle output	5,808,000	3,995,000	2,212,000	984,000	12,999,000
Output per plant	161,333	210,263	170,154	98,400	166,654
Output share (%)	44.7	30.7	17.0	7.6	100.0
1992					
Assembly plants	30	21	12	13	76
Vehicle output	4,416,000	3,455,000	1,851,000	2,039,000	11,761,000
Output per plant	147,200	164,524	154,250	156,846	154,750
Output share (%)	37.5	29.4	15.7	17.3	100.0
1996 Forecast					
Assembly plants	26	21	12	14	73
Vehicle output	4,727,000	3,990,000	2,237,000	3,115,000	14,069,000
Output per plant	181,808	190,000	186,417	222,500	192,726
Output share (%)	33.6	28.4	15.9	22.1	100.0

Note: Big Three data exclude joint-venture operations with other producers. Ford includes Hermosillo, Mexico: Chrysler includes Toluca, Mexico, and All Other Producers includes VW Mexico output for U.S./Canada. Industry is total of Big Three and other producers; independent heavy-truck producers are excluded. Production for 1996 is forecast by Data Resources Inc. (DRI); other figures are Ward's data.

Source: *Ward's Automotive Yearbook 1993*, p. 184.

their newly established European production base to begin a long-term campaign to boost their sales and market share in Europe. Japanese production in Europe was projected to reach 1.5 million vehicles by 1997. Observers believed the Japanese companies aimed to increase their European share from 12 percent in 1992 to 18 percent by 1998. The 12-member European Community, which started functioning as a unified market in 1992, was committed in principle to abolishing all national automotive quotas eventually, and the current system of Japanese import quotas was due to be phased out in the year 2000.[1] The stakes in Europe were big because of its size and growth prospects; Europe's six biggest automotive companies—Volkswagen-Audi, Fiat, Peugeot-Citroen, Mercedes-Benz, Renault, and Volvo were not all expected to survive in their present form. The European-based subsidiaries of General Motors and Ford—GM Europe and Ford Europe—were among the top six European market share leaders in 1993; GM Europe ranked third behind Volkswagen-Audi and Peugeot/Citroen while Ford Europe trailed Renault and was just ahead of sixth-ranked Fiat. Europe's six market share leaders had volumes ranging from 1.4 to 2.8 million vehicles annually; the remaining European manufacturers produced under 700,000 vehicles annually (see Exhibit 1). In 1994 the European producers lagged behind both Japanese and American companies in several competitive respects and only Mercedes-Benz, BMW, and Volkswagen-Audi could be considered global competitors.

THE GEOGRAPHY OF MOTOR VEHICLE PRODUCTION

Motor vehicles, with their 10,000 to 15,000 parts, were one of the most complex products to manufacture and were a telling measure of a country's industrial capabilities. As of the early 1990s, 70 percent of all motor vehicles were produced in six countries—Japan, the United States, Germany, France, Spain, and South Korea. In the years immediately following World War II, U.S.-based companies produced 75 percent of the world's motor vehicles, but the percentage had eroded steadily as companies in other countries gained the technical skills needed for vehicle manufacture and geared up production to meet growing demand in their geographic areas. In 1993, motor vehicle production in the U.S. accounted for about 20 percent of world output. Japan surpassed the United States as the largest production base for motor vehicles in 1980. U.S. production hit an all-time peak of 12.8 million vehicles in 1978 and since then had fluctuated between 6.9 million and 11.6 million vehicles annually. While production in the U.S. stalled, production in Japan and Western Europe was on the upswing throughout much of the 1980s—see Exhibits 4, and 5a 5b. Total production in South America had been stuck in the 1 to 1.5 million range since 1975. Since 1982 South Korea's vehicle production had grown eightfold to 1.7 million units in 1992, one-third of them for export.

In 1994 Japan was the world's leading exporter of motor vehicles, a position it had held since the mid-1970s. In the 1950s Japanese producers had begun pursuing export sales as a way of escaping the economy-of-scale limitations of a small home country market; by the mid-1980s Japanese companies were exporting over 6 million vehicles annually, chiefly to the U.S. and Europe. Since then, however, the steadily

---

[1] The 12 member nations of the European Community were Great Britain, France, Germany, the Netherlands, Italy, Portugal, Greece, Luxembourg, Spain, Belgium, Turkey, and Ireland.

EXHIBIT 4 | **Trends in World Motor Vehicle Production by Geographic Location, 1960–92**

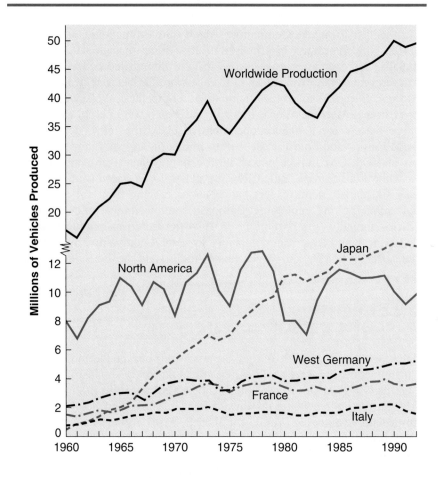

Continental Production and Assembly

	North America	Europe	Asia	South America
1980	9,874,206	15,412,235	11,279,395	1,454,124
1985	14,006,178	15,901,217	12,880,368	1,104,300
1990	12,613,497	15,574,234	14,802,864	912,392
1991	11,784,585	16,867,200	17,186,659	1,215,382
1992	12,843,857	17,186,659	16,871,843	1,487,229

Definitions: North America—Canada, Mexico, U.S.; Europe—Western Europe and Eastern Bloc including former USSR; Asia—India, Japan, Korea; South America—Argentina, Brazil.
Source: *Automotive News,* 1990 Market Data Book Issue, pp. 3 and 6; 1993 Issue, pp. 3 and 4.

rising value of the Japanese yen coupled with a growing threat of protectionism (most countries were gravely concerned about the job losses associated with rising Japanese imports) had prompted the Japanese companies to curtail their strategic reliance on exports and, instead, establish production bases in North America and

Europe. By 1994 Japanese vehicle producers had built 11 assembly plants in North America (with annual production capacity of 3,000,000 vehicles) and 4 in Europe (with annual capacity of 1,000,000 vehicles), cutting their exports from a peak of 6.7 million in 1985 to 5.6 million in 1993.

Most of the vehicles exported by Germany (about 2.2 to 2.6 million annually) and France (about 2 million annually) went to other European countries, although about 10 percent of Germany's exports were for the U.S. market. Virtually all of Canada's motor vehicle exports (about 1.6 million annually) went to the United States. Among the U.S. automakers, only Chrysler competed in foreign markets via the export route; its plants were all located in the U.S., Canada, and Mexico. General Motors and Ford had big subsidiary operations in Europe, and each had captured about 12 percent of the European market with their European-produced makes. Worldwide, GM had facilities in 32 countries and Ford operated in 25 countries. Virtually all of the world's leading manufacturers were exploring ways to increase their global reach through exports, by establishing foreign production bases, or by forming strategic alliances with a foreign producer.

EXHIBIT 5A | **Where Motor Vehicles Are Produced**

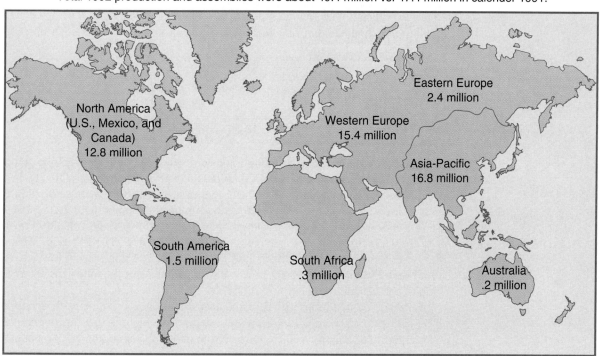

World Vehicle Production by Continent

Total 1992 production and assemblies were about 49.4 million vs. 47.4 million in calender 1991.

North America (U.S., Mexico, and Canada) 12.8 million

Eastern Europe 2.4 million

Western Europe 15.4 million

Asia-Pacific 16.8 million

South America 1.5 million

South Africa .3 million

Australia .2 million

EXHIBIT 5B | **Where Motor Vehicle Producers Ranked According to Production in Each Country, 1992**

Leading Motor Vehicle Producers Ranked According to Production in Each Country, 1992									
Manufacturer	Country	Cars	Trucks	Total	Manufacturer	Country	Cars	Trucks	Total
Toyota	Japan	3,171,311	760,030	3,931,341	Isuzu	Japan	118,391	354,887	473,278
General Motors	U.S.A.	2,392,256	1,356,719	3,748,975	Chrysler	Canada	50,623	413,878	464,501
Ford	U.S.A.	1,333,578	1,496,412	2,829,990	Ford	England	302,148	157,749	459,897
Nissan	Japan	1,750,829	418,781	2,169,610	Honda	U.S.A.	458,254	—	458,254
Peugeot SA*	France	1,821,397	129,157	1,950,554	Rover Group	England	378,797	20,864	399,661
Renault	France	1,504,111	308,166	1,812,277	General Motors	Spain	366,400	10,600	377,000
Volkswagen	Germany	1,549,503	108,120	1,657,623	SEAT	Spain	329,500	25,000	354,500
Fiat Group	Italy	1,465,258	152,654	1,617,912	Volkswagen	Brazil	288,784	58,825	347,609
Mitsubishi	Japan	939,590	456,285	1,395,875	Ford	Spain	310,800	—	310,800
Mazda	Japan	1,037,133	243,917	1,281,050	Fiat	Brazil	244,652	65,620	310,272
Honda	Japan	1,067,289	132,531	1,199,820	Vauxhall	England	287,884	14,112	301,996
Opel	Germany	1,071,544	14,499	1,086,043	Nissan	U.S.A.	171,244	128,924	300,168
Chrysler	U.S.A.	259,112	760,713	1,019,825	Ford	Mexico	198,258	58,942	257,200
Hyundai	S. Korea	701,654	157,596	859,250	NUMMI	U.S.A.	180,958	75,287	256,245
Suzuki	Japan	535,171	309,240	844,411	Chrysler	Mexico	154,645	80,152	234,797
Mercedes-Benz	Germany	531,457	156,596	688,053	General Motors	Brazil	173,333	40.042	213,375
VAZ (Lada)	Russia	623,000	64,000	687,000	Daewoo	S. Korea	172,484	6,536	179,020
General Motors	Canada	327,945	338,940	666,885	Mazda	U.S.A.	167,940	—	167,940
Ford	Germany	622,377	—	622,377	Ford	Brazil	107,556	45,727	153,283
Daihatsu	Japan	392,478	217,864	610,342	Volvo	Sweden	111,100	11,560	122,660
BMW	Germany	580,295	—	580,295	Saab	Sweden	72,763	37,590	110,353
Fuji	Japan	366,502	147,423	513,925	Ford	Australia	91,707	5,453	97,160
Kia	S. Korea	315,459	186,768	502,227					
Ford	Canada	366,299	127,852	494,151					
Audi	Germany	492,085	—	492,085					

Sources: *Automotive News,* 1993 Market Data Book Issue, pp. 3–5; *1993 Ward's Automotive Yearbook,* p. 59.

THE WORLD MARKET FOR MOTOR VEHICLES

In 1994 there were about 550 million motor vehicles in operation worldwide—about 415 million passenger cars and 135 million pickup trucks and commercial vehicles—and the total was growing 2 to 3 percent annually. The U.S. was far and away the biggest consumer of motor vehicles from a country standpoint with 123.3 million passenger cars and 58.2 million trucks in operation. There was one vehicle in operation in the U.S. for every 1.4 persons there, one for every 2.5 persons in Western Europe, one for every 2.6 persons in Japan, one for every 11 persons in Mexico, and one for every 13 persons in Brazil; in less-developed nations, the ratios ranged all the way up to one vehicle for every 500 persons.

New-vehicle demand ran 8 to 10 percent of the number of vehicles in operation; over 92 percent of new-vehicle sales represented replacement in one form or another. The average life of a motor vehicle ranged from about 8 years in the U.S. to about 15 years in countries where travel by vehicle was much less prevalent. Comparative sizes of the various major markets were as follows:

	New Car and Truck Sales (in millions)		Percent of World Market	
	1988	1992	1988	1992
United States	15.7	12.9	32.3%	28.4%
Western Europe	14.4	14.6	29.6	32.1
Japan	6.7	7.0	13.8	15.4
U.S.S.R. (former)	1.6	.9	3.3	2.2
Canada	1.5	1.2	3.1	2.6
Brazil	.7	.6	1.4	1.8
Australia	.5	.4	1.0	.9
South Korea	.5	1.2	1.0	2.6
Argentina	.2	.2	.4	.7
Taiwan	.2	.5	.4	1.1
South Africa	.2	.3	.4	.7
All other country markets	6.4	5.3	13.2	11.6
Total	48.6	45.5	100.0%	100.0%

In terms of passenger cars, Western Europe was the largest market with new car sales of 13 to 14 million units versus 9 to 10 million in the United States and nearly 4 million in Japan. The U.S. was the world's biggest market for trucks and commercial vehicles with annual sales of 5 million units; Japan was second with 3 million units annually; and Western Europe was third with annual sales just under 2 million trucks. The Japanese truck market, like the Japanese car market, was pretty much closed to foreign companies; imports of foreign-made trucks into Japan amounted to less than 1 percent of total sales.

MARKET GROWTH

Demand for motor vehicles was quite cyclical (see Exhibit 4). Since 1978, worldwide demand had grown at a 1.3 percent average annual rate. Sales in any given country market tended to be strongest during periods of economic prosperity and weakest during recessionary periods. Forecasters expected slim annual growth rates of 1 to 1.5 percent worldwide during the 1990s, with annual demand approaching 55 million units by the year 2000. The fastest rates of growth were expected to come in newly developing and Third World countries where there were substantially fewer vehicles in operation relative to total populations. The vehicle markets in North America, Western Europe, and Japan were the most mature—annual demand in these three largest markets of the world was projected to increase by no more than 2 million units throughout the entire decade of the 1990s. Producers regarded Europe as the most attractive of the three major markets in the 1990s because of the opening up of Eastern Europe, the formation of the European Community as a unified trade area of 320 million consumers, and the potential for further growth in vehicle use across Europe. Ford had predicted annual car sales in Europe could reach 18 to 20 million by the year 2000. The Southeast Asia market (Thailand, Indonesia, Vietnam, China, Malaysia, Taiwan, and the Philippines) was also expected to boom, jumping from 4.7 percent of global unit sales in 1987 to 10 percent by 2000.

Some analysts predicted that lesser-known producers in Asia, South America, and Eastern Europe could be making 18 to 20 percent of the world's cars and trucks by the year 2000, up from 12.5 percent in 1986. But most producers in developing countries were small and lacked the technology to match the sophistication of vehicles made by the major producers in the U.S., Japan, and Western Europe; moreover, the technology gap was widening. A more probable scenario was that the major global producers would locate parts production and assembly plants in developing countries to take advantage of their attractive potential for sales growth. In 1994 Japan was the leading exporter of vehicles to developing and Third World nations, followed by France and then the United States.

THE TRUCK SEGMENT

Worldwide, light- and heavy-duty trucks, buses, taxis, vans, sports-utility vehicles, and assorted types of other commercial vehicles accounted for 25 percent of total automotive sales. However, the division between passenger-car sales and truck-bus–commercial vehicle sales varied significantly from market to market. In Western Europe, eight passenger cars were sold for every one truck-bus-commercial vehicle. In the U.S. and Japan, the breakdown was 65 percent passenger cars and 35 percent trucks, buses, and commercial vehicles. In China, trucks outsold passenger cars 4 to 1; in the Middle East, sales were equally divided between cars and trucks.

Truck sales had grown a bit faster than passenger-car sales worldwide since 1980, partly because they provided a cheaper form of transportation. In the U.S., where truck demand had grown the most, light-truck sales (mostly pickups and 4-wheel-drive utility vehicles) grew from 2.2 million units in 1980 to 4.6 million units in 1992, equal to a 6.3 percent compound growth rate; sales of light trucks in the U.S. were expected to reach 6 million vehicles annually by the late 1990s. Worldwide, most producers saw the market for light pickup trucks, vans, and sports-utility vehicles (like the Ford Explorer and Jeep Cherokee) continuing to grow 1 or 2 percentage points faster than the passenger-car market. The base demand for heavy trucks was about 150,000 vehicles annually in the U.S. and about 250,000 vehicles worldwide.

Japanese and U.S. producers controlled 70 percent of the world's truck and commercial vehicle sales. General Motors and Ford were the coleaders in the overall truck-bus-van–commercial vehicle segment but 8 of the world's 12 largest truck producers were Japanese companies:

Company (Country Base)	Estimated 1992 Sales
General Motors (U.S.)	1.8 million
Ford (U.S.)	1.7
Chrysler (U.S.)	1.2
Toyota (Japan)	1.1
Nissan (Japan)	.6
Mitsubishi (Japan)	.5
Suzuki (Japan)	.4
Isuzu (Japan)	.4
Daihatsu (Japan)	.3
Mazda (Japan)	.3
Renault (France)	.3
Fuji (Japan)	.2

In Europe, the leaders in heavy trucks were Renault, Daimler-Benz (Mercedes), and Volvo; in Japan, the heavy-truck leaders were Hino and Nissan Diesel; and in the U.S., the leaders were Navistar (the maker of International trucks), PACCAR (the maker of Peterbuilt and Kenworth brands), Mack, Daimler-Benz (Mercedes and Freightliner brands), and GM Volvo. Truck exports from Europe and the U.S. had declined in recent years whereas Japanese truck exports had increased.

Exhibit 6 shows vehicle sales for the world's 12 largest producers during the 1990s and Exhibit 7 shows the passenger-car and light-truck market shares of the leading producers in the world's three largest geographic markets.

MAKES AND MODELS

Automakers produced a variety of models and styles to cater to differing driver tastes and user needs. Exhibit 8 shows the percentage composition of the various segments. While every vehicle was factory-equipped with certain "standard" features (included in the base price), it was common practice to offer such add-on options as air-conditioning, stereo sound systems, compact disk players, high-performance tires, deluxe wheel covers, sunroofs, airbags, and trim packages; these, along with a choice of interior and exterior colors, permitted a vehicle to be customized to a buyer's tastes and pocketbook. Optional equipment could boost the base price by $1,000 to $4,000 per vehicle.

In recent years, the number of models on the market had proliferated in response to increasingly diverse buyer needs and preferences. Whereas in the 1970s, car owners across the U.S. mainly bought full-size family sedans, by the 1990s buyer preferences had splintered into an array of distinct segments—subcompacts, compacts,

EXHIBIT 6 | **The Top 12 Motor Vehicle Producers, 1990–93**

	1990		1991		1992		1993	
	Units Produced	% Share	Units Produced	% Share	Units Produced	% Share	Units Produced	% Share
General Motors	7,454,000	14.8	7,015,000	14.8%	7,146,000	14.5%	7,299,000	15.1%
Ford Motor Co.	5,872,389	11.7	5,359,000	11.3	5,764,374	11.7	5,700,000	11.8
Toyota Motor Co.	4,889,414	9.7	4,719,000	9.9	4,695,633	9.5	4,450,309	9.2
Volkswagen AG	3,057,598	6.1	3,128,328	6.6	3,499,139	7.1	3,000,000	6.2
Nissan Motor Co.	3,063,186	6.1	3,082,491	6.5	2,982,937	6.0	2,818,017	5.8
Fiat Group	2,697,800	5.4	2,461,000	5.2	2,231,000	4.5	1,600,000	3.3
Chrysler Corp.	1,645,457	3.3	1,480,819	3.1	2,159,000	4.4	2,348,030	4.8
Peugeot-Citroen PSA	2,219,900	4.4	2,057,553	4.3	2,049,800	4.1	1,751,600	3.6
Renault SA	1,783,341	3.5	1,790,709	3.8	2,041,829	4.1	1,761,306	3.6
Mitsubishi Motors	1,793,387	3.6	1,907,694	4.0	1,832,000	3.7	1,875,000	3.9
Honda Motor Co.	1,993,000	4.0	1,995,000	4.2	1,828,000	3.7	1,827,800	3.8
Mazda Motor Corp.	1,607,054	3.2	1,551,255	3.3	1,460,000	3.0	1,241,564	2.6
All others	12,298,590	24.4	10,893,713	23.0	11,743,763	23.8	12,755,733	26.3
World total	50,375,116	100.0%	47,441,562	100.0%	49,433,475	100.0%	48,428,359	100.0

Source: *Automotive News,* 1994 Market Data Book, p. 3.

EXHIBIT 7 | **Market Share Leaders in Passenger Cars and Light Trucks, Three Largest Geographic Markets, 1989 and 1992**

Passenger-Car Market Shares (%)								
Western Europe	**1989**	**1992**	**United States**	**1989**	**1992**	**Japan**	**1989**	**1992**
Fiat-Lancia	14.9%	11.9%	General Motors	34.8%	34.6%	Toyota	43.9%	35.5%
Peugeot	12.9	12.2	Ford	22.1	21.6	Nissan	23.2	20.2
VW-Audi	14.8	17.5	Chrysler	10.3	8.3	Honda	10.8	10.3
Ford	11.9	11.3	Honda	7.9	9.4	Mazda	5.9	7.3
GM-Opel	10.4	12.4	Toyota	7.3	9.3	Mitsubishi	4.9	7.6
Renault	10.1	10.6	Nissan	5.2	5.1	Daihatsu	2.4	5.4
Rover Group	3.4	2.5	Mazda	2.7	3.0	Subaru	2.1	3.9
Mercedes-Benz	3.4	3.0	Hyundai	1.8	1.3	Suzuki	1.7	5.5
Nissan	2.9	3.2	Volkswagen	1.6	1.1	Isuzu	1.5	.4
BMW	2.7	3.3	Subaru	1.4	1.3	All imports	3.6	4.0
Toyota	2.1	2.5	Volvo	1.0	.8			
Volvo	2.1	1.5	All other imports	3.9	4.2			
			All Japanese imports	26.0	30.1			
			All European imports	4.9	4.0			

Light-Truck Market Shares (%)								
Western Europe			**United States**	**1989**	**1992**	**Japan**	**1989**	**1992**
Not available			General Motors	35.7%	33.3%	Toyota	16.2%	27.0%
			Ford	30.0	30.1	Suzuki	15.4	11.7
			Chrysler	21.0	22.2	Mitsubishi	14.6	16.9
			Toyota	4.7	5.7	Daihatsu	14.5	7.8
			Nissan	3.3	3.6	Nissan	11.0	12.9
			Isuzu	2.2	2.1	Fuji	8.3	5.6
			All other imports	3.1	3.0	Honda	7.1	5.3
			All Japanese imports	13.3	14.2	Mazda	6.3	6.5
			All European imports	0.1	.1	Isuzu	4.9	6.1
						Imports	0.04	.1

Sources: *Automotive News, Business Japan,* and *Ward's Automotive Yearbook.*

mid-size, family-size, personal luxury models, 2-doors, 4-doors, pickup trucks, vans, sports-utility vehicles, 4-wheel drive vehicles, and so on. In 1994, for example, U.S. car buyers could choose from 500 models offered by 3 American makers, 14 European makers, 8 Japanese makers, and 2 Korean makers. Market fragmentation greatly reduced the sales volume any one model achieved. Whereas in the 1970s sales volumes of popular-selling models amounted to 400,000 to 700,000 units annually, in 1994 annual sales volumes of 350,000 units per model were "large" and annual volumes of only 10,000 units per model were not uncommon. Market fragmentation and the diversity of buyer needs made it competitively important for would-be market leaders to be full-line producers, offering a variety of models and price ranges for buyers to choose from. Increasingly frequent shifts in buyer preferences had put a premium on a manufacturer's ability to read market trends accurately and put freshly designed models with sales appeal into showrooms quickly.

The most profitable models were full-size sedans, luxury cars, pickup trucks, vans,

EXHIBIT 8 | Size of U.S. Passenger-Car and Light-Truck Market Segments, 1992

Passenger-Car Segments	Percent of Total Market	Light-Truck Segments	Percent of Total Market
Subcompacts	25.5%	Compact pickup	21.9%
Compacts	15.2	Regular-size pickup	25.2
Intermediates	37.3	Compact van	20.9
Full-size	7.6	Regular-size van	7.8
Luxury	9.0	Compact utility vehicle	21.1
Near-luxury	3.8	Regular-size utility vehicle	3.1
Specialty	1.6		
	100.0%		100.0%

Source: *Automotive News,* 1993 Market Data Book Issue, p. 26.

and 2-wheel or 4-wheel-drive utility vehicles. Profit margins on light trucks and utility vehicles were above-average because these vehicles were less costly to produce than cars. Luxury and full-size cars were high-margin items because the extra prices they commanded far exceeded their incremental production costs.

Japanese producers were at a disadvantage in competing for the light-truck and sports-utility segments of the U.S. market. Japanese companies did not produce full-size pickup trucks for sale in Japan because Japanese streets were too narrow to accommodate them. Moreover, the U.S. imposed a 25 percent import tax on all 2-door trucks—pickups, minivans, and sports-utility vehicles. To detour the import tax, the Japanese had introduced 4-door model vans and utility vehicles; in 1993 Toyota introduced a full-size pickup truck in the U.S., but early sales had been disappointing.

BUYER PREFERENCES AND PURCHASING HABITS

In selecting the make and model to purchase, buyers typically took many considerations into account: vehicle size, the number of passengers that could be transported, comfort and roominess, styling appeal, drivability and handling, price, the manufacturer's reputation for quality, fuel economy, the length of warranty periods, financing terms, dealer service, prior experiences with makes and models, word-of-mouth reports from acquaintances, and ratings of independent consumer groups. Older buyers tended to be more brand loyal than either younger or better-educated buyers; older buyers also favored domestic brands over imports. First-time buyers were disposed toward economically priced small cars and tended to shop the market more thoroughly, looking at several brands and models. In metropolitan areas buyers often preferred compact, fuel-efficient vehicles for commuting to work in rush-hour traffic. Outdoor enthusiasts and rural residents frequently were owners of a pickup truck or a 4-wheel-drive vehicle. In areas where snow conditions were often severe, 4-wheel drive utility vehicles were big sellers. Households with more than one vehicle normally opted for different models to better accommodate the needs of individual family members. The hottest products in the U.S. in the 1990s were minivans and sports-utility vehicles, whose sales had jumped from about 200,000 in 1983 to 2.3 million in 1993. Along with pickups, they were classified as light trucks because of their weight and interior space.

On the whole, buyers were increasingly prone to brand switching and model switching, especially as their transportation needs changed due to the number and ages of family members, commuting requirements, place of residence, and adjustments in lifestyle. It was common for buyers to trade up to more luxurious or sporty and expensive vehicles as their incomes rose. Some buyers switched models and brands with each purchase for the sake of variety or because they found the styling and design of certain new models particularly appealing. Others were trend conscious and opted for whatever new models were "in." Prestige-conscious buyers purchased brands and models best suited to the image they wanted to project. The biggest buyer segment consisted of those whose top priority was practical, dependable transportation at an economical price. Because of rising vehicle prices, greater use of 48-month financing plans, and improving vehicle quality, many drivers were making a new-vehicle purchase over a longer life-cycle, and the average age of vehicles in operation was rising. A number were also shifting from passenger cars to pickup trucks because the latter had lower sticker prices and comparable options and features. Leasing was growing rapidly in popularity because of lower monthly payments. In the U.S., repurchase of the same make of car ranged from about 30 percent for buyers above age 65 down to 13 percent for buyers under age 25.

In the world's major motor vehicle markets, buyers were relatively sophisticated about the features they wanted their vehicles to have and about the driving performance they expected. Buyers placed a high value on mechanical reliability, quality manufacture, and trouble-free operation. High-tech gadgetry tended to be a plus, serving as a sign of cutting-edge automotive know-how on the manufacturer's part. Squeaks and rattles irritated owners and were the most frequently cited reasons for brand switching. Manufacturers' recalls to repair defective parts and consumer satisfaction surveys identifying the "best" and "worst" models were well covered by the news media.

The two most widely reported surveys were done by J. D. Power & Associates and *Consumer Reports* magazine. The J. D. Power survey reported customer satisfaction levels and repair problems of a statistically representative sample of buyers during the first 90 days of new-car ownership; Japanese cars had dominated the quality ratings for the past 10 years, and 10 of the 12 highest-rated models in the 1993 survey were Japanese-made (see Exhibit 9). *Consumer Reports* based its quality ratings on readers' responses to its questionnaire survey about their repair experiences during the whole time they had owned their present vehicles. The results of the *Consumer Reports* 1993 survey are presented in Exhibit 10.

VEHICLE DESIGN

Typically, the task of designing a new model began with a concept based on extensive market research, assessment of buyer tastes and needs, a feel for the market, and manufacturing capability. Once preliminary sketches won approval, designers developed full-sized mock-ups, drawings, and specifications. Very large investments could be involved in introducing a new model—development and tooling for Ford's Escort approached $3 billion and GM spent $4 billion to launch Saturn. Redesigning existing models was a less-expensive proposition, but modification of a single component could so affect the interface with related parts and components that entire systems would have to be redesigned and parts production lines retooled at considerable

E X H I B I T　9　┃　**J. D. Power and Associates Customer Satisfaction Study^{TM}**

1993 Car Customer Satisfaction Index

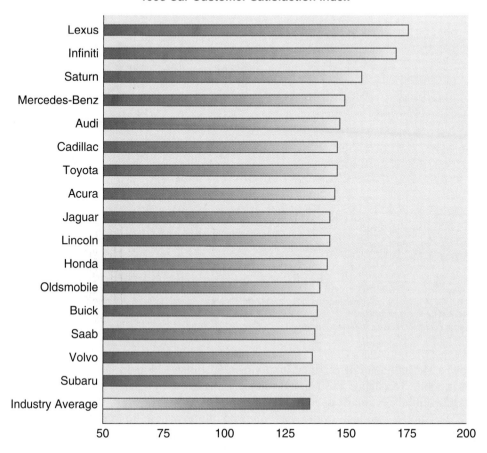

Note: J. D. Power and Associates does not reveal the performance of those car and truck lines ranking below the industry average.

Source: 1993 J. D. Power and Associates, New Car Customer Satisfaction Index Study, Spring 1993.

The length of a vehicle maker's design cycle was competitively significant. Compressing the time it took to design, engineer, and manufacture new models enabled an automaker to respond more quickly to sales trends and changing buyer preferences, and reduced the time it took to incorporate new product features and manufacturing improvements. In 1990 Japanese automakers could design, engineer, and manufacture completely new models in 42 months; the design-to-production cycle ran 50 to 60 months for U.S. automakers and 60 to 84 months for European companies. Moreover, Japanese automakers were redesigning 80 percent of their models every five years compared to U.S. companies' practice of changing just 40 percent in a five-year span. For instance, the Ford Taurus, introduced in 1985, was not scheduled for revamping until 1995. Honda had launched three new Accords since 1985. When stodgy designs caused a downturn in Nissan's sales in the mid-1980s, it accelerated redesign of practically its entire lineup of models. In contrast, when General Motors

E X H I B I T   1 0 | *Consumer Reports'* Overall Reliability Ratings of 1991–93 Cars and Trucks Marketed in the United States

	Number of 1991–93 Car and Truck Models with Repair Frequencies Rated				
Manufacterurer	Much Better than Average	Better than Average	Average	Worse than Average	Much Worse than Average
General Motors	0	3	19	17	1
Ford Motor Company	0	1	15	6	2
Chrysler	0	0	16	13	3
Toyota	7	7	0	0	0
Nissan	2	6	4	0	0
Honda	0	4	0	1	0
Mazda	0	3	4	1	0
Mitsubishi	0	0	4	3	0
BMW	0	1	1	0	0
Volkswagen-Audi	0	1	0	1	0
Mercedes-Benz	0	1	0	0	0
Volvo	1	1	0	0	0

Note: Data provided by survey respondents did not permit statistically reliable ratings to be developed for all of the models produced by each manufacturer.

Source: *Consumer Reports,* April 1994, pp. 256–57.

downsized its lineup of personal luxury cars (Cadillac Eldorado, Buick Riviera, and Oldsmobile Toronado) in 1985 and sales plummeted, GM stuck with the same basic styling until the regularly scheduled redesign in 1992.

The shorter product cycles had allowed the Japanese to make technological improvements faster and to introduce new designs more often. However, by 1994 U.S. producers had revamped their approaches to design and cut their cycle times significantly. Chrysler brought its new Dodge Neon models to market in 31 months, Ford's resurrection of the Mustang took 35 months, and GM's 1995 Chevrolet Lumina models had a design-to-market time of 38 months. European manufacturers had cut their cycle times significantly as well; Mercedes had implemented a crash program and managed to bring out its new C-class series in under four years, but European producers as a group still trailed Japanese and U.S. producers on cycle times by 6 to 15 months.

In 1994 Toyota and Honda were regarded as the world's best and most efficient at bringing new models to market, not because they were speedier or had superior design capabilities, but because they had higher engineering productivity, better internal teamwork, and stronger supplier relationships—which translated into using fewer people and having lower costs. Several instances demonstrated the extent to which the Japanese automakers had product-introduction costs and model-redesign costs below those of rival U.S. and European producers. When Toyota decided to introduce its luxury-car line, it spent $700 million to develop the all-new Lexus LS400, added a second Lexus model for about $350 million, and introduced design and production technologies for the Lexus program that could be adapted for the company's lesser-priced car lines. When Ford decided it wanted another luxury brand, it bought British-based Jaguar for $2.5 billion in 1989 and invested another $500 million to modernize Jaguar's factories and rejuvenate Jaguar's faltering product line. Most recently, Ford had spent a reported $6 billion to design and produce its new "world car," known as Mondeo in Europe and the Ford Contour and Mercury Mystique in the United States. In 1994 U.S. and European automakers were more prone than Japanese automakers to try to recover their higher model-redesign costs by stretching out redesign cycles so as to spread restyling and retooling costs over bigger volumes; this strategy worked so long as car buyers did not tire of a model's looks for six to eight years and sales held up in the latter stages of the design cycle.

RESEARCH AND DEVELOPMENT

Automotive R&D covered a broad front, ranging from manufacturing technology to cost reduction to improved features and quality to high-tech frontiers. As automakers began 1994, R&D efforts were aimed at reducing engine pollution emissions, boosting fuel economy, developing robots to replace assembly workers, improving power-train efficiency, exploring the use of ceramics in engine components, enhancing corrosion protection, improving crashworthiness and occupant safety, and expanding onboard self-service/diagnostic systems and the use of computerized controls. Typical vehicles contained $900 worth of electronics in 1990; the amount was expected to reach $2,000 by the late 1990s. Engines and transmissions of the newest models were being equipped with a variety of sophisticated control systems. All companies were working on lighter, cheaper, more powerful, and lower-polluting engines. Development of vehicles powered by electric batteries and natural gas was accelerating; California had passed air-pollution legislation requiring that 2 percent of major manufacturers' sales in California be electric cars by 1998. The National Energy Policy Act of 1992 required fleet owners to have at least 2 percent of their fleets powered by natural gas or electric batteries by 1998. In 1993 President Clinton announced a partnership with GM, Ford, and Chrysler to produce a clean, fuel-miserly car; the program's goal was to triple the mileage of a typical car within 10 years.

In general, Japanese and European manufacturers spent 4 to 6 percent of company revenues on R&D compared to 3 percent for U.S. companies. The Japanese government encouraged joint R&D efforts and cost sharing among the Japanese automakers to boost both R&D efficiency and R&D effectiveness. An MIT study showed that in 1985 Honda spent $670 million on R&D and General Motors spent $3.7 billion; each company ended up with about 300 patents. Some European manufacturers cooperated on basic research in such areas as fuel economy and materials usage. Virtually all automakers relied on the research efforts of parts suppliers for improved parts performance, advances in components design, development of new materials such as ceramics, and new applications for electronic components and computerized controls. Japanese automakers and parts suppliers were active in opening automotive-related engineering research centers and making grants to engineering research programs at U.S. universities to gain early access to American developments in automotive technology.

PARTS AND COMPONENTS SUPPLIERS

Motor vehicles had between 10,000 and 15,000 parts. Some were made in-house and some were sourced outside. Reliance on outside suppliers varied greatly from manufacturer to manufacturer. The two extremes were GM, which sourced about 30 percent of its components externally, and Honda, which sourced 80 percent externally; Ford sourced about 50 percent of its parts externally, Toyota about 73 percent, and Chrysler about 75 percent. Make-or-buy decisions were normally driven by cost and investment considerations. External sourcing dominated when component manufacture required large investments, highly specialized know-how or equipment, big experience curve effects, or scale economies such that the volume of components a manufacturer needed was too small to permit low-cost production in-house. Even where in-house components manufacture was cost justified, automakers sometimes produced only 60 to 80 percent of their requirements for a particular component internally so that ups and downs in the volume needed could be accommodated by ordering more or less from outside suppliers. Worldwide, the trend among vehicle producers was toward both greater outsourcing and reliance on fewer numbers of suppliers.

Worldwide, there were over 100,000 suppliers providing original-equipment parts and accessories for new vehicles and replacement parts for the "aftermarket." Most were small enterprises employing fewer than 100 people, but the number also included major companies with sales of $1 billion or more. Original-equipment parts were the backbone of the business, accounting for 75 to 90 percent of total parts sales, but aftermarket parts sales were more lucrative. Because vehicle makers demanded low-cost parts meeting precise specifications and delivery schedules, suppliers were under great pressure to be both efficient and reliable as to quality and delivery. Many parts companies were nonunionized. To keep costs down, they ran plants continuously with three shifts and overtime, kept the sizes of their engineering and administrative staffs to an acceptable minimum, watched overhead expenses like hawks, and substituted less-expensive materials where possible. In 1994, suppliers were being pressured to accept more responsibility for R&D efforts to improve their products, and they were under strong mandates to provide better and better quality assurance. Vehicle makers were increasingly delegating the design and engineering on new-model parts to suppliers to accelerate the introduction of new car lines and to divide the heavy development expense.

PARTS SUPPLY STRATEGIES OF U.S. VEHICLE MAKERS

About 40,000 suppliers were engaged in furnishing parts to vehicle makers in the United States. GM, Ford, and Chrysler usually divided supply contracts for a part among several suppliers, both to insure uninterrupted deliveries in case one particular supplier had difficulties and to foster strong price competition among rival suppliers. As a rule, U.S. auto companies were reluctant to source a complete system from outside suppliers if it was a high-volume item or if the component was considered critical (engines, transmissions, axles). Typically, a higher percentage of newly introduced components was purchased from outside suppliers than was the case for components used for many years running. Vehicle makers purchased primarily on the basis of low price, but they also looked for consistent quality, a track record of reliability, and technological capabilities. Most U.S. plants maintained bigger parts inventories than Japanese plants because they had not mastered just-in-time inventory practices as well as the Japanese; in many instances, arriving parts were inspected. Recently, U.S. companies had begun sourcing parts from fewer, more technologically capable suppliers and granting contracts for three to five years in return for price concessions; this contrasted with the past practices of buying most outside parts under annual contracts covering the model year and frequent switching of suppliers to gain a lower price. Suppliers had also started locating production facilities near new assembly plants to assure manufacturers of their commitment to meeting the manufacturer's requirements on a long-term basis and to facilitate coordination. Clustering parts-supply manufacture near assembly plants also proved economical when shipping costs were significant.

General Motors, Ford, and Chrysler had goals of standardizing more parts and systems across their car and truck models in order to capture the economies of longer production runs and simplify the task of designing, engineering, and manufacturing many models. Parts standardization yielded substantial cost and quality benefits, as well as making it cheaper and easier to supply replacement parts for after-the-sale repairs. U.S. carmakers were also approaching parts suppliers to design and build entire systems rather than individual parts. For instance, rather than using outside suppliers to stamp out door handles, they were moving toward having suppliers design and build entire door systems, complete with armrests, interior trim, latches, and wiring. While a few auto parts suppliers had such capabilities, many smaller parts manufacturers were not equipped to design and build systems.

There was ferocious competition between candidate material suppliers in a host of applications: plastic versus steel in body panels, aluminum versus copper in radiators, rubber versus plastic versus chrome in interior and exterior trim. Gaining a vehicle maker's acceptance for a new material or innovative component was sometimes arduous; vehicle makers often insisted on several years of testing for reliability, and in situations where the incumbent component was made in-house they were reluctant to quickly switch to outside suppliers if it meant incurring early write-offs on their existing parts-making investments. Even if an outside supplier developed a patented position on a desirable new part, U.S. vehicle makers seldom accepted a sole-source arrangement past the early stage of the innovation's acceptance.

PARTS SUPPLY STRATEGIES OF JAPANESE VEHICLE MAKERS

There are some 400 Japanese parts makers, plus another 10,000 parts-making enterprises that operated as subcontractors to the major parts companies. Over 96 percent of Japanese parts production was controlled by companies with 500 or more employees. Most Japanese parts suppliers belonged to a major automaker family (or *keiretsu*) and located their plants relatively close to the associated automaker's final assembly plant.[2] The smallest subcontractors in the family tended to be responsible for one simple item. Their production was shipped to a minor-components family member who assembled an assigned component from the several parts it received plus those made in-house; these minor-components assemblers channeled their output on up the line to a bigger systems or major-components assembler who delivered it just-in-time (*kanban*) to the automaker—it was not unusual for suppliers to make several deliveries daily, allowing parts inventories at work stations to be as small as a two-hours' supply. Japanese automakers, especially Toyota and Nissan, sourced most of their parts from within their families, but they also purchased small percentages from suppliers in other families to promote healthy competition among the various parts makers. Honda, Mazda, Mitsubishi, and other small-share companies had fewer auto parts manufacturers in their keiretsus than Toyota and Nissan and thus sourced a bigger fraction of their parts and components from members of other keiretsus and unaffiliated suppliers. Parts makers affiliated with Toyota and Nissan were regarded as more technologically sophisticated and competent than auto parts suppliers in

---

[2]The *keiretsu* system, common to many Japanese industries involved intricate alliances, interlocking company structures, and ownership of each other's stock such that separate companies in the same keiretsu often cooperated closely on matters of mutual business interest. Competition and arms-length business transactions tended to be more intense across keiretsus than within keiretsus.

competitors' families. The keiretsu system had so far effectively blockaded U.S. and European parts manufacturers from supplying more than a token volume of parts to Japanese assembly plants located in Japan—in 1992 U.S. auto parts suppliers had less than a 1 percent market share in Japan. However, political and trade pressures were building on the Japanese automakers in 1994 to agree to source more parts from U.S. manufacturers.

Japanese vehicle makers also preferred to source parts from Japanese suppliers at their North American and European plants. While they sometimes bowed to pressures to use local parts suppliers at their foreign-based assembly plants, their policy was to encourage their Japan-based suppliers to develop export markets and to be capable of supplying their foreign assembly plants. To support the Japanese assembly plants in North America, Japanese parts suppliers had established more than 300 parts-making operations in the U.S., Canada, and Mexico; Japanese parts suppliers were likewise developing European locations to supply the Toyota, Honda, and Nissan plants in Great Britain and the Mazda plant in Spain and to solicit business from other European-based vehicle producers. In many instances, the Japanese parts suppliers had entered into joint ventures with host country partners to help them become comfortable in dealing with government officials, construction companies, labor unions, and other organizations that had to be dealt with in starting up new plant operations outside Japan. Virtually all of the Japanese parts suppliers in North America and Europe were eagerly seeking customers other than the Japanese assembly plants and were stressing the engineering support they would provide to customers.

Suppliers to Japanese assembly plants were expected to meet rigorous just-in-time delivery schedules and to be scrupulous about quality—Japanese automakers maintained no mechanisms for inspecting arriving parts. Japanese producers guaranteed their suppliers long-term contracts, extended them credit, and often had a minority ownership stake. Vehicle manufacturers held extensive discussions with their suppliers about their production plans, volume requirements, impending technological changes, potential new specifications, and ways for making improvements. When gearing up to make a new part, it was standard practice for suppliers to work closely with automakers in phasing parts production *gradually* up to full capacity so that parts quality would be high all along the way to maximum line speeds.

Japanese automakers provided technical assistance to their suppliers in modifying equipment or the parts-making process when needed, but suppliers were pressured hard to stay abreast of advanced components technology, to pay special attention to parts design and engineering, and to pursue continuous improvement in their parts manufacturing and parts quality. Automakers expected that the prices they paid for parts should normally be declining over time and they exerted continual downward pressure on suppliers' prices. Many Japanese parts suppliers, as a consequence, were less profitable than the Japanese automakers, paid their employees lower wages, did not guarantee lifetime employment, and occasionally laid off workers if business slackened. But in terms of defects per million parts, they were widely regarded as the world's best on quality. In 1994, all the major Japanese automakers were engaged in programs to reduce the variety of parts in their respective models.

PARTS SUPPLY IN EUROPE

Most European vehicle makers sourced 60 to 80 percent of their components externally, chiefly from suppliers within their own national boundaries. U.S. parts suppliers operating in Europe typically sold to vehicle manufacturers all over Europe, however, as well as to the European assembly plants of Ford and GM.

The German supplier industry was dominated by large, technologically advanced firms that produced well-engineered, high-quality components. They maintained sizable research and engineering staffs and participated broadly in joint R&D efforts with automakers and related suppliers. Exports were often substantial.

Fiat dominated the Italian supplier industry, producing key components in-house and purchasing the balance from hundreds of small, family-owned suppliers. Fiat was the most integrated European manufacturer.

French auto parts suppliers were mostly small- and medium-sized firms lacking in resources to invest in modern facilities and advanced research. Many had problems keeping quality up and unit costs down and nearly all were heavily dependent on orders from Renault and Peugeot/Citroen.

MANUFACTURING AND ASSEMBLY

Motor vehicle assembly was an intricate process requiring the coordination of outside suppliers, in-house parts manufacture, skilled craftsmen, semiskilled assembly-line workers, and mechanized techniques. Assembly plants were typically huge complexes, requiring anywhere from $200 million to $2 billion dollars in capital investment and employing thousands of workers. In years past when producers could sell 500,000 or more units of the same model, efficient, low-cost production depended on capturing scale economies and experience curve benefits. More recently though, as demand fragmented and model sales under 100,000 units became commonplace, efficient assembly depended on flexible manufacturing techniques that allowed the same plant to turn out several models with minimal changeover costs. The new keys to overall low costs were achieving economical parts production, utilizing plant layouts and equipment that permitted assembly of different models, maintaining a high level of capacity utilization (to spread high fixed costs out over more units), making use of state-of-the-art automated equipment, minimizing downtime for model changeovers when parallel assembly lines were infeasible, continually pursuing ways to improve work methods and boost assembly line productivity, and gaining full worker cooperation in performing tasks more efficiently. Minimum efficient plant sizes for passenger-car assembly were in the neighborhood of 100,000 to 200,000 units annually. Even with automated techniques, it took 16 to 20 hours of labor time to assemble a vehicle, thus making wage rates and union work rules a significant cost determinant. Union rules traditionally put narrow bounds on the tasks a worker in a particular job classification could be assigned; this was tolerable in a mass-production situation where tasks were repetitive, but such restrictions were a major obstacle to high labor productivity on assembly lines where worker flexibility was needed in assembling different models and accomplishing efficient changeovers. Flexible assembly methods, to be low cost, demanded far more of plant management in the way of manufacturing know-how and people-management skills than did routinized mass production of a single model.

High-quality manufacture and assembly was a pervasive concern at all auto companies. Nothing irritated buyers more than a rash of problems with a newly purchased vehicle; there was always much publicity surrounding models with defects and high repair frequencies, and it could take a producer years to overcome the stigma of turning out problem-causing vehicles.

Japanese producers were the most adept at high-quality, low-cost manufacture and assembly. They started their quality-control effort at the design stage, stressing the need for design engineers to make their designs "manufacturable." Parts and components suppliers were expected to push hard for both zero defects and low costs. Following Toyota's pioneering efforts, most Japanese assembly plants employed lean production systems that required less manufacturing space, less investment in tools, and fewer workers than the assembly processes at U.S. and European plants. Toyota's lean production system, which other Japanese producers had emulated, stressed continuous improvement (the concept of *kaizen*), reduction of costs through just-in-time techniques (the concept of *kanban*), teamwork between employees and managers, worker initiative and involvement, and accountability for quality. Japanese companies saw high labor productivity as dependent on proper plant layout, appropriate work methods, and how people were organized and managed. Advanced technology and automation were used only when they enhanced quality. The production goals at Japanese assembly plants were continually declining costs, zero defects, zero parts and components inventories, and superior fits and finishes. Strict quality-control procedures were in place everywhere. Attention to detail, pride of workmanship, and a strong quality consciousness pervaded the workforces at Japanese assembly plants. When problems were identified, they were attacked aggressively and corrected. There were few (usually two to four) job classifications for assembly-line workers, allowing workers to perform multiple tasks.

Managers at Japanese plants worked closely with employees to master the art of making gradual, minute, incremental labor-saving changes in production operations (the concept of kaizen). According to an official at Honda's Marysville, Ohio, plant:

> We don't set out to double the output of our number two stamping line. We look for only the next step. We shorten the time it takes to stamp our largest body panel by two seconds. And when we accomplish that, we shorten the time on the next largest panel, and then all the panels. And then we do the same thing on the next stamping line. When we've gone through the whole process, perhaps we've made the entire stamping plant 20 percent more efficient.

It was standard Japanese management practice to pursue continuous improvement, year after year, in workforce methods, process technology, and use of more efficient equipment. Employees who put forth good suggestions for improvement were rewarded. Managers concentrated on creating a gung-ho work environment, and every plant was focused on continuous cost reduction. The efficiency of Japanese automaking plants in North America and Europe was on a par with comparable plants in Japan.

A 1987 MIT study of 40 assembly plants in 13 countries showed that the average assembly plant in Japan used 20.3 hours of labor to produce a car versus 24.4 hours for the average North American plant and 32.9 hours at European plants. Exhibit 11 shows comparative operating efficiency for a GM assembly plant, a Toyota assembly plant in Japan, and a California assembly plant operated by Toyota management in a joint venture with GM. The statistics provide dramatic evidence of the advantages of Japanese assembly processes and work practices.

Since the mid-1980s, both U.S. and European vehicle producers had begun programs to overhaul their assembly plants and work practices to be competitive with the Japanese producers. In 1994 Ford was said to have the best assembly plant productivity among U.S. and European producers. The labor time for assembly at two Ford plants was under the Japanese average in the MIT study and Ford's Taurus-Sable assembly plant in Atlanta was the most labor efficient U.S. plant, based on the most recent data available. During the 1990s, labor productivity at many older assembly plants in the U.S. and Europe had improved dramatically. After GM bought

EXHIBIT 11 | **Comparative Operating Efficiency of a GM Assembly Plant versus a Toyota GM Plant in California versus a Toyota Plant in Japan, 1987**

Efficiency Measure	GM's Framingham Assembly Plant (Closed in July 1989)	GM–Toyota Plant in California*	Toyota's Takaota Plant
Assembly hours per car	31	19	16
Square feet of assembly space per car produced	8.1	7.0	4.8
Assembly defects per 100 cars	135	45	45
Average inventory of parts maintained in assembly plant	2 weeks	2 days	2 hours

*Operated by Toyota management with heavy reliance on techniques and approaches employed by Toyota in Japan.

Source: James P. Womack and Daniel T. Jones, *The Machine That Changed the World* (New York: Macmillan, 1990), as reported in *The New York Times Magazine,* September 23, 1990, p. 23.

EXHIBIT 12 | **Comparisons of Quality of Japanese, American, and European Cars, 1980, 1989, and 1993**

	Number of Defects per Car		
Car Manufacturer	1980	1989	1993*
Chrysler	8.1	1.8	NA
General Motors	7.4	1.7	1.08
Ford	6.7	1.5	NA
U.S. average	7.3	1.6	1.13
Japanese average	2.0	1.2	0.84 (estimate)
European average	2.8	2.1	1.28

*During first 90 days of ownership.

Sources: Harbour & Associates for 1980 and 1989; J. D. Power & Associates for 1993 as reported in *The Wall Street Journal.*

a 50 percent interest in Sweden's Saab in 1989, it cut the labor time for assembly from a shocking 120 hours per car to 57 hours in 1992 and to a planned 30 hours on its 1994 Saab 900 models. Ford had cut the assembly time by 50 percent at its Jaguar assembly plant in Britain.

Exhibit 12 presents data on the number of new-car defects for Japanese companies compared to American and European companies. The most common auto defects were faulty electrical accessories, blemishes in paint and trim, engine trouble, and squeaks and rattles.

PRODUCTION COSTS

Production costs of similar vehicles varied widely from manufacturer to manufacturer owing to differences in the geographic locations of plants, the age of plant equipment, plant sizes, whether the workforce was unionized, local wage rates (see Exhibit 13), labor productivity, the ease/difficulty with which a vehicle's design could be manufactured and assembled, the costs of raw materials and components, the extent of automation, and the manufacturing approaches and practices employed by management. Furthermore, shifts in currency exchange rates could result in inefficient plants in one country actually being cost competitive with efficient plants in another country. During the 1990s, for example, significant increases in the value of the yen against both the dollar and European currencies in the 1992–93 period wiped out the production cost advantages the Japanese producers enjoyed at their very efficient plants in Japan and undermined their strategy of exporting cars made in Japan to foreign markets and selling them at prices below the comparable models of U.S. and European producers.

In 1994 labor costs for assembly ranged from a low of about $480 at an efficient Toyota Corolla plant in Japan (16 hours at an average hourly cost of $30, including fringes) to $900 for a Ford Taurus (20 hours at $45 per hour, including fringes) to $27,000 for a Rolls Royce (900 hours at an average cost of $30 per hour). For an $18,000 Ford Taurus, the direct assembly expense for labor ran about 5 percent of the sticker price. Assembly labor costs for most models were comfortably under 10 percent of current sticker prices. By comparison, marketing and distribution costs ran about 30 to 35 percent of the sticker price. GM, for example, spent $30 million for an introductory advertising campaign for its new Aurora models, which, based on projected sales of 30,000 units annually, equaled $1,000 per vehicle just for advertising.

Until the 1990s, the Japanese automakers had been able to win market share gains in the U.S. and Europe because their quality was higher and their prices were lower. Production costs at Japan-based assembly plants were sufficiently lower than Japanese producers could make vehicles in Japan, export them to the U.S., and sell them at prices $1,000 to $2,500 below the comparable models of U.S. producers, or export

EXHIBIT 13 | **Average Hourly Compensation Rates in the Motor Vehicle Industry, Selected Countries, 1991**

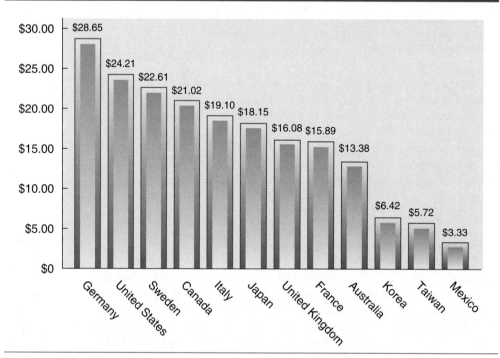

Note: This tabulation is based on average earnings, including benefits and bonuses.
Source: U.S. Bureau of Labor Statistics, as reported in 1993 *Ward's Automotive Yearbook*, p. 59.

them to Europe and undercut the prices of European producers by $500 to $750 per vehicle. But in 1992 and 1993, the yen appreciated 15 to 20 percent against the dollar, effectively raising the cost of cars made in Japan and sold in the U.S. by 15 to 20 percent. Japanese producers were forced into raising sticker prices on their U.S. models by sizable amounts, since over half the Japanese vehicles sold in the U.S. were made in Japan—the percentage made in Japan for any one model varied from under 10 percent for models made in the Japanese producers' new North American plants (like the Honda Accord and the Toyota Camry) to 100 percent for models made exclusively in Japan (like Lexus, Infiniti, Acura, and Nissan Maximas). Moreover, by 1994 both U.S. and European producers had made major headway in revamping assembly-line processes, improving labor efficiency, and otherwise getting their production costs more in line with Japanese standards.

In 1994, Japanese models were selling anywhere from $1,000 to $18,000 above comparable U.S. models. Toyota's top-of-the-line Lexus LS400, made in Japan, had a price $18,000 above GM's new American-made Oldsmobile Aurora, a luxury sedan with essentially equivalent technology, styling, and features (though the Aurora didn't have the Lexus's quality image and reputation). However, Japanese manufacturers still had a $300 to $600 cost advantage over U.S. producers on cars built at newly constructed Japanese assembly plants in North America and a similar advantage over European producers for models made at their newly built European plants. Several reasons accounted for these continuing cost advantages. One was the low interest rates available to Japan automakers from Japanese banks. Between 1986 and 1991 Toyota had borrowed $6.2 billion at interest rates of 1.2 percent to 4 percent; GM and Ford had paid 9 percent and more on their borrowings during the same time frame. Another reason related to lower costs for pension benefits and health care premiums of retirees—in 1992, for instance, GM was not only paying for health care costs of 386,000 U.S. employees and their dependents but also the health care costs of 358,000 retirees and their dependents, plus pension benefits for these retirees. The North American and European plants of the Japanese producers were too new to have such retiree cost burdens. Other contributors to the Japanese producers' cost advantage in North America and Europe were their lower costs for model redesign and new-model development, their lean production systems, and their lower plant-investment costs.

Toyota was the low-cost producer among Japanese automakers. Chrysler was the overall low-cost producer among U.S. automakers, followed by Ford and then General Motors. In 1993, based on North American production only, Chrysler produced 25.6 vehicles per employee, Ford turned out 24.6 vehicles per employee, and GM made 14.0 vehicles per employee. General Motors' standing as the high-cost producer was in sharp contrast to its position throughout the 1950s and 1960s when long production runs of fewer basic models and a commanding 50 percent market share had made it the world's low-cost producer. Fiat and GM were the low-cost producers among European carmakers even though Volkswagen-Audi was regarded as the world's leader in assembly-line automation.

Still, in 1994, GM, Ford, and Chrysler had not succeeded in producing low-end models for the North American market at a cost that enabled them to make a profit. All three U.S. makers were sourcing low-priced models (Ford Probe, Geo Prism and Metro, Eagle Talon, Plymouth Laser) from Korean producers and from North American assembly plants either operated in partnership with or owned by Japanese producers. While GM's Saturn models had been well received in the market, Saturn had not achieved the sales volumes of 350,000 to 400,000 units it needed annually to be profitable. It remained to be seen whether Chrysler could earn a profit on its just-introduced Neon subcompact line.

CAR RETAILING AND DEALERSHIPS

Worldwide, most new motor vehicles were retailed to buyers through independent franchised dealers. The one big exception to relying totally on retail dealer channels was in Japan where vehicles were marketed chiefly through affiliated distributors and manufacturers' direct sales forces. Toyota had over 30,000 salespeople and Nissan employed over 25,000. Distributors sold on average more than 5,000 vehicles annually and marketed only one producer's brands—dual or multiple franchises were prohibited. Sales staffers were organized into teams of seven or eight people who were trained in all aspects of the job. Every day started and ended with a team meeting. Team members drew up profiles of every household within the geographic area around the distributorship; after calling for an appointment, sales agents made house-calls. During a visit, the customer's profile would be updated and, based on the new answers, the agent would suggest the most appropriate specifications for a new vehicle. If the household decided to consider purchasing a new car, there were discussions regarding optional equipment, colors, trade-in price, a financing package, insurance, and delivery date. Since the vast majority of new cars sold in Japan were manufactured to order and delivered to the buyer within five days or less, dealers kept only three or four demonstrator models on hand. When sales lagged, the sales team put in extra hours (the team was paid on a group commission), and if sales lagged to the point where the factory did not have enough orders to sustain full output, production workers were transferred over to sales. Dealers fixed all defects the owner encountered with the cars at no cost to the owner (even after the end of the formal warranty); however, the owner was responsible for normal maintenance and for repairs needed to pass Ministry of Transport inspections. The first inspection had to be passed when the car was three years old; thereafter, inspections became more frequent and more demanding. Dealers' service areas were primarily used for handling the inspection process.

The prime objective of Japanese dealers was to build brand loyalty by creating long-term relationships with their customers, making them feel part of the manufacturer's "family," treating them well, and charging them fair prices. Sales agents called their customers regularly, stayed up-to-date on when sons and daughters might be needing their first cars, and sent owners birthday cards. Car sales agents in Japan were so attentive and persistent that, so the saying went, the only way to escape them was to leave the country.

Outside Japan, the vast majority of new-vehicle sales were handled by independent franchised dealers (some manufacturers made factory-direct fleet sales to rental car companies and to large corporations that utilized many vehicles in day-to-day operations). Retail dealers also handled final inspection and preparation of vehicles for delivery, warranty claims, repairs and service, trade-ins, and financing. Manufacturers supported their dealerships by conducting nationally advertised sales campaigns, developing sales literature, sponsoring training programs for repair mechanics, cooperating in local sales promotions, providing new-car financing, and offering incentives to stimulate sales when showroom traffic slacked off. About 30 to 35 percent of the retail price of a vehicle represented dealers' markups and the marketing and distribution costs incurred by manufacturers. With the gap in perceived product quality in the industry narrowing, industry observers were predicting that the competitive edge in automotive retailing would swing to dealers with the widest selection, best on-the-spot delivery capabilities, and best prices.

In the U.S., multibrand dealerships were common. In smaller towns dealers had long been franchised to carry two brands of the same domestic manufacturer (Oldsmobile-Cadillac, Lincoln-Mercury, Chrysler-Plymouth). More recently, though, dealers had added one or more import brands to supplement sales of their original domestic brand and to spread their economic risk and large overhead costs. Most foreign manufacturers had built their dealer networks by getting domestic dealers with lagging sales to take on an import brand. The popularity of import brands in the U.S., coupled with fewer numbers of import dealers, had resulted in the best-selling import brands having substantially bigger unit sales volumes per dealer than was the case for domestic brands—for instance, the 1,350 Toyota dealers in the U.S. averaged 700 new vehicles per year whereas the 4,500 Chevrolet dealers averaged only 525 vehicles annually. The average U.S. car dealership sold 1,200 new and used vehicles annually and had annual revenues of about $15 million. Large "superdealers," with multiple franchises and multiple locations in metro-areas, had revenues of $100 to $800 million on volumes of 20,000 to 70,000 vehicles (some of which usually included fleet sales).

In 1993, there were 16,000 car dealers in the U.S., who had 48,800 franchises (an average of 3 brands per dealer), and who operated 24,000 new-car sales outlets; by 2000 it was anticipated that there would be just 8,000 dealer principals operating 18,000 retail sales outlets. In trucks, there were 9,150 dealers and 26,400 new-truck franchises, an average of 2.9 brands per dealer. Several of the largest and most successful U.S. dealerships also operated outlets in foreign countries, and the numbers were expected to increase during the 1990s. Consolidation among retail dealers was occurring because of growing popularity of multiple-franchise dealerships and thinner dealer profit margins. To offset the decline in profits from new-vehicle sales, dealers were relying on income from car financing, extended warranty contracts, paint protectors, rustproofing and undercoating, installation of optional deluxe trim packages, and no-haggle pricing (which required fewer salespeople).

European producers generally had their strongest dealer networks in their own countries. However, the leading companies all had dealer outlets scattered across Europe. Mercedes-Benz, Volvo, BMW, Volkswagen-Audi, and Porsche had between 200 and 800 dealers in the U.S., plus distribution capabilities in selected other countries. Dual or multiple franchising was restricted in most European nations, particularly in Britain.

STRATEGIC ALLIANCES AND JOINT VENTURES

During the 1980s and early 1990s, automakers and parts suppliers formed dozens of joint ventures to conduct automotive research, produce components and engines, and assemble new car and truck models. Such alliances not only allowed investment risks and operating costs to be shared but they also gave the partners attractive new avenues for accessing manufacturing methods, management practices, technology, and global markets. Japanese-American, Japanese-European, and European-European ventures were the most common. General Motors and Toyota were 50-50 partners in an assembly plant in Fremont, California; GM and Toyota had also teamed up in Australia. GM owned a 39 percent stake in Isuzu Motors and was a 50-50 partner with Suzuki Motor Co. in a Canadian assembly plant that turned out Geo Metro models for GM and Suzuki Swift models for Suzuki. Sweden's Volvo and France's state-owned Renault had bought minority ownerships in each other and were planning to combine their design facilities, parts production, and engine manufacture. Ford, which owned a 25 percent stake in Mazda, had arranged for up to 120,000 Ford Probes a year to be produced at Mazda's new Flat Rock, Michigan, assembly plant where Mazda was producing two of its own models for the U.S. market. Nissan was handling the imports of Volkswagen in Japan and Volkswagen was marketing Nissan's 4-wheel-drive vehicle in Germany. Volkswagen had ties with 11 other companies including Volvo, Daimler-Benz (the maker of Mercedes cars and trucks), Nissan, Porsche, and Ford. VW and Ford were partners in a plant in Portugal that built minivans. Korea's Daewoo Motor Corp., which had recently suffered through a breakup of its 50–50 joint venture with General Motors, had entered into an alliance with Honda to produce the next-generation Acura Legend; the deal gave Daewoo access to Japanese luxury-car technology and granted Honda the Korean foothold it had long wanted.

THE WORLD CAR CONCEPT

The concept of a world car sold in multiple markets had intrigued manufacturers since the 1970s because of the potential for dramatically reducing development and production costs by spreading R&D, tooling, and engineering expenses across worldwide operations and economizing on the number of models. Scale economies were generally greater in component manufacture than in assembly operations. Components for a world car could be produced in large, modern plants located in low-wage countries and shipped to smaller assembly plants located in or near regional and large country markets. Designs for the world car would be similar in most countries and would incorporate as many of the same components as feasible; limited modifications would accommodate differing consumer tastes and regulatory requirements across country markets. So far, however, automakers had met with only moderate success in manufacturing and marketing a world car because buyer demand had historically been fairly divergent across national markets due to different styling preferences, uneven buyer sophistication regarding options and driving performance, disparate income levels and buying power, dissimilar gasoline prices, and widely varying road systems. Additionally, there had been problems regarding local content rules, transcontinental shipping costs, political instability in key low-wage countries, differing pollution emission standards, and the logistical complexity of integrating production, distribution, and marketing across such a wide geographic expanse. Truckmakers faced much the same obstacles in trying to market a global truck.

So far, Toyota had come closest to executing a world car concept; Toyota essentially built one version of each model at its huge assembly complex in Japan, making only minor country-specific modifications when needed. The company had sold nearly 1 million of its Corolla models in 1992. Toyota engineers were careful to design cars that were suitable for multiple markets. Honda made the same car at its U.S. plants that were made at its Japanese plants and exported cars made at its Marysville, Ohio, plant back to Japan. Ford was the only U.S. manufacturer that had pursued the concept of a world car; the company's collaboration with Mazda to produce a world car had proved unsuccessful when the resulting models had ended up with an insignificant number of common parts. However, Ford had high hopes that its $6 billion investment in a mid-size world car—named the Mondeo in Europe and the Ford Contour and Mercury Mystique in the United States—would pay off.

COMPETITIVE CONDITIONS IN 1994

Both American and European automakers viewed the Japanese companies as their strongest competitive threats. Even though the rising value of the Japanese yen had pushed up the average prices of Japanese cars to levels $1,000 to $18,000 above comparable U.S.-made cars, U.S. consumers were still attracted to Japanese-made vehicles. In 1993 Japanese companies captured 40 percent of passenger-car sales in California, 23 percent of the total U.S. passenger-car market, and 14 percent of the U.S. truck market. Analysts were predicting that Japanese carmakers' North American production capability and continued vehicle exports to the U.S. could yield them 30 to 35 percent of the U.S. passenger-car market before the year 2000.

Despite the Japanese automakers' success in penetrating global markets and in becoming full-line producers, they faced formidable challenges in 1994. Exports fell in 1993 for the eighth straight year; declining exports, coupled with a full-blown recession in Japan, had put pressure on profit margins and employment levels at Japan-based plants. In 1992, profit margins averaged just 0.8 percent of revenues, equal to a profit of about $100 per vehicle—well below the $600 to $700 average of the mid-1980s. The long-term debt of Japan's 11 motor vehicle manufacturers exceeded $80 billion; Isuzu and Mazda both had debt-to-equity ratios exceeding 100 percent. At the same time, trade frictions had worsened with the U.S. under the Clinton Administration. The sudden turn in their near-term market prospects and fortunes had all the Japanese producers looking for ways to standardize components, cut costs, and restore profitability. Japanese producers had announced several plant closings and personnel cutbacks, formed a number of partnerships to produce both parts and models, lengthened product cycles, reduced the number of model options and variations, and delayed the introduction of several new models. Isuzu announced its withdrawal from passenger car-products—electing to put more emphasis on its truck business (it was the Japanese leader in diesel engines and was second in medium-size trucks). Talk of mergers and consolidations among the Japanese producers was widespread. A Honda executive said in mid-1993, "In the future, no one company will be responsible for all of its own products. I believe the industry will be split into department store manufacturers and boutique manufacturers."

While in 1990 the U.S. producers had been floundering in the wake of Japan's unrelenting gains in the U.S. market and elsewhere, in 1993 and 1994 they showed signs of competitive resurgence worldwide. Worldwide production of Japan's vehicle producers fell 2.7 percent in 1993 while production at GM, Ford, and Chrysler was up 6 percent. A recession in Japan had hurt Japanese companies' sales at home and a stronger yen had blunted their export sales worldwide. Japanese companies' share of the U.S. market dropped from nearly 28 percent in 1991 to 25.1 percent in 1992 and to 23.1 percent in 1993. Several factors were at work: the big increases on the sticker prices of most Japanese models; growing evidence that the quality of U.S. models was almost equal to Japanese models (as measured by the number of new-car defects reported in the first 90 days); a strong "buy American" feeling among many consumers; and popularity of several newly introduced and restyled U.S. models. Ford's Taurus replaced Honda's Accord as the top-selling model in the United States in both 1992 and 1993.

Since 1989 GM, Ford, and Chrysler had made major strides in factory productivity, customer service, and product development. All three had an array of new and redesigned models in the marketplace and more in the pipeline for 1995 and 1996. Chrysler had transformed itself into a world leader in product development; both Ford and GM were profitable in 1993 following losses in 1992. Company-for-company, the U.S. auto industry was the strongest in the world in 1994. Despite subpar sales of 14.2 million cars and trucks in 1993, the three U.S. companies had combined operating profits of $9.6 billion whereas most Japanese and European producers posted losses or, at best, token profits. Experts believed that the Japanese would have to initiate further price increases to achieve satisfactory profits. Japanese automakers believed the long-term solution of yen-driven price increases and buy-American sentiment was to build a bigger fraction of their vehicles in the U.S.; in 1993, roughly half the Japanese car brands sold in the U.S. were U.S.-built.

In Europe, a steep recession had cut deeply into 1993 sales levels. European automakers were all launching renewed efforts to cut costs and boost workforce productivity to try to catch up to the gains U.S. and Japanese companies had made several years earlier. Stymied somewhat by import restrictions and a stronger yen, Japanese producers were concentrating on getting their European production bases operating at full efficiency and contemplating whether to expand their European production capacity or depend on exports from Japan to support market share gains. BMW was constructing an assembly plant in South Carolina and Mercedes-Benz was building a plant to produce sports-utility vehicles in Alabama.

In post–Eastern Europe, two companies in Germany, Trabant and Wartburg, had ceased production and closed their hopelessly obsolete factories. A plant in Serbia, which had exported the low-price, low-quality Yugo to the U.S. until 1992, quit making cars and started making weapons for the war in Bosnia. Russian producers had asked U.S. companies for technology to upgrade their models; GM had agreed to provide sophisticated engine control systems to VAZ to make the Lada. Volkswagen-Audi had acquired Skoda in the Czech Republic. In 1992 Fiat acquired Poland's largest producer, FSM, which built two old Fiat designs; Fiat was updating FSM's models. GM was in negotiations with Poland's second-largest producer, FSO, regarding an alliance or possible acquisition. Germany's BMW had negotiated a deal to acquire Britain's Rover Group.

In Asia, 11 small Taiwanese companies had begun assembling models supplied by partners from Japan, the U.S., and Europe to satisfy rising domestic demand. Volkswagen-Audi, Peugeot, GM, and Chrysler had begun to manufacture vehicles in China; Honda and Ford were said to be looking for partners in China. Car production in China had tripled in 1992 to 120,000 units, and Chinese demand for motor vehicles was expected to mushroom over the next several decades. All of South Korea's major automakers had increased their export targets considerably, to a total of 625,000 to 650,000 in 1993-94. Korean vehicle producers were actively investing in new production capacity. Vehicle production in Korea had increased 800 percent since 1982. Korean manufacturers, chiefly Hyundai, Daewoo Motors, and Kia Motors, planned to expand their Korean-based capacity from the present 1.7 million units annually to 5 million units annually by 2000. The Korean companies were eager to duplicate the Japanese success and were pushing hard to boost their production know-how, manufacturing efficiency, and vehicle quality. In late 1993, Kia followed Hyundai and introduced a bargain-priced sedan in the U.S. market.

Whereas during the 1985–93 period, competition had centered around assembly-plant productivity, defect-free product quality, and the time it took to bring out a new or redesigned model, many observers believed that production and assembly were not going to be such important keys to competitive success in the future. This was because all major vehicle manufacturers were going all-out to achieve competitiveness on manufacturing cost, quality, and product development cycles, eliminating much of the competitive advantages in these areas held by the Japanese companies. In the years ahead, observers predicted, the challenges would lie in reducing marketing and distribution costs (which ran 30 to 35 percent of sticker prices), reducing corporate overhead costs, and creating a network of superefficient suppliers with the capability both to design and to manufacture complete, preassembled systems (doors with all the wires and mechanical gadgetry installed, complete dashboards, entire front and rear seating, electronic controls, and so on) rather than just deliver individual parts and components for assembly by the car manufacturer. Involving suppliers in the earliest stages to help plan and design new components would shift many design and technology developments upstream in the value chain to suppliers, allowing manufacturers to concentrate on managing the integration of the vehicle, creating unique lines of models from an array of modular components. It would also permit greater parts and components standardization across models and would streamline assembly times. Chrysler, which already sourced over 70 percent of its parts and components from outside suppliers, was moving the fastest to entrust the design and production of component systems to suppliers.

PROFILES OF SELECTED JAPANESE AUTOMAKERS

Exhibit 14 shows the worldwide production volumes for Japan's motor vehicle producers during the most recent five years.

HONDA MOTOR COMPANY

Founded in 1948, Honda was a maverick among Japanese carmakers. It was less tied to its keiretsu than the other Japanese producers and it was not prone to coordinate its actions with Japan's Ministry of International Trade and Industry, which guided the long-term strategic thrusts of Japanese companies. Rather, Honda's success had been engineered by the entrepreneurial instincts of its founder, Soichiro Honda, who died in 1991. First in motorcycles and later in automobiles, Soichiro Honda had come up with state-of-the-art products that surpassed, in one way or another, the models previously on the market. Honda first made a name for itself in the 1950s and 1960s when it emerged as the world's leading producer of motorcycles, scooters, and mopeds. The company did not start making automobiles until the 1960s.

Honda Motor was the most multinational of all the Japanese automakers. It had over 50 plants in 31 countries and its product line included cars, trucks, motorcycles, portable power generators, garden tillers, lawnmowers, and several other power equipment items—all of which used gasoline engines of one type or another. Over 60 percent of sales were outside Japan and automobiles accounted for 75 percent of total revenues. Honda products were designed with a global sense, to conquer world markets rather than just Japanese markets. In 1991 Honda reorganized the company into three product groups—autos, motorcycles, and power equipment—and did away with its consensus-style management; the heads of each product line were given considerable autonomy. The company earned $307 million on sales of $33.4 billion in 1992 and $220 million on sales of $35.8 billion in 1993.

EXHIBIT 14 | **Japanese Manufacturers' Worldwide Production of Cars and Trucks, 1989–1993**

	1989	1990	1991	1992	1993
Toyota	4,068,342	4,312,790	4,175,350	4,010,523	3,632,672
Cars	3,055,101	3,345,885	3,180,054	3,171,311	2,882,698
Trucks and Buses	920,801	866,488	905,027	760,030	679,052
Hino Trucks and Buses	92,440	100,417	90,269	79,182	70,922
Nissan	2,428,423	2,478,703	2,391,472	2,169,610	1,859,356
Cars	1,972,508	2,020,523	1,946,173	1,750,829	1,524,541
Trucks and Buses	455,915	458,180	445,299	418,781	334,815
Mitsubishi	1,249,510	1,332,938	1,405,647	1,395,875	1,362,447
Cars	708,418	833,265	914,178	939,590	944,247
Trucks and Buses	541,092	499,673	491,469	456,285	418,200
Mazda	1,270,085	1,422,624	1,385,941	1,281,050	1,029,128
Cars	967,665	1,118,036	1,085,400	1,037,113	864,468
Trucks and Buses	302,420	304,588	300,541	243,937	164,660
Honda	1,363,214	1,383,711	1,358,415	1,199,820	1,150,849
Cars	1,155,682	1,223,389	1,215,054	1,067,289	1,021,814
Trucks and Buses	207,532	160,322	143,361	132,531	129,035
Suzuki	868,318	838,969	858,268	844,411	796,661
Cars	430,053	511,832	531,343	535,171	510,265
Trucks and Buses	438,265	327,137	326,925	309,240	286,396
Daihatsu	664,339	636,449	670,481	610,342	560,320
Cars	263,631	373,110	420,313	392,478	352,855
Trucks and Buses	400,708	263,339	250,168	217,864	207,465
Fuji	556,590	516,759	528,333	513,925	437,924
Cars	310,623	319,585	330,107	366,502	322,622
Trucks and Buses	245,967	197,174	198,226	147,423	115,302
Isuzu	556,463	563,194	470,950	473,278	397,793
Cars	188,725	202,347	130,447	118,391	73,584
Trucks and Buses	367,738	360,847	340,503	354,887	324,209
Total	13,025,284	13,486,137	13,244,857	12,498,834	11,227,150
Total cars	9,052,406	9,947,972	9,753,069	9,378,694	8,497,094
Total Trucks and Buses	3,972,878	3,538,165	3,491,788	3,120,160	2,730,056

Source: *Automotive News*, 1993 Market Data Book, p. 3; *Automotive News*, 1994 Market Data Book, p. 3.

Honda was the first Japanese company to build abroad after World War II, starting with a moped plant in Belgium in 1962. It was the first Japanese automaker to open an assembly plant in the U.S. (1982) and Honda was the top-selling Japanese nameplate in the American market. Honda's Marysville, Ohio, plant was something of a sensation, generating numerous stories in the media about its immaculate appearance and astonishing features: the workers clad in white uniforms, the division of line workers into only two job classifications (production associate and maintenance associate), the on-site sports complex, the one cafeteria where everyone ate, and the prolific employee-suggestion system. Honda managers believed that the expert on any task was the person who did it every day on the assembly line. Honda made sure that employees who made the best suggestions for improvement were visibly recognized. Honda's U.S. plants made the use of U.S.-made parts a top-priority practice; the company said the local content of its 1994 Honda Accord models was 73 percent. In 1994 the Justice Department charged Honda of America with having engaged in corrupt practices and racketeering in operating its wholesale network during the 1980–93 period; embarrassed by the scandal, Honda management dismissed several executives.

Honda's reputation for manufacturing quality and customer satisfaction was a big factor in the company's success. In the J. D. Power reports on consumer satisfaction with automobile quality and dealer service, Honda's Acura brand had been the top-rated nameplate in 1987, 1988, and 1989. The Honda nameplate (Accord, Prelude, Civic, and CRX) had achieved top-5 rankings in each of the five J. D. Power surveys from 1985 through 1989. The Honda Accord had made *Car and Driver* magazine's list of the "Ten Best" cars every year since 1981. However, the Accord models were not nearly as popular in Japan. In 1992 and 1993, the Honda Accord was displaced by the Ford Taurus as the best-selling U.S. model. A newly restyled Accord was introduced in 1994. Toyota's Lexus and Nissan's Infiniti were both more highly rated than the Honda Accord or the Acura Legend models in recent J. D. Power surveys.

Although Honda shunned alliances with other automotive companies, it had collaborated with Britain's Rover Group on a variety of projects since 1979. In 1989 Honda and Rover Group initiated a joint project to construct a 100,000-vehicle-per-year assembly plant next to an existing Honda engine plant in Swindon, England; shortly thereafter, Honda purchased a 20 percent ownership in Rover and Rover bought a 20 percent stake in Honda's British plant. However, when Rover agreed to be acquired by BMW in 1994, Honda announced it would divest its ownership of Rover.

NISSAN MOTOR COMPANY

As early as 1983 Nissan was making cars and trucks in eight countries outside Japan: the U.S., Mexico, Peru, Australia, Spain, Italy, Thailand, and the Philippines. In addition, Nissan had affiliates in a dozen other countries where its vehicles were being assembled or made under license and had formed a number of strategic alliances to strengthen its access to foreign markets. In 1986 Nissan became the first Japanese producer to open an assembly plant in Britain. Nissan was strongly committed to establishing fully integrated operations in Europe, from vehicle design and development to manufacturing to sales and service.

In the early 1990s Nissan had introduced three new models in the U.S.—a minivan (Quest), the Infiniti J30 sports sedan, and a stylish 4-door Altima sedan. The company was reinventing its image; it wanted to be known as a 4-door sedan company—the most popular model type. Nissan's strategy was to develop snappy cars that people would talk about and to compete as a full-line producer of cars and trucks. In Japan the company was trying to increase its market share from 24 percent to 30 percent; to do this it had increased the number of models in its lineup to 29—the same as Toyota—and offered customers a choice of 2,280 variations. However, Nissan's unit sales had declined for two straight years (see Exhibit 14). In 1992, the company reported losses of $448 million on sales of $50.2 billion; it lost $806 million on sales of $53.8 billion in 1993. Observers attributed the losses to Nissan's being stretched out trying to match Toyota in Japan, the U.S., and Europe simultaneously. In 1993 and 1994 the company was engaged in restructuring its operations to restore profitability. It had set a target of eliminating 5,000 jobs by 1996 through attrition.

TOYOTA MOTOR COMPANY

Toyota was Japan's largest industrial enterprise, the world's third-largest automaker, and the largest of 14 interlocking Japanese auto-and-truck-related companies known as the Toyota group. Included in the Toyota group were Hino Motors, Japan's biggest maker of heavy trucks, and Daihatsu, Japan's eighth-largest automaker; Toyota owned 11 percent of Hino Motors and 15.7 percent of Daihatsu. Toyota had a 40 percent-plus market share in Japan and earned $1.4 billion on sales of $85.3 billion in 1993.

Toyota made 85 percent of its vehicles at a rural location called Toyota City, 150 miles outside Tokyo. Toyota City had all the trappings of a company town—company housing, a company hospital that provided free health care to workers, and a huge recreational center. The production facilities at Toyota City were the most efficient in the world, making Toyota the world's low-cost vehicle producer. Toyota produced 45 percent as many vehicles as GM with a workforce one-tenth the size of GM's. In 1994, Toyota opened an addition at its Georgetown, Kentucky, plant that doubled capacity to 500,000 units; the expansion enabled Toyota to add production of its new-generation 4-door Cressida model. The Georgetown plant was scheduled to be Toyota's worldwide source for the low-luxury Cressida; the plant also built Toyota Camrys. Next to the Georgetown plant, Toyota had a $300 million facility to supply pistons, valves, cylinder heads, and 4-cylinder engines for the cars produced in Georgetown. Toyota's 50-50 venture with GM at the New United Motor Manufacturing, Inc. (NUMMI), plant in Fremont, California, provided Toyota with 100,000 Corollas a year; a Canadian plant also made Corollas. Independently of GM, Toyota opened a second assembly line at NUMMI in 1991 to produce 100,000 Toyota trucks annually. In Britain, Toyota had a 200,000-vehicle plant and had plans for expanding and integrating its operations throughout Europe.

Toyota was a full-line producer. Its Lexus models were considered the world benchmark for luxury cars. The company had made an extensive effort to be no. 1 in customer satisfaction. However, the company's operating profit margins had fallen from a healthy 6.7 percent in 1990 to a meager 1.3 percent in early 1993. In 1992 Toyota launched an emergency program to reduce costs by 80 billion yen (about $714 million). Toyota's white-collar workforce had increased 45 percent since the early 1980s compared to an 18 percent increase in production workers.

MITSUBISHI MOTORS

Mitsubishi Motors was one of 28 companies constituting the Mitsubishi group; the Mitsubishi keiretsu included Mitsubishi Bank, Mitsubishi Electric, Asahi Glass, Kirin Brewery, Mitsubishi Heavy Industries, Tokio Marine and Fire Insurance (Japan's largest property and casualty insurer), and Nippon Kogaku (the maker of Nikon cameras). Mitsubishi Motors was the third-largest Japanese auto producer (up from fifth in 1989). In 1992, the company reported profits of $207 million on sales of $25.5 billion. It dominated Japan's growing sports-utility and station-wagon segments and confidently talked of pursuing additional market share in Japan. Mitsubishi had introduced one upscale, near-luxury model, the Diamante, creating an entirely new sub-market in Japan. Its Galant and Diamante models were selling well in the U.S.; the company had a 230,000-unit plant in Illinois that made compact models for both its own brand and for Chrysler. It had spent a paltry $4.5 million to upgrade a 49-year-old plant in Japan and raise automation on final assembly by 18 percent; the upgrading was being studied worldwide as an example of how to do more for less. Mitsubishi Motors earned $52 million on sales of $27.3 billion in 1993.

THE SMALLER JAPANESE AUTOMAKERS

The makers of the four lowest-volume Japanese nameplates—Subaru, Daihatsu, Isuzu, and Suzuki—were struggling to remain competitive. Subaru, a division of Fuji Heavy Industries, was forging closer cooperative ventures with Nissan (Fuji and Nissan were both members of the same Japanese trading conglomerate and Nissan owned 5.9 percent of Fuji's stock). Subaru was also said to be considering teaming up with Suzuki, with whom it already had a joint venture in the United States. Suzuki had been hurt when *Consumer Reports* in June 1988 called its Samurai 4-wheel-drive model unsafe and urged a model recall; in 1989 Suzuki's sales in the U.S. dropped from 81,349 to 30,181 vehicles, despite the introduction of two new models. Its U.S. sales had never recovered. Suzuki's strategic focus was on making low-cost minicars and subcompacts for less-affluent country markets where cars were not used much. Suzuki had a 76 percent share of the automobile market in India and a 66 percent share in Pakistan. It was the second-leading Japanese supplier in Indonesia (behind Toyota) and the leading Japanese supplier in China. One of Daihatsu's mainstays was minicars; it built about 450,000 annually, second in Japan behind Suzuki. Daihatsu was a member of the same keiretsu as Toyota. Toyota owned 15.7 percent of Daihatsu and was said to be considering increasing its stake. In 1993 Toyota assigned production of a new engine to Daihatsu and relations between the two were expected to grow closer in the future.

PROFILES OF THE AMERICAN AUTOMAKERS

Exhibit 15 presents selected operating and financial data for the three major U.S. motor vehicle producers. In 1993 in the U.S., Detroit's Big Three had 731,000 employees; another 900,000 were employed by auto parts suppliers and some 650,000 people worked at car dealerships.

GENERAL MOTORS

In 1994 General Motors was in the midst of a turnaround. Despite being the world's largest industrial corporation (1993 revenues of $134 billion) and the longtime leader in the world automotive industry, GM's share of the U.S. passenger-car market had eroded steadily from 45 percent in the mid-1970s to 35 percent in the early 1990s. In 1992, GM's outside directors joined forces to oust GM's CEO and several other top executives, replacing them with a new team headed by John F. "Jack" Smith who had revived GM's European operations in the 1980s. GM had lost $4.45 billion in 1991 and $2.6 billion in 1992 excluding special charges. The special charges, however, were significant and included a one-time charge against earnings of $20.5 billion to accrue the health care benefit expenses for future retirees, a one-time charge of $749 million to restructure its Hughes Aircraft subsidiary, and a $749 million write-down of the value of its National Car Rental subsidiary—adding up to an all-time world record single-year loss of $23.5 billion. GM also had unfunded pension liabilities of

EXHIBIT 15 | **Selected Operating Results for U.S. Vehicle Producers, 1988–93** *(Dollar values in millons)*

	1988	1989	1990	1991	1992	1993
General Motors						
Unit sales	8,108,000	7,907,000	7,454,000	7,025,000	7,146,000	7,785,000
North America	5,915,000	5,533,000	5,013,000	4,554,000	4,856,000	5,206,000
Rest of world	2,193,000	2,374,000	2,441,000	2,471,000	2,290,000	2,579,000
Revenues	$ 123,642	$ 126,932	$ 124,705	$ 123,056	$ 132,429	$ 138,219
Net income	$ 4,856	$ 4,224	$ (1,986)	$ (4,453)	$ (23,498)	$ 2,109
Worldwide payroll	$ 27,549	$ 28,684	$ 29,251	$ 29,641	$ 30,340	$ 29,806
Total assets	$ 164,063	$ 173,297	$ 180,237	$ 184,326	$ 191,013	$ 188,201
Ford Motor Company						
Unit sales	6,441,000	6,337,000	5,805,000	5,345,000	5,764,000	5,964,000
North America	4,264,000	4,036,000	3,536,000	3,113,000	3,594,000	4,078,000
Rest of world	2,177,000	2,301,000	2,269,000	2,232,000	2,170,000	1,886,000
Revenues	$ 92,446	$ 96,146	$ 97,650	$ 88,286	$ 100,132	$ 108,521
Net income	$ 5,300	$ 3,835	$ 860	$ (2,258)	$ (7,385)	$ 2,529
Worldwide payroll	$ 13,010	$ 13,327	$ 14,014	$ 12,810	$ 13,800	$ 13,800
Total assets	$ 143,367	$ 160,893	$ 173,663	$ 174,429	$ 180,545	$ 198,938
Chrysler Corporation						
Unit sales	2,567,000	2,381,000	1,984,000	1,866,000	2,175,000	2,476,000
North America	2,220,000	2,108,000	1,734,000	1,573,000	1,840,000	2,300,000
Rest of world	347,000	273,000	250,000	293,000	335,000	176,000
Revenues	$ 34,421	$ 35,186	$ 30,620	$ 29,370	$ 36,897	$ 43,830
Net income	$ 1,009	$ 323	$ 68	$ (795)	$ 723	$ (2,551)
Worldwide payroll*	$ 5,162	$ 4,949	$ 4,140	$ 3,968	$ 4,798	$ 5,367
Total Assets	$ 48,291	$ 51,112	$ 46,374	$ 43,076	$ 40,653	$ 43,830

*Excludes benefits
Source: *1993 Ward's Automotive Yearbook*, p. 121.

$17 billion. Except for its North American operations, where operating losses equaled $7.9 billion in 1991 and $4.5 billion in 1992, GM was profitable. In 1992 GM's international automotive operations earned $1.2 billion, its automotive and dealer financing business earned $1.2 billion, the Hughes Aircraft division earned $748 million (excluding special charges), and its Electronic Data Systems subsidiary, purchased from Ross Perot, earned $635 million.

GM was a full-line vehicle manufacturer, had 750,000 employees worldwide, 571,000 automotive employees, 8,600 dealers, over 20,000 suppliers in 26 countries, and some 200 plants and facilities in 34 countries. The company for decades had produced and marketed five brands of passenger cars for the North American market—Chevrolet, Pontiac, Oldsmobile, Buick, and Cadillac. In 1989 it introduced the subcompact Geo line sold through Chevrolet dealers; the various Geo models were produced for GM by Toyota, Isuzu, and Suzuki. In 1990 a seventh brand was launched by the company's all-new, showcase Saturn division. Both the Geo and Saturn lines were intended to compete head-on against low-end Japanese models. Trucks were sold under the GMC and Chevrolet names; GM was tied with Ford for the world lead in sales of light trucks. In Europe, GM's Opel and Vauxhall lines had achieved a 12.4 percent market share, up from 10.5 percent in 1989; Opel/Vauxhall had doubled its passenger-car sales in Western Europe since 1981. GM's European operations were profitable. In 1989 GM had purchased 50 percent of the auto division of Saab-Scania. GM's overall market share outside the U.S. was 8.5 percent; international sales accounted for 26 percent of total sales, up from 11 percent in 1985.

During the 1980s GM had invested $77 billion to refurbish its factories, install new equipment, and improve labor productivity—the most massive modernization and rebuilding ever undertaken by any corporation. Another $2 billion was spent on employee training and education. Hourly employment was reduced by 125,000 workers between 1984 and 1992 and salaried employment had been cut by 50,000, mainly through early retirement programs. Nonetheless, in 1994 GM was still stuck as the high-cost U.S. producer, partly because the company's labor contract with the UAW required GM to provide nearly full pay to laid-off workers and partly because health care costs for employees and retirees averaged about $9,500 per active employee (up from $3,500 per active employee in 1982). GM's average manufacturing labor cost per vehicle was about $2,400 in 1993, compared to $1,800 for Chrysler and $1,500 for Ford.

To launch the company on the comeback trail, GM's new management in 1992 initiated a series of moves:

- Speeding up cost reduction and quality improvement initiatives.
- Initiating a single global strategy for sourcing parts and components.
- Implementing a major reorganization to consolidate and streamline all of GM's North American operations under a single executive and strategy team. The new North American operations (NAO) group absorbed GM's three existing vehicle divisions and set objectives for downsizing the workforce, eliminating parts and model redundancies, reducing product-development time and cost, spreading best practices throughout the whole corporation, instituting more flexible decision-making processes, and shifting from a goal of "market share with profitability" in North America to "profit first" with less emphasis on market share.
- Announcing plans to discontinue production at 19 parts plants and 4 assembly plants to bring GM's North American capacity down to 5.4 million units annually by 1996.
- Cutting the size of the central headquarters staff from 13,500 to 2,300 employees and reducing the salaried workforce in North America from 91,000 to 71,000 by 1994.
- Refocusing the strategy of GM's automotive components group worldwide (ACGW) to aggressively pursue sales to non-NAO customers, to emphasize parts and components systems with the greatest potential for global growth, and to concentrate its resources on products where ACGW could be competitive against the best producers in the world. ACGW was the largest automotive parts and components supplier in the world, with sales of about $15 billion to NAO and $5.4 billion to GM's overseas subsidiaries and to a variety of outsider customers that included every other major vehicle manufacturer. ACGW subsequently selected seven major product categories that offered it long-term strategic growth potential: ride and handling systems, engine management systems, power and signal distribution systems, occupant control systems, lighting systems, thermal management systems, and energy storage and management systems. In each of these categories, which collectively accounted for 86 percent of ACGW's sales, the group's major products ranked first or

second in global market share or else offered GM a technology advantage over competitors. ACGW products not part of these seven categories (14 percent of current sales) were scheduled to be offered for sale, placed into joint ventures, consolidated, or exited.

- Designing all future passenger car models around three platforms, accelerating components sharing across models, and creating a Vehicle Launch Center to concentrate and coordinate GM's engineering, design, and technological capabilities.

- Developing a separate marketing strategy for each car and truck division to promote greater styling, image, and price differentiation and to avoid look-alike models that appealed to essentially the same kinds of customers.

- Putting much more emphasis on reaching out to customers and emulating Saturn's success in achieving customer satisfaction; actions included a GM MasterCard that allowed users to build up annual credits of 5 percent on each item charged toward the future purchase or lease of a new GM vehicle, a roadside assistance program, toll-free customer assistance centers, a new program to enhance dealer service, and efforts to extend Saturn's no-haggle pricing approaches to other dealers.

- Protecting GM's profitable position in full-size trucks and large luxury cars and strengthening its position in mid-size cars and compact trucks. To enhance its 32 percent market share in the U.S. light-truck segment, GM planned major styling and product enhancement changes over the next several years that would give buyers many of the conveniences and features of cars, improve ease of entry and exit, boost fuel economy, and enhance powertrains.

GM's new management team believed its mandate was to restore GM's profitability quickly, satisfy customers with better products, and grow the business in future years.

FORD MOTOR COMPANY

Ford was the most successful U.S. automaker of the 1980s. It began the decade by losing $3 billion. It ended the decade more profitable than GM in three of the last four years, leading U.S. manufacturers in productivity gains, cost reductions, quality improvements, and fuel-efficient aerodynamic styling. At least two of Ford's plants were the equal of Japanese plants in labor efficiency. Several of Ford's new models had been market successes and Ford's car and truck market share had risen 6 percentage points during the 1980s to 24.6 percent. In 1993 Ford's share of the U.S. passenger car market was 21.8 percent and its truck share was 31.9 percent. Five of the 10 best-selling vehicles in the U.S. in 1993 were Ford products—the F-series pickup (the overall leader for the 12th consecutive year at 565,100 units), the Ford Taurus (third with 360,400 units), the Ford Ranger (fourth with 340,200 units), the Ford Explorer (sixth with 302,200 units), and the Ford Escort (ninth with 269,000 units). The company was a full-line producer but had only four car and truck brands (Ford, Mercury, Lincoln, and Jaguar) versus GM's nine. Ford was the world's fourth-largest industrial corporation and the automobile industry's second-largest producer. In 1993 Ford named Alex Trotman as its new chairman and CEO; Trotman was the first foreign-born executive to head a U.S. automobile company.

Ford had invested heavily in plant modernization and Japanese-style production methods to improve its cost competitiveness. Ford had learned much from its partnership with Mazda Motors and was deeply involved in changing the ways it built vehicles to mimic Japanese approaches. At the company's stamping and assembly plant in Wayne, Michigan, Ford had installed giant Japanese-made presses that allowed workers to change dies in as little as two minutes—compared to 6 to 12 hours in a traditional Ford stamping plant. Plant managers wore the same uniforms as hourly workers and pocket patches emphasized first names; the plant contract with the UAW called for 1 job classification for nonskilled workers, allowing workers to swap responsibilities, instead of the usual 12 job classifications that spelled out precisely what a worker could and could not do. Workers ate beside managers in the cafeteria and parked in the same lots. Ford's goal was to achieve a 50 percent increase in worker efficiency between 1993 and year-end 1996.

Ford had recently introduced a program to cut material costs and product-development costs. The company also had a new flexible manufacturing plant that permitted building more than a dozen engine sizes and configurations on a single assembly line and shifting production from one engine type to another to meet changing sales patterns (previously, Ford had dedicated each of its engine plants to building a single engine type). Virtually all of Ford's North American cars and light trucks were scheduled to have all-new or substantially improved engines and transmissions by the end of 1996; the powertrains in Ford's European lines were also in the process of being equipped with mostly new powertrains.

Worldwide, Ford's automotive operations lost $1.5 billion in 1992 on sales of $84.4 billion. In the U.S., Ford lost $405 million on sales of $51.9 billion (versus a loss of $2.2 billion in 1991 on sales of $40.6 billion). Outside the U.S., Ford lost $1.1 billion on sales of $32.5 billion, compared with a loss of $970 million in 1991 on sales of $31.4 billion; Ford's foreign losses were almost totally associated with its European operations. In 1993 Ford reported after-tax profits of $2.5 billion on sales of $109 billion.

Ford had an 11.5 percent share of the European car market and a truck share of 12.1 percent; in 1992 it was the market share leader in Britain and ranked third in Italy and fourth in France, Germany, and Spain. The company had about 8,000 dealers across Europe, tops among any European seller. Management expected that the new European Mondeo models would improve European performance. Ford was laying the foundation to become the company's key player in the newly independent countries of Eastern Europe where it had already franchised 100 dealers and opened plants to produce components. The company was committed to being a global player and had strengthened its competitive positions in Taiwan, China, Australia, New Zealand, and Latin America, achieving higher volume in all these areas in 1992.

Ford was working to make a success of its $2.5 billion acquisition of Jaguar. Ford had invested $700 million to modernize Jaguar's plant, reduce costs, and improve manufacturing quality. So far, defects had been reduced 77 percent on the XJ6 models and 87 percent on the XJS models; payroll costs had been reduced nearly 50 percent by cutting the workforce from 12,000 to 6,000. Jaguar lost $400 million in 1992. Unit volume in 1993 was 27,400 cars, compared to a peak of 49,500 cars in 1988.

Ford had 16 new cars and trucks scheduled for introduction in the 1995–97 period, including a new minivan to compete against Chrysler's popular models. A program was in place to cut the development time for new models to 36 months (development time for the 1996 Ford Taurus models was 42 months). All of the company's new-model work was being assigned to 700-person project development teams; the big teams included specialists from all disciplines and were divided into as many as 25 subteams. Specialists moved from project team to project team as their duties for a particular model were completed. Ford was constructing a $150-million facility to house as many as 15 new-model teams under one roof.

Ford was the most aggressive of the major vehicle manufacturers in promoting vehicle leasing. It had very attractive 24-month leasing packages and was test marketing a leasing program where customers could lease a new Ford vehicle every 2 years for a total of 12 years; at the end of the 12-year period the sixth vehicle would be owned outright by the customer. Ford saw this as a way to develop long-term relationships with customers: allow them to drive a new vehicle every 2 years for a single monthly payment and refocus marketing efforts on providing a simple, hassle-free transportation service instead of trying to woo customers back each time they purchased a new vehicle. Some Ford and Lincoln-Mercury dealers had begun opening free-standing neighborhood service facilities, called Ford Auto Care Centers, that were equipped with the latest service technology, had skilled dealership personnel, and used only Ford parts. Ford was also using its service-bay diagnostic technology to test brand-new vehicles and improve new-vehicle quality.

CHRYSLER CORPORATION

Going into 1994 Chrysler was the world automotive industry's success story of the 1990s. Saved from bankruptcy by Lee Iacocca in the early 1980s, the company had begun the 1990s with dated models, costs that were still not competitive, a weak financial condition, and total dependence on a North American production base. Many industry experts predicted the company would not survive in its present form. But Chrysler had introduced three successful models in 1992 and 1993—the Jeep Grand Cherokee, the Dodge Intrepid and other LH sedans, and a restyled Dodge Ram pickup truck—to complement its strong minivan lines (Plymouth Voyager and Dodge Caravan); the new lineup boosted Chrysler's U.S. market share in cars and trucks to 14.8 percent in 1993, compared to 12.0 percent in 1991. In 1993 Chrysler had operating profits of $2 billion and earned more in North America from automotive operations than Ford and GM combined or all of Japan's automakers combined. Chrysler had improved operating efficiency and capacity utilization to the point where it was the lowest-cost U.S. producer. Industry analysts estimated that in 1993 Chrysler made an average gross profit of $8,140 on each of the more than 200,000 Grand Cherokees it sold, $5,735 on each of the 200,000 LH sedans it sold, and about $5,100 on each of 500,000 Voyagers and Caravans.[3]

One of the keys to Chrysler's success was its pioneering use of cross-functional teams to design, engineer, and bring new models to market. The teams included professionals with all the needed skills to develop a new model; the teams were delegated ample decision-making authority and were held responsible for both project costs and model success in the marketplace. In 1991 Chrysler created teams for small cars, large cars, minivans, and Jeep/trucks; in 1992 all four teams were housed in a new $1 billion technology center that had been built with spacious floors so each team could work together. Chrysler's new Neon models were developed in 31 months at a cost of $1.3 billion. The team for Chrysler's new 1995 sedan (code-named JA), which was aimed at young parents, consisted of younger engineers, designers, and marketers who called themselves the thirtysomethings. Chrysler believed its totally reengineered minivan, scheduled for introduction in 1996, would

---

[3]Alex Taylor, "Will Success Spoil Chrysler?" *Fortune,* January 10, 1994, pp. 90–91.

be a generation and a half beyond Ford's 1995 Windstar minivan both aesthetically and functionally.

Chrysler's unit volume was about one-third of Ford's and one-fifth of GM's. It was the world's 28th-largest industrial corporation and the eighth-largest motor vehicle manufacturer. The company's chairman and CEO was Robert J. Eaton, 53, who had been recruited from his job as head of GM Europe in 1992 to succeed Lee Iacocca; Chrysler's president, chief engineer, and chief manufacturing executive had also been lured away from jobs at rival companies. Management was not a fan of long-term strategic alliances and, so far, had elected to concentrate production and sales in North America; the company had plans, however, to double exports of assembled vehicles from 100,000 in 1993 to 200,000 by the late 1990s. In the early 1990s, Chrysler had held merger talks with Fiat; it had been burned in a joint venture with Renault; and it had sold its 50 percent interest in the Diamond Star assembly plant in Illinois to former partner Mitsubishi. Chrysler purchased 70 percent of its parts and components from outside suppliers, compared to 50 percent at Ford and 30 percent at GM.

Chrysler's biggest weakness in 1994 was product quality. All of the company's brands were "below average" in the 1993 J. D. Power survey of defects recognized by customers in the first 90 days of ownership. Dodge, Chrysler's most popular brand, averaged 1.55 defects per car, compared with an average of 1.08 for all U.S. cars and .7 for top-rated Lexus. Between October 1993 and April 1994, every one of Chrysler's recently launched models had been recalled (although the problems were minor). To improve production quality, Chrysler began a five-year, $1.5 billion program in Fall 1993 to provide quality training for workers, improve equipment, replace older machinery, and install test tracks at each factory to roadtest each newly assembled vehicle prior to shipment.

PROFILES OF SELECTED EUROPEAN AUTOMAKERS

Exhibit 16 shows market share trends for passenger cars for all the major producers active in the European market.

DAIMLER-BENZ

Daimler-Benz was a $60 billion manufacturer of Mercedes-Benz cars and trucks (67 percent of sales), aerospace and defense products (16 percent of sales), and electronics and technology systems (15 percent of sales). The company was the world's largest producer of heavy trucks (over six tons), the largest bus manufacturer in Europe, the world's 19th-largest vehicle producer, and the world's largest maker of diesel-engine cars. Its Mercedes line of luxury cars was world renowned for engineering excellence and had surpassed Cadillac as the world's top-selling luxury car in the early 1970s. Mercedes cars symbolized wealth, prestige, and quality. The least-expensive Mercedes cost about $30,000 and the most expensive model was about $135,000. Mercedes-Benz was regarded as the premier brand in the automotive industry even though other models like the famed Rolls-Royce and Italy's Lamborghini commanded bigger price tags. Traditionally, Mercedes cars ranked high on customer satisfaction surveys and had high resale value. Owner loyalty was quite high. Daimler-Benz produced 500,000 to 600,000 passenger cars annually, about 2 percent of the worldwide total; all of its cars were made in German plants and about half

EXHIBIT 16 | European Market Shares of Major Automakers, Passenger-Car Segment, 1985–92

	1985		1990		1991		1992		1993	
	Units	Percent Share	Units	Percent Share	Units	Percent Share	Units	Percent Share	Units	Percent Share
VW group	1,529,415	15.2%	2,070,267	15.6%	2,214,477	16.4%	2,357,747	17.5%	1,815,900	15.9%
VW	1,113,124	11.0	1,377,740	10.4	1,448,949	10.7	1,565,044	11.6		
Audi	260,840	2.6	360,043	2.7	396,422	2.9	413,645	3.1		
SEAT	155,451	1.5	307,845	2.3	321,550	2.4	328,362	2.4		
Fiat group	1,304,494	12.9	1,884,023	14.2	1,731,319	12.8	1,604,407	11.9	1,273,000	11.1
Ford total	1,267,830	12.6	1,532,930	11.5	1,604,338	11.9	1,521,346	11.3	1,315,300	11.5
Ford Europe	1,266,970	12.6	1,514,573	11.4	1,592,256	11.8	1,510,654	11.2	1,304,600	11.4
Jaguar	—	0.0	18,357	0.1	12,082	0.1	10,692	0.1	10,700	0.1
Peugeot group	1,226,179	12.2	1,712,257	12.9	1,628,170	12.1	1,644,658	12.2	1,401,500	12.2
Peugeot	661,258	6.6	1,081,040	8.1	1,081,942	8.0	996,335	7.4		
Citroen	476,322	4.7	631,217	4.8	609,228	4.5	648,323	4.8		
GM total	1,212,339	12.0	1,569,932	11.8	1,629,706	12.1	1,679,480	12.4	1,451,800	12.7
Opel/Vauxhall	1,205,915	12.0	1,512,397	11.4	1,577,320	11.7	1,628,714	12.1		
GM other	6,424	0.1	57,535	0.4	52,386	0.4	50,766	0.4		
Renault	1,139,305	11.3	1,307,317	9.8	1,352,451	10.0	1,433,145	10.6	1,200,900	10.5
Mercedes	394,015	3.9	435,878	3.3	451,592	3.3	409,759	3.0	351,200	3.1
Austin Rover	420,052	4.2	389,178	2.9	355,751	2.6	330,842	2.5	358,600	3.1
Nissan	306,614	3.0	377,262	2.8	437,132	3.2	437,839	3.2	395,800	3.5
Toyota	247,580	2.5	354,189	2.7	359,120	2.7	337,964	2.5	318,300	2.8
BMW	290,565	2.9	366,457	2.8	411,688	3.1	441,375	3.3	369,600	3.2
Volvo	254,697	2.5	233,257	1.8	198,706	1.5	200,652	1.5	170,900	1.5
Mazda	203,477	2.0	275,905	2.1	285,211	2.1	268,868	2.0	193,500	1.7
Mitsubishi	116,345	1.2	172,337	1.3	191,095	1.4	161,076	1.2	138,700	1.2
Honda	—	—	159,608	1.2	165,986	1.2	175,498	1.3	161,500	1.4
All others	161,330	1.6	434,974	3.3	476,234	3.5	493,828	3.7	533,900	4.7
Total passenger car market	10,074,237	100.0%	13,275,771	100.0%	13,492,976	100.0%	13,498,484	100.0%	11,450,400	100.0%
Japanese makes	1,140,401	11.3%	1,540,525	11.6%	1,663,834	12.3%	1,589,315	11.8%	1,378,700	12.0%

Sources: *1989 Ward's Automotive Yearbook,* p. 87; *1993 Ward's Automotive Yearbook,* p. 82; *Automotive News,* Jan. 24, 1994.

were exported. One out of three cars had a diesel engine. The company produced about 225,000 trucks, about one-third of which were produced in foreign plants scattered across 10 countries. When Daimler-Benz bought Freightliner, a U.S. maker of heavy-duty trucks, for $260 million in 1981, Freightliner had only a 9 percent market share and ranked seventh out of eight manufacturers. In 1994 Freightliner was the market share leader with revenues of about $3 billion and was often first to introduce innovative new components and features.

However, Mercedes faced major challenges in 1994. Daimler-Benz reported a loss of $1.1 billion on sales of $59.5 billion in 1993. Mercedes-Benz's share of the German market had fallen from 11.6 percent in 1985 to 6.4 percent in 1992, only partly due to recessionary conditions. Since 1986 Mercedes-Benz's U.S. sales had eroded from a peak of nearly 100,000 cars annually to around 60,000. The company had been slow to respond to market signs that it was overengineering and overpricing its cars and had virtually ignored the mounting challenges from Toyota's Lexus, Nissan's Infiniti, Ford's Jaguar, GM's Cadillac Seville, and BMW. The company had a 30 percent cost disadvantage against Japanese and U.S. competitors. Wage rates in Germany for skilled auto workers were among the highest in the world and productivity at Mercedes plants in Germany was comparatively low.

Helmut Werner, Mercedes' new CEO who became president in early 1993, had moved quickly to institute major strategic changes to reinvent the company and make it an exclusive, full-line manufacturer offering high-quality vehicles of all shapes and sizes. Werner's strategy was to cut costs, lower prices, broaden the product line, and maintain the qualities of safety, technology, and performance that had allowed Mercedes to charge a price premium. The company had announced it would cut 25,700 jobs from its workforce of 169,000 by the end of 1994; the cuts included 4,000 headquarters employees—the first white-collar layoffs in Mercedes' 107-year history. A new C-Class sedan series, with base prices of $29,900 to $34,900, had recently been introduced to attract entry-level luxury-car buyers; prices were also trimmed on a number of models to make them competitive with Toyota's top-of-the-line Lexus models and to demonstrate commitment to providing better value. To save on costs, Mercedes had begun assembling cars in Mexico and South Korea. The company was building a $570-million plant in Spain to produce minivans and a $300-million plant in Alabama to produce sports utility vehicles. Werner had also indicated that Mercedes was developing plans for a subcompact city car. In the future, Mercedes' sticker prices were to be governed by a market-driven target price; designers, engineers, and manufacturing personnel were expected to meet cost targets that would produce a satisfactory profit.

VOLKSWAGEN-AUDI

Volkswagen-Audi was Germany's second-largest company and the largest European exporter of cars to the United States. In English, Volkswagen translated into "the people's car." The company had made a name for itself worldwide with its VW Beetle, the most successful model of any car ever produced. More than 21 million Beetles were produced at plants in Germany, Brazil, and Mexico. More than 5 million Beetles had been sold in the U.S., and the Beetle had been the best-selling model in Brazil. Volkswagen's share of the U.S. market peaked in 1970 at 7.2 percent when 570,000 vehicles, mostly Beetles, were sold. When the Beetle met its market demise in the late 1970s, Volkswagen elected to erase its reputation as a builder of small, inexpensive cars and move instead to selling "classless" vehicles. The strategy worked well in Europe and the VW Golf became the best-selling car in Europe. But the Golf never caught on with U.S. buyers, some of whom had been burned by the high price and poor quality of the Volkswagen Rabbit, the first successor to the Beetle. In 1975 Volkswagen lost its import leadership to the Japanese in the U.S. market, and it had never been able to stage a comeback. In 1992, VW's share of the U.S. car market was 1.1 percent. Even so, Volkswagen-Audi was the most multinational of the European auto companies, engaging in overseas manufacture, joint ventures and acquisitions, as well as exporting, to build its global visibility. In Japan, Nissan made VW's Santana model under license. In Germany, VW and Toyota had teamed up to make pickup trucks. In Latin America, Ford and VW had merged their operations in Argentina and Brazil into a new company called Autolatina, which had 15 plants and annual capacity of 900,000 vehicles. VW acquired the biggest auto company in Spain, SEAT, in 1986.

Volkswagen was the overall market leader in Europe. Volkswagen had suffered from low profitability during much of the 1980s. In 1992 VW earned $49 million on sales of $56.7 billion. The company's new CEO, appointed in 1993, had embarked on a program to make the company more cost competitive; plans were in place to cut the work force by 12 percent and reduce payroll costs by $1 billion, to trim investment outlays by one-third, simplify and strengthen the product line, and change the corporate culture by recruiting top talent from competitors. VW's new production director, recruited from GM, was accused of stealing GM's trade secrets and strategic plans for Europe when he and seven co-workers left GM in early 1993. The scandal was one factor in VW's 11 percent drop in sales in the first half of 1993; the company lost $1.2 billion on sales of $46.3 billion in 1993.

FIAT

Fiat was the largest company in Italy's private sector and the world's sixth-biggest automaker in terms of total revenues and eleventh-largest in terms of 1992 unit volume. About 40 percent of Fiat's stock was owned by the Agnelli family, which had founded Fiat; the Agnellis had major shareholdings in a host of other Italian enterprises. According to London's *Financial Times,* companies in which the Agnellis had ownership interests accounted for one-third of the total capitalization of all stocks traded on the Milan Bourse (the Italian stock exchange); an article in the *Financial Times* said, "Fiat is to the Italian state what the Duke of Burgundy was to medieval kings of France—technically part of the kingdom, but barely less powerful than they were." Giovanni Agnelli, grandson of the founder of Fiat, had superstar recognition in Italy.

Fiat was a world leader in the use of robots and computers; the automated technology was provided by Fiat's machine tool subsidiary, Comau, which was a world leader in the development of automated production lines. GM, Ford, Chrysler, Daimler-Benz, BMW, and Volvo were all users of Comau robots. One of Comau's most impressive installations was a $300-million engine plant that had five parallel assembly lines each equipped with 148 robots controlled by 600 personal computers, which in turn were coordinated by 103 larger computers; the plant turned out 2,600 engines per day with a workforce of 950 people. Fiat opened one of Europe's most advanced assembly plants in 1993. On the whole, Fiat's plants were the most highly automated of any vehicle producer, and Fiat, among the European-based companies, was considered to be the low-cost producer. The company's main production facilities were in Italy, Portugal, and Brazil, with additional operations in Yugoslavia, Poland, Spain, Turkey, Indonesia, Thailand, Argentina, Zambia, Morocco, Egypt, and South Africa.

Fiat enjoyed a 55 percent market share in Italy, but had limited distribution outside Italy. Ford and GM were barred from building auto plants in Italy. Japanese imports were restricted to 2,500 cars per year, but this restriction did not apply to Japanese models made in Europe—a factor that had allowed Japanese producers to capture 3.7 percent of the Italian passenger-car market in 1992. The company's product line was broad, ranging from minicars at the bottom to Ferrari sports cars at the top. Fiat's efforts to penetrate the U.S. market had been disastrous and the company withdrew in 1983. In 1986 Ford and Fiat joined forces and merged their heavy-truck operations in Europe; talks between the two companies to merge their European car operations had fallen through in 1985. Merger talks with Chrysler failed in 1991. Fiat had been jockeying with Volkswagen-Audi, GM, Ford, and Peugeot for market share leadership in Europe since the mid-1980s. The company had 16 new models scheduled for launch during 1994–95.

Fiat earned $447 million on sales of $48 billion in 1992. But the company was financially strapped for cash in 1993, announcing that it needed to raise $3.2 billion in a combination of asset sales and capital infusion. Fiat's unions were restive over the small wage increases they had received recently. Fiat was also embroiled in a major investigation of corruption. Almost a dozen of Fiat's top executives had been implicated in alleged bribes to Italian politicians and their political parties; several had admitted wrongdoing. In 1993, Fiat reported losses of $1.1 billion on total sales of $34.7 billion.

PEUGEOT

Peugeot was the second-oldest automobile manufacturer in the world and the largest company in France *not* owned by the French government. In the 1970s, Peugeot had embarked on a strategy to become "the General Motors of Europe," a move loudly applauded by the French government. Peugeot executives reasoned that to compete against the Americans and the Japanese, Peugeot would have to be big and have an international reach. Peugeot proceeded to merge with Citroen, the third-largest French auto company, in 1976. In 1978 Peugeot purchased all of Chrysler's European operations, which included plants in Britain, France, and Spain. These acquisitions catapulted Peugeot into the ranks of the world's largest automotive companies and made it the biggest European producer. Peugeot had tried to use Chrysler's dealer network in the U.S. to establish a strong base in the American market, a feat no French carmaker had ever accomplished. It turned out to be a nightmare. The Chrysler factories in Europe were antiquated and turned out unappealing cars; even though Peugeot changed the name of Chrysler's products to Talbot (giving Peugeot three nameplates—Peugeot, Citroen, and Talbot), the facelift didn't work. Peugeot lost money for five straight years. Between 1978 and 1987 Peugeot retrenched, closing plants, consolidating operations, and cutting its workforce by 100,000 (abandoning its 170-year-old policy of never laying off its workers). Production dropped from 2.2 million cars at the time of the mergers to 1.6 million in 1985, and Peugeot fell to fourth place in Europe behind Volkswagen, Ford, and Fiat.

A new chief executive and two new small cars that were market successes helped get Peugeot back in contention by 1988. Factories were modernized, robots installed, the size of the workforce cut by 20 percent, and parts production for Peugeot and Citroen models merged into common plants. Sales in 1989 were back up to 2.1 million vehicles and had fluctuated between 1.8 and 2.3 million in the years since. In 1993 the company lost $250 million on sales of $25.7 billion. Peugeot held about a 35 percent market share in France, just ahead of Renault's 30 percent share. Peugeot was also strong in Spain, Portugal, and Belgium-Luxembourg. Peugeot's new CEO aspired to overtake Volkswagen-Audi as the European leader by 1993. His plan was to produce two full lines of cars—four models each of Peugeot and Citroen, ranging in size from subcompacts to luxury sedans.

RENAULT

Despite profits of $1.1 billion in 1992, Renault was financially and competitively vulnerable. It was both owned and heavily subsidized by the French government, often having served over the years as a laboratory of socialist ideas for the government. The company had $10 billion in debt and a debt-to-equity ratio of 2 to 1. About 90 percent of its cars were sold in France, Italy, and Spain, all highly protected markets. Quality and labor productivity had both improved in recent years. In 1990 Renault and Volvo formed a strategic alliance. Under the pact, Renault owned 25 percent of Volvo Car Corp. and 45 percent of Volvo's truck operations; Volvo owned 20 percent of Renault. The alliance with Volvo had produced several strategic benefits. Volvo was strong in luxury cars. Renault had strength in small cars. Volvo turned out heavy trucks; Renault made small and medium commercial vehicles. Together, the two companies had a 26 percent market share in heavy-duty trucks. By standardizing gearshifts, subassembly units, and other parts, the two companies achieved substantial savings on design, product development, and components production. In early 1993, secret merger discussions with Fiat produced no agreement. In late 1993 Renault and Volvo negotiated a merger, but mounting opposition from Volvo stockholders nixed the deal. Renault had several promising new models, including a new subcompact priced at about $10,000. According to one analyst, "Renault has done its leaning and been the European company most closely following Japanese precepts." When the Volvo merger failed, Renault's CEO indicated that Renault would begin to seek other joint-venture partners. Some analysts predicted the alliance with Volvo would not survive.

TOYOTA MOTOR CORPORATION IN 1994

Jana F. Kuzmicki, Indiana University Southeast

One of the dreams I have is to see our automobiles being driven in every corner of the world, allowing people to lead fuller lives. I intend to undertake every effort so that Toyota will be able to meet whatever challenges may emerge and continue to build attractive products.

Shoichiro Toyoda, Chairman,
Toyota Motor Corporation

Toyota Motor Corporation, the third-largest automaker in the world, was acknowledged by both industry observers and its competitors as the "best carmaker in the world." Headquartered in Toyota City, approximately 150 miles west of Tokyo in central Japan, Toyota was the largest industrial enterprise in Japan and the fifth-largest in the world, according to *Fortune's* Global 500. In fiscal 1993, Toyota had sales of $95.4 billion, a net profit of $1.6 billion, and about $15.6 billion in cash, earning it the nickname of the "Bank of Toyota"; overseas revenues were 26 percent of the company's total revenues in 1993. Under the leadership of current President Tatsuro Toyoda, Toyota Motor's most significant accomplishments included

- Developing a fundamentally new approach to manufacturing, admired and emulated by competitors, that was predicted to eventually transform the way things were made in virtually every industry.
- Maintaining its status as the most efficient automaker in the world, having achieved this feat in 1965.
- Being the undisputed quality leader in automotive manufacturing, making three of the four cars with the fewest defects sold in the U.S. in 1990.
- Introducing one of the most successful luxury automobiles, the Lexus, which was consistently ranked no. 1 in quality in the U.S.
- Having outstanding labor relations.

Toyota had plants in more than 20 countries, including the United States and the United Kingdom. In 1992, Toyota held 35.5 percent of the Japanese car market, about 9.5 percent of the global market, and 8 percent of the U.S. vehicle market. Toyota's sales of autos and trucks in the U.S. had consistently exceeded 1 million since 1990. Toyota's goals included producing 6 million vehicles and securing 10 percent of the global vehicle market (the "Global 10" strategy) by the turn of the century. Articulated as early as 1969 by then President Taizo Ishida, Toyota's long-term ambition was to become worldwide what it was in Japan—*Ichiban* or no. 1—thus guaranteeing a battle with GM, the current global leader, for the world's top spot by the turn of the century.

As the mid-1990s approached, changes in the domestic and global competitive markets presented unique challenges to Toyota's management: declining domestic demand, continuing appreciation of the yen, increasing government pressure to reduce annual work hours of employees (combined with a declining labor force), persisting trade frictions with both the U.S. and Europe, and intensifying competition from a revitalized U.S. auto industry. Exhibit 1 presents the global market shares of the companies vying for world leadership of the auto industry. Exhibit 2 presents summary financial information for Toyota.

COMPANY HISTORY AND BACKGROUND

Toyota's beginnings could be traced to Sakichi Toyoda, an inveterate tinkerer, who eventually received a total of 84 patents for his inventions. The automatic loom, his most famous invention, resulted in the establishment of Toyoda Automatic Loom Works in 1926. Early in his career in 1910, Sakichi Toyoda became discouraged with his work and decided to visit the U.S., where he spent six months inspecting the factories. Several years after his return, Sakichi Toyoda stated to a group of engineers:[1]

> To tell you the truth, I felt that my eyes had been opened. As I viewed the plants in cities all across the United States, and felt the tremendous energy of the Americans, I got angry at myself for being so blind. I was ashamed for having been ready to throw everything away after only a few failures.

Kiichiro Toyoda, son of Sakichi Toyoda, inherited his father's inquisitive nature, but his interest lay in the fledgling auto industry. Like his father, Kiichiro Toyoda visited the U.S. in 1930 to study the art of automaking. Armed with $500,000 from the sale of the automatic loom patent to a British company in 1929, Kiichiro Toyoda pursued the development of a small passenger car. Initially, he concentrated on learning the techniques of mass production. For inspiration, Kiichiro Toyoda often turned to Henry Ford's book, *My Life and Work,* urging others in the company to read it. By the middle 1920s, both Ford and GM had built assembly plants in Japan, turning out 18,000 vehicles a year. The auto quickly caught on in Japan, resulting in early dominance of the Japanese auto market by American automakers.

Kiichiro Toyoda was handicapped in his endeavors by the underdeveloped Japanese parts and machinery industries. Typically, these firms were family enterprises, and their products were either unreliable or high priced. Undaunted, Kiichiro Toyoda focused on what kind of and how many automobiles to build to develop a successful

---

[1]Milton Moskowitz, *The Global Marketplace: And 101 Other Global Corporate Players* (New York: Macmillan, 1987), p. 601.

EXHIBIT 1 | Global Market Shares of the Top Twelve Motor Vechicle Producers, 1987-92*

Company	1992	1991	1990	1989	1988	1987
General Motors	14.5%	14.8%	14.8%	16.5%	17.0%	16.7%
Ford	11.7	11.3	11.7	13.3	13.7	13.2
Toyota	9.5	9.9	9.7	9.3	8.1	7.9
Volkswagen	7.1	6.6	6.1	6.1	5.9	5.9
Nissan	6.0	6.5	6.1	6.3	5.7	4.9
Fiat Group	4.5	5.2	5.4	5.1	4.5	4.2
Chrysler Corp.	4.4	3.1	3.3	5.0	5.4	4.8
Peugeot-Citroen	4.1	4.3	4.4	4.6	4.4	4.2
Renault SA	4.1	3.8	3.5	4.3	4.1	3.9
Honda	3.7	4.2	3.9	3.9	3.7	3.4
Mitsubishi	3.7	4.0	3.6	2.3	2.7	2.7
Mazda	3.0	3.3	3.2	3.1	2.6	2.6

*Based on total production of all vehicles, including cars, trucks, buses, tractors, and commercial vehicles.

Sources: *Automotive News,* 1993 Market Data Book Issue, p. 3; *Automotive News,* 1990 Market Data Book Issue, pp. 3 and 6; *Automotive News,* 1989 Market Data Book Issue, p. 6.

EXHIBIT 2 | Summary Financial Information, Toyota Motor Corporation, 1989-93 (US$ 000)

	06/30/93	06/30/92	06/30/91	06/30/90	06/30/89
Sales	$95,368,396	$80,798,839	$71,548,258	$60,488,874	$55,826,452
Net income	1,648,174	1,890,828	3,132,327	2,903,767	2,409,984
Market capital	52,835,246	42,599,881	44,510,677	52,070,549	50,310,907
Common equity	43,771,975	37,300,899	33,168,907	27,872,018	25,818,656
Total assets	87,220,451	75,968,284	65,186,974	55,476,605	49,784,087

enterprise. He decided it was essential to mass produce a passenger car of the size most in demand in Japan; according to Kiichiro Toyoda:[2]

> Instead of avoiding competition with Ford and Chevrolet, we will develop and mass produce a car that incorporates the strong points of both and that can rival foreign cars in performance and price. Although we will base our method of production on the American mass-production system, it will not be an exact imitation but will reflect the particular conditions in Japan.

Kiichiro Toyoda's persistent efforts culminated in the production of Toyota's first passenger-car prototype in 1935.

Meanwhile, the government took steps to stimulate domestic auto production. In 1936, the Law Concerning the Manufacture of Motor Vehicles was passed to promote the establishment of the Japanese auto industry and to curb vehicle imports from abroad. The law required that companies manufacturing more than 3,000 units annually within Japan be licensed by the government, that a majority of the stock-

---

[2]*Toyota: A History of the First 50 Years* (Toyota City, Japan: Toyota Motor Corporation, 1988), p. 45.

holders in such companies be Japanese, and that 100 percent domestic production of all vehicle parts be a goal. Ford and GM were never granted a license, resulting in the eventual end of their Japanese auto operations.

Toyoda Automatic Loom Works was granted a license, officially designating it as a company eligible to make motor vehicles. Aware of the importance of a brand name, Kiichiro Toyoda held a public contest, which drew 27,000 entries, for a new Toyoda logo. "Toyota" was the winning entry; as a design, the Japanese symbol imparted a sense of speed, was considered aesthetically superior, and required eight (8 is considered a lucky number in Japan) strokes to write it. The automotive department was separated out as a new company in August 1937, resulting in the formation of the Toyota Motor Company. The Toyoda precepts, embodying the philosophy and convictions of Sakichi Toyoda, were to serve as guidelines for the operations of the companies in the Toyota group (see Exhibit 3). In the following year, Toyota completed construction of its first major plant located in Koromo (today's Toyota City).

In designing the Koromo plant, Kiichiro Toyoda's ideas provided the foundation for what was to become known as the Toyota production system. Kiichiro Toyoda's approach to vehicle manufacturing, codified into a manual four-inches thick, described in meticulous detail the flow-production system, or "just-in-time" concept. By this he meant, "Just make what is needed in time, but don't make too much." The manufacturing system Kiichiro Toyoda designed was predicated on four principles:[3]

- Have the 30 or more factory buildings of various sizes laid out so that their proximities to one another will be conducive to the smooth production of complete automobiles.
- Locate machinery in the plant so the layout will facilitate work flow from one machine to the other.
- Build machines that will be flexible enough in function to meet any requirement, bearing in mind that they are to be used for 20 or 30 years.
- Forget the commonly held notion that warehouses are essential in a plant.

"Creating product quality within the process" was another idea of Kiichiro Toyoda. The goal was not to just differentiate between good and bad products, but to find a way to correct whatever needed fixing, be it machinery, equipment, or tools, to prevent defects from happening in the first place. Implementing the system involved thorough training of the employees and getting them to abandon their old ways of doing things.

E X H I B I T 3 | **The Toyoda Precepts**

1. Be contributive to the development and welfare of the country by working together, regardless of position, in faithfully fulfilling your duties.
2. Be at the vanguard of the times through endless creativity, inquisitiveness, and pursuit of improvement.
3. Be practical and avoid frivolity.
4. Be kind and generous; strive to create a warm, homelike atmosphere.
5. Be reverent, and show gratitude for things great and small in thought and deed.

Source: *Toyota: A History of the First 50 Years* (Toyota City, Japan: Toyota Motor Corporation, 1988), pp. 37–38.

---

[3]Ibid., p. 70.

World War II disrupted Kiichiro Toyoda's vision of producing passenger cars. Automakers were obliged to concentrate on producing trucks for the military due to governmental limitations on the building of small vehicles. Scarce raw materials, such as iron and steel, were a major problem, and Toyota spent more energy scavenging for materials than building vehicles. Wartime production of trucks and buses peaked in 1941 with 42,813 units built by all Japanese automakers; in that same year, Toyota produced only 208 passenger cars. In 1945, Toyota produced 3,275 trucks and buses and no passenger cars.

POST–WORLD WAR II OPERATIONS

Following World War II, the Japanese auto industry had to begin anew. Determined to enter car and truck production on a full-scale basis, Toyota executives faced several obstacles: producing a variety of vehicles appropriate for a small domestic market; coping with obsolete production equipment and facilities in disrepair; dealing with a native Japanese workforce no longer content to be treated as an expendable factor of production; being unable to purchase the latest U.S. and European technology because of lack of capital; and growing interest of expansion-minded foreign motor vehicle producers in building plants in Japan or, at least, serving the Japanese market with vehicles exported from their own domestic plants.

Kiichiro Toyoda firmly believed the era of the small passenger car had arrived. Research on a small car became Toyota's top priority:[4]

> The passenger car that will be appropriate for Japan will be not an American-style large car, but rather a small car. In Japan, there is some experience accumulated in the area of small cars, yet when it comes to development on the basis of the functions which are peculiar to a small car, the record is quite short. As a result, existing small cars suffer from many problems, such as cramped interiors, excessive weight, low horsepower, and excessive vibration. If these problems could be solved, then naturally people would come to evaluate the utility of small cars on the same level as that of large ones. And undoubtedly, along with such advantageous characteristics would come the possibility of exporting small cars.

When permission was received to produce a limited number of small vehicles in mid-1947, Toyota launched a small passenger car, named the Toyopet.

Adverse economic conditions in 1949 resulted in a financial crisis at Toyota. A consortium of banks agreed to provide aid to Toyota if the sales department was incorporated as an independent company (Toyota Motor Sales) and substantial personnel cuts were made. In 1950, Eiji Toyoda, Kiichiro Toyoda's cousin, visited the Ford facilities in the U.S. to study the U.S. approach to automaking. Upon his return, when asked how long it would take to catch up to Ford, Eiji Toyoda responded: "Ford's not doing anything we don't already know." If a difference existed, it was due to a large gap in production scale, not in technological know-how.

Eiji Toyoda's reports provided the basis for a five-year modernization plan, affecting all aspects of Toyota's operations. The ultimate goal was to increase production capacity to 3,000 units per month. The Toyota creative ideas and suggestions system, based on the suggestion system used by Ford, was implemented to support company-wide improvements in production methods and efficiency. One outcome of this program was the company slogan, "Good thinking, good products." After 13 years in business, Toyota had produced 2,685 automobiles, compared with the 7,000 that

---

[4]Ibid., p. 101.

Ford's Rouge plant was producing in a single day. By the early 1950s, Toyota's financial situation had improved, enabling it to direct profits into research and development and to expand its capital base.

ROLE OF THE GOVERNMENT

Rapid growth in the development of the Japanese auto industry was aided by government policies. Targeted as one of the high-priority industries after World War II in the government's economic reconstruction program, the government pursued two major initiatives to promote automobile self-sufficiency in the quasi-closed economy. First, the Ministry of International Trade and Industry (MITI) limited imports to about 1 percent of the Japanese market. Second, a plan was proposed to "rationalize" the auto industry through mergers and specialization. Although the plan never materialized, it resulted in heavy investment by the auto companies, enabling them to become more competitive.

Additional government measures to strengthen and protect the ability of the industry to compete included protective tariffs; restrictions on foreign capital participation and loans; accelerated depreciation; special import arrangements for machinery and technology; and long-term, low-interest loans for the auto parts industry. Unprecedented economic growth (average annual rate of 15 percent) in Japan in the 1960s, combined with the spread of private car ownership, caused the Japanese auto industry to boom.

The Crown line of Toyota cars, with a top speed of 65 mph, debuted on January 1, 1955, to an enthusiastic reception by the Japanese public. Barely able to keep up with orders due to brisk demand for the Crown, Toyota decided to construct the Motomachi Plant, which would produce 5,000 units per month. According to Eiji Toyoda, the plant was viewed as a big gamble, but enabled Toyota to[5]

> [rise] head and shoulders above its domestic competitors . . . So we gained a decisive edge right from the start. Ever since then, we've continually pressed on for fear of being overtaken, rapidly putting up one new factory after another . . . to keep pace with the wave of motorization that hit Japan in the 1960s. By that time, we had won the confidence of the banks and no longer had difficulty raising capital or securing loans for new construction.

THE TOYOTA PRODUCTION SYSTEM

In the late 1940s, top Toyota executives determined that traditional mass production systems used in the U.S. and Europe were inappropriate for building autos suitable for the Japanese market. That decision, followed by four decades of experimenting with and improving on Kiichiro Toyoda's flow-production system, steered Toyota on a course that resulted in the Toyota production system (TPS). The TPS was a customer-focused, lean production approach to motor vehicle manufacturing—a system so novel and efficient that it represented a reinvention of modern manufacturing techniques. The total system began with and was totally geared to the needs of customers and dealers. In contrast, with the mass production approach, the needs of the factory came first, and dealers and customers were expected to make any necessary accommodations.

---

[5]Eiji Toyoda, *Toyota: Fifty Years in Motion* (New York: Harper & Row, 1985), p. 127.

The TPS combined the best features of both craft and mass production, while avoiding the high cost of the former and the rigidity of the latter. Emphasis on teamwork, communication, efficient use of resources, elimination of waste, and continuous improvement guided the development of the TPS. The system focused on excellence—continually declining costs, zero defects, zero inventories, and growing ability to expand product variety. The TPS melded the activities of everyone from top management to line workers, suppliers, and dealers into a tightly integrated process, capable of responding almost instantly to customer demand. The TPS had six components:

- A motivated and extremely productive workforce.
- Low-cost, high-quality factory operations guided by just-in-time deliveries of parts and flow-production techniques.
- Long-term partnerships with suppliers.
- Careful market research and short design-to-showroom cycles to keep models closely aligned with market demand.
- Custom-order production and superior customer service.
- A management approach focused on continuous improvement, teamwork, and decentralized decision-making.

The following sections describe each of these in more detail.[6]

WORKFORCE PRACTICES

Prodded by the Japanese government, Toyota (and many other Japanese companies) agreed to guarantee lifetime employment for employees. Toyota provided a pay scale based on seniority, not job classification, with bonus payments tied to company profitability. In return, employees agreed to be flexible in their work assignments and to commit to initiating improvements rather than merely responding to problems.

A major implication was that the workforce was a significant long-term fixed cost much like the company's plants and machinery. Toyota needed to get the most out of its human resources over their working lifetimes. Thus, it was only logical to continuously enhance employees' skills and to gain the benefit of their knowledge and experience, as well as their physical strength.

Mutual trust, communication, and continuous training characterized the employment relationship. A labor-management declaration, signed in 1962, symbolized the mutual trust relationship. Eiji Toyoda believed that maintaining a relationship of mutual trust with the employees was largely responsible for improvements in labor-management relations:[7]

> Mutual trust is the basis of labor relations. Labor relations at Toyota were initially marked by doubts and disbelief, but with time differences were ironed out. The labor-management declaration we signed was simply a written statement of this rapprochement. The purpose of this document was to uphold and sustain the trust that had been built up between management and labor, and to prevent backsliding by either side from this position. It also was intended as a reminder to those who came after to guard the fruits won through the sacrifices made by both sides. The spirit of this declaration still lives on at Toyota.

---

[6]The following discussion of the Toyota production system draws heavily on James P. Womack, Daniel T. Jones, and Daniel Roos, *The Machine That Changed the World* (New York: Macmillan, 1990).

[7]Toyoda, *Toyota: Fifty Years in Motion*, p. 128.

Management consistently worked hard at maintaining good relations. Establishing quality circles was integral to the overall relationship. The goal of these employee groups was not just to look for ways to improve product quality, but to improve all facets of production—unit cost, speed of assembly, and delivery schedules. Additionally, management initiated elaborate orientation programs and actively promoted informal contact between employees at all levels of the company. The result was enthusiastic, devoted, conscientious employees who often hung around the assembly line after-hours offering suggestions on improvements in work methods. During a recent year, Toyota received 860,000 employee suggestions for improvement; approximately 94 percent of the ideas were adopted, resulting in estimated savings in excess of $30 million per year.

FACTORY OPERATIONS

Toyota management regarded final assembly of a vehicle in a typical mass production plant as extremely inefficient. Mass production involved wasted materials, effort, and time. For example, during the late 1940s and early 1950s, an assembly plant might operate normally for only 10 days, while remaining idle for 20 days due to a lack of parts. Toyota's goal was to manufacture only what was needed, when it was needed, and in the quantity needed.

Technologically advanced machinery, teams of workers, a high level of work standardization, and small inventories and repair areas typified the factory system. Toyota implemented several innovations to improve production efficiency:

- *Multiskilled assembly workers:* Organizing workers into teams, each team was responsible for determining the necessary operations associated with building a vehicle. Each employee was responsible for operating an average of five machines (multimachine handling). As productivity continued to increase, the teams assumed additional responsibilities, such as housekeeping, minor tool repair, and quality checking, thus reducing the need for engineering and production specialists to perform these functions.

- *Andon boards (electrical signs):* These were installed at strategic locations in a plant to track daily production, signal overtime requirements, and identify trouble spots along the line. Individual workers had smaller versions to tell them, for example, whether a bolt was attached tightly enough.

- *Just-in-time or "flow" production:* The objective here was to smooth the flow between the processes supervised by various employees and to drastically reduce the inventories of parts and components. The *kanban* system, using the exchange of various-sized cards, was developed to transfer information between processes. Each card showed the number of parts and parts numbers of items needing replacement. This system was called the "supermarket method," since it imitated the practice in U.S. supermarkets where customers went to stores to buy what they wanted when they wanted it (rather than to store goods) while the supermarket restocked items as they were sold. Thus, a "pull" system evolved—each employee went back to the previous station on the assembly line to retrieve work-in-process, just at the necessary time, getting only the amount needed for immediate processing.

- *Zero defects or built-in quality:* Implementation of a problem-solving system, "the five why's," involved a worker being trained to systematically trace every error back to its ultimate cause (by asking "why" as each layer of the problem was uncovered) and then devising a fix so it would not occur again. Cords were installed above the production line to be pulled by any employee at any time to stop the line if complications arose. Each employee served as the customer for the process just before his and in essence became a quality-control inspector.

Implementation proceeded gradually as employees learned the system. Adjusting production speed, improving production layouts, and gaining experience in error detection and correction resulted in fewer errors occurring.

SUPPLIER RELATIONSHIPS

Auto assembly plants accounted for approximately 15 percent of Toyota's total manufacturing process, with the rest attributed to the production of the 10,000 or so discrete parts going into a single car. Toyota's suppliers were divided into two tiers, each having different responsibilities. Toyota dealt only with its primary suppliers, numbering approximately 175, on a development project. These suppliers were each assigned a whole component, such as car seats or the electrical system. These suppliers would then contract with secondary suppliers to provide individual parts or subsystem components.

First-tier suppliers were treated as an integral part of Toyota's product development team and were given performance rather than engineering specifications for their assigned component parts. For example, a supplier was told to design a set of brakes that would stop a 2,200-pound car going 60 miles per hour in the space of 200 feet, and do it 10 times in succession without fading. Both the space within which the brakes had to fit and the price were specified. A prototype had to be delivered to Toyota for testing, and if it worked, a production order was awarded. When production of the new model began, suppliers delivered the component parts directly to Toyota's assembly lines, typically several times per day (occasionally ever hour or two), with no inspection of incoming deliveries.

Other aspects of Toyota's approach to supplier relationships included:

- Becoming completely familiar with every supplier's operations, including having Toyota design engineers stationed at supplier plants.
- Making equity investments in suppliers' businesses (often, Toyota and its suppliers had substantial holdings of each other's stock).
- Establishing supplier associations that met regularly to share new findings on better ways of making parts.
- Reaching agreements with suppliers that allowed Toyota representatives access to the supplier's costs and profit margins and that provided these representatives opportunities to suggest to the supplier how cost savings might be achieved.
- Providing loans to suppliers, if needed, to purchase cost-saving or quality-enhancing equipment.
- Fostering cooperative, stable, long-term business relationships with suppliers.

PRODUCT DESIGN AND DEVELOPMENT

Leadership, teamwork, communication, and simultaneous development formed the basis of Toyota's approach to designing and engineering a new model. Customer needs and attitudes were carefully analyzed and teams of functional specialists, under the guidance of a *shusa* (chief engineer), were responsible for all activities related to the development of a new product—design, engineering, selection of all suppliers, and marketing strategies. Although they maintained ties with their functional departments, the specialists were committed to the project until their phase of the project was completed. At the inception of the project, team members signed formal pledges to do exactly what everyone agreed upon as a group. If conflicts about resources and priorities occurred, it was at the beginning rather than the end of the process. At the outset of a project, all relevant functional specialties were represented, resulting in the most people being involved at the initial stages. The job of the *shusa* was to force the group to face all the difficult trade-offs they would have to make to reach consensus.

Simultaneous development involved product and manufacturing engineers working closely together under the *shusa* so factory machinery was developed in tandem with prototype testing. Typically, prototype testing led to changes in the car that required alterations in the assembly line; since design and production processes proceeded simultaneously, last-minute changes infrequently stalled production plans.

Fewer tools, lower inventories, a higher proportion of projects going into production on time, no productivity penalty, higher quality, and less human effort resulted in short development times per new car when compared with non-Japanese automakers—less than 40 months for Toyota versus about four years for U.S. automakers and seven years for many European producers. According to one study, Toyota employed slightly more than half as many engineers in designing a new model compared to U.S. companies. As a consequence, Toyota offered a wider variety of models, introducing them to the marketplace more quickly and cheaply than traditional mass producers. By the early 1990s, Toyota produced 26 separate lines of cars, more than most any other auto manufacturer.

CUSTOMER AND DEALER RELATIONS

Cooperative links between Toyota, its dealers, and customers were seen as integral to long-term success. In Japan, Toyota had five nationwide dealer "channels" (Toyota, Toyopet, Auto, Vista, and Corolla), each of which marketed a portion of the Toyota line. For example, one channel sold less-expensive models while another sold sportier models. The five dealer channels had different labels and model names for their cars, but the main distinction among them was their focus on different types of customers. The major purpose of the channel was to develop a direct link between the manufacturing system and vehicle owners.

A description of the Corolla channel illustrates how Toyota's distribution system in Japan functioned. Established in 1961, the channel sold the Corolla, Camry, Supra, Celica, and several truck models. The channel consisted of 78 dealer firms, operating from approximately 17 different sites. Corolla owned 20 percent of the dealerships outright and had a partial ownership in others, but most dealerships were financially independent. Corolla provided training to the approximately 30,000 people who made up the sales staffs at the 78 dealerships and also offered a full range of services and sales assistance to the dealerships it did not own. In 1989, the Corolla dealer channel, with a staff of some 30,400 people, sold about 635,000 cars and trucks (an average of just over 21 vehicles per staff member). With the exception of the showroom, few similarities existed between a Japanese and a U.S. dealership. A typical Corolla channel dealership in Japan had only three or four demonstrator models and no parking lots of unsold vehicles for prospective buyers to look at. Nor was there a battle over the walk-in customer by the sales staff since the sales team was paid on a group commission, rather than on an individual commission basis.

The sales staff at each Corolla dealership were multiskilled, having been trained in all aspects of sales—product information, order taking, financing, insurance, and data collection—and were divided into teams of seven or eight members. A team meeting began and ended each work day. After developing a profile of all households in the dealership's geographic area and calling for an appointment, members of the sales team made door-to-door sales calls. Updating the household profile was one objective; if the family was ready to purchase a car, a custom order—every Toyota sold in Japan was tailor-made to customer specifications—was placed with the factory via an on-line computer. Haggling over price was almost nonexistent, and the deal was not concluded until arrangements regarding financing, trade-in of the old car, and insurance were made. The sales representative delivered the new car directly to the owner's house.

Additional services provided were registration, arrangements for regular maintenance, taking care of rigorous government inspections, fixing any problems encountered by the owner even after the formal warranty expired, providing a car while the car was being repaired, sending birthday cards, and sending condolence cards in the event of a death in the family. The principal objective was not just a one-time sale; rather it was to make the customer feel a part of the Toyota "family," to establish a long-term relationship with the customer, and to build strong brand loyalty. The success of the sales system employed by Toyota (and other Japanese automakers) was reflected by the fact that brand switching was much less common in Japan than in other countries.

The door-to-door sales system was gradually being phased out. Younger buyers, more interested in shopping around than older buyers, wanted to purchase their cars directly from a dealership. Toyota, along with other Japanese automakers, was also having difficulty recruiting salespeople willing to sell cars door-to-door.

Toyota was exploring the use of information technology to cut the high costs associated with the sales system. This involved installing an extensive computer system in the dealerships. A current Corolla owner entering a Corolla dealership inserted his membership card in the system, which displayed all the pertinent information of the owner's household. The owner made relevant changes in the information, and the system then suggested the most appropriate models for the owner's needs, with prices included. The owner also had access to databases dealing with such things as financing, car insurance, and parking permits. If seriously interested in buying, the owner approached the sales team to discuss specific details. The number of cars sold in this way was steadily increasing in Japan, and Toyota hoped to deal with most existing owners using this method. The sales force could then concentrate on "conquest" sales—those to owners currently purchasing other brands.

Customer Relations outside Japan Toyota's sales approach to customers in the U.S. and Europe currently resembled the dealer networks used by American and European producers. Customized orders were not accepted due to the distance involved in supply. Instead, Toyota sold through a network of franchised dealers; to make sure its models were equipped to buyer preferences, Toyota focused on adding a variety of options as standard equipment on their exports, resulting in customers' having more choices. As Toyota established independent production facilities in countries outside Japan, the company planned to investigate the feasibility of building cars to customer order and delivering them almost immediately, imitating the approach used in Japan.

TOYOTA'S APPROACH TO MANAGING ITS PRODUCTION SYSTEM

Management of Toyota's production system required different career paths when compared with mass production. In mass production, career progression was virtually nonexistent for production employees, and specialists in engineering, marketing, and finance were promoted on the basis of technical expertise while general managers progressed through the numerous layers in the corporate hierarchy.

At Toyota, however, union members had an opportunity to move into the company's management structure. Each employee's first assignment at Toyota entailed working on the production line. Decentralized decision-making was reflected in the career opportunities of all employees, regardless of their career paths. For employees remaining in the factory, the reward system consisted of performance bonuses and pay increases based on seniority. Since fewer layers of management existed, resulting in less opportunity for promotions, the ability to solve increasingly difficult problems was emphasized as the most important aspect of any job, even if job titles did not change. Technical specialists and engineers were assigned to product-development teams; often they had to learn new skills as they progressed through their careers. The goal was to expose these specialists to the day-to-day activities of the company and have them study intensively the changing moods, tastes, and driving habits of vehicle buyers. Responsibilities of general managers consisted of tying supplier organizations to the assembly operations and tying geographically dispersed units of the company together. Often, managers were rotated among the company's various operations, including foreign operations, or they might be assigned to management positions in the supplier organizations.

Overall, the TPS was an exercise in trying to achieve perfection—it focused each employee on anticipating problems and finding preventive solutions. Implementation of the TPS had been a long, gradual process. Begun in the early 1950s, and only after much trial and error, it was in place in all Toyota plants by 1963; subsequently, the TPS was introduced to parts and materials suppliers. By the 1970s, the entire system was firmly ingrained in Toyota's operations and was formally named the "Toyota Production System."

Guided by the philosophy of *kaizen* ("continuous improvement"), Toyota's management constantly pushed for improvements to the TPS and for better and better execution. In the 1980s, Toyota launched bold efforts to make the TPS work more efficiently, responsively, and flexibly to the increased proliferation in car models and to changes in the kinds of cars that consumers wanted. After years of leaving technological innovation to Nissan and Honda, Toyota tripled its R&D spending from $750 million in 1984 to $2.2 billion in 1989. Enhancements to the TPS included construction of new integrated facilities, incorporating the most advanced production technology; increased emphasis on maintenance of machinery and equipment; and expansion of automation. Automation involved the introduction of on-line computers for production control; increased use of robots to perform such jobs as spot welding, painting, arc welding, and attaching nuts; and computerization of Toyota's entire operation through the installation of the CAD/CAM (computer-aided design/computer-aided manufacturing) system.

Toyota's overriding objective was to produce only the products demanded in the volumes required. To avoid extreme fluctuations in production volumes associated with changes in customer preferences, Toyota produced the same model simultaneously at more than one plant and produced a number of different models at each plant. Toyota gradually introduced "flexible body lines" (assembly of a number of distinct models on the same product line without decreasing productivity or quality) at its plants, beginning in 1985. Since each line handled mixed production, the time needed to switch to new models was considerably shortened.

As the mid-1990s approached, increasing costs (labor, capital, depreciation, raw materials, and marketing) associated with auto manufacturing in Japan, combined with a plateau in productivity and a labor shortage, spurred Toyota to focus on "modernizing the original idea." Toyota reorganized its product-development activities and embarked on the biggest automation drive in its history. The number of *shusas* had reached about three dozen, which resulted in excessively cumbersome product-development operations. Under the new system, three chief engineers were accountable for the following categories of vehicles: front-wheel drive, rear-wheel drive, and trucks. Each chief engineer was responsible for encouraging cooperation among the *shusas* to achieve the goal of reducing the number of unique vehicle parts by 30 percent. Although employees were to remain at the hub of the production process, use of computers and robots was expected to increase. One plan involved increasing the amount of mechanized work in Toyota's engine-assembly plants from 73 percent to 85 percent by 1993. Expanded use of automated design and manufacturing processes was estimated to decrease the design-to-production time from 24 to 22 months. Additional improvements to the TPS included implementing three-crew scheduling systems, which achieved six-day-a-week production at a factory (without overtime), and gradually reducing the variety of models.

Results of Toyota's most recent enhancements to the TPS were clearly evident at the Tahara manufacturing plant where two luxury models—the Crown Majesta and Aristo (Lexus GS300)—were assembled:[8]

> [The] no. 4 [line at Tahara] is immaculately maintained, remarkably clean, and surprisingly quiet. Since electric vehicle carriers have replaced clangy chain-driven conveyors, people can converse normally. The strains of Beethoven's "Fur Elise" waft through the air over the public-address system.
>
> At Tahara workers are hard to find; machines are everywhere. Large motorized platforms called automatic guided vehicles carry steel body panels to the giant stamping presses. Two video cameras help robots perfectly align hoods with engine compartments. Engines, transmissions, and front and rear suspensions rise from the floor, the body descends from above, and the two mate automatically. Machines wielding wrenches attach the bolts. A light board shows when they have achieved proper tightness.

According to the general manager of the plant, the goal of automation was "to make a comfortable working environment for employees and to reduce costly turnover of expensively trained workers."[9] Manufacturing experts indicated that although Tahara's no. 4 line was less automated than some European auto factories, its productivity was unmatched. In the final assembly area, a single shift of 197 employees turned out 192 cars per day. When welding and painting were added in, 16 employee hours were involved in assembling a fully equipped luxury car. Although the time was analogous to producing the Ford Taurus, it was less than half the time necessary for comparable luxury cars: 34 hours for a Lincoln Town Car, 40 hours for a Cadillac Seville, and in excess of 100 hours for a large Mercedes-Benz or BMW.

---

[8] Alex Taylor III, "How Toyota Copes with Hard Times," *Fortune,* January 25, 1993, pp. 80–81.
[9] Ibid., p. 81.

According to an MIT study conducted in the 1980s, the TPS used less of everything—"half the human effort in the factory, half the manufacturing space, half the investment in tools, half the engineering hours to develop a new product"—when compared with the traditional mass production methods relied on by American and European manufacturers.[10] Toyota's reinvention of the manufacturing process resulted in a high-quality car or truck built to customer specifications and delivered within 10 days to three weeks.

DOMESTIC OPERATIONS

Nagoya, Japan, home of Toyota City, was the hub of Toyota's worldwide operations network. Toyota City had all the trappings of a "company" town—12 manufacturing plants (4 were dedicated to assembly), factories for nearly 140 of its parts suppliers, company housing (dormitories, apartments, and houses), a huge Toyota sports center (Olympic-size pool, two football fields, four baseball diamonds, two gymnasiums), a Toyota Hospital (free medical care was provided), and clubs of all kinds. Top executives worked out of a flat-roofed three-story structure smaller than a typical U.S. high school.

In 1969, Toyota became the fifth-largest automaker in the world, surpassing Fiat. In 1970, Toyota passed Chrysler, advancing to fourth place; in 1971, it jumped ahead of Volkswagen to become the third largest. In 1985, Toyota was producing 40 percent as many cars as GM with a workforce slightly more than one-tenth the size of GM's (part—but only part—of the difference was due to Toyota's greater use of subcontractors). In 1993, Toyota had 108,000 employees, producing nearly 5 million vehicles worldwide. Toyota's share of the passenger car market in Japan was 35.5 percent in 1991; Toyota's closest rival, Nissan, had a 20.5 percent share (see Exhibit 4).

The competitive environment of the 1980s and 1990s introduced several factors (some unique to Japanese automakers) that affected the ability to compete both domestically and internationally:

- Slowing economic growth both globally and in Japan (from an inflation-adjusted average annual rate of nearly 5 percent in the late 1980s, the Japanese economy was expected to grow at an average rate of about 3 percent during the decade of the 1990s).
- Continuing trade frictions due to trade imbalances between Japan and other countries and the lack of openness of the Japanese market to imports.
- Declining exports to the U.S. and Europe due to import restrictions and strict domestic content laws in other countries.
- Continuing appreciation of the yen (whereas it took 260 yen to equal a dollar in early 1985, by late 1993 it took only 107 yen to equal a dollar).
- Escalating competition in the low-priced car market marked by the entrance of several newly industrialized countries (abundant low-cost labor and rising levels of technology placed them on the heels of the Japanese auto industry).
- Increasing overcapacity in the mature, global auto industry.
- Declining sales and profits, combined with increasing costs, in the Japanese auto market.

---

[10]Womack, Jones, and Roos, *The Machine That Changed the World,* p. 13.

EXHIBIT 4 | **Domestic Market Share of the Five Largest Japanese Automakers, 1970–91***

Year	Toyota	Nissan	Honda	Mazda	Mitsubishi	All Others
1970	29.8%	24.7%	10.6%	6.6%	8.9%	19.4%
1975	39.2	31.3	5.9	6.5	6.2	10.9
1978	37.9	29.2	6.0	6.0	9.1	11.8
1980	37.3	29.0	5.9	6.9	8.8	12.1
1981	38.3	28.1	6.5	7.7	8.2	11.2
1982	38.6	27.1	7.9	8.1	7.4	10.9
1983	39.8	26.6	7.8	7.8	6.0	12.0
1984	41.2	26.0	7.9	6.9	6.4	11.6
1985	42.6	25.2	9.6	6.1	5.4	11.1
1986	43.9	24.3	9.7	6.2	4.6	11.3
1987	44.4	23.4	10.3	6.1	4.8	11.0
1988	43.9	23.2	10.8	5.9	4.9	11.3
1989	40.0	22.6	10.4	6.7	5.3	15.0
1990	37.1	20.7	10.1	7.8	6.2	18.1
1991	35.5	20.5	10.6	7.4	6.9	19.1

*Total new passenger car registrations.
Source: Motor Vehicle Manufacturers' Association, *World Motor Vehicle Data,* 1993 edition, pp. 69–71, and 1989 edition, pp. 69–71.

To strengthen its position in the highly competitive, global auto market, Toyota focused on enhancing several aspects of its corporate operations. Toyota Motor Company and Toyota Motor Sales were combined in 1982. According to a joint statement by Eiji Toyoda, the new chairman, and Shoichiro Toyoda, the new president of Toyota Motor, the major reasons for the merger were to develop Toyota's international operations and to achieve greater efficiencies in management operations:[11]

> To cope with the turbulent 1980s and to progress further along the path we have taken thus far, a need has emerged to integrate our production and sales functions, which are in fact two sides of the same coin, so that they can augment each other more comprehensively and organically.

Toyota launched the "T-50 Operation" in June 1986, to commemorate the 50th anniversary of its first passenger car. Competitors interpreted the intent of the "operation" as meaning that Toyota aspired to a 50 percent share of the Japanese passenger car market. According to a manager of a mid-level automaker, "It is a shame for the auto industry to permit Toyota to grab a share of 50 percent. Toyota, as the leader of Japan's auto industry, should behave in a more adultlike manner."[12] Redoubled sales efforts by the other automakers succeeded in keeping Toyota's share at 49.2 percent (its highest in history) of all new cars registered in June. This compared with the respective shares of Nissan at 22.8 percent, Honda at 11 percent, and Mazda at 5.6 percent. Typical comments by rival automakers and dealers, who requested anonymity, regarding Toyota's performance included[13]

---

[11]*Toyota: A History,* p. 314.
[12]As quoted in *Business Japan,* October 1986, p. 44.
[13]Ibid., pp. 44–45.

"Toyota is formidable. There is a qualitative difference in its sales system."

"To be honest, we have received a tremendous jolt. We cannot but ask Toyota to relent a little more."

"Dealers down to the periphery are exhorted to adhere to orderly sales practices. But such developments may inevitably lead to drastic price-cutting tactics."

"To be frank, we have no other course but defense. We cannot understand why Toyota cars sell so well. Our parent company (Nissan) insists on fair play and discipline, but we can no longer stick to all our scruples. It is a miracle that Toyota has not adopted the incentive system."

According to rivals, Toyota's strength lay in technical development, enabling it to supply cars exactly matched to customer needs; a powerful distribution system; and near-perfect user services.

By the latter 1980s, Toyota's success was, according to industry observers, beginning to breed complacency due to *dai-kigyo-byo* (big company disease) and lagging corporate morale. Former President Shoichiro Toyoda commented: " . . . things have changed. The days when every employee committed himself completely—and with utter satisfaction—to his job and his company are gone. People are much more varied in their expectations today."[14] Shoichiro Toyoda implemented a "put the customer first" campaign aimed at challenging the company's total approach to making cars and recertifying that customer satisfaction was the first priority. The committee responsible for this customer-satisfaction drive was given three years—one thousand days—to get Toyota on the move again and institute *kaizen* on a corporate scale. Additional actions by Shoichiro Toyoda included eliminating two layers of middle management, stripping 1,000 executives of their staffs, and reorganizing product development, putting himself in charge. Toyota's top management stated it was willing to restrain its growth; according to Shoichiro Toyoda:[15]

We manufacturers realize that we must reexamine and redefine Japan's role in the world, provide positive support, and, taking into account the necessity of contributing to the economies of our trade partners, never forget "coexistence and coprosperity" [the need for *kyozon-kyoei* or both competition and cooperation].

The time has come for the industry, taken as a global unit, to learn to live together. In the past, competition was the rule, and some firms went to the wall as a consequence. We cannot have a repeat of this today. The new goal of the car industry must be collective prosperity, not cutthroat competition.

The competitive environment in Japan in the early 1990s found the Japanese automakers mired in their worst slump in 40 years. Appreciation of the yen had converted a Japanese price advantage of about $1,000 per car in 1985 into a $2,000 price disadvantage by late 1993; effects of the global recession had resulted in declining vehicle production to 11.5 million vehicles, nearly 2 million less than in 1990; consequences of the "market-share paradox" had resulted in the halving of profit margins although Japanese automakers had tripled sales during the past two decades (losses by at least 4 of the 11 automakers were expected in 1993); and capacity utilization was estimated to be only 80 percent.

As the dominant Japanese automaker, Toyota faced intensifying pressures from the government, rival competitors, and labor unions to take a leadership role in restructuring its strategies. Known as *risutora* (when translated into English, it meant

---

[14] As quoted in *Tokyo Business Today,* August 1989, p. 17.

[15] As quoted in *Business Japan,* September 1985, p. 18, and *Tokyo Business Today,* August 1989, p. 16.

pruning people, products, and plants), Toyota was urged to lengthen product cycles, raise prices, and call off its drive for market share overseas. Toyota responded by instituting the following changes:

- Implementing changes in the TPS.
- Commencing a companywide cost-cutting campaign, beginning in 1992 (administrative costs were slashed by 30 percent, which involved cutting expense account budgets for entertainment and business dinners in half, eliminating white-collar overtime, and restricting travel; as part of the "business revolution," 20 percent of Toyota's 4,000 white-collar administrative employees were shifted from regular jobs to 70 business-reform teams, ostensibly set up to look for corporate inefficiencies).
- Adopting a new corporate slogan—"Making quality cars and friends around the world" (Toyota's actual corporate slogan, printed in a production-methods handbook, was "Taking our destiny into our own hands").
- Slicing the average employee's annual work hours by 50 hours to 2,050 in 1992 while aiming for additional cuts to 1,900 hours in 1993 (this was slightly less than the average of 1,920 annual hours for U.S. autoworkers).
- Adopting U.S. human resource methods (this included using specific job descriptions, implementing merit pay, cutting managers' bonuses, and creating a new category of temporary professional employees; for example, newly hired automotive designers were hired for one-year contracts, with an annual salary of $89,800 based on individual merit, not seniority).
- Reducing capital spending from an average of $500 billion yen to around $350 billion yen, beginning in April 1993.
- Increasing prices of its vehicles in the U.S. market.
- Announcing an International Cooperation Program, a three-pronged plan aimed at increasing imports, boosting local purchasing by its overseas operations, and furthering cooperation with foreign automakers.
- Building or expanding six assembly plants worldwide with a total capacity of one million vehicles (five were in export markets outside Japan—Britain, Pakistan, Thailand, Turkey, and the U.S.—while a new factory was being built on the southern island of Kyushu).

FINANCIAL OPERATIONS

Toyota Motor Corporation was the largest entity in an affiliation of 13 interlocking companies known as the Toyota group (see Exhibit 5). The Toyota group was affiliated with the Mitsui *keiretsu*. A Japanese *keiretsu,* a form of business alliance, typically consisted of about 20 major companies, one in each major industrial sector, but there was no holding company at the top of the organization. Key companies in a keiretsu were banks, insurance companies, and trading companies. The companies were not legally part of a common corporate structure but were held together by cross-locking equity structures—each company owning a portion of every other company's equity—and a sense of reciprocal obligation. Although a key purpose was to help each other raise investment funds, members were also provided protection against hostile takeovers. Another advantage was the ability of group members to obtain low-cost financing from banks in their keiretsu.

Toyota was regarded as ultraconservative, a trait which was especially reflected in its cash hoard and strong balance sheet. Successful utilization of *zaiteku* (financial

EXHIBIT 5 | The Toyota Group Companies, 1993

Toyota Motor Corporation
Sales: $10,163.4 billion (06/93)
Tatsuro Toyoda, President
Shoichiro Toyoda, Chairman

Toyota Auto Body
Sales: $605.3 billion (03/93)
Saburo Bito, President

Toyota Motor owns 43.0%

Aisin Seiki Co., Ltd.
(Auto parts)
Sales: $838.5 billion (03/93)
Shigeo Aiki, President

Toyota Motor owns 21.9%

Toyoda Spinning & Weaving
(Textiles, auto parts)
Sales: N/A

Toyota Motor owns 8%

Hino Motors, Ltd.
(Heavy Trucks)
Sales: $632.4 billion (03/93)
Tomio Futami, President

Toyota Motor owns 11.2%

Daihatsu Motor Co., Ltd.
(Automaker)
Sales: $875.4 billion (03/93)
Takashi Toyozumi, President

Toyota Motor owns 48.7%

Kanto Auto Works Ltd.
(Auto parts)
Sales: $421.9 billion (03/93)
Fumio Agetsuma, President

Toyota Motor owns 48.7%

Toyota Central Research & Development Laboratories
Sales: N/A

Toyota Motor owns 54%

Aichi Steel Works, LTD.
Sales: $164.0 billion (12/92)
Masaaki Ohhashi, President

Toyota Motor owns 21.8%

Toyoda Gosei Co., Ltd.
(Auto parts)
Sales: $269.5 billion (04/93)
Sheji Ban, President

Toyota Motor owns 40.9%

Toyoda Machine Works, Ltd.
(Machine tools)
Sales: $202.8 billion (03/92)
Toyo Kato, President

Toyota Motor owns 21.1%

Nippondenso Co., Ltd.
(Electronic auto parts)
Sales: $1,523.8 billion (12/92)
Tsuneo Ishimaro, President

Toyota Motor owns 23.6%

Toyoda Automatic Loom Works, LTD.
Sales: $583.4 billion (03/92)
Yoshitoshi Toyoda, President

Toyota Motor owns 23.4%

Sources: *Business Week*, November 4, 1985, p. 45; *1989 International Directory of Corporate Affiliations* (Illinois: National Register Publishing), p. 475.

management of surplus cash) resulted in Toyota earning more profits on its financial investments than it did from selling cars. Toyota allocated its investment funds to financial institutions offering the best interest rates, regardless of the type of product, via its competitive bidding system. Thus, Toyota commanded the highest possible interest rates on its cash balances, referred to as the "Toyota rate" in Japanese financial circles, and its interest income had risen over the last several years. Toyota was considered one of Japan's most powerful financial institutions. Toyota's cash-management system closely resembled its *kanban* production system and was typical of its efforts to reduce to a minimum cost inefficiencies. According to one account, Toyota limited employees to one pencil at a time and a sign over the towel dispenser in the restroom at headquarters read: "Visitors Only."

In 1988, Toyota established the Toyota Finance Corporation to provide financing for installment sales and facility leasing for Toyota dealers and affiliated companies. Beginning in 1992, credit brokering and guaranteeing services were furnished to Toyota dealers. Projected services included extending automobile loans to its retail customers, extending housing loans, issuing credit cards, and installing automated teller machines in dealerships. One of Toyota's long-term objectives was to manage its own pension fund.

Toyota's potential plans for its excess cash included building new factories around the world; diversifying through acquisitions in electronics, telecommunications, factory automation, financial, and aerospace; and creating joint ventures with other automakers. According to one high-ranking Toyota executive:[16]

> If an acquisition looks right, we'll look at the candidates positively. We wouldn't like to refuse some food without even tasting it. Such an acquisition would be for the purpose of winning the survival race in the world automotive business, which is getting more and more heated. It's not that we want to beat General Motors, it's that we want to make sure they won't beat us.

Exhibit 6 presents financial statistics of Toyota Motor Corporation.

PRODUCT STRATEGY

By the latter 1960s, Toyota's strategy resembled General Motors'—blanketing the market with a variety of nameplates, each one a step above the other in size and cost. Initial emphasis was on cars for the family market, rather than specialized models. The Publica, the least-expensive model, was intended for buyers moving up from motorcycles or minicars. Next, in ascending order, was the Corolla (similar in size and price to the VW Beetle), the best-selling Corona, the Corona Mark II (Cressida), and the six-cylinder Crown (about the size of an American compact). Additional limited-production prestige models built, but not exported, were the eight-cylinder luxurious Century and the 2000GT, a two-seater similar to the Jaguar XKE. A limited range of trucks complemented Toyota's autos.

Although new, sportier models (Celica) aimed at the youth market were subsequently introduced, Toyota had lagged behind other Japanese automakers in introducing new models because of its concentrated efforts to meet the emission control standards of the 1970s. Additionally, the oil crises of the 1970s dictated a new approach to developing passenger cars appropriate to the international market—small, fuel-efficient, front-wheel drive passenger cars. Toyota's first products in this area were

---

[16]As quoted in *Fortune,* November 21, 1988, p. 198.

E X H I B I T   6 | **Selected Financial Data, Toyota Motor Corporation, 1984–93 (In thousand of Yen)**

	Fiscal Year Ending				
	06/30/93	06/30/92	06/30/91	06/30/90	06/30/89
Net sales	10,210,749,000	10,163,376,000	9,855,132,000	9,192,838,000	8,021,042,000
Cost of goods sold[1]	8,462,160,000	8,352,360,000	8,226,964,000	7,139,641,000	6,409,881,000
Gross income	1,264,487,000	1,339,003,000	1,595,377,000	1,713,784,000	1,316,118,000
Depreciation and amortization[2]	484,102,000	472,013,000	32,791,000	339,413,000	295,043,000
Selling, general, and administrative expenses[3]	1,082,589,000	1,120,490,000	1,095,516,000	1,070,789,000	848,178,000
Total operating expenses	10,028,851,000	9,944,863,000	9,355,271,000	8,549,843,000	7,553,102,000
Operating income	181,897,000	218,511,000	499,859,000	642,995,000	467,940,000
Nonoperating interest income	139,709,000	203,070,000	226,709,000	NA	NA
Other income/expenses—net	53,991,000	55,622,000	34,129,000	313,496,000	241,845,000
Interest expense	53,389,000	49,348,000	51,153,000	119,162,000	84,130,000
Pretax income	322,208,000	427,855,000	709,544,000	837,329,000	625,655,000
Income taxes	161,437,000	212,542,000	301,000,000	415,213,000	297,479,000
Minority interest	2,737,000	1,640,000	2,811,000	1,461,000	620,000
Equity in earnings	18,341,000	24,314,000	25,716,000	20,647,000	18,706,000
Net income	176,464,000	237,840,000	431,450,000	441,301,000	346,262,000
Cash and equivalents	1,438,508,000	1,944,163,000	1,753,698,000	2,204,580,000	1,935,887,000
Net receivables[4]	2,222,715,000	2,419,839,000	2,384,198,000	2,624,625,000	933,979,000
Inventories	391,185,000	421,867,000	404,662,000	337,985,000	334,226,000
Total current assets	4,529,754,000	5,180,390,000	4,849,393,000	5,167,190,000	4,343,971,000
Property, plant, equipment—gross	5,745,093,000	5,351,231,000	4,529,224,000	3,860,399,000	3,437,261,000
Accumulated depreciation	3,181,346,000	2,875,127,000	2,543,871,000	2,307,155,000	2,062,606,000
Other assets	90,265,000	71,737,000	40,464,000	360,656,000	1,434,260,000
Total assets[5]	9,338,378,000	9,555,759,000	8,978,922,000	8,431,095,000	7,152,886,000
Total current liabilities	2,592,596,000	2,980,864,000	2,625,877,000	2,691,260,000	1,958,583,000
Long-term debt	1,738,514,000	1,575,359,000	1,481,580,000	1,221,274,000	1,219,463,000
Other liabilities	294,264,000	283,837,000	283,102,000	265,557,000	249,832,000
Total liabilities	4,625,374,000	4,840,060,000	4,390,559,000	4,178,091,000	3,427,878,000
Minority interest	26,496,000	23,762,000	19,643,000	17,135,000	15,431,000
Capital surplus	276,894,000	276,542,000	272,359,000	263,177,000	NA
Retained earnings	4,160,013,000	4,117,147,000	3,986,018,000	3,676,352,000	NA
Common shareholders' equity[6]	4,686,507,000	4,691,937,000	4,568,720,000	4,235,869,000	3,709,577,000
Total liabilities and equity	9,338,378,000	9,555,759,000	8,978,922,000	8,431,095,000	7,152,886,000

[1]1991—Includes depreciation.
[2]1991—Excludes depreciation included in cost of goods sold.
[3]1990—Includes some nonoperating expense (income).
[4]1993, 1992, 1991, 1990—Includes other current nontrade receivables and/or other current assets.
[5]1992, 1991—Adjusted to exclude foreign currency translation gains/losses.
[6]1993, 1992, 1991—Adjusted to include foreign currency translation gains/losses.

EXHIBIT 6 | **Selected Financial Data, Toyota Motor Corporation, 1984–93 (In thousand of Yen)** *Continued*

		Fiscal Year Ending		
06/30/88	06/30/87	06/30/86	06/30/85	06/30/84
7,215,798,000	6,675,411,000	6,646,243,000	6,770,250,000	5,908,973,000
5,730,922,000	5,355,276,000	5,172,934,000	5,095,031,000	4,551,097,000
1,226,498,000	1,074,693,000	1,254,226,000	1,484,299,000	1,172,521,000
258,378,000	245,442,000	219,083,000	190,920,000	185,355,000
758,772,000	708,014,000	753,196,000	783,522,000	678,834,000
6,748,072,000	6,308,732,000	5,777,915,000	6,069,473,000	5,415,286,000
467,726,000	366,679,000	868,328,000	700,777,000	493,687,000
NA	NA	NA	NA	NA
164,825,000	170,542,000	-183,650,000	167,166,000	138,489,000
22,296,000	19,041,000	17,442,000	18,542,000	22,503,000
610,255,000	518,180,000	667,236,000	849,401,000	609,673,000
315,027,000	258,526,000	320,636,000	441,912,000	307,646,000
1,477,000	-1,050,000	1,066,000	1,683,000	2,219,000
17,658,000	NA	NA	NA	NA
310,952,000	260,704,000	345,534,000	405,806,000	294,808,000
1,387,721,000	1,262,158,000	1,070,941,000	1,225,561,000	1,055,449,000
803,540,000	698,624,000	654,872,000	642,584,000	602,973,000
261,719,000	259,047,000	268,143,000	307,084,000	265,174,000
2,807,201,000	2,530,168,000	2,248,320,000	2,429,816,000	2,137,375,000
3,086,031,000	2,865,971,000	2,588,990,000	2,318,172,000	2,158,278,000
1,872,704,000	1,724,380,000	1,549,106,000	1,430,078,000	1,319,509,000
1,429,848,000	337,614,000	294,525,000	242,150,000	53,906,000
5,450,376,000	4,870,832,000	4,348,104,000	4,279,218,000	3,686,269,000
1,596,290,000	1,380,921,000	1,277,396,000	1,439,787,000	1,258,488,000
330,493,000	220,996,000	5,306,000	8,135,000	10,235,000
225,259,000	208,389,000	191,340,000	176,069,000	158,995,000
2,152,042,000	1,810,306,000	1,474,042,000	1,623,991,000	1,427,718,000
13,074,000	15,439,000	16,764,000	16,772,000	15,979,000
NA	NA	NA	NA	NA
NA	NA	NA	NA	NA
3,285,260,000	3,045,087,000	2,857,295,000	2,638,455,000	2,242,572,000
5,450,376,000	4,870,832,000	4,348,104,000	4,279,218,000	3,686,269,000

the Tercel and Camry. When the Camry debuted in 1982, it was hailed by auto enthusiasts as the first in a new generation of front-wheel drive cars; however, some critics thought it lacked elegance owing to its functional styling and plain interior. Toyota entered the high-performance, specialty-car market with the MR2 and Supra, introduced in the 1980s. New models were regularly introduced, and by the 1990s, Toyota had vehicles in virtually all market segments. Toyota was beginning to be viewed as a fashion leader, putting to rest its reputation for fuddy-duddy design, evidenced by the introduction of the following vehicles: the Sera (a glass-topped minicoupe with gull-wing doors) and Mark II (a midsize car), sold only in Japan; the jellybean-shaped Previa, designed in California and a hit with U.S. buyers; and the Lexus, sold in Japan and several overseas markets. One impartial indicator of the attractiveness of Toyota's cars was their price in the used-car market. According to one study, Toyota's vehicles retained more than 70 percent of their value five years after being purchased. Only three other brands were in this category. Exhibit 7 displays Toyota's overall motor vehicle production.

EXPORT ACTIVITIES

Toyota established an export department in 1950 to explore the feasibility of overseas exports. Toyota's early export efforts were characterized by trial and error since the company was generally unfamiliar with the competitive conditions and import restrictions in foreign countries. Toyota targeted Southeast Asia, Latin America, and the Caribbean as its first export channels because of their proximity and interest. With an increase in local content laws prohibiting the export of completely built autos to several countries, such as Brazil and Mexico, Toyota experimented with a knockdown (KD) system, beginning in the latter 1950s. A KD set was one whose shipment price was less than 60 percent of the total cost of component parts making up a whole car. Problems, such as unavailability of local parts or assembly with

E X H I B I T 7 | **Motor Vehicle Production, Toyota Motor Corporation, 1935–92**

Year	Cars	Trucks and Buses	Total
1935	0	20	20
1940	268	14,519	14,787
1945	0	3,275	3,275
1950	463	11,243	11,706
1955	7,403	15,383	22,786
1960	42,118	112,652	154,770
1965	236,151	241,492	477,643
1970	1,068,321	540,869	1,609,190
1975	1,714,836	621,217	2,336,053
1980	2,303,284	990,060	3,293,344
1981	2,248,171	972,247	3,220,418
1982	2,258,253	886,304	3,144,557
1983	2,380,753	891,582	3,272,335
1984	2,413,133	1,061,116	3,429,249
1985	2,569,284	1,096,338	3,665,622
1986	2,684,024	976,143	3,660,167
1987	2,708,069	930,210	3,638,279
1988	2,982,922	985,775	3,968,697
1989	3,055,101	920,801	3,975,902
1990	3,345,885	866,488	4,212,373
1991	3,180,054	905,027	4,085,081
1992	3,171,311	760,030	3,931,341

Sources: *1993 Ward's Automotive Yearbook*, p. 66; *1991 Ward's Automotive Yearbook*, p. 78; *1990 Ward's Automotive Yearbook*, p. 285; *Toyota: A History of the First 50 Years* (Toyota City, Japan: Toyota Motor Corporation, 1988), p. 461.

incorrect or missing parts, hampered the early exports of KD sets. Toyota revamped the KD system and resumed knockdown exports to several countries beginning in 1962. Toyota continued to export KD sets to several countries, including Africa and Southeast Asia, as part of its export strategy. Toyota's total vehicle exports are displayed in Exhibit 8.

UNITED STATES

Toyota's top management initially opposed exporting to the United States. Numerous doubts existed regarding the suitability of the Toyota car in terms of performance, reliability, and price. Several factors influenced Toyota to begin exporting to the U.S.: growth of the small car market (European competitors, primarily Volkswagen, had captured almost 10 percent of this market by the late 1950s); U.S. automakers'

EXHIBIT 8 | **Motor Vehicle Exports, Toyota Motor Corporation, 1965–91**

	Passenger Cars	Trucks	Buses	Total
1965	33,297	29,855	368	63,520
1966	70,545	33,993	607	105,145
1967	111,461	45,308	1,113	157,882
1968	203,169	73,287	2,631	279,087
1969	287,369	104,376	3,357	395,102
1970	346,462	130,932	4,498	481,892
1971	604,923	176,880	4,484	786,287
1972	555,430	165,037	4,085	724,552
1973	525,056	191,273	4,311	720,640
1974	605,433	242,299	8,533	856,265
1975	612,744	247,788	7,820	868,352
1976	835,817	330,998	10,499	1,177,314
1977	968,270	433,138	11,827	1,413,235
1978	900,366	465,407	16,401	1,382,174
1979	905,392	458,120	20,136	1,383,648
1980	1,149,420	604,673	31,352	1,785,445
1981	1,063,385	615,711	37,390	1,716,486
1982	1,062,841	581,532	21,420	1,665,793
1983	1,069,053	580,368	14,940	1,664,361
1984	1,100,353	672,082	28,488	1,800,923
1985	1,198,982	746,532	34,441	1,979,955
1986	1,210,200	650,677	14,886	1,875,763
1987	1,192,146	560,490	18,301	1,770,937
1988	1,231,906	557,719	26,096	1,815,721
1989	1,139,680	512,461	16,989	1,669,130
1990	1,215,519	440,916	20,692	1,677,127
1991	1,223,917	450,186	29,486	1,703,589

Source: Motor Vehicle Manufacturer's Association, *World Motor Vehicle Data,* 1993 edition, p. 63.

not building small cars; and the probability the U.S. would adopt import restrictions. According to a Toyota executive, "If the U.S. goes ahead and restricts imports, Toyota will be cut out of the American market for good. We've got to get in there now or never."

Toyota shipped two Crown Toyopets to the U.S. in 1957. The Crown was a flop. Lacking power to travel on high-speed roads, it vibrated badly at speeds over 100 kph and overheated when driven over mountains and on desert roads. It was unable to traverse a California hill to the dealer showroom where it was to debut. Shoichiro Toyoda labeled it a "junk" car, unsuitable for American roads.

In late 1960, Toyota halted passenger-car exports to the U.S. Determined to make a comeback, it vigorously set about designing and building the right cars for the U.S. market. When Toyota introduced the Corona to the U.S. in 1965, it was a hit with the American consumer. Toyota's strategy involved offering a comparatively luxurious, well-built small car with acceleration superior to other economy imports. Outfitted with a 90-horsepower engine, it was nearly twice as powerful as a VW Beetle. With a larger engine, it was possible to offer options, such as automatic transmission and air-conditioning. Toyota also strengthened its dealer network, after-sales service, and advertising promotions, and concentrated its initial sales efforts in Los Angeles. In 1968, Toyota introduced the smaller Corolla which conformed to its policy at that time of avoiding direct competition with the U.S. automakers. Toyota sold 6,388 vehicles in the U.S. in 1965; by 1969, volume exceeded 100,000. By 1975, the U.S. was Toyota's largest export market, and Toyota had usurped Volkswagen as the best-selling foreign import. Aided by the growth in the small-car market (from 43 percent in 1973 to about 60 percent in 1980), Toyota's exports climbed rapidly until the early 1980s when the combination of several events conspired to contain the invasion of Japanese vehicle imports.

Allegations of dumping surfaced when a Volkswagen executive stated that Volkswagen was selling its models in the U.S. at losses ranging from $250 to $600 each. A dumping investigation, directed at automakers in eight countries, was conducted. Although Toyota was included in this investigation, it was officially cleared of these charges; however, suspicions that dumping was a common practice among certain automakers persisted. In 1980, based on a change in "definition," the U.S. increased its customs duty on trucks from 4 percent to 25 percent. In the same year, the UAW and Ford argued that Japanese vehicle imports had resulted in increasing unemployment among U.S. auto workers and was harming the domestic auto industry. They petitioned the ITC to require Japanese automakers to build plants in the U.S. and to apply volume restrictions on their exports. Although the ITC ruled that there was no direct causal relation between the increase in auto imports and the difficulties experienced by the U.S. auto industry, voluntary restraints on exports were established by the Japanese government, beginning on May 1, 1981. Under the VRA (voluntary restraint agreement), the nine Japanese automakers were limited to a U.S. market share equal to their level of imports during 1974–75. Initially slated to last three years, the voluntary restraints were extended:

1981–83:	1,680,000 vehicles
1984:	1,850,000 vehicles
1985–91:	2,300,000 vehicles
1992:	1,650,000 vehicles

Initially, the quotas actually benefited Toyota. Forced to limit exports, Toyota not only increased prices, it also began to replace its small, inexpensive export cars with larger, more expensive ones loaded with options. Toyota was able to sell all of its allotted quota and often found itself without enough vehicles to sell. Plans for U.S. production of its most popular models, the Camry and Corolla, were implemented, resulting in new and redesigned models being consistently introduced. By the 1990s, vehicles were available in all major market segments, including big trucks and luxury cars.

T100   The T100 was Toyota's first foray into the big truck market, which experienced a 12 percent growth rate in 1992, making it the fastest-growing U.S. vehicle segment (four of the top six vehicles sold in the U.S. in 1993 were in this market, which included pickups, minivans, and sport-utility vehicles). Designed expressly for the U.S. market and built in Japan, the T100 debuted in November 1992. Overpriced (an import fee of as much as $2,500 was tacked on) and underpowered, it met with a less-than-enthusiastic reception by the American consumer, with sales progressing at a rate much less than the planned 50,000 annual units. The design of the T100 was a compromise since Toyota hoped to avoid a Detroit backlash. It was intermediate-sized, falling midway between three-quarter-sized and full-sized trucks offered by the Big Three, and was powered by a standard V-6 engine. Future enhancements, including a V-8 engine option and an extended cab version, were planned. Talks had ensued between Toyota and GM about Toyota using one of G.M.'s idle U.S. plants to build the T100, but it was unlikely that an agreement would be reached in the immediate future.

Lexus   Having mastered the formula for producing and selling low- and mid-priced cars, Toyota hoped to repeat this success in the luxury car market. A dream of chairman Eiji Toyoda, who felt that Toyota did not get the respect it deserved, was to "develop the best car in the world." In 1983, he challenged the Toyota engineers, using Mercedes and BMW as the benchmarks, to pursue this dream and to do what no other automaker had achieved: design a sedan that would travel 150 mph while carrying four passengers in relative quiet, comfort, and safety—without incurring the American gas-guzzler tax. The overall strategy involved marketing a high-performance car equal in quality to Mercedes and BMW, but priced below them and above the U.S. luxury models, Cadillac and Lincoln.

The first step involved the purchase of the competitors' cars—four Mercedes, a Jaguar XJ6, and two BMWs—which were subjected to grueling test drives and then taken apart for further study. Next, 11 performance goals, relating to such things as aerodynamics, weight, noise levels, and fuel efficiency, were established. Overall, the extensive development process involved six years, an investment of over $500 million, creation of a flexible organizational structure to oversee the project, development of a new engine, and establishment of separate marketing and advertising entities, involving a separate dealership organization to sell the car. In contrast to European automakers, which utilized extensive hand labor to achieve quality, Toyota installed the most elaborate automation that was feasible, believing that only mechanized processes could meet Lexus's stringent assembly standards.

Incorporating such advanced features as hydraulic active suspension, a two-stroke engine, and traction control, the Lexus was faster, more fuel efficient, and less expensive than its German competitors:

Acceleration speed (0–60 mph):
    Lexus   – 8.6 seconds
    BMW   – 10.3 seconds
    Mercedes– 9.3 seconds
Official highway gas mileage:
    Lexus   – 23.5 mpg
    BMW   – 19.0 mpg
    Mercedes– 18.0 mpg
Price:
    Lexus   –$35,000
    BMW   –$54,000
    Mercedes–$61,210

The Lexus 400 was analyzed by the engineers of all of Toyota's rivals; reputedly, no evidence of technical shortcuts was found. Some industry observers suggested that Toyota had low-balled the prices of its Lexus models; Toyota claimed it was earning its usual profit on the car.

According to Shoichiro Toyoda, the success of the Lexus depended on how well it was made. "Our biggest challenge will be to have no defects and to build a reliable car that won't break down."[17] The size of the luxury segment (1 million units annually in the latter 1980s) was projected to grow annually by about 10 percent, reaching about 1.5 million units by the mid-1990s. Growth, combined with gross margins of 20 percent (versus 12 percent to 16 percent on less-expensive models), were additional incentives for Toyota to enter this market.

The LS400 was launched in the U.S. in September 1989; three months after its introduction, three minor glitches, including one that could cause the cruise-control system to remain on after the driver attempted to turn it off, were found in the LS400s, resulting in Toyota's recalling about 8,500 units. Toyota responded by personally calling each owner with two options:[18]

> Bring the car in yourself to be fixed on the spot, or have Lexus pick it up at night and return it ready-to-go the next morning. Either way, Lexus not only fixed the defect but also washed the car, cleaned the inside and filled it with gasoline. Some dealers even placed a small gift, such as an ice scraper, on the front seat. Owners were mollified, and many were impressed.

After-sales service was also a top priority:[19]

> A customer who had just purchased an LS400 rushed back to the dealer, saying he was furious that a new car should break down so fast. When we looked for the problem, we found that the emergency brake was on. When the "faulty car" was replaced at no cost, the customer was so thrilled with the unexpected service that he bought another car.

---

[17] As quoted in *Fortune,* August 14, 1989, p. 65.
[18] As quoted in *The Wall Street Journal,* July 20, 1990, p. A8.
[19] As quoted in *Tokyo Business Today,* February 1990, p. 28.

According to one industry analyst, "When the Lexus LS400 first came out, people said it was a better value than a comparable Mercedes or BMW. Now they are saying flat out that it is a better car than a Mercedes or BMW."[20] By late 1993, Toyota offered three models—the ES300, priced at $30,600; the SC300, priced at $38,000; and the LS400, priced at $49,900. The Lexus had consistently been ranked no. 1 in the J. D. Power's Initial Quality Survey of new cars since its introduction. With an estimated market share of almost 10 percent in the luxury segment projected for 1993, Lexus ranked third behind Cadillac and Lincoln.

Endaka (the rising yen), a desire to reduce trade friction, and declining profits prompted Toyota to increase prices on virtually all of its models several times during 1992 and 1993. Exhibit 9 provides price comparisons of U.S. and Japanese cars as of March 1993. Industry analysts estimated that Japanese cars were priced at $2,500 more than comparable U.S. cars, on average, with Toyota's models being pricier than most other Japanese automakers. Toyota's predicament was partly attributed to its shifting cars dramatically upscale in terms of size and quality. One source indicated that Toyota's new and redesigned models were overengineered, offering too much quality for the money. According to one U.S. dealer, "They've built too much quality into the cars, and the public's not willing to pay for it." A second price hike in 1993 involved increases ranging from a low of 2.5 percent on its least-expensive models to a high of 12.7 percent on its pricier models, and a third increase added about 3 percent more to all models. Toyota was also using American-style incentives to secure sales, including a leasing program for its vehicles and rebates to dealers or buyers. Exhibit 10 shows the U.S. market share of the major automakers.

E X H I B I T 9 | **Price Comparisons of Similarly Equipped American versus Japanese Cars, March 1993**

Compact Cars	
Toyota Corolla	$14,458
Chevrolet Geo Prism	13,030
Sport Coupes	
Mazda MX-6	$21,375
Ford Probe GT	18,886
Mid-Size Cars	
Toyota Camry LE	$21,433
Ford Taurus GL	18,902
Honda Accord LX	
anniversary edition	18,780
Dodge Intrepid	18,729
Oldsmobile Cutlass Supreme	16,445

Source: *The Wall Street Journal,* March 4, 1993, p. A1.

---

[20]As quoted in *Fortune,* July 2, 1990, pp. 60 and 64.

EXHIBIT 10 | U.S. Market Share of the Major Automakers, 1973–92*

Year	General Motors	Ford	Chrysler	Toyota	Honda	Nissan	All Imports
1973	44.9%	24.4%	13.7%	2.5%	.4%	2.0%	15.2%
1974	42.4	25.9	14.1	2.7	.5	2.1	15.7
1975	43.8	23.6	12.3	3.3	1.2	3.0	18.2
1976	47.6	22.6	13.7	3.4	1.5	2.7	14.8
1977	46.3	23.4	12.0	4.4	2.0	3.5	18.3
1978	47.8	23.5	11.1	3.9	2.4	3.0	17.8
1979	46.3	20.8	10.1	4.8	3.3	4.4	22.7
1980	45.9	17.2	8.8	6.5	4.2	5.8	28.2
1981	44.6	16.6	9.9	6.7	4.4	5.5	28.8
1982	44.2	16.9	10.0	6.6	4.6	5.9	29.6
1983	44.3	17.2	10.4	5.9	4.4	5.7	27.5
1984	44.6	19.2	10.4	5.0	4.9	4.7	24.9
1985	42.7	18.9	11.3	5.3	5.0	5.2	25.9
1986	41.2	18.2	11.5	5.3	6.1	4.8	28.2
1987	36.6	20.2	10.8	6.0	7.2	5.2	32.2
1988	36.3	21.7	11.3	6.2	7.3	4.5	31.2
1989	35.2	22.3	10.4	6.9	8.0	5.2	31.8
1990	35.6	20.8	9.3	8.4	9.2	4.9	26.4
1991	35.6	20.0	8.6	9.1	9.8	5.1	25.7
1992	34.6	21.6	8.2	9.3	9.4	5.1	24.3

*U.S. passenger car sales.

Sources: *1993 Ward's Automotive Yearbook*, p. 205; *1990 Ward's Automotive Yearbook*, p. 208; *1984 Ward's Automotive Yearbook*, p. 101; *Automotive News*, 1993 Market Data Book Issue, p. 19.

EXPORT ACTIVITIES OUTSIDE THE U.S.

Strict import restrictions, idiosyncratic tastes of European consumers in their choice of autos, intense competition in countries having their own automakers, and the great diversity among the European countries hindered Toyota's ability to penetrate the Western European auto market. By the latter 1970s, several countries had established import restrictions. Toyota's maximum share of the British market was set at 2 percent (later increased to 11 percent) of the total market, and France set the maximum share for all Japanese vehicles at 3 percent of the total market. Quotas in Italy and Spain limited Japan's share to less than 1 percent. In 1981, the EEC placed passenger cars on the list of import items from Japan to be monitored.

The main attraction of early Toyota vehicles to Europeans was their novelty and simplicity of mechanical structure, making them relatively trouble-free. By the early 1980s, virtually all new European cars were front-wheel-drive models. They displayed excellent driving performance, had luxury-class specifications, and offered numerous options. European automakers were discounting their prices in bold competitive moves, and Toyota's exports to Europe were negatively affected. Shoichiro Toyoda outlined Toyota's market strategy at a European dealers meeting in late 1982:[21]

---

[21]*Toyota: A History*, p. 351.

The European market holds much potential for Toyota, and it demands only the finest products . . . We feel strongly that Toyota must be a leader with vision in Europe and elsewhere, and the first step in becoming a leader is to regain the number one position among Japanese automakers as early as possible, and after that to widen the gap between ourselves and others . . . In short, Toyota's success in Europe becomes possible only when your thinking and our thinking are the same, when we share the same goal.

In 1986, Western Europe overtook the U.S. as the largest market for new car sales in the world. With the emergence of the European Community (EC 1992), the region was expected to be a competitive battlefield. Although sales plunged in the early 1990s, they were projected to reach 14.4 million passenger cars by 1995 and 15.2 million in 2000. If potential sales in Eastern Europe were factored in, some industry insiders were suggesting that European sales (excluding the former Soviet Union) could approach 20 million by 2000. A 1991 agreement between Japan and the EC limited imports of Japanese vehicles to about 11 percent until 1998; however, in 1993 the Japanese agreed to reduce their exports even further in response to the declining market.

Meanwhile, Toyota was battling Nissan for the role of the no. 1 Japanese importer. Toyota was the top-selling Japanese automaker in Belgium, Finland, Denmark, Ireland, Norway, and Sweden, and had obtained 9.7 percent of the market in Greece, 3.1 percent in Germany, and 2.1 percent in the United Kingdom. In Italy, France, and Spain, Toyota had minimal presence, holding less than 1 percent of the market in each country. Beginning in Spring 1992, Toyota began exporting its U.S.-built Camry wagons to Europe.

To combat the Japanese, European carmakers were exploring possible new relationships with each other to become more competitive. However, with the European carmakers experiencing some of the same problems (inefficiency, quality problems, and slowness of bringing new cars to market) as the U.S. automakers, the Japanese threat was viewed as formidable by European automakers. Toyota had recently begun exporting its luxury and sports cars to Europe, such as the Lexus, and European production of a mass-market model had recently begun. Exhibit 11 shows the European market share of the major automakers.

Toyota gradually expanded its exports to other countries during the 1960s and 1970s. Distinctive factors associated with some of these countries, including worsening economic conditions, political interests, high foreign debt, and stringent domestic content laws, resulted in declining exports to several countries by the 1990s. However, Toyota had been able to lay solid foundations in several countries, including Australia, Malaysia, India, Taiwan, Brazil, and Columbia, through joint-venture partnerships or companies in which it held an equity interest. By the 1990s, Toyota's major thrust toward global expansion appeared to be focused on establishing production capacity in overseas markets.

OVERSEAS PRODUCTION OPERATIONS

The necessity for establishing local production bases outside Japan became evident to Toyota in the early 1980s. Prior to 1982, Toyota had not engaged in any major strategic alliances or independent overseas production, but the rapidly changing competitive situation prompted the company to reevaluate its posture. Prominent concerns of Toyota executives included the nature of labor-relations practices, the degree

EXHIBIT 11 | **European Market Share of the Major Automakers, 1982–92***

Company	1992	1991	1990	1989	1988	1987	1986	1984	1982
VW Group	17.5%	16.4%	15.6%	15.2%	14.9%	15.0%	14.7%	12.0%	12.0%
Fiat Group	11.9	12.8	14.2	14.8	14.8	14.2	14.0	12.7	12.3
Peugeot Group	12.2	12.1	12.9	12.6	12.9	12.1	11.4	11.5	12.3
General Motors	12.4	12.1	11.8	11.4	11.0	11.2	11.0	11.1	9.6
Ford	11.3	11.9	11.6	11.7	11.4	12.1	11.7	12.8	12.3
Renault	10.6	10.0	9.9	10.3	10.1	10.6	10.6	10.9	14.4
Mercedes	3.1	3.4	3.3	3.2	3.4	3.5	3.7	3.2	3.2
Austin Rover	2.5	2.6	2.9	3.0	3.4	3.4	3.5	3.9	3.9
Nissan	3.2	3.2	2.8	2.9	2.9	2.9	3.0	2.8	2.9
BMW	3.3	3.1	2.8	2.8	2.7	2.4	2.6	3.0	2.7
Toyota	2.5	2.7	2.7	2.6	2.7	2.8	2.9	2.2	2.3
Mazda	1.9	2.1	2.1	1.8	1.9	1.9	2.0	2.0	—
Volvo	1.5	1.5	1.8	2.0	2.1	2.2	2.3	2.3	2.0
Mitsubishi	1.2	1.4	1.3	1.2	1.2	1.2	1.2	—	—
Honda	1.3	1.2	1.2	1.0	1.1	1.0	1.2	—	—

*Total new passenger car registrations.

Sources: *1993 Ward's Automotive Yearbook*, p. 82; *1990 Ward's Automotive Yearbook*, p. 269; *1986 Ward's Automotive Yearbook*, p. 65; *1984 Ward's Automotive Yearbook*, p. 54.

to which various components of the TPS could be transferred to facilities in other countries, and the ability to manage an operation on another continent.

UNITED STATES

Lagging behind the other leading Japanese automakers, Honda and Nissan, in establishing production facilities in the U.S., it was inevitable that Toyota would establish an alliance with a U.S. automaker. Talks of a tie-in with Ford had occurred on four occasions, beginning in 1939, with the last discussion of building a plant together (this time in the U.S. and not Japan) to develop and produce small cars occurring in 1980. According to Eiji Toyoda, the roles were reversed:[22]

> As before, Toyota did the proposing, but the nature of the proposal was different. In 1960, we had asked Ford to teach us everything they could about small cars, but in 1980 the situation had changed. This time, we were offering to jointly produce our vehicle at Ford. The student had traded places with the teacher. This only goes to show how much the world can change in the short space of 20 years.

Like prior discussions, this one did not culminate in an agreement.

Toyota linked up with GM in 1984 to establish NUMMI, its first base of operations in the U.S. The 50-50 joint venture initially produced Chevy Novas and Toyota Corollas at a shuttered GM plant in Fremont, California. In the latter 1980s, the Nova was replaced by the GEO Prism model line, and in 1990 approximately 205,000 Geo Prisms and Corollas were produced; production of a Toyota compact pickup truck was slated to begin in the early 1990s. GM contributed the manufacturing plant and was responsible for marketing and selling the GEO. Toyota managed NUMMI, and

---

[22]Toyoda, *Toyota: Fifty Years in Motion*, p. 130.

former UAW workers were rehired for the production jobs. From Toyota's perspective, the venture would enable it to reduce its risk, allowing it to gain valuable experience associated with local production. Specifically, Toyota wanted to evaluate the competency of U.S. suppliers, the adequacy of the transportation systems, and options for dealing with unionized labor in the U.S.

To implement certain components of the TPS, Toyota's top priority was to establish stable labor relations with the UAW. Mutual trust and respect between management and labor was emphasized in the negotiated contract, which provided affirmative action before laying off any employee, allowed any employee to stop the production line to fix a problem, eliminated multiple-job classifications to encourage flexible workers, and arranged workers into teams. Team leaders were carefully selected, with on-site training provided in Toyota City. Indoctrination included courses on Toyota's history, corporate policies, production philosophy, quality control circle activities, and the concept of teamwork. Hands-on training involved exposure to production activities and worksite management at the Takaoka Plant for two weeks. Nine groups of 257 trainees participated in this training. American production employees were not typically promoted to management level jobs. In contrast, NUMMI established a contract with the UAW to introduce a foreman-promotion system. As of 1990, 110 employees had been promoted.

The Fremont facility was extensively remodeled with simplicity guiding the process. Renovation entailed (1) replacing old equipment; (2) restructuring the body, painting, and assembly lines into a series of short parallel lines that were less complex and less robotic intensive than the long, complex, and highly automated assembly lines typical of most GM plants; (3) installing line-stop switches; and (4) establishing the *kanban* system of production control.

The philosophy in selecting suppliers was to abandon the traditional adversarial nature of supplier-buyer relationships. NUMMI established a practice of almost never switching vendors and used only one or two suppliers for each component. Vendors were carefully selected, were expected to utilize the practices of *kanban* or just-in-time inventory control, and had little chance of losing their contracts if they fulfilled the agreed-upon terms. There was no competitive bidding in awarding contracts, and suppliers were expected to meet rigid standards in return for security. At the opening ceremony in April 1985, NUMMI's president commented:[23]

> Principally as a result of the efforts of the team members of NUMMI and the people in so many related companies who have cooperated in this project, we have built here in Fremont a first-class assembly plant. Thanks to our cooperative parts suppliers and our 1,200 employees, we are now producing cars of world-class quality. Our slogan at NUMMI this year is "Quality assurance through teamwork." People working together means teamwork, and I believe it is teamwork that will be the key to our success.

The following practices were implemented at NUMMI—an "open office" floor plan, a single cafeteria, common parking facilities, announcement of managerial decisions to the union before implementation, personal announcements of company policy by the president, and a suggestion system focusing on work improvements for use by all employees. Employee attendance reached 97 percent during the first year of operation. By 1989, productivity levels were 40 percent higher than typical GM plants, and NUMMI had the highest quality levels GM had ever known.

---

[23]*Toyota: A History,* p. 336.

At about the time NUMMI was launched, Toyota announced plans to begin independent production in North America with the construction of plants in the U.S. and Canada. Toyota's decision to locate the Toyota Motor Manufacturing (TMM) plant in Georgetown, Kentucky, was based on several factors: parts procurement, transportation convenience, land prices, electricity supplies, labor resources, and tax and other preferential treatment (a $125 million financial incentive package was offered by Kentucky officials). Commenting on the selection decision in late 1985, Shoichiro Toyoda stated:[24]

> We view today's official announcement of our plant site selection as one of the highlights in our company's history . . . In fact, choosing the site for our American plant was one of the most difficult decisions we've ever had to make at Toyota. After considering all of the factors involved, however, we decided that Kentucky is the best location for our American plant. At the same time, we wish to thank all the other states that presented site proposals. More than 25 years have passed since we started our exports to the United States, and since then we have moved steadily forward toward realizing our dream of building a perfect partnership with our American friends. As we continue to move into the future, we intend not only to contribute toward creating more job opportunities and promoting economic growth, but also to try and build a new relationship that will serve everyone's needs.

Opened in 1988, TMM represented an investment of $1.1 billion dollars to construct an assembly plant and related facilities to build 240,000 Camrys annually, in addition to engines, axles, and steering components. By 1990, the 4-door Camry was being built at a rate of one every 75 seconds or about 170 per day on a single shift. Domestic content of the vehicle was at 60 percent but was projected to reach about 75 percent when the powertrain plant under construction reached full production in 1991.

While quality was high at Georgetown, productivity was initially about 10 percent below Toyota's plants in Japan. According to a Toyota executive, U.S. suppliers were the problem. Although Toyota preferred to purchase major parts from the 250 Japanese suppliers who had established plants in the U.S., political concerns, increasing quality of U.S. parts, and the rising yen prompted Toyota to increase its purchases of American-made parts. For example, during the start-up year of operations at Georgetown, Toyota bought $1.1 billion of U.S.-made parts; in 1994, it expected to purchase about $5.3 billion of parts and materials from U.S. suppliers.

Flooded with over 50,000 applicants for the 3,000 factory jobs, Toyota devised an extensive selection system, which focused on employee potential, rather than on education and work experience. The process consumed about 18 hours per applicant and involved tests and simulations that assessed technical, interpersonal, and leadership skills. One new employee (a former hairdresser) likened getting a job at Toyota to winning a lottery. "The odds were tremendous, but I would have swept floors."

In 1990, TMM received the Gold Plant Award from J. D. Power & Associates and announced expansion plans. A second assembly plant was to be built at Georgetown, increasing production capacity by 200,000 vehicles and increasing jobs to more than 5,000. When completed in early 1994, the Georgetown complex was expected to assemble the Avalon, a new top-of-the-line sedan, in addition to the Camry. TMM achieved another first in August 1992, when it began exporting the first U.S.-built vehicle, the Scepter (a new right-hand-drive version of the Camry station wagon), for

---

[24]Ibid., p. 338.

sale in Japan. According to TMM's president, Toyota's commitment to Georgetown was "a tribute to all team members at Toyota . . . Being able to expand operations here is especially rewarding to us."

As the mid-1990s approached, Toyota was on its way to becoming an almost stand-alone U.S. producer, able to research and engineer, as well as to design and assemble, its cars in the U.S. Toyota had established the Calty Design Center in California in the early 1970s. Several models, including the Celica and the new Previa minivan, were developed at the Center, specifically to suit the tastes of U.S. consumers. In 1991, Toyota embarked on a $220 million program to significantly expand its U.S.-based design and research activities. The program included opening the Toyota Technical Center USA Inc. (Toyota's U.S. R&D arm), a $46 million prototype-vehicle evaluation facility in Torrence, California; beginning construction of a $110 million vehicle proving facility near Phoenix, Arizona; opening a $19 million expansion of the Calty Design Center; and opening a $41 million evaluation laboratory at its technical center in Ann Arbor, Michigan. Thus, Toyota maintained separate U.S. subsidiaries for sales, manufacturing, engineering, and R&D, each reporting individually to Toyota City.

Toyota was gaining the ability to execute its lean distribution approach of built-to-order cars, but this critical component of the TPS had yet to be achieved. Toyota had expanded its distribution network during the 1980s in the U.S.—in 1983, it had 1,093 new car franchises, and by 1990, the number had increased to 1,248. In contrast, the total number of U.S. car dealerships had steadily declined—from 30,800 in 1970, the number had fallen to 25,100 by 1989. Implementing the lean approach to distribution appeared to be part of the plan.

According to one Japanese auto executive, "The system makes no sense unless cars are built to order and delivered almost immediately. We can do this only as we develop a complete top-to-bottom manufacturing system in North America and Europe by the end of the 1990s."[25] According to one authority, Toyota had not reached its full potential in the U.S. since the TPS worked best when "the entire complement of car-production activities are performed as close as possible to the point of final production."[26]

OVERSEAS OPERATIONS OUTSIDE THE U.S.

Calls for protectionism echoed loudest on the European continent. Strict import restrictions had limited the Japanese share to a consistent 11 percent of the market. By the early 1990s, Honda, Nissan, and Toyota had each opened production facilities in the United Kingdom, using proven formulas from Japan and the U.S. in areas such as site selection and employee training, with most of the output to be exported to mainland Europe. By 1995, the Japanese were expected to be producing 775,000 cars annually in Europe; it was estimated the Japanese automakers could secure about 20 percent of the European market by 2000. In early 1993, Toyota rolled off its first cars, the mid-size Carina E (its first car designed specifically for the European market), at its new Burnaston plant in Great Britain. Plans called for eventual employment of 3,000 employees and production of 200,000 cars annually by 1997. Toyota had ambitious plans to establish additional production capacity in Europe through equity

---

[25]Womack, Jones, and Roos, *The Machine That Changed the World,* p. 188.

[26]As quoted in *Fortune,* September 10, 1990, p. 80.

equity investments, joint ventures, or independent production; countries being targeted included Germany and Spain.

Toyota's emphasis on establishing overseas production facilities was not restricted to the U.S. and Europe. Restricted by rigorous domestic content laws in several Asian countries, Toyota (along with other Japanese automakers) had a virtual monopoly in the region where the presence of U.S. and European automakers was almost unknown. Auto sales in Asia were projected to grow from 4.7 percent of global sales in 1987 to 8.7 percent by 1995. Millions of dollars of investment, combined with long-term thinking, persistence, and flexibility, had aided in Toyota's securing a leadership role.

In countries that banned auto imports, such as South Korea, Toyota had taken minority stakes in Korean auto companies and provided technology or parts supplies. In countries affected by political instability or uncertain economic prospects, such as

EXHIBIT 12 | **Overseas Production Companies, Toyota Motor Corporation, 1994**

Geographic Region	Countries Where Facilities Are Located	Local Name of Toyota's Subsidiary
North America	U.S.A.	Toyota Motor Manufacturing, U.S.A., Inc.
		New United Motor Manufacturing, Inc.
		(50-50 Joint Venture with GM)
	Canada	Toyota Motor Manufacturing Canada Inc.
South America and the Caribbean	Brazil	Toyota do Brasil S.A., Industria e Comercio
	Peru	Toyota del Peru S.A.
	Colombia	SOFASA-Renault SA (Toyota owned 17.5%)
	Venezuela	Servicios de Ensamblaje, C.A.
	Trinidad and Tobago	Amar Assembly Plant '85 Ltd.
	Uruguay	Ayax S.A.
	Ecuador	MARE S.A.
Europe	United Kingdom	Toyota Motor Manufacturing (U.K.) Ltd.
	Portugal	Salvador Caetano I.M.V.T., S.A.
Southeast Asia and Oceania	Australia	Toyota Motor Corporation Australia Ltd.
		United Australian Automotive Industries Ltd.
		(50-50 Joint Venture with GM)
	New Zealand	Toyota New Zealand (Thames) Ltd.
		Toyota New Zealand (Christchurch) Ltd.
	Indonesia	P. T. Toyota Astra Motor
	Thailand	Toyota Motor Co. Thailand, Ltd.
	Malaysia	UMW Toyota Motor Sdn. Bhd.
		(Toyota owned 28%)
	Taiwan	Kuozui Motors, Ltd.
		Fung Yong Co., Ltd.
	Philippines	Toyota Motor Philippines Corporation
Middle East	India	DCM Toyota Ltd.
	Turkey	Haci Omer Sabanci Holding A.S.
		(Toyota owned 40%)
	Pakistan	Indus Motor Co. Ltd. (Toyota owned 12.5%)
Africa	South Africa	Toyota South Africa Manufacturing Ltd.
	Kenya	Associated Vehicle Assemblers Ltd.
	Zambia	Rover (Zambia) Ltd.
	Zimbabwe	Willowvale Motor Industries (Pvt.) Ltd.

Sources: *Toyota: A History of the First 50 Years* (Toyota City, Japan: Toyota Motor Corporation, 1988), pp. 464–65; and various other sources.

the Philippines, Toyota had signed on with local partners, cautiously expanding its presence. Toyota had also assisted in building local auto industries in some East Asian countries to alleviate concerns over Japanese domination. Overall, the Japanese automakers had been successful at establishing a regional auto production base. Although major profits had not yet been achieved from the Asian strategy, the pieces were in place, and the region was poised for sustained economic growth. Exhibit 12 displays the location of selected Toyota overseas production facilities.

TOYOTA'S FUTURE

Toyota surpassed Ford in the production of cars in the global market in 1990. By 1995, Toyota anticipated selling 1.5 million vehicles in the U.S., 50 percent of them built in the U.S.; Toyota planned on selling 2 million vehicles in the U.S. by 2000, hoping to surpass Ford. According to one industry analyst's projection, Toyota would be producing 6.3 million vehicles annually by 2000. Toyota had recently introduced the newly remodeled Mark II, Chaser, and Cresta luxury cars to the Japanese market while a redesigned Celica coupe, a new mid-size Lexus, and a 300-horsepower Supra sports car were slated for the U.S. market. Toyota's future plans were clearly focused on global expansion, with production facilities located at the center of large overseas markets, including North America, Europe, Southeast Asia, and Oceania, with products being exported to neighboring countries.

However, intensified competition in the global auto industry presented Toyota with significantly different challenges as the mid-1990s approached. The company's ability to achieve its objectives was jeopardized by several factors—declining profits and exports, deteriorating market share in both Japan and the U.S. (declining to less than 8 percent by the end of 1993), and decelerating growth in numerous industrialized country markets. During the 1980s, the Detroit auto manufacturers had drastically overhauled their operations, enabling them to significantly narrow the gap in the areas of product quality and customer satisfaction compared to the Japanese automakers. Chrysler had become a world leader in product development, while Ford had established the pace in manufacturing productivity; although GM was still grappling with transition problems, it remained the leader in the global marketplace. In addition, the U.S. automakers had returned to profitability, reaping $9.6 billion in operating profits in 1993 while the Japanese and European automakers lost billions of yen and deutsche marks. However, Donald N. Smith of the University of Michigan (a long-term Toyota observer) commented, "The worst mistake any competitor can make is to not assume that Toyota will be markedly better five years from now."[27]

_____

[27] As quoted in *Fortune,* January 25, 1993, p. 81.

DCM-TOYOTA LTD. OF INDIA

Madhav S. Shriram, DCM Shriram Industries, Ltd.
Alan G. Robinson, University of Massachusetts at Amherst
Dean M. Schroeder, Valparaiso University

In the five years since the start of the joint venture between DCM Limited of India and the Toyota Motor Company of Japan to produce light commercial vehicles (LCVs), a great deal of progress had been made. The DCM–Toyota Ltd. (DTL) plant in Surajpur was now building a world-class vehicle, one that Mr. Awasthi, the company's executive director, believed to be by far the best of its kind manufactured in India. The DTL LCV, called the Dyna, was equipped with an engine that was more powerful, rugged, and fuel efficient than its competitors. It had a sturdy construction, and its plush interior and exterior finish were superior to those of most Indian-built cars. The Dyna embodied the latest in LCV technology from Japan; in fact, certain components had been improved and strengthened for the harsh Indian driving conditions.

The DTL plant was modern, well engineered and well managed, and operated under the Toyota production system. The employees were highly motivated, well educated, and thoroughly trained. Even Toyota was impressed with the plant and with the high productivity of its Indian workers. And yet the company had been slow to make a profit. The strong yen and stiff competition were making things difficult. In 1984, when DTL was in the planning phase, the exchange rate was 21 yen to the rupee. In February 1989, the rupee bought only 8.25 yen. Critical LCV components imported from Japan, and priced in yen, were now costing two and a half times more than planned. Consequently, in fiscal year 1988, DTL lost Rs 57,133,420[1] on Rs 904,902,313 in total sales. The company's performance continued to improve gradually, however; it reported a modest profit of Rs 3 million in the first quarter of 1989. This profitability was attributed largely to a new marketing strategy of price increases that broke ranks with the competition. Unfortunately, this strategy also resulted in a

Copyright © 1992 by the *Case Research Journal* and Dean M. Schroeder.
[1]The February 1989 exchange rate for rupees (Rs) was approximately 15 rupees per U.S. dollar.

loss of eight percentage points of market share and dropped DTL from first place in vehicle sales volume to last among the top three 3.5-tonne^2 LCV manufacturers.

It was unclear what the long-term effects would be of the shift in marketing strategy from price competition to competing on the basis of superior quality. Many Indian buyers were unfamiliar with the high technology in the DTL vehicles and were unaccustomed to the level of quality they represented. Furthermore, it was not clear that the nation's infrastructure could support such a high-technology and quality vehicle. There was no nationwide network with the necessary skills and technology to fully service the vehicle. Finally, Indian law put DTL on a strict schedule to increase the domestic content of its LCV to 90 percent, and it was uncertain whether domestic manufacturers could meet the required high standards critical to retaining the DTL vehicle's exceptional quality.

BACKGROUND

DCM LTD.

In 1989, DCM Ltd. was the 14th-largest multiproduct manufacturing company in India. Its product line included textiles, sugar, both industrial and potable alcohol, fertilizers, edible oils, business machines, cement, polyvinylchloride (PVC), and foundry products. In 1989, its sales were approximately Rs 6.5 billion and it employed 25,000 people.

DCM was founded in 1889 as Delhi Cloth Mills Ltd., largely through the efforts of Gopal Rai, the company's first secretary (i.e., top manager). The venture, which produced textiles, was so successful it paid its first dividend to investors only six months later. When Gopal Rai's health failed in 1906, his younger brother, Madan Mohan Lal, took over as secretary. Shortly thereafter, the company began to falter, primarily because of the high prices it had to pay for raw cotton. The poor performance persisted until Shri Ram, son of Madan Mohan Lal, became actively involved in the company. Shri Ram was the dominant figure in the growth of DCM into a successful conglomerate.

When he was in high school, Shri Ram got a job selling cloth as a shop assistant. Although it was then standard practice to stretch the cloth on the measuring table and shortchange customers by two inches per yard, Shri Ram gave his customers not only the full yard, but an extra two inches as well. The shop owner was furious when he found out, but soon realized that customers kept coming back and his volume of business was growing quite rapidly. Shri Ram would later bring to DCM this philosophy of treating people fairly.

When Shri Ram first came to work at DCM, the firm was losing money. Shri Ram persuaded his father to appoint him head of ginning, which had the worst record of all the departments. By introducing a system of worker incentives (a radical idea at that time in India), Shri Ram turned the department around in short order. The sudden increase in production and profits persuaded an initially reluctant board of directors to approve the companywide implementation of these incentives. After this success, Shri Ram was able to talk the board into giving him control of the other departments

---

^{2} A tonne, or metric ton, is equal to approximately 1.13 tons.

as well. Within three years of his joining the company, Shri Ram became the de facto secretary of DCM and his father a mere figurehead.

World War I brought the company an important break. The British, who had previously repressed the Indian textile industry to protect their domestic manufacturers, now encouraged it to produce as much as possible. Through the manufacture of canvas tents for troops, DCM grew rapidly and was able to lay down a financial base from which to continue its growth. During World War II, DCM started to manufacture hurricane lamps and to diversify into agricultural products such as sugar and fertilizers. These moves were very natural, for two reasons. First, the economy of India was largely based in agriculture (which, even in 1989, accounted for 80 percent of GNP). Second, the government, which wished to increase domestic production to reduce imports, was encouraging all companies to diversify as much as possible. By the time India became independent from Great Britain in 1947, DCM had grown into one of the five largest business houses in India. Since Shri Ram's death in 1965, the firm had remained under the control of the Shriram family. In 1985, Bansi Dhar, a grandson of Shri Ram, was appointed chairman and managing director. Throughout all of DCM's divisions, the company always strove to deliver the high quality and extra value implicit in Shri Ram's "2 extra inches." For example, the company's two sugar plants adhered to the rigid international quality standards for crystal size, purity, opacity, evenness of grain, and speed of dissolution in water, rather than the much less stringent Indian standards.

THE BUSINESS CLIMATE

In 1989, India, a nation of over 800 million people, was the largest democracy in the world. It was an emerging nation with a wide gap between rich and poor. While the average Indian worker earned less than Rs 15 ($1) per day, India boasted a world-class scientific community, excellent academic institutions (including five institutes of technology and the world-famous Tata Institute), as well as the ability to produce nuclear weapons and loft satellites into geosynchronous orbit. India had a tightly regulated and mixed economy. Although the private sector was very active, most of the core industries—such as mining and extraction (of coal, iron ore, and gold), steel, banking, electric power, airlines, shipping, railways, communications, and the postal service—were nationalized. Some industries had been taken over by the state owing to fears of exploitation by foreigners or monopolies, others because of their immense capital requirements or the desire to subsidize their products and services for the general public. By and large, these state-run industries were inefficient and poorly managed. For example, in 1989, the world price of steel was half of what it cost to produce it in India.

India's infrastructure could make industrial business operations quite challenging. The absence of reliable electric power provided a good example. Because it was subject to frequent outages and disruptions, most medium-to-large firms had captive power generation plants to avoid the problems that an interruption in the power supply of even a fraction of a second could cause to equipment and instrumentation. An infrastructural issue of special concern to DTL was the quality of the Indian road system. Many of the roads had been built shortly after independence from Britain and designed to last for only five years. In March 1989, *India Today* called attention to the poor condition of these roads, and to the poor management that compounded the problem:

Though India ranks fourth in the world after the U.S., Brazil, and the Soviet Union in road length, the quality of the road network would embarrass many small African countries. And the World Bank has categorized India as a country where both the road network and road-building technology are obsolete. . . .

The fact that many officials connected with the road sector have been busy feathering their own nests has further added to the collapse of the system. The states' public works departments (PWDs), which are responsible for both okaying road-building contracts and approving the work, are notorious for corruption. . . . Senior officials estimate that often as much as half the money allocated for the construction of roads may disappear into the pockets of corrupt officials and private contractors. There have been instances of roads being built only on paper in remote areas—all the money having been creamed off.

It has not helped matters that other officials connected with the road sector are equally corrupt. Overloaded trucks are a major cause of road deterioration, yet truckers defy the law with impunity by bribing the highway police. All-India Motor Transport Congress Secretary General Chitaranjan Das points out that bribing the police is now such an established practice that even trucks which are not overloaded have to fork over money. The income department even accepts these payments as legitimate expenses incurred by truck operations.[3]

Poor road conditions, in their turn, inflicted heavy damage on the nation's vehicles—an estimated Rs 20 billion annually in excess wear and tear.

In 1947, India inherited a comprehensive system of licensing from the departing British. The system had been set up during World War II to ensure the efficient and equitable allocation of scarce resources such as power, coal, steel, cement, foreign exchange, petroleum products, and rail capacity. Although the system worked well initially, it gradually became more bureaucratic and complex. Nothing could be done until all the appropriate officials had approved and granted licenses. Typical business operations required clearances from the government for foreign exchange, power usage, raw materials, imports, and loans.

In 1980, however, Indira Gandhi was elected prime minister and began liberalizing the private sector. She also encouraged joint ventures with foreign companies, not only for technology transfer, but to open export markets as well. Licenses for joint ventures with foreign companies could now be obtained with greater speed and ease, and hundreds of foreign joint ventures were formed. In the motor vehicle industry, they were begun with such companies as Toyota, Mitsubishi, Mazda, Nissan, Honda, and Suzuki.

In 1984, Mrs. Gandhi was assassinated, and her son, Rajiv Gandhi, became the new prime minister. He continued to improve the Indian business climate: marginal income tax rates were reduced from as high as 97.75 percent down to 50 percent, quotas on imports of many capital goods and raw materials were abolished, and tariffs were lowered. These moves resulted in the rapid growth of exports and foreign investment in India. Industrial investment jumped 50 percent in the first year of the new policies.[4] The stock market rose to over 250 percent above its 1980 level and hit new highs throughout fiscal year 1986, and interest rates declined dramatically. New capital raised in the market by the private sector rose from almost none in 1980 to Rs 10.6 billion in fiscal year 1985, and again to Rs 24.3 billion in fiscal year 1987. Capi-

---

[3]*India Today,* March 18, 1989, pp. 78–79.
[4]*The Economist,* February 25, 1989, pp. 75–76.

tal raised in the 1990 market was expected to set a new record. Other signs of increasing sophistication in the private financial markets—as reported in 1989 by *The Economist Intelligence Unit*—included a rapidly growing number of institutional investors and new opportunities for foreign investors through mutual fund portfolios of Indian stocks.[5]

Although the business climate had improved considerably since 1980, many problems remained. Business leaders were calling for increased privatization of government-controlled firms to increase the quality and efficiency of the country's infrastructure as well as to help lower the national debt. Nevertheless, moves in these directions met with considerable resistance, since privatization was heresy to many powerful special interest groups in India.[6] Another factor with the potential to slow India's future growth was a projected shortage of electric power brought on by the increased economic activity. Scheduled hydroelectric projects, which required long lead times under the best conditions, were being slowed by environmental concerns, as were new coal-burning power plants. Current government policy was shifting toward generating electric power with natural gas, to make use of some recent major natural gas discoveries in India, and because the plants were cleaner and could be brought on-line quickly. Unfortunately, because of severe limitations on the capital available to make the needed improvements in the electric power infrastructure, power shortages remained a threat to continued rapid industrial development.

THE LCV MARKET

Although the alternatives available for transportation in India included ox carts, river barges, railways, and airplanes, in 1989 the road system was providing most of the extra transportation capacity required by India's rapidly growing economy. In 1951, only 11 percent of Indian goods were being transported by road; the rest moved by rail or water. By 1986, this figure had grown to 50 percent; it was projected to reach 62 percent by the year 2001. The government-controlled railroads were usually slow. Oddly enough, airfreight was not much faster, owing to a national policy requiring it to be thoroughly searched and to sit on the ground for at least 24 hours, as a precaution against terrorist bombings. Consequently, the demand for commercial vehicles had been rising. Yet until 1980, there was a large gap in the product range of trucks available. The only trucks on the market were either small pickup trucks of less than 1 tonne capacity, or full-sized trucks with a capacity of 7 tonnes or greater. Very few LCVs—trucks with capacity ranging from 2 to 6 tonnes—were manufactured in India. (Exhibit 1 provides a picture of the DTL LCV in various configurations and lists body options and configurations.) The government projected a national market of 24,000 LCVs annually by 1985, which it expected to grow to 47,000 by 1991. Exhibit 2 gives the annual sales of LCVs since 1984 and the projections through 1991 made by DTL's marketing staff.

Over the previous decade, eight companies, four of them joint ventures with Japanese firms, began producing LCVs in India. The Indo-Japanese joint ventures were those of DCM and Toyota, Eicher Motors and Mitsubishi, Swaraj and Mazda, and Allwyn and Nissan. Exhibit 3 gives product volume and market share information for all eight firms. In 1989, five of them manufactured LCVs rated at 2 tonnes; the others produced 3.5-tonne LCVs. The market for 2-tonne trucks was dominated

---

[5]*The Economist Intelligence Unit,* Country Report no. 1, India (1989).
[6]Ibid.

EXHIBIT 1 | **Various Dyna Body Options**

DCM-Toyota range: Body options and configurations for specific jobs.

- Fixed-side deck
- Drop-side deck
- High-side deck
- Tipper/Dumper
- Bottle carrier
- Garbage compactor
- Troop carrier

- Aluminum closed van
- Aluminum high-side deck
- Personnel carrier
- Standard bus
- Deluxe bus
- Mobile clinic
- Others

The DYNA 600 is on the short list of the UNDP (United Nations Development Programme) for supply of factory-made configurations to UN organisations worldwide.

Body Options

Bottle carrier

High-side deck

Bus (super-long wheel-base)

Troop carrier

Aluminum closed van

Mobile clinic

Tipper/Dumper

E X H I B I T 2 | **Sales of Light Commercial Vehicles (*Number of vehicles sold and projected sales on April–March basis*)**

Class	1984–85	1985–86	1986–87	1987–88	1988–89	1989–90	1990–91
LCV (2T)	23,409	22,881	23,918	30,569	30,651	32,000	34,000
LCV (3.5T)		2,653	5,287	8,375	10,997	12,000	13,000

Source: DTL market research from government documents.

by two domestic companies, Bajaj and the Tata Engineering and Locomotive Company (TELCO). Bajaj was known in India for its (relatively small) three-wheeled delivery vehicles, while TELCO held a hefty 75 percent of the full-size truck market. Mahindra, Standard, and Allwyn-Nissan (the only Indo-Japanese joint venture that produced a 2-tonne vehicle) all had relatively small market shares. All three of the 3.5-tonne LCV manufacturers were Indo-Japanese joint ventures and produced very similar vehicles. DTL was the first of these companies to begin production; Eicher-Mitsubishi and Swaraj-Mazda followed less than a year behind.

All the Indo-Japanese joint ventures suffered from the rapid rise in the yen. Eicher-Mitsubishi, for example, experienced a production cost increase, attributable entirely to the stronger yen, of Rs 24,000 per vehicle from May to November 1988.

TELCO TELCO had been manufacturing large trucks in India since 1964; the LCV was the smallest vehicle it had ever produced. Most of TELCO's truck manufacturing technology was derived from former commercial ties with Daimler-Benz of West Germany in the 1960s. In 1989, TELCO was an entirely Indian company that relied exclusively on Indian design and engineering technology. TELCO produced two kinds of LCV: Models 407 and 608. The Model 608, a 3-tonner, had yet to be successfully launched into the market. It had been introduced several times but had been

E X H I B I T 3 | **Number of Vehicles Sold and Market Share for Light Commercial Vehicles in 1987–88 and 1988–89**

Manufacturers	1987–88 July–June	Market Share (Percent)	1988–89 July–March	Market Share (Percent)
LCVs (2-tonne class)				
Bajaj	12,663	42%	9,513	40%
Mahindra	5,276	17	3,567	15
Standard	1,689	6	857	4
TELCO 407/608	8,680	28	8,013	34
Allwyn-Nissan	2,132	7	1,632	7
Total (LCV—2T)	30,440	100	23,582	100
LCVs (3.5-tonne class)				
DCM-Toyota	3,417	37	2,439	29
Eicher-Mitsubishi	3,373	36	3,496	41
Swaraj-Mazda	2,498	27	2,529	30
Total (LCV—3.5T)	9,288	100	8,464	100

Source: DTL market research from government documents.

pulled back because of technical problems with the gearbox and other components. The Model 407, priced at Rs 174,000, was much less expensive than the Indo-Japanese joint-venture LCVs, all of which were priced around Rs 230,000. In addition, the 407 was simple and rugged in design. Although rated for loads of up to only 1.5 tonnes, it was capable of carrying up to 4 tonnes. Its technology was older and common. When a 407 broke down, which happened frequently, it could be fixed in almost any village shop. The 407 got relatively poor gas mileage of 8 to 10 km/litre, whereas all of the Indo-Japanese joint venture vehicles delivered approximately 12 km/litre. Its dominance of the LCV market was credited to its low cost, rugged construction, ease of repair, and to TELCO's name recognition—the company's full-sized trucks were the most common on India's highways.

Bajaj Bajaj manufactured two-wheeled scooters and three-wheeled delivery vehicles. Scooters were the primary mode of transportation for a large percentage of the population of India. Bajaj entered the 2-tonne LCV market by purchasing the Matador line from the Firodia family. The Bajaj LCV came in two standard configurations: a small bus or delivery van, and a fixed-sided truck. The company's strategy was to pursue market share by maintaining the very low price of Rs 100,000. Although the Matador had front-wheel drive and a fairly fuel-efficient engine, DTL executives did not regard it as state of the art and reported that the vehicles often developed severe maintenance problems after about three years.

Mahindra Mahindra manufactured four-wheel drive vehicles, including jeeps, which it supplied to the Indian armed forces. The military was also a primary market for Mahindra's LCV. However, the company was doing poorly in the civilian LCV market. It had recently entered into a technical collaboration with Peugeot to produce an efficient diesel engine and had just purchased Allwyn-Nissan.

Allwyn-Nissan Allwyn-Nissan's vehicle was rated at 2 tonnes, which put it in more direct competition with the TELCO 407 than with the products of the other Indo-Japanese joint ventures. Allwyn was a state-owned company; the joint venture was also run by the government, which provided most of its business. Sales were reported to be very low. Rumor had it that workers were called in to manufacture trucks only after the company received orders. Up until 1989, Allwyn-Nissan had not been much of a factor in the LCV market.

Standard Standard was an automobile manufacturer based in Madras in southern India. It sold primarily in the south, and was not a major player in the LCV market. In fact, its LCV operation was now virtually shut down.

Eicher-Mitsubishi Eicher-Mitsubishi was the last to enter the field, beginning production in July 1986, and was so far the most successful of the four Indo-Japanese joint ventures. Eicher was one of the finest tractor manufacturers in India. By avoiding such expensive capital purchases as air-conditioning, conveyor belts, automated equipment, and a modern new plant, great short-term savings and a low break-even point were made possible. Its 3.5-tonne vehicle was almost identical to the DTL Dyna and had been, until recently, sold for the same price. (Unlike the

Dyna, however, its trucks were not undercoated or painted electrostatically.) Much of the credit for Eicher-Mitsubishi's success was given to its chairman and managing director, Vikram Lal, who had been described as a "human dynamo." Another factor was the company's dealership network; its trucks were sold through its tractor dealerships, which were well established throughout India. Not surprisingly, the company made many individual sales of trucks to farmers and independent truckers.

Swaraj-Mazda   Swaraj-Mazda was a government-owned tractor manufacturer in the state of Punjab, a rich agricultural region of northern India. The company, which dominated the Punjab tractor market, was intending to anchor its LCV market there as well. It began producing LCVs in October 1985. Although these trucks were almost identical to the Dyna, DTL had nevertheless managed to be quite successful in Punjab, primarily because of an aggressive local DTL dealer.

THE DCM-TOYOTA JOINT VENTURE

HISTORY

In 1980, DCM Ltd. proposed to Toyota a joint venture to manufacture LCVs in India. The two companies were well matched in several respects. Both had similar backgrounds in textiles from which each had diversified, and each had a long tradition of high-quality manufacturing and providing excellent value to the customer.

Established in 1937, the Toyota Motor Corporation was by 1989 the largest automobile manufacturer in Japan and the third largest in the world. Interestingly, its parent company, Toyoda Automatic Loom Works, once sold textile manufacturing machinery to Delhi Cloth Mills in 1930. In addition to 11 plants in Japan, the company had 30 plants in 15 other countries. It employed over 86,000 people and sold its vehicles in 140 countries. Non-Japanese sales accounted for almost half of its total production.

After the partners verified the high market potential with their own extensive surveys, DCM-Toyota Ltd. (DTL) was incorporated on August 1, 1983, with its registered offices at the DCM building in New Delhi. Toyota took 26 percent of the equity and DCM 33 percent; the remaining 41 percent was raised in the Indian stock market, where it was oversubscribed sevenfold. The new company built a facility designed to manufacture 15,000 (18,000 with overtime) LCVs per year. It was sited in Surajpur, a town of approximately 20,000 people, located about 35 kilometers[7] southwest of New Delhi. Because it was in an area targeted for economic development by the government, DTL benefited from considerable tax breaks. All research and development costs were 100 percent deductible in perpetuity, 25 percent of DTL's profits were tax exempt for 7 years after plant startup, and 20 percent of the profits derived from the LCV business were exempt from taxes for 10 years after the first LCV was sold.

THE PLANT, TECHNOLOGY, AND TRAINING

Of all the LCV producers, DTL had the most modern plant and production system. Its plant had nine production lines: chassis and final assembly, frame assembly, hub and drum machining, axle assembly, engine assembly, and the welding, painting,

---

[7]A kilometer is approximately six-tenths of a mile.

trim, and deck lines. A diagram of the plant illustrating the process flow is given in Exhibit 4.

The latest production technologies, although rare in India, were used in the manufacture of the Dyna. On the paint line, for example, phosphate undercoating was deposited through electrolysis in a dip tank for complete coverage, electrostatic spray painting was employed for uniformity, and painted components were baked to harden the finish. On the hub and drum line, advanced five-axis computer-controlled machining centers assured high precision in parts. Engines were assembled in a specially controlled clean room.

The plant operated on the Toyota production system (TPS), a "pull" system that was the original just-in-time (JIT) system. All operations were pulled on, ultimately, by the final assembly line; the other lines had only to keep small buffers of their finished products full. Instruction sheets fed in at the beginning of each of the trim, deck, and chassis and final assembly lines assured they were all synchronized. All work-in-process movement was on dollies custom-designed for each specific operation.

To learn the TPS, foremen and managers from all levels in DTL had been sent to Toyota City in Japan for training. During their absence, the personnel department had carefully selected workers from the local area who fitted desired profiles. TPS selection guidelines required all workers to have a high school education or an ITT (a technical school) diploma. They were required to be under 23 years of age, since older applicants were considered too inflexible and fixed in their thinking. Local villagers were preferred and constituted some 120 of the 143 production workers. In addition to undergoing tests of intelligence, aptitude, and dexterity, applicants were also given a complete medical examination, including psychological screening to assess whether each applicant was a "good person in heart and mind."

The workers were trained in the Toyota style, beginning with talks and video shows about Toyota. They were taught the aims and values of the TPS, which were rooted in the motto "good thinking, good product." They learned about quality circles, *kaizen* (continuous improvement), *muda* (waste), *poka-yoke* (mistake-proof devices), *kanban* (control cards), and all the other tools of the TPS, and they also received training on truck assembly and the DTL plant. The goal of this training was to instill a strong sense of responsibility for high quality in the workers, who were taught to stop the assembly line if any quality problems arose. Not only were no penalties incurred for interrupting production, but stopping the line was encouraged, since it exposed problems that could be solved once and for all. Because the TPS made all workers responsible for quality control (QC), DTL kept only a skeleton QC department of six people. Great care was taken to demonstrate to the workers their vital importance to the organization. To emphasize this, all personnel and guests ate together in DTL's one cafeteria.

The meticulous training paid off. In the planning stage, it was expected that the productivity of DTL's Indian workers would be only 20 to 35 percent of that of the workers in Toyota City. It soon became clear that this had been a gross underestimate; the Indian workers were 65 percent as productive as their Japanese counterparts and continued to improve. This figure was quite impressive since the Japanese plants were more highly automated than DTL's. Interestingly, DTL's target of zero defects before shipment was actually achieved on some days. As in Japan, the line and office workers were all strongly committed to the company; they frequently stayed after hours (without pay) for quality circles or when additional production was needed. If the company needed extra workers on the line in peak periods, instead of

EXHIBIT 4 | **DTI's Surajpur Plant**

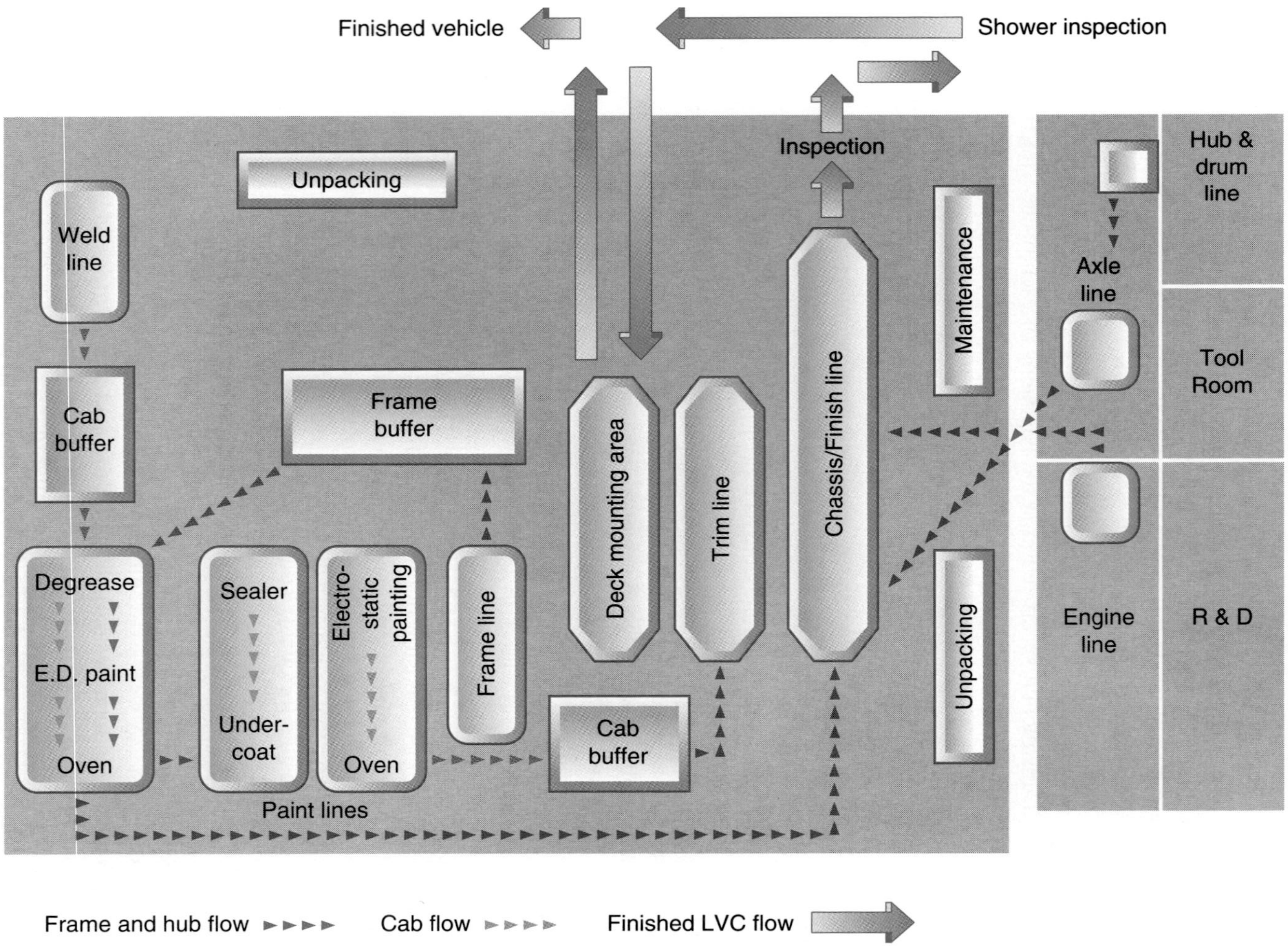

Hub & drum line

Tool Room

R & D

Axle line

Engine line

Shower inspection

Maintenance

Unpacking

Inspection

Chassis/Finish line

Trim line

Deck mounting area

Cab buffer

Finished vehicle

Unpacking

Frame buffer

Frame line

Electro-static painting

Oven

Sealer

Under-coat

Paint lines

Weld line

Cab buffer

Degrease

E.D. paint

Oven

Finished LVC flow

Frame and hub flow ▲ ▲ ▲   Cab flow ▲ ▲ ▲

the normal Indian practice of hiring temporaries, clerical staff was assigned there to help. Even Toyota executives were impressed by the productivity and high-quality output of the Surajpur plant.

THE DYNA TRUCK

The DTL vehicle, the Dyna, came in two basic models—the Dyna-1 and the Dyna-3. The Dyna-3 was a complete truck with a standard cab and deck. The Dyna-1, a mechanically complete truck without the cab or deck, was for customers who wanted to finish it for their own special purposes. Both models are shown in Exhibit 5, together with their technical specifications. Production information for the Dyna models for fiscal year 1988 and the first three quarters of 1989 is given in Exhibit 6.

Approximately 20 percent of the vehicles manufactured by DTL were Dyna-1 models. The Dyna-1 customer could either have DTL custom-finish the vehicle or could take it to a private "body builder" to be finished inexpensively with wood or other materials. The Dyna-1 trucks finished by DTL were sold mainly to government agencies or institutional buyers with special requirements. Custom cabs and decks were built by DTL to conform to both customer specifications and Toyota's quality standards. Examples of these special purpose vehicles (SPVs) were delivery vehicles for soft-drink distributors, armored vehicles for the police and security forces, ambulances for emergency services, and buses. A variety of SPV configurations can be seen in Exhibit 1. SPV sales could be very seasonal for certain markets, such as soft-drink manufacturers, which had high summer demand, and for which it was very hard to build inventories because of planning uncertainty. For example, the factory of Campa Cola, the largest soft-drink manufacturer in northern India, was burned during demonstrations following Mrs. Gandhi's assassination. This led to a slump in demand for Dyna bottle carriers.

The capacity of the Dyna was 3.5 tonnes, but the truck was actually designed for up to 6 tonnes and had been operated with loads as high as 10.5 tonnes. It was built for low-fuel-cost transport of goods, possibly perishable, which needed to travel quickly. One advantage of a medium-size truck like the Dyna was that it could travel city streets 24 hours a day, whereas bigger trucks could not because of laws against their daytime use in certain populated areas.

Experience quickly showed that the Dynas took a lot more punishment than was originally anticipated. They were often overloaded by 100 to 150 percent and driven at great speed over bad roads. The resulting burst tires, broken axles, fractured leaf springs, bent frames, and completely stripped gears meant that, early in the venture, a lot of the parts needed to be upgraded. Also, the vehicles were frequently involved in high-speed accidents and were often dented owing to aggressive driving, since many drivers were unaccustomed to the speeds and acceleration the Dyna could attain. The upgraded Dyna was a far more rugged vehicle than its Japanese counterpart. In fact, when riding with Indian drivers testing it under normal Indian road conditions, Japanese engineers never failed to express amazement at the punishment the Dyna could take.

SUPPLIERS

In early 1989, 25 percent by value of the component parts of DTL's vehicles were still imported from Japan. This was either because, like the engine components and transmission gears, they required precision and high quality, or because, like the large frame and cab members, they had to be stamped using dies and presses larger than

EXHIBIT 5 | **Dyna Standard Configuration**

Technical Specifications

Engine

Model	: 14B
Type	: 4-cylinder in line DI diesel engine
Bore & stroke (mm)	: 102×112
Piston displacement (cc)	: 3660
Comp. ratio	: 18
Max. power (DIN)	: 94 HP at 3400 rpm
Max. torque (DIN)	: 24 kgm at 1800 rpm
Air cleaner	: Oil bath type with precleaner
Fuel system	: Bosch type, rotary distribution pump with centrifugal mechanical governor and automatic timer

Transmission

Clutch	: Hydraulically operated single dry plate with diaphragm spring
Gear box	: 5 forward-speed all synchromesh
Final drive	: 12-inch Crown Wheel

Steering
Recirculating ball nut–type with variable ratio of 30:1 to 34:1

Front axle
Reverse Elliot I-beam

Rear axle
Full-floating in banjo-type housing

Suspension
Semielliptic laminated leaf springs with auxiliary leaf springs at the rear and double-acting hydraulic telescopic shock absorbers on all four wheels

Brakes

Service brake	: Hydraulically operated drum brakes with tandem master cylinder and vacuum booster
Parking brake	: Internal expanding at rear of gear box
Exhaust brake	: Vacuum-assisted with ON-OFF operating lever

Electrical
Battery: 12V, 70AH
Alternator: 12V-45A

Frame
Ladder-type with reinforced C-channel section

Tires
Front: 2; Rear: 4; Spare tire: 1
Size: 7.50×16—12 PR

Dimensions	Cab and Chassis with Optional Rear Deck LWB	Cowl and Chasis Version for Bus Applicator SLWB
Wheel base (mm)	3290	3785
Overall length (mm)	6000	6440
Overall width (mm)	1995	1995
Overall height (mm)	2215	2025
Deck (internal $L \times W \times H$)		
Drop-side (mm)	$4350 \times 2030 \times 610$	NA
Fixed-side (mm)	$4350 \times 1850 \times 530$	NA
High-side (mm)	$4350 \times 1850 \times 1175$	NA
Min. turning radius (m)	6.1	6.9
Ground clearance (mm)	210	210
GVW (kg)	5990	5990

Standard Configurations

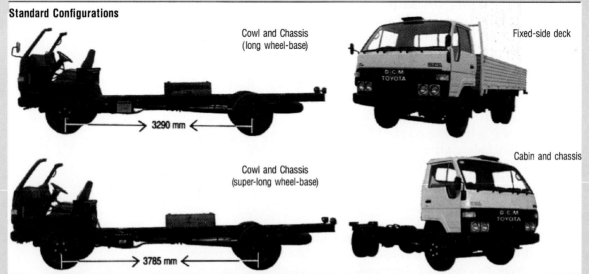

Cowl and Chassis (long wheel-base) — 3290 mm

Fixed-side deck

Cowl and Chassis (super-long wheel-base) — 3785 mm

Cabin and chassis

Source: Company records.

EXHIBIT 6 | **DCM–Toyota Limited LCV Sales by Model during 1988–89** *(Including exports)*

Models	July 1987–June 1988	July 1988–March 1989
–1 Based models		
–1 (cowl and chassis)	297	191
Bus	193	141
SPV (special purpose vehicle)	32	13
Total	522	345
–3 Based models		
–3 (cabin and chassis)	397	205
High-side deck	1,069	710
Drop-side deck	415	359
Fixed-side deck	917	772
SPV	230	164
Total	3,028	2,210
Grand total	3,550	2,555

Source: DTL marketing staff.

those commonly available in India. DTL began with 42 percent local content, reached 75 percent local content by the end of 1988, and had to attain 90 percent by the end of 1991 or face severe penalties from the government. The problem DTL was encountering in its indigenization efforts was to develop a base of domestic suppliers with the technology and inclination to produce certain high-quality components. Some of the major challenges in this regard were as follows.

- Large, high-quality metal stampings and plastic-molded components were not readily available in India because of a shortage of presses and molding machines capable of handling the sizes of dies required.
- The technology to bond rubber to metal—which was necessary for engine mounts, alternator mounts, and other critical components—was in its infancy in India.
- The precision required for some parts to meet Japanese standards was not achievable in India, where much of the technology in use was very old.

Fortunately, DTL had one advantage over the other Indo-Japanese joint ventures: the company's Indian parent, DCM Ltd., operated a world-class foundry. Plans were in the works to have the engine blocks manufactured there. Pistons might be supplied by Shriram Pistons and Rings Ltd., another firm controlled by the Shriram family. DTL was also considering redesigning the dashboard to be manufactured in six parts instead of one. This would have allowed it to be produced domestically with smaller machines but raised concerns of increased assembly costs and lower quality.

To date, DTL had successfully indigenized three-quarters of the Dyna. The domestic suppliers used could be divided into three classes: the large well-established suppliers, the Indo-Japanese joint-venture suppliers, and the small, local, independent suppliers. The big manufacturers typically produced high-quality products, had excellent delivery, and were very responsive. Some of these companies, such as the tire suppliers, had affiliations with large international companies and operated in competitive markets. Others, such as Automotive Axles Ltd., which manufactured axle housings and gears, were near-monopolies because no other Indian companies could match their technology. The Indo-Japanese joint-venture suppliers fell into two categories: (1) those established to serve DTL, and (2) those established to serve the Indian government's joint venture with Suzuki to produce automobiles. The former delivered to DTL on a JIT basis and had excellent quality, though they tended to be high priced. DCM and Toyota established a collaboration, independent of DTL, and located two kilometers from the Surajpur plant, to supply wiper motors, starters, and alternators. The joint ventures set up to serve Suzuki did not always deliver reliably, largely because DTL was such a small customer (relative to Suzuki). The small local manufacturers supplied various special nuts, bolts, and small metal and plastic components. Delivery was usually not a problem, but quality could be. These suppliers made extensive use of DTL's ancillary development department (ADD) to improve their quality.

Parts supplied by all vendors were handled initially by the ADD, whose major tasks were to help indigenize the DTL vehicle, to integrate suppliers into the firm as JIT "partners," and to provide suppliers with advice on techniques to improve their quality. Sometimes suppliers genuinely did not understand why higher quality was needed. For example, DTL had to work hard to persuade its bus body builders that the vehicle needed to be watertight, should have no sharp edges, and should not rattle. One of them was quoted as saying: "This is a bus, not a car."

DTL MARKETING

The DTL sales department was staffed with 20 people in the head office and 5 salespeople stationed in regional offices around the country. Customers for LCVs ranged from large institutions operating entire fleets of vehicles to individuals who may have owned farms or small businesses. To reach them, the sales staff was divided into two groups: international/institutional and domestic. Institutional customers included large companies and state and local governments. (DTL was waiting for clearance to sell to the national government and armed forces, potentially a very large market.) Institutional selling was done directly to the institutions involved. The orders were generally for fleets of vehicles and often for customized Dyna-1 models such as buses, armored vehicles, or bottle trucks. DTL was traditionally strong in this market. Competitors could not match the quality and engineering of the special purpose Dyna-1s. DTL also exported to Bangladesh, Nepal, Sri Lanka, Bhutan, Mauritius, and Pakistan and was trying to gain business in countries in the Middle East. The Indian government provided financial support and other export-related assistance to all LCV manufacturers. DTL's export potential was somewhat limited because Toyota did not want the Dyna exported to nations that it was serving already.

Trucks were sold domestically through DTL's network of 53 main dealerships and 57 subdealers or branches. These were also supported by an additional 33 authorized service centers. Dealership status was granted only to those who could meet Toyota's rigorous standards, which required that facilities be staffed with factory-trained technicians with the knowledge and tools to do all required service and repairs to LCVs. Dealers also had to maintain large inventories of spare parts. (Subdealers were those who were not yet fully qualified dealers.) The entire dealership network, established from scratch starting in 1985, included some dealers that sold exclusively DTL products and some that sold other complementary products as well. DTL provided free training to service technicians and helped dealers import service equipment. The dealer's profit on a typical LCV sale was about Rs 5,000. The normal procedure was for a dealer to get a customer order and forward it to the factory; delivery usually occurred within a month.

Until mid-1988, DTL competed on the basis of price with Eicher-Mitsubishi and Swaraj-Mazda, its two major rivals in the 3.5-tonne LCV market. All three companies produced vehicles of similar sizes and capacities. Even though DTL executives viewed their vehicle as superior to the others in quality, engineering, and performance, price was still used as the basis for competition. As a result, DTL held a slightly higher market share than either of the other two companies. In mid-1988, the marketing manager was transferred to another post in DCM, and the marketing staff was restructured. The new marketing management initiated a different strategy that called for disengagement from the "price wars" and the marketing of the Dyna based on its superior quality. The Dyna was then priced about Rs 10,000 higher than its competitors. Eight points of market share were lost over the next nine months. However, the strategy shift resulted in one significant benefit: unlike its rivals, DTL was now profitable for the first time in its history. Vikram Lal, chairman of Eicher-Mitsubishi, then the market leader in the 3.5-tonne LCV class, was quoted as stating that his company would lose "about Rs 3 Crore [30 million] this year."[8]

THE DYNA'S FIT WITH THE MARKET

Of the four Indo-Japanese joint ventures, DTL alone used a JIT manufacturing system and conveyorized assembly lines. In addition, DTL had more modern painting facilities, with electrodeposition of primer and electrolytically deposited paint. While this provided DTL a competitive advantage in manufacturing technology and product quality, it was uncertain whether the added expense was justified, for three reasons.

First, consumers were wary of the new technology in the Dyna trucks, particularly with the unfamiliar Toyota name on them. The new truck came with a higher price tag than people expected and was built to much higher standards than customers were accustomed to. The Dyna did not break down every few days, and problems common to older designs of LCVs—ruptured fuel lines and broken fan belts, for example—had, by and large, been eliminated. Tire wear was one of the major costs of truck ownership, because tires were very expensive in India. Unlike the older truck designs, including TELCO's, the Dyna was designed to have its wheels aligned and tires balanced on computerized equipment, which greatly reduced tire wear. Quite apart from the generally high standards to which the entire vehicle was manufactured, this reduced tire wear alone made the Dyna a less expensive vehicle to operate in the long term than the other LCVs.

The second reason for concern was that service for the Dyna was not available in many parts of the country. India is vast, and the number of dealers capable of providing full service for the vehicle was relatively limited. The DTL dealership network was new, having been established only in the last four years, whereas competitors had been able to take advantage of long-standing truck or tractor dealership networks spread throughout India. Consequently, DTL had been less successful than the other LCV manufacturers in selling to individual buyers.

The third concern for DTL was that its high standards made indigenization of components quite difficult. Since there were only a handful of suppliers in India capable of manufacturing certain necessary components to DTL's quality standards,

---

[8]*India Today,* March 31, 1989, p. 80.

DTL's ability to negotiate price concessions was limited. For some components, there were no domestic manufacturers that could meet the quality standards.

Despite these challenges, in June 1989, S. G. Awasthi, DTL's executive director, remained a steadfast supporter of his company's current strategy:

> The management policy adopted by DTL so far has paid rich dividends and this policy is likely to yield even richer dividends in the future. I am confident that the corporate strategy adopted by DTL would be a model for other automobile manufacturers in the years to come.

Vivek Bharat Ram, grandson of Shri Ram and the current managing director of DTL, shared this view of the company's future:

> The basic principle on which DTL has always operated is that of following the customer-first philosophy. This is the policy I intend to firmly adhere to in the future also.

While DTL was clearly committed to developing and implementing strategies that offered the equivalent of Shri Ram's "2 extra inches" to the LCV market, there was concern about market acceptance of such a product. The shift in strategies from one of matching the pricing moves of competitors to one of value pricing based on the Dyna's higher quality led to the company's first profitable quarter, but it also resulted in a loss of eight points of market share. DTL moved from first in market share among the three 3.5-tonne LCV manufacturers to last (see Exhibit 4) as a result of breaking ranks on pricing. Concerns focused on whether the market share could, or should, be regained and what the longer-term consequences of a shift in market position would mean.

REFERENCES

Singh, K., and A. Joshi. *Shri Ram: A Biography* (London: Asia Publishing House, 1968).
The Economist, March 4, 1989, p. 34.

NUCOR CORPORATION

Charles Stubbart, University of Massachusetts
Dean Schroeder, Valparaiso University
Arthur A. Thompson, Jr., University of Alabama

It's the closest thing to a perfect company in the steel industry.

Daniel Roling
Analyst for Merrill Lynch

In August 1990, Ken Iverson, Nucor's chief executive officer, believed that the company had the technology and the cost advantage it needed to achieve 15 to 20 percent annual growth in its steel business over the next five years despite a sluggish demand for steel products industrywide. A few years earlier Wall Street analysts had been predicting that Nucor's rapid growth was not sustainable. Iverson had disagreed with the assessment, believing that if Nucor could perfect a promising new technology to cast thin slabs of steel, then it could produce steel plate and flat-rolled sheet steel very efficiently and open up sizable expansion opportunities.

Following Iverson's strong convictions about the potential in thin-slab casting, Nucor led all other steel companies during the mid-1980s in investing in R&D efforts to develop thin-slab casting technology. By 1988 Iverson was satisfied the company could make the technology work and Nucor initiated construction of a mill in Crawfordsville, Indiana, to make sheet steel products using the innovative thin-slab casting process. It was the first mill of its kind in the world. Production start-up began in August 1989; over the next 10 months Nucor spent nearly $45 million working out numerous technological bugs in the process and improving the metallurgical quality of the mill's steel output. By June 1990 the Crawfordsville plant reached break-even and was able to turn out prime-quality sheet steel consistently. Nucor's potential in the flat-rolled sheet steel market was vast since the mill was sized to produce only

Prepared with the research assistance of University of Alabama PhD candidate Tracy R. Kramer. Copyright © 1990 by the authors.

800,000 to 1,000,000 tons per year in a market where demand was 40 million tons per year and since the efficiency of Nucor's thin-slab casting process gave it a 25 percent cost advantage over both foreign and domestic competitors. Already, Nucor was designing a second mill to come on-line in 1992.

Since 1980, Nucor's revenues had grown at a compound annual rate of 11 percent. Annual steel production at Nucor had risen from 1,040,000 tons in 1980 to 2,500,000 tons in 1989; production in 1990 was expected to surpass 3,000,000 tons. Iverson believed that Nucor could become a major player in the steel industry in the United States before the year 2000. Exhibit 1 provides a financial overview of Nucor's recent performance.

THE STEEL INDUSTRY IN THE UNITED STATES

Four types of companies competed in the U.S. market for steel products in 1990: the major domestic integrated producers, minimill companies, specialty steel producers, and foreign manufacturers. The major domestic integrated producers included the giants of the industry—USX Corp. (formerly U.S. Steel Corp.), Bethlehem Steel, Inland Steel, Armco Steel, LTV Corp., and several others, all of whom operated capital-intensive plant complexes that processed iron ore through a series of production stages into finished steel products of any size and variety. Integrated mills were scaled to turn out several million tons of steel products annually, and the largest integrated producers each had 10 to 25 million tons of annual capacity. Integrated producers had a combined market share of about 50 percent.

Specialty steel producers manufactured low-volume steel products for specialized markets and applications; about 5 percent of total steel shipments involved specialty steels such as stainless steel. Imported steel, chiefly from Europe, Japan, Korea, Canada, and Latin America, accounted for 20 percent of domestic steel sales, and the percentage had been declining since 1984 when imports accounted for a 26 percent market share.

The minimill companies employed small-scale electric arc furnaces to melt ferrous scrap and recycle it into a relatively limited line of commodity steel items like reinforcing bars, wire rods, roof bolts for underground mines, and light-to-medium structural steel. Minimills ranged in size from a one-plant company with annual capacity as low as 150,000 tons up to multiplant companies with 500,000-ton plants and companywide capacities of 3 million tons per year. The leading minimill producers included North Star Steel, Lukens, Nucor, Oregon Steel Mills, Insteel Industries, Chaparral Steel, Florida Steel, and Birmingham Steel. Exhibit 2 presents comparative statistics for 17 of the leading producers in the United States.

In recent years, minimills had prospered, largely by capturing market share from higher-cost integrated producers. New state-of-the-art minimill plants could be constructed for under $200 per ton of capacity (versus about $2,000 per ton for an integrated mill), and an aging foundry could be modernized and converted to an efficient minimill operation for under $30 million (less than $100 per ton of capacity). Minimills typically were located either near supplies of scrap metal or near product markets to minimize shipping expenses; and they normally enjoyed low labor costs per ton produced. As a consequence, minimills tended to be very cost efficient, able to compete head-to-head against even the most efficient foreign producers. The minimills' share of total steel shipments in 1990 was about 25 percent and trending upward.

EXHIBIT 1 | Summary of Nucor's Financial Performance, 1984–89

	1984	1985	1986	1987	1988	1989
For the Year						
Net sales	$660,259,922	$758,495,374	$755,228,939	$851,022,039	$1,061,364,009	$1,269,007,472
Costs and expenses:						
Cost of products sold	539,731,252	600,797,865	610,378,369	713,346,451	889,140,323	1,105,248,906
Marketing, administrative, and other expenses	45,939,311	59,079,802	65,900,653	55,405,961	62,083,752	66,990,065
Interest expense (income)	(3,959,092)	(7,560,645)	(5,288,971)	(964,823)	2,558,914	11,132,657
	581,711,471	652,317,022	670,990,051	767,787,589	953,782,989	1,183,371,628
Earnings from operations before federal income taxes	78,548,451	106,178,352	84,238,888	83,234,450	107,581,020	85,635,844
Federal income taxes	34,000,000	47,700,000	37,800,000	32,700,000	36,700,000	27,800,000
Earnings from operations	44,548,451	58,478,352	46,438,888	50,534,450	70,881,020	57,835,844
Gain on sale of Research Chemicals	—	—	—	—	38,558,822	—
Net earnings	$ 44,548,451	$ 58,478,352	$ 46,438,888	$ 50,534,450	$ 109,439,842	$ 57,835,844
Earnings per share:						
Earnings per share from operations	$2.10	$2.74	$2.17	$2.39	$3.34	$2.71
Gain per share on sale of Research Chemicals	—	—	—	—	1.82	—
Net earnings per share	2.10	2.74	2.17	2.39	5.16	2.71
Dividends declared per share	.24	.27	.31	.36	.40	.44
Percentage of earnings from operations to sales	6.7%	7.7%	6.1%	5.9%	6.7%	4.6%
Percentage of earnings from operations to average equity	16.0%	17.8%	12.5%	12.5%	15.4%	10.4%
Capital expenditures	$ 26,333,882	$ 28,701,463	$ 86,201,391	$189,990,476	$ 345,632,411	$130,200,982
Depreciation	28,899,421	31,105,788	34,931,520	41,793,009	56,264,631	76,571,240
Sales per employee	176,069	197,011	181,983	189,116	218,838	241,716
At Year-End						
Current assets	$253,453,373	$334,769,147	$295,738,255	$234,717,237	$ 247,758,616	$ 280,033,934
Current liabilities	100,533,684	121,255,828	118,440,973	147,473,270	216,107,302	193,560,545
Working capital	152,919,689	213,513,319	177,297,282	87,243,967	31,651,314	86,473,389
Current ratio	2.5	2.8	2.5	1.6	1.1	1.4
Property, plant, and equipment	228,735,092	225,542,041	275,869,389	419,372,902	701,903,094	753,797,578
Total assets	482,188,465	560,311,188	571,607,644	654,090,139	949,661,710	1,033,831,512
Long-term debt	43,232,384	40,233,769	42,147,654	35,462,500	113,248,500	155,981,500
Percentage of debt to capital	12.6%	10.1%	9.9%	7.7%	17.5%	21.1%
Stockholders' equity	299,602,834	357,502,028	383,699,454	428,009,367	532,281,449	584,445,479
Per share	$ 14.10	$ 16.65	$ 18.16	$ 20.19	$ 25.00	$ 27.31
Shares outstanding	21,241,618	21,472,508	21,131,298	21,196,088	21,287,691	21,399,620
Stockholders	22,000	22,000	22,000	27,000	28,000	25,000
Employees	3,800	3,900	4,400	4,600	5,100	5,400

EXHIBIT 2 | Financial and Operating Highlights for Selected Integrated and Minimill Steel Producers, 1980 and 1988

	Revenues ($ millions)			Net Profits ($ millions)		
	1980	1988	Average Compound Change	1980	1988	Average Compound Change
Integrated Producers						
Bethlehem Steel	$6,743	$5,489	−2.5%	$121	$403	16.2%
LTV Steel	8,010	7,325	−1.1	128	456	17.2
USX Corp. (U.S. Steel division)	8,738	5,800	−5.0	58	501	30.8
Armco, Inc.	5,678	3,227	−6.8	265	165	−5.8
Inland Steel	3,256	4,068	2.8	30	249	30.4
National Steel	3,945	2,599	−5.1	84	66	−3.0
Weirton Steel (formed 1984)	—	1,384	N/A	—	(2)	—
Wheeling-Pittsburgh	1,054	1,103	0.6	15	149	33.5
Minimill Producers						
Bayou Steel (formed 1988)	—	190	N/A	—	23	N/A
Birmingham Steel (formed 1985)	—	344	N/A	—	25	N/A
Chaparral Steel	131	376	14.1	13	61	21.2
Florida Steel	287	476	6.6	19	20	0.8
Lukens	376	450	2.3	5	63	38.3
New Jersey Steel (formed 1985)	—	139	N/A	—	16	N/A
Northwestern Steel	426	497	1.9	23	29	3.2
Nucor	482	1,061	10.4	45	71	5.8
Oregon Steel (formed 1985)	—	190	N/A	—	18	N/A

N/A = not applicable.

Sources: Compiled by the casewriters from a variety of sources including company annual reports, company 10-K reports, *Value Line Industry Surveys, Metal Statistics,* and telephone interviews.

Even though steelmaking was a "basic" industry, worldwide demand for steel products was viewed as both stagnant (slow-growth or no-growth) and cyclical. Steel production in the United States had been in a cyclical downtrend since 1972 (see Exhibit 3). Integrated U.S. producers, burdened with aging facilities and high-cost labor contracts, had suffered the most in terms of lost market share, falling production, and unprofitable operations. Since 1979 the U.S. steel industry as a whole had incurred losses in 6 out of 10 years. However, minimill producers were generally profitable throughout the 1980s; it was the big integrated producers who found themselves forced to close down plants and retreat from markets where their high costs prevented them from competing profitably. LTV Corp., the second largest integrated U.S. producer, had filed for Chapter 11 reorganization and was operating under protection of the courts. Since 1978 closings of inefficient and obsolete plants by the

EXHIBIT 2 | **Financial and Operating Highlights for Selected Integrated and Minimill Steel Producers, 1980 and 1988 (*continued*)**

Production of Raw Steel (000 tons)			Shipments of Finished Steel Products (000 tons)			Number of Mills	
1980	1988	Average Compound Change	1980	1988	Average Compound Change	1988	Principal Products
15,000	12,855	–1.9%	11,080	10,303	–0.9%	2	Sheet, strip, bars, rods, structured shapes, plates
9,760	10,461	0.9	7,000	8,963	3.1	4	Hot/cold-rolled sheet, strip, coated goods, tubulars
23,280	15,545	–4.9	17,200	12,175	–4.2	7	Sheet, strip, tin, plates, piling, pipe and tubular, bars
7,300	5,771	–2.9	5,400	4,903	–1.2	3	Carbon flat-rolled and sheet, electrical and stainless, bar, rod, wire
7,049	6,126	–1.7	5,286	5,020	–0.6	1	Sheet, strip, plate, bar, and structural
7,600	5,393	–4.2	6,600	4,970	–3.5	3	Hot/cold-rolled sheet, strip, tin, galvanized
	3,155	N/A	—	2,729	—	1	Hot/cold flat-rolled sheet
3,119	2,527	2.6	2,210	2,235	0.1	1	Hot/cold-rolled sheet, strip, galavanized, tin, rail
—	540	N/A	—	504	N/A	1	Flats, angles, beams, wide flange, unequal angles
—	1,275	N/A	—	1,031	N/A	6	Rebar, rounds, squares, flats, angles, billets
387	1,360	17.0	381	1,230	15.8	1	Rebar, angles, channels, beams, rounds, special bar, quality steel
827	1,374	6.6	736	1,223	6.6	5	Rebar, rounds, flats, angles, rods, merchant
734	741	0.1	—	660	N/A	2	Carbon and alloy steel plates
—	744	N/A	—	433	N/A	1	Rebar, light structurals
1,302	1,754	3.8	1,049	1,455	4.2	2	Beams, angles, channels, flats, rods, coiled rebar, wire
1,150	2,030	7.4	672	1,347	9.1	6	Angles, channels, flats, rounds, billets, beams, rod, rebar
—	420	N/A	—	344	N/A	3	Plate and pipe

integrated producers had reduced steelmaking capacity in the United States from 158 million tons to 112 million tons, yet capacity utilization rates in the United States were still running below 90 percent.

STEEL TYPES AND STEEL PRODUCTS

Steel was made primarily of iron and carbon. Thousands of varieties of steel could be turned out by varying the content of iron, carbon, and alloying elements such as chromium, nickel, manganese, silicon, vanadium, and molybdenum. The most common varieties of steel had carbon contents between 0.25 and 2.0 percent; harder grades of steel had a higher carbon content. The use of alloying elements made steel more resistant to heat, corrosion, and wear. Stainless steel was the most popular of the alloy steels; it contained 8 percent nickel and 18 percent chromium.

EXHIBIT 3 | Selected Statistical Highlights for the U.S. Steel Industry, 1978-89

Year	Production Capacity (million tons)	Raw Steel Production (million tons)	Operating Rate (percent)	Shipments of Steel Products (million tons)	Exports (million tons)	U.S. Imports (million tons)	Apparent Supply (million tons)	Imports as a Percent of Supply	Average Number of Employees	Employment Cost per Hour (all employees)
1989	115.9	97.9	84.5%	84.1	4.6	17.3	96.8	17.9%	169,000	$25.35
1988	112.0	99.3	88.7	84.0	2.1	20.9	102.8	20.3	168,898	25.30
1987	112.2	89.2	79.5	76.6	0.9	20.4	96.1	21.2	163,338	24.23
1986	127.9	81.6	63.8	70.3	0.9	20.7	90.0	23.0	174,783	23.56
1985	133.6	88.3	66.1	73.0	0.9	24.3	96.4	25.2	208,168	23.26
1984	135.3	92.5	68.4	73.7	0.9	26.2	98.9	26.4	236,002	21.82
1983	150.6	84.6	56.2	67.6	1.2	17.1	83.5	20.5	242,745	22.49
1982	154.0	74.6	48.4	61.6	1.8	16.7	76.4	21.8	289,437	23.60
1981	154.3	120.8	78.3	88.4	2.9	19.9	105.4	18.9	390,914	20.70
1980	153.7	111.8	72.8	83.9	4.1	15.5	95.2	16.3	398,829	18.79
1979	155.3	136.0	87.8	100.3	2.8	17.5	115.0	15.2	453,181	16.38
1978	157.9	137.0	86.8	97.9	2.4	21.1	116.6	18.1	—	—

Source: American Iron and Steel Institute.

Steel was produced in a broad variety of shapes, thicknesses, and lengths—there were round bars, flat bars, thick plates, coiled sheets, steel rails, I beams, steel pipes and tubing, and wire and cable of all dimensions, alloys, and grades. Container companies used tin sheets to make tin cans and flat-rolled sheet steel for oil drums and pails. The automobile companies used flat-rolled thin sheet steel in automobile bodies, structural steel in the frames and chassis, and iron castings for the engine block and other parts. Construction companies used steel beams, reinforcing rods, steel siding, and steel decking. Electrical equipment companies were big buyers of wire and cable. Drilling companies used steel pipes and tubing in drilling oil and gas wells. Major steel users typically bought their supplies directly from the producing mill. Small users and occasional users purchased from local steel service centers and distributors that made their business from stocking a variety of shapes and grades and being able to deliver them on short notice. About 20 percent of total steel production was marketed through area service centers and distributors. Exhibit 4 shows steel shipments by major product category. Exhibit 5 shows the markets for steel products by major end-user category.

Some steel products, like reinforcing bars, were commodities and had essentially the same metallurgical properties no matter which plant or company produced them. Other products, however, were made to the customer's specifications and had to meet sometimes stringent metallurgical requirements so that the steel would perform properly in the intended application. Automakers, for instance, required prime-quality sheet steel with no surface defects that could be bent and shaped without cracking and that withstood rust corrosion. Customers with rigid specifications required a mill to produce samples for testing and scrutinize the quality of its output for several months before deciding to include a mill on their list of acceptable steel suppliers. As one steel buyer for Ford Motor Co. put it, "We like to buy from people with an established record . . . our first sourcing criterion is quality, not price."

EXHIBIT 4 | **Steel Shipments in the U.S. by Major Product Category, 1982–89** (*In thousands of net tons*)

Products	1982	1983	1984	1985	1986	1987	1988	1989
Semifinished steel	3,693	3,861	4,407	4,345	4,954	5,456	5,978	6,236
Shapes and piling	3,563	3,622	4,156	4,699	4,528	5,120	5,209	5,355
Plates	4,146	3,816	4,339	4,327	3,565	4,048	7,328	7,384
Rails	517	634	965	704	461	366	497	458
Other railroad products	265	250	274	228	179	149	118	104
Bars and tool steel	10,812	11,700	13,232	12,668	12,171	13,575	14,489	14,171
Pipe and tubing	5,026	3,242	4,276	4,096	2,836	3,570	4,443	4,011
Wire products	1,308	1,359	1,222	1,136	1,080	1,105	1,073	1,002
Tin mill products	4,321	4,308	4,062	3,773	3,802	3,988	4,069	4,126
Sheets—hot rolled	9,052	11,619	13,133	12,952	12,167	13,048	12,589	13,281
Sheets—cold rolled	1,132	13,781	13,664	13,574	13,250	13,859	13,871	13,854
Sheets—galvanized	6,063	7,380	7,867	8,669	9,299	12,320	11,511	12,071
Electrical sheets and strip	445	458	490	413	416	465	524	484
Hot- and cold-rolled strip	1,222	1,554	1,652	1,462	1,555	1,587	2,144	1,572
Net total steel products	61,567	67,584	73,739	73,043	70,263	76,654	83,840	84,109

Source: American Iron and Steel Institute.

EXHIBIT 5 | **Purchase of Steel Mill Products by Major End-User or Customer Category, 1984–89**
(In millions of net tons)

End-Use/Customer Category	1984	1985	1986	1987	1988	1989	Average Annual Compound Change, 1984–89
Appliances	1,635	1,466	1,648	1,633	1,638	1,623	–0.15%
Automotive	12,882	12,950	11,889	11,343	12,555	12,000	–1.41
Construction	10,153	11,230	10,614	11,018	12,101	12,464	4.19
Containers	4,352	4,089	4,113	4,371	4,421	4,465	0.51
Converting and processing	5,136	5,484	5,635	7,195	8,492	7,982	9.22
Electrical equipment	2,365	1,869	2,113	2,373	2,459	2,533	1.38
Machinery	2,886	2,271	2,076	2,277	2,798	2,630	–1.84
Oil and gas	2,003	2,044	1,023	1,489	1,477	1,107	–11.18
Steel service centers	18,364	18,439	17,478	19,840	21,037	19,564	1.27
Other domestic and commercial equipment	1,339	1,215	1,173	1,149	1,199	1,187	–2.38
Other	4,389	3,725	3,121	3,252	4,071	3,867	–2.50
Nonclassified	7,807	7,767	8,885	10,199	10,359	10,773	6.65
Exports	428	494	495	514	1,233	1,700	31.76
Total	72,739	73,043	70,263	76,654	83,840	81,895	2.12%

Source: American Iron and Steel Institute.

SUBSTITUTE PRODUCTS

A portion of the stagnant demand for steel industry products was attributable to the challenge from substitute products. The substitution of aluminum for steel in beverage cans had cut steel's share of the can market from 87 percent in 1972 to 26 percent in 1988. In 1977 the typical U.S.-made passenger car contained 2,535 pounds of iron and steel; by 1988, the average passenger car contained 1,897 pounds. Some users of plastics, aluminum, and steel had flexible enough production systems to switch from one material to another within a short time frame whenever prices changed enough to make switching advantageous. Within the past few years, switching away from steel had slowed considerably, since many of the most attractive substitution possibilities had run their course.

Assembled and finished plastic parts were generally less expensive than steel parts because of cheaper tooling costs and because one plastic part could take the place of several steel parts that had to be welded or bolted, thus allowing labor savings in assembly. Plastics were also lighter and more corrosion resistant. On the other hand, steel had several advantages over plastics—superior surface finish, better paintability, and more adaptability to faster production speeds. The auto industry expected that steel would remain the material of choice for body skins well into the 1990s; so far, plastic body panels had not gained great acceptance among vehicle owners.

STEELMAKING TECHNOLOGY

Although the pace had quickened recently, steelmaking technology had evolved slowly over several centuries. The first blast furnace in the United States was built in the 1600s; until the 1900s the principal improvements involved increased size, better design, and speedier operation. Blast furnaces made molten iron from iron-ore pellets, crushed limestone, and coke. In the early 1900s the open hearth furnace (OHF) came into use; OHFs involved loading molten iron from the blast furnace, scrap steel, and limestone into a shallow steelmaking hearth open to flames from both ends. The process resulted in higher-quality steels needed in automobiles and certain other applications. The percentage of steel made in OHFs peaked in 1968 and fell to under 5 percent by 1990.

The technological replacement was the basic oxygen furnace (BOF), developed in Austria following World War II. The BOF utilized molten iron ore (pig iron) from a blast furnace, scrap steel, and oxygen fed into the vessel to produce a vigorous chemical reaction that accelerated the steelmaking process. Whereas the open hearth process consumed several hours, a basic oxygen furnace did the job in 45 minutes. In 1990 about 60 percent of domestic steel output was produced using BOFs.

The third steelmaking approach involved electric arc furnaces (EAFs). EAF technology bypassed the need for iron-ore preparation, coke ovens, and blast furnaces required in OHF and BOF technology (see Exhibit 6). The only raw material needed was scrap iron and steel. In EAFs an electric current arcs from one electrode to another inside the furnace to melt ferrous scrap; the molten steel is then formed into the desired shapes or poured into slabs for further processing. As of 1990, about 35 percent of the total raw steel production in the United States was produced in EAFs, up from 20 percent in 1975.

Integrated steel mills employed OHF and BOF technology. Electric arc furnaces were the mainstay of the minimills. Minimills producers were particularly cost efficient when a company could source its electric power economically and when scrap steel prices were relatively low. Moreover, minimills were designed in a manner that made technical updating and rebuilding a fairly simple, economical undertaking; this was in sharp contrast to integrated mills, where changing the production scheme called for major investments. The primary drawback to EAFs was the limited range of steel products that could be produced. Whereas the use of OHFs and BOFs gave integrated producers the ability to make all grades and shapes of steel products, minimills with EAFs were restricted to low-grade commodity steel products.

Continuous Casting Continuous casting was a relatively new production approach that greatly increased the efficiency of steelmaking by converting molten steel directly into solid shapes ready for rolling and finishing. Without continuous-casting equipment, the steel ingot produced by the furnace (be it OHF, BOF, or EAF), had to go through additional time-consuming production steps, including costly reheating, before it was converted to semifinished steel shapes. In mills with continuous-casting equipment, molten steel coming out of the furnace was transferred quickly into a ladle and poured into a container at the top of the caster where it was fed continuously into the caster. The molten steel then flowed downward through the caster in a continuous ribbon. As it moved through a series of water-cooled molds in the caster, it was sprayed with water, cooled, and turned into a more solidified state. Guided by rollers and channels, the solidifying steel was gradually directed onto a horizontal plane where, now solid, it was cut into 8- to 10-inch slabs of predetermined lengths. Exhibit 6 provides a simplified overview of the production steps in integrated mills as compared to minimills.

Continuous casting reduced operating costs about $30 per ton compared with the older ingot/slab process and, also, resulted in higher-quality steel. In the mid-1970s only about 15 percent of the steel produced in the United States was continuously

EXHIBIT 6 | **Comparative Steelmaking Methods**

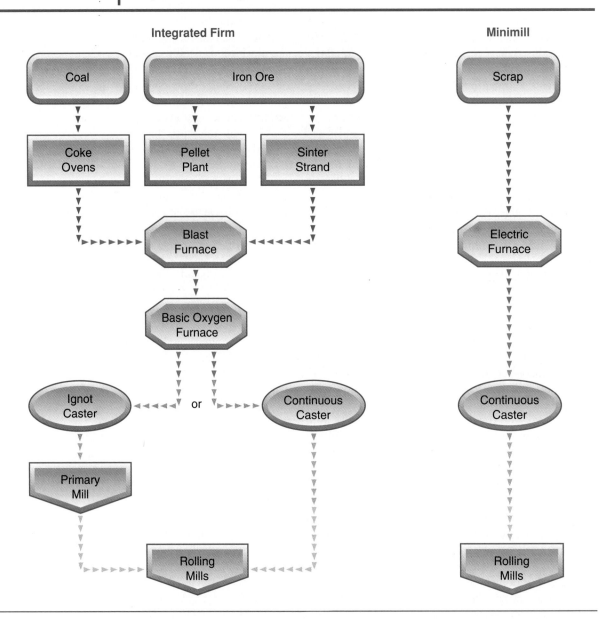

cast; by 1990, however, U.S. steelmakers had installed additional continuous-casting capability and boosted the percentage of continuously cast products to 70 percent— versus over 90 percent in Japan and over 80 percent in Europe. Over 95 percent of U.S. minimills used continuous casting.

THE RISING STATURE OF MINIMILLS

Minimill companies first began to be a force in the steel industry in the 1970s. The strategy of early minimills was to locate plants some distance away from integrated mills but relatively close to customer markets and scrap metal sources. Each plant was dedicated to the production of just one or two products. Product specialization boosted operating efficiency and simplified the marketing task. Most minimills operated with nonunion work forces to avoid union work rule restrictions and gain the flexibility to organize work in the most efficient manner. Workers were usually paid an hourly wage below the union scale but many companies used incentive pay schemes linked to worker output that pushed the compensation of minimill workers close to what union workers earned. Using their substantial cost advantage (anywhere from $25 to $200 per ton), minimills captured business by underpricing the integrated producers.

During the late 1970s and the 1980s, minimills in the United States prospered. A number of new minimill companies were formed and existing minimill firms opened new plants. Scrap remained in plentiful supply and for much of the period scrap prices declined relative to iron-ore prices. Output per worker at minimills ran about double the worker output at integrated mills; since the wages of minimill workers were comparable to workers' earnings in the unionized plants of large integrated producers, labor costs per ton at minimills were about half the labor costs of integrated companies. The market success of minimills was limited, however, to lower-grade commodity steel products like reinforcing bars (rebar) used in construction—angle steel, flats, rounds, channels, and I beams. By the mid-1980s minimills dominated the U.S. market for commodity steel (about 25 percent of total domestic steel shipments); no integrated producer had a significant market share in commodity steel and most had ceased production of such items entirely. In 1988, for the first time, the biggest minimill producer outshipped the ninth largest integrated producer. Going into 1990 minimills supplied 100 percent of the rebar market, 75 percent of the wire rod market, 60 percent of the hot-rolled bar market, and 30 percent of the light-to-medium structural steel market.

Because the minimills were running out of market share to take away from the integrated producers in commodity steel products, most were searching for opportunities to penetrate the markets for large structural steel products and flat-rolled sheet steels—segments traditionally dominated by domestic and foreign integrated producers. Chaparral Steel, a Texas-based minimill, had announced a 300,000-ton capacity expansion to increase its structural size capability from 18 inches to 24 inches. Nucor had formed a joint venture with a Japanese firm, Yamato, to produce 10-inch- to 24-inch-wide flange steel beams at a new 650,000-ton plant in Arkansas; the plant design could accommodate another 300,000 tons with improvements. Another minimill was considering opening a 700,000-ton plant to produce structurals in Texas. Such significant capacity additions would put additional competitive pressure on USX Corp. and Bethlehem Steel, the two biggest U.S. integrated producers in the medium and heavy structural steel market. The market for heavy structurals ranged from 4.8 to 6.3 million tons, with imports capturing up to 33 percent of shipments.

INNOVATIONS IN THIN-SLAB CASTING

However, the most significant market opportunity for minimills was in adapting the continuous-casting process to produce thin slabs rather than the customary thick slabs. With thin-slab casting, minimills could compete in the market for sheet- and strip-mill products (45 to 50 percent of total industry shipments) that had come to be the heart of the integrated producers' business. Without thin-slab casting, minimills were effectively precluded from making flat-rolled steel products because of the prohibitively high cost of building a hot strip mill to roll thick steel slabs into thin sheet and strip-steel products; conventional rolling equipment cost about $600 million to install and required a volume of 3 million tons annually for efficient operation. Thin-slab casting gave minimills entry access because thinner slabs, coming directly from the continuous caster, greatly reduced the capital costs for the necessary equipment and cut the volume needed to operate efficiently. Nucor's new mill at Crawfordsville was the first attempt by a U.S. minimill company to use newly developed thin-slab casting techniques to produce flat-rolled steel products. Most modern integrated mills used casting equipment that turned out slabs 8 inches to 10 inches thick; a few mills in the world could turn out 6-inch-thick slabs. Nucor's Crawfordsville plant utilized a novel machine that produced a 2-inch-thick slab that could be rolled, hot, into sheets with thicknesses of 0.1 to 0.5 inches, as specified by customers. Three other minimill companies had announced plans to follow Nucor's lead in building new plants to turn out flat-rolled steel products, though none as yet had commenced construction.

So far, competitors had not moved aggressively to embrace thin-slab casting technology, perhaps waiting for Nucor's pioneering effort to prove successful. Most recently, USX Corp., the largest integrated producer, had opted for a conventional slab casting machine for one of its plants. Birmingham Steel had canceled plans for a thin-slab plant using different equipment from that at Crawfordsville. The conventional industry view was that the metallurgical qualities of a thin cast would be poor. Integrated producers were said to be hesitant to take on the risks of an unproven technology, given the difficulty of realizing all the potential labor savings with a unionized work force; they also had the additional problem of how to engineer the technology into the configuration of an existing integrated mill at an acceptable cost.

COMPETITIVE CONDITIONS

The demand for steel products varied up and down with overall industrial production and economic activity. Steel prices generally rose during periods of strong demand. Price discounting was prevalent in slack times as mills tried to maintain production efficiency by operating as close to full capacity as possible. Once buyers were satisfied that the metallurgical properties and quality of a mill's products were satisfactory, purchase decisions hinged upon price and ability to meet delivery schedules. Steel users were price sensitive and nearly always shopped among the acceptable suppliers for the best price. Unless market demand was especially strong and mills were struggling to meet delivery schedules, price was usually decisive in choosing which mill to purchase from.

In 1989 and early 1990 market demand was soft, with shipments running about 5 percent under 1988 levels. The prices of many steel products had dropped as much as $50 per ton, shaving producers' profit margins significantly and reflecting active price competition and price discounting. Public spending for construction was off by 7 percent and industrial/commercial construction had been in a downtrend since 1987. Automakers were not expecting 1990 to be a strong year for automobile and truck sales. Increased scrap prices since late 1987 had eroded much of the raw material cost advantage that minimills previously had had over integrated producers.

THE POTENTIAL FOR COMPETITIVE CHANGE

A number of factors had the potential to alter the competitive structure of the steel industry, especially as concerned the position of the minimill producers. To begin with, entry barriers were low into the minimill segment; new minimills could be constructed and existing steel facilities could be converted into a cost-efficient minimill option for under $50 million. A number of entrepreneurial companies and investor groups, both inside and outside the minimill segment, were known to be looking at new start-up or conversion opportunities to make steel products for specialized market niches.

Second, the cost gap between minimills and fully integrated producers was narrowing in several respects. Integrated producers had cut their costs by downsizing their white-collar and blue-collar work forces, modernizing their plants, and gaining wage and work rule concessions in newly negotiated labor contracts. Meanwhile, minimills were confronted with rising prices and tighter supplies for high-quality scrap metal (see Exhibit 7). Widening use of continuous casting had reduced the supply of scrap generated in-house at fully integrated mills and prompted integrated producers to become bigger buyers of scrap on the open market. At the same time, with more and more flat-rolled sheet steel being zinc-coated to meet auto industry requirements for rustproofing, minimills were confronted with bigger dust disposal and heavy-metal pollution problems associated with recycling auto bodies. Industry observers believed that the quality of the available scrap supplies would progressively deteriorate, not only driving scrap prices higher but also forcing minimills to incur higher transportation costs as they had to go farther and farther out from mill-sites to obtain quality scrap supplies. Further complicating the scrap problem was the

EXHIBIT 7 | **Trends in the Consumption and Prices of Scrap Steel in the United States, 1972–88**

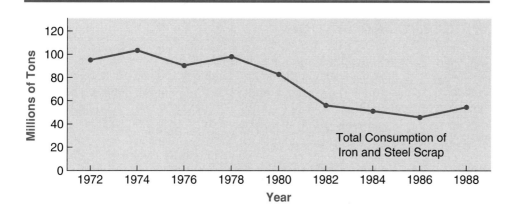

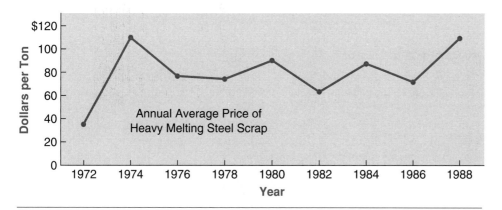

fragmented nature of the scrap metal junkyard business, a factor that forced scrap users to seek out needed supplies from a comparatively large number of dealers under highly competitive conditions.

A third force for competitive change was the fact that there were strong signs of overcapacity in certain commodity steel products, promoting the outbreak of frequent price discounting and the narrowing of profit margins during periods of weak demand. And last, the emergence of new steelmaking technologies having relative low capital costs to implement—like Nucor's innovative efforts in thin-slab casting—was opening up new product markets to small-scale production methods. Among the products being studied or already in production by at least one minimill were sheet steels, medium and heavy structural steels, seamless tubing, and special-quality bar steels. To the extent that technological changes opened more and more product doors to economic small-scale production and entailed low attendant capital costs, it was likely that an industry once dominated by a few integrated giants would gradually fragment into more and more small production units specializing in niche markets. Product specialization reduced downtime for product changeovers and equipment adjustments, required fewer operating skills, and economized on sales and engineering staffs—all of which translated into cost advantages for a minimill producer as compared to a fully integrated producer. Minimill companies led the steel industry in the United States in worker productivity, the use of state-of-the-art manufacturing technologies, guaranteed quality programs, new product development, and innovative marketing practices.

NUCOR CORPORATION

Although Nucor was the third largest minimill company in the United States, it was widely recognized as *the* leader of the minimill industry and one of the best-run steel companies in the world. The company built its first minimill in 1968 in Darlington, South Carolina; the mill had annual capacity of 120,000 tons. By 1990 the company was operating six minimills with combined capacity close to 3,600,000 tons. In addition, the company produced and marketed steel joists, girders, and steel deck through its Vulcraft Division. Five other small divisions produced steel bars, steel grinding balls, bolts, steel bearings and machined parts, and metal buildings. Management believed that Nucor was among the lowest-cost steel producers in the world. For a number of years, the prices charged by Nucor had been competitive with the prices of imported steel products. Nucor had operated profitably every quarter of every year that it had been in the minimill business.

Nucor's Steel Division

Nucor's steel division consisted of four mills—one each in South Carolina, Nebraska, Texas, and Utah—which produced steel reinforcing bars and light structural carbon and alloy steels. At all four mills steel scrap was melted in electric arc furnaces and poured directly into continuous-casting systems that produced steel billets (thick, long slabs of steel). Highly sophisticated rolling mills converted the billets into a wide range of chemistries and sizes of steel angles, straight-length and coiled round reinforcing rods, channel steel, flat bars, and other shapes. The mills were major suppliers of steel angles. Nucor Steel Division customers were primarily steel service centers, building construction firms, and the manufacturers of farm equipment, oil and gas equipment, mobile homes, bed frames, transmission towers, hand tools, automotive parts, highway signs, machinery, and industrial equipment.

Nucor's Darlington, South Carolina, mill had been expanded and extensively modernized since its construction in 1968. The other three mills were constructed between 1973 and 1981. A new continuous caster, a new reheat furnace, and a new high-speed rolling mill had recently been installed at the Nebraska mill at a cost of $35 million. All four Nucor plants were among the most modern and efficient mills in the United States. The total cost of all four mills, including expansions, improvements, and modernizations, averaged less than $175 per ton of current annual capacity.

Productivity was quite high at all four mills; the average Nucor worker produced 700 to 800 tons of steel per year versus 450 tons per employee at the mills of unionized integrated companies; labor costs at Nucor's mills ran about 15 percent of revenues, compared to 25 to 35 percent at integrated companies. All employees had a significant part of their compensation based on their productivity. Employee turnover in all mills was extremely low.

Scrap steel was the most significant cost item for Nucor, running $60 to $120 per ton depending on scrap prices and averaging 25 to 35 percent of selling price per ton. Energy costs amounted to about $45 per ton; Nucor management bargained aggressively with its power company suppliers to obtain the lowest possible rates on electric power. Exhibit 8 presents selected operating statistics for Nucor's four steel minimills.

Nucor used a far simpler pricing system than most other steel companies: All customers were charged the same announced price, regardless of quantity ordered. Management believed this allowed customers to maintain the lowest practical inventory. In contrast, other steel suppliers commonly granted quantity discounts and many made special price concessions to win a particular order. Nucor's steel prices were very competitive, generally being equal to or below the prices of imported steel. In years past a big portion of Nucor's sales growth had come at the expense of integrated and foreign producers. However, now that minimills had used their low-cost advantage to force integrated companies and imports out of the market for commodity steel products, Nucor was increasingly competing with other low-cost minimills for the available business in commodity steel products. Kenneth Iverson, Nucor's CEO, observed:

> We are now head-to-head against much tougher competition in the market for commodity steel products. It was no contest when we were up against the integrated companies. Now we are facing minimills who have the same scrap prices, the same electrical costs, and who use the same technologies.

It was this lack of further growth opportunity for low-end commodity steel products that prompted Iverson to push the development of thin-casting technology at Nucor and to form a joint venture with a Japanese partner to enter into the production of structural steel beams—two altogether new product markets for Nucor.

The New Crawfordsville Mill   In 1989 Nucor completed construction of a $270 million steel mill to produce 800,000 tons per year of hot- and cold-rolled sheet steel products near Crawfordsville, Indiana. This mill was the largest single project Nucor had ever undertaken and represented a capital intensity ($335 per ton of annual capacity) that was much larger than usual for a minimill operation. It used a new process for casting a thin slab 2 inches thick by 52 inches wide. Without reheating, the slab was

EXHIBIT 8 | **Actual and Estimated Performance of Nucor's Steel Division, 1984–93**

	1984	1985	1986	1987	1988	1989E	1990E	1991E	1992E	1993E
Capacity (000s of tons)										
Darlington, South Carolina	500	500	500	500	500	513	525	538	552	566
Norfolk, Nebraska	600	600	615	615	621	559	573	587	602	617
Jewett, Texas	600	600	615	630	646	650	666	683	700	717
Plymouth, Utah	400	400	410	550	594	609	624	640	656	672
Total	2,100	2,100	2,140	2,296	2,361	2,330	2,389	2,448	2,510	2,572
Raw Steel Production										
(000s of tons)										
Darlington	393	465	416	400	500	475	475	525	525	525
Norfolk	393	402	412	460	500	485	475	550	575	575
Jewett	465	451	443	446	550	480	500	625	650	650
Plymouth	291	375	435	474	545	560	600	575	600	600
Total	1,542	1,693	1,706	1,790	2,095	2,000	2,050	2,275	2,350	2,350
Operating Rate										
Darlington	79%	93%	83%	80%	100%	93%	90%	98%	95%	93%
Norfolk	66	67	67	75	80	87	83	94	96	93
Jewett	78	75	72	72	85	74	75	92	93	91
Plymouth	73	94	106	86	92	92	96	90	92	89
Average	73%	81%	80%	78%	89%	86%	86%	93%	94%	91%
Shipments of Steel Products										
(000s of tons)	990	1,152	1,140	1,313	1,437	1,450	1,460	1,677	1,744	1,735
Average Price/Ton	$282	$273	$278	$288	$340	$340	$320	$323	$326	$330
Operating Cost/Ton										
Scrap	$88	$79	$77	$76	$117	$112	$100	$102	$104	$106
Energy	43	44	44	45	44	44	44	45	45	46
Labor	55	52	52	51	50	52	52	52	52	52
Other direct production costs	54	54	50	51	50	55	53	53	53	53
Total	$240	$228	$223	$223	$261	$263	$249	$251	$254	$256
Divisional Revenue-Cost-Profit										
Performance (in millions of $)										
Revenues	$398.32	$439.35	$442.94	$501.12	$712.30	$680.00	$656.00	$735.28	$767.12	$774.79
Operating costs	338.89	367.45	355.25	387.39	547.20	529.01	510.47	572.05	596.75	602.71
Depreciation and administration	19.75	20.74	21.77	23.30	24.93	25.93	29.82	31.90	34.14	36.53
Division cost	358.64	388.18	377.03	410.69	572.13	554.94	540.28	603.95	630.89	639.23
Division profit	$ 39.68	$ 51.16	$ 65.91	$ 90.43	$140.17	$125.06	$115.72	$131.33	$136.23	$135.56

Source: R. Douglas Moffat, Robinson-Humphrey Equities Research, February 21, 1990.

cut to length and processed immediately on rolling equipment into sheets 0.096 to 0.500 inches thick, then coiled for shipment or further processing. The plant was equipped with state-of-the-art electric arc furnaces and rolling mill equipment, plus it enjoyed a substantial labor cost advantage arising from labor productivity of 0.75 to 1.0 man-hours/ton compared with 2.5 man-hours/ton at the most efficient integrated steel plants. Nucor was operating the plant with its customary incentive-compensated, nonunion labor force. The plant was in the heart of the sheet steel–consuming section of the United States, had an unusually attractive 10-year contract for electric power that yielded the lowest electric energy costs per ton of any Nucor plant, had ample supplies of high-quality scrap steel available locally, and was served by two railroads. Overall, Nucor management estimated that its production costs at Crawfordsville would run about $100 per ton lower than the costs incurred by integrated producers. Exhibit 9 presents actual and estimated operating performances for the mill.

Despite high start-up and debugging costs (about $45 million), the new thin-slab process at Crawfordsville had turned out quality steel during its first 10 months of operation, with some 90 percent of the latest months' output being prime quality metallurgically. A variety of superficial surface defects, however, were holding back production and delaying the qualification process with potential purchasers. Several sections of the plant had to be redesigned and reequipped to eliminate some of the

EXHIBIT 9 | Actual and Estimated Performance of Nucor's Crawfordsville Mill, 1989–93

	1988	1989E	1990E	1991E	1992E	1993E
Production (000s of tons)						
Hot rolled		40	170	450	500	600
Cold rolled		0	300	350	400	400
Total		40	470	800	900	1000
Price/Ton						
Hot		$320	$345	$400	$425	$450
Cold		475	450	500	525	550
Average	$450	$320	$412	$444	$469	$490
Production Costs/Ton						
Scrap	$142	$112	$110	$122	$129	$131
Labor	50	60	48	40	35	35
Energy	44	44	30	30	30	30
Hot rolling	135	115	111	95	95	95
Cold rolling	60	54	55	35	33	32
Total	$431	$385	$354	$322	$322	$323
Overall Revenues-Costs-Profits						
(in millions of $)						
Revenues	$ 0.00	$ 12.80	$193.65	$355.00	$422.50	$490.00
Operating costs	0.00	15.41	166.15	257.60	290.06	322.71
Operating profit	0.00	(2.61)	27.51	97.40	132.44	167.29
Depreciation and administration	0.00	12.00	21.00	24.00	24.00	24.00
Start-up cost	12.00	33.40	0.00			
Division profit	$(12.00)	$(48.01)	$6.50	$73.40	$108.44	$143.29

Source: R. Douglas Moffat, Robinson-Humphrey Equities Research, February 21, 1990.

trouble spots; this had lengthened the time frame to break in the plant and increased start-up costs. As of August 1990, weekly production had not exceeded 10,000 tons, versus a planned capacity of about 16,000 tons weekly. Nucor management was confident that the problems it was having mastering the technology would be worked out and that the plant would be close to capacity production by the end of 1990.

Nucor had spent $5 million on engineering for a second plant; the second plant design incorporated numerous improvements based on experiences at Crawfordsville, and management was anticipating that the second plant could be brought up to capacity production in perhaps half the time needed at Crawfordsville and with less expense. Air-quality monitoring at several potential sites was already in progress in order to fast-track the construction of additional plants. Nucor was also working on ways to expand the width of the sheets its new flat-rolled process could turn out. At 52 inches wide, Crawfordsville's steel was too narrow for hoods, doors, and other body parts that accounted for 60 to 70 percent of the steel consumption of the motor vehicle industry.

NUCOR-YAMATO'S STRUCTURAL BEAM MILL

Nucor and Yamato Kogyo, one of Japan's major producers of wide-flange steel beams, were partners in a new 650,000-ton minimill in Blytheville, Arkansas, that produced wide-flange steel beams and heavy structural steel products. The plant had cost $220 million. Nucor had 51 percent ownership in the joint venture. For more than 10 years Yamato Kogyo had used a special continuous-casting method that turned out a semifinished beam closer in shape to a finished beam than could be achieved by traditional methods; Yamato's technology was being used in the Arkansas mill. Operations had started in the second half of 1988; within six months the mill was operating profitably. By early 1990 the mill was at capacity production and had orders for all of its output. Virtually all of the sales came at the expense of integrated producers; approximately 100,000 tons were exported to Japan, Indonesia, Norway, and several other countries.

Nucor employed 406 people at the Blytheville plant. It took approximately 1 man-hour of labor to produce a ton of steel, compared with 1.7 to 2.0 man-hours per ton typical at Japanese plants. The mill enjoyed very favorable electric rates, a factor that was critical in selecting the Blytheville location. Melting capacity was between 900,000 and 1,000,000 tons annually, but the capacity of the rolling mill was 750,000 tons. Nucor planned to continue exporting as long as it could price competitively and as long as melting capacity for producing semifinished beams and blooms (slabs suitable for forming semifinished shapes) exceeded the mill's capacity to roll finished shapes. Studies were under way to expand this mill's capacity. The mill was laid out for an easy expansion to 1 million tons per year at an incremental capital investment of $25 million; very few additional workers would be needed.

Direct production costs averaged just over $300 per ton in 1989 but had dropped to $275 per ton in early 1990 as additional operating experience produced internal efficiency gains. Further efficiencies, driving costs down to $250 to $265 per ton, were expected. Nucor's costs allowed it to be competitive in Japan at current exchange rates. Margins were attractive, despite the fact that market prices had dropped from $400 to $355 per ton during 1989, as Nucor took the industry lead in cutting prices to win orders for the new mill's output. Exhibit 10 provides estimates of the mill's costs and profit contribution.

EXHIBIT 10 | **Actual and Estimated Performance of Nucor-Yamato's Structural Beam Mill, 1988–93**

	1988	1989E	1990E	1991E	1992E	1993E
Production (000s of tons)	65	625	650	750	850	1,000
Average Price/Ton	$400	$380	$350	$390	$395	$400
Costs/Ton						
Scrap	$117	$112	$100	$102	$104	$106
Energy	30	25	20	20	20	20
Labor	80	33	20	28	28	28
Rolling	140	125	100	100	100	100
Other	25	10	10	10	10	10
Total	$392	$305	$250	$260	$262	$264
Overall Revenues-Costs-Profits (in millions of $)						
Revenues	$ 26.00	$237.50	$227.50	$292.50	$335.75	$400.00
Operating costs	25.48	190.63	162.50	195.00	222.73	264.12
Operating profit	0.52	46.88	65.00	97.50	113.02	135.88
Depreciation	2.93	23.13	24.05	27.75	31.45	37.00
Start-up costs	36.60	0	0	0	0	0
Division profit	$(39.01)	$ 23.75	$ 40.95	$ 69.75	$ 81.57	$ 98.88

Source: R. Douglas Moffat, Robinson-Humphrey Equities Research, February 21, 1990.

The wide-flange beam market was an estimated 4 million tons in 1990, with imports accounting for a 27 percent market share. Domestic producers had 3 million tons of capacity in place. Chaparral Steel was bringing a new 500,000-ton plant on-line in 1991, and Northwestern Steel and Wire was planning to reopen a 500,000-ton mill in Houston obtained from Armco Steel. Chaparral's plant had a novel thin-casting feature that produced a semifinished beam even closer to final shape than Blytheville's product, but its output was thought to be aimed more at the lighter structural segment, whereas the beams at Blytheville were for heavy structural uses.

THE VULCRAFT DIVISION

Nucor's Vulcraft Division was the largest U.S. producer of steel joists and joist girders; these products formed support systems for warehouses, retail stores, shopping centers, manufacturing buildings, schools, churches, and, to a lesser extent, multistory buildings and apartments. The division also produced steel deck for floor and roof systems; steel deck was specified in 90 percent of the buildings using steel joists and joist girders. Vulcraft was Nucor's original steel business and it was management's desire to supply Vulcraft's basic steel needs internally that prompted the company to integrate backward into minimills and steelmaking. Material costs, primarily steel, represented about 50 percent of Vulcraft's sales dollar; about 95 percent of Vulcraft's steel requirements were obtained from Nucor's steel plants. Vulcraft's strategy was to be the low-cost supplier of joists. The division competed with a large number of other joist manufacturers. Competition centered around timely delivery and price.

Vulcraft's products were produced and marketed nationally from six plants. Joists were manufactured on assembly lines. The steel moved on rolling conveyors from station to station. Teams of workers at each station cut and bent the steel to shape, welded joists together, drilled holes in them, and painted the finished joists. Almost all Vulcraft production employees worked under a group incentive system that offered weekly bonuses for above-standard performance. The division had a fleet of 150 trucks to ensure on-time delivery.

Joist and joist girder sales were obtained by competitive bidding. Vulcraft provided price quotes on 80 to 90 percent of the domestic buildings using joists and joist girders; in 1989 Vulcraft's market share was about 35 percent of total domestic sales. Vulcraft's joist sales had been in the 445,000-ton-per-year range for the past three years; current joist production capacity was just over 600,000 tons. Vulcraft's sales of steel deck were in the 140,000-ton range, with increases to the 260,000-ton range expected by 1993; operating profits from deck sales in 1989 were about $7 million, and increases to about $14 million by 1993 were being anticipated. Exhibit 11 provides data on the costs and profitability of Vulcraft's joist and deck products.

NUCOR COLD FINISH BAR DIVISION

Nucor had three facilities that produced turned, ground, and polished steel bars in round, hexagon, square, and flat rectangular shapes; such cold-finished steel products were used extensively in making machine shafts and precision parts. All three facilities were among the most modern in the world and used in-line electronic testing to ensure outstanding quality. The division obtained its steel from nearby Nucor minimills. Costs were low enough to permit competitive pricing. Nucor's current share of this segment was 16 percent. Total market segment size was about 1,000,000 tons. Total capacity at Nucor's three facilities was close to 200,000 tons. Nucor management expected sales and earnings of this division to increase over the next several years (see Exhibit 12).

OTHER DIVISIONS

Nucor had four other small divisions with combined sales of about $90 million in 1989. Nucor Grinding Balls produced steel grinding balls in Utah for the mining industry; the division was a low-cost producer and was able to charge very competitive sales prices. Nucor Fastener operated a state-of-the-art bolt-making facility having annual capacity of 45,000 tons; the plant was highly automated and had fewer employees than comparable facilities. Nucor Fastener competed in a highly competitive market dominated by foreign suppliers; the plant ran close to capacity in 1989, with the division capturing a 12 percent market share. Nucor Machined Products, acquired in 1986, produced high-quality steel parts and bearings for a variety of large industrial users; a portion of its steel came from Nucor Cold Finish. Nucor Building Products commenced operations in 1988 to produce metal buildings and metal framing; much of its steel was supplied by Nucor's minimills. By 1993 these divisions were expected to be generating combined revenues of about $135 million and combined operating profits of about $13 million. A fifth division, Research Chemicals, was sold in 1988 at a profit of $38.6 million. In 1989 Nucor's minimills supplied about 525,000 tons of steel (about 20 percent of total production) to the company's Vulcraft, Cold Finish, Grinding Balls, and other divisions.

KEN IVERSON AND THE NUCOR CULTURE

Kenneth Iverson took over the reins of Nucor in 1965 before Nucor's entry into minimills. He had previously been general manager of Vulcraft, then the only profitable part of Nucor. It was Iverson who decided that Nucor ought to be making steel to supply Vulcraft. Iverson's goal was to be able to match the prices of imported steel:

EXHIBIT 11 | Actual and Estimated Performance of Nucor's Vulcraft Division, 1984–93

Joist Products	1984	1985	1986	1987	1988	1989E	1990E	1991E	1992E	1993E
Production (000s of tons)	424	471	453	444	446	446	430	430	430	430
Percent change	21.93%	9.98%	(3.97)%	(2.03)%	0.00%	(3.26)%	0.00%	0.00%	0.00%	0.00%
Average price/ton	$590	$595	$575	$559	$595	$608	$590	$613	$636	$655
Cost / ton										
Steel	$275	$263	$268	$278	$330	$330	$310	$313	$316	$320
Conversion	163	158	152	152	152	152	152	156	161	166
Freight	50	23	45	45	45	45	45	45	45	45
Total	$488	$444	$464	$475	$527	$527	$507	$515	$522	$531
Overall joist revenues-costs-profits (in millions of $)										
Revenues	$250.16	$280.15	$260.48	$248.20	$264.14	$261.40	$253.66	$263.42	$273.47	$281.67
Operating costs	206.91	208.99	210.39	210.82	233.91	226.53	217.93	221.27	224.67	228.15
Depreciation and administration	8.50	9.35	10.00	10.70	11.45	12.26	13.11	14.03	15.01	16.07
Division profit	$ 34.75	$ 61.90	$ 40.08	$ 26.67	$ 18.77	$ 22.61	$ 22.61	$ 28.12	$ 33.78	$ 37.45

Deck Products	1984	1985	1986	1987	1988	1989E	1990E	1991E	1992E	1993E
Production (000s of tons)	118	169	176	154	147	135	149	201	231	266
Price/ton	$600	$600	$600	$575	$670	$670	$620	$670	$690	$711
Cost/ton										
Steel	455	457	456	447	520	515	450	500	525	500
Conversion	45	45	45	47	45	45	47	47	47	47
Freight	35	35	34	35	35	35	37	39	41	43
Total	$535	$537	$536	$529	$600	$595	$534	$586	$613	$640
Overall deck revenues-costs-profits (in millions of $)										
Revenues	$70.80	$101.40	$105.60	$88.55	$98.49	$90.61	$92.23	$134.56	$159.38	$188.79
Operating cost	63.13	90.76	94.27	81.53	88.23	80.50	79.47	117.70	141.58	170.00
Depreciation and administration	2.49	2.74	2.88	3.02	3.17	3.33	3.50	3.67	3.85	4.05
Division profit	$ 5.18	$ 7.90	$ 8.45	$ 4.00	$ 7.09	$ 6.78	$ 9.26	$ 13.18	$ 13.95	$ 14.74

EXHIBIT 12 | **Actual and Estimated Performance of Nucor's Cold Finish Bar Division, 1984–93**

	1984	1985	1986	1987	1988	1989E	1990E	1991E	1992E	1993E
Production (000s of tons)	90	87	108	133	155	160	160	168	176	185
Price/ton	$450	$440	$462	$456	$515	$515	$505	$505	$505	$505
Costs/ton	$378	$368	$449	$421	$451	$460	$450	$450	$450	$450
Division performance (in millions of $)										
Revenues	$40.60	$38.38	$49.90	$60.65	$79.83	$82.48	$80.80	$84.82	$89.06	$93.51
Operating cost	34.00	32.00	48.50	55.95	69.91	73.54	71.91	75.53	79.31	83.28
Division profit	$ 6.60	$ 6.38	$ 1.40	$ 4.70	$ 9.92	$ 8.94	$ 8.89	$ 9.39	$ 9.75	$10.23

Source: R. Douglas Moffat, Robinson-Humphrey Equities Research, February 21, 1990.

"We had some vision that if we were successful, we could expand and create another business by selling steel in the general marketplace."

During his tenure as CEO, Iverson had consciously modeled Nucor on certain bedrock values: productivity, simplicity, thrift, and innovation.

Productivity Iverson liked to contrast Nucor to integrated companies. He recounted a field trip he had taken to an integrated steel plant when he was a student at Purdue: "This was the late afternoon. We were touring through the plant, and we actually had to step over workers who were sleeping there. I decided right then that I didn't want to work for a big steel plant." As Nucor's CEO, Iverson saw to it that workers had a strong incentive to be as productive as possible. Work teams had production standards and were paid bonuses proportional to the amount their output exceeded the standard—production 25 percent above the standard resulted in a 25 percent wage bonus, paid the following week.

Simplicity and Thrift Iverson and other managers at Nucor had developed practices and symbols that conveyed simplicity and reinforced the company's low-cost producer strategy. One of their notable achievements was lean staffing and a streamlined organizational structure. Only four levels separated the official hierarchy: workers, department managers, division managers, corporate. Iverson said:

> You can tell a lot about a company by looking at its organization charts . . . If you see a lot of staff, you can bet that it is not a very efficient organization . . . Secondly, don't have assistants. We do not have that title and prohibit it in our company . . . And one of the most important things is to restrict as much as possible the number of management layers . . . It is probably the most important single factor in business.

Nucor's spartan values were most evident at its corporate headquarters. Instead of having a handsome, expensive showcase building sited on landscaped grounds, Nucor rented a few thousand square feet of the fourth floor of a nondescript office building with an insurance company's name on it. The only clue that Nucor was there was its name (listed in ordinary-size letters) in the building directory. The office decor was spartan, simple, and functional. Under 30 people worked in the headquarters as of 1990, up from 16 in 1985. The latest additions were attributable to Nucor's growth and planned expansions. The company assiduously avoided the normal paraphernalia of bureaucracy. No one had a formal job description. The company had no written mission statement and no written strategic plan. There was little paperwork, few regular reports, and fewer meetings. Iverson commented on his staff and how it functioned:

> They are all very sharp people. We don't centralize anything. We have a financial vice president, a president, a manager of personnel, a planner, internal auditing, and accounting . . . With such a small staff there are opportunities you miss and things you don't do well because you don't have time . . . But the advantages so far outweigh the disadvantages . . . We focus on what can really benefit the business . . . We don't have job descriptions, we just kind of divide up the work.

Innovation Nucor was a leading innovator among steel minimills and also in the joist business. The company aggressively searched for ways to improve its production methods and was noted for its experimentation with new technologies. Internally, much emphasis was placed on improving efficiency and achieving lower costs. Cost-saving opportunities were pursued relentlessly and all plant managers were quick to install cutting-edge technologies and improve production practices to boost efficiency and drive costs down. As a consequence, Nucor plants tended to be kept in state-of-the-art condition despite their having been constructed years earlier. The new Crawfordsville mill was the result of over five years of research and engineering study into pioneering thin-slab casting; Nucor had invested almost $25 million of its own money to develop the technology and had monitored experimental efforts worldwide. Iverson and other Nucor executives had kept pushing R&D to make thin-slab casting commercially feasible despite widespread skepticism across the industry that such an effort would pay off.

KEN IVERSON: PUBLIC FIGURE

Nucor's success had made Iverson a public figure. He had been interviewed by newspapers, magazines, radio, and TV; he spoke to industry groups and business schools; and he had been called to testify before Congress. He explained why he was willing to devote his time to these extracurricular activities:

> Generally, our policy is to stay as far away as we can from government . . . except that I felt so strongly about protectionism that I thought I should make my views known—especially because our view is so different from the other steel mills . . . Talking to investors is an important part of the company's relationship with the marketplace . . . The company gets a direct benefit and it makes good sense . . . I do some talks at business schools just from the standpoint that I get pleasure out of that . . . We do occasionally hire MBAs, but we haven't had much success with them.

Iverson had a casual, informal, and unaffected style. His office was neither large nor furnished with expensive decorations. For lunch he took visitors across the street to a delicatessen—their "executive dining room"—for a quick sandwich. Nucor had no executive parking spaces, no executive restrooms, no company cars. Everyone, including Iverson, flew coach class. When Iverson went to New York he rode the subway instead of taking a limousine or taxi. Other Nucor managers followed Iverson's example, shunning ostentation, luxury, and status symbols common among other successful companies.

ORGANIZATION

Following Iverson's "lean management" philosophy, only four levels of management separated Iverson from the hourly employees. At corporate headquarters they joked that with four promotions, a janitor could become CEO! Exhibit 13 depicts Nucor's

EXHIBIT 13 | **Nucor's Organization Structure, 1990**

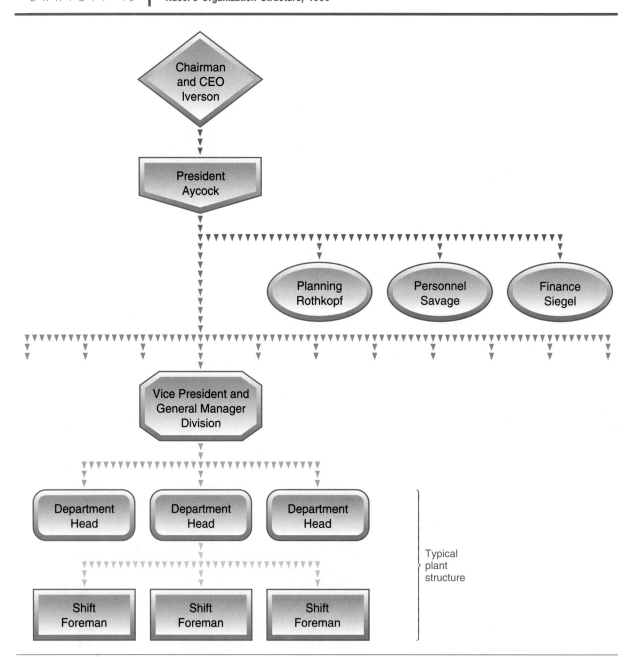

Note: Nucor's six steel mills (divisions), six joist plants, fastener division, and machined products division were each headed by a vice president and general manager.

organization chart. Below the corporate level the company was organized into divisions. These divisions roughly corresponded to plant locations.

In 1984, under the pressure of the growing size of the company and Iverson's busy public role, the jobs of president and CEO were separated. By trying to be "everything to everyone," Iverson was spreading himself a little thin. Dave Aycock was promoted from a plant manager's job to president, responsible for day-to-day operations of Nucor. Aycock talked about his role:

I worked at Vulcraft when it was acquired by Nucor in 1955 . . . I've been in this new job for about a year . . . It's very exciting . . . If I had actually known roughly half of what I thought I knew, I would probably have been more valuable . . . Most of my time has been spent learning the personalities, the reactions, and philosophies of the operating personnel . . . Many of them were glad to see the change because they thought Ken was overworked.

Division Management Because Nucor had a very small headquarters staff (about 30 people in 1990) and because of top management's great confidence in operating personnel, division managers played a key role in decision-making. Iverson said of the division managers: "They are all vice presidents, and they are behind our success. They make the policies of this company. Most of them have been with Nucor at least 10 years. But their pay is based on how this company does—not on how well their division does—it's the group concept again."

Corporate-Division Interaction Contact between divisions and corporate headquarters was limited to a report of production volume, costs, sales, and margin—the "monthly operations analysis." Each month every division received the "smiling face" report, comparing all the divisions across about a dozen categories of efficiency and performance. One division manager described how Iverson delegated and supervised:

> Mr. Iverson's style of management is to allow the manager all the latitude in the world. His involvement with managers is quite limited. As we have grown, he no longer has the time to visit with division managers more than once or twice a year . . . In a way I feel like I run my own company because I don't get marching orders from Mr. Iverson. He lets you run the division the way you see fit, and the only way he will step in is if he sees something he doesn't like, particularly bad profits, high costs, or whatever. But in the four years I've worked with him I don't recall a single instance where he issued an instruction to me to do something differently.

The casewriters asked a division manager how the corporate officers would handle a division that wasn't performing as it should:

> I imagine Dave Aycock would call first and come out later, but it would be appropriate to the situation. Ken and Dave are great psychologists. Right now, for instance, the steel business is showing a lower return on assets, but I don't feel any pressure on me because the market is not there. I do feel pressure to keep my costs down, and that is appropriate. If something went wrong Dave would know.

How does Nucor respond to problems in management performance?

> We had a situation where we were concerned about the performance of a particular employee . . . a department manager. Ken, Dave, and I sat down with the general manager to let him know where we were coming from. So now the ball is in his court. We will offer support and help that the general manager wants. Later I spent a long evening with the general manager and the department manager. Now the department manager understands the corporate concern. Ken will allow the general manager to resolve this issue. To do otherwise would take the trust out of the system . . . We are not going to just call someone in and say, "We're not satisfied. You're gone." But eventually, the string may run out. Ken will terminate people. He takes a long time to do it. I respect that. Ken would rather give people too much time than too little.

Important issues merited a phone call or perhaps a visit from a corporate officer. A division manager told the casewriters that he talked to headquarters about once a week. Divisions made their own decisions about hiring, purchasing, processes, and equipment. There was no formal limit on a division manager's spending authority.

Sales policy and personnel policy were set at the corporate level. Divisions didn't produce a plan, but: "People in this company have real firm ideas about what is going on and what will be happening . . . mostly by word-of-mouth." Relationships between the divisions were close. They shared ideas and information; the steel mills worked closely to meet the steel needs of the steel products divisions.

Decision-Making Division managers met formally in a group with corporate management three times a year at the "Roundtable." Sessions began at 7 AM and ended at 8 PM. At these meetings, budgets, capital expenditures, and changes in wages or benefits were agreed on, and department managers were reviewed. Iverson waited for a consensus to emerge about an alternative before going ahead with a decision. He did not impose decisions. Corporate officers described Nucor's decision-making processes:

> Over a long period of time, decisions in this company have been made at the lowest level that they can—subject to staying within the philosophy of the company. We get a lot of work done without too many managers. Ken has the business courage to stay out of the small things. It takes a lot of courage for general managers to resist the temptation to control every event.
>
> I can walk into Ken's office anytime and talk about anything I want to talk about. Agree or disagree with anything he has done. I don't agree with every decision that is made. I have the right to disagree. Sometimes I disagree strongly. Ken hears me out. Ken listens to other people. He does not feel that he is always right. Sometimes he will change his mind.
>
> I remember when I first started to work for Nucor and I was sitting down with Ken Iverson. He told me, "John, you are going to make at least three mistakes with this company in the first few years that you are with us. Each one of these mistakes will cost us $50,000. I want you to be aggressive, and I want you to make decisions. One word of caution. We don't mind you making the mistakes, but please don't make them all in one year."
>
> Ken defers a decision when the executives are strongly divided to give people a chance to consider it more. Ken is a superb negotiator. He might look at the various positions and say, "I have a compromise," and lay that out. Many times he can see a compromise that everyone is comfortable with.

FINANCE AND CAPITAL BUDGETING

The theme of simplicity also extended to financial matters. Sam Siegel, Nucor's vice president of finance, did not use a computer. He told the casewriters:

> When you make too many calculations they get in the way of business. Each of the divisions uses computers for many purposes, including financial analysis. You could make an economic case for centralizing some of that here at corporate headquarters. We could save money and create all kinds of information, but then we would have to hire more people to study that information.

No financial analysts worked at corporate headquarters. Nucor did not use sophisticated models of discounted cash flow or complicated formulas to govern capital expenditures, preferring an eclectic capital investment policy. Iverson commented: "Priority? No. We don't even do that with capital expenditures. Sometimes we'll say . . . we won't put up any buildings this year . . . But in recent years we've been able to fund anything we felt we needed. We don't do it by priorities." During the 1987–89 period, capital expenditures had totaled $665 million, versus $141 million over the preceding three years; the majority of the spending had gone for the Crawfordsville plant ($270 million) and for the new plant at Blytheville to build steel beams ($220 million). These projects were the two largest ever undertaken by the company; funds had been provided from operations and new long-term debt. In 1989, Nucor's ratio of long-term debt to total capital (long-term debt plus stockholders' equity) was 0.21; the company's objective was to keep the ratio below 0.3. Management believed the company had the financial ability to borrow significant additional funds without going above its leverage target. Capital expenditures for 1990 were projected to be in the range of $75 million, and the percentage of long-term debt to total capital was projected to fall below 20 percent by year-end 1990.

> We look at it from the standpoint of whether it's replacement and if it's modernization, what the payback period is, or if it is a new facility. In many cases the payback on a new steel mill is longer than you would like, but you can't afford not to do it. I think maybe that is where other manufacturing companies go wrong—where they have these rigid ideas about investments. If you don't put some of these investments in, after four or five years you are behind . . . You can't afford to fall behind, even if you don't get the payback. That's why the integrated steel companies didn't put in continuous casters, because they couldn't get the payback they wanted . . . Now they have got to do it . . . From an economic point of view they didn't do anything wrong, they didn't make a mistake.

Financial Reporting Each division had a controller who reported directly to the division manager and indirectly to Siegel. Siegel saw the role of his controllers as being broad: "Controllers who merely do financial work are not doing a good job. A controller should become involved with key plant operations . . . should learn the whole operation." Siegel spent only about one-half of his own time on strictly financial matters, contributing the other half toward "problems, issues, and projects" of importance to the company.

HUMAN RESOURCES

Nucor was known for its human resources practices. The casewriters visited a Vulcraft plant and talked with a department manager who had worked at Vulcraft for 16 years about what made Nucor different:

> Our plants are located strategically. The company puts them in rural areas, where we can find a good supply of quality labor-people who believe in hard work. We have beaten back three unionizing campaigns in the last 10 years. These employees are very loyal. In fact, we had to hire a guard to protect the union organizers from some of our workers. We see about 3 percent turnover and very little absenteeism. They are proud of working with us. It's fun when they come to you and ask for work.

Why did Nucor do so well with employees?

> Most companies want to take their profits out of their employees. We treat employees right. They are the ones who make the profits. Other companies aren't willing to offer what is needed to allow people to work. They can't see the dollar down the road for the nickel in their hand. Nucor's people make it strong.

Nucor's incentive systems had been a subject of much discussion and comment. *Fortune* estimated in 1981 that Nucor's workers earned an average of $5,000 more than union steelworkers. Nucor workers were among the highest-paid manufacturing, blue-collar employees in the United States.

> **Casewriter:** But aren't Nucor's wages high—how can a low-cost producer afford to pay top dollars for labor?

Iverson: They earn every bit of it! Sure, it's generous . . . There's a reason for it. It's hot, hard, dirty, dangerous, skilled work. We have melters who earn more than $40,000, and I'm glad they earn it. It's not what a person earns in an absolute sense, it's what he earns in relation to what he produces that matters.

The incentive system at Nucor had several key elements. John Savage, manager of personnel services, explained the company's personnel philosophy:

Our employee relations philosophy has four primary components . . . Management's first and foremost obligation to employees is to provide them the opportunity to earn according to their productivity . . . Next, we are obligated to manage the company in such a way that employees can feel that if they are doing their job properly, they will have a job tomorrow . . . Third, employees must believe that they are treated fairly . . . Lastly, employees must have an avenue of appeal if they believe they are being treated unfairly, to Mr. Iverson himself if necessary.

Everyone at Nucor participated in incentive plans. These incentives took several different forms depending on the type of work involved.

Production Incentives Production groups of 25 to 30 employees were assigned clearly measurable production tasks and the time needed to perform each task was based on historical time standards. If, for example, a group produced a joist in 50 percent less than standard time, they got a 50 percent bonus. Bonuses were paid at the end of the following week. When equipment sat idle, no bonus accrued. If an employee was absent for a day, he or she lost a week's bonus—a difference amounting to as much as $7 per hour. Although workers often earned wages far above the average for manufacturing, the system was very tough:

If you work real hard and you get performance, the payment is there next week . . . You worked like a dog and here is the money . . . There are lots of people who don't like to work that hard, and they don't last for long. We have had groups get so mad at a guy who wasn't carrying his weight that they chased him around a joist plant with a piece of angle iron and were gonna kill him . . . Don't get the idea that we're paternalistic. If you are late even five minutes you lose your bonus for the day. If you are late by more than 30 minutes because of sickness or anything else, you lose your bonus for the week. We do grant four "forgiveness" days a year. We have a melter, Phil Johnson, down in Darlington. One day a worker arrived at the plant and said that Phil had been in an auto accident and was sitting by his car on Route 52 holding his head. The foreman asked, "Why didn't you stop to help him?" The guy said, "And lose my bonus?"

Many Nucor workers earned between $30,000 and $50,000 per year. Nucor's monetary incentives made the company attractive to job seekers (see Exhibit 14). Iverson told a story about hiring new workers:

We needed a couple new employees for Darlington, so we put out a sign and put a small ad in the local paper. The ads told people to show up Saturday morning at the employment office at the plant. When Saturday rolled around, the first person to arrive at the personnel office was greeted by 1,200 anxious job seekers. There were so many of them that the size of the crowd began to interfere with access into and out of the plant. So the plant manager called the state police to send some officers over to control the crowd. But the sergeant at the state police barracks told the plant manager that he couldn't spare any officers. You see, he was shorthanded himself because three of his officers were at the plant applying for jobs!

Managerial Compensation Department managers received a bonus based on a percentage of their division's contribution to corporate earnings. In an operating division such bonuses could run as high as 50 percent of a person's base pay. In the corporate

EXHIBIT 14 | **Excerpts of Interviews with Hourly Employees at Nucor**

Jim

(Jim is 32 years old, did not finish school, and has worked at Vulcraft for 10 years. He works at a job that requires heavy lifting. Last year he earned about $38,500.)

"This is hard physical work. Getting used to it is tough, too. After I started working as a spliceman my upper body was sore for about a month . . . Before I came to work here I worked as a farmer and cut timber . . . I got this job through a friend who was already working here . . . I reckon I was very nervous when I started here, but people showed me how to work . . . The bonuses and the benefits are mighty good here . . . and I have never been laid off . . . I enjoy this work . . . This company is good to you. They might let employees go if they had problems, but first they'd give him a chance to straighten out . . . In 1981 things were slow and we only worked three or four days a week. Sometimes we would spend a day doing maintenance, painting, sweeping . . . and there wasn't no incentive. I was glad I was working . . . I was against the union."

Kerry

(Kerry is 31 years old, married, and expecting a child. He has worked on the production line for about three years.)

"I was laid off from my last job after working there five years. I went without work for three months. I got this job through a friend. My brother works as a supervisor for Nucor in Texas . . . This is good, hard work. You get dirty, too hot in the summer and too cold in the winter. They should air-condition the entire plant (laughs). On this joist line we have to work fast. Right now I'm working 8 1/2 hours a day, six days a week . . . I get good pay and benefits. Vulcraft is one of the better companies in Florence (South Carolina) . . . Everyone does not always get along, but we work as a team. Our supervisor has his off days . . . I want to get ahead in life, but I don't see openings for promotion here. Most of the foremen have had their jobs for a long time, and most people are senior to me in line . . . This place is very efficient. If I see a way to improve the work, I tell somebody. They will listen to you."

Other comments from hourly workers:

"I am running all day long. It gets hot and you get tired. My wife doesn't like it because sometimes I come home and fall asleep right away."

"When something goes down, people ask how they can help. Nobody sits around. Every minute you are down, it's like dollars out of your pocket. So everybody really hustles."

office the bonus could reach 30 percent of base pay. Plant employees who didn't work on the production line got a bonus based on either their division's profit contribution or corporate return on assets.

Senior officers had no employment contracts or company-paid pension plan. More than half of their compensation was based on company earnings. Their base salaries were set at about 70 percent of market rates for similar jobs. Ten percent of pretax earnings were set aside and allocated to senior officers according to their base salary. The base level was tied to a 12 percent return on shareholders' equity. Half the bonus was paid in cash, and half was deferred in the form of Nucor stock. In a profitable year officers could earn as much as 190 percent of their base salary as bonus and 115 percent on top of that in stock.

Other Compensation Incentives Nucor also operated a profit sharing trust. The plan called for 10 percent of pretax earnings to be assigned to profit sharing each year. Of that amount, 20 percent was paid to employees in the following year, and the remainder was held to fund the worker retirement program. Vesting in the trust was 20 percent after one year and 10 percent each following year. The arrangement had the effect of making the retirement income of Nucor employees depend on the company's success. Additionally, Nucor paid 10 percent of whatever amount an employee was willing to invest in Nucor stock, gave employees five shares of stock for each five years of employment, and occasionally paid extraordinary bonuses.

Lastly, Nucor ran a scholarship program for children of full-time employees. In 1985 over 300 children were enrolled in universities, colleges, and vocational schools. One family had educated eight children on Nucor's plan.

No Layoffs Nucor had never laid off or fired an employee for lack of work. Iverson explained how the company handled the need to make production cutbacks:

> When we have a difficult period, we don't lay anybody off . . . We call it our "share the pain program . . . The bonus system remains in place, but it's based on four days' production instead of five. The production workers' compensation drops about 25 percent, the department managers' drops 35 to 40 percent, and the division managers' can drop as much as 60 to 80 percent. Nobody complains. They understand. And they still push to get that bonus on the days they work.

The Downside Nucor's flat structure and steep incentives also had certain negative side effects. First, the incentive system was oriented toward the short term. If a general manager was thinking about a major capital investment project, he was also thinking about reducing his short-term income. Iverson described how the ups and downs of the incentive plans affected officers: "If the company can hit about 24 percent return on equity, an officer's salary can reach 300 percent of the base amount. It maxed out in 1979 and 1980. In 1981 total officers' compensation dropped way off. In 1980 I earned about $400,000, but in 1981 I earned $108,000. So officers have to watch their life-style!" Iverson's 1981 pay made him, according to *Fortune,* the lowest paid CEO in the Fortune 500 industrial ranking. Iverson commented that it was "something I was really a little proud of." In 1989 Iverson's salary was $220,000 and he earned an additional $107,750 in cash and stock incentive compensation. The company's 16 most senior officers earned a combined $2.7 million in salary and incentives in 1989.

Second, promotions came very slowly. Many managers had occupied their current jobs for a very long time. Nucor had experienced some problems in developing the skills of its firstline supervisors.

Many other companies studied Nucor's compensation plans. The casewriters asked John Savage about the visits other companies made to study Nucor's system:

> Many companies visit us. We had managers and union people from General Motors' Saturn project come in and spend a couple of days. They were oriented toward a bureaucratic style . . . You could tell it from their questions. I was more impressed with the union people than with the management people. The union people wanted to talk dirty, nitty-gritty issues. But the management people thought it was too simple, they didn't think it would work. Maybe their business is too complex for our system . . . We never hear from these visitors after they leave . . . I believe it would take five to seven years of working at this system before you could detect a measurable change.

High wages and employment stability got Nucor listed in the book *The 100 Best Companies to Work for in America.* A division manager summed up the Nucor human relations philosophy this way: "It's amazing what people can do if you let them. Nucor gives people responsibility and then stands behind them." Exhibit 14 presents selected excerpts from interviews with hourly employees about their jobs at Nucor.

STRATEGIC PLANNING AND NUCOR'S FUTURE

Nucor followed no written strategic plan, had no written objectives (except those stated in the incentive programs), and had no mission statement. Divisions were not asked to do formal strategic plans. We asked Sam Siegel about long-range strategic planning. He confided: "You can't predict the future . . . No matter how great you may think your decisions are, the future is unknown. You don't know what will happen . . . Nucor concentrates on the here-and-now. We do make five-year projections, and they are good about three months. Five to 10 years out is our philosophy." We also asked Bob Rothkopf (planning director) about planning at Nucor:

> I work on the strategic plan with Ken twice a year. It's formulated out of the projects we are looking at. He and I talk about the direction we feel the company is going . . . The elements of the most recent plan are that we take the basic level of the company today and project it out for five years. We look at net sales, net income, under different likely scenarios. We add new products or projects to that baseline.

Rothkopf had responsibility for generating most of the information he used in his forecasts. He often used consultants or other companies to get the information he needed. None of the other senior executives or division managers got deeply involved in developing long-term projections. Rothkopf described how decisions to pursue new projects were reached:

> Projects come from all over. Some come from our general managers, or from our suppliers, our customers . . . or come walking in the door here. Iverson is like a magnet for ideas, because of who he is and what Nucor is . . . We evaluate each project on its own, as it comes up. As each opportunity arises, we go in and investigate it. Some investigations are short; we throw out quite a few of them. We don't make any systematic search for these ideas.

Rothkopf compared Nucor's strategic decision-making approach to formal strategic planning done by other companies:

> Our businesses are all related and easy to keep track of. When a big decision comes up we discuss it. That's easy because of the simple structure of the company . . . Planning has disadvantages . . . time-consuming . . . expensive . . . hard to get the information for it . . . tends to get bureaucratic.

NUCOR'S FUTURE

Nucor's top strategic priority for the 1990s seemed straightforward and clear-cut: Assuming all went well in perfecting the thin-slab casting technology at Crawfordsville, then proceed to build additional mills for flat-rolled sheet steel products as fast as circumstances allowed. But Iverson wondered whether it was really that simple. What was there to worry about? How could the expansion opportunities best be financed? What threats were there to Nucor's strategy and how could these be defended against? Was Nucor's cost advantage sustainable?

HUSH PUPPIES CHILE

Allen J. Morrison, American Graduate School
of International Management
James Bowey, Bishop's University

In July 1992, Ricardo Swett, age 50, could look back on a decade of exceptional growth of his family-owned Hush Puppies line of casual shoes and retail outlets in Chile. Unlike the parent company, which had experienced serious difficulties in the 1980s, Hush Puppies in Chile had seen profits climb and sales explode by an average of 30 percent per year since 1985. By emphasizing excellence in design and by developing a chain of upscale retail shoe stores as well as an efficient factory, Hush Puppies had become the favorite brand of upper-class Chilean men. Expansion into women's and children's shoes during the last three years had also been successfully implemented.

As the company's market position in Chile soared, Ricardo Swett, who served as general manager of Hush Puppies in Chile, began to contemplate further expansion in other Latin American markets. The company had recently established a limited presence in Uruguay, Bolivia, and Paraguay and was beginning to enter Argentina with its line of Brooks athletic shoes. Ricardo was uncertain how fast the company should expand in these countries or whether efforts should be focused instead on promoting exports to North America or on consolidating the company's market position in Chile. Ricardo was also wondering about expanding into other retailing concepts in Chile, including athletics and outdoor clothing stores as well as children's shoes and apparel. Contemplating how and when to proceed, Ricardo recognized that key family members were waiting for a recommendation.

COMPANY BACKGROUND

Hush Puppies Chile began operations in 1980 through the concerted efforts of three brothers, Alfonso, Ricardo, and Juan Pablo Swett. In the early 1960s, the three brothers formed NORSEG, a start-up company that supplied safety equipment to industrial

Certain identifying information has been disguised to protect confidentiality. Copyright © 1993 by The American Graduate School of International Management-Thunderbird and Bishop's University.

and mining sites throughout Chile. With rising sales and a healthy cash flow, the brothers gradually expanded operations to include real estate development, several agricultural projects, and a 10 percent equity position in Elecmetal S.A., one of the largest industrial companies in Chile. Over time, these operations were organized as separate companies under the family-owned Costanera S.A.C.I. Holding Co.

WOLVERINE WORLD WIDE

In the spring of 1979, the three Swett brothers were informed by their advertising agency, Veritas, Ltd., that Wolverine World Wide was interested in expanding into Chile. Wolverine, based in Rockford, Michigan, controlled a portfolio of footwear brands including Hush Puppies casual shoes, Wolverine work and outdoor boots, Bates uniform shoes, and Brooks athletic shoes. Incorporated in 1954, Wolverine traced much of its initial success in footwear markets to its reliance on the production of casual pigskin shoes. In the mid-1950s, Wolverine developed a new elaborate pigskin tannage technology to take advantage of the characteristics of fine-grain pigskin and in 1958 introduced Hush Puppies casual pigskin shoes.

During the 1960s and 1970s, Hush Puppies emerged as a major brand with particular strength in the men's segment. The infamous basset hound became a widely recognized symbol for quality and comfort. Success in the United States was followed by international expansion, initially in Canada and Europe. In the early 1980s, spurred by fears that the U.S. government might lift import quotas on low-cost shoes from the Far East and Latin America, Wolverine moved to accelerate its international expansion. By 1992, Wolverine World Wide had established joint ventures or licensing agreements in over 40 countries, including most of Europe, Japan, and South America.

In Chile, Wolverine was looking for an agent to import or manufacture Hush Puppies branded shoes under license. In response to Wolverine's initiatives, the Swett brothers commissioned market research studies, which revealed that the Chilean shoe market was dominated by formal, dressy products and that no companies effectively met the demand for casual shoes. The market research also indicated that Bata, a large Canadian-owned shoe company with worldwide operations, controlled an estimated 60 percent share of the market in Chile. Bata Chile operated primarily as a manufacturing company and sold the bulk of its output to small independent stores throughout the country. Independent retailers had considerable power over manufacturers in controlling which brands to promote and which styles to display. Bata also operated several dozen of its own retail stores throughout Chile and was rumored to be considering further expansion.

Ricardo, Alfonso, and Juan Pablo believed that the open market of 1980 provided an ideal opportunity to start a new business. The brothers were particularly interested in the upper-class market in Chile which, they believed, had been exposed to the Hush Puppies brand through international travel and was familiar with its high quality and unique designs. Wolverine World Wide also appeared to be an open company; its managers were supportive and personable. The brothers agreed that any venture with Wolverine would succeed.

A MOVE TO RETAILING

The Swett brothers decided early on that retailing provided the key for getting Hush Puppies into Chile. According to Renato Figueroa, commercial manager of Hush Puppies Chile in 1980:

> Manufacturers risked their efforts, their capital, and their futures, while the retailers had control of the market . . . Retailers treated all brands alike, not giving special treatment to any brand in particular. [We came to the conclusion that] the best way was to build our own store chain . . . Our decision was based on the notion that we would be able to influence and handle the market. We would know our consumers. This would enable us to place Hush Puppies in a different position from the rest of the competition in Chile.

After negotiations with Wolverine, Hush Puppies Chile was given exclusive rights to import Hush Puppies shoes and develop retail outlets in Chile. Although no upfront fees were paid to Wolverine, the brothers committed themselves to opening as many as 25 retail stores within three years. Expectations were that the costs for the first 5 stores, including leasehold improvements, training, inventories, and so on, would total about $2 million. Of this amount, about $1 million would be borrowed. The remaining $1 million represented a substantial risk to the brothers.

It was agreed that stores would be designed as family concept outlets in which both parents and children could find comfortable, casual shoes. The best Hush Puppies shoes would be imported from around the world, with about 80 percent coming from the United States. The target market was identified as high-income consumers (referred to as the "ABC 1" market) or the top 10 percent of wage earners in Chile. Given the stratification of wealth in Chile, these consumers were comparable to upper-middle class and upper-income U.S. consumers, making the target market in Chile substantially more upscale than that in the United States.

Stores were situated in large, convenient locations primarily in the Santiago metropolitan area. The sales staff was extensively trained to relate to the upscale customers and were well compensated, reflecting the Swett brothers' desire for continuity and professionalism. Shoe prices were set at a 10 percent premium over average shoe prices and were the same in every store. In distant locations in Chile, the plan was for Hush Puppies Chile to grant franchises to independent retailers. As agreed upon by the brothers, Ricardo assumed responsibility as the general manager of Hush Puppies Chile. Juan Pablo Swett assumed responsibility as the general manager of NORSEG Chile. Alfonso was involved in major investment decisions and strategic planning for all family-owned businesses as well as some day-to-day decision-making at Hush Puppies Chile. By early 1982, Hush Puppies Chile had established seven shoe stores in the greater Santiago area.

A MOVE TO MANUFACTURING

After several years of promising economic growth, the bottom fell out of Latin American economies in 1982. Hit by slumping commodity prices, massive national debt, soaring interest rates, and worldwide recession, the Chilean economy, like every other in Latin America, plunged into a state of depression. In Chile, the GDP fell by 14 percent in 1982 alone. Between 1982 and 1985, unemployment officially hovered around 14 percent; unofficially, it surpassed 30 percent. During the same period, the Chilean peso lost two-thirds of its value against the U.S. dollar, leading to a commensurate rise in import costs.

With Hush Puppies Chile totally reliant on imported shoes, the company was devastated by the economic downturn. Only two options appeared possible: shut down in the face of massive losses or move into manufacturing. According to Alfonso and Ricardo:

> We believed in the brand. The consumer liked it. As a result, we had no choice but to get into manufacturing. All our businesses have always been very conservative with low debt load. So we weren't at real risk in the downturn. We saw the business in the long

term. Besides, we could get into manufacturing inexpensively since everyone else was getting out; real estate was cheap.

In April 1982, the Swett brothers made the decision to move Hush Puppies Chile into shoe manufacturing. In November 1982, a partnership was formed between Wolverine World Wide and Hush Puppies Chile, with 70 percent of the manufacturing joint venture owned by Hush Puppies Chile and 30 percent owned by Wolverine. Both partners agreed to contribute representative amounts of capital to ensure that manufacturing output met growth targets.

From Wolverine's perspective, a manufacturing facility in Chile made sense for a number of reasons. In 1981, import quotas ended in the United States and Wolverine moved aggressively to shift production overseas. Under the joint venture agreement with Hush Puppies Chile, Wolverine would have access to a new source of shoes made with low-cost Chilean labor. The U.S. company would also receive royalties on Hush Puppies sales as well as benefit from profit sharing from the Chilean production facility. Finally, Wolverine's wholly owned Puerto Rican affiliate would become an ongoing supplier of some selected components for the Chilean operation.

In February 1983, a small new manufacturing facility was opened in suburban Santiago that included approximately 10,000 square meters of manufacturing capacity, a two-story executive office complex, and a factory retail outlet. Manufacturing, import, and export sales were handled by Hush Puppies Chile, Ltd. Retail operations were organized under the separate company name of Commercial Puppies, Ltd.

Hush Puppies Chile and Commercial Puppies were both organized with their own boards of directors, which included the three Swett brothers as well as a small group of trusted Western-educated managers from the operating companies. Most directors served on two or three boards. Strategic decisions were made at the board level and passed down to the operating company general managers. While both Hush Puppies Chile and Commercial Puppies were recognized as separate companies with their own functional structures, managers worked closely together to coordinate activities.

RAPID GROWTH

By 1985, the Chilean economy started to turn around and from 1985 to 1990 the company enjoyed rapid growth. In 1985, Hush Puppies Chile added Brooks athletic shoes to fill out its product line. Brooks athletic shoes were owned by Wolverine and sales of the Brooks' brand in the United States had been boosted by the upsurge in interest in physical fitness. While some Brooks shoes were to be manufactured in Santiago, most were to be imported from the Far East. It was anticipated that about 70 percent of the Brooks shoes distributed in Chile would be sold to outside retailers; the remaining 30 percent would be sold in Hush Puppies shoe stores.

As overall sales picked up, Hush Puppies Chile and Commercial Puppies focused more on building and maintaining key brands. The objective was to develop a reputation for excellence in marketing by emphasizing advertising, service, and style. Feedback from retail stores proved a major strength in focusing design and manufacturing on consumer needs. Hush Puppies Chile managers regarded the company as market oriented, as opposed to manufacturing oriented, thus differentiating the company from many Far East suppliers. By the end of 1985, Commercial Puppies was managing 22 company-owned stores and Hush Puppies Chile was supervising four franchise stores.

To strengthen marketing efforts, advertising budgets were expanded, reaching 5 percent of sales in 1987. In 1987, the company started a major advertising program entitled "the pleasure of walking" that proved particularly appealing to increasingly health-conscious upper- and upper-middle-class Chileans. Follow-up multicolor ads promoting Hush Puppies' line of outdoor casual and hiking boots were placed in major newspapers and top magazines throughout the country (see Exhibit 1). Television advertisements were also developed, which focused on Hush Puppies as statements of quality and style. During the late 1980s and early 1990s, Hush Puppies Chile won three annual Wolverine World Wide awards for the quality of its advertising campaign and marketing strategy.

The company's strategy to strengthen the Hush Puppies brand succeeded. By the end of 1987, the production of shoes reached 265,000 pairs, an increase of 18 percent over 1986. In 1988, production increased an additional 15 percent to 305,000 pairs; in 1989, shoe production was up 29 percent to 392,000 pairs. Despite these impressive gains, the company remained relatively weak in two important categories: women's shoes and children's shoes. In an effort to reposition itself in these fast-growing segments, several bold initiatives were undertaken in the late 1980s.

A MOVE TO WOMEN'S AND CHILDREN'S SHOES

To strengthen the company's position in the women's shoe market, more effort was devoted to product design and marketing. The women's product manager, Cardina Schmidt, believed that prior to 1990 the women's product line had not adequately

EXHIBIT 1 | **Sample Advertisement Placed by Hush Puppies Chile in Major National Magazines**

satisfied the style and fashion demands of Chilean women. Good design was particularly important in the women's segment where styles changed nearly every six months. Women in the target segment were particularly fashion conscious and were generally familiar with the newest fashions in Europe and North America.

In order to make Hush Puppies more appealing to women, high-fashion shoes were imported from Italy, France, and Argentina. Hush Puppies Chile also hired exclusive designers to develop its own collection of women's shoes. Designers and managers regularly visited Hush Puppies stores to question women on desired design features like colors and styles. New window displays were designed to establish a more stylish image, and a major television advertising campaign was launched. As a result of these efforts, sales growth in the women's segment increased dramatically.

During this same period, the company also undertook a major initiative in children's shoes. The history of the company's efforts with children's shoes was reported to the casewriters by Sebastian Swett, a second-generation Swett and a product manager for kids' shoes:

> Surveys detected great opportunities for us in the children's market. The market was very traditional. It offered old models in brown or white . . . The market seemed willing to pay a higher price for shoes with aggressive colors and concepts, such as comfort and security . . . We had a few advantages, such as the excellent Hush Puppies image, which was attractive for children and easily identified . . . We also had several disadvantages. Our stores were not appropriate for selling kids' shoes; other competitors had years in the market; [and finally] we didn't have the machinery to develop a great collection for kids below 12 years in age.

In early 1990, Hush Puppies for Kids was launched, consisting of four different categories that varied according to the age of the child. Soft Puppies shoes were introduced for infants; Little Puppies were designed for children age 1 to 3 years; Young Puppies were introduced for children aged 4 to 8 years; and finally, Junior Puppies were designed for children age 9 to 14 years. The introduction was accompanied by extensive television advertising. In spite of the Swetts' lack of a history with children's shoes, Hush Puppies for Kids was an immediate success.

STRENGTHENING THE ATHLETIC SHOE POSITION

By the summer of 1989, Brooks was positioned as the number three brand in the Chilean athletic shoe market after Diadora and Adidas. In the United States, however, Brooks was a relatively weak brand, a fact not altogether lost on fashion-conscious Chilean adolescents, and L.A. Gear was emerging as the top trend shoe for adolescents. L.A. Gear was a relative newcomer in the athletic shoe industry and, to capitalize on its increasing popularity, had begun to search for international distributors. The opportunity to market L. A. Gear's more fashionable brand was clear and Alfonso approached the company in the summer of 1990.

After considerable discussion, L.A. Gear agreed in the fall of 1990 to work with Hush Puppies Chile to bring the L.A. Gear brand to Chile. L.A. Gear shoes would be imported from U.S. inventories or directly from the manufacturers in Korea and China, thus sparing Hush Puppies any manufacturing risks. Hush Puppies Chile's intention was to consolidate the L.A. Gear operations with those of Brooks; however, L.A. Gear insisted that Hush Puppies Chile create a distinct sales company to maximize the brand's potential. Wolverine World Wide was also very concerned about the impact that the L.A. Gear initiative would have on Brooks in Chile. In response, Costanera created Top Sport to handle sales of L.A. Gear shoes. A separate company, Coast Sport, was organized to manage all Brooks sales. It was hoped that creating separate companies for the two lines of athletic shoes would promote greater strategic focus on each brand as well as encourage new sales initiatives for athletic shoes.

WOLVERINE'S MANUFACTURING POSITION IS PURCHASED

In December 1991, Costanera acquired the 30 percent of Hush Puppies Chile operations owned by Wolverine World Wide. The buyout was prompted by Wolverine's failure to support Hush Puppies Chile's ambitious expansion plans. During late 1989 and 1990, manufacturing facilities were expanded over 30 percent in Chile to keep pace with booming demand. Plans called for production capacity to be increased by another 20 percent in 1991. New investment requirements in Chile as well as other countries, combined with the need to reinvest profits, translated into a negative cash flow for Wolverine. At the same time, Wolverine was facing changes in the business in the United States and was struggling to conserve capital. As a result, a buyout became an attractive option for both parties. The purchase of Wolverine's 30 percent share of manufacturing was estimated to have cost Costanera approximately $3.6 million. With the buyout complete, Hush Puppies Chile changed its name to Forus, S.A. In January 1992, the name of Commercial Puppies was changed to For-Shop, Ltd. Exhibit 2 provides a full organization chart for Costanera Holding.

Under the terms of the acquisition, Wolverine extended its licensing agreement to Forus for 20 years. In addition, Forus pushed for and received the rights to manufacture and sell Hush Puppies brands in Bolivia, Paraguay, and Uruguay. Forus was also licensed to sell—but not manufacture—Brooks athletic shoes in Bolivia, Paraguay, Uruguay, Argentina, and Peru. Outside these countries, sales of Hush Puppies or Brooks-branded products could only be made to other Wolverine licensees. For Wolverine, Costanera's program for growth, given its success in Chile, made it a logical strategic partner for building sales in Latin America. Increased sales in the region would mean higher royalties to Wolverine as well as an increase in the export of raw materials.

After the buyout, the relationship between Costanera and Wolverine remained strong. Both companies continued to share designs and coordinate product introductions. Forus also remained a major purchaser of leather and leather products as well as Brooks shoes. Exhibit 3 reports the extent of business relations between Forus and Wolverine World Wide over a six-year period.

GROWTH IN RETAIL OPERATIONS

By the end 1991, Forus had succeeded in significantly broadening the market appeal of its Hush Puppies brands. In the ABC1 men's market, Hush Puppies was number one in market share; in the ABC1 women's market, Hush Puppies was number five in terms of market share; and in the ABC1 children's market, Hush Puppies was number four in market share. Market mix for the ABC1 segment and Hush Puppies branded sales ratios on a unit volume basis are included in Exhibit 4.

At year-end 1991, total annual retail sales of Hush Puppies, Brooks, and L.A. Gear shoes amounted to 328,000 pairs. About 74 percent of these shoes were sold in 25 company-owned stores. An additional 9 percent of sales was generated through "Hush Puppies Corners," which had been established in shoe departments of 14 major retail department stores. In promoting Hush Puppies Corners, For-Shop agreed

EXHIBIT 2 | **Costanera Holdings: Organization Chart**

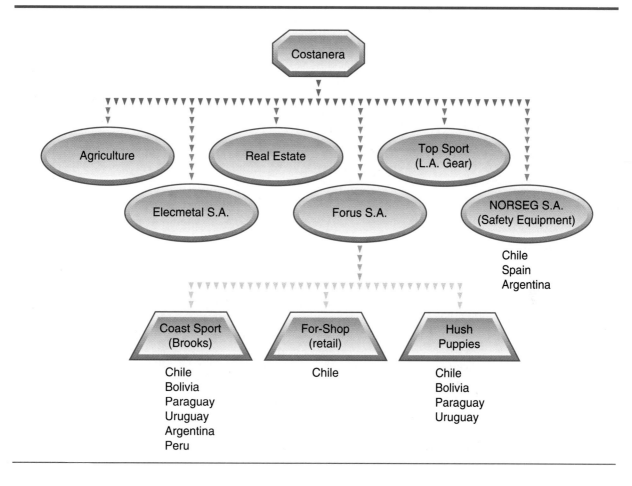

EXHIBIT 3 | **Business Relations with Wolverine World Wide** (*Thousands of U.S. dollars*)

	Total 1987–91	Projected 1992
Purchases		
Leather and raw material	$ 6,302	$2,000
Hush Puppies finished shoes	557	640
Brooks shoes	3,960	1,400
Total	$10,819	$4,040
Royalties		
Hush Puppies	$ 1,032	$ 500
Brooks	441	120
Total	$ 1,473	$ 620

to train sales employees and assist in designing and setting up displays. About 10 percent of the company's sales was also generated through small independent retail outlets. Franchise sales represented approximately 7 percent of total retail sales. In 1991, the company had five franchise stores located in isolated cities in Chile. By the summer of 1992, the number of company-owned retail stores in Chile had increased to 26, with 4 more planned by year-end. Exhibit 5 presents retail sales data for 1990 and 1991, as well as projections for 1992.

INTERNATIONAL EXPANSION

Although the Swett brothers were pleased with Hush Puppies' overall growth in Chile, they were constantly reminded of the vulnerability lessons of 1982. Certainly Costanera was a much more balanced company by mid-1992 than it had been 10 years earlier. It had a healthy balance sheet, a portfolio of popular American brand

EXHIBIT 4 | **ABC1 Segment Mix and Hush Puppies Sales Mix** (*December, 1991*)

ABC1 Market Mix%		Hush Puppies Sales Mix (%)		Hush Puppies Market Share (%)	
Men	24%	Men	46%	Men	30%
Women	47	Women	30	Women	8
Children	29	Children	24	Children	11

EXHIBIT 5 | **For-Shop: Retail Sales, 1990–92**

	1990	1991	1992*
Number of stores	25	25	26
Sales (pairs 000s):			
Hush Puppies men's	152	164	188
Hush Puppies women's	69	74	125
Hush Puppies children's	37	49	61
Sports shoes	31	41	44
Total pairs	289	328	418
Sales (US$000s):			
Total shoes	$8,575	$12,163	$17,260
Total accessories	519	841	1,226
Total	$9,094	$13,004	$18,486
Average US$ retail price (pair)	$29.67	$37.08	$41.29
Average monthly inventory (pairs 000s)	122	129	158
Annual inventory turnover	2.4	2.5	2.7
Number of employees	154	177	203

*1992 sales are estimates.

names, improving manufacturing capabilities, world-class design skills, and substantial marketing expertise. Despite these advantages, Ricardo and several managers began to realize that the depth of Hush Puppies Chile's market penetration, particularly in the ABC1 men's casuals, would lead to increased competition from new European and American brands.

With these concerns in mind, Ricardo began considering other alternatives for growth. A move into men's dress shoes was rejected, because the segment was already highly competitive and because managers at Hush Puppies Chile did not believe that their skill base would provide the company with a significant competitive advantage. However, other opportunities for growth were being seriously studied. These included growth by expanding exports to North America and Europe and growth through product and market diversification in South America.

EXPORT OPPORTUNITIES—NORTH AMERICA

Ever since it had begun manufacturing almost 10 years earlier, Hush Puppies Chile had always hoped to develop a strong export business, particularly to North America and Europe. Success in exports seemed likely, given Chile's comparative advantage of low-cost labor and Hush Puppies Chile's excellent styling and product-development skills. Hush Puppies Chile's manufacturing labor costs in 1991 averaged $2.00 per hour, including all benefits; in neighboring Argentina, wages in the shoe industry averaged from $2.25 to $2.50 per hour. In addition to being at least comparable in terms of costs, the quality and consistency of Chilean labor was generally regarded as superior to that available in neighboring countries.

From a company perspective, an emphasis on exporting seemed to make sense for two reasons. First, sales to the northern hemisphere could potentially offset cyclical sales in the southern hemisphere. Forus was typically over capacity in the period leading up to fall/winter (February through July) and under capacity in spring/summer (August through January). Any additional export sales during the off-season would provide a better utilization of plant and equipment while minimizing fluctuations in employment levels. Second, the additional export sales volume would allow the ever-increasing manufacturing and new-product development overheads to be spread over a larger volume, thereby boosting overall profits.

Despite the appeal, exports to North America and Europe remained relatively modest. One problem was that exports from Chile were expected to compete with much lower-cost footwear from China, India, and the Philippines. Hush Puppies' domestic target market was also the high-end segment, which added design and service costs that negated many of Chile's labor cost advantages. Also, Hush Puppies Chile's very diversified product line increased per-unit production costs through short production runs while at the same time removing opportunities for high volume exports. A final problem was that direct and indirect labor costs represented only about 25 percent of total manufacturing costs, thus limiting the company's ability to pursue a low-cost exporting strategy. Because of these difficulties, several managers in the company believed that an export strategy built on superior design and marketing had the most chance to succeed. Others disagreed, arguing that if Hush Puppies Chile were serious about substantially increasing exports to North America and Europe it would have to develop lower-priced shoes. Such a move would also open additional mass-market opportunities for the company in Chile.

The company had never seriously considered shifting manufacturing to lower-cost Asian countries. Difficulties in controlling overseas production and the need to respond to rather fickle customer needs undermined the potential savings of overseas manufacturing. Managers at Hush Puppies Chile also believed the company had no competitive advantage in importing. Estimates for 1992 were that the company would import about US$3.0 million in raw materials (mostly soles and leathers) and about US$1.7 million in finished shoes. The United States would supply approximately 25 percent of these imports, with the rest coming from the Far East, Argentina, Brazil, Italy, Spain, Germany, Mexico, and the United Kingdom.

OPPORTUNITIES IN LATIN AMERICA

From 1987 to 1991, the average annual sales growth for Forus, For-Shop, and Coast Sport was 20 percent per year. From 1990 to 1991, sales growth accelerated to a staggering 35 percent, encouraged in part by the rapid growth of the Chilean economy. Strict adherence to free markets and free trade had led to booming economic growth in Chile, with the economy expanding an average of 6 percent per year from 1987 to 1992. Many economists were predicting GDP growth of 10 percent per annum throughout the remainder of 1992, making Chile one of the fastest-growing economies in the world and an engine of economic growth in the region. (For a brief overview of Chile's economic development over the last two decades, see Exhibit 6.)

EXHIBIT 6 | **The Chilean Economy: A Brief Overveiw**

Political polarization under the left-wing government of President Salvador Allende (1970–73) brought the country close to a civil war and ended in September 1973 with a coup d'etat led by General Augusto Pinochet. During his 17-year rule, Pinochet turned to the writings of free market advocate and Nobel Prize-winning economist Milton Friedman to guide national industrial policy. Immediately after seizing power, martial law was imposed, the economy was liberalized, and foreign corporations were invited to return to Chile. Pinochet's 1980 blueprint for political democratization was completed on December 14, 1989, when a national plebescite was held and Patricio Alwin, the Christian Democratic leader of a center-left coalition, was elected president. He took office on March 11, 1990. While in mid-1992 Augusto Pinochet remained commander of the nation's armed forces, the emerging democracy seemed stable and strong to most observers.

The success of Chile's free market reforms after a decade of stagflation and debt crisis amazed many observers. Most economists attributed Chile's enviable economic growth to its unrelenting dedication to free markets. By mid-1992, the bulk of the Chilean left was no longer anticapitalist, and a remarkable degree of consensus existed in the country about the need to maintain a liberal market economy and prudent fiscal policies. The main dividing issues related to a new labor code granting more rights to unions, and the question of what to do about serious human rights violations that had occurred under the Pinochet regime.

Economic Data—Chile: 1983–91

	1983	1985	1987	1989	1991
GDP ($ billions)	$ 19.8	$ 15.6	$ 18.9	$ 25.4	$ 30.0
Population (millions)	11.7	12.1	12.5	13.0	13.1
GDP per head ($)	$1,692	$1,289	$1,512	$1,954	$2,239
Inflation (%)	23.1%	26.4%	21.5%	21.4%	18.7%
Unemployment (%)	17.4	10.9	8.0	4.8	5.2
Total debt/GDP (%)	91.9	130.7	109.3	68.4	63.1

Despite its interest in open markets, Chile has shunned involvement in Mercosur or the free trade zone that neighboring Paraguay, Uruguay, Argentina, and Brazil hoped to have running by 1994. Confident after nine years of stability and growth, Chile in 1992 was aspiring to become the first Latin American county to join the NAFTA. If NAFTA membership were to prove elusive, the government intended to pursue a free trade agreement with Japan, Chile's top export market after the United States.

The company's initiative in Latin America began in earnest in May 1989, when Hush Puppies Chile began exporting Hush Puppies shoes to Uruguay. With air freight to Uruguay averaging about US$0.55 per kilogram, transportation costs appeared favorable for exports. By the end of 1989, the company had sold more than 19,000 pairs of shoes in a country with a total population of just three million. In 1990, Hush Puppies Chile granted exclusive franchise rights to the Moliterno family, a diversified industrial company based in the capital city of Montevideo. Moliterno quickly established Hush Puppies Uruguay as a wholly owned subsidiary. During 1990, three Hush Puppies retail outlets were opened, two in Montevideo and one in Maldonado.

Despite high ambitions, sales remained weak. Ricardo Swett was convinced that Moliterno, with little experience in retailing, had chosen less than optimal retail locations. Stores were poorly maintained, and Moliterno spent essentially nothing on Hush Puppies advertising and promotion. Sales were also hurt by competition from low-priced footwear exported by financially strapped manufacturers in Argentina and Brazil.

In the spring of 1991, Forus purchased 55 percent of Hush Puppies Uruguay. According to Ricardo, Hush Puppies Chile had always wanted to be a partner with Moliterno. The original agreement included an option to buy a majority stake in Hush Puppies Uruguay that Forus decided to exercise. Under the terms of the investment, Forus and Moliterno contributed US$400,000 to create a new company called Hush Puppies Uruguay S.A., which in turn purchased the Hush Puppies-related assets of Moliterno. After gaining effective control over retailing, Hush Puppies Chile moved to strengthen operations. Sales employees received additional training, and new store locations were sought. By the end of 1991, three more Hush Puppies Uruguay stores were opened, bringing to six the total number of Hush Puppies locations in that country.

Essentially no Hush Puppies shoes were exported to Paraguay in 1991, and no changes were planned for 1992. Customs duties on shoes averaged 70 percent in Paraguay but were being slowly cut under pressure from the GATT, as well as broader initiatives undertaken in creating the Southern Cone Economic Market. Ricardo Swett believed that as the economy opened up in 1993, Forus would begin some modest exports.

In Bolivia, a country of seven million, Forus established a licensing agreement with Global Trading Company of La Paz. Although the agreement had been in place for less than a year, two stores had been opened and Hush Puppies Corners had been set up in two department stores. Ricardo estimated that exports for 1992 would amount to about 15,000 pairs, or about US$525,000. Because of prevailing import tariffs, retail prices in Bolivia were set at a 10 percent premium over Chilean net prices. Although it was too early for managers at Forus to evaluate the long-term effectiveness of Global Trading Company in Bolivia, Forus had an option to buy up to a 50 percent equity position in the company at a time of its choosing.

In 1992, the company's efforts in Argentina were focused exclusively on promoting its Brooks line of athletic shoes. Coast Sport Argentina was established in 1991 and acted exclusively as a wholesaler for a variety of independent retail outlets in the country. Eighty percent of the new company was owned by Coast Sport Chile and 20 percent by NORSEG Argentina, which had, as a majority owner, NORSEG Chile. Brooks shoes were imported directly from factories in the Far East or from Coast Sport inventories in Chile. Ricardo estimated that in 1992 in Argentina the company would sell about 32,500 pairs of Brooks shoes, worth approximately US$1 million.

RECENT DEVELOPMENTS

After witnessing almost a decade of accelerating growth and profits, Ricardo Swett was reflective. Projections indicated that 1992 would be the best year ever for the company, with after-tax profits at over 15 percent of sales and return on equity surpassing 35 percent. (Financial statements for 1990 and 1991 are reported in Exhibit 7.) With such growth and profitability, it was easy to feel confident.

By the summer of 1992, Ricardo was weighing a number of options to recommend to Alfonso and Juan Pablo for consideration. One major thrust under consideration was to move aggressively into apparel retailing. Although Costanera had little experience with clothing, apparel seemed to fit well with the company's other retail

EXHIBIT 7 | **Financial Statements for Forus, S. A.** *(For the years ended December 31, 1990, and 1991)*

Income Statement		
	1990 (Ch. $)	1991 (Ch. $)
Operating revenues	$3,917,656,542	$5,092,329,385
Operating costs	(2,874,204,603)	(3,507,627,947)
Gross margin	1,043,451,939	1,584,701,438
Administrative and sales expenses	(534,015,090)	(666,112,679)
Operating results	509,436,849	918,588,759
Nonoperating expenses	(113,686,107)	110,645,279
Income before tax	395,750,742	1,029,234,038
Income tax	16,273,224	49,547,770
Net income	$ 379,477,518	$ 979,686,268
US $1 = $ Chilean	337.09	374.09

Balance Sheet		
	1990 (Ch. $)	1991 (Ch. $)
Assets		
Total current assets	$1,678,518,025	$2,561,279,678
Total fixed assets	2,084,031,742	2,387,101,951
Less accumulated depreciation	(544,166,086)	(699,091,557)
Net fixed assets	1,539,865,656	1,688,010,394
Investment in related companies plus other assets	1,632,891,422	1,966,126,263
Total assets	$4,851,275,163	$6,215,416,335
Liabilities and Stockholders' Equity		
Total current liabilities	$1,530,707,772	$1,756,973,367
Long-term liabilities:		
Bank debt	377,752,696	608,837,630
Other accounts payable	130,702,501	152,427,111
Total long-term liabilities	508,455,197	761,264,741
Total stockholders' equity	2,812,112,194	3,697,178,227
Total liabilities and equity	$4,851,275,163	$6,215,416,335

operations. It was thought that the best way to proceed would be to open a chain of stores, combining both Brooks and L.A. Gear athletic shoes with branded sports clothing. While the combination of athletic-shoe and clothing stores had proved a major hit in Europe, Japan, and North America, it had yet to be effectively pursued in Chile. A combination outlet would have the advantage of allowing the company to move incrementally into apparel while concurrently expanding athletic-shoe sales. Costs for a retail space in a typical upscale Santiago shopping mall were estimated at 7 percent of net sales with leasehold improvements averaging about US$30,000. The company did not have a store name under consideration and was wondering how to aggressively proceed.

A second option being considered was to open a chain of outdoor clothing stores. The outdoor clothing and accessory market was particularly attractive, because it was a segment that appeared to have been neglected in Chile. Through visits to the United States, all three Swett brothers had become familiar with a variety of fast-growing outdoor clothing stores, such as Timberland, Eddie Bauer, and North-by-Northwest. Market research in Chile indicated that outdoor clothing sales could grow rapidly, and Ricardo wondered if he should recommend a major move into this segment. What was uncertain was the extent to which the skills learned in marketing shoes could be transferred to outdoor clothing.

A third option for the company was the introduction of a new retailing concept for children's shoes and apparel. While first Hush Puppies Chile and then Forus had been selling children's shoes for the past 10 years, the introduction of Hush Puppies for Kids had been a major hit in the marketplace. In July 1992, managers at Hush Puppies Chile were debating whether to extend the Kids line to include branded children's clothing and accessories. A full line of merchandise would accompany a full move into children's retailing by filling out stores and providing an added draw for consumers. Wolverine had been trying for years to introduce Hush Puppies branded clothes for children in the United States, but the efforts had not gone well. To better develop a recognizable brand in the United States, Wolverine had just recently adopted the Hush Puppies for Kids logo that had been developed in Chile. While Ricardo realized the potential for new retail concepts, he was also fully aware that a movement into retailing would have serious consequences for the company.

Behind the increasing interest in diversifying the retail base of the company was the recognition that retailing was becoming more specialized. The need for even greater specialization was articulated by Renato Figueroa, general manager of ForShop's retail operations: "As the market becomes more globalized, our next move must be to specialize in our stores. Where we have family stores, we must in the future have men's stores, kids' stores, women's stores, and life-style stores."

Ricardo was also faced with the decision of focusing management efforts on increasing sales in Chile or on expanding sales in other Latin American countries. Some in the company argued that Costanera could do both at the same time. Others disagreed by highlighting the risk that foreign operations would increasingly siphon critical resources away from core Chilean operations.

For Ricardo Swett, the critical issue was management:

> Our big problem with growth is people. How can the management of the company keep up with such rapid growth? We need good middle managers . . . On average, about 60 percent of our senior managers have had formal university training in management. When we exclude manufacturing managers, this number climbs to about 80 percent. Still, we spend a lot of effort training our managers. On average, each of our managers receives about two and a half weeks of training per year.
>
> Sometimes I feel that we are moving too slowly. The world is changing so fast that it

is increasingly difficult to stay abreast of what is going on internationally. What worries me is that our managers might not be reacting fast enough. There needs to be a daily commitment to learning.

Clearly, Ricardo had much to consider. While any major decision would require the support of both Alfonso and Juan Pablo, Ricardo realized that they would be relying on him for direction. Ricardo seemed to have more questions than answers. How fast should they move and where should they target expansion?

NORTHERN TELECOM JAPAN, INC.

Adrian Ryans, The University of Western Ontario

In late May 1988, Howard Garvey, the newly appointed president of Northern Telecom Japan, Inc. (NTJI), was reviewing the financial projections for the subsidiary's next three years of operation. After two months of studying the operations of the company, Garvey was planning to address a committee, consisting of the presidents of all the Northern Telecom (NT) companies, regarding the current state of NTJI. In his presentation, he would have to either accept the current three-year operating plan or present his proposed revisions. If he accepted the plan, he would be responsible for delivering the forecasted results. If he rejected the plan, he would have to explain why his forecasts differed from those of his predecessors.

With the meeting scheduled to be held in Toronto, Canada, in a month, Garvey decided to review the projections in light of what he had seen during his first six weeks in Japan.

THE TELECOMMUNICATIONS INDUSTRY

The decade of the 80s brought about major changes in the telecommunications industry. Of the approximately 30 major telecommunications manufacturers that had existed in the late 70s, only 15 remained in 1988. The impetus for this change was the rising cost of research required to remain a competitor in this industry. Digital switching, existing only in the minds of engineers at the turn of the decade, had become a necessity for doing business. By 1988, the estimated cost of developing a state-of-the-art digital central-office switch was $1 billion.

With the need for greater research dollars came the need for volume. Companies could no longer exist by relying on their national markets alone. Some analysts, extrapolating this trend into the future, were predicting that by the year 2000 only 5

Certain names and other identifying information have been disguised to protect confidentiality. Copyright © 1990 The University of Western Ontario.

of the current 15 companies would remain, as any one company would need at least a 10 percent share of the world market to continue to compete. Exhibit 1 lists the top eight telecommunications manufacturers in 1988.

By 1988, the major thrust in the industry was in the development of ISDN systems. ISDN was an internationally agreed-upon protocol for an Integrated Service Digital Network: a network that would support the simultaneous transmission of data, voice, and image. ISDN technology united the computer, telephone, and television into one network and could eventually devolve these three devices into one.

NORTHERN TELECOM

NT first began manufacturing telecommunications instruments in Canada in 1884. The company, then named Northern Electric, began operations as the Canadian subsidiary of Western Electric, the equipment manufacturing subsidiary of American Telelphone and Telegraph (AT&T). In 1956, the U.S. Department of Justice implemented the AT&T Consent Decree forcing AT&T to sever all relationships with firms outside the United States. The purpose of this action was to prevent AT&T from leveraging its monopoly in the United States to build strong competitive positions in the rest of the world. Western Electric, as the manufacturing arm of AT&T, was forced to sever its relationship with Northern Electric in the same way that AT&T was forced to severe its relationship with Bell Canada. With this action NT became a wholly owned subsidiary of Bell Canada.

Historically, both Bell Canada and NT had relied on AT&T's research facility, Bell Labs, to keep them at the forefront of the industry. With these relationships now severed, the long-term survival of NT, as a producer of telecommunications equipment, became contingent upon the development of its own research facility. In 1959, NT established an internal research and development division, which specialized in designing products for the Canadian market. In 1971, the division was spun off into a jointly owned subsidiary of both NT and Bell Canada. The new company, named Bell Northern Research (BNR), provided research and development for both Bell Canada and NT.

The tricorporate structure provided an ideal environment for the growth of all three companies. Bell Canada, operating as a monopoly in the provinces of Ontario

EXHIBIT 1 | **The Top Eight Manufacturers of Telecommunications Equipment, 1988**
(*Revenues in US $ billions*)

1. Alcatel	(France)	$11.5
2. AT&T	(United States)	11.3
3. Siemens	(West Germany)	10.8
4. NEC	(Japan)	6.5
5. Northern Telecom	(Canada)	5.2
6. LM Ericsson	(Sweden)	4.2
7. Hitachi	(Japan)	3.4
8. Futjitsu	(Japan)	2.9

Note: The chart shows only revenues attributed to telecommunications sales. Sales for each company may be significantly higher.

and Quebec,[1] worked closely with BNR and NT to develop the equipment needed to meet its future requirements. While Bell Canada served as the operating telecommunications company specialist and BNR as the development specialist, NT provided the manufacturing and marketing expertise.

By the mid-70s it had become apparent that research and development expenses required to keep NT at the forefront of the telecommunications industry would require revenues greater than those available in Canada alone. NT had to decide to become a small niche player in the industry or to expand its operations globally. In 1976, NT management set themselves an ambitious goal. In an attempt to increase NT's share of the U.S. market, they focused their research on digital technologies with the hope of becoming the first telecommunications company in the world to offer a complete digital switching system. They thought success in this endeavor would help to springboard them into the world market.[2] In 1976, NT invited executives from North American telephone operating companies to a conference at Disney-World (Florida). The Canadian company's announcement that the Digital World had arrived as a consequence of NT's development of the first truly digital switches started the major thrust toward digital switching in North America.

In the early 80s, the U.S. Department of Justice ruled that AT&T would have to be broken up in order to promote greater competition within the U.S. telephone market. In 1984, Judge Green announced the "Modification of Final Judgment," which ruled specifically how AT&T would be divided, and ordered that the 22 Bell subsidiaries be grouped together to form seven independent, regional telephone companies.

This event provided NT with an unprecedented opportunity for growth in the U.S. market. Many of the engineers within these newly formed companies were familiar with the benefits offered by digital switching and were anxious to begin incorporating this technology into their networks. With these companies now free to purchase their equipment from any supplier, not just from AT&T-owned Western Electric, NT was able to make substantial inroads.

By the beginning of 1988, NT had become the world's leading supplier of fully digital telecommunications systems, with sales of $4.85 billion.[3] Bell Canada remained the majority shareholder with a 53 percent holding, while the remaining shares were traded on the New York, Toronto, London, and Tokyo exchanges. On a geographic basis, revenues were derived as follows: 62 percent from Northern Telecom, Inc. (NTI), the U.S. subsidiary; 33 percent from Northern Telecom Canada, Ltd.; and 5 percent from Northern Telecom World Trade Corporation, the umbrella company that oversaw all international subsidiaries, including Japan. (See Exhibit 2 for the consolidated financial statements.) NT was positioned as the fifth-largest telecommunications manufacturer in the world, with a 6.5 percent share of the global market for telecommunications equipment and related services. NT operated 41 manufacturing facilities worldwide. Of these, 24 were located in Canada, 13 in the United States, 2 in Malaysia, 1 in the Republic of Ireland, and 1 in France. Research was conducted at 24 of these plants as well as at 10 BNR labs, including 4 in Canada, 5 in the United States, and 1 in the United Kingdom.

---

[1]The provinces of Ontario and Quebec accounted for 68 percent of the population and roughly 80 percent of the Canadian telecommunications market.

[2]For a more detailed account of this decision please refer to Western Business School case #9-83-4031 (rev. 10/85), "Northern Telecom (A)."

[3]All dollar figures in this case are U.S. denominated.

EXHIBIT 2 | **Consolidated Financial Statements of Northern Telecom Limited**
(For the year ended December 31, in US $ millions)

	1984	1985	1986	1987
Earnings and related data:				
Revenues	$3,374.0	$4,262.9	$4,383.6	$4,853.5
Cost of revenues	2,074.1	2,708.9	2,730.5	2,895.8
Selling, general, and administrative expense	603.2	701.9	764.6	917.8
Research and development expense	333.1	430	474.6	587.5
Depreciation	162.8	203.3	247.3	264.1
Provision for income taxes	120.8	132.8	127.9	141.5
Earnings before extraordinary items	255.8	299.2	313.2	347.2
Net earnings applicable to common shares	243.2	273.8	286.8	328.8
Earnings per common share ($) before extraordinary items	1.06	1.18	1.23	1.39
Dividends per share ($)	0.16	0.18	0.20	0.23
Financial position at December 31:				
Working capital	$ 859	$ 933.9	$1,188.7	$ 570.7
Plant and equipment (at cost)	1,458	1,737.5	1,975.2	2,345.6
Accumulated depreciation	591.5	672.4	877.3	1,084.2
Total assets	3,072.9	3,490.0	3,961.1	4,869.0
Long-term debt	100.2	107.6	101	224.8
Redeemable retractable preferred shares	293.6	277.5	281	153.9
Redeemable preferred shares	—	73.3	73.3	73.3
Common shareholders' equity	1,379.8	1,614.6	1,894.9	2,333.3
Return on common shareholders' equity	19%	18.3%	16.3%	15.6%
Capital expenditures	$ 437.8	$ 457.3	$ 303.8	$ 416.7
Employees at December 31	46,993	46,549	46,202	48,778

Source: Northern Telecom, Ltd., annual report, 1987.

On the technological front, NT was well positioned for competing in the upcoming decade, and NT maintained its lead in ISDN development with a successful test of more than 20 business, government, and residential applications during a trial in Phoenix, Arizona. In addition, NT's SuperNode software technology, which allowed software modules to be added as needed, provided the most powerful and flexible digital switches in the business.

The management of the company chose 1988 to announce to its employees and shareholders "Vision 2000," outlining NT's ambitious goal of becoming the world's leading supplier of telecommunications equipment by the year 2000 (see Exhibit 3).

THE JAPANESE MARKET

The Japanese, impressed by the technological developments that had occurred at Bell Labs in the United States, had modeled their domestic telephone company after AT&T. Their version, Nippon Telegraph and Telephone (NTT), had been established as a government-owned monopoly with the mandate of providing domestic telecommunications services throughout Japan. Another government-owned company, Kokusai Denshin Denwa (KDD), provided all international long-distance service. NTT's

EXHIBIT 3 | **Vision 2000: The Challenge of Leadership**

Between now and the year 2000, the global market for telecommunications equipment and associated services is going to explode—from about $75 billion in 1987, to approximately $300 billion, a growth rate unmatched by any other industry.

Northern Telecom's own growth will be equally dramatic. It will be based on the steps we are taking now to ensure the achievements of Vision 2000—our goal of leadership in the worldwide telecommunications marketplace into the next century.

The global information network has already become one of the world's most effective means of increasing productivity. From the remote oil fields of the People's Republic of China, to the financial institutions of the United Kingdom, to the high-tech innovators of California's Silicon Valley, communications provides the advantages for competitive success and improved quality of life.

This is recognized by enlightened governments around the world, which have singled out telecommunications as a major priority for development and modernization.

Traditional voice services and rapidly increasing requirements for data transmission are outstripping the ability of existing networks to meet the competitive pressures of global business needs and the growing demands of society. At the same time, new technologies and new generations of equipment are creating additional demands for services previously only dreamed of.

While new products, services, and technologies are propelling the growth of telecommunications worldwide, we are focusing on markets where the opportunity is greatest. Beyond North America, we are concentrating on such markets as Australia, China, France, Japan, New Zealand, West Germany, and the United Kingdom, where deregulation and growth are creating market opportunities that have already led to strategic sales of our products. In these seven countries alone, the market will grow from $20 billion to $100 billion by the year 2000.

We expect our business outside North America to rise to about 15 percent of our total revenues in the early 1990s and continue to increase through the rest of that decade.

Northern Telecom's vision of the year 2000 involves a number of imperatives. It means continually generating sustainable advantages over our competitors through excellence in creating value for our customers, which in turn enhances their growth and profitability.

It requires our corporation to be global in reach and thinking, while showing flexibility, sensitivity, and good corporate citizenship in diverse markets.

And it demands that Northern Telecom deliver products and systems of the highest quality and reliability, on time, tailored to the varying needs of our customers. We must also provide the highest level of service in the industry.

The conditions of leadership are clear. In a fiercely competitive international marketplace, leadership will go to that corporation with the clearest global vision, the fastest response, and the capability and the commitment to satisfy the ever more complex market requirements of the future.

Northern Telecom intends to be that corporation.

Source: Northern Telecom, Ltd., annual report, 1987.

research facility worked very closely with the Ministry of International Trade and Industry, operating more as a national research center than as a corporate research facility. Jointly sponsored research conducted at the lab was largely responsible for helping Japan catch up to the United States in semiconductor technologies.

Unlike AT&T in the United States, NTT did not have any manufacturing facilities. Instead, it relied on four major Japanese suppliers, Nippon Electric Company (NEC), Hitachi, Oki, and Fujitsu, to manufacture its equipment. The Big Four worked closely with NTT researchers to jointly design all the switches for the Japanese telecommunications network. Under this arrangement, each of them manufactured identical equipment and received roughly a 25 percent share of NTT's business. Through these relationships Japan was able to build and support a significant manufacturing base for telecommunications equipment.

In 1982, an ad hoc commission of administrative reform was set up by the Japanese government to study ways of introducing competition into the Japanese telecommunications system. In 1985, the committee released a report calling for deregulation of the entire telecommunications industry and the privatization of government-owned NTT. One of the most important results of the report was the establishment of the new common carriers (NCCs). The NCCs were firms that would be licensed to compete in both the domestic and international long-distance telephone markets in a manner similar to Sprint and MCI in the United States. October 1, 1989, was the date set for the beginning of service by the NCCs.

The NCCs presented an opportunity for foreign telecommunications equipment suppliers, as many of these new firms were building their own networks from scratch. Furthermore, these companies didn't have existing relationships with the domestic suppliers and were looking outside Japan to see how they could gain a competitive advantage over the existing NTT/KDD networks.

In 1988, the Japanese telecommunications market, estimated at $25 billion, was the third largest in the world, and one of the fastest growing. The three main segments that made up this market were telephone companies (telcos), corporations, and households.

Telcos Telcos, providing the network for telecommunications, had needs ranging from wiring and optical fiber to large-scale switching equipment, from underwater cables to satellite or microwave transmission equipment. Sales to telcos were usually made through tenders, often called four to five years in advance of the required installation date (see p. 674 for an explanation of NTT's procurement process).

Success in this market required not only state-of-the-art hardware but also an extensive service organization. Highly trained servicemen and an inventory of spare parts had to be kept within easy access of all areas of the network, since any problems had to be fixed within hours. In 1988, sales to telcos represented 50 percent of the total Japanese telecommunications market. Sales to NTT represented roughly 90 percent of this segment.

Corporations As the networking and communications needs of companies grew throughout the 80s, so did the market for private branch exchanges (PBXs). A PBX was the brain of a large organization's own internal phone system. It allowed companies with only a few outside lines to provide internal phone service to all of their employees, thus reducing overall telephone costs. PBXs had become increasingly more sophisticated and complex over the years by offering such facilities as voice mail, automatic callback, and direct-in-ward dialing. Sales of PBX systems were usually made through a competitive bidding process.

One factor that distinguished the Japanese market from other world markets, however, was the existence of keiretsu. A keiretsu was a group of firms loosely connected through part ownership. (See "A Note on the Japanese Keiretsu" on page 675 for more information.) These firms had a tendency to purchase equipment from within their keiretsu group whenever possible. With the Big Four Japanese telecommunications suppliers having sewed up most of the business in their own keiretsu, the size of the market that was left for NT to compete for was questionable.

Households In Japan, most individuals purchased their own telephones, rather than renting them from NTT. Phones were sold through three primary distribution outlets: department stores, electronics specialty chain stores, and numerous large and small independent electronics stores. Along with the Big Four, many of Japan's leading consumer electronics companies also manufactured telephones. The resulting market

EXHIBIT 4 | Telephone and PBX Sales in Japan in 1988

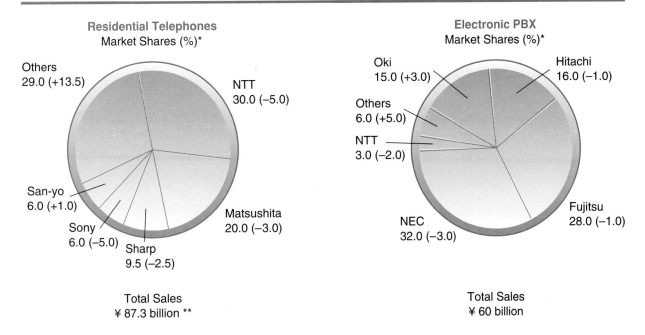

Residential Telephones
Market Shares (%)*

Others 29.0 (+13.5)
NTT 30.0 (−5.0)
San-yo 6.0 (+1.0)
Sony 6.0 (−5.0)
Sharp 9.5 (−2.5)
Matsushita 20.0 (−3.0)

Total Sales
¥ 87.3 billion **

Electronic PBX
Market Shares (%)*

Oki 15.0 (+3.0)
Hitachi 16.0 (−1.0)
Others 6.0 (+5.0)
NTT 3.0 (−2.0)
NEC 32.0 (−3.0)
Fujitsu 28.0 (−1.0)

Total Sales
¥ 60 billion

* Numbers in brackets indicate change in share from previous year.
** 125 Japanese Yen = $1 U.S. (1988).

Source: *Information & Communication in Japan,* InfoCom Research, Inc., Tokyo, 1990, p. 171.

was extremely competitive. (See Exhibit 4 for market data.) Competition among producers tended to occur along three dimensions: product features, design, and price. In the spirit of kaizen,[4] phones were being continually introduced with new features. Many of the best-selling phones were heavily advertised.

THE COMPETITION

There were numerous competitors in the Japanese telecommunications market (see Exhibit 5). However, NT faced only four primary domestic competitors in selling to NTT.

Nippon Electric Company   NEC, the fourth-largest telecommunications producer in the world, reported overall revenues of $22 billion in 1988. The company was organized into four divisions:

1. Communications systems and equipment.
2. Computer and industrial electronic systems.
3. Electronic devices.
4. Home electronic products.

Communications systems and equipment contributed 28 percent of the overall revenue. NEC was well known for the high quality of its hardware. However, adding

---

[4]*Kaizen* is a Japanese word used to describe the Japanese philosophy of continuous incremental improvement.

EXHIBIT 5 | **Competition in the Japanese Telecommunications Markets in 1988**

Company	Telephone Sets	PBXs	Digital Switches
Alphone Co., Ltd.	X		
Alcatel NV	X	X	X
Anritsu Corporation	X		
Iwasaki Tsushiniki Co., Ltd.	X	X	
AT&T International Japan	X	X	X
Oidenki Co., Ltd.		X	
Oki Electric Industry Co., Ltd.	X	X	X
Kanda Tsushin Kogyo	X		
Canon, Inc.	X	X	
Kyushu Matsushita	X		
Kenwood Corporation	X		
International Electronics	X		
Sun Telephone Co.	X		
Sanyo Electric Co., Ltd.	X	X	
Siemens K.K.	X		X
Sharp Corporation	X	X	
Shinwa Tsushinki	X		
Sony Corporation	X		
Taiei Manufacturing, Ltd.		X	X
Taiko Electric	X	X	X
Takachiho, Ltd.	X		
Takamizawa Electric Co.		X	
Omron Electronics Co.	X	X	
Tamura Electric Works, Ltd.	X		
Toshiba Corporation	X	X	
Nakayo Telecommunications, Ltd.	X	X	X
Nitsuko Corporation	X	X	
NEC Corporation	X	X	X
Victor Company of Japan	X		
Northern Telecom	X	X	X
Pioneer Electronic Corporation	X		
Hitachi, Ltd.	X	X	X
Fujitsu, Ltd.	X	X	X
Matsushita Corporation, Ltd.	X	X	
Mitsubishi Electric Corporation	X	X	
Ricoh Co., Ltd.	X		

Source: *Information & Communications in Japan,* InfoCom Research, Inc., Tokyo, March 1990, pp. 173–78.

advanced features to NEC's product was difficult, because the company's software was less flexible than NT's.

Hitachi　With revenues of $40 billion in 1988, Hitachi was the largest overall company of the four competitors. A highly diversified company, its product range extended from nuclear power plants to semiconductors. The company was divided into five principal business groups:

1. Power systems and equipment.
2. Consumer products.
3. Information and communication systems and electronic devices.
4. Industrial machinery and plants.
5. Wire and cable and chemicals.

The "information and communication systems and electronic devices" division encompassed businesses from computers to semiconductors and telecommunications equipment. This division accounted for 33 percent of revenues in 1988. Hitachi was ranked as the seventh-largest telecommunications manufacturer in 1988. In 1987 the company opened a subsidiary to produce PBX units in the United States.

Fujitsu Fujitsu, IBM's most aggressive worldwide competitor in the mainframe computer market, was divided into four primary business groups:

1. Computers and data processing.
2. Telecommunications.
3. Semiconductors.
4. Components.

Telecommunications represented 12.5 percent of the company's $16 billion in revenue in 1988. The company was strong in all areas of the telecommunications business, from fiber optic cable to digital switching equipment. In March 1988, the company released an ISDN system linking computers, word processors, and networks into one package.

Internationally, Fujitsu had formed an alliance with General Electric in the United States to manufacture and market PBX systems.

Oki Oki, the smallest of the Big Four Japanese suppliers, was strong internationally in cellular telephones and fax machines. Revenues in 1988 amounted to $3.6 billion, with 26.9 percent of this amount resulting from sales of telecommunications systems. The company was divided into three principal groups:

1. Telecommunications systems.
2. Information processing systems.
3. Electronic devices.

NORTHERN TELECOM JAPAN, INC.

In the early 80s, NT initiated a program whereby senior managers were sent as ambassadors to various telecommunications markets around the world. These managers met with potential customers and assessed the prospects of the market from NT's perspective. Japan, at that time representing the third-largest telecommunications market in the world, was selected early as one of the countries to be visited. In 1982, Edmund Fitzgerald, president of Northern Telecom, Ltd., went to Japan as NT's ambassador.

Fitzgerald, although not an expert in doing business in Japan, knew that the Japanese loved baseball as much or more than most Americans. Having owned the Milwaukee Brewers at one point, he was well connected in baseball circles and shared with the Japanese their enthusiasm for the sport. Thinking that it might help, he asked his good friend Bowie Kuhn, the ex-commissioner of major league baseball in the United States, to join him for the trip.

Through Kuhn's connections with Japanese baseball officials, and with those officials' connections in Japanese business circles, Fitzgerald was able to get a letter of introduction to Dr. Shinto, the president of NTT. Through a combination of his personality, his baseball stories, many gifts of Inuit carvings, and his sincerity in wishing to do business in Japan, he was able to win the respect of his Japanese counterparts, thus laying the groundwork for building NT's relationship with NTT.

While in Japan, Fitzgerald employed the services of a well-known Japanese businessman/consultant to look into NTT's operations and various government and legal issues. The work of the consultant uncovered two significant facts for NT. First, NTT needed to replace a significant number of small community dial office systems in the rural areas of its network. Second, the recent trade friction between the United States and Japan was making the Japanese government very uncomfortable. It seemed very plausible that NTT, as a government-regulated monopoly, would feel pressure to open up to foreign suppliers—especially to those from the United States.

Armed with this information, NT, acting through its American subsidiary, NTI, prepared an unsolicited proposal for NTT, to supply the Japanese company with NT's DMS-10, the world's first fully digital switching system. With a capacity of up to 10,000 lines, the DMS-10 was ideally suited for use as a community dial office. The bid to NTT was made in 1982. At the same time, NT established an office in Japan with the arrival of a single expatriate. Although the bid to NTT was well received, it did not immediately translate into a direct order.

In 1983, NT committed itself to the Japanese market with the legal registration of NTJI. In the latter part of the year, NT received an invitation from NTT to participate in a competitive bid for a single emergency switching system. This switch, which was to be mounted in a trailer, would be used to provide emergency switching capability if an earthquake or other type of disaster left a community without telephone service. Coincidently, the specifications for this switch were very similar to those of NT's DMS-10. The slightly modified DMS-10 was named the KS-2, and NT succeeded in beating the competition to become the first foreign telecommunications company to supply to NTT. Although the one-time sale represented less then $400,000, the associated benefits for NT were far greater. The sale allowed NT to learn more about NTT, its needs, and its methods of doing business. At the same time, the opportunity for NTT to evaluate NT's quality and technology helped to strengthen the relationship that had been developing over time.

In 1984, NTT announced a competitive tender to replace a large number of rural electromechanical community switching exchanges. A decision by NT to bid for this tender would have to include a commitment to establish a full-service network in Japan, as the vendor was required to provide ongoing servicing of the equipment. NT, believing in the long-term potential of the Japanese market, entered a bid, once again featuring the DMS-10.

Designing flexible software systems was one area where North American producers had a competitive advantage over their Japanese rivals. A feature of NT's proposal extended to NTT the right to modify the software operating system of the switch, for the purpose of developing market-specific feature applications. This arrangement required NT to provide NTT with documentation on its operating software. AT&T, also bidding on this contract, was reluctant to include this right, fearing that NTT might divulge this information to the four domestic manufacturers.

NT management, after assessing the long-term opportunity of doing business with NTT, determined that the risk was minimal, as the software programs within the switch were reaching maturity. More important, however, they wanted to develop a relationship between NT and NTT based on reciprocal trust.

On May 19, 1986, Northern's bid was selected by NTT and Northern Telecom committed to building and maintaining a subsidiary in Japan capable of installing and servicing 1,500,000 lines over a five-year period, beginning in late 1988. The contract was worth $250 million for the new subsidiary Northern Telecom Japan, Inc. (NTJI).

THE PENETRATION STRATEGY

With the establishment of NTJI, NT embarked on a long-term strategy of becoming a supplier of its full line of switching equipment to NTT. Because this relationship would take time to develop, a short-term penetration strategy was also developed for attacking the two other main segments of the Japanese telecommunications market: telephones and PBX units.

Telephones NTJI entered the Japanese telephone market in 1984 with the launch of its Contempra model, an upscale designer telephone set. Initial sales were encouraging, as the Contempra filled a niche at the top of the market. However, shortly after this product was introduced into the middle segment of the market, NT found that the competition was extremely severe. Without the volume of the more standard telephone sets to support the administrative overhead, NT realized that the telephone segment provided little opportunity for profit. As a consequence, efforts to market these products were discontinued.

PBX Unit: The SL-1 NTJI's disappointment in the telephone set segment of the market was not a complete surprise to upper management in Northern Telecom, Ltd., as NTI, the U.S. subsidiary, was also experiencing similar stiff competition. What upper management did not anticipate, however, were the problems that NTJI experienced in trying to sell its PBX systems in Japan. The SL-1, NT's digital PBX system, was the world's best-selling PBX system. Because of its successful sales throughout North America, NT had expected that the SL-1 would be a success in Japan as well. When actual sales fell considerably short of forecasts, management decided to investigate.

Examination of this issue uncovered a multitude of miscalculations in NT's marketing approach. First, NT had seriously underestimated the strength of the domestic competition and their keiretsu relationships. Second, NTJI had not studied how Japanese companies actually used their phone systems and, therefore, did not realize that its product did not meet the basic needs of Japanese corporate users. To the Japanese, direct access dialing was not a desirable feature, as every call to the company should be answered and greeted by the company's receptionist. She would then call ahead to check if the person was in before either transferring the call or taking a message. Consequently, NT's highly advanced product offered little advantage to the Japanese customer. Third, the product was being marketed at a premium price. On average, NT's system was priced 20 percent higher than the local competition's product. Finally, all of the promotional materials for the SL-1 were in English, and the product was being sold through a distributor who had not been given sufficient product training to promote the SL-1 adequately in Japanese. His failure to communicate this to NTJI officials resulted in the relationship between NT and the distributor becoming very strained.

Despite the problems encountered in the telephone set and PBX markets, NTJI continued its efforts to penetrate the Japanese telco market and, in January 1988, signed an agreement with International Digital Communications (IDC), one of the newly sanctioned NCCs, to provide the switching equipment needed to run their network. IDC chose NT's DMS-250 tandem switching system and DMS-300 international gateway switch. This decision was influenced by NT's previous success in selling these switches to MCI and Sprint in the United States, as NT supplied 50 percent of MCI's and 100 percent of Sprint's switching equipment. IDC was licensed to begin operations on October 1, 1989, and NT was committed to installing a complete network to be ready by that date.

By early 1988, NTJI had 87 full-time employees. Of these, roughly 40 were expatriates from NTI and the remaining were local Japanese.

HOWARD GARVEY

Howard Garvey joined NT in 1955 as an installer. He worked his way through the Canadian organization and, after 18 years of service, was appointed assistant to the vice president, sales, of NTI—the U.S. subsidiary. In 1978, he was appointed NTI's first national account manager and subsequently generated the first $50 million supply contract in the United States. In March 1982, he was appointed vice president, sales, with responsibility for AT&T and the Bell operating companies. His promotion coincided with a new thrust to market digital systems to the Bell system in the United States, eventually leading to almost $100 million in sales for NTI.

By 1988, sales in his division were exceeding $1.2 billion, and Garvey was recognized as one of the key people instrumental in achieving NT's success in penetrating the U.S. market. In March of that year Desmond Hudson, the president of Northern Telecom World Trade (NTWT), asked Garvey if he would do in Japan what he had done so well in the United States. Garvey accepted a three-year posting and was told he had until July to learn all he could about Japan. Shortly afterward, Edmund Fitzgerald, the chairman and CEO of Northern Telecom, on returning from a trip to Japan, prompted Hudson to accelerate Garvey's assignment. A few weeks later, in April 1988, Garvey arrived in Japan as president of NTJI.

GARVEY'S IMPRESSIONS OF NTJI

In commenting on NTJI, Garvey pointed out that

> In January of 1988, the chairman and several other key executives within Northern Telecom took stock of where the company was in respect to the Japanese market. We had a major contract with NTT to install 1,500,000 lines worth $250,000,000. We had a major contract with IDC with a date staring us in the face that not only meant part of our future but also IDC's future was at stake. If that thing went down then we were dead in Japan. We also had an unprecedented opportunity over here, as we were moving into a new marketplace with the NCCs.

When NT's management had reviewed the NTJI operation they noticed that there were an increasing number of bypasses around NTJI. The customers, apprehensive about the local organization's ability to service their needs, often dealt directly with North America. It was concluded that the situation required a change in the management of NTJI.

> Because of my background and experience in increasing our market share in the United States, into the Bell system in particular, and because there was such a similarity

between the structures of AT&T in North America and NTT in Japan, I was given the opportunity to come and see what needed to be done to make sure that we didn't jeopardize the opportunity that was facing us.

During April and May, Garvey examined the operations of NTJI in an effort to find areas upon which he could improve. The following were his observations:

The organization that existed in Japan was essentially being run from the United States. Executives in NTI, proud of their accomplishment as one of the few American companies that had successfully broken into the Japanese market, had not been proactive in developing NTJI into a stand-alone subsidiary. There was a sense that NTI owned NTJI and the practice was that representatives of NTI were continually flying over to Japan to interact with various NTT officials.

As a result NTJI was still heavily dependent on the United States. This created within Japan an organization very limited in technical, marketing, and management skills, even though the organization had been in Japan for over four years.

There were people in the local management group that were not compatible with Japanese customers. As an example, there was a fellow that was in charge of service, the leading edge in your customer relationship, with a domineering attitude based upon years in the U.S. military . . . he didn't fit very well.

There was a heavy expatriate presence and that relates back to the dependency on the United States. The ex-pats of course could call back to the United States for anything they wanted. Over and above that, there was no support infrastructure within the Japanese organization. The company was growing with minimum sense of direction and a complementary management hierarchy was lacking within the company.

Another major shortcoming was that the organization that existed in Japan was facing the United States. In other words, the organization was plugged into the organizational structure that existed in NTI in the United States, into a marketing group in the United States, into a service group in the United States, into a technical support group in the United States, without consideration of turning around and facing the customer and adapting to their organization.

As a result of the existing organization in Japan, engineers in some divisions within NTT would have to interface with two or three different divisions within NTJI [see Exhibit 6]. For example, members of NTT's software engineering center would have to regularly contact people in NTJI's design, design follow-up, and engineering divisions. Even more troublesome though, managers of NTT regional centers, who managed the outlying areas of NTT's network, would at times have to interface with almost every division within NTJI. This presented great problems for the regional manager, who inevitably called the wrong person within NTJI and spent the rest of the day playing telephone tag with various people before finding the right person to solve his problem.

When we talk about how to succeed in business, we hear more and more these days that you'd better be aware of your customer's needs. You can't have your back to the customer as NTJI did here. The company was structured to do business more conveniently with the United States than with our customers.

An additional problem within the company at the time was that there was a lack of business discipline. For example, local purchasing went virtually uncontrolled. The existing approval system was very loosely monitored. In fact, almost anyone could travel anywhere with minimal approvals.

Because of these factors, there existed a great deal of client apprehension. Customers didn't see any effective marketing, technical, or management support within NTJI. They were justifiably concerned about how NTJI was going to meet the obligations that it had here in Japan, as the company appeared to be run from the other side of the world.

There was also a perceptible split between the ex-pats and the nationals, and I again refer back to trying to do business in Japan and facing the customer. It was to the point

EXHIBIT 6 | An Example of Structural Problems in NTJI

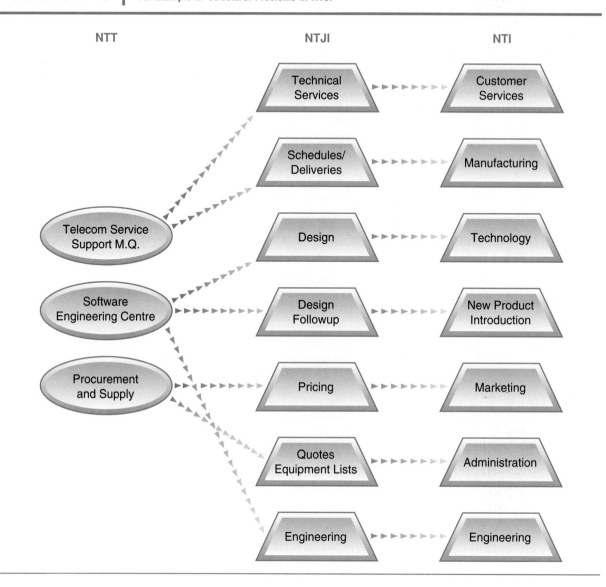

where there was minimal reciprocal dialogue between the national employees and the ex-pats. Unfortunately, the ex-pats were predominantly in management positions in NTJI, and many decisions were made without any discussion or involvement with the Japanese employees. They were usually in the situation of "do as we tell you, we know best." Of course that cost us an awful lot of employee discontent. It carried over into the recognition that we had to start growing some local experienced talent, but our reputation presented further difficulties in trying to recruit people.

There was an inadequate definition of responsibilities within the organization. The nationals particularly did not know what their jobs were. They took day-to-day directions from the ex-pats. Their responsibilities changed because the ex-pats were able to go to any individual, regardless of what his job was, and say "do this" or "go here." It was very unsettling for them. There was a definite lack of definition of responsibilities, and little sense of belonging to NTJI for the national employees.

Lastly, there was a serious lack of focus on where we were going in NTJI. For example, many of the people required for the installation and maintenance of NTT's contract for DMS-10s had not yet been hired or trained. The company's objectives in Japan and how they were going to be achieved were not communicated well to the employee population.

THE FINANCIAL PROJECTIONS

In late May 1988, Garvey was reviewing the current operating projections for NTJI (see Exhibit 7). He was aware of several developments that had occurred since the original projections had been made in January 1988.

First, NT had received an order from NTT for a single DMS-200. The order was the first central office switch sold to NTT by a non-Japanese vendor. It was commissioned by NTT to be used as an overflow switch to handle the surge in telephone traffic that occurred every year following "golden week."[5] In previous years, NTT had come under severe criticism as its network became jammed with calls and many people could not get through. The DMS-200–based system, to be installed in November 1989, would eventually contribute $20–30 million in revenue. However, it would also require a similar-sized investment in development costs by NT to adapt the DMS-200 to work within the Japanese public network and to develop the necessary supply infrastructure.

Second, it appeared that additional development costs would have to be incurred to modify NT's DMS-250 and DMS-300 for the IDC network. Garvey estimated the costs of these modifications within a range of $10–20 million.

Furthermore, Garvey had the benefit of being able to compare the first quarter's actual results against the projections. Revenues for the first quarter were slightly lower than projections and costs were slightly higher. From his earlier assessment of the company, he calculated that the forecast seriously underestimated the costs of product development, servicing, and support that companies like NTT demanded. Garvey estimated that over the next two years an additional $5 million would be needed for increased technical support from the United States, and at least $2 million would be needed for training local personnel.

With these factors in mind, Garvey began planning his presentation for the executive committee.

EXHIBIT 7 | **Financial Projections for NTJI (for the year ended December 31)** (*in US $ million*)

	1988				Totals		
	Q1	Q2	Q3	Q4	1988	1989	1990
Orders					43	126	173
Sales	$2.1	$2.3	$3.0	$9.1	$16.5	$75	$130
Earnings					$(6)	$ 3	$ 9
Headcount					136	196	232

[5]"Golden week," falling in April, is so named because it contains three public holidays within the span of seven days. Many Japanese companies close for the entire week, making this a very popular time for Japanese people to travel.

NTT'S PROCUREMENT PROCESS

OUTLINE OF PROCEDURES

Based on the policy of "open, fair, and nondiscriminatory" procurement, NTT procures products required to operate its business following competitive procedures.

At NTT, procurement procedures are divided into five different categories, according to the nature of the products to be procured. These are Tracks I, II, III, II-A, and III-A.

When NTT purchases or hires any products in excess of $130,000 per year (equivalent to 24 million yen[1] for FY 1988), the products are procured according to one of the above-mentioned procedures.

Track I covers the procedures for the procurement of specific products which fall under the Agreement on Government Procurement. NTT selects suppliers by public bid in conformity with GATT[2] rules.

Tracks II, III and Tracks II-A, III-A cover the procedures for the procurement of products, other than those specified for Track I. In addition, NTT procurement procedures are transparent and nondiscriminatory in compliance with the spirit of GATT.

WHAT IS A TRACK?

Track I   Track I covers the procedures for the procurement of specific products offered to GATT by NTT as items that fall under the Agreement on Government Procurement.

As a general rule, NTT issues a public announcement in *Kampo* (the Japanese official gazette) when purchasing Track I products, and product suppliers are selected by competitive bids. Bids or "tenders" are usually conducted every one or two years.

There are two types of Track I bids. One type is the *open tender,* where bids are submitted by anyone who desires to participate in the tender, and successful tenderers are selected upon evaluation following tender opening. The other type is the *selective tender;* for this type of tender, anyone who desires to participate in the tender is required to pass prequalification.

Notice of prequalification is provided publicly in advance of the tender notice. Those applicants who have passed the prequalification are eligible to participate in the selective tender.

Tracks II and III   Tracks II and III cover the procedures for initial procurement of new products, other than those procured through Track I.

Track II covers the procedures for initial procurement of such new products produced on a commercial basis or that can be used as is or with minor modification.

NTT selects applicants offering the most attractive proposals to NTT as suppliers for Track II products, based on the results of the evaluation of the proposals submitted by the applicants following the instructions provided in the public notice.

Track III covers the procedures for procurement of products that are not produced on a commercial basis and that need to be newly developed. Joint development partners are selected from among the applicants submitting application documents fol-

---

[1]125 Japanese yen = $1.00 U.S. (1988).
[2]GATT: General Agreement on Tariffs and Trade.

lowing the instructions provided in the public notice. Joint development partners may be requested to manufacture a prototype for testing to confirm function and performance of the newly developed product.

Tracks II-A and III-A   Tracks II-A and III-A cover the procedures for repeat procurement of products already procured previously through Track II and Track III. Track II-A and III-A procedures are also applied to new applicants who have not been qualified but who desire to supply such products. NTT, at all times, welcomes proposals from new applicants. When a new applicant is judged to be superior to a qualified supplier, NTT will also award a contract to such superior applicant as a newly selected supplier.

PRODUCTS PROCURED BY NTT

NTT procures various categories of products as required to provide telecommunication services:

- Switching equipment.
- Transmission equipment.
- Radio equipment.
- Data communication equipment.
- Power supply equipment.
- Customer equipment.
- Cables.
- Others (i.e., office equipment, vehicles, etc.).

Of the products listed above, those that fall under the category of Track I procurement include:

- Equipment and materials for plants (i.e., vehicles, poles, modems, computers, facsimiles, etc.).
- Paper and other products for office use, including clothing.
- Equipment for research and development.
- Equipment for training.
- Equipment for medical use.

Flow chart diagrams of all procurement procedures were attached to this document.

A NOTE ON THE JAPANESE KEIRETSU[4]

KEY CHARACTERISTICS

A *keiretsu* is a family of different companies linked together by ownership of each other's stock, common board of directors members, and often vender-customer relationships. The keiretsu structure evolved from Japan's postwar *zaibatsu,* which origi-

[4]This note was largely written by Allan Kwan, Northern Telecom Japan, Inc., in February 1991, with assistance from Professor C. B. Johnston for the sole purpose of providing material for class discussion at The Western Business School. Any reproduction, in any form, of the material in this note is prohibited except with the written consent of the School. Copyright 1992 © The University of Western Ontario.

inated in the family-controlled groups whose member firms were subsidiaries of a holding company. The concept of zaibatsu, or "group capitalism," formed internalized markets for such scarce resources as capital, technology, and labor. As a result, member firms could achieve economies of scale and pursue joint entry into new ventures while fortifying each unit in the group.

In 1947, Japan's antimonopoly law made holding companies illegal, which forced the prewar zaibatsu to change its structure. Once reconstructed, the keiretsu that evolved had one major difference from the zaibatsu—a lack of any central holding company or controlling entity. Instead, the member companies have limited equity ownership in one another. The shares that a firm might own of another may be only 1 or 2 percent but, when combined with the percent owned by other family members, aggregate family ownership is large enough to provide the mutual security of interdependence.

Each keiretsu contains a major bank and a leading marketing and procurement company, often referred to as a trading company.

The current-day keiretsu provides its members with effective diversification and a large and stable in-house market for existing and new products, and it facilitates the phasing out of business activities that have become uncompetitive.

Six features characterize the Japanese keiretsu:

- Cross-shareholding of stock and interlocking boards of directors (it is customary for senior executives to sit on the boards of several member companies).
- The formation of a president's club in which top executives meet regularly to map out coordinated business strategies and work together on matters of mutual interest.
- Joint investment among member companies in projects of mutual interest.
- Keiretsu member banks provide financing to keiretsu member companies.
- Members often source needed materials, components, supplies, and equipment from other members, with the sales often brokered by the trading company.
- The businesses of member companies, when aggregated, constitute a subeconomy of diverse, but linked, business interests.

TYPES OF KEIRETSU

Capital Keiretsu Capital-connected keiretsu include the well-known former zaibatsu (financial combines) Mitsui, Mitsubishi, Sumitomo, and the Fuyo group and the bank-centered groups led by the Dai-Ichi Kangyo Bank and the Sanwa Bank. These six groups are essentially loose federations of powerful, independent firms, clustered around a bank and a general trading company (Exhibit 8). Cross-shareholding is very common among member firms, as is exchange of corporate directors. The core bank provides priority funds to member firms. The trading companies, such as Mitsubishi Corporation and Mitsui and Company, sit on large cash reserves and have hundreds of subsidiaries. The custom of buying from fellow group members is strong.

Another component of the capital-connected keiretsu is the "industrial keiretsu." The industrial keiretsu, also known as "new groups," include such huge firms as Hitachi, Matsushita Electric Industries Company, NEC Corporation, and Fujitsu, Ltd. (Exhibit 9). These and other large manufacturing firms have converted former divisions and plants into separate subsidiaries, which are integrated in a pyramid structure. This new breed of keiretsu tends to be more specialized and is usually based on a single large manufacturer. The industrial keiretsu are included in the category because the interfirm ties are cemented essentially by capital.

EXHIBIT 8 | **Sample Members of Six Major Industrial Groups***

	Mitsui	Mitsubishi	Sumitomo	Fuyo (Fuji)	Sanwa	Dai-Ichi Kangyo
Number of member firms	24	29	19	29	44	46
Employees	235,198	238,309	152,877	322,936	381,368	471,238
Assets ($ billion)	$ 532	$ 791	$ 757	$ 710	$ 808	$ 780
Banking and insurance	Mitsui Bank Mitsui Trust and Banking Mitsui Mutual Life Insurance Taisho Marine and Fire Insurance	Mitsubishi Bank Mitsubishi Trust and Banking Meiji Mutual Life Insurance Tokio Marine and Fire Insurance	Sumitomo Bank Sumitomo Trust and Banking Sumitomo Life Insurance Sumitomo Marine and Fire Insurance	Fuji Bank Yasuda Trust and Banking Yasuda Mutual Life Insurance Yasuda Fire and Marine Insurance	Sanwa Bank Toyo Trust and Banking Nippon Life Insurance	Dai-Ichi Kangyo Bank Asshi Mutual Life Insurance Fukoku Mutual Life Insurance Nissan Fire and Marine Insurance Taisei Fire & Marine Insurance
Trading	Mitsui and Co.	Mitsubishi Corp.	Sumitomo Corp.	Marubeni Corp.	Nichimen Corp. Nisho Iwai Corp. Iwatani International	C. Itoh and Co. Kanematsu-Gosho, Ltd. Nissho Iwai Corp. Kawasho Corp.
Electric machinery	Toshiba Corp.	Mitsubishi Electric	NEC Corp.	Hatachi, Ltd. Oki Electric Industry Yokogawa Electric	Hitachi, Ltd. Iwatsu Electric Sharp Corp. Kyocere Corp. Nitto Denki Corp.	Hitachi, Ltd. Fuji Electric Yasukawa Electric Works Fujitsu, Ltd. Nippon Columbia
Transportation, communication, and the like	Mitsui-OSK Lines Mitsui Warehouse	Nippon Yusen Mitsubishi Warehouse	Sumitomo Warehouse	Tobu Railway Keihin Electric Express Showa Line	Hankyu Corp. Nippon Express Yamashita-Shinnihon Steamship	Nippon Express Kawasaki Kisen Shibusawa Warehouse

*As of 1988.

The six largest keiretsu (Exhibit 8)—Mitsui, Mitsubishi, Sumitomo, Fuyo (Fuji), Sanwa, Dai-Ichi Kangyo—account for 61 percent of the Tokyo stock market's capitalization and assets of $4.4 trillion, while 40 smaller keiretsu account for 17 percent of Tokyo market capitalization and assets of $366.4 billion.

Production Keiretsu The production keiretsu is typically observed in the automotive industry, and it is characterized by the vertical integration of manufacturers and their suppliers. A large manufacturing firm will source major components from keiretsu-affiliated primary suppliers, which in turn distribute work to dozens, maybe hundreds, of small keiretsu-affiliated subcontractors. All the major suppliers are integrated into the manufacturer's production process and receive extensive technological, managerial, and financial support. They are issued precise instructions on production runs, prices, and delivery schedules, which they are expected to meet.

Manufacturers and their suppliers are tied by reciprocal obligation: the supplier to high quality and low costs; the manufacturer to providing a steady flow of orders and financial and technical resources.

EXHIBIT 9 | **Size of Keiretsu Groups**

Keiretsu	Number of Subsidiaries
Hitachi	688
Bridgestone	647
C. Itoh and Co.	628
Mitsui and Co.	513
Mitsubishi Corp.	459
Marubeni	378
Honda	352
Matsushita	340
Nisho Iwai Corp.	293
Sumitomo Corp.	287
Toshiba	215
Nippon Meat Packers	211
Onoda Cement	198
Dainippon Ink	164
Sony	163
Toray Industries	160
Kubota	160
Fujitsu	152
Daiei (supermarket chain)	152
Jusco	150

Source: *The Economist,* January 5, 1991.

Sales-Distribution Keiretsu   The sales-distribution keiretsu involves the vertical integration of product distribution from factory door to retail outlets. The companies that engage in this type of keiretsu, such as Matsushita and Hitachi (Exhibit 10), are often involved in capital-connected and production keiretsu.

The distribution keiretsu is in decline, whereas the production keiretsu, particularly as it is applied in the automotive industry, seems destined to be "internationalized." This is a result of two factors, the first being the high prices charged by the keiretsu stores; consumers have switched to discount stores in search of lower prices, and the share of the retail market controlled by keiretsu stores has consequently declined. Second, maintaining keiretsu retail stores causes inefficiencies in the manufacturer's production system, because each store must stock a full line of company products, regardless of the pace of sales. Overall, from the standpoint of the manufacturer, the keiretsu stores are causing increased sales costs, higher product costs, and weakened product planning and development. As a result, manufacturers are moving to reduce the number of keiretsu stores, to concentrate on the most productive stores, and to improve relations with mass retailers.

How the Keiretsu Conduct Business

Traditional Views   Keiretsu often turn inward for business partnerships as a result of the high level of vertical and horizontal integration. Cooperation between member companies is a matter of conducting joint business. It is estimated that as much as 50 percent of the business transactions conducted by group members is with other affiliates of the same keiretsu.

E X H I B I T 10 | **Sample Structures of Sales-Distribution Keiretsu**

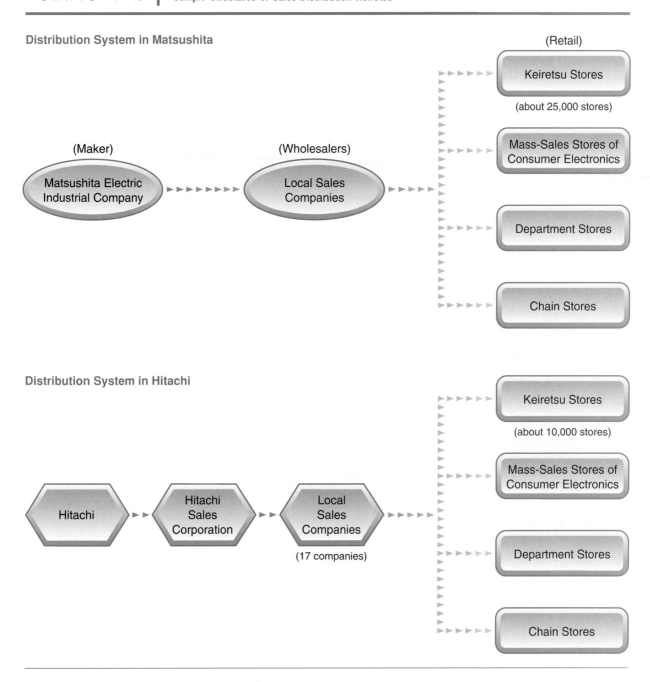

Modifications to Traditional Views   In Japan, traditionally mergers and outside acquisitions have been infrequent. However, recent developments indicate the Japanese corporations now seek M&A targets in Japan to speed up their diversification and globalization. The second most popular targets are companies in the EEC where market unification is imminent.

The majority of Japanese corporate purchases in the past involved targets with which the buyer had a trading partnership or personal relationship between top executives. Now most acquisitions involve companies in the same line of business and in related and peripheral fields.

Recently, a consortium, including the Osaka city government, C. Itoh and Company, and a group of other large Japanese corporations, developed a plan to establish an International Trade Mart at Osaka's Asia and Pacific Trade Center. The mart will bring under one roof some of Japan's main distributors and retailers, together with exporters from around the globe. The trade mart is designed to bypass the traditional Japanese distribution system and provide foreign sellers with an immediate outlet for their merchandise.

THE KEIRETSU MODEL OF PROCUREMENT

The big keiretsu that acquire smaller companies consider them part of the "family" and expect loyalty. Thus, in sourcing needed supplies, materials, components, equipment, and services, member companies give preferential treatment to the products/services of other keiretsu members. While such interaction is common, no one member of a group would follow the "buy group products" concept to the point that it harms its own interests.

In a keiretsu, no single company predominates. Since one core member of a keiretsu rarely owns more than 10 percent of another, it doesn't do business with another unless it makes economic sense. Just as they hold only minority financial shares in each other, most member companies depend on other members for no more than 15 to 20 percent of their supplies or sales.

CRAFTING STRATEGY IN DIVERSIFIED COMPANIES

PEPSICO AND THE FAST-FOOD INDUSTRY

Joseph Wolfe, University of Tulsa

As the PepsiCo Corporation entered the early 1990s, Wayne Calloway, the company's chairman and chief executive officer, had every right to be optimistic. From 1991 to 1992 sales had increased 14 percent, earnings were up 21 percent, and per share dividends had increased 20 percent. Moreover, PepsiCo's three major business units—soft drinks, snack foods, and quick-service restaurants—had turned in sales increases of 10 percent, 17 percent, and 16 percent, respectively. Since 1987 PepsiCo's sales had increased at a 16.8 percent compound rate annually, and income from continuing operations had grown at an 18 percent rate. Calloway had set a new goal for the corporation's 338,000 employees by asking the question "How does a $20 billion company add another $20 billion in just five years?"

Calloway believed PepsiCo had two major growth opportunities: (1) expand the global reach of Pepsico's present products and businesses and (2) add new businesses to the company's portfolio and redefine its areas of strategic interest:

> Not too long ago we would have described ourselves as a company in the business of soft drinks, snack chips, and quick-service restaurants. Today we're in the business of beverages, snack foods, and quick-service food distribution. A soft drink company sells only carbonated colas and the like; a beverage company might sell things like water and tea or fruit-based drinks. Also, a restaurant company is restricted to certain physical locations. A food distribution company can take its products wherever there's a customer, without necessarily making an investment in a large restaurant. We also reconsidered our geographic limitations. Up until a few years ago we were basically a strong U.S. company with a solid but limited international presence. Not so today. In 1991 nearly one out of every four sales dollars came from our international operations. When you consider that 95 percent of the world's population is outside the U.S., you can see what that means in terms of opportunity. And this is doubly true of our kinds of products, which are in great demand everywhere on earth, with almost no economic or cultural barriers.

Although Calloway saw numerous opportunities for PepsiCo, many industry observers had noted that recent domestic soft-drink sales gains had been marginal and that the cola segment was saturated. Even though cola sales amounted to $34 billion in 1992, growth had been only 1.5 percent—far lower than the 5 to 7 percent annual growth rates experienced in the 1980s, despite changes in packaging, logotypes, and advertising campaigns by both Coke and Pepsi. The market for diet soft drinks, for years a growth segment, in 1992 showed its first annual decline in share of total soft-drink sales from 29.8 percent in 1991 to 29.4 percent, and overall consumption of soft drinks rose only marginally, from 47.8 gallons to 48.0 gallons per capita. In the United States, Coca-Cola maintained its 40.7 percent share of the soft-drink market while PepsiCo slipped from 31.5 percent to 31.3 percent. In Europe, the first-mover advantages claimed by Pepsi in the former Warsaw Pact nations quickly evaporated after Coca-Cola launched its 18-month, $400 million "Operation Jumpstart" campaign in central Europe's post-socialist countries. Health concerns had generally affected the sales of both snack foods and fast-food dining and had strong implications for PepsiCo's Frito-Lay, Pizza Hut, Taco Bell, and Kentucky Fried Chicken divisions. Although new product formulations had been introduced by almost all snack chip and cracker manufacturers, and new, leaner burgers and menu assortments had been introduced by most leading fast-food chains, customer responses and sales results had been mixed.

Although PepsiCo was known worldwide for its soft drinks (Pepsi, Diet Pepsi, Mountain Dew, and—outside the U.S.—7-Up), the company derived 28 percent of its revenues from Frito-Lay and another 37 percent from its restaurant operations—Pizza Hut, Taco Bell, and Kentucky Fried Chicken. While sales in PepsiCo's three restaurant divisions had been rising, their costs and profit performances had been spotty. Nonetheless, Calloway's outlook for these business units was optimistic:

> A steadily growing interest in eating away from home and the continued gravitation to convenience foods are creating an atmosphere of excitement for our restaurants. Our strategy is to take advantage of these trends by accelerating our growth in existing markets and introducing our products to new markets. At Pizza Hut, we'll continue to expand delivery aggressively. We're testing alternatives to our traditional dine-in concept and we're adding innovative distribution channels. Taco Bell is also continuing its break with tradition. Alternative distribution points and the increasing use of technology to drive costs down make Taco Bell the market innovator. The situation at KFC in the U.S. is challenging. We're in the process of restructuring our business to greatly improve productivity and customer service. We're reorganizing our kitchens, upgrading our units, and adding nontraditional distribution points.

PEPSICO INC.

In 1993 PepsiCo was an international company operating in three industries—soft drinks, snack foods, and restaurants. As shown in Exhibit 1, it had followed an evolutionary path to its current status as a $20 billion company. From humble beginnings in 1893 as a soda fountain drink known as "Brad's drink," the trademark Pepsi-Cola was created in 1902 when the Pepsi-Cola Company became a North Carolina corporation. Profitable operations ensued until heavy losses on sugar inventories caused its bankruptcy in 1922. A new "Pepsi-Cola Corporation" was formed the following year and all operations were moved to Richmond, Virginia. The Virginia operation lost money for the next five years and then was only marginally profitable until it bankrupted in June, 1931.

Using the assets and borrowing power of the New York-based Loft, Inc., candy company, Charles Guth subsequently purchased Pepsi-Cola's proprietary rights for

EXHIBIT 1 | **Significant Events In Pepsico's Corporate History**

1893	"Brad's Drink" concocted in Caleb B. Bradham's pharmacy in New Bern, North Carolina.
1902	Pepsi-Cola Company incorporated in North Carolina.
1908	First bottling franchise created.
1920	Sugar prices rise dramatically from 5 1/2¢ to 26 1/2¢ per pound. Bradham invests heavily in sugar inventories. Prices drop to 3 1/2¢ per pound in December and the company reports a $150,000 loss on operations.
1922	Company files for bankruptcy. Bradham forced to resign and R. C. Megargel & Company forms "The Pepsi-Cola Company" as a wholly owned Delaware corporation. This company lapses on March 18, 1925, for nonpayment of taxes.
1923	Craven Holding Corporation of North Carolina purchases all of Pepsi-Cola's assets and its trademark. Roy C. Megargel forms the "Pepsi-Cola Corporation" in Richmond, Virginia, after purchasing Pepsi's trademark, business, and goodwill from the Craven Holding Corporation for $35,000. Operations in New Bern closed and moved to Richmond.
1928	Company is merged with the "National Pepsi-Cola Corporation," which was 90% owned by Megargel.
1931	Company goes bankrupt. Charles Guth uses $10,500 from the Loft, Inc., candy and candy-store company to buy Pepsi's proprietary rights. A new Pepsi-Cola Company is founded in Long Island City and loses money for the next three years.
1933	Company begins to bottle its soft drinks in used 12-oz. beer bottles. Within five months over 1,000 cases a day are being sold.
1935	Loft, with support from Phoenix Securities Corporation, sues Guth for control of Pepsi-Cola. Guth loses the suit but appeals the decision. Company is managed by a court-appointed team during the appeal process.
1938	Coca-Cola files a trademark violation suit against Pepsi over its use of the word Cola. Coke loses the lawsuit.
1939	Charles Guth loses his appeal. All legal and financial control of the company reverts to Phoenix Securities, which has a dominant stock interest in Loft. "Pepsi-Cola hits the spot" jingle created.
1941	Pepsi jingle played on over 469 radio stations and voted America's best-known tune in 1942.
1946	Sales level off at about $45 million for the next few years and earnings drop 70%.
1950	Pepsi nears bankruptcy. Alfred N. Steele leaves Coca-Cola to become Pepsi's president and vows to "Beat Coke." Pepsi's Cuban sugar plantation sold for $6 million. Over the next five years $38 million is invested in new plants and equipment.
1955	Steele marries film star Joan Crawford. Pepsi's advertising budget is $14 million or 18% of the industry's total. Advertising theme is "Be Sociable with Light Refreshment." Sales have risen 112% since 1950. Company owns 120 plants in over 50 countries.
1958	Steele attempts to merge company with Pabst Brewing Company.
1959	Steele dies of a heart attack after completing "Adorama," a $200,000 national sales promotion tour. Donald Kendall, head of Pepsi's overseas operations, photographs Nikita Khrushchev drinking six cupfuls of Pepsi at a Moscow trade fair. Drink becomes an instant hit with the Russians and the East European world.
1962	Advertising theme is "Now, it's Pepsi, for those who think young."
1963	Coke introduces diet Tab and Pepsi-Cola introduces Patio Diet Cola and later Diet Pepsi to fill low-calorie segment pioneered by Royal Crown's Diet Rite Cola.
1964	Advertising theme is "Come Alive, You're in the Pepsi Generation." Company establishes the Pepsi-Cola Equipment Corp. to lease trucks and equipment to bottlers. Company later acquires and adds to this unit Lease Plan International, a trucking concern,

$10,500. The drink was reformulated to Guth's tastes and Pepsi syrup was sold mainly to Loft's own candy stores; the operation continued to lose money. Mired in the depths of the Great Depression, the company began to bottle its soft drink in used 12-oz. beer bottles and promoted the slogan "Two large glasses in each bottle." Customers were attracted by Pepsi's offering of almost twice as much for the same 5¢ charged by Coca-Cola for its 6 1/2-oz. container. Sales and profits rose dramatically, but court battles were soon waged against the firm on two fronts. The Loft Company's management, with the help of its major stockholder Phoenix Securities, sued Guth to gain control of Pepsi, while Coca-Cola simultaneously filed a trademark infringement suit over Pepsi's use of the world "Cola." After four years of court-appointed management, Charles Guth lost all his claims. In the intervening period Coca-Cola also lost its lawsuit against Pepsi despite having successfully sued many other soft-drink manufacturers for the same violation and having seen more than 1,100 other cola manufacturers go out of business.

EXHIBIT 1 | **Significant Events In Pepsico's Corporate History** (Continued)

	National Trailer Convoy, North American Van Lines, Lee Way Motor Freight, and Chandler Leasing. Pepsi-Cola United Bottlers buys Rheingold Breweries for $26 million; PepsiCo later acquires a 51% interest in the United Bottlers operation. Company acquires Tip Corp., the Virginia manufacturer of Mountain Dew.
1965	Develops Devil Shake to compete with the Yoo-Hoo chocolate drink. Company attempts to buy controlling interest in Miller Brewing Co. Company purchases Wilson Sporting Goods from LTV. Pepsi-Cola Company merges with Frito-Lay of Dallas to become PepsiCo, Inc. Herman W. Lay becomes PepsiCo's largest stockholder and chairman of its board.
1966	Advertising theme is "Taste That Beats the Others Cold. . . Pepsi Pours It On." Company closes its upstate New York sugar refinery after losing $12 million on operations.
1969	Pepsi's late-year advertising theme becomes "You've Got a Lot to Live, and Pepsi's Got a Lot to Give." Soft-drink sales are $940 million compared to Coke's $1.3 billion.
1970	Corporation moves from its Manhattan Headquarters to the suburb of Purchase, New York.
1974	Company fined $50,000 for conspiring to fix sugar cane prices in 1972 and 1973.
1977	Company acquires Pizza Hut for about $300 million. Coca-Cola outbids PepsiCo for Taylor Wines of New York for $96 million. Pepsi's management admits that its overseas executives have made $1.7 million in questionable payments to local officials; Coke's questionable payments had been $1.3 million.
1978	Company acquires Taco Bell, Inc., the nation's largest Mexican fast-food chain, for $148 million in stock.
1982	Lee Way Motor Freight loses $12.8 million.
1984	Taco Bell unit experiments with La Petite Boulangerie, a franchised chain of bakeries. Introduces Slice to compete in the "natural fruit" drink segment. Sells Lee Way Motor Freight for a $15 million after-tax loss.
1985	Sells North American Van Lines for an after-tax gain of $139 million. Sells Wilson Sporting Goods for an $18 million after-tax loss.
1986	Acquires Kentucky Fried Chicken, the world's largest chicken chain. Acquires Mug Root Beer and 7-Up for distribution in all non-U.S. markets.
1989	Acquires the United Kingdom's Smiths Crisps Limited and Walkers Crisps Holdings Limited for $1.34 billion. Acquires General Cinema's domestic bottling operations for $1.77 billion.
1991	Taco Bell acquires Hot 'n Now hamburger franchiser.
1992	Acquires Evercrisp Snack Productos de Chile SA and Mexico's Kas SA and Knorr Elorza SA. Buys out joint-venture partners Hostess Frito-Lay in Canada and Gamesa Cookies in Mexico. Acquires a 50% interest in California Pizza Kitchen Inc. and an equity position in Carts of Colorado, Inc.
1993	Pepsi-Cola International begins to distribute Cadbury Schweppes products in central Europe through a franchise partnership. Increased distribution of H2Oh! sparkling water and Avalon still water in the United States. PepsiCo creates a $600 million European snack-food joint venture with General Mills after failing in its bid to purchase the company's European operations. PepsiCo's snack companies in Spain, Portugal, and Greece are joined with General Mills's French, Belgium, and Dutch operations into Snack Ventures Europe.

For the next 20 years the company operated as a soft-drink firm, battling against already entrenched Coca-Cola. Another bankruptcy was narrowly averted in 1950 and various diversifications were attempted or consummated from the late 1950s to the mid-1960s. Upon its merger with Frito-Lay in 1965, the company became PepsiCo, Incorporated. During the next 25 years PepsiCo's growth was fueled by acquisitions, new-product introductions, product-line extensions, and geographic expansion—see Exhibit 1.

PEPSICO'S BUSINESS PORTFOLIO IN 1993

In 1993 PepsiCo's soft-drink division marketed Pepsi-Cola, Mountain Dew, and Slice in regular and diet versions in both the U.S. and international markets, and 7-Up outside the United States. The soft-drink division also operated various joint bottling and distribution ventures with Ocean Spray and Lipton Tea in the United States; Canada's Avalon spring water in areas along the Eastern seaboard; A&W's root beer, Squirt,

Squirt, and Vernors in Asia; and Knorr Elorza SA in Spain. Crystal Pepsi and Diet Crystal Pepsi, touted as clear, uncolored "New Age" soft drinks, were introduced during Super Bowl XXVII with 90 seconds of advertising at $28,000 a second. The division was slowly rolling out All Sport in an effort to crack the $800-million-a-year sports-drink category in the U.S. beverage market.

The company's snack-foods division, Frito-Lay, made and distributed products throughout the world. Its major offerings were Lay's Potato Chips, Cheetos, Doritos, Crunch Tators, Tostitos, Ruffles, Rold Gold Pretzels, Fritos corn chips, and Santitas Tortilla Chips. New snack and chip products included Sun-Chips multigrain snacks, Suprimos wheat-based snack chips, McCracken's cracker crisps, and Sonric (a sweet snack marketed in Mexico). Frito-Lay had recently introduced a line of salsa and picante sauces, winning an 11 percent share of a $500-million market by 1992. In 1993 the division introduced a premium brand of salsa and picante named after its popular Tostitos restaurant-style chips. Major manufacturing and processing operations were located in the United Kingdom, Spain, Mexico, Portugal, and Brazil. Joint ventures were under way in Mexico with the Gamesa Company in the cookie business and with Poland's Wedel in the sweet-snack segment. Frito-Lay had just assumed complete ownership of the Arnotts snacks and cracker company in Australia, after initially operating as a joint venture. The U.S. snack food industry was growing 3 to 5 percent annually compared to an 8 to 10 percent growth rate internationally. Snack foods were a $35 billion industry in the United States. The market for snack foods was less well developed internationally; snack chip retail sales outside the U.S. were an estimated $10 to $12 billion. Profit margins in the snack foods industry averaged 4 to 5 percent.

PepsiCo also operated the world's largest system of restaurants through its Pizza Hut, Taco Bell, and KFC chains. Included in this division was PepsiCo Food Systems Worldwide (PFS), which supplied all company-owned and franchised units with food, paper goods, equipment, and promotional materials. The restaurant division's rev-

EXHIBIT 2 | **PepsiCo's Consolidated Income Statements, 1989–92**
(In millions of dollars)

	1992	1991	1990	1989
Net sales	$21,970.9	$19,607.9	$17,802.7	$15,242.4
Cost of goods sold	10,492.6	9,395.5	8,549.4	7,421.7
Gross profit	11,477.4	10,212.4	9,253.3	7,820.7
Selling and general administration	8,840.3	7,880.8	7,008.6	5,887.4
Pretax operating income	2,637.1	2,331.6	2,244.7	1,933.3
Nonoperating income	113.7	(45.4)	111.2	26.8
Interest expense	586.1	615.9	688.5	609.6
Pretax income	2,164.7	1,670.3	1,667.4	1,350.5
Provision for taxes	597.1	590.1	576.8	449.1
Less exceptional items and discontinued operations*	374.3	-0-	13.7	-0-
Net income	$ 1,193.3	$ 1,080.2	$ 1,076.9	$ 901.4

*1990 net charges for discontinued operations; 1992 net charges for required accounting changes for retiree health benefits and unfunded pension costs for retirees.
Source: Adapted from company 10-K report and *News from PepsiCo Inc.,* February 2, 1993, p. 2.

EXHIBIT 3 | **PepsiCo's Consolidated Balance Sheets, 1989–92** *(in millions of dollars)*

	1992	1991	1990	1989
Assets				
Cash	$ 169.6	$ 186.7	$ 170.8	$ 76.2
Marketable securities	1,888.5	1,849.3	1,644.9	1,457.7
Receivables	1,588.5	1,481.7	1,414.7	1,239.7
Inventories	768.8	661.5	585.8	546.1
Other current assets	426.6	386.9	265.2	231.1
Total current assets	4,842.3	4,566.1	4,081.4	3,550.8
Property, plant, and equipment	7,442.0	6,594.7	5,710.9	5,130.2
Advances to subsidiaries	1,707.0	1,681.9	1,505.9	970.8
Intangibles	6,959.0	5,932.4	5,845.2	5,474.9
Total assets	$20,951.2	$18,775.1	$17,143.4	$14,126.7
Liabilities and Shareholder Equity				
Notes payable	$ 706.8	$ 228.2	$ 1,626.5	$ 866.3
Accounts payable	1,164.8	1,196.6	1,116.3	1,054.5
Income taxes	387.9	492.4	443.7	313.7
Other current liabilities	2,064.9	1,804.9	1,584.0	1,457.3
Total current liabilities	4,324.4	3,722.1	4,770.5	3,691.8
Deferred charges	1,682.3	1,070.1	942.8	856.9
Long-term debt	7,964.8	7,806.2	5,600.1	5,777.1
Other long-term liabilities	1,624.0	631.3	925.8	909.8
Total liabilities	15,595.5	13,229.7	12,239.2	11,235.6
Common stock	14.4	14.4	14.4	14.4
Capital surplus	667.6	476.6	365.0	323.9
Retained earnings	5,439.7	5,470.0	4,753.0	3,978.4
Less treasury stock	667.0	745.9	611.4	491.8
Currency adjustment	(99.0)	303.3	383.2	66.2
Total shareholder equity	5,355.7	5,545.4	4,904.2	3,891.1
Total liabilities and net worth	$20,951.2	$18,775.1	$17,143.4	$14,126.7
Dividends paid	$395.5	$343.2	$293.9	$241.9

Source: Adapted from company 10-K report and *1992 Annual Report,* pp. 32 and 46.

enues came from company-owned store sales, initial franchising fees, royalty and rental payments from franchisees, and net wholesale sales to franchisees by PFS. In 1993, Pizza Hut and KFC each operated in over 60 countries and Taco Bell was in 11 countries. Pizza Hut had recently opened new outlets in Aruba, Cyprus, and Gibraltar; KFC, in France and Chile; and Taco Bell, in Aruba, Korea, and Saudi Arabia. Taco Bell was experimenting in Charleston, South Carolina, and Fresno, California, with its Hot 'n Now acquisition, an express drive-through burger concept; all three restaurant chains were testing new items for possible addition to their menus. Exhibits 2 and 3 present PepsiCo's recent financial statements. Exhibit 4 provides information regarding PepsiCo's international activities. Exhibits 5 and 6 show financial breakdowns by business segment and global area. Exhibit 7 indicates recent write-offs and special charges associated with PepsiCo's restaurant-division operations.

EXHIBIT 4 | PepsiCo's Sales and Profits By Geographic Area, 1989–92   *(in million of dollars)*

Area	Net Sales				Operating Profit			
	1992	1991	1990	1989	1992	1991	1990	1989
United States	$16,551.0	$15,167.8	$14,046.9	$12,519.4	$2,059.6	$1,842.2	$1,853.3	$1,601.9
Europe	1,349.0	1,486.0	1,344.7	771.7	52.6	61.8	108.5	53.8
Canada and Mexico	2,214.2	1,434.7	1,089.2	899.0	251.0	198.7	164.2	117.1
Other	1,855.8	1,519.4	1,321.9	1,032.3	138.6	123.8	98.4	122.9
Total	$21,970.0	$19,607.9	$17,802.7	$15,222.4	$2,501.8	$2,226.5	$2,224.4	$1,895.7

Source: *1990 and 1991 Stockholder's Reports,* p. 35, and *1992 Annual Report,* p. 29.

EXHIBIT 5 | PepsiCo's Sales and Operating Profits By Business Segment, 1989–92   *(in millions of dollars)*

Business Segment	Net Sales				Operating Profit			
	1992	1991	1990	1989	1992	1991	1990	1989
Beverages: Domestic	$ 5,485.3	$ 5,171.5	$ 5,034.5	$ 4,623.3	$ 686.3	$ 746.2	$ 673.8	$ 577.6
International	2,120.4	1,743.7	1,488.5	1,153.4	112.3	117.1	93.8	98.6
Total	7,605.6	6,915.2	6,523.0	5,776.7	798.6	863.3	767.6	676.2
Snack Foods: Domestic	3,950.4	3,737.9	3,471.5	3,211.3	775.5	616.6	732.3	667.8
International	2,181.7	1,827.9	1,582.5	1,003.7	209.2	171.0	202.1	137.4
Total	6,132.7	5,565.8	5,054.0	4,215.0	984.7	787.6	934.4	805.2
Restaurants: Domestic	7,115.4	6,258.4	5,504.0	4.684.8	597.8	479.4	447.2	356.5
International	1,116.9	868.5	684.8	545.9	120.7	96.2	75.2	57.8
Total	8,232.3	7,126.9	6,188.8	5,230.7	718.5	575.6	522.4	414.3
Total: Domestic	16,551.0	15,167.8	14,010.0	12,519.4	2,059.6	1,842.2	1,853.3	1,601.9
International	5,419.0	4,440.1	3,755.8	2,703.0	442.2	384.3	371.1	293.8
Grand Total	$21,970.0	$19,607.9	$17,765.8	$15,222.4	$2,501.8	$2,226.5	$2,224.4	$1,895.7

Source: *1990 and 1991 Annual Reports,* p. 35, and *News from PepsiCo, Inc.,* February 2, 1993, p. 5.

EXHIBIT 6 | PepsiCo's Identifiable Assets by Division and
Geographic Area, 1989-92   *(in millions of dollars)*

Division and Area	1992	1991	1990	1989
Soft drinks	$7,857.5	$6,832.6	$6,465.2	$6,198.1
Snack foods	4,628.0	4,114.3	3,892.4	3,310.0
Restaurants	5,097.1	4,254.2	3,448.9	3,070.6
Total	$17,582.6	$15,201.1	$13,806.5	$12,578.7
United States	$11,957.0	$10,777.8	$9,980.7	$9,593.4
Europe	1,948.4	2,367.3	2,255.2	1,767.2
Canada and Mexico	2,395.2	917.3	689.5	409.5
Other	1,282.0	1,138.7	881.1	808.6
Total	$17,582.6	$15,201.1	$13,806.5	$12,578.7

Source: *1990 and 1991 Stockholder's Reports,* p. 35, and *1992 Stockholder's Report,* p. 29.

EXHIBIT 7 | Special Charges or Write-Offs at PepsiCo's Restaurant Businesses, 1989–91 (*in millions*)

Pizza Hut	1990—$9.0 for closing underperforming domestic units; $8.0 to consolidate domestic field operations; $2.4 to relocate headquarters
Taco Bell	1989—$5.5 to consolidate domestic field operations
	1990—$4.0 for closing underperforming domestic units
KFC	1989—$8.0 for reorganization
	1990—$4.0 for closing underperforming domestic units
	$0.6 for closing underperforming international units
	1991—$32.8 to restructure domestic operations
	$1.2 to restructure international operations
	$9.0 for delay of Skinfree Crispy introduction

Source: *1990 and 1991 Annual Reports,* p. 35.

THE FAST-FOOD INDUSTRY

In the U.S., consumers ate about 750 million meals a day. Since the 1960s, the proportion of food consumed in the home had declined. By the 1990s U.S. consumers were spending almost as much on restaurant fare as for prepared and nonprepared grocery store food—see Exhibit 8. Prepared foods had become the fastest-growing category because they relieved the cooking burdens on working parents; Exhibit 9 shows the market shares of different prepared-food providers. In 1993 restaurant sales were a projected $268 billion, a substantial portion of which was consumed off-premises—see Exhibit 10.

The 1980s was a decade of high growth for restaurant businesses, with average sales increases amounting to 8.7 percent a year. In the 1990s, however, real growth was projected to slow (Exhibit 11). After adjusting for inflation, industry sales increased only 11.8 percent in 1991 and price wars among certain competing chains had recently broken out in response to outlet proliferation and the lingering 1991 recession. Discounting was starting to become a common promotional tactic to generate traffic and the major chains were redefining the nature of a "bargain" through "value meals" that offered sandwich-fries-drink combinations at a special price. Pizza Hut and KFC had both introduced value-priced all-you-can-eat lunch buffets. Despite slowing overall growth, there were several fast-growth segments based on menu type (Exhibit 12). From 1985 to 1990 the fast-food industry's sandwich segment rose from 4.9 percent of total sales to 5.7 percent of sales while hamburger chain sales fell from 53.4 percent to 50.5 percent of all sales. In 1991 the 100 largest restaurant chains in the U.S. added only 413 hamburger outlets but pizza makers opened 1,095 additional restaurants. By the beginning of 1992 there were about 18,600 pizza and 26,600 burger restaurants in the United States. Ice cream and yogurt outlets were ranked third in number but this category had a net loss of 142 outlets in 1991. A number of factors contributed to the pizza category's growth: the variety of crusts and toppings appealed to a range of tastes, the cheese base was rich in protein, and pizza was more suitable for home delivery or drive-by pickup than burgers or fries because it held up over longer distances and carried a ticket price that made home delivery feasible for pizza firms. Exhibit 13 lists the five fastest-growing fast-food chains in the United States.

EXHIBIT 8 | Grocery Store Sales versus Restaurant Sales in the United States, 1976-91

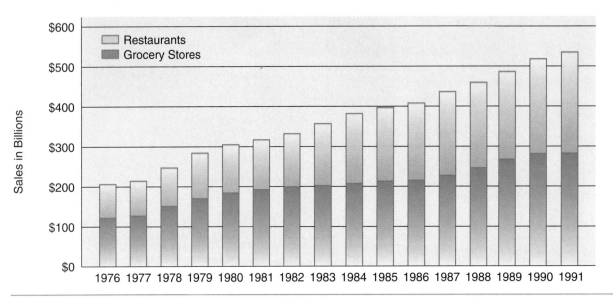

Source: Derived from graph data presented in Eben Shapiro, "A Page from Fast-Food's Menu," *New York Times,* October 14, 1991, p. D1.

EXHIBIT 9 | Market Shares of Major Prepared Food Providers, 1989-91

Year	Food Source			
	Fast-Food Restaurants	Table-Service Restaurants	Supermarkets	Other
1991	51.0%	23.0%	14.0%	12.0%
1990	46.0	27.0	14.0	13.0
1989	41.0	33.0	12.0	14.0

Source: Adapted from Charles S. Clark, "Fast-Food Shakeup," *CQ Researcher* 1, no. 25 (November 8, 1991), p. 837.

Although the upscale, casual dining segment had lost market share in recent years, popular restaurants in good locations generated relatively high profits by serving high-margin meals, encouraging bar and table liquor sales, and offering appetizers and desserts at good markups. General Mills, Inc., had been especially successful in the casual dining, ethnic-theme restaurant segment. To leverage the know-how and expertise gained from its successful but mature Red Lobster seafood restaurant chain, in 1982 General Mills simultaneously inaugurated a series of new Olive Garden restaurants based on an Italian theme, purchased a North Carolina fern-bar restaurant chain named Darryl's, acquired a California health-food restaurant chain called The Good Earth, and purchased Gallardo, a Mexican-food chain. Of the four concepts, the Olive Garden appeared to have the greatest potential because Italian cuisine was the most popular ethnic food in the United States. By 1992 General Mills's Olive Garden chain

EXHIBIT 10 | **On-Premises versus Off-Premises Sales at Restaurants, 1992**

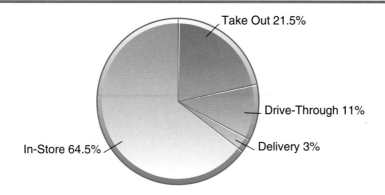

Take Out 21.5%

Drive-Through 11%

Delivery 3%

In-Store 64.5%

Source: From data and graphs in "Forget Candlelight, Flowers—and Tips: More Restaurants Tout Take-out Service," *Wall Street Journal,* June 18, 1992, p. B1.

EXHIBIT 11 | **Combined Sales and Expenses for Selected Restaurant Chains, 1989–91, with Estimates for 1992–97 (*in millions of dollars*)**

	1989	1990	1991	1992*	1993*	1995–1997*
Sales	$12,048.0	$12,943.0	$13,330.0	$14,085.0	$15,315.0	$21,275.0
Cost of sales	9,445.6	10,017.9	10,277.4	10,845.5	11,716.0	16,062.6
Gross profit	2,602.4	2,925.1	3,052.6	3,239.6	3,599.0	5,212.4
Administrative overhead	426.0	459.1	473.0	325.8	401.0	640.7
Depreciation	604.9	758.9	800.8	845.0	895.0	1,155.0
Pretax profit	1,571.5	1,707.1	1,778.7	2,068.7	2,303.0	3,416.7
Less taxes	573.6	602.6	601.2	713.7	783.0	1,161.7
Net profit	$ 997.9	$ 1,104.5	$ 1,177.5	$ 1,355.0	$ 1,520.0	$ 2,255.0
Net worth	$ 4,937.7	$ 5,762.3	$ 6,624.8	$ 7,640.0	$ 8,860.0	$13,075.0

*Estimated.

Note: Summary results for Bob Evans Farms, Carl Karcher Enterprises, Frisch's Restaurants, International Dairy Queen, JB's Restaurant, Luby's Cafeterias, McDonald's, Morrison Restaurant, National Pizza, Perkins Family Restaurant, Piccadilly Cafeterias, Ryan's Family Steak Houses, Shoney's, Sizzler International, TCBY Enterprises, Vicorp Restaurants, and Wendy's International.

Source: William G. Barr, "Restaurant Industry," *Value Line,* September 25, 1992, p. 295.

EXHIBIT 12 | **Comparative Growth Rates of Major Fast-Food Menu Categories, 1991**

Food Segment	Growth
Pizza	5.4%
Chicken	6.8
Fish	11.6
Mexican	12.6
Oriental	28.4

Source: Adapted from PepsiCo's *1991 Annual Report,* p. 31.

EXHIBIT 13 | **Five Fastest-Growing Fast-Food Chains, 1991**

Chain	Menu/Theme	1990 Sales (in millions)
Taco Bell	Inexpensive Mexican food	$2,600
Subway	Deli-style submarine sandwiches	1,400
Sonic	1950s-style drive-ins	515
Sbarro	Fast Italian food	277
Rally's	Double drive-throughs/burgers	216

Source: Lois Therrien, "The Upstarts Teaching McDonald's a Thing or Two," *Business Week,* October 21, 1991, p. 122.

had grown to 320 restaurants with combined sales of $808 million. Olive Garden's success did not come easily, however, as management spent five years and about $28 million before settling on the chain's optimal recipes, flavorings, and decor. Although uniformity and consistency were the hallmarks of fast-food chains, the Olive Garden found it had to recognize regional taste differences if it was to cater to the white-collar, evening dinner crowd. It discovered through taste tests and trial menus that chunky tomato sauce did not do very well in St. Louis but patrons in California loved it; in Rhode Island veal saltimbocca was a popular menu item.

In 1993 General Mills was in its third year of testing Chinese cuisine at its China Coast restaurant in Orlando, Florida. The company had first experimented with oriental cuisine at its Minneapolis-based Leeann Chin buffet and take-out chain in 1985. Disappointed with the results, the company hired Terry Cheng, a Chinese-American chef and food biologist, to produce a more satisfying menu for American tastes. The China Coast's menu featured six main dishes, including moo goo gai pan, fried rice, egg rolls, and sweet-and-sour chicken. Exhibit 14 presents a listing of national chains employing various ethnic menus and upscale dining accommodations, along with their ratings from a 1992 *Consumer Reports* reader survey.

In addition to price promotions and niche hunting as strategies for dealing with the fast-food industry's slowing growth, company strategies were being aimed at developing more appealing outlet designs, alternative food delivery methods, attempts to capture the after-six eating crowd, and increased penetration of foreign markets where the popularity of fast-foods was just developing.

THE OFF-PREMISES FAST-FOOD SEGMENT

Because of the growing popularity of restaurant take-out, drive-through, and delivery service, off-premises sales at fast-food enterprises grew 5.9 percent in 1991 whereas total on-premises sales were flat. Some chains had been more successful than others in the off-premises segment. At Wendy's, off-premises sales accounted for 65 percent of volume in 1992 (up 30 percent since 1988); off-premises sales accounted for 70 percent of Burger King's volume. Despite the attractiveness of providing take-out service, certain dangers were involved. According to George Rice, chairman of GDR Enterprises, "Off-premises sales are a great opportunity, but they can also screw up your business." He recommended owners view off-premise sales as a separate business and ask such questions as "Who's going to take orders? How's the kitchen going to integrate take-out with on-premise orders? Where are take-out

EXHIBIT 14 | **Selected National Restaurant Chains by Type, 1992**

Family Restaurants

Big Boy
963 units. Originally known for its hamburgers but now offers a variety of meals and a soup, salad, and fruit bar. Worst-rated restaurant in this category. Value and prices were average.

Denny's
1,391 units. 24-hour service, well-known for breakfast menu and grilled sandwiches. Menus for senior citizens and children. Alcohol served at many locations. Food taste and selection rated less than average for average-priced fare.

International House of Pancakes
500 units. Traditional breakfast stop with a wide variety of all-day meals of average value and price. Menus for seniors and children. Most patrons were seated immediately.

Po Folks
137 units. Large portions of "home style cookin'." Special menus for seniors and children. Has a take-out service and catering facilities. Considered a good value with lower than average prices. Received the highest overall rating in this category of restaurants.

Village Inn
229 units. Focuses mainly on breakfast with a limited selection of lunch and dinner meals. Senior citizen discount and low fat/calorie breakfasts. Most diners were seated immediately.

Steak/Buffet Restaurants

Golden Corral
458 units. Mostly steak but limited grilled chicken and seafood. Food, salad, and dessert bar with over 100 items. Menus for seniors and children. Bar. Prices and food value judged better than average.

Mr. Steak
60 units. Steak, chicken, and seafood. Take-out service and a children's menu. Received the highest rating for this type of restaurant.

Sizzler
634 units. Features chicken, steak, and seafood with a large salad, soup, taco, and pasta bar. Senior citizen and children's menus. Entertainment lounge and wine. Take-out service. Taste, food selection, price, and value rated average.

Casual Dinner Houses

Bennigan's
223 units. Menu varies throughout the U.S. but emphasizes Southwestern dishes and finger foods. Children's menu. Take-out. Bar. Received the lowest ratings for this type of restaurant. Value and prices were much worse than average although the atmosphere was rated much better than average.

Chili's
267 units. Southwest grill, Tex-Mex, burgers, and salads. Seniors and children's menus. Bar. Fare was rated above average in tastiness. Rated about average for this group.

El Torito
169 units. Clearly Mexican featuring fajitas, quesadillas, and chimichangas, and daily specials. Sunday brunch. Bar. Dinner portions were considered larger than average.

Houlihan's
54 units. Steaks, burgers, and fajitas. Kids menu. Bar and lounge. Value and prices were rated much worse than average for this group.

Olive Garden
Homemade pasta, regional Italian meat and seafood specialties. Large Italian wine list. Children's menu, take-out service and catering. The highest-rated restaurant in this category with much better than average taste and better than average menu selection. Dinner portions were larger than average and the food's quality was more consistent. At least 25% of the raters had to wait more than 10 minutes to be seated for dinner.

Red Lobster
550 units. Seafood, chicken, and steak with catch-of-the-day specials. Children's menu, take-out service, and bar. Prices rated much higher than average although its fare was rated above average in taste and selection. 25% of the raters had to wait more than 10 minutes to be seated.

Ruby Tuesday
151 units. Menu varies throughout the U.S. with international appetizers and main courses. Salad bar and weekend brunch. Senior citizen discounts and children's menus. Bar. Rated below average for price and value.

Steak and Ale
158 units. Well-appointed atmosphere featuring steak, seafood, pasta, and chicken. Salad bar. Bar. Food rated much tastier than average and above average in selection; Prices were much higher than average. Rated the second-highest restaurant in this group.

T.G.I. Friday's
202 units. Very eclectic menu. Also has "lite" and children's menus. Take-out service and bar. Prices were much higher than average although tastiness and selection were better than average.

Tony Roma's
122 units. Barbecued ribs and chicken entrées. Take-out, bar, and children's menu. Food rated higher than average in tastiness although rated below average in value and cost.

Source: Adapted from "Best Meals Best Deals," *Consumer Reports* 57, no. 6 June, 1992, pp. 361–62.

customers going to stand while they wait? Will they make the restaurant look crowded?" Many sit-down restaurant chains resisted doing take-outs and, instead, were using their ambiance as a competitive weapon against the plastic-boothed and spartan-appearing fast-food chains. Ann Durning of the Olive Garden chain observed, "We make take-out available, but our feeling is that there's more to a full-service restaurant than food. There is also good service, Italian music, and fresh flowers on the table."

One strategy for eliminating the problems of offering both on- and off-premises dining from the same location was the creation of outlets that prepared meals exclusively for off-premises consumption. Pizza Hut had opened Fastino's, a chain that sold pasta and pizza on a take-out and drive-through basis only. A number of Pizza Hut operations had opened a special outlet that only made pizzas for delivery. Other chains were experimenting with double-drive-through designs. In Raleigh, North Carolina, McDonald's had a location with tandem drive-through windows on the side of a small food preparation and cashiering building; the outlet had no counter or seating, was one-third the size of a typical McDonald's 4,500-square-foot restaurant, and had 35 employees instead of the more normal 60-person crew. To accelerate food preparation and simplify order taking, most such outlets had a limited menu that excluded salads and breakfast entrees such as pancakes. Taco Bell and Arby's were among the other companies experimenting with exclusive drive-through designs and menus.

THE DEVELOPMENT OF SMALLER-SCALE OUTLETS

To access market niches and locations that could not support full-size or traditional fast-food operations, several major chains had developed smaller outlets suitable for small-town locations and were experimenting with the use of kiosks and portable food carts. Taco Bell had operated one-person kiosks in supermarkets in Phoenix and its first Mexico City outlet was a two-person food cart started in June 1992; two more such locations were planned for Mexico City and one was slated for Tijuana. Pizza Hut already had 500 carts in operation and had plans to set up more than 10,000 carts in the United States and more than 100,000 in overseas locations. KFC had opened a cart unit in a General Motors plant in January 1992, and had plans for carts in train stations, office buildings, sports stadiums, and amusement parks. PepsiCo was negotiating with Wal-Mart to put fast-food units in the mass merchandiser's chain throughout the United States. In early 1992, PepsiCo purchased a minority interest in Carts of Colorado Inc. McDonald's had opened niche outlets in airports and hospitals and small-scale units in rural towns that were about half the size of a standard McDonald's, seated about 50 people, and had drive-through service. Wendy's had an outlet in the lobby of an Atlanta Day's Inn, and many Marriott hotels had placards in their rooms offering room delivery of Pizza Hut pizzas prepared in their own kitchens even though guests could go downstairs and eat a meal in the hotel's restaurant or order from the regular room service menu. Hotels and motels were often able to generate attractive sales volumes and to charge slight price premiums for the fast-food products of major chains compared to their own in-house versions because of the chains' consistent quality reputations and buyer familiarity with their products. Economy hotels and motels that either did not have dining facilities or were losing money on them were viewed as attractive market targets by the fast-food industry. Economy or budget hotels accounted for about 38% of the nation's 44,500 hotels and motels and were the fastest-growing segment of the lodging industry.

EFFORTS TO ATTRACT DINNER CUSTOMERS

Fast-food chains were struggling to find ways to attract after-six dinner customers and to capitalize on the rise of the "casual dining out experience." Fast-food was not viewed as an attractive option by most dinner customers. Norman K. Stevens, former marketing chief for Hardee's, said, "People's expectations at dinner are totally different from at lunch." People who ate out at night saw dinner as more of a leisurely event, not something to be gotten over with as quickly as possible, and they generally weren't interested in having typical fast-food fare. While McDonald's had been able to attract breakfast customers to complement its popular lunch trade, it had been notably unsuccessful drawing dinner customers. The company's 1987 "Mac Tonight" campaign featuring a piano-playing Moonman character intended to induce customers to have an evening meal at a McDonald's produced little result. In 1993 only about 20 percent of McDonald's sales came after 4:00 PM.

Burger King had initiated a dinner menu and table service to try to revive its stagnant sales and attract a different dinner customer. In certain outlets tablecloths and napkin rings were provided to heighten the ambiance. Starting at 4:00 PM patrons could order four main courses priced from $3.00 to $5.00—a hamburger, a steak sandwich, fried shrimp, or a fried chicken filet in a dinner basket served with either a baked potato or french fries, and a salad or cole slaw. Customers were given a tray, beverage cups, and a numbered plastic marker along with free popcorn. When customer orders were ready, they were brought to the table. Management believed its sitdown dinner service was a major factor in increasing the company's operating profit over 9% from 1991 to 1992. While table service and expanded menu selections for dinner were innovations for sandwich-oriented chains, KFC and Pizza Hut already had heavy dinner traffic—about 65 percent and 73 percent of KFC's and Pizza Hut's respective sales were in the evening.

To combat slowing industrywide sales growth and increasing market saturation in various food segments in the United States, many restaurant chains had begun to focus more attention on opportunities in foreign markets. McDonald's had 3,696 foreign restaurants (versus 8,772 in the U.S.) and was opening 400 to 450 foreign units annually. McDonald's biggest restaurant was a 700-seat facility in Beijing, China. One analyst estimated that McDonald's overseas profits would surpass its domestic profits by 1995, given the growing number of foreign units it operated and the high unit volumes they produced. KFC opened its first East European store in Budapest, Hungary, in partnership with the Hungarian franchisee Hemingway Holding AG in October 1992 after working nearly two years to develop local suppliers. Pizza Hut opened two restaurants in Moscow in September 1990, with one selling pizzas for hard currency and the other selling them for rubles; the two outlets served about 20,000 customers a week, roughly the number served by 10 Pizza Huts in the United States.

HEALTH AND NUTRITIONAL CONCERNS

To many consumers fast-food had always meant "bad food." PepsiCo had attempted to downplay the stereotype of "fast" not being "good" by calling its chains "quick service" restaurants. McDonald's stressed the enjoyment of eating fast, tasty meals with friends, family, and co-workers. To address health and nutritional concerns, fast-food chains were introducing low-fat and low-calorie items to their standard fare as well as emphasizing the nutritional value of fast-food dining. In early 1990 McDonald's introduced its McLean Deluxe, a 91-percent fat-free hamburger containing carrageenan, a seaweed-based additive. Two years later, as part of a public information effort, the company aired a dozen animated 55-second TV spots called "What's on Your Plate" that explained the basics of well-balanced eating and how it could be accomplished. In each restaurant McDonald's posted nutritional information, and leaflets about its food were available for the asking. Burger King displayed posters with the calorie, fat, cholesterol, and sodium content of all its menu items. The company was also test marketing menus exclusively based on Weight Watchers foods in 350 stores and experimenting with foods under 300 calories, including chicken on angel-hair pasta and chocolate mocha pie. About 60 percent of Taco Bell's company-owned outlets provided complete nutritional product information. Wendy's policy was to match its competitors regarding the amount of nutritional information it supplied.

Many critics, however, were not satisfied with the industry's efforts at providing healthy menu selections. Michael Jacobson, executive director of the Center for Science in the Public Interest, said, "The charts and posters don't convey much to the average person. The information is presented as a matrix with 10 or 15 numbers for every food. Most people aren't going to lose their places in line to read about nutritional values." Bonnie Liebman, director of nutrition at the Center for Science in the Public Interest, observed about Subway's "fattiest" sandwich, a six-inch meatball sub, "It's not particularly healthy, but it has only half as much fat as a McDonald's Big Mac."

Exhibit 15 displays the nutritional content of typical fast-food restaurant fare for an entire day. The average adult needed between 1,200 and 3,000 calories daily for weight maintenance. Approximately 50 to 60 percent of those calories were recommended to come from carbohydrates, 15 to 20 percent from protein, and no more than 25 to 30 percent from fat. It was also recommended that

EXHIBIT 15 | **Nutritional Content of Selected Meals at Selected Fast-Food Chains**

Meal	Nutrition				
	Carbohydrates	Protein	Fat	Cholesterol	Calories
Breakfast at McDonald's					
Orange juice	19 g	1 g	0 g	0 g	80
McMuffin sausage/egg	28	23	27	263	440
Hashbrown potatoes	15	1	7	9	130
Total	62	25	34	272	650
Lunch at Pizza Hut					
3 slices medium size pepperoni pizza	75	42	36	75	750
1 regular Pepsi	40	0	0	0	159
Total	115	42	36	75	909
Supper at KFC					
3 drumsticks	12	39	27	201	438
Cole slaw	13	2	7	5	119
2 buttermilk biscuits	56	10	24	2	470
1 regular Pepsi	40	0	0	0	159
Total	121	51	58	208	1,186
Grand total	298	118	128	555	2,745

Note: Carbohydrates, protein, fat, and cholesterol listed in grams.

Source: *Eating Out Made Simple* (Tulsa, OK: St. Francis Hospital, 1991), pp. 16–17, 22, 25–26.

healthy adults limit their sodium intake to 3,000 milligrams per day and cholesterol to 300 milligrams.

FRANCHISOR-FRANCHISEE RELATIONSHIPS

Since the early 1960s McDonald's had pioneered and proven the virtues of franchising as a way to gain rapid penetration of local retail markets. Frandata Corp. of
Washington, DC, estimated there were more than 3,000 franchisers in the United
States operating about 540,000 franchised outlets—a new outlet of some type opened
about every 16 minutes. In 1992, franchised business sales totaled $757.8 billion,
about 35 percent of all retail sales. Restaurants, which constituted the franchising
industry's largest single group, experienced 1991 per-store sales increases of 6.2 percent versus an overall restaurant industry growth rate of 3.0 percent.

Despite generally favorable sales and profits, franchisor-franchisee relationships
were strained at several prominent fast-food chains. When Britain's Grand Metropolitan PLC purchased Burger King from the Pillsbury Co. in 1989, it ordered changes
in floor tile designs, background music, and cutbacks in field management help. It
also created an advertising campaign that many Burger King franchisees felt was
unsuccessful. In 1991 Burger King's management group met with a disgruntled,
1,300-member National Franchisee Association for the first time in seven years. The
association's grievances were so great it even explored buying Burger King from
Grand Metropolitan.

Almost all of Taco Bell's franchisees joined an independent group in January 1992
to oppose Taco Bell management's aggressive price-cutting strategy and to challenge
a contract clause that allowed Taco Bell to open company-owned stores within a
franchisee's market. To protest the advertised prices Taco Bell set for its company-
owned stores, about 30 percent of the franchised Taco Bell units priced certain menu
items higher than the nationally promoted prices in September 1992. Taco Bell
officials had announced in March 1992 the chain's intention to maintain the 59-cent,
low-price strategy that many believed started the industry's promotional discounting
in late 1988.

Although the low-price strategy had helped Taco Bell achieve 50 percent sales
increases to $2.4 billion in two years, the division's profit growth dropped from gains
of 108 percent and 19 percent for the first two quarters of 1991 to 2 percent and 5
percent in the following two quarters. Moreover, Taco Bell's discounting prompted
McDonald's to launch a retaliatory price-cutting campaign in 1991. A McDonald's
franchisee in Tampa, Florida, that had 29 McDonald's restaurants reported price cutting increased his customer count by 15 percent but overall sales increased only 4 to
5 percent and profits fell 10 to 15 percent. Franchisees at other chains had similar
experiences with promotional pricing campaigns, creating a widespread belief that
franchisees were bearing the brunt of the price wars being conducted by their chains'
headquarters management. The Taco Bell franchisees wanted higher-priced items
featured in advertisements, but Tim Ryan, the system's senior vice president of marketing, said, "Our customers' focus on price is unchanged. Value continues to be the
primary driver." Taco Bell's corporate marketing group was testing a Value Menu
that was priced 10 cents lower than the present discounted items. Actions by Taco
Bell's Hot 'n Now management group had also provoked franchisee protests. All Hot
'n Now units had been encouraged to feature 39-cent prices for hamburgers, french
fries, and soft drinks. Claiming that they could not make a profit at these prices and
that the company's advertisements were confusing, 15 franchisees formed an independent association to stand up to PepsiCo in October 1992.

PEPSICO'S QUICK-SERVICE RESTAURANT DIVISION

Under Wayne Calloway's leadership, PepsiCo's success had been characterized as "Love change. Learn to dance. And leave J. Edgar Hoover behind." Calloway believed change was inevitable and that it was better to initiate change than to be constantly reacting to new situations: "The worst rule of management is 'If it ain't broke, don't fix it.' In today's economy, if it ain't broke, you might as well break it yourself, because it soon will be." Calloway wanted PepsiCo to deal with customers in new ways and he allowed each chain a wide degree of latitude. To promote new ways of thinking at PepsiCo's business subsidiaries, he was not averse to moving managers from one division to another. For example, the president of Frito-Lay was shifted to the presidency of Kentucky Fried Chicken and the head of Pepsi's World-wide Beverages was appointed president of Frito-Lay—both changes were made in 1991. Over the past eight years, three senior soft-drink sales and marketing vice presidents had left the company after failing to produce results acceptable to Calloway. One of Calloway's key strategic objectives was to double PepsiCo's revenues from quick-service businesses during the 1990s: "For us the restaurant business is the most compelling action around. We're not going to prosper if we just wait for busy people to come to our restaurants. We want to move toward the day when pizzas, chicken, and tacos are as convenient and readily available as a bag of Doritos is now." Exhibits 16 through 19 provide recent operating results for PepsiCo's restaurant businesses.

KENTUCKY FRIED CHICKEN

KFC's same-store sales had not risen for the past two years (Exhibit 16) and it had met with a number of failures in trying to diversify its menu offerings away from fried chicken on-the-bone. A number of factors, however, were operating in KFC's favor. Michael Mueller, a restaurant analyst with Montgomery Securities, observed, "Regular hamburger customers, for health and variety, are switching to chicken." Restaurant industry sales of chicken entrees and sandwiches had climbed to 12.4 percent of all transactions in 1990 and 10.9 percent in 1987; during the same period, sales of hamburgers had fallen from 19 to 17 percent of total industry sales. KFC's two closest rivals, Church's and Popeye's, had recently merged and then subsequently been forced to file for reorganization under Chapter 11 of the bankruptcy code to try to escape financial insolvency.

KFC dominated the chicken segment of the U.S. fast-food industry with a 50 percent market share (Exhibit 17), but many fast-food chains had introduced chicken-

EXHIBIT 16 | **Same-Store Sales Growth by Chain, 1989–92**

Chain	1992	1991	1990	1989
Pizza Hut	0.0%	0.5%	5.5%	9.2%
Taco Bell	6.0	4.1	11.5	15.3
KFC	0.0	0.0	7.0	2.0

Source: Derived from E. S. Ely, "Some High Hurdles Loom for Pepsico's Fast-Food Hotshots," *New York Times,* February 16, 1992, sec. 3, p. 5, and *News from PepsiCo, Inc.,* February 2, 1993, pp. 7–9.

EXHIBIT 17 | **Restaurant Division's U.S. Market Shares by Food Category, 1990**

PepsiCo Chain	Food Category	Market Share	Total Market (in billions)
KFC	Chicken	48.6%	$ 7.0
Pizza Hut	Italian	26.2	16.4
Taco Bell	Mexican	69.6	4.6

Source: Based on data presented in *1992 Annual Report,* p. 23.

EXHIBIT 18 | **Number of Company-Owned and Franchised Units, by Chain, 1992**

Area	Pizza Hut	Taco Bell	KFC
United States			
Company-owned	4,301	2,498	1,994
Franchised	2,905	1,446	3,074
Total	7,608	4,078	5,089
Overseas			
Company-owned	539	5	726
Joint Venture	370	0	474
Franchised	937	24	2,440
Total	1,846	75	3,640
Grand total	9,454	4,153	8,729

Note: Unit totals include 477 primarily Pizza Hut kiosks and 293 other special concepts. Taco Bell U.S. unit count includes 99 company-owned and 38 franchised Hot 'n Now restaurants. U.S. count does not include 29 California Pizza Kitchen, Inc., units.

Source: Abstracted from *1992 Annual Report,* p. 24.

EXHIBIT 19 | **Comparative Sales and Operating Profits for PepsiCo's Three Restaurant Chains, 1989–92** (*in millions of dollars*)

Chain	Net Sales				Operating Profits			
	1992	1991	1990	1989	1992	1991	1990	1989
Pizza Hut	$3,603.5	$3,258.3	$2,949.9	$2,453.5	$335.4	$314.5	$245.9	$205.5
Taco Bell	2,460.0	2,038.1	1,745.5	1,465.9	214.3	180.6	149.6	109.4
KFC	2,168.8	1,830.5	1,530.3	1,331.3	168.8	80.5	126.9	99.4
Total	$8,232.3	$7,126.9	$6,225.7	$5,250.7	$718.5	$575.6	$522.4	$414.3

Source: Data found in *1990* and *1991 Annual Reports,* p. 35, and *News from PepsiCo, Inc.,* February 2, 1993, p. 6.

based meals to broaden the appeal of their menus. Wendy's had introduced a grilled chicken sandwich and Burger King had come out with a BK Broiler sandwich. McDonald's began offering chicken fajitas in mid-year 1991 and it was testing both grilled chicken sandwiches and oven-baked chicken on-the-bone. Taco Bell introduced four chicken products in April 1991, and Pizza Hut began testing marinated, rotisserie-cooked chicken in mid-1992. Two of Taco Bell's items were 79-cent chicken tacos and 99-cent chicken-and-cheese-filled tortillas called MexiMelts. Taco

Bell management did not expect its chicken products to cannibalize business from KFC; according to one of its executives, "What we're offering fills a void, a different niche."

Industry experts saw KFC's reliance on fried chicken products as its main menu problem. Although chicken was lean and potentially healthy, the batters and frying processes employed usually offset those advantages. The chain had changed its name to KFC to disassociate itself from the "fried chicken" label. A new skinless, but still fried, product called Lite 'N Crispy was introduced in Spring 1991; it suffered a number of embarrassing marketplace setbacks because of its higher price, lack of taste, and franchisee protests of low margins. Initially announced as a phased national introduction, it was renamed Extra Crispy and withdrawn until 1992 to resolve production and taste problems. The delay ultimately resulted in charges of $9 million against domestic operations in 1991. Some industry observers said that Lite 'N Crispy's flop was a symptom of bigger problems; a Paine Webber analyst stated, "There doesn't seem to be a strategic direction. There is a disjointedness, and the skin-free chicken is a microcosm of that." The introduction of Lite 'N Crispy was intended as the first in a series of moves to broaden KFC's chicken menu to include flavored chicken, such as lemon, barbecue, hot 'n spicy, and teriyaki, and other non-fried fare.

KFC introduced Popcorn Chicken in July 1992; it consisted of small pieces of marinated, breaded, and fried chicken. The Center for Science in the Public Interest, in its *Nutrition Action Healthletter,* described Popcorn Chicken as "nuggets of grease-drenched breading that are oozing with fat and salt." A standard 5.3-ounce serving contained 45 grams of fat, almost twice as much as in two Big Macs, and 1,775 mg of sodium. Other new products were stalled in KFC's test kitchens and a line of eight new sandwiches failed while in test market. The sandwiches, including barbecue, spicy, and chicken salad designed for the lunch trade, increased sales only when heavily promoted. Moreover, they cannibalized KFC's higher-margin chicken-on-the-bone sales.

William McDonald, KFC's senior marketing vice president, said reformulating the chicken was not easy: "It's not a no-brainer. We've learned a product has got to be unbelievably indulgent, special, and unique, and not eminently substitutable at home." The chain had experimented with baking, open-hearth grilling, char-grilling, and broiling—with minimal success. It had recently scrapped a version of Monterey Broil, its latest effort, and was starting over again to make it stand out from home-prepared chicken by spicing up its flavor; perfecting the recipe was expected to take anywhere from 6 to 18 months. Tests were also under way on a spicy, rotissiere-broiled chicken recipe.

The chain had also been working on store appearance and overhaul advertising, in addition to making menu changes. As one KFC official put it, "KFC has a 1960s image and it's the 1990s. We've got to turbo-charge." By early 1992, 85 percent of its U.S. stores had invested an average of $7,500 for new landscaping, new atriums, a coat of fresh red roof paint, and brighter wallpaper. Beginning in Spring 1992, KFC had initiated a new ad campaign featuring the make-believe town of Lake Edna and its single KFC restaurant. The campaign's purpose was to capture the positive, feel-good aspects associated with good food and the traditional values and security found in small towns. KFC spent almost $120 million on advertising in 1991, compared to $387 million for McDonald's, $118 million for Pizza Hut, and $93 million for Taco Bell.

When John Cranor moved from Frito-Lay to head up KFC's turnaround efforts in 1991, he recruited several Pizza Hut executives to help him learn the fast-food business. Cranor and his new management team had implemented a number of actions to streamline the KFC organization and reduce costs. As an economy measure KFC had begun to use more frozen products in its cooking to reduce in-house chicken preparation labor costs. In another move, Cranor eliminated about one-half of KFC's managers and support staff at both the 800-employee Louisville, Kentucky, headquarters and its 700-employee field management offices. The downsizing resulted in middle managers' supervising more stores and headquarters' becoming more involved in field operations. Although the restructuring resulted in annual savings of $25 million after a one-time charge of $43 million, observers were skeptical of the long-term benefits. Ron Paul, president of Technomic Inc., said, "All this does is improve their margins in the short run. It does not fundamentally change the menu and the way consumers view the store."

KFC also had franchisee problems. Franchisees controlled about two-thirds of KFC's outlets in the U.S.; many were independent minded and had outlets in middle- or low-income neighborhoods where customers were less concerned about nutrition and were partial to fried food. Long-time franchise owners were loyal to Colonel Sanders' original Kentucky Fried Chicken recipe, having initially purchased their franchises because of its taste, and were antagonistic toward some of the new products headquarters had created for them. Their skepticism and dissatisfaction had been expressed in many ways on numerous occasions. PepsiCo had been in court for three years litigating and defending against various contract disputes with franchisees. KFC had begun to buy out some disgruntled franchisees as a partial solution to dealing with these frustrations.

When asked how KFC's turnaround had progressed under his leadership, Cranor responded, "I didn't expect turning KFC around was going to be an easy proposition. We're all impatient with everything. We need direction, we need a unified focus. We just want to make sure we don't screw up a $6 billion business while we decide how to get from there to $10 billion." One fast-food industry analyst saw KFC's challenge as one of "attracting new users without losing its current loyal following."

PIZZA HUT WORLDWIDE

Steven S. Reinemund, Pizza Hut's president and former Marriott Corporation executive, viewed the division as a pizza distribution company. Pizza Hut had been very aggressive in pursuing both off- and on-premises pizza sales. Pizza Hut began delivering pizza in 1987 and had built a number of outlets dedicated to delivery and carry-out. George Rice, a food-service consultant, commented, "Since 1984 the entire growth in restaurant sales has been in take-out, delivery, and other consumption outside the stores. That makes Pizza Hut one of the industry's best-positioned companies." Although Pizza Hut had captured about 25 percent of the pizza delivery market (Exhibit 16), it was well behind Domino's and just even with Little Caesar's in the number of stores devoted to take-out and delivery service. Currently, Little Caesar's was adding such units at a faster rate than Pizza Hut.

In 1992, to combat declining in-store sit-down sales, Pizza Hut initiated all-you-can-eat lunch buffets for $3.99. The buffets were tested for four months at Pizza Huts in Dallas, Indianapolis, Savannah, and Tulsa, and then rolled out to 2,000 restaurants. Reinemund said, "We're into it hot and heavy. It is phase one of our effort to revitalize our dine-in business." The buffets featured pastas, salads, and pizza. To maintain product quality, Pizza Hut designed a screen that sat inside a pan and allowed air to circulate around the pizza; this allowed pizzas to stay hot and fresh at the buffet table for as long as 20 minutes.

Pizza Hut management was exploring the upscale pizza market with a concept called Pizza Hut Cafes. Management believed a market existed for this concept even though there were several small chains and many owner-managed restaurants that featured pastas, gourmet pizzas, and desserts in casual dining atmospheres. Its cafe, which had been tested in Wichita, Kansas, featured tablecloths, desserts, sauteed chicken, and a wider variety of pizzas than found in regular Pizza Huts.

TACO BELL WORLDWIDE

Under John Martin's leadership, Taco Bell had become the fast-food industry's value leader. In late 1988 the chain introduced its 59-cent Value Menu, boosting sales 50 percent in two years to $2.4 billion. Continuing the trend of offering everyday bargains, Taco Bell in 1990 reorganized most of its menu into three price tiers—59 cents, 79 cents, and 99 cents. Although Taco Bell later backed off rigid adherence to these tiers in response to franchisee pressures for higher margins, Taco Bell management believed offering value menus was the chain's key to success. John Martin had said Taco Bell alone could one day be as big as the entire PepsiCo Corporation was in 1992.

To be a low-cost provider, Taco Bell had shifted as much food preparation to outside suppliers as possible. Its ground beef was precooked outside the store and then reheated; its tortillas were already fried; precooked dishes were provided in boil bags for easy reheating; and all its onions were pre-diced in a factory. These actions had reduced labor requirements by 15 hours daily at every outlet and cut kitchen space from 70 percent to 30 percent of a typical building. According to a Taco Bell executive, "Our entire Taco Bell restaurant can fit into a McDonald's kitchen." Other operating efficiencies had come from greater automation, simplified food production, and menu items that were quick to prepare. Management had reconfigured the menu to emphasize plain tacos and burritos that took only 8 seconds to make versus the 20 seconds needed to make a Mexican pizza or a taco salad. With the new efficiencies, a new Taco Bell restaurant in 1992 could handle twice the volume with half the labor compared to what a Taco Bell restaurant had been able to do in 1987. Taco Bell was currently testing taco-making robots in a further effort to lower operating costs. While the emphasis on low-cost efficiency made Taco Bell the industry's low-price leader, various industry analysts questioned the strategy because rock-bottom pricing hurt profit margins, cannibalized the sales of full meals, could leave customers unfilled, and created an image of low quality.

CALLOWAY'S STRATEGIC VISION FOR PEPSICO

In 1993 Wayne Calloway's overall goal for PepsiCo was "to be the best consumer products company in the world." He went on to explain:

> In 1992 we took dramatic steps to keep us on a strong growth path. Our domestic beverage division is being completely restructured to serve our customers better. And our aggressive acquisition activity, over 50 in all, is doing a lot to expand and strengthen our core businesses. We're entering 1993 with solid momentum and well positioned to address changing consumer needs. Low-cost Mexican food is still a novelty to most Americans, there are more ways to sell pizza, and new products and value combinations at KFC will bring customers back more often.

PHILIP MORRIS COMPANIES, INC.

Tracy Robertson Kramer, George Mason University
Arthur A. Thompson, Jr., The University of Alabama

The business makeup of the Philip Morris Companies in 1993 was markedly different from what its long-time heritage in cigarettes might suggest. In the early 1950s, Philip Morris' business centered entirely on cigarettes, and the company had only a 9.2 percent market share—fourth among the six U.S. manufacturers and far behind R. J. Reynolds (the leader with a 34 percent market share) and second-place American Brands (with a 25.6 percent market share). But the company's management resolved to strengthen PM's position in cigarettes and, beginning in 1956, management launched a major diversification program—the first such move among the U.S. cigarette firms. Philip Morris' basic strategy was to use surplus cash flows from cigarette operations to acquire companies with potential to become market leaders in their industries. Most of the acquired companies represented opportunities to grow the sales of previously undermarketed consumer products with the aid of PM's considerable marketing know-how in cigarettes.

Between 1957 and 1993, Philip Morris made numerous acquisitions, including investments in or acquisitions of more than 20 companies in 1992 alone (see Exhibit 1). The early acquisitions were small packaging companies whose products were used in cigarette manufacturing. During the 1960s, the company began diversifying into consumer products with the purchase of companies such as American Safety Razor, Clark Chewing Gum, Miller Brewing Company, and 7-Up. Not all the acquisitions met Philip Morris's growth expectations, and several were subsequently divested, often at substantial gains over the original acquisition prices.

Under the guidance of Joseph F. Cullman III, who became chief executive officer in 1957, Philip Morris' sales grew from $400 million in 1957 to $14.1 billion in 1984, a compound annual growth rate of over 14 percent. Cullman took the company from 170th on *Fortune's* list of the 500 largest industrial corporations in the U.S. in 1957 to 32nd in 1984, engineering 16 acquisitions and creating an international cigarette division. Of the company's $13.7 billion growth in revenues between 1957 and 1984, $6 billion came from gains in domestic cigarette sales, $3.8 billion from the

E X H I B I T 1 | **Philip Morris Acquisitions and Divestitures, 1957–1993**

Acquisition Date		Divestiture Date
1957	Acquired Milprint, Inc., a flexible packaging plant, and its subsidiary, Nicolet Paper Company, which manufactured greaseproof paper used by the packaging industry	1985
1958	Acquired Polymer Industries, Inc., a manufacturer of industrial adhesives and textile chemicals	1982
1960	Acquired American Safety Razor Products Corporation	1977
1963	Acquired Burma-Nita Company	1973
	Acquired Clark Bros. Chewing Gum Company	1973
1969	Acquired 53 percent ownership of Miller Brewing Company from W. R. Grace & Company at a price of $130 million	
1970	Acquired control of Mission Viejo Company, a California community development and home-building firm	
	Acquired remaining 47 percent of stock of Miller Brewing Company from De Rance Foundation in Milwaukee	
	Acquired Plainwell Paper Company	1985
1971	Acquired Armstrong Coated Products	1982
	Acquired Lindeman (Holdings) Ltd., an Australian wine company	
1972	Completed 100 percent acquisition of Mission Viejo Company for maximum total price of $48 million	
	Acquired Wikolin Werk Willi E. Kohlmeyer G.M.B.H., a West German specialty chemical manufacturer	1982
1973	Formed Surtech Coating Company	1978
1977	Acquired Wisconsin Tissue Mills, Inc., for 314,984 shares of common stock	1985
1978	Acquired 97 percent of the Seven-Up Company for $520 million	1986
1980	Acquired a 31 percent ownership interest of British-based Rothmans International, Ltd., the world's third-largest cigarette producer; also obtained the rights to market major Rothmans brands in the United States and South America	1989
1985	Acquired General Foods for $5.7 billion in a hostile takeover	
1988	Acquired Kraft Foods for $12.9 billion in a hostile takeover	
1989	Acquired Oroweat Baked Goods, Anderson Clayton, Catelli Magic Moments and Light Touch Desserts, DiGiorno Pasta, and Louis Kemp Seafood to fill gaps in its food segment	

new international cigarette division, $2.9 billion from beer sales, and $1 billion from the remaining acquisitions including 7-Up and the packaging firms.

Hamish Maxwell replaced Cullman as CEO in 1985. The son of a third-generation tobacco leaf dealer in London, Maxwell took a position with PM in 1954 as a cigarette salesman in Richmond. He headed the development of PM's international operations in the 1960s, and his first major move as CEO was the $5.6 billion purchase of General Foods Corporation in 1985. By 1988 PM, under Maxwell's direction, had purchased Kraft Foods and merged the two companies into a $23 billion food-processing company, the second largest in the world. In 1989 and 1990, PM acquired Jacobs Suchard, the second-largest European chocolatier, and six smaller food companies that complemented the Kraft General Foods product line. Under Maxwell's management, PM's revenues grew from $16.3 billion in 1985 to $44.8 billion in 1989

EXHIBIT 1 | **Philip Morris Acquisitions and Divestitures, 1957–1993 (continued)**

Acquisition Date		Divestiture Date
1990	Acquired Jacobs Suchard, a Swiss-based coffee and chocolate manufacturer and distributor of the Toblerone brand of chocolates	
1990	Acquired Dresden Cigarette Company, the largest cigarette-manufacturing operation in Eastern Europe	
	Sold Venezolana Empacadora, a meat processing subsidiary in Denmark, to Plumrose	1991
	Acquired Alimentos Especiales, a food processing company in Argentina	
1992	Acquired Quesera Menorquina, a Spanish food processor	
	Acquired a 55% ownership interest in Freia Marabou, a major Norwegian chocolatier and confectioner, for $1.5 billion	
	Acquired a 30% stake of Czechoslovakian tobacco company, Tabak, for $104.4 million	
	Acquired an 80% share of Zigarettenfabrik Eger, a Hungarian cigarette manufacturer	
	Acquired RJR Nabisco's cold cereal business for $450 million	
	Acquired German buscuits manufacturer, Bahlsens Keksfabrik, for DM 1.9 billion	
	Acquired a 7.9% share in Fomento Economico Mexicano, a Mexican brewer and snack food company	
1993	Acquired Terry Group from United Biscuits Holding in UK for $318.8 million	
	Acquired Pet Foods' stake in Swedish snack food company, Estrella, for $87.5 million	
	Increased its share in Tabak (Czech) to 82% at a cost of approximately $300 million	
	Acquired 49% of Krasnodar Tobacco Factory, Russia for $4.9 million	
	Acquired 65% of Klapedia Tobacco, Lithuania, for $40 million	
	Targeted a 49% investment in a state-owned tobacco company from Kazakhstan, Russia	
	Sold its ice cream brands (Sealtest, Breyer's, and Früsen Gladje) to Unilever	1993
	Put its *Birds Eye* frozen foods division up for sale	1993

(a 29 percent annual growth rate), making PM the seventh-largest company on the Fortune 500 list. By 1990, domestic and international tobacco combined was 40 percent of sales, beer was 8 percent, and food was 51 percent.

In March of 1991, Hamish Maxwell announced that he was stepping down from his position at PM and that Michael A. Miles had been chosen to succeed him as chairman and chief executive. At the time, Miles was heading up the merger of Kraft General Foods and had been with the company only since 1989. The appointment of Miles represented the first time in Philip Morris' 144-year history that a "nontobacco man" was at the company's helm.

Miles, a nonsmoker often considered cool, aloof, and all-business by colleagues, was an "ad-man" by training and a "fix-it man" by trade. He graduated from Northwestern University's Medill School of Journalism where he majored in advertising, and immediately upon graduation secured a position with the Leo Burnett advertising agency. His reputation as a turnaround artist began when he crafted a strategy that emphasized quality and service to heal the ailing Kentucky Fried Chicken chain, which at the time was owned by Heublein, Inc. When Heublein was acquired by RJR Nabisco in 1982, Miles accepted the presidency of Dart & Kraft, Inc. There he divested many of the nonfood businesses, instituted cost-cutting programs, and began to modernize many of the companies' brands through both brand extensions and aggressive advertising campaigns. Industry experts suggested that the appointment of Miles as the new leader of PM was an indication that future growth in the company would come via line extensions and acquisitions.

As of 1993, Philip Morris had leading businesses in three large industries—cigarettes, beer, and food processing—and produced over 3,000 items. Philip Morris' business portfolio consisted of

- The largest cigarette company in the U.S. market, with a 42.3 percent market share (up from 30.8 percent in 1980 and 16.7 percent in 1970).
- The world's largest international tobacco company, selling 421.2 billion units outside the U.S. representing 160 brands in more than 170 countries and territories.
- The world's second-largest brewer of beer—Miller Brewing Company.
- The world's second-largest food-processing company—Kraft General Foods Group.
- A capital division that included credit financing for PM subsidiaries, customers, and suppliers; leveraged leasing of major equipment; and Mission Viejo, a land planning, development, and sales division.

Exhibit 2 shows PM's diversified structure and business portfolio makeup going into 1993. Exhibit 3 provides sales and operating profit breakdowns by business unit and Exhibit 4 provides a 10-year financial summary.

EXHIBIT 2 | **The Business Portfolio Makeup of Philip Morris, 1992** *(Operating revenues and operating profits in billions of dollars)*

Cigarettes	Beer	Food	Financial
Philip Morris U.S.A.	**Miller Brewing Company**	**Kraft General Foods**	**Philip Morris Capital Corporation**
Revenues: $12.0	Revenues: $4.0	Revenues: $29.0	Revenues: $.28
Profits: $5.2	Profits: $.26	Profits: $2.6	Profits: $.17
Brands: Marlboro, Virginia Slims, Bucks, Benson & Hedges, Merit, Cambridge, Parliament, and Alpine	Brands: Miller Lite, Miller High Life, Miller Genuine Draft, Milwaukee's Best, Lowenbrau, and Sharp's	Brands: Kraft cheeses, Maxwell House coffees, Louis Rich turkey, Oscar Mayer luncheon meats, hot dogs, and bacon, Louis Kemp seafood products, Post cereals, Jell-O, Kool-aid, Sealtest, Breyers, and Light'n Lively dairy products, Kraft salad dressings and box dinners	Products: Major equipment leasing financial programs for customers and suppliers
Philip Morris International			**Mission Viejo**
Revenues: $13.7			Revenues: $.15
Profits: $2.0			Profits: $.05
Brands: Marlboro, Philip Morris, Lark, Chesterfield, Galaxy, Peter Jackson, Merit, Parliament, Muratti			Products: Land planning, developing, and sales

Source: Company annual report.

EXHIBIT 3 | Selected Financial Highlights of Philip Morris Companies, 1990-92

Data by Segment for the Years Ended December 31 (in millions)			
	1992	1991	1990
Operating revenues:			
Tobacco	$25,677	$23,840	$21,090
Food	29,048	28,178	26,085
Beer	3,976	4,056	3,534
Financial services and real estate	430	384	460
Total operating revenues	$59,131	$56,458	$51,169
Operating profit:			
Tobacco	$7,193	$6,463	$5,596
Food	2,769	2,016	2,205
Beer	258	299	285
Financial services and real estate	219	178	196
Total operating revenues	10,439	8,956	8,282
Unallocated corporate expenses	380	334	336
Operating income	$10,059	$8,622	$7,946
Identifiable assets:			
Tobacco	$9,479	$8,648	$7,770
Food	32,672	31,622	32,336
Beer	1,545	1,608	1,612
Financial services and real estate	5,297	4,538	3,886
Total	48,993	46,416	45,604
Other assets	1,021	968	965
Total assets	$50,014	$47,384	$46,569
Depreciation expense:			
Tobacco	$291	$294	$282
Food	507	480	438
Beer	141	139	141
Financial services and real estate		1	1
Capital additions:			
Tobacco	$460	$438	$324
Food	947	955	860
Beer	134	144	99

Miles had a number of obstacles to overcome in the latter half of the decade. The traditional measure of success at Philip Morris was a 20 percent annual increase in earnings—a difficult task at best. But Miles's charge was more demanding for several reasons: all of PM's businesses were in mature industries; its cash cow, the tobacco business, was experiencing shrinking profit margins because of negative industry conditions; and changing consumer shopping habits, increased price sensitivity, and plant closings caused by excess capacity were threatening its food revenues.

PM'S DOMESTIC TOBACCO SBU

For over 30 years, Philip Morris had been the most successful of all the U.S. cigarette manufacturers, boosting domestic cigarette sales from approximately 46 billion units in 1960 to 214 billion units in 1992 and domestic cigarette profits from $47 million

EXHIBIT 4 | Selected Financial Data For Philip Morris Companies, Inc., 1982–92   *(In million of dollars, except per-share data)*

	1992	1991	1990	1989	1988	1987	1986	1985	1984	1983	1982
Summary of Operations:											
Operating revenues	$59,131	$56,458	$51,169	$44,080	$31,273	$27,650	$25,542	$16,158	$14,102	$13,256	$11,720
United States export sales	3,797	3,061	2,928	2,288	1,863	1,592	1,193	923	925	970	978
Cost of sales	26,082	25,612	24,430	21,868	13,565	12,183	11,901	6,709	5,840	5,665	5,532
Federal excise taxes on products	2,879	2,978	2,159	2,140	2,127	2,085	2,075	2,049	2,041	1,983	1,180
Foreign excise taxes on products	6,157	5,416	4,687	3,608	3,755	3,331	2,653	1,766	1,635	1,527	1,435
Operating income	10,059	8,622	7,946	6,789	4,397	3,990	3,537	2,664	1,908	1,840	1,547
Interest and other debt expense, net (consumer products)	1,451	1,651	1,635	1,731	670	646	772	311	276	230	244
Earnings before income taxes and cumulative effect of accounting change	8,608	6,971	6,311	5,058	3,727	3,344	2,765	2,353	1,632	1,610	1,303
Pretax profit margin	14.6%	12.3%	12.3%	11.5%	11.9%	12.1%	10.8%	14.6%	11.6%	12.1%	11.1%
Provision for income taxes	$ 3,669	$ 3,044	$ 2,771	$ 2,112	$ 1,663	$ 1,502	$ 1,287	$ 1,098	$ 743	$ 706	$ 521
Earnings before cumulative effect of accounting change	4,939	3,927	3,540	2,946	2,064	1,842	1,478	1,255	889	904	782
Cumulative effect of accounting change		(921)			273						
Net earnings	4,939	3,006	3,540	2,946	2,337	1,842	1,478	1,255	889	904	782
Earnings per share before cumulative effect of accounting change	5.45	4.24	3.83	3.18	2.22	1.94	1.55	1.31	.91	.90	.78
Per share cumulative effect of accounting change		(.99)			.29						
Net earnings per share	5.45	3.25	3.83	3.18	2.51	1.94	1.55	1.31	.91	.90	.78
Dividends declared per share	2.35	1.91	1.55	1.25	1.01	.79	.62	.50	.43	.36	.30
Weighted average shares (millions)	906	925	925	927	932	951	954	959	981	1,008	1,005

EXHIBIT 4 | Selected Financial Data For Philip Morris Companies, Inc., 1982–92 *(In million of dollars, except per-share data) (continued)*

	1992	1991	1990	1989	1988	1986	1985	1984	1984	1983	1982
Capital expenditures (consumer products)	$1,573	$1,562	$1,355	$1,246	$1,024	$718	$678	$347	$298	$566	$918
Depreciation (consumer products)	963	938	876	755	608	564	514	367	341	294	250
Property, plant and equipment, net (consumer products)	10,530	9,946	9,604	8,457	8,648	6,582	6,237	5,684	4,014	4,381	4,178
Inventories (consumer products)	7,785	7,445	7,153	5,751	5,384	4,154	3,836	3,827	2,653	2,599	2,834
Total assets	50,014	47,384	46,569	38,528	36,960	21,437	19,482	18,712	9,880	9,908	9,756
Total long-term debt	14,583	14,213	16,121	14,551	16,812	5,983	6,887	8,035	2,239	2,549	3,776
Total debt—consumer products	16,269	15,289	17,182	14,887	16,442	6,355	6,889	7,887	2,566	3,054	3,728
—financial services and real estate	1,934	1,611	1,560	1,538	1,504	1,378	1,141	944	436	141	83
Total deferred income taxes	2,248	1,803	2,083	1,732	1,559	2,044	1,519	1,233	907	825	627
Stockholders' equity	12,563	12,512	11,947	9,571	7,679	6,823	5,655	4,737	4,093	4,034	3,663
Common dividends declared as a % of net earnings	43.0%	58.7%	40.5%	39.3%	40.3%	40.6%	39.9%	38.1%	46.8%	40.5%	38.6%
Book value per common share	$14.07	$13.60	$12.90	$10.31	$8.31	$7.21	$5.94	$4.96	$4.21	$4.03	$3.64
Market price of common share—high/low	$86\frac{5}{8}$-$69\frac{1}{2}$	$81\frac{3}{4}$-$48\frac{1}{4}$	52-36	$45\frac{1}{2}$-25	$25\frac{1}{2}$-$20\frac{1}{8}$	$31\frac{1}{8}$-$18\frac{1}{8}$	$19\frac{1}{2}$-11	$11\frac{7}{8}$-9	$10\frac{3}{8}$-$7\frac{3}{4}$	9-$6\frac{3}{4}$	$8\frac{1}{2}$-$5\frac{1}{2}$
Closing price of common share at year-end	$77\frac{7}{8}$	$80\frac{1}{4}$	$51\frac{3}{4}$	$41\frac{5}{8}$	$25\frac{1}{2}$	$21\frac{3}{8}$	18	11	$10\frac{1}{8}$	9	$7\frac{1}{2}$
Price/earnings ratio at year-end	14	19	14	13	11	11	11	8	11	10	9
Number of common shares outstanding at year-end (millions)	893	920	926	929	924	947	951	955	971	1,000	1,007
Number of employees	161,000	166,000	168,000	157,000	155,000	113,000	111,000	114,000	68,000	68,000	72,000

Source: *1992 Annual Report.*

to $5.2 billion to become the largest cigarette producer in the U.S. In 1992, for the third consecutive year, Philip Morris U.S.A. accounted for more than half the cigarette industry's U.S. profits, and nearly all its profit growth. Between 1960 and 1993, PM increased its share of U.S. sales from 10 percent to an industry-leading 42 percent. With an operating profit margin of 43 percent in 1992, PM's domestic cigarette business was its primary source of cash surpluses. This segment contributed only 20 percent of PM's total revenues, but 47 percent of total operating profits.

U.S. CIGARETTE INDUSTRY TRENDS

Ever since the Surgeon General's report in 1964 citing cigarette smoking as a health hazard, the cigarette industry in the U.S. had been struggling to protect its sales and customer base. During the 1990s, however, the industry had been under sustained assault on many fronts. A report by the Environmental Protection Agency citing the risks of passive smoking, the threat of substantial increases in cigarette taxes, the passage of many no-smoking ordinances, aggressive antismoking campaigns, a slight downturn in per capita cigarette consumption, and downward pressure on cigarette pricing had made the $44 billion tobacco industry a declining business by 1993.

Demographics   U.S. consumers smoked approximately 24.9 billion packs of cigarettes in 1992, in the neighborhood of 498 billion cigarettes. This figure represented a 2.4 percent decrease over 1991 consumption figures. Per capita smoking in the U.S. had been declining for three decades at the rate of almost 3 percent per year (see Exhibit 5). In 1993 only about 30 percent of those over 18 smoked, versus about 50 percent in the mid-1950s. The smoking population was increasingly composed of lower-income and less-educated groups. Thirty-four percent of smokers had less than a high school education, and only 16 percent were college graduates. Smoking demographics had also changed significantly along gender and racial lines, with more women and blacks smoking and more white males quitting.

EXHIBIT 5 | **U.S. Per-Capita Consumption of Tobacco Products, 1983–1992**

	Units		Pounds			
Year	Cigarettes*	Large cigars & cigarillos[†]	Smoking tobacco[†]	Chewing tobacco[†]	Snuff*	Total tobacco products*
E 1992	2,629	24.1	0.17	0.74	0.29	5.28
1991	2,713	24.9	0.18	0.79	0.28	5.40
1990	2,817	26.2	0.20	0.79	0.28	5.48
1989	2,926	28.4	0.22	0.82	0.27	5.68
1988	3,096	29.1	0.25	0.86	0.26	6.11
1987	3,197	31.7	0.27	0.89	0.25	6.30
1986	3,274	35.8	0.29	0.93	0.26	6.56
1985	3,370	37.9	0.32	1.01	0.28	6.81
1984	3,446	41.9	0.35	1.05	0.27	6.85
1983	3,488	43.8	0.40	1.05	0.27	7.19

*Consumption per capita, 18 years and over
[†]Consumption per male, 18 years and over
E-Estimated
Source: Department of Agriculture.

Antismoking Concerns In addition to a shrinking smoking population, social, political, and legal pressures against cigarette smoking were increasing. In January 1993, the Environmental Protection Agency (EPA) announced that secondhand or passive smoke (the ambient smoke emitted by cigarette smokers) was responsible for as many as 9,000 deaths due to lung cancer annually (see Exhibit 6). This announcement had a profound impact on the tobacco industry, causing intolerance and hostility toward cigarette smoking to increase dramatically. The report became the primary ammunition in the campaign to convince businesses, restaurants, local governments, and sports stadiums to ban or severely restrict smoking on their premises. The U.S. Surgeon General was campaigning for a ban on smoking in all public places by the year 2000. By 1993, the U.S. government had banned smoking in most federal workplaces, including military installations, and 42 states had prohibited smoking in public places. In June 1993 the U.S. Postal Service, citing the EPA report as justification, banned smoking in all its facilities. McDonald's Corp., the fast-food industry giant, imposed sweeping no-smoking policies. Thomas Lauria, a spokesman for the Tobacco Institute, understated the situation when he commented: "We're certainly getting slammed."[1]

While the EPA report did not mandate any particular action, the Food and Drug Administration (FDA) was lobbying to regulate tobacco. FDA commissioner Dr. David Kessler, a zealous antismoker, threatened to ban cigarettes unless Congress granted the FDA the right to regulate tobacco as a controlled substance. Kessler cited new evidence that nicotine was addictive, a claim that the tobacco industry had been denying for years. He suggested that nicotine was possibly as addictive as illegal drugs such as cocaine and heroine. He cited as practical evidence the fact that 17 million adults attempt to quit smoking annually, but only 1 in 10 succeeds. Furthermore, Kessler contended that tobacco manufacturers were guilty of manipulating the nicotine levels in cigarettes to keep smokers hooked. In congressional testimony, Kessler quoted a 1972 company memo by a PM scientist who wrote: "Think of the cigarette as a dispenser for a dose unit of nicotine."[2] And from a patent filing by a tobacco manufacturer, he referenced the following: "It is a further object of this invention to provide a cigarette which delivers a larger amount of nicotine in the first few puffs of the cigarette than in the last few puffs."[3]

California Representative Henry Waxman reported that in 1983 a Philip Morris study found that nicotine induces addictive behavior in rats and that the paper was accepted for publication in a scientific journal but was suppressed by the company.

E X H I B I T 6 | **Selected Statistics on Smoking, 1993**

Total annual number of tobacco-related deaths	419,000
Of those, cardiovascular-disease deaths	180,000
Lung-cancer deaths	120,000
Annual number of deaths from secondhand smoke	9,000
Male smokers, 1965	28.9 million
Male smokers, 1993	24.0 million
Female smokers, 1965	21.1 million
Female smokers, 1993	22.3 million

---

[1] *U.S. News and World Report,* April 18, 1994, p. 33.
[2] Ibid., p. 35.
[3] Ibid.

This prompted Waxman to launch an investigation into the practices of tobacco industry participants. Additionally, a class-action suit was filed in New Orleans charging the tobacco industry with concealing evidence about the dangers of smoking.

Kessler's lobbying efforts to regulate tobacco culminated in an antismoking bill presented by Representative Mike Synar, Democrat of Oklahoma. The bill had the following provisions:

Manufacturers required to disclose the approximately 700 chemical additives (5 of which have been declared hazardous substances) in tobacco products.

A reduction or elimination in the levels of harmful additives, including ammonia and ethyl furoid.

A warning label regarding the addictive nature of nicotine.

Restriction of tobacco advertising and promotion, especially that aimed at minors.

FDA control of the nicotine levels in cigarettes.

The tobacco industry responded immediately and aggressively. Following the EPA report, the *Wall Street Journal* announced in June 1993 that a coalition composed of Philip Morris, RJR's R. J. Reynolds Tobacco Co., two tobacco-growers organizations, Gallins Vending Co. (a cigarette vending machine company), and Universal Leaf Tobacco Co. (a tobacco supplier), had filed a lawsuit seeking a permanent injunction to overturn the EPA findings. The coalition charged that the EPA had resorted to manipulating statistics and "cherry picking" data in order to "falsely disparage" cigarettes. Specifically, the lawsuit contended that the EPA's results were flawed because they failed to incorporate the findings from two major studies that found contradictory results.

The tobacco industry also wielded enormous political lobbying power. The industry contributed $1.6 million in campaign contributions in 1993, excluding contributions to favored charities and causes of pro-tobacco legislators. The tobacco industry traditionally helped finance the Congressional Black Caucus, underwrote the annual retreat of House Democrats to the Greenbrier resort, and found support from Virginia Representative Tom Bliley who had a strong influence over the Energy and Commerce Committee's GOP votes.[4]

Individual tobacco companies were fighting back as well. Philip Morris had recently filed a libel suit against ABC-TV's program "Day One," which had accused the industry of adding nicotine to cigarettes, specifically citing the Philip Morris company. Tobacco industry spokesman, Thomas Lauria, denied that cigarette manufacturers added or manipulated levels of nicotine. He noted that cigarettes contain 66 percent less nicotine today than they did 30 years ago and disputed the notion that nicotine was addictive: "Nobody has checked into the Betty Ford Clinic to get off cigarettes."[5]

However, Robert Robinson, the assistant director for program development at the Office on Smoking and Health, stated that antismoking campaigns had experienced a paradigm shift: "The solution to the problem needs to rely less on targeting individuals in cessation programs than targeting legislatures . . . [The solution is] no longer seeing the smoker as the problem but rather seeing the tobacco industry as the problem. Instead of how to get the smoker to change behavior, the focus now is how can we get the tobacco industry to change its behavior."[6]

---

[4]Ibid., p. 38.
[5]Ibid., p. 36.
[6]*Washington Post Magazine,* February 20, 1994, p. 28.

Antismoking sentiments and pending legislation represented serious threats to the industry. The tobacco industry had avoided regulation in the past by defeating legislative attempts to enact restrictions. Kessler's new evidence was aimed at demonstrating that the product was a drug and clearly under the jurisdiction of the FDA. It was rumored that if Synar's bill failed, Kessler would "be forced" to declare cigarettes unsafe and demand that they be phased out before banning them completely.[7] All parties concerned, both antismoking activists and tobacco manufacturers, hoped to avoid abolishing the product. Many were concerned with the black market that would be created to supply the demand. According to Mr. Arnold Trebech, director of the Washington-based Drug Policy Foundation, "We would have a black market in cigarettes that would make the current black market in cocaine and heroin look like a Sunday-school picnic."[8]

In addition to feeling the heat from antismoking campaigns in general, the industry was being criticized by Surgeon General Joycelyn Elders for its advertising that targeted underage smokers. According to the Office on Smoking and Health, more than 1 million Americans under the age of 18 became regular smokers each year—about 3,000 a day. In 1993, 3.1 million teenagers were regular smokers. Eighty percent of all adult smokers began smoking before the age of 20, with an average starting age of 14.5 years. Antismoking activists contended that Philip Morris' Marlboro Man and RJR's Joe Camel were the main culprits in sending powerful messages to American youth. According to the activists, cigarette manufacturers played on adolescent fears and aspirations by connecting cigarettes with images of social acceptance and giving them a ready-made identity in the form of the hip Joe Camel or the rebellious, sexy Marlboro Man.

In December 1991 scientists from the Medical College of Georgia published a study in the *Journal of the American Medical Association* (JAMA) showing that 91 percent of six-year-olds included in their study could match Joe with a Camel cigarette—96 percent were able to match Mickey Mouse with the Disney Channel. A University of Massachusetts Medical School report indicated that 43 percent of surveyed teenagers thought that Joe was "cool," while only one in four adults agreed. Additionally, another report in JAMA stated that Camel's market share among underage smokers had increased from 0.5 percent to 32.8 percent since the advent of the Joe Camel campaign in 1987. A survey of teenagers by *U.S. News and World Report* found that Camels appealed to teenagers' desire for acceptance, while Marlboros appealed to their impulse to be defiant. Sixty-nine percent of teenage smokers smoked the most advertised brand, Marlboro, compared to only 24 percent of the adult population.

The Federal Trade Commission (FTC) was under pressure to ban the Joe Camel campaign from several powerful sources, including the American Lung Association, the American Heart Association, the American Cancer Society, former Surgeons General Antonia C. Novella and C. Everett Koop, and the attorneys general of 27 states. The FTC received a letter from the Coalition on Smoking and Health stating, "Using a cartoon camel modeled after James Bond, 'Miami Vice,' 'Top Gun,' and many other figures that appeal to young people, this campaign represents one of the most egregious examples in recent history of tobacco advertising targeted at children."[9]

R. J. Reynolds credited the Joe Camel campaign with revitalizing its 75-year-old brand. Joe was believed responsible for changing the brand's image from a hot, harsh smoke preferred by an older generation to a "smooth character" image. The company

---

[7]*U.S. News and World Report,* April 18, 1994, p. 36.
[8]Ibid.
[9]*Washington Post Magazine,* February 20, 1994, p. 12.

had no plans to alter the campaign, citing the stabilization of the brand's market share at 4.4 percent as justification. R. J. Reynolds spokeswoman Maura Payne Ellis stated that the Joe Camel campaign was targeted at Marlboro smokers in their 20s and 30s in order to encourage them to switch brands and was "absolutely not—never has and never will be" targeted at adolescents.[10] According to Ellis, Reynolds did not keep track of its market share among underage smokers: "We don't do research among young smokers because we don't think young people should smoke."[11]

Pricing   In 1970 the average price per 20-unit pack was $.41; by 1993 that price had escalated to an average $1.80 per pack. Historically, cigarette demand had been price inelastic, such that cigarette consumption levels were not substantially altered by price changes, allowing cigarette producers to pass along cost increases and rising excise taxes, as well as to widen profit margins, through price increases. Throughout the 1980s, cigarette manufacturers were able to keep their profit margins in the 20 percent range (see Exhibit 7), as compared to a 10 to 15 percent range for most other packaged goods. Cigarette price increases were as much as 16 cents per pack greater than the standard price increases caused by inflation (see Exhibit 8). However, by the early 1990s consumers were becoming more price sensitive, forcing cigarette manufacturers to trim the size of further price increases.

Buyer resistance to the prices of major cigarette brands was said to be a prime reason that sales of lower-priced generic and discount brands were growing rapidly. The fastest-growing new brands were those that sold for less. Price-value brands claimed over 30 percent of the total cigarette market in 1992 (see Exhibit 9). Ironically, the industry leaders in the premium segment, Philip Morris and R. J. Reynolds, supplied the majority of the discount segment as well. However, manufacturers' profit margins

EXHIBIT   7 | **Tobacco Companies' Profit Margin**   *(in percent)*

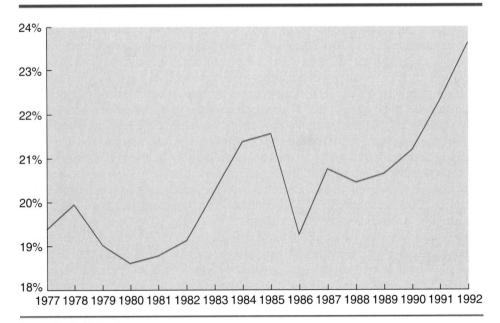

Source: Standard & Poor's.

---

[10]Ibid.

[11]Ibid., p. 13.

EXHIBIT 8 | **Tobacco Product Prices versus the CPI** *(1982–84 = 100)*

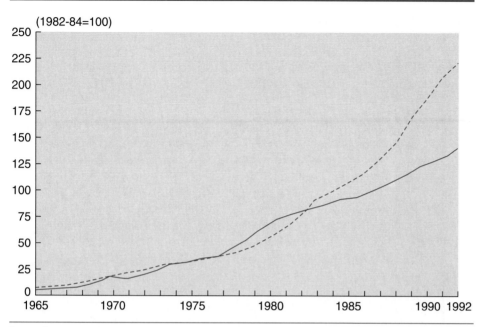

Source: Department of Labor.

on the cut-rate brands were only about one-tenth of their full-priced counterparts since manufacturers still paid high packaging and promotion costs. Profits on the lower-priced brands averaged about 5 cents a pack in 1993, compared to 55-cent-per-pack profitability for premium brands.

Market Segmentation   Quick to recognize the changing demographics, the tobacco companies used market segmentation strategies to attempt to increase market share. The companies segmented on the basis of gender, race, age, income, and type of cigarette. Lorillard's Newport focused on young, urban blacks. PM's Dunhill and RJR's Ritz targeted upscale smokers. PM's Virginia Slims and Brown & Williamson's Capri aimed at women, and American Brand's filtered Pall Mall aimed at the price conscious. Kool and Salem shared the majority of the menthol segment, although most popular brands such as Marlboro and Winston offered a menthol version.

Tobacco companies tried to grab market share from their competitors by launching new products or by recasting existing brands. In 1993 there were over 420 brand versions on the U.S. market. The levels of tar and nicotine in cigarettes were varied to differentiate products. The manufacturers also experimented with the size and shape of cigarettes. Capri, a Brown & Williamson brand, was very successful in marketing an ultraslim cigarette to women and PM had also entered this market with a Virginia Superslims brand. One innovation, RJR Nabisco's smokeless cigarette, was said to look and taste like any other cigarette and to emit much less tar and ambient smoke. However, the product had been a market failure. Other unusual ideas included RJR's vanilla-scented Horizon brand and Lorillard's lemon-scented Spring Lemon Lights; both brands achieved only nominal market shares.

Diversification   firms in the tobacco industry had diversified for two main reasons: (1) their tobacco businesses were cash cows and produced very sizable cash flow surpluses year after year, and (2) cigarettes were increasingly seen as a health hazard

EXHIBIT 9 | **The Discount Segment of the Cigarette Market**

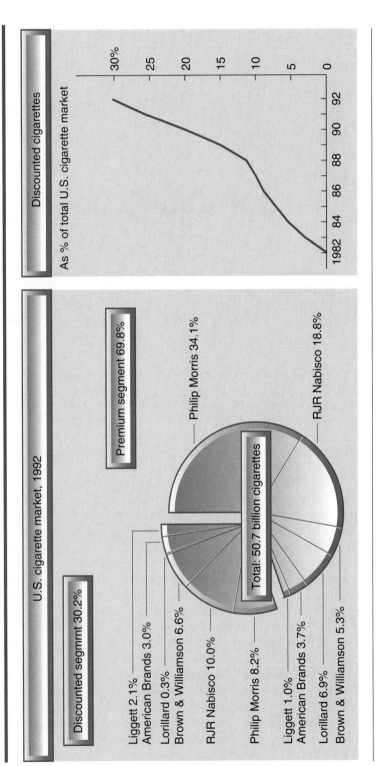

U.S. cigarette market, 1992

Discounted segmrnt 30.2%

Premium segment 69.8%

Liggett 2.1%
American Brands 3.0%
Lorillard 0.3%
Brown & Williamson 6.6%

RJR Nabisco 10.0%

Philip Morris 8.2%

Liggett 1.0%
American Brands 3.7%
Lorillard 6.9%
Brown & Williamson 5.3%

Philip Morris 34.1%

RJR Nabisco 18.8%

Total: 50.7 billion cigarettes

Discounted cigarettes

As % of total U.S. cigarette market

30%
25
20
15
10
5
0

1982 84 86 88 90 92

Source: *Maxwell Consumer Report.*

cigarette sales were drifting in a slow long-term decline. The eventual decline in cigarette sales, anticipated by industry executives for many years, had prompted other cigarette manufacturers besides Philip Morris to diversify their business portfolios during the 1960s and 1970s. Philip Morris had been moderately successful in reducing its dependence on tobacco revenues. In 1970 tobacco contributed 85 percent of sales and 90 percent of income; in 1980 it was down to 65 percent of sales and 86 percent of income; and in 1993 tobacco products, domestic and international combined, contributed only 43 percent of PM's sales and roughly 66 percent of operating income. But whereas Philip Morris moved mainly into consumer goods businesses where its cigarette marketing skills could be transferred into a major competitive asset, other tobacco manufacturers chose to diversify more broadly (see Exhibit 10).

EXHIBIT 10 | **Degree of Diversification and Range of Business Interests of Major Tobacco Manufacturers**

American Brands	RJR Nabisco, Inc.	B.A.T. Industries (Parent of Brown & Williamson)	Loews Corp. (Parent of Lorillard)	Liggett Group
American Tobacco Co.	R. J. Reynolds Tobacco Co. (cigarettes, pipe and chewing tobacco)	Tobacco products	Tobacco	Cigarettes
American Cigar Co.		Retailing	CNA Financial (insurance)	NFL trading cards
Gallagher Ltd. (international cigarette operation)	Nabisco Brands, Inc.	Paper	Loews hotels	Confectionery licensing
James B. Beam Distilling Co.	Planters Lifesavers Co. (nuts, popcorn, candy, gum)	Packaging and printing	Loews theaters	
Swingline, Inc.	Biscuits: cookies, crackers (Oreo, Chips Ahoy)	Cosmetics	Bulova Watch Co.	
Acushnet Co. (golf products, Titlist)		Home furnishings	Residential development	
Franklin Life Insurance Co.	Grocery products: cereals (Shredded Wheat), margarine, A-1 steak sauce, Milkbone dog biscuits, Grey Poupon mustards, and Royal desserts			
Master Lock Co.				
Wilson Jones Co. (office supplies)				
ACCO World (fasteners)	Del Monte Tropical Fruit Co. (canned fruits, vegetables, fruit juices, desserts)			
Day-timers				
Waterloo Industries (tool storage products)				
Twentieth Century (do-it-yourself plumbing)	Sports marketing			
Aristokraft (kitchen and bath cabinets)	Containerized ocean freight shipping (Sea-Land Service, Inc.)			
Polland & Atchison (optical goods and services)	Signal Petroleum			
Forbuoy's (U.K. candy, tobacco, and news agent chain)	Aminoil			
T. M. Group (U.K. vending machine company)	Packaging products			

Source: Compiled from 1989 annual reports for each company.

Industry Profitability Yet in 1993 the tobacco producers, notwithstanding all their diversification moves into new industries, still derived a large fraction of their sales and earnings from cigarettes. The strong sales and profit performance of the cigarette producers was principally a consequence of hefty price increases over the years (averaging 10 percent annually from 1970 through 1993), rather than increased sales volume; industry volume peaked in 1982 at 640 billion units and had declined about 3 percent annually since then. While the industry was declining in terms of volume sales, it was nevertheless a very profitable industry, with an average return on sales of 17 percent. Cigarette production required low capital investments; thus the large profit margins generated substantial cash flows. PM's capital additions were only 6 percent of segment profits and each dollar invested in assets generated $2.71 in revenues in 1992 (see Exhibit 3).

COMPETITION IN THE DOMESTIC CIGARETTE INDUSTRY

The overall market shares of the six competitors in the U.S. cigarette industry in 1993 are listed below:

Manufacturer	1952	1961	1970	1980	1989	1992
R. J. Reynolds	26.2%	34.0%	31.7%	32.8%	28.5%	28.8%
Philip Morris	9.7	9.2	16.7	30.8	41.9	42.3
Brown & Williamson	5.9	9.3	16.7	13.7	11.4	11.9
American Brands	32.3	25.6	19.7	10.7	8.0	6.8
Lorillard	5.6	10.5	8.5	9.8	7.0	7.2
Liggett Group	17.8	10.8	6.5	2.2	3.2	3.0
All others	2.5	0.6	0.2	0.0	0.0	0.0

Philip Morris' 42 percent market share derived from its having 6 of the 20 best-selling brands, including the number one brand, Marlboro. R. J. Reynolds Tobacco Company had brands in the top 20, but had experienced a steady decline in market share over the past two decades. Like PM, RJR had diversified primarily into consumer goods—R. J. Reynolds acquired Nabisco Company in 1985 for $4.9 billion and changed its name to RJR Nabisco to reflect the change in direction. RJR Nabisco was subsequently acquired by RJR Nabisco Holdings, a wholly owned subsidiary of Kohlberg Kravis & Roberts, which took the company private in 1988. In 1993, the company had revenues of $15.1 billion, with an operating income of 17.2 percent.

American Brands diversified through unrelated acquisitions, such as golf products, office products, insurance companies, optical services, and retailing. Its operating income was 11.9 percent of its $13.7 billion in revenues in 1993. Brown & Williamson was owned by B.A.T. Industries, a British company and the world's largest cigarette producer. Lorillard was a subsidiary of Loews Corporation, a $13.7 billion conglomerate with businesses in hotels, theaters, and watches. The Newport brand represented 60 percent of Lorillard's sales. Cigarettes represented only 16 percent of the company's revenues, but was its most profitable unit. The company posted a total net income of only $122 million in 1993—cigarette income was $524 million but its property and casualty insurance business (58 percent of the company's sales) lost money.

The Liggett Group had experienced several ownership turnovers in the last decade. In 1980, Liggett Group was acquired by the British conglomerate, Grand

Metropolitan. By 1986 the group was sold in a private buyout and operated independently. The company had 4 full-price brands (Chesterfield, Eve, L&M, and Lark), 2 price-value brands (Chesterfield filter Lights and Savvy), and 1 extra-low-price brand (Pyramid), none in the top 20. Liggett Group's only diversification moves were two licensing rights: one for confectionery products and one for National Football League trading cards.

Competitive Weapons There were three primary competitive weapons used by cigarette manufacturers—advertising, new product innovations, and pricing. Although Philip Morris excelled at marketing its cigarettes, other manufacturers also anchored their marketing efforts in establishing an image and a position for each brand. Since all cigarette advertising was banned from TV and radio in 1971, print, billboard, and promotional advertising was used extensively by all six domestic manufacturers to create and reinforce brand images and personalities—currently, the six U.S. manufacturers were spending a combined $650-$700 million annually on media advertising.

New variations of a successful brand, such as different filters, lengths, and packaging, were commonly used tactics to expand a brand's appeal—in 1993 PM marketed 20 versions of Marlboro and R. J. Reynolds offered 6 versions of Winstons. According to an industry consultant, "Line extensions are the way to go. It costs only $30 million to $50 million to launch a line extension but $200 million to $300 million for a free-standing brand."[12] Other innovations included smoke-free or nicotine-free cigarettes, but these had met with little market success so far. In general, attempts to create brand appeal and build brand loyalty paid off because smokers' brand loyalties were among the strongest relative to other consumer goods products.

As mentioned previously, the price-value cigarettes were the fastest-growing segment. Manufacturers had developed new brands to offer at a lower price to price-conscious smokers. The Liggett Group was aggressively competing in this segment and was the first to offer an extra-low-price brand, Pyramid. PM introduced Bristol and Alpine in 1989 in the discount category and introduced the Buck brand in 1990. RJR and PM had invested heavily in the price-value segment in recent years and in 1990 held 33.2 percent and 27.1 percent of this segment, respectively. (See Exhibit 11 for comparative market share figures.) Tobacco analysts said the companies were forced to compete in this segment or watch their rivals steal away the penny-pinching smokers and drive down prices. The downside of being a major player in this segment was that the advertising promotions for the price-value brands encouraged smokers to trade down, cannibalizing sales from Marlboro and other full-priced brands.

PERFORMANCE OF THE PHILIP MORRIS U.S.A. DIVISION

In the 1970s and 1980s, Philip Morris U.S.A. led all U.S. tobacco manufacturers in growth in both unit cigarette sales and market share. During the 1970s Philip Morris U.S.A.'s cigarette unit sales grew at an average annual compound rate of 8.5 percent— five times the industrywide rate of 1.7 percent. During the 1980s, PM's unit sales of cigarettes rose from 191 billion units to 220 billion units, a compound annual growth rate of 1.6 percent, even though industrywide unit sales dropped from 619 to 525 billion units (an average of -0.3 percent). The division's market share went from 16.7

---

[12]*Advertising Age,* February 3, 1992.

EXHIBIT 11 | **Market Share Data by Cigarette Category, 1992**

Cigarette Market Shares	
Philip Morris	42.3%
RJR	28.8
Brown & Williamson	11.9
Lorillard	7.2
American Tobacco	6.8
Liggett	3.0
Premium Cigarette Market Shares	
Philip Morris	48.8%
RJR	27.0
Lorillard	9.9
Brown & Williamson	7.6
American Tobacco	5.3
Liggett	1.4
Discount Cigarette Market Shares	
RJR	33.2%
Philip Morris	27.1
Brown & Williamson	21.9
American Tobacco	10.0
Liggett	6.9
Lorillard	0.9

Source: *Forbes,* May 10, 1993, p. 110, from *Maxwell Consumer Report.*

percent in 1970 to an all-time company high of 43.4 percent in 1991. This ability to take market share away from rivals made the Philip Morris U.S.A. division a growth business in an industry where sales had declined industrywide from the 600 to 620 billion range in the late 1970s to about 507 billion cigarettes in 1992. William Campbell, CEO of PM U.S.A., voiced PM's outlook for the division: "We have always viewed PM U.S.A. as a growth company, and, basically, I continue to believe that's a relevant vision . . . The charge I have from senior management is that we continue to deliver superior income performance in the context of continued share and volume gains."[13]

In 1993, PM's Marlboro brand was the world's best-known brand and best-selling cigarette. The company sold 124 billion Marlboro cigarettes in the U.S. in 1992, which lined up end to end would reach to the moon and back 27 times.[14] Marlboro's national lead had been widening every year since 1975 when Marlboro sales overtook Winston for the number one position. Furthermore, the sales of the Marlboro brand in the U.S. alone exceeded revenues of large well-known companies such as Campbell Soup, Kellogg, and Gillette.[15] U.S. sales of Marlboro were 58 percent of PM's total domestic sales of 214.3 billion units and commanded a market share of over 24 percent. PM's Benson & Hedges brand held 3.1 percent of the market; Merit, Virginia Slims, Cambridge, a price-value brand, and Parliament had market shares under 3 percent.

---

[13]*Wall Street Journal,* November 1990.

[14]*Fortune,* May 3, 1993, p. 68.

[15]Ibid.

Cigarette Marketing at PM Philip Morris developed its marketing competencies by consistently implementing a precise sequence of marketing strategies. As the industry matured and sales declined, PM (and other U.S. manufacturers) began to exploit market niches. The company was alert to demographic trends that signaled the emergence of a new market segment opportunity. When a new segment of ample size was identified, PM would create a new brand or alter an existing brand and try to grow it into a segment leader.

In addition to offering a product designed to appeal to the entire smoking population, PM developed products and tailored advertising to identify with a particular segment of the market. PM offered cigarettes targeted at women, blacks, and the upper-, middle-, and lower-income levels. Philip Morris followed up on its market segmentation and product positioning strategies by first defining and communicating a brand's individual image and personality and then tenaciously reinforcing and enhancing the brand's personality via colors, imagery, packaging, consistent advertising, and point-of-sale displays. Each product offered was given the attention and advertising support necessary to attempt to grow the product into a segment leader. PM rarely changed its basic advertising theme and image for a brand, although it was common to add new wrinkles and variations.

Top management in the cigarette division was composed almost exclusively of marketing specialists and people with strong marketing experience and backgrounds. The key skills were shrewd market segmentation, imaginative marketing, trend awareness and trend anticipation, and ability to translate perceptions of "the moods of the time" and what was happening in the marketplace into bold actions to exploit new market niches. Because of PM's large advertising budgets for its cigarette brands, PM marketing specialists were able to exercise considerable buying power in negotiating media purchases, enabling PM to capture advertising economies of scale.

Marlboro Marlboro was initially introduced in 1924 in two varieties: an ivory tip, and a red tip that was targeted primarily at women. In 1954 the company saw the opportunity to capitalize on the changing consumer preference for filtered cigarettes. PM repackaged the brand with a red-and-white geometric-designed box and the Marlboro man was born. The product associated itself with an image of universal appeal. The cowboy—in Stetson hat and leather chaps, often on horseback, always silent and always serious—conveyed the image of American independence and frontiersman spirit. R. W. Murray, PM's President and COO, described the Marlboro man: "The cowboy has appeal to people as a personality. There are elements of adventure, freedom, being in charge of your destiny."[16] PM had changed neither the package nor the image for over 35 years.

The Marlboro man was perhaps PM's greatest asset. Although all cigarette advertising was banned from television in 1971, Marlboro ads appeared extensively in magazines, on billboards, and at point-of-purchase displays. Hollywood westerns paved the way for the Marlboro man internationally, where foreigners were eager to associate themselves with the American image. One Munich-born-and-raised immigrant said, "If Americans want to be chic like a European, they have to buy a Mercedes or BMW. For us it is easier; all we have to do is smoke Marlboros and wear jeans."[17]

---

[16]*Forbes,* February 9, 1987.
[17]Ibid.

PM kept the Marlboro image alive through the use of line extensions, rather than by altering the image. The company responded to changing customer preferences by adding Marlboro 100s in 1967, a longer cigarette; Marlboro Lights in 1972, a low tar and nicotine option; Marlboro 25s in 1985, which had 25 cigarettes per pack; in 1989 Marlboro Ultra Lights; and in 1991 Marlboro Mediums, a milder version of Marlboro targeted at males who found Marlboro Lights unmanly or associated with women.

Other Brands   In 1968 PM introduced Virginia Slims to appeal to the increasing number of women smokers. Using the same logic that was successful with the Marlboro brand, PM linked the brand to the image of the modern woman. The Virginia Slims woman was attractive, fashionable, carefree, and very liberated. The ads always contrasted the Virginia Slims woman with the subjugated woman of the past, accompanied with the tag line, "You've come a long way baby." Susan Jannetta, Virginia Slims' brand manager, said, "[Virginia Slims] ads have historically tried to convey fun, fashion, and flattery . . . The Virginia Slims woman is confident, yet approachable."

The Benson & Hedges brand cultivated an image designed to appeal to the yuppie generation. The ads featured young adults in leisure situations, sometimes alone, sometimes in groups. This brand was also popular with the black smoking population and ads often featured black jazz musicians. Benson & Hedges held 3.1 percent of the total market in 1992.

PM introduced the Bucks brand in 1990 to appeal to the growing numbers of price-conscious smokers. Author Goldfarb, brand manager, said, "Bucks is positioned to capture price-sensitive male smokers who are looking for an alternative brand choice." This brand was associated with a fully antlered stag on a red or white background for regular or light cigarettes, respectively. Magazines and billboards pictured the buck with engaging tag lines such as "The Buck stops here," "Buck the system," "The almighty Buck," or "Herd of Bucks?" The company pitched the brand to retailers through trade magazine advertisements that exclaimed, "There's more than one way to make a Buck." These ads claimed to help retailers "rack up sales to price-sensitive smokers" by offering consumers full, rich flavor for a money-saving low price and by handsome packaging and "off-beat promotions" and "catchy advertising."

Production Efficiencies   In addition to marketing competencies, Philip Morris also had competitive strength in production efficiency. PM's management made conscious efforts to learn how all the bits and pieces of the cigarette business fit together and how they could be better integrated into a smoothly functioning manufacturing, distribution, and sales promotion process. PM strived to keep margins up by stringently controlling costs and producing at maximum efficiency. According to the company's 1993 annual report, "Our position as the low-cost producer in the U.S. cigarette industry should help us continue to increase our profits from our domestic tobacco business."

The demand generated by advertising allowed PM to achieve manufacturing economies of scale. The company had 10 tobacco manufacturing and processing facilities in the U.S.: 7 in or near Richmond, Virginia, 1 in North Carolina, and 2 in Kentucky. These facilities produced 214.3 billion units in 1992, 26 percent of which were purchased by PM's international division for export.

PM had invested over $5.3 billion since 1978 in plants, equipment, and facilities (a figure that was less than 10 percent of total domestic tobacco revenues). Two new state-of-the-art facilities were built—one opened in 1983 in North Carolina and one opened in 1986 in Kentucky. The company also made capital expenditures to expand or modernize its eight existing plants, with a goal of achieving maximum production efficiencies. State-of-the-art equipment increased capacity to as much as 500 million cigarettes per day per plant. These technologies, combined with rigid cost controls, helped PM position itself as a low-cost producer with an average total cost, including marketing and administrative overhead, of 2.2 cents per unit sold.

FUTURE PROSPECTS FOR TOBACCO

In April 1989, in response to concerns expressed by certain stockholders that the company was "dealing in death" by promoting sales of its cigarettes to consumers, PM's board of directors added a resolution to the agenda at the annual stockholders meeting proposing that the company discontinue all production and distribution of cigarettes by the year 2000. Management was opposed to this proposal and the resolution was soundly defeated by the stockholders.

Management was bullish about PM's future in domestic tobacco. According to William Murray:

> As we look to the future, there is every reason to believe that we can continue to grow our global tobacco business. We have vitality and momentum. We have a unique portfolio of trademarks. Our modern, state-of-the-art factories manufacture low-cost, high-quality products in ever increasing quantities. And we are investing in research and development in order to have a constant stream of new products available to meet changing consumer needs.
>
> Together, these factors bring us cash flows matched by few companies in any industry anywhere in the world, and give us confidence in the future of our tobacco business.

However, on April 2, 1993, PM U.S.A. announced that it was reducing the price of its Marlboro brand by 20 percent. Management believed this move was the correct strategy in light of several market conditions. first was the impact that lower-priced cigarettes had had in recent years. Marlboro's 10-percent-per-year price increases, which were more than double inflation rates, had increased the margin between premium and value smokes to "unreasonable" levels. Additionally, PM had seen its market share erode from a high of 26 percent in 1989 to as low as 22 percent in April 1993. PM's management predicted that the $.40 per pack price reduction would drop the segment's operating profits by as much as 40 percent, or $2 billion, which it said was an acceptable loss for long-term gains in market position.

Investors and industry analysts were skeptical about the new pricing strategy. The following day Philip Morris' stock price nosedived over $20 per share. The drop—referred to as Marlboro Friday—represented a loss in stock value of $13.4 billion, the largest one-day decline by a single company since October 19, 1987.[18] Other critics of the move referred to it as "an ill-conceived and foolishly executed decision in an attempt to recover from years of surprising mismanagement."[19] These critics contended that the decision was based on a single test market in Portland, Oregon.

---

[18]*Fortune,* May 3, 1993.
[19]Ibid.

A few weeks later, at the company's 1993 shareholders' meeting, Michael Miles made the following comments regarding the company's decision to cut the price of its Marlboro brand:

> The first and most significant concern [about this business] is about domestic cigarette pricing and profitability.
>
> The discount segment of the U.S. cigarette market has been growing steadily for several years. That growth accelerated dramatically last summer, when certain of our domestic competitors put on a major drive behind discount brands priced to retail at 99 cents.
>
> With consumer confidence at historic low levels, these very low-priced cigarettes offered a compelling value-for-money to an increasing number of smokers. And as the growth of the deep discount products mushroomed, the industry's premium brands—including ours—declined.
>
> Over the period since the widespread appearance of 99-cent packs last summer, we have attempted to deal with the discount pricing challenges tactically, with short-term promotions and other actions. Initially, these efforts seemed to be succeeding, and as recently as just this past January, research data indicated that discount growth was slowing, and that our Marlboro share was stabilizing. But by late March it was clear that the deep discount products were again surging in volume, and premium brand shares again came under pressure.
>
> Although our full margin brands—Marlboro, Benson & Hedges, Virginia Slims, and Merit—fared better than our competitors' premium products, the declines of our brands, especially the most recent declines in February and March, were simply unacceptable to us in the context of the long-term performance of our business.
>
> Accordingly, the company had to make a basic business decision, one for which I believe there was only one right answer. Given the choice between whether to let volume and share for our strongest global brand continue to decline, or to invest in the defense of Marlboro and our other key trademarks, we took action to defend and build our key brands for the sake of the company's future growth.
>
> More specifically, on April 2 we announced a significant change in pricing strategy designed to make our premium products more affordable, and thus encourage consumers to make purchase decisions based on brand preference rather than price . . .
>
> Regrettably, this change in strategy does involve a significant reduction in 1993 profitability for Philip Morris U.S.A., and to a lesser degree for Philip Morris Companies as a whole. Because of the impact on our 1993 profits, it was obviously a very difficult decision for us to make. I can assure you that it was not made precipitously, but only after careful analysis of all the available options.
>
> We do believe that our strategy sets the stage for renewed stability and profitability in our full-margin cigarette business, and for overall volume, share, and profit growth for Philip Morris U.S.A. in the longer term.

PM's pricing strategy instigated a price war among premium brands as each strove to maintain its competitive position. By early 1994 both Camel and Winston brands had similar pricing strategies.

PM'S INTERNATIONAL TOBACCO SBU

All cigarette production and sales outside the U.S. were handled by Philip Morris International. This segment represented 23 percent of PM's total revenues, 28 percent of total tobacco revenues, and 19 percent of total operating income in 1992. From 1988 through 1992, PM International's revenues grew at a compound rate of 20.4 percent and operating income grew at 25 percent (as compared with 9.5 percent and 15 percent, respectively, for PM U.S.A.). PM executives saw the greatest opportunities for PM's cigarette business in international markets and were rapidly increasing its presence through acquisitions and exports.

CONDITIONS IN THE INTERNATIONAL TOBACCO MARKET

Because antismoking sentiments were weaker outside the United States than inside, worldwide tobacco consumption was still growing approximately 2 to 2.5 percent per year. This combined with the downward pressure on prices in the U.S. market made the overseas market more attractive, despite the lower profit margins associated with international sales. The average pretax profit to PM on domestic cigarettes was 30 cents per pack in 1993 compared with a pretax average of only 11.5 cents per pack on international sales.

In 1993 several political and economic conditions offered challenges and opportunities for tobacco manufacturers. The demise of communism, the reunification of Germany, and improved trade relations between the U.S. and China resulted in new markets for the 1990s. In 1980, the total demand for cigarettes excluding the U.S. was 3.9 trillion units—a market which Western companies had access to only about 40 percent. In 1993 the demand had increased to approximately 4.9 trillion units, 95 percent of which Philip Morris and other competitors had access to.

In 1993 cigarette consumption was rising most strongly in formerly socialist bloc countries (see Exhibit 12). Western cigarette manufacturers as well as Eastern governments had much to gain from supplying the large demand of the area: cigarette consumption in the former Eastern bloc countries was estimated at 700 billion units, as compared to 500 billion in the U.S. and 600 billion in Western Europe. The Western cigarette manufacturers saw the opening of an enormous market as well as the potential to establish low-cost production facilities to service the European Community. The governments of these countries viewed the arrangement as a potential source of revenue to relieve their cash-strapped budgets. In 1992, tobacco taxes generated $990 million in Poland, $380 million in the Czech Republic, and $310 million in Hungary. In countries such as Turkey, Hong Kong, and Taiwan, taxes made the prices of imported cigarettes double that of the government's brands. However, citizens were able to use protest signatures to get a 200 percent tax increase reduced to a 100 percent increase in Hong Kong, and Turkish officials agreed to reduce tariffs once companies such as Philip Morris began production on Turkish soil using Turkish workers.

Both PM and RJR had entered the Eastern European markets through a combination of exports and acquisitions of local tobacco companies. By 1993, Philip Morris International had acquired an interest in eight tobacco companies in the former Soviet bloc and was targeting expansion in Turkey and Bulgaria (see Exhibit 1). RJR had acquired five East European operations and opened a $33 million plant in Warsaw capable of producing 8 billion Camel and Winston cigarettes annually. Germany's Reemtsma and B.A.T. were also strong contenders via acquisitions in the Eastern European region.[20]

Although tobacco consumption was relatively flat in Japan, a large percentage of the population smoked, trade barriers were lowered in 1986, and consumers were agreeable to switching or upgrading to U.S. brands. These circumstances made the Japanese markets very attractive to U.S. manufacturers. finally, the development of a unified European community in 1992 offered the opportunity to decrease the market

---

[20]*The Economist,* August 21, 1993, pp. 52–53.

EXHIBIT 12 | **U.S. Cigarette Exports to Leading Destinations***
(Ranked by 1992 Shipments)

	Shipments (billions of units)			
Destination	1989	1990	1991	1992
1. Japan	45.10	47.60	54.00	57.70
2. Belgium-Luxembourg	33.20	53.50	48.20	53.30
3. Hong Kong	19.10	16.50	16.10	17.60
4. Former Soviet Republics	†	2.70	4.60	12.20
5. Saudi Arabia	5.30	6.00	7.50	7.60
6. Turkey	0.80	3.10	9.90	7.60
7. United Arab Emirates	7.00	7.00	7.50	6.70
8. South Korea	3.80	3.40	4.00	3.90
9. Cyprus	2.00	0.60	1.40	3.90
10. Singapore	4.50	4.20	3.50	3.80
11. Taiwan	2.30	3.70	3.50	2.90
12. Israel	1.80	1.80	1.80	2.20
13. Paraguay	0.90	1.20	2.50	2.20
14. Morocco	1.00	1.10	1.80	1.70
15. Netherlands Antilles	1.40	1.20	1.50	1.50
16. Kuwait	1.60	1.10	0.80	1.50
17. Panama	1.50	1.20	1.10	1.40
18. All other locations	10.50	8.40	9.50	17.90
Total	141.80	164.30	179.20	205.60

*Year ending June. †Included in all other locations.
Source: Bureau of Census.

fragmentation in Europe. From 1990 through 1993, the sales volume for PMI's European Community operations had increased by 25 percent.

Of the 5 trillion cigarettes sold worldwide, U.S. manufacturers held less than a 20 percent share in 1993. PM and RJR were expanding their international volumes by 5 to 6 percent per year. Unlike the U.S. market, the international cigarette market was highly fragmented in terms of producers. Many of the foreign producers restricted their operations to a single country or small group of countries. Therefore, there were many more competitors in the international markets, creating a fragmented competitive environment.

Major Competitors

In the international arena, Philip Morris competed against 13 major companies. Philip Morris' largest rival was B.A.T. Industries Ltd. (formerly British-American Tobacco Co.), which was the world's largest tobacco company, with roughly a 10 percent worldwide market share—compared to second-place PMI's share of 9 percent. B.A.T. Industries was represented in over 160 countries and divided its portfolio of businesses into a financial services group and a tobacco group. The financial services group had three large insurance companies as its principal operating companies. The tobacco group consisted of Brown & Williamson in the U.S.; British-American Tobacco in over 40 countries in Europe, Australia, Latin America, Asia, and Africa; B.A.T. Cigarettenfabriken in West Germany; Souza Cruz in Brazil; Imperial Tobacco in Canada; Skandinavisk in Denmark; and ITC in India. Brown & Williamson, with brands such as Kool, Viceroy, Kent, Capri, Richland, Belair, and Lucky Strike, held 11.9 percent of the U.S. market; Imperial held nearly 58 percent of the Canadian market.

Rothmans, formerly in partnership with PM, was a major competitor in the U.K., the European countries, Australia, and Greece. In France, the nationally owned SEITA held 51 percent of the market. Likewise, Greece's state-owned cigarette manufacturers held 66 percent of its domestic market. R. J. Reynolds, the fourth-largest tobacco company worldwide, was the only other U.S.-based manufacturer with a global presence. RJR's Winston brand accounted for most of its international sales.

In 1993 Philip Morris had a 9 percent share of an estimated total 5-trillion-unit worldwide cigarette market and was the leading U.S. cigarette exporter. PM International owned or leased over 30 facilities outside the U.S. and distributed products to more than 170 countries or territories.

PM's International Cigarette Strategy

PM's basic strategy for building critical mass in the international markets was a combination global/multicountry approach. Philip Morris International followed a production strategy that was primarily a multicountry approach—PMI produced cigarettes in facilities located throughout the world and offered brands or products that were tailored for a particular market or region. However, there were also some global aspects to PM's international strategy. The plants and facilities owned and leased by PMI were by no means autonomous; PM headquarters maintained a network of control and coordination among the various overseas facilities. Additionally, PM followed a global approach to producing and marketing some brands internationally, particularly its Marlboro brand. PMI purchased nearly 110 billion units (primarily Marlboros), approximately 26 percent of all international sales, from PM U.S.A., and transferred the brand image it had built in the U.S. to foreign markets.

Acquisitions PM acquired local cigarette manufacturers as a way of gaining entry to foreign markets. PM's primary interest in local companies was in acquiring rights to market their brands and to use them to serve as vehicles for introducing other PMI brands into the local markets. As of 1993 PM had acquired or had interest in over 30 plants located throughout the world. Philip Morris had a 100 percent controlling interest in plants in the following locations:

Australia	1 plant
Belgium	2 plants
Brazil	2 plants
Germany	3 plants
Italy	1 plant
The Netherlands	1 plant
Switzerland	2 plants

PM International's average market share in several critical markets was

Germany	35%
Italy	43
France	27
Switzerland	45
Japan	12
Argentina	52

The company held at least a 20 percent share of the markets in Australia, Belgium, Brazil, and the Netherlands.

PMI was the leading foreign cigarette manufacturer in terms of volume and market share in the European Community (Belgium, France, Germany, Greece, Italy, Luxembourg, Malta, the Netherlands, Portugal, and Spain). Within this area, PMI brands held 25 percent of the market. Every cigarette sold by PMI in the EC area was manufactured in one of PMI's four EC-located facilities: Bergen op Zoom, Netherlands; Brussels, Belgium; and Munich and Berlin, Germany.

In 1978, PM International acquired the overseas rights to all the cigarette brands of Liggett, a move that further strengthened PM's international market position. Liggett brands covered by the purchase included Lark, L&M, Chesterfield, Eve, and Decade. The Lark brand was the leading imported brand in Japan in 1989. In 1981, Philip Morris and Rothmans International announced a $350 million deal whereby PM acquired an immediate 22 percent ownership interest in Rothmans along with the U.S. marketing rights for Rothmans brands (Dunhill, Peter Stuyvesant, and Rothmans). Rothmans specialized in top-of-the-line brands and British-style, Virginia-blend cigarettes, which had a deluxe or superpremium image. In April 1989, PM and Rothmans agreed to combine their cigarette sales and distribution in Britain in an effort to revive profits and market share and achieve production and marketing synergies. The combined operations would have resulted in 14 percent of the British market and generated $256 million in cigarette revenues annually. In November 1989, however, PM sold its stake to Switzerland's Compagnie financiere Richemont AG. Industry analysts said the move was made because PMI management had concluded that the venture did not deliver the market penetration potential that PM had initially hoped for.

In 1991, PM acquired Dresden Cigarette Manufacturing Company, the largest cigarette manufacturing operation in eastern Germany. This purchase added four additional brands to PMI's product line, one of which accounted for about 25 percent of all cigarettes sold in eastern Germany. Dresden's combined share was approximately 35 percent of the market. This purchase followed an agreement in which PM agreed to supply more than 20 billion cigarettes to the Russian Republic—the largest republic in the former Soviet Union. PMI resisted the urge to tone down the harsh taste of the f6 and revamp its package; it was rewarded for not "Westernizing" the product with a three point increase in share.

In return for providing technical assistance to improve tobacco manufacturing in Russia, PMI secured an agreement in principle to supply cigarettes to the Russian Republic from 1992 to 1995. In 1991, the company shipped 22 billion cigarettes to the former Soviet Union, and had plans to sell 80 to 100 billion cigarettes in the area by 1997. In addition to exports, the company had made equity investments in three cigarette firms in the country. It acquired a 49 percent stake in Krasnodar Tobacco in 1992 for $5 million and planned to spend another $60 million expanding and updating the plant with the goal of producing 12 billion cigarettes in the plant by 1996. The company was also negotiating to build a plant in St. Petersburg capable of producing 10 billion Marlboro cigarettes annually. Industry analysts noted that smokers in the eastern European communities on average spent 8 to 10 percent of their income on cigarettes. During the height of the Soviet cigarette shortage (analysts predicted the supply was approximately 50 billion units short of the 400 billion demand), packs of Marlboros were sold on the black market for as much as 25 rubles each, or approximately $40 at the official exchange rate. Under PMI's agreement with Russia, the company barters cigarettes for products—most likely gold and oil—

that can be exchanged for U.S. dollars in markets outside Russia, thereby avoiding hard currency exchange difficulties.

PMI also secured an acquisition in the Czech Republic after a bidding war with four other international contenders. The company paid $400 million for a 77 percent share in the company. Unique to this deal, however, was the 1950 Czech monopoly law granting exclusive tobacco production rights. This gave PMI control over 80 percent of the Czech tobacco market—its highest share of any market in the world.

Capacity PM's strategy was to renovate the newly acquired facilities, install state-of-the-art equipment, and bring the manufacturing process up to PM's production and efficiency standards. Generally, production continued status quo at the newly acquired facilities, while PM imported Marlboros and other brands until the plant upgrades were completed. At that point, PM ceased most of its imports and began production of both its major brands and the newly acquired brands in the newly renovated facilities. This strategy increased the lengths of the production runs at the upgraded plants and reduced costs in those facilities by allowing PM to allocate fixed costs over a greater number of units and by lowering the distribution costs of its major brands in the area. However, this also meant that the lengths of the production runs at the plants that were originally supplying the imports were reduced; so the net cost advantage was less than the plant-level advantage.

Brands Brand marketing and advertising were primarily global, with adjustments for country-level market conditions. PM used the Marlboro cowboy image, with very few exceptions, uniformly in each of the 170 countries and territories to which it distributed. The Marlboro brand, which had been the world's largest-selling cigarette brand since 1972, represented over 50 percent of PM's international volume. Marlboro was the number one cigarette in France, Greece, West Germany, and the Netherlands in 1992.

As in the U.S., the company followed a market segmentation strategy and heavy reliance on media advertising to create a brand image and to build customer loyalty. PM transferred its marketing skills and competences into developing new brands designed to meet the needs of a specific country, such as the Muratti brand in Italy and Peter Jackson in Australia. PM also used its marketing know-how to increase the market share of the newly acquired brands.

FUTURE PROSPECTS FOR INTERNATIONAL TOBACCO

The management at PM saw great potential in its international tobacco strategic business unit. Worldwide, cigarette consumption was still a growing industry, while domestic consumption was slowly declining. International politics, trade agreements with Japan and China, the emergence of a unified European Community, the fall of communism, and the rise of capitalism were opening doors to markets that had previously been closed to PM International. These markets were characteristically dominated by government-run monopolies that had little incentive to offer consumers a wide variety of cigarette types and brands. Too often, these monopolies were poorly managed and consumers were faced with severe cigarette shortages. PMI anticipated using its global brand images and strategic plant locations to capitalize on the unmet consumer demand, to offer smokers a wider brand selection, and to rapidly grow its worldwide share.

PM President and Chief Operating Officer William Murray made the following remarks at the 1993 annual meeting:

Our international tobacco business continues to grow strongly in markets throughout Western and Eastern Europe, the Middle East, Asia and Latin America.

We are gaining market share and strengthening our number one position in the highly profitable markets of the European Community.

In addition, we are rapidly increasing volume in regions of the world where large and growing cigarette markets give us new and exciting opportunities for growth. For example, since the dissolution of the eastern Bloc, we have made acquisitions or investments in eastern Germany, Hungary, the Czech Republic, Russia, and Lithuania. Just a few years ago, these markets appeared closed to us forever. Today they are the site of dynamic business growth that should continue well into the next century . . .

The large and rapidly growing economies of Asia provide many other significant opportunities for us. For example, four markets—Japan, Taiwan, Korea, and Thailand—have become accessible to us only during the past six years. Combined, their cigarette volume is already the size of the U.S. market. We have already become the leading foreign competitor in each country. More importantly, our overall 9 percent market share in these four countries leaves us plenty of room for growth.

We are capitalizing on our vast opportunities by building on our brand portfolio . . . But even as we work to improve and expand all our trademarks, our first priority is Marlboro—one of the only truly global brands in the world.

Marlboro is steadily building on its position as the world's best-selling cigarette. The continued strength of the Marlboro family is clearly essential for us to realize our full potential in the global cigarette market in the years to come.

PM'S MILLER BREWING SBU

Philip Morris' acquisition of Miller Brewing Company in 1969 was motivated largely by PM's desire to use the excess cash flows from its profitable cigarette business to exploit the company's cigarette marketing expertise in other consumer product categories. Following the acquisition, PM spent several years sizing up Miller's situation, replacing Miller's management with some of PM's top-flight cigarette personnel, and giving the newly installed management team time to learn and understand the beer business. Then PM began to put strategic changes at Miller into high gear.

Essentially, Miller's new management relied on the same classic consumer marketing techniques that had lifted PM from fourth to first place in the tobacco business and that had made Marlboro the leading cigarette brand: it looked upon the beer market as being divided into segments, brought out new products and packaging for those segments, and then spent heavily on advertising and merchandising to reach the targeted segments. PM's approach to marketing strategy was a radical departure from the beer industry's traditional approach to treating the beer market as a homogeneous entity that could be served by one product in one type of package. "Philip Morris changed the ground rules by introducing consumer marketing to the popular price segment," said John Bissell, senior vice president of Stroh's Brewery.[21]

In 1970, the first year of operation under PM, Miller Brewing contributed $199 million in revenues and held only a 4.3 percent share of the domestic beer market. In 1992, Miller Brewing Company had 22.3 percent of the domestic market, with four brands in the top 10–ranked beers (Miller Lite, Miller High Life, Miller Genuine Draft, and Milwaukee's Best) and sales of 42.2 million barrels. In 1992, 6.7 percent of Philip Morris' revenues and 2.5 percent of profits were contributed by its Miller Brewing division.

---

[21]*Marketing and Media Decisions,* May 1985.

U.S. BEER INDUSTRY TRENDS

Demographics Demographic trends in the 1980s tended to have an adverse affect on the levels of beer consumption. The 1980s heralded the maturity of the so-called baby boomers and was referred to as the fitness decade—a period during which physical fitness and nutrition awareness were significantly heightened. As a result, domestic drinking habits had changed. Exhibit 13 indicates the changing composition of beverage consumption. Almost all beverages lost market share to soft drinks and bottled water during the 1980s, an indication of the marketing skill of the soft-drink manufacturers and the increased health consciousness of the decade.

Americans spent $51.3 billion on over 180 million barrels of domestic beer in 1992 (see Exhibit 14). Consumption levels of beer per capita had been declining and the levels of beer production in barrels were relatively flat throughout most of the 1980s, with a slight peak in volume in 1990:

Year	Consumption (millions of barrels)	Per Capita Consumption (gallons)
1980	178.0	24.5
1981	181.9	24.7
1982	182.4	24.3
1983	183.8	24.3
1984	182.7	24.0
1985	183.0	23.8
1986	187.5	24.1
1987	187.3	23.9
1988	187.9	23.7
1989	186.9	23.3
1990	191.6	23.6
1991	189.4	23.2
1992	189.0	22.8

Source: Compiled by the case authors from a variety of sources, including *Beverage Industry,* January 1990 and January 1991; *Beverage World,* May 1993; and *1993 Modern Brewery Age.*

Overall, total domestic beer sales increased by a compound annual growth rate of just 1 percent between 1986 and 1990. The market decreased by 1.2 percent between 1990 and 1991 and decreased again slightly in 1992. Forecasts called for annual decreases of perhaps as much as 1 percent annually.

Beer drinkers also changed their preferences for beer types. Exhibit 15 shows that from 1981 to 1990 the light beer segment grew from 25.2 million barrels, 13.8 percent of the beer consumed in the U.S., to 53.6 million barrels and 28 percent of the market. The only other product category to experience growth was imports, which grew from 2.9 percent to 4.5 percent of the total market.

In addition to competition from other beer brands, brewers faced competition from beer substitutes and small, regional brewers. Microbreweries gained popularity in the 1980s. These breweries were small, often locally owned, and produced a draft beer that was served in-house only. Often these breweries were combined with a restaurant to create a publike atmosphere that appealed to young professionals. The no-alcohol segment was advertised as a substitute beer for either the designated driver on evenings out or as a low-calorie option for the health conscious. This segment

EXHIBIT 13 | **Per Capita Beer Gallonage Consumption 1991 versus 1992**

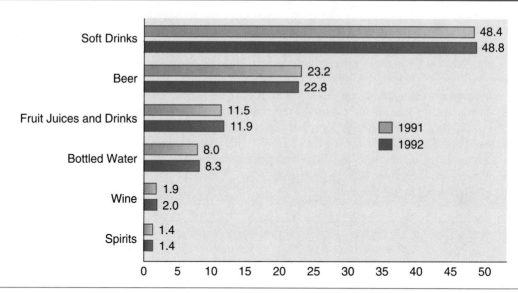

Source: *Beverage World* estimates based on industry contacts.

EXHIBIT 14 | **U.S. Beer Sales—1992 versus 1991**

	1992 Barrelage	1991 Barrelage	% Change
Domestic	180,705,000*	181,446,000*	−0.4
Imports	8,322,884	7,926,000	5.0
Exports	5,495,000*	4,611,000	19.2
Total	194,522,884*	193,983,000	0.3

*Estimated without adjustment for warehouses and malt coolers. Includes sales to U.S. military abroad.

grew between 10 and 15 percent annually between 1985 and 1992. Samuel Adams was one example of a successful microbrewery strategy. The company promoted its product on the basis of its quality ingredients and careful production, using slogans such as "[The big name brewers] spill more in a year than I make."

Nonalcoholic beer was increasing in popularity. It was developed to provide a socially acceptable alternative to spirits and was considered a social responsibility coup for the beer manufacturers. Another side benefit of the product category was that it was not subject to excise taxes and therefore was a more profitable product. Most major brewers had a nonalcoholic brew on the market. Heileman's Kingsbury brand was the no-alcohol industry leader, but Anheuser-Busch's O'Doul's and Miller's Sharp's were gaining share as were Coors's Cutters and Molsen's Excell.

Antialcohol Movement   Beer consumption was also affected by government regulations and social issues. In 1984 Congress directed states to raise their legal drinking age to 21 or lose federal highway funds. This move eliminated the 18-to-20-year-old youth market, the segment that traditionally consumed more gallons per capita than

EXHIBIT 15 | **Malt Beverage Market Breakdown by Product Category, 1981–90** *(In millions of barrels and market share)*

	Superpremium		Premium		Light		Popular		Malt Liquor		Imported	
Year	Barrels	Share	Barrels	Share	Barrels	Share	Barrels	Share	Barrels	Share	Barrels	Share
1981	12.7	6.9%	93.9	51.6%	25.2	13.8%	39.0	21.4%	5.9	3.2%	5.2	2.9%
1982	12.8	7.0	88.4	48.5	32.3	17.7	36.7	20.1	6.4	3.5	5.8	3.2
1983	11.5	6.3	86.3	47.0	34.0	18.5	39.2	21.3	6.5	3.5	6.3	3.4
1984	9.1	5.0	82.2	45.0	36.4	19.9	42.0	23.0	5.8	3.2	7.2	3.9
1985	7.9	4.3	80.1	43.6	37.6	20.5	44.4	24.2	5.7	3.1	7.9	4.3
1986	7.1	3.6	80.6	43.0	41.4	22.1	44.0	23.4	5.6	3.0	6.6	4.7
1987	6.7	3.6	77.6	41.5	44.9	24.0	42.7	22.3	5.8	3.1	9.4	5.0
1988	6.0	2.6	76.6	40.8	48.0	25.6	42.1	23.2	5.5	2.6	9.4	5.0
1989	5.2	2.8	75.8	40.3	50.5	26.9	42.2	22.4	5.6	3.0	8.7	4.6
1990	4.7	2.4	71.4	37.3	53.6	28.0	41.9	21.9	5.7	3.0	8.6	4.5

Source: *Beverage Industry,* January 1991.

any other. In addition to the rise in the legal drinking age, some states banned happy hours in bars and imposed stiffer penalties on drunk drivers, to the detriment of away-from-home consumption.

In 1988 Congress mandated that beginning October 1990 warning labels must appear on alcoholic beverage packages. The labels read: "Government Warning: According to the Surgeon General, women should not drink alcohol during pregnancy because of risk of birth defects. Consumption of alcoholic beverages impairs your ability to drive a car or operate machinery and may cause other health problems." This regulation represented a potential for increased product liability lawsuits for the industry. Campaigning by groups such as Mothers Against Drunk Driving (MADD) kept antialcohol sentiments high, but the industry responded with advertising campaigns that stressed moderation and introduced low- or no-alcohol products. Other groups sought to ban all beer advertising on the premise that the advertisements unduly influenced young drinkers. However, the brewers countered that their advertising was designed to differentiate among brands, not increase consumption.

COMPETITION IN THE BEER INDUSTRY

Throughout most of the 1970s, the beer industry experienced substantial contraction in the number of breweries in operation and by 1980 had fallen to approximately half the levels in 1970. However, the number gradually crept back up to more than double the 1970 levels by 1991:

Year	Number of Brewing Facilities	Year	Number of Brewing Facilities
1970	154	1987	120
1980	86	1988	183
1982	82	1989	245
1984	96	1990	286
1986	103	1991	333

Source: U.S. Bureau of Alcohol, Tobacco, and Firearms.

These new facilities were built primarily to accommodate the volume gains experienced by Anheuser-Busch, Miller, and Coors and the growing popularity of microbreweries that sprang up in the late 1980s. There were 170 brewers in the U.S. in 1993, but the five largest companies controlled 88 percent of the market. (See Exhibits 16 and 17 for market share data by company.) In general, throughout the 1990s, the incremental gains in market share of the "big three"—Anheuser-Busch (A-B), Miller, and Coors—came at the expense of the smaller brewers. Stroh Brewery, with only one beer in the top 10, was losing volume at an average rate of decline of nearly 10 percent annually. Heileman Brewing, with no beers ranked in the top 10,

E X H I B I T   16   **| 1992 Market Share—Top Five Brewers**   *(Includes imports)*

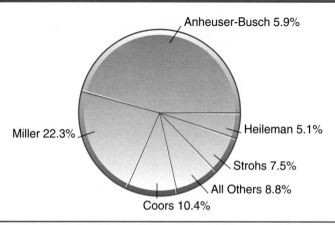

Source: *1993 Modern Brewery Age.*

E X H I B I T   17   **| Domestic Market Share—Top Five Brewers, 1982–92**

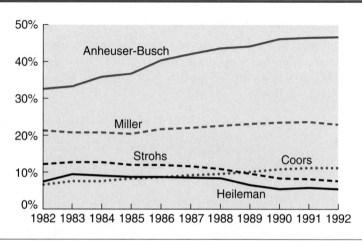

Source: *1993 Modern Brewery Age.*

lost 6.1 percent in 1990, but its market share position, while still declining, had ceased its rapid plunge by 1992; its sales were falling at a rate of less than 1 percent per year.

Competitive Weapons   Advertising was a principal competitive weapon in the beer industry. Brewers relied heavily on media ads to create brand loyalty, establish brand image, and introduce new brands to the public. New products developed for market niches were also important. Miller was attempting to create a market for bottled draft beer with its Miller Genuine Draft brand; A-B was trying to establish a segment for dry beers via introduction of Michelob Dry and Bud Dry; and A-B had entered the light-alcohol segment with its L.A. brand, but had had little success.

Pricing was another competitive weapon. flat consumption rates and the growing buyer sensitivity to price forced brewers to hold price increases to a minimum and try to boost profits through cost reduction. The larger brewers, A-B, Miller, and Coors, benefited from high capacity utilization and economies of scale because of larger volumes. A-B was pricing aggressively to gain market share. It sacrificed profits for volume by reducing prices 15 to 40 cents per 12-pack of Budweiser on a market-by-market basis in order to achieve its stated objective of 50 percent market share by 1995.

The increase in the federal excise taxes on beer that went into effect January 1, 1991, was predicted to decrease annual consumption by 2 percent. The increase in the per bottle cost was from $0.16 to $0.32. This in turn was expected to increase the level of competitive rivalry. The "big three" breweries were expected to continue to dominate the domestic beer industry at the expense of the smaller breweries throughout the 1990s.

THE COMPETITORS

Anheuser-Busch Companies, Inc.   Anheuser-Busch was the industry leader in 1993 with 46 percent of the total market and 6 brands in the top 10-ranked beer brands. The market share for its flagship brand, Budweiser, was greater in 1992 (25.7 percent) than all of Miller's brands combined (22.3 percent). A-B was also adept at using advertising to create brand image and loyalty and at developing new products. A-B attempted to replicate Miller's success with Lite and Genuine Draft by creating a niche for dry beers. Michelob Dry was introduced in 1988 and Bud Dry in 1989. In 1990, the dry beer segment represented 3 percent of the domestic market. Bud Dry held 53 percent and Michelob Dry held 20 percent of the dry beer segment, equal to 1.6 percent and 0.6 percent, respectively, of the total beer market.

A-B was a vertically integrated company. Through its Busch Agricultural Resources, Inc., subsidiary, the company supplied one-third of its malt needs, 50 percent of both its brewing rice and malting barley requirements, and 7 percent of its hops needs. The company supplied more than 45 percent of its own container requirements with eight canning plants and three lid plants. It owned 13 domestic brewing facilities with a production capacity of 95 million barrels in 1993. The company had 900 independent beer wholesalers and 10 company-owned wholesale operations. A-B was diversified outside of beer production (the Busch Gardens Amusement Parks, Eagle Brand Foods, and the St. Louis Cardinals major league baseball team).

A-B had a strong international presence. Anheuser-Busch International was formed in 1981 to expand beer sales outside the U.S. In 1993 the company's brands were distributed in over 50 countries through its exporting networks or one of its five foreign production facilities. The company used strategic alliances to facilitate its entry into some markets including an 18 percent stake in Mexico's leading brewer, Grupo-Modelo; a joint venture with Kirin Brewing Company, Ltd., in Japan; a licensing agreement with Oriental Brewing Co., Ltd., of Seoul, South Korea; as well as numerous licensing and exporting arrangements throughout the European countries.

The Adolph Coors Company The Adolph Coors Company was a privately held company that competed in the premium, superpremium and light beer segments. The company held 10.4 percent of the domestic market, and its Coors Light and Coors brands were ranked 2nd and 10th, respectively, in the top 10-ranked beers. Coors's advertising focused on the quality of the product (ingredients, water, manufacturing process, etc.) rather than the "good times" theme of other brewers' advertisements.

The company had five stated objectives: 1) to optimize growth and profitability of its existing brand portfolio; 2) to research, develop, and capitalize on domestic and international new business ideas directly related to the production and marketing of malt-based beverages; 3) to minimize costs while maximizing quality and value to the customer; 4) to develop a highly motivated work force that provided skills and talents needed to achieve the goal of the company; and 5) to preserve and defend the right to do business in a fair and equitable way. Coors was considered a very socially responsible company, both as a manufacturer of an alcoholic beverage and an influence on its environment. Coors literature cites savings of over 700,000 trees, 29 million gallons of water, and 120,000 cubic yards of landfill space in response to its efforts to increase the recycled content of its cans, bottles, cardboard packages, and point-of-purchase displays. As an employer, Coors used cross-functional teams to manage its employees.

Coors was pursuing a number of international expansion strategies, including export opportunities, licensing agreements, and equity participation arrangements with other brewers. In 1993 it exported to 12 foreign countries as well as 16 U.S. military bases. It had a licensing agreement with Asahi Breweries, Ltd., to brew and distribute original Coors in Japan. It also had a licensing agreement for Molson Breweries to distribute Coors and Coors Light in Canada (however, the nature of that agreement was unknown as a result of Molson's changing allegiances). In 1992 Scottish and Newcastle Breweries of Scotland began to brew Coors Extra Gold for distribution in the United Kingdom. The company also formed a joint venture with Jinro Limited of Korea to build and operate the Jinro-Coors Brewing Company in South Korea in 1994.

The company had two primary brewing facilities, one in Golden, Colorado, and the other in Memphis, Tennessee, with a total brewing capacity of 23 million barrels. Its primary packaging facility located in Elkton, Virginia, combined with some packaging capabilities in Memphis, yielded a packaging capacity of 28 million barrels. The company had aggressive plans to introduce one successful new product per year. In 1993 it introduced Coors Extra Gold Light. Coors experienced a .25 percent increase in sales from 1991 to 1992, the majority coming from an increase from 11.7 million barrels to 12.3 million barrels in its light brand.

The Stroh Brewing Company The Stroh Brewing Company, the fourth-ranked brewery with 7.5 percent of the market, had experienced steady and dramatic losses in market share during the 1980s. Stroh's 1993 structure was the result of two major acquisitions in the early 1980s. The company acquired F&M Schaefer Brewing in 1980 and Joseph Schlitz Brewing in 1982. This resulted in company ownership of six breweries and two container manufacturing plants. In 1992 the company lost money for the ninth straight year. The company was responding to its market share losses by reducing the number of brands it offered and concentrating advertising and distribution on the remaining offerings. Stroh's product line was increasingly targeted at the price-conscious and blue-collar segments of the market.

Heileman Heileman's initial strategy was to acquire smaller, declining brands, decrease capital expenditures and advertising to the bare minimum, and ride out the life of the brand. This strategy was relatively successful, but future success depended on the availability of declining brands. Heileman was purchased in a leveraged buyout by Bond Holding Corporation in 1989 and in 1991 was struggling under the tremendous debt load incurred as a result of the takeover. The company announced plans to sell two breweries and eight brands in March 1990. Heileman President and COO Murray Cutbush said the divestiture was prompted for strategic fit reasons, but industry analysts said Heileman was unloading unused capacity. In 1990 Heileman Brewing filed a Chapter 11 bankruptcy claim and Cutbush resigned as president of Heileman in early 1991; the resignation was apparently prompted by Cutbush's inability to maneuver the company with its declining volume and its heavy debt load. By 1993 the company had slowed its death plummet, although it was still suffering market share erosion and was struggling to regain some semblance of profitability under its new leadership structure.

THE PERFORMANCE OF MILLER BREWING COMPANY

Throughout the 1970–75 period when the strategic changes were first initiated and implemented, Miller gained dramatically in market share but not in profitability. Miller spent heavily for advertising—roughly $3 per barrel compared with an industry average of just more than $1 per barrel. Miller's operating profits in the five-year period 1971–75 averaged less than $7 million per year—a 3.1 percent annual return on the $227 million that Philip Morris had spent in purchasing Miller, a figure that did not take into account either interest expenses or the expenditures for capital additions undertaken by PM during this same period. In the next five years Miller's operating profits rose sharply, and its market share also continued to climb. Since 1980 market share had flattened out, but sales and operating profit margins continued to improve:

Year	Miller's Operating Revenues ($millions)	Miller's Operating Profits ($millions)	Miller's Share of Beer Sales	Miller's Operating Profit Margin
1970	$ 198.5	$ 11.4	4.3%	5.7%
1975	658.3	28.6	8.6	4.3
1980	2,542.3	144.7	21.1	5.7
1985	2,914.0	132.0	20.8	4.5
1986	3,054.0	154.0	21.3	5.0
1987	3,105.0	170.0	21.6	5.5
1988	3,262.0	190.0	21.4	5.8
1989	3,435.0	226.0	22.4	6.6
1990	3,534.0	285.0	22.0	8.1
1991	4,056.0	301.0	22.4	7.4
1992	3,976.0	260.0	21.5	6.5

Source: PM annual reports.

Miller High Life　　Upon being acquired, Miller's first move was to reposition the Miller High Life brand, the flagship brand Miller had when PM made the acquisition. The new ads touted "Miller Time" and "If you have the time, we have the beer." This repositioning of High Life's identity and image was a resounding success. By 1978 Miller High Life had become the second-largest selling beer in the U.S.; Anheuser-Busch's Budweiser brand ranked first.

Miller High Life reached an all-time high of 18.6 percent in 1979. By 1989 the brand's share had fallen to 4.1 percent. The company had to rely on new products to keep capacity utilization at an acceptable level. Reflecting on Miller's performance of the previous decade, Maxwell said, "I think the steam went out of Miller in the 1980s, partly because the competition, especially Anheuser-Busch, became more determined. And maybe because of some other things. Perhaps we overreached on pricing. So the business trailed off. We built a brewery too many [the inactive Trenton, Ohio, facility was built for $450 million]."[22] By the end of the decade the company had come full circle and was again repositioning the High Life brand. A new advertising campaign, "Buy that man a Miller," was introduced in 1989, but by early 1994 it was clear that PM had little hope of regaining the brand's position in the premium beer segment.

Miller dropped the prices on the High Life brand, revived the old "Miller Time" campaign, and repositioned the brand as a higher-grade alternative to store brands and other low-priced beers that appealed to the price conscious. As a mid-tier brand, Miller was expecting to spend less on promotional advertising and to extract residual benefits from nostalgic campaigns. The brand's sales increased 9 percent following a 20 percent price reduction. By early 1994, a 12-pack of Miller High Life that had cost $6.99 two years before could be purchased for only $4.99.[23]

Miller Lite　　In January 1975 Miller introduced Lite on a national basis with a blitz advertising campaign costing an estimated $10 million. The campaign for Lite stressed the "less filling" advantage of a reduced calorie beer that "tastes great" like other premium beers. To dramatize the theme, Miller used sports personalities (Whitey Ford, Wilt Chamberlain, Dick Butkus, Joe Frazier) to tout the message. The response to Lite exceeded Miller's expectations, and demand quickly matched Miller's capacity to brew and distribute the Lite brand. More than a few rival brewers belittled Miller's attempt "to enter a market that did not exist," but the success of Lite was so dramatic that within a short time 30 other brands of low-calorie beers were rushed onto the market by other brewers. Nonetheless, Miller's Lite brand remained the leading low-calorie brand by a wide margin and became the most successful new beer brand introduced in the century (a record previously held by Anheuser-Busch's Michelob brand). By 1983 Lite was the second-best-selling brand of beer, a position it still held in 1994. Lite was the international favorite low-calorie beer for the ninth consecutive year in 1993.

Other Brands　　In 1974 Miller moved to challenge Michelob—Anheuser-Busch's most profitable product—which dominated the superpremium segment. Miller was attracted to this segment by both the higher margins and the more than 30 percent annual growth in Michelob sales. Miller acquired exclusive import rights for the

---

[22]*Fortune,* May 8, 1989.
[23]*Business Week,* March 2, 1994.

world-famous Lowenbrau brand of German beer. Anheuser-Busch's reaction to the entry of Lowenbrau was summed up neatly by August A. Busch III: "This is Lowenbrau made in the United States, not the beer imported from Europe, and the consumers are not going to be fooled by that little game." Miller did not achieve the success in the superpremium category that it had enjoyed in the premium and light categories. Michelob's market share had stabilized around the 2.2 percent range while Lowenbrau was still less than 1 percent.

In the mid- to late 1980s, Miller's performance was aided by the introduction of three new brands—Meister Brau, Milwaukee's Best, and Genuine Draft. Meister Brau was introduced in 1983 and Milwaukee's Best in 1984 in an attempt to gain share in the popular segment. These brands put Miller Brewing in head-on competition with Anheuser-Busch's Busch brand, which was the popular-beer segment leader. However, Miller was more successful with this endeavor, and by 1990 Milwaukee's Best held 4.2 percent of the market, close behind Busch's 5 percent share.

With the introduction of the Miller Genuine Draft brand, Miller Brewing hoped to create and dominate a new beer category the way Miller Lite did light beers. Noting that packaged draft beer represented one-third of Japanese beer consumption, the company acquired the technology from Sapporo Brewery in Japan for using ceramic filters to remove impurities. The product was introduced in the spring of 1986 and by year-end had achieved sales of more than 1.5 million barrels. By 1990, volume had risen to 5.7 million barrels, a 3.0 percent market share. This volume boost encouraged Miller to refit its inactive Trenton plant for production of Genuine Draft. By 1993 Genuine Draft was ranked as the sixth most popular beer in the U.S., making it the most successful beer introduced in the past 10 years.

In 1990 Miller introduced a light version of Genuine Draft that industry analysts predicted would steal share away from the Genuine Draft brand. Hamish Maxwell's response to these concerns was: "Every new product you ever bring out takes business away. The issue is, if you have a good idea, do it yourself. Because if you don't and somebody else does it, you're a total loser."[24]

In 1992 the company introduced on a national basis Miller Reserve and Miller Reserve Light, two 100 percent barley packaged draft beers. It also introduced Colders 29 and Colders 29 Light in 17 states and in Washington, D.C. Each of these products represented attempts to broaden Miller's product line, find untapped niches in the market, and in general, revitalize the business unit.

International Strategies   In April 1993 Miller finalized an important strategic alliance with Molson Breweries, Canada's leading beer company. Molson Breweries was a joint venture between Molson Companies Ltd. of Canada and Foster's Brewing of Australia. Through a 20 percent interest in Molson and full ownership of Molson's U.S. operations, Miller gained the ability to participate in the Canadian beer market and to acquire a group of imports with strong brands to market in the U.S. Miller's investment made it a partner in Molson's Canadian operations and, more significantly, gave it full rights to market and distribute the entire line of Molson beers and Foster's Lager in the U.S.

Miller also made a substantial investment in Mexico—the eighth-largest and one of the fastest-growing beer markets in the world. The company acquired a 7.9 percent interest in Fomento Economico Mexicano, S.A. de C.V., or FEMSA as it was

---

[24]*Business Week,* August 8, 1988.

known. FEMSA was one of Mexico's two leading brewing companies and was estimated to hold approximately 49 percent of the Mexican beer market. The company's brands included: Carta Blanca, the number two Mexican beer; Tecate, the third most popular; Superior, which held market position number four; and XX Lager ("Dos Equis") beer. FEMSA also held a chain of convenience stores in Mexico with which, when combined with the beverage company, Miller hoped to gain a greater presence in the large and growing Mexican market.

FUTURE PROSPECTS FOR THE BEER SEGMENT

Miller's president and chief operating officer, Jack D. MacDonough, joined Miller in September 1992 from Anheuser-Busch, where he had headed the company's international marketing. Mr. MacDonough said of Miller's future: "We plan to build Miller every way we can, including North American and global expansion. But our focus always has to be the United States. It's both our home market and the largest single beer market in the world."

PM'S FOOD PRODUCTS BUSINESS UNIT

PM's entry into the food-processing industry was its latest, and largest, diversification effort. This segment contributed 49 percent of the company's revenues and 30 percent of the operating profits in 1992. PM entered this segment via two major acquisitions—General Foods acquired in 1985 and Kraft, Inc., acquired in 1988, both hostile takeovers.

GENERAL FOODS

In 1985, shortly after Hamish Maxwell took over as CEO, Philip Morris made a tender offer for General Foods. Maxwell saw in GF another opportunity to use PM's cumulative knowledge of marketing in a huge consumer market. The offer was initially rejected, but Maxwell's tenacity and PM's cash offer of $5.7 billion won out.

Prior to acquisition by PM, General Foods had sales of $9 billion in 1985. The company operated in four worldwide product groupings:

Segment	Percent of Net Sales	Brands
Packaged grocery products	42%	Entenmanns pastries; Crystal Light; Kool-Aid; Grape Nuts; Log Cabin; Jell-O, Stove-Top; Shake 'n Bake; Birds Eye frozen foods; Hostess cakes
Grocery coffee	28	Maxwell House; Sanka; Brim
Processed meats	18	Oscar Mayer and Louis Rich turkey products
Food service products	12	Jell-O; Crystal Light; Oscar Mayer

At the time of the acquisition, GF labored under a stifling bureaucracy that Philip Morris worked to reduce to make the company more responsive to marketing and market trends. Although GF had well-known brands, significant market share in some areas, and strategic positioning in others, the operating earnings indicated that only the processed meats division had experienced consecutive years of growth from 1980 through 1985. Oscar Mayer was GF's best performer and had shown the ability to spot and exploit market opportunities, such as the acquisition of Louis Rich in

1979. The division operated independently of PM for the first two years after acquisition while PM executives learned the food-processing business.

In 1987 General Foods contributed approximately 36 percent to PM's operating revenues. This represented a major step in Hamish Maxwell's plan to restructure Philip Morris as a consumer-products company and substantially reduce dependence on tobacco. GF was just beginning to move out from under the bureaucracy when GF Chairman Smith left PM to lead Pillsbury, leaving a restructuring project unfinished. Maxwell needed a leader at GF who would instill some of PM's marketing values and began looking around for someone to head GF.

KRAFT FOODS

Maxwell targeted Kraft Foods for takeover to fill in the gaps at General Foods, to broaden its product line in foods, and to increase its share in the food-processing industry, in addition to providing potential leadership for the entire food segment. The company had a portfolio of well-known brands that when combined with General Foods' translated into more shelf space and increased pricing power for PM. Like PM, Kraft focused on brand building, brand extension, and new product development.

Kraft also brought with it capable managers and superior profit margins. Under the direction of Chairman John Richman and President Michael Miles, Kraft Foods had recently completed a restructuring program aimed at increasing market focus, decreasing costs, and, ironically, avoiding a takeover attempt. In 1987, the company's net sales were $9.9 billion with operating profits of $910 million. The company had sold its profitable Duracell battery division as part of a campaign to return to an "all food" company and was aggressively acquiring new food businesses.

Kraft was divided into three business units:

Segment	Percent of Net Sales	Brands
U.S. consumer foods	46%	
Refrigerated products		Kraft cheeses: Philadelphia Brand cream cheese; Velveeta; Cheez Whiz
Grocery products		Miracle Whip; Kraft mayonnaise; Seven Seas; Kraft macaroni & cheese dinners; Parkay margarine
Frozen foods		Tombstone pizza; Lender's bagels; Budget Gourmet dinners
Dairy		Breyers; Sealtest; Frūsen Gladje; Light 'n Lively; Breakstone
International food	23	All Kraft international sales
U.S. commercial food	31	
Food service		
Food ingredients		

Philip Morris acquired Kraft in October 1988 for $12.9 billion in a hostile takeover. Industry analysts said that the Kraft acquisition was smoother than that of General Foods because the management at Kraft, after the initial resistance, was committed to making the merger work.

TRENDS IN THE FOOD INDUSTRY

In 1992 U.S. consumers spent over $350 billion on retail food products, of which about $250 billion was spent in supermarkets and convenience stores. This market was fragmented in terms of the number of product groups, the number of categories within groups, and the number of competitors within each category. The major product groups were baked goods, dairy, frozen foods, fresh and cured meat, fish and poultry, produce, and dry and canned goods.

The U.S. food industry was a mature market with an average annual growth of 1 to 2 percent. Including the small, independent, single-product food producers, there were hundreds of participants in this market. New competitors in the industry tended to be large, diversified organizations. Companies such as Philip Morris and R. J. Reynolds, which owned subsidiaries in several industries, were entering the food segment to further diversify their portfolios. PM acquired General Foods in 1985 and Kraft Foods in 1988, while RJR acquired Del Monte Foods in 1979 and Nabisco, Inc., in 1985.

New Product Innovations There were several changes in the industry that represented growth opportunities for food companies by offering new products or reformulated products to meet changing customer needs. first, consumers' eating habits had changed during the last decade. In the 1990s people wanted products that were lower in calories, lower in cholesterol, more nutritious, and lower in salt. The increased number of working mothers, the smaller households, and the decline in the traditional family household created a demand for products that were quick and easy to prepare, serve, and clean up. There was an emphasis on new products throughout the industry, either through extensions of existing products or entirely new offerings. Food producers also met the changing demands by offering specialty products that had particular value to a portion of the consumers, such as low-fat foods for the weight and health conscious. These products generally had higher profit margins than average and companies found that new product innovations could create new niches as well as enable them to establish leadership within the niche by being first in the segment.

Entry Barriers In recent years barriers to entry had been increasing due to the volume of sales necessary to obtain production economies and gain shelf space. Most new competitors were entering via acquisition, since distribution channels, shelving, and brand recognition were already in place. Substitution was also a problem for food processors. Every company faced competition not only from brand substitutes within a category but substitution from other categories as well—all under one roof. For instance, a consumer interested in purchasing peas could choose fresh, frozen, or canned peas, then choose between Birds Eye brand or Green Giant brand frozen peas.

COMPETITION IN THE FOOD INDUSTRY

Throughout the 1980s, larger companies acquired or merged with smaller food producers to broaden their product lines, consolidate market share or, as in PM's and RJR's cases, to diversify. Pillsbury, Inc., was acquired in 1988 for $5.7 billion in a hostile takeover by Grand Metropolitan (a previous owner of the Liggett Group cigarette company). Companies such as Grand Metropolitan, Philip Morris, and R. J. Reynolds brought strong financial positions and considerable cash reserves to the food-processing industry. In 1990 the industry was dominated by the major players listed in Exhibit 18, which also indicates the relevant financial information per company.

Marketing Market leadership was crucial because volume sales were necessary to reduce per unit costs, share advertising and distribution costs, and wield bargaining power with chain grocers. Food companies competed for shelf space in grocery

EXHIBIT 18 | **1993 Sales and Profit Data for the Major U.S. Food Processing Companies ($ in millions)**

Company	Sales	Net Profit
Borden	$ 5,506.3	$ 38.4
CPC International	6,738.0	454.5
Campbell Soup	6,586.2	557.2
Dean Foods	2,274.3	68.4
Flowers Industries	962.1	39.2
General Mills	8,134.6	563.4
H. J. Heinz	7,425.0	600.0
Hershey Foods	3,488.2	256.6
Hormel	2,854.0	100.8
Kellogg Co.	6,295.0	675.0
Quaker Oats	5,730.6	300.8
Ralston Purina	5,915.4	322.5
Sara Lee	14,580.0	704.0

stores. Position in the store, placement on the shelf, the number of facings on the shelf, and end-of-aisle displays were important in obtaining and maintaining volume. A company's ability to gain shelf space for its products was a function of brand recognition, brand loyalty, and breadth of product line. Companies with broad product lines were in a better position to negotiate shelf space than single product producers, because brand recognition tended to have a cumulative effect so that as the product line increased, the leverage that food processors wielded over grocers also increased.

Brand recognition and brand loyalty were created primarily through advertising. In addition to access to shelf space, brand strength was critical to generating volume sales, achieving pricing leverage, and facilitating new product innovations. Brand loyalty gave producers some latitude to increase prices without severely affecting volume. Greater volume translated directly into lower per-unit costs. These cost savings either generated surplus cash for the producers or were used to lower prices to further increase volume. Additionally, brand recognition facilitated new product introductions. Food producers were often able to capitalize on brand success through shared advertising and distribution costs. The major players spent over $4.9 billion on advertising in 1992 to generate brand loyalty and carve out competitive positions.

THE PERFORMANCE OF THE KRAFT GENERAL FOODS BUSINESS UNIT

Kraft Foods and General Foods were merged into the Kraft General Foods Group in 1989 under the direction of Michael Miles. The combined companies represented the second-largest food company worldwide, behind Nestlé, and sold 14 of the top 50 U.S. food brands. One of the first changes after the merger was the organization of the food business into two individual companies: North American Food and International Food. By 1992, when Miles took over the leadership of PM, total food revenues had grown at a compound annual rate of slightly over 9 percent while operating income had grown at 15 percent compounded annually, a strong indication of Miles's ability to decrease costs and improve the profitability of the organization.

Michael Miles commented in the 1989 annual report on the expectations of the merger:

The combination of Kraft and General Foods created more than the second-largest food company in the world. It created an organization determined to be the leader in its industry.

To lead the industry we must rank first in quality, with products and services that consistently meet all our customers' and consumers' needs and expectations, setting the standards for taste, nutrition, convenience, variety, and value.

We intend to lead in productivity as well as quality. In 1989, Kraft General Foods people achieved more than $425 million in savings by operating more efficiently. These are permanent cost reductions, providing ongoing benefits for our company.

The real opportunity now is synergy—working together so that the Kraft General Foods of the future adds up to more than the sum of its parts in the past.

With our family of brands, and the support of Philip Morris, we have immense strengths and even more potential. We are going to use them to grow still more.

NORTH AMERICAN FOOD

Altogether the KGF group, including KGF Canada (another KGF operating unit under the North American Food umbrella and Canada's largest packaged food company), had a 10 percent share of the American packaged food market. Exhibit 19 indicates the diverse product mix at KGF.

PM's high expectations hinged on building brand loyalty through advertising while ruthlessly cutting costs and improving overall productivity. A consultant to Kraft told *Adweek,* "Kraft believes General Foods is an overstuffed manicotti. They're going to make it a much leaner, tougher company. That's going to mean a lot of changes."[25] Miles was put in charge of the $22.9 billion operation and began with demands for improved productivity and an intensive search for ways to milk more from existing assets. One executive recruiter who had outplaced several executives

EXHIBIT 19 | **Philip Morris' North American Food 1992 Retail Operating Revenues by Category**

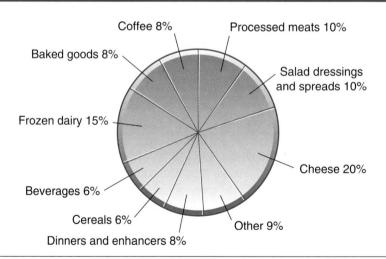

---

[25] *Adweek,* January 27, 1989.

from both Kraft and General Foods said of Miles: "He's famous for trimming to the bone."[26] Miles began with consolidating some of KGF's 200 domestic plants and 70 distribution centers. By 1990, KGF subsidiaries were pared to 132 domestic manufacturing and processing facilities and 56 major distribution centers.

In 1992 the company restructured its frozen foods business, taking a one-time restructuring charge on its financial statements of $455 million. It sold its U.S. frozen desserts business, with brands such as Breyers and Sealtest, to Unilever United States, Inc., and was negotiating the sale of its Birds Eye frozen vegetables business. Additionally, its main frozen-foods line, the $300 million Budget Gourmet Brand, was experiencing loss of share to ConAgra Inc.'s Healthy Choice frozen entrees. The company consolidated the frozen-foods and Oscar Mayer meats divisions, laid off over 1,000 employees, and proceeded with its plans to consolidate Kraft and General Foods distribution into one system. As evidence of the success of KGF's streamlining efforts, the unit's profit margins had increased each year:

Year	Margin
1989	9.40%
1990	9.58
1991	10.23
1992	10.80

Product Innovations   Michael Miles was well known for his ability to rejuvenate existing brands through advertising, but brand extensions and new product innovations were his trademark. The KGF Group introduced a total of 300 new products in 1989, including those jointly developed, winning the 1990 New Products Company of the Year award presented by *Prepared Foods Magazine.* During 1992, under Miles's leadership, Philip Morris Companies introduced almost 200 new products and over 400 line extensions—for food, tobacco, and beer products combined. KGF's line extensions included such products as Philadelphia Brand neufchatel cheese, Cholesterol Free Miracle Whip, Kraft Cholesterol Free mayonnaise, new flavors of its General Foods International Coffees, and flavor variations for its Shake 'n Bake coatings.

In light of growing interest in health and nutrition, fat replacement technologies represented a major growth opportunity. KGF successfully adapted a variety of proprietary fat replacement technologies to a host of products, from Sealtest Free nonfat ice cream to Kraft pourable salad dressings and Entenmann's reduced calorie, fat-free and cholesterol-free cakes. The company also attempted to attract health-conscious consumers with products such as Post Honey Bunches of Oats, Lender's Oat Bran bagels, Oroweat Oat Nut bread, Freihofer's Hearthstone breads, Louis Kemp seafood products, and Light 'n Lively products. By 1993, the company offered 14 reduced-fat Oscar Mayer meats and 22 fat-free or reduced-fat Kraft cheese products.

In a drive based on the fact that 72 percent of the homes in the United States had microwave ovens and that convenient meal preparation was essential, the company introduced Kraft microwave entrees, Oscar Mayer Zappetites snacks, Minute microwave meals, and Jell-O microwave pudding. Growth in sales of ready-to-eat desserts led KGF to acquire the Catelli Magic Moments and Light Touch mini-

---

[26]*Marketing Week,* January 27, 1989.

dessert lines, increasing market share in Canada to 65 percent. In addition, Oscar Mayer bolstered its U.S. convenience-store presence through contracts with Circle K and Emro Marketing Co., and continued to expand Oscar Mayer Lunchables lunch combinations nationally. The company also supplied Boboli breads for on-site supermarket pizza preparation, and increased capacity in the food service operation helped to keep growth apace with the expanding restaurant food market. Between 1992 and 1993, KGF acquired Jack's pizza and RJR Nabisco's entire cereal line to further strengthen its product line.

Combined Marketing Efforts　The merger of Kraft and General Foods increased PM's total advertising and promotional spending to over \$2 billion, making the company the world's largest advertiser. Philip Morris had not merged the advertising expenditures of KGF, Miller, and PM's tobacco business because of divergent audience interests. While KGF was primarily a broadcast-oriented advertiser, PM's cigarette companies were banned from the airwaves. And while Miller was a significant broadcast buyer, its sports/male viewer orientation was not very compatible with that of KGF's family/prime-time audience.

KGF was able to achieve cost savings by grouping the Kraft and GF brands into product lines (such as refrigerated foods, frozen foods, and packaged dinners) and by combining its sales forces along product categories (such as cheeses, coffees, and cereals). Previously, a particular territory required two salespersons per product category—one for GF and one for Kraft. With the combined sales force, one salesperson could service the entire territory, which substantially reduced KGF's sales force costs. Grouping the Kraft and GF brands together increased the number of brands that each salesperson had to offer, thus giving salespersons more clout with retailers in bargaining over the shelf space allocated to KGF brands. KGF also derived synergies by advertising several products together, such as the "Great American Breakfasts" campaign, which featured 10 key brands: Post Raisin Bran, Post Bran flakes, Lender's bagels, Maxwell House coffee, Parkay margarine, Oscar Mayer bacon, Philadelphia Brand cream cheese, Velveeta, Log Cabin syrup, and Kraft cheeses. KGF realized advertising savings with this promotion as well, since the cost of 1 large promotion was less than the sum of 10 individual promotions. Ron Toyama, promotion manager of Kraft U.S.A., said, "This is another example of how Kraft and General Foods brands can combine forces to create a program that's bigger than the sum of its parts."

Purchasing　Following the merger of GF and Kraft, management moved to reduce raw materials costs by combining GF and Kraft purchasing functions and thereby gain greater leverage with suppliers. KGF realized \$36 million in savings by jointly negotiating purchasing contracts on behalf of various KGF companies. The KGF Group formed an executive purchasing council, including PM U.S.A. and Miller Brewing, to provide guidance and policy direction for purchasing decisions. Rick Studemann, vice president for purchasing at KGF, said, "We set goals and instituted an aggressive program to deliver the savings. All prospective suppliers are evaluated first in terms of quality, technology, cost, and service—we don't just run after the low-cost supplier. The benefits of scale follow from this assessment."

Recent Performance　During the early 1990s, KGF's North American Foods confronted problems often associated with a mature industry. Many of the company's core products were under severe price competition from private-label brands. Kraft's cheese division, a \$2.5 billion jewel in its crown, suffered operating losses up to 20 percent in 1992 when the increasing costs of milk combined with downward pressures on prices caused substantial losses in volume and share. Predatory pricing prompted the company to divest its frozen dessert business and attempt to sell its frozen vegetable business. The company was forced to abandon its luxury pricing strategy and drastically reduce its retail prices on many of its cheese products—for example, the company cut its prices on its Cracker Barrel products by 14 percent.

Richard Mayer, who became CEO of KGF North American Foods following Miles's appointment as corporate CEO, said of the division's current pricing approach: "We see a much more price-sensitive consumer, a narrowing of the quality gap between private-label and branded manufacturers' goods, and profound changes in the retail trade toward low-price operators."[27]

KGF INTERNATIONAL FOODS

In 1992, 15 percent of PM's revenues and 10 percent of profits were contributed by the KGF International operating unit. This represented 30 percent of total food revenues and 33 percent of total food profits. International Foods marketed KGF's strong U.S. brands, such as Kraft cheeses and Maxwell House coffees, as well as products with regional appeal, in Europe, Asia/Pacific, and Latin America. KGF's International Foods had 78 plants, facilities, and warehouses outside the U.S. PM's strategy was to replicate its success in international cigarettes by acquiring established brands and using their distribution channels to market KGF brands in foreign markets. According to Miles: "When you see the enormous success the international tobacco company has had, it provides that much more inspiration for our food managers to stick with the fight, to chase the opportunity. And inspiration is a very important part of what motivates people."[28]

Exhibit 20 reports the company's investments or acquisitions in International Food to either strengthen existing businesses or for geographic growth.

International Foods comprised three core businesses: coffee, which accounted for 34 percent of the division's sales; confectionery, with 24 percent of sales; and cheese, with 17 percent. The final 25 percent of the division's business was from general products, not specifically categorized with one of the core businesses. Philip Morris was the world leader in roast and ground coffee and in processed cheese.

Jacobs Suchard AG   As recently as 1981, Jacobs Suchard had been a single-product company. Under the direction of Klaus Jacobs, the company grew from the largest coffee supplier in West Germany to a worldwide food distributor primarily through acquisitions. In 1982 Jacobs Coffee, a German-based privately held firm, merged with Swiss-based Suchard and Tobler chocolate companies to form Jacobs Suchard. In 1986 Jacobs Suchard acquired the Van Houten Company, a Dutch producer of chocolate and cocoa goods. In 1987 the company entered the Belgium chocolate-manufacturing market by acquiring Cote d'Or, the last remaining independent Belgian chocolate manufacturer. Jacobs moved into the U.S. and Canadian markets with the purchase of Andes Candies and in 1987 acquired U.S.-based E. J. Brach. In 1988 it attempted to enter the British market by acquiring Roundtree chocolates, but lost out in a takeover battle for Roundtree to Nestlé.

---

[27]*Fortune,* April 6, 1992, p. 90.
[28]Ibid., p. 92.

In 1990 Philip Morris made a takeover bid to acquire 80 percent of Swiss coffee and chocolate maker Jacobs Suchard for $3.8 billion. Jacobs Suchard had 12 percent of the European chocolate market, behind Mars (with 17 percent), and Nestlé (23 percent).

At the time of PM's acquisition, Jacobs Suchard had ambitious plans. It hoped to use Brach's distribution network of 400 salespeople to win share in the U.S. and Canadian markets. The strategy was to introduce brands with an established international appeal into the U.S. market. It hoped to have 100 salespeople in the Tokyo area by the end of 1990 to push the six varieties of Milka brand in the growing Japanese market. During 1990 the company streamlined European operations by reducing the number of plants in Europe from 22 to 6.

Philip Morris kept the European coffee and chocolate operations and sold back the other businesses including E. J. Brach to Mr. Jacobs. The move gave PM market leadership in coffee in West Germany and France and 12 percent of the European chocolate market, plus access to European distribution channels for food products. PM management saw the Jacobs Suchard acquisition as a vehicle through which it could compete as a major player in the European market for food products.

In 1993 PM merged the cheese and grocery operations of Kraft General Foods Europe with the coffee and confectionery businesses of Jacobs Suchard into a new company, Kraft Jacobs Suchard, based in Zurich, Switzerland. This newly merged entity would operate in 20 countries and had combined annual revenues of approximately $9 billion. The move was considered an important step in improving the company's efficiency and competitive position in the European food industry.

Freia Marabou　　In April 1993 International Foods acquired Freia Marabou, the leading chocolate and sugar confectionery and snack food manufacturer in Scandinavia. Freia Marabou was also the largest Nordic company focused on branded foods. Jack

E X H I B I T　20　| 　**Philip Morris' International Food Acquistions and Investments**

Strengthen Existing Businesses	Geographic Growth
International food:	**International food:**
Grand'Mère (France)	Freia Marabou (Scandinavia)
El Almendro (Spain)	Maarud (Norway)
El Caserio (Spain)	Splendid (Italy)
Fiesta (Greece)	Figaro (Slovakia)
Guangtong (China)	Csemege (Hungary)
Tianmei (China)	
Twin Valley Fromage Frais (Australia)	
ETA peanut butter (Australia)	
La Montevideana (Argentina)	
Alimentos Especiales (Argentina)	
Domestic food:	
Jack's pizza	
RJR Nabisco cereals	

Note: Made or announced since January 1, 1992; some await regulatory approval.

Keenan, president and CEO of KGF International, said of the acquisition: "Even combined, KGF International and Jacobs Suchard were still relatively small in Scandinavia. Freia Marabou significantly increases our presence in the Nordic countries, and puts us in a much better position to compete in the region."

Prior to the acquisition, Freia Marabou's total 1992 sales were approximately $900 million—three times that of KGfi in the region. The company's line of chocolates offered a stronger cocoa flavor that KGfi felt would complement the Jacobs Suchard line and would be very well received across Europe. Its sugar confectionery products, including Toy, figaro, and Rollo brands, held leading positions in Denmark. The company was the region's market leader in snack foods, with number one positions in Norway and Sweden and number two positions in Denmark and finland.

The Terry Group Philip Morris made another addition to its confectionery company in 1993 with the purchase of the Terry group from United Biscuits. The Terry group was the fourth-largest chocolate and sugar confectionery company in the United Kingdom. Its Callard & Bowser brands of toffee, butterscotch, licorice, and mints were already widely distributed in the U.S. It also had other well-known brands, such as Nuttalls, Smith Kendon, and Chocometz. The acquisition was considered strategically important because the U.K., as the second-largest confectionery market in Europe, was the largest and most profitable European market in which KGfi lacked a significant position. The Terry group was perceived as providing the essential established production and distribution platforms for penetration of the British confectionery market. The merger of Jacobs Suchard, Freia Marabou, and the Terry group created the third-largest confectionery company in Europe.

FUTURE PROSPECTS FOR PM'S FOOD BUSINESS UNIT

William Murray had the following comments on Philip Morris' food divisions:

> In our North American food business, we entered 1992 with large price gaps that could not be sustained without unacceptable market share and volume losses in some of our key categories. Over the course of the year, we took aggressive steps to reduce these price gaps in several key categories, most notably cheese and red meats. These initiatives have positioned us well for future growth . . .
>
> Although we still face a number of challenges, we are making clear progress in many key categories. Our North American food operations have good momentum, and they are poised for improved performance in the future . . .
>
> With $8.7 billion in 1992 revenues, we already have a much larger international food business than any other U.S.-based company. As a stand-alone company, our overseas food business would rank 59th among the Fortune 500 . . .
>
> Through acquisition . . . as well as internal growth, our international food operations have generated substantial annual income gains since we combined Kraft and General Foods in 1989.
>
> We have built an international food business with strong leadership positions in three global categories. As we pool the strengths of our operations with those of our recently acquired companies and brands, we look forward to continued profitable growth.

THE FINANCIAL SERVICES AND REAL ESTATE SEGMENT

This segment of Philip Morris operated as a separate corporate division, not as a wholly owned subsidiary. It contributed less than 1 percent of PM's revenues and 2 percent of operating profits in 1992. The division operated as Philip Morris Capital

Corp. (PMCC), with a primary subsidiary, Mission Viejo. PMCC invested in third-party leveraged and direct finance leases and securities of third parties, primarily preferred stocks, and engaged in various financing activities for customers and suppliers of the company's subsidiaries. The division's recent revenues and operating profit performance indicated that while revenues were relatively flat, income from operations was both rising and attractively large:

Year	Revenue (millions)	Operating Income (millions)
1985	$303	$ 66
1986	474	32
1987	488	68
1988	629	163
1989	527	173
1990	460	196
1991	384	178
1992	430	219

Philip Morris Capital Corporation PMCC was formed in 1982 primarily to provide credit financing for customers of PM's operating companies. The financial activities of PMCC also included leveraged lease transactions for major equipment. PMCC contributed $284 million in revenues to PM's total operations in 1992.

Mission Viejo PM completed its acquisition of Mission Viejo in 1972 at a price of approximately $48.5 million and was organized as a subsidiary of PMCC in 1983. The company was initially engaged in community and residential development and the development of and investment in commercial properties. Its main base of activity was the development of a completely preplanned community named Mission Viejo on approximately 11,000 acres in Orange County, California. Mission Viejo was a major factor in homebuilding in California throughout the 1970s, but by the late 1980s the company began a planned withdrawal from homebuilding. This move was partly a reaction to the soft residential housing market that characterized the 1980s and partly a desire to concentrate on financial activities that had a greater strategic fit. In 1992 Mission Viejo contributed $146 million in revenues to PM's total operations.

FUTURE PROSPECTS FOR PHILIP MORRIS COMPANIES

In 1992 the management at Philip Morris Companies adopted a new mission: To be the most successful consumer packaged goods company in the world. It crafted six strategies for generating steady and sustainable growth. The "strategies to be the best" were

1. To maintain the highest quality of people.
2. To protect and build the company's brand franchises.
3. To grow profitable new business.
4. To maximize productivity and synergy in all businesses at all times.

5. To make total quality management a reality in every aspect of PM's operations.

6. To manage with a global perspective.

Chairman and CEO Miles commented on the strategies and PM's prospects for the future:

The majority of the company's businesses are performing well and have good momentum. Our brands remain strong, our financial condition is excellent, and our long-term outlook is very positive.

The first of our strategies is to maintain the highest quality of people . . . We are, and will remain, dedicated to helping all our employees achieve their full career potential within Philip Morris Companies.

Our second strategy is to protect and build our brand franchises. We have the world's strongest portfolio of brands, and we invested approximately $11 billion in worldwide marketing activities last year alone to keep them strong.

Our third strategy is to grow profitable new business with line extensions, new products, geographic expansion, acquisitions, and joint ventures and strategic alliances. Last year, we introduced almost 200 new products and more than 400 line extensions in our tobacco, food, and beer businesses . . .

I want to assure you that we are not just growing in size. We are gaining strength in—and access to—markets where we have significant potential for volume and profit growth in the future.

Our fourth strategy is to maximize productivity and synergy in all businesses at all times. Last year, our productivity and synergy initiatives generated approximately $750 million in savings. We expect still greater savings this year.

Our fifth strategy is to make total quality management a reality in every aspect of our everyday operations. In part, this means using cross-functional teams to improve some of our key products. These teams are both shortening product development cycles and making the product closer to the consumer's ideal.

Our sixth strategy is to manage with a global perspective. This means going to the best source for everything—human resources, capital, product development, and raw materials—through worldwide purchasing councils and other coordinated efforts . . .

Considering that 95 percent of the world's population and 75 percent of its economic activity are outside the United States, we have immense opportunities for future growth.

There is no mystery to these strategies. They involve simple ideas, such as good people and profitable growth. But over time these strategies have made Philip Morris a company of formidable strength. And that strength, and our long-term vision of how to use it, have enabled us to increase stockholder wealth significantly over the years.

A PROSPECTIVE ACQUISITION AT FIGGIE INTERNATIONAL

James J. Dowd, University of Virginia
Michael D. Atchison, University of Virginia
John H. Lindgren, Jr., University of Virginia

Harry E. Figgie, Jr., founder and CEO of Figgie International, was flying home to Cleveland after a very quick trip to California. Only the day before, he had received a call from Marvin May, the founder of Mayco Pump Corporation in Los Angeles. Mr. May had been urged by one of Mr. Figgie's divisional executives to call Mr. Figgie before he sold his company to a large German competitor. Mr. May told Mr. Figgie that he expected to close the German deal within 48 hours, but that he would prefer to deal with Figgie, who had expressed interest in buying Mayco five years earlier. In response, Mr. Figgie had flown to California, and now he had to decide whether to proceed with this prospective acquisition.

A few years earlier, this would have been an easy decision, just another "tuck-in acquisition" like so many others he had completed over the last ten years. Combining Mayco Pump with his Huber Essick division seemed to make good strategic sense.

In August 1991, however, the decision was not so easy. The economic downturn in the United States was adversely affecting almost all of Figgie International's businesses. Especially hard hit were the corporation's six construction-related businesses, whose sales and earnings had plummeted over the past year.

Of these six divisions, Huber Essick was the weakest. Less than a year ago Figgie had tried to sell the division, and now he was contemplating making a sizable investment to build it up, without any sign of improvement in the market it served. As he considered this opportunity, however, he asked himself a question: Is this acquisition a master stroke that will guarantee dominance in this segment of the construction equipment industry, or am I buying a stateroom on the Titanic?

This case was prepared for the 12th McIntire Invitational Case Competition held at the University of Virginia on February 3–6, 1993. We gratefully acknowledge the General Electric Foundation and the McIntire School of Commerce for their support of the MICC and of our case preparation. We are also grateful to Harry E. Figgie, Jr., for allowing us to develop this case and for his continuing support of business education.

EXHIBIT 1 | **Selected Financial Highlights for Figgie International, 1986–90**

	Year Ended December 31					
	1990	1989	1988	1987	1986	Percent Change 1986–90
Financial Data (in thousands of dollars)						
Revenue[1]	$1,360,959	$1,313,484	$1,185,414	$1,037,194	$952,854	43%
Income from continuing operations	39,662	62,857	60,116	46,931	40,857	–3
Income from discontinued operations	—	69	1,759	2,409	1,569	–100
Net income	39,662	62,926	61,875	49,340	42,426	–7
Total assets[1]	1,065,590	1,027,206	927,047	750,089	674,236	58
Key working capital[2]	364,600	388,282	337,924	272,549	255,079	43
Total debt:[1]						
Manufacturing and Service Companies	421,010	375,035	227,856	124,535	113,598	271
Insurance and Leasing Companies	15,516	20,018	25,000	15,000	8,000	94
Figgie International Inc. and Subsidiaries	436,526	395,053	252,856	139,535	121,598	259
Per Share Data (in dollars)						
Earnings per common share—primary and fully diluted[3]						
Continuing operations	$ 2.28	$ 3.04	$ 2.92	$ 2.23	$ 2.03	12%
Discontinued operations	—	—	.09	.11	.07	—
Net income	2.28	3.04	3.01	2.34	2.10	9
Cash dividends per Class A	.50	.40	.38	.30	.26	92
common share[3] Class B	.50	.40	.34	.26	.23	117
Net tangible book value per common share[3]	14.23	13.31	12.80	13.36	12.50	14
Other Data						
Common stock outstanding[3]	18,701,649	18,909,822	22,290,009	20,352,213	21,232,203	
Holders of common stock	11,141	10,887	9,212	7,557	8,419	
Number of employees	16,000	17,000	17,400	16,400	16,300	

[1]Restated to reflect finance subsidiary as a discontinued operation.

[2]Key working capital consists of trade receivables, net, plus inventories less accounts payable.

[3]In November 1989, the company declared a three-for-one stock split effected as a 200 percent stock dividend on its class A and class B common stock to stockholders of record on January 15, 1990, payable on January 22, 1990. All share and per share amounts are reflected on a post-split basis.

Source: *Figgie International Annual Report,* 1990, p. 1.

GROWTH AND DEVELOPMENT OF FIGGIE INTERNATIONAL

In 1991 Figgie International was a large, widely diversified conglomerate, reporting 1990 revenues of $1.36 billion. Exhibits 1 and 2 present summary financial data on the corporation and its industry segments.

With 36 principal divisions and subsidiaries organized in seven product groups, Figgie International served consumer, industrial, technical, and service markets worldwide. Its best-known product lines included Rawlings sporting goods and American LaFrance fire trucks. Exhibit 3 provides an overview of the product groups and their major divisions in 1991.

EXHIBIT 2 | **Financial Information for Figgie International by Business Segment, 1988–90   (In thousands of dollars)**

	Year Ended December 31		
	1990	1989	1988
Sales to/revenue from unaffiliated customers:			
Consumer	$ 198,945	$ 175,342	$ 185,068
Industrial			
Fire protection/safety/security	490,655	461,536	372,313
Machinery and allied products	379,630	384,411	339,006
Total industrial	870,285	845,947	711,319
Technical	252,546	265,119	263,866
Services	39,183	27,076	25,161
Total sales and revenues	$1,360,959	$1,313,484	$1,185,414
Operating profit:			
Consumer	$ 18,238	$ 20,582	$ 22,461
Industrial			
Fire protection/safety/security	52,344	54,042	43,541
Machinery and allied products	37,199	47,597	46,658
Total industrial	89,543	101,639	90,199
Technical	24,472	38,445	27,826
Services	9,040	11,200	12,463
Total segments	141,293	171,866	152,949
General corporate expenses	(34,821)	(39,867)	(36,690)
Interest expense, net	(42,001)	(32,791)	(20,923)
Income before taxes on income	$ 64,471	$ 99,208	$ 95,336
Identifiable assets:			
Consumer	$ 118,457	$ 108,140	$ 81,653
Industrial			
Fire protection/safety, security	188,107	180,816	164,952
Machinery and allied products	259,206	260,473	239,445
Total industrial	447,313	441,289	404,397
Technical	140,751	156,554	150,754
Services	211,845	181,647	170,167
Corporate	116,435	111,585	79,943
Discontinued operation	30,789	27,991	40,133
Total assets	$1,065,590	$1,027,206	$927,047
Capital expenditures:			
Consumer	$ 2,447	$ 2,446	$ 3,261
Industrial			
Fire protection/safety/security	6,849	6,415	6,970
Machinery and allied products	25,589	28,308	12,766
Total industrial	31,438	34,723	19,736
Technical	4,224	4,108	4,528
Services	25,147	26,646	29,742
Corporate	14,214	9,753	7,833
Total capital expenditures	$77,470	$77,676	$65,100
Depreciation and amortization:			
Consumer	$ 2,094	$ 2,099	$ 2,544
Industrial			
Fire protection/safety/security	6,843	6,070	6,066
Machinery and allied products	9,953	8,532	8,983
Total industrial	16,796	14,602	15,049
Technical	5,226	5,317	5,498
Services	7,705	6,715	5,293
Corporate	4,032	6,378	3,065
Total depreciation and amortization	$35,853	$35,111	$31,449

Source: *Figgie International Annual Report*, 1990, pp. 42–43.

754

EXHIBIT 3 | **Figgie International's Product Groups, Major Divisions, and Major Products, 1991**

Consumer Group

Rawlings Sporting Goods: baseballs, gloves, basketballs, other sporting goods.

Sherwood-Drolet: Sher-Wood and Chimo hockey sticks.

Fred Perry Sportswear: fashionable tennis and sportswear apparel.

Thermometer Corporation of America: thermometers and barometers for the home and similar instruments for industrial and scientific applications.

Interstate Engineering: Compact and Tri-Star vacuum cleaners, fire alarms, and aluminum zinc die castings.

Figgie Consumer Products Licensing Division: worldwide licensing of consumer product trademarks.

Industrial—Fire Protection and Safety

"Automatic" Sprinkler Corporation of America: fire sprinkler protection systems.

American LaFrance: fire trucks, fire apparatus, and battery-powered vehicles for the airline industry.

Badger-Powhatan: fire extinguishers and brass products for the fire industry.

ASCOA Fire Systems: manufacturer of fire protection sprinkler systems and special hazard systems.

Scott Aviation: chemical/biological protective masks and helmets, self-contained breathing apparatus for firefighters.

Industrial—Machinery and Allied Products Group

Geo. J. Meyer Manufacturing: bottling and packaging equipment.

Alfa Packaging Equipment: high-speed labeling equipment and weight fillers.

Consolidated Packaging Machinery: automatic capping equipment and rotary piston fillers for various industries; case packers, uncasers, electronic bottle inspectors.

Logan Co.: conveyor products and systems, and parcel and baggage sortation systems.

Safway Steel Products: tubular steel scaffolding for new construction, remodeling, and maintenance projects.

Huber Essick: light construction equipment, with special emphasis on mixing, finishing, pumping, and spraying equipment, including plaster, mortar, and cement mixers, material pumps, vibratory road rollers, and road maintainers.

Snorkel-Economy: powered mobile work platforms and scissorlifts for construction and industrial maintenance.

SpaceGuard Products: woven wire partitions and other iron products for industry.

Closetech International: maker of high-speed can closing machines for beverage industries.

Technical Group

Interstate Electronics Corporation: sophisticated telemetry, detection and display systems for U.S. Navy's fleet ballistic missile programs, and flat-panel and cathode ray tube displays for the military and satellite communications receivers for NASA.

Hartman Electrical Manufacturing: high-reliability electrical components, including power relays, protection relays, circuit breakers switches and automatic control panels.

CASI-RUSCO: computer-based CARDENTRY access control equipment and monitoring systems for security, parking, time and attendance, and fuel management control.

Services Group

Figgie Leasing Corporation: vehicle and equipment leasing; fleet management services.

Figgie Properties: real estate development, services, and management.

Waite Hill Holdings: wholly owned subsidiary, which owns two insurance companies and a claims investigation and safety services firm.

Figgie Natural Resources: oil and gas investments.

Advance Security: uniformed security officers, investigative services, and security consultation.

Investigations Corporation of America: full-service investigations company specializing in corporate, internal, and personnel background investigations.

Automation Group

S-P Manufacturing: precision power chucks, rotary chuck actuators, and other workholding products for the machine tool industry.

Lin-Act/Carter: aluminum and steel hydraulic and pneumatic cylinders, valves, pumps, actuators, and related fluid power products.

Figgie Hydraulics/Stallman Gear: cast-iron gear-type pumps, motors, and components, custom gears and hydraulic pump gears.

Greer Hydraulics: accumulators, surge suppressors, and pulsation dampeners.

Safety Product Distribution Group

Safety Supply America: independent distributor of industrial health and safety products.

Sources: *Figgie International Annual Report,* 1990; "This is Figgie International. . . ," company publication, 1988.

HARRY E. FIGGIE, JR.

Known in his company as "the Chairman," Harry Figgie served in the infantry in World War II and returned home to complete his education. Under the G.I. Bill he earned a metallurgical degree at Case Institute of Technology and an MBA at Harvard Business School. Later, while working at three different companies in northern Ohio, he attended night classes and simultaneously completed a master's degree in industrial engineering from Case and a law degree from John Marshall Law School.

He complemented this broad-based education with nine years of management consulting experience with Booz Allen & Hamilton, where he specialized in profit improvement and cost reduction, as well as corporate reorganizations and acquisitions. He was a partner and later president of their industrial engineering subsidiary. In 1962 he left consulting to join A.O. Smith Corporation as group vice president for its industrial products group. Within two years, he doubled sales and increased profits fivefold for the four, and later, five divisions in this group.

THE FIRST ACQUISITION: "AUTOMATIC" SPRINKLER

On December 31, 1963, Harry Figgie took the first step in building his own company with a leveraged buyout of the "Automatic" Sprinkler Corporation of America.[1] With annual sales of $22 million, the company had not turned a profit in five years and was on the verge of bankruptcy. By concentrating on deep cost cutting and completely revamping the way the company did business, Figgie was able to turn a 9.6 percent pretax profit on revenues of $25 million in his first year.

Figgie referred to his first year with "Automatic" Sprinkler as "phase one, the fight for survival." He described the subsequent development of his company in three phases.

PHASE TWO: NUCLEUS ACQUISITIONS (1965–69)

In its first two years the corporation was highly leveraged, financed largely with short-term debt. In November 1965 Harry Figgie took his company public, paid off the short-term debt, and the company entered phase two of its development with $7 million in long-term debt and $7.5 million in equity.

In building a large, diversified corporation, Harry Figgie relied on a theory he had developed during his years in consulting. Figgie's "nucleus theory" advocated acquiring one company and adding to it other companies in the same general industry. Within the nucleus group, the combined knowledge of and experience in an industry would enable each individual company to increase its market penetration.

Figgie saw "Automatic" Sprinkler as the nucleus division around which he could build a group of companies in the fire protection, safety, and security markets. The nucleus groups that guided Figgie acquisitions in these years were consumer/recreation, electrical/electronics, packaging machinery/material handling, and construc-

---

[1] In 1985 Harry E. Figgie, Jr., was the guest of honor and speaker at a 1985 Virginia meeting of the Newcomen Society of the United States for the study of the history of engineering and technology. His speech, "A Dream Comes True, The Story of Figgie International," was later published as Newcomen publication no. 1264, copyright 1986 by Figgie International Inc., and is the source for the information presented here on the history of the company through 1985.

tion/mining. These were perceived as niche markets that would be relatively resistant to foreign competition in the formative years.

The strategy was to identify distressed companies in these markets that the Figgie management team could turn around; they could not afford to buy larger, well-run companies. In the five-year period of phase two, the company added 36 companies with 52 divisions. Most were small companies, averaging about $7 million in sales, and all of them fit within one of the five nucleus groups. At the end of this acquisition period, total sales were $356 million, with profits of $8.6 million.

PHASE THREE: CONSOLIDATION (1970–83)

Having reached a size Figgie believed was large enough to withstand economic and market pressures, the corporation turned inward to nurture and consolidate its divisions. To strengthen the weak divisions, Figgie focused on cost control and on building a strong management team.

During this consolidation phase, 99 percent of the company's sales growth was generated internally. During this period the corporation increased its emphasis on international business and on services. Overseas sales volume increased sevenfold in this period. Several corporate staff groups were transformed into freestanding business units, including the leasing group, the licensing group, and the insurance department, which became Waite Hill Holdings.

PHASE FOUR: TUCK-IN ACQUISITIONS (1983–90)

Making its way back to the acquisition market, Figgie International began making "tuck-in" acquisitions to increase the size and improve the performance of existing divisions with potential. In 1989, for example, the company purchased five businesses for just under $7.4 million, and in 1990, it bought four businesses for $7.1 million. In all, 38 acquisitions totalling $194 million were completed during this phase, and two new product groups were formed: the automation group and the safety distribution group.

At the same time, the corporation would focus for future growth on fewer, larger divisions. In 1987 it stated a five-year goal of having 6 divisions with over $100 million in sales or $10 million in profits, and 12 divisions with over $50 million in sales or $5 million in profits. The remaining divisions were expected to post sales over $20 million; divisions unable to achieve those targets would be spun off or consolidated.

Also, with an eye on fluctuations in the economy and a desire for greater financial stability, the corporation established a target for its debt-to-equity ratio. From a high of 6 to 1 in its earliest years, the ratio had reached .84 to 1 in 1985. In that year, Figgie set a goal of reaching a .35-to-1 ratio in 1987. In 1987, the corporation achieved a ratio of .37 to 1. In 1988, however, Figgie International became a takeover target, which led to steep increases in corporate borrowing and raised the debt-to-equity ratio to 1.24 to 1. At the end of 1990, the ratio was at 1.1 to 1.

In its annual report for 1990, Figgie International reported its rankings among America's leading corporations as determined by *Fortune* magazine's "Fortune 500." In that group, Figgie International ranked 62nd in total return from 1979 to 1989, and 187th in EPS growth for the same decade. Within the industry group "industrial and farm equipment," of 28 companies Figgie International ranked 1st in total return and 3rd in EPS growth from 1979 to 1989. The Chairman was proud of these results, and of the corporation's own market research showing that on a worldwide basis, of 150 products made by Figgie International, over 50 percent ranked 1st, 2nd, or 3rd in their markets in 1991.

GOALS FOR THE 1990s

The same annual report for 1990 also reported some sobering results. Noting the impact of the economic recession on the company's performance, especially those divisions most closely tied to the construction industry, the corporation reported a very small increase in sales and significant declines in profits and in per-share earnings.

Despite the unfavorable business climate, Figgie International remained committed to its strategic goals. Consolidation of smaller divisions into larger units would continue. Already the corporation had exceeded its target by forming seven divisions with over $100 million in sales. In that context, the Chairman announced that the company would not be making any acquisitions in the near future. Recalling the earlier period of consolidation, he wrote in his letter to shareholders in the 1990 annual report:

> It may cost us some enticing acquisitions, but we have shut down our merger and acquisition activities, as we did in 1970, and we are concentrating heavily on improved working capital utilization, debt paydown, and selective operating improvements.

Later in the Report, he added:

> At some point in the future, we will resume our tuck-in acquisition program, largely to drive our big divisions to become bigger and better. But for the present, we have declared a moratorium on acquisitions until we see which way the economy is going, and until we materially drop our debt-to-equity ratio.

The annual report reiterated Figgie's continuing commitment to preparing for the future by achieving world-class manufacturing technology and process. This was a major strategic thrust to achieve significant improvements in product design, engineering, and manufacturing, allowing for significant improvements in customer service and delivery time, all while substantially reducing operating costs, especially for material and labor.

At the company's annual stockholder meeting in June 1991, the Chairman described the company's plan for the future as consisting of four key points:

1. Continue consolidating plants and investing in modern manufacturing equipment and technology.
2. Remain diversified with emphasis on larger divisions.
3. Reduce key working capital and bring down the company's debt-to-equity ratio to .35 to 1.
4. Continue expanding overseas markets—Figgie's foreign sales had risen from $70 million in the mid–1980s to $250 million in 1990.

MANAGING IN THE RECESSION: FIGGIE INTERNATIONAL IN 1991

At the end of every year, each Figgie division completed a five-year strategic plan. Prepared and signed by all management staff in the division, the five-year plan described the division's current competitive position, reviewed its most recent results, and detailed its plans and goals. Each year the Chairman and the responsible group executive from headquarters met with each division president to examine and approve the plans. Once approved, the plan targets for the coming year were regarded as a rock-solid, hardcore commitment for which the division president would be held accountable. Accordingly, the five-year plan and the entire planning process became known as "the hardcore" at Figgie International.

The U.S. economic recession in 1990–91 posed a serious challenge to these plans. As part of the "hardcore" process, each division prepared an alternate plan accounting for unfavorable contingencies in the coming year. By the end of June 1991, 27 divisions had been told by the Chairman to go to their alternate plans.

Between the third quarter of 1990 and the third quarter of 1991 the corporation underwent five separate cost-cutting programs. The first two affected all divisions, while a third and a fourth initiative were later focused on 19 struggling divisions. The fifth round of cuts occurred in 7 of those 19 divisions still not responding. As a whole, the corporation was about 50 percent off budget, and 90 percent of that decline was due to the six construction-related divisions.

THE CONSTRUCTION EQUIPMENT MARKET

According to the U.S. Department of Commerce, there were four end markets for construction: building construction, public works, surface mining, and exports. Within these markets there were four categories of construction equipment:

Earthmoving machinery, including tractors, crawler dozers, loaders, scrapers, graders, hydraulic excavators and backhoes, pipelayers, and off-highway trucks, used primarily in building construction, but also in road and dam construction.

Cranes and excavators, including small backhoes mounted on tractors, large walking draglines and power shovels, used on virtually all types of construction projects; replacement parts account for considerable sales in this category.

Underground mining machinery, including conventional equipment such as cutters, drills, loaders, and conveyors; also continuous miners and longwall systems.

Other construction equipment, including asphalt and concrete pavers; mixing, spreading and finishing machines; compactors; air compressors and air tools; and pumps, hoists, and rock-crushing equipment.

The market for construction equipment was highly sensitive to fluctuations in the economy. Exhibits 4, 5, and 6 describe recent trends in private and public construction in the United States. Commercial construction was suffering in part due to a surplus of office buildings and retail centers in metropolitan New York, Los Angeles, Chicago, and Boston. Vacancy rates in these markets were high and there was no sign of a downward trend in the near future.

The construction equipment market was regarded as highly competitive, with manufacturers vying for shares of a constricted global market by increasing international expansion. In recent years U.S. manufacturers had increased exports to international markets. Seeking to avoid restrictive trade regulations, they had also entered into deals with overseas companies. The Middle East, Eastern Europe, Asia, and the European Community all seemed to offer good prospects.

FIGGIE INTERNATIONAL'S CONSTRUCTION-RELATED DIVISIONS

The company had competed in the construction equipment industry since the mid-1960s, when it acquired Safway Steel, a manufacturer of tubular scaffolding. Safway became the nucleus around which other construction companies were added, including Snorkel, initially a maker of mobile work platforms for the fire service. After

EXHIBIT 4 | **New U.S. Residential Construction Starts by Quarter, 1988–91** (*in thousands of units*)

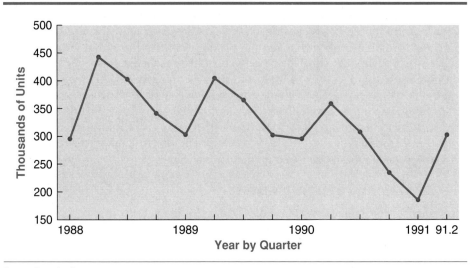

Source: Coworks, Inc.

EXHIBIT 5 | **U.S. Private Nonresidential Construction in Place by Quarter, 1988–91**

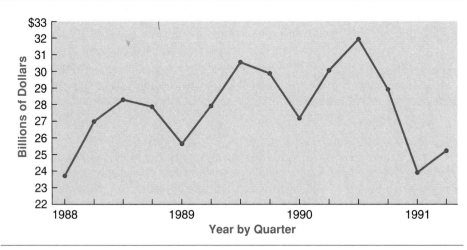

Source: Coworks, Inc.

expanding their product lines, Safway and Snorkel went on to become two of Figgie's best divisions, consistently profitable despite the cyclical nature of booms and busts in the industry.

In the third quarter of 1990, however, the construction market as a whole entered a decline unlike any previous downturn. As one Figgie executive described it, "It used to be a gentle slide, but in September 1990 the whole market went right off a cliff." Between the third quarter of 1990 and the third quarter of 1991 sales and profits for the six construction-related divisions at Figgie International, including Safway and

EXHIBIT 6 | **U.S. Public Construction in Place by Quarter, 1988–91**

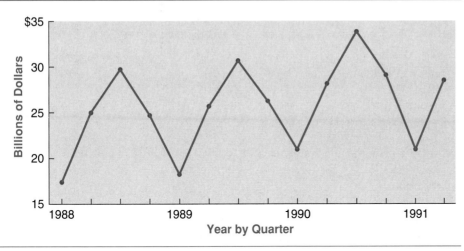

Source: Coworks, Inc.

Snorkel, experienced drastic declines. In that context, the future of Huber Essick, a perennial problem division in this group, quickly became a major concern.

THE HUBER ESSICK DIVISION

In 1991 the Huber Essick division manufactured light construction equipment, including mixing, finishing, pumping, and spraying equipment, as well as vibratory rollers and small road maintainers. The division was in transition from its older lines of earthmoving equipment to smaller, newer products that moved, mixed, or pumped plaster, cement, and similar materials. Special emphasis was placed on the division's line of concrete and plaster mixers and pumps, and its exterior insulation finishing system (EIFS) hydrospray pump for fireproofing materials. A market overview for the division's major products appears in Exhibit 7, and financial statements for the division are shown in Exhibits 8 and 9.

EXHIBIT 7 | **1990 Market Overview for Figgie's Huber Essick Division: Products, Market Sizes, and Market Shares of Major Competitors**

Product Category	Concrete & Plaster Mixers	Plaster & Fireproofing Pumps	MCP Concrete Pump	Hydrospray Pump 50xt	Rollers	Huber Maintainer
Estimated Market Sizes	$30 million	$8 million	$8 million	$2-3 million	$50 million	$4-5 million
Estimated Market Shares	Essick 20% Stone 40–45% Stow 15–20% others 15–20%	Essick 10–15% Mayco 35–40% Thomsen 35–40% others 5–10%	Essick, under 10% Mayco 70–80% others 10%	Essick 40% Spray King 50% others 10%	Essick, under 1% many others	Huber 10–15% Athey 10–15% Puckett 30% Lee 10% Fiat Allis 30%

Source: Huber Essick hardcore estimates, October 1990.

EXHIBIT 8 | **Balance Sheet, Huber Essick Division, 1989–91**
(*In thousands of dollars*)

	1989 Actual	1990 Actual	1990 Projected per Hardcore	1991 Projected per Hardcore	1991 Projected Revised
Assets:					
Cash	$ (61)	$ 65	$ (100)	$ (100)	$ (30)
Net accounts receivable	1,126	579	745	792	484
Inventory and contracts	3,652	3,757	3,556	3,289	2,562
Other current assets	23	13	25	25	105
Total current assets	$4,740	$4,414	$4,226	$4,006	$3,121
Net properties	410	640	648	564	288
Other assets	217	272	226	226	577
Total assets	$5,367	$5,326	$5,100	$4,796	$3,986
Liabilities:					
Accounts payable	$ 731	$ 652	$ 575	$ 605	$ 375
Other current liabilities	(252)	(241)	(132)	505	(345)
Total current liabilities	$ 479	$ 411	$ 443	$1,110	$ 30
Leases	29	270	340	301	262
Long-term debt	0	0	0	0	0
Total liabilities	$ 508	$ 681	$ 783	$1,411	$ 292
Equity:					
Intercompany current	$ 356	1,461	$ 917	$ 63	$1,693
Retained earnings	(1,739)	(3,058)	(2,842)	(2,920)	(4,241)
All other equity	6,242	6,242	6,242	6,242	6,242
Total equity	$4,859	$4,645	$4,317	$3,385	$3,694
Total liabilities and equity	$5,367	$5,326	$5,100	$4,796	$3,986

Concrete mixers were basically motorized cylinders on wheels. Ingredients to make concrete were put in at the top of the mixer and the cylinder turned to mix the concrete. Plaster and mortar mixers were similar, with blades added inside the cylinder to mix ingredients to a finer consistency. Essick mixers were sized to be towed to a construction site and used to mix the concrete for footings, postholes, curbs, or blocks.

Motorized material pumps were used to pump plaster, mortar, stucco, or fireproofing materials. Depending on the model, Essick pumps could deliver these materials to job sites 80 stories straight up or as far as five hundred yards away. For example, in constructing a high-rise building the material would be mixed on the ground and then pumped to the desired floor of the building.

The Huber name was an old one in the industry, dating back to 1863. Originally located in Marion, Ohio, Huber manufactured heavy equipment for road construction, including motor graders, vibrating rollers, and maintainers. In 1977 Huber was moved to Charleston, South Carolina, and consolidated with the Scott division's crane line to form the Scott Huber division. In 1984 the Essick division, a manufacturer of plaster, mortar, and concrete mixers, was consolidated to form Scott Huber Essick. All three product lines were manufactured in the Charleston plant, which exceeded 400,000 square feet, until 1987, when the Scott line was discontinued.

EXHIBIT 9 | **Income Statement, Huber Essick Division, 1989–91**
(In thousands of dollars)

	1989 Actual	1990 Actual	1990 Projected per Hardcore	1991 Projected per Hardcore	1991 Projected Revised
Net sales	$11,696	$ 9,358	$ 9,765	$10,485	$ 6,226
Direct material	6,221	4,867	5,069	5,015	3,080
Direct labor	764	580	638	534	336
Fixed costs/overheads	2,502	2,227	2,342	1,840	1,722
Other	730	552	532	512	597
Total cost of sales	10,217	8,226	8,581	7,901	5,735
Gross profit	$ 1,479	$ 1,132	$ 1,184	$ 2,584	$ 491
Selling expense	1,168	1,227	1,184	999	853
G&A expense	547	621	612	468	444
R&D expense	561	380	380	278	253
Debt service	708	744	744	648	684
Total operating expense	2,984	2,972	2,920	2,393	2,234
Operating profit	$(1,505)	$(1,840)	$(1,736)	$ 191	$(1,743)
Interest (expense)	(37)	(83)	(82)	(65)	(61)
Lease interest (expense)	0	(29)	(40)	(32)	(29)
Other income (expense)	(20)	10	17	20	77
Intercompany income (expense)	(71)	(57)	(48)	(1)	(37)
Profit before state tax	(1,633)	(1,999)	(1,889)	113	(1,793)
State tax	0	0	0	8	0
Profit before F.I.T	(1,633)	(1,999)	(1,889)	105	(1,793)
Federal income tax	(555)	(680)	(642)	38	(610)
Profit after tax	$(1,078)	$(1,319)	$(1,247)	$ 67	$(1,183)

For the years 1988, 1989, and 1990, Huber Essick failed to meet its hardcore targets for sales and profit before tax. As 1990 sales plummeted in the latter half of the year, fixed costs were cut to bare minimum levels, but it was clear that the division would post an operating loss for the year.

Since the product line names were still well known and well regarded, the Chairman met with the board of directors and recommended selling the division. No formal announcement was made, but an investment advisory firm was engaged to put out informal feelers for prospective buyers. In November 1990 the Chairman was told that Stow, one of Huber Essick's major competitors in concrete mixers, had expressed interest in buying the division.

Preliminary analysis supported the merger in concept. Where Stow was strong in rentals, especially in the Northeast, Huber Essick's strengths were in sales through dealers, especially in the Southeast. Also, Stow products were priced at the low end of the market, while Huber Essick's were sold at higher prices.

It soon became clear, however, that Stow, a family business, had neither the cash to purchase Huber Essick, nor the credit to finance a leveraged buyout. Instead, Stow's young president, Mark Hotchkiss, proposed working out a joint venture to capitalize on their strengths. The Chairman agreed, and in February 1991 negotiations began.

As they explored a possible joint venture, the two companies disagreed on where the manufacturing operations would be located: at Stow's plant in Binghamton, New York, or at Huber Essick's in Charleston, South Carolina. Dr. Harry E. Figgie III, the vice chairman for technology and strategic planning, visited the Binghamton plant and concluded that the Charleston site, where progress toward world-class manufacturing was already under way, was unquestionably superior. An independent consulting firm was retained to study the two sites. Its report confirmed that it would take far more time and money to achieve world-class manufacturing standards in Binghamton, and recommended locating the joint venture in Charleston.

Hotchkiss still did not agree. The Chairman invited him to visit the Figgie International Tech Center to see the new manufacturing technology at work, but the visit did not change his mind.

The Chairman then told Hotchkiss he would never agree to a joint venture in Binghamton, and then offered to buy Stow. He asked the young man to think about it and call him later. A few weeks later, Mr. Figgie called Hotchkiss, who said he would not sell the company, and the relationship came to an end.

MAYCO PUMP CORPORATION: ANOTHER OPPORTUNITY

Several weeks later the Chairman received a call from Chuck Hutchinson, Huber Essick's vice president of sales, who had heard that Mayco Pump Corporation might be for sale. Only five years earlier, the Chairman had tried to buy Mayco as a tuck-in acquisition for Huber Essick, but the company had not been for sale. According to Hutchinson, the recession had hit Mayco hard, and Marvin May, its president, was looking to sell the company and retire. Hutchinson wondered if the Chairman was still interested in acquiring Mayco.

Mayco Pump Corporation was a division of a family business founded in 1951. Based in Los Angeles, Mayco had a strong reputation for quality and exceptional service. It was the industry's largest producer of trailer-mounted concrete and fireproofing pumps, and it had recently invented a sludge pump for use in industrial and municipal sewage and waste water treatment systems. Dominant in West Coast construction, Mayco had its own retail store in Los Angeles. It was the first U.S. firm to sell concrete pumps in Japan, and it also exported to other markets in the Pacific Rim, Europe, and the Middle East.

At Hutchinson's urging, Mr. May called Mr. Figgie. The two men spoke for awhile about the economy, and Figgie learned that Mayco sales were off 60 percent. May confirmed that Mayco Pump was for sale, but informed Figgie that a German competitor was to make a final offer in only two days.

Figgie flew to California the next day. He visited the factory leased by Mayco. Because it bought all the parts for its products, its manufacturing operations consisted primarily of welding and assembly, with very little machining work.

May provided income statements for the previous three years, and a balance sheet and income statement through June 30, 1991 (see Exhibits 10, 11, and 12) As an "S" corporation, in lieu of retained earnings, Mayco profits had been paid out as dividends to the shareholders and then reinvested in the company as interest-bearing loans. While reflected on the income statement as interest expense, interest on these loans would normally be the equivalent of after-profit shareholder dividends.

In addition, May pointed out that in the previous two years his company had made three major investments:

EXHIBIT 10 | Income Statement, Mayco Pump, 1988–90

	1990	1989	1988
Sales	$11,560,198	$11,715,538	$9,826,860
Cost of materials	6,423,555	6,880,595	5,862,170
Labor and manufacturing expense	1,961,522	2,061,496	2,017,467
Gross profit	$ 3,175,121	$ 2,773,447	$1,947,223
Selling/delivery	1,063,186	927,502	556,833
General and administrative	1,746,696	1,226,363	1,102,421
Proft before interest payments to owners	$ 365,239	$ 619,582	$ 287,969
Interest payments to owners	374,421	426,042	290,130
Net profit before taxes	$ (9,182)	$ 193,540	$ (2,161)

EXHIBIT 11 | Balance Sheet, Mayco Pump, June 30, 1991

Assets:	
Cash	$ (100,785)
Accounts receivable	1,266,301
Notes receivable	221,249
Prepaids and other current assets	154,685
Inventory	2,889,051
Total current assets	$4,430,501
Net property, plant and equipment	170,421
Other noncurrent assets	114,477
Total assets	$4,715,399
Liabilities and equity:	
Accounts payable	$ 664,497
Accrued and other current liabilities	116,019
Total current liabilities	$ 780,516
Other loans	232,469
Other long-term liabilities	41,741
Total liabilities	$1,054,726
Loans from shareholders	4,067,518
Capital stock	110,000
Retained earnings	(516,846)
Total shareholder loans and equity	$3,660,672
Total liabilities and shareholder equity	$4,715,398

- The establishment of an export division, with foreign distributors in Europe, Asia, and the Middle East.
- Development and introduction of larger models of concrete pumps.
- Entrance into the sludge pump market, making Mayco the only U.S. manufacturer in this market.

EXHIBIT 12 | **Income Statement, Mayco Pump, January 1 to June 30, 1991**

Sales	$3,794,957
Cost of materials	2,186,305
Labor and manufacturing expense	922,812
Gross profit	$ 685,840
Engineering	162,227
Selling/delivery	503,885
General and administrative	471,517
Profit before interest payments to owners	$ (451,789)
Interest payments to owners	202,395
Net profit before taxes	$ (654,184)

TO BUY OR NOT TO BUY

Flying back to Cleveland, Mr. Figgie considered the situation. Because manufacturing processes were similar, he believed the Mayco product line could easily be made in the Charleston plant, reducing materials costs by as much as 50 percent. Consolidation at Charleston would also reduce labor and manufacturing expenses between 14 percent and 16 percent, and decrease selling and general administrative expenses between 10 percent and 13 percent. These reductions could be achieved, he believed, with no significant cost increase for product shipments.

May had also assured him that Mayco's key product development engineer would remain with the company through the acquisition, as would the key international marketing executive. When the economy recovered, and when the construction market turned around, the combined businesses would dominate the market.

May wanted $7 million for the company, a price the Germans were reportedly willing to pay. Mr. Figgie had 24 hours to decide whether to match this reported offer.

ROCKY MOUNTAIN HELICOPTERS, INC.

Romuald A. Stone, James Madison University

Rocky Mountain Helicopters, Inc. (RMHI), was one of the largest providers of helicopter support services in the United States and was the industry leader in providing air medical transport (AMT) services to health care facilities. Between 1988 and 1993, RMHI's revenues grew at a 14 percent annual compound rate to reach $85 million, with the air medical segment contributing 60 percent of total revenues. Despite its growth, RMHI's president and CEO, J. Russel Spray, faced several important strategic issues in 1993.

After earning $814,000 on corporate revenue of $81.79 million in 1992, RMHI reported a loss of $12.9 million and suffered a working capital deficit of $28.4 million in 1993. Stemming the flow of red ink was one of Mr. Spray's top priorities. The poor performance in 1993 put the company in a position of noncompliance with certain covenants concerning its long-term debt. Related concerns involved meeting short- and long-term obligations and how to finance continued growth. Although recent efforts at diversification had been failures and some of these operations had been terminated, Mr. Spray also had to evaluate which other unproductive operations and assets were candidates for divestiture. Increasing shareholder wealth was another major issue. RMHI's stock had plunged from a high of $7 5/8 when the company went public in 1990 to a low of $1 5/8 during the fourth quarter of fiscal 1993 (see Exhibit 1).

THE AIR MEDICAL INDUSTRY

In 1992, the hospital-based air medical transportation industry celebrated its 20th anniversary. Founded on helicopter evacuation principles used in the Korean and Vietnam conflicts, air ambulances made the difference between life and death for thousands of severely injured service members. The practice of using medically

---

The generous cooperation of Rocky Mountain Helicopters, Inc., in providing information for this case is gratefully acknowledged.

EXHIBIT 1 **Rocky Mountain Helicopters' Stock Prices by Quarter, 1990–93**

	Price Range	
Quarter Ended	High	Low
April 30, 1993	$3	$1 5/8
January 31, 1993	4 1/4	2 3/4
October 31, 1992	4 1/2	3 1/2
July 31, 1992	4 3/4	3 3/4
April 30, 1992	5 1/2	4
January 31, 1992	5 7/8	3
October 31, 1991	6 1/4	4 1/2
July 31, 1991	5 3/8	4 3/8
April 30, 1991	6 3/8	4
January 31, 1991	6 7/8	3 3/8
October 31, 1990	7 5/8	6

Source: Company records.

equipped helicopters to fly critically ill or injured people from accident sites or remote or rural locations to the care they needed had contributed to improved trauma patient survival. More than 300 hospitals now supported some form of air medical transport. Industry analysts believed the notion of a helicopter as just a conventional flying ambulance would increasingly become obsolete in the 1990s. They expected that the latest in medical and flight technologies would be applied to developing airborne intensive care units, making them acute health care facilities first, helicopters second.[1]

The first civilian medical emergency helicopter program began in Switzerland in the late 1960s. The first U.S. hospital-based helicopter program was established in 1972 at Saint Anthony's in Denver, Colorado. By 1980, there were 26 hospital-based helicopters providing medical evacuation services. By 1992, the number of emergency hospital-based helicopter programs had grown to 189. According to a recent survey by WinterGreen Research, Inc., annual revenues for hospital-based helicopter programs were $254.8 million in 1991 and were projected to grow to $1.2 billion by the year 2001.[2] WinterGreen also predicted that the number of programs would increase by 63 percent to 290 by 2001, with the number of hospitals participating increasing to 783 in 2001 from 303 in 1991.

However, the competitive environment was not all that rosy. Emergency air medical service operators were facing numerous business pressures in the 1990s that included tougher competition in the marketplace and a fast-changing health care industry environment. Coupled with aging fleets, higher operating costs, shrinking profits, resistance to price increases by customers, and increasing demands for cost containment, profitable industry growth would be a challenge.

A recent industry survey revealed 163,701 patients were flown by air medical aircraft (both fixed wing and helicopter) in the United States in 1991 (see Exhibit 2). Fixed-wing transports accounted for 24,281 patients or 66 per day. The heli-

[1]Westergaard Institutional Network report on AMI, February 11, 1993.

[2]Ibid.

copter segment transported 139,420 patients or an average of 382 patients per day. A history of total helicopter transports since 1984 is shown in Exhibit 3. Overall growth of helicopter-transported patients for the 1984–91 period was 13.3 percent. However this trend had slowed dramatically—the growth from 1990 to 1991 was almost zero.

Over the period 1986 to 1989, a total of 36 new hospital-based air medical programs were opened in the U.S. But from 1990 to 1992, only four new programs were added. "Growth as measured in terms of aeromed start-up programs has plateaued," according to Nina Merrill, executive director of the Association of Air Medical Services (AAMS). "We see one or two new programs start up every year and one or two canceled."[3] Exhibit 4 provides recent statistical highlights for hospital-based helicopter programs and the growth slowdown that seemed to be in progress.

However, W. Terrance Schreier, CEO and chairman of Air Methods, did not agree with the predictions that the industry had entered the maturity stage:

> These predictions aren't based on what's happening in health care right now. The bottom line is that hospitals are going to close as the nation redistributes its health care system. Aircraft are going to be used to improve patients' access to the health care they

EXHIBIT 2 | **Patient Flights by Air Medical Aircraft, 1991**

	Helicopter	Fixed-Wing	Total
Hospital	124,326	19,199	143,525
Nonhospital	15,094	5,082	20,176
Total	139,420	24,281	163,701

Source: "Annual Transportation Statistics," *The Journal of Air Medical Transport,*

EXHIBIT 3 | **Hospital-Based Helicopter Transport Statistics, 1984–91**

Year	Total Patients	Transport Average per Program	% to Scene*	% to Sponsor**	% at Night	Average Number of Miles One-way
1991	124,326	709	29	71	37	58
1990	123,599	705	27	71	37	60
1989	113,200	697	25	68	37	58
1988	108,900	698	25	70	38	61
1987	97,900	623	23	68	36	61
1986	87,607	590	23	67	39	61
1985	68,694	570	24	64	37	63
1984	51,855	553	26	64	35	61

*Percentage of missions in which a patient was transported directly from a location *outside* of a hospital or clinic facility to a receiving facility/airport.
**Percentage of missions in which a patient was returned to the facility from which the flight originated.
Source: "Annual Transportation Statistics," *The Journal of Air Medical Transport,* March 1992, p. 27.

---

[3]B. Wagstaff, "Aeromed Transport: Poised for Growth," *Aviation International News,* September 1, 1993, p. 102.

EXHIBIT 4 | **Statistical Highlights for Hospital-Based Helicopter Programs, 1986–92***

General	1992	1991	1990	1989	1988	1987	1986
Programs	178	178	174	165	155	145	129
Cities	139	143	137	136	131	125	111
Helicopters	231	225	231	213	195	184	151
Operators	31	29	27	32	33	31	37
Patients (000)	125	124	119	111	104	93	78

*Reflects survey conducted July to July of each year.
Source: *The Journal of Air Medical Transport,* July 1992, p. 28.

need. The AMT market isn't "saturated," "mature," or "flat." The market is shifting due to external forces and growth is pausing as a reaction to that shift. If the market is so stagnant, how come three of the four new contracts we signed recently were start-up operations?"[4]

The overall number of helicopters in the industry had changed little over the past three years, remaining at 231 aircraft in 1992. There was a noticeable trend toward use of more twin-engine helicopters and a decline in use of single-engine helicopters.

The average per-flight charge for various regions of the United States for helicopter and fixed-wing aircraft was reported each year in the *Journal of Air Medical Transport.* The transport charges for 1992 by AAMS regions are shown in Exhibits 5 and 6. The calculations include base fee per mile, hourly fees, and medical team professional fees (if any). For helicopters the nationwide average transport charge was $2,381, an increase of 9 percent over the 1991 average of $2,182. States with the highest fee structures are shown in Exhibit 7.

HEALTH CARE REFORM AND THE AIR MEDICAL INDUSTRY

A key driving force affecting the air medical transport industry was the national health care crisis. After World War II only 10 percent of the population was insured as compared to 85 percent today. In short, having someone else pay the bills pushed both the demand for and the supply of medical care through the roof. It was well-documented that health care costs had spiraled out of control. The nation's medical tab was $900 billion in 1993, up from $250 billion in 1980. At 14.4 percent of GDP, the U.S. spent significantly more on health care than any other industrialized nation.

President Clinton had made curtailing medical costs a top priority his first year in office: "All our efforts to strengthen the economy will fail . . . unless we also take this year . . . bold steps to reform our health care system."[5] The president sent his Health Security Act to Congress in October 1993 as a first step toward rebuilding the nation's health care system. The 1,342-page bill called for sweeping changes that would affect all Americans. The fallout of the bill would certainly impact the AMT

---

[4]Ibid., p. 104.
[5]H. Stout, "Health Care Experts Devising Clinton Plan Face Sticky Questions," *Wall Street Journal,* March 11, 1993, p. A1.

EXHIBIT 5 | **Association of Air Medical Services (AAMS) Regions**

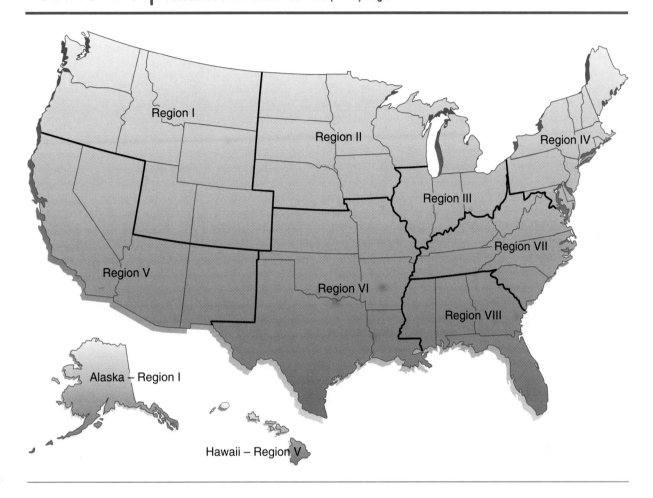

industry, but most operators were uncertain how health care reform would affect them and the industry.

In a recent survey of helicopter air medical directors by *Rotor & Wing,* two key problems affecting emergency service operators emerged: reimbursement and justification for air medical transport services. Many operators faulted Medicare and Medicaid for not paying enough. *Rotor & Wing* reported in its October 1993 issue:

> According to Mary Davis, program director of Mercy Air Rescue in Southern California, "Medicare reimbursement is so poor we can't afford to take assignments. An assignment is an agreement where health care providers accept whatever Medicare pays as their *only* reimbursement, which precludes billing the patient or any other party for the balance.] The government has forced us into this position. Proposed medical cuts in California are so drastic that we might not be able to transport [aid] recipients." She adds: "That may put more providers out of business."[6]

---

[6]P. Rickey, "Industry's Three Rs for Health Care Reform," *Rotor & Wing* 27, no. 10 (October 1993), p. 23.

EXHIBIT 6 | Annual Transport Charges for Air Medical Services by Regions, 1992*

AAMS Region Programs	Helicopter (N=136)	Fixed-Wing		
		Piston (N=21)	Turboprop (N=52)	Turbojet (N=52)
Region 1	$2,072	$3,877	$3,987	$4,485
Region 2	2,124	2,335	3,288	2,903
Region 3	2,801	1,637	1,782	1,948
Region 4	3,530	—	3,650	2,328
Region 5	3,100	5,338	4,551	4,400
Region 6	1,696	1,563	2,761	1,632
Region 7	2,680	855	3,219	2,083
Region 8	1,859	1,550	3,375	2,644
Nationwide				
Low	$ 730	$ 855	$ 742	$1,590
High	6,130	6,725	6,400	7,258
Average	2,381	2,743	3,662	3,109
Round-trip miles	120	600	600	600

*This is the tenth survey compiled by *The Journal of Air Medical Transport.*
Charges include base fee per mile, hourly fees, and medical team professional fees (if any).
Source: *The Journal of Air Medical Transport,* May 1992, p. 25.

EXHIBIT 7 | Highest Average Helicopter Fees for Air Medical Services by State, 1992

Rank	State	Average Fee
1	Massachusetts	$6,130
2	Illinois	4,114
3	Nevada	3,905
4	Pennsylvania	3,889
5	New York	3,343
6	California	3,258
7	Kentucky	3,174
8	South Carolina	3,123
9	Indiana	2,948
10	Oregon	2,940
	National Average	$2,381

Source: *The Journal of Air Medical Transport,* May 1992, p. 25.

In many hospital-based programs, hospitals were absorbing the difference between what insurers paid and what the air transportation cost. This approach was cost-justified if the patient stayed at the facility long enough for the hospital to make up the deficiency on its other charges.

For air medical transport services that were not hospital based, the situation was more acute. For example, the CalStar program in San Francisco received only 50 percent of its cost from government insurance programs—one-half of the patients in the Bay area were on Medicare or Medicaid. CalStar CEO Joseph Cook described his frustration: "This is not a Ford van we're driving; it's a multimillion dollar ship."[7] Cook saw the air medical industry contributing to the current dilemma in two key areas. He suggested too many flights were not medically justified. In addition, he believed too many hospital-based programs were not charging what it truly cost them to transport a patient. Consequently, when nonhospital-based program operators submitted their bills that represented full costs (including a reasonable profit), insurers sometimes challenged the charges as too high, given the benchmarked charges of hospital-based fees. Cook believed the air medical industry was vulnerable and called "for ways to provide this service in a more cost-efficient manner."

In addition to the reimbursement issue, insurers wanted to know whether a patient transfer by air was really necessary. For example, did the service make a medical difference in terms of patient survivability/morbidity? To address this issue, many operators were pressing for uniformly accepted standards to determine which patients required air medical transport. There was a paucity of studies that substantiated the survivability benefits of flying patients to a trauma or tertiary care center.

In view of these concerns and pending changes in health care on the horizon, the air medical transporters were working hard to ensure they continued to have a place in the health care industry. According to one report: "Members of the AAMS executive board and others are calling on congressmen; many program directors actively participate in local and state groups that are setting transport and trauma standards. Others are allowing more media access to their facilities to gain public support."[8]

In July 1993, the AAMS executive board issued an executive summary that addressed the Clinton administration's health care reform package in three key areas: access to, quality of, and cost of care. The summary listed key advantages of air medical transport in today's hospital system and in the integrated system expected to emerge following health care reform.[9] Exhibit 8 presents an abridged version of the AAMS's main position and its rationale.

Another related force affecting the industry was that hospital bed utilization was only running at approximately 65 percent. Less invasive surgical procedures were expected to further reduce hospital stays and create even more empty beds. The only way to reduce excess capacity was to close a large number of hospitals. Mergers and consolidations were another viable way to save administrative and other duplicative service costs.[10] It appeared the health care industry would be forced to drive down costs without meaningfully impairing the quality of health care services.[11]

On a positive note for the AMT industry, specialized services (e.g., cardiac, trauma, burn, neonatal) were becoming more common and were often offered in separate facilities. Moreover, as more hospitals evolved into regional acute care providers, transportation became an important issue in moving patients to the place of treatment. Often, ground transportation was not adequate to move patients with life threatening injury or illness quickly enough. Helicopters provided the only means

---

[7]Ibid., p. 24.
[8]Ibid., p. 26.
[9]Ibid.
[10]Extracted from information provided by WinterGreen Research, Inc., on the air medical transport industry.
[11]M. McNamee, "Surprise! Health Care's Fever May Have Finally Broken," *Business Week,* April 26, 1993, p. 31.

E X H I B I T   8 | **Summary of AAMS Position on Health Care Reform**

Health Care Access Thesis

Air medical transport significantly improves access to health care services, resulting in documented decreases in patient morbidity and mortality.

The rationale points to limited access of rural patients to specialized health care, due to both the costs for rural hospitals to maintain such services and the closure of smaller hospitals. Air medical transport provides access to advanced life-support (ALS)—in transport and in delivering patients to major hospitals, while also offering speed and range substantially greater than ground ambulances.

Cost Containment Thesis

Air medical transport supports health care cost containment.

The rapid, high-quality medical service provided by air medical transport results in improved patient outcomes, shorter hospitalization, and enhanced cost containment. Air medical helicopters save costs by providing ALS care where ground ALS services are cost-prohibitive, and fixed-wing air medical services provide national/international access and repatriation in a cost-effective manner, while providing appropriate care enroute. The availability of air medical rapid transport also supports development of regional medical systems, which cut costs by eliminating duplicate services.

Health Care Integrator Thesis

Historically air medical transportation has facilitated health care collaboration.

Air medical services have already fostered interfacility relationships and services between primary and tertiary care hospitals. The trend is continuing toward cost-effective multihospital delivery systems, and cost containment will encourage integration of air and ground emergency medical services (EMS). Air medical services can be a focal point for government attention on EMS issues.

Source: Adapted from P. Rickey, "Industry's Three Rs for Health Care Reform," *Rotor & Wing* 27, no. 10 (October 1993), p. 26.

of integrating a network of specialized hospitals on a regional basis.[12] Ed Eroe, president of West Michigan Air Care, aptly described the role helicopters play in this environment:

> In much the same way that airlines organize themselves into hub-and-spoke systems, hospitals develop networks of affiliation with local hospitals and clinics . . . Today, this traditional way of doing health care business is getting a shot in the arm via the distance-canceling use of copter; that community's ambulance can stay where it's needed and the critical care patient gets where he needs to go.[13]

Many hospitals were reevaluating their emergency air medical programs. Those that discontinued their programs did so for economic reasons; helicopter programs were expensive and often did not break even. For example, at Fairfax Hospital, the largest hospital in northern Virginia, the cost to operate, maintain, and be on constant stand-by availability was an average $5,000 per launch for the hospital's twin-engine Bell 412 medical helicopter.

For the future, it was expected few hospitals would initiate air medical programs on their own; instead, it was expected that hospitals would turn to independent operators or joint-venture arrangements. "The ones that survive will be the very strong, shared services programs," according to Nina Merrill, executive director of the AAMS.[14] Currently, 20 percent of all air ambulance programs were run by hospital consortiums rather than single hospitals.

---

[12]Information provided by WinterGreen Research, Inc.

[13]Wagstaff, "Aeromed Transport," p. 103.

[14]S. Lutz, "Fewer Hospitals Giving Helicopters a Whirl," *Modern Healthcare,* August 1992, p. 30.

COMPANY HISTORY[15]

Rocky Mountain Helicopters, Inc. (RMHI), was founded in 1970 in Provo, Utah, by aviation enthusiasts James B. Burr and his brother Robert C. Burr. Beginning as a two-man, one-helicopter operation, the company's initial focus was on providing aviation support services to seismic energy exploration companies in the Rocky Mountain region. As demand for additional helicopter support services increased in this market, RMHI expanded its aviation assets through direct purchase and lease of additional aircraft. However, beginning in the late 1970s and early 1980s, the downturn in the oil market coupled with a related decrease in seismic energy exploration in the Rocky Mountain region made this segment of the energy business increasingly unattractive. RMHI gradually reduced its involvement in energy operations by selling off aircraft and related equipment.

In 1975, RMHI entered the aeromedical market by acquiring all the assets of the operator of the first aeromedical transport program in the United States, located at St. Anthony Hospital in Denver, Colorado. This acquisition marked RMHI's entry into the aeromedical transport market; the company's involvement in aeromedical transport continued to grow steadily and represented 60 percent of its revenue base in 1993.

In 1975, RMHI acquired Western Helicopters, Inc., a helicopter support services and charter company based in Rialto, California. Other subsidiaries of RMHI included RMH Aeromedical and RMH Development; the latter subsidiary was formed in 1981 for the purpose of engaging in research and development projects. Currently, RMH Development was marketing helicopter rotor blades on a limited basis.

In 1985, RMHI acquired 95 percent of the shares of Air Today, Inc., a Denver-based freight forwarding company serving various locations in the Rocky Mountain region. However, this operation was discontinued in early 1989.

In May 1990, RMHI formed Advantage Aviation, Inc., to operate RMHI's Donaldson Airport fixed base operation (FBO) in Greenville, South Carolina. Advantage Aviation sold fuel, parts, and maintenance to private aircraft flying in and out of Donaldson Airport and provided maintenance support to the company's fleet of helicopters and aircraft.

In Feburary 1991, RMHI acquired Avtech Systems, Inc., which produced parts for aerospace and defense-related contracts. In 1992, Avtech lost $4,000 on sales of $4,734,000; Avtech accounted for approximately 5.5 percent of RMHI's $84.9 million total revenue in 1992. Avtech was divested in August 1993 with an estimated loss on disposal of $1,884,000. Approximately $1,039,000 of that amount represented operating losses in 1993 alone.

In early 1992, RMHI acquired two lumber remanufacturing plants which processed raw timber year-round, producing knot-free wood for manufacturers of window and door components, paneling, decorative moldings, and similar wood products. According to then President James B. Burr, "This acquisition provided us with the opportunity to increase the value-added in each phase of our timber operation, from freshly harvested timber to the finished product."[16] However, both lumber

---

[15]This section extracted from company records.

[16]E. Walters, "Rocky Mountain Helicopters Acquires Lumber Remanufacturing Company," *Business Wire,* January 28, 1992, p. 1.

remanufacturing operations were sold in early 1993 after incurring operating losses of $1,822,000 in fiscal 1993.

In 1992, RMHI formed a new division known as Advantage Airlines to provide regional commuter airline service between Portland International Airport and the cities of Eugene and Medford, Oregon, and Pasco, Washington. However, operations were suspended and discontinued in July 1992 just two months after first launching the service. The operation became a quick casualty of the fare wars it helped spawn. In a newspaper article announcing suspension of the airline service, RMHI President J. Russell Spray was quoted as saying, "We are in the midst of the most heated fare war the airline industry has ever known . . . We feel it is in the best interest of the company as a whole not to continue operating our airline from any location at this time."[17] But as one of Advantage's rivals noted, "They didn't have anything new going for them that wasn't being offered by a competitor . . . They weren't bringing anything new to the party."[18] Operating losses for the year totaled $1,951,000.

Since its founding 23 years earlier, RMHI had grown into a comprehensive aviation support services company, employing approximately 840 employees, including 300 pilots and 220 mechanics. The company's operating fleet consisted of 116 aircraft, of which 99 were helicopters and 17 were fixed-wing aircraft. Through its subsidiary operations and various divisions, RMHI's business portfolio in 1993 included aeromedical transportation services, sale of aircraft fuel and parts, helicopter logging, remote construction and utility work, charter flight services, aviation parts manufacturing, and aircraft maintenance, repair, and refurbishment. RMHI main business segments are profiled in the following sections. Exhibit 9 depicts RMHI's organization chart. Exhibit 10 presents RMHI's revenues by business segment from 1991 to 1993.

AIR MEDICAL OPERATIONS

RMHI had played a key role in pioneering the use of helicopters and airplanes equipped with patient life-support systems to transport persons requiring intensive medical care from either the scene of an accident or general care hospitals to highly skilled trauma centers, tertiary care centers, or teaching hospitals. From its humble beginnings in 1975 with its first hospital-based air medical program, the company had matured to become the largest provider of air medical transport services in the U.S.

The company currently operated 72 helicopters and 10 fixed-wing aircraft tied to supporting air medical programs at 52 hospitals located in 27 states. RMHI provided aircraft configured to customer specifications for air medical transport as well as flight crews (pilots and mechanics) who lived near the hospitals they served. Hospitals managed their own air medical programs and provided all the necessary medical personnel and equipment to support such operations.

Air medical services were generally provided under three-to-five-year contracts that generated a monthly fixed fee plus an hourly usage fee. The contracts contained an annual fee adjustment clause related to changes in cost of living, parts prices, and insurance rates. In addition, helicopter medical contracts often required that hospitals pick up the tab for helicopter jet fuel used in the course of providing air transport services. In 1990, fuel represented only 4.3 percent of the company's total operating expenditures.

---

[17]K. Knutson, "Intense Summer Air-Fare Wars Have Indefinitely Grounded a Fledgling Portland-Based Airline," *Tri-City Herald,* September 30, 1992.

[18]T. Shannon, "Advantage Airlines Suspends Flights," *Eugene Register-Guard,* July 17, 1992.

EXHIBIT 9 | Rocky Mountain Helicopters, Inc. Organization Chart, 1993

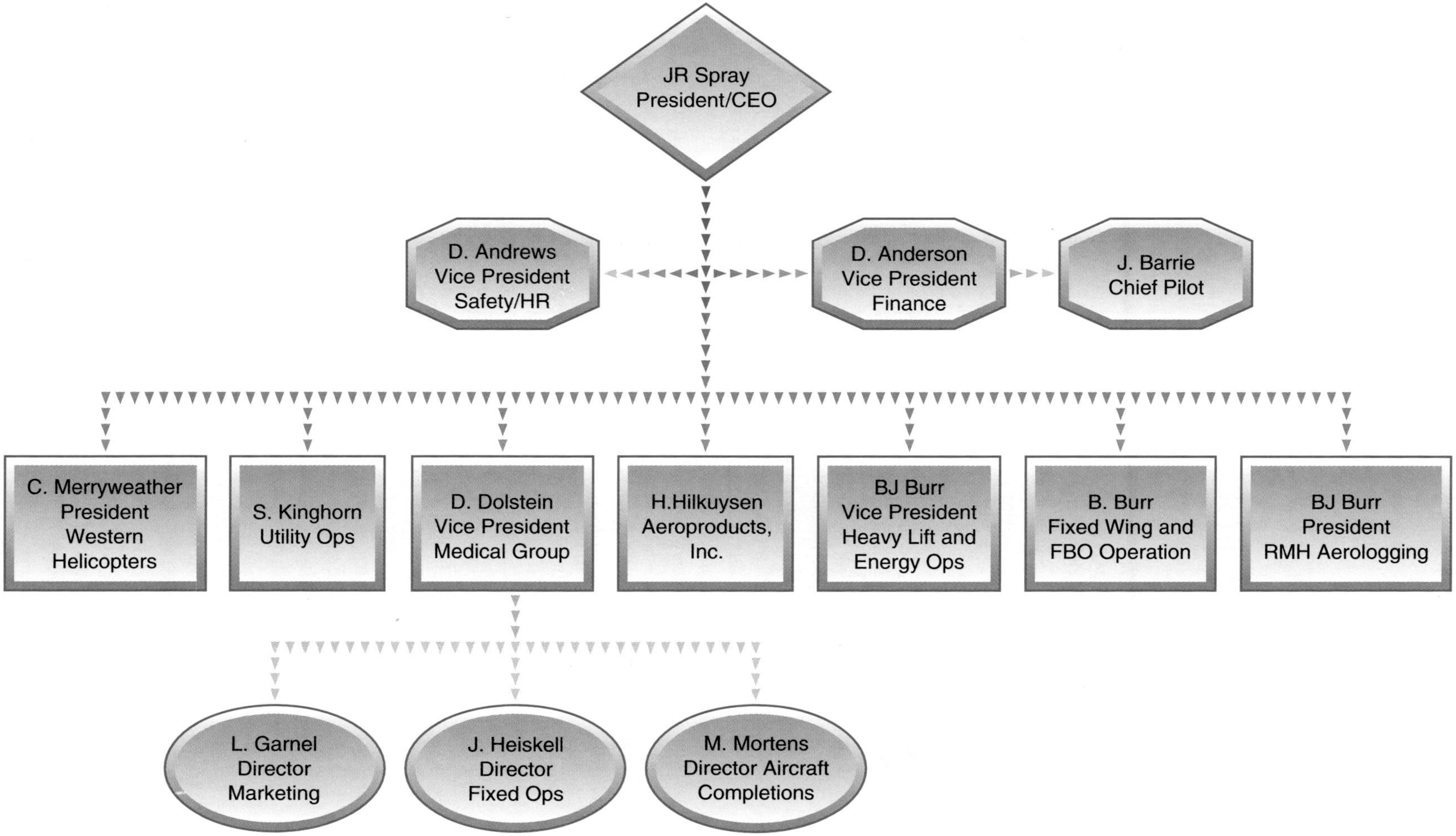

JR Spray
President/CEO

D. Anderson
Vice President
Finance

J. Barrie
Chief Pilot

D. Andrews
Vice President
Safety/HR

C. Merryweather
President
Western
Helicopters

S. Kinghorn
Utility Ops

D. Dolstein
Vice President
Medical Group

H. Hilkuysen
Aeroproducts,
Inc.

BJ Burr
Vice President
Heavy Lift and
Energy Ops

B. Burr
Fixed Wing and
FBO Operation

BJ Burr
President
RMH Aerologging

L. Garnel
Director
Marketing

J. Heiskell
Director
Fixed Ops

M. Mortens
Director Aircraft
Completions

EXHIBIT 10 | **Revenues from Continuing Operations for 1991–1993, Fiscal Years Ended April 30**

Business Segment	1993		1992		1991	
	Dollars	%	Dollars	%	Dollars	%
Air medical	$50,997	60%	$48,082	59%	$44,676	61%
Aerologging	19,398	23	18,519	23	13,557	18
Utility	3,367	4	3,409	4	5,024	7
Fixed wing/ parts/sales/other	6,173	7	5,881	7	5,300	7
Western Helicopters	2,819	3	3,068	4	2,798	4
Gain on equipment sales	2,219	3	2,728	3	1,841	3
Total revenues	$84,973	100%	$81,687	100%	$73,196	100%

Source: RMHI 10–K.

New contracts and some renewals were awarded following a competitive bidding process, which took into account various factors including price, industry experience and reputation, maintenance and support capabilities, quality of pilots, and availability of specified aircraft equipment and medical interior configurations.

RMHI's air medical operations were managed by a divisional director who supervised a director of marketing, a director of flight operations, and an aircraft completions manager. The division was divided into seven geographical regions each headed by a regional manager. Each program was in turn supervised by a designated program pilot who was responsible for the operation of the service at each hospital.

AEROLOGGING OPERATIONS

Helicopter logging operations involved cutting, flying, and loading timber onto customers' trucks. RMHI management believed that the demand for aerologging services exceeded the current supply of such services. The main market for RMHI's aerologging operations was centered in Alaska, but some operations also took place in Idaho and Montana. The principal customers were Alaskan native corporations and major wood products companies. These companies in turn remarketed the wood to Pacific Rim customers in unmanufactured (raw timber) form. Pacific Rim customers were willing to pay a premium price for such wood products. Current governmental regulations restricted export of timber from government lands in an unmanufactured form to foreign countries. Timber from privately owned forests could be exported in an unmanufactured state. Prices for export timber tended to follow higher quality domestic structural timber prices but could be influenced by foreign economies, foreign inventory levels, and housing starts in foreign countries.

Timber contracts were generally awarded following a competitive bidding process. Rates were established based upon level of competition and geographic locality of the helicopters. Payment was based upon scaled board feet delivered to the customer. The aerologging operation maintained a marketing and operations support office in Ketchikan, Alaska. Currently, four Sikorsky S-61 and four Bell Jet Ranger helicopters were used for aerologging services.

Aerologging was done primarily in areas previously considered uneconomical to log because of road building costs, areas not accessible, areas of catastrophic damage (e.g., fire, disease, blowdown), and areas classified as environmentally sensitive.

UTILITY OPERATIONS

RMHI's utility operations centered on providing helicopter support services in connection with power-line and ski-lift construction and seismic exploration conducted in the Rocky Mountain region. Related operations included work as a subcontractor for major oil and telecommunications companies, independent seismic companies, and companies operating ski resorts. Each year RMHI also bid to provide contract fire-fighting support services to the U.S. Forest Service during the summer months in the western United States. Contracts were awarded project by project and generally lasted one to three months (usually in the summer). However, because of the geographic availability of aircraft, aircrew experience, and equipment support capabilities, many of the same customers were retained year after year.

Competition among helicopter operators for utility and energy exploration projects was keen. Contract bidding was price-driven. Operations tended to be more profitable during the summer than the remainder of the year.

FIXED WING AND FIXED BASE OPERATIONS (FBO)

Fixed wing aircraft (twin turbine or jet engine powered) were used to support air medical helicopter operations whenever flight distance precluded use of helicopter flights. Other fixed-wing aircraft were used in support of RMHI's own operations as well as for charter flights.

RMHI's FBO businesses provided charter support services for the air medical, aerologging, and energy operations as well as for general corporate needs. RMHI currently had FBOs at Donaldson Airport in Greenville, South Carolina, and at Rialto Municipal Airport in Rialto, California. Generally, FBOs served the local charter market, sold aircraft parts and fuel, and provided flight instruction. Jet charter services were available from its hanger and office facilities at the Salt Lake International Airport.

WESTERN HELICOPTERS, INC.

Acquired in 1975, Western Helicopters provided a wide range of helicopter flight services from its base in Rialto, California. With a fleet of seven helicopters and three fixed-wing aircraft, the subsidiary sold parts and fuel to the general aviation public, provided law enforcement flight training and seismic exploration support services, engaged in aerial filming and stunt flying for the motion picture industry, marketed aviation services to federal and state forestry operations, provided pipe and power-line patrol, and offered corporate charter and aircraft maintenance services. In April 1993, Western Helicopters entered into an agreement with Mercy Air, Inc., to jointly operate Mercy's air ambulance service in Southern California, Nevada, and Arizona and jointly manage Western's operations. Profits and losses were to be shared equally among the partners.

AEROPRODUCTS INTERNATIONAL, INC. (AII)

Aeroproducts International, Inc., was incorporated during fiscal 1993 to design and market kits for retrofitting Lama, A-Star, and Bell 222 helicopters with alternative engines. AII was located in Provo, Utah. While the company believed this program had market potential, a market for retrofitted aircraft had not yet developed.

REPAIR, MAINTENANCE, TESTING, AND COMPLETION SERVICES

Located in Provo, Utah, RMHI operated its own comprehensive repair, maintenance, testing, and aircraft modification facility. This facility provided the full spectrum of aviation services necessary to support RMHI's fleet of 116 aircraft and resulted in significant cost savings over having the work done by outside sources. Helicopter operations generally required two to three times the maintenance that fixed-wing aircraft required on a per-flight-hour basis. For fiscal years 1993, 1992, and 1991, maintenance and repair expenses were $15,275,000, $13,385,000, and $11,509,000, respectively, or approximately 17 percent of total operating expenses. These costs were based on flight hours flown and estimated flight-hour cost for each aircraft. The increase in this expense was attributed to the increase in overall flight hours, the increased use of more sophisticated twin-engine aircraft in air-medical operations, and the growing number of operational aircraft.

Services available included component testing and rebuilding, engine overhaul, avionics installation, custom interior configurations, and complete overhaul with all the ancillary activities necessary for such support. The facility was also certified as a helicopter repair facility for many of the world's helicopter manufacturers.

RMHI's MANAGEMENT TEAM

When James B. Burr announced his retirement in March 1993 after serving for 23 years as chairman and CEO, the board of directors appointed J. Russell Spray as acting chairman, president, and CEO of the company. Previously, Mr. Spray had served as RMHI's president and chief operating officer since March 1992. Commenting on Mr. Spray's appointment, Mr. Burr said, "With [Mr. Spray's] success in guiding the company's medical division toward becoming the largest hospital-based air ambulance operator in the world, it seems logical to tap his attributes as they apply to the company's operation in all areas."[19] A brief biographical sketch of each of the key officers in the company follows.

J. Russel Spray Mr. Spray, 46, joined RMHI in 1979 as a lead pilot of one of the company's emergency air transportation programs. His advancement in the company progressed quickly. In 1980 he was appointed eastern regional manager for the medical division, and in 1982 he was promoted to executive director of the division. Since 1986, he had served as RMHI's vice president of the medical division and director of operations. Mr. Spray had over 28 years of experience in the helicopter industry with more than 17 years in management positions.

David R. Anderson Mr. Anderson, 50, joined RMHI in July 1991 after having served as senior vice president of administration and chief financial officer of Valtek Incorporated, a manufacturer of industrial products. He had been with Valtek since 1972. Previously, Mr. Anderson was an auditor at KPMG Peat Marwick, an international accounting firm.

Donald G. Andrews Mr. Andrews, 60, had been the vice president of safety/human resources since May 1982. From 1980 to 1982 he served as the director of safety for

---

[19]E. Walters, "Rocky Mountain Helicopters Announces Appointment of a New Chief Executive Officer," *Business Wire,* March 24, 1993, sec. 1, p. 1.

the company. Prior to joining the company, Mr. Andrews was a professor at Brigham Young University. He was currently the chairman of the safety committee of the Helicopter Association International.

Clair T. Merryweather Mr. Merryweather joined RMHI in 1980 and had served as president of Western Helicopters, Inc.

Bryan J. Burr Since 1989, Mr. Burr, 35, had served as vice president of heavy lift and energy operations, and president of RMH Aerologging, Inc., since May 1991. In 1986 he was appointed operations manager of the company's heavy lift operations. Mr. Burr was the son of the former chairman and CEO, James B. Burr.

John R. Barrie Mr. Barrie had been chief pilot of the company since March 1988. Prior to joining RMHI, he served as operations inspector for the Federal Aviation Administration for over 12 years.

David L. Dolstein Mr. Dolstein joined RMHI in 1981 as a pilot and was promoted to regional manager of the medical group in 1982. In 1984, he was promoted to director of marketing—medical group.

John M. Heiskell Mr. Heiskell had been director of flight operations—medical group since 1985. He joined the company in 1981 as a lead pilot.

RMHI'S FINANCIAL POSITION

Exhibits 11, 12, and 13 present income statements, balance sheets, and cash flow statements for the five-year period ending April 30, 1993. For 1993, RMHI suffered a net loss of $12,902,000 on total revenue of $84,973,000. This record deficit consisted of a net loss from continuing operations of $6,803,000 and a net loss of $6,099,000 from discontinued operations. Although revenue increased by $3,286,000 or 4 percent over 1992, operating expenses increased by almost 17 percent from $76,320,000 to $89,207,000.

The largest contributor to the revenue increase in 1993 was the air medical division, which generated $2,915,000, or 89 percent of all revenue increases. Air Medical renewed or extended nine contracts, expanded four transport systems with additional aircraft, developed two new programs, and terminated two Air Medical contracts. Overall, the air medical segment's contribution margin declined $2,676,000 from $5,770,000 in 1992 to $3,094,000 in 1993. Despite the provision for annual escalation clauses in its long-term medical contracts, some of Air Medical's costs for aircraft and liability insurance, workers' compensation insurance, repair, and maintenance had increased faster than the escalation clauses provided.

In 1993, aerologging operations generated $19.4 million in revenue or approximately 5 percent over 1992 revenues. However, despite this growth, aerologging operations suffered more than $8.3 million in operating losses, compared to losses of $2.7 million in 1992. Approximately $5 million of the 1993 losses were attributed to underbidding aerologging contracts by 31 percent. About $835,000 of the $8.3 million loss could be traced to discounts given by RMHI to RMH Aeroservices, Inc., a corporation owned by two former employees of the company who were sons of

EXHIBIT 11 | **Consolidated Income Statements, Rocky Mountain Helicopters, Fiscal Years 1989–93**

	1993	1992	1991	1990	1989
Revenues					
Operating	$82,754,000	$78,959,000	$71,355,000	$64,376,000	$51,742,000
Gain on equipment sales	2,219,000	2,728,000	1,841,000	1,495,000	339,000
Total revenues	84,973,000	81,687,000	73,196,000	65,871,000	52,081,000
Operating expenses					
Direct operating	36,975,000	29,718,000	26,328,000	22,729,000	19,923,000
Aircraft leases	11,168,000	10,018,000	10,019,000	8,659,000	7,613,000
Pilots and mechanics	16,746,000	14,745,000	13,748,000	12,244,000	10,194,000
Depreciation and amortization	17,220,000	16,163,000	14,014,000	12,388,000	8,470,000
Cost of fuel used	2,391,000	2,401,000	2,202,000	1,959,000	1,222,000
Logging contract judgment	1,300,000	—	—	—	—
General and administrative	3,407,000	3,275,000	2,553,000	2,468,000	1,908,000
Total operating expenses	89,207,000	76,320,000	68,864,000	60,447,000	49,330,000
Operating income (loss)	(4,234,000)	5,367,000	4,332,000	5,424,000	2,751,000
Net interest expense	4,367,000	3,911,000	2,715,000	2,419,000	1,941,000
Income (loss) before income taxes	(8,601,000)	1,456,000	1,617,000	3,005,000	810,000
Income tax provision (benefit)	(1,798,000)	263,000	400,000	351,000	178,000
Net income (loss) from continuing operations	(6,803,000)	1,193,000	1,217,000	2,654,000	632,000
Discontinued operations					
Income (loss) from operations	(4,149,000)	(379,000)	153,000	0	(555,000)
(Loss) on disposal	(1,950,000)	0	0	0	(342,000)
Total discontinued operations	(6,099,000)	(379,000)	153,000	0	(897,000)
Net income (loss)	($12,902,000)	$ 814,000	$ 1,370,000	$ 2,654,000	($265,000)
Earnings per common share					
Income (loss) from continuing operations	($1.49)	$0.34	$0.39	$1.02	$0.24
Income (loss) from discontinued operations	(1.33)	(0.11)	0.05	0.00	(0.34)
Net income (loss)	($2.82)	$0.23	$0.44	$1.02	($0.10)
Weighted average shares outstanding	4,578,938	3,544,901	3,139,457	2,614,030	2,614,030

Source: Company records.

James B. Burr, the former chairman and CEO. After two accidents in 1992 involving single-engine helicopters, the company switched to using twin-engine Sikorsky S-61s, which offered a greater margin of safety and reliability. However, these aircraft had higher operating costs than single-engine helicopters and RMHI ran into difficulty financing an adequate amount of spare parts to keep its four aerologging S-61s flying. In fact, the company flew 400 fewer hours in the fourth quarter of 1993 as compared to the same period in 1992. In an effort to raise cash needed to buy spare parts and keep these helicopters flying, RMHI sold off some sawmill equipment. Even more critical to the aerologging operation were the high fixed costs that included land, land-based and floating camps, heavy equipment, operating and support helicopters, fixed-wing aircraft, and rented hangar and office space.

Collectively, operating revenues for the utility, fixed wing/parts/sales, and Western Helicopters business units remained relatively unchanged with $12,359,000 in 1993, as compared to $12,358,000 for 1992. Parts sales included the operations of the Aero-Products International division, which incurred losses of approximately $900,000.

Weather and seasonal conditions played a big role in RMHI's revenue stream. If weather conditions were adverse, operational flights were restricted, if not totally grounded. The winter months especially had a detrimental effect on flight volume. Since flight volume was one of the key determinants of the company's profitability, a decrease in flight hours translated into a decrease in revenues. Generally, the company was profitable during the summer months (April 15 to October 15) and lacked sufficient flight volume to be profitable during the winter period.

Gains from equipment sales totaled $2,219,000 and $2,728,000 in 1993 and 1992, respectively, for a net decline of $509,000. The 1993 gains resulted from the sale of two aircraft and the crash of three helicopters in the air medical segment. In 1992, five aircraft were sold and four others crashed—two in air medical and two in aerologging operations. Gains from equipment sales were a normal and recurring part of RMHI's business and occurred as the result of aircraft sales and insurance proceeds from helicopter accidents.

Direct operating expenses rose approximately 25 percent to $36,975,000 in 1993. The rise in operating expenses included increases of approximately $1.63 million in cost of goods sold (mostly attributed to $1.58 million increased contract costs related to aerologging operations), $1.99 million in insurance costs, $1.86 million in repair and maintenance expenses, and $1.85 million in workers' compensation insurance, payroll taxes, and employee benefits. The increases in workers' compensation and

EXHIBIT 12 | **Consolidated Balance Sheets, Rocky Mountain Helicopters, Fiscal Years 1989–93**

	1993	1992	1991	1990	1989
Assets					
Current assets					
Cash	$ 52,000	$ 305,000	$ 140,000	$ 205,000	$ 335,000
Accounts receivable, net	10,290,000	9,982,000	9,256,000	7,534,000	7,900,000
Related party receivable	193,000	256,000	263,000	141,000	393,000
Stock subscription receivable				350,000	
Inventories	24,421,000	23,548,000	20,821,000	17,001,000	15,899,000
Prepaid expenses and deposits	1,138,000	517,000	433,000	361,000	196,000
Total current assets	36,094,000	34,608,000	30,913,000	25,592,000	24,723,000
Property and equipment					
Land	851,000	390,000	246,000	122,000	122,000
Buildings and office equipment	9,835,000	8,912,000	6,723,000	4,847,000	2,769,000
Helicopters and other aircraft	60,337,000	50,393,000	44,579,000	30,874,000	26,820,000
Other operational equipment	9,600,000	8,423,000	6,274,000	3,879,000	2,870,000
	80,623,000	68,118,000	57,822,000	39,722,000	32,581,000
Less accumulated depreciation and amortization	(23,237,000)	(18,777,000)	(16,413,000)	(15,179,000)	(13,404,000)
Net property and equipment	57,386,000	49,341,000	41,409,000	24,543,000	19,177,000
Other assets					
Related party notes receivable	29,000	145,000	148,000	674,000	610,000
Miscellaneous	1,531,000	1,941,000	1,779,000	1,186,000	905,000
Total other assets	1,560,000	2,086,000	1,927,000	1,860,000	1,515,000
Total assets	$95,040,000	$86,035,000	$74,249,000	$51,995,000	$45,415,000

(continued)

EXHIBIT 12 | **Consolidated Balance Sheets, Rocky Mountain Helicopters, Fiscal Years 1989–93 (Continued)**

	1993	1992	1991	1990	1989
Liabilities and Equity					
Current liabilities					
Accounts payable	$ 9,049,000	$ 8,259,000	$ 5,546,000	$ 3,736,000	$ 6,061,000
Accrued liabilities	12,350,000	10,416,000	9,521,000	7,864,000	6,563,000
Related party note payable	750,000	0	0	0	0
Current maturities of long-term debt	2,676,000	6,585,000	5,119,000	3,185,000	3,070,000
Current portion of obligations under capital leases	900,000	821,000	622,000	641,000	465,000
Debt and lease obligations in default	38,782,000	0	0	0	0
Total current liabilities	64,507,000	26,081,000	20,808,000	15,426,000	16,159,000
Long-term debt, net of current portion	12,087,000	30,945,000	26,364,000	18,061,000	17,484,000
Obligations under capital leases, net of current portion	3,413,000	5,065,000	3,815,000	2,075,000	1,706,000
Accrued aircraft maintenance costs	3,892,000	3,052,000	3,429,000	3,984,000	3,422,000
Deferred income taxes	0	1,798,000	1,535,000	1,135,000	949,000
Deferred gain on sale, configuration and leaseback of aircraft	1,661,000	2,076,000	2,668,000	2,400,000	1,622,000
Deferred lease accrual	2,856,000	3,093,000	2,938,000	2,367,000	1,530,000
Stockholders' equity					
Common stock, $.02 par value; authorized 10,000,000 shares; issued 1993—5,372,291; 1992—4,155,568 shares 1991—3,139,457	107,000	83,000	81,000	63,000	53,000
Additional paid-in capital	12,580,000	7,003,000	6,586,000	1,829,000	489,000
Retained earnings (accumulated deficit)	(5,671,000)	7,231,000	6,417,000	5,047,000	2,393,000
	7,016,000	14,317,000	13,084,000	6,939,000	2,935,000
Less treasury stock at cost, 543,760 shares	(392,000)	(392,000)	(392,000)	(392,000)	(392,000)
Total stockholders' equity	6,624,000	13,925,000	12,692,000	6,547,000	2,543,000
Total liabilities and stockholders' equity	$95,040,000	$86,035,000	$74,249,000	$51,995,000	$45,415,000

Source: Company records.

insurance costs were directly related to the company's past safety record in helicopter operations and timber-related accidents. To minimize these costs, the company had continued to emphasize safety and had started contracting out for many of its timber-related tasks. Other direct operating expenses such as aircraft leases, pilot and mechanic salaries, fuel, depreciation, and interest expense were a function of the size of the company's fleet, type of aircraft flown, and number of flight hours flown.

General and administrative expense increased by 4 percent to $132,000 in 1993. The largest contributor to this increase was travel-related costs. The company believed that travel costs should diminish in the future due to discontinuation of several operations.

RMHI's total debt position at the end of fiscal year 1993 was $86,755,000 of which $38,782,000 represented debt and lease obligations in default. Because the company could not comply with certain covenants related to its loan agreements with certain long-term lenders, the defaulted debt appeared as current debt on the consolidated balance sheet.

EXHIBIT 13 | Consolidated Statements of Cash Flows, Rocky Mountain Helicopters, Fiscal Years 1989–93

	1993	1992	1991	1990	1989
Cash Flows from Operating Activities					
Net income (loss) continuing operations	($ 6,803,000)	$ 1,193,000	$ 1,217,000	$ 2,654,000	($ 265,000)
Adjustments to reconcile net income (loss) to net cash provided by (used in)					
Operating activities:					
Discontinued operations	(5,518,000)	(641,000)	(477,000)	0	0
Depreciation and amortization	17,220,000	16,163,000	14,009,000	12,388,000	8,470,000
Addition to aircraft components	(9,215,000)	(12,825,000)	(12,110,000)	(9,662,000)	(7,534,000)
Recognition of deferred gains	(50,000)	(324,000)	(214,000)	(165,000)	(133,000)
Deferred income taxes	(1,798,000)	263,000	400,000	186,000	59,000
Gain on disposition of aircraft	(2,219,000)	(2,728,000)	(1,841,000)	(1,495,000)	(339,000)
Common stock issued to company pension plan	340,000	301,000	68,000	0	0
Change in assets and liabilities net of effects of discontinued operations:					
Inventories	(1,664,000)	(3,169,000)	(3,430,000)	(1,102,000)	(3,374,000)
Accounts receivable	600,000	(797,000)	(873,000)	618,000	(1,323,000)
Prepaid expenses and deposits	(665,000)	1,000	(48,000)	(165,000)	(68,000)
Miscellaneous other assets	(53,000)	(85,000)	74,000	(417,000)	(35,000)
Accounts payable	1,684,000	2,193,000	1,694,000	(2,325,000)	2,576,000
Accrued liabilities	221,000	360,000	2,018,000	2,864,000	1,207,000
Total adjustments	(1,117,000)	(1,288,000)	(730,000)	725,000	(494,000)
Net cash provided by (used in) operating activities	$(7,920,000)	$(95,000)	$487,000	$3,379,000	$(759,000)
Cash Flows from Investing Activities					
Capital expenditures	(12,308,000)	(14,425,000)	(19,463,000)	(9,507,000)	(5,105,000)
Proceeds from aircraft dispositions	6,820,000	9,316,000	7,034,000	3,093,000	1,826,000
Payments to lessors on aircraft dispositions	(2,192,000)	(423,000)	(2,291,000)	(275,000)	(1,101,000)
Net cash used in investing activities	(7,680,000)	(5,532,000)	(14,720,000)	(6,689,000)	(4,380,000)
Cash Flows from Financing Activities					
Proceeds from sale of common stock	155,000	119,000	4,333,000	1,000,000	0
Additional long-term liabilities	21,924,000	17,279,000	18,070,000	5,842,000	7,711,000
Principal payments	(6,732,000)	(11,709,000)	(8,837,000)	(4,605,000)	(3,373,000)
Deferred gain from completion of aircraft	0	103,000	602,000	943,000	742,000
Net cash from financing activities	15,347,000	5,792,000	14,168,000	3,180,000	5,080,000
Net increase (decrease) in cash	(253,000)	165,000	(65,000)	(130,000)	(59,000)
Cash, beginning of year	305,000	140,000	205,000	335,000	394,000
Cash, end of year	$ 52,000	$ 305,000	$ 140,000	$ 205,000	$ 335,000

Source: Company records.

Working capital needs were financed under a revolving credit line with Washington Square Capital, Inc., up to $14.5 million. RMHI was currently in an over-advance position on its credit line. Washington Square had permitted over advances in the past by agreement. Interest on the line of credit was paid monthly based on the outstanding balance based on a weighted average of the prime rate at three large commercial banks plus 2⅜ percent. Currently, RMHI and Washington Square were negotiating refinancing the line of credit and increasing the line to $18.5 million.

While it had managed to restructure some of its other debt obligations, RMHI still remained in default with many other creditors. As a result, some of the company's vendors had imposed cash-on-delivery terms. With respect to income taxes, the company had available income tax credits and operating loss carryforwards of $18.97 million to offset future income taxes payable.

As noted previously, RMHI's diversification strategy resulted in the acquisition of two lumber remanufacturing plants, the start-up of a regional commuter airline, and a machine tool company. However, these operations proved unprofitable and siphoned off cash from other profitable operations, putting added strain on an already tenuous financial situation. In 1993, RMHI divested these unprofitable operations. Collectively, the three discontinued operations used $5.5 million, $641,000, and $477,000 in cash in 1993, 1992, and 1991, respectively. RMHI's new corporate strategy was to concentrate on core business competencies and to continue efforts to divest nonperforming operations and nonproductive assets.

Cash flows from operations had been inadequate to support the company's substantial investments in capital equipment and the expansion of operations. RMHI had a negative net cash flow from operations in 1993 of $7.92 million. Key sources of cash flow included additional long-term borrowings of $21.9 million, depreciation and amortization expenses of $17.2 million, and proceeds from aircraft dispositions of $6.82 million.

LITIGATION

RMHI was a party to various legal actions. As the result of a helicopter crash that killed and injured several employees in 1992, the company was the defendant in a wrongful death and personal injury claim. The lawsuit sought damages in excess of the company's insurance coverage. In another court case involving an alleged breach of an oral contract related to helicopter logging services, the company lost the case but was appealing. The consolidated financial statements included an accrual for $1.3 million pending outcome of the appeal.

RMHI'S STRATEGY

RMHI intended to continue to be a major player in the air medical services industry. Although future growth was expected to be slower than during the 1980s as the industry adjusted to change, management believed the demand for medical helicopter air transportation services would still remain attractive. As such, the company planned to selectively seek new contracts to provide safe, fast, and cost-efficient transportation of the critically ill and injured. The company hoped to build on its reputation for excellence and leadership in the air medical transportation industry.

With respect to its aerologging business, RMHI planned to continue focusing on building long-term exclusive contractual relationships with the major timber companies located in southeast Alaska. A key strategic goal was to become a major player in this industry.

As for the energy markets, the firm planned to maintain its share of this segment, but did not plan to expand in this area for the near term.

Management planned for fixed-wing assets and the FBOs to continue to support the air medical operations segment. The FBOs expected to continue to sell fuel and parts, and provide charter service and flight instruction. RMHI also planned to market its repair, maintenance, testing, completion, and engine retrofitting services to nonaffiliated customers as well as to use such services to support existing company operations.

RMHI'S MAJOR COMPETITORS IN AIR MEDICAL SERVICES

The air medical service industry consisted of a number of capable operators providing aviation services to the health care industry. RMHI's principal competitors in the air medical market were Air Methods Corporation in Englewood, Colorado; Corporate Jets, Inc., in Pittsburgh, Pennsylvania; Omniflight Helicopters, Inc., in Charleston, South Carolina; and Petroleum Helicopters, Inc., in Layfayette, Louisiana. Exhibit 14 presents the major competitors and their respective market positions.

Air Methods Corporation[20] Air Methods Corporation (AMC) considered itself one of the largest, exclusive providers of state-of-the-art emergency air medical systems and services to hospitals throughout the United States and North America. It operated and managed 30 helicopters and 12 airplanes serving 54 hospitals in 14 states. AMC differentiated itself from many of its competitors by exclusively using Instrument Flight Rules ("IFR")-certified equipment and IFR-rated pilots. This provided client hospitals with higher degrees of navigational capability (including flying in adverse weather), flight safety, and navigational accuracy than was ordinarily available using more limited Visual Flight Rules ("VFR")-certified equipment and pilots without instrument ratings. Pilots and helicopter support crews were based at client hospitals to facilitate operations and maintain a high level of readiness. Because AMC was privately-held, no data was available concerning its operating and financial performance.

Corporate Jets, Inc. Corporate Jets, Inc. (CJI), was a private corporation founded in 1969 by Fred S. Shaulis, who remained its sole stockholder and chairman. CJI entered the medical aviation field in 1981 when it began providing specialized jet

E X H I B I T 14 | **Number of Contracts to Provide Air Medical Services, 1986–92**

Operator Contracts	1992	1991	1990	1989	1988	1987	1986
Rocky Mountain	43	43	43	42	38	35	31
Omniflight	28	40	40	22	21	18	15
Air Methods	15	12	12	9	9	8	7
Corporate Jets	13	11	11	unknown	unknown	unknown	unknown
Petroleum	9	8	9	9	8	4	2
St. Louis	6	6	6	6	5	5	4
Metro Aviation	5	5	6	6	5	4	4
Keystone	6	6	5	5	4	3	2
Indianapolis	7	4	unknown	unknown	unknown	unknown	unknown
Hospital Air	2	2	4	4	3	4	2
Other*	22	19	22	22	23	19	25
Hospital**	19	18	14	14	13	17	11

*Operators with two or less contracts.
**Hospitals with own flight department.
Source: *Journal of Air Medical Transport,* July 1992, p. 28.

[20]Extracted from AMC 10-K, 1992.

transportation for the Pittsburgh Transplant Foundation's organ procurement program. Since then, CJI had grown to become one of the nation's largest airborne emergency medical service companies with approximately 625 employees. The company currently managed 17 hospital-based programs utilizing 30 helicopters and one airplane. Helicopter air medical services accounted for 26 percent of the company's estimated total revenue of approximately $19 million in 1993.[21]

Omniflight Helicopters, Inc. Omniflight Helicopters, Inc., was a subsidiary of Omniflight, Inc., a private corporation founded in 1962. As a private organization, the company had a policy of not disclosing information on the company or its operations to the public. However, the *1993 Directory of Corporate Affiliations* estimated Omniflight's revenues to be in the $49 to $59 million range. Omniflight had approximately 450 employees and 82 helicopters (an unknown number of which were assigned to air medical transport services).

Petroleum Helicopters, Inc.[22] Petroleum Helicopters, Inc. (PHI), was established in 1949 and provided helicopter transportation service to companies engaged in offshore oil and gas development and production. For the fiscal year ending April 30, 1993, this primary business segment represented approximately 77 percent of PHI's operating revenues of $171.8 million. The remaining 23 percent of operating revenues came from aeromedical, international, and technical services.

Overall demand for PHI's offshore oil and gas transportation services began to decline in 1991 as a result of reduced exploration and production activity in the domestic Gulf. This trend continued into early 1993, which negatively impacted operating revenues over this period by $20.8 million. Management responded to these trends by expanding marketing efforts in the aeromedical and international arenas and by significantly reducing PHI's helicopter fleet and workforce. As a result of the increased marketing emphasis, aeromedical and international flight activities increased 14.8 percent over 1992 levels to $29 million in 1993.

PHI operated the largest commercial helicopter fleet in the world, a total of 258 helicopters, of which 226 were based in the U.S. Gulf of Mexico region. In 1993, PHI had 1,838 employees, including 549 pilots, 865 mechanics, and 424 in flight operations and administration.

RMHI'S COMPETITORS IN AEROLOGGING

RMHI's main competitor and industry leader in the aerologging helicopter industry was Columbia Helicopters, based in Portland, Oregon. Several other competitors in this industry were significantly smaller than Columbia Helicopters and none was considered a major competitor of RMHI.

Columbia Helicopters, Inc.[23] Columbia Helicopters, Inc. (CHI), was a private corporation founded in 1957 by Wes Lematta when he bought a used Hiller 12B helicopter. The first year of operation was slow. Between occasional rides given at county fairs

---

[21]Company profile developed from information provided by David P. Franc, air medical systems liaison at CJI.
[22]Extracted from PHI *Annual Report* and 10-K, 1993.
[23]CHI's profile extracted from information provided to the casewriter by CHI.

and some construction projects, Lematta somehow managed to pay his bills. In 1958, his fledgling operation got a shot in the arm when Lematta gained national recognition after rescuing 17 seamen from a sinking dredge off Coos Bay, Oregon, with his Hiller 12B. That recognition set the stage for new customers and continuing growth of the company.

By 1962, CHI's business included basic helicopter charter, contract services, and helicopter flight training. During the 1960s CHI continued to grow and to add additional helicopter assets to its fleet. CHI's entry into the aerologging business followed shortly after it acquired seven Boeing BV-107 tandem rotor helicopters in 1972 from the then defunct New York Airways. CHI had since become the leader in the aerologging industry, harvesting more timber per year than all other aerologging operators combined. A single BV-107 helicopter could log over 2 million pounds, or approximately 40 log truck loads, of timber per day. In 1992, CHI transported a total load of over 1.6 million tons, a load equivalent to 64,000 log truck loads. Currently, CHI's logging helicopter fleet consisted of 12 Boeing BV-107s and five Boeing Chinook 234s, also tandem rotor heavy-lift machines.

CHI's distinctive advantage in this industry centered on its fleet of heavy-lift helicopters and its flight crews who were highly skilled and experienced at long line (external load) operations. This process involved moving heavy loads of logs at the end of lines up to 300 feet long with speed and precision. In addition, the company's logging department was staffed by professional logging engineers who traveled worldwide on timber appraisals involving aerologging. CHI's logging crews were trained to know log scaling procedures, log weights, defect, and grade.

Aerologging represented a significant portion of CHI's business. Normally 60 to 70 percent of its fleet was engaged in logging operations. The remainder of its helicopter resources were dedicated to supporting oil drilling rigs in remote locations around the world, electric power transmission line construction, rooftop placement of heavy equipment, and fire fighting. Because it was a private company, specific financial and operating figures for CHI were not available.

RMHI's Competition in Other Business Segments

RMHI's competitors in the energy exploration market in the Rocky Mountain area consisted only of several small operators. RMHI set itself apart from the competition by emphasizing its service and support capabilities, fleet flexibility, and expertise in reducing flight time and aircraft downtime.

As for fixed-wing operations and FBOs, the competition consisted of other FBOs in the same local markets. Competition for charter services was keen and often based on lowest cost.

RMHI'S FUTURE

Considering the company's dismal performance in 1993, Mr. Spray was confronted with some tough decisions if RMHI was to remain competitive. As he reviewed his company's present situation, he pondered his most pressing concerns: restructuring the company's debt and satisfying its lenders, developing and maintaining profitable operations, and generating positive cash flows to sustain the future viability and growth of the firm.

IMPLEMENTING AND EXECUTING STRATEGY

ROBIN HOOD

Joseph Lampel, New York University

It was in the spring of the second year of his insurrection against the High Sheriff of Nottingham that Robin Hood took a walk in Sherwood forest. As he walked he pondered the progress of the campaign, the disposition of his forces, the Sheriff's recent moves, and the options that confronted him.

The revolt against the Sheriff had begun as a personal crusade. It erupted out of Robin's conflict with the Sheriff and his administration. However, alone Robin Hood could do little. He therefore sought allies, men with grievances and a deep sense of justice. Later he welcomed all who came, asking few questions, and demanding only a willingness to serve. Strength, he believed, lay in numbers.

He spent the first year forging the group into a disciplined band, united in enmity against the Sheriff, and willing to live outside the law. The band's organization was simple. Robin ruled supreme, making all important decisions. He delegated specific tasks to his lieutenants. Will Scarlett was in charge of intelligence and scouting. His main job was to shadow the Sheriff and his men, always alert to their next move. He also collected information on the travel plans of rich merchants and tax collectors. Little John kept discipline among the men, and saw to it that their archery was at the high peak that their profession demanded. Scarlock took care of the finances, converting loot to cash, paying shares of the take, and finding suitable hiding places for the surplus. Finally, Much the Miller's son had the difficult task of provisioning the ever-increasing band of Merrymen.

The increasing size of the band was a source of satisfaction for Robin, but also a source of concern. The fame of his Merrymen was spreading, and new recruits poured in from every corner of England. As the band grew larger, their small bivouac became a major encampment. Between raids the men milled about, talking and playing games. Vigilance was in decline, and discipline was becoming harder to enforce. "Why," Robin reflected, "I don't know half the men I run into these days."

Copyright © 1991 by Joseph Lampel.

The growing band was also beginning to exceed the food capacity of the forest. Game was becoming scarce, and supplies had to be obtained from outlying villages. The cost of buying food was beginning to drain the band's financial reserves at the very moment when revenues were in decline. Travelers, especially those with the most to lose, were now giving the forest a wide berth. This was costly and inconvenient to them, but it was preferable to having all their goods confiscated.

Robin believed that the time had come for the Merrymen to change their policy of outright confiscation of goods to one of a fixed transit tax. His lieutenants strongly resisted this idea. They were proud of the Merrymen's famous motto: "Rob from the rich and give to the poor." "The farmers and the townspeople," they argued, "are our most important allies. How can we tax them, and still hope for their help in our fight against the Sheriff?"

Robin wondered how long the Merrymen could keep to the ways and methods of their early days. The Sheriff was growing stronger and becoming better organized. He now had the money and the men, and was beginning to harass the band, probing for its weaknesses. The tide of events was beginning to turn against the Merrymen. Robin felt that the campaign must be decisively concluded before the Sheriff had a chance to deliver a mortal blow. "But how," he wondered, "could this be done?"

Robin had often entertained the possibility of killing the Sheriff, but the chances for this seemed increasingly remote. Besides, killing the Sheriff might satisfy his personal thirst for revenge, but it would not improve the situation. Robin had hoped that the perpetual state of unrest, and the Sheriff's failure to collect taxes, would lead to his removal from office. Instead, the Sheriff used his political connections to obtain reinforcement. He had powerful friends at court, and was well regarded by the regent, Prince John.

Prince John was vicious and volatile. He was consumed by his unpopularity among the people, who wanted the imprisoned King Richard back. He also lived in constant fear of the barons, who had first given him the regency, but were now beginning to dispute his claim to the throne. Several of these barons had set out to collect the ransom that would release King Richard the Lionheart from his jail in Austria. Robin was invited to join the conspiracy in return for future amnesty. It was a dangerous proposition. Provincial banditry was one thing, court intrigue another. Prince John had spies everywhere and he was known for his vindictiveness. If the conspirators' plan failed, the pursuit would be relentless, and retribution swift.

The sound of the supper horn startled Robin from his thoughts. There was the smell of roasting venison in the air. Nothing was resolved or settled. Robin headed for camp promising himself that he would give these problems his utmost attention after tomorrow's raid.

QUEENSLAND MINERALS LIMITED

Peter Killing, The University of Western Ontario

Don Jackson, vice president of the metals division of Amcon Corporation and the manager of the company's worldwide toranium business, put down the telephone with a smile. He had just learned that the company's recently expanded toranium smelter in Pittsburgh had successfully met all of its emission and economic targets for its first six months of operation. Pittsburgh's performance was good news for the metals division as it was the first full-scale test of the division's new Micron refining process, and it appeared to be an unqualified success.

Jackson's smile grew particularly broad as he considered Amcon's plans for a major expansion of Queensland Minerals. Located in Australia, Queensland operated the world's largest toranium mining and smelting operation and was equally owned by Amcon and Victoria Heavy Industries (VHI). In the past, Jackson had had difficulty convincing VHI that Queensland should be expanded, but, with the low emission levels and energy savings offered by the Micron process, he thought that he should now be able to carry the day.

THE PARENT COMPANIES

Amcon Corporation and Victoria Heavy Industries were among the world's largest natural resource companies. Approximately the same size, the two companies competed around the world in a variety of markets. They also frequently cooperated. Although the Queensland venture was their largest alliance, Amcon and VHI worked together in a variety of other joint exploration ventures in remote corners of the world.

Amcon had been founded by an American prospector whose extravagant ways and propensity to gamble on unproven mineral deposits had brought the company to the

Certain names and other identifying information may have been disguised to protect confidentiality. Copyright 1992 © The University of Western Ontario. Used with permission.

point of bankruptcy more than once. After one particularly harrowing experience, disgruntled shareholders united to eject the entrepreneur and hire professional managers, with a mandate to bring more discipline to the organization. Amcon subsequently developed an industrywide reputation for sound financial management practices, and for always having its homework done. VHI, on the other hand, often reminded Amcon managers of their own company in its earlier days. Amcon managers saw their VHI counterparts as less disciplined than themselves and operating with a greater degree of autonomy than would have been possible in Amcon. Whether these generalizations were true or not, what was evident for all to see was that Amcon and VHI were the two most profitable companies in the industry, and the rivalry between them was high.

As indicated in Exhibit 1, both Amcon and VHI had a metals division, and, in each company, this division accounted for more than 50 percent of total revenue and profit. Don Jackson and Sam Ziff ran the toranium business in their respective companies, and each had prime responsibility for Queensland Minerals.

QUEENSLAND MINERALS

Queensland Minerals was believed to be the lowest-cost toranium-producing facility in the world. Its profits were of major importance to the metals divisions of both Amcon and VHI.

Although each parent owned 50 percent of Queensland, the venture agreement called for VHI to operate the company, which it had done since the birth of the alliance eight years earlier. In practice, this meant that the venture was staffed and managed on a day-to-day basis by VHI. The board of directors, which contained four members from each parent company, met quarterly to review performance and approve the annual operating and capital budgets. Don Jackson was on the board, along with John Pitman, the president of Amcon's metals division, Len Major, the vice president of finance for Amcon Corporation, and David Ringwood, the president of Amcon's Australian subsidiary.

Queensland's outlook was promising, as demand for toranium was growing, particularly in Japan, and, in the opinion of Jackson, expanding the output of the facility had been a viable economic proposition for the past four years. VHI had resisted Jackson's continued recommendations for expansion, however, arguing that the environmental issues were too great and expansion would never be approved by the government. To make matters worse, a request for permission to expand would focus the attention of environmental groups on the operation. When the Micron process was first completed, Jackson had tried to convince Sam Ziff that the time was right for expansion. Although Ziff had seemed to favor the idea, he had come back with the comment that his fellow managers wanted to see Amcon first use the process in one of its own smelters, to make sure that it really worked. Now, two years later, Jackson had the evidence that he needed, and the time for the long overdue expansion in Australia had arrived.

ARRIVAL IN MELBOURNE

Two weeks later, Don Jackson was in Melbourne, meeting with David Ringwood.

Don Jackson: As I told you over the phone, David, the Pittsburgh expansion has gone according to plan, and we are now in a position to make a solid proposal to VHI and Queensland for a 30 percent expansion of the Queensland

EXHIBIT 1 | **Partial Organization Charts**

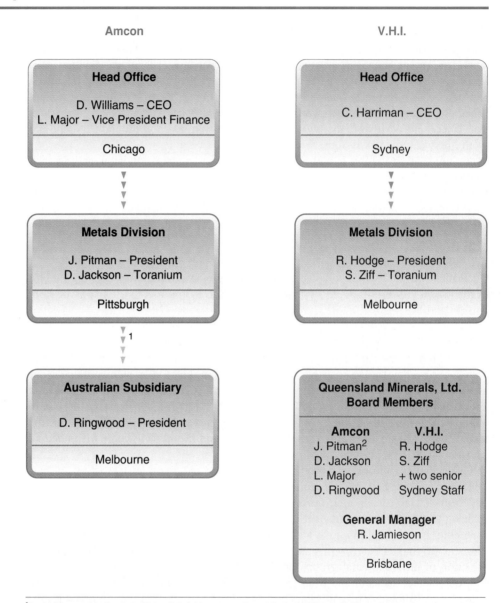

[1]David Ringwood had a dotted-line relationship to a number of Amcon divisions, as his company operated in multiple product areas. Queensland was, however, Amcon's most important investment in Australia.
[2]J. Pitman was currently chairman of the Queensland board. In eight months, the position would move to R. Hodge as part of a regular two-year cycle.

mining operation and the smelter. I would like Ralph Samson [a Pittsburgh-based staff analyst] to work with one of your people to update the numbers on the project, but I don't believe that will take very long. The projected return on investment for the expansion will be higher than any other project that we have in the pipeline, and I would guess that will be true for VHI as well. I think we should plan to make a proposal to them in about a month. My feeling is that we should target Jamieson (Queensland Minerals' general manager) and his management team first, and then let them sell it to VHI's Queensland board members. Meanwhile, I will get Pitman and Major up to speed so they know what we are pushing for. Does this sound OK to you, David?

David Ringwood: I don't think that this is going to be as simple as that, Don. I know that, historically, VHI executives have always said that they did not want to expand Queensland, because of the environmental issues, but now there is a lot more to it than that. As you know, for the past two years, VHI has been trying to expand one of their coal mines in northern Australia, and they are now in the middle of an acrimonious dispute regarding aboriginal rights and sacred ground in the outback. The last thing that they want is to present the Australian government with another expansion proposal, no matter how environmentally improved it is.

I have proposed that I talk directly to the government to explain the benefits of the Micron process, but VHI does not want me to. They have made it clear that this is their country, and they do not want us wandering the halls of power interfering in their existing relationships.

Anyway, Don, even without this problem, I would argue that Jamieson is having so much difficulty operating the mine at current levels that we should not push for expansion right now. Since VHI reorganized their metals division a year ago to make it meaner and leaner, the efficiency of Queensland has been falling steadily. Remember that discussion at the last board meeting, about the fact that operating costs have risen from $45 to $48 per ton over the past six months? I think that we are going to see that trend continue, unless we get some changes made.

What seems to be happening is that the VHI metals division staff backup that Jamieson's people had relied on is no longer there, and it is making a difference—although they will not admit it. I am trying to get Jamieson to take more Amcon people into his operation—we have six in there at the moment—but they see our people as meddling in their affairs. Jamieson has made it clear that *they* are the operators, and the operation is theirs to run.

Don Jackson: Yes, I remember the cost discussion, but didn't Jamieson explain that costs were rising because they were now taking material from a more difficult area of the mine . . . they have done the easy stuff was the way I think he put it.

David Ringwood: That's what he said, but it is only partly true. The real problem, which I have learned from the engineers that we have in Queensland, is that Jamieson has a couple of supervisors two levels below him that are doing a poor job and need to be replaced. Of course no one will listen to their opinion. I even brought the matter up with Ziff, privately, but got nowhere. He says that issues like that are not the concern of the board. In his view, Jamieson is making good money, and the way prices are going, he is going to make even better money. He says it's not our job to tell him how to manage his people. I think that we had better bring the issue up at the next board meeting . . . and I think, Don, that this definitely has to take precedence over the expansion issue.

Don Jackson: David, I appreciate that we have to keep on top of Jamieson with respect to the existing operation, but this expansion *has* to happen. Williams and Pitman are both counting on it, and that means my head is on the line. Everyone knows that the Micron process is a winner, and I can't just go back and say that the Australians don't want it. That's not good enough. Anyway, if we don't move very soon, I am sure that Torcan, our Canadian competitor, is going to expand their mine in Ontario. I want to forestall that if I can, by announcing our own expansion.

I understand that VHI has some problems with their coal mine expansion, but Sam Ziff has not said anything to me to the effect that this will hold up the expansion of Queensland. I'll discuss the issue with him tomorrow.

MEETING WITH SAM ZIFF

The following morning Don Jackson met with Sam Ziff in Ziff's Melbourne office, which was about two blocks from the office tower in which Amcon's Australian head office was housed. Ziff said that he was delighted to learn of the success of the Micron process, but explained that, while he fully supported the expansion of the Queensland operation, the timing was not ideal.

Sam Ziff: I understand your impatience, Don, but please bear with us on this. We have a number of sensitive negotiations under way with the government at the moment, and adding one more might well destroy what is already a very shaky situation . . . and both our companies would be losers if that happened. Remember that we have 20 years of reserves in the Queensland mine, and a year or so here or there is not going to make much difference in the overall success of the project. In fact the way toranium prices are moving up . . . and are likely to continue to increase . . . selling our output later at a higher price might not be a bad idea.

LATER THE SAME DAY

Later the same day a very frustrated Don Jackson was back in David Ringwood's office discussing the situation with Ringwood and Peter Harper, a mining engineer who had been working for Queensland for a year, although he remained on the payroll of Amcon Australia.

Don Jackson: I cannot believe these people! Who does Ziff think he is, saying that the timing is "not ideal"! He has known for two years that this was coming. Did he hope that the Micron process would fail? Pitman is going to have my head.

David Ringwood: I think that you should give up on the expansion for the time being, Don. VHI will not give in on this one, no matter how high you go up the ladder. They have too much at stake, and for them the expansion of Queensland is not a major issue. Did you tell him that Jamieson needs to fire a couple of people?

Don Jackson: I decided not to get into it. Ziff and the other VHI directors give Jamieson a very free hand . . . so there did not seem to be much point. They simply do not control things as tightly as we do. Unfortunately that 15-page agreement that we signed 10 years ago to establish this venture does not help much. If we were doing this deal today we would have 200 pages, and a lot more disclosure and control!

David Ringwood: Well, maybe it is time for a change in the agreement. I have been thinking for some time that our lives would be a lot easier if we operated the Queensland venture ourselves. If we were the operator, we could solve these immediate production issues, and we could influence the timing of the expansion as well. Given the Australian government's attitude to foreign investment, I don't think that we should try for 51 percent ownership, but we should be able to keep the ownership at 50 percent and have us as the operator. What do you think, Peter?

Peter Harper: I think that would be great. Trying to influence Queensland managers from positions like mine inside the venture is hopeless. We do our technical homework and sometimes they use it, but more often they ignore it. We don't usually get invited to the meetings where the decisions are made, and we only find out afterward if our arguments carried the day.

If we were the operator, we could end the constant frustration and wasted effort that this relationship currently involves. Time after time we have done our homework and they have not, and time after time they ignore us. I don't just mean me, Don; I am thinking of your lack of results with Ziff a couple of years ago, and I could quote lots of other examples. We are always right, and we can prove it, but they don't care! I don't know how to get them to listen.

I have tried to get them to accept more of our engineers—after all, we are not costing them anything—but it is pretty clear that we have reached the limit. They see us as Amcon spies who add some value, but are often more trouble than we are worth, because of what we report back to you guys. As operator, we could really clean this place up.

Don Jackson: Do you two think that this is realistic? Why would VHI give up being the operator? There is a lot of pride involved here. If the positions were reversed, we certainly would not yield. What arguments could we use? Having said that, I do think that you two are right. Maybe it is time for a fundamental change in this relationship. Setting aside a move to us as the operating partner, we have three choices. (moving to flipchart)

1. We buy out VHI's interest. Would they sell? Would the government let it happen? Would Pitman and Williams go for it?
2. We sell our interest in Queensland. Would they buy? Could we get a good price? Would Williams and Pitman go for it?
3. Establish a new 50-50 management structure. Would it work? Could we sell the idea to both sides?

What I mean by the third alternative is that we would change the management structure to reflect the fact that we are equal partners in this venture. So far, they have dominated everything. What if we changed the arrangement so that half of Jamieson's management team were our people. We could also supply half the engineers, half the operating people, and so on. Then we could influence the operating issues and the strategic stuff, like this expansion. This makes a lot more sense than trying to influence them from the outside, as we are at present. The board would also start getting better information. At the moment, Jamieson tells us whatever he wants to. I never feel that we get the full picture.

I think that this last alternative is the best. David, will you help me work up a proposal for Pitman on this?

SHENANDOAH POWER COMPANY: WESTHAVEN DISTRICT

Faculty of the Global Utility Institute, Samford University

On the morning of July 12, 1993, Rick Barton, manager of the Westhaven district of Shenandoah Power Company, was reading a memorandum addressed to all budget heads. The memorandum indicated that the State Utility Rate Commission (URC) had disallowed certain promotional expenditures by Shenandoah's corporate marketing department. The result of this ruling would likely cause a reduction of Shenandoah's revenues for the current year. The memorandum indicated that Shenandoah was likely to appeal the ruling; however, the revenues in question would be held in escrow pending a final resolution of the conflict with the URC.

The memorandum also pointed out what Rick had previously recognized, that the abnormally warm winter and rainy spring had reduced Shenandoah's revenues by about 7 percent below budget through June 30. The current load forecast for the remainder of the year, while improved over the first half, suggested that Shenandoah would fall short of its revenue target by about 4 percent for the year.

The combination of the reduced load and the recent URC ruling had prompted Shenandoah's senior management to request that budget heads "examine all possible avenues of cost reduction, to permit the company to reach its earnings targets for 1993!"

Rick examined the district's financial reports for June (see Exhibits 1 and 2). "I wish they'd make it clear what they want me to do," he muttered to himself. He went on thinking:

> The only costs I can effectively reduce are my direct costs, and yet these amount to less than 5 percent of my total operating revenue. I could slash those by 10 percent and not make much contribution to the corporate targets. Over 75 percent of the cost on my contribution report is tied up in generation and transmission costs. That's where the company could achieve real cost reduction. I'm going to raise this issue the next time I talk with Bob Quinn (vice president, Northern area).
>
> At least now we get credit for the revenues generated within the district. Our contribution for the last two months has been up, largely because of some added growth in the eastern part of the district and because of hot weather the last three weeks of June. But we're still running behind what we had budgeted for the first six months. And this

---

Names, places, and certain other information have been disguised. Copyright, 1994, by the Samford University Foundation and Southern Company College.

EXHIBIT 1 | **Contribution Report for Westhaven District, June 1993** *(In $000)*

	June Year -To- Date			Yearly Totals		
	1993 Actual Amount	1993 Budget Amount	1992 Actual Amount	1993 Forecast Amount	1993 Budget Amount	1992 Actual Amount
Electricity sales (in kilowatt hours)	602,003	607,897	578,283	1,226,273	1,231,013	1,172,012
Booked retail kwh sales	$38,004	$38,385	$36,474	$77,425	$77,800	$73,998
Other revenues	327	325	245	775	775	710
	38,331	38,710	36,719	78,200	78,575	74,708
Less:						
Variable generation and transmission	10,881	10,990	10,543	23,060	23,190	22,247
Fixed generation and transmission	18,600	18,600	17,675	37,200	37,200	35,373
Generation and transmission costs	29,481	29,590	28,218	60,260	60,390	57,620
Gross margin	8,850	9,120	8,501	17,940	18,185	17,088
Less:						
Direct controllable costs	1,874	1,810	1,739	3,725	3,700	3,626
Demand services costs	232	230	224	465	460	446
District asset costs	1,452	1,450	1,395	2,875	2,900	2,814
Total District O&M costs	3,558	3,490	3,358	7,065	7,060	6,886
Operating margin	5,292	5,630	5,143	10,875	11,125	10,202
Less: Allocated direct support costs	1,470	1,430	1,397	2,900	2,860	2,774
Contribution	3,822	4,200	3,746	7,975	8,265	7,428
Total costs	$34,509	$34,510	$32,973	$70,225	$70,310	$67,280

EXHIBIT 2 | **Percent Comparison for Westhaven District, June 1993**

	June Year To Date			Yearly Totals		
	1993 Actual to Budget	1993 Actual to Last Year	1992 Budget to Last Year	1993 Forecast To Budget	1993 Forecast to Last Year	1992 Budget to Last Year
Electricity sales (in kWhs)	−1.0%	4.1%	5.1%	−0.4%	4.6%	5.0%
Booked retail KWH sales	−1.0	4.2	5.2	−0.5	4.6	5.1
Other revenues	0.6	33.5	32.7	0.0	9.2	9.2
	−1.0	4.4	5.4	−0.5	4.7	5.2
Less:						
Variable generation and transmission	−1.0	3.2	4.2	−0.6	3.7	4.2
Fixed generation and transmission	0.0	5.2	5.2	0.0	5.2	5.2
Generation and transmission costs	−0.4	4.5	4.9	−0.2	4.6	4.8
Gross margin	−3.0	4.1	7.3	−1.3	5.0	6.4
Less:						
Direct controllable costs	3.5	7.8	4.1	0.7	2.7	2.0
Demand services costs	0.9	3.6	2.7	1.1	4.3	3.1
District asset costs	0.1	4.1	3.9	−0.9	2.2	3.1
Total District O&M costs	1.9	6.0	3.9	0.1	2.6	2.5
Operating margin	−6.0	2.9	9.5	−2.2	6.6	9.0
Less: Allocated direct support costs	2.8	5.2	2.4	1.4	4.5	3.1
Contribution	−9.0	2.0	12.1	−3.5	7.4	11.3
Total Costs	0.0	4.7	4.7	−0.1	4.4	4.5

potential loss of additional revenues because of the URC ruling (not yet shown on the financial statements) clearly jeopardizes our shot at budgeted performance and a year-end bonus (see Exhibit 3 for the district's performance goals for 1993).

As standard procedure within the Westhaven district, the management team assembled each month the day after the financial reports arrived to conduct a quick-and-dirty review of the contribution report and supporting statements (see Exhibit 4 for the organization chart for the Westhaven district, and Exhibit 5 for the expense detail). This month's meeting, scheduled for 1:30 PM, would have the added pressure of the memorandum.

Rick anticipated that the meeting would not be pleasant as the managers reviewed the statements and the budget directive. The reports for June indicated that the district's expenditures were a bit above expectations, and, coupled with the decreased revenue due to the weather, this had produced a district contribution to date that was below target. The ruling would only make the situation worse. The impact of the bad news would likely cause a stir among the department heads.

Rick recalled a conversation over lunch the previous week with Bill Berry, power delivery manager for the district, in which Bill had remarked how pleased he was with the performance of his department in containing costs and meeting customer needs. Bill had indicated that he had commended his supervisors for their contributions to this effort. Rick wondered about the demoralizing affect the latest news would have on Bill and the other department heads.

SHENANDOAH POWER COMPANY

Shenandoah Power was a moderately large electric utility company serving over 900,000 customers across a large portion of a state in the mid-Atlantic region. The company had sold in excess of 33 billion kilowatt hours of electrical power in 1992

EXHIBIT 3 | **Westhaven District 1993 Goals**

	1993 Goal	Minimum Level	Bonus Percent
Contribution	$8,265,000	$7,428,102	2%
Customer satisfaction	60%	57%	3%
Employee readiness index	85%	80%	1%

Note: Shenandoah's Bonus Program paid out as much as 10% of annual compensation according to the following requirements:

1. Each business unit (i.e., district, plant, etc.) must meet or exceed its previous year performance in all three categories listed above, i.e., meet or exceed the *minimum*, to qualify for any corporate or business unit bonus.
2. A corporate bonus of 4% would be paid if Shenandoah Power met its corporate goal in two key areas—2% for the corporate ROE goal, and 2% for the corporate customer satisfaction goal. The two bonus categories were independent, i.e., a bonus would be paid for ROE, even if Shenandoah failed to reach its customer satisfaction goal.
3. Business unit bonuses of up to 6% would be paid if the business unit met or exceeded its unit goals in the three areas listed above. These three bonus categories were independent, i.e., Westhaven could earn a 1% bonus for performance in employee readiness even if it failed to meet the 1993 goals for contribution and customer satisfaction.

Bonuses were awarded to individual business unit personnel based on an assessment of their individual performance and contribution to the business unit achievement. Business unit managers (i.e., district managers, plant managers, etc.) were *not* included in this bonus plan, but were awarded separate bonuses based on an evaluation of their performance by their superiors.

EXHIBIT 4 | **Westhaven District Management Team**

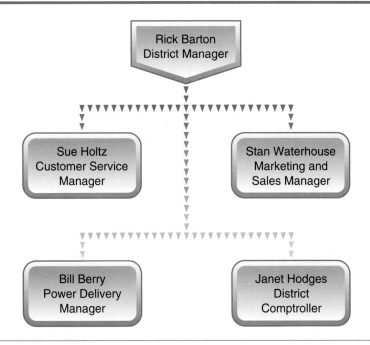

and earned $235 million on revenues of $2.1 billion. Return on equity was 12.9 percent in 1992, within the allowable range of 12.5 to 13.5 percent set by the URC. Shenandoah had targeted 13.2 percent as the goal for 1993.

Shenandoah Power was organized into three primary functions: power generation, which coordinated the company's five fossil fuel steam and nine hydroelectric generating plants; transmission, which operated and maintained the statewide transmission lines that fed power from the plants to local distribution centers; and district operations, which performed the marketing and distribution functions to retail consumers of electric power. Total employment across these functions was in excess of 7,000.

Shenandoah competed in a utility environment that consisted mainly of regulated monopolies with strong vertical integration and well-defined franchise service territories. However, recent federal legislation (the National Energy Policy Act of 1992) had opened competition in generation and given all power producers rights to use the transmission networks of electric utilities in making bulk power sales. Within the state, large industrial customers could make a one-time choice among several competing electrical utility suppliers. Thus, the environment was changing, and utilities—including Shenandoah—were facing competitive pressures to reduce costs and increase customer satisfaction.

Major strategic directions and companywide policies were set by Shenandoah's 12-person board of directors. Of these, five were members of Shenandoah's management team, including the president, executive vice president of operations, chief financial officer, and vice presidents of marketing and external affairs. These five, along with the three area vice presidents, constituted Shenandoah's executive committee, which directed the company's day-to-day activities.

As a regulated utility granted exclusive rights to supply power in designated areas of the state, Shenandoah filed financial statements with the state URC, the Federal Energy Regulatory Commission (FERC), and, because it was a publicly held corporation, the Securities and Exchange Commission. While an estimated 10 percent of

EXHIBIT 5 | **Cost Detail for Westhaven District, June 1993**

	Current Month			Year to Date		
Direct Controllable	Labor	Other	Total	Labor	Other	Total
Distribution O&M	$ 67,331	$ 22,562	$ 89,893	$400,818	$ 139,415	$ 540,233
Customer accounting	44,901	20,113	65,014	271,622	118,253	389,875
Uncollectible accounts	0	23,007	23,007	0	130,431	130,431
Customer service and information	2,426	19,777	22,203	14,830	119,839	134,669
Sales	0	9,949	9,949	0	59,695	59,695
Administrative & general	2,213	10,118	12,331	13,280	60,706	73,986
Other (including benefits, tax, etc.)	0	103,720	103,720	0	545,007	545,007
Total direct controllable	$116,871	$209,246	$326,117	$700,550	$1,173,346	$1,873,896
Demand Services*						
Courier service			$ 423			$ 1,987
Print shop			490			9,663
Fleet transportation expenses			29,113			165,045
Storeroom			1,036			2,990
Information services			8,487			49,946
Repair shop expenses			456			2,706
Total demand services			$ 40,005			$ 232,337
District asset costs:						
Depreciation expense			$210,534			$1,263,207
Property insurance			1,610			9,657
Property taxes			29,908			179,446
Total district asset costs			$242,052			$1,452,310
Total district O&M			$608,174			$3,558,543

*Demand services were activities/functions performed for all districts by various Shenandoah corporate-level units.

the total shares of stock outstanding was held by employees, Shenandoah shares were widely held by individual investors as well as pension, endowment, and mutual funds. In recent years, however, Shenandoah management had come under increasing pressure from the financial and investor communities, because its dividend payout had not kept pace with inflation since 1986.

As interest rates declined throughout 1992 and into the first six months of 1993, the company took steps to refinance its bond and debt obligations to reduce its interest expenses, but the weather impact on revenues and continued high fixed costs of operations had limited increases in profitability. In fact, for the first six months of 1993, Shenandoah's profits lagged 6 percent behind those earned in the first half of 1992—well below the budgeted increase of 3 percent—a total shortfall of 9 percent.

DISTRICT OPERATIONS

District operations had divided the state into three areas and 21 geographic districts, each with a staff responsible for selling and delivering power to local customers residing within its prescribed territorial limits. Each district was responsible for building and maintaining the distribution system within its territory. In most cases, district operations also shared responsibility with the company-centralized transmission function for maintenance of the transmission assets within its territory. A significant percentage of district personnel were involved in these operating functions.

Administratively, each district was grouped with an area, also organized geographically. District managers within an area reported directly to the area vice president. Area staff provided operations and marketing support to districts, particularly in the areas of transmission operations and economic development.

Billing and customer accounting were centralized at corporate headquarters. However, districts were responsible for the field service function, which performed the meter-reading tasks required to generate customer billing. In addition, districts administered the customer service function, which handled customer requests for service and/or maintenance, complaints, inquiries regarding bills, collections, and most other customer contact. Since a large percentage of customers paid their bills in person, districts often maintained a number of local offices at convenient locations to facilitate bill payments and provide personalized service.

While the marketing organization at the district level worked with developers to promote electrical power use for space heating, water heating, cooking, and clothes drying, marketing did not have primary contact with residential customers. Generally, these customers initiated requests for service with the customer service department. Marketing, however, played a vital role in the development of new commercial and industrial business. Both district, area, and corporate marketing staff were often involved with large potential customers. Because these customers frequently had specialized power requirements, marketing often worked in tandem with the operations group in developing programs to respond to these requirements.

Historically, utilities, like banks and other institutions that provided services held vital to the public interest, played an important role in the economic and social development of the regions in which they operated. District employees, particularly the district manager and those in the marketing function, were expected to be involved in their communities and to play key roles in local chambers of commerce, industrial development authorities, and civic organizations.

WESTHAVEN DISTRICT

The Westhaven District was a study in contrasts. While the district had one of the highest rates of population growth within the Shenandoah system, (about 4 to 5 percent annual growth), the growth was not uniform throughout the district boundaries. The western part of the district remained generally rural and had experienced little or no increase in residential, commercial, or industrial activity in the past 10 years. The terrain was rugged with farming valleys interspersed between several ranges of heavily wooded mountains. There was little or no commercial activity in the western section, but a modest industrial load from the several wood products firms located in the region justified Shenandoah Power's presence.

The eastern portion of the district was more urban, consisting of a number of residential communities, supplemented with many shopping centers, office buildings, and industrial parks. Population growth in the two counties which constituted this area of the district had averaged in excess of 7 percent per annum over the last five years and showed no signs of abatement.

Total revenues for the district as a whole exceeded $74 million in 1992 with sales of kilowatt hours just under 1.2 billion. Commercial revenue comprised about 45 percent of the total revenue of the district, and virtually all of this was concentrated in the two eastern counties. No single customer, however, accounted for more than 2 percent of total revenue. Commercial sales were the fastest growing segment of the district's revenue base.

The district had a limited industrial customer base. Most were wood products–related operations and were located in the western portion of the district. Industrial revenues represented less than 15 percent of the district's total revenues. The largest customer was Piney Woods Timber, which produced lumber products for building materials distributors. Piney Woods had completed two years of record performance, however, and was contemplating plans for construction of additional facilities within the region.

The Westhaven district was part of the Northern area of Shenandoah Power's district operations organization. Rick Barton, district manager, reported directly to Bob Quinn, vice president in charge of the Northern area.

1993 GOALS AND PERFORMANCE

In 1993, the district had established goals to increase revenue by approximately 5 percent over the previous year and hold district direct controllable O&M costs to a modest 2 percent increase. As a result, the 1993 annual contribution had been budgeted at $8.3 million, an 11 percent increase over 1992, in anticipation that the cost of product and the district's other costs would increase only modestly as well. (See Exhibits 1 and 2 for a comparison of the 1993 budget with the previous year's results.)

Results for the first half of the year had been a bit disappointing. Contribution was up only 2 percent over that for the same time last year, despite a 4 percent increase in revenues. The revenue increase was slightly below expectation, however, because of the inclement weather.

The management team had carefully redesigned the district organization structure and used a combination of personnel changes and retirements to reduce the district's head count by ten, a reduction of about 5 percent. These personnel reductions had been controversial, as many had felt that district staffing was already below what was needed to offer superior customer service. Rick and his management team had spent many hours talking with district personnel, educating them on the need for the company to become more cost competitive, and had finally gained agreement to the staff reductions.

These staff reductions had led to some severance costs (included in the Other category in expense detail shown in Exhibit 5), which had caused an increase in the year-to-date district direct controllable cost of almost 8 percent. However, district management was confident that these reductions in personnel would reap savings in the second half of the year and that, barring any surprises or further reductions, district direct controllable cost would approach its 1993 goal of only a 2 percent increase.

The district had also placed major emphasis on two additional initiatives during its goal-setting process. In concert with a similar emphasis throughout Shenandoah Power, the district had set a goal to increase its customer satisfaction indexes from the 1992 level of 57 percent to over 60 percent during 1993. The most recent surveys administered in June had shown little progress, however; those in the highest category of satisfaction remained near the 57 percent figure. District management continued to explore ways to ascertain customer needs and develop programs to increase customer satisfaction.

In addition, in response to some rather disappointing results on the employee readiness survey, the district had developed several projects intended to improve employee morale, job performance, and teamwork. Staff reductions had placed added urgency on these productivity efforts. The management team had worked hard the first six months to improve communication and to promote Shenandoah's vision statement as a guide to employee action and decision making. Rick felt that his district had made a lot of progress in this area. He wondered what impact the budget directive and further cuts might have on employee morale.

PLANS FOR THE REMAINDER OF THE YEAR

The current load forecast for the second half of the year, while in line with budgeted revenues for this half, would not make up for the lower revenues experienced in the first half of the year. As a result, Rick estimated that, with no changes in major initiatives, revenues for the Westhaven district would finish the year about 0.5 percent less than budget—a 4.7 percent increase over the previous year. While total costs—including generation, transmission, district, and allocated costs—were forecast to be a shade below budget, the net impact on contribution was that it would fall almost $300,000 below budget, reducing the year-end bonus payouts for district personnel to a mere 1 percent.

While the budget memorandum did not precisely identify the impact of the URC ruling on Westhaven's revenues, any additional shortfall would have a devastating impact and would eliminate the bonus entirely. It seemed that revenue enhancements and/or cost reduction were the only possible responses.

Rick recalled that in a previous staff meeting, Stan Waterhouse, district sales manager, and Sue Holtz, customer service manager, had proposed a review of demand services expenditures, particularly fleet and printing charges. Each had suggested that acquiring services locally, rather than from corporate, would save some money and possibly add to local goodwill. Rick had authorized the study, although he had cautioned the staff to investigate usage, quality, and service as well. He wondered if the study had been completed.

Janet Hodges, district controller, had also raised the issue of fuel costs, citing a study that suggested that a reduction in the systemwide coal pile inventory from 60 to 40 days could reduce the Westhaven district's annual cost of product by as much as $250,000 per year! Rick wondered how he, and other district managers, might initiate some actions that could lead to reductions in the product cost transferred from generation and transmission.

Janet had also questioned the allocation to the Westhaven district of some corporate marketing expense related to a "Smart Park" to be located at the other end of the state. Rick had been concerned that the allocation to his district ($225,000) was higher than the perceived value. He wondered if he should fight this allocation to help his district reach its contribution goal.

As the clock struck 11:00 AM, Rick retrieved from his bookshelf the thick notebook containing the district's ongoing projects for 1993. The notebook contained a brief description of all of the major projects either under way, or expected to be launched before the end of the year (see Exhibit 6 for extracts from the notebook). Rick also noticed the loose sheet in the notebook—a letter from Mitchell Construction (specialists in distribution line relocation)—indicating that due to cutbacks in another state, the company had eight crews and attendant equipment available for immediate use.

Rick hoped that the management team would look carefully at these projects for the district to meet its customer satisfaction and contribution goals and respond to the budget directive.

EXHIBIT 6 | **Extracts of Selected Projects in the Westhaven District for 1993[1]**

1. Feeder Relocation for Highway 333

Relocation of feeder due to widening of Highway 333. Highway 333 runs in an arc of 22.83 miles in the southwest portion of the district. The widening was originally scheduled for the dates indicated below; however, the state highway department had recently notified the district that the project had been delayed for six months.

The project had been scheduled to use six Westhaven crews. Some outages had been experienced on this line due to the age of the conductors; the conductors would be replaced when the line was moved. The revenues and costs indicated below had been included in the original budget for 1993.

Dates	September 15–November 12
Revenue impact for 1993:	
State reimbursement	$ 353,430
Recovery of revenues lost in outages	50,000
O&M expense:	
Labor	253,139
Materials	84,400
Capital expenditures:	
Labor	810,045
Material	552,416
Total project cost:	$1,700,000
Original contractor bid:	$1,976,000

2. Vehicle Rebuilds

The vehicles in the following list (i.e., "bucket trucks") had been scheduled for rebuilding in 1993 and included in the budgeted O&M costs.

Dates	January–December
Revenue impact	None
O&M expense:	
Labor	$90,200
Materials	9,000
Capital expenditures:	
Labor	$57,800
Materials	91,000

Vehicle Number	Month	Cost
4139	January	$12,000
4143	January	12,000
4567	February	18,000
4568	March	18,000
4662	February	12,000
4663	March	12,000
5141	October	32,000
5142	November	12,000
5143	December	12,000

[1]While capital projects employed assets with differing lives and depreciation schedules, Shenandoah charged all projects and departmental budgets a flat 8 percent investment cost charge to cover an allowance for associated depreciation expense, property taxes, and insurance.

EXHIBIT 6 | **Extracts of Selected Projects for 1993** *(Continued)*

Vehicle Number	Month	Cost
5147	December	$12,000
5150	July	12,000
5521	September	12,000
5522	August	18,000
5563	April	18,000
5764	June	12,000
5799	June	12,000
5817	May	12,000

3. Pole Count

Inventory district poles and pole attachments. This project had been scheduled to be performed by a contractor, but had not been included in the budget.

Dates	December
Revenue impact	$130,000
O&M expense:	
Contractor bid	$ 25,000
Capital expenditures	None

4. Chipper Mill Feeder Construction

Piney Woods Lumber, a customer of Shenandoah Power and the Westhaven district, was in the final stages of constructing a new chipper mill in the Loring Valley in the extreme western part of the district. Initially, the company had considered a site in the middle of Shenandoah's service territory, but later chose the site across the mountain range near Loring. Piney Woods then contracted to buy its power from the Westvale Electric Member Cooperative, which was to supply the power from their Chambley River Hydroelectric Plant in the northwest corner of Westhaven district.

Shenandoah had pursued the Piney Woods plant even after the change to the Loring site, but its bid had reflected the additional cost of isolation transformers necessary to protect its line from surges caused when the chipper struck large knots in the timber processed. The plant's load had been projected at 15–20,000 kilowatts annually with incremental revenues of three quarters of a million dollars. Moreover, it was expected to bring in 150 additional jobs to the valley.

The Westvale EMC had planned to supply power to the chipper mill through a 44 kv feeder that would cross the Chambley River. Recently, Piney Woods had notified Rick Barton that Westvale had failed in its efforts to obtain a permit from the Environmental Protection Agency and had abandoned the project. Piney Woods had petitioned Shenandoah Power for electrical service and offered an exclusive contract if the work could be completed by November.

Westhaven's engineers indicated that the project would require six crews for approximately two months of work to construct the required 4 miles of feeder. Since the Shenandoah feeder would not have to cross the river, no problems were expected from the EPA. Because the original bid to provide service had been lost to the EMC, the revenue and cost impacts below had *not* been included in the current budget.

Dates	ASAP
Revenue impact (this year)	$ 135,000
O&M expense	None
Capital expenditures	$1,321,250

5. Local Office in Layonton

The Westhaven district planned to lease approximately 3,900 square feet of office space, 10,000 square feet to house vehicles, and 10,000 square feet of warehouse space on five acres in the Layonton Industrial Park for use as a local office. The park was located in one of the fastest growing areas in the eastern part of the district. Improvement in customer service had been the primary justification.

Staffing for the office would include:

Office manager	Transfer
Customer service representatives (2)	New hires
Three-person crews (4)	Transfers
Section chief	New hire
Meter reader	Transfer
Field person	New hire

EXHIBIT 6 | **Extracts of Selected Projects for 1993** *(Continued)*

The lease was offered at 75% of the current market value of the facilities and was available at this rate for 60 days. An alternative that had been considered earlier would have involved the purchase of 10 acres of land for $2,000,000, coupled with construction costs of $800,000 to erect and equip the needed facilities. The revenue/expense estimates below had been included in the budget.

Dates	September 15
Revenue impact	None
O&M expense:	
Lease	$150,000
Labor	60,000
Capital expenditures:	
Trucks (2)	$ 22,000

6. Reclearing 230 kv Feeder

Reclearing of a right-of-way for the 230 kv feeder that cut through 75 miles of the southwest portion of the district. The right-of-way involved mountainous and swampy terrain.

The contractor had indicated that the right-of-way could be cleared with a hydro-axe. The project had begun on that basis. If the remainder of the project were postponed, however, manual clearing would be required, which would increase the cost by 40%. In most of the swampy terrain yet to be completed, tree growth had reached within 10 feet of conductors. The revenue/expense estimates included below had been included in the current budget.

Dates:	March 1–September 10
Revenue impact	None
O&M expense:	
Contractor Bid*	$500,000
Capital Expenditures	None

*Approximately $275,000 had been spent through June 30.

7. Expansion of Tree Trimming

Add two 4-person contract tree-trimming crews for the year to eliminate the backlog of tree trimming. The revenue/expense estimates included below had been included in the current budget.

Dates	January 1–December 31
Revenue impact	
(revenue recovery from outages)	$ 90,000
O&M expense:	
Contractor bid*	$240,000
Capital expenditures	None

*Approximately $80,000 had been spent through June 30.

8. Customer Service Office Hour Expansion Pilot

The district had intended to initiate a pilot program in the latter half of the year to expand the operating hours of customer service in an attempt to positively impact customer satisfaction. The pilot had been developed as a response to customer comments that had appeared in the active customer satisfaction surveys.

Current office hours were from 9:00 AM to 4:00 PM, Monday through Friday. The pilot would keep the office open from 7:30 AM through 7:30 PM, Monday through Friday and from 8:30 AM through noon on Saturday. The expense estimate shown below had *not* been included in the original budget.

Dates	August 1–December 31
Revenue impact	None
O&M expense:	
Labor	$37,000
Capital expenditures	None

EXHIBIT 6 | **Extracts of Selected Projects for 1993** *(Continued)*

9. Phone Mail

Corporate services had announced the availability of phone mail—a new capability to be provided in the telephone system. This was designed to increase productivity across all of the district offices in Shenandoah Power. Districts were expected to utilize the service and would be billed according to usage. The expense estimate shown below had *not* been included in the original budget.

Dates	September 1–December 31
Revenue impact	None estimated
O&M expense (projected this year)	$34,000
Capital expenditures	None

10. District Communication System Replacement

The Westhaven and Darlington districts had negotiated a contract with Emerson Electric for a new FM radio system to replace old, often malfunctioning, existing systems. The final letter of commitment (which required a 20% downpayment) was due in the fall. The operational date for the new system would be March 1, 1994. The expenses shown below had been included in the current budget.

Dates	October 1
Revenue impact	None estimated
O&M expense (savings)	$ (20,000)
Capital expenditures	$4,000,000

11. Study of Demand Services Expenditures

An earlier study of demand services expenses had been initiated by Stan Waterhouse and Sue Holtz. Rick Barton had asked for additional analysis (not yet completed) which would focus on usage, quality, service, and availability. The data provided in the table below reflected current utilization.

Expense Category		Corporate	Outside Bid
Printing services	Fixed	$ 6,000	$ 8,000
	Variable	15,000	10,000
Fleet	Fixed	$100,000	$40,000
	Variable	250,000	250,000
Office computer maintenance		$ 11,515	$10,000

12. Uncollectible Accounts Task Force

Rick Barton had formed a task force headed by Sue Holtz, customer service manager, to deal with the deteriorating situation of uncollectible accounts. The task force had not yet produced its report and recommendations for action.

The following table indicates the district's recent history with uncollectible accounts.

Month and Year	Expenditures	
	Month	Year to Date
December, 1991		$181,023
December, 1992		376,385
January, 1993	$39,353	39,353
February, 1993	26,475	65,828
March, 1993	11,657	77,485
April, 1993	9,548	87,033
May, 1993	20,391	107,424
June, 1993	23,007	130,431

THE SOLID SHIELD AMERICAS PROJECT

Paul J. Schlachter, Florida International University

It was a late morning in early September 1990. Thick gray clouds had settled over Costa Rica's central highlands where the airport headquarters of Aerocoop (Cooperativa de Servicios Aero Industriales, R. L.) was located. On the work floor of the Automotive division, people's spirits were as unsettled and heavy as the atmosphere outside. Aerocoop's joint venture with Foremost Emergency Vehicles was barely 6 months old, and assembly work on the Solid Shield ambulance prototype had reached a crucial stage.

Tom Kearney, a technical consultant for Foremost, had arrived from Florida to review progress on the prototype. He didn't hear what he wanted to hear and didn't like what he saw. Even though the Costa Ricans had put in additional time beyond the hours they had budgeted for assembly work, the demonstration vehicle was far from ready. In addition, Aerocoop's engineers had not documented their work as they progressed. Kearney noted that some of the finishing did not measure up to Foremost's standards, and plywood pieces for the interior cabinets had not been cut to Foremost's specifications.

David Sastre was a veteran member of Aerocoop and served as the Solid Shield project coordinator for the Costa Ricans. He asked Kearney what he thought, as they walked across the floor to the plant office. Kearney voiced his concerns about where the project was headed: "The way it's going, I'm really not sure our truck will be finished in time for the dealers to see it." Foremost sales staff and distributors were scheduled to arrive from the United States in two weeks to see the vehicle, as everyone involved in the project was aware. Sastre realized that the fortunes of the Automotive division rested on the joint venture, and he asked Kearney what he thought

Originally presented at a meeting of the North American Case Research Association, November 1991. This case was written with complete cooperation of management, solely for the purpose of stimulating student discussion. Data are based on field research in both organizations; all events are real, though the names of the organizations and the individual managers have been disguised. Copyright © 1993 by the *Case Research Journal* and Paul Justin Schlachter.

should be done. Kearney said he was calling Ted Wise, Foremost's general manager of operations and head of logistics for the joint project, to fill him in on the situation.

Inside Sastre's office, Kearney expressed himself more frankly:

> There's no way it can be completed on time and to our specifications unless Wise comes down and supervises the rest of the work. I'll try to convince him. He doesn't like being away from our plant too long. But I'm telling you, that truck has to be ready for the salespeople. We won't accept any delay.

Kearney asked Sastre whether that option would be acceptable to Automotive's management. Sastre replied that he understood the urgency of the situation and would explain matters to the others. He began to ponder which approach he could use to convince the other Automotive managers to let the American take charge. He could imagine vividly their reactions, particularly those of his own boss Alfonso Cortes.

FOREMOST AND THE EMERGENCY VEHICLE INDUSTRY

Foremost Emergency Vehicles was located in an industrial-residential suburb in Florida, and had completed more than a decade of successful operations. It had always built custom vehicles for specific users. Its customers were private and public sector emergency services, located mostly in the middle-Atlantic and Northeastern states.

From his early days in emergency medical services as an owner of a fleet of ambulances, J. L. Burrows understood the user's point of view. In 1978 he began to build his own vehicles, becoming the founder and sole owner of Foremost. One of his first hires was the marketing manager, Bill Timms, an ambulance dealer who brought a firsthand knowledge of the product and valuable personal contacts. Ted Wise arrived in 1984; he had started as a production worker before becoming general manager of operations, and after six years he knew the various building processes in great detail. Although these three men were at different levels in the company's formal hierarchy, they interacted a great deal in practice because they contributed complementary skills to the management of Foremost.

The skilled workforce of computer-aided designers, builders, and painters totalled 110. Turnover at beginning worker levels was moderate, but it was not considered a problem because the skilled individuals remained longer and they formed the backbone of the company's building expertise. Foremost had a lean administration and support staff of only 10 persons, including secretaries, all of whom worked in small, functional offices on one end of the plant. A simplified diagram of the organization and lines of authority at Foremost is in Exhibit 1.

Foremost began in a garage with output of one vehicle a month, and grew gradually into a solid player in a very competitive and volatile industry. By 1990, output had reached 15 to 18 units per month, and annual sales were $10 million. Product knowledge was a given throughout the industry, because society expected and purchasers demanded durable and reliable vehicles. Timms felt very strongly that his company succeeded because it knew its product, relied on internal financing, and tracked its product costs carefully. Considering the small, decentralized, specialized market for ambulances and rescue vehicles, an ambulance maker's accounting and cost control could be critical to its success.

E X H I B I T 1 | **Simplified Organization Chart for Foremost Emergency Vehicles**

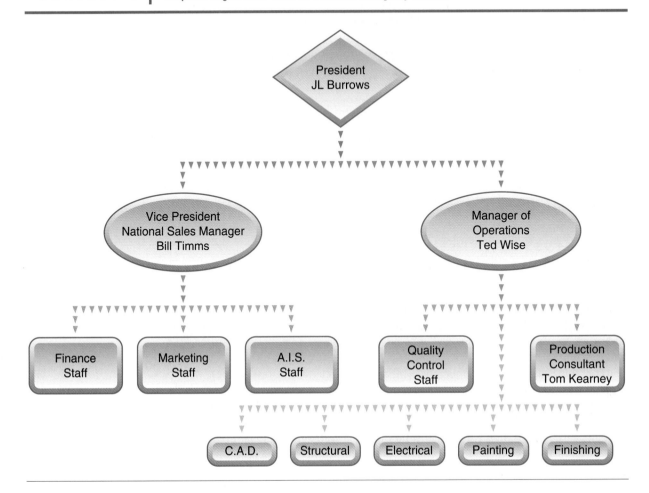

The emergency vehicle industry in the United States was comprised in 1990 of about 40 manufacturers. Precise figures on the emergency vehicle industry were hard to come by, because companies were privately held and did not provide data to their industry association, the National Truck Equipment Association. Timms characterized the industry as cutthroat, full of competitors ready to underprice each other. Only a few of these businesses built standard-size ambulances and rescue vehicles for inventory and sale to dealers. For the most part companies built vehicles on order to customer specifications, providing a completed turnkey product with logo and all. These vehicles were built to last 15 years or more and so would not be replaced quickly. Customers included county and city governments as well as private emergency services, all of them located in the United States. Typical buyers had a small shopping list, normally buying only one unit at a time for $40,000 or higher; some acquired two to five. Total domestic orders in the entire industry varied between 3000 and 4200 units in a given year, and competition for these orders was unrelenting.

Custom work could be more profitable per unit than mass production of vehicles, but it could entail unforeseen additional engineering time and production hours, plus rework. It was not unusual for a customer who was visiting the plant just to see its vehicle in progress to ask for changes in the light bars or for additional accessories. External appearance counted for a lot in the emergency vehicle industry, and seeing the vehicle on the plant floor gave infrequent buyers a different perspective from what they saw at the blueprint stage. Despite the fact that the trucks would probably get scratched all over during the first few emergency calls, customers wanted them flawless at pickup time.

Accurate cost accounting was crucial because the contract bidding process encouraged producers to accept lower margins. Bill Timms felt that the desire to win contracts had led to pricing policies that did not allow recovery of overhead costs. In that climate, Foremost needed rapid feedback on its jobs in process, especially the labor inputs. Work time data, identified by kind of work and job, were entered into a time clock linked to the company's minicomputer. The computer also processed materials inventory and financial reporting data, and would soon be used to plan work schedules.

Foremost had followed a conservative financing policy through the years, growing mostly from within. As Timms saw it, greater financial risk existed in the emergency vehicle industry than in the general economy. Business slumps for that industry might originate from both the supplier and the customer sides. The Big Three automakers might stop supplying engines and chassis, as had happened twice in the past decade, and hold up production for months. Every buyer in the entire country might limit purchases to emergency replacements during a 24-month period, and then companies with outstanding debt would go bankrupt.

Internally inspired efforts to assure product quality in the emergency vehicle industry were reinforced from two external sources. The first was the automotive companies that manufactured the chassis. These companies conducted on-site training and inspections of the production processes used by the emergency vehicle builders. Since Foremost purchased its truck and van chassis from Ford, Foremost personnel received an annual training course on-site from Ford representatives, and annual inspections were carried out. Satisfying these two requirements led to membership in Ford's qualified vehicle modifier (QVM) program, and Foremost was a charter member.

Second, all emergency vehicles in the United States had to meet U.S. Department of Transportation (DOT) certification, specifically the KKK-A-1822C standards. These set minimum performance standards, including acceleration speed, flashing light sequence, smoothness of ride, and quick access to emergency equipment. DOT inspectors visited the Foremost plant to inspect and test one of each general vehicle type. Foremost had five types of vehicle certified to the KKK-A-1822C standards.

Because these two external organizations were mostly concerned with patient safety and minimum performance levels, and conducted minimal sampling of product, they could not provide sufficient stimulus for Foremost to attain the kind of product quality that its customers wanted and needed. Foremost had to be concerned about the aluminum tube, sheet, and other materials, the thoroughness of the job (e.g., continuous rather than spot welding, properly wired harnesses, and perfectly fitting doors and molding), the appearance of the paint, logo, shine, and other finishing features, not to mention the performance reliability of the lights and other equipment installed in the vehicles.

Although each worker was responsible for a particular phase of the building process, no worker operated in isolation. Foremost had no quality control department as such, and instead used teams of workers themselves to check work completed at certain intervals.

Timms said that Foremost was stimulated to maintain its level of quality product through ongoing feedback from customers. The company's low-volume, labor-intensive, job-order approach, as well as the small user market, implied close contact with customers:

> Our customers come here to pick up the trucks and look them over right on the floor. They stay for hours looking for any defect before they drive them away. This rubs off on all our people, because no one wants to have to answer for something they did wrong.

In this competitive environment, where everyone had to meet strict standards, companies could differentiate themselves by their service reputation. Timms placed a top priority on customer loyalty, for reasons beyond a marketing manager's concern for customers:

> My customers compete with other government services for user and taxpayer dollars, and they have to justify their purchase to their constituencies. To this end they seek name recognition as well as a quality vehicle.

They also expected quick response when a part failed and needed replacement. J. L. Burrows said that he started Foremost after another company let him down:

> I bought an ambulance from them. Then one of the switches burned out, and I called them about it. They said they weren't responsible, even though it happened during the first week. Can you imagine! For a simple little switch, they not only lost my business, they gained a competitor!

BACKGROUND ON AEROCOOP

Aerocoop was begun in Costa Rica in 1963 by the employees of an aircraft repair company that had just gone bankrupt. From the beginning it was an employee-owned cooperative, constituted in accord with Costa Rican law. In the ensuing years, thanks to its prime location at Juan Santamaria International Airport, in a hangar leased from the government, and thanks also to protective legislation restricting other aircraft repair facilities from operating within a 40-kilometer radius, Aerocoop had grown into a multiservice organization. Recently, it had received further government support when its facilities at the airport were declared to be a duty-free zone. Historically, then, the cooperative had carried on business relatively free of domestic competition. A simplified chart of the organization and lines of authority at Aerocoop is provided in Exhibit 2.

Aerocoop's principal line of business was its traditional aircraft repair services, organized as the Aviation division. Its large logo was clearly visible to all arriving air passengers. Its aircraft mechanics and other personnel performed routine repairs and overhauls in a work area large enough to handle four aircraft at a time, either full-sized jets (e.g., 727s) or older propeller craft. Aviation employed a total of 500 people, and generated about two-thirds of Aerocoop's revenues, all in hard currency.

In an adjacent shop area 120 skilled workers made up Aerocoop's Automotive division. They built frames and equipped and painted full-size buses, minibuses, and vans, mostly for use in interurban transit inside Costa Rica. An administrative staff of more than 20 persons served Automotive, attending to quality control, cost reporting, planning, and design; they had just begun to install CAD equipment. David Sastre and the other operational support people had offices inside the plant itself, but most

EXHIBIT 2 | **Simplified Oraganization Chart for Aerocoop, R. L.**

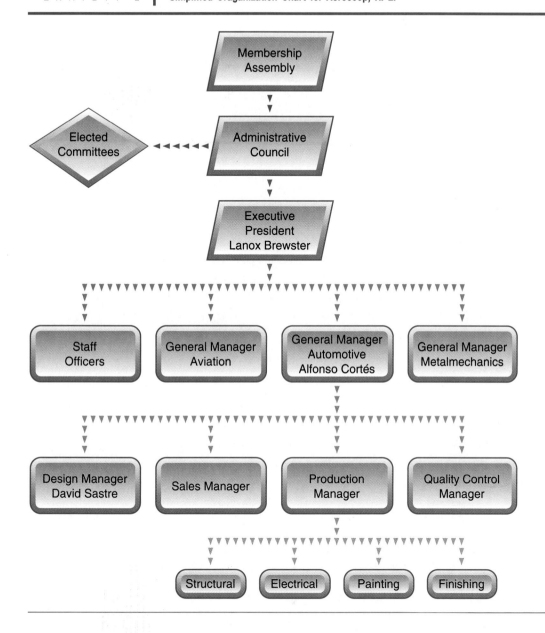

of the managers, including division general manager Alfonso Cortés, worked in a separate office building.

The Automotive division, begun in the mid-1960s, had become the chief domestic producer of buses. It also built specialized vehicles in small batches, in response to requests from government agencies. For example, Automotive provided the *papamovil,* the enclosed booth attached to a pickup truck body which was used by Pope John Paul II during his visit to Central America in 1983. The division's annual revenues, about one-fourth of Aerocoop's total, were almost all in *colones,* Costa Rica's relatively weak national currency.

EXHIBIT 3 | Aerocoop, R. L., Common-Size Balance Sheets, 1989–91

	Percent of Total Assets			Percent Change in Absolute Totals	
	9/30/89	9/30/90	3/31/91	90/89	91/90
Assets					
Cash	(0.1)%	(1.3)%	(1.0)%	(961.5)%	(1.4)%
Short-term investments	2.8	4.5	0.1	69.2	(97.0)
Net receivables	31.9	32.8	20.5	8.6	(23.1)
Net inventories	27.3	21.8	35.8	(15.6)	101.5
Work-in-process	5.0	7.5	3.1	56.5	(49.3)
Other current	1.1	1.5	12.1	44.1	891.4
Total current assets	68.2	66.9	70.5	3.8	30.0
Net fixed assets	29.1	30.0	26.3	9.1	7.6
Other fixed assets	1.3	1.0	1.3	(18.7)	59.8
Long-term investments	1.3	1.8	1.5	50.7	0.0
Interdivisional accounts	0.1	0.2	0.4	111.4	145.8
Total assets	100.0%	100.0%	100.0%	5.7%	22.9%
Liabilities and Stockholders' Equity					
Payables	23.6%	30.3%	43.4%	35.6%	76.0%
Accounts payable	NA	NA	11.6	NA	11.4
Notes payable	NA	NA	31.8	NA	123.7
Other current	22.5	21.4	14.2	0.3	(18.6)
Total current liabilities	46.1	51.7	57.6	18.4	37.0
Long-term debt	19.7	8.6	12.9	(54.1)	85.4
Provisions	14.1	17.7	8.4	32.3	(41.6)
Total liabilities	80.0	78.0	78.9	3.0	24.4
Equity					
Social capital	14.6	10.6	8.8	(23.3)	1.8
Adjustments for quasi-reorganization	0.0	6.6	5.3	NA	0.0
Reserves	3.9	3.7	3.0	0.0	0.0
Prior period surplus	0.9	0.7	0.9	0.0	121.2
Current surplus	0.0	0.5	3.0	NA	703.9
Total equity	20.0	22.0	21.1	16.5	17.7
Total liabilities and stockholders' equity	100.0%	100.0%	100.0%	5.7%	22.9%

Automotive did not have the same external stimulus to achieve product quality as did Foremost. Mandated performance standards were far less numerous and stringent for buses than for ambulances. In a country like Costa Rica, where secondhand and thirdhand buses were widely used, brand-new vehicles had little trouble passing government inspections. Besides, high tariffs kept the number of imported new buses at a low level. As in the case of Foremost, consumers of Aerocoop products were very few in number, but the lack of viable alternative producers in Costa Rica took away much of their leverage. In such an environment, the workers' own abilities and pride were what most contributed to quality, both in individual work and group reviews. The Automotive division had two quality-control supervisors, who played their part in "inspecting in" quality as work progressed inside the plant.

EXHIBIT 4 | Aerocoop, R. L., Common-Size Income Statement
Earning Performance, 1989–91

	1989	1990	1991 (6 months)
Common-Size Income Statement (percent of total sales)			
Sales	100.0%	100.0%	100.0%
Less cost of sales	59.4	56.2	54.4
Less fixed expenses	19.4	16.1	16.9
Less selling expenses	2.5	4.3	4.5
Less administrative expenses	14.9	13.6	2.5
Operating income	3.7	9.8	21.7
Financial income	5.0	10.5	9.5
Other income	9.7	6.4	7.9
Less financial expenses	8.8	8.5	11.9
Less other expenses	8.6	17.8	4.9
Net income	1.0%	0.4%	22.3%
Less central administrative expenses	NA	NA	16.1
Liquid income	NA	NA	6.2%
Earnings Performance by Division (percent)			
Aviation division			
Share of revenues	68.6%	68.9%	54.7%
Return on sales	12.8	11.8	8.8
Return on assets	NA	18.7	6.8
Automotive division			
Share of revenues	26.2%	23.3%	32.4%
Return on sales	(25.1)	(13.5)	0.9
Return on assets	NA	NA	0.3
Metalmechanic division			
Share of revenues	5.2%	7.7%	12.9%
Return on sales	(23.0)	3.8	8.2
Return on assets	NA	NA	2.1

Including the small Metalmechanics division and the newly centralized administrative departments, Aerocoop had a total of 800 employee-members. Since 1988 it had maintained total assets equivalent to about US$10 million at a gradually depreciating exchange rate. Its total services in 1988 generated revenues equivalent at the time to $10 million. Revenues in 1989 and 1990 were in the vicinity of 1,200 million colones, representing a modest increase in dollars to $12 million. Exhibits 3 and 4 provide a common-size summary of consolidated balance sheets and earnings statements for Aerocoop for the years 1989 to 1991.

THE DEEPENING ECONOMIC CRISIS

Throughout its existence, Aerocoop had been a dependable source of hard currency for a Costa Rican economy impacted for decades by negative trade balances. Since the late 1970s the *colon* had suffered an annual devaluation against the dollar of 25 percent or more. Costa Rica's traditional sources of foreign exchange, among them coffee, bananas, and livestock, had declined gradually in price all during that time. In the face of the economic crisis, international lenders and consultants had recommended that the country lower its tariffs on imports, diversify its production, and seek to export competitively. Both the private and public sectors in Costa Rica encouraged a more diversified production, offering to potential exporters incentives such as marketing studies and tax exemption.

Historically a protected organization, Aerocoop was heavily challenged by the new economic environment. As airlines began to invest in newer, more fuel-efficient aircraft (Boeing 767s, Airbus 310s and 320s), Aerocoop's aviation mechanics needed to become certified to work on those planes or the cooperative would lose its most profitable business. If Automotive continued to build a single line of buses for all its customers, the division would face the same fate as Henry Ford's black Model Ts. The tourism and interurban bus lines were buying newer, sleeker models from countries like Brazil and Mexico, and paying less for them.

The costs of running the cooperative had also risen steadily over the years. A succession of socially conscious governments had authorized generous benefit packages for all employees in the country. Aerocoop's worker-members approved additional benefits for themselves during that time. But government contracts and other support gradually receded. The low-volume jobs that Automotive fulfilled for the government yielded lower margins as materials and labor costs increased. As its funds from operations turned negative, Aerocoop took on debt and became subject to domestic interest rates in excess of 35 percent.

Government meanwhile became smaller and leaner in response to IMF requirements. In 1990 the citizens voted into power a new administration that looked more favorably on privatization and showed less sympathy for the cooperative movement. It even promised tax breaks for interurban bus companies seeking to import new vehicles from Mexico.

A NEW, EXPORT-ORIENTED MANAGEMENT

In mid-1989 the cooperative's governing council (Consejo de Administración) chose CPA Lenox Brewster as its new executive president. Brewster was a native Costa Rican, fluent in both Spanish and English, and he had held managerial positions with the wax giant S. C. Johnson. The choice of a person well-versed in financial matters reflected concern inside Aerocoop about its precarious financial situation. Brewster himself reminded everyone that the tax exemption and protected status that Aerocoop enjoyed should have translated into stable dollar revenues and comfortable margins on products and services. He felt that the cooperative could be a very profitable concern, rather than just breaking even, and he intended to convince the associate members that he was right.

From the start Brewster insisted to Automotive personnel that their division could not continue as it had in the past. He based his argument on the new economic order, in which imports would compete with Aerocoop for the limited domestic bus market. He emphasized that the rest of Aerocoop's membership would not accept an indefinite period of losses by the Automotive division. Finally, he recommended that Automotive adopt a vigorous export strategy. In response, division personnel adopted a medium-range export goal of 75 percent of the division's total output.

To help find export opportunities, Brewster approached CINDE (Costa Rican Investment and Development),[1] a quasi-private-sector promoter of Costa Rican exports in other countries. A market study commissioned by CINDE pointed to opportunities in the specialized vehicle markets. In August 1989 an official of CINDE in Miami helped to arrange a meeting of Automotive's general manager with Burrows and Timms at the Foremost headquarters.

WHY FOREMOST DECIDED TO GO TO CENTRAL AMERICA

For some time Foremost management had wanted to broaden its customer base beyond the customized market. Vice President Timms worked with his staff to create designs for a series of standardized vehicles with the trade name "Solid Shield." These designs formed the basis of bids that Timms had submitted on the larger-volume contracts. "I've never won one of those bids," Timms said, "because my competitors underbid me, but they don't include all their overhead in their estimates."

Timms knew the risks involved in tying up the company's working capital in unsold ambulances, especially because Foremost was relatively small and had always financed its growth internally. At the same time he saw advantages in having a finished goods inventory: "I can persuade my customers to purchase a truck on the spot if they see it parked in the lot, ready to drive away."

Foremost management realized that the company could only compete on the standardized vehicle bids by reducing product costs. Because the company purchased in relatively small quantities, it could do little about the cost of truck chassis and other building materials. Management did not feel that further efficiency in labor inputs could be achieved at their Florida facility. They had considered finding a low-cost source of skilled metalworking offshore that would match the company's quality standards as well as general industry standards. Because management was unaware that any such source existed, it put the project on temporary hold.

EARLY CONTACTS

About that time, the CINDE official and Aerocoop's Automotive division manager came to Foremost. They told Burrows and Timms about the skilled workers at Aerocoop, their lower wage levels, and their location only six shipping days away in an industrial duty-free zone. They also described the Costa Rican government's incentives for nontraditional exports, including facilitated movement of materials components into and out of the country. Burrows and Timms in turn described their own search for a low-cost source of skilled labor. Both sides decided to explore Automotive's potential role in assembling standardized modules for Foremost.

The following spring, as the political climate in Central America improved, Timms flew to Costa Rica. He was impressed by the caliber of mechanical skills of

---

[1]CINDE began in the early 1980s as a means of introducing producers in Costa Rica to those in other countries, especially the United States. Its original source of funding, the U.S. Agency for International Development, has since been supplemented from several private-sector organizations. From its offices in San Jose, Costa Rica, and Miami and other cities in the United States, its technicians work as intermediaries between businesspersons, sponsoring conferences as well as commissioning market studies for specific industries.

Aerocoop's member-workers. In addition, the Automotive plant facilities were more than double those at Foremost. Although the Automotive people had never built emergency vehicles for export or even worked with aluminum, their bus and cab experience was evident. Timms described the Solid Shield project to the management of Automotive and showed them his plans. Both sides agreed to build jointly a prototype of the simplest type I model (see Exhibit 5). Foremost and Aerocoop workers would start work on the prototype in Florida, then Aerocoop would complete it in Costa Rica and return the finished product for sale in the United States.

The negotiators then discussed the terms of payment. Before going to Costa Rica, Timms had prepared cost and price estimates for the type I vehicle. He knew that direct labor in Florida was costing Foremost $22 per hour, and that he would have to contract at a much lower price in order to make a profit. Foremost personnel had often worked on similar kinds of modules, and Ted Wise gave him a reliable estimate of 500 labor hours, which they then inflated by 20 percent to allow for the extra learning time that Aerocoop workers would need for the prototype.

Aerocoop for its part had done its own calculation. Because Automotive workers had never built this kind of vehicle, division management made its work-time estimate at the higher end to lower the risk of loss. Although they held out for a time allowance of 800 to 850 hours per vehicle, Timms stuck firmly to his own number. As he recalled later,

> I saw that we weren't getting anywhere, so I told them that the deal was off and I started to leave the room to go back home. But they surrounded me to prevent me from leaving, and asked me not to break off the talks.

Eventually they accepted his offer of a labor standard of 600 work hours per type I vehicle and a rate of $7 per hour. This more than covered a typical hourly rate for wages and benefits and other support costs, guaranteeing a substantial profit margin for Aerocoop if its workers met the standard.

EXHIBIT 5 | **Solid Shield Ambulance Series**

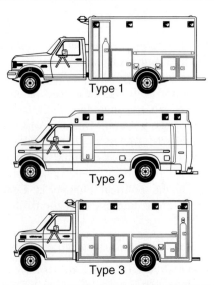

VEHICLE CONSTRUCTION

The joint project, including the prototype and the units that would follow, required a sizable initial investment. Foremost management financed this from the company's own ongoing operations, just as they had done in other projects. Burrows and Timms expected to recover the funds (and other first-year investments) after two years of regular production and sales of the finished vehicles.

The ambulance body which Aerocoop workers began to build was an example of the common type I vehicle, in which a module made of reinforced aluminum was attached to a pickup truck chassis (see Exhibit 5). The type II, a modified van, had tended to be too crowded for its uses and was not in great demand. In contrast, the type III was a heavier aluminum module mounted on a van chassis with free movement between module and cabin. The Solid Shield project would eventually include both type I and type III models.

The two parties also decided how to divide responsibilities for the type I prototype. Foremost would supply the chassis and all other raw materials and provide the technical assistance necessary to build the module according to plan. Production would begin in Florida, where personnel from both firms would work jointly on welding and structure. Automotive would complete the prototype in Costa Rica, painting it and installing the plywood cabinets. Once it passed inspection by a Foremost agent, it would be returned to Florida for sale in the United States. Foremost personnel would build the electrical wiring for the prototype, but Aerocoop would assume responsibility for wiring of subsequent modules.

David Sastre, Automotive's director of design, agreed to supervise the project from the Aerocoop side, while at Foremost continuing oversight came from Ted Wise's office. Neither firm hired additional workers or managers at the prototype stage, but instead gave added responsibilities to their more reliable personnel. Six of Automotive's best welders learned the aluminum welding technology, and four others were trained in cabinetmaking.

On May 20, 1990, four project members from Aerocoop arrived at the Foremost plant to begin work on the prototype. They include Sastre and three foremen from the structural phase of the operation. They were accompanied by CINDE's consultant for the metalworking industry, who translated for both sides. The foremen had received training in aluminum welding in Costa Rica, and everyone on the team had studied the technical specifications for the module.

During their two weeks in Florida the Costa Ricans worked with Foremost personnel to build the frame, position the plates, then mount the unpainted module on a truck chassis. They observed and participated in the initial stages, including the building of structure, skin, and roof, and they helped to install aluminum compartments. They gradually learned to work with aluminum and make efficient welds on surfaces and edges.

The Foremost managers did not know Spanish, and few of the Aerocoop personnel closely involved in the project spoke English fluently. Although diagrams and technical terms were self-explanatory to some extent, communication on a basic level proved to be difficult. This did not affect the work in Florida, because the Costa Ricans observed and taped the process and relied on their interpreter. New communication problems emerged after they returned to Costa Rica, however, when they faced issues of product quality and finishing. Sastre resolved this temporarily by asking his nephew, Javier Laguna, to visit the plant and act as interpreter. Laguna also translated the type I specifications into Spanish for them. His language ability and knowledge of vehicle assembly impressed Wise during a visit he made to Aerocoop in early August.

THE COSTA RICAN PHASE

When Foremost shipped the prototype module to Costa Rica in mid-June, the frame and plating work was completed and the module mounted on the truck chassis. The Foremost electricians had assembled the electrical harnesses in Florida and sent them along with the module. These were complex wiring networks designed for the emergency vehicle's electrical circuits. Seven harnesses with 10 to 15 wires each were used in the prototype, some of them six feet in length. More intricate work remained to be done. The Automotive workers had to smooth down the welds and the metal finish in general, build and insert additional metal storage compartments, assemble the plywood counters, spray-paint the module, apply the gloss, and do other required finishing work. Wise had detailed instructions prepared for all the work and he sent them down with the module. Included was a cut list specifying the number and size of pieces to be cut for the plywood cabinets.

The module was placed in a separate working area in the middle of the Automotive plant, dedicated to vehicles for export. The smoothing and compartment work and wiring installation took place there. No one was assigned full time to the prototype because the buses had priority; as a result crews were scheduled on the module at intervals. When the time came to install the cabinets and spray-paint the vehicle, it would be moved, in turn, to the required locations. The cabinet shop was located at one side of the plant; its personnel cut, sanded, and fitted the plywood pieces there. The painting area was located on the opposite side, and buses took up most of its schedule.

FINAL INSPECTION TIME

Back in Florida Bill Timms began the marketing phase of the project. Wanting to generate the maximum publicity from the one vehicle they were building, he considered alternative scenarios for his first public announcement. Because he was impressed by Costa Rica and the Aerocoop operation, and because offshore assembly of ambulances was untried and even unheard of in North America, he thought that Aerocoop itself would make an ideal showplace. For that reason, he decided to invite all of Foremost's U.S. dealers to Costa Rica on September 20, to see the completed type I prototype. Ted Wise told him it should be ready by then, based on his last visit and on reports he had received.

Three weeks before the dealers were scheduled to go, Tom Kearney made a short inspection trip. Kearney was a technical consultant who worked part-time for Foremost, and he planned to help with the installation of the electrical harnesses. Sastre met him, described the project status, and accompanied him through the plant as interpreter. Sastre told him that Brewster and the governing council were putting pressure on Automotive to show some progress on its exporting strategy, to help Aerocoop weather its worsening liquidity crisis.

It took only an hour for Kearney to realize that the impression Wise had gotten from the fax reports was mistaken. The Solid Shield prototype still needed much finishing, cabinet installation, and painting work. Meanwhile, Automotive had reported 750 labor hours to that point, 25 percent above the time standard on which the cooperative would be paid. Kearney was very disappointed that no one from Automotive's staff had documented the work carefully. He also discovered that the cabinetmaking personnel were cutting the plywood pieces according to their subjective hunches rather than following the cut list Wise had sent them in June.

Kearney saw plenty that day to give him concern over the project. He expressed his concern to Sastre, and said he intended to call Ted Wise and suggest that he come right away. He thought Wise would have to supervise on-site the finishing work on the prototype. Sastre agreed that the project had reached a critical point, but he wondered to himself whether any of the options were satisfactory. For example, theoretically they *could* decide to abort the project, but that seemed unthinkable. As for more delays, Kearney had said that Foremost had ruled those out. And if Wise came down to take over, that would effectively leave him in control of several distinct activities in the plant in addition to the prototype. The other Automotive managers would not be thrilled at that prospect.

However, Sastre could remember one other time when an outsider had directly supervised a project at Aerocoop. Back in the 1960s, the United Nations Economic Commission for Latin America (CEPAL) had sent a Spanish management consultant to visit the cooperative and recommend ways to expand and diversify. That same visitor had recommended starting a unit that eventually became the Automotive division, and he had served as its general manager for 15 years.

Sastre was aware that the Automotive workers knew Timms and Wise from their past visits to Costa Rica and that they respected the professionalism of the North Americans. Sastre thought there would be only token resistance to the arrangement Kearney suggested. However, he wanted to announce the proposal formally to the other Automotive managers, and would try to schedule a meeting that afternoon or the following morning. And he looked Kearney right in the eye when he said, "Tom, I hope you can stay for the meeting. You can persuade them better than I can about how important this is."

VILLAGE INN

Diana Johnston, University of South Florida
Russ King, University of South Florida
Jay T. Knippen, University of South Florida

The Village Inn, located on Bermuda Boulevard in San Diego, was only a few blocks away from San Diego State University and was within several miles of some of California's largest tourist attractions. Visiting lecturers, speakers, professors interviewing for jobs, and people attending conferences at the university provided a considerable amount of business for Village Inn.

The inn was also near a concentrated area of light and heavy industry. The largest shopping mall in San Diego was under construction across the street from the inn. A relatively new Veterans Administration hospital and the University Community Hospital were both located within one mile. The inn's very favorable location, together with the fact that it was a franchise of a major national chain, had made it a profitable investment. During the past 12 months, the inn had had an average occupancy rate of between 65 and 70 percent, some 15 or more percentage points above the break-even occupancy rate of 50 percent.

Although the Village Inn had only modest competition from other hotel or motel facilities in the immediate vicinity, a new Quality Inn was under construction next door. The other closest competitors were nearly three miles away at the intersection of Bermuda Boulevard and Interstate 8. Village Inn offered a full range of services to its guests, including a restaurant and bar. The new Quality Inn next door was going to have just a coffee shop. Insofar as its restaurant/bar business was concerned, the Village Inn's strongest competitor was the popular-priced University Restaurant, two blocks away. Village Inn did not consider its own food service operations to be in close competition with the area's fast-food franchises or with higher-priced restaurants.

OWNERSHIP OF VILLAGE INN

Mr. Johnson, a native of Oregon, opened the first Village Inn in San Diego in 1958. Since that time he had shared ownership in 15 other Village Inns, several in the San Diego area. He opened the Bermuda Boulevard Inn in October 1966. Prior to his focusing on the motel and restaurant business, Johnson had owned and operated a furniture store and a casket manufacturing plant. A suggestion from a business associate in Oregon influenced his decision to seek Village Inn franchises and get into the motel business. In some of his Village Inn locations, Johnson leased the restaurant operations; however, Johnson felt that because the occupancy rate at the Bermuda Boulevard location was so favorable, it was more profitable to own and operate the restaurant and bar himself.

MANAGEMENT OF THE INN

Johnson had employed Mrs. Deeks as the innkeeper and manager of the entire operation. She had worked at Village Inn for the past seven and one-half years. Previously, Deeks had done administrative work for San Diego General Hospital and before that she had been employed as a photo lab technician for two years. Her experience in the motel/restaurant business included working for several restaurants and lounges for five years as a cocktail waitress just before joining Village Inns.

Deeks stated that her main reason for first going to work for Village Inn was that she felt there was more money to be made as a waitress than anything else she had tried. Her formal education for her present position of innkeeper consisted of a three-week training course at the Home Office Training Center in Louisville, Kentucky, and one-week refresher courses each year at the center.

Recently the assistant innkeeper had been promoted and transferred to another location. Both Johnson and Deeks agreed that there was a pressing need to fill the vacancy quickly. It was the assistant innkeeper's function to supervise the restaurant/bar area, and this was the area that always presented the toughest problems to management. Unless the food was well prepared and the service was prompt, guests were quick to complain. Poor food service caused many of the frequent visitors to the area to prefer to stay at other motels. Moreover, it was hard to attract and maintain a sizable lunchtime clientele without having well-run restaurant facilities. With so many restaurant employees to supervise, menus to prepare, and food supplies to order, it was a constant day-to-day struggle to keep the restaurant operating smoothly and, equally important, to see that it made a profit. Deeks, with all of her other duties and responsibilities, simply did not have adequate time to give the restaurant/bar enough close supervision by herself.

While searching for a replacement, Johnson happened to see a feature article in the *Village Inn Magazine,* a monthly publication of the Village Inns of America chain—copies of which were placed in all of the guest rooms of the inns. The article caught Johnson's attention because it described how a successful Village Inn in San Bernardino had gained popularity and acclaim from guests because of the good food and fast service provided by the head chef of the restaurant operations. After showing the article to Deeks, Johnson wasted no time in getting in touch with the head chef of that inn, Mr. Bernie, and persuading him to assume the new role of restaurant/bar manager for the Bermuda Boulevard Village Inn in San Diego.

FOOD SERVICE FACILITIES AND LAYOUT

Exhibit 1 depicts the arrangement of the lobby area and food service facilities at the inn. A brief description of the restaurant/bar area follows.

Restaurant   The restaurant itself consisted of a dining room that seated 74 people, a coffee shop that seated 62 people, and a bar that seated 35 people. The inn's banquet facilities were just behind the main dining room and could seat 125 people.

EXHIBIT 1 | Partial Layout of Village Inn

Main Building

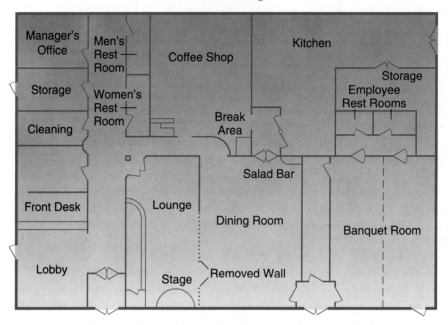

The essential role of the restaurant and bar area was to provide pleasant and convenient facilities for the inn's guests. The contractual franchise agreements with the national chain required all owners to provide these services in conjunction with the overnight accommodations. There were periodic inspections of the facilities by a representative from Village Inn's corporate office. Village Inn required each franchisee to comply with minimum standards for its food service facilities in an effort to promote comparability and ensure attractiveness. Restaurant services were to be available to guests from 6:30 AM until 11 PM.

Coffee Shop   The coffee shop was open from 6:30 AM to 11 AM to serve breakfast to motel guests. At 11 AM, these facilities were closed and the main dining area was opened. The coffee shop was occasionally used beyond scheduled hours to serve customers for lunch and dinner when there was an overflow from the dining area. Tables in both the coffee shop and the dining room were decorated and set uniformly.

Dining Room   The dining area was open from 11 AM until 11 PM. It was located next to the lounge and was physically separated from the coffee shop by a wall. The lunch and dinner offerings featured a salad bar with menu items that were somewhat uniform with other Village Inns and were prescribed by the franchise agreement. However, menu deviations were allowed if approved by corporate representatives from Village Inn's central office.

Bar   The bar, separated from the dining room by a partition, was open for business from 10 AM until 1 AM. It had tables and booths, and customers who preferred to do so could have their food served to them in the bar area. A small dance floor was located in front of the entertainer stage near the front window; a jukebox furnished music when there was no live entertainment. A small bar stockroom was located at one end of the bar counter. The cash register area was centrally located to receive payments from customers in all three areas—dining room, coffee shop, and bar.

Kitchen The kitchen facilities, located beside the coffee shop and dining room, had a stainless steel counter at the entrance door from the restaurant area. It was here that waitresses turned orders in to the cooks and that the cooks served the orders up to the waitresses. The cooking area was located in the center of the room and sinks were located along the sides of the kitchen.

RESTAURANT OPERATIONS

As was to be expected, customer traffic in the restaurant fluctuated widely. Busy periods were generally at the traditional meal hours, but the peak load at any given mealtime period often varied by as much as an hour from one day to the next. At lunchtime, for example, customers sometimes seemed to come all at once, while on other days the arrival times were more evenly distributed throughout the 11:30 AM to 1:30 PM interval. Experience had shown that these peaks were hard to anticipate and that the staff had to be prepared for whatever occurred. Moreover, on Monday, Tuesday, Wednesday, and Thursday evenings, the customers were mostly businesspeople, sales representatives, and university visitors, whereas on weekends there were more family travelers. Because of the inn's location, its clientele consisted somewhat more of the former than the latter.

The inn's restaurant business was also subject to some seasonal fluctuations. There were always a certain number of people who spent the winter in Southern California to escape the harsh northern and Canadian winters; these included not only winter tourists but also the Canadian "snow birds" who came to Southern California to work in the late fall and returned to Canada in March or April. In addition, the inn's business picked up noticeably during the June graduation exercises at San Diego State University and during the week when the fall term opened. By and large, the daily fluctuations were harder to predict than the seasonal fluctuations.

RESTAURANT STAFFING

Because of the alternating peak periods and slack periods, the employees in the food service area tended to work together, take breaks together, and eat their meals together. In commenting on the kinds of people who tended to work in hotel-motel operations, Deeks indicated to the casewriters that employees were typically gregarious and were there because they wanted to be. They had to contend with an uneven work pace, a low wage scale (often no more than the minimum wage), and irregular working hours. Since waitresses earned only a token wage and relied mainly on tips for their income, they could not afford many slow days or bad days at work. Their livelihood was dependent on how well they greeted customers, how prompt was the service they delivered, and, in general, their ability to make customers feel satisfied with the attention they received. When the food was cold or ill prepared or the service poorer than expected, customers left smaller tips and the waitresses' disgruntlement carried over to the kitchen staff, the hostess, and the busboys. When customers complained directly to the inn's management, the pressure and anxiety was felt by the whole restaurant staff. Deeks noted that people who could not adjust to the tempo and temperament of the restaurant business usually did not stay in it long. She noted further that it was extremely difficult to standardize the human service aspects of the restaurant business and that trying to attract and keep a good, experienced food-service staff was a challenging task.

Deeks supplied the following job descriptions of the restaurant staff. These descriptions came only from her thoughts and perceptions and had never been formally set forth in writing to the inn's employees:

Bartender Cut up fruit for drinks, wash glasses, serve counter drinks, clean behind bar, stock liquor and mixes, stock beer, fill room service orders, ring up checks, balance register, and help with inventory.

Hostess/Cashier Take room service orders, seat guests, deliver menu, direct seating, supervise waitresses and busboys, perform any functions within her prescribed area that speed service, check out customers from dining area, check out register, file cash register receipts, and assign stations.

Waitresses Take food orders, deliver orders to kitchen, pick up and serve food orders, serve beverages, and perform any functions that speed service as directed by the hostess.

Busboys Bus tables, put clean place settings on tables, clean dining rooms, stock supplies, take ice to all areas, get supplies for cooks, help set up banquets, deliver room service orders, help with maintenance, and perform any functions that speed service as directed by the hostess and manager.

Dishwasher Wash dishes, pots, pans, and sweep and mop floors.

Cook Prepare meals, schedule meals for prep cook, assist management in ordering supplies, receive food supplies, supervise and direct kitchen help, and assist management in menu changes. Report to management any changes or problems that occur.

Prep Cook Prepare all food that the cook needs for the dinner and evening meals, assist cook in any meal preparation that is necessary to expedite service to guests, inform cook of any problems that need attention, and help cook see that facilities are clean at all times.

Breakfast Cook Open the kitchen in the morning, prepare breakfast food for motel guests, and provide information necessary to maintain in-stock supplies.

MR. BERNIE

When Mr. Bernie arrived to assume his new duties as restaurant/bar manager, he wasted no time demanding and receiving total obedience from the personnel under his direction. He made it clear that he would not tolerate insubordination and that the consequences would be immediate discharge. Although Bernie stayed in his new job less than three months (from January to March), he nonetheless created an almost instantaneous climate of ill will and hatred from his subordinates. The intense dislike for Bernie was voiced by nearly every employee. One example of this was a statement by Elaine, the day hostess/cashier who had been employed in this capacity for the past two and one-half years: "I enjoy my job because I like people. But Mr. Bernie was something else! I generally do not use this term in my vocabulary, but Mr. Bernie was a bastard from the day he arrived until the day he left."

Bernie's unpopularity was brought out further by a busboy's impromptu comment. Elaine, trying to possibly justify Bernie's temperament by pointing out that he was not of American extraction, and unable to recall his nationality, inquired of a nearby busboy if he could remember. The busboy immediately and sincerely replied, "He crawled out from under a rock."

Bernie spent considerable time trying to impress upon his staff the "right way" (his way) of accomplishing tasks (see Exhibits 2 and 3). Most of the employees resented Bernie's close supervision. Ann, a veteran employee and waitress, describing her resentment, said, "No one really needs to supervise us, especially the way Mr. Bernie stood over us. Usually the hostess is the supervisor, but all the old girls know what they are doing and everyone does their job."

Although an intense dislike for Bernie was foremost in the minds of the employees, he did make a number of improvements and innovations. Physical changes became obvious within all departments under his authority. In the kitchen, a general cleanup campaign was instituted, an order spindle was added, and new oven

EXHIBIT 2 | Memo Number 1 from Mr. Bernie to Food Service Staff

People,
Please help keep the floor clean.
If you drop something, pick it up.
Wipe table off into a trash can.
If you spill something, the mops and brooms are outside.
It's no fun scrubbing the floor Saturday, and if you don't believe it,
be here Saturday night at 11:00 PM

"Mr. B"

EXHIBIT 3 | Memo Number 2 from Mr. Bernie to Food Service Staff

March 11

To All Food and Beverage Employees:

I wish to thank each and every one of you for the very good job you have done in the past two weeks. The service has greatly improved on both shifts. There has been a better customer-employee relationship, but there is a long way to go yet. We are nearing the end of our winter season so it is most important to all of us that we concentrate on more service in order to obtain a local year-round business. Appearance, neatness, and good conduct on the floor will obtain this, along with good food.

A waitress and busboy are like salesmen. The hostess-cashier can determine the quality of service in this organization.

I expect my waitresses while on duty to be on the dining room cafe floor at all times. I should find waitresses and busboys at the cashier stand only when getting a ticket or paying a check.

I smoke myself—probably more than the rest of you put together. Your service area is beginning to look like a cigarette factory. I do not expect people to give up their smoking habits, but I do expect them to conform to the rules and regulations of Village Inn, Inc., and those of the health department, "No Smoking on Premises." I would not like to enforce the law.

In the last two weeks I have walked into the operation after a busy breakfast or dinner and found everyone sitting around the first three booths of the cafe. I do not say it cannot be used, but when I find no waitresses on either floor day or night and customers have to call for service because waitresses are off the floor, I believe each waitress and busboy on all shifts should ask themselves one thing: what kind of service would I like if I were a guest? There is only one thing I know, in this part of California when the tourist is gone, half of the employees work on a part-time basis, which is not good on anyone's pocketbook. Therefore, I say let's not be second best but let's be first.

With regard to employees taking their meal breaks, I do not wish to schedule them but I cannot have everyone eating at once. Busboys will eat one at a time.

Thank you once again for your good performance.

"Mr. B"

equipment installed. In the coffee shop and restaurant, new silverware, china, and glasses were purchased, and the menu was improved and complemented by the use of a salad bar. Explicit work duties were written and verbally defined to all employees under Bernie.

Bernie separated the cashier/hostess function into two distinct jobs. The cashier was confined to the cash register station and given instructions as to the duties she was to perform in that area. The hostess was given instructions to greet people, seat them, and supply menus. When Bernie was absent, he instructed the hostess to see that the waitresses and busboys carried out their jobs efficiently and effectively. According to Gay, one of the two day hostesses:

> When Mr. Bernie was here I never had any employee problems. Waitresses and busboys did what I asked. But now if we have a busboy absent or we are crowded, some of the waitresses inform me they will not bus tables. Today there's no one in charge of anything. We need more employees here. It is always better to have more help than not enough. That's one thing Mr. Bernie did, he doubled the help the day he came.

The changes that Bernie instituted regarding the waitresses were significant in several aspects. All waitresses were required to wear fitted uniforms. This necessitated their driving across town for a uniform fitting. Bernie's detailed scrutinizing consisted of specific instructions on how to serve customers and which station locations each waitress would serve. He even went so far as to show them how to wrap the silverware and the napkins and give explicit instructions to veteran waitresses on how to fill out the order tickets.

Bernie had the wall between the dining room and bar taken down. He then brought in an entertainer who supplied dinner music for both the restaurant and bar guests. Today the waitresses are getting some dysfunctional effects from this innovation; according to one:

> Mr. Bernie brought in an organ player. While this was conducive to a more pleasant dining atmosphere, the organist was not good enough to keep the people beyond their meal. But now that Mr. Bernie is gone our new entertainer is causing some serious problems. For example, last night I had a family of five sit at a table in my station for two and a half hours after their dinner. If people won't leave and they won't buy drinks, I can't make tips.

Bernie instilled an atmosphere of insecurity and day-to-day doubt in the minds of the employees as to how long they could weather the barrage of innovation and directives. To some, just remaining on the job became a challenge in itself. Elaine (the day hostess) phrased it in this manner:

> I have been employed with the Village Inn for almost two and one-half years. I have worked most of my life and have never felt insecure in any of my jobs. The last job I held was a swimming instructor for 10 years with the Academy of Holy Names in San Diego. The reason I had to leave there was because of the change in the educational background requirement, which called for a college degree.
>
> My children are all college graduates with highly responsible positions. They achieved this by hard work. I instilled this in their minds because I am a hard worker. But when Mr. Bernie was here, I experienced for the first time in my life the feeling of not knowing from one day to the next if my job would be there when I came to work. What few personnel he failed to drive away, he fired.

Linda, who was a bartender in the lounge area, commented further on Bernie's supervisory tactics:

Bernie was a rover. When he walked into an area, including my area, he could not stand to see someone not involved with busy work. He even made me clean under the bar on the customers' side. I'm not a maid and I often wanted to tell him so. But the way he was hiring and firing employees, I just kept my mouth closed and did as he told me. My experiences with Mr. Bernie were nothing compared to the relationship he had with the busboys. From the bar he would sneak around and watch them in the dining area. If they did anything the least bit out of line, he would call them aside and give them lectures that could last for half an hour. He really treated the busboys like the scum of the earth. When the boys did get a break, they would come over to the bar and get a coke and ice. You know, he even started charging them 25 cents for that!

Sam, a cook hired by Bernie, offered a slightly different perspective of Bernie:

My wife was working here as a hostess and I used to bring her to work every day. One day I came in with her and for some reason they were short of help in the kitchen. They needed a dishwasher. I was sitting in the coffee shop and Mr. Bernie walked over and asked me if I could use a job. I had been interested in cooking ever since I was in the Navy. There are two things you can do in your spare time in the Navy . . . drink and chase women, or find a hobby. I found a hobby, which was cooking. On my two days off, I used to go down in the galley and help the cooks. There I learned everything I know today. When I got out of the service I worked as a prep cook in a restaurant in Pennsylvania for a year or so. My real specialty is soups, though. Anyway, I had been a dishwasher here for about two days when the cook walked off the job after three years of service here. Mr. Bernie came in and asked how I'd like to be the new cook and here I am today. Mr. Bernie really taught me a lot. He taught me that a restaurant has three things it must give a customer: service, good food, and a pleasing environment to dine. If you have these three, customers will return.

I've spent most of my working career in the automotive business doing such things as driving trucks. But I'm really into this cooking thing. Mr. Bernie taught me that about 50 percent of the customers who come in and order from the menu have no idea what they are ordering. The menu is too complicated. The customer doesn't know what he thinks he ordered and what you think he ordered. Another thing that fascinates me is trying to think like the customer. His definition of rare, medium, and well done is altogether different from my idea of how it should be. One addition by Mr. Bernie was the salad bar. This is a tremendous help to my job. If the waitress can get to the customer before they go to the salad bar and take their order, this gives me plenty of lead time to be sure the meal will be cooked right and served in the attractive manner that Mr. Bernie was so particular about. This lead time is especially important on those days that we are unusually busy. For example, I have prepared as many as 250 meals on some days and as few as 40 on others.

The employees who left or were dismissed by Bernie included two hostesses, two waitresses (one had an employment record at the inn that dated back five years), and two busboys. Two of the personnel that Bernie fired have since returned to their old jobs. One of the waitresses that subsequently was rehired described her reason for leaving as follows:

I really enjoy being a waitress and have been here for about five years. The work isn't really too hard and the pay is good. I took all the "directives" I could take from Mr. Bernie! A week before he left, I gave my resignation and took a vacation. When I returned, I learned of his departure and here I am again. I'm really glad things have worked out as they did.

Deeks's opinion of Bernie's performance was one of general dissatisfaction with the way he handled his dealings with employees.

Mr. Bernie was highly trained, but he was an introvert who stood over his subordinates and supervised everything they did. Cooks are a rare breed of people all to themselves. The help situation has changed greatly in the past few years. It used to be that you could give orders and tell people what they were supposed to do. Now, you have to treat them with kid gloves or they'll just quit and get a job down the street. This problem is particularly true with cooks. They are very temperamental and introverted and they expect to be treated like prima donnas.

Mr. Johnson and I really tried to work with Mr. Bernie during his 90-day trial period. We knew that terminating him without a replacement would be hard on us, but we had no choice. We are now without a restaurant/bar manager or assistant innkeeper. We have been looking for a replacement, but finding a person that is knowledgeable in both the hotel and restaurant management is something of a chore.

CONDITIONS AFTER MR. BERNIE'S DEPARTURE

Since Bernie had departed, the restaurant personnel were in general agreement that their operation was understaffed. Often guests were seated in both the dining area and coffee shop waiting to be served; even though the waitresses were apparently busy, many customers experienced waits of 20 to 30 minutes. Elaine, one of the two hostesses, explained the lack of prompt service as follows:

> The coffee shop is supposed to take care of the guests until 11 AM and then the restaurant part is to be opened. Mr. Bernie handled the situation differently than we do now. When he was here, he would not open the dining hall in the morning no matter how crowded the coffee shop was. I can remember mornings when people were lined into the hallway and all the way outside the front door. I guess he knew two girls and two busboys could not handle two rooms.
>
> But today we handle the situations differently. If the coffee shop gets crowded or we have many dirty tables, we open up both rooms. This really makes it hard on the girls trying to serve both rooms. What we generally have when this happens is poor service to all concerned and consequently some guests leave unhappy and without tipping the waitresses.

Ralph, a busboy, indicated the problem was not felt in the restaurant only. He seemed to feel the lack or absence of a manager was the primary problem:

> Mrs. Deeks just can't run this operation by herself. It is physically impossible for her to be here seven days a week from 6:30 AM until 11 PM and manage the kitchen, restaurant, bar, coffee shop, front desk, maid service, and maintenance crew all at the same time.

Some of the employees perceived their duties and functions differently. For instance, the restaurant's two day hostesses alternated work shifts. Elaine would seat customers, give them their menus, take beverages to customers to help out the waitresses, help out busing tables when it was very busy, and have very little to say in supervising the waitresses and busboys. On the other hand, the other day hostess, Gay, would seat customers and give them menus but would not do what she perceived to be the duties of waitresses and busboys. Instead, she exercised supervisory authority over these personnel and when they were not able to get everything done, she would try to find out why not, rather than doing things herself.

There were similar discrepancies in the ways the waitresses and busboys performed their duties. In some cases, waitresses would help busboys clear tables during overcrowded periods and busboys would also help out the waitresses by bringing water and coffee to the people who were waiting to be served. The other side of the coin came up also. Some of the waitresses, particularly those who had been employed for some time, felt that it was the busboys' responsibility to clear tables and would not lift a finger to help them. In these instances, the busboys did not go out of their way to help the waitresses.

Gene, the other bartender, offered yet another view of the inn's problems:

> You know, I could tell management a few things about the restaurant business if they asked me. I knew from the first day Mr. Bernie arrived that he wouldn't work out. But Mr. Bernie is not the only problem they had. One of the biggest problems they have with this restaurant is in the banquets they have. We have a luncheon here every week with such clubs as the Sertoma, Kiwanis, and the like. Their luncheons start at noon and last until 1:30 or so. Have you ever noticed how they park outside? Well, I'll tell you they park all over the front parking lot and when local people drive by they assume our restaurant is full and go on down the street. These businessmen tie up most of our help and yet the dining room may be empty. These banquet people don't buy drinks with lunch like the local businessmen do who take clients out to lunch and often have a bigger bar bill than their restaurant checks. There's only one successful way to have a banquet business and that's not next to your dining room. If the banquet room was on the opposite side of the restaurant, then it would be OK.

EMPLOYEE TRAINING

The Village Inn provided a minimal amount of job training for employees with the exception of the management staff. The contractual agreement between franchise owners and Village Inns of America required all innkeepers, assistant innkeepers, and restaurant managers to attend the Home Office Training Center within a year of being hired. They also had to attend refresher courses on a yearly basis.

The restaurant personnel, in contrast, were given little job training. Instead, efforts were made to hire cooks, waitresses, and bartenders who had previous experience in the field. But in practice, this policy was not always adhered to—as was exemplified by the way Linda became a bartender:

> My training on the job was really short and sweet. Mr. Bernie came in one day and inquired, "How would you like to be a bartender?" At the same time he handed me a book on mixing drinks. I went home and studied it and "poof" I was a bartender.
>
> Within a short time on the job, I began getting a lot of help and advice from the waitresses who came over to the bar for drink orders. Sometimes when we do get a drink mixup they are very nice about it. I've even had people from other departments in the inn to help me when the situation called for it. One night I had two ladies in here, one from the "crazy house" and the other her bodyguard. After a few "shooters," as they referred to the drinks, they asked for their check. They wanted to use a credit card instead of paying cash. This was not a problem, but so I would get my tip I offered to carry the check and credit card to the front desk. Then they said I would cheat them on their bill once I was out of their sight. The front desk man heard the hassle and came in and escorted the ladies to the desk. This type of working together happens here all the time. Mrs. Deeks, my boss, is really a nice person to work for. She doesn't come around very much, except if she needs information or to advise me about something.

PAY SCALES

Management indicated that there was a shortage of good employees and that a low pay scale was characteristic of the restaurant business. Some of the employees expressed their awareness of this also.

(Bartender) Linda: The pay scale is really low compared to other areas. My first job as a cocktail waitress in San Diego was in a dive downtown. They paid us $2 an hour plus tips, but the tips were lousy. Here they're paying $3 an hour plus tips, which is somewhat better, but it's still way below the wages elsewhere. I really don't feel like I'm suited for this work, but I make more money at the bar than I did as a cocktail waitress.

(Hostess) Gay: I make $4 an hour here. With all the responsibility and experience I've had, the pay scale here compared to other parts of the country is deplorable. The busboys make almost as much as I do. They make $3.50 an hour plus 15 percent of the waitresses' tips. Even though the pay scale is low, there is always overtime available to most all of the employees who want it. My husband who is a cook here has worked 145 hours so far in this two-week pay period and he still has five more days to go.

Barb, one of the waitresses, further substantiated the availability of overtime by saying she got at least one hour overtime each day. She attributed the extra hours of overtime to the fact that the inn's restaurant staff always seemed to have at least one person unexpectedly absent each day.

The problem in the restaurant was apparently compounded by the fact that it was operating with a minimum number of employees. Timmy, a busboy, indicated the wide range of activities that were expected of him and the other busboys:

We do everything; I clean and bus tables, sweep floors, and do janitorial work. I don't mean in just my area either. If the front desk needs a porter or runner or if some type of room service is needed, I do that too. Mr. Bernie was really hard to work under, but he always confined us to restaurant duties. When he was here, we didn't do all those jobs outside our area. Those duties were handled by a front-desk porter. But I'd still rather have to do things all over the place than have to put up with Mr. Bernie.

SEARCHING FOR
MR. BERNIE'S REPLACEMENT

In outlining her thoughts on trying to replace Bernie, Deeks stated:

I really had a good track record with personnel before Mr. Bernie came along. I strongly objected to his dictatorial supervision. In my experience I have learned employees perform their jobs better when left alone most of the time. I once tried to set up off-job activities for my employees. I reserved a room at the hotel for employees to meet together after working hours to play cards and drink coffee. Unfortunately, the room was not used enough to merit keeping it on reserve. However, I still support functions that the employees suggest. We are presently sponsoring a bowling team that two of my waitresses belong to.

Most of the waitresses would rather work night shifts if they have their choice. Some of the girls have children and husbands that require them to be home at night. This balances the shifts real well. One reason I prefer to schedule the waitresses is because of peculiar problems which occur. For example, I have two extremely good waitresses that will not work on Saturdays and Sundays. The other waitresses do not know this, and I feel if I were to allow the hostess to do the scheduling I would have some immediate personnel problems. To further complicate any benefits that might be derived by allowing the hostesses to make out schedules, it would be necessary to reveal my awareness of the slower waitresses we have which I schedule on Saturday and Sunday—our slower business days.

I am really more active in management and day-to-day problems than most of the employees realize. Any significant changes in rules or policies are usually passed in the form of a written memo. I prefer to handle communication in this way for two reasons:

first, there is no room for distortion, and second, it does not give the employees a feeling that they are being closely supervised. However, I do need an assistant to help me manage this place. I have verbally put the word out to other inns and motels. I'm really not concerned whether I get a restaurant manager or an assistant innkeeper so long as he has a knowledge of the food and beverage service. I'm really going to be cautious in the selection of this person as I don't want to jump out of the frying pan into the fire.

REFLOTRON (A)

Joyce Miller, International Institute for Management Development

In the spring of 1990, Helmut Henkel, the head of international product management for patient and doctor's office systems in Boehringer Mannheim's diagnostics division, was considering how to move forward with the Reflotron project, an innovative system that provided on-the-spot analysis of a blood sample in the confines of the doctor's office. Within a year of Reflotron's launch in 1985, sales had lagged and the project still faced losses, partly because of internal supply bottlenecks but also because of changes in reimbursement patterns in several key markets. At this point, Henkel wondered how the potential for a product that provided such benefits to physicians, particularly in terms of enhancing patient service, could have been so misjudged by the organization.

THE CLINICAL CHEMISTRY ANALYZER MARKET

Over the past two decades, physicians had come to rely increasingly on laboratory test results as a guide to diagnosing patients, and the market for clinical chemistry analyzers had soared.

From a medical point of view, doctors wanted to obtain accurate diagnostic results as fast as possible, preferably at the site where they were seeing the patient. From a cost standpoint, however, it was impossible to have every necessary piece of sophisticated equipment available in their own laboratories, offices, or host hospitals. As a result, blood samples were typically transported to a hospital or medical center that serviced the surrounding doctors' offices and clinics. If the equipment or manpower to conduct particular tests was not available, the vials were sent on to another hospital or specialized diagnostic laboratory. Once the blood sample was analyzed, the

This case was prepared under the supervision of Professor Mary Rose Greville. Copyright © 1992 by the International Institute for Management Development (IMD), Lausanne, Switzerland.

results were delivered back to the originating physician, who could then arrive at a diagnosis and prescribe treatment.

The market for clinical chemistry analyzers represented the largest segment of the overall *in vitro* diagnostics market. In the United States alone, the analyzer industry was valued at $730 million in 1989. Analyzers, together with the chemical reagents required to analyze specimen samples, were available to meet a range of diagnostic needs. Large central laboratories required systems capable of handling a throughput of thousands of tests hourly, whereas systems that performed 10 to 15 tests per hour were sufficient for most doctors' offices (see Exhibit 1).

MARKET SEGMENTATION

The high end of the analyzer market was characterized by instruments capable of performing 50 or more 20-test profiles per hour. Such products were suitable for only the largest hospital medical centers and regional or national reference labs. Analyzers with a throughput of 600 to 800 tests per hour, or about 15 patient profiles hourly, represented the largest and most profitable segment of the market. These units were targeted to hospitals with 200 to 400 beds, independent laboratories, and large group practices.

A few years earlier, explosive growth in the demand for analyzers used in doctors' offices had been predicted. According to officials at the Center for Disease Control in

EXHIBIT 1 | Overview of the Clinical Chemistry Analyzer Market in the United States, 1989

	Market Type				
	Ultra Large	Large Hospital/ Reference Lab	Mid-Size Hospital	Small Hospital	Doctor's Office
Analyzer throughput (tests/hour)	3000–5000	1000–2000	600–800	150–600	20–150
Annual sales	$30 million	$80 million	$280 million	$280 million	$60 million
Suppliers	Models Offered				
Ames Technicon	DAX 72	DAX 24, Chem 1	Axon	RAXT	RA 500, Seralyzer
Boehringer Mannheim	Hitachi 736	Hitachi 737	Hitachi 717	Hitachi 704	Reflotron
Olympus	5000 061	5000 031	Reply	—	—
American Monitor	Excel	Perspective	—	—	—
Beckman	—	CX7	CX5, Astra Ideal	CX4	—
Ciba-Corning	—	580	570	550	—
Abbott	—	—	EPX	Spectrum	Accett, Vision
Coulter	—	—	Optichem 500	Optichem 180	Optichem 120
Baxter	—	—	Paramax 720	Paramax 520	—
Kodak	—	—	710	500	Ektachem DT-60
Fischer-IL	—	—	Monarch	—	—
DuPont	—	—	—	Dimension	Analyst
Roche	—	—	—	Mira S	—
Pharmacia ENI	—	—	—	Gem Profiler	Gem Tab, Gem Star
Kyoto Daiichi	—	—	—	—	Spotchem
Bio Auto Med	—	—	—	—	ASCA

Source: Theta Corporation.

Atlanta, Georgia, in-office testing would become the primary site for providing clinical laboratory tests in the United States. Chemistry tests accounted for the bulk of routine tests ordered, and many of these could now be easily performed in the doctor's office (see Exhibit 2). One consultant estimated that 100,000 to 125,000 practices in the U.S. were capable of profiting substantially from in-office testing.

For the most part, however, the anticipated growth in the demand for analyzers in the physician's office segment had failed to materialize. An American market researcher elaborated:

> With low-end chemistry analyzers capable of only a small hourly throughput, utilizing high-cost reagents and expensive technicians or nursing time, the retention of profits is unrealistic. Most small physician groups or solo practitioners find that their most pressing need in managing their practices is hiring and keeping good help. A recurring statement by physicians who were asked if they would consider offering lab testing in their office was, "I can't even find nurses to help me with the medical aspects of my practice . . . my staff doesn't have the time to worry about instruments and testing." Another typical response was, "I am very busy practicing medicine. My professional reputation is on the line every day. I send diagnostic work to a quality lab where I know the results are reliable."

EMERGING TRENDS

Over the past few years, there had been increasing pressure in many industrialized countries to reduce health costs. In Germany, the government had recently mandated significant cost reductions in the health care system. In the U.S. the 1984 Deficit Reduction Act had established a freeze on Medicare reimbursement for physicians' services, and hospitals were being forced to cut costs as well. In their cost-saving efforts, one of the first measures had been to scrutinize clinical testing request practices, and to look at in-house laboratory services as a cost center rather than as a profit center.

Several of the firms active in the analyzer market sold across the spectrum of instrument size, although most had tended to focus on the middle sectors (refer to

EXHIBIT 2 | Types of Lab Tests Performed in the Office by U.S. Physicians Who Do In-Office Testing

Type of Lab Test	Percent of Physicians Who Perform Test, by Specialty							
	General/ Family	Osteopath	Internist	Cardiologist	Gastroenterologist	Urologist	Ob/Gyn	Pediatrician
Chemistry	67%	51%	74%	61%	60%	15%	9%	30%
Hematology	76	54	61	65	92	19	73	89
Microbiology	44	46	53	22	32	49	24	67
Therapeutic drug monitoring	9	7	26	35	12	2	0	11
Urinalysis	98	93	95	100	92	98	94	96
Serology	16	15	16	13	28	9	6	17
Immunology	4	2	16	13	8	4	0	9
RIA	13	10	24	13	12	4	6	2
Other	9	5	3	22	8	11	21	4

Source: Theta Corporation.

Exhibit 3 for profiles of some of the industry's main competitors). Boehringer Mannheim was one of the companies that offered the entire range of chemistry analyzers. Through a 1978 agreement, Boehringer Mannheim imported, distributed, supplied, and maintained analyzers produced in Japan by Hitachi Ltd., together with its own reagents that were used in these systems. Recently, however, Boehringer Mannheim had made efforts to build up its in-house expertise on the instrumentation side. An industry observer remarked:

> Boehringer Mannheim was used to being the only company supplying the big labs with wet chemistry, and they had an excellent cost base to work from. However, developments in dry chemistry had a lot of potential in both the lab and the doctor's office, and by the mid-1980s, the whole industry had opened up. For instance, by exploiting its expertise in the films business, Kodak had developed a system to have blood interfere with reagents coated in dry form onto a clear sheet of film to obtain a specific diagnostic result. Such an approach eliminated the traditional step where reagents had to be manually constituted. Moreover, less-skilled operators could be used, which translated into savings in manpower costs.
>
> By 1985, Kodak was positioned to make strong inroads in the U.S. where there was more pressure for cost containment in health care, and it was easier to fire people. However, the feeling was that Europeans would not be as receptive to a closed system, particularly given that Kodak's reagents were twice as expensive as the existing technology. They liked having open systems where they could use any reagent on any instrument. Kodak would have to do a good job of getting customers to perceive the high convenience of its system to gain a position in Europe.

BOEHRINGER MANNHEIM

The Boehringer Mannheim family of companies was privately held by Corange Ltd., a Bermuda-registered holding company managed by an executive committee under the direction of Curt Engelhorn. Boehringer Mannheim's expertise spanned the range of diagnostics, pharmaceuticals, orthopedics, and biochemicals. Set up in a matrix style, the organization was divided by strategic function, geographic area, and product line (see Exhibit 4). The role of Corange was to provide cohesive long-term financial management for the group. Individual subsidiaries had a great deal of independence in formulating their own strategies and managing their own operations and marketing. Germany represented the largest market for Boehringer Mannheim's activities, followed by the U.S., Italy, and Spain.

CORPORATE HISTORY

Boehringer Mannheim traced its beginnings back to Stuttgart, Germany, where the company was founded in 1859 by Christian Friedrich Boehringer. In 1873, the company moved to Mannheim where it was involved primarily in the production and sale of quinine. Dr. Friedrich Engelhorn, a research chemist whose father had founded Badische Anilin und Sodafabrik (BASF), joined the company in 1882 and subsequently became a partner in the firm. The Engelhorn family gained control of the company a decade later when the managing director of the company died, leaving no heirs.

Over the intervening years, Boehringer Mannheim became involved in the manufacture of a broad range of chemicals and pharmaceuticals developed in its own laboratories. In the mid-1940s in the small Bavarian town of Tutzing, a small team of scientists began working to isolate biochemical substances from animal and vegetable

EXHIBIT 3 | **Selected Company Profiles**

Abbott Laboratories

With headquarters in Illinois, Abbott was a major manufacturer of health care products, employing nearly 40,000 people and doing business in more than 160 countries. In 1988, the company generated revenues of $4.9 billion, with net earnings of $752 million.

Abbott gained a position in the diagnostic laboratory products industry with its 1968 acquisition of Courtland Laboratories, a small regional blood bank reagent producer. The company had since become the leading factor in the market primarily through internal development. Abbott's diagnostics division manufactured and sold the complete line of test kits, reagents, and instrumentation for performing chemistry, immunology, and radioimmunoassay analyses.

Ames Technicon

Technicon had long been a leader in the clinical laboratory market, although it had fallen from prominence by the late-1980s under the ownership of Cooper Biomedical Corp. In 1989, Technicon was acquired by Ames, a German-owned conglomerate with annual revenues of $3.5 billion. This combination was expected to make Ames Technicon second only to Abbott in the clinical diagnostic field.

In 1982, Ames introduced the Seralyzer, the first analyzer utilizing dry reagent technology and reflectance photometry. This format was similar to the one used in Kodak's Ektachem DT-60 and Boehringer Mannheim's Reflotron. Approximately 2,000 units had been placed primarily in doctors' offices. The Seralyzer currently listed for about $3,500. Thirteen test parameters were available and another 8 were under development.

Baxter Healthcare Corporation

Baxter was the world's largest supplier of medical and diagnostic products with 1988 sales of $6.8 billion. The company was founded in 1931 by Dr. Donald Baxter, a pioneer in the commercial manufacture of intravenous solutions. Baxter offered a full line of intravenous solutions, infusion devices, ultrasonic diagnostic equipment, medical and surgical gloves, and renal dialysis equipment.

Currently, Baxter marketed several configurations of its longstanding Paramax automated chemistry analyzer to clinical laboratories. Approximately 1,000 units had been placed in the United States over the past four years. In 1988, Baxter's diagnostic area accounted for revenues of $125 million.

Ciba-Corning

Formed in 1981 as a joint venture between Ciba-Geigy, the Swiss-based pharmaceutical company, and Corning Glass, which owned Metpath Laboratories and Gilford Instruments, Ciba-Corning marketed a full range of laboratory equipment, including chemistry analyzers.

Sales of diagnostic products accounted for $40 million, or 14% of the company's total sales in 1988. Ciba-Corning had a strong position in the two largest segments of the clinical diagnostic instrument market, although the company did have plans to cover the entire product range.

DuPont

Founded in 1801, DuPont was the world's largest chemicals producer and manufactured a broad range of fibers, plastics, and specialty products. DuPont launched an internally developed ACA clinical analyzer line in 1970, which was currently in place in more than 4,500 institutions worldwide, about 22% of them outside the United States. In 1988, DuPont's diagnostics systems division accounted for revenues of $110 million.

On introduction, the ACA analyzer was quickly accepted as an indispensable instrument in hospital labs. Over time, prices were routinely increased and captive customers had no choice but to pay since no other reagent systems could be used with the ACAs. By 1989, DuPont had all but phased out the ACA series, replacing it with the Dimension and Analyst, aimed at the small hospital and doctor's office respectively. These were both closed reagent systems, unlike many of the competitive systems currently on the market.

Kodak

Eastman Kodak's life sciences division was formed in 1984 with a mandate to expand the company's activity in clinical chemistry analysis and diagnostic imaging. By 1988, Kodak was obtaining $30 million annually from the sale of diagnostic products.

Drawing on its expertise in film, Kodak had developed a distinctive system that used colorimetric slides to perform clinical tests on serum or plasma specimens. This approach eliminated sample and reagent carryover, which occasionally occurred with many competitive systems. Kodak's 700 series analyzer was well accepted in the mid-size hospital laboratory market, and its recently launched Ektachem DT-60 was making inroads in the doctor's office segment.

Kyoto Daiichi (KDK)

Based in Kyoto, KDK had revenues of ¥7 million in 1989, 80% of which were generated in Japan. The company offered both instruments and reagents for urinalysis systems, diabetes systems, and dry-chemistry systems, such as the Spotchem.

Introduced in early 1990, KDK's Spotchem was hailed as a revolution in clinical chemistry analyzers designed specifically for the physician's office. Based on the principle of photometry, the Spotchem was able to simultaneously perform individual and profile analysis for up to 12 tests. The system could complete 72 to 120 tests per hour and retailed in the range of $15 to $20,000. The Spotchem was marketed directly in Japan and available through distributors in the rest of the world. Analysts speculated that, with its larger throughput and higher price, the Spotchem could face even more challenges than Boehringer's Reflotron in terms of trying to change doctors' diagnostic behavior.

EXHIBIT 4 | Organizational Chart for the Boehringer Mannheim Family of Companies

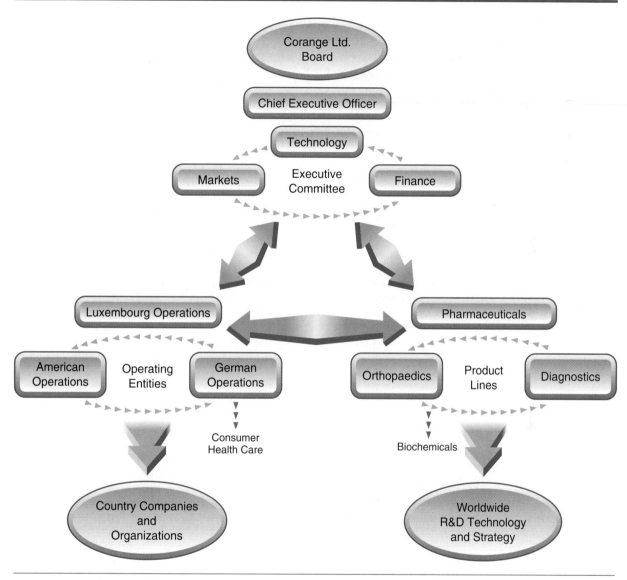

Source: Boehringer Mannheim.

materials. This work laid the foundation for the diagnostic business that subsequently became the major activity of the company.

A state-of-the-art biochemicals manufacturing facility was built in 1972 in Penzberg, 25 kilometers from Tutzing. Over the years, Penzberg had developed into one of the world's leading research centers for therapeutics, diagnostics, biochemicals, and reagents. Over 200 test methods in more than 400 forms of application had been developed in-house up to the production stage. As an example, Boehringer Mannheim had pioneered the use of test strips for multiple determinations based on a urine sample. Boehringer Mannheim was also a leader in the field of diabetes diagnosis, having developed a highly innovative system in the early 1970s for determining blood glucose levels based on "dry chemistry," as opposed to the wet chemistry approach that had been traditionally used in diagnostic systems. This system was seen as the most significant advance in diabetes management since the advent of insulin, and it sparked a proliferation of competitive blood glucose meters that could be used for home or bedside monitoring.

In 1974, Boehringer Mannheim acquired Bio-Dynamics Inc., based in Indianapolis, Indiana, which became the cornerstone of Boehringer Mannheim America. For years, Bio-Dynamics had been the most formidable factor in the U.S. physician's office-testing market, supplying instrumentation and materials to perform clinical chemistry hematology, bacteriology, and coagulation testing. In addition, Bio-Dynamics had packaged products to serve the at-home, self care market.

In 1986, a decision was made to transform Boehringer Mannheim's U.S. operation from primarily a sales and marketing company into a fully staffed corporation. An R&D unit was established with the mandate to develop a new generation of diabetes products, building on work that had been done years earlier in Mannheim. The scaling-up phase took about 18 months. A senior manager recalled:

> We needed to come up with a new diabetes product, and the U.S. management team felt strongly about building up their organization strategically. They had to build up from technicians and engineers to scientists. Several people came to Germany for training, and some Mannheim people moved to Indianapolis on two-to-three-year assignments. To start out with such a complex technical project in a new organization was a huge challenge.
>
> By 1988, there was a feeling that this activity was not coming along quickly enough, and that what was under development would get more difficult. We were desperate for a product. The self-testing market had a large potential with high profitability, and the window was closing. We were conscious that it was not unusual for an R&D effort to fail, and we wanted to minimize the risk. Although it was controversial, we began a parallel activity in Mannheim to develop a diabetes product based on a different technical approach.
>
> There were good reasons for doing it this way. The alternative of doing it in joint teams wasn't really feasible. Sufficient people were not ready to move to Germany or the U.S. for three to four years for a specific project. Furthermore, there would have been questions of communication on a day-to-day basis, and ultimately this would have delayed the project for several months. Having different approaches in different locations was only possible financially because Boehringer Mannheim was doing so well. The idea was to minimize the risks and to get products into the marketplace as soon as possible. Arguments that customers in Europe and the U.S. were different, that they had different needs, preferences for delivery, and so on, were also sometimes heard. The result is that we now have two areas, each with a high local sales volume and a full R&D structure developing a different system, and each with a different view on how the business should develop. The biggest challenges are getting people to understand the needs of their counterparts and to accept and keep compromises toward getting complementary parallel development, and dealing with internal competition.

Investment in R&D was seen as key to remaining competitive internationally. On average, Boehringer Mannheim injected about 13 percent of its sales income into R&D, which was one of the highest rates in the industry. In 1989, this amounted to DM242 million, almost half of which was channelled into the diagnostics area.

BOEHRINGER MANNHEIM AND DIAGNOSTICS

Building on its pioneering work in biotechnology and the use of reagents in clinical diagnosis, Boehringer Mannheim had become a leading supplier of test kits used in such varying fields as medicine, molecular genetics, foodstuff analysis, and the diagnosis of plant viruses. Early on, the company had established a number of strategic health care objectives for its diagnostics business, which included simple fast analyses for the clinical laboratory, screenings for the general public, rapid examinations by doctors, and practical self-monitoring instruments for patients.

Currently, the diagnostics division contributed close to half of the group's almost DM2 billion revenues and generated approximately 70 percent of the group's operating profit. Upwards of 10,000 people were employed in this area, which represented about half of Boehringer Mannheim's workforce worldwide. The work of this division could be divided roughly into systems for large medical laboratories (centralized diagnostics), and products for the home care market and doctor's office (decentralized diagnostics).

THE REFLOTRON PROJECT

In the late 1970s, an idea was born in Boehringer Mannheim's marketing department to assemble six to seven basic parameters together with a small photometer to form a portable system for on-the-spot analysis of blood in medical practices and at emergency sites. At this time, decentralized in-office testing was only a minor part of the market. Chugai and Bio-Dynamics had a combined installed base of 25,000 wet chemistry analyzers in doctors' offices in Japan and the United States, respectively. In Europe, Eppendorf had experienced some success in placing photometer systems, but this market was still relatively undeveloped. Jörg Karlen, the head of product management for doctor's office systems, commented:

> The doctor's office market was seen as an important segment for Boehringer Mannheim. Initially, we had a very positive experience with our glucose meter, Reflomat/Stat Tek. Using our in-house instrument know-how, we developed its successor, Reflocheck, which was well accepted in the professional market. Within a limited time period, we were able to build a functioning, reliable instrument that worked with a single parameter, using reflectance photometry. Meanwhile, it became apparent that our cholesterol parameter for the Reflomat system was temperature dependent, and the uric acid parameter had failed as well. So we started with a new project, Reflotron, which stemmed from the vision to improve patient care in the doctor's office.
>
> Our core competency was in reagent strips. In the early 1980s, a decision was made to build up our skill in instrumentation as well. The vision was to ultimately bring all the necessary instrument power in-house. This meant taking on several hurdles at the same time, and we knew that we would be on a steep learning curve. However, we had great confidence in our abilities. We'd had success in the instrument area, and the Reflotron project had the full support of management and a team of highly skilled, highly committed people were dedicated to it.

The idea behind Reflotron was to develop a highly convenient "information box" that could handle whole blood analysis. Placing a single drop of blood onto a special diagnostic strip built out of several layers and membranes caused an enzymatic reaction that induced alternations of color, which were measured and interpreted inside the accompanying device. The biochemical result was shown on a display and printed out on paper. Whereas the classical central laboratory typically took an entire day to deliver an analysis, Reflotron provided a result within 5 to 10 minutes in the doctor's office. The system had fairly simple requirements for installation, training, and use, and its precision and reliability were comparable to the traditional labs.

Reflotron would enable physicians to conduct a comprehensive diagnosis in the presence of the patient. Obtaining results in a single visit helped ease the patient's mind and provided a benchmark for ordering supplemental tests. Rather than demand long lists of different parameters from the central labs as they had done in the past, doctors would now be able to target key additional data. Reflotron had the potential to considerably increase diagnostic efficiency and decrease diagnostic costs.

Helmut Henkel, the current head of international product management for patient and doctor's office systems in Boehringer Mannheim's diagnostics division and one of the original champions of the Reflotron project, reflected:

> This was a revolution—not having to use liquids, not having to be calibrated by the user, and not having to wait for the results from a central lab. This was a way to deliver better medicine. In a way, Reflotron was 10 years ahead of its time. We thought that Reflotron would alter the diagnostic habits of doctors all over the world. We envisioned that as people became convinced of its comforts and benefits, Reflotron would be pulled by patient demands and pushed by competitive pressures into the physician's office. Doctors would buy Reflotron in order to provide patients with information immediately, and they would receive an income from each assessment. No one could imagine how we'd have any difficulties placing this wonderful instrument on the market. We knew that Kodak and Technicon were developing dry chemistry systems, which were a threat to our wet chemistry business, and we needed to take action.
>
> At the time, we were all chemists and physicians in marketing. We were all enthusiastic about the project, about the scientific and technological challenges and possibilities. We'd done some market research in Germany, Switzerland, and the United States, and we extrapolated our findings to other countries. The final customer target was generally understood although not quantitatively stated in specific detail. Based on our in-house expertise and experience, and the feedback coming in from the sales force, we felt that we had sufficient knowledge about market conditions and customers. The general opinion was that the market was there, and few voices were raised against us. In-office diagnostic testing was commonly accepted in Germany, Japan, and the United States. This was an opportunity to add the doctor's office market, which we had strategically identified, to our already well-established positions in hospital diagnostics and patient self-testing.
>
> I had complete conviction in the power of the Reflotron technology, and I still do. If we had it to do over again, I would have proceeded faster and invested even more in the early years of the development process. We should have been on the market in 1983.

The original intention was to introduce a nine-parameter system at Medica 82, the industry's major trade show in Düsseldorf. However, Reflotron's launch was delayed for two years while some fundamental problems relating to the instrument's ability to handle whole blood were sorted out. This capability was the source of Reflotron's competitive advantage. Other manufacturers were either not doing this, or could not; Jörg Karlen elaborated:

> Reflotron ended up being quite complex technically because the instrument actually touches the reagent carrier, and it's difficult to absolutely control this process. No other company could run this product; it's too complicated.
>
> During this time, some of our wet-chemistry people felt threatened by the developments in dry chemistry. There was a lot of discussion about whether we should design a supplemental product line or one that would be in direct competition with our own resources. We had major capacities working on the CS2000 project, a dry-based technology aimed at central labs, and the cooperation between our R&D departments in Mannheim and Indianapolis was not so good at this time. When CS2000 was shelved, these resources were put on Reflotron. This looked fortuitous at the time.
>
> In the beginning, we thought about just having the essential parameters available on Reflotron's test menu. We talked to customers, and our dreams developed in an upward wave to the point where we aimed to have 30 to 40 clinical chemistry parameters on the

palette, including basic immunology and coagulation tests. The level had to be cut down to 20 to 25 once we saw how difficult this would be to achieve. This had a major calming effect on the wet-chemistry group. These people realized that dry chemistry would not be a substitute for all of their activities. As well, by 1985, the use of central labs and private labs run by GPs was growing, and the doctor's office market was stagnating. In a way, there was already less for them to lose.

Despite the technological setbacks, we still felt that there was an opportunity for Reflotron. We believed that physicians would be receptive and would, in fact, prefer to do basic testing themselves. We had this vision—Reflovision—we believed that even if it cost users more money, even if it required them to make an investment for the machine, they would still want Reflotron because of its potential to bring the capabilities of the lab for doing basic diagnostics into the doctor's office.

At the outset, the market potential was estimated at 400,000 doctors working in their own practices. Worldwide placements during the first five years were initially expected to be about 40,000. After seeing the positive response of customers, this level was raised to 96,000. Reinhardt Spengler, responsible for product management at the time, added:

These numbers became fixed in everyone's brain; these were the levels we were aiming for. Our targets were based on existing reimbursement schemes and information gathered from talking with customers. At the time, we did see some obstacles in converting the centralized markets like France, Spain, and Italy, which were legislatively behind Germany in terms of decentralized testing, but we thought we'd overcome this on the basis of having an easy-to-use high-quality product, and by showing physicians and medical opinion leaders a favorable cost/benefit analysis.

In 1987, the early placement forecasts for Reflotron were revised downward to a more realistic target of 63,000, assuming that the parameter menu would be extended to 24 within five years. The Reflotron system was to retail at the equivalent of DM9,500, which was deemed sufficient to cover the project costs. Profits would be linked to the supplements business. It was estimated that each doctor would utilize at least 2,000 reagent strips annually. Priced at DM2.50 to 3.50, the reagent carriers would yield Boehringer Mannheim a sound margin. At this time, the average cost for central lab service was DM1.50. Reimbursement for in-office testing was stable, and more stringent quality assurance regulations were not anticipated.

REFLOTRON RECEIVES HIGH PRAISE IN THE MARKETPLACE

In late 1985, Reflotron was launched amid high acclaim from potential customers and Boehringer Mannheim's own sales organizations. Representatives of medical and professional associations, as well as politicians and economists, publicly expressed their approval. Boehringer Mannheim subsequently received the 1985 national German innovation award for the Reflotron system.

Positioned as a "pocket lab" conveniently at hand for the physician and increasing the comfort of the patient, Reflotron was initially purchased by doctors who were attracted to innovative, high-tech medical products. At its introduction, Reflotron could handle six basic diagnostic parameters. In 1986, sales were on plan, with 12,000 units placed worldwide. Reflotron was poised to achieve significant success in the highly decentralized markets—such as Switzerland and some U.S. states, where on-the-spot testing was generally accepted and an excellent margin was available to doctors under existing reimbursement schemes. In Germany, Austria, and Japan, in-office testing was possible but the margin was limited and at times only covered the cost of the system. In Italy, Spain, and Denmark, there was increasing acceptance of decentralized testing but, as yet, no standards for reimbursement had been set. In the majority of countries, such testing had to be done in commercial or hospital laboratories by law.

Given Boehringer Mannheim's major position in other segments of the domestic diagnostics market, it was expected that Germany would provide a large part of Reflotron's revenue base, particularly given the affluence, relative insensitivity to the price of health care, and the growing number of practicing physicians. By the time Reflotron was on the market, however, there was increasing pressure to contain national health costs, and increasing awareness of revenue and income on an individual level. Reimbursement organizations, attuned to the advances in technology, realized that less work was required to analyze results and were reducing payments accordingly, although no actual limits had been placed on the number of tests that could be ordered. In late 1986, the average repayment for a single parameter was cut from DM6.50 to DM3.50. Around this time, Boehringer Mannheim conducted several cost/benefit studies in Germany showing that DM300 million could be saved annually with the Reflotron system by reducing the total number of diagnostic parameters ordered nationally. Insurance companies and politicians alike expressed strong support for such an outcome.

Throughout this time, central labs in several countries had formed lobbies aimed at toughening the conditions for using Reflotron as a substitute for their activities. As an example, the French chemical laboratories, together with the national nuclear, medical, and immunological centers, had organized a boycott of Reflotron and had made it virtually impossible to place the systems in France. Reinhardt Spengler recounted:

> Given the historical context behind the evolution of the technology, we really didn't see the lobbies coming at us. We were driven by a genuine love for the technology. We were enamored by the sheer quality of the Reflotron system. Internally, we hadn't anticipated the strength of the resistance from the central labs. The French biochemists threatened to stop buying all other Boehringer Mannheim products if we introduced Reflotron. Our country manager in France agreed to their demands, but it took some time to cool down the emotions. Today, we manage to niche out a position for Reflotron in the French veterinary market.

THE RATE OF SALES GROWTH BEGINS TO FALL

Just over a year after Reflotron's introduction, sales began leveling off. Moreover, reagent consumption was about half the level that had been forecasted. Although Reflotron was considered the most innovative dry-chemistry analyzer on the market and covered all regularly required tests, doctors were disappointed that it could not perform all the parameters that could be done using wet chemistry in the central labs. This was particularly a problem in the U.S. where GPs, dealing with increasingly sophisticated patients and wary of malpractice allegations, wanted to build an extensive profile on which to base therapeutic consequences. At the outset, about 80 salespeople were dedicated to Reflotron on a national basis. Distributors were subsequently taken on to cover the U.S. market when it became apparent how much capacity was required to sell Reflotron to individual physicians.

The high expectations for Reflotron's market penetration were also not achieved because of several internal factors. Dr. Henkel explained:

> From the beginning, we had to manage bottlenecks and stockouts in the supply of the instruments and the reagents, which weakened our position as a reliable partner for the

sales organizations. We had quality crashes on both sides stemming from the complicated technology, which also caused a huge overrun on our R&D budget. Reflotron has moving parts, staggered motors, and a pressing mechanism where the inherent tolerances are too high. We were getting different measures for homogeneous materials. The product design is exciting for engineers and chemists, but it's too difficult for routine production. We're really producing engineering models not mass products. We can only do it with a tremendous effort, which means high manufacturing costs. Annually, we were spending millions in R&D and not getting the learning curve we expected. Because of the lengthening development cycle, each new parameter was costing DM10 million to develop, and we had to scale back the offering and introduce certain parameters later than we had planned.

A Repositioning for Reflotron

In Switzerland, the concept of "patient management" was well established. In 1986, there were 6,000 licensed GPs in Switzerland offering a broad range of services in the doctor's office. Dr. Ulrich Hürlimann, the general manager for Switzerland, elaborated:

The whole condition of the doctor's office in Switzerland was ideal for Reflotron, and we placed 1,500 systems within 18 months of introduction. Reflotron is a good door-opener for the salespeople. The Swiss are quite receptive to new technology and have a high respect for precision, and they receive a good remuneration for handling this complexity. The attitude of the GP is, "That's my patient and I will try to cover whatever he has before transferring him to a specialist." With its capabilities for on-the-spot analysis, Reflotron was seen as an excellent tool for patient management, and the Swiss were satisfied with having just 10 basic screening parameters.

Of course, the big labs were concerned about this development, and they began exerting pressure to lower the reimbursements and tighten the market, but we commissioned a third party assessment that showed Reflotron's quality was equivalent to centralized diagnosis. Still, we're facing the same pressure for cost containment that is happening globally in health care. We're limited by the desire of governments and other bodies to save money. It's easier to reduce the volume of tests being ordered than to influence the whole cost structure of a hospital. In 1986, the reimbursement ranged from SF8 to SF20 per test. By 1993, this level could be reduced considerably.

The experience in Switzerland became the key for repositioning Reflotron in other markets. Reflotron would no longer be a disappointing lab system but rather a supplemental tool in the doctor's office. Several countries took up the idea and repositioned Reflotron as a "chemical stethoscope" that enhanced the relationship between doctor and patient by providing immediate feedback of diagnostic results during a patient's first visit, based on a few essential parameters. Reflotron was initially launched by Boehringer Mannheim's diagnostics sales force as a dry-chemistry analyzer, but, once the new positioning was established, in many cases it was turned over to the therapeutics salespeople, who had closer contacts with the GPs. Their message to physicians was that Reflotron was an important income tool, given that a direct financial contribution was available out of each determination. As well, Reflotron had several additional advantages:

- Potential to increase patient volume through health checkups and in-office risk-factor assessment.
- Ability to enhance medical image through better patient service.
- Ability to improve patient binding through more efficient therapy.

However, the indirect financial benefits of patient management proved less compelling in the markets. In some instances, Reflotron even came to be perceived as something of a professional toy, a luxury medical product. As a result, the range of potential customers shrank from virtually every physician to a small segment of price-insensitive doctors with a particular concern for patient comfort or technological performance.

In 1987, Reflotron's sales took off in the United States. Boehringer Mannheim's U.S. sales organization saw an opportunity for Reflotron in the growing public interest in cholesterol testing. At one point, Reflotron systems were being placed in pharmacies, drug stores, and even supermarkets to enable individuals to check their own cholesterol levels. Ultimately, the product's image inside the medical community was severely downgraded. Reflotron became the equivalent of an intelligent cholesterol meter rather than a professional flexible diagnostic tool.

A STRATEGIC PLAN TO BREAK EVEN

In early 1988, the diagnostics division was restructured from a functional organization into two business units: lab systems and decentralized diagnostics. This was part of a move to become more profit-oriented and even more attuned to customers and markets.

As part of the new decentralized diagnostics unit, a physician's office systems team was created. This group was given a mandate to develop the doctor's office business and was asked to present a plan for breaking even on the Reflotron project in 1991, while holding R&D spending at the current level. "Break Even 1991" hinged on four outcomes:

- Increased volume of instrument placements.
- Increased test throughput (reagent consumption) per instrument.
- Increased efficiency of R&D.
- Decreased production costs.

The first two goals were to be achieved through close cooperation between central marketing and the country organizations. Continuity in product planning and the implementation of tough project management were seen as the keys to improving R&D efficiency. It was anticipated that manufacturing costs would be considerably reduced by the introduction of a new, redesigned Reflotron device that was more robust and convenient and with better EDP capabilities. On the reagent carrier side, lower production costs would be achieved through increased sales, product support projects, and higher yields per lot. At this time, the U.S. was the largest national market for Reflotron, representing 66 percent of the cost of sales.

FROM OPTIMISM TO DISAPPOINTMENT

By the spring of 1990, it had become apparent that the Reflotron project would not reach the break-even point in the near future because of developments in several key markets. In the United States, the cholesterol testing market had deteriorated because of the activities of screening entrepreneurs. Interested only in windfall profits, they were not meeting the minimum quality assurance requirements. In Germany, there was ongoing activity to lower reimbursements and increase quality regulations. As well, the cost for central lab diagnosis had been steadily decreasing, to reach an average of DM0.50 per test. In France, the opportunities for decentralized testing had been roadblocked, and in Italy, payments for in-office testing had been curtailed. Furthermore, the high expectations for the Japanese market would not be achieved because of difficulties with the local marketing partner (see Exhibit 5 for additional details on the market potential in the main regions). Throughout this time, there were internal delivery problems with reagents, and the introduction of the redesigned Reflotron had also been delayed. Dr. Henkel remarked:

> In hindsight, it's hard to believe we judged that we needed a new instrument. The feeling was that the salespeople wouldn't be interested in selling a five-year-old device. The idea was to save production costs and enhance the interface features at the same time. But we ran into the same problems with this development as we had had before. We were reinventing the wheel. This was supposed to be a performance issue, not an engineering issue. Moreover, we pushed the new project too hard and ended up debugging in the market. As a result, people tended to be looking inward and troubleshooting.

EXHIBIT 5 | Market Potential, Market Share, and Competition

Region	United States	Europe	Japan	% group possibly to reach
Central Structures No Reimbursement		Swiss / Germany / Italy / France		0 – 5%
Changing Conditions				5 – 10%
Decentralized Structures Low/Reasonable Reimbursement				10 – 25%
Decentralized Structure/Good Reimbursement				25 – 50%
+ Strong Distribution	but KODAK ABBOTT AMES		but FUJI KONICA KDK	> 50%

Source: Reflotron Team.

WAL-MART STORES, INC.

Arthur A. Thompson, The University of Alabama
Kem Pinegar, Birmingham-Southern College
Tracy Robertson Kramer, George Mason University

In 1994, Wal-Mart seemed well on its way toward achieving Sam Walton's vision of becoming a $125 billion company by the year 2000. Wal-Mart's three-person leadership team, consisting of Chairman of the Board S. Robson Walton (Sam and Helen Walton's oldest son), Vice Chairman and Chief Operating Officer Donald G. Soderquist (a veteran Wal-Mart executive whose role went back to the company's formative years), and President and CEO David D. Glass (handpicked by Sam Walton to succeed him as CEO), could look with justifiable pride on the company's remarkable climb to having become the world's largest discount retailer:

	1960	1970	1980	1990	1994
Sales	$1.4 million	$31 million	$1.2 billion	$26 billion	$67 billion
Profits	$112,000	$1.2 million	$41 million	$1 billion	$2.3 billion
Stores	9	32	276	1,528	2,136

In the months since Walton's death in 1992, Wal-Mart's sales had grown from $44 billion annually to over $67 billion annually. Every week, more than 40 million people shopped in a Wal-Mart store. Each year, Wal-Mart sold 55 million sweatsuits, 27 million pairs of jeans, and nearly 20% of all the telephones bought in the United States. Procter & Gamble supplied more goods to Wal-Mart than it sold in all of Japan.

Wal-Mart had made *Fortune's* list of the 10 most admired corporations several times and in late 1989 was named "Retailer of the Decade" by *Discount Store News*. No company in the world could match Wal-Mart's revenue growth of over $65 billion in 14 years. Owners of Wal-Mart's stock had fared spectacularly well: a

Copyright © 1994 by Arthur A. Thompson, Jr.

100-share $1,650 investment in Wal-Mart stock in 1970, when shares first began trading, was worth $2.7 million in 1994; a 100-share investment at $47 per share in 1983 had become, after stock splits, a 3,200-share investment worth $91,000 in 1994. The market value of Wal-Mart's common stock (equal to the stock price times the number of outstanding shares) was the sixth highest of all U.S. companies as of March 1994. The Walton family owned about 35 percent of Wal-Mart's stock, worth about $23 billion.

Exhibit 1 provides a summary of Wal-Mart's financial and operating performance for fiscal years February 1984 through January 1994.

SAM WALTON

Sam Walton graduated from the University of Missouri in 1940 with a degree in economics and took a job as a management trainee at J.C. Penney Co. His career with Penney's ended with a call to military duty in World War II. When the war was over, Walton decided to open a Ben Franklin retail variety store in Newport, Arkansas, rather than return to Penney's. Five years later when the lease on the Newport building was lost, Walton decided to relocate his business in Bentonville, Arkansas, where he bought a building and opened Walton's 5 & 10 as a Ben Franklin-affiliated store. By 1960 Walton was the largest Ben Franklin franchisee, with nine stores.

In 1961 Walton started to become concerned about the long-term competitive threat to variety stores posed by the emerging popularity of giant supermarkets and discounters. An avid pilot, he took off in his plane on a cross-country tour studying the changes in stores and retailing trends, then put together a plan for a discount store of his own. Walton went to Chicago to try to interest Ben Franklin executives in expanding into discount retailing; when they turned him down, he decided to go forward on his own. The first Wal-Mart Discount City opened July 2, 1962, in Rogers, Arkansas.

Sam Walton's talent for discount retailing surfaced early. Although he started out as a seat-of-the-pants merchant, he had great instincts, was quick to learn from other retailers' successes and failures, and was adept at garnering ideas for improvements from employees and promptly trying them out. As the company grew, Sam Walton proved an effective and visionary leader. His folksy manner and his talent for motivating people, combined with a very hands-on management style, produced a culture and a set of values and beliefs that kept Wal-Mart on a path of continuous innovation and rapid expansion. Wal-Mart's success and Walton's personable style of leadership generated numerous stories in the media that cast the company and its founder in a positive light and soon made both famous. As Wal-Mart emerged as the premier discount retailer in the United States, an uncommonly large cross-section of the American public came to know who Sam Walton was and to associate his name with Wal-Mart.

WAL-MART'S STRATEGY

The hallmarks of Wal-Mart's strategy were low everyday prices, wide selection, a big percentage of name-brand merchandise, a customer-friendly store environment, low operating costs, disciplined expansion into new geographic markets, innovative merchandising, and customer satisfaction guarantees. On the outside of every Wal-Mart store in big letters was the message "We Sell for Less." The company's advertising

EXHIBIT 1 | Financial and Operating Summary for Wal-Mart Stores, Inc., Fiscal Years 1984–1994

(Dollar amounts in thousands except per share data)	1994	1993	1992	1991
Operating Results				
Net sales	$67,344,574	$55,483,771	$43,886,902	$32,601,594
Net sales increase	21%	26%	35%	26%
Comparative store sales increase	6%	11%	10%	10%
Rentals from licensed departments and other income—net	640,970	500,793	402,521	261,814
Cost of sales	53,443,743	44,174,685	34,786,119	25,499,834
Operating, selling, and general and administrative expenses	10,333,218	8,320,842	6,684,304	5,152,178
Interest costs:				
Debt	331,308	142,649	113,305	42,716
Capital leases	185,697	180,049	152,558	125,920
Provision for federal and state income taxes	1,358,301	1,171,545	944,661	751,736
Net income	2,333,277	1,994,794	1,608,476	1,291,024
Per share of common stock*:				
Net income	1.02	.87	.70	.57
Dividends	.13	.11	.09	.07
Financial Position				
Current assets	$12,114,602	$10,197,590	$ 8,575,423	$ 6,414,775
Inventories at replacement cost	11,483,119	9,779,981	7,856,871	6,207,852
Less LIFO reserve	469,413	511,672	472,572	399,436
Inventories at LIFO cost	11,013,706	9,268,309	7,384,299	5,808,416
Net property, plant, equipment, and capital leases	13,175,366	9,792,881	6,433,801	4,712,039
Total assets	26,440,764	20,565,087	15,443,389	11,388,915
Current liabilities	7,406,223	6,754,286	5,003,775	3,990,414
Long-term debt	6,155,894	3,072,835	1,722,022	740,254
Long-term obligations under capital leases	1,804,300	1,772,152	1,555,875	1,158,621
Preferred stock with mandatory redemption provisions	—	—	—	—
Shareholders' equity	10,752,438	8,759,180	6,989,710	5,365,524
Financial Ratios				
Current ratio	1.6	1.5	1.7	1.6
Inventories/working capital	2.3	2.7	2.1	2.4
Return on assets**	11.3%	12.9%	14.1%	15.7%
Return on shareholders' equity**	26.6%	28.5%	30.0%	32.6%
Other Year-End Data				
Number of Wal-Mart stores	1,953	1,850	1,714	1,568
Number of Supercenters	68	30	6	5
Number of Sam's Clubs	419	256	208	148
Average Wal-Mart store size (square feet)	83,900	79,800	74,700	70,700
Number of associates	528,000	434,000	371,000	328,000
Number of shareholders	257,946	180,584	150,242	122,414

*Reflects the two-for-one stock split distributed February 1993.
**On beginning of year balances.
Source: Company annual report for 1994. (The company's fiscal year ends in January.)

EXHIBIT 1 | **Financial and Operating Summary for Wal-Mart Stores, Inc., Fiscal Years 1984–1994** *(continued)*

1990	1989	1988	1987	1986	1985	1984
$25,810,656	$20,649,001	$15,959,255	$11,909,076	$8,451,489	$6,400,861	$4,666,909
25%	29%	34%	41%	32%	37%	38%
11%	12%	11%	13%	9%	15%	15%
174,644	136,867	104,783	84,623	55,127	52,167	36,031
20,070,034	16,056,856	12,281,744	9,053,219	6,361,271	4,722,440	3,418,025
4.069,695	3,267,864	2,599,367	2,007,645	1,485,210	1,181,455	892,887
20,346	36,286	25,262	10,442	1,903	5,207	4,935
117,725	99,395	88,995	76,367	54,640	42,506	29,946
631,600	488,246	441,027	395,940	276,119	230,653	160,903
1,075,900	837,221	627,643	450,086	327,473	270,767	196,244
.48	.37	.28	.20	.15	.12	.09
.06	.04	.03	.02	.02	.01	.01
$ 4,712,616	$ 3,630,987	$ 2,905,145	$ 2,353,271	$1,784,275	$1,303,254	$1,005,567
4,750,619	3,642,696	2,854,556	2,184,847	1,528,349	1,227,264	857,155
322,546	291,329	202,796	153,875	140,181	123,339	121,760
4,428,073	3,351,367	2,651,760	2,030,972	1,388,168	1,103,925	735,395
3,430,059	2,661,954	2,144,852	1,676,282	1,303,450	870,309	628,151
8,198,484	6,359,668	5,131,809	4,049,092	3,103,645	2,205,229	1,652,254
2,845,315	2,065,909	1,743,763	1,340,291	992,683	688,968	502,763
185,152	184,439	185,672	179,234	180,682	41,237	40,866
1,087,403	1,009,046	866,972	764,128	595,205	449,886	339,930
—	—	—	—	4,902	5,874	6,411
3,965,561	3,007,909	2,257,267	1,690,493	1,277,659	984,672	737,503
1.7	1.8	1.7	1.8	1.8	1.9	2.0
2.4	2.1	2.3	2.0	1.8	1.8	1.5
16.9%	16.3%	15.5%	14.5%	14.8%	16.4%	16.5%
35.8%	37.1%	37.1%	35.2%	33.3%	36.7%	40.2%
1,399	1,259	1,114	980	859	745	642
3	—	—	—	—	—	—
123	105	84	49	23	11	3
66,400	63,500	61,500	59,000	57,000	55,000	53,000
271,000	223,000	183,000	141,000	104,000	81,000	62,000
79,929	80,270	79,777	32,896	21,828	14,799	14,172

tag line reinforced the low-price theme: "Always the low price. Always." Its low-price image was bolstered with ads urging customers to bring in "any competitor's local ad—we'll match it." Major merchandise lines included housewares, consumer electronics, sporting goods, lawn and garden items, health and beauty aids, apparel, home fashions, paint, bed and bath goods, hardware, automotive repair and maintenance items, toys and games, and groceries (mostly nonperishable items such as packaged products, household supplies, snack foods, and canned goods). As of 1994, store sizes averaged about 84,000 square feet, with a range of 40,000 to 180,000 square feet. In-store fixtures were basic, but the atmosphere was bright, cheery, and fresh, with ample aisle space and attractively presented merchandise displays. Store personnel were friendly and helpful; the aim was to make each shopper's experience pleasant and satisfying. In 1993 Wal-Mart announced plans to replace 100 of its standard snack bars with franchise-owned McDonald's restaurants.

Penny-pinching cost consciousness pervaded every part of Wal-Mart's operations—from store construction to pressuring vendors and suppliers for low prices on every item Wal-Mart stocked to supplying stores via an efficient distribution system to keeping corporate overhead costs down. The cost savings Wal-Mart achieved were passed on to customers in the form of lower retail prices.

WAL-MART'S GEOGRAPHIC EXPANSION STRATEGY

One of the most distinctive features of Wal-Mart's business strategy was the manner in which it expanded outward into new geographic areas. Whereas many chain retailers achieved regional and national coverage quickly by entering the largest metropolitan centers before trying to penetrate less populated markets, Wal-Mart always expanded into *adjoining* geographic areas, saturating each area with stores before moving into new territory. New stores were usually clustered within 200 miles of an existing distribution center so that deliveries could be made cost effectively on a daily basis; new distribution centers were added as needed to support store expansion into additional states. But the really unique feature of Wal-Mart's geographic strategy involved opening stores in small towns surrounding a targeted metropolitan area *before* moving into the metropolitan area itself—an approach Sam Walton termed "backward expansion." Wal-Mart management believed that any town with a shopping area population of 15,000 or more persons was big enough to support a Discount City store. Once stores were opened in towns around the most populous city, Wal-Mart would locate one or more stores in the metropolitan area and begin major market advertising.

By clustering new stores in a relatively small geographic area, the company's advertising expenses for breaking into a new market could be shared across all the area stores, a tactic Wal-Mart used to keep its advertising costs under 1 percent of sales (compared to 2 or 3 percent for other discount chains). Don Soderquist explained why the company preferred its backward expansion strategy:[1]

> Our strategy is to go into smaller markets first before we hit major metro areas because you've got a smaller population base to convince over. So you begin to get the acceptance in smaller markets and the word begins to travel around and people begin to travel further and further to get to your stores.

In the small towns Wal-Mart entered, it was not unusual for a number of businesses that carried merchandise similar to Wal-Mart's lines to fail within a year or two after Wal-Mart's arrival. Wal-Mart's low prices tended to attract customers away from apparel shops, general stores, pharmacies, sporting goods stores, shoe stores, and hardware stores operated by local merchants. The "Wal-Mart effect" in small communities was so big that it had spawned the formation of consulting firms specializing in advising local retailers how to survive the opening of a Wal-Mart.

---

[1] *Discount Store News,* December 18, 1989, p. 162.

EXPERIMENTATION WITH NEW STORE FORMATS

A second element of Wal-Mart's growth strategy involved employing different store formats to build market share within a given area. Sam's Wholesale Club marked Wal-Mart's first major venture in expanding its merchandising reach. The company saw excellent strategic fit between its Wal-Mart discount operations and the concept of wholesale club merchandising.

Sam's Wholesale Club Sam's Wholesale Clubs were membership-only, cash-and-carry warehouses, approximately 100,000 square feet in size, which carried frequently used, brand-name items in bulk quantities as well as some big-ticket merchandise (TVs, tires, household appliances, computers, and electronic equipment). To qualify for membership, one had to be the owner of a business, self-employed, a government employee (federal, state, or local), a Wal-Mart stockholder, or be buying on behalf of a civic or community service organization; a federal tax I.D. or a business license was often used to establish an applicant's membership eligibility. The annual membership fee was $25. Sam's catered to the needs of small businesses for general merchandise and supplies for internal use. The advertising tag line for Sam's was "Our business is your business."

Most goods at Sam's were displayed in the original cartons stacked in wooden racks or on wooden pallets. Where feasible, incoming merchandise was premarked and palletized, allowing it to be moved from delivery trucks into the selling/display area by forklifts. In the greatly downscaled apparel department, merchandise was displayed on tables, in boxes, and hanging from metal racks. Many items stocked were sold in bulk quantity (five-gallon containers, bundles of a dozen or more, and economy-size boxes). Prices tended to be 10 to 15 percent below the prices of Discount City stores since merchandising costs and store operation costs were substantially lower.

The first Sam's was opened in 1983 and by 1994 there were 419 Sam's Clubs open in 49 states. Sales in fiscal year 1993 exceeded $12.3 billion, averaging just over $48 million per unit. Wal-Mart was experimenting with several modifications of the Sam's Wholesale Club format, including increasing the size from 100,000 to 130,000 square feet, creating more excitement in merchandise presentation, and offering such service and merchandise enhancements as a bakery, a butcher shop, a produce department, an optical facility, and an express shipping service.

The Supercenter Format Wal-Mart's newest store variation was the Supercenter, a format that Wal-Mart began testing in 1987. Supercenters were intended to give Wal-Mart improved drawing power in its existing markets by providing a one-stop shopping destination. Supercenters had the full array of general merchandise found in Wal-Mart stores, plus a full-scale supermarket, deli, fresh bakery, and such specialty/convenience shops as a hair salon, portrait studio, dry cleaners, and optical wear department. Supercenters were about 125,000 to 150,000 square feet in size and were targeted for locations where sales per store of $30 to $50 million annually were thought feasible.

Wal-Mart management believed the Supercenter format was quite promising; numerous experiments were under way in the 68 Supercenters already open and the company was planning to open 50 additional Supercenters in the remaining months of 1994. In trying to perfect the Supercenter concept, Wal-Mart management was focusing on improving merchandise layouts and displays and on learning all it could about grocery marketing and grocery distribution. To enhance its knowledge of the

EXHIBIT 2 | Wal-Mart Retailing Locations, February 1994

	Wal-Mart Stores	Sam's Clubs	Supercenters	Distribution Centers	McLane's	Western
Alabama	70	8	4	1		
Alaska		3				
Arizona	29	6		1	1	
Arkansas	66	4	11	6		
California	66	26		1	2	
Colorado	34	8		1	1	1
Connecticut	2	3				
Delaware	2	1				
Florida	124	36	1	1	1	
Georgia	83	14		1	1	1
Hawaii		1				
Idaho	7	1				
Illinois	101	24	1		1	
Indiana	69	14		2		
Iowa	45	4		1		
Kansas	42	7	1			
Kentucky	67	4	1			
Louisiana	72	9	2			
Maine	14	3				
Maryland	13	9				
Massachusetts	7	5				
Michigan	30	21				
Minnesota	29	8				
Mississippi	52	3	5	1	1	
Missouri	91	12	14			
Montana	4	1				
Nebraska	17	3				

supermarket business and develop the organizational ability to execute the Super-center concept with a high degree of proficiency, Wal-Mart had acquired a grocery distribution company in Texas, McLane Company, which had nationwide distribution capabilities and also operated food processing facilities. McLane was a major supplier to The Southland Corporation's 7-Eleven chain of convenience stores and to independent grocers. In 1993 McLane had sales of $2.9 billion.

In addition, Wal-Mart had a small number of Bud's Warehouse Outlets, which specialized in close-out goods, and was experimenting with a new concept called vendor stores that involved selecting key suppliers in a major category and giving them wide latitude in merchandising their products; suppliers participating in the vendor store trials included Rubbermaid, Black & Decker, Cannon, Pioneer, Gitano, Toshiba, and Wrangler. In 1993 Wal-Mart had opened a farm, home, and garden store called County Farms that focused on the business needs of farmers; the stores had refrigerated vaccines to treat animal ailments, selected farm and garden equipment, a market quote board for commodity prices, a conference room 4H clubs could use for meet-

EXHIBIT 2 | Wal-Mart Retailing Locations, 1994 *(continued)*

	Wal-Mart Stores	Sam's Clubs	Supercenters	Distribution Centers	McLane's	Western
Nevada	6	2				1
New Hampshire	11	4				
New Jersey	9	5				
New Mexico	19	3				
New York	28	14			1	
North Carolina	79	12				
North Dakota	8	2				
Ohio	49	21		1		
Oklahoma	72	6	9			
Oregon	15					
Pennsylvania	37	12		1		
Puerto Rico	3	2				
Rhode Island	2	1				
South Carolina	49	6		2		
South Dakota	8	1				
Tennessee	84	8	2			
Texas	214	52	17	4	3	2
Utah	11	4		1	1	
Virginia	41	8		1	1	
Washington	3	2			1	
West Virginia	12	4				
Wisconsin	48	10		1		
Wyoming	9	2				
USA Total	**1,953**	**419**	**68**	**27**	**15**	**5**
Mexico	14*	7	2		1	
Grand Total	**1,967**	**426**	**70**	**27**	**16**	**5**

*Includes 2 Superamas, 10 Boedegas, and 2 Aurreras.

meetings, a small-engine parts and service center, and an array of lawn, garden, and feed products.

Exhibit 2 shows the number of Wal-Mart stores in each state as of 1994.

MERCHANDISING INNOVATIONS

Wal-Mart was unusually active in experimenting with and testing new merchandising techniques. From the beginning, Sam Walton had been quick to imitate good ideas and merchandising practices employed by other retailers. According to the founder of Kmart, Sam Walton "not only copied our concepts, he strengthened them. Sam just took the ball and ran with it."[2] Wal-Mart prided itself on its "low threshold for change" and much of management's time was spent talking to vendors, employees, and customers to get ideas for how Wal-Mart could improve. Suggestions were actively solicited from employees. Almost any reasonable idea was tried; if it worked well in stores where it was first tested, then it was quickly implemented in other stores. Experiments in store layout, merchandise displays, store color schemes, mer-

[2]As quoted in Bill Saporito, "What Sam Walton Taught America," *Fortune,* May 4, 1992, p. 105.

chandise selection (whether to add more upscale lines or shift to a different mix of items), and sales promotion techniques were always under way. Wal-Mart was regarded as an industry leader in testing, adapting, and applying a wide range of cutting-edge merchandising approaches.

THE COMPETITIVE ENVIRONMENT

Discount retailing was an intensely competitive business. Wal-Mart's two closest competitors were Kmart and Sears. Both firms had comparable strategies and store formats but throughout the 1980s Wal-Mart had grown far faster than Kmart (see Exhibit 3). In 1989 Sears, concerned with lagging sales and Wal-Mart's rise to industry leadership, switched to an everyday-low-price strategy and started stocking leading brand-name merchandise to complement its own private-label goods. In 1994, nearly all discounters were using some form of everyday low pricing.

Competition among discount retailers centered around pricing, store location, variations in store format and merchandise mix, store size, shopping atmosphere, and image with shoppers. Wal-Mart was the only top-10 discount retailer that located a majority of its stores in rural areas. Surveys of households comparing Wal-Mart with Kmart and Target indicated that Wal-Mart had a strong competitive advantage. According to *Discount Store News:*[3]

> When asked to compare Wal-Mart with Kmart and Target, the consensus of households is that Wal-Mart is as good or better. For example, of the households with a Wal-Mart in their area, 59 percent said that Wal-Mart is better than Kmart and Target; 33 percent said it was the same. Only 4 percent rated Wal-Mart worse than Kmart and Target. . . . When asked why Wal-Mart is better, 55 percent of the respondents with a Wal-Mart in their area said lower/better prices. . . . Variety/selection and good quality were the other top reasons cited by consumers when asked why Wal-Mart is better. Thirty percent said variety; 18 percent said good quality.

Wal-Mart's reputation extended to areas where it did not have stores, reducing the costs of pushing outward into new geographic areas. Numerous stories in the media about Sam Walton and Wal-Mart's merchandising prowess had given the company a favorable image and name recognition among consumers.

THE WAREHOUSE CLUB SEGMENT

The two largest competitors in the warehouse club segment were Price/Costco and Sam's Wholesale Clubs. These two accounted for a combined total of 80 percent of total sales among wholesale clubs and 55 percent of total store outlets (see Exhibit 4). In November 1990, Wal-Mart acquired Wholesale Club in a $172 million transaction, a move that increased the size of the Sam's chain to 168 stores by adding 27 stores in six Midwestern states. The per-store cost of the acquisition was just over $6 million compared to $5.5 million to build and open a new Sam's. Analysts said the acquisition cut a year off the time it would have taken to enter these states and, at the same time, provided an established customer base. With the acquisition, Sam's became the undisputed leader of the warehouse club segment.

There was an industrywide effort among wholesale club competitors to differentiate themselves on the basis of service. Service differentiation was intended to make

---

[3]*Discount Store News*, December 18, 1989, p. 168.

EXHIBIT 3 | Comparative Financial Performance of Sears (Merchandise Group Operations only), Kmart, and Wal-Mart, 1980–1993

	Sales (In millions of dollars)			Net Income (In millions of dollars)			Net income as a Percentage of Sales		
Year	Sears*	Kmart	Wal-Mart**	Sears*	Kmart	Wal-Mart**	Sears*	Kmart	Wal-Mart**
1980	$18,675	$14,118	$ 1,643	$ 229	$ 429	$ 56	1.2%	3.0%	3.4%
1981	20,202	16,394	2,445	285	311	83	1.4	1.9	3.4
1982	20,667	16,611	3,376	432	408	124	2.1	2.5	3.7
1983	25,089	18,380	4,667	781	859	196	3.1	4.7	4.2
1984	26,508	20,762	6,401	905	835	271	3.4	4.0	4.2
1985	26,552	22,035	8,451	766	757	327	2.9	3.4	3.9
1986	27,074	23,812	11,909	736	1,028	450	2.7	4.3	3.8
1987	28,085	25,627	15,959	787	1,171	627	2.8	4.6	3.9
1988	30,256	27,301	20,649	524	1,244	837	1.7	4.6	4.1
1989	31,599	29,533	25,811	647	1,155†	1,076	2.1	3.9	4.2
1990	31,986	32,070	32,602	257	1,146	1,291	0.8	3.6	4.0
1991	31,433	34,580	43,887	486	1,301	1,608	1.5	3.8	3.7
1992	31,961	31,031	55,484	(2,977)	941	1,995	(9.3)	2.7	3.6
1993	29,565	34,156	67,345	752	(328)	2,333	2.5	(1.0)	3.5

*Sears' data represents Merchandise Group Operations only; revenues and income for other Sears' businesses (insurance, finance, and so on) have been eliminated so that data will be comparable across companies.

**Wal-Mart's fiscal year ends January 31 of each year; data for the period January 31, 1980 through January 31, 1981 are reported in Wal-Mart's annual report as 1981 results. Because Wal-Mart's fiscal year results really cover 11 months of the previous calendar year, this exhibit shows Wal-Mart's 1981 fiscal results in the 1980 row, its 1982 fiscal results in the 1981 row, and so on. This adjustment makes Wal-Mart's figures correspond more to the same time frame as the calendar year data for Sears and Kmart.

†Before a pre-tax provision of $640 million for restructuring.

Source: Company annual reports, 1980–1993.

club membership appealing to a broader segment of the market. Prior to the late 1980s, none of the major warehouse clubs operated in the same geographic markets. However, the success of the club concept had fueled geographic expansion by all competitors. As competitors saturated the geographic areas surrounding their initial stores, they were expanding outward to increase market coverage and were trying to beat rival clubs to the most attractive market areas. By the 1990s, warehouse club competitors had moved into rivals' markets and were competing head-on for the first time, forcing mergers and producing slowdowns in sales growth. In 1994, the wholesale club market in the U.S. was regarded as mature.

WAL-MART'S APPROACHES TO STRATEGY IMPLEMENTATION

To implement its strategy, Wal-Mart put heavy emphasis on forging solid working relationships with both suppliers and employees, paying attention to even the tiniest details in store layouts and merchandising, capitalizing on every cost-saving opportunity, and creating a high-performance spirit. The characteristics that often stalled the growth and success of large companies—too many layers of management, lack of internal communication, and an unwillingness or inability to change—were absent at Wal-Mart.

EXHIBIT 4 | Comparative Statistics for Leading Membership Warehouse Retailers, 1991–92

Chain, Parent, Headquarters	Revenues[a] (in millions)		Percent Change	Operating Income (in millions)		Percent Change
	1992	1991		1992	1991	
Sam's Club Wal-Mart Stores Bentonville, AR	$12,339	$ 9,430	30.8%	$270*	$233	15.9%
Price Club[1] The Price Co., San Diego, CA	7,480	6,740	10.9	223	213	4.7
Costco Wholesale[2] Costco Wholesale Corp. Kirkland, WA	6,620	5,305	24.8	184	136	35.3
Pace Membership Warehouse Kmart Corp., Aurora, CO	4,358	3,646	19.5	30*	39	(23.1)
BJ's Wholesale Club Waban Inc., Natick, MA	1,760	1,432	22.2	30*	17	76.5
Smart & Final Smart & Final Inc. Santa Barbara, CA	752*	683	13.4	21*	18	16.7
Mega Warehouse Foods Megafoods Stores, Inc. Mesa, AZ	293	245	19.6	3.5*	3	16.7
Warehouse Club[3] Warehouse Club Inc., Skokie, IL	241	250	(3.6)	0.2	(0.4)	—
Wholesale Depot Wholesale Depot Inc. Natick, MA	200*	100*	100	NA	NA	—
Club Aurrora[4] Wal-Mart Stores/Cifra S.A. Mexico City	60*	—	—	—	—	—
Price Club de Mexico[5] Price Club de Mexico S.A. de C.V. Mexico City	40*	—	—	—	—	—
Total:	$34,143	$27,811	23.2%	—	—	—

[a]Sales and membership fees where applicable. *DSN estimate. ( ) decrease. NA: not available or not applicable.

[1]Includes sales from 17 Canadian clubs; revenues include membership fees and other income of $160M in 1992 and $142M in 1991; excludes real estate income. Merged with Costco in 1993.

[2]Includes sales from 12 Canadian clubs; revenues include membership fees and other income of $121M in 1992 and $90M in 1991. Merged with Price in 1993.

[3]Revenues included membership fees and other income of $7M in 1992 and 1991.

[4]Revenues, club count not included in Sam's Club statistics.

[5]Revenues, club count not included in Price Club statistics.

Sam's Club fiscal year ended Jan. 31, 1993.
Price Club fiscal year ended Aug. 31, 1992.
Costco Wholesale fiscal year ended Aug. 30, 1992.
Pace Membership Warehouse fiscal year ended Jan. 27, 1993.
BJs Wholesale Club fiscal year ended Jan. 30, 1993.
Source: Discount Store News, March 1, 1993, p. 18.

Smart & Final fiscal year ended Jan. 4, 1993.
Mega Warehouse Foods fiscal year ended Dec. 31, 1992.
Warehouse Club fiscal year ended Oct. 3, 1992.
Wholesale Depot fiscal year ended Dec. 31, 1992.

EXHIBIT 4 | Comparative Statistics for Leading Membership Warehouse Retailers, 1991–92

| Number of Stores | | | Average | | |
1/92	1/93	1/94*	Club Size	Membership	Merchandise
208	256	305	115,000	Paid; restricted	General merchandise/food
88	94	102	117,000	Paid; restricted	General merchandise/food
91	100	110	115,000	Paid; restricted	General merchandise/food
87	115	137	115,000	Paid; restricted	General merchandise/food
29	39	54	110,000	Paid; restricted	General merchandise/food
116	125	139	16,000	Free; unrestricted	Food/janitorial/ packaging
14	22	31	52,000	Free; unrestricted	Food/household and business consumables
10	10	10	100,000	Paid; restricted	General merchandise/food
4	8	15	64,000	Paid; restricted	General merchandise/food
2	3	8	75,000	Paid; restricted	General merchandise/food
8	1	3	100,000	Paid; restricted	General merchandise/food
649	773	914	—	—	—

THE EVERYDAY-LOW-PRICE THEME

While Wal-Mart did not invent the everyday-low-price strategy, it had done a better job than any other discount retailer in executing the concept. The company had the reputation of being the everyday-lowest-priced general-merchandise retailer in its market. In areas where Wal-Mart had a store, consumer surveys showed 55 percent of the households considered Wal-Mart's prices as lower or better than competitors; an impressive 33 percent of the households not having a Wal-Mart store in their area had the same opinion.[4] Wal-Mart touted its low prices on its store fronts ("We Sell

[4]Ibid.

for Less"), in advertising, on signs inside its stores, and on the logos of its shopping bags.

ADVERTISING

Wal-Mart relied less on advertising than any of its competitors. The company distributed only one or two circulars per month (versus an average of one per week at Kmart) and ran occasional TV ads, relying primarily on word-of-mouth to communicate its marketing message. As a percentage of sales, Wal-Mart's advertising expenditures were the lowest in the discount industry, several percentage points below what Kmart spent. Wal-Mart's spending for radio and TV advertising was so low that it didn't register on national ratings scales. Most Wal-Mart broadcast ads appeared on local TV and local cable channels. However, Wal-Mart had been successful in supplementing its low ad expenditures with media publicity concerning several programs it had initiated. Wal-Mart's policy of giving preferential treatment to products made in the United States generated thousands of local newspaper articles, nearly all of which quoted Wal-Mart statistics that its Buy American plan had saved or created thousands of American jobs. Wal-Mart had also gotten free media publicity with its program to spotlight products with environmentally safe packaging. The company often allowed charities to use its parking lots for their fund-raising activities.

DISTRIBUTION

Over the years, Wal-Mart management had turned the company's centralized distribution systems into a competitive edge. David Glass said, "Our distribution facilities are one of the keys to our success. If we do anything better than other folks that's it."[5] Wal-Mart got an early jump on competitors in distribution efficiency because of its rural store locations. Whereas other discount retailers relied upon manufacturers and distributors to ship directly to their mostly metropolitan-area stores, Wal-Mart found that its rapid growth during the 1970s was straining suppliers' ability to use independent trucking firms to make frequent and timely deliveries to its growing number of rural store locations. To improve the delivery of merchandise to its stores, the company in 1980 began to build area distribution centers and to supply stores from these centers with its own truck fleet. Wal-Mart added new distribution centers when new, outlying stores could no longer be reliably and economically supported from an existing center. In 1994, the company had 22 distribution centers covering 21.5 million square feet. Together the centers employed 16,000 workers who handled over 850,000 truckloads of merchandise annually with a 99 percent accuracy rate on filling orders. Wal-Mart's distribution centers made extensive use of automated systems:[6]

> The conveyor system starts with walk-pick modules where order selection occurs. The cartons move on a conveyor to a central merge where an operator releases cartons onto a sortation system. A laser scanner reads a bar code and tells the automatic sorter where to divert cartons at rates in excess of 120 per minute. The cartons are diverted to various shipping doors.

---

[5]Ibid., p. 54.
[6]Ibid.

A study of 1988 data indicated Wal-Mart's distribution cost advantage over Sears and Kmart was significant:

	1988 Sales (in millions)	Distribution Costs (in millions)	Distribution Costs as a Percent of Sales
Sears	$50,251	$2,513	5.0%
Kmart	27,301	956	3.5
Wal-Mart	20,649	263	1.3

Source: *Discount Store News,* December 18, 1989, p. 201.

Whereas Wal-Mart had the capability to make daily deliveries to nearly all its stores, Kmart delivered to its stores about once every four to five days and Target delivered every three to four days.

THE USE OF CUTTING-EDGE TECHNOLOGY

Wal-Mart was aggressive in applying the latest technological advances to increase productivity and drive costs down. The company's technological goal was to provide employees with the tools to do their jobs more efficiently and to make better decisions. Technology was not used as a means of replacing existing employees. Moreover, Wal-Mart's approach to technology was to be on the offensive—probing, testing, and then deploying the newest equipment, retailing techniques, and computer software programs ahead of most, if not all, other discount retailers.

In 1974 the company began using computers to maintain inventory control on an item basis in distribution centers and in its stores. In 1981, Wal-Mart began testing point-of-sale scanners and committed itself to chainwide use of scanning bar codes in 1983—a move that resulted in a 25 to 30 percent faster checkout of customers. In 1984, Wal-Mart developed a computer-assisted merchandising system that allowed the product mix in each store to be tailored to its own market circumstances and sales patterns. Between 1985 and 1987 Wal-Mart installed the nation's largest private satellite communication network, which allowed two-way voice and data transmission between headquarters, the distribution centers, and the stores and one-way video transmission from Bentonville's corporate offices to distribution centers and to the stores; the system was less expensive than the previously used telephone network. The video system was used regularly by company officials to speak directly to all employees at once.

In 1989 Wal-Mart established direct satellite linkage with about 1,700 vendors supplying close to 80 percent of the goods sold by Wal-Mart; this linkup allowed the use of electronic purchase orders and instant data exchanges. Wal-Mart had also used the satellite system's capabilities to develop a credit card authorization procedure that took five seconds, on average, to authorize a purchase, speeding up credit checkout by 25 percent compared to the prior manual system. The company had exemplary data processing and information systems. Not only had the company developed the computer systems to provide management with detailed figures on almost any aspect of Wal-Mart's operations, but the company was also regarded as having one of the lowest-cost, most efficient data processing operations of any company its size in the world. The company's rapid adoption of cutting-edge retailing technologies across many areas of its business had given Wal-Mart a technology advantage over most other discounters.

CONSTRUCTION POLICIES

Wal-Mart management worked at getting more mileage out of its capital expenditures for new stores, store renovations, and store fixtures. Ideas and suggestions were solicited from vendors regarding store layout, the design of fixtures, and space needed for effective displays. Wal-Mart's store designs had open-air offices for management personnel that could be furnished economically and featured a maximum of display space that could be rearranged and refurbished easily. Because Wal-Mart insisted on a high degree of uniformity in the new stores it built, the architectural firm Wal-Mart employed was able to use computer modeling techniques to turn out complete specifications for up to 12 new stores a week. Moreover, the stores were designed to permit quick, inexpensive construction as well as to allow for low-cost maintenance and renovation. All stores were renovated and redecorated at least once every seven years. If a given store location was rendered obsolete by the construction of new roads and highways and the opening of new shopping locations, then the old store was abandoned in favor of a new store at a more desirable site. As of 1994, Wal-Mart was expanding or relocating stores at the rate of 100 per year.

In keeping with the low-cost theme for facilities, Wal-Mart's distribution centers and corporate offices were also built economically and furnished simply. The offices of top executives were modest and unpretentious. The lighting, heating and air-conditioning controls at all Wal-Mart stores were connected via computer to Bentonville headquarters, allowing cost-saving energy management practices to be implemented centrally and freeing store managers from the time and worry of trying to hold down utility costs. Wal-Mart mass-produced a lot of its displays in-house, not only saving money but also cutting the time to roll out a new display concept to as little as 30 days.

RELATIONSHIPS WITH SUPPLIERS

Wal-Mart was noted for driving a hard bargain with its suppliers, bringing all of its considerable buying power to bear. The company's purchasing department was austere and utilitarian. Purchasing agents were dedicated to getting the lowest prices they could, and they did not accept invitations to be wined or dined by suppliers. The marketing vice president of a major vendor told *Fortune* magazine:[7]

> They are very, very focused people, and they use their buying power more forcefully than anybody else in America. All the normal mating rituals are verboten. Their highest priority is making sure everybody at all times in all cases knows who's in charge, and it's Wal-Mart. They talk softly, but they have piranha hearts, and if you aren't totally prepared when you go in there, you'll have your ass handed to you.

Even though Wal-Mart was tough in negotiating for absolute rock-bottom prices, the company worked closely with suppliers to develop mutual respect and to forge long-term partnerships that benefited both parties. Vendors were invited to tour Wal-Mart's distribution centers to see firsthand how things operated and to learn what kinds of problems Wal-Mart had in achieving greater efficiency. Vendors were also encouraged to voice any problems in their relationships with Wal-Mart and to become involved in Wal-Mart's future plans. For example, in 1987 after Sam Walton asked Procter & Gamble executives to view a focus group of Wal-Mart executives talking about their prickly relationship with P&G, P&G responded by stationing a

---

[7]*Fortune,* January 30, 1989, p. 53.

team of people near Wal-Mart headquarters to work with Wal-Mart on a continuing basis.[8] One top-priority project involved an effort to supply more P&G items in recyclable packaging to meet Wal-Mart's publicly stated goal of selling products that were environmentally safe. Another concerned linking the two companies' computers to set up a just-in-time ordering and delivery system for many products P&G supplied to Wal-Mart stores; when Wal-Mart's stocks reached the reorder point, a computer automatically sent a resupply order by satellite to the nearest P&G factory, which then shipped more of the item to a Wal-Mart distribution center or, in the case of disposable diapers, directly to the store. P&G and Wal-Mart saw the automatic reordering arrangement as a win-win proposition because with better coordination P&G could plan efficient manufacturing runs, streamline distribution, and lower its costs, passing some of the savings on to Wal-Mart.

Wal-Mart looked for suppliers who were dominant in their categories (thus providing strong brand-name recognition), who could grow with the company, who had full product lines (so that Wal-Mart buyers could both cherry-pick and get some sort of limited exclusivity on the products it chose to carry), who had the long-term commitment to R&D to bring new and better products to retail shelves, and who had the ability to become more efficient in producing and delivering what they supplied. As one supplier remarked, "Wal-Mart wants suppliers who can keep up." Several suppliers described Wal-Mart's approaches to doing business with them:[9]

> They challenge us constantly. Can we do this? How about if we tried that? They're constantly on the lookout for ways to improve themselves.
>
> They approach problems as opportunities, not as complaints. They're completely genuine in meetings . . . all cards are on the table.
>
> No matter how good your products are, if they don't tell the story on the shelf, they won't do well at Wal-Mart. They're looking for dynamic, creative packaging that will act as a salesman.
>
> They know their stores, their products, and their markets, and they have an uncanny ability to predict what their customer wants. Their advice about products is valuable to us.
>
> We have to do what we say we're going to do . . . Wal-Mart's demands can be staggering, like when they need many thousands of VCRs for a promotion. If we can't be sure that we can have the stock *in their warehouses* on a given day, we let them know that, [and] suggest moving the promotion back a month.
>
> They honor their commitments and they expect the same in return. If we gear up for a promotion, and the circular gets cancelled, they'll still take the goods. That's how they do business.

WAL-MART'S "BUY AMERICA" POLICY

In a March 1985 letter sent to about 3,000 domestic suppliers, Sam Walton discussed the serious threat of the nation's balance of trade deficit and conveyed the company's desire to carry more U.S.-made goods in Wal-Mart's stores:

> Our Wal-Mart company is firmly committed to the philosophy of buying everything possible from suppliers who manufacture their products in the United States. We are convinced that with proper planning and cooperation between retailers and manufacturers many products can be supplied to us that are comparable, or better, in value and

---

[8]Saporito, "What Sam Walton Taught America," p. 104.
[9]*Discount Store News,* December 18, 1989, pp. 109 and 156.

quality to those we have been buying offshore . . . Wal-Mart believes our American workers can make the difference if management provides the leadership.

Walton then sent a now-famous edict to Wal-Mart buyers and merchandise managers: "Find products that American manufacturers have stopped producing because they couldn't compete with foreign imports." Wal-Mart kicked off its Buy America program publicly with newspaper and TV ads featuring the slogans "We Buy American Whenever We Can So You Can, Too" and "Wal-Mart—Keeping America Working and Strong." Wal-Mart's stores displayed "Bring It Home to the USA" banners hanging from store ceilings; special "Made in America" posters and small placards citing job-creating statistics were put on fixtures that held American-made goods—see Exhibit 5. In the company's 1993 annual report, management explained the Buy America program and cited instances of products that were now being made in U.S. plants:

> The Buy America program demonstrates a long-standing Wal-Mart commitment to our customers that we will buy American-made products whenever we can *if* those products deliver the same quality and affordability as their foreign-made counterparts. It also exemplifies a *partnership* that we have developed with our American vendors and suppliers to seek out products that can be manufactured here competitively and to help facilitate their reintroduction to the American marketplace.
>
> We have never said that we always buy American. We wish we could. But many times we have paid a premium to get products that were previously made overseas to be manufactured here.
>
> Last year, Wal-Mart challenged Kalikow Brothers, a long-time vendor-partner, to move production of popular men's shorts back from the Orient to the States. By working together, we were able to relocate the manufacturing to a plant in Lake Butler, Florida. Over 125 jobs were added. A second plant has been rejuvenated in the process.
>
> A maker of ladies' foundation garments in Blackwell, Oklahoma, Southwest Cupid, adapted modular concepts introduced at a seminar sponsored by Wal-Mart and one of the vendor's fabric suppliers. As a result of these efforts, they were able to bring production back from Haiti and Jamaica. Because of our increased orders for their Lady Manhattan brand, they are opening a new plant in concert with the Native American community located in Hominy, Oklahoma.
>
> These are just two examples of conversions that Wal-Mart has helped facilitate from offshore to domestic manufacturing. There are many more.
>
> Whatever can be competitively made in the USA, should be. It won't happen overnight. It might not happen in every industry and every category. But to keep trying is the right thing to do, and Wal-Mart will not let up in its efforts.

Wal-Mart claimed the program had resulted in its reducing its purchases of foreign-made goods from about 35 percent to about 30 percent of everything it sold. According to industry analysts, however, Wal-Mart still imported about twice as much of what it sold as Kmart. Yet because of the manner in which Wal-Mart had implemented and communicated its Buy America policy, consumer awareness of Wal-Mart's efforts was high in comparison with awareness of other companies' efforts that had followed Wal-Mart's lead in promoting American-made products.

WAL-MART'S ENVIRONMENTALLY SAFE POLICY

In 1989 Wal-Mart became the first major retailer to embark on a program urging vendors to develop products and packaging that would not harm the environment.

EXHIBIT 5 | Examples of Wal-Mart's Signs and Ads Advocating American-Made Products and Environmental Consciousness

Bring It Home To The U.S.A.

At Wal-Mart, we are committed to forming partnerships with American manufacturers to produce products we are currently buying from foreign markets.

PREVIOUSLY IMPORTED
NOW PURCHASED IN THE USA

Girls Flannel Shirts
Hampton Girl - Greenville, NC.
26 Jobs Created

.6 Cubic Foot Microwave
Magic Chef Inc. - Anniston, AL.
633 Jobs Created

JOBS FOR AMERICANS!
With your support, since 1985, we have created or retained over... **43,000** Manufacturing Jobs for Americans

Our Commitment To Land, Air, & Water

You Can Make A Difference

- **Run washing machine and dishwasher only when full.**
- **Plant trees.**
- **Put in a toilet dam and reduce water use by 50%.**
- **Start a compost pile in your backyard.**
- **Keep a coffee mug at work.**
- **Water lawns and plants in the morning to minimize evaporation.**
- **Don't litter.**
- **Request a low-cost home energy audit from your utility company.**
- **Take glass, aluminum, paper to recycling centers. Each U.S. citizen produces 4 to 6 pounds of waste per day, 80% of which ends up in land fills.**
- **Look for the three-arrow recycling symbol on packages.**

RECYCLE

Management negotiated with its suppliers of signs, shopping bags, and other such items to convert them to environmentally safe products. It started posting shelf signs beside merchandise with environmentally safe features. The company took its campaign public with full-page ads in *USA Today* and *The Wall Street Journal* using the theme "We're Looking for Quality Products That Are Guaranteed Not to Last." The policy was implemented because Wal-Mart's top management saw the environment as a top-priority national issue; David Glass, Wal-Mart's president, told an audience:[10]

> I believe that retailers and suppliers must now be socially conscious in a way that we haven't before. Those of you who don't believe that we have a terrible problem with the environment are naive. We are running out of land to bury things. We are quickly spoiling our drinking water and eroding the ozone layer. . . .
>
> We need to take a responsibility for the role we play and for our own actions. What we will do is identify these products in our showrooms and ask our customers to buy those rather than other products that are not safe for the environment. . . . We believe we can bring [environmentally safe products] to market at the same kind of price.

The company further described its policy and efforts in its 1993 annual report:

> As serious as environmental challenges are becoming—pollution, waste of resources and others—the real hurdle is the mistaken collective belief that we simply can't do anything about them.
>
> At Wal-Mart, we *know* we can do something, because we know our people. They have *proven* they can make a difference. So all of us are working harder to understand the environmental issues, to communicate them more effectively, and to do the right things in all of our stores across America.
>
> It is important to note that our program was not designed to sell a particular product, promote a private label, or capitalize on a politically correct cause. The truth is reason enough: The health of our planet is at stake. Our customers know it, and we know it.
>
> Last year our stores together with their communities recycled approximately 442,000 tons of paper and plastic. In partnership with our vendors, we now print *all* of our circulars on recycled paper. Each year, we buy more products made of recycled materials, and we challenge our vendor-partners to find alternatives that are more environmentally responsible. These efforts have resulted in hundreds of product or packaging improvements.
>
> Our customers want to help, too. So we help them by collecting motor oil and batteries and establishing neighborhood recycling centers, often placing bins in our store parking lots until permanent centers can be established. To encourage environmental efforts by our schoolchildren, we are involved with programs like Kids for a Clean Environment. To date, this international organization has over 30,000 members in local clubs across America. We print and distribute materials and newsletters, and we help fund an 800 number. In one of our most ambitious efforts, we are building an experimental Wal-Mart store of the future.
>
> Opening in the spring of 1993 in Lawrence, Kansas, this unique store is designed to be environmentally friendly in every way possible. We believe it will create new markets for recycled products and construction techniques. It will serve as a working laboratory for students. It will become a dynamic experiment in testing new environmental ideas.
>
> We realize we have barely begun. But with the support of Wal-Mart's customers, shareholders, and our vendor-partners, we are certain we can create a cleaner and a safer environment for our children.

Despite some cynical observations that Wal-Mart's policy was a publicity and marketing ploy, Wal-Mart had succeeded in influencing suppliers to spend more on R&D to develop products with more environmentally safe ingredients and to find ways to use recyclable packaging materials. Procter & Gamble was among the first suppliers to be responsive to Wal-Mart's environmental program; by 1990 all of

---

[10]*Discount Store News,* December 18, 1989, pp. 109 and 156.

P&G's soap and detergent packages had been converted to 100 percent recycled cartons, and its plastic containers were being coded so they could be efficiently separated for recycling. The head of P&G's team servicing the Wal-Mart account commented, "They're trying to do the right thing and to educate the consumer."

WAL-MART'S APPROACH TO PROVIDING SUPERIOR CUSTOMER SERVICE

Wal-Mart tried to put substance behind its pledge of "Satisfaction Guaranteed" and do things that would make customers' shopping experience at Wal-Mart pleasant. A "greeter" was stationed at store entrances to welcome customers with a smile, thank them for shopping at Wal-Mart, assist them in getting a shopping cart, and answer questions about where items were located. Clerks and checkout workers were trained to be courteous and helpful and to exhibit a "friendly, folksy attitude." All store personnel took an oath of friendliness: "I solemnly promise and declare that every customer that comes within ten feet of me, I will smile, look them in the eye, and greet them, so help me Sam." Wal-Mart's management stressed five themes in training and supervising store personnel:

1. Think like a customer.
2. Sell the customer what they want to buy.
3. Provide a genuine value to the customer.
4. Make sure the customer has a good time.
5. Exceed the customer's expectations.

One of the standard Wal-Mart chants drilled into all employees was

> Who's number one? The customer.
> The customer is the boss.

Wal-Mart's newest stores had wider aisles and significantly more customer space. In all stores, efforts were under way to present merchandise in easier-to-shop shelving and displays. Floors in the apparel section were carpeted to make the department feel homier and to make shopping seem easier on customers' feet. Store layouts were constantly scrutinized to improve shopping convenience and make it easier for customers to find items. Store employees wore blue vests to make it easier for customers to pick them out from a distance. Fluorescent lighting was recessed into the ceiling, creating a softer impression than the exposed fluorescent lighting strips used at Kmart stores. Management stressed making the decor of Wal-Mart's stores convey feelings of warmth and freshness as a way of signaling customers that Wal-Mart was a bit more upscale and carried a little better quality merchandise than rivals. Yet nothing about the decor conflicted with Wal-Mart's low-price image; retailing consultants considered Wal-Mart very adept at sending out an effective mix of vibes and signals concerning customer service, low prices, quality merchandise, and friendly shopping environment.

Wal-Mart's management believed that the attention paid to all the details of making the stores more user-friendly and inviting caused shoppers to view Wal-Mart in a more positive light. A reporter for *Discount Store News* observed:[11]

---

[11]Ibid., p. 161.

The fact is that everything Wal-Mart does from store design to bar coding to lighting to greeters—regardless of how simple or complex—is implemented only after carefully considering the impact on the customer. Virtually nothing is done without the guarantee that it benefits the customer in some way. . . . As a result Wal-Mart has been able to build loyalty and trust among its customers that is unparalleled among other retail giants.

SAM WALTON'S LEADERSHIP STYLE AND BUSINESS PHILOSOPHY

Mr. Sam, as he was fondly called and remembered, was not only Wal-Mart's founder and patriarch but also its spiritual leader. Despite great wealth, he was a man of simple tastes and genuine affection for people. His folksy personality, unpretentious manner, and interest in people and their feelings caused people inside and outside the company to hold him in high esteem. Regarded by many as "the entrepreneur of the century" and "a genuine American folk hero," he enjoyed a reputation for being concerned about employees, being community-spirited, and being a devoted family man who epitomized the American dream and demonstrated the virtues of hard work. Casewriter interviews with Wal-Mart associates in 1986 indicated how he was regarded by the rank-and-file:

> He's a beautiful man. I met him when this store opened. He came back two and one-half years later and still remembered me. He walked over to this department and said, "Grace, you and I have been around a long time, I'm gonna hug your neck."
>
> I was just . . . I was thrilled [to meet him]. He's a very special person. He is a very outgoing person, and it kind of motivates you just to sit and listen to him talk. He listens—that's another thing.
>
> He's just an everyday person . . . When you meet him he's just like one of us. You can talk to him. Anything you want to ask him—you can just go right up and ask.
>
> He's really down-to-earth. He'll put his arm around you, hug you, and tell you you're doing a good job.
>
> Mr. Walton cares about his employees. You get the feeling that you're working for him instead of Wal-Mart. And although he may not need the money, he's good to us and we try to be good to him.

Four key core values and business principles underpinned Sam Walton's approach to managing the company:[12]

- Treat employees as partners, sharing both the good and bad about the company so they will strive to excel and participate in the rewards.
- Build for the future, rather than just immediate gains, by continuing to study the changing concepts that are a mark of the retailing industry and be ready to test and experiment with new ideas.
- Recognize that the road to success includes failing, which is part of the learning process rather than a personal or corporate defect or failing. Always challenge the obvious.
- Involve associates at all levels in the total decision-making process.

He practiced these principles diligently in his own actions and insisted other Wal-Mart managers do the same. Until his health failed badly in 1991, he spent several

---

[12]Ibid., p. 29.

days a week visiting the stores, gauging the moods of shoppers, listening to employees discuss what was on their minds, learning what was or was not selling, gathering ideas about how things could be done better, complimenting workers on their efforts, and challenging them to come up with good ideas. Charles Cates, a former manager of the second store Wal-Mart opened, described what happened on a typical Sam Walton visit to a Wal-Mart store:[13]

> First, you get a telephone call from Sam. He says, "Charlie, can you pick me up at the airport?" Then, in the car, he wants to know who your assistant managers are . . . the names of their children, wives, and what's happening in their lives. So you brief him on your assistants and their families.
>
> When he gets to the store, he wants to take a tour. He goes to each department manager. He'll say, "The department looks good," and ask, "Why are we out of merchandise? What are your sales this year? What's your markup? What's your best-selling item?
>
> He pats them on the back, shakes their hands, and thanks them for doing a good job. He's always motivating people. The associates feel like they're working directly for Sam Walton.
>
> After the tour, he'll meet with the associates in the store lounge. He commends them for the store's sales increases and he talks about merchandise. He has contests with merchandise. He'll tell a department manager: "You all find an item and I'll find an item and we'll see which item sells better."
>
> He's always challenging us. He'll look at another item and ask, "It's priced at $5. How many more can we sell at $4?"

Following Walton's lead, it became established practice for Wal-Mart managers at all levels to spend much time and effort motivating employees to achieve excellence, motivating them to offer ideas, to get involved, and to function as partners. A theme reiterated over and over again was that every cost counted and every worker had a responsibility; the slogan that every employee heard repeatedly was, "The customer is boss and the future depends on you." David Glass explained the philosophy underlying this approach:[14]

> Wal-Mart is unique because we require involvement. There's a pressure to get involved. Whatever level you're at, you'll perform far better if you're involved and believe that you can make a difference.

Wal-Mart fostered the concept of involvement by referring to all employees as "associates," a term Sam Walton had insisted on from the company's beginnings because it denoted a partnerlike relationship.

The values, beliefs, and practices that Sam Walton tried to instill in Wal-Mart's culture were reflected in statements made in his autobiography, completed weeks before his death in April 1992:[15]

- Everytime Wal-Mart spends one dollar foolishly, it comes right out of our customer's pockets. Everytime we save a dollar, that puts us one more step ahead of the competition—which is where we always plan to be.
- One person seeking glory doesn't accomplish much; at Wal-Mart, everything we've done has been the result of people pulling together to meet one common goal.

---

[13]Ibid., p. 235.
[14]Ibid., p. 83.
[15]Sam Walton with John Huey, *Sam Walton: Made in America* (New York: Doubleday, 1992), pp. 10, 12, 47, 63, 115, 128, 135, 140, 213, 226–29, 233, 246, 249, 254, and 256.

- I have always been driven to buck the system, to innovate, to take things beyond where they've been.

- We paid absolutely no attention whatsoever to the way things were supposed to be done, you know, the way the rules of retail said it had to be done.

- My role has been to pick good people and give them the maximum authority and responsibility. . . . I'm more of a manager by walking and flying around, and in the process I stick my fingers into everything I can to see how it's coming along. . . . My appreciation for numbers has kept me close to our operational statements and to all the other information we have pouring in from so many different places.

- The more you share profit with your associates—whether it's in salaries or incentives or bonuses or stock discounts—the more profit will accrue to your company. Why? Because the way management treats the associates is exactly how the associates will then treat the customers. And if the associates treat the customers well, the customers will return again and again.

- The real challenge in a business like ours is to become what we call servant leaders. And when they do, the team—the manager and the associates—can accomplish anything.

- There's no better way to keep someone doing things the right way than by letting him or her know how much you appreciate their performance.

- I like my numbers as quickly as I can get them. The quicker we get that information, the quicker we can act on it.

- The bigger we get as a company, the more important it becomes for us to shift responsibility and authority toward the front lines, toward that department manager who's stocking the shelves and talking to the customer.

- We give our department heads the opportunity to become real merchants at a very early stage of the game . . . we make our department heads the managers of their own businesses . . . we share everything with them: the costs of their goods, the freight costs, the profit margins. We let them see how their store ranks with every other store in the company on a constant, running basis, and we give them incentives to want to win.

- We're always looking for new ways to encourage our associates out in the stores to push their ideas up through the system. . . . Great ideas come from everywhere if you just listen and look for them. You never know who's going to have a great idea.

- A lot of bureaucracy is really the product of some empire builder's ego . . . we don't need any of that at Wal-Mart. If you're not serving the customers, or supporting the folks who do, we don't need you.

- I believe in always having goals, and always setting them high . . . the folks at Wal-Mart have always had goals in front of them. In fact, we have sometimes built real scoreboards on the stage at Saturday morning meetings.

- You can't just keep doing what works one time, because everything around you is always changing. To succeed, you have to stay out in front of that change.

- I feel like it's up to me as a leader to set an example.

Walton's success flowed from his cheerleading management style, his ability to instill the principles and management philosophies he preached into Wal-Mart's culture, the close watch he kept on costs, his relentless insistence on continuous improvement, and his habit of staying in close touch with both consumers and associates. It was common practice for Walton to lead cheers at annual shareholder meetings, store visits, managers' meetings, and company events. His favorite Wal-Mart cheer was

> Give me a W!
> Give me an A!
> Give me an L!
> Give me a squiggly! (Here, everybody sort of does the twist.)
> Give me an M!
> Give me an A!
> Give me an R!
> Give me a T!
> What's that spell?
>
> **Wal-Mart!**
> **Who's number one?**
> **The CUSTOMER!**

He observed, "If I'm leading the cheer, you'd better believe we do it loud." Walton was also noted for his rendition of "calling the hogs"—the University of Arkansas Razorbacks' cheer. The company had a number of cheers and chants, and Walton used them to create a "whistle while you work" atmosphere, loosen everyone up, inject fun and enthusiasm, and get sessions started on a stimulating note.

SOLICITING IDEAS FROM ASSOCIATES

Associates at all levels of the company were challenged to come up with ideas and suggestions to make the company better. An assistant store manager explained:[16]

> We are encouraged to be merchants. If a salesclerk, a checker, or a stockman believes he can sell an item and wants to promote it, he is encouraged to go for it. That associate can buy the merchandise, feature it, and maintain it as long as he can sell it.

That same assistant store manager, when he accidentally ordered four times as many Moon Pies for an in-store promotion as intended, was challenged by the store manager to be creative and figure out a way to sell the extra inventory. The assistant manager's solution was to create the first World Championship Moon Pie Eating Contest, held in the store's parking lot in the small town of Oneonta, Alabama. The promotion and contest drew thousands of spectators and was so successful that it became an annual store event.

Listening to employees was a very important part of each manager's job. All Wal-Mart executives relied on MBWA (management by walking around); they visited stores, distribution centers, and support facilities regularly, staying on top of what was happening and listening to what employees had to say about how things were going. It was a practice Sam Walton initiated and ardently believed in:[17]

---

[16]*Discount Store News,* December 18, 1989, p. 83.
[17]Sam Walton with John Huey, *Sam Walton: Made in America,* p. 248.

The folks on the front lines—the ones who actually talk to the customer—are the only ones who really know what's going on out there. You'd better find out what they know. This really is what total quality is all about. To push responsibility down in your organization, and to force good ideas to bubble up within it, you must listen to what your associates are trying to tell you.

Walton always insisted that most of the company's best ideas came from Wal-Mart associates and that visiting stores and listening to associates was a valuable use of his time. Wal-Mart's use of people greeters at the entrance of each store was one of those ideas; according to Wal-Mart's Tom Coughlin:[18]

Back in 1980, Mr. Walton and I went into a Wal-Mart in Crowley, Louisiana. The first thing we saw as we opened the door was this older gentleman standing there. The man didn't know me, and he didn't see Sam, but he said, "Hi! How are ya? Glad you're here. If there's anything I can tell you about our store, just let me know."

Neither Sam nor I had ever seen such a thing so we started talking to him. Well, once he got over the fact that he was talking to the chairman, he explained that he had a dual purpose: to make people feel good about coming in, and to make sure people weren't walking back out the entrance with merchandise they hadn't paid for.

The store, it turned out, had had trouble with shoplifting, and its manager was an old-line merchant named Dan McAllister who knew how to take care of his inventory. He didn't want to intimidate the honest customers by posting a guard at the door, but he wanted to leave a clear message that if you came in and stole, someone was there who would see it.

Well, Sam thought that was the greatest idea he'd ever heard of. He went right back to Bentonville and told everyone we ought to put greeters at the front of every single store. A lot of people thought he'd lost his mind.

Our folks felt that putting someone at the door was a waste of money. They just couldn't see what Sam and Dan McAllister were seeing—that the greeter sent a warm, friendly message to the good customer, and a warning to the thief. They fought him all the way on it. Some people tried hard to talk him out of it. They tried to ignore it.

Sam just kept pushing and pushing and pushing. Every week, every morning, he'd talk about greeters. He'd throw fits whenever he went into a store and didn't find one. Gradually, he wore everyone down and got his way. I'd say it took about a year and a half because they really resisted it. But Sam was relentless.

I guess his vindication had to be the day in 1989 when he walked into a Kmart in Illinois and found that they had installed people greeters at their front doors.

A Wal-Mart store manager told one of the casewriters that up to 90 percent of his day was spent walking around the store communicating with the associates—praising them for a job well done, discussing how improvements could be made, listening to their comments, and soliciting suggestions. Task forces to evaluate ideas and plan out future actions to implement the ideas were common, and it was not unusual for the person who developed the idea to be appointed the leader of the group. Store managers asked each associate what she or he could do individually and what could be changed to improve store operations. Associates who believed a policy or procedure detracted from operations were encouraged to challenge and change it.

The company had a fleet of 12 airplanes that enabled Wal-Mart executives to make weekly visits to the field and regularly tour all company facilities.

---

[18]Ibid., pp. 229–30.

THE WORK ATMOSPHERE AT WAL-MART

Throughout company literature, comments could be found referring to Wal-Mart's "concern for the individual." Such expressions as "Our people make the difference," "We care about people," and "People helping people" were used repeatedly by Wal-Mart executives. According to one of the company's management recruiters,

It's a special feeling you get when you walk into a Wal-Mart store. And when you're working there is when you really notice it because the people care about each other. It's like being with a successful football team, that feeling of togetherness, and everyone is willing to sacrifice in order to stay together.

Wal-Mart associates at a rural store location told the casewriters about how they liked working at Wal-Mart and about the family-oriented atmosphere that prevailed among store associates:

There is no comparison between Wal-Mart and other places I've worked. Wal-Mart is far above. They just treat customers and associates really nice.

It's more of a family-oriented place than anywhere I've worked. They seem to really care about their employees. It's not just the money they're making, but a true concern for the people working here.

We're just like a family. Everybody cares for each other. The management is fantastic. You can go to them for anything and feel free to contradict them if you want to.

I care about my responsibilities. You're just more proud of it. You're more apt to care about it. You'll want people to come in and see what you've done. I guess the pats on the back let you know what you've done is appreciated. And when they show their appreciation you're going to care more and do better.

We're a united group. We may be from different walks of life but once we get here we're a group. You may leave them at the door, but when you're in here you're part of a family. You help each other; you try to be everybody's friend. It's a united feeling.

Yet, Wal-Mart still had vestiges of some "old-fashioned" beliefs and employment practices that seemed out of step in an otherwise progressive company. Restrictions on hiring persons over 65 were not formally lifted until Sam Walton himself approached the mandatory retirement age of 65. There were relatively few women in store management positions even though the majority of the employees in many stores were female. Only three of the company's top 113 executives were women. Associates were not allowed to date one another without authorization from the executive committee, a requirement that had resulted in several lawsuits against the company.

At the close of interviews with Wal-Mart associates at two Alabama stores, the casewriters asked associates to relate what made Wal-Mart special from their perspective:

They tell us that we are the best.

I like working at Wal-Mart better than any other place. I'm freer to handle the work better . . . I can go at my own speed and do the work the way I want to do it.

I enjoy Wal-Mart; I've been here eight years. Of course, we work, but that's what we're here for. You've got potential with Wal-Mart.

I think Wal-Mart is one of the best companies there is. I wouldn't want to work for anyone else.

The editors of the trade publication *Mass Market Retailers* paid tribute to Wal-Mart's associates in 1989 by recognizing them collectively as the "1989 Mass Market

Retailers of the Year." They summed up the contributions and efforts of Wal-Mart's employees:

> The Wal-Mart Associate. In this decade that term has come to symbolize all that is right with the American worker, particularly in the retailing environment and most particularly at Wal-Mart.

COMPENSATION AND INCENTIVES

Wal-Mart had installed an extensive system of incentives that allowed associates to share monetarily in the company's success.

The Profit-Sharing Plan   Wal-Mart maintained a profit-sharing plan for full and part-time associates; individuals were eligible following one year of continuous employment provided they had worked 1,000 hours or more. Annual contributions to the plan were tied to the company's profitability and were made at the sole discretion of management and the board of directors. Wal-Mart's contribution to each associate's profit-sharing account became vested at the rate of 20 percent per year beginning the third year of participation in the plan. After seven years of continuous employment the company's contribution became fully vested; however, if the associate left the company prior to that time, the unvested portions were redistributed to all remaining employees. Most of the profit-sharing contributions were invested in Wal-Mart's common stock, with the remainder put into other investments. Associates could begin withdrawals from their accounts upon retirement or disability, with the balance paid to family members upon death. Company contributions to the plan totaled $98.3 million in 1991, $129.6 million in 1992, and $166 million in 1993. In early 1994 the value of the profit-sharing fund exceeded $2 billion and the plan included approximately 300,000 participants.

Stock Purchase Plan   A stock purchase plan was adopted in 1972 to allow eligible employees a means of purchasing shares of common stock through regular payroll deduction or annual lump-sum contribution. Prior to 1990, the yearly maximum under this program was $1,500 per eligible employee; starting in 1990 the maximum was increased to $1,800 annually. The company contributed an amount equal to 15 percent of each participating associate's contribution. Long-time employees who had started participating in the early years of the program had accumulated stock worth over $100,000. About one-fourth of Wal-Mart's employees participated in the stock purchase plan in 1993.

In addition to regular stock purchases, certain employees qualified to participate in stock option plans; options expired 10 years from the date of the grant and could be exercised in nine annual installments. At year-end 1993 there were nearly 29 million shares reserved for issuance under stock option plans. The value of options granted in recent years was substantial: $96 million (1990), $128 million (1991), $143 million (1992), and $235 million (1993).

Base Compensation and Benefits   Although only full-time associates were eligible to participate in Wal-Mart's benefits programs, Wal-Mart did not deliberately use large numbers of part-time employees to avoid having to pay benefits. Part-time jobs were most common among salesclerks and checkout personnel in the stores where customer traffic varied appreciably during days of the week and months of the year.

Associates at Wal-Mart were hired at higher than minimum wage and could expect to receive a raise within the first year at one or both of the semiannual job evaluations. An associate told a casewriter that at least one raise was guaranteed in the first year if Wal-Mart planned to keep the individual on the staff. The other raise depended on how well the associate worked and improved during the year. At Wal-Mart only the store managers were salaried. All other associates, including the department managers, were considered hourly employees.

Sales Contests and Other Incentive Programs　One of Wal-Mart's most successful incentive programs was its VPI (Volume Producing Item) contests. In this contest, departments within the store were able to do a special promotion and pricing on items they themselves wanted to feature. Management believed the VPI contests boosted sales, breathed new life into an otherwise slow-selling item, and helped keep associates thinking about how to bolster sales; two sales associates commented on the VPI incentive scheme:

> We have contests. You feature an item in your department and see how well it sells each week. If your feature wins, you get a half day off.
>
> They have a lot of contests. If you're the top seller in the store you can win money. For four weeks in a row I've won money. That gives you a little incentive to do the very best you can. You kind of compete with other departments even though we're a big family in the long run. You like a little competition, but not too much.

Associate incentive plans were in place in every store, club, distribution center, and support facility. Associates received bonuses for good ideas, such as how to reduce shoplifting or how to improve merchandising. Wal-Mart instituted a shrinkage bonus in 1980. If a store held losses from theft and damage below the corporate goal, every associate in that store was eligible to receive up to $200. As a result, Wal-Mart's shrinkage ran about one percent compared to an industry average of two percent.

Another motivational tactic that Wal-Mart employed involved dress-up days in which associates dressed according to a theme (for instance, Western days or Halloween); these added fun and excitement for associates, and the festive mood carried over to the customer.

TRAINING

At Wal-Mart we guarantee two things: Opportunity and hard work.

Bill Avery, Wal-Mart management recruiter

Management Training　Wal-Mart managers were hired in one of three ways. Hourly associates could move up through the ranks from sales to department manager to manager of the check lanes into store management training. Second, people with outstanding merchandising skills at other retail companies were recruited to join the ranks of Wal-Mart managers. And third, Wal-Mart recruited college graduates to enter the company's training program.

Casewriter interviews with Wal-Mart associates revealed a positive attitude concerning advancement opportunities and the company's work climate:

> You have the option to go as far as you want to go if you do a good job.
>
> It's up to you; if you do the work, you'll get the raises. I think it's a good place to work. There's a lot here (as far as advancement) if you want to work for it. It's a good open relationship with management. The benefits are good and the pay is above average for most discount stores.

The management training program involved two phases. In the first phase the trainee completed a 16-week on-the-job training program:

Phase I	
Week 1	Checkouts/service desk
Week 2	Cash office
Weeks 3 & 4	Receiving
Week 5	Invoicing
Weeks 6, 7, & 8	Hard goods merchandising
Weeks 9 & 10	Merchandise office
Weeks 11, 12, & 13	Home and seasonal merchandising
Weeks 14, 15, & 16	Apparel merchandising

At designated times during Phase I, trainees were tested and evaluated by the store managers. During this time, the individual was encouraged to complete a self-critique of his/her own progress and also a critique of the calibre of guidance being received from the training effort. At the end of Phase I, the trainee moved at once into Phase II.

The initial three weeks of Phase II were structured to cover such management topics as internal/external theft, scheduling, store staffing, retail math, merchandise replenishment, and the Wal-Mart "Keys to Supervision" series, which dealt with interpersonal skills and personnel responsibilities. After completion of the first three weeks of Phase II, the trainee was given responsibility for an area of the store. The length of time during the remainder of Phase II varied according to the rate at which each trainee progressed. After showing good job performance, demonstrated leadership, and job knowledge, the trainee was promoted to an assistant manager. As an assistant manager, training continued with the retail management training seminar, which was designed to complement the in-store training with other vital management fundamentals. With the quickly paced growth rate of Wal-Mart stores, the above-average trainee could progress to store manager within five years. Through bonuses for sales increases above projected amounts and company stock options, the highest performing store managers earned around $70,000 to $100,000 annually.

To further promote management training, in November 1985 the Walton Institute of Retailing was opened in affiliation with the University of Arkansas. Within a year of its inception every Wal-Mart manager from the stores, the distribution facilities, and the general office was expected to take part in special programs at the Walton Institute to strengthen and develop the company's managerial capabilities.

Associate Training   Wal-Mart did not provide a specialized training course for its hourly associates. Upon hiring, an associate was immediately placed in a position for on-the-job training. From time to time, training films were shown in the Friday morning associates' meetings, but no other formalized training aids were provided by Wal-Mart headquarters. Store managers and department managers were expected to train and supervise the associates under them in whatever ways were needed.

A number of associates commented on the Wal-Mart training programs:

Mostly you learn by doing. They tell you a lot; but you learn your job every day.

They show you how to do your books. They show you how to order and help you get adjusted to your department.

We have tapes we watch that give us pointers on different things. They give you some training to start off—what you are and are not supposed to do.

The training program is not up to par. They bring new people in so fast—they try to show films, but it's just so hard in this kind of business. In my opinion you learn better just by experience. The training program itself is just not adequate. There's just not enough time.

We have all kinds of films and guidelines to go by, department managers' meetings every Monday, and sometimes we have quizzes to make sure we're learning what we need to know.

The most training you get is on the job—especially if you work with someone who has been around awhile.

MEETINGS

The company used meetings both as a communication device and as a culture-building exercise. Wal-Mart claimed to hold the largest annual stockholders' meeting in the world. Shareholders' meetings were held in the University of Arkansas Razorback basketball arena and were usually attended by 5,000 to 8,000 people, including associates and vendors. The necessary formalities of the meeting were typically conducted very promptly; the remainder of the meeting typically resembled a two-hour corporate pep rally featuring company cheers, skits, and a parade of vendors and associates who were cited for special accomplishments. Vendors were recognized for having met tight delivery deadlines, for having lowered prices, or for having cooperated extensively. Associates who had exceeded goals, helped people in distress, or written new cheers or songs were brought up and recognized on stage, with scenes of their accomplishments appearing on the screens behind them.

The Year-End Managers' Meetings Held in February in a convention hall set up like a Wal-Mart store with new displays and product lines, these three-day meetings brought together Wal-Mart managers from the store department level on up. Geography and numbers had recently forced Wal-Mart to have four meeting sessions held at two different sites. Everyone, including wives, wore Wal-Mart name tags with first names in big letters and last names in fine print. The meetings included presentations by managers and vendors, discussions of expansion plans and company goals, training videos, achievement awards, Wal-Mart cheers, a banquet, and entertainment. Wal-Mart's senior executives viewed these meetings as a way to reinforce the bonds of teamwork within the management ranks.

The Saturday Morning Headquarters Meetings At 7:30 AM every Saturday morning since 1961, the top officers, the merchandising staff, the regional managers who oversaw the store districts, and the Bentonville headquarters' staff—over 100 people in all— had gathered to discuss the week's sales, store payroll percentages, special promotion items, and any current problems. Reports on store construction, distribution centers, transportation, loss prevention, information systems, and so on were also given to keep everyone up-to-date. In his autobiography, Sam Walton reflected on the meetings and their role in Wal-Mart's culture:[19]

From the very start we would get all our managers together and critique ourselves. . . . We would review what we had bought and see how many dollars we had committed to

---

[19]Ibid., pp. 62 and 164.

it. We would plan promotions and plan the items we intended to buy. Really, we were planning our merchandising programs. And it worked so well . . . it just became part of our culture. . . . We wanted everybody to know what was going on and everybody to be aware of the mistakes we made. When somebody made a bad mistake—whether it was myself or anybody else—we talked abut it, admitted it, tried to figure out how to correct it, and then moved on to the next day's work.

The Saturday morning meeting is where we discuss and debate much of our philosophy and our management strategy; it is the focal point of all our communication efforts. . . . Its purpose is to let everyone know what the rest of the company is up to. If we can, we find heroes among our associates in the stores and bring them in to Bentonville, where we praise them in front of the whole meeting. . . . For the meeting to work, it has to be something of a show.

The meetings were deliberately very informal and relaxed. Those attending might show up in tennis or hunting clothes so that when the meeting was over they could go on to their Saturday activities. The meetings tended to be upbeat and usually began with several Wal-Mart cheers.

The Friday Morning Store Meetings   On Friday morning, general store meetings were held in each Discount City store and wholesale club. Associates at every level could ask questions and expect to get straightforward answers from management concerning department and store sales and cost figures, along with other pertinent store figures or information. The meeting might also include information on new company initiatives, policy change announcements, and perhaps video training films. Often, the meeting would begin or end with one or more Wal-Mart cheers.

Each week, department and store figures were posted in the meeting area. That way associates could see how their departments ranked against other departments and how the store was doing overall. If the figures were better than average, associates were praised verbally and given pats on the back; associates in departments that regularly outperformed the averages could expect annual bonuses and raises. When departmental performances came out lower than average, then the store manager would talk with department associates to explore ways to improve. On the door leading into the employee area in each store was a sign that said, "Today's stock price is _____, tomorrow's depends on you."

The Friday Merchandising Meeting   Another Wal-Mart tradition was a weekly meeting of the buyers and merchandising staff headquartered in Bentonville and the regional managers who directed store operations. David Glass explained the purpose:[20]

In retailing, there has always been a traditional, head-to-head confrontation between operations and merchandising. You know, the operations guys say, "Why in the world would anybody buy this? It's a dog, and we'll never sell it." Then the merchandising folks say, "There's nothing wrong with that item. If you guys were smart enough to display it well and promote it properly, it would blow out the doors." So we sit all these folks down together every Friday at the same table and just have at it.

We get into some of the doggonedest, knock-down drag-outs you have ever seen. But we have a rule. We never leave an item hanging. We will make a decision in that meeting even if it's wrong, and sometimes it is. But when the people come out of that room, you would be hard-pressed to tell which ones oppose it and which ones are for it. And once we've made that decision on Friday, we expect it to be acted on in all the

---

[20]Ibid., pp. 225–26.

stores on Saturday. What we guard against around here is people saying, "Let's think about it." We make a decision. Then we act on it.

Another technique Wal-Mart used to keep buyers in touch with customers and attuned with store operations involved sending each buyer out to a different store every three months to act as manager for two to three days in the department he or she bought merchandise for—referred to by Wal-Mart as the Eat What You Cook program.

All these meetings plus the in-the-field visits by Wal-Mart management created a strong bias for action. A *Fortune* reporter observed, "Managers suck in information from Monday to Thursday, exchange ideas on Friday and Saturday, and implement decisions in the stores on Monday."[21] General Electric CEO Jack Welch described his experiences at Wal-Mart:

> Everybody there has a passion for an idea and everyone's ideas count. Hierarchy doesn't matter. They get 80 people in a room and understand how to deal with each other without structure. I have been there three times now. Every time you go to that place in Arkansas, you can fly back to New York without a plane. The place actually vibrates.[22]

WAL-MART'S FUTURE

In 1988 Sam Walton, at the age of 70, reduced his role in active day-to-day management, relinquishing the title of chief executive officer to David Glass, but nonetheless retaining the title of chairman of Wal-Mart's board of directors. Until his death in April 1992, Walton continued to make appearances at major company events and to serve as company patriarch, but the task of leading the company into the 1990s was turned over to Glass and his next-in-command, Donald Soderquist, who functioned as chief operating officer. Both were highly regarded inside and outside the company, and both were seen as having the full complement of retailing savvy and management skills to follow in Walton's footsteps. The management team under Glass and Soderquist was believed by retailing experts to be very talented and very deep in the skills needed to sustain Wal-Mart's success.

At Wal-Mart's 1990 annual stockholders' meeting, Sam Walton expressed his belief that by the year 2000 Wal-Mart should be able to double the number of stores to about 3,000 and to reach sales of $125 billion annually. At the time, some retailing analysts were even more bullish on Wal-Mart's long-term prospects, predicting that the number of stores, clubs, and Supercenters could number over 4,300 and could generate nearly $200 billion in sales by the turn of the century. Wal-Mart's four biggest sources of growth potential were seen as (1) expanding into states where it had no stores, (2) continuing to saturate its current markets with new stores, (3) perfecting the Supercenter format to expand Wal-Mart's retailing reach into the whole grocery and supermarket arena—a market with annual sales of about $375 billion, and (4) moving into international markets. Wal-Mart had recently begun opening stores in Mexico. In 1994, the company was operating 18 stores in Mexico in a joint venture with CIFRA, Mexico's largest retailer, and two Wal-Mart Supercenters. Wal-Mart had plans for aggressive expansion of its CIFRA joint-venture operations as well as opening additional Wal-Mart Supercenters in Mexico City, Monterrey, and

---

[21]Bill Saporito, "What Sam Walton Taught America," p. 105.
[22]Ibid.

other major population centers in Mexico. In early 1994, Wal-Mart announced plans to acquire 120 Woolco stores in Canada and spend $100 million to revamp them to the Wal-Mart format.

However, in early 1994 there were signs of an impending slowdown in Wal-Mart's growth, and in addition the company had suffered through a series of embarrassing events that cast a dubious light on some of its operating practices. Throughout much of 1993, sales gains at Wal-Mart stores that had been open more than a year ran in the 4 to 7 percent range, compared to historical annual gains of 10 to 15 percent (see line 3 of Exhibit 1); sales at some Sam's Wholesale outlets actually declined from levels a year earlier. Companywide, sales grew only 22 percent in 1993 versus revenue growth of 25 to 35 percent annually in earlier years.

A report on CBS's "60 Minutes" showed instances of Wal-Mart stores' posting Made in America signs on racks of apparel that actually came from foreign sources; the "60 Minutes" program also told of instances where Wal-Mart had sourced merchandise from foreign manufacturers that utilized child labor and sweatshop tactics in their factories to hold down costs and meet the price levels that Wal-Mart's buyers insisted on. Gitano, a major Wal-Mart supplier headquartered in Italy, was under investigation for racketeering, falsifying corporate records, and numerous other criminal and civil violations. An Arkansas Chancery Court in October 1993 ordered Wal-Mart to stop selling health and beauty care products and over-the-counter drugs below cost at its Conway Supercenter. The suit was brought by the owners of three Conway drugstores who contended Wal-Mart was trying to injure competition and drive them out of business. In depositions taken in 1992 Wal-Mart employees said the chain set prices based on how much competition it faced—for strong competition, lower prices, and for weak competition, higher prices. At the trial, David Glass acknowledged that Wal-Mart sold some merchandise below cost but he denied that the reason was to drive competitors out of business. Wal-Mart had appealed the judge's verdict. Because 22 other states had statutes similar to the one in Arkansas barring pricing practices that could injure competitors, observers speculated that any retailer who discounted and/or underpriced competitors to draw shoppers or who used different prices in different areas based on market conditions and competition could be accused of predatory pricing.

In Vermont several communities had resisted giving store construction permits to Wal-Mart following strong protests by local residents and businesspeople that the opening of a Wal-Mart in their communities was inconsistent with preserving Vermont's rural character and that such stores would (1) adversely impact both local shopkeepers and the environment (due to added traffic, visual pollution, and soil erosion) and (2) impair the state's ability to attract tourists seeking a peaceful rural getaway. Wal-Mart's stock price, which had historically risen each year, fell 13 percent during 1993 and in early 1994 was trading in the $23 to $28 range—substantially below the record high of $33 reached in early 1993.

MARY KAY COSMETICS, INC. (A)

Robin Romblad, The University of Alabama
Arthur A. Thompson, Jr., The University of Alabama

In spring 1983 Mary Kay Cosmetics, Inc. (MKC), the second-largest direct-sales distributor of skin care products in the United States, encountered its first big slowdown in recruiting women to function as Mary Kay beauty consultants and market the Mary Kay cosmetic lines. As of April, MKC's sales force of about 195,000 beauty consultants was increasing at only a 13 percent annual rate, down from a 65 percent rate of increase in 1980. The dropoff in the percentage of new recruits jeopardized MKC's ability to sustain its reputation as a fast-growing company. MKC's strategy was predicated on getting even larger numbers of beauty consultants to arrange skin care classes at the home of a hostess and her three to five guests; at the classes consultants demonstrated the Mary Kay Cosmetics line and usually sold anywhere from $50 to $200 worth of Mary Kay products. MKC's historically successful efforts to build up the size of its force of beauty consultants had given the company reliable access to a growing number of showings annually.

Even though MKC's annual turnover rate for salespeople was lower than that of several major competitors (including Avon Products), some 120,000 Mary Kay beauty consultants had quit or been terminated in 1982, making the task of recruiting a growing sales force of consultants a major, ongoing effort at MKC. Recruiting success was seen by management as strategically important. New recruits were encouraged to spend between $500 and $3,000 for sales kits and start-up inventories; the initial orders of new recruits accounted for over one-third of MKC's annual sales. The newest recruits were also instrumental in helping identify and attract others to become Mary Kay beauty consultants.

Richard Rogers, MKC's cofounder and president, promptly reacted to the recruiting slowdown by announcing five changes in the company's sales force program:

- The financial incentives offered to active beauty consultants for bringing new recruits into the Mary Kay fold were increased by as much as 50 percent.

The assistance and cooperation provided by many people in the Mary Kay organization are gratefully acknowledged. Copyright © 1986 by Arthur A. Thompson, Jr.

- A new program was instituted whereby beauty consultants who (1) placed $600 a month in wholesale orders with the company for three consecutive months and (2) recruited five new consultants who together placed $3,000 in wholesale orders a month for three straight months would win the free use of a cream-colored Oldsmobile Firenza for a year (this program was in addition to two other programs that awarded beauty consultants with even better performances the use of a pink Buick Regal or pink Cadillac).
- The minimum order size required of beauty consultants was increased from $400 to $600.
- The prices at which MKC wholesaled its products to consultants were raised by 4 percent.
- The requirements for attaining sales director status and heading up a sales unit were raised 25 percent; a sales director had to recruit 15 new consultants (instead of 12), and her sales unit was expected to maintain a monthly minimum of $4,000 in wholesale orders (up from $3,200).

In addition, MKC's 1984 corporate budget for recruiting was more than quadrupled and, as a special recruiting effort, the company staged a National Guest Night in September 1984 that consisted of a live closed-circuit telecast to 78 cities aired from Dallas, Texas, where MKC's corporate headquarters was located. Mary Kay salespeople all over the United States were urged to invite prospective recruits and go to one of the 78 simulcast sites.

NATIONAL GUEST NIGHT IN BIRMINGHAM

Jan Currier, senior sales director for MKC in the Tuscaloosa, Alabama, area, invited two other women and one of the casewriters to drive to Birmingham in her pink Buick Regal to attend what was billed as "The Salute to the Stars." On the way, Jan explained that as well as being entertaining, the evening's event would give everyone a chance to see firsthand just how exciting and rewarding the career opportunities were with MKC; she noted with pride that Mary Kay Cosmetics was one of the companies featured in the recent book *The 100 Best Companies to Work for in America*. As the Tuscaloosa entourage neared the auditorium in Birmingham, the casewriter observed numerous pink Cadillacs and pink Buick Regals in the flow of traffic and in the parking lot. Mary Kay sales directors were stationed at each door to the lobby, enthusiastically greeting each person and presenting a gift of Mary Kay cosmetics. Guests were directed to a table to register for prizes to be awarded later in the evening.

Inside the auditorium over 1,500 people awaited the beginning of the evening's program. A large theater screen was located at center stage. The lights dimmed promptly at 7 PM and the show began. The casewriter used her tape recorder and took extensive notes to capture what went on:

Mark Dixon [*national sales administrator for the South Central division, appears on stage in Birmingham*]: Welcome, ladies and gentlemen, to National Guest Night, Mary Kay's Salute to the Stars. Tonight, you're going to be a part of the largest teleconference ever held by a U.S. corporation.

Now please help me welcome someone all of us at Mary Kay love very dearly, National Sales Director from Houston, Texas, Lovie Quinn.
[*The crowd stands and greets Lovie with cheers and applause.*]

Lovie Quinn [*comes out on stage in Birmingham to join Mark Dixon. Lovie is wearing this year's Mary Kay national sales director suit of red suede with black mink trim.*]: Good evening, ladies and gentlemen, and welcome to one of the most exciting events in the history of Mary Kay. An evening with Mary Kay as she salutes the stars . . . During the evening you'll learn about career opportunities. There will be recognition of our stars. We'll see the salute to them with gifts and prizes you hear about at Mary Kay. You'll hear about . . . pink Cadillacs . . . pink Buick Regals, and Firenza Oldsmobiles.

You're going to hear about and see diamond rings and beautiful full-length mink coats. And of course we'll talk about MONEY.

If you've never attended a Mary Kay function you might very easily get the impression that we brag a lot. We like to think of it as recognition . . . But we would not be able to give this recognition of success if you, the hostesses, our special guests, did not open up your homes so we may share with you and some of your selected friends the Mary Kay skin care program. For that reason we would like to show our appreciation at this time. Will all the special guests please stand up.

[*About 40 percent of the audience stands up and the remainder applaud the guests.*]

Lovie Quinn: Now I need to have all our directors line up on stage. [*Each one is dressed in a navy blue suit with either a red, green, or white blouse—the color of the blouse signifies director, senior director, or future director status.*] Enthusiasm and excitement are at the root of the Mary Kay philosophy. This is why we always start a meeting like this with a song. We invite all of you to join with the directors and sing the theme song, "That Mary Kay Enthusiasm." [*Lovie motions for the audience to stand; the choir of directors begins to clap and leads out in singing. The audience joins in quickly.*]

> I've got that Mary Kay enthusiasm up in my head, up in my head, up in my head.
> I've got that Mary Kay enthusiasm up in my head, up in my head to stay.
> I've got that Mary Kay enthusiasm down in my heart, down in my heart, down in my heart.
> I've got that Mary Kay enthusiasm down in my heart, down in my heart to stay.
> I've got that Mary Kay enthusiasm down in my feet, down in my feet, down in my feet.
> I've got that Mary Kay enthusiasm down in my feet, down in my feet to stay.
> I've got that Mary Kay enthusiasm up in my head, down in my heart, down in my feet.
> I've got that Mary Kay enthusiasm all over me, all over me to stay.

[*The song concludes to a round of applause. The crowd is spirited.*]

Lovie Quinn: Now we'd like to recognize a group of very special consultants. These ladies have accepted a challenge from Mary Kay and have held 10 beauty shows in one week. This is something really terrific. It demonstrates the successful achievement of a goal. We have found when you want to do something for our chairman of the board, Mary Kay Ash . . . you don't have to give furs. The most special gift you can give to Mary Kay is your own success.

[*All of those recognized are seated in the first 10 rows with their guests; seating in the front rows is a special reward for meeting the challenge. The crowd applauds.*]

Lovie Quinn: It is almost time for the countdown to begin, but before it does one more special group must be recognized. These ladies are Mary Kay's Gold Medal winners. In one month they recruited *five* new consultants.

[A number of ladies stand; they beam with pride and each has been awarded a medal resembling an Olympic gold medal. The audience gives them a nice round of applause.]

Lovie Quinn [*Lovie continues to fill the crowd with excitement and anticipation.*]: The countdown is going to be in just a few moments. It will be a treat for those of you that have not met Mary Kay before. Please help me count down the final 10 seconds before the broadcast.

[But the crowd is so excited it starts the countdown when one minute appears on the screen. As the seconds wind down, the crowd gets louder with anticipation and then gets in sync chanting: "10, 9, 8, 7, 6, 5, 4, 3, 2, 1." More screams and applause.

On the screen a gold Mary Kay medallion appears, then the production lines at the plant are shown, and then trucks shipping the products. The audience claps as they see these on the screen. Headquarters is shown. Now a number of the Mary Kay sales directors are shown framed in stars on the screen. People clap when they recognize someone from their district. Loud applause fills the auditorium when Mary Kay Ash, MKC's chairman of the board and company cofounder, is shown in a star.

The Dallas-based part of the simulcast opens with female dancers dressed in pink and male dancers dressed in gray tuxedos. They perform the "Mary Kay Star Song," which includes a salute to various regions in the United States. The Birmingham crowd cheers when the South is highlighted.

A woman is chosen out of the audience in Dallas. Her name is Susan; the audience is told that at various intervals in the broadcast we will see her evolution into a successful Mary Kay Beauty consultant. Initially we see her get a feeling that maybe she can be a Mary Kay star. The message is that personal dreams of success can come true. Will she be successful? The answer comes back, "Yes, She Can Do It."

Mary Kay Ash is escorted on stage by her son Richard Rogers. She is elegantly dressed with accents of diamonds and feathers. The applause, the loudest so far, is genuinely enthusiastic and many in both the Dallas and Birmingham audiences are cheering loudly.]

Mary Kay Ash: Welcome everyone to our very first Salute to the Stars, National Guest Night. How exciting it is to think that right now over 100,000 people are watching this broadcast all over the United States . . . Even though I can't see all of you, I can feel your warmth all the way to Dallas.

During the program this evening one expression you're going to hear over and over again is *you can do it* . . . This is something we really believe in. What we have discovered is the seeds of greatness are planted in every human being . . . Tonight we hope to inspire you, to get you to reach within yourself, to bring out some of those star qualities that I know you have. And no matter who you are and no matter where you live, I believe you can take those talents and go farther than you ever thought possible and we have a special place waiting just for you.

Now I would like to introduce someone who has a special place in my heart. Someone who has been beside me from the very beginning. Without him Mary Kay Cosmetics would not be what it is today. Please welcome your president and cofounder of our company, my son, Richard Rogers.

Richard Rogers [*steps to the microphone, accompanied by respectful applause*]: When we started this company over 20 years ago my mother and I never dreamed we would be standing here talking live to over 100,000 of you all across the country . . . Tonight we've planned a memorable evening just for you. A program that conveys the spirit of Mary Kay. Going back 21 years ago, Mary Kay saw a void in the cosmetics industry. The observation she made was that others were just selling products. No one was teaching women about their skin and how to care for it . . . This is the concept on which she based her company. So on September 13, 1963, Mary Kay Cosmetics opened its doors in Dallas, Texas.

Throughout the decade Mary Kay's concepts continued to flourish . . .

By the end of the 60s, Mary Kay Cosmetics had become a fully integrated manufacturer and distributor of skin care products. In 1970 the sales force had grown to 7,000 consultants in Texas and four surrounding states.

California was the first state MKC designated for expansion. When we first went there, no one had ever heard of Mary Kay Cosmetics. Within three years California had more consultants selling Mary Kay Cosmetics than the state of Texas . . . With this success, expansion continued throughout the United States . . . By 1975 MKC had grown to 700 sales directors, 34,000 consultants, and $35 million in sales.

International expansion was initiated in 1978 by selling skin care products in Canada. In just 36 months MKC became the fourth-largest Canadian cosmetic company . . . Since that time, Mary Kay has expanded to South America, Australia, and in September we opened for business in the United Kingdom.

At the end of 1983, MKC had over 195,000 consultants. Sales had reached over $600 million around the world . . . With total commitment to excellence setting the pace, MKC is still working toward achieving the goal of being the finest teaching-oriented skin care organization in the world . . . Mary Kay is proud to have the human resources necessary to meet this goal. At Mary Kay P&L means more than profit and loss. It also stands for People and Love. People have helped MKC reach where it is today, and they will play a big part in where it will be tomorrow.

Tonight we're proud to announce the arrival of a book that expresses the Mary Kay philosophy of Golden Rule management, a book that outlines the management style that has contributed to the success of Mary Kay Cosmetics. The new book is *Mary Kay on People Management*. [*The crowd applauds at this announcement.*]

Mary Kay Ash [*reappears on stage*]: We're so excited about the new book. I am pleased to have the opportunity to talk with you about it tonight. Actually, I started to write that book over 20 years ago. I had just retired from 25 years of direct sales. I wanted to share my experiences, so I wrote down my thoughts about the companies I had worked for. What had worked and what had not . . . After expressing my ideas, I thought how wonderful it would be to put out these ideas of a company designed to meet women's needs into action. That is when Mary Kay Cosmetics was born . . . The company helps women meet the goals they set for themselves . . . I feel that is what has contributed to the success of the organization. Everyone at MKC starts at the same place, as a consultant, and everyone has the same opportunities for success.

[*The broadcast returns to the scenario of Susan as she becomes a new Mary Kay consultant. Susan sings about the doubts people have about her joining Mary Kay. She disregards this and decides to climb to success. At the end of the scene, she projects a positive, successful image that her friends and family recognize. The audience responds favorably.*]

Dale Alexander [*national sales administrator for Mary Kay Cosmetics appears on stage in Dallas*]: It is a great honor to be with you tonight and I want to add my most sincere welcome . . . Recognition is one of the original principles on which our company is based. It's an essential ingredient in the Mary Kay formula for success . . . I want to start out by recognizing the largest group. The group of independent businesswomen who are out there every day holding beauty shows, teaching skin care, selling our products, and sharing the Mary Kay opportunity. At this time will all of the Mary Kay beauty consultants across the nation stand to be recognized? [*In Birming-*

ham the lights go up and the crowd applauds the consultants in the audience.] Next we want to recognize the Star Consultants . . . Will these ladies stand?

Many of our people are wearing small golden ladders. This is our Ladder of Success. Each ladder has a number of different jewels awarded for specific accomplishments during a calendar quarter. Star consultants earn rubies, sapphires, and diamonds to go on their ladders. The higher they climb, the more dazzling their ladders become. A consultant with all diamonds is known at Mary Kay as a top Star Performer. It is like wearing a straight-A report card on your lapel.

In addition to ladders, consultants have an opportunity to earn great prizes each quarter . . . This quarter's theme is Salute to the Stars . . . and these prizes are out of this world.

[*The scene shifts to a description of the fall 1984 sales program; it utilizes a "Star Trek" theme, and across the screen is emblazoned "Starship Mary Kay in Search of the Prize Zone." Captain Mary Kay appears with members of her crew on Starship Mary Kay. She remarks their mission is to seek out prizes to honor those that reach for the sky. They are approaching the prize zone. The awards and prizes are flashed onto the screen.*

[*Even though this "space" presentation of prizes is humorous, the ladies know that the rewards are real; they respond as the scene ends with a round of applause and a buzz of excitement. The scene concludes with the message, "When you reach for the sky you bring home a star."*]

The Prize Zone Bonus Prizes Available Based on Fourth-Quarter Sales	
$1,800 wholesale sales	Cubic zirconia necklace and earrings or travel set with hair dryer
$2,400 wholesale sales	Leather briefcase with matching umbrella
$3,000 wholesale sales	Diamond earrings with 14K gold teardrops
$3,600 wholesale sales	Telephone answering machine
$4,200 wholesale sales	Sapphire ring
$4,800 wholesale sales	Electronic printer by Brother—fits in a briefcase
$6,000 wholesale sales	Diamond pendant—nine diamonds—.5 karat on a 18K gold chain

Mary Kay [*returns to the stage*]: You can climb that ladder of success at Mary Kay. It is up to you to take that very first step . . . There are so many rewards for being a Mary Kay consultant. There are top earnings, prizes, and lots of recognition. But there is even more to a Mary Kay career and that is the fulfillment of bringing beauty into the lives of others . . .

When a woman joins our company she knows she can do it. But not alone. She'll receive support from many people. A big sister relationship will form between a new consultant and her recruiter . . . Whoever invited you tonight thought you were a special person. She wanted to share this evening and introduce you to our company and let you see for yourself the excitement and enthusiasm Mary Kay people have when they are together . . . The enthusiasm of our consultants and directors is responsible for our success.

[*The scenario about Susan returns to the screen. This time she is thinking about concentrating her efforts on recruiting. After five recruits, she will become a team leader.*

A good goal to strive for, she thinks. A woman that had doubted Susan's career earlier is the first one recruited. Then four more ladies are recruited: a waitress, a teacher, a stewardess, and a nurse. All kinds of people can be Mary Kay consultants. Susan has reached her goal—she is a team leader. The crowd applauds her success.

Dale Alexander [*returns to the microphone in Dallas*]: There is the perfect goal of a Mary Kay career. And now it is time to recognize a very special group of individuals who are proof of this point. Will all the team leaders please stand and remain standing for a few moments? [*The lights go up and team leaders stand. All are wearing red jackets.*]

To qualify for a team leader, each consultant must recruit five new consultants . . . And now will you please recognize these ladies' achievements with a round of applause? [*The audience applauds.*] Now it is time to draw for the prizes. In each of the 75 locations, two names will be drawn. These lucky people will both win this exquisite 14K diamond earring and pendant set. [*The crowd oohs and aahs when the jewelry is shown on the screen.*] These two winners will also be eligible for the prize to be given by Mary Kay when the broadcast resumes.

[*The lights go up in the Birmingham auditorium. Lovie draws two tickets from a big box. When she calls out the names, the winners scream and run on stage to accept their gifts. The crowd applauds the winners.*]

Lovie Quinn [*on the stage in Birmingham*]: Please join me in counting down the final seconds left before we rejoin the broadcast.

[*Everyone stands and enthusiastically counts off "11, 10, 9, 8, 7, 6, 5, 4, 3, 2, 1." The crowd applauds and cheers.*]

Mary Kay [*appears on the screen as the broadcast from Dallas is rejoined*]: I wish I could be there to congratulate each winner . . . The two lucky winners in each of the 75 cities are eligible to win the grand prize . . . It used to be you just drew a number out of a hat. Now that is considered old-fashioned. Tonight, we'll use a computer. All I have to do is push a button and a city will be randomly selected. The local winners in that city will also win this .75 carat diamond ring. [*The crowd buzzes as a close-up of the ring is shown on the giant screen.*] Are you ready? OK. Here goes. [*Mary Kay presses a button.*] The lucky city is Philadelphia. [*The crowd applauds.*] Congratulations, Philadelphia, and we will be sending each of you a ring real soon.

By the way, while we are talking about prizes, would you happen to have a spare finger for a diamond ring? [*The crowd cheers.*] Or could you squeeze into your closet room for a full-length mink coat? [*The crowd is really excited.*] Or is there by any chance a space in your driveway for a car? [*The crowd cheers and applauds. One member of the audience remarks how she would be glad to get rid of that old blue thing she is driving.*] Well, all you have to do is set your Mary Kay career goals high enough to achieve the recognition and rewards available just for you . . .

I remember the first sales competition I set my goals to win. I worked so hard and all I won was a flounder light. [*The audience laughs.*] Does anyone know what you do with it? It is something you use when you put on waders and gig fish. [*The audience laughs again.*] I thought the prize was awful . . . but my manager was a fisherman and he thought it was great.

Winning that flounder light taught me a lesson. I decided if I was ever in a position to give awards, they would be things women appreciate, *not* flounder lights . . . things women would love to have. Absolutely no washing machines and certainly no ironing boards. [*The audience shows their approval by cheers and applause.*] At MKC, you are rewarded for consistent sales and recruiting performance . . . This past spring, a new program was added . . . We call it our VIP program. It stands for Very Important

Performer . . . This program allows a person to win a cream-colored Oldsmobile Firenza with rich brown interior . . . A consultant is eligible for this prize only three months after joining MKC.

Mary Kay Cosmetics can offer several unique career opportunities:

- A 50 percent commission on everything you sell.
- A 12 percent commission on all the sales made by your recruits.
- You work your own hours.
- After three months, you can be eligible for a car. The car is free. MKC pays the insurance.
- When you do well, you get a lot of recognition. Not dumb old things like turkeys and hams. We're talking diamonds and furs.
- You work up to management because of your own efforts and merit.

Other companies would think these things are part of a dream world. At Mary Kay, we do live in a dream world and our dreams do come true. [*The audience applauds loudly. The broadcast then returns to the scenario about Susan. She sets a goal to be a VIP. Through song and dance, her group illustrates setting goals and receiving recognition. Step by step they climb the ladder of recognition. The audience applauds this short scene on succes.*]

Dale Alexander [*comes back to the Dallas stage*]: We have some VIPs among us tonight . . . Mary Kay's Very Important Performers. Will all the VIPs now stand? [*The lights go up in Birmingham; the VIPs stand and the audience applauds.*] Through her enthusiasm and hard work, each VIP has worked hard to achieve this status. And to recognize her accomplishments, she was awarded an Oldsmobile Firenza to show off her achievement and success. Now let's give all our VIPs a round of applause. [*The Birmingham and Dallas audiences respond with more applause.*]

Mary Kay Ash [*comes onto the stage in Dallas and the crowd in Birmingham turns its attention to the screen.*]: With Mary Kay you can achieve success . . . All you have to do is break down your goals into small manageable steps . . . You are able to move on to bigger accomplishments as you gain confidence in yourself.

Let's look at some of the provisions of the Mary Kay career plan and see how it works:

- Your products are purchased directly from the company.
- Generous discounts are offered on large orders.
- There are no territories. You can sell and recruit wherever you want.
- We provide our customers the best possible way to buy cosmetics. They can try the products in their own home before they buy.
- All Mary Kay products are backed by a full 100 percent money-back guarantee.

Mary Kay is a good opportunity to go into business for yourself . . .

There are many benefits of running your own business . . . You meet new people and at the same time you enjoy the support of the Mary Kay sisterhood . . . Plus you earn financial rewards as well as prizes . . .

Now we need to talk about the position of Mary Kay sales director. Directors receive income not only from shows, facials, and reorders but also from recruit commissions . . . In addition they earn unit and recruiting bonuses from Mary Kay . . . Some earn the privilege to drive pink Regals and Cadillacs . . . Each year, hundreds of sales directors earn over $30,000 a year. And today in our company we have more women earning over $50,000 a year than any other company in America. [*The audience applauds.*] At the very top are our national sales directors . . . Their average is about $150,000 a year in commissions. How about that? [*The audience applauds.*] Everyone at Mary Kay starts at the same place with the same beauty showcase. I've always said you can have anything in this world if you want it badly enough and are willing to pay the price. With that kind of attitude anyone can succeed at Mary Kay. [*The vignette about Susan comes back onto the screen. Susan sets a goal to achieve sales director. She sings about how invigorating her new career is and how she now wants to be a coach, a teacher, a counselor, and a friend to others. Everyone around her recognizes how her success has positively affected her whole life. The scene ends and the audience applauds.*]

Dale Alexander [*comes onto the screen from Dallas.*]: Those individuals that advance on to directorship lead our organizations. They set the pace for their units. Will all our sales directors please stand? [*The sales directors stand as the lights go up in Birmingham and the audience applauds.*] Among all our directors there are some that have reached a very special level. They have earned the privilege of driving one of Mary Kay's famous pink cars . . . One thing is guaranteed. Whenever you see one of those pink cars on the road, you know there is a top achiever behind the wheel. At this time, we want to honor all these ladies. [*First the Regal drivers stand and then the Cadillac drivers. The audience recognizes each group with applause.*] Finally, there is one last group we want to recognize. A group whose members have already committed to a future with Mary Kay . . . They are our DIQs or directors in qualification. They are working toward meeting the goals to qualify for directorship . . . Will all the DIQs stand for a round of applause?

[*The lights go up and the DIQs stand. They are recognized with applause from the audience. The lights fade and the scene shifts back to Dallas.*]

Mary Kay: I want to congratulate these ladies. Next week I'll have the pleasure of hostessing our traditional tea for the DIQs at my home. [*The audience applauds.*] Our DIQs are a perfect example of one of the points we have tried to make this evening . . . You can set your goals and achieve them if you want them badly enough.

I've always felt our most valuable asset is not our product but our people . . . I wish I could tell you all the success stories of consultants at MKC . . . We have chosen a few stories we think best represent Mary Kay consultants. The first person you'll meet is Rena.

[*The audience applauds; Rena is recognized by the Mary Kay people present. The narrator of the film clip tells us that Rena has been with MKC for 17 years. She has been Queen of Unit Sales four consecutive years, an honor that was earned when the sales unit she managed exceeded $1 million in sales in one year. Her reward was four $5,000 shopping sprees at Neiman-Marcus Co. in Dallas. When she started, she was living on $300 a month in government housing with her husband and three small children. One day a friend offered to buy her dinner and pay for a babysitter if she would attend a meeting. She couldn't pass up this offer so she went to the Mary Kay meeting. The meeting inspired her and she joined MKC. At the end, we learn that Rena has had cancer for the last eight years, a fact that is not well known; the point is made that it has never affected her ability to succeed with Mary Kay Cosmetics. The crowd applauds her success story.*

Next comes a film clip about Ruel; the audience is told that Ruel was raised in Arkansas, a daughter of a sharecropper. She joined Mary Kay in 1971. By 1976 she was a national sales director. A career with Mary Kay has given her confidence. She has two children in medical school and one of her sons just won a national honor, the]

Medal of Valor. All of this she attributes to Mary Kay. Her children saw her achieve and they knew they could too. Her career with Mary Kay has allowed her to climb up the scale from a poor sharecropper's daughter to become financially independent. Along the way, she has had the opportunity to meet many wonderful people. As her success story ends, the audience applauds.

The third story is about Arlene. Arlene has been a national sales director since 1976. She achieved this just five years after joining MKC. She had been at home for 13 years and wanted to have her own business, set her own hours, and write her own checks. She found she could achieve these goals in a career with Mary Kay. Arlene, we are told, has been able to reach inside herself and achieve great success. Arlene testifies that one of her biggest rewards at Mary Kay has been helping other women achieve the goals they set. The audience loudly applauds the last of the success stories.]

Mary Kay: I am so proud of these ladies . . . It makes me feel good to be able to offer all these wonderful opportunities to so many women.

Every journey begins with a single step. All you have to do is make up your mind that *you* can do it! Isn't it exciting. You *can* do it.

All you need to start a Mary Kay career is a beauty case. It carries everything: vanity trays, mirrors, products, and product literature.

Tonight it becomes easier . . . If you join us as a beauty consultant tonight, we will give you your beauty showcase. [*The audience interrupts with a round of applause.*] When you submit your beauty consultant agreement along with your first wholesale order, you will receive the beauty case free, an $85 value.

At Mary Kay you'll make lasting friends and you'll achieve a feeling of growth . . . Tonight we wanted to give you a feel for Mary Kay Cosmetics. We have a place for you to shine . . . Believe in yourself and you can do anything.

[*The broadcast from Dallas concludes; the audience stands and applauds the program.*]

Lovie Quinn [*comes on stage in Birmingham*: I started at Mary Kay just to earn money for Christmas. I told Mary Kay I could only work four hours a week. Believe it or not Mary Kay welcomed me into the organization.

Things were different then. There were no manuals or guides. I was given my first cosmetics in a shoe box. Mary Kay Cosmetics has come a long way. Each consultant has her own beauty case and is trained in skin care.

Last year I earned over $112,000. This does not include my personal sales . . . I am now driving my 13th pink Cadillac . . . For three years I have been in the half-million dollar club. The prizes for this honor include either a black mink, a white mink, or a diamond ring, all worth $10,000 each. I have all three.

Mary Kay Cosmetics offers many opportunities to women . . . Tonight, if you join MKC, I would be honored to sign your agreement. This will let Mary Kay know you made your commitment tonight.

[*Lovie invites the new consultants to meet her up front. The audience applauds her. Many of the women eagerly go up to meet Lovie and have their agreements signed.*]

THE DIRECT-SALES INDUSTRY

In 1984 Avon was the acknowledged leader among the handful of companies that chose to market cosmetics to U.S. consumers using direct-sales techniques; Avon, with its door-to-door sales force of 400,000 representatives, had worldwide sales of about $2 billion. Mary Kay Cosmetics was the second-leading firm (see Exhibit 1).

Other well-known companies whose salespeople went either door-to-door with their product or else held "parties" in the homes of prospective customers included Amway Corp. (home cleaning products), Shaklee Corp. (vitamins and health foods), Encyclopedia Britannica, Tupperware (plastic dishes and food containers), Consolidated Foods' Electrolux division (vacuum cleaners), and StanHome (parent of Fuller Brush). The direct-sales industry also included scores of lesser-known firms selling about every product imaginable—clothing, houseplants, toys, and financial services. Although Stanley Home Products invented the idea, Mary Kay and Tupperware were the best-known national companies using the "party plan" approach to direct selling.

The success enjoyed by Avon and Mary Kay was heavily dependent upon constantly replenishing and expanding their sales forces. New salespeople not only placed large initial orders for products but they also recruited new people into the organization. Revenues and revenue growth thus were a function of the number of representatives as well as the sales productivity of each salesperson. Market size was

E X H I B I T   1 | **Estimated Sales of Leading Direct-Selling Cosmetic Companies, 1983**

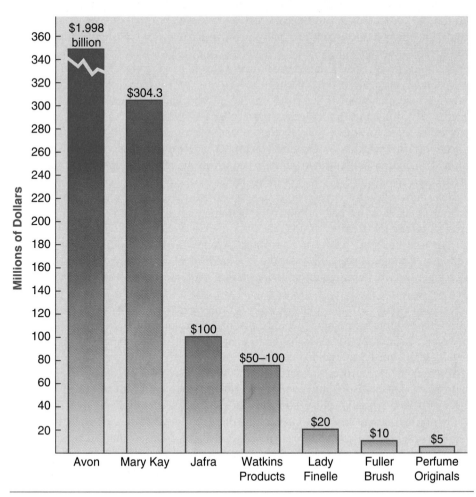

Source: "Reopening the Door to Door-to-Door Selling," *Chemical Business,* February 1984.

not seen as a limiting factor for growth because direct-sales companies typically reached fewer than half the potential customer base.

Direct selling was grounded in capitalizing on networking relationships. Salespeople usually got their starts by selling first to relatives, friends, and neighbors, all the while looking for leads to new prospects. Direct-sales specialists often believed that party-plan selling was most successful among working class, ethnic, and small-town population groups where relationships were closer knit and where the social lives of women had a high carryover effect with work and high school. However, industry analysts saw several trends working against the networking approach and party plan type of direct selling—rising divorce rates, the scattering of relatives and families across wider geographic areas, weakening ties to ethnic neighborhoods, declines in the number and strength of the "old girls" networks in many towns and neighborhoods, increased social mobility, the growing popularity of apartment and condominium living where acquaintances and relationships were more transient, and the springing up of bedroom communities and subdivisions populated by commuters and/or by families that stayed only a few years.

In the 1980s, direct-selling companies began to have problems recruiting and retaining salespeople. During the two most recent recessionary periods in the United States, it was thought that the pool of potential saleswomen available for recruitment into direct-sales careers would expand owing to above-normal unemployment rates. It didn't happen. As it turned out, many women became the sole family support and even greater numbers sought steady, better-paying jobs in other fields. Part-time job opportunities mushroomed outside the direct-sales field as many service and retailing firms started hiring part-time permanent workers rather than full-time permanent staffs because part-time workers did not have to be paid the same extensive fringe benefits that full-time employees normally got. When the economy experienced upturns, the pool for direct-sales recruits shrank even more as people sought security in jobs offering regular hours and a salary; in 1983 all direct-sales companies reported increased difficulty in getting people to accept their part-time, sales-oriented, commission-only offers of employment.

Avon and Mary Kay were both caught offguard by these unpredicted events. Staffing plans at Avon had originally called for expansion in the number of sales force representatives from 400,000 in 1983 to 650,000 by 1987; in 1984 the company revised the 1987 goal down to 500,000 representatives. Four straight years of declining earnings convinced Avon that the traditional strategy of utilizing an ever-larger number of representatives to generate increased revenues was no longer effective.

Sarah Coventry, a home-party jewelry firm, decided in 1984 that relying solely upon direct-selling approaches would not only be a continuing problem but also a growing problem. The company began to look for ways to supplement its direct-sales methods and shortly announced a plan to begin to sell Sarah Coventry products in retail stores. Fuller Brush, a long-standing door-to-door seller, began to distribute mail-order catalogs displaying a wider line of "househelper" products.

As of 1984, virtually every company in the direct-sales industry was critically evaluating the extent to which changes in the economy and in employment demographics would affect the success of direct selling. Many firms, including Avon and Mary Kay, were reviewing their incentive programs and sales organization methods. A number of industry observers as well as company officials believed some major changes would have to be made in the way the direct-sales industry did business.

MARY KAY ASH

Before she reached the age of 10, Mary Kay had the responsibility of cleaning, cooking, and caring for her invalid father while her mother worked to support the family. During these years, Mary Kay's mother encouraged her daughter to excel. Whether at school or home, Mary Kay was urged to put forth her best efforts. By the time she was a teenager, Mary Kay had become a classic overachiever, intent on getting good grades and winning school contests. Over and over again, she heard her mother say "you can do it." Years later, Mary Kay noted on many occasions, "The confidence my mother instilled in me has been a tremendous help."[1]

Deserted by her husband of 11 years during the Great Depression, Mary Kay found herself with the responsibility of raising and supporting three children under the age of eight. Needing a job with flexible hours, she opted to try a career in direct sales with Stanley Home Products, a home-party housewares firm. One of the first goals Mary Kay set at Stanley was to win Stanley's Miss Dallas Award, a ribbon honoring the employee who recruited the most new people in one week; she won the award during her first year with Stanley. After 13 years with Stanley, Mary Kay joined World Gift, a direct-sales company involved in decorative accessories; a few years later she was promoted to national training director. Her career and life were threatened in 1962 by a rare paralysis of one side of the face.

After recovery from surgery, she decided to retire from World Gift; by then she had remarried and lived in a comfortable Dallas neighborhood. She got so bored with retirement she decided to write a book on her direct-sales experiences. The more she wrote, the more she came to realize just how many problems women faced in the business world. Writing on a yellow legal pad at her kitchen table, Mary Kay listed everything she thought was wrong with male-run companies; on a second sheet she detailed how these wrongs could be righted, how a company could operate in ways that were responsive to the problems of working women and especially working mothers, and how women could reach their top potential in the business world. Being restless with retirement, she decided to do something about what she had written on the yellow pad and began immediately to plan how she might form a direct-sales company that had no sales quotas, few rules, flexible work hours, and plenty of autonomy for salespeople.

Finding a product to market was not a problem. In 1953, when she was conducting a Stanley home party at a house "on the wrong side of Dallas," she had noticed that all the ladies present had terrific-looking skin. It turned out that the hostess was a cosmetologist who was experimenting with a skin care product and all the guests were her guinea pigs. After the party, everyone gathered in the hostess's kitchen to get samples of her latest batch. The product was based on a formula that the woman's father, a hide tanner, developed when he accidentally discovered that some tanning lotions he made and used regularly had caused his hands to look much younger than his face. The tanner decided to apply these solutions to his face regularly, and after a short time his facial skin began looking more youthful too. The woman had since worked with her father's discovery for 17 years, making up batches that had the chemical smell of tanning solutions, putting portions in empty jars and bottles, and selling them as a sideline; she gave out instructions for use written in longhand on notebook paper. Mary Kay offered to try some of the hostess's latest batch and,

---

[1]Mary Kay Ash, *Mary Kay* (New York: Harper & Row, 1981), p. 3.

despite the fact that it was smelly and messy, soon concluded that it was so good she wouldn't use anything else. Later, she became convinced that the only reason the woman hadn't made the product a commercial success was because she lacked marketing skills.

In 1963, using $5,000 in savings as working capital, she bought the formulas and proceeded to organize a beauty products company that integrated skin care instruction into its direct-sales approach. The company was named Beauty by Mary Kay; the plan was for Mary Kay to take responsibility for the sales part of the company and for her second husband to serve as chief administrator. One month before operations were to start, he died from a heart attack. Her children persuaded her to go ahead with her plans, and Mary Kay's 20-year-old son, Richard Rogers, agreed to take on the job of administration of the new company. In September 1963, they opened a small store in Dallas with one shelf of inventory and nine of Mary Kay's friends as saleswomen. Mary Kay herself had limited expectations for the company and never dreamed that its sphere of operations would extend beyond Dallas.

All of Mary Kay's lifelong philosophies and experiences were incorporated into how the company operated. The importance of encouragement became deeply ingrained in what was said and done. "You Can Do It" was expanded from a technique used by her mother to a daily theme at MKC. Mary Kay's style was to "praise people to success." She put into practice again the motivating role that positive encouragement had played in her own career; recognition and awards were made a highlight of the sales incentive programs that emerged. By 1984, recognition at MKC ranged from a single ribbon awarded for a consultant's first $100 show to a $5,000 shopping spree given to million-dollar producers.

The second important philosophy Mary Kay stressed concerned personal priorities: "Over the years, I have found that if you have your life in the proper perspective, with God first, your family second, and your career third, everything seems to work out."[2] She reiterated this belief again and again, regularly urging employees to take stock of their personal priorities and citing her own experience and belief as a positive example. She insisted on an all-out, firmwide effort to accommodate the plight of working mothers. Mary Kay particularly stressed giving beauty consultants enough control over how their selling efforts were scheduled so that problems with family matters and sick children were not incompatible with a Mary Kay career. A structure based on no sales quotas, few rules, and flexible hours was essential, Mary Kay believed, because working mothers from time to time needed the freedom to let work demands take a backseat to pressing problems at home.

Fairness and personal ethics were put in the forefront, too. The Golden Rule (treating others as you would have them treat you) was high on Mary Kay's list of management guidelines:

> I believe in the Golden Rule and try to run the company on those principles. I believe that all you send into the lives of others will come back into your own. I like to see women reaching into themselves and coming out of their shells as the beautiful person that God intended them to be. In my company women do not have to claw their way to the top. They can get ahead based on the virtue of their own ethics because there's enough for everyone.[3]

---

[2]Ibid., p. 56.

[3]As quoted in "The Beauty of Being Mary Kay," *Marketing and Media Decisions,* December 1982, pp. 150, 152.

To discourage interpersonal rivalry and jealousy, all rewards and incentives were pegged to reaching plateaus of achievements; everybody who reached the target level of performance became a winner. Sales contests based on declaring first place, second place, and third place winners were avoided.

MKC, INC.

The company succeeded from the start. First-year wholesale sales were $198,000; in the second year, sales reached $800,000. At year-end 1983, wholesale revenues exceeded $320 million. Major geographical expansion was initiated during the 1970s. Distribution centers were opened in California, Georgia, New Jersey, and Illinois, and the company expanded its selling efforts internationally to Canada, Argentina, Australia, and the United Kingdom.

Early on, Mary Kay and Richard decided to consult a psychologist to learn more about their personalities. Testing revealed that Mary Kay was the type who, when encountering a person bleeding all over a fine carpet, would think of the person's plight while Richard would think first of the carpet. This solidified their decision for Mary Kay to be the company's inspirational leader and for Richard to concentrate on overseeing all the business details.

In 1968 the company name was changed to Mary Kay Cosmetics, Inc. Also during 1968 the company went public and its stock was traded in the over-the-counter market; in 1976 MKC's stock was listed on the New York Stock Exchange. Income per common share jumped from $0.16 in 1976 to $1.22 in 1983. An 11-year financial summary is presented in Exhibit 2; Exhibits 3 and 4 provide additional company data.

Richard Rogers, president, gave two basic reasons for the success of MKC:

We were filling a void in the industry when we began to teach skin care and makeup artistry and we're still doing that today. And second, our marketing system, through which proficient customers achieve success by recruiting and building their own sales organization, was a stroke of genius because the by-product has been management. In other words, we didn't buy a full management team, they've been trained one by one.[4]

One of the biggest challenges MKC had to tackle during the 1970s was how to adapt its strategy to deal with the influx of women into the labor force. Full- and part-time jobs interfered with attending beauty shows during normal working hours, and many working women with children at home had a hard time fitting beauty shows on weeknights and weekends into their schedules. To make the beauty show sales approach more appealing to working women, the company began to supplement its standard "try before you buy" and "on-the-spot delivery" sales pitch themes. Consultants were trained to tout the ease with which MKC's scientifically formulated skin care system could be followed, the value of investing in good makeup and attractive appearance, the up-to-date glamour and wide selection associated with MKC's product line, the flexibility of deciding what and when to buy, and the time-saving convenience of having refills and "specials" delivered to one's door instead of having to go out shopping. Mary Kay consultants quickly picked up on the growing popularity of having beauty shows on Tuesday, Wednesday, and Thursday nights; a lesser proportion of weekday hours were used for morning and afternoon showings, and a greater proportion came to be used for seeking and delivering reorders from ongoing users.

---

[4]Mary Kay Cosmetics, Inc., "A Company and a Way of Life," company literature.

EXHIBIT 2 | Selected Financial Data, Mary Kay Cosmetics, Inc., 1973–83 *(In thousands, except per-share data)*

	1973	1974	1975	1976	1977	1978	1979	1980	1981	1982	1983
Net sales	$22,199	$30,215	$34,947	$44,871	$47,856	$53,746	$91,400	$166,938	$235,296	$304,275	$323,758
Cost of sales	6,414	9,054	10,509	14,139	14,562	17,517	27,584	52,484	71,100	87,807	88,960
Selling, general, and administrative expenses	9,674	13,128	15,050	19,192	21,394	27,402	45,522	86,998	120,880	154,104	168,757
Operating income	6,111	8,033	9,388	11,540	11,900	8,827	18,304	27,456	43,316	62,364	66,041
Interest and other income, net	377	443	202	501	175	660	493	712	1,485	2,763	3,734
Interest expense	58	54	60	43	212	504	958	635	1,014	1,284	2,886
Income before income taxes	6,430	8,422	9,530	11,998	11,863	8,983	17,839	27,533	43,787	63,843	66,889
Provision for income taxes	3,035	3,973	4,480	5,854	5,711	4,110	8,207	12,398	19,632	28,471	30,235
Net income	$ 3,395	$ 4,449	$ 5,050	$ 6,144	$ 6,152	$ 4,873	$ 9,632	$ 15,135	$ 23,155	$ 35,372	$ 36,654
Net income per common share	$.09	$.11	$.13	$.16	$.17	$.15	$.33	$.52	$.82	$1.18	$1.22
Cash dividends per share	$.01	$.03	$.03	$.05	$.05	$.06	$.06	$.09	$.10	$.11	$.12
Average common shares	38,800	38,864	38,982	39,120	35,480	33,408	29,440	28,884	29,324	29,894	30,138
Total assets	$19,600	$24,743	$27,996	$34,331	$35,144	$36,305	$50,916	$ 74,431	$100,976	$152,457	$180,683
Long-term debt	$ 756	$ 87	$ 42	—	$ 5,592	$ 3,558	$ 4,000	$ 3,000	$ 2,366	$ 4,669	$ 3,915
Return on average stockholders' equity			21%	23%	24%	20%	38%	48%	48%	45%	32%
Stock prices											
Year high			$2¾	$2⅞	$2⅝	$1⅞	$3⅞	$8¾	$18¾	$28½	$47⅞
Year low			1⅞	1¾	1½	1¼	1¼	3	6⅛	8⅜	13⅛

Source: Mary Kay Cosmetics, Inc., *1983 Annual Report.*

EXHIBIT 3 | Growth in the Number of MKC Sales Directors and Beauty Consultants, 1973–83

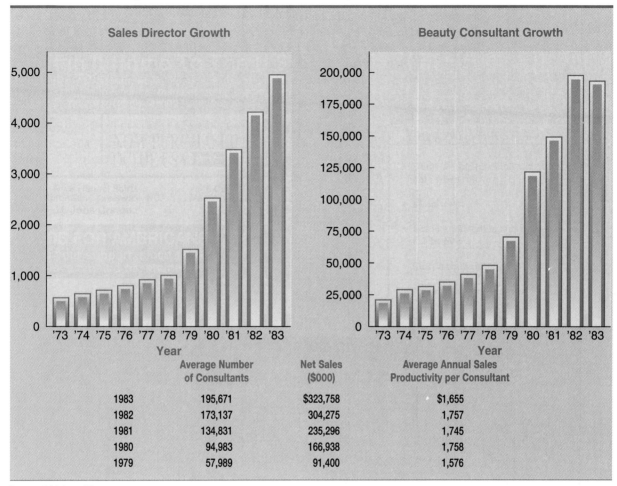

	Average Number of Consultants	Net Sales ($000)	Average Annual Sales Productivity per Consultant
1983	195,671	$323,758	$1,655
1982	173,137	304,275	1,757
1981	134,831	235,296	1,745
1980	94,983	166,938	1,758
1979	57,989	91,400	1,576

Source: *1983 Annual Report.*

EXHIBIT 4 | Percentage Breakdown of Product Sales at Mary Kay Cosmetics, 1979–83

	1979	1980	1981	1982	1983
Skin care products for women	49%	52%	49%	46%	44%
Skin care products for men	1	2	1	1	1
Makeup items	26	22	26	26	30
Toiletry items for women	10	10	10	12	11
Toiletry items for men	2	2	2	2	2
Hair care	2	2	2	2	2
Accessories	10	10	10	11	10
Total	100%	100%	100%	100%	100%

Source: *1983 Annual Report.*

MKC's corporate sales goal was to reach $500 million in revenues by 1990. As of 1984, about 65 percent of total sales were made to customers at beauty shows. However, it was expected that as the size of the company's customer base grew, the percentage of orders from repeat buyers would rise well above the present 35 percent level. MKC estimated that the average client spent over $200 a year on cosmetics. The company saw its target clientele as middle-class women in the 18 to 34 age group primarily and in the 35 to 44 age group secondarily and believed that a big percentage of its customers consisted of suburban housewives and white-collar clerical workers. The company's literature always pictured upscale women, dressed in a classy and elegant yet understated way, in either the role of a Mary Kay beauty consultant or the role of a user of Mary Kay cosmetics. As company figurehead, Mary Kay Ash personally made a point of being fashionably and expensively dressed, with perfect makeup and hairstyle—a walking showcase for the company's products and a symbol of the professionally successful businesswoman (Exhibit 5).

EXHIBIT 5 | **Mary Kay Ash in 1983**

Source: *1983 Annual Report* (picture on front cover).

MANUFACTURING

When Mary Kay Cosmetics commenced operations in 1963, the task of making the products was contracted out to a private Dallas-based manufacturing company. Mary Kay explained why:

> In 1963 I had no previous experience in the cosmetics industry; my forte was recruiting and training salespeople. After I acquired the formulas for the skincare products, the first thing I did was seek out the most reputable cosmetics manufacturer I could find. Specifically I wanted a firm that not only made quality products, but observed the Food and Drug Administration's regulatory requirements to the letter. I knew it would be a fatal mistake to attempt to cut corners. With the right people in charge, we would never have to concern ourselves with that aspect of the business.[5]

In 1969, MKC built a 300,000-square-foot facility adjacent to corporate headquarters. Packaging, warehousing, purchasing, and research labs were all housed in this location. Also included was a printing setup that created Mary Kay labels in English, Spanish, and French. Many of the operations were automated.

The company's scientific research approach to skin care was supported by a staff of laboratory technicians skilled in cosmetic chemistry, dermatology, physiology, microbiology, and package engineering. Ongoing tests were conducted to refine existing items and to develop new products. Laboratory staffs were provided with the comments and reactions about the products that came in from the beauty consultants and their customers. Consultants were strongly encouraged to report on their experiences with items and to relay any problems directly to the laboratory staff. About 80 percent of the R&D budget was earmarked for improving existing products.

MKC believed that it was an industry leader in researching the properties of the skin (as concerned skin elasticity and moisture) and the anatomy of skin structure. Much of the research at MKC was performed in cooperation with academic institutions, particularly the University of Pennsylvania and the University of Texas Health Science Center.

PRODUCT-LINE AND DISTRIBUTION POLICIES

As of 1984, the Mary Kay product line consisted of the basic skin care program for various skin types, the glamour collection, the body care products line, and a line of men's products called Mr. K. Most of the women's products were packaged in pink boxes and jars. When the company first began operations, Mary Kay personally put a lot of thought into packaging and appearance:

> Since people do leave their toiletries out, I wanted to package our cosmetics so beautifully that women would *want* to leave them out. So I was looking for a color that would make a beautiful display in all those white bathrooms. There were some shades of blue that were attractive, but the prettiest complementary color seemed to be a delicate pink. It also occurred to me that pink is considered a more feminine color. But my main reason for choosing it was that delicate pink seemed to look prettier than anything else in those white tile bathrooms. And from that I gained a *pink* reputation.[6]

[5]Mary Kay Ash, *Mary Kay on People Management* (New York: Warner Books, 1984), p. 13.
[6]Ash, *Mary Kay,* pp. 150–51.

Mr. K, the men's line, was introduced in the 1960s in response to a number of confessions from men who used their wives' Mary Kay products. A rich chocolate brown package accented with silver was chosen for Mr. K. The men's line included a basic skin care program as well as lotions and colognes. The majority of Mr. K purchases were made by women for their husbands and boyfriends.

Consultants bought their supplies of products directly from MKC at wholesale prices and sold them at a 100 percent markup over wholesale. To make it more feasible for consultants to keep an adequate inventory on hand, the product line at MKC was kept streamlined to about 50 products. Mary Kay consultants were encouraged to carry enough products in their personal inventories that orders could be filled on the spot at the beauty shows. As an incentive to support this practice, MKC offered special awards and prizes when consultants placed orders of $1,500 or more.

A consultant could order as many or as few of the company's products as she chose to inventory. Most consultants stockpiled those items that sold especially well with their own individual clientele, and consultants also had the freedom to offer special promotions or discounts to customers. Nearly 50 percent of sales were for the skin care products that had evolved from the hide tanner's discovery. Consultants were required to pay for all orders with cashier's checks or money orders prior to delivery. MKC dealt only on a cash basis to minimize accounts receivables problems; according to Mary Kay, "Bad debts are a major reason for failure in other direct-sales companies." In 1984, the average initial order of new consultants for inventory was about $1,000 ($2,000 in retail value). Consultants who decided to get out of the business could resell their inventories to MKC at 90 percent of cost.

During the company's early years, consultants were supplied only with an inventory of items to sell; shipments arrived in plain boxes. There were no sales kits and no instruction manuals to assist in sales presentations. However, by the 1970s, each new recruit received training in skin care techniques and was furnished with a number of sales aids. Later, new consultants were required to buy a beauty showcase containing everything needed to conduct a beauty show (samples, pink mirrors, pink trays used to distribute the samples, and a step-by-step sales manual that included suggested dialogue). In 1984 the showcase was sold to new consultants for $85. Along with the showcase came a supply of beauty profile forms to use at showings; guests filled out the form at the beginning of the show, and from the information supplied a consultant could readily prescribe which of the several product formulas was best suited for the individual's skin type.

In addition to the income earned from product sales, consultants earned bonuses or commissions on the sales made by all the recruits they brought in. MKC paid consultants with one to four recruits a bonus commission equal to 4 percent on the wholesale orders of the recruits. A consultant with five or more recruits earned an 8 percent commission on the orders placed by recruits, or 12 percent if she also placed $600 a month in wholesale orders herself. MKC consultants who were entitled to a 12 percent commission and who had as many as 24 recruits were averaging about $950 monthly in bonuses and recruitment commissions as of 1984.

MKC's Sales Organization

The basic field organization unit for MKC's 195,000-person force of beauty consultants was the sales unit. Each sales unit was headed by a sales director who provided leadership and training for her group of beauty consultants. The top-performing sales directors were designated as national sales directors, a title that signified the ultimate achievement in the Mary Kay career sales ladder. A corporate staff of seven national sales administrators oversaw the activities of the sales directors in the field and their units of beauty consultants.

The sales units were not organized along strict geographical lines, and sales directors were free to recruit consultants anywhere; Mary Kay explained the logic for this approach:

One of the first things I wanted my dream company to eliminate was assigned territories. I had worked for several direct-sales organizations in the past, and I knew how unfairly I had been treated when I had to move from Houston to St. Louis because of my husband's new job. I had been making $1,000 a month in commissions from the Houston sales unit that I had built over a period of eight years and I lost it all when I moved. I felt that it wasn't fair for someone else to inherit those Houston salespeople whom I had worked so hard to recruit and train.

Because we don't have territories at Mary Kay Cosmetics, a director who lives in Chicago can be vacationing in Florida or visiting a friend in Pittsburgh and recruit someone while there. It doesn't matter where she lives in the United States; she will always draw a commission from the company on the wholesale purchases made by that recruit as long as they both remain with the company. The director in Pittsburgh will take the visiting director's new recruit under her wing and train her; the recruit will attend the Pittsburgh sales meetings and participate in the local sales contests. Although the Pittsburgh director will devote a lot of time and effort to the new recruit, the Chicago director will be paid the commissions. We call this our "adoptee" program.

The Pittsburgh recruit may go on to recruit new people on her own. No matter where she lives, she becomes the nucleus for bringing in additional people for the director who brought her into the business. As long as they're both active in the company, she will receive commissions from the company on her recruit's sales activity.

Today we have more than 5,000 sales directors, and most of them train and motivate people in their units who live outside their home states. Some have beauty consultants in a dozen or more states. Outsiders look at our company and say, "Your adoptee program can't possibly work!" But it does work. Each director reaps the benefits from her recruits in other cities and helps other recruits in return.[7]

THE BEAUTY CONSULTANT

Nearly all of MKC's beauty consultants had their first contact with the company as a guest at a beauty show. A discussion of career opportunities with Mary Kay was a standard part of the presentation at each beauty show. As many as 10 percent of the attendees at beauty shows were serious prospects as new recruits.

All beauty consultants were self-employed and worked on a commission basis. Everyone in the entire MKC sales organization started at the consultant level. The progression of each consultant up the "ladder of success" within the MKC sales organization was tightly linked to (1) the amount of wholesale orders the consultant placed with MKC, (2) her abilities to bring in new sales recruits, and (3) the size of the wholesale orders placed by these recruits. There were five rungs on the ladder of success for consultants, with qualifications and rewards as follows:

1. *New beauty consultant* (member of Perfect Start Club).

   Perfect Start Club qualifications:

   Study and complete perfect start workbook.

---

[7]Ash, *Mary Kay on People Management,* pp. 2–3.

Observe three beauty shows.

Book a minimum of eight shows within two weeks of receiving beauty showcase.

Awards and recognition:

Receives perfect start pin.

Earns 50 percent commission on retail sales (less any discounts given to customers on special promotions).

Becomes eligible for a 4 percent recruiting commission on wholesale orders placed by active personal recruits (to be considered active, a consultant had to place at least a $600 minimum wholesale order during the current quarter).

2. *Star consultant.*

Qualifications:

Must have three active recruits.

Be an active beauty consultant (place a minimum wholesale order of $600 within the current calendar quarter).

Awards and recognition:

Earns a red blazer.

Earns a star pin.

Earns Ladder of Success status by placing $1,800 in wholesale orders in a three-month period.

Earns 50 percent commission on personal sales at beauty shows.

Earns 4 percent recruiting commissions on wholesale orders placed by active personal recruits.

Is eligible for special prizes and awards offered during quarterly contest.

Receives a Star of Excellence ladder pin by qualifying as a star consultant for 8 quarters (or a Double Star of Excellence pin for 16 quarters).

3. *Team leader.*

Qualifications:

Must have five or more active recruits.

Be an active beauty consultant.

Awards and recognition:

Earns 50 percent commission on sales at own beauty shows.

Earns a Tender Loving Care emblem for red blazer.

Earns an 8 percent personal recruiting commission on wholesale orders of active personal recruits.

Earns a 12 percent personal recruiting commission if (a) five or more active personal recruits place minimum $600 wholesale orders during the current month and (b) the team leader herself places a $600 wholesale order during the current month.

Receives team leader pin in ladder of success program.

Is eligible for quarterly contest prizes and bonuses.

4. *VIP (Very important performer).*

Qualifications:

Must have obtained team leader status.

Must place wholesale orders of at least $600 for three consecutive months.

Team must place wholesale orders of at least $3,000 each month for three consecutive months.

Awards and recognition:

Earns the use of an Oldsmobile Firenza.

Earns 50 percent commission on sales at own beauty shows.

Earns a 12 percent personal recruiting commission.

Receives VIP pin in ladder of success program.

Is eligible for quarterly contest prizes and bonuses.

5. *Future director.*

Qualifications:

Must have qualified for team leader status.

Must have 12 active recruits at time of application.

Must make a commitment to Mary Kay to become a sales director by actually giving her letter of intent date.

Awards and recognition:

Earns a future director crest for red jacket.

Plus all the benefits accorded team leaders and VIPs, as appropriate, for monthly and quarterly sales and recruiting performance.

New recruits were required to submit a signed beauty consultant agreement, observe three beauty shows conducted by an experienced consultant, book a minimum of eight beauty shows, and hold at least five beauty shows within their first two weeks. Each consultant was asked to appear in attractive dress and makeup when in public and to project an image of knowledge and confidence about herself and the MKC product line. Mary Kay felt the stress on personal appearance was justified: "What we are selling is beauty. A woman is not going to buy from someone who is wearing jeans and has her hair up in curlers. We want our consultants to be the type of woman others will want to emulate."[8]

Consultants spent most of their work hours scheduling and giving beauty shows. A showing took about two hours (plus about an hour for travel time), and many times the hostess and one or more of the guests turned out to be prospective recruits. New consultants were coached to start off by booking showings with friends, neighbors, and relatives and then network these into showings for friends of friends and relatives of relatives.

Consultants were instructed to follow up each beauty show by scheduling a second facial for each guest at the showing. Many times a customer would invite friends to her second facial and the result would be another beauty show. After the

---

[8]Rebecca Fannin, "The Beauty of Being Mary Kay," *Marketing & Media Decisions* 17 (December 1982), pp. 59–61.

follow-up facial, consultants would call customers periodically to check on whether the customer was satisfied, to see if refills were needed, and to let the customer know about new products and special promotions. Under MKC's "dovetailing" plan, a consultant with an unexpected emergency at home could sell her prearranged beauty show to another consultant and the two would split the commissions generated by the show.

THE SALES DIRECTOR

Consultants who had climbed to the fifth rung of the consultants' ladder of success were eligible to become sales directors and head up a sales unit. In addition to conducting her own beauty shows, a sales director's responsibilities included training new recruits, leading weekly sales meetings, and providing assistance and advice to the members of her unit. Sales directors, besides receiving the commission on sales made at their own showings, were paid a commission on the total sales of the unit they headed and a commission on the number of new sales recruits. In June 1984, the top 100 recruiting commissions paid to sales directors ranged from approximately $660 to $1,900. It was not uncommon for sales directors to have total annual earnings in the $50,000 to $100,000 range; in 1983, the average income of the 4,500 sales directors was between $25,000 and $30,000.

There were six achievement categories for sales directors, with qualifications and awards as shown below:

1. *Director in qualification (DIQ).*

   Qualifications:

   > Must have 15 active personal recruits.
   > Submits a letter of intent to obtain directorship.
   > Gets the director of her sales unit to submit a letter of recommendation.
   > Within three consecutive months:
   >
   > - Must recruit an additional 15 consultants for a total of 30 personal active recruits.
   > - The unit of 30 personal active recruits must place combined wholesale orders of $4,000, $4,500, and $5,000 for months one, two, and three, respectively.

   Awards and recognition:

   > Earns personal sales and personal recruiting commissions (as per schedules for at least team leader status).
   > Eligible for prizes and bonuses in quarterly contests.

2. *Sales director.*

   Qualifications:

   > Sales unit must maintain a minimum of $4,000 in wholesale orders each month for the sales director to remain as head of her unit.

   Awards and recognition:

   > Receives commissions of 9 percent to 13 percent on unit's wholesale orders.

Receives monthly sales production bonuses.

- A $300 monthly bonus if unit places monthly wholesale orders of $3,000-$4,999.
- A $500 monthly bonus if unit places monthly wholesale orders of $5,000 and up.

Receives a monthly recruiting bonus (for personal recruits or for recruits of other consultants in the sales unit).

- $100 bonus if three to four new recruits come into unit.
- $200 bonus if five to seven new recruits come into unit.
- $300 bonus if 8 to 11 new recruits come into unit.
- $400 bonus for 12 or more recruits.

Is given a designer director suit.

Is entitled to all commission schedules and incentives of future sales directors.

3. *Regal director.*

Qualifications:

Members of sales unit must place wholesale orders of at least $24,000 for two consecutive quarters.

Must qualify every two years.

Awards and recognition:

Earns the use of a pink Buick Regal.

Is entitled to all the commission percentages, bonuses, and other incentives of a sales director.

4. *Cadillac director.*

Qualifications:

Sales unit members must place at least $36,000 in wholesale orders for two consecutive quarters.

Must qualify every two years.

Awards and recognition:

Earns the use of a pink Cadillac.

Is entitled to all the commission percentages, bonuses, and other incentives of a sales director.

5. *Senior sales director.*

Qualifications:

One to four sales directors emerge from her unit.

Awards and recognition:

Earns a 4 percent commission on offspring directors' consultants.

Is entitled to all the commission percentages, bonuses, and other incentives of at least a sales director.

6. *Future national director.*

Qualifications:

Five or more active directors emerge from her unit.

Awards and recognition:

Is entitled to all the commission percentages, bonuses, and other incentives of a senior sales director.

As of late 1983, the company had about 700 Regal directors and about 700 Cadillac directors; in one recent quarter, 81 sales directors had met the qualifications for driving a new pink Cadillac.

THE NATIONAL SALES DIRECTOR

Top-performing sales directors became eligible for designation as a national sales director, the highest recognition bestowed on field sales personnel. NSDs were inspirational leaders and managers of a group of sales directors and received commissions on the total dollar sales of the group of sales units they headed. In 1984, MKC's 50 national sales directors had total sales incomes averaging over $150,000 per year. A 1985 *Fortune* article featured Helen McVoy, an MKC national sales director since 1971, as one of the most successful salespeople in the United States; in 1984 she earned $375,000. McVoy began her career with Mary Kay in 1965 at the age of 45. Her family was on a tight budget, having lost all of their savings in a bad mining investment. To support her plant-collecting hobby, Helen started selling Mary Kay products on a part-time basis—two hours a week. Her original investment was for a beauty case; by the end of her first year she had made $17,000. From 1970 through 1984, she was the company's top-volume producer.

TRAINING

Before holding a beauty show, a new consultant had to observe three beauty shows, attend orientation classes conducted by a sales director, and complete a self-study set of MKC training materials. This training covered the fundamentals of conducting skin care shows, booking future beauty shows, recruiting new Mary Kay consultants, personal appearance, and managing a small business. Active consultants were strongly encouraged to continue to improve their sales skills and product knowledge. In addition to weekly sales meetings and frequent one-on-one contact with other consultants and sales directors, each salesperson had access to a variety of company-prepared support materials—videotapes, films, slide shows, and brochures.

In 1983, a new educational curriculum was introduced to support each phase of a Mary Kay career. A back-to-basics orientation package provided a foundation for the first stage of career development. A recruitment notebook provided dialogue of mock recruiting conversations, and sales directors were provided with an organizational kit to help them make a smooth transition from being purely a consultant to being a sales manager as well as a consultant.

Additional learning opportunities were provided in the form of special product knowledge classes, regional workshops, and annual corporate-sponsored seminars.

MOTIVATION AND INCENTIVES

New sales contests were introduced every three months. Prizes and recognition awards were always tied to achievement plateaus rather than declaring first-, second-, and third-place winners. Top performers were spotlighted in the company's full-color monthly magazine, *Applause* (which had a circulation of several hundred thousand).

Mary Kay Ash described why MKC paid so much attention to recognition and praise:

I believe praise is the best way for a manager to motivate people. At Mary Kay Cosmetics we think praise is so important that our entire marketing plan is based upon it.[9]

Praise is an incredibly effective motivator; unfortunately, many managers are reluctant to employ it. Yet I can't help feeling that they know how much praise means, not only to others, but to themselves . . . I believe that you should praise people whenever you can; it causes them to respond as a thirsty plant responds to water.[10]

The power of positive motivation in a goal-oriented structure such as ours cannot be overstated. This is what inspires our consultants to maximize their true potentials.[11]

As a manager you must recognize that everyone needs praise. But it must be given sincerely. You'll find numerous occasions for genuine praise if you'll only look for them.[12]

Because we recognize the need for people to be praised, we make a concentrated effort to give as much recognition as possible. Of course with an organization as large as ours, not everyone can make a speech at our seminars, but we do attempt to have many people appear on stage, if only for a few moments. During the Directors' March, for example, hundreds of directors parade on stage before thousands of their peers. In order to appear in the Directors' March, a director must purchase a special designer suit. Likewise we have a Red Jacket March, in which only star recruiters, team leaders, and future directors participate. Again, a special uniform is required for participation.[13]

How important are these brief stage appearances? Frankly I think it means more for a woman to be recognized by her peers than to receive an expensive present in the mail that nobody knows about! And once she gets a taste of this recognition, she wants to come back next year for more![14]

SEMINAR

MKC staged an annual "Seminar" as a salute to the company and to the salespeople who contributed to its success. The first seminar was held on September 13, 1964 (the company's first anniversary); the banquet menu consisted of chicken, jello salad, and an anniversary cake while a three-piece band provided entertainment. By 1984, the seminar had grown into a three-day spectacular repeated four consecutive times with a budget of $4 million and attended by 24,000 beauty consultants and sales directors who paid their own way to attend the event. The setting, the Convention Center in Dallas (see Exhibit 6), was decorated in red, white, and blue in order to emphasize the theme, "Share the Spirit." The climactic highlight of the seminar was

[9]Ash, *Mary Kay on People Management*, p. 21.
[10]Ibid., p. 23.
[11]Ibid., p. 26
[12]Ibid., p. 27.
[13]Ibid., p. 25.
[14]Ibid., p. 26.

EXHIBIT 6 | **Share the Spirit, 1984 Annual Seminar, Mary Kay Cosmetics**

Source: Mary Kay Cosmetics, Inc., *Interim Report,* 1984.

Awards Night, when the biggest prizes were awarded to the people with the biggest sales. The company went to elaborate efforts to ensure the awards night was charged with excitement and emotion; as one observer of the 1984 Awards Night in Dallas described it, "The atmosphere there is electric, a cross between a Las Vegas revue and a revival meeting. Hands reach up to touch Mary Kay; a pink Cadillac revolves on a mist-shrouded pedestal; a 50-piece band plays; and women sob."

Mary Kay Ash customarily made personal appearances throughout the seminar period. In addition to awards night, the seminar featured sessions consisting of informational and training workshops, motivational presentations by leading sales directors, and star entertainment (Paul Anka performed in 1984, and in previous years there had been performances by Tennessee Ernie Ford, John Davidson, and Johnny Mathis). Over the three days, Cadillacs, diamonds, mink coats, a $5,000 shopping spree at Neiman-Marcus for any director whose team sold $1 million worth of Mary Kay products, and lesser assorted prizes were awarded to the outstanding achievers of the past year. Gold-and-diamond bumblebee pins, each containing 21 diamonds and retailing for over $3,600, were presented to the Queen of Sales on Pageant Night; these pins were not only the company's ultimate badge of success, but Mary Kay felt they also had special symbolism:

It's a beautiful pin, but that isn't the whole story. We think the bumblebee is a marvelous symbol of woman. Because, as aerodynamic engineers found a long time ago, the bumblebee cannot fly! Its wings are too weak and its body is too heavy to fly, but fortunately, the bumblebee doesn't know that, and it goes right on flying. The bee has become the symbol of women who didn't know they could fly but they *did!* I think the women who own these diamond bumblebees think of them in their own personal ways. For most of us, it's true that we refused to believe we couldn't do it. Maybe somebody else told us, "You can do it!" So we did.[15]

CORPORATE ENVIRONMENT

The company's eight-story, gold-glass corporate headquarters building in Dallas was occupied solely by Mary Kay executives. An open-door philosophy was present at MKC. Everyone from the mailroom clerk to the chairman of the board was treated with respect. The door to Mary Kay Ash's office was rarely closed. Often people touring the building peeked in her office to get a glimpse of the pink-and-white decor. Mary Kay and all other corporate managers took the time to talk with any employee.

First names were always used at MKC. Mary Kay herself insisted on being addressed as Mary Kay; she felt people who called her Mrs. Ash were either angry at her or didn't know her. In keeping with this informal atmosphere, offices didn't have titles on the doors, executive restrooms didn't exist, and the company cafeteria was used by the executives (there was no executive dining room).

To further enhance the informal atmosphere and enthusiasm at MKC, all sales functions began with a group sing-along. Mary Kay offered several reasons for this policy:

> Nothing great is ever achieved without enthusiasm . . . We have many of our own songs, and they're sung at all Mary Kay get-togethers, ranging from small weekly meetings to our annual seminars. Our salespeople enjoy this activity, and I believe the singing creates a wonderful esprit de corps. Yet outsiders, especially men, often criticize our singing as being "strictly for women." I disagree. Singing unites people. It's like those "rah-rah-rah for our team" cheers. If someone is depressed, singing will often bring her out of it.[16]

The company sent Christmas cards, birthday cards, and anniversary cards to every single employee each year. Mary Kay personally designed the birthday cards for consultants. In addition, all the sales directors received Christmas and birthday presents from the company.

THE PEOPLE MANAGEMENT PHILOSOPHY AT MKC

Mary Kay Ash had some very definite ideas about how people ought to be managed, and she willingly shared them with employees and, through her books, with the public at large. Some excerpts from her book *Mary Kay on People Management* reveal the approach taken at Mary Kay Cosmetics:

> People come first at Mary Kay Cosmetics—our beauty consultants, sales directors, and employees, our customers, and our suppliers. We pride ourselves as a "company known for the people it keeps." Our belief in caring for people, however, does not conflict with our need as a corporation to generate a profit. Yes, we keep our eye on the bottom line, but it's not an overriding obsession.[17]

---

[15]Ash, *Mary Kay,* p. 9.
[16]Ash, *Mary Kay on People Management,* p. 59.
[17]Ibid., p. xix.

Ours is an organization with few middle-management positions. In order to grow and progress, you don't move upward; you expand outward. This gives our independent sales organization a deep sense of personal worth. They know that they are not competing with one another for a spot in the company's managerial "pecking order." Therefore the contributions of each individual are of equal value. No one is fearful that his or her idea will be "stolen" by someone with more ability on the corporate ladder. And when someone—anyone—proposes a new thought, we all analyze it, improve upon it, and ultimately support it with the enthusiasm of a team.[18]

Every person is special! I sincerely believe this. Each of us wants to feel good about himself or herself, but to me it is just as important to make others feel the same way. Whenever I meet someone, I try to imagine him wearing an invisible sign that says: MAKE ME FEEL IMPORTANT! I respond to this sign immediately and it works wonders.[19]

At Mary Kay Cosmetics we believe in putting our beauty consultants and sales directors on a pedestal. Of all people, I most identify with them because I spent many years as a salesperson. My attitude of appreciation for them permeates the company. When our salespeople visit the home office, for example, we go out of our way to give them the red-carpet treatment. Every person in the company treats them royally.[20]

We go first class across the board, and although it's expensive, it's worth it because our people are made to feel important. For example, each year we take our top sales directors and their spouses on deluxe trips to Hong Kong, Bangkok, London, Paris, Geneva, and Athens to mention a few. We spare no expense, and although it costs a lot extra per person to fly the Concorde, cruise on the Love Boat, or book suites at the elegant Georges V in Paris, it is our way of telling them how important they are to our company.[21]

My experience with people is that they generally do what you expect them to do! If you expect them to perform well, they will; conversely, if you expect them to perform poorly, they'll probably oblige. I believe that average employees who try their hardest to live up to your high expectations of them will do better than above-average people with low self-esteem. Motivate your people to draw on that untapped 90 percent of their ability and their level of performance will soar![22]

A good people manager will never put someone down; not only is it nonproductive—it's counterproductive. You must remember that your job is to play the role of problem solver and that by taking this approach of criticizing people you'll accomplish considerably more.

While some managers try to forget problems they encountered early in their careers, I make a conscious effort to remember the difficulties I've had along the way. I think it's vital for a manager to empathize with the other people's problem, and the best way to have a clear understanding is to have been there yourself![23]

Interviews with Mary Kay consultants gave credibility to the company's approach and methods. One consultant described her experience:

I had a lot of ragged edges when I started. The first time I went to a Mary Kay seminar, I signed up for classes in diction and deportment; believe me, I needed them. I didn't even have the right clothes. You can only wear dresses and skirts to beauty shows, so I sank everything I had into one nice dress. I washed it out every night in Woolite and let it drip dry in the shower.

---

[18]Ibid., pp. 11–12.
[19]Ibid., p. 15.
[20]Ibid., p. 19.
[21]Ibid., p. 20.
[22]Ibid., p. 27.
[23]Ibid., p. 6.

But I was determined to follow all the rules, even the ones I didn't understand— *especially* the ones I didn't understand. At times, it all seemed foolish, especially when you consider that all my clients were mill workers and didn't exactly appreciate my new grammar. But I kept telling myself to hang in there, that Mary Kay knew what was good for me.

When I first started, I won a pearl-and-ruby ring. A man or a man's company may say I'd have been better off with the cash, but I'm not so convinced. Mary Kay is on to something there. From the moment I won that ring, I began thinking of myself as a person who deserved a better standard of living. I built a new life to go with the ring.[24]

Another consultant observed:

The essential thing about Mary Kay is the quality of the company. When you go to Dallas, the food, the hotel, and the entertainment are all top notch. Nothing gaudy is allowed in Mary Kay.[25]

When asked if she didn't think pink Cadillacs were a tad gaudy, she responded in a low, level tone: "When people say that, I just ask them what color car their company gave them last year."

On the morning following Awards Night 1984, a group of Florida consultants was in the hotel lobby getting ready to go to the airport for the flight home.[26] One member had by chance met Mary Kay Ash in the ladies' room a bit earlier and had managed to get a maid to snap a Polaroid photograph of them together. She proudly was showing her friends the snapshot and was the only one of the group who had actually met Mary Kay. The consultant said to her friends, "She told me she was sure I'd be up there on stage with her next year. She said she'd see me there." Her sales director, observing the scene, commented, "She's got the vision now. She really did meet her. And you've got to understand that in Mary Kaydom that's a very big deal."

THE BEAUTY SHOW

It was a few minutes past 7 on a weeknight in Tuscaloosa, Alabama. Debbie Sessoms and three of her friends (including the casewriter) were seated around the dining room table in Debbie's house. In front of each woman was a pink tray, a mirror, a pencil, and a blank personal Beauty Profile form. Jan Currier stood at the head of the table. She welcomed each of the ladies and asked them to fill out the personal Beauty Profile form in front of them.

When they were finished, Jan started her formal presentation, leading off with how MKC's products were developed by a tanner. She used a large display board to illustrate the topics she discussed. Next Jan told the group about the company and the founder, Mary Kay Ash. She showed a picture of Mary Kay and explained she was believed to be in her 70s—though no one knew for sure because Mary Kay maintained that "a woman who will tell her age will tell anything." Jerri, one of the guests, remarked that she couldn't believe how good Mary Kay looked for her age. Jan told her that Mary Kay had been using her basic skin care formulas since the 1950s.

Jan went on to talk about the growth of the sales force from 9 consultants to over 195,000 in 1984. She explained how the career opportunities at MKC could be adapted to each consultant's ambitions. A consultant, she said, determined her own work hours

---

[24] As quoted in Kim Wright Wiley, "Cold Cream and Hard Cash," *Savvy,* June 1985, p. 39.
[25] Ibid., p. 41.
[26] Ibid.

and could choose either a full-time or part-time career. Advancement was based on sales and recruiting abilities. The possible rewards included diamonds, minks, and Cadillacs.

Before explaining the basic skin care program, Jan told the women that with the Mary Kay money-back guarantee, products could be returned for any reason for a full refund. Jan distributed samples to each of the guests based on the information provided in the personal beauty profiles. Under Jan's guidance, the ladies proceeded through the complete facial process, learning each of the five basic skin care steps advocated by Mary Kay. There was a lot of discussion about the products and how they felt on everyone's skin.

When the presentation reached the glamour segment, each guest was asked her preference of makeup colors. Jan encouraged everyone to try as many of the products and colors as they wanted. Jan helped the guests experiment with different combinations and worked with each one personally, trying to make sure that everyone would end up satisfied with her own finished appearance.

After admiring each other's new looks, three of the women placed orders. Jan collected their payments and filled the orders on the spot. No one had to wait for delivery.

When she finished with the orders, Jan talked with Debbie's three guests about hostessing their own shows and receiving hostess gifts. Chris agreed to book a show the next week. Debbie was then given her choice of gifts based on the evening's sales and bookings. To close the show, Jan again highlighted the benefits of a Mary Kay career—being your own boss, setting your own hours—and invited anyone interested to talk with her about these opportunities. Debbie then served some refreshments. Shortly after 9 PM, Jan and Debbie's three guests departed.

Walking to Jan's car, the casewriter asked Jan if the evening was a success. Jan replied that it had been "a pretty good night. Sales totaled $150, I got a booking for next Wednesday, I made $75 in commission in a little over two hours, the guests learned about skin care and have some products they are going to like, and Debbie got a nice hostess gift."

THE WEEKLY SALES MEETING

Jan Currier, senior sales director, welcomed the consultants to the weekly Monday night meeting of the members of her sales unit.[27] After calling everyone's attention to a mimeographed handout on everybody's chair, she introduced the casewriter to the group and then invited everyone to stand and join in singing the Mary Kay enthusiasm song. As soon as the song was over, Jan started "the Crow Period" by asking Barbara, team leader, to stand and tell about her achievement of VIP status. Barbara told of setting and achieving the goals necessary to win the use of an Oldsmobile Firenza. Her new goal was to assist and motivate everyone on her team to do the same. Jan recognized Barbara again for being both the Queen of Sales and the Queen of Recruiting for the previous month.

Jan began the educational segment by instructing the consultants on color analysis and how it related to glamour. She continued the instruction by explaining the proper techniques of a man's facial.

---

[27]Most sales directors had their sales meeting on Monday night, a practice urged upon them by Mary Kay Ash. Mary Kay saw the Monday night meeting as a good way to start the week. "If you had a bad week—you need the sales meeting. If you had a good week, the sales meeting needs you! When a consultant leaves a Monday meeting excited, she has an entire week to let excitement work for her." Ash, *Mary Kay,* p. 40.

Next everyone who had at least a $100 week in sales was asked to stand. Jan began the countdown "110, 120, 130 . . . 190." Barbara sat down to a round of applause for her $190 week in sales. "200, 220 . . . 270." Melissa sat down. The ladies applauded her efforts. Mary was the only one left standing. There was anticipation of how high her sales reached as the countdown resumed. "280, 290, 300 . . . 335." Mary sat down. Everyone applauded this accomplishment of a consultant who had only been with MKC for four months and who held a 40-hour-a-week full-time job in addition to her Mary Kay sales effort.

At this time Jan asked Linda and Susan to join her up front. She pinned each lady and congratulated them on joining her team. The Mary Kay pin was placed upside down on the new consultant's lapel. Jan explained this was so people would notice and ask about it. When they did, a consultant was to respond by saying: "My pin is upside down to remind me to ask you if you've had a Mary Kay facial." The pin would be turned right side up when the consultant got her first recruit. Each of the new consultants also received a pink ribbon. This marked her membership in the Jan's Beautiful People sales unit. Both Linda and Susan were given some material Jan had prepared (Exhibit 7); Jan said she would go over it with them after the meeting.

EXHIBIT 7 | **Example of Material Provided *to* New Beauty Consultants at Weekly Sales Meeting**

The Mary Kay Opportunity	Yearly Total
3 shows per week with $150.00 sales per show	
Less 15 percent hostess credit = $191.25 profit (per week)	$ 9,945
Three persons buying per show, three shows per week =	
468 prospective customers per year	
Average selling to 7 out of 10 = 327 new customers per year	
Call each customer at least six times per year	
Average $15.00 in sales per call	
Yearly reorder profits will be	14,715
1 facial per week—52 prospective customers per year	
Average selling to 7 of 10 = 36 new customers	
If each buys a basic, your facial profits will be	792
36 new customers from facials	
Call each customer six times per year	
Average $15.00 in sales per call	
Your yearly *reorder* profit will be	1,620
Recruit one person each month	
Each with at least a $1,500 initial order (wholesale)	
Ordering only $500.00 every month thereafter	
Your 4 percent–8 percent commission checks from these 12 recruits	3,490
Your yearly profits will be approximately	$30,472

This is a simple guideline designed to show you, in figures, approximately how much you can benefit from your Mary Kay career. These figures may vary a little, due to price changes. These totals are based on orders placed at our maximum discount level and do not include referrals, dovetail fees, and prizes.

Working hours per week for the above should not exceed 20 hours, if your work is well planned. Attitude and consistency are the keys to your success.

Jan Currier
Senior Sales Director

Next a new competition was announced. This contest focused on recruiting. For each new recruit, a consultant would receive one stem of Romanian crystal. So everyone could see how beautiful the rewards were, Jan showed a sample of the crystal.

A final reminder was made for attendance at the upcoming workshop on motivation. Jan sweetened the pot by announcing she would provide a prize to the first one in her unit to register and pay for the seminar. Next week she would announce the winner.

The meeting was adjourned until next Monday evening.

An Interview with Jan Currier

One night shortly after attending the meeting of Jan's Beautiful People sales unit, the casewriter met with Jan to ask some questions.

Casewriter: How many are in your unit?

Jan: We're down right now. I had a small unit to start with. I only had 56 . . . A decent unit has got a hundred, 75 to 100 at least.

Casewriter: Is it the size of the town that hampers you?

Jan: No, no it's me who hampers me. The speed of the leader is the speed of the unit. If I'm not out there doing it, then they're not going to be doing it. If I'm recruiting, they're recruiting.

Casewriter: What about your leader, is your leader not fast?

Jan: No, it's me; see, when you point a finger, three come back.

Casewriter: How do you handle a situation where a consultant would like to do well, but she doesn't put in the time necessary to do well?

Jan: You have to go back to that premise, that whole philosophy that you're in business for yourself but not by yourself. So if a girl comes in and says I want to make X number of dollars, then I will work with her and we will do it. I try to get them to set goals and really look at them every week and work for it. One gal comes in and wants to make $25 a week and another says, "I have to support my family." There's a big difference.

Casewriter: How do you handle those that only want to make $25 a week?

Jan: If you get rid of the piddlers, you wouldn't have a company. It's the piddlers that make up the company. There are only going to be one or two superstars.

Casewriter: How do you motivate the people in your unit?

Jan: The only way you can really motivate is to call, encourage, write notes, and encourage recognition at the sales meetings and recognition in the newsletter. If they're not doing anything, they usually won't come to the sales meeting, but once in a while maybe; they'll find excuses.

Casewriter: What do you do when a person hits that stage?

Jan: Everybody has to go through that phase . . . If you're smart, you'll go to your director, read your book, and go back to start where you were before—with what was working to begin with, and you'll pull out of it. There are a lot of them who never pull out of it. They came in to have fun.

Casewriter: And the fun wears out.

Jan: Let's face it. This is a job. It's work, it's the best-paying hard work around, but it's work. I just finished with one gal last week who ended up saying, "Well, I just thought it would be fun. I thought it was just supposed to be fun." And I said, "Yes, but it's a job."

Casewriter: Can you tell before a person starts if she'll be successful?

Jan: There's no way to predict who's going to make it; the one you think is going to be absolutely a superstar isn't. You give everybody a chance. I measure my time with their interest and I tell them that. I'll encourage them, but they are going to pretty much do what they want to do. I learned that the hard way. There is no point laying guilt trips, no point pestering them to death, and pressure doesn't work.

Casewriter: Do you feel recognition is the best motivator?

Jan: Absolutely, recognition and appreciation. I think appreciation more than anything else. Little notes, I'm finally learning that too. Some of us are slow learners . . . So I'll write little notes telling someone, I really appreciate your doing this, or I'm really proud of you for being a star consultant this quarter, or I'm so glad you went with us to Birmingham to the workshop.

Casewriter: Does it upset you when people don't come to the sales meetings?

Jan: I used to grieve when they wouldn't come to sales meetings. I'd ask what am I doing wrong . . . Finally I realized that no matter how many people aren't there, the people who are there care and they are worth doing anything for. It's strange, we seem to get a different batch every meeting.

Casewriter: I get the impression that you are always looking for new recruits.

Jan: Yes, I've gotten more picky. I'm looking more for directors. I'm looking for people who really want to work. I look for someone who is older, not just the 18-year-olds because they don't want to work. They want to make money, but they don't want to work . . . I'd like to build more offspring directors.

Casewriter: What kind of people do you look for?

Jan: Not everybody's right for Mary Kay. It takes somebody who genuinely cares about other people.

Casewriter: Is there a common scenario that fits most new recruits?

Jan: Mary Kay attracts a lot of insecure women who are often married to insecure men. And that woman is told over and over by Mary Kay how wonderful she is and how terrific she is and how she can do anything with God's help. She can achieve anything. And like me she is dumb enough to believe it and go along with it.

Casewriter: What do you feel is the reason for the slowdown in recruiting at Mary Kay?

Jan: The key to this drop has been partly the economy, but partly a lot of people are weeding out. That's OK because the cream is going to rise to the top. I really believe that. We're going to have a stronger, much better company. I could see it at leadership (conference). The quality of people was much higher. It gets higher every year.

MKC'S FUTURE

MKC's sales in 1984 fell 14 percent to $278 million (down from $324 million in fiscal year 1983). The company's stock price, after a two for one split at about $44, tumbled from $22 in late 1983 to the $9 to $12 range in 1984. Profits were down 8 percent to $33.8 million. The declines were blamed on a dropoff in recruiting and retention (owing to reduced attractiveness of part-time employment) and to the expense of starting up the European division. As of December 31, 1984, the company had about 152,000 beauty consultants and 4,500 sales directors as compared to 195,000 beauty consultants and 5,000 sales directors at year-end 1983. Average sales per consultant in 1984 amounted to $1,603, versus $1,655 in 1983 and a 1980 to 1982 average of $1,753; only 60,000 of the 152,000 consultants were thought to be significantly productive. A cosmetic analyst for one Wall Street securities firm, in talking about the company's prospects, said, "Brokers loved this stock because it had such a great story. But the glory days, for the time being, are certainly over."[28]

The company's mystique was upbeat, however. Mary Kay Ash was on the UPI list of the most interviewed women in America. And when the Republicans chose Dallas for their 1984 convention, the Chamber of Commerce had to persuade Mary Kay to change the date of the 1984 Seminar, which was slated for the same week in the same convention center. Positive anecdotes about Mary Kay Ash and how MKC was operated were cited in numerous books and articles.

Mary Kay Ash indicated that the company had no plans for changing the main thrust of the company's sales and recruiting strategies:

> This is an excellent primary career for women, not just a way to get pin money. We see no need to alter our basic approach. It's taken us this far.[29]
>
> We have only 4 percent of the total retail cosmetics market. The way I see it, 96 percent of the people in the United States are using the wrong product. There's no reason why we can't become the number one cosmetics company in the United States.[30]

---

[28]As quoted in Wiley, "Cold Cream and Hard Cash," p. 40.
[29]Ibid.
[30]As quoted in *Business Week,* March 28, 1983, p. 130.

LEXMARK INTERNATIONAL, INC.

John E. Gamble, Auburn University at Montgomery

Early in 1994, Marvin Mann, chairman and chief executive officer of Lexmark International, Inc., initiated a series of meetings with employees worldwide to discuss the company's progress during its first three years and the outlook for the new year. He told employees that extremely tough competition, compounded by a continued soft world economy, had hurt the company's financial performance in 1993. Market conditions in the chief product areas where Lexmark competed—personal printers, personal computer keyboards, and typewriters—had changed dramatically over the past 12 months. New printer product announcements by the competition, coupled with significant price reductions, had put pressure on Lexmark's printer revenue and profit margins, even though sales volumes were increasing. The same was true in the keyboard business. As personal computer manufacturers slashed prices, they put pressure on their components suppliers for price concessions. Although unit volumes of printers and keyboards were increasing, the demand for typewriters was declining worldwide. While typewriter sales had been declining for years, the 1993 drop was faster than Lexmark's management had projected. Against this backdrop, Chairman Mann told employees that Lexmark had ended 1993 with a stronger product line and that customer satisfaction had improved in most businesses. The chairman said that he was committed to changing whatever needed to be changed at Lexmark and that it was time to take the next step.

IBM ANNOUNCES IT WILL DIVEST ITS INFORMATION PRODUCTS UNIT

On August 1, 1990, the employees of the IBM information products (IP) business unit located in Lexington, Kentucky, apprehensively assembled for an employee

Researched and written under the direction of Professors A. J. Strickland and Arthur A. Thompson, Jr., The University of Alabama.

meeting. IBM Chairman and CEO John F. Akers was present to discuss the future of the unit and the Lexington facility. Employees were aware that IBM was having financial difficulty as net income had fallen by more than $2 billion in 1989 and knew that some type of restructuring was going to take place. Rumors and press reports had been circulating around Lexington for months that the facility that had manufactured IBM typewriters since 1956 and IBM printers since the early 1980s would either be closed or sold, possibly to the Japanese. Akers told the gathering that IBM planned to sell the entire information products unit to a New York investment firm in order to focus more on systems integration and solutions for customers; he said that the information products business was no longer strategic to IBM's long-term emphasis on systems integration. (The business had less than 10 percent market share in desktop printers, sales of approximately $1.6 billion, and approximately 5,500 employees; the unit's main products were desktop printers—which produced approximately half of the division's revenues, typewriters, office equipment supplies, and keyboards. Its manufacturing and development facilities were in Lexington, Kentucky; Boulder, Colorado; and Boigny, France.) Akers told the assembled employees that selling the information products business unit would enhance competitiveness and efficiency for both IBM and the new company.

Akers introduced IBM Vice President Marvin Mann as the chief executive officer of the new stand-alone company that would develop, manufacture, and market IBM desktop printers, typewriters, related supplies, and keyboards under the IBM brand until 1996 and under its own brand thereafter. CEO Mann said to the employees:

> In the past decade, the information products group at IBM has made tremendous progress on the product development and manufacturing side of the business. In becoming a stand-alone business, we will have the dedicated resources and independent focus needed to expand our sales volume. We intend to increase our investment on advertising and promotion, greatly improve our dealer support programs, and incorporate a sales force with information products as its only priority.

Mann's entire career had been with IBM. Upon graduating from The University of Alabama, he had joined IBM in 1958 as a marketing representative. Mann's 33-year career had included executive positions in marketing, finance and planning, product management, and various general management positions. From 1988 to 1990 he had been president of IBM's service sector division with responsibility for development and marketing of hardware and software solutions for customers within the financial services, securities, insurance, retail, wholesale distribution, and services industries. He had been general manager of IBM's venture in electronic systems for retail stores and supermarkets. He became president and chief executive officer of Satellite business systems in 1984 and in 1986 president of IBM's information products division, the business that became Lexmark after it was sold.

Although Mann stated that all employees were to be treated fairly throughout the buyout process, the IBM employees in Lexington—most of whom had counted on spending the rest of their careers working for IBM—were understandably apprehensive, fearing the security provided by IBM's long-standing policy of no layoffs and continuous employment was a thing of the past. Mann was aware of the anxiety and job insecurity that existed and realized it would take positive leadership to guarantee a smooth transition. Employees knew that those who elected to stay on with the new enterprise could not expect the same kind of financial safety net and long-term job security they had enjoyed as IBM employees. In closing his speech, Mann pledged that the new company would make every effort to keep everyone on and avoid lay-offs, but that all Lexington employees would be given two options:

1. Employees could stay on and join in an effort to create a viable new company.
2. Some employees could take advantage of the Lexington transition payment program, which was an opportunity to leave IBM with a cash settlement and pursue other employment opportunities.

IBM HISTORY AND CULTURE

International Business Machines, which in 1989 had over 375,000 employees world-wide, over $77 billion in assets, and over $62 billion in revenue, was founded in 1914 as the Computing-Tabulating-Recording Company by Charles R. Flint. The company, renamed International Business Machines (IBM) in 1924, was a consolidation of 13 small businesses that manufactured and marketed business machines. It was the company's first CEO, Thomas J. Watson, Sr., who started IBM on the road to becoming the undisputed world leader in computers and office technology.

Watson believed in the potential greatness of the individual. The idea that every individual should be treated with respect was a novel one in the business world of the early 1900s. Most corporations did not view their sales forces with any more esteem than they did their production workers at that time, and salesmen, especially traveling salesmen, were one of the least-respected occupations. Furthermore, little emphasis was placed on after-the-sale service back then; all sales were considered final and companies expected customers to solve their own problems when it came to using the products they had bought.

Watson had very strong convictions about how he should lead his personal life and he applied these same convictions to the way he conducted business. He felt that for a company to achieve greatness, its management must pursue excellence in everything: how it treated individuals inside the company and outside the company, its employees and its customers; and how everyone in the company should be expected to meet the challenges of their jobs. Watson established three principles that came to permeate IBM's culture for the next 60 years:

- The individual must be respected.
- The customer must be given the best possible service.
- Everyone in the company must achieve excellence and superior performance.

Watson's principles were never platitudes or mere rhetoric at IBM. The business principles he developed for IBM were adopted to create the profitable company that he envisioned IBM could become; they had nothing to do with trying to create a utopian workplace. Watson believed a highly productive and outstanding workforce was key to IBM's long-term success. He believed that if the company treated its workforce well and showed respect for each individual that each employee, in turn, could be expected—indeed, required—to pursue excellence in whatever they were assigned to do. Watson could be tyrannical and unforgiving when he felt that an employee was not putting forth the very best effort.

Watson believed that it was necessary for IBM to build a sales force different from other sales forces, that a poorly dressed traveling salesman with little self-esteem would not be able to convince company presidents or executives to choose IBM equipment. Watson wanted every salesman's mother to be proud of her son's career.

He felt that if a person had a career that he was proud of, he would come to work invigorated, ready to sell more than he had sold the day before. In Watson's view, professionalism, self-respect, and dignity were essential when IBM sales representatives called on the people in companies who made the purchasing decisions.

Watson's second principle stated that the company would provide the highest level of customer service of any company in any industry, not just the highest customer service among its primary rivals. Watson knew that if IBM could provide excellent service after the sale, the sales force could make repeat sale after repeat sale to IBM customers. Watson insisted that IBM be a customer-oriented company. Every company operation focused on customer requirements. Job descriptions focused on providing superior service to prospects, customers, and vendors.

Watson's third principle demanded excellence in all aspects of the business: sales, customer service, and product development. IBM was never content to make incremental changes to the product line or imitate the products of rival firms. Each new line had to be significantly superior to the existing line of products. Watson thought it was vital for IBM to be known as the company that set the standard for product innovation and quality. Exponential growth would only be possible with a product line whose capabilities greatly exceeded competing products. Watson understood that a customer was unlikely to pay a premium price for an IBM product if there were a number of comparable products available in the market at lower prices.

Compensation of employees was an important component of IBM's emphasis on personal excellence. It was stressed that every employee could make a difference, and every employee who did was compensated well. There were no automatic annual raises or cost-of-living adjustments at IBM. Superior performance was rewarded with higher levels of compensation. Watson treated employees fairly, but expected IBM employees to push themselves toward excellence. Salesmen who met their quotas joined the One Hundred Percent Club. Salesmen who did not qualify for the club were chastised for cheating themselves and their families by not devoting adequate interest to their work. Those who repeatedly failed to qualify were weeded out.

Watson felt that it was important to promote through the ranks to reward good performance. The company recruited the brightest students from the best schools and then provided extensive training to help them succeed. These individuals all started their careers with IBM as marketing representative trainees. The best performers moved quickly to higher positions. Usually, the unsatisfactory performers were identified within the first few years and dismissed early on. Watson was successful in creating a culture that drove individuals to excellence. In return, IBM offered career-long employment. The company did not institute layoffs until 1993, when it was forced to take drastic measures to turn around the company after net losses of $7.8 billion during 1991 and 1992. Because of the high level of job satisfaction and job security at IBM, no labor union had ever been successful in organizing any group of IBM employees.

After Tom Watson, Sr., died in 1956, the company continued to follow his three principles. Tom Watson, Jr., who became CEO of IBM in 1956, said:

> For any organization to survive and achieve success, there must be a sound set of principles on which it bases all of its policies and actions. But more important is its faithful adherence to those principles.[1]

---

[1] F. G. Rodgers, *The IBM Way* (New York: Harper & Row, Publishers, 1986), p. 18.

Buck Rodgers, a career IBMer, who began as a marketing rep trainee in 1950 and eventually served as IBM vice president of marketing with worldwide responsibility from 1974 to 1984, stated:

> The only sacred cow in an organization is its principles. A company must never change them. No matter what its nature or size, there must be certain bedrock beliefs to serve as its guiding force. While a company must be flexible, always regrouping and changing with the times, its beliefs must remain irrevocable, deeply embedded throughout time. IBM's three basic beliefs are so fundamental to success that any deviation is unthinkable.[2]

Al Williams, IBM president from 1961 to 1966, saw the company's philosophy as more than a measure of company size and profitability.

> It is not bigness we seek, it is greatness. Bigness is imposing. Greatness is enduring.[3]

IBM's INDUSTRY LEADERSHIP

It has been said that "no one was ever fired for buying IBM." IBM gained such a dominant market share that the company was twice scrutinized by the U.S. Justice Department for possible monopoly violations. The company defended itself on the grounds that there were numerous other computer companies in the market, and that it was able to maintain its large market share as a result of its superior products and service. IBM's share of the mainframe computer market was estimated to be as high as 90 percent in an antitrust complaint filed by Control Data in 1967.

Not only superior products and service, but also the company's leasing arrangement contributed to its market share leadership. Mainframe computers could not be purchased from IBM, only leased. This arrangement not only made financing for purchases of IBM computers convenient and accessible, but helped lock in customers, sustaining IBM's large market share. Lease extensions, continued annual lease renewals, along with negotiation of leases on new models, made it fairly routine for IBM salespeople to reach quota. While a salesman, Tom Watson, Jr., reached his annual sales quota on January 2 due to continuing lease agreements. In order to resolve an antitrust suit brought by the government in 1952, IBM signed a consent decree in 1956 that allowed for the sale as well as lease of IBM mainframe computers. A second antitrust suit was filed against IBM on the last day of the Johnson administration in 1969. IBM vehemently denied any restraint of trade and the U.S. Justice Department finally dropped the case in 1982 after it had determined that the suit was "without merit."

Developments in computer technology during the 1970s and early 1980s brought about fundamental changes in the computer industry. Computer technology improved at a pace that made leasing the same computer equipment for long periods impractical. Computers features and capabilities were changing so rapidly that leased equipment could potentially become obsolete during the term of a lease. In the 1980s, IBM discontinued leasing as a sales strategy and began to sell all leased equipment. IBM had significant growth in revenues and earnings through 1984 as customers made lump-sum payments for the residual value of the equipment they were leasing. Finally, IBM was able to retain market share because prohibitive switching costs

---

[2]*Ibid.*, p. 18.
[3]*Ibid.*, p. 19.

effectively tied customers to IBM. If an IBM customer switched computer manufacturers, it was forced to reenter all stored data to conform to the new operating system. This enabled IBM to realize gross profit margins on its mainframe sales as high as 90 percent and to justify the costs of its large, highly trained, highly compensated marketing staff and entrenched corporate bureaucracy.

In 1981, IBM introduced a personal computer line that changed the complexion of the computer marketplace. Personal computers (PCs) created a new market of computer users for IBM. But as they became more powerful they eventually triggered a trend among some mainframe users to shift to intermediate systems and PCs, particularly as their speed and storage capacity increased. PC sales came from nowhere to capture a projected $34 billion in industry sales in 1992. Sales volume for mainframe computers was projected at $13 billion in 1992.[4] Exhibit 1 shows the changes in the computer market by segment from 1987 to 1991. In addition to impacting the mainframe computer business, the PC had a major effect on the typewriter industry. There were very few word processing functions that could be performed better by a typewriter than by a personal computer. As a result very few users continued to purchase new typewriters once they had purchased a PC.

CRACKS IN IBM's PERFORMANCE AND MARKET POSITION

During the mid-1980s, IBM lost market share as IBM-compatible mainframes and PCs were introduced to the market by a variety of small computer companies. IBM's decision to outsource key components of the personal computer such as the operating system had allowed a large number of companies to produce IBM-compatible PCs. These manufacturers were able to produce personal computers very similar to IBM's that actually utilized the same operating system. Through the sourcing agreement, IBM allowed the disk operating system (DOS) to be sold widely by the operating system developer, Microsoft. The availability of DOS to other manufacturers eliminated the need to reenter data if an IBM PC owner later purchased an IBM-compatible PC produced by a different manufacturer. IBM turned down an offer from Microsoft Chairman Bill Gates to sell IBM the rights to DOS for about $75,000 in 1980. Changes in IBM's computer market share by segment from 1984 to 1988 are shown in Exhibit 2.

The small companies that manufactured IBM clones were swifter in responding to rapid technological and market changes than IBM's hierarchical structure. IBM's organizational structure often had nine levels between the CEO and production workers. This tall structure contributed to lengthy product-development times. A top IBM product developer, who left in frustration, expressed sentiments held by many at IBM concerning decision making: "If it takes you 10 months to figure out what you want to do, and you go through six changes of direction as you develop it, you can expect a 34-month development process."[5]

As product differentiation became more difficult and new entrants arrived in the market, prices dropped dramatically on mainframes and PCs. During the late 1980s, it was common knowledge among mainframe customers that IBM would discount its retail price by 25 to 40 percent in order to conclude a sale. Personal computer prices had dropped over 75 percent since 1984 while the capabilities of the PC had steadily

---

[4]*S & P Industry Survey,* December 31, 1992, p. C77.
[5]Paul Carroll, "Hurt by a Pricing War, IBM Plans Write-Off and Cut of 10,000 Jobs," *Wall Street Journal,* December 6, 1989, p. A1.

EXHIBIT 1 | Shipments of Computers by Market Segment, 1987 versus 1991

1987
Total Value of Shipments –$63 billion

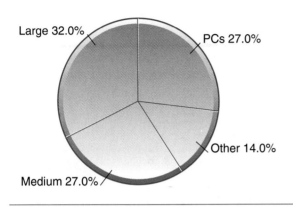

1991
Total Value of Shipments –$93.4 billion

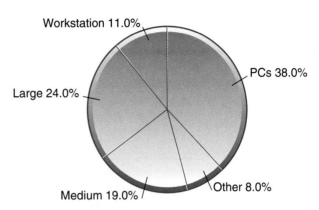

Source: International Data Corp. and Datamation.

EXHIBIT 2 | IBM's Share for Various Sizes of Computers, 1984 and 1988

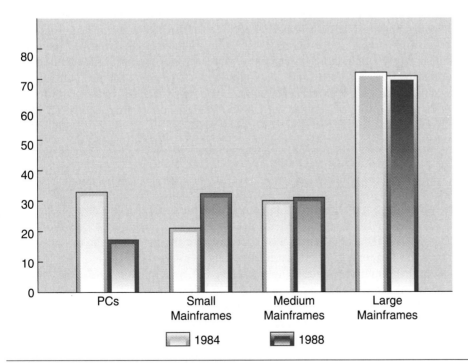

Source: International Data Corp. and Standard & Poor's estimates.

increased. As prices continued to decrease, IBM and other computer manufacturers had to increase the number of units sold to maintain the same level of revenue. As IBM's market vulnerability became clear, IBM executives were driven to take increasingly strong actions to stem IBM's declining stock price and maintain revenues and earnings.

IBM'S ATTEMPTS TO RESTRUCTURE

In December 1989, IBM took its first actions to respond to the dramatic changes that had manifested themselves in the industry. Chairman John Akers announced that IBM would reduce its work force by 10,000 through attrition and incentives—not layoffs—and that the company would consolidate operations in order to reduce manufacturing costs. IBM stated that a restructuring charge of $2.42 billion against 1989 fourth-quarter earnings would reduce future costs by $1 billion annually. The $2.42 billion restructuring charge included the following components:

Costs of facility consolidations and capacity reductions	$1,335 million
Costs of employee separations and relocations	500 million
Adoption of new guidelines to provide for the earlier recognition of costs in both hardware and software due to the pace of technological change	585 million

IBM also realized that in order to protect against further erosion of its once-dominant market position, it needed to focus its resources and strategic priorities on a smaller number of product and market arenas. IBM chose to spin off its information products business into a wholly owned subsidiary that would be sold to Clayton, Dubilier & Rice (CD&R), a New York investment firm. IBM retained a 10 percent equity position in the new company. Faithful to its philosophy of ensuring fairness to its employees, IBM chose CD&R as the purchaser of the business because of its reputation for improving the operations of its acquisitions through improved management rather than by liquidating assets and discharging employees. IBM intentionally did not put the business up for bid, but sought out a buyer that had a reputation for having concern for its employees and that had a record of success. Exhibit 3 provides IBM revenues by business segment for 1989 to 1991; revenues from typewriter sales are included under the category "other workstations."

THE LEVERAGED BUYOUT

The leveraged buyout of the IBM Information Products Corporation (IPC), the wholly owned subsidiary created to implement the sale to CD&R, became official on March 27, 1991, eight months after IBM had announced its intention to sell the business. CD&R paid IBM approximately $1.5 billion for 90 percent of the business; 70 percent of the acquisition cost was financed by a group of six major worldwide banks. Marvin Mann was named chairman and Lexmark International, Inc., began independent operations with approximately $1.6 billion in worldwide revenues and approximately 4,000 employees. Ownership of Lexmark was divided between an equity fund managed by CD&R, Lexmark management and employees, IBM, and other large institutional investors such as Equitable Capital Management. The CD&R fund owned more than 50 percent of the shares, IBM owned 10 percent, institutional investors owned near 25 percent, and 15 percent of the shares were set aside for

EXHIBIT 3 | IBM's Revenues by Business Segment and Product Category, 1989–91 *($ in millions)*

	Consolidated			U.S. Only		
	1991	1990*	1989*	1991	1990*	1989*
Information technology:						
Processors†	$14,954	$16,433	$16,236	$ 4,717	$ 5,744	$ 5,941
Workstations†						
Personal systems	8,505	9,644	8,409	3,210	3,887	3,667
Other workstations**	3,216	4,076	3,876	1,040	1,349	1,323
Peripherals†						
Storage	7,184	8,967	7,362	2,825	3,413	2,477
Printers	1,010	1,263	1,454	308	413	519
Other peripherals	2,284	2,960	2,642	1,116	1,353	1,313
Software	10,524	9,952	8,424	3,767	3,639	3,139
Maintenance	7,414	7,198	6,791	2,884	2,886	2,959
Other	7,749	6,602	5,526	2,615	2,525	2,417
	62,840	67,095	60,720	22,482	25,209	23,755
Federal systems	1,952	1,923	1,990	1,952	1,923	1,990
Total	$64,792	$69,018	$62,710	$24,434	$27,132	$25,745

*Reclassified to conform with 1991 presentation.
**Includes typewriters.
†Hardware only; excludes functions not embedded, software, and maintenance.
Source: 1991 International Business Machines annual report.

management and employees. IBM became Lexmark's largest customer, purchasing all of its personal printers and keyboards from Lexmark. Lexmark was licensed to use the IBM trademark for five years on all products manufactured or under development at the time of the sale.

The negotiations between CD&R and IBM over the sale of the information products business nearly broke down several times. Contract negotiations involved staff members from several IBM functional areas and at times the IBMers would "nonconcur" on issues—IBM jargon for inability to reach an agreement. All "nonconcur" issues on IBM's side of the negotiation table were pushed up to a higher level of management for resolution. Donald Gogel, a partner in Clayton, Dubilier & Rice, stated that the transaction would not have been completed had it not been for Akers's commitment to making the divestiture work. After the sale was finalized, Mr. Gogel devised a board game called "Nonconcur" and gave out 350 copies to the parties involved in the negotiations.

IMPLEMENTATION OF THE NEW STRATEGY AT LEXMARK

While IBM and Clayton, Dubilier & Rice were negotiating the terms of the transaction, the information products management team, led by Marvin Mann, began immediately after the August 1, 1990, announcement to restructure the printer, typewriter, keyboard, and supplies businesses into independent businesses. Because the desktop printer industry, like the PC computer industry, was a very competitive marketplace characterized by deep price cuts, narrow profit margins, and short product life-cycles,

Lexmark's new management team knew that the new company would need a radically different strategy to compete successfully. IBM had relied on a differentiation strategy keyed to proprietary technology rights and customer service. Lexmark's managers believed that the new company would have to bring down costs and learn to get new printer products to market faster. Early on, Mann established three internal operating imperatives:

- The new company must reduce its workforce through incentives for voluntary severance.
- The company must flatten its organizational structure.
- The company must change the existing IBM culture into a culture more focused on costs, teamwork, and speed—this was thought to be essential in an industry driven by technology and lower prices.

By the end of 1991, 1,700 Lexington employees had left the business under the Lexington transition payment program announced at the August 1, 1990, employees meeting. The transition program provided two weeks' pay for each six months' service up to 104 weeks' pay, plus $25,000 for any employee wishing to leave the new company. Mann sent a letter to all employees who wished to remain with the new company, indicating that most of the benefits and personnel programs for the new company would be modeled after the IBM programs in effect. He also announced a transitional retirement leave program that permitted retirement-eligible and five-year-leave-of-absence employees in Boulder and Lexington to work for the new company but ultimately retire from IBM.

LEXMARK ORGANIZATIONAL STRUCTURE AND CULTURE

Although many employees left the company, most key manufacturing and development executives chose to remain, thus preserving continuity during the restructuring period. During the restructuring, employees developed a concise vision of what the company should be. Lexmark's vision statement is shown in Exhibit 4.

Between the time the intent to sell the unit was announced and the time the LBO was finalized, the information products business was restructured into four business units—personal printers, typewriters, keyboards, and related office-equipment supplies. Each unit was given the authority and resources needed to successfully direct its business. Each unit operated under broad Lexmark strategy guidelines but was given the ability to make independent development, manufacturing, pricing, forecasting, and business planning decisions. Chairman Mann described the strengths of the new Lexmark structure and how it allowed the company to become more competitive.

> We quickly broke the company down into parts which were manageable—decentralizing the authority and control functions. We broke the business down into four business units—one for personal printers, one for typing workstations, one for input technologies, and one for office equipment supplies. We gave each of these units the development, manufacturing, pricing, forecasting, business planning, and financial functions that they needed to drive the business. We teamed them with marketing units in each of the major geographies of the world and gave them a common set of objectives and measurements that caused them to work together around the world. These cross-functional teams work together to develop strategic plans, discuss which products to develop, and how we are going to price and market them. They are all highly motivated to help each other because they are paid based on the performance of their business on a worldwide basis.

EXHIBIT 4 | **Vision Statement for Lexmark International, Inc., 1991**

Lexmark International, Inc.

Our Vision

Lexmark's future is full of promise for the company and for its employees. Our vision is based on mutual commitments by Lexmark and its employees. If consistently and strongly supported, the principles and tenets of our vision will become powerful forces. The Lexmark vision can be summarized as follows:

- We satisfy our customers with superior service and environmentally sound products that meet or exceed their expectations.
- We are well–informed, self–motivated, highly trained, and empowered to continually improve in everything we do.
- We measure our success by the satisfaction of our customers, by our enthusiasm, by the respect of our neighbors, and by our company's financial results.

In a more expanded form, our vision embodies the following values:

Our Customers

We are committed to the satisfaction and success of our customers and business partners. We listen to our customers. They are our top priority. We understand, anticipate, and satisfy their wants and needs.

We have partnerships with our customers. This includes both our traditional customers who buy our products, and our internal customers who are our fellow employees. We also have partnerships with our suppliers. These partnerships are based on teamwork, commitment, and trust. As a result, customers want our products and return for repeat business.

Our Company

We are a leading company at providing the highest–quality and best–value products and service to our customers

We are recognized as a world leader in quality and technology in our markets. We often win national and international awards. We use these award criteria as guides to achieving our vision.

We adhere to the highest ethical standards.

Ourselves

We take ownership of our jobs and demonstrate pride in our accomplishments. We are well trained and informed. We care about, respect, and trust each other. We teach and help each other, and gain satisfaction from working together as a team.

Our Workplace

We have a safe and productive workplace. Every job is essential to achieving our vision.

Innovation, initiative and decisiveness are encouraged and rewarded. We make decisions quickly, based on facts and prudent risk taking with minimum checks, balances and reviews. Our work is based on efficient, effective processes that are tested and refined with customer feedback.

Communication is free and open in an environment of empowerment where employees contribute their best while continually improving themselves, and the company. As a result, Lexmark is a satisfying place to work.

Our Neighbors

Our company is a responsible corporate citizen in each country and community where it operates. Our company encourages and assists us to be actively involved in a wide range of charitable, environmental, and community–related activities. We show concern for others through action. Our products and processes reflect a special concern for protecting the environment.

LEXMARK.

The development of a worldwide marketing and sales organization was of particular importance to Lexmark during the restructuring period because under IBM the information products business had been involved only with manufacturing and development. The IBM sales force marketed all IBM products. The use of a single sales force responsible for the entire IBM product line had placed information products at an extreme disadvantage. The IBM sales force had devoted little time and resources to the printer business, partly accounting for why the division had failed to gain a market share consistent with its product quality.

Lexmark management believed a dedicated, focused sales force created an opportunity for the business to achieve greater market share. Lexmark chose to team marketing units with each product unit in each major geographic area of the world. Three geographic regions were identified as profit centers:

- The United States.
- Canada, Latin America, and Asia Pacific.
- Europe, the Middle East, and Africa.

These marketing units were headed by an executive in each region who was responsible for revenue, profit, and cash flow in the region. Worldwide market managers in each product area coordinated marketing efforts across the regions.

In developing strategic plans, the organizational structure included cross-functional worldwide teams that worked together in defining new products and in determining marketing and pricing strategies. All functional areas were driven to accomplish the same organizational objectives and were evaluated by common measurements. Strategic planning was accomplished by bringing together market managers and employees from the various functional areas. Each of these managers had the common objective of developing a strategic plan that would maximize revenue and operating profits for the duration of the plan. Lexmark executives believed it was important that every functional area of the company share the same objectives. In their view, conflicting objectives within the organization would eventually lead to reduced organizational performance. Common objectives and common measurement techniques were a dramatic departure from the way things had been managed under IBM's structure. IBM had relied on a functional alignment that included a broad product set within each functional area; a central organization was responsible for establishing objectives—varying between functional areas—related to products as diverse as typewriters and high-end computers.

REDUCING THE LAYERS THROUGH EMPLOYEE EMPOWERMENT

By March 1991, Lexmark had eliminated layers of management, reduced the number of people in manufacturing and support by 40 percent, and reduced the number of managers in manufacturing and support by 60 percent. Lexmark's corporate headquarters in Greenwich, Connecticut, had fewer than 20 employees. Chairman Mann explained how the company could operate effectively with so many fewer people:

> You might ask how we manage to get by with 2,000 fewer manufacturing and support employees and make the progress we have. The answer is in what we call empowered teamwork. The day of a manager deciding what everybody is going to do and telling them what to do next has passed. The key is getting employees to participate, to help set the direction, to help set goals, and then work together to meet them.

Mann believed employee empowerment and participation would increase efficiency. The flatter structure had a maximum of four levels between the employees and the CEO. An entrepreneurial spirit quickly appeared in the company. Many employees wanted to implement changes because they knew the protected environment provided by IBM's policy of career-long employment was gone forever and their job security was tied to the success of the new company. Under IBM, their ideas had been subjected to scrutiny by many levels of management and proposed changes had always been delayed or killed at the first sign of "nonconcurrence." Many of the division's proposals and recommendations had been stifled because headquarters executives regarded information products as too small a portion of IBM's business to justify giving IP much attention, funding, or resource priority.

Lexmark's philosophy was to give employees the leeway to make decisions they believed were in the best interest of the organization. Major decisions were not made by the chairman, but by the people close to production and the marketplace. Long-term strategic plans were developed by the people directly involved with production, development, and marketing; it was their responsibility to identify the segment that appeared most attractive and to come up with a plan to succeed in the target market. Mann and the unit heads reviewed, discussed, and ultimately approved strategic plans, but empowered employees and teams were responsible for developing, recommending, and implementing plans.

Employees were given latitude in other decision-making situations as well. For instance, a Lexmark market manager who wanted Mann's advice concerning a pricing issue called him and discussed the issue over the telephone for 15 or 20 minutes and reached an agreement. Under IBM's "contention" system, individuals from development, production, and marketing would have gone through a formal process of forecasting and analysis. Arguments would have been made by each group and there would have been a series of review processes. If an agreement could not be reached between the functional areas, suboptimal compromises would have been made. Lexmark saw this contention system as one of the major impediments to success and made every effort to avoid lengthy presentation and review processes.

Even with the contention system eliminated, it was evident that Lexmark's competitors were using far more resources for product development and that the new company would have to learn to bring innovative products to market even more quickly. Lexmark benchmarked its product-development techniques against other companies' and brought in people to provide advice on expeditious approaches to the development process. Strategic alliances were formed with suppliers who manufactured key components and they were made partners in the development process. Lexmark organized the workers into small cross-functional development teams that had significant autonomy and the ability to move quickly. As a result, in its first year Lexmark introduced nine new laser and dot matrix printers, four new models of typewriters and typing workstations, four new advanced computer keyboards, and broadened its line of supplies.

Lexmark also reaped the benefits of empowerment for floor-level employees. For example, production workers were asked to reengineer the typewriter assembly line. The workers were able to redesign the process so that one typewriter could be produced in one hour and 15 minutes. Under the IBM assembly process it had required eight hours. This new assembly process also contributed to a 50-percent reduction in warranty costs for a product that was already the world standard of excellence. Lexmark dramatically reduced the size of the purchasing department that had the responsibility for delivering parts to the production areas. The new production process allowed workers in some cases to order parts over the telephone as they were needed.

Production workers were given input into decisions regarding how their work was to be performed and were held accountable for their decisions. Roger Hopwood, Lexmark's laser printer production manager, told line workers that they would be given the responsibility for signing the requisition form for a new laser printer assembly line. Before signing the requisition, the workers saw areas of improvement and hammered out changes to the assembly line with the industrial engineers. This level of responsibility took some workers by surprise, and it also took some workers a while to get used to the idea that they had ownership in the company and that their decisions directly impacted the profitability of the company. In a related incident, Mr. Hopwood was asked by a worker to sign for $26,000 of ionizing equipment. Mr. Hopwood told the worker that he trusted his judgment and that he should sign the form. The worker returned shortly afterward and stated that he had decided that only $6,000 of equipment was needed.

Lexmark wanted empowered employees who could work with their co-workers to bring efficiency to existing processes. The company decided it was important to eliminate the IBM suggestion program that rewarded individuals for their ideas. The company felt it would benefit more from employees getting together and discussing ideas and working on changes together as a team.

In one instance, a group of eight production workers in Lexington had an idea to change a procedure for shipping typewriters to Europe that ended up saving several million dollars per year. The workers developed and implemented a process enabling production workers in Lexington to customize typewriters for German, French, Italian, and other languages. Previously, Lexmark had produced only English-language typewriters in the Lexington plant and had shipped them to exporters for customizing and packaging.

LEXMARK'S INCENTIVE COMPENSATION SYSTEM

In March 1992, Lexmark introduced an incentive plan tying bonus pay to firm performance. Under the original plan, 25 percent of the incentive was based on achieving company financial objectives, 50 percent on achieving business unit financial objectives, and 25 percent on the individual employee's unit or team performance. In May 1992, Mann announced that Lexmark employees who had worked at least six months in 1991 would receive a bonus equal to two-and-one-half week's base salary as a reward for the company's strong 1991 financial performance. Mann commented on the impact of Lexmark's policies regarding compensation and employee ownership:

> Our employees realize that the future of Lexmark depends on them. This cultural change has driven productivity, creativity, and innovation. We have put every employee on an incentive plan. Every employee owns stock in the company and every employee has stock options. We have done everything we know how to do to make the employees feel like they own the company and they are responsible for it. And let me tell you, it is paying real dividends.

LEXMARK'S APPROACH TO MARKETING AND BRAND AWARENESS

Lexmark's new marketing and sales organization faced several challenges. Because Hewlett-Packard had developed significant brand awareness and brand loyalty through its dominant market share in personal printers (see Exhibit 5), Lexmark countered with a proactive intercept strategy where salespeople called on users, in addition to dealers, to encourage users to replace their existing printers with Lexmark printers. Lexmark believed direct sales calls on users would be an important way to generate new sales and create more awareness of the Lexmark name. Most dealers carried a variety of printer brands and were not pushing one brand over another.

While Lexmark had the initial advantage of using the IBM logo—the world's ninth most powerful brand—on most of its products, it would have to discontinue the use of the logo in 1996. The company had formulated a rebranding strategy to bring the Lexmark name to the forefront gradually—see Exhibit 6. The company planned to introduce the branding changes around new product offerings rather than to rebrand existing products. Exhibit 7 shows a sample print ad promoting Lexmark's 4039 line introduced in April 1993. The company also initiated a corporate campaign to educate and inform targeted audiences about Lexmark. Lexmark earmarked $5 million of its $20-million worldwide 1992 advertising budget for image building. These ads were initially placed in U.S. print media such as *Business Week, The Wall*

EXHIBIT 5 | **PC Printers, Market Shares for 1992**

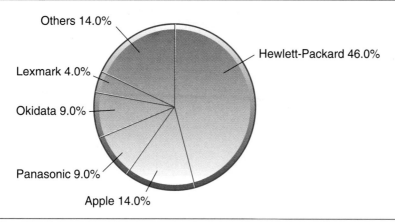

Source: Burnstein Research.

Street Journal, Forbes, and various trade journals and then coverage was gradually broadened worldwide. One of Lexmark's image-building ads is shown in Exhibit 8.

AN OVERVIEW OF THE MARKETS FOR LEXMARK'S PRODUCTS

PRINTERS

The most attractive business unit in Lexmark's portfolio was the personal printer business—the printers themselves and associated supplies (toner and ribbons). Supplies were to the printer business what razor blades were to the razor. Added profitability came from selling supplies to the owner of the printer. Even though competition in the industry was fierce, Lexmark's printer business offered the best opportunity for company growth. The potential for the desktop printer business had made the IBM information products unit an attractive buy for CD&R.

The dot matrix printer was the most widely sold printer for use with the PC because of its low cost to end users. There was little differentiation among dot matrix printers, and manufacturers were forced to compete primarily on price. Most dot matrix printers retailed between $175 and $400, depending on features. IBM had found it difficult to price dot matrix printers aggressively due to the company's vast overhead. Lexmark felt that it would be better positioned to compete in this market by restructuring to lower costs. Price reductions in other printing technologies such as laser and ink jet were taking market share away from the dot matrix, and dot matrix sales were expected to decline over time. U.S. dot matrix printer sales peaked in 1991 at approximately 5.1 million units. Lexmark had identified a specialized market that actually was growing—the heavy-duty forms printing market. Lexmark sold literally hundreds of thousands of its 2300 family of wide- and narrow-carriage forms printers with their unique design for printing multipart continuous applications.

One of the main contributors to the declining dot matrix market share was a reduction in laser printer prices. Laser printers broke below the $1,000 price level in 1990 due to the decreased cost of printer "engines" and other components. Laser printer demand was projected to grow at an annual rate of over 10 percent. Exhibits 9, 10,

EXHIBIT 6 | **Staged Changes in Lexmark's Branding of Its Products**

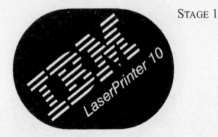

LEXMARK PRODUCT NAME PLATE TRANSITION

STAGE 1

STAGE 2

STAGE 3

STAGE 4

and 11 provide the forecasted demand for printers in units and dollar volume for the years 1992 through 1996.

Hewlett-Packard, the market leader in laser printers, began a price war in 1991 by reducing prices 14 percent. Price competition was strongest in the low-end laser printer segment. Low-end laser printers were defined by the industry as those printing seven pages per minute (ppm). A recent addition to the low-end printer segment was the portable printer for use with laptops and notebook computers. A 2.5-pound printer offered by GCC Technologies, for use with the Macintosh PowerBook, was among the smallest. Portable printer sales in 1992 were 466,000 units, but demand

EXHIBIT 7 | **Sample Lexmark Product Ad**

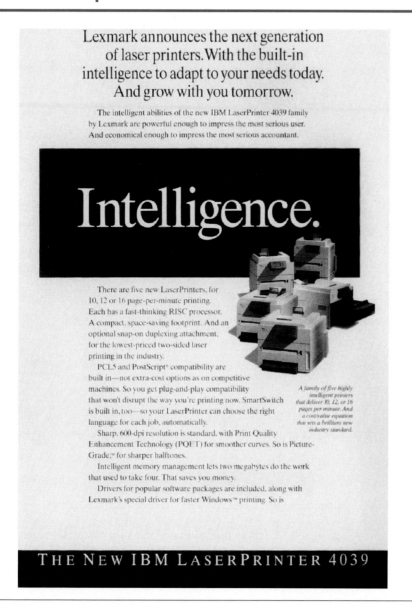

was expected to reach 1.1 million by 1995. As prices continued to drop on low-end units, channels of distribution were expanded to include superstores and consumer electronics stores. Industry analysts suspected that the traditional dealer network would play a smaller role in distribution of low-end printers but would remain the primary channel for network-capable printers and color printers.

Lexmark was the first to offer laser units with 600 dots per inch (dpi) resolution, but was followed within one year by Hewlett-Packard and later by a few other manufacturers. Lexmark's strategy was to focus on market segments that required more functionality in printers. The challenge was to profitably match or undercut HP on price and still offer printers that provided more functionality. The point of attack was on selected business segments that needed special-application printers.

EXHIBIT 8 | **Sample Lexmark Image-Building Ad**

A printer was designed for banks that had as a part of its internal memory all the forms used by a loan officer in making loans. When a customer made an application for a loan, the loan officer entered the individual's name, address, and other pertinent information, and the printer generated a completed form. For a hospital application, the printers located at the nurses' stations could be equipped with an alarm when an emergency item was printed that required immediate attention. Lexmark's strategy for its printer business had three major components:

- Get new models to market faster than competitors.
- Be closer to the customers and their individual needs.
- Be the low-cost producer by outdesigning the competition.

The image quality of 600 dpi printers was comparable to traditional offset printing methods, thereby making 600 dpi printers the gateway to a new method of publishing for some organizations. Although text printed at 300 dpi was acceptable in most applications, graphics quality was substantially superior when printed at 600 dpi. Lexmark priced its 600 dpi printer similarly to most competitors' 300 dpi models.

EXHIBIT 9 | Forecasted U.S. Printer Demand in Units and Dollar Volume, 1992–96

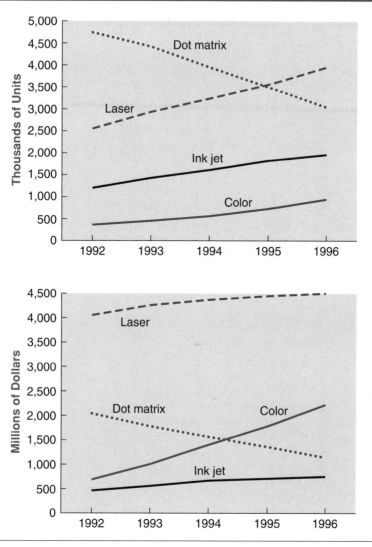

Source: Forecasted demand was determined by conducting interviews with industry analysts.

Another trend brought about by the increase in popularity of laser printers was the use of laser printers on local area networks (LANs). Several workers could be attached to the same printer by a network, thereby reducing the organization's expenditures on printers. A new class of laser printer was developed to alleviate problems associated with multiple users sending print files to a printer designed for a single user. LAN-capable laser printers offered higher engine speed, printing at up to 30 ppm, and could meet more diverse language emulation, font, and output requirements than non-LAN-capable laser printers. The LAN-capable printers were also designed to have longer duty cycles, up to 75,000 pages per month, and offered expanded paper-handling capabilities. Whereas traditional laser printers utilized 200-sheet input bins and output bins holding as few as 100 sheets, LAN-capable printers offered up to 1,500-sheet input bins and 500-sheet output bins. Although the LAN-

EXHIBIT 10 | **Forecasted European Printer Demand in Units and Dollar Volume, 1992–96**

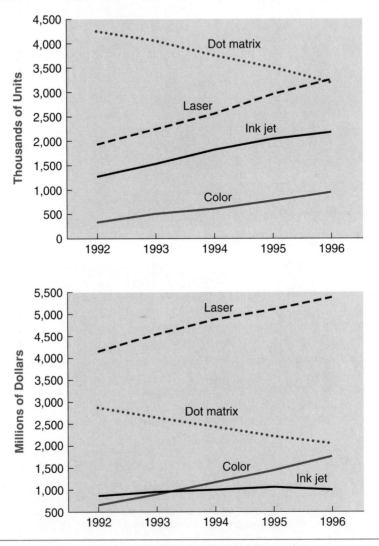

Source: Forecasted demand was determined by conducting interviews with industry analysts.

capable printers ranged from $3,500 to $8,000, the units were particularly attractive to organizations with large work groups. One 30-ppm LAN-capable laser printer could do the work of four or five 8-ppm laser printers without built-in work group features. Lexmark received good reviews on its new series of LAN-capable laser printers—the 4039 line—introduced in April 1993. The series offered entry-level models that had reduced speed for $1,599. The line also included models designed for high usage and function for as little as $3,399. These prices were slightly below the prices of Hewlett-Packard's comparable models and, in line with Lexmark's strategy, offered more capability.

The ink jet printer was a technology that had been around for a few years but was gaining popularity due to its high image quality, low price, and color capability. Most

E X H I B I T   11 | **Forecasted Rest-of-World Printer Demand in Units and Dollar Volume, 1992–96**

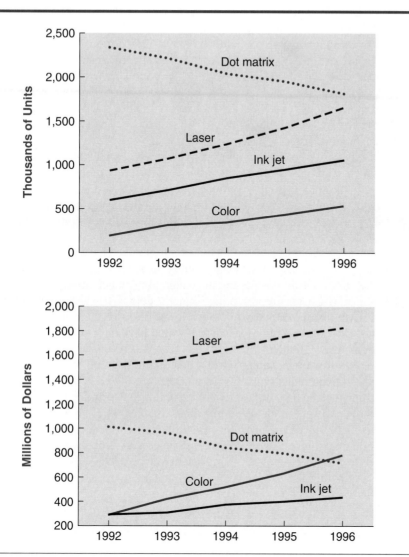

Source: Forecasted demand was determined by conducting interviews with industry analysts.

ink jet printers offered near–laser print quality and sold for about $400 retail. Ink jet printers were most appropriate for low-volume printing needs because of their slow printing speed. Ink jet also represented the low end of the color segment. Hewlett-Packard, Lexmark, and Canon USA all introduced color ink jet printers during 1992. Color ink jet printers were relatively inexpensive—Hewlett-Packard's color ink jet sold for less than $2,000—but the print quality was far inferior to other color technologies.

Canon had developed a variation of ink jet it called the bubble jet. Bubble jet printers operated in a slightly different manner from ink jets but had the ability to print at resolutions as high as 400 dpi. Canon's lower-end bubble jet printers (200 dpi) sold for approximately $400 retail. Canon was also developing color–bubble jet technology. Masaaki Iwasaki, vice president and general manager of Canon USA, stated, "The future of bubble jet technology is extremely bright." He expected continued improvements in "resolution, speed, flexibility, color printing, and the eventual reduction of the cost of printer ownership."[6]

Thermal dye transfer printers did not hold a substantial market share but did have the ability to produce very good color graphics. This printing process was able to produce a highly detailed continuous color image. The low market share was primarily due to its slow speed and expense of operation. Thermal transfer ribbons and printheads were expensive and needed to be replaced often. Kodak, who led in thermal transfer technology, expected the process to capture a larger percentage of the printer market by the end of the 1990s as speed and cost of operation improved. Most thermal transfer units listed between $4,000 and $10,000.

The highest-quality color technology available was produced by dye sublimation printers, which were also referred to as dye diffusion printers. Dye sublimation offered near photographic-quality printing but was extremely expensive. Most units sold for approximately $20,000 retail, but some models were offered for as low as $10,000. The models offered at the lower prices required a memory upgrade costing as much as $4,000.

Some industry analysts expected electro-photographic (E-P) or "true" laser technology to offer the highest growth opportunity in color printing. Hewlett-Packard, Canon, and Xerox were all developing the technology, which affixed dry toner to the page using scattered beams representing different colors. It was anticipated that E-P units could reach the marketplace at a much lower cost to the consumer than thermal transfer units. One market analyst stated E-P would have three times the market share of thermal transfer by 1995.

Advances in software technology had a potential impact on the demand for printers of all types. Some industry analysts predicted that at some point a paperless society might emerge created by new software capabilities. Electronic mail (E-mail), PC-based facsimile software, high-speed modems, and electronic libraries were growing technologies that reduced the need for printed material to some extent. International Data Corporation, a market research firm, predicted that E-mail would increase from 6 million users in 1991 to over 35 million users by 1996. Lexmark management believed that growing use of electronic communications would not deter users from wanting a hard copy of correspondence on file.

TYPEWRITERS

The demand for typewriters had steadily declined since the introduction of the personal computer. No significant changes in typewriter technology were anticipated by those in the industry, but users still had some needs that could be met only by the typewriter. Increased capabilities of word processing software and the increased paper-handling capabilities of laser printers were quickly encroaching on most typewriter functions, but multipage forms, envelopes, and labels could still be handled easier on a typewriter than on a personal computer. Industry analysts had found it difficult to accurately forecast the demand for office typewriters. Exhibits 12 and 13 present the variations between 1992 and 1993 forecasts for 1993–96 office typewriter demand in the U.S. and Europe.

---

[6]"Non-Impact Printers Too Good to Pass Up," *Purchasing,* January 16, 1992, p. 139.

EXHIBIT 12 | **Variations in Forecasted U.S. Demand for Office Typewriters, 1993–96** *(In thousands of units)*

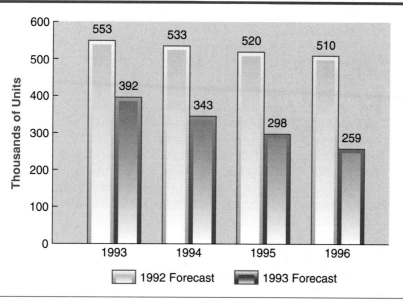

Source: Venture Development and InfoSource.

EXHIBIT 13 | **Variations in Forecasted European Demand for Office Typewriters, 1993–96** *(In thousands of units)*

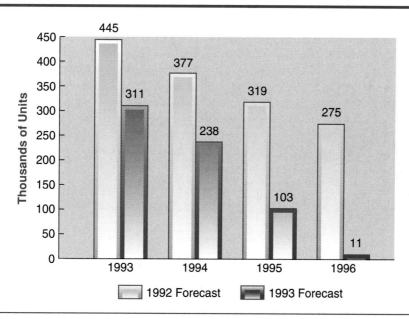

Source: Venture Development and InfoSource

Lexmark was the market leader in typewriter sales with approximately 50 percent market share based on sales revenue. The business continued to be very profitable for the company due to its relatively low cost and stable pricing. The IBM brand's reputation for quality allowed Lexmark to price typewriters at a substantial differential over the competition's pricing. Although demand for typewriters was steadily decreasing, Lexmark management expected to stabilize revenue from typewriter sales by expanding the channels of distribution in the U.S. and opening new markets in less-developed countries. The company's strategic objective in the typewriter industry was for Lexmark to be "the last vendor left standing."

Lexmark's vast preferred-dealer network contributed to price cutting in the declining U.S. typewriter market. Lexmark eliminated half of its 1,000-dealer network and authorized selected dealers to resell to smaller dealers in order to ensure that its best-performing dealers would remain profitable in typewriter sales. Lexmark also added office superstores to the distribution network to expand its coverage of the market, but provided the superstores with a different line of models.

KEYBOARDS

As the price of personal computers continued to decrease, computer manufacturers pressed original-equipment manufacturers (OEMs) to reduce the price of keyboards. The computer manufacturers had lowered tolerance and specification requirements for keyboards in order to purchase keyboards at lower prices. It was imperative that OEMs aggressively manage cost in order to compete at the $18 industry-average wholesale keyboard price. Foreign manufacturers of keyboards were at an advantage in supplying keyboards to PC manufacturers due to their lower cost of labor. One U.S. company, Key Tronic Corporation, was able to eliminate the offshore labor cost advantage by decreasing the number of parts included in the keyboard assembly process from 150 to only 17. The parts reduction generated labor-cost savings of 65 percent.

Even though IBM was having financial difficulties, it was still the market leader in personal computer sales. Lexmark was IBM's sole supplier of keyboards and therefore was the market share leader among the 75 to 100 keyboard manufacturers. IBM would be allowed by the terms of the sale of the information products unit to solicit bids from other keyboard suppliers after an unspecified time following the conclusion of the leveraged buyout. Lexmark had established a small sales force that had secured contracts to supply keyboards to other PC manufacturers. Although Lexmark keyboards were highly rated in terms of product quality and innovation, this contributed to a higher cost position than rival keyboard manufacturers. Lexmark's keyboards were actually overdesigned for the requirements of many personal computer manufacturers.

Lexmark and others had introduced new input devices such as magnetic-stripe readers, touch screens, pointing devices (mouse), scanners, and bar code readers. Most of these were relatively new technologies that had not gained sales volumes approaching that of keyboards.

OFFICE EQUIPMENT SUPPLIES

Lexmark's share of the office equipment supplies market was a function of the number of Lexmark printers and typewriters in use. In order for Lexmark to increase sales of office equipment supplies—primarily toner cartridges and ribbons—the sales force needed to put more Lexmark printers and typewriters into use. Lexmark's office equipment supplies were priced at approximately a 15 percent premium over competitors' products because of superior quality and high user loyalty. Lexmark offered a warranty return policy that replaced defective supplies purchased by users. Lexmark had achieved a defect rate of less than 0.2 percent.

All Lexmark office equipment supplies had distinctive packaging prominently displaying the IBM brand. The company saw the brand transition as a critical element of sustained success because of IBM's reputation for quality and brand loyalty. Lexmark intended to maintain the same coloring and graphics on all packaging even though the IBM name would have to be discontinued by 1996.

Rival manufacturers of cartridges and ribbons were successful in taking a portion of Lexmark's market share of some products once an item had been on the market for a year or more. Impact products—ribbons—were an example of a supply item for which Lexmark's market share had decreased as a result of diminishing user loyalty and competitive pricing by rivals. Lexmark's 1993 market share in ribbon products stood at 25 percent to 100 percent, depending on the technology. IBM had maintained over 50 percent to 100 percent market share in the 1980s. Lexmark had not lost substantial market share in nonimpact products—toner cartridges—due to the level of the technology required to produce high-quality cartridge products. There were very few manufacturers other than Lexmark and Canon who had the technology available to produce toner or ink jet cartridges.

Environmental concerns in Europe and the U.S. were also impediments to new entrants to the toner cartridge industry. Germany had laws in place in 1994 that required toner manufacturers to take back used toner and cartridges after use in copiers or printers. Lexmark had developed Operation Resource in order to comply with such legislation. All toner cartridge packaging was designed in a way that allowed the used cartridge to be returned to Lexington in the same packaging. A Lexington shelter workshop was allowed to recycle the parts of the cartridges and keep the profits from recycling. Manufacturers were also required to display the percentage of recyclable content on the toner cartridge packaging in the Europe and the U.S. This requirement required repackaging for sale in different countries because there were 13 different recycling symbols worldwide.

THE FUTURE

Lexmark management felt that it had made progress in creating a culture conducive to innovation in production, product development, and marketing. Lexmark had been able to bring a number of cutting-edge products to market in a very short time. Several computer publications rated Lexmark products as among the best on the market and *PC Magazine* awarded the company its "technical excellence" award. Lexmark had also been able to get its production costs and overhead expenses in line to ensure that its products would be priced competitively. Few innovations in the industry were not quickly imitated, which made price a deciding factor for many customers. Lexmark did manufacture all key components of its printers, including the vital printer engine. However, Lexmark was unable to achieve the economies of scale enjoyed by Hewlett-Packard and others who had much higher manufacturing volumes. Lexmark was able to offset some of this economies-of-scale disadvantage through more innovative and cost-effective engineering design.

The marketing team had been successful in expanding market share to make Lexmark the fourth-largest printer manufacturer by early 1993. Fifty percent of Lexmark's printers were being operated with non-IBM PCs. Still, the company's weak 1993 financial performance made it clear that Lexmark's future was far from secure.

WATERFORD CRYSTAL, LTD.

Philip H. Anderson, University of St. Thomas

In September 1991, Paddy Galvin, chief executive of Waterford Crystal, announced the launch of a new brand of crystal called "Marquis by Waterford Crystal." The announcement was very significant because it was a completely new brand of crystal that would be sourced out of Yugoslavia, Portugal, and Germany. Initial distribution would be limited to the U.S. market. The new brand would be priced below and distributed separately from Waterford's traditional line crystal, but still sold in many of the same retail outlets.

A BRIEF OVERVIEW OF THE CRYSTAL BUSINESS

MANUFACTURING

The crystal manufacturing business is by nature very labor intensive. Each piece of crystal goes through the processes of mixing, blowing, cutting, and polishing. Mixing involves the heating of raw materials in a furnace to temperatures in excess of 1400 degrees centigrade to create molten crystal. Blowing forms the molten crystal into a basic item such as a wine goblet or vase. The cutting process etches a design pattern into the blank piece. Finally, the piece is polished to smooth the edges of the cuts and give the piece the luster and sparkle for which crystal is known. Labor costs typically represent 50 to 55 percent of the cost of manufacturing crystal.

Blowing is done either by machine or by mouth by a skilled craftsman. Similarly, crystal pieces can be cut by machine or be hand cut. Three different technologies are used in the crystal-cutting process. They are (1) fully hand cut, (2) semiautomated and slow-speed automated, and (3) high-speed automated. Crystal pieces that are both mouth blown and hand cut have the highest image of quality of all crystal products.

Copyright © by Philip H. Anderson.

Developing craft skills is a key element in a manufacturer's ability to increase production output. This is particularly critical in the case of mouth-blown and hand-cut products. In addition to the wages paid to blowers and cutters, an intensive apprenticeship program must be maintained. Apprenticeships typically last for four or more years. Each craftsman usually oversees several apprentices. The availability of craft and design skills is a major factor in establishing and maintaining competitive advantage. Relative to the labor component involved in manufacturing crystal, raw materials are inexpensive and readily available.

Labor-cost efficiency was not a significant issue until the late 1970s. At that time, pressure on prices forced manufacturers to focus on costs in order to maintain gross profit margins. The pressure on prices came from multiple sources. Primary among these were general economic conditions, an increasing number of competitors (most of them European), and new technology. The technology of glass blowing had changed little since crystal making began. The traditional tools, hollow irons and wooden templates, were still used by glass blowers to create the crystal pieces that were then passed on to cutters who hand cut the design patterns. Recently, improved processing of machine-cut crystal had been introduced into the industry. While the quality of machine-cut crystal had improved, its level varied and was not equal to hand-cut crystal. Machine-cut crystal was lower in price relative to hand-cut crystal.

Lead crystal manufacturing is not a fixed capital intensive business. However, it does require a significant level of investment and its working capital needs are high. High-value finished inventories have to be maintained throughout the distribution channels. In addition, work-in-progress inventories contain a high value-added component which must be financed, reflecting significant cash requirements.

MARKETING

The technology differences used in the manufacture of crystal products translate into three market segments: high-end, medium, and low-end. These three segments are based on price and brand name recognition. Exhibit 1 shows the principal manufacturers for each of these market segments in the United States. It also provides an example of the price structure of these segments in 1988. The Irish Trade Board estimated that in 1988 Waterford/Wedgwood controlled 66 percent of the high-end market, followed by Orrefors (9.6 percent) and Baccarat (7.8 percent). The estimate of Waterford Crystal's share of this market was considered low by some in the industry. No other manufacturer had over 5 percent of the U.S. high-priced market. Based on price, St. Louis, Baccarat, and Lalique were targeting the very top end of the high-priced market. Lenox controlled an estimated 40 percent of the middle-priced market.

Each of these market segments can be further divided into three subgroups; stemware and giftware, premium and incentive, and catalog mail order. Stemware and giftware includes the bridal market, which accounted for 41 percent of all U.S. crystal sales in 1988. Bridal gifts represented the initial ownership of crystal for most people. Computerized bridal registration at major retail outlets has encouraged sales of this segment. Total giftware sales were estimated to make up approximately two-thirds of the high-end U.S. crystal market. This segment generated sales of $111 million. Prior to the recession of 1991, the primary growth for crystal sales occurred in the giftware segment of the business.

The premium and incentive market in the United States consisted of three sectors: trade (sales and dealer incentives), consumer premiums, and business gifts. The busi-

EXHIBIT 1 | **Major Manufacturers of Crystal Products for Market Segments in the United States, 1988**

Manufacturer	Average U.S. Retail Price of Better-Selling Stemware Line
High-End:	
Lalique (France)	$60–70 per piece
St. Louis (France)	60–70
Baccarat (France)	50–60
Waterford/Wedgwood (Ireland)	35–50
Orrefors (Sweden)	35–45
Middle:	
Galway Crystal (Ireland)	$30–40
Lenox (United States)	25–35
Gorham (W. Germany)	25–35
Noritake (W. Germany)	25–35
Saski	25–35
Miller Rogaska (Yugoslavia)	20–30
Mikasa (W. Germany)	15–25
Low-End:	
Colony	$10–20
Durand (France)	5–15
Bormioli (Italian)	5–10
Toscany	5–10

Source: Coras Trachtala–Irish Export Board market report, 1988.

ness gifts sector was projected to offer the greatest growth potential for the crystal industry. In 1988 this market was estimated to have a value of $1.5 billion.

The United States catalog mail-order business was projected to grow at about 8 to 9 percent per annum. While some product sectors in this market (e.g., sporting goods) were expected to grow faster, the medium and high-end gift sector was predicted to have average growth rates. According to the Direct Marketing Association, 8.5 billion catalogs were distributed throughout the U.S. by the postal service in 1988. That year there were at least 3,200 different catalogs in circulation, a majority of these published by 250 to 300 companies. The number of catalogs a company published varied considerably. For example, Spiegel distributed 35 catalogs in 1988, Nieman Marcus issued 28, and Horchow issued 7.

Department stores are the dominant channel of distribution for crystal in the U.S. market (see Exhibit 2). There is an increasing trend, particularly of high-end crystal manufacturers, to open their own retail stores.

Separate from the markets described above is the lightingware market. This market consists of both residential and business lighting fixtures. Crystal products for this market include items such as table lamps and chandeliers. The table lamp sector represented the major component of the residential market.

THE ORIGIN OF WATERFORD CRYSTAL, LTD.

Crystal glass had its origins in the development of "flint glass" in the mid-1600s. It was glass with a lead content that gave it a durable crystalline appearance. When cut, it reflected light like a prism. The manufacture of crystal glass in a regularly operat-

EXHIBIT 2 | **Major Distribution Channels of Crystal Products, 1988**

Category	Percent of Retail Sales
Department stores	51%
Jewelry stores	17
Manufacturer-owned retail stores	8
Specialty stores	9
Mail order	5
Door to door	5
Craft stores	3
Others	2
	100%

Source: Coras Trachtala–Irish Export Board market report, 1988.

ing factory in Ireland dates back to 1729. Almost 50 years later in 1783, two brothers, George and William Penrose, started the most famous of all Irish crystal companies, Waterford Glass. (The company later changed its name to Waterford Crystal.) The crystal produced by the original Waterford factory quickly gained a prestige status. The purity of its color was seen as superior to any other crystal produced in Ireland or England. The Penrose brothers continued crystal production until 1799, when they sold Waterford to the Gatchell family.

The repeal of restrictions on Irish commerce by the British parliament in 1799 allowed the crystal industry to flourish. By 1825 there were eleven companies in Ireland manufacturing glassware. Collectively, these companies enjoyed a large export trade throughout Europe, North America, and South America. In that year, the United Kingdom government imposed severe export duties on Irish crystal. The high export duties, accompanied by a general economic depression and a consequent lack of capital, forced the Irish glass manufacturers to close, one by one. The Gatchells closed their Waterford factory in 1851. It was one of the last to close, leaving the Irish lead-glass crystal-making industry dormant for nearly a century.

In spite of its relatively short company history, the Waterford Glass Company had established a reputation for quality around the world, and particularly throughout North America. The American Declaration of Independence was signed beneath a Waterford chandelier, which still hangs in the same location. Another Waterford chandelier hangs in the Kennedy Center in Washington, D.C. After Waterford ceased operations, Waterford's image increased as its crystal products became more difficult to obtain. Old Waterford glass is now a collector's item, of almost priceless value.

THE REBIRTH OF THE WATERFORD GLASS COMPANY

In 1946 Charles Bacik left Czechoslovakia looking for a location to reestablish his quality glass manufacturing business. He had been imprisoned by the Germans during World War II and following the war his glass factory had been nationalized by the communists. Bacik went to Dublin to meet with Bernard Fitzpatrick, one of his customers before the war. Knowing the history and worldwide reputation that still existed for Waterford crystal, the two men decided to reestablish the old glass company. Together they set up a factory in the city of Waterford, Ireland, in 1947.

Bacik recruited Miroslav Havel, an artist in Prague, to come to Ireland to serve as the designer for Waterford Glass. Havel studied the old Waterford crystal pieces in the National Museum in Dublin, replicating their designs for the first sets of stemware produced by the company. Many of those designs are still in production today.

The initial craftsmen for Waterford Glass came from throughout Europe: Germany, France, Estonia, Poland, and Scotland, in addition to Ireland. Almost 100 years of inactivity in the industry had left Ireland with few crystal craftsmen. This forced Bacik to look outside the country to find sufficient numbers of craftsmen with the skills he needed. The European craftsmen came searching for work in postwar Europe, and stayed because they enjoyed making "the finest crystal that money can buy" with its 33 percent lead content, unique thickness, deep cuts, and sparkle. Many of these craftsmen were still there 40 years later.

1950–85: THE MCGRATH FAMILY ERA

A critical point in the company's history came in 1950. Joe McGrath, who had made his fortune helping to found the Irish Hospitals Sweepstakes, recognized the value in the Waterford image. McGrath was also co-owner of Irish Glass Bottle Company and he understood the glass business. He invested the capital necessary to transform Waterford Glass from a small manufacturing company to one with the capacity to become a major producer in the crystal industry. McGrath's funds were used to build a new factory with new furnaces for melting and blowing glass in Waterford. Total sales revenues at the time were about IR£500,000 and profits were relatively modest. McGrath's investment in Waterford Glass gave his family control over the company's operations that would last for the next 35 years.

Joe McGrath was deeply committed to Ireland, its culture, and its heritage. He participated in Ireland's War of Independence with Britain (1916–22). McGrath was actively involved in the founding of the state and became a minister in the first Irish government formed after achieving independence. For McGrath running Waterford Glass was not just a business venture, it was also a means of providing jobs for his country, which had a long history of high unemployment. Growing the company was what was most important to Joe McGrath. Profits were not his primary concern.

The depressed state of the Irish economy in the 1950s, the small population base, and the high levels of Irish emigration led McGrath to focus on growing the company through exports to the increasingly affluent U.S. marketplace. In 1961, a marketing subsidiary was established in the United States. Three years later, a distributing company was established in the United Kingdom.

By the end of 1965 sales revenues had grown to IR£3 million with profits of IR£400,000. Employment had grown to 800 people and the company had recently moved its operations from a 3-acre site in Waterford city to a 40-acre site at Kilbarry on the city's outskirts. (The company's headquarters are still in the same location.)

The financing of this growth came from a number of sources. McGrath's Irish Glass Bottle Company gave loans totalling IR£200,000 between 1955 and 1958. Another IR£300,000 was raised when the company went public on the Irish Stock Exchange in 1966. In 1969, a one-for-twelve rights issue raised another IR£400,000. Between 1971 and 1984, the Industrial Development Authority (I.D.A.) granted payments totaling IR£5.7 million.

Paddy McGrath took over management of Waterford Glass from his father in 1966. At that time, the McGrath family controlled, either directly or indirectly, 40 percent of the company's equity. In addition to direct family ownership, the McGraths were members of a trust, along with two other families, that held 20 percent of the company's shares outstanding. The company had enjoyed growth and profits under Joe McGrath's leadership. Under the direction of Paddy McGrath as chairman and Noel Griffin as managing director (until his death in 1981), that success continued (see Exhibit 3).

Demand for Waterford crystal was strong during this period, typically exceeding Waterford's production capacity. A new factory at the Kilbarry site was opened in 1967. Four more factory units were planned for construction for the 1968 to 1984 time period. Demand increased at such a rate that all four of these plants were built by 1972. An additional plant was built in Dungarvan (also in the Waterford area) later that year.

Paddy McGrath inherited his father's dedication and broad sense of responsibility to his homeland. He believed his responsibilities extended beyond just the managing of Waterford Glass to providing service to his country. One of Ireland's goals since achieving independence had been to reduce its chronically high unemployment levels and the consequent high emigration of Irish in the search for work. Like his father, Paddy McGrath sought to provide employment opportunities for his Irish countrymen. The success of Waterford Glass allowed McGrath to pursue his goal of investing in Ireland. For Paddy McGrath that meant creating new or protecting existing jobs in Ireland while maintaining the Irish lifestyle.

McGrath's pursuit of employment for Ireland translated into the acquisition of multiple businesses by Waterford Glass. Under Paddy McGrath's leadership, Waterford Glass expanded into areas beyond the manufacture and sale of high-quality crystal. Between 1970 and 1977 the company took over ownership of a number of Irish companies. Management also changed the official name of the company to Waterford Glass Group to reflect its expanded business interests. In 1974 a newspaper article described Waterford as "the crystal, fine bone china, car assembly, and department store" company. By 1983 Waterford Glass owned or partially owned over 30 companies ranging from a postcard manufacturing company, the Renault automobile franchise for Ireland, and four retail department stores located across Ireland in the cities

EXHIBIT 3 | **Sales and Profits of Waterford Glass Group, 1975–84***

	Sales	Before Tax Profits	E.P.S. (pence)
1975	60.0	4.7	3.24p
1976	79.7	6.8	3.97p
1977	100.5	9.0	4.60p
1978	116.7	10.6	6.08p
1979	135.5	11.6	4.43p
1980	154.1	8.1	2.99p
1981	190.2	10.4	4.10p
1982	203.8	8.5	3.76p
1983	212.3	10.2	4.47p
1984	245.1	14.6	5.58p

*Sales and profit figures are stated in IR£ in millions.
Source: Waterford Glass, annual reports, 1975–84.

of Dublin, Cork, Limerick, and Galway (see Exhibit 4). During this period employment of the company grew to approximately 6,000 employees. Almost 50 percent of these employees were involved in businesses outside the crystal industry.

Blowers and cutters, representing approximately one-half the factory workers, were paid on a piece-rate basis. Management of the shop floor involved working with a strong trade union which had negotiated high piece rates and restrictive labor prac-

EXHIBIT 4 | **Waterford Glass Group and Associated Companies, 1983**

Company	Equity	Principal Business
Glass and China Division		
Waterford Crystal Limited	100%	Crystal glass manufacturer
Dungarvan Crystal Limited	100	Crystal glass manufacturer
Waterford Crystal (Lightingware) Limited	100	Crystal glass manufacturer
Waterford Glass Group (U.K.) Limited	100	Subsidiary holding company
Aynsley China Limited	100	Fine bone china manufacturer
Waterford-Aynsley (U.K.) Limited	100	Distributing company
Waterford Crystal Inc.	100	Distributing company
William Smith & Sons Limited	100	Distributing company
Waterford Crystal S.A.	100	Distributing company
Finance Division		
Waterford Glass (Group Services)	100%	Group management services
Purchase Corporation of Ireland Limited	100	Subsidiary holding company
Southern Industrial Trust (Ireland)	100	Finance company
C. H. Arthur Limited	100	Finance company
Sales Finance Limited	100	Finance company
Retail Division		
Waterford-Harrods Limited	60%	Subsidiary holding company
Switzer & Company Limited	60	Department store
Cash & Company Limited	60	Department store
William Todd & Company Limited	60	Department store
Alexander Moon Limited	60	Department store
Printing Division		
John Hinde Limited	100%	High-quality color printer
John Hinde (Distributors) Limited	100	Distributing company
John Hinde Curteich Inc.	100	Distributing company
Motor Division and Related Activities		
The Smith Group Limited	100%	Subsidiary holding company
Smiths (Engineering) Limited	100	Car assembler
Smiths (Distributors) Limited	100	Motor assembler
Smiths (Wholesale) Limited	100	Motor factoring and builders' provider
Smiths (Group Services) Limited	100	Group management services
Murdochs Stores Limited	100	Retail store
Rucon Limited	100	Construction company
Smiths Self Motoring Limited	100	Contract car hire
C.R.V. Group Limited	100	Vehicle assembler
Norco Limited	50	Light engineering

Source: Waterford Glass, annual report, 1983, pp. 14–15.

tices. By the mid-1980s labor rates for Waterford Glass were 77 percent above the average industrial salary in Ireland. Further, when blowers would finish a "pot of glass" toward the end of a shift it was sometimes uneconomical to start a new pot. In these instances the blowing team working out of that pot would leave work early. The average number of hours a factory employee worked each week was in the low 30s. Even so, they earned a comfortable standard of living, given the piece-rate system in operation.

Early in 1985, management signed a three-year labor agreement that raised labour-related costs (wages, pensions, pay-related social insurance taxes, and other benefits) by 44 percent over the life of the agreement. Also included in the agreement were restrictions on labor practices that resulted in the increased use of overtime to meet company production goals. In addition, the agreement introduced a profit-sharing scheme that made every employee eligible for stock bonuses. This resulted in eligible employees receiving IR£550 worth of shares in 1985, IR£400 in 1986, and IR£400 in 1987. The cost to Waterford for this scheme totaled over IR£4 million over the three years of the agreement.

The fact that the agreement covered a three-year period was in itself significant. In Ireland, the typical labor agreement is renegotiated yearly. To lock in an agreement that extends beyond this time frame is rare. If an agreement is not successfully rene-gotiated, it continues in effect until the next agreement is signed. Labor's preference is to be able to renegotiate if inflation, and so on, have worsened, but to have the option to let the current agreement continue in effect if economic conditions continue to favor the union membership.

Early in 1984 Avenue Investments, the holding company through which the McGraths and two other families maintained control of Waterford Glass, made some poor investments and it was rumored the families needed access to cash. In August 1984, Avenue Investments sold its 20 percent stake in Waterford Glass to London-based Globe Investment Trust, for IR£17 million. Though Waterford Glass had a world-famous reputation, its profit levels and dividend payments did not meet Globe's standards for performance. As Globe pressed for improvement, Waterford suddenly found itself having to meet an external standard for return on invested capi-tal for the first time in over three decades. Shortly following the sale by Avenue Investments, McGrath resigned as chairman of Waterford Glass.

1985–89: THE PADDY HAYES YEARS

Prior to Paddy McGrath's departure, Globe began a search for an executive from out-side Waterford Glass Group to replace him. On May 5, 1985, concurrent with the announcement of McGrath's resignation, the Waterford Board of Directors announced the appointment of Paddy Hayes as chairman and CEO of Waterford Glass Group. Prior to coming to Waterford Glass, Hayes had been with Ford Motor of Ireland for 30 years, the last 14 years as chairman and CEO. Hayes had also served as chairman of Aer Lingus (Ireland's national airline), and had been appointed by the Irish govern-ment to serve on various boards of government agencies.

Hayes had the reputation of a strong manager, one that knew how to run a tight manufacturing business and make tough decisions. In 1984 Ford Motor management moved to consolidate European operations and consequently decided to close its Ford assembly plant in Cork, Ireland. Hayes was given the task of shutting down the operations, which resulted in the loss of 600 jobs.

Hayes took over leadership of a company beset with a number of problems. Chief among these problems was the cash drain caused by the assortment of businesses not associated with the crystal industry. By early 1985, borrowings for Waterford Glass had reached almost IR£50 million, and more than 50 percent of this was for the noncore businesses. The low profitability and the poor cash flow of these noncore businesses led Hayes to move quickly to sell them off. The retail division holdings were sold in 1985 for IR£7.4 million, the motor division holdings in 1986 for nominal considerations, Aynsley China in 1987 for IR£19.7 million, and the printing division in 1988 for IR£5.7 million. In each of these cases, the selling price also included the transfer of the individual company's debt to the purchaser, increasing the value of the sale for Waterford.

Within his first 18 months at Waterford Glass, Hayes had eliminated nearly all the company's debt through the sale of these noncore companies. In 1985 alone, the debt/equity ratio for Waterford Glass was reduced from 1984's 48 percent to 27 percent, and outstanding debt dropped to IR£22 million. By 1989 the company (now called Waterford Wedgwood, following the acquisition of Wedgwood China in 1986) consisted of four divisions, all focused on the manufacture and sale of crystal and china (see Exhibit 5).

The company's balance sheet was further strengthened by a successful ADS (American depository shares) issue on the U.S. NASDAQ market in June 1986. The company issued 21.4 million new ordinary shares in the form of 2.14 million American depository shares at an initial public offering price of $20.04 per ADS. (The

EXHIBIT 5 | **Waterford Wedgwood and Associated Companies, 1989**

Company	Principal Business
Crystal and China Manufacturing	
Waterford Crystal Limited	Crystal glass manufacturer
Josiah Wedgwood & Sons Limited	Ceramic tableware manufacturer
Distribution	
Waterford Crystal Gallery Limited	Product display and sales center
Waterford Wedgwood Australia Limited	Distributor
Waterford Wedgwood Canada, Inc.	Distributor
Waterford Wedgwood U.S.A., Inc.	Distributor
Waterford Wedgwood Japan Limited	Distributor
Waterford Wedgwood Retail Limited	Retailer
Josiah Wedgwood & Sons (Exports) Ltd.	Exporter
Waterford Wedgwood Trading Singapore Pte. Limited	Retailer
Waterford Wedgwood N.V.	Distributor
Finance	
Waterford Glass (Group Services) Limited	Group management services and finance
Statum Limited	Finance
Other	
Waterford Wedgwood U.K. plc	Subsidiary holding company
Waterford Wedgwood Holdings, Inc.	Subsidiary holding company
Waterford Glass Research and Development Limited	Research and development
Dungarvan Crystal Limited	Nontrading

Note: All companies are 100% owned with the exception of Dungarvan Crystal Limited in which the Group holds 100% of the ordinary voting shares (the "A" class shares).
Source: Waterford Wedgwood, annual report, 1989, p. 35.

NASDAQ market trades in European securities by bundling them into groups of 10 for trading as ADS shares.) All shares were subscribed for, raising IR£28 million after expenses. These funds were used to virtually eliminate Waterford Glass's debt by the fall of 1986.

Hayes also enhanced Waterford's marketing operations. Free-standing Waterford Glass retail shops were established in the United States. The number of crystal designers the company employed almost doubled by 1989, leading to the introduction of many new products and more contemporary designs. During this time the company also increased its emphasis on the fast-growing gift market, developing crystal products such as clocks and picture frames. In 1988, Waterford controlled 66 percent of the high-quality, prestige end of the U.S. crystal market.

WEDGWOOD CHINA ACQUISITION

On November 28, 1986, Waterford Glass moved to solidify its position in the fine tableware industry with the acquisition of Wedgwood for IR£255.5 million. Wedgwood was a 200-year-old manufacturer and marketer of fine bone china, famous in the British and Japanese markets. It had a prestigious, high-quality image in a market dominated by porcelain china. In contrast to porcelain china, fine bone china is very thin (yet strong) and translucent, giving it the image of delicacy, elegance, and refinement. Wedgwood had been under the pressure of a hostile takeover attempt by London International Group, a condom manufacturer.

Hayes was named chairman and CEO of the combined companies. Colm O'Connell was named managing director of the crystal manufacturing division. Three directors of Wedgwood continued on as directors of the new, combined board of the two companies. They were Sir Arthur Bryan (former chairman), James Moffat (former managing director), and Alan Wedgwood (nonexecutive director and descendant of the founder, Josiah Wedgwood). Moffat subsequently resigned from the Waterford Glass board on March 31, 1987, "to make more time available to pursue other interests." Hayes recruited Paddy Byrne to become CEO of the china company. Byrne had been general sales manager with Hayes at Ford Ireland prior to becoming chief executive of Ford Motor in Portugal, and later in Spain.

Exhibit 6 shows an organizational chart of Waterford Glass Group, following the Wedgwood acquisition. In addition, sales and distribution offices were located in the U.S.A., Canada, United Kingdom, Ireland, Japan and the Far East, and Europe. Each of these offices had a functional reporting relationship with Brophy (finance) and O'Donoghue (sales and marketing), as well as a direct reporting relationship with Hayes.

At the time of the acquisition, Wedgwood had 18 factories and approximately 6,600 employees. The majority of these were in Stoke-on-Trent in England. This compared to Waterford's 1986 employment level of about 5,300 employees, 3,400 of whom worked in Ireland.

Almost two-thirds (IR£166.6 million) of the Wedgwood acquisition was financed through the issuance of Waterford ordinary shares. Waterford shares were exchanged for Wedgwood shares at the rate of 14 Waterford shares for every 3 Wedgwood shares. This yielded Wedgwood shareholders a share value of 565p for shares which had been valued at 380p on October 6, 1986. The issuance of the new Waterford shares for the Wedgwood shares resulted in only 35 percent of Waterford Glass shares being held in the Republic of Ireland. The remaining shares were held in the United Kingdom (55 percent) and in the United States (10 percent). Prior to the sale, 42 percent of Waterford shares were held in Ireland. As recently as 1983, 79 percent

EXHIBIT 6 | Waterford Glass, Organizational Chart, 1987

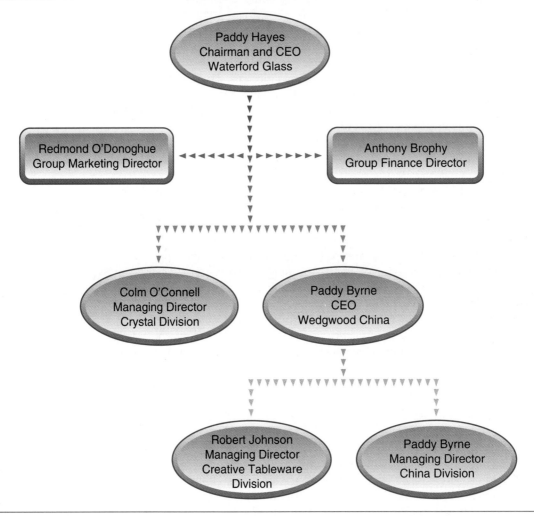

Source: Waterford Glass Group, annual report, 1987.

of Waterford's outstanding shares were held in the Republic of Ireland and 20 percent were held in the United Kingdom.

The acquisition of Wedgwood was partly offset by the sale of some of Wedgwood's assets that were not part of its primary business of manufacturing and selling fine bone china. In 1987, Waterford Glass management sold Trent Sanitaryware (a manufacturer of bathroom decor and fixtures) for IR£26.5 million, the 2,000-acre Ranton estate (a hunting preserve) for IR£2.8 million, and two facilities in Australia for IR£2.4 million. In addition, a Wedgwood joint venture with English Country Crystal was terminated. Following the disposal of these assets, Wedgwood was reorganized into two divisions—fine china and earthenware. At the end of 1987, Wedgwood employment levels were reduced by 986 people as the result of these restructuring efforts.

The Wedgwood acquisition led Waterford management to dispose of its Aynsley China business at the end of 1987. Aynsley China's market was in the United Kingdom and was primarily made up of British customers. Waterford management wanted to broaden the marketing of its china products and chose to focus the resources it would allocate to the china industry on Wedgwood china. A management led buyout of Aynsley China netted Waterford another IR£19.7 million.

The Wedgwood acquisition was viewed by Waterford management as a good fit for Waterford Glass on two levels: brand name image and channels of distribution. Waterford crystal and Wedgwood china were both aiming for the high-quality, prestige end of the market. Additionally, the distribution systems of the two companies complemented each other. Both sold their products through high-end retail shops. Waterford management estimated the synergistic benefits of integrating the worldwide distribution network could produce savings of IR£10 million. The elimination of redundant warehouse facilities could yield even further savings.

The acquisition gave Waterford immediate access to distribution in 150 Wedgwood shops in Britain and the Wedgwood sales network in Japan. At the same time, Wedgwood could use Waterford's sales network in North America. The combined sales of Waterford and Wedgwood was almost double its nearest competitor, Lenox Corporation, which was based in the United States. The initial plan was to market the two brands to the public as two separate companies, maintaining separate advertising programs, but to use the same distribution system.

While the methods of distribution were similar, the images the two companies had in their respective markets were quite different. Although the two companies were aiming at the top end of the prestige markets, they had not always been successful in achieving this image. Waterford crystal was seen as the premier brand in the United States, but did not carry the same status into its European and Japanese markets. Wedgwood's bone china image in its various markets was quite different from Waterford's image. Its prestige image was strongest in England and Japan, moderate throughout Europe, and weakest in the United States. Sales growth in Japan had averaged 58 percent per year from 1984 to 1987. Waterford management saw this as an opportunity to combine the two marketing programs throughout the world and benefit from each other's brand name strengths. They believed they could strengthen the market image and presence of both companies, using one company's strong image in a particular market to improve the weaker image of the other company. For example, the Wedgwood base in Japan was used to increase Waterford crystal's penetration into that market in October, 1987. By the end of 1987 Waterford crystal was being sold in more than 60 of Japan's leading department stores.

The acquisition of Wedgwood was not without its problems. Wedgwood management moved to change its marketing strategy in the United States. Advertising was increased and given a more upscale focus. However, discounting had been a frequently used tactic by Wedgwood distributors and retailers to maintain sales volumes and they often continued this practice in spite of the new advertising campaign. This left Wedgwood's less than prestigious image in the United States little changed.

Action was also taken to combine the marketing of the two products under a single Waterford Wedgwood brand name. Unfortunately, this marriage of the brand names caused some difficulties in the distribution channels. For example, in the United States Waterford crystal had been successful in prestigious shops, requiring no discounting while maintaining uniform price points for its products. Wedgwood's image in the United States would not support these same marketing tactics. Retailers were reluctant to place Wedgwood products in the same retail area and maintain pricing without discounts. Problems also arose in markets where Wedgwood was strong and Waterford lacked the prestige image. While discounting of Waterford crystal products did not occur, their image was not sufficient to command equal respect when placed side by side with Wedgwood china products.

The manufacturing operations of the two companies were kept separate following the Wedgwood acquisition. Waterford's crystal production remained in Ireland and Wedgwood's bone china production in England. Although both companies used a piece-rate system as part of their compensation program, the wage scales of the two were dramatically different. At the time of the acquisition, the average wage for Waterford workers was more than three times that of the Wedgwood worker. These differences were a reflection of the labor union histories of the companies, the local economies, and Ireland's high personal tax rates. Wedgwood worker salaries were about equal to the average industrial salary in England.

The purchase of Wedgwood also significantly affected Waterford Glass's debt burden. After reducing its debt by the fall of 1986 to near zero, the Wedgwood acquisition resulted in a year-end debt level of IR£67.3 million. This reflected nearly a 50 percent increase from the 1984 debt level of IR£45.4 million that had existed prior to the sell-off of Waterford's noncore business. It also signaled the beginning of a series of increases in net debt levels and, consequently, the company's annual interest expense (see Exhibit 7).

In spite of these difficulties, the Wedgewood division was a consistent contributor to Waterford Glass operating profits. Its marketing problems not withstanding, Wedgwood's overall cost structure allowed it to maintain profitable operations (see Exhibit 8).

In 1989, as a reflection of Wedgwood's importance to Waterford Glass's operations, the company's name was officially changed to Waterford Wedgwood. Three divisions were created under this corporate umbrella, the Waterford Crystal division, the Wedgwood division, and the Creative Tableware division. The Creative Tableware division represented products acquired with the Wedgwood purchase that were not high-prestige, bone china. They included earthenware brands such as Johnson Brothers and Bull-in-a-China-Shop.

CRYSTAL DIVISION PROBLEMS

In contrast to Wedgwood, continuing profitable operations were not the case with the crystal division. By 1987, the labor agreement signed by the prior Waterford management in 1985 (described above) had caused labor-related costs to increase by 44 per-

EXHIBIT 7 | Waterford Wedgwood, Net Debt and Interest Expense *(IR£ in millions)*

	Net Debt	Interest Expense
1983	54.6	x.x
1984	45.4	x.x
1985	21.9	11.7
1986	67.3*	5.3
1987	84.3	6.4
1988	109.5	11.0
1989	125.0	19.5
1990	38.0	13.0
1991	50.2	6.5

*Reflects borrowings related to Wedgwood acquisition completed on November 28, 1986.
Source: Waterford Glass and Waterford Wedgwood, annual reports, 1983–91.

EXHIBIT 8 | Wedgwood Division Profit Contribution   (IR£ in millions)

	Division Sales	Operating Profit
1986	NA*	NA*
1987	168.0†	25.1†
1988	190.4†	27.5†
1989	164.7	16.3
1990	156.3	17.7
1991	219.1‡	10.3‡

*NA = Not applicable; acquired November 28, 1986.
†Includes Creative Tableware results which are reported separately beginning in 1989.
‡Reflects the new reporting structure put into effect January 1, 1991.
Source: Waterford Glass and Waterford Wedgwood, annual reports, 1986–91.

cent. Making the situation worse, during that same three-year time period the value of the U.S. dollar relative to the Irish punt declined by over 30 percent, from \$.95 to \$.67. The effect of the dollar devaluation on Waterford revenues was dramatic. For example, when the dollar was at parity with the Irish punt, a crystal goblet that sold in the United States for \$40 was booked back in Ireland as IR£40 in revenue. Following the devaluation of the dollar, the same \$40 sale in the United States was now worth only 28 Irish punts. Exhibit 9 shows the average exchange rates for the principal currencies impacting the company's business.

The impact of the U.S. dollar's devaluation on Waterford was especially severe because 85 percent of its sales depended on the American market. Direct exports to the United States accounted for over 65 percent of Waterford's crystal output and another 20 percent came from sales to Americans visiting other countries. Many of these were tourists in Ireland, but Waterford also generated sales through unique distribution channels such as Caribbean cruise ships where Americans bought their crystal without ever setting foot in Ireland. (Exhibit 10 shows the distribution of the company's sales by geographical area.)

EXHIBIT 9 | Average Exchange Rates for the Principal Currencies with Which the Company Does Business

Year	Irish Punt Versus:		
	U.S. Dollar	British Pound	Japanese Yen
1984	1.05	.80	NA*
1985	1.07	.82	NA
1986	1.34	.91	NA
1987	1.49	.91	214.8
1988	1.52	.86	195.3
1989	1.42	.87	195.7
1990	1.66	.93	239.6
1991	1.61	.91	217.1

*NA = Not applicable.
Source: Waterford Glass and Waterford Wedgwood, annual reports, 1984–91.

EXHIBIT 10 | **Waterford Wedgwood, Sales by Geographic Area**

	1987	1988	1989	1990
Waterford Crystal				
United States	66.4%	69.1%	69.6%	66.8%
United Kingdom	8.5	8.2	7.9	9.0
Ireland	12.4	12.3	13.4	13.7
Europe	3.1	1.1	1.0	.9
Far East	1.7	3.5	3.5	2.6
Other	7.9	5.8	4.6	7.0
Total	100.0%	100.0%	100.0%	100.0%
Wedgwood/Creative Tableware				
United States	19.7%	17.1%	16.5%	15.7%
United Kingdom	46.8	46.8	45.8	45.0
Ireland	.4	.7	.7	.7
Europe	8.6	9.1	10.4	12.9
Far East	10.7	12.6	12.9	14.0
Other	13.8	13.7	12.7	11.7
Total	100.0%	100.0%	100.0%	100.0%
Total Sales of Group Products				
United States	34.0%	33.9%	34.4%	31.0%
United Kingdom	35.0	34.3	33.0	34.2
Ireland	4.0	4.4	5.0	4.6
Europe	6.9	6.5	7.2	9.3
Far East	7.9	9.7	10.4	10.6
Other	12.2	11.2	10.0	10.3
Total	100.0%	100.0%	100.0%	100.0%

Source: Davy Stockbrokers, Equity Research–Waterford Wedgwood, October 23, 1991, p. 5.

The decrease in revenues caused by the dollar's devaluation, combined with increased labor costs, effectively eliminated Waterford's profit margins in its major market. Even price increases in the United States of 21 percent between 1984 and 1987 could not prevent this profit erosion. In a 1987 interview, Hayes stated that "at the present price, the U.S. dollar exchange rate means that we are losing money on every item we produce for the U.S." As would be expected, these price increases affected demand. Sales volume dropped 10 percent in 1986 and was down another 18 percent by mid-1987. Not only did direct sales to the United States decline, but sales to U.S. tourists travelling in Ireland also dropped as the weak dollar diminished the benefits of buying crystal in Ireland for shipment back to the United States.

By mid-1987, the need for significant, major corrective action was readily apparent. The focus centered on the reduction of labor costs for two reasons. First, in 1987 labor costs made up more than 80 percent of overall production costs in Waterford Glass. Waterford management estimated this to be 20 percent higher than that of its competitors. Second, there was little likelihood of a strengthening of the dollar in the near future. Even the optimistic view did not expect favorable movement by the dollar until after the November 1988 presidential elections, if even then. The company had hedged its bets on the dollar by selling dollars forward against future U.S. sales. (See Exhibit 11.) But this practice was not a viable long-term strategy. The successful

EXHIBIT 11 | **Foreign Currency Hedging*** *(All currency figures are in millions)*

	1985	1986	1987	1988	1989	1990	1991
U.S. dollars	60.8	109.7	90.1	91.7	93.2	68.3	67.0
Canadian dollars	—	1.5	5.2	14.2	10.0	6.0	4.0
British pounds	6.0	1.8	—	10.0	2.0	—	—
Japanese yen	—	—	560	1173	550	500	1550
Australian dollars	—	—	3.6	11.0	7.5	—	6.0
Hong Kong dollars	—	—	—	8.8	7.7	5.0	2.0
Singapore dollars	—	—	—	2.2	—	2.0	.8

*Reflects forward currency contracts purchased to hedge the risk of exchange rate increases on anticipated foreign currency transactions.
Source: Waterford Glass and Waterford Wedgwood, annual reports, 1985–91.

hedging could only delay the effects of the U.S. dollar's devaluation on its financial performance, not eliminate it.

THE REDUNDANCY PROGRAM

By mid-1987, Waterford Glass management had settled on a redundancy program (i.e., early retirement) for its skilled workers as a means to cut its labor costs. While not unheard of in Ireland (the government had recently been retrenching), this was a first-time experience for Waterford's workers. The union refused to negotiate with the company on this issue so the company took their redundancy offer directly to the workers.

Given the traditional militancy of the trade union and the lack of earlier use, gaining approval of the workers for the initiation of redundancies was expensive. The agreement reached with the workers was seven weeks of pay for every year of service. Some long-term workers received as much as a single payment of IR£62,000 (after taxes). Others received a combined package which paid them as much as IR£40,000 tax free, plus an additional IR£210 per week tax free in retirement benefits. While the company had a goal of reducing its labor force by 750 workers, over 1,000 left the company. Of these, 800 were full-time employees who accepted the redundancy offer; the remainder were temporary and contract staff.

The major effects of the restructuring associated with the redundancy program, as outlined in the company's 1987 annual report, were

- A reduction of a third of the workforce from 3,010 to 2,005.
- A reduction of wage costs of IR£18 million per annum, which was expected to lead to a 20 percent decrease in unit production costs.
- The installation of new diamond cutting wheels.
- The installation of a continuous melting tank furnace in Dungarvan by June that would enhance productivity and quality.
- Increased flexibility and mobility within craft sections.
- Excess costs of production during the restructuring period and stock provisions amounting to IR£14.8 million.
- Extraordinary item costs (i.e., voluntary redundancy, early retirement, and productivity payments) totalling IR£35 million.

The impact of this redundancy program on the city of Waterford was considerable. More than a third of the city's workforce was employed at the glass factory. These workers were also much better paid than most workers (77 percent above the average industrial salary in Ireland). Consequently, local officials estimated Waterford workers' discretionary income made the loss of one crystal worker equal to the loss of almost two industrial jobs to the Waterford city economy. This purchasing power added to the ripple effect the loss of these jobs had on the local economy.

Some of the blowers and cutters gained employment with other Irish crystal manufacturers. For example, 13 of Tipperary Crystal's 34 employees in July, 1989, were ex-Waterford employees. Regardless, Waterford was still the dominant crystal manufacturer in Ireland, representing over 80 percent of all Irish crystal workers. Exhibit 12 shows the 1992 employment levels of the other Irish crystal companies. Few of these companies do their own blowing of the crystal glass. Most buy "blanks" that are machine blown by other crystal manufacturers and then do the cutting on their premises.

Expectations were that the restructuring program would be a success. The diamond cutting wheels had a number of advantages over the old carborundum wheels. Besides their longer life, the diamond wheels made smoother, cleaner cuts, making them twice as fast as the old carborundum wheels. This increased efficiency was expected to have a corresponding effect on the labor cost associated with cutting the crystal designs. While the redundancy program caused the company to incur significant extraordinary charges against earnings totaling almost IR£50 million, the goal of employment reduction had been reached and surpassed. In fact, the company later rehired about 100 of its blowers on a contract basis. Still, the expectation was that lower labor costs and more efficient labor would combine to return Waterford to profitability.

EXHIBIT 12 | **Crystal Manufacturers in Ireland, February 1992** *(Excluding Waterford Crystal)*

Company	Number of Employees	Year Established
Tyrone Crystal (Northern Ireland)	200	1971
Cavan Irish Crystal	75	1969
Galway Irish Crystal	64	1967
Tipperary Crystal	63	1987
Clarenbridge Crystal Ltd.	28	1975
Duiske Handcut Glass	32	1974
Connemara Celtic Crystal	21	1972
Failte Crystal	20	1979
Cork Crystal	16	1983
Frances Studio	12	1981
Penrose Glass	11	1976
Jerpoint Glass Studio Ltd.	11	1979
Blackwater Crystal	7	1989
Kilkenny Crystal	5	1969
Shandon Crystal	3	1991*

*Originally established in 1980. Ownership changed in July 1991.

Source: *Kompass Register of Irish Industry & Commerce, 1990,* table 33-62.0 31, and telephone inquiries, February 1992.

Initially these expectations appeared to be achievable. In May, 1988, Hayes reported to shareholders that Waterford was "reaching a production rate equal to 100 percent of the normal, historic rate of production—with a 30 percent drop on employee numbers." But, as Hayes soon discovered, all was not as it seemed regarding the situation at the glass company.

Rather than use this period of change as a time to tighten labor practices, manufacturing management at Waterford tried to appease the anxiety and unhappiness in the remaining workforce by accepting informal agreements relaxing the new labor standards and policies that had been negotiated as part of the redundancy program. While this served to placate the workers, it also worked against the goals of the redundancy program. Labor efficiencies were not achieved and labor costs, rather than decreasing, continued at levels that precluded profitability.

Unfortunately these informal agreements and their effect on labor costs were not communicated to Hayes and the board of directors. Later, when these agreements and their associated costs caused progress on the restructuring program to fall short of the levels planned and budgeted for, incorrect information was submitted to Hayes. Some costs were deferred and material inventories were overvalued by IR£20 million to hide the lack of efficiency in the factory.

Based on information submitted to the board and approved by the company's external auditors, which proved to be incorrect, Hayes made mid-year earnings projections as part of the company's public reporting process. By the end of 1988 these discrepancies became apparent and losses, rather than profits, for the company were reported. In January, 1989, both the managing director of the crystal manufacturing division (Colm O'Connell) and the group finance director (Anthony Brophy) resigned from Waterford's board and retired from the company later that year. Four months later, Hayes resigned as the pressure increased for wholesale management changes from major institutional shareholder groups.

1989 TO THE PRESENT: THE PADDY GALVIN YEARS

Following Hayes's resignation, the Waterford Wedgwood board made a number of management changes. In April 1989, Howard Kilroy (a director since 1985) became nonexecutive chairman of Waterford Wedgwood and Paddy Byrne (CEO of the Wedgwood division) was appointed as CEO of Waterford Wedgwood. Byrne also continued to hold his position as CEO of Wedgwood. Richard Barnes assumed the position of managing director of the Wedgwood division and Robert Johnson continued as managing director of the Creative Tableware division.

The search for a replacement to manage the Waterford Glass operations had begun in January after O'Connell's resignation. At that time, Hayes began recruiting Paddy Galvin to become chief executive of the crystal company. Following Hayes's resignation, the Waterford Wedgwood board continued discussions with Galvin. In May, 1989, Galvin accepted the offer to become chief executive of the Waterford Crystal division. An organization chart reflecting these changes is shown in Exhibit 13.

Galvin came to Waterford Wedgwood from Guinness Ireland Ltd., where he had been operations director. He also had served as executive chairman of Guinness Dublin, Irish Ale Brewers Ltd., and Harp Ireland Ltd. While at Guinness, Galvin oversaw the reduction of 1,600 workers and initiated a IR£100 million capital investment program.

EXHIBIT 13 | Waterford Wedgwood, Organizational Chart, May 1989

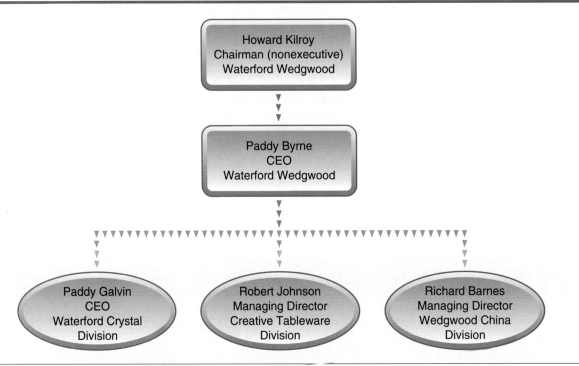

Source: Waterford Wedgwood, annual report, 1989.

In June 1989, in an attempt to regain control over its costs, Waterford management convinced the workers to accept a number of changes to their contract. This included

- A pay freeze until the end of 1991.
- The introduction of a new cutters' piece rate.
- A tightening up of sickness and benefit programs.
- An extension of the retirement age from 55 to 58 years of age for craft workers and from 60 to 63 for all other staff. (Note: The retirement age affected when workers could retire with the *full* retirement benefits negotiated by their trade union. Retirement at a relatively young age meant the company had to increase its contribution to the workers' general retirement fund to keep it actuarially sound. Similarly, any increase in retirement age increased the number of years the workers contributed to the funding of their retirement benefits. Prior to 1989, the workers made no contribution to their retirement fund.)
- A reduction in the number of full-time employees spending company time on union matters. At the time there were 60 shop stewards who the company estimated spent about IR£600,000 worth of company time annually on union business.

In return, the management agreed to a profit sharing agreement where workers would receive 5 percent of profits, once profits reached IR£10 million per annum. This profit sharing would be distributed to the workers either in share options, cash, or through increased contributions to their pensions.

The year 1989 ended with continued operating losses for the crystal division. It lost IR£21.3 million on sales of IR£111.8 million. This compared with 1988 crystal sales of IR£93.7 million that yielded an operating loss of IR£20.5 million (see Exhibit 14). Given these results, Waterford management moved to cut costs in two areas, debt service and labor.

ADDITIONAL EQUITY INVESTMENT

By the beginning of 1990, Waterford Wedgwood's debt level had grown to IR£125.0 million, requiring an interest expense of IR£19.5 million. This was almost twice the IR£11 million paid in 1988 (see Exhibit 7). In order to lower their debt level, Waterford Wedgwood management sought out additional equity investors in the company. On March 28, 1990, shareholder approval was given for the issue of 212 million new shares to a consortium created by two investment companies, Morgan Stanley (Boston, U.S.A.) and Fitzwilton, plc (Ireland). The Morgan Stanley/Fitzwilton consortium (organized under a legal entity called Shuttleway Holdings, Inc.) agreed to pay 37.5 pence per share (IR£79.5 million) for their 29.9 percent share of the company. At the time, Waterford Wedgwood shares were trading for approximately 50

EXHIBIT 14 | **Waterford Wedgwood, Consolidated Profit and Loss Account** *(IR£ in millions)*

	1987	1988	1989	1990
Sales revenues				
Waterford Crystal	76.4	93.7	111.8	87.0
Wedgwood China	183.2	190.4	164.7	156.3
Creative Tableware	NA	NA	55.6	47.8
Other	18.1	16.9	17.0	16.8
Discontinued operations	4.7	3.4	—	—
Total	282.4	304.4	349.1	307.9
Less: cost of sales	(162.0)	(164.7)	(202.3)	(168.8)
Gross profit	120.4	139.7	146.8	139.1
Less: distribution costs	(69.7)	(85.0)	(100.0)	(80.0)
Less: administration costs	(42.7)	(48.6)	(49.3)	(47.9)
Plus: other operating income (loss)	2.9	.7	1.4	(1.2)
Operating profit (loss)				
Waterford Crystal	(18.7)	(20.5)	(21.3)	(5.0)
Wedgwood	26.9	27.5	16.3	17.7
Creative tableware	NA	NA	4.6	(.4)
Other	1.6	(1.3)	(.7)	(2.3)
Discontinued operations	1.1	1.1	—	—
Total operating profit (loss)	10.9	6.8	(1.1)	10.0
Exceptional gains (costs)	(14.8)	(7.0)	—	(18.4)
Net interest paid	(6.4)	(11.0)	(19.5)	(13.0)
Profit (loss) before taxes	(10.3)	2.7	(20.6)	(21.4)
Taxes	(7.6)	(7.9)	(8.4)	(5.7)
Extraordinary items	(29.9)	10.5	—	(1.1)
Net profit (loss)	(47.8)	(5.2)	(29.0)	(28.2)
Earnings (loss) per share	(4.05p)	(1.19p)	(6.56p)	(4.29p)

Notes: "Other" comprises non-Group manufactured crystal and china products. "Discontinued operations" include John Hinde Ltd. and Johnson Tiles Pty (1987) and Aynsley China (1988).

Source: Waterford Glass and Waterford Wedgwood, annual reports, 1987–90.

pence per share. An additional IR£22.8 million was raised from Waterford Wedgwood's existing shareholders through the issue of one new share (at a price of 27.5 pence per share) for every five shares already held. After fees were paid to the investment banker, the company netted IR£96.2 million. As part of the agreement, the Morgan Stanley/Fitzwilton group appointed four members to the Waterford Wedgwood board of directors and agreed not to attempt any takeover of Waterford Wedgwood during the next 30 months.

This injection of equity capital had two significant effects. It gave Waterford Wedgwood the cash it needed to reduce its high debt to an acceptable level, lowering the interest expense which was hampering a return to profitability. It was estimated at the time of the investment that net debt would be reduced to between IR£40 and IR£50 million by the end of 1990. Exhibit 15 shows the strengthened balance sheet resulting from this equity investment.

The investment also signaled the continuing shift of ownership of the company to sources further outside of Ireland. Both Morgan Stanley and Fitzwilton were driven by financial results rather than by Irish interests. The consortium's 29.9 percent share of Waterford Wedgwood's outstanding stock far outweighed that of any other group or individual. Following the equity investment, five other companies owned a sufficient number of shares to require reporting them as substantial shareholders in the company's 1990 annual report. Two companies had shareholdings between 5 percent and 10 percent and three companies owned between 3 percent and 5 percent of Waterford Wedgwood outstanding shares. Exhibit 16 provides a listing of these companies.

The Fitzwilton group was headed up by Tony O'Reilly, one of Ireland's most successful businesspeople. Following considerable success developing a number of Irish companies, O'Reilly convinced the head of Heinz-UK to invest in Ireland, resulting in the establishment of Heinz-Erin in 1966. O'Reilly's performance managing Heinz-Erin led to his appointment two years later as CEO of the Heinz-UK operations. In 1970 he moved to the United States as senior vice president of Heinz North America and Pacific and in 1979 succeeded Burt Gookin as president of Heinz. While O'Reilly had strong Irish roots, many of Fitzwilton's investors did not. They invested their money to achieve good financial returns and would not be influenced by feelings of Irish nationalism. This, in combination with Morgan Stanley's involvement, meant major decisions affecting Waterford Glass's current and future operations would not be controlled by a local Irish resident.

Concurrent with management's efforts to correct Waterford Wedgwood debt levels, management were also working to further cut the company's high operating costs. In January the company announced its intention to eliminate the workers' attendance bonus and the controversial "bonanza scheme" for cutters, citing the effect of these programs on the high cost of labor for Waterford Glass. At the time, labor costs represented 70 percent of total production costs for the company. Both of these programs had been in effect since the McGrath era.

The attendance bonus paid all factory workers an additional 2 percent of their wages for showing up for work. It was estimated this program cost the company IR£800,000 per year. The cutters' "bonanza weeks" represented to management a clear example of the control that had been lost to the union. The bonanza weeks were introduced so that cutters, who were on a piece-rate basis, would not lose wages in a week when the country had a "bank holiday", that is, a public holiday. (Ireland had four bank holidays a year.) In order to determine the proper payment the cutter was to receive for the holiday, his production over a two-week period was measured. This

EXHIBIT 15 | **Waterford Wedgwood, Consolidated Balance Sheet** *(IR£ in milions)*

	1987	1988	1989	1990	1991
Assets					
Current assets					
Cash and deposits	53.7	88.5	42.4	35.8	27.2
Accounts receivable	59.8	66.8	55.5	51.5	47.3
Stocks					
Raw materials	8.8	12.4	13.5	13.4	10.1
Work-in-progress	17.7	24.3	21.0	14.9	13.7
Finished goods	63.6	74.6	75.7	65.6	72.3
Net current assets	203.6	266.6	208.1	181.2	170.6
Fixed assets					
Net plant and equipment	36.2	55.5	53.7	50.6	47.3
Net freehold land and buildings	69.0	68.1	58.5	58.3	55.8
Net leasehold land and buildings	11.8	10.7	10.1	8.0	6.5
Investments and loans	4.4	2.9	1.7	1.4	1.8
Net fixed assets	121.4	137.2	124.0	118.3	111.4
Total assets	325.0	403.8	332.1	299.5	282.0
Liabilities and Stockholders' Equity					
Current liabilities					
Notes payable	130.9	166.9	152.0	99.2	57.8
Long term liabilities					
Long term debt	87.0	102.7	82.1	40.4	74.4
Capital grants deferred	2.2	2.0	1.9	1.8	1.8
Finance lease obligations	1.3	6.6	5.1	6.1	5.1
Other	11.4	12.6	7.2	7.7	4.3
Net LT liabilities	101.9	123.9	96.3	56.0	85.6
Total liabilities	232.8	290.8	248.3	155.2	143.4
Stockholders' equity					
Called up share capital	23.5	23.7	23.8	42.1	42.3
Share premium account	211.6	55.0	55.5	133.8	133.8
Revaluation reserve	17.3	21.7	20.7	20.7	20.2
Other reserves	2.2	1.9	1.9	1.9	1.9
Goodwill on consolidation	(156.9)	—	—	—	—
Profit and loss account	(5.5)	.7	(28.1)	(54.2)	(59.6)
Minority interests	—	10.0	10.0	—	—
Total stockholders' equity	92.2	103.0	83.8	144.3	138.6
Total liabilities and stockholders' equity	325.0	403.8	332.1	299.5	282.0

Source: Waterford Glass and Waterford Wedgwood, annual reports, 1987–91.

figure was used as the base for calculating the cutter's production target for the two weeks covering the holiday period. This base was reduced by 20 percent to adjust for the lost day of production over the two-week period. It was only necessary for the cutter to achieve the reduced target in order to receive the pay level equivalent to the typical two week period. Production above the reduced target would yield commensurate additional pay. This scheme effectively gave cutters a 10 percent holiday

EXHIBIT 16 | **Waterford Wedgwood, Substantial Ordinary Shareholders, May 1991**

Greater than 10%
Shuttleway Holdings, Inc.—29.9%

Between 5% and 10%
Irish Life Assurance, plc—6.9%
A.I.B. Investment Nominees Limited—7.5%

Between 3% and 5%
British Coal Pension Funds
Standard Life Assurance Company
Friends Provident Group
Fidelity Magellan Fund
M & G Investment Managers

*Source: Waterford Wedgwood, annual report, 1991, p. 11.

"bonanza" since they were only losing 10 percent of production time (1 day out of a 10 working day period) but received a 20 percent reduction in how much they had to produce to achieve full pay. Waterford management estimated the cost of the bonanza program at IR£750,000 per year.

THE STRIKE

When cutters did not receive their bonanza payments following the March bank holiday (St. Patrick's Day), the union called a mass meeting and voted for a strike. Two days later, on April 5, 1990, the strike began. Even though the bonanza scheme did not affect all the workers (625 of the 2,300 union employees were cutters), the strike had broad support among the workers. The elimination of the bonanza scheme was seen by the union as an attempt to divide and conquer. The workers also believed the action by the company was the tip of a wedge to be used to take back the benefits they had earned over the years. The strike was the first full-scale strike in the company in 21 years. (There had been periodic, short, impromptu work stoppages as recently as the past January, but not a union sanctioned strike.) The strike lasted 14 weeks.

The effect of the strike extended beyond the company and the workers to the local community. The crystal company created between 10 percent and 15 percent of the employment for the city of Waterford, either directly or indirectly. Waterford had a population of approximately 40,000 in 1990. Workers from Waterford Crystal injected about IR£600,000 into the local economy each week. The company itself spent about IR£18 million a year buying Irish goods and services, IR£3.5 million of that was spent locally. In addition, the crystal company attracted 100,000 visitors for factory tours each year. Money these visitors spent in hotel stays, restaurants, bars, and souvenirs was critical to Waterford city's economy.

Beyond the monetary effects of the strike were the social costs. While these costs were not measurable, they were no less painful. The dispute divided friends and family as supervisory staff passed union members on the picket line. Many people in the city saw the Waterford workers as highly paid, perhaps even overpaid and spoiled, who should be willing (and certainly would be able) to do with less for the good of their families, the city of Waterford, and the surrounding communities that were dependent on the crystal company.

Business reactions to the strike were varied. Banks and utility companies agreed to restructure or suspend mortgage and utility payments until the strike ended, although this often just delayed foreclosures that occurred later. Local businesses were asked to contribute to the union's strike fund and defer payments on outstanding debts. Some businesspeople felt they had no choice but to contribute, even if they disagreed with the strike. They feared failure to support the union could result in lost business once the strike was over.

There were many claims on both sides of the conflict. Management argued labor costs were high because of unreasonable labor practices and restrictions. As examples, they cited the Christmas and summer holiday bonuses, which gave every worker an extra two weeks pay twice a year, costing the company IR£2.5 million a year. These two bonuses were in addition to a worker's normal holiday pay. The attendance bonus and cutters' bonanza schemes were also targeted by management, as were such practices as giving the workers a half hour off to attend mass on every holy day of obligation and paying workers IR£10 a day allowance if they were temporarily assigned to work in the company's factory that was a mile away from the main plant. These issues, plus agreements made in June 1989 that had not yet been implemented, formed the heart of management's concerns that needed to be corrected for successful resolution of the strike.

The union cited the company's refusal to refer their grievance over the elimination of the bonanza program to the country's Labor Court for arbitration. They claimed this indicated the company's true intention was to break the union's power. Jim Kelly, chairman of the union's branch for Waterford Crystal, noted the union's willingness to work with the company in the past, citing IR£8.8 million in cuts members agreed to a year earlier to help the company achieve profitability. (Galvin countered that IR£12 million in cuts had been agreed to, but only IR£8.8 million achieved because of labor reticence.)

The union agreed to return to work in July, after 14 weeks of tough negotiations. Six outstanding points were submitted to the Irish Labor Court for binding arbitration, four of which were:

1. Payments to be made to the workers for a buyout of the bonanza program. The company offered single payments of between IR£750 and IR£1,500 to each cutter. The union sought IR£2.25 million.

2. The status of the 2 percent attendance bonus. The union wanted it retained, the company wanted it eliminated.

3. The retirement age for craftsmen. The union wanted it kept at 58. The company wanted it raised to 61.

4. An increase in the length of the work week by 90 minutes to 39 hours, without added pay. The union wanted this limited to three years, the company sought five years.

The Labor Court was also to rule on two issues for separate sections of the union. These dealt with compensation for lost overtime and the retention of breaks for women workers. The Court decided in favor of the company on all six points.

THE FOREIGN SOURCING PROGRAM

In September 1990, Waterford Glass announced an agreement with a German-based company to produce a limited number of test pieces. The German company was able to meet Waterford's design and specifications requirements, while producing the items for one-third less than the cost of an equivalent piece made in the Waterford plant. The German-produced items were to be test-marketed in the United States at different price points from the existing lines of Waterford crystal. Management said that results of the test marketing would be determined at the end of the year.

In announcing the German sourcing, Paddy Byrne stressed that these "very limited" number of products would be "complementary" rather than "supplementary" to products made in Waterford city factories. Citing a dependence on a narrow line of products, Byrne emphasized the need for a greater range of product offerings. He stated that in order to widen the price line, other sources were necessary, but that this "mustn't damage the brand."

At the end of November, Waterford management announced plans to put "short-time" working conditions into effect the following year. The short-time program, if implemented, would mean workers would be laid off one week in each of the months of March and May through July. From August through December, the workers would follow a schedule of working one week on followed by one week off. This meant workers would only work a total of 38 weeks in 1991.

The Restructuring Program

In December 1990, Waterford Wedgwood announced that the company would split Waterford Crystal and Wedgwood into two independent, stand-alone, operating entities. Paddy Galvin was to continue as chief executive of Waterford Crystal, but with more autonomy and worldwide responsibility for crystal operations. Each division would have its own board, management, capital investment resources, and balance sheet. Even in the United States, where sales and distribution management were previously shared, the two companies were separated. Because British tax laws prevented losses in Ireland from being applied against earnings in England, the splitting of the companies was also seen as allowing the allocation of some costs to Wedgwood to reduce its overall tax bill. An organization chart reflecting the company's structural reorganization, as well as further management changes announced in July of 1991 (and discussed below), is shown in Exhibit 17.

One effect of this split was that interest charges and head office costs would be directly assigned to each company, rather than shared. Given the disparity in performance of the two divisions, this move was seen as an attempt to bring Waterford's financial performance under sharper review. As one investment fund manager stated, "I assume this restructuring is to make it clear to the crystal workforce and the unions that the umbilical cord with Wedgwood, that has kept them afloat for the past few years, is now broken."

At the same time as the restructuring was announced, Paddy Byrne resigned as CEO of Waterford Wedgwood. A company statement said, "Mr. Byrne fully supports this reorganization, but sees no appropriate role for himself." As stated by a company member, the planned restructuring eliminated the need for a group CEO and a move by Byrne back as chief executive of Wedgwood would be seen as a demotion.

Results for 1990 saw losses before taxes of IR£21.4 million compared to a pretax loss of IR£20.6 million in 1989. Management attributed IR£10 million of the loss directly to the strike. Sales for Waterford Wedgwood fell from IR£349.1 million to IR£307.9 million. Waterford divisional performance showed a substantial improvement for the crystal business. Crystal operating losses were reduced from IR£21.3 million in 1989 to IR£5.0 million in 1990, even though sales for the division fell from IR£111.8 million to IR£87.0 million (see Exhibit 13). In spite of this

EXHIBIT 17 | **Waterford Wedgwood, Organizational Chart, July 1991**

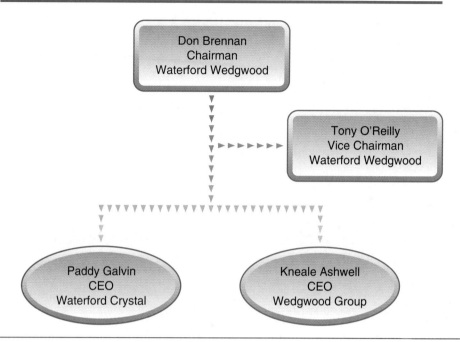

Source: Waterford Wedgwood, annual report, 1991.

improvement, share prices for Waterford Wedgwood continued to decline (see Exhibit 18).

EVENTS IN 1991

Problems for Waterford and its workers continued into 1991. The Gulf War, a weak U.S. dollar, the U.S. and U.K. economies both suffering through a recession, and reduced tourist activity, resulted in soft sales for the first half of the year. Sales for the first six months fell from IR£37.5 million in 1990 to IR£27.1 in 1991. Although the restructuring at the end of 1990 had created two autonomous divisions, financial reporting was still done on a consolidated basis. As a consequence, net results were still unclear because the proportion of debt attributable to each division was not reported. Exhibit 19 shows the company's consolidated profit and loss report for 1991, reflecting the restructured reporting system.

The low demand meant widespread short-time working conditions were put into effect for Waterford's 2,300 workers. Cutters were scheduled to be off for 18 weeks during 1991, blowers were scheduled for 14 weeks off. (Note: Allowing for holidays, craft workers averaged a net of 28 weeks of work in 1991. Cutters experienced more short-time working conditions than other workers.) Short-time work, combined with lost wages due to the strike in 1990, left the workers with severe financial problems of their own. Many were faced with repossession of their homes and crystal workers were now considered a bad credit risk.

In May, Howard Kilroy announced his retirement as chairman of Waterford Wedgwood. Kilroy cited the need to devote time to his new position as Governor (Chairman) of the Bank of Ireland as a crucial factor in his decision. Don Brennan, Morgan

EXHIBIT 18 | **Waterford Wedgwood, Share Price**

	Irish Exchange		London Exchange		U.S. NASDAQ (ADSs)* Exchange	
	High	Low	High	Low	High	Low
1980	35p	26p	NA	NA†	—	—‡
1981	29	21	NA	NA	—	—
1982	25	18	NA	NA	—	—
1983	32	16	NA	NA	—	—
1984	60	28	NA	NA	—	—
1985	86	40	NA	NA	—	—
1986	158	80	144p	69p	$22.12	$15.38
1987	151	58	136	53	22.00	9.88
1988	136	68	115	59	20.00	11.00
1989	104	42	85	42	14.88	7.12
1990	60	18	57	17	9.62	3.00
1991	41	20	37	20	7.00	3.38

*One American depository share (ADS) = 10 Waterford Wedgwood shares.
†NA = Not available.
‡Company shares were not traded on the New York (NASDAQ) exchange until 1986.
Source: Waterford Glass and Waterford Wedgwood, annual reports, 1980–91.

Stanley managing director, was appointed to replace Kilroy. Brennan's appointment signaled a strengthening of Morgan Stanley's control over its Waterford Wedgwood investment and a further lessening of local Irish control. Additional management changes included the appointment of Tony O'Reilly as vice-chairman of Waterford Wedgwood, and chairman of the Wedgwood division and Kneale Ashwell as CEO of the Wedgwood division (see Exhibit 17). Brennan's appointment was for two years, with O'Reilly assuming the position of chairman for two years beginning in May 1993.

In September, Waterford launched the new brand of crystal called "Marquis by Waterford Crystal." The Marquis crystal brand was priced lower than the traditional Waterford crystal. Marquis stemware was priced at $29–$39, compared with $50 or more for traditional Waterford stemware. It was lighter, more contemporary in design, less ornate in the cutting, and had its own branding and packaging. It was hand cut in factories in Germany, Yugoslavia, and Portugal. Marquis crystal had separate advertising and was marketed separately from the classic Waterford. It had its own logo, packaging, and in-store merchandising. Marquis crystal was shipped directly to distribution points. No Marquis line inventories were maintained at Waterford city facilities.

Paddy Galvin described the Marquis line as targeted at younger, more price-sensitive buyers at a lower entry point, giving them a stepping stone for purchasing the classic Waterford crystal at a later date. Initial consumer reaction was described as "encouraging." For competitive reasons, the company did not report annual sales of the Marquis line separately from its traditional lines of crystal.

As the recession continued and the demand for Waterford crystal remained low, there were reports in October that the U.S.-based directors were pressing to institute redundancies at the Waterford plants. (Exhibit 20 provides a description of the Water-

EXHIBIT 19 | **Waterford Wedgwood, Consolidated Profit and Loss Account** *(IR£ in millions)*

	1990	1991
Sales revenues		
Wedgwood group		
Wedgwood and Johnson Brothers	201.7	193.2
Waterford Crystal distribution	13.0	10.8
Non-group	16.5	15.1
Total Wedgwood group	231.2	219.1
Waterford Crystal	76.7	73.0
Total group sales	307.9	292.1
Less: cost of sales	(168.8)	(164.5)
Gross profit	139.1	127.6
Less: distribution costs	(80.0)	(76.2)
Less: administration costs	(47.9)	(42.9)
Plus: other operating income (loss)	(1.2)	.6
Operating profit (loss)	10.0	9.1
Wedgwood group		
Wedgwood and Johnson Brothers	17.9	12.8
Waterford Crystal distribution	(1.1)	(.8)
Non-group	(2.0)	(1.7)
Total Wedgwood group	14.8	10.3
Waterford Crystal	4.8	(1.2)
Total operating profit (loss)	10.0	9.1
Exceptional gains (costs)	(18.4)	(5.2)
Net interest paid	(13.0)	(6.5)
Profit (loss) before taxes	(21.4)	(2.6)
Taxes	(5.7)	(2.5)
Extraordinary items	(1.1)	—
Net profit/(loss)	(28.2)	(5.1)
Earnings (loss) per share	(4.29p)	(.73p)

Source: Waterford Glass and Waterford Wedgwood, annual report, 1991.

ford Wedgwood board of directors in June 1991.) While Galvin reported that "nothing has been finalized yet," rumors put the job losses at between 600 and 750 workers. One thing was clear, according to Galvin. If there were to be any redundancies, the financial terms would not be anywhere near those given in 1987.

EXHIBIT 20 | **Waterford Wedgwood, Board of Directors, April 1992**

Donald P. Brennan (chairman)*	Gerald P. Dempsey*	Sonia Land*
Anthony J. F. O'Reilly*	E. Patrick Galvin	Kevin C. McGoran*
Kneale H. Ashwell	Christopher J. S. Johnson	Robert H. Niehaus*
David I. Dand*	P. Redmond O'Donoghue	F. Alan Wedgwood*

*Descriptions of Nonexecutive Directors

Donald P. Brennan (nonexecutive chairman)
Appointed to the board on May 22, 1991.
Managing director of Morgan Stanley and Co., Inc. (head of Morgan Stanley merchant banking division, member of Morgan Stanley and Co. management committee, chairman of Morgan Stanley leveraged equity fund II, Inc.) and a director of Shuttleway Holdings, Inc., and other companies.

Anthony J. F. O'Reilly (deputy chairman)
Appointed to the Board on April 25, 1990.
Chairman and CEO of H.J. Heinz Company, chairman of Fitzwilton Public Limited Company, and a director of Shuttleway Holdings, Inc., and other companies.

David I. Dand
Appointed to the Board on July 5, 1985.
Chairman and CEO of Gilbey's of Ireland group.

Gerald P. Dempsey
Joined the Group on March 1, 1986.
Appointed nonexecutive chairman of the Waterford Crystal business in 1991. Director of Canada Life Assurance Co. (Ireland) Ltd., Gilbeys of Ireland Group Ltd., and other companies.

Sonia Land
Appointed to the Board on March 25, 1992.
Director and chief executive of Sheil Land Associates Limited. Director of Peach Publishing Limited, Marsh and Sheil Limited, and Merlion Publishing Limited.

Kevin C. McGoran
Appointed to the Board on April 25, 1990.
Deputy chairman and CEO of Fitzwilton Public Limited Company.

Robert H. Neihaus
Appointed to the Board on April 25, 1990.
A managing director of Morgan Stanley and Co., Inc., and a director of Shuttleway Holdings, Inc., and other companies.

F. Alan Wedgwood
Appointed to the Board on November 28, 1986.
Senior scientist at Harwell and a director of Wedgwood since 1966.

Source: Waterford Wedgwood, annual report, 1991.

STRATEGY, ETHICS, AND SOCIAL RESPONSIBILITY

BARRY DAVIS AND TEXACO CORP.

Arthur A. Thompson, Jr., The University of Alabama

In 1993 Barry Davis had the distinction of being Texaco's all-time high-volume independent retail gasoline dealer. Mr. Davis operated three Texaco service stations in the Salem, Oregon, area and in 1992 earned profits of nearly $470,000 at the three sites. The land for the stations was leased from Texaco. Not only did Mr. Davis's three stations pump enough gasoline to make him the biggest of Texaco's 1,122 independent dealers, his stations routinely outperformed stations owned and operated by Texaco. Mr. Davis had a folder full of thank you's and commendations from Texaco officials impressed by the exceptional sales performance his stations achieved.

In his conversations with Texaco managers over the years, Mr. Davis was frequently asked to explain his "secret" for how his three stations pumped such high volume. During a lunch with Texaco officials in 1992, Mr. Davis credited God for the unusual success of his stations: "I told them God takes care of me and mine. Everything I've asked for, I've gotten." In a different conversation with Texaco officials, Mr. Davis revealed that God had once appeared in one of his service station bays in the form of a green cloud, along with thunder and lighting. Mr. Davis, 50 years old, described himself as a "nondenominational Christian." He had eight children and lived in a hilltop house with a discreet wooden cross on the door.

In late 1992, Mr. Davis announced that God had told him to shut his three stations each week for the 24-hour biblical Sabbath—sunset Friday to sunset Saturday. The closings began on Friday, January 1, 1993. At sunset on Fridays, four-foot-high signs were posted in the windows at all three stations saying in Texaco red, "Closed for the Sabbath." The stations reopened after sunset on Saturdays. Even though the Friday evening to Saturday evening time frame was a period when many drivers stopped in for gasoline, Mr. Davis believed his stations would easily make up lost

---

This case is based on information reported by Bill Richards, "Can Texaco Win a Battle if the Lord Is on the Other Side?" *The Wall Street Journal,* February 24, 1993, pp. A1 and A8.

sales on the other six days. Mr. Davis thought that Texaco would understand his actions, saying, "Texaco is the most religious oil company in the nation. Bottom line, I win and God wins."

Texaco representatives immediately met with Mr. Davis to try to reverse his decision, pointing out that the Sabbath closings were a clear violation of provisions in his contract that specified a seven-day-a-week, 24-hour-a-day operation. Negotiations were unsuccessful. In February 1993, Texaco filed suit in federal court in Portland, Oregon, demanding that Mr. Davis comply fully with his contract with Texaco. In its filing Texaco said that while Mr. Davis had a right to his religious beliefs, the company had a right to expect compliance or else be free to terminate his contract. Texaco's court filing stated, "Defendant has repeatedly claimed he has direct communication with God about his closures." Texaco attorneys indicated the company had suggested alternatives to closing the stations during the Sabbath period, including donating any profits on sales during the period to a religious cause. According to the company's affidavit, "Mr. Davis said he asked God about that and God said it was unacceptable." Texaco attorneys further noted that January 1993 sales at Mr. Davis's stations were down 26 percent.

Federal Judge Helen Frye granted Texaco's request for a preliminary injunction, directing Mr. Davis to fulfill his contractual obligations and remain open all day, seven days a week. The judge agreed with Texaco's contention that the matter involved a contractual dispute and had nothing to do with religious freedom.

Mr. Davis, in his court filing, contended that Texaco's demands to remain open amounted to "involuntary servitude" for his religious beliefs. While the 1964 federal civil rights act protected employees against religious discrimination by employers, Mr. Davis was a contractor, not a Texaco employee. Mr. Davis's attorneys argued, however, that while the civil rights act might not apply to Texaco in this instance, Mr. Davis's religious freedom was violated by the judge's order to remain open against his religious beliefs. Pending appeal of the judge's order, Mr. Davis ignored the preliminary injunction to reopen on the Sabbath.

Texaco executives at the company's White Plains, New York, headquarters monitored the situation closely, concerned that the incident could snowball into something bigger. Texaco had already received letters from customers supporting Mr. Davis's stand. Michael Sherlock, executive director of the Oregon Gasoline Dealers Association, which represented independent operators of 1,800 service stations in the state, commented to a *Wall Street Journal* reporter that while Mr. Davis's pact with God was a bit unusual, "We have plenty of dealers who would like to close on Sundays because of their own religious beliefs." Representatives of the Seventh Day Adventist Church, with approximately one million members nationwide, had offered to assist Mr. Davis in defending against Texaco's lawsuit; attorneys for the church said two or three Adventists were denied or lost jobs each day because church doctrine didn't allow them to work on the Sabbath. Furthermore, relationships between major oil companies and their independent retail dealers had been growing increasingly uneasy for a decade as the number of company-owned outlets grew and the number of dealer-operated outlets fell.

Mr. Davis was taken aback by Texaco's reaction to his station closings. He had discussed God with Texaco representatives on numerous occasions. Davis said, "We're not talking an unknown quality here. For years I was a hero. Now suddenly they're treating me like the wacko from Waco."

FOOD LION AND "PRIMETIME LIVE"

Joseph Wolfe, University of Tulsa

On Thursday evening, November 5, 1992, Diane Sawyer of the ABC network's top-rated investigative program "PrimeTime Live" leveled her hazel-eyed gaze into the television cameras and announced,

> Tonight we have a story about what the consumer sees in the supermarket and what goes on behind the scenes . . . a "PrimeTime" investigation.
>
> Food Lion is the fastest-growing grocery chain in the nation, a remarkable success story in an industry where profit margins tend to be perilously low. But six months ago we started talking to current and former employees. Seventy agreed to go on the record, people from different states, who didn't know each other, yet [all] told us similar stories about sanitation and food handling in some departments in their stores.
>
> Before we begin, a word about the Food Lion employees that were filmed with hidden cameras. They're hard working people who care about their jobs. But what this report will show is the kind of thing that *can* happen when the pressure for profit is great and you break the rules.

Following the "PrimeTime" report shown that evening and also the next week, Food Lion was thrown into a maelstrom of negative publicity and market reactions. In Friday trading, the prices of Food Lion's two classes of common stock fell 10.8 percent and 13.8 percent, respectively, and were the NASDAQ's most active over-the-counter issues. Even before trading opened on Friday morning in New York, the price of Food Lion's parent corporation's stock fell 6.2 percent in very heavy trading on the Brussels stock exchange. As concerned investors bailed out of Food Lion's stock, newspapers and TV stations in cities and towns where Food Lion had stores carried follow-up stories on "PrimeTime Live's" report. Customer traffic in Food Lion's stores fell off significantly. In March 1993 Standard & Poor's placed up to

An earlier version of the case was presented at the November 1993 meeting of the North American Case Research Association. Copyright © 1994 by the case author.

$500 million of Food Lion's debt on its credit watch list and later that month Moody's Investors Service lowered the chain's senior long-term debt rating. In downgrading Food Lion's bond rating, Moody's cited the "PrimeTime" investigation's negative publicity, the company's falling sales and growth rates, and the fact that the swift recovery Moody's felt would occur after the expose "isn't happening and further pressures on earnings could occur."

To make matters worse, the televised expose came at a time when Food Lion was struggling to make a success of its expansion into Texas and Oklahoma. After opening 42 stores in the Dallas/Fort Worth area to disappointing sales in 1991, it was a week away from opening 7 new stores in the Tulsa, Oklahoma, area and trying to make major inroads against strong local and national supermarkets operating in Tulsa. Food Lion officials in both Tulsa and its Salisbury, North Carolina, headquarters tried to minimize the television program's long-term consequences but they admitted the publicity was causing concern. Two months before the "PrimeTime Live" report aired, when Food Lion learned the investigation was under way, it had filed a lawsuit against Capital Cities/ABC Inc. over the methods used in preparing its investigation and in April, 1993, the suit was amended to include a civil racketeering (RICO) action for damages amounting to at least $30 million.

In the months following the "PrimeTime Live" report, other problems at Food Lion started to surface. The chain's same-store sales had been falling at an increasing rate over recent years and it had made a number of low-growth, defensive expansions to ward off new competition in its home territories. Although Food Lion felt it was both unfairly targeted and blameless regarding the food handling and employment practices detailed in the expose, various industry observers believed the report merely highlighted the harsh realities of doing business in the supermarket industry and the exploitative practices the company had employed in its quest to expand the number of its stores and gain market penetration across a wider geographic area.

FOOD LION, INC.

Food Lion was started by Ralph Ketner, Brown Ketner, and Wilson Smith in 1957 as a one-store independent called Food Town. The cofounders, all former Winn-Dixie employees, struggled for the next 10 years to build a market base in their home state of North Carolina. A number of stores were opened and closed as the small 16-unit chain fought to win customers and create a successful merchandising format. It was only when Ralph Ketner came up with a strategy of everyday low prices that the chain began to prosper. Food Town went public in 1970. Four years later the Belgium grocery combine of Establissements Delhaize Freres et Cie (Delhaize Le Lion) purchased a controlling stock interest in the company, and shortly thereafter its representatives were elected to half the seats on Food Lion's board of directors. With Delhaize Le Lion's financial backing, rapid expansion ensued. The chain changed its name to Food Lion when in 1983 it expanded into a territory already having a number of stores called Food Town.

DELHAIZE LE LION GROUP

Delhaize Le Lion was Belgium's second largest retailing conglomerate. It was also Belgium's most internationally oriented company, with over 60 percent of its sales coming from outside the country—principally the United States. The company had adopted its overseas diversification strategy mainly because of Belgium's 1975 "loi de cadenas" or padlock law, which attempted to protect the country's small, independent retailers by limiting the domestic expansion of the country's larger retail chains. Speaking to a group of entrepreneurs in June, 1981, Delhaize Le Lion's Guy Beckers described his company's thinking at the time of the law's passage:

> The number of domestic supermarkets could not increase indefinitely and the rate of increase of the turnover of existing supermarkets would diminish some time or another. First, we took it for granted that manufacturing was not our job. We looked at the situation in a number of European countries. Everywhere the same constraints were evident—control by the state, pressure from the trade unions, and not many potential openings as far as sales points were concerned. This made us look toward the United States. We were looking for a region with a growing population and an expanding economy. We chose the Sun Belt, which fulfilled these requirements: (1) lower energy consumption—with air-conditioning there is no problem about heat affecting the quality of work; (2) unemployment—the South is better situated from this point of view than other regions of the United States; (3) the South is the best region for lower wage scales; (4) increase of population—the South comes at the top of the list; (5) the South is at the top of the list for capital investments for equipment and next to the top for nonresidential investments.

Within Belgium, Delhaize Le Lion operated over 100 of its own supermarkets and had 144 franchisees and affiliates, including 64 AD Delhaize supermarkets, 41 neighborhood Delhaize food stores, a number of traditional stores with whom it had long-term supply agreements, a chain of 51 Dial discount stores, and a chain of over 60 DI drug stores. Exhibit 1 summarizes Delhaize Le Lion's holdings and operations in both Western Europe and the United States.

Operating control of Food Lion was delegated to an American group headed by Tom E. Smith, the U.S. company's current CEO. His first affiliation with Food Lion came from working in the company's first store as a bagboy in 1958 when he was 17. After graduating from Catawba College in 1964 with an A.B. in business administration he worked for Del Monte Foods for six years and subsequently became Food Lion's only buyer. In his role as buyer, Smith developed the company's strategy of making mass purchases at discount prices and simplifying store operations by stocking fewer brands and sizes than the chain's competitors. He became the company's vice president for distribution in 1974 and its executive vice president in 1977. In 1981, at the age of 39, Smith was promoted to president of Food Lion and then assumed the added title of CEO in 1986. In 1992 his company-related compensation included dividends on his 1,534,089 shares of Food Lion stock and a base salary of $628,788 (a 20% raise from the previous year), plus a $272,955 performance bonus based on record 1991 earnings. In late December, 1991, the company's Class A and B common stocks were both trading in the $24 to $26 range.

FOOD LION'S OPERATING CHARACTERISTICS

Food Lion was a regional supermarket chain operating primarily in the Southeastern section of the United States; it had recently expanded north into Pennsylvania and westward into Louisiana, Texas, and Oklahoma. Average store size approximated 25,000 square feet; the company's older stores were concentrated in rural areas, many serving a trading area of fewer than 7,000 people. The simplicity and standardization of store operations had been a key factor in the company's success. Food Lion stores usually did not carry nongrocery items, shelved approximately 16,000 stock-

EXHIBIT 1 | **Delhaize Le Lion's Business Activities and Holdings**

Belgium Retail and Wholesale Operations

106 Delhaize Le Lion company-owned supermarkets

64 AD Delhaize franchised supermarkets

41 Delhaize neighborhood food stores

39 independent stores supplied through food distribution arrangements

51 Dial discount food stores

62 DI drug stores

4 warehouses operated by Delhaize Le Lion Coordination Center SA

Full or Partial Operating Control through Ownership Interests

Delimmo—a real estate company providing long-term leases to 14 of its supermarkets in Belgium. Owned by Delhaize Le Lion SA through a 99.9% stock interest.

Delned—a holding corporation 100% owned by Delimmo. Through Delned (BV Delhaize The Lion Nederland) Delimmo has a 50% interest in Shipp's Corner Shopping Center, Virginia Beach, Virginia, and the Debarry Center, Jacksonville, Florida.

Wambacq & Peeters—a transportation company delivering goods from Delhaize Le Lion's Belgium distribution centers; controlled by Delhaize through a 55% stock ownership.

Pingo Doce—a 31-store supermarket chain operating in the Portuguese cities of Lisbon and Porto of which Delimmo has a 38.8% stock interest.

Artip SA—an airline ticket reseller 33.14% owned by Delhaize Le Lion.

Deficom SA—an affiliate of the Defi holding company in the telecommunications industry of which Delhaize Le Lion has a 10% ownership interest.

Food Lion Inc. USA—controlled by Delhaize Le Lion's 50.3% ownership of Food Lion's Class A nonvoting shares and a 44.2% ownership of its Class B voting shares either directly or indirectly through its wholly owned American subsidiary Delhaize The Lion America Inc. USA.

Delhaize the Lion America—a wholly owned company of Delhaize Le Lion SA (Detla).

Super Discount Markets Inc.—a seven-superstore food chain operating in Atlanta, Georgia, under the name Cub Foods of which Delhaize The Lion America Inc. USA has 60% ownership.

Source: Summarized from "Retailer Profile No. 1: Delhaize Le Lion," *Marketing in Europe,* July 1990, pp. 95–99.

keeping units (SKUs), and were 20 to 35 percent smaller than the stores of such competitors as Winn-Dixie and Kroger. Because of their smaller size and simple shelf-and-display layouts, Food Lion stores were cheaper to build—about $650,000 each versus $1.5 million for the average supermarket. Exhibit 2 presents data on store operations.

Prior to the 1990s Food Lion had leased stores from local developers. In 1991 the company began assuming ownership of newly constructed stores. Tom Smith attributed the shift in its construction/ownership policy to "a credit crunch that has made it difficult, if not impossible, for developers to build Food Lion stores and lease them to us as they have done in the past." Food Lion had financed its Dallas/Fort Worth, Texas, stores with internally generated funds but had indicated it would continue to use debt to finance future store growth. In 1992 Food Lion spent approximately $200 million on new store construction and renovation of older units.

To economize on inbound shipping costs, Food Lion built its regional distribution centers adjacent to rail lines; it got about 25 percent of its goods by rail, a bigger percentage than most rival supermarket chains. In 1991 it opened three new 700,000-square-foot dry/refrigerated facilities, and through an additional expansion in 1992, its total amount of distribution center space amounted to 8.7 million square feet. In 1993 Food Lion operated distribution centers in 9 locations:

EXHIBIT 2 | **Food Lion Stores in Operation, 1988–92**

	1992	1991	1990	1989	1988
Number of stores	1,012	881	778	663	567
Total square footage (000)	26,428	22,480	19,424	16,326	13,695
Scanning stores	1,012	801	508	315	130

Source: 1991–92 annual reports, pp. 4–5, and press release, February 11, 1993, p. 3.

Salisbury, North Carolina

Dunn, North Carolina

Prince George County, Virginia

Elloree, South Carolina

Green Cove Springs, Florida

Plant City, Florida

Greencastle, Pennsylvania

Roanoke, Texas

Clinton, Tennessee

Food Lion carefully nurtured its reputation as a low-cost, efficient operation that passed cost savings on to its customers in the form of lower prices. Company lore had it that the firm's name was changed from Food Town to Food Lion because only two letters had to be replaced on store signs. All advertisements were prepared in-house, a practice that helped keep marketing costs to 0.5 percent of sales, compared to the industry's average of about 1.1 percent. Tom Smith appeared in about half of the company's advertisements extolling, "At Food Lion, when we save, you save." The strategy was to attract customers with everyday low prices rather than running costly weekly price-special advertisements in newspapers. As one competitor acknowledged, "They do a good job of promoting their everyday low-price image. They promise to deliver one thing—price—and they do, on groceries and frozens." He also added, however, "Their feature prices on produce are not that dramatic." When resetting or remodeling older stores, Food Lion placed an adhesive covering over its old shelves rather than installing new shelving, a practice that saved up to $10,000 a store. This method also sped up the renovation process by one week, saving an additional $4,000 per renovation. By 1992 Food Lion had installed scanning equipment at the checkout counters in all stores. Store visits by brokers and direct sales representatives were recorded on the store's computer to track whether each store was visited every four weeks as requested. To minimize "shrinkage" or theft, Food Lion was testing an electronic article surveillance (EAS) system in 25 of its stores. Food Lion's director of loss prevention, Clayton Edwards, commented,

> We tagged health and beauty aids, cigarettes, meat, and, where applicable, wine. After six months, our gross profits were up nearly 10 percent. The biggest change was in the attitude of store management. With EAS, they feel as if they finally have a way of fighting theft. It makes for a safer shopping environment. We found that once word gets out—and it gets out very quickly—that a particular store is using EAS, the bad apples or undesirables tend to go elsewhere. I think that supermarkets willing to invest in electronic tagging systems will definitely have a competitive advantage in years to come.

At the headquarters level, all buying was centralized and all stores were run in the same fashion, creating a tightly disciplined, consistent, centralized operation. Centralized buying had resulted in both lower procurement costs and food prices for the chain. One vendor said Food Lion has "the best buyers in the business. They will buy a year's worth of product if they can cut a deal and hold the price. Individual buyers have the authority to buy millions of dollars worth of a product with no second opinions needed. There is no buying committee. It's awesome." All stores were relatively small, layouts were almost identical, and store and district managers were told exactly what to do. According to one competitor, Food Lion's "store managers have a checklist of what they should do, and they had better follow it. There's only one way to do things. Managers may have some leeway in supporting local charities, but that's about it. You can go into a Food Lion store in Florida and find the same end displays and plano-grams as in a store in North Carolina." Because of low overhead costs and efficient store operations, a typical Food Lion unit could make a profit on weekly volumes as low as $100,000.

Food Lion had one of the industry's most liberal employee benefits packages. Its stock purchase plan was open to all full-time employees over 18 and all part-timers who had been employed for at least one year. Other benefits included a profit-sharing plan, vision care, and a comprehensive medical and dental plan. Despite the company's progressive benefits, some observers said Food Lion's overall management system encouraged loyalty but discouraged initiative. Many managers had reportedly quit the company after a few years "because they felt the company was cold and impersonal, and they had no real feeling of security there." Others claimed Food Lion saved money by dismissing workers before they were fully vested in the company's profit-sharing plan. One worker, assisted by the United Food and Commercial Workers Union (UFCW), which was engaged in a long-term struggle to organize Food Lion's workers, had filed a civil action suit against Food Lion alleging that the company did not provide dismissed workers with an extension of their health insurance coverage as required by federal law.

EXPANSION ACTIVITIES AND PLANS

During each of the past five years, Food Lion had added over 100 stores per year to its chain. The method Food Lion employed in entering the Jacksonville, Florida, market was typical of how it tried to achieve a foothold in new geographic areas. First the company blanketed the Jacksonville market with ads alerting shoppers "Food Lion is coming to town, and prices will be going down." Then, when its stores opened, Food Lion touted its low prices, often running price comparison ads. After operating in Jacksonville for one year, Food Lion's five stores had 2.4 percent of the market; by 1991 the company had added 32 more stores and had achieved a 14 percent share. The chain's entry into the market, however, did not go unchallenged. Months before Food Lion's new stores opened in Jacksonville, Winn-Dixie lowered its prices 5 percent across the board; by the time Food Lion opened its stores, food prices in the Jacksonville area were down almost 15 percent. Although Food Lion obtained a 14 percent market share, Winn-Dixie still led with a 28 percent share (down from about 38 percent) after Food Lion completed its Jacksonville expansion.

Given Winn-Dixie's experience with Food Lion, rival chains had begun to learn how to withstand the company's entry into their markets. When Food Lion came to the already crowded Dallas/Fort Worth area in December, 1990, many competitors quickly responded to news announcements of the company's planned entry. Because Food Lion did not emphasize service, many local grocers went to 24-hour operations, promoted home delivery, and added such services as FAX machines, Western Union money transfers, and money orders. Some stores emphasized the selection and variety of food offered, especially perishables and deli-bakery sections where Food Lion was felt to be at a competitive disadvantage. Most also lowered prices in one form or another—opting for everyday low pricing, advertising hot specials in weekly shopping guides, running 1-cent sales, or offering triple coupons. Nearly all market participants experienced rising advertising and in-store promotional costs. Some used end-of-aisle displays, banners, and flags to compare their stores' prices to Food Lion's; others advertised they would meet Food Lion's prices on comparable items; and many, such as Tom Thumb Food Stores and Kroger, ran advertisements twice a week rather than weekly. Kroger additionally guaranteed the lowest milk prices in town or triple the difference in cash.

The Organization of Economic Cooperation and Development (OECD), an international agency that promoted mutually beneficial trade practices among countries, began receiving formal complaints against Delhaize/Food Lion in 1985 for not employing fair marketing practices and for operating in ways that threatened the host country's standard of living. The OECD asked its trade union advisory committee to investigate and its summary findings were:

> Food Lion routinely opens a store in a town and launches a competitive war based on lower prices in order to take the market away from the already established supermarkets. The already established grocers are forced into closure or to lower their prices, which they can only do by lowering wages and benefits they pay in line with the level set by Food Lion.

After one year in the Dallas/Fort Worth market, and its attendant price war, Food Lion had garnered a 4 percent market share, less than half its 10 percent objective. Although Food Lion's management expressed initial pleasure with its results, a local real estate broker observed, "In 75 percent of their stores they are extremely pleased, but in 25 percent they are extremely unhappy. They are in some terrible locations." Many of the company's successes were in rural locations and less affluent neighborhoods with less sophisticated shoppers and weaker competition. Vince Watkins, Food Lion's operations vice president, had an explanation for the chain's relatively weak results in Texas. "The competition out there was much better organized in preparing for our entry than perhaps they had been in other areas." Additionally, because of Food Lion's obsession with standardization, its Texas stores ignored local food preferences and stocked popular eastern brands not normally found in the Southwest. Belatedly, Food Lion management relaxed its standardization policy and allowed its Dallas/Fort Worth stores to stock such regional favorites as ranch beans, various peppers, corn husks, plantain, and a select grade of beef popular with Texans.

Despite these results, Food Lion had designated its "primary expansion areas" for the 1990s as being Kansas, Louisiana, Oklahoma, Missouri, Arkansas, Mississippi, and Alabama. In 1993 Food Lion planned on opening about 110 new stores, primarily in Virginia, Maryland, West Virginia, and Texas. The general mobilizing cry of "2,000 stores by the year 2000" was a common theme throughout the chain. Exhibit 3 presents economic and population growth data for states where the company had existing and planned store locations. Exhibit 4 profiles rival supermarket chains in Food Lion's projected new markets and Exhibit 5 presents comparative financial and operating data for these same chains.

COMPANY CORPORATE RESPONSIBILITY AND COMMUNITY RELATIONS EFFORTS

Food Lion was proud of its recognition as a good corporate citizen. In 1986 the company received the Martin Luther King Award for its humanitarian efforts. Some of the actions that led to the award included Food Lion's donating trucks to aid southeastern farmers during the 1985 drought to transport hay from Indiana to save farm-

EXHIBIT 3 | **Population Statistics for States with Existing and Targeted Food Lion Stores**

Operations	1990 Per Capita Income	1991 Population (000)	1991 Population Rank	1980–90 Percent Growth	2000 Projected Population* (000)
Current states:					
Delaware	$20,039	680	46	12.1	802
Florida	18,586	13,277	4	32.7	16,315
Georgia	16,944	6,623	11	18.6	8,005
Kentucky	14,929	3,713	24	0.7	3,689
Maryland	21,864	4,860	19	13.4	5,608
North Carolina	16,203	6,737	10	12.7	7,717
Pennsylvania	18,672	11,961	5	0.1	12,069
South Carolina	15,099	3,560	25	11.7	3,962
Tennessee	15,978	4,953	18	6.2	5,424
Texas	16,769	17,349	3	19.4	17,828
Virginia	19,746	6,286	12	15.7	7,275
West Virginia	13,747	1,801	34	–8.0	1,651
Projected states:					
Alabama	$14,826	4,089	22	3.8	4,358
Arkansas	14,218	2,372	33	2.8	2,509
Kansas	17,986	2,495	32	4.8	2,534
Louisiana	14,391	4,252	21	0.3	4,141
Mississippi	12,735	2,592	31	2.1	2,772
Missouri	17,497	5,158	15	4.1	5,473
Oklahoma	15,444	3,175	28	4.0	2,924

*Series A migration assumptions employed.

Sources: *Statistical Abstract of the United States 1992* (Washington, DC: U.S. Department of Commerce, Economics, and Statistics Administration, Bureau of the Census, 1992), pp. 22–23; *Current Population Reports: Population Estimates and Projections*, series P-25 (Washington, DC: U.S. Department of Commerce, Social and Economic Statistics Administration, Bureau of the Census, 1989), p. 13; *Information Please Almanac 1992* (New York: Dan Golenpaul Associates, 1993), p. 52.

ers' cattle, providing equal-opportunity employment, and establishing express lanes for handicapped customers.

When dealing with controversy, the company had traditionally met the criticism head on. During one attack by Winn-Dixie in Jacksonville, Food Lion produced a television advertisement featuring Tom Smith in his office assuring consumers that "Winn-Dixie would have you believe that Food Lion's low prices are going to crumble and blow away. Let me assure you that as long as you keep shopping at Food Lion, our lower prices are to stay right where they belong—in Jacksonville." In 1984 Smith reacted quickly when a number of rumors in eastern Tennessee linked the Food Lion logotype to Satanic worship. Grand Ole Opry star Minnie Pearl was hired by the company to appear in local advertisements until the stories disappeared.

RECENT OPERATING RESULTS

Despite the fallout from the "PrimeTime Live" report, Food Lion stated that its general plans for expansion in 1993 were still in effect (see Exhibit 6). Tom Smith's objective was to double Food Lion's revenues by 1997, even though near-term sales and profit projections had been dampened by recent events—see Exhibits 7 and 8.

EXHIBIT 4 | **Profiles of Selected Actual and Potential Food Lion Competitors**

Albertson's Inc.—operates over 650 grocery stores in 19 western and southern states. Store formats include about 250 combination food/drugstores employing approximately 58,000 square feet of selling space per store, 250 superstores of about 42,000 square feet each, 118 27,000-square-ft. conventional supermarkets, and 32 warehouse stores. The company operates 9 full-line distribution centers, which handle about 65% of the merchandise carried in its stores. In May, 1992, Albertson's acquired 74 Jewel Osco stores. Future sales growth is expected to come from store space expansions planned at about 10% a year and population increases found in its Florida and West Coast markets. The company competes through a strong private brand program, everyday low pricing, and superior service. Albertson's is 40% unionized.

Bruno's Inc.—operates more than 250 supermarkets in Alabama, Florida, Georgia, Mississippi, and Tennessee under the names Food World, Consumer Warehouse, Bruno's, Food Max, and Piggly Wiggly. Its stores average about 35,000 square feet each. In 1992 same-store sales fell 1% and it has been buffeted by high store opening costs and increased advertising expenditures caused by increased competition in some of its hotly contested markets. Bruno's plans to open 33 new units in 1993 and will be installing in-store computers to reduce inventory shrinkage and increase labor productivity.

Delchamps, Inc.—is affiliated with the Topco cooperative grocery purchasing organization. The chain operates 115 supermarkets along the Gulf coasts of Alabama, Florida, Louisiana, and Mississippi as well as 10 liquor stores in Florida. All stores are leased under long-term agreements and measure about 35,345 square feet each. Sales fell in 1992 due to food price deflation and competitive pressures. Delchamps responded to heavy local competition by doubling the value of coupons up to 60¢ and by making cash donations to schools equalling 1% of the cash receipts collected by the schools. The chain has begun to reduce its selling costs by cutting its nighttime store hours and obtaining greater labor productivity.

Giant Food—this is a highly integrated chain of 154 supermarkets concentrated in Washington, DC, Baltimore, and adjoining areas in Virginia and Maryland. It has its own warehouses and distribution network and a construction and maintenance company. Giant Food also produces its own privately labelled ice cream, baked goods, dairy products, soft drinks, and ice cubes. Same-store sales, which have averaged about $22.7 million per store, fell in 1992 but the chain's high degree of vertical integration adds about 1% to its overall margins.

The Kroger Co.—America's largest grocery chain with major market shares in the Midwest, South, and West. Kroger operates about 1,265 stores, of which 657 are combination food and drug units and 520 are superstores. The chain also operates over 940 convenience stores. Kroger acquired the Mini-Mart convenience store chain in 1987 and sold its free-standing drug stores in the same year. In October 1988 it accomplished a major restructuring. To foil a takeover bid at that time Kroger declared a special dividend, which left the company with much debt. Much of its current cashflow is now being used to retire that debt. Kroger processes food at 37 plants and offers over 4,000 privately labelled goods. The company is heavily unionized and has faced stiff competition in Houston, Cincinnati, Dayton, and Tennessee.

Weis Markets—has most of its 127 food outlets in southern Pennsylvania but also a few units in Maryland, Virginia, West Virginia, and New York. Other food retailers, including a number of low-price warehouse club chains, have moved into Weis's markets, forcing it to cut prices. Same-store sales and operating margins have fallen annually for the past few years. Weis owns about 55% of its sites, is debt free, and sells nationally branded merchandise plus 1,800 items under its trademarks Big Top, Carnival, and Weis Quality. The company also operates five Amity House Ice Cream Shoppes and the Weis Food Service institutional supply company.

Winn-Dixie Stores—this company is America's fifth largest grocery chain and the largest one in the Sunbelt. It operates about 1,200 supermarkets under the names Winn-Dixie and Marketplace. The chain is nonunionized and has its own distribution centers, processing and manufacturing plants, and a fleet of trucks. In 1990 Winn-Dixie began emphasizing everyday low prices in addition to its usual high service orientation. Store sizes average 31,400 square feet.

EXHIBIT 5 | **Comparative Statistics for Selected Food Lion Competitors, 1992**

	Albertson's	Bruno's	Delchamps	Giant Food	Kroger	Weis Markets	Winn-Dixie
Sales	$10,095.0	$2,618.2	$949.8	$3,550.0	$22,085.0	$1,320.0	$10,074.0
Gross margin	26.0%	22.2%	26.5%	31.5%	22.5%	27.7%	22.8%
Net profit margin	2.67%	2.34%	.60%	1.85%	.37%	5.90%	2.09%
Inventory turnover	13.0	11.2	10.0	16.0	15.0	14.5	10.9
Long-term debt	$ 575.0	$ 172.2	$ 42.4	$ 255.0	$ 4,250.0	$ 0.0	$ 90.3
Net worth	1,340.0	422.4	112.8	650.0	−2,749.0	692.0	952.2

Note: All data in millions of dollars except for margin percentages and inventory turns per year.
Sources: Value Line company surveys, November 20, 1992, pp. 1498, 1501, 1503–05, 1508, 1515–16.

EXHIBIT 6 | **Food Lion's Estimated New Store Expenditures, 1993**

Capital Item	Expenditure (000,000)
Construction	$ 60.0
Store equipment	85.0
Land costs and distribution center expansion	10.0
Total	$155.0

EXHIBIT 7 | **Food Lion's Same-Store Sales Volume Changes, 1989–92**

Year	Growth
1989	8.6%
1990	4.5
1991	2.7
1992	−0.4

EXHIBIT 8 | **Monthly Changes in Same-Store Sales at Food Lion, November 1992–March 1993**

Period	Decrease
November, 1992	9.5%
December, 1992	6.2
January, 1993	7.6
February, 1993	5.4
March, 1993	5.7

Source: Food Lion, Inc. 1992 annual report, p. 15.

The company's switch from leasing to owning newly opened stores had pushed long-term debt from 27 percent of capital to 35 percent in 1992, but Smith intended to start selling and leasing back new stores as soon as the real estate market rebounded. Exhibits 9 and 10 present the company's balance sheets and income statements for 1989–92 while Exhibit 11 presents comparative quarterly sales and profit results for comparable periods before and after the "PrimeTime Live" expose.

ABC's "PRIMETIME LIVE" EXPOSE

The food handling and sanitation practices at Food Lion were first brought to "Prime-Time Live's" attention by the Government Accountability Project, a group that provided support to company whistle-blowers. Subsequently, ABC producer Lynn Neufer-Litt began to gather materials for the expose by talking to 70 current and past Food Lion employees who had worked at 200 different company stores. To obtain independent confirmation of the various employee claims, several investigators, one of whom was Lynn Neufer-Litt, applied for jobs in over 20 different Food Lion stores. Two were hired and worked in 3 stores in two meat departments and a deli. Via both hidden-camera footage and employee interviews conducted by Diane Sawyer, viewers were provided a behind-the-scenes look at Food Lion's food handling methods, labeling practices, actions to protect profit margins, and the kinds of shortcuts employees used to cope with the company's time management system.

Food Freshness and Food-Handling Practices   Razor-thin profit margins and intense price competition made all supermarket chains conscious of ways to trim costs, avoid spoilage, and maintain shelf-life freshness. Since merchandise costs were about 79 percent of total expenses, any savings Food Lion could achieve in this area could prove to be of major importance. Food Lion's upper management went to great lengths to demonstrate frugality and come up with ways to squeeze out cost savings. Area managers and even vice presidents would sometimes get into trash barrels and dumpsters to retrieve discarded food, stating, "You're throwing away profits." Bryan Rogers, an ex–produce manager, told Diane Sawyer, "I've seen them *in* the dumpster, not just leaning over into it, climb *in* it, I mean be up in it," to get merchandise and have it recycled. "Just take a head of cauliflower, for instance, I mean to where it's just got tiny black spots all over the top of it, and they'd bring it back in and want you to take a, like a Brillo pad type of thing, and scrub it to get the little black stuff off and stick it in a tray and reduce it and try to get something for it."

A meat manager stated, "We try to sell everything we can to keep from throwing anything away." Another worker, shown on camera trimming off discolored portions of outdated pork, announced, "OK, these are conversions, they look just as good as fresh." Jean Bull, a meat wrapper who had worked in 12 different Food Lion stores over a 13-year period, said,

> I have seen my supervisor take chicken back out of the bone can, make us wash it, and put it back out, and it was rotten. It's just unreal what they'll do to save a dime. They take *that* pork that's already starting to get a slime to it, it gets what they call a halo to it, a kind of green tinge to it, and they take and put that into a grinder with sausage mixture, and they put it back out for anywhere from 7 to 10 days as fresh, homemade sausage. And it's rotten.

Another tale of trimming away spoilage to salvage questionable meat and of the pressures placed on employees to perform was told by Larry Worley, an ex-market

EXHIBIT 9 | **Food Lion Balance Sheets, 1989–92** *(in $ millions)*

	Fiscal Year Ending Nearest Saturday to December 31			
	1992	1991	1990	1989
Assets				
Current assets:				
Cash and cash equivalents	$ 105.1	$ 4.3	$ 10.4	$ 15.7
Receivables	96.0	97.1	77.0	72.9
Income tax receivable	2.2	0.0	0.0	0.0
Inventories	896.4	844.5	673.6	577.9
Prepaid expenses	15.5	36.5	6.7	4.7
Total current assets	1,115.2	982.5	767.7	671.2
Property at cost less depreciation and amortization	1,373.6	1,036.8	791.8	610.5
Total assets	$2,488.8	$2,019.3	$1,559.5	$1,281.7
Liabilities and Shareholders' Equity				
Current liabilities:				
Notes payable	$ 459.6	$ 122.5	$ 127.5	$ 131.7
Accounts payable, trade	324.1	343.2	290.1	237.0
Accrued expenses	196.8	184.0	148.9	104.3
Long-term debt—current	.6	1.1	3.4	12.8
Capital lease obligations—current	5.1	4.1	3.1	3.2
Income taxes payable	0.0	22.0	29.8	21.8
Total current liabilities	986.3	676.9	602.8	510.8
Long-term debt	248.1	247.2	97.9	99.9
Capital lease obligations	245.7	195.2	153.8	95.0
Deferred charges/income	51.4	67.4	36.3	37.4
Deferred compensation	1.7	1.7	0.0	0.0
Total liabilities	1,533.1	1,188.4	890.9	743.2
Shareholders' equity:				
Common stock net common	241.9	161.2	161.1	161.0
Capital surplus	.2	2.0	1.2	.7
Retained earnings	713.6	667.9	506.3	376.7
Total shareholders' equity	955.7	831.1	668.6	538.5
Total liabilities and shareholders' equity	$2,488.8	$2,019.3	$1,559.5	$1,281.7
Dividends paid	$ 53.8	$ 48.0	$ 43.0	$ 32.5

Sources: Company 10-K report; February 11, 1993, press release; company annual reports for 1991–92.

manager: "We'd have this pack of cheese, sliced American cheese, and rats would get up on top of that and just eat, eat like the whole corner off of it. You'd have to trim it up and put it back out. You *had* to because if we didn't make our gross profit we were out the door."

"PrimeTime Live" cited other instances of how Food Lion extended the shelf life of outdated products through repackaging or reformulation. Whole ham that was two weeks past the meat packer's "sell-by" date was sliced up, placed in trays, and put on sale as fresh meat. Another worker was observed unwrapping old ground beef and

E X H I B I T   10 | **Food Lion Statements of Income, 1989–92**   *(in \$ millions)*

	Fiscal Year Ending Nearest Saturday to December 31			
	1992	1991	1990	1989
Net sales	\$7,196.0	\$6,438.5	\$5,584.4	\$4,717.1
Cost of goods sold	5,760.0	5,103.0	4,447.2	3,772.5
Gross profit	1,436.4	1,335.5	1,137.2	944.6
Selling and administrative expenses	975.1	855.8	738.7	619.9
Interest expense	49.1	34.4	32.6	29.2
Depreciation and amortization	121.6	104.6	81.4	65.0
Income before taxes	290.6	340.7	284.5	230.5
Provision for income taxes	112.6	135.5	111.9	90.7
Net income	\$ 178.0	\$ 205.2	\$ 172.6	\$ 139.8

Source: Company 10-K report and February 11, 1993, press release.

E X H I B I T   11 | **Quarterly Sales and Income Results at Food Lion before and after the "PrimeTime Live" Report**   *(in \$ millions)*

Quarter	Sales	Net Income
4/1991	\$2,300.0	\$60.8
4/1992	2,020.0	27.3
1/1992	1,600.0	49.6
1/1993	1,660.0	21.9

Sources: "Food Lion's Payout Is Delayed Following Fallout of News Story,"*The Wall Street Journal,* February 3, 1993, p. B2; and "Firm Posts 56% Decrease in 1st-Quarter Earnings," *The Wall Street Journal*, April 8, 1993, p. C6.

mixing it with fresh ground beef. Bonnie Simpson, a five-year Food Lion veteran meat wrapper, told of the time outdated ham was soaked in bleach to remove its foul odor and then cut into small squares and sold as cubed pork; she also told of how fish was treated to preserve the appearance of freshness:

> Fish has a three-day shelf life, OK? After three days you're supposed to reduce it and sell it or throw it away. But we didn't do that. We soaked the fish in baking soda and then we'd squirt lemon juice on it, then put it back in the case and sell them for three more days. The fish would be so rotten it would crumble in your hand.

In an on-camera segment a manager in the meat department was shown working with some cellophane-wrapped packages of outdated chicken parts, telling workers, "Open them up and put a soaking pad, a couple of them in the tray. This way we can put three days' date on them." He then proceeded to spread barbecue sauce on the chicken parts and sent them to the gourmet section for sale at full price.

Diane Sawyer noted that despite these practices, no cases of food poisoning had been connected to Food Lion or any other grocery chain in North Carolina where these practices were observed. And Johanna Reese, an official of North Carolina's division of environmental health, said Food Lion had an "average to above-average record" regarding health inspections.

Time Management and Unsanitary Work Practices   To try to be as labor efficient as possible, Food Lion utilized a time-management system called "effective scheduling" that was developed by a consulting firm. Under this system all work had been timed and standards established dictating the work's pace. For example, a meat cutter was expected to cut one box of meat every 32 minutes and a meat wrapper was allotted one hour to unload and stock 50 boxes of product. Based on these standards, each store received from headquarters a schedule mandating the work each department should accomplish in 40 hours. Tom Smith was a supporter of controlling labor costs through this means: "We don't work our employees hard. We work them smart."

However, many Food Lion employees found it hard to complete the work in the allotted time and resorted to skipping work breaks and working illegally "off the clock" to complete their assigned workloads. Three workers interviewed by Diane Sawyer on camera said their weekly unpaid work amounted to 10 to 25 hours each week and the work pace was grueling. Mark Riggs, a former manager of two Food Lion stores, said on camera that he felt pressured by higher management to get performance from his employees: "I felt guilty, incredibly guilty, for the things I made people do. It was the biggest reason for me leaving [Food Lion]. I couldn't look at myself in the mirror at the end of the day. You had to push people, push people."

Some Food Lion employees were said to take shortcuts to save time and meet work-load expectations; these shortcuts sometimes resulted in unsanitary workplace conditions. In one meat department the ground beef grinder was not cleaned in either the morning or evening and the department's bandsaw blades and wheels were not disassembled at the end of the workday to eliminate spending time reassembling them the next morning. In these instances, meat residues were later deposited on newly ground meat the next day. In one on-camera scene, a deli clerk, casting a baleful eye around her work station's area, commented after the hidden camera showed dirty trays and baking tins and a meat cutter "ice skating" on a grease-covered floor:

> Well the floor and the meat slicer . . . God, comin' into a place and the glunk on the slicer is thick. The floor's got all kinds of crap all over it. I don't think it's real appealing for a deli.

Another expose segment pointed out shipping problems associated with Food Lion's advance-purchasing system that was used to obtain discounts from manufacturers. Although Food Lion's centralized advance-purchases and volume buying resulted in lower incoming product costs, occasional shipping delays or problems getting merchandise from distribution centers in a timely manner sometimes resulted in meat products arriving in stores near their "sell-by" dates. In one on-camera sequence the following dialogue transpired:

> **Meat manager:** You *know* that the lamb that you cut on Monday is not gonna run, is not gonna go through Wednesday. Because the damn stuff is old when it comes in.
>
> **"PrimeTime":** What do you mean it's old when it comes in?
>
> **Meat manager:** It's ——— lamb. I have been on their ass for three years to get some decent lamb, if they want to sell lamb.

FOOD LION'S RESPONSES

Prior to its broadcast, "PrimeTime Live" provided Food Lion with a report on its investigation and invited a company spokesperson to be an interview subject. Rather than appearing under "PrimeTime's" conditions, Food Lion immediately began running television advertisements. Tom Smith was shown strolling through a Food Lion store where he mentioned the company's "A" sanitation rating and the chain's pride in its cleanliness standards. On the morning of the telecast employees in Salisbury held a rally where pro-company petitions and letters were prepared; these expressions were later sent to congresspeople and Capital Cities/ABC Inc. In Tulsa, a newspaper story was published the same morning discussing the program's possible effect on Tulsa's new stores; in the story Vince Watkins was quoted as saying, "It is our understanding that this program will make some very serious and potentially devastating allegations about our company. These allegations will make excellent television but they will not be the truth."

The next day Food Lion distributed a media "fact sheet" outlining its position regarding food handling and employee scheduling practices. The company began visiting each store shown in the segment and interviewing the employees involved. The announcement promised to quickly accomplish the following:

1. Establish more stringent periodic testing of employees to ensure complete and clear understanding of all of Food Lion's policies and procedures.

2. Increase internal and external audits and internal inspections by management to ensure that these policies and procedures were rigorously implemented.

3. Continue to ensure that if there ever was any problem in any Food Lion store, anywhere, at any time, it would be fixed.

Other operating procedures were changed immediately. The company's previous meat handling policy had been to open the packages on their "sell-by" date to check for freshness. Any spoiled meat was to be discarded while still-fresh meat would be repackaged and sold at a discount. "So as not to create any further suspicions" about repackaging, Food Lion said price reductions would be taken while the meat remained in the case at which time it could be sold for only one day longer.

Although the chain expressed a belief that the furor would quickly subside, such was not the case. A Food Lion executive admitted, "Our stock price is down, but we expected that to happen and we expect it to go back up to its previous level. The reason Food Lion has been so successful is because our customers are happy with the job we're doing." In an effort to stem the company's sliding stock price, Tom Smith made a 50-minute conference call to Wall Street securities analysts in which he told them most of the program's sources lacked credibility and were union sympathizers. He also made a television commercial where he said, in part, "You've heard some shocking stories about Food Lion. We do have sound policies and procedures. However, occasionally a problem can exist." The headquarters' public relations staff sent 60,000 videotapes of Food Lion's responses to the broadcast out to each employee and urged them to show it to their families, friends, and local groups. It was also suggested that along with showing the tapes employees "might want to have a party with their friends and serve them food from Food Lion's delis."

During the ensuing weeks Food Lion launched a counteroffensive in the press and on television against what it considered unfair, careless, and dishonest reporting on the "PrimeTime Live" segment. As one Food Lion executive put it, "When unwarranted attacks are made on a company, you don't say, `We'll take our hit and move on.' You come back with the truth." Food Lion questioned whether allegedly out-of-date meat loaf shown on camera was actually nine days old since it would have become visibly black to the television cameras after only four days. Various products were displayed in one televised "PrimeTime Live" sequence, such as Colombo yogurt and Healthy Choice lunch meats, but these items had never been carried by Food Lion. Also, Beef America products were shown on the "PrimeTime Live" report, but it was Montford beef that had been shipped 6 to 7 weeks old in vacuum sealed packages. The time period on those products was well within the allotted 12 to 14 week freshness period. And in the very damaging barbecue-sauce segment, the chicken products changed from scene to scene.

Additionally, Food Lion management raised questions about the union's integrity, as well as the motivations of 3 of the program's interviewees. A total of 65 of the 70 people interviewed by "PrimeTime Live" were supplied by the UFCW and 6 of the 7 people identified in the story were involved in UFCW-initiated lawsuits against Food Lion. Joe Sultan, the former perishables manager, was reprimanded for poor conditions in his department and fired for requiring off-the-clock work from his people. Bryan Rogers, while denigrating the company's produce in the telecast, had shopped at a Food Lion the night of the "PrimeTime Live" program. Jean Bull, who talked about selling slime-covered pork, shopped with her family at Food Lion each week; she had been reprimanded for passing bad checks and had a lawsuit pending against Food Lion.

Numerous legal actions were also begun by Food Lion. The company filed a suit charging ABC with fraud because ABC's producers lied to Food Lion to get jobs at its stores. Through this lawsuit, Food Lion gained access to the program's unedited footage as well as the right to question the program's producer. A Food Lion official said, "Some of the things we are finding out from our depositions make it plain to us they engaged in extensive illegal acts and violated state and federal laws in doing so." As a result, Food Lion amended its original suit in April 1993 to include claims the network violated federal racketeering laws in conducting its expose, alleging that ABC employees engaged in racketeering, trespassing, illicit eavesdropping, and wire fraud; under provisions of the law, Food Lion asked that triple damages be assessed against ABC. ABC's response to this emendation noted that "Food Lion does not challenge the truth of the ABC report. It challenges only the undercover methods used by ABC. We believe Food Lion's charges of racketeering are outrageous. We believe this is a legally baseless complaint."

In another lawsuit filed February 12, 1993, against the UFCW, Food Lion alleged the union had waged a smear campaign in an attempt to unionize the company. In seeking actual and punitive damages, Food Lion charged the union with "abuse of process," use of "economic guerrilla tactics" to tarnish its image, and the filing of frivolous lawsuits to obtain proprietary information about company operations and finances.

Some observers questioned the wisdom of Food Lion's public relations strategy; a Fort Worth retailing consultant said, "From a public relations standpoint, they were their own worst enemy. I would have advised a massive mea culpa as opposed to the defensive posture that they're taking." Food Lion, however, believed it was pursuing the right strategy, citing General Motors' vindication and subsequent network retraction and apology following a flawed NBC "Dateline" report on safety hazards supposedly associated with one of GM's pickup truck models. A Food Lion official said that GM's experience "illustrates that TV tabloid-type programs will go to extraordinary lengths to concoct or stage events."

Although Food Lion had often relied on court actions to defend its business interests, on several occasions the company's practice had been subjected to federal investigation and judicial scrutiny. The company began meeting with the U.S. Labor Department in January 1993 to head off possible federal charges of child-labor and overtime violations; the Labor Department investigation resulted from a 183-person class action suit filed in September 1991 that asked for $388 million in back pay and damages. The suit was filed with the help of UFCW officials; none of the Food Lion workers on behalf of whom the suit was filed were members of the UFCW. Francis D. Carpenter, who claimed to have regularly worked 60- and 70-hour weeks during his seven years at Food Lion's Southern Pines, North Carolina, grocery store, said "It got to the point where I just couldn't take it anymore. My supervisor would always say 'Do what you have to do to get the job done, but don't let me catch you working off the clock.' I took that to mean 'Work off the clock, but don't get caught.'" In its suit the union concluded employees often worked up to 13 hours a week off the clock. Food Lion had already lost one decision of this nature when a North Carolina U.S. District Court judge ordered Food Lion to pay two former employees a total of $53,000 in overtime wages and damages.

Food Lion was also being investigated by the Labor Department regarding some 1,400 incidents of alleged violations of child-labor laws; 1,200 of the incidents involved teenagers working with or near potentially dangerous equipment; the case was one of the largest of its kind involving a single employer. Food Lion believed that about 90 percent of the incidents related to teenagers putting cardboard boxes into package balers that were turned off. A federal ban on teenagers doing that type of work had gone into effect just months prior to the suit's filing and the grocery industry as a whole was fighting the ban's breadth. To help achieve compliance with the new federal requirement, Food Lion had instituted a company policy that required teenage employees to sign statements acknowledging their awareness of the ban. They also wore a blue dot on their name tags identifying themselves as teenagers so that managers would not unknowingly ask underage employees to perform forbidden work. A Food Lion vice president said, "I don't think anybody violated it intentionally and I don't think anyone in management asked them to do it."

FOOD LION'S TULSA OPERATIONS

Over a short period Food Lion had opened seven stores in the Tulsa metropolitan area. This had virtually coincided with the "PrimeTime Live" report. The stores were built in the city's fastest-growing localities and each faced different combinations of competitors within a two-mile shopping radius. Exhibit 12 lists the major supermarkets operating in the Tulsa market; additional competition came from at least three warehouse clubs and 135 convenience stores.

EXHIBIT 12 | **Food Lion's Supermarket Competition in Tulsa**

Company	Stores
Albertson's	4
Bud's Food Stores	4
Consumer's IGA	2
Homeland	25
Payless Food Store	2
Price Mart	3
Price Rite Reasor's/Reasor's Foods	2
Super H Discount Foods	5
Warehouse Market	12

Food Lion's stores were open from 7:00 AM to 11:00 PM and they were clean, well lit, easily accessed, and utilitarian in their appearance. They were 28,000- to 32,000-square-foot stores and cost $1 to $2 million each to construct depending primarily on the real estate values associated with each unit. All were similarly configured. The company employed its usual low-price strategy which was announced through comparative advertising of the type shown in Exhibit 13. Well in advance of Food Lion's store openings, however, established competitors began cutting prices and featuring cents-off end displays and shelf specials. Several reinstituted double redemptions on

EXHIBIT 13 | **Content of Typical Food Lion Price Comparison Advertisement in Tulsa**

Comparison reveals:

Food Lion Prices Lower in Tulsa

Food Lion's extra low prices are lower everyday on the items families buy most. Below are just a few examples. These represent thousands of items you can buy for less at Food Lion every day of the week. Visit Food Lion today and discover how much you can save each week on your total food bill.

	Price Mart	Homeland	Food Lion
Libby's lite sliced peaches (16 oz.)	$ .89	$ 1.19	$ .79
Del Monte cut green beans (8 oz.)	.43	.53	.34
Del Monte creamed corn (8.75 oz.)	.43	.53	.34
Veg All (16 oz.)	.59	.59	.48
Del Monte green peas (8.5 oz.)	.43	.53	.30
Bush's baked beans (16 oz.)	.69	.69	.50
Van Camp's Beanee Weenees (7.75 oz.)	.74	.85	.55
Hunt's whole peeled tomatoes (14.5 oz.)	.73	.79	.48
Mahatma yello rice (5 oz.)	.41	.39	.33
Campbell's vegetable soup (10.5 oz.)	.64	.65	.55
Campbell's cream of chicken soup (10.75 oz.)	.69	.75	.64
Spam deviled spread (3 oz.)	.59	.65	.56
Underwood's deviled ham (4.5 oz.)	1.29	1.39	1.09
Libby's Vienna sausages (5 oz.)	.63	.75	.43
Bush's hot chili beans (16 oz.)	.49	.55	.38
Franco American spaghetti (14.75 oz.)	.65	.69	.50
Franco American Spaghetti O's w/meatballs (14.75 oz.)	1.13	1.16	.89
Chef Boyardee Beef-o-Getti (15 oz.)	1.13	1.16	.89
Chef Boyardee beef ravioli (15 oz.)	1.13	1.16	.79
Chef Boyardee micro. spaghetti w/meatballs (7.5 oz.)	.99	1.09	.79
Prego spaghetti sauce w/mushrooms (30 oz.)	1.89	2.27	1.69
Old El Paso taco dinner (12/9.75 oz.)	2.39	2.59	1.99
Kraft deluxe macaroni (14 oz.)	1.69	1.77	1.39
Crisco shortening (16 oz.)	1.28	1.39	1.23
Totals	$21.95	$24.11	$17.92

America's Fastest Growing Supermarket Chain
This price comparison was made December 17, 1992. Some prices may have changed since that time.

coupons, a practice that had been previously discontinued in the Tulsa market, and some guaranteed they would match Food Lion's prices on a product-by-product basis.

In addition to the competitive actions taken by other supermarkets, another challenge to Food Lion came immediately from the UFCW's Local 76. John Stone, the local's president, felt the "PrimeTime Live" expose's effect would be short-lived and would be effective for about three weeks. To keep its own message before the public, and to keep the controversy alive, Stone's UFCW local mailed "informational literature" to households in each Food Lion store's ZIP-code area and passed out leaflets at each store's parking lot entrance for a number of weeks. Postcard literature mailed to households during the week of December 3, 1992, was headlined "FOOD LION IS FOREIGN OWNED!" and stated, "Every dollar in profit goes overseas to Belgium!" The card said, "Food Lion cheats its employees to gain an illegal advantage over American businessmen who obey the law! Don't let a foreign company dump its garbage on American consumers! SHOP AMERICAN! DON'T SHOP AT FOOD LION!" The leaflets passed out at the entrances to store parking lots reiterated the "Buy American" theme and decried the company's abusive labor practices.

WHAT NOW?

Addressing shareholders at the company's 1993 annual meeting, Tom Smith acknowledged that problems surrounded its southwestern market expansion, of which Tulsa served only as an example:

> Operating results in this market have been less than originally expected and are significantly below the average for the company's stores in other markets. We will closely monitor and evaluate performance in this market in light of the company's performance objectives and will continue to do all things reasonably necessary to increase performance. However, at the present time, the company does not plan any significant additional growth in the Southwest and is studying alternative strategies for this market.

Asked what Smith's remarks meant, a Food Lion vice president scoffed at any idea of selling the southwestern stores or the 1.1-million-square-foot Roanoke, Texas, distribution center: "We intend to battle hard for market share out there."

Meanwhile the company disclosed in late April 1993 the filing of three shareholder suits against it. One suit alleged Food Lion's top executives conspired to inflate the market price of the company's securities. The second lawsuit maintained executives made misstatements or omissions in its company reports dating back to September 1991, and the third claimed the company's 1992 proxy statement was false and misleading when it failed to disclose the improper food-handling procedures reported by "PrimeTime Live." During 1993, Food Lion stock traded in the $5 to $8 range on the NASDAQ, far below the $25 to $30 price range that it had traded in during the months preceding the "PrimeTime Live" report.

E. & J. GALLO WINERY

Daniel C. Thurman, U.S. Air Force Academy
A. J. Strickland III, The University of Alabama

In the mid-1980s, alcohol consumption in the United States had been declining in virtually every category except low-priced wines. A number of producers in the wine industry did not believe they should be producing what they called skid-row wines (wines fortified with additional alcohol and sweetener and sold in screw-top, half-pint bottles). Richard Maher, president of Christian Brothers Winery in St. Helena, California, who once was with E. & J. Gallo Winery, said he didn't think Christian Brothers should market a product to people, including many alcoholics, who were down on their luck. "Fortified wines lack any socially redeeming values," he said.

Major producers of the low-end category of wines, called "dessert" or "fortified" (sweet wines with at least 14 percent alcohol), saw their customers otherwise. Robert Hunington, vice president of strategic planning at Canandaigua (a national wine producer whose product, Wild Irish Rose, was the number one low-end wine), said 60 percent to 75 percent of its "pure grape" Wild Irish Rose was sold in primarily black, inner-city markets. Hunington described Wild Irish Rose's customer in this $500 million market as "not supersophisticated," lower-middle class, low-income blue-collar workers, and mostly men. However, Canandaigua also estimated the annual national market for dessert category wine to be 55 million gallons; low-end brands accounted for 43 million gallons, with as much as 50 percent sold in pints (typically the purchase choice of alcoholics with a dependency on wine). Daniel Solomon, a Gallo spokesperson, said Gallo's Thunderbird had lost its former popularity in the black and skid-row areas and was consumed mainly by retired and older people who didn't like the taste of hard distilled products or beer.[1]

Tony Mayes, area sales representative for Montgomery Beverage Company, Montgomery, Alabama, said one-third of the total revenue from wine sales in the state of Alabama was from the sale of one wine product—Gallo's Thunderbird. Sales

---

[1] Alix M. Freedman, "Misery Market—Winos & Thunderbird Are a Subject Gallo Doesn't Like to Discuss," *The Wall Street Journal*, February 25, 1988, pp. 1, 18.

crossed all demographic lines. According to Mayes, a consumer developed a taste for wine through an education process that usually began with the purchase of sweet wines from the dessert category. He attributed the high sales of Thunderbird to the fact that the typical wine drinker in Alabama was generally not the sophisticated wine drinker found in California or New York.

COMPANY HISTORY AND BACKGROUND

The E. & J. Gallo Winery, America's biggest winery, was founded by Ernest and Julio Gallo in 1933. More than 55 years later, the Gallo Winery was still a privately owned and family-operated corporation actively managed by the two brothers. The Gallo family had been dedicated to both building their brands and the California wine industry.

The Gallos started in the wine business working during their spare time in the vineyard for their father, Joseph Gallo. Joseph Gallo, an immigrant from the Piedmont region in northwest Italy, was a small-time grape grower and shipper. He survived Prohibition because the government permitted wine for medicinal and religious purposes, but his company almost went under during the Depression. During the spring of 1933, Joseph Gallo killed his wife and chased Ernest and Julio with a shotgun. He killed himself following their escape. Prohibition ended that same year, and the Gallos, both in their early 20s and neither knowing how to make wine, decided to switch from growing grapes to making wine. With $5,900 to their names, Ernest and Julio found two thin pamphlets on wine-making in the Modesto Public Library and began making wine.[2]

The Gallos had always been interested in quality and began researching varietal grapes in 1946. They planted more than 400 varieties in experimental vineyards during the 1950s and 1960s, testing each variety in the different growing regions of California for its ability to produce fine table wines. Their greatest difficulty was to persuade growers to convert from common grape varieties to the delicate, thin-skinned varietals because it took at least four years for a vine to begin bearing and perhaps two more years to develop typical, varietal characteristics. As an incentive, in 1967, Gallo offered long-term contracts to growers, guaranteeing the prices for their grapes every year, provided they met Gallo quality standards. With a guaranteed long-term "home" for their crops, growers could borrow the needed capital to finance the costly replanting, and the winery was assured a long-term supply of fine wine grapes. In 1965, Julio established a grower relations staff of skilled viticulturists to aid contract growers. This staff counseled growers on the latest viticultural techniques.[3]

Private ownership and mass-production were the major competitive advantages contributing to Gallo's success. Gallo could get market share from paper-thin margins and absorb occasional losses that stockholders of publicly held companies would not tolerate. Gallo was vertically integrated, and wine was its only business. While Gallo bought about 95 percent of its grapes, it virtually controlled its 1,500 growers through long-term contracts. Gallo's 200 trucks and 500 trailers constantly hauled wine out of Modesto and raw materials in. Gallo was the only winery to make its own bottles (two million a day) and screw-top caps. Also, while most of the com-

---

[2] Jaclyn Fierman, "How Gallo Crushes the Competition," *Fortune,* September 1, 1986, pp. 24–31.
[3] "The Wine Cellars of Ernest & Julio Gallo, a Brief History," a pamphlet produced by Ernest & Julio Gallo, Modesto, Calif.

petition concentrated on production, Gallo participated in every aspect of selling its product. Julio was president and oversaw production, while Ernest was chairman and ruled over marketing, sales, and distribution. Gallo owned its distributors in about a dozen markets and probably would have bought many of the more than 300 independents handling its wines if laws in most states had not prohibited it.

Gallo's major competitive weakness over the years had been an image associated with screw tops and bottles in paper bags that developed because of its low-end dessert wine, Thunderbird.[4] There were stories, which Gallo denied, that Gallo got the idea for citrus-flavored Thunderbird from reports that liquor stores in Oakland, California, were catering to the tastes of certain customers by attaching packages of lemon Kool-Aid to bottles of white wine to be mixed at home.[5]

Thunderbird became Gallo's first phenomenal success. It was a high-alcohol, lemon-flavored beverage introduced in the late 1950s. A radio jingle sent Thunderbird sales to the top of the charts on skid rows across the country. "What's the word? Thunderbird. How's it sold? Good and cold. What's the jive? Bird's alive. What's the price? Thirty twice." Thunderbird had remained a brand leader in its category ever since. In 1986, Gallo spent $40 million on advertising aimed at changing its image to one associated with quality wines.

Information on Gallo's finances was not publicly available, and the brothers maintained a tight lid on financial details. In a 1986 article, *Fortune* estimated that Gallo earned at least $50 million a year on sales of $1 billion. By comparison, the second leading winery, Seagram's (also the nation's largest distillery), had approximately $350 million in 1985 wine revenues and lost money on its best-selling table wines. *Fortune* stated that several of the other major Gallo competitors made money, but not much.[6]

Gallo produced the top-selling red and white table wines in the country. Its Blush Chablis became the best-selling blush-style wine within the first year of its national introduction. Gallo's award-winning varietal wines were among the top sellers in their classifications. The company's Carlo Rossi brand outsold all other popular-priced wines. Gallo's André Champagne was by far the country's best-selling champagne, and E & J Brandy had outsold the number two and three brands combined. Gallo's Bartles & Jaymes brand was one of the leaders in the wine cooler market.[7]

THE U.S. WINE INDUSTRY

Wine sales in the United States grew from about 72 million gallons in 1940 to nearly 600 million gallons by 1986, accounting for retail sales in excess of $9 billion (see Exhibit 1). This retail sales volume had exceeded such major established grocery categories as detergents, pet foods, paper products, and canned vegetables. While wine consumption had grown at an astonishing rate, trends toward moderation and alcohol-free life-styles made this growth rate impossible to maintain. Nevertheless, annual growth was projected to be 3.2 percent through 1995.

Per-capita consumption of wine was low in the late 1950s and early 1960s because wine drinking was perceived as either the domain of the very wealthy or the extreme

---

[4]Jaclyn Fierman, "How Gallo Crushes the Competition."
[5]Alix M. Freedman, "Misery Market."
[6]Jaclyn Fierman, "How Gallo Crushes the Competition."
[7]"Gallo Sales Development Program," a pamphlet produced by Ernest & Julio Gallo, Modesto, Calif.

opposite. "Fortified" dessert wines were the top-selling wines of the period. The first surge in consumption in the late 1960s was the result of the introduction of "pop" wines, such as Boones Farm, Cold Duck, and Sangrias. These wines were bought by baby boomers, who were now young adults. Their palates were unaccustomed to wine drinking and these wines were suited to them. By the mid-1970s, the pop wine drinkers were ready to move up to Lambruscos and white wine "cocktails," and per-capita consumption increased (see Exhibit 2). The wine spritzer became the trend, still the alternative to more serious wines for immature palates. Just as this surge

EXHIBIT 1 | The National Wine Market, 1977–86

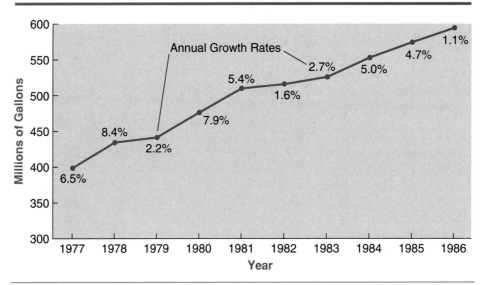

Source: *National Beverage Marketing Directory,* 10th ed., 1988.

EXHIBIT 2 | Per-Capita Consumption of Wine in the United States

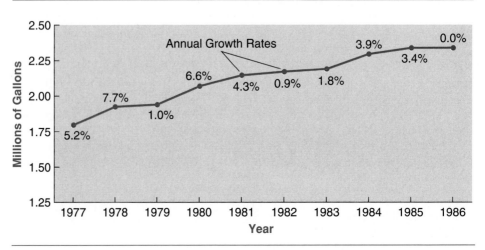

Source: *National Beverage Marketing Directory,* 10th ed., 1988.

began to wane, wine coolers were introduced in 1982 and exploded on the market in 1983. Wine coolers were responsible for a 5 percent market surge in 1984 and experienced four consecutive years of very high growth rates, rising 6 percent in 1987 to 72.6 million nine-liter cases.

The imported wines category enjoyed an upward growth rate from 6.6 percent of the market in 1960 to a high of 27.6 percent in 1985 (see Exhibits 3 and 4). The category lost market share to 23.1 percent in 1986 primarily because of the shift from Lambruscos to wine coolers. Additional factors were the weakening dollar and an overall improved reputation for domestic wines.

There were about 1,300 wineries in the United States. *Fortune* identified the major market-share holders in the U.S. market in a September 1986 article. It showed Gallo as the clear leader, nearly outdistancing the next five competitors combined (see Exhibit 5).

A number of threats had faced the wine industry, not the least of which had been the national obsession with fitness and the crackdown on drunk driving. Americans drank 6.5 percent less table wine in 1985 than in 1983 (see Exhibits 6 and 7), and consumption was projected to be down another 5 percent in 1986. The industry answer to this problem had been the introduction of wine coolers—Gallo's Bartles

E X H I B I T 3 | **Wine Production by Place of Origin** *(Millions of nine-liter cases)*

Origin	1970	1975	1980	1985	1986	Average Annual Compound Growth Rate			Percent Change 1985–86
						1970–75	1975–80	1980–85	
California	82	115	139.5	133.2	133.3	7.0%	3.9%	−0.9%	0.1%
Other states*	18	19	18.7	16.9	17.3	1.4	−0.3	−2.0	2.4
United States	100	134	158.2	150.1	150.6	6.1	3.3	−1.0	0.3
Imports	13	21	43.1	57.2	45.3	10.5	15.8	5.8	−20.8
Total†	113	155	201.3	207.3	195.9	6.6%	5.4%	0.6%	−5.5%

*Includes bulk table wine shipped from California and blended with other state wines.
†Addition of columns may not agree because of rounding.
Source: *Impact* 17, no. 11 (June 1, 1987), p. 4.

E X H I B I T 4 | **Market Share Trends in Wine Production**

Place Produced	1970	1975	1980	1985	1986	Share Point Change		
						1970–80*	1980–85	1985–86
California	73%	74%	69.3%	64.2%	68.0%	3.7	−5.0	3.8
Other states	15	12	9.3	8.2	8.9	−6.7	1.1	0.7
United States	88	86	78.6	72.4	76.9	−9.4	6.2	4.5
Imports	12	14	21.4	27.6	23.1	9.4	−6.2	−4.5
Total	100%	100%	100.0%	100.0%	100.0%	—	—	—

*1980 based on unrounded data.
Source: *Impact* 17, no. 11 (June 11, 1987), p. 4.

EXHIBIT 5 | **1985 Share of U.S. Wine Market**

Company	Percent
E. & J. Gallo Winery	26.1%
Seagram & Sons	8.3
Canandaigua Wine	5.4
Brown-Forman	5.1
National Distillers	4.0
Heublein	3.7
Imports	23.4
All others	24.0
Total	100.0%

Source: Jaclyn Fierman, "How Gallo Crushes the Competition," *Fortune,*

EXHIBIT 6 | **Shipments of Wine Entering U.S. Trade Channels by Type** *(Millions of nine-liter cases)*

Type	1970	1975	1980	1984	1985	1986	Average Annual Compound Growth Rate			Percent Change*
							1970–75	1975–80	1980–85	1985–86
Table	55.9	88.9	150.8	170.9	159.2	147.1	9.9%	11.2%	1.1%	−7.4%
Dessert	31.1	28.2	19.1	15.5	14.3	14.7	−2.0	−7.5	−5.7	3.2
Vermouth	4.2	4.2	3.7	3.0	2.9	2.7	—	−2.5	−4.8	−6.9
Sparkling	9.3	8.4	12.7	19.7	19.4	18.7	−1.9	8.6	8.6	−4.5
Special natural	11.8	24.0	13.6	10.9	10.7	10.9	15.3	−10.7	−4.7	1.9
Imported specialty[†]	0.3	1.0	1.5	1.0	0.9	1.8	25.4	8.1	−9.7	104.7
Total[‡]	112.6	154.7	201.3	221.0	207.3	195.9	6.6%	5.4%	0.6%	−5.5%

*Based on unrounded data.
[†]Imported fruit wines and wine specialties (includes sangria and fruit-flavored wines).
[‡]Addition of columns may not agree because of rounding.
Source: *Impact* 17, no. 11 (June 11, 1987), p. 3.

EXHIBIT 7 | **Shares of Market Trends in Shipments of Wine Entering U.S. Trade Channels by Tpye**

Type	1970	1975	1980	1984	1985	1986	Share Point Change		
							1970–80*	1980–85	1985–86
Table	50%	57%	74.9%	77.2%	76.8%	75.1%	25	1.9	−1.7
Dessert	28	18	9.5	7.0	6.9	7.5	−18	−2.6	0.6
Vermouth	4	3	1.8	1.4	1.4	1.4	−2	−0.4	[†]
Sparkling	8	5	6.3	9.0	9.4	9.5	−2	3.0	0.2
Special natural	10	16	6.8	5.0	5.2	5.6	−3	−1.6	0.4
Imported specialty	[‡]	1	0.7	0.5	0.4	0.9	+	−0.3	0.5
Total[†]	100%	100%	100.0%	100.0%	100.0%	100.0%	—	—	—

*1980 based on unrounded data.
[†]Addition of columns may not agree because of rounding.
[‡]Less than 0.05%.
Source: *Impact* 17, no. 11 (June 11, 1987), p. 3.

and Jaymes coolers were number one until they lost the lead by only a slight margin to a Seagram's brand in 1987.

Another trend had been a shift toward a demand for quality premium wines made from the finest grapes. Premium wines increased market share from 8 percent in 1980 to 20 percent in 1986. Again, Gallo had sold more premium wine than any other producer, but Gallo's growth had been limited by its lack of snob appeal.[8]

Although more than 80 percent of the U.S. adult population enjoyed wine occasionally, Gallo's research indicated that by global standards most Americans were still infrequent wine drinkers. Only about one in four Americans drank wine as often as once a week. Per-capita consumption in the United States was less than 2.5 gallons per year, compared to about 20 gallons in some Western European countries.[9]

Though the health consciousness and alcohol awareness of the 1980s had a moderating influence on wine growth patterns as consumers traded up in quality and drank less, long-term growth was expected to be steady but slower than that of the 1970s and early 1980s. Exhibit 8 provides drinking patterns for 1986. Personal disposable income was expected to grow in the United States through 1995, busy lifestyles to contribute to more dining out, and sale of wine in restaurants to increase. As the aging baby boomers grew in number and importance, their wine purchases were expected to increase. All these factors contributed to the projected average yearly increase in growth rate of 3.2 percent through 1995.[10]

THE DESSERT WINE INDUSTRY

Dessert wine represented a 55-million-gallon, $500-million-a-year industry. As mentioned earlier, the dessert wine category, also called fortified wines, included wines that contained more than 14 percent alcohol, usually 18 to 21 percent. They were called fortified because they usually contained added alcohol and additional sugar or sweetener. This category included a group of low-end-priced brands that had been the brunt of significant controversy. Canandaigua's Wild Irish Rose had been the leading seller in this category, with Gallo's Thunderbird claiming second place, followed by Mogen David Wine's MD 20/20.[11]

Dessert wines had shown a decreasing trend both in amount of wine consumed and in market share from 1970 through 1985. However, the trend changed in 1986 when dessert wine's market share rose six-tenths of a share point to 7.5 percent of the total wine market (see Exhibit 7). The rise was attributed in large measure to the 19 percent federal excise tax increase on distilled spirits. An additional factor in the increase in the dessert wine category was the shift to fruit-flavored drinks, which also affected the soft drink industry and wine coolers.[12]

A number of factors indicated that the growth trend would continue for the $500 million dessert wine category. The desire to consume beverages that contained less alcohol than distilled spirits and were less expensive than distilled spirits, the desire for fruit flavor, and the American trend toward eating out at restaurants more often contributed to the trend toward increased consumption of dessert wines. Additionally,

[8]Jaclyn Fierman, "How Gallo Crushes the Competition."

[9]"Gallo Sales Development Program."

[10]"Coolers Providing Stable Growth," *Beverage Industry Annual Manual*, 1987.

[11]Alix M. Freedman, "Misery Market."

[12]"U.S. News and Research for the Wine, Spirits, and Beer Executive," *Impact* 17, no. 11 (June 1, 1987); and *Impact* 17, no. 18 (September 15, 1987).

EXHIBIT 8 | **Beverage Consumption Patterns, 1986**

1986 National Beverage Consumption by Gender (percentage of volume)

Gender	Malt Beverages	Wine	Distilled Spirits	Coolers	Total Nonalcoholic Beverages	Total Beverages
Male	80.8%	51.6%	62.6%	44.9%	51.1%	52.7%
Female	19.2	48.4	37.4	55.1	48.9	47.3
Total	100.0%	100.0%	100.0%	100.0%	100.0%	100.0%

1986 National Alcoholic Beverage Consumption by Household Income (percentage of volume)

Household Income	Malt Beverages	Wine	Distilled Spirits	Coolers	Total Alcoholic Beverages
Under $15,000	26.1%	11.7%	19.7%	22.3%	26.5%
$15,000–$24,999	19.1	13.9	18.1	19.5	21.3
$25,000–$29,999	10.8	14.2	6.6	10.9	12.1
$30,000–$34,999	11.7	9.9	14.7	7.9	10.3
$35,000 and over	32.3	50.3	40.9	39.4	29.8
Total	100.0%	100.0%	100.0%	100.0%	100.0

1986 National Beverage Consumption by Time of Day (percentage of volume)

Time of Day	Malt Beverages	Wine	Distilled Spirits	Coolers	Total Nonalcoholic Beverages	Total Beverages
Breakfast/morning	2.7%	2.1%	4.6%	1.5%	32.7%	30.6%
Lunch	6.8	5.8	4.2	4.4	20.8	19.8
Snack	27.5	19.0	31.9	27.0	10.9	12.0
Dinner	14.2	45.8	15.5	13.7	22.9	22.6
Evening	48.8	27.3	43.8	53.4	12.7	15.0
Total	100.0%	100.0%	100.0%	100.0%	100.0%	100.0%

1986 National Beverage Consumption by Location of Consumption (percentage of volume)

Location	Malt Beverages	Wine	Distilled Spirits	Coolers	Total Nonalcoholic Beverages	Total Beverages
Total home	64.6%	75.8%	61.4%	76.9%	76.1%	75.5%
Total away from home	35.4	24.2	38.6	23.1	23.9	24.5

Source: *Impact* 17, no. 18 (September 15, 1987), pp. 3–4.

the dessert wine category had survived relatively well with virtually no promotion or advertising. This had been possible because, of the category's 55 million gallons, low-end brands accounted for 43 million gallons, approximately 50 percent of which was sold in half pints; and this market had not been accessible by traditional advertising or promotion.

The dessert wine category had been a profitable venture because many of the wines in this category were made with less expensive ingredients, packaged in less expensive containers, and had usually been sold without promotion. Canandaigua estimated that profit margins in this category were as much as 10 percent higher than those of ordinary table wines. Gallo said this was not true for its products, but it would not reveal the figures.

The low-end dessert wines were a solid business. *The Wall Street Journal* reported that, of all the wine brands sold in America, Wild Irish Rose was the number 6 best seller, Thunderbird was 10th, and MD 20/20 was 16th. In contrast to the growth expectations of other brands and categories, sales of these low-end brands were expected to be up almost 10 percent. Yet the producers of these top-selling wines distanced themselves from their products by leaving their corporate names off the labels, obscuring any link to their products. Paul Gillette, publisher of the *Wine Investor,* was quoted in a discussion of this unsavory market as saying: "Makers of skid-row wines are the dope pushers of the wine industry."[13]

[13] Alix Freedman, "Misery Market."

THE STRIDE RITE CORPORATION

Arthur A. Thompson, Jr., University of Alabama

Stride Rite Corp., the maker of Keds, Sperry Top-Siders, and Stride Rite children's shoes, has a sterling reputation for being a socially responsible employer and a good corporate citizen. In 1971, years before family issues began to be considered in major U.S. companies, Stride Rite established the first corporate day care center in the United States. Stride Rite opened the center primarily for the children living near Stride Rite's distribution center and corporate offices in Boston's Roxbury neighborhood. The day care center was located in an old factory building where Stride Rite, until a few years earlier, had made all of its children's shoes. Arnold Hiatt, Stride Rite's president and chairman from 1968 until 1992, explained why the center was started:[1]

> The neighborhood was falling apart around us. Businesses were pulling out, housing was in disrepair, crime and violence were more and more common. And every time I looked out my window, I saw lots of small children with nothing to do and no place to go.
>
> It didn't take a great deal of imagination to make the connections. We were in the children's shoe business. We were in a decaying neighborhood surrounded by children in need. We had resources available in the form of empty manufacturing space.

Employees were surprised by the company's action to open a day care center. Initially, almost all the children enrolled in the center were black. Over time, as employees saw that the center's programs were effective, more workers started to enroll their children. Eventually, Stride Rite decided to establish an enrollment policy of 50 percent community children and 50 percent employees' children.

In the years that followed, Stride Rite undertook many other socially progressive initiatives:

---

[1] As quoted in Nan Stone, "Building Corporate Character: An Interview with Stride Rite Chairman Arnold Hiatt," *Harvard Business Review,* March–April 1992, p. 96.

- Instituting a board-approved policy of allocating a percentage of the company's pretax profits to support its social and community programs. Initially pegged at 1 percent, the percentage was gradually increased; in 1991 Stride Rite's board approved an allocation of 5 percent, equal to $4.5 million in 1991 and over $5 million in 1992.
- Starting a family leave policy where either mothers or fathers could take time off to care for a newborn child.
- Opening an intergenerational day care center that brought both children and the elderly together in a common environment.
- Beginning a program that permitted Stride Rite employees to volunteer two hours a week to work one-on-one with disadvantaged children and teenagers in two Cambridge, Massachusetts, public schools; the program provided personal attention, academic support, and career awareness.
- Starting a Stride Rite Scholars Program at Harvard University and Northeastern University to help inner-city students get a college education. In return for $5,000 per year scholarships, recipients served as mentors to other inner-city youths, helping them with schoolwork and spending summers in housing projects. After graduation, the scholarship recipients could continue their public service for a year under a $15,000 fellowship.
- Donating 100,000 pairs of sneakers to poverty-stricken residents of Mozambique.
- Paying Harvard graduate students to work in a Cambodian refugee camp.
- Establishing a smoke-free work environment.
- Becoming the sole corporate sponsor of "Long Ago and Far Away," a highly acclaimed public television series that introduced children to the joys and wonders found through reading.

In 1992, *Working Mother* magazine named Stride Rite one of its Top 100 Companies committed to programs that benefit both mothers and children; it was Stride Rite's fifth year in a row to win the award. Also in 1992 Stride Rite joined 54 other companies to form Businesses for Social Responsibility. Stride Rite had won admirers among many critics of U.S. businesses. A founder of Action for Children's Television, which lobbied for better TV programming for children, said Stride Rite was "a case study of giving something back to the community." Since 1990, Stride Rite had received 14 public service awards, including ones from the National Women's Political Caucus, the Northeast Human Resources Association, and Harvard University, which praised Stride Rite for "improving the quality of life" in Cambridge and the nation.

COMPANY BACKGROUND

Stride Rite shipped its first children's shoes to retailers in 1919. The company's commitment was "to produce an honest quality product in an honest way and deliver it as promised." The company built its reputation in baby shoes and children's shoes; its classically designed, well-made shoes soon became a brand trusted by quality-conscious mothers. Stride Rite had been considered a leader in the children's shoe segment of the U.S. footwear industry since the 1930s. The company never wavered from its commitment to "manufacturing and marketing the best footwear for healthy growing feet." Stride Rite's philosophy was "to offer the best possible quality at the lowest possible price." The company's character and business practices reflected traditional, conservative values: classic designs, good taste, simplicity, comfort, quality, durability, fit, and affordability. The company did not see itself as being in the fashion business and it evidenced no interest in setting trends in contemporary shoe styles. Stride Rite deliberately avoided faddish designs and styling on the theory that it was not smart enough to know what the next fad was going to be.[2]

For many years, Stride Rite sold its shoes exclusively through "Main Street" family shoe stores and leading urban department stores. The company worked closely with its dealers to ensure good service and professional fitting and eventually put together a code of conduct for dealers. Dealers that weren't able to meet Stride Rite's standards for service lost their franchise. The company had an extensive dealer training program: training videos, special classes for new dealers, twice-yearly seminars for all dealers, and an on-site, hands-on course for every new dealer in how to run a children's shoe department. When shopping malls started to catch on in the early 1970s, Stride Rite saw them as a threat to its network of Main Street family shoe store dealers, many of whom viewed malls as an expensive and uninviting prospect, but at the same time an opportunity to exploit a whole new distribution channel. The company leased space in malls and developed the first children's shoe store chain in the United States. As Stride Rite proved the viability of speciality shoe stores for children, expansion-minded Stride Rite dealers began to open mall stores, too.

To combat slowing growth, Stride Rite purchased Sperry Top-Sider in 1979, and a few years thereafter it purchased Keds from Uniroyal. Sperry Top-Siders were the first shoe developed especially for boating, and the Sperry Top-Sider brand was widely recognized and respected among boating enthusiasts. To leverage Sperry's reputation for quality, comfort, performance, style, and durability and to grow sales of the brand, Stride Rite added new collections of casual and dress casual shoes to complement its marine collection.

The Keds acquisition posed some tough challenges. Keds was losing market share in its most important line, athletic shoes for boys and young adults.[3] Throughout the 1950s, 1960s, and early 1970s, the Pro Keds high-top basketball sneaker was the clear market leader and the brand of choice of most teenagers and basketball teams. But by the late 1970s and early 1980s, while Keds kept turning out the same shoes it had made since the 1950s, the teenage and young adult market had defected to high-performance models made by Nike and Adidas. Stride Rite concluded that the Keds brand had lost its credibility in the athletic shoe market and decided to get out of the performance shoe business altogether even though it constituted half of Keds's revenues. Stride Rite saw performance shoes as a fad business, dependent on fashion and styling; moreover, the imperatives of endorsements by professional athletes and heavy media advertising made it costly to promote performance shoes. The company elected to concentrate on building the canvas-top sneaker part of Keds's business where the emphasis was on the same traditional themes that had made Stride Rite successful in the children's shoe business.

In 1993, Stride Rite had total sales approaching $625 million annually, more than double the 1986 level. The company was organized around four divisions: the Stride Rite children's group, the Keds division, the Sperry Top-Sider division, and Stride Rite International, which marketed all three of the company's brands in about 30

---

[2]Ibid., pp. 103–4.
[3]Ibid.

countries in Europe, Asia, and Latin America. The Keds division was by far the largest. The children's group was the leading marketer of high-quality children's shoes in the U.S.; its shoes were marketed through franchised dealers, 132 company-owned Stride Rite Bootery stores, and 41 leased departments within leading department stores. The children's group's major competitor was Brown Shoe, which marketed Buster Brown Shoes. Keds's major competitors were Nike, Reebok, and Converse. The Sperry Top-Siders division faced competition from Bass, Rockport, Florsheim, and Timberland. Exhibit 1 presents a five-year financial summary.

ARNOLD HIATT, STRIDE RITE'S PRESIDENT AND CEO, 1968–92

Arnold Hiatt's first job was as an executive trainee at Filene's Department Store in Boston.[4] Competing with 15 other candidates for five positions three steps up in Filene's executive ranks did not appeal to Hiatt. In 1952, when a small children's shoe company in Lawrence, Massachusetts, filed Chapter 11, Hiatt saw an opportunity to get out of the corporate rat race and run his own business. With loans from the Bank of Boston and his father, at the age of 26 he purchased Blue Star Shoes, a supplier of private-label children's shoes for major department store chains. Hiatt gradually built up Blue Star's list of department store accounts and later created the company's own Blue Star branded line as a lower-priced alternative for parents who didn't want to pay for Stride Rite quality. Once Blue Star started making money, Hiatt instituted a profit-sharing plan for all employees. Hiatt was impressed with the results:[5]

> All of a sudden, I had a lot of partners. I never saw a last on the floor again. I didn't see any crooked back seams when I went into the packing room. People started to take pride in what they were doing because they had a sense of ownership.

Stride Rite executives, admiring Hiatt's entrepreneurial qualities and needing executive-level leadership, made offers to acquire Blue Star starting in 1964. Hiatt resisted because he didn't want to give up his independence. In 1967 Stride Rite made an offer so lucrative that Hiatt couldn't turn it down; at the time Blue Star's sales were about $5 million annually. Hiatt was elevated to president of Stride Rite in 1968 and later to chairman and chief executive officer. Regarded as a staunch political liberal, Hiatt served as treasurer for Senator Eugene McCarthy's 1968 Democratic presidential campaign against Richard Nixon.[6] It was under Arnold Hiatt that Stride Rite built its reputation as a progressive, socially responsible company.

In a 1992 interview conducted by the managing editor of the *Harvard Business Review,* Arnold Hiatt identified the business principles and practices that he nurtured and encouraged during his 24 years as a senior executive at Stride Rite:[7]

- Respect for people and working conditions that reflect that respect—"You just treat people the way you want to be treated".

---

[4]Ibid., p. 98.
[5]Ibid., p. 97.
[6]Joseph Periera, "Social Responsibility and Need for Low Cost Clash at Stride Rite," *The Wall Street Journal,* May 28, 1993, p. A6.
[7]Nan Stone, "Building Corporate Character," pp. 96, 97, 101–3.

EXHIBIT 1 | Selected Financial Highlights for The Stride Rite Corp., 1988–92[1]

	1988	1989	1990	1991	1992
Net sales	$378,788	$454,373	$515,842	$574,379	$585,926
Income from continuing operations[2]	34,740	46,166	55,541	65,960	61,506
Loss from discontinued operations	(4,677)	(494)	—	—	—
Net income[2]	31,786	45,672	55,541	65,960	61,506
Income before nonrecurring charges[3]	34,740	46,166	55,541	65,960	72,593
Common stock dividends	7,470	9,302	10,382	13,050	15,872
Working capital	124,257	155,208	168,738	223,031	246,561
Total assets	244,464	251,676	266,023	332,090	383,524
Long-term debt	6,667	5,833	5,000	4,167	3,333
Stockholders' equity	134,030	166,662	181,359	240,427	271,535
Common shares outstanding at end of year	53,746	53,408	50,857	51,481	50,908
Per common share:					
Income from continuing operations[2]	.63	.86	1.05	1.28	1.19
Loss from discontinued operations	(.08)	(.01)	—	—	—
Net income[2]	.58	.85	1.05	1.28	1.19
Cash dividends	.138	.175	.20	.255	.31
Book value	2.49	3.12	3.57	4.67	5.33
Number of employees	4,000	3,900	3,700	3,600	3,100
Number of shareholders	2,500	3,000	3,000	2,900	4,100

[1]Financial data is in thousands, except for per share information.

[2]Income from continuing operations in 1988 excludes the cumulative effect of a change in accounting principle related to inventories. Net income and net income per common share in 1988 include the cumulative effect of the accounting change, which amounted to $1,723,000 and $.03, respectively.

[3]Nonrecurring charges in 1992 of $18,319,000 (an after-tax charge of $11,087,000 or $0.22 per share) were primarily caused by expenses associated with the relocation of the Company's distribution facilities.

Source: 1992 company annual report.

- Providing opportunities for all employees to make a contribution and to see that their actions as individuals could make a difference.
- Meeting the company's obligations to its customers—"If customers are going to be committed to Stride Rite, we have to earn their commitment. We can't do that with magazine ads or television spots. We can only do it in the store by measuring the child's foot carefully, by making sure we have the right size, the right width, the right product in stock, and by disciplining ourselves *not* to make a sale if the child's old shoe still fits. Expertise and restraint are crucial parts of Stride Rite's identity. They are how we deliver professional service to parents without having to say that that's what we are about."
- A one-price-for-everyone policy—no quantity discounts and no special off-price deals for certain customers.
- A strong commitment to traditional values: quality products, classic styles,

affordable prices, professional service, dependability, and integrity in relationships with suppliers, dealers, and consumers.

- Sufficiently outstanding financial results and earnings that allowed stockholders to feel good about their investment.
- Conservative financial policies and a careful system of financial controls and financial reporting.
- A belief that business was obligated to be socially responsible and use some of its resources to address societal ills—"You can't run a healthy company in an unhealthy society for long."

Hiatt introduced a stock purchase plan that allowed all Stride Rite employees to buy the company's shares at a discount. He also developed an incentive plan that rewarded senior managers for exceeding short-term and long-term profit goals. Under Hiatt, Stride Rite's financial performance had been strong. Earnings grew every year during the 1973–92 period except for 1984 and 1992. The stock price rose sixfold between 1986 and June 1993. The company's return on investment ranked in the upper 1 percent of all public companies for most of the 1985–92 period. Stride Rite's stock was a favorite among socially conscious investors.

Arnold Hiatt retired as Stride Rite's chairman in mid-1992. His handpicked successor was 51-year-old Ervin R. Shames. Shames had joined the company in 1990 when Ronald J. Jackson, a toy industry executive hired in 1989 as Mr. Hiatt's heir apparent, left after six months to head Fisher-Price Inc.[8] Mr. Shames, who was runner-up to Mr. Jackson in the initial search to find a replacement for Mr. Hiatt, was then hired as president and chief executive. Mr. Shames took on the additional title of chairman when Arnold Hiatt retired in 1992. Hiatt remained as a member of Stride Rite's board of directors and he also continued as chairman of the Stride Rite Charitable Foundation. The Foundation oversaw Stride Rite's social responsibility programs and directed how the monies Stride Rite's board allocated for such programs (currently 5 percent of pretax profits) would be spent.

STRIDE RITE'S ACTIONS TO CLOSE ITS INNER-CITY FACILITIES AND MOVE PRODUCTION OVERSEAS

Even as Stride Rite was nurturing its progressive social and community programs, it began a long-term program of closing outmoded production facilities in Maine and New Hampshire and shifting production to lower-wage rural areas and, increasingly, to sites in Asia.[9] While the moves were made slowly and reluctantly, Stride Rite's executives believed they were necessary to protect the company's competitiveness. In the 1970s, a substantial fraction of the company's shoe production was shifted from its main Harrison Avenue plant, adjacent to the headquarters offices in Boston's Roxbury, out to the Lawrence, New Hampshire, plant (which had made Blue Star shoes before its acquisition) and to new plants in Auburn, Maine, and Tipton, Missouri. Arnold Hiatt attributed the move to declining production quality at the Harrison Avenue plant; prior to the move, management tried to stem the erosion of Stride Rite's production standards with several quality improvement programs but was

[8]Joseph Pereira, "Stride Rite Is Caught Flat-Footed by CEO's Departure," *The Wall Street Journal*, June 29, 1993, p. B2.
[9]Joseph Pereira, "Social Responsibility and Need for Low Cost Clash at Stride Rite," p. A6.

unsuccessful. In 1981 Stride Rite moved its corporate offices from Roxbury to a nicer, cross-city Boston suburb—an attractive building on Kendall Square in Cambridge; Hiatt explained why:

> We held out as long as we could, but it became clear that people that had the more skilled jobs at Stride Rite were coming from other parts of the city and were increasingly reluctant to go into Roxbury.[10]
>
> . . . We were also starting to lose employees either because they'd experienced something unpleasant themselves or because they'd become frightened by the growing number of purse-snatchings, attempted thefts, and the like. Then one day a bullet came through my window. I knew it was time to go.[11]

To soften the impact on the Roxbury community, Stride Rite closed its distribution centers in Atlanta and in Salem, N.H., and moved their operations to Roxbury.

In 1984, management decided to cease all production at the Harrison Avenue plant and closed the factory. All that remained in Roxbury was the distribution center employing about 175 people—a far cry from the 2,500 people once employed at Stride Rite's Roxbury facilities. Two other plants were also closed in 1984. Altogether, Stride Rite laid off 2,500 of its U.S. employees in that one year.

To replace the production at the closed plants and to accommodate rising sales volumes, Stride Rite turned to manufacturers in South Korea to supply its shoes. The company avoided long-term contracts with its Korean suppliers, preferring to shop for the best price it could get consistent with its quality standards.[12] Stride Rite generally sourced its shoes from producers who had upgraded their factories and workforce to craft levels. To give it bargaining leverage and strong influence over quality control, Stride Rite placed large orders with its South Korean suppliers—often 40 percent to 60 percent of their production. By the early 1980s, Stride Rite was sourcing one-half of its shoes from Korean suppliers. Later, orders were placed with contractors and subcontractors in Taiwan and China.

In 1989 Arnold Hiatt and Stride Rite's head of sourcing flew to Thailand to visit prospective suppliers and check out their facilities. They were particularly impressed by one supplier and its president. The supplier was wary, however, having had the experience of building a factory to supply another U.S. shoe company only to have orders cut when the buyer's sales fell off; many workers had to be laid off and one young worker committed suicide. To lessen the supplier's concerns that Stride Rite might do the same thing, Hiatt proposed a joint-venture arrangement that involved Stride Rite investing company funds in the factory. The supplier accepted, including agreeing to Hiatt's request to build and operate a day care center. Hiatt described the factory in his 1992 interview with *HBR*:

> Today the factory is a major complex located near the Cambodian border. It employs 1,200 people and produces close to 20,000 pairs of Keds each day. It is also the nicest manufacturing facility I have ever seen, with landscaped gardens and pools and little windmills to circulate air through the plant.[13]

During the 1984–93 period, Stride Rite closed 15 U.S. factories, mostly in the Northeast and several in depressed areas. In June 1992 the Tipton, Missouri, plant was closed and 280 workers permanently laid off. (Three other nearby shoe factories

---

[10]Ibid.
[11]Nan Stone, "Building Corporate Character," p. 96.
[12]Ibid., p. 101.
[13]Ibid.

also closed, idling 1,400 additional workers; with these closings shoe-factory employment in Missouri was down from 25,000 in 1968 to 8,250 in 1992.) In 1993 Stride Rite announced plans to close its New Bedford, Massachusetts, warehouse, which employed about 300 people; at the time, the unemployment rate in New Bedford was 14 percent. In the weeks following the announcement, two suspicious fires at the New Bedford warehouse caused $250,000 damage and three Stride Rite workers were under investigation. Stride Rite also announced it would close the Roxbury distribution center in 1994, which employed 175 workers; the unemployment rate in the Roxbury area was close to 30 percent due to several other community plant closings.

The distribution center operations in New Bedford and Roxbury were being moved to a new facility under construction in Louisville, Kentucky, that was expected to employ 275 people.[14] Louisville was chosen over sites in Indiana, Ohio, and Massachusetts because Kentucky offered a $24 million tax break over 10 years; the Massachusetts offer was only $3 million. Lower wage rates also played a role. Stride Rite expected to save millions on its inbound and outbound shipping costs by moving its warehousing operations from the Northeast to the Midwest. Most Stride Rite shoes produced in Asia were shipped to Los Angeles and Seattle, then trucked to Boston and New Bedford, where they were sorted, labeled, boxed, and dispatched by common carrier to retailers nationwide. The new distribution center in Louisville would reduce labor requirements for warehousing operations by 40 percent, eliminate 800 to 1200 miles on some truck routes, and speed delivery to retailers by two to four days. A big fraction of Stride Rite's sales was to dealers located in the South and Midwest. Arnold Hiatt argued forcefully against the Roxbury closing and the move to Louisville, but was overruled by the new CEO, Ervin Shames, and Stride Rite's Board of Directors.

In 1993 Stride Rite made only 10 percent of its shoes in the United States, at its two remaining factories in Missouri.[15] The company employed 2,500 people, down from a peak of 6,000. Stride Rite's U.S. workers averaged $1,200 to $1,400 per month in wages and had modest fringe benefit packages. By comparison, skilled shoe-factory workers in China earned $100 to $150 a month, working 50 to 65 hours a week; unskilled Chinese workers that performed packing and sorting jobs were paid $50 to $70 a month.

Stride Rite executives contended that the company had no alternative to shifting its shoe production overseas and taking full advantage of cheap Asian labor to lower its production costs. Arnold Hiatt said, "To the extent that you can stay in the city, I think you have to; [but] if it's at the expense of your business, I think you can't forget that your primary responsibility is to your stockholders."[16] His successor, Ervin Shames, commented, "Putting jobs into places where it doesn't make economic sense is a dilution of corporate and community wealth."[17]

Others were not so sure, however. Donald Gillis, executive director of Boston's Economic Development and Industrial Corp., which tried to get Stride Rite to keep its Roxbury facilities open, said, "The most socially responsible thing a company can do is to give a person a job."[18] Gilda Haas, an economic and urban-planning lecturer

---

[14]Joseph Pereira, "Social Responsibility and Need for Low Cost Clash at Stride Rite," p. A6.
[15]Ibid., pp. A1 and A6.
[16]Ibid., p. A6.
[17]Ibid.
[18]Ibid., p. A1.

at UCLA, observed: "What exactly did the corporate sector mean when they spoke of the need for inner-city jobs last year as Los Angeles burned?"[19] Alberto Andrade, a 60-year-old immigrant with eight children, who had worked for eight years at the Roxbury distribution center and needed 14 hours of overtime weekly to make ends meet, was distressed about his job prospects when Roxbury closed in 1994: "Who will feed my children?"[20] Anita and Donny Bracht, parents of four children and both former Stride Rite employees at the Tipton plant, were still unemployed over a year after the plant's closing; with their unemployment benefits about to run out and no job prospects in sight, Anita said, "I'm about ready to panic."[21] Although federal job retraining programs had been made available in Tipton, the Brachts could not afford the $80 per week for a babysitter while they attended retraining classes; besides, the union hall had a waiting list of 500 people for any union jobs that became available.

---

[19]Ibid.
[20]Ibid., p. A6.
[21]Ibid.

CASE INDEX